The
Book of
Common
Prayer

and Administration of the Sacraments
and Other Rites
and Ceremonies of the Church

Together with The Psalter or Psalms of David

According to the use of
The Episcopal Church

The Church Hymnal Corporation, New York
and The Seabury Press

Certificate

I certify that this edition of The Book of Common Prayer
has been compared with a certified copy of the Standard Book,
as the Canon directs, and that it conforms thereto.

Charles Mortimer Guilbert
Custodian of the Standard Book of Common Prayer
September, 1979

ISBN: 0-89869-080-3 Pew Edition, Red
0-89869-081-1 Pew Edition, Black
0-89869-082-X Chancel Edition

Table of Contents

The Ratification of
The Book of Common Prayer (1789)

By the Bishops, the Clergy, and the Laity of the Protestant Episcopal Church in the United States of America, in Convention, this Sixteenth Day of October, in the Year of Our Lord One Thousand Seven Hundred and Eighty-Nine.

This Convention having, in their present session, set forth *A Book of Common Prayer, and Administration of the Sacraments, and other Rites and Ceremonies of the Church,* do hereby establish the said Book: And they declare it to be the Liturgy of this Church: And require that it be received as such by all the members of the same: And this Book shall be in use from and after the First Day of October, in the Year of our Lord one thousand seven hundred and ninety.

Preface

It is a most invaluable part of that blessed "liberty wherewith Christ hath made us free," that in his worship different forms and usages may without offence be allowed, provided the substance of the Faith be kept entire; and that, in every Church, what cannot be clearly determined to belong to Doctrine must be referred to Discipline; and therefore, by common consent and authority, may be altered, abridged, enlarged, amended, or otherwise disposed of, as may seem most convenient for the edification of the people,"according to the various exigency of times and occasions."

The Church of England, to which the Protestant Episcopal Church in these States is indebted, under God, for her first foundation and a long continuance of nursing care and protection, hath, in the Preface of her Book of Common Prayer, laid it down as a rule, that "The particular Forms of Divine Worship, and the Rites and Ceremonies appointed to be used therein, being things in their own nature indifferent, and alterable, and so acknowledged; it is but reasonable that upon weighty and important considerations, according to the various exigency of times and occasions, such changes and alterations should be made therein, as to those that are in place of Authority should, from time to time, seem either necessary or expedient."

The same Church hath not only in her Preface, but likewise in her Articles and Homilies, declared the necessity and expediency of occasional alterations and amendments in her Forms of Public Worship; and we find accordingly, that, seeking to keep the happy mean between too much stiffness in refusing, and too much easiness in admitting variations in things once advisedly established, she hath, in the reign of several Princes, since the first compiling of her Liturgy in the time of Edward the Sixth, upon just and weighty considerations her thereunto moving, yielded to make such alterations in some particulars, as in their respective times were thought convenient; yet so as that the main body and essential parts of the same (as well in the chiefest materials, as in the frame and order thereof) have still been continued firm and unshaken.

Her general aim in these different reviews and alterations hath been, as she further declares in her said Preface, to do that which, according to her best understanding, might most tend to the preservation of peace and unity in the Church; the procuring of reverence, and the exciting of piety and devotion in the worship of God; and, finally, the cutting off occasion, from them that seek occasion, of cavil or quarrel against her Liturgy. And although, according to her judgment, there be not any thing in it contrary to the Word of God, or to sound doctrine, or which a godly man may not with a good conscience use and submit unto, or which is not fairly defensible, if allowed such just and favourable construction as in common equity ought to be allowed to all human writings; yet upon the principles already laid down, it cannot but be supposed that further alterations would in time be found expedient. Accordingly, a Commission for a review was issued in the year 1689: but this great and good work miscarried at that time; and the Civil Authority has not since thought proper to revive it by any new Commission.

But when in the course of Divine Providence, these American States became independent with respect to civil government, their ecclesiastical independence was necessarily included; and the different religious denominations of Christians in these States were left at full and equal liberty to model and organize their respective Churches, and forms of worship, and discipline, in such manner as they might judge most convenient for their future prosperity; consistently with the constitution and laws of their country.

The attention of this Church was in the first place drawn to those alterations in the Liturgy which became necessary in the prayers for our Civil Rulers, in consequence of the Revolution. And the principal care herein was to make them conformable to what ought to be the proper end of all such prayers, namely, that "Rulers may have grace, wisdom, and understanding to execute justice, and to maintain truth;" and that the people "may lead quiet and peaceable lives, in all godliness and honesty."

But while these alterations were in review before the Convention, they could not but, with gratitude to God, embrace the happy occasion which was offered to them (uninfluenced and unrestrained by any worldly authority whatsoever) to take a further review of the Public Service, and to establish such other alterations and amendments therein as might be deemed expedient.

It seems unnecessary to enumerate all the different alterations and amendments. They will appear, and it is to be hoped, the reasons of them also, upon a comparison of this with the Book of Common Prayer of the Church of England. In which it will also appear that this Church is far from intending to depart from the Church of England in any essential point of doctrine, discipline, or worship; or further than local circumstances require.

And now, this important work being brought to a conclusion, it is hoped the whole will be received and examined by every true member of our Church, and every sincere Christian, with a meek, candid, and charitable frame of mind; without prejudice or prepossessions; seriously considering what Christianity is, and what the truths of the Gospel are; and earnestly beseeching Almighty God to accompany with his blessing every endeavour for promulgating them to mankind in the clearest, plainest, most affecting and majestic manner, for the sake of Jesus Christ, our blessed Lord and Saviour.

Philadelphia, October, 1789.

Concerning the Service
of the Church

The Holy Eucharist, the principal act of Christian worship on the Lord's Day and other major Feasts, and Daily Morning and Evening Prayer, as set forth in this Book, are the regular services appointed for public worship in this Church.

In addition to these services and the other rites contained in this Book, other forms set forth by authority within this Church may be used. Also, subject to the direction of the bishop, special devotions taken from this Book, or from Holy Scripture, may be used when the needs of the congregation so require.

For special days of fasting or thanksgiving, appointed by civil or Church authority, and for other special occasions for which no service or prayer has been provided in this Book, the bishop may set forth such forms as are fitting to the occasion.

In all services, the entire Christian assembly participates in such a way that the members of each order within the Church, lay persons, bishops, priests, and deacons, fulfill the functions proper to their respective orders, as set forth in the rubrical directions for each service.

The leader of worship in a Christian assembly is normally a bishop or priest. Deacons by virtue of their order do not exercise a presiding function; but, like lay persons, may officiate at the Liturgy of the Word, whether in the form provided in the Daily Offices, or (when a bishop or priest is not present) in the form appointed at the Eucharist. Under exceptional circumstances, when the services of a priest cannot be obtained, the bishop may, at discretion, authorize a deacon to preside at other rites also, subject to the limitations described in the directions for each service.

In any of the Proper Liturgies for Special Days, and in other services contained in this Book celebrated in the context of a Rite One service, the contemporary idiom may be conformed to traditional language.

Hymns referred to in the rubrics of this Book are to be understood as those authorized by this Church. The words of anthems are to be from Holy Scripture, or from this Book, or from texts congruent with them.

On occasion, and as appropriate, instrumental music may be substituted for a hymn or anthem.

Where rubrics indicate that a part of a service is to be"said," it must be understood to include"or sung,"and *vice versa*.

When it is desired to use music composed for them, previously authorized liturgical texts may be used in place of the corresponding texts in this Book.

Scriptural citations in this Book, except for the Psalms, follow the numeration of the Revised Standard Version of the Bible.

The Calendar
of the Church Year

The Church Year consists of two cycles of feasts and holy days: one is dependent upon the movable date of the Sunday of the Resurrection or Easter Day; the other, upon the fixed date of December 25, the Feast of our Lord's Nativity or Christmas Day.

Easter Day is always the first Sunday after the full moon that falls on or after March 21. It cannot occur before March 22 or after April 25.

The sequence of all Sundays of the Church Year depends upon the date of Easter Day. But the Sundays of Advent are always the four Sundays before Christmas Day, whether it occurs on a Sunday or a weekday. The date of Easter also determines the beginning of Lent on Ash Wednesday, and the feast of the Ascension on a Thursday forty days after Easter Day.

1. Principal Feasts

The Principal Feasts observed in this Church are the following:

Easter Day   All Saints' Day, *November 1*
Ascension Day   Christmas Day, *December 25*
The Day of Pentecost   The Epiphany, *January 6*
Trinity Sunday

These feasts take precedence of any other day or observance. All Saints' Day may always be observed on the Sunday following November 1, in addition to its observance on the fixed date.

2. Sundays

All Sundays of the year are feasts of our Lord Jesus Christ. In addition to the dated days listed above, only the following feasts, appointed on fixed days, take precedence of a Sunday:

The Holy Name
The Presentation
The Transfiguration

The feast of the Dedication of a Church, and the feast of its patron or title, may be observed on, or be transferred to, a Sunday, except in the seasons of Advent, Lent, and Easter.

All other Feasts of our Lord, and all other Major Feasts appointed on fixed days in the Calendar, when they occur on a Sunday, are normally transferred to the first convenient open day within the week. When desired, however, the Collect, Preface, and one or more of the Lessons appointed for the Feast may be substituted for those of the Sunday, but not from the Last Sunday after Pentecost through the First Sunday after the Epiphany, or from the Last Sunday after the Epiphany through Trinity Sunday.

With the express permission of the bishop, and for urgent and sufficient reason, some other special occasion may be observed on a Sunday.

3. Holy Days

The following Holy Days are regularly observed throughout the year. Unless otherwise ordered in the preceding rules concerning Sundays, they have precedence over all other days of commemoration or of special observance:

Other Feasts of our Lord

The Holy Name   Saint John the Baptist
The Presentation   The Transfiguration
The Annunciation   Holy Cross Day
The Visitation

Other Major Feasts

All feasts of Apostles   Saint Mary the Virgin
All feasts of Evangelists   Saint Michael and All Angels
Saint Stephen   Saint James of Jerusalem
The Holy Innocents   Independence Day
Saint Joseph   Thanksgiving Day
Saint Mary Magdalene

Fasts

Ash Wednesday   Good Friday

Feasts appointed on fixed days in the Calendar are not observed on the
days of Holy Week or of Easter Week. Major Feasts falling in these weeks
are transferred to the week following the Second Sunday of Easter, in the
order of their occurrence.

Feasts appointed on fixed days in the Calendar do not take precedence of
Ash Wednesday.

Feasts of our Lord and other Major Feasts appointed on fixed days,
which fall upon or are transferred to a weekday, may be observed on any
open day within the week. This provision does not apply to Christmas
Day, the Epiphany, and All Saints' Day.

4. Days of Special Devotion

The following days are observed by special acts of discipline and
self-denial:

Ash Wednesday and the other weekdays of Lent and of Holy Week,
except the feast of the Annunciation.

Good Friday and all other Fridays of the year, in commemoration of the
Lord's crucifixion, except for Fridays in the Christmas and Easter
seasons, and any Feasts of our Lord which occur on a Friday.

5. Days of Optional Observance

Subject to the rules of precedence governing Principal Feasts, Sundays, and Holy Days, the following may be observed with the Collects, Psalms, and Lessons duly authorized by this Church:

Commemorations listed in the Calendar
Other Commemorations, using the Common of Saints
The Ember Days, traditionally observed on the Wednesdays, Fridays, and Saturdays after the First Sunday in Lent, the Day of Pentecost, Holy Cross Day, and December 13
The Rogation Days, traditionally observed on Monday, Tuesday, and Wednesday before Ascension Day
Various Occasions

Provided, that there is no celebration of the Eucharist for any such occasion on Ash Wednesday, Maundy Thursday, Good Friday, and Holy Saturday; and provided further, that none of the Propers appointed for Various Occasions is used as a substitute for, or as an addition to, the Proper appointed for the Principal Feasts.

January

1	A	**The Holy Name of Our Lord Jesus Christ**
2	b	
3	c	
4	d	
5	e	
6	f	**The Epiphany of Our Lord Jesus Christ**
7	g	
8	A	
9	b	
10	c	William Laud, Archbishop of Canterbury, 1645
11	d	
12	e	
13	f	Hilary, Bishop of Poitiers, 367
14	g	
15	A	
16	b	
17	c	Antony, Abbot in Egypt, 356
18	d	**The Confession of Saint Peter the Apostle**
19	e	Wulfstan, Bishop of Worcester, 1095
20	f	Fabian, Bishop and Martyr of Rome, 250
21	g	Agnes, Martyr at Rome, 304
22	A	Vincent, Deacon of Saragossa, and Martyr, 304
23	b	Phillips Brooks, Bishop of Massachusetts, 1893
24	c	
25	d	**The Conversion of Saint Paul the Apostle**
26	e	Timothy and Titus, Companions of Saint Paul
27	f	John Chrysostom, Bishop of Constantinople, 407
28	g	Thomas Aquinas, Priest and Friar, 1274
29	A	
30	b	
31	c	

February

1	d	
2	e	**The Presentation of Our Lord Jesus Christ in the Temple**
3	f	Anskar, Archbishop of Hamburg, Missionary to Denmark and Sweden, 865
4	g	Cornelius the Centurion
5	A	The Martyrs of Japan, 1597
6	b	
7	c	
8	d	
9	e	
10	f	
11	g	
12	A	
13	b	Absalom Jones, Priest, 1818
14	c	Cyril, Monk, and Methodius, Bishop, Missionaries to the Slavs, 869, 885
15	d	Thomas Bray, Priest and Missionary, 1730
16	e	
17	f	
18	g	
19	A	
20	b	
21	c	
22	d	
23	e	Polycarp, Bishop and Martyr of Smyrna, 156
24	f	**Saint Matthias the Apostle**
25	g	
26	A	
27	b	George Herbert, Priest, 1633
28	c	
29		

March

1	d	David, Bishop of Menevia, Wales, c. 544
2	e	Chad, Bishop of Lichfield, 672
3	f	John and Charles Wesley, Priests, 1791, 1788
4	g	
5	A	
6	b	
7	c	Perpetua and her Companions, Martyrs at Carthage, 202
8	d	
9	e	Gregory, Bishop of Nyssa, c. 394
10	f	
11	g	
12	A	Gregory the Great, Bishop of Rome, 604
13	b	
14	c	
15	d	
16	e	
17	f	Patrick, Bishop and Missionary of Ireland, 461
18	g	Cyril, Bishop of Jerusalem, 386
19	A	**Saint Joseph**
20	b	Cuthbert, Bishop of Lindisfarne, 687
21	c	Thomas Ken, Bishop of Bath and Wells, 1711

14 22 d James De Koven, Priest, 1879
3 23 e Gregory the Illuminator, Bishop and Missionary of Armenia, c. 332

24 f

11 25 g **The Annunciation of Our Lord Jesus Christ to the Blessed Virgin Mary**

26 A

19 27 b Charles Henry Brent, Bishop of the Philippines, and of Western New York, 1929

8 28 c

29 d John Keble, Priest, 1866

16 30 e

5 31 f John Donne, Priest, 1631

April

	1	g	Frederick Denison Maurice, Priest, 1872
13	2	A	James Lloyd Breck, Priest, 1876
2	3	b	Richard, Bishop of Chichester, 1253
	4	c	
10	5	d	
	6	e	
18	7	f	
7	8	g	William Augustus Muhlenberg, Priest, 1877
	9	A	William Law, Priest, 1761
15	10	b	
4	11	c	**George Augustus Selwyn, Bishop of New Zealand, and Litchfield, 1878**
	12	d	
12	13	e	
1	14	f	
	15	g	
9	16	A	
17	17	b	
6	18	c	
	19	d	Alphege, Archbishop of Canterbury, and Martyr, 1012
	20	e	
	21	f	Anselm, Archbishop of Canterbury, 1109
	22	g	
	23	A	
	24	b	
	25	c	**Saint Mark the Evangelist**
	26	d	
	27	e	
	28	f	
	29	g	Catherine of Siena, 1380
	30	A	

May

1	b	**Saint Philip and Saint James, Apostles**
2	c	Athanasius, Bishop of Alexandria, 373
3	d	
4	e	Monnica, Mother of Augustine of Hippo, 387
5	f	
6	g	
7	A	
8	b	Dame Julian of Norwich, c. 1417
9	c	Gregory of Nazianzus, Bishop of Constantinople, 389
10	d	
11	e	
12	f	
13	g	
14	A	
15	b	
16	c	
17	d	
18	e	
19	f	Dunstan, Archbishop of Canterbury, 988
20	g	Alcuin, Deacon, and Abbot of Tours, 804
21	A	
22	b	
23	c	
24	d	Jackson Kemper, First Missionary Bishop in the United States, 1870
25	e	Bede, the Venerable, Priest, and Monk of Jarrow, 735
26	f	Augustine, First Archbishop of Canterbury, 605
27	g	
28	A	
29	b	
30	c	
31	d	**The Visitation of the Blessed Virgin Mary**

The First Book of Common Prayer, 1549, is appropriately observed on a weekday following the Day of Pentecost.

June

1	e	Justin, Martyr at Rome, c. 167
2	f	The Martyrs of Lyons, 177
3	g	The Martyrs of Uganda, 1886
4	A	
5	b	Boniface, Archbishop of Mainz, Missionary to Germany, and Martyr, 754
6	c	
7	d	
8	e	
9	f	Columba, Abbot of Iona, 597
10	g	Ephrem of Edessa, Syria, Deacon, 373
11	A	**Saint Barnabas the Apostle**
12	b	
13	c	
14	d	Basil the Great, Bishop of Caesarea, 379
15	e	
16	f	Joseph Butler, Bishop of Durham, 1752
17	g	
18	A	Bernard Mizeki, Catechist and Martyr in Rhodesia, 1896
19	b	
20	c	
21	d	
22	e	Alban, First Martyr of Britain, c. 304
23	f	
24	g	**The Nativity of Saint John the Baptist**
25	A	
26	b	
27	c	
28	d	Irenaeus, Bishop of Lyons, c. 202
29	e	**Saint Peter and Saint Paul, Apostles**
30	f	

July

1	g	
2	A	
3	b	
4	c	**Independence Day**
5	d	
6	e	
7	f	
8	g	
9	A	
10	b	
11	c	Benedict of Nursia, Abbot of Monte Cassino, c. 540
12	d	
13	e	
14	f	
15	g	
16	A	
17	b	William White, Bishop of Pennsylvania, 1836
18	c	
19	d	
20	e	
21	f	
22	g	**Saint Mary Magdalene**
23	A	
24	b	Thomas a Kempis, Priest, 1471
25	c	**Saint James the Apostle**
26	d	The Parents of the Blessed Virgin Mary
27	e	William Reed Huntington, Priest, 1909
28	f	
29	g	Mary and Martha of Bethany
30	A	William Wilberforce, 1833
31	b	Joseph of Arimathaea

August

1	c	
2	d	
3	e	
4	f	
5	g	
6	A	**The Transfiguration of Our Lord Jesus Christ**
7	b	John Mason Neale, Priest, 1866
8	c	Dominic, Priest and Friar, 1221
9	d	
10	e	Laurence, Deacon, and Martyr at Rome, 258
11	f	Clare, Abbess at Assisi, 1253
12	g	
13	A	Jeremy Taylor, Bishop of Down, Connor, and Dromore, 1667
14	b	
15	c	**Saint Mary the Virgin, Mother of Our Lord Jesus Christ**
16	d	
17	e	
18	f	William Porcher DuBose, Priest, 1918
19	g	
20	A	Bernard, Abbot of Clairvaux, 1153
21	b	
22	c	
23	d	
24	e	**Saint Bartholomew the Apostle**
25	f	Louis, King of France, 1270
26	g	
27	A	
28	b	Augustine, Bishop of Hippo, 430
29	c	
30	d	
31	e	Aidan, Bishop of Lindisfarne, 651

September

1	f	
2	g	The Martyrs of New Guinea, 1942
3	A	
4	b	
5	c	
6	d	
7	e	
8	f	
9	g	
10	A	
11	b	
12	c	John Henry Hobart, Bishop of New York, 1830
13	d	Cyprian, Bishop and Martyr of Carthage, 258
14	e	**Holy Cross Day**
15	f	
16	g	Ninian, Bishop in Galloway, c. 430
17	A	
18	b	Edward Bouverie Pusey, Priest, 1882
19	c	Theodore of Tarsus, Archbishop of Canterbury, 690
20	d	John Coleridge Patteson, Bishop of Melanesia, and his Companions, Martyrs, 1871
21	e	**Saint Matthew, Apostle and Evangelist**
22	f	
23	g	
24	A	
25	b	Sergius, Abbot of Holy Trinity, Moscow, 1392
26	c	Lancelot Andrewes, Bishop of Winchester, 1626
27	d	
28	e	
29	f	**Saint Michael and All Angels**
30	g	Jerome, Priest, and Monk of Bethlehem, 420

October

1	A	Remigius, Bishop of Rheims, c. 530
2	b	
3	c	
4	d	Francis of Assisi, Friar, 1226
5	e	
6	f	William Tyndale, Priest, 1536
7	g	
8	A	
9	b	Robert Grosseteste, Bishop of Lincoln, 1253
10	c	
11	d	
12	e	
13	f	
14	g	
15	A	Samuel Isaac Joseph Schereschewsky, Bishop of Shanghai, 1906
16	b	Hugh Latimer and Nicholas Ridley, Bishops, 1555, and Thomas Cranmer, Archbishop of Canterbury, 1556
17	c	Ignatius, Bishop of Antioch, and Martyr, c. 115
18	d	**Saint Luke the Evangelist**
19	e	Henry Martyn, Priest, and Missionary to India and Persia, 1812
20	f	
21	g	
22	A	
23	b	**Saint James of Jerusalem, Brother of Our Lord Jesus Christ, and Martyr, c. 62**
24	c	
25	d	
26	e	Alfred the Great, King of the West Saxons, 899
27	f	
28	g	**Saint Simon and Saint Jude, Apostles**
29	A	James Hannington, Bishop of Eastern Equatorial Africa, and his Companions, Martyrs, 1885
30	b	
31	c	

November

1	d	**All Saints**
2	e	Commemoration of All Faithful Departed
3	f	Richard Hooker, Priest, 1600
4	g	
5	A	
6	b	
7	c	Willibrord, Archbishop of Utrecht, Missionary to Frisia, 739
8	d	
9	e	
10	f	Leo the Great, Bishop of Rome, 461
11	g	Martin, Bishop of Tours, 397
12	A	Charles Simeon, Priest, 1836
13	b	
14	c	Consecration of Samuel Seabury, First American Bishop, 1784
15	d	
16	e	Margaret, Queen of Scotland, 1093
17	f	Hugh, Bishop of Lincoln, 1200
18	g	Hilda, Abbess of Whitby, 680
19	A	Elizabeth, Princess of Hungary, 1231
20	b	
21	c	
22	d	
23	e	Clement, Bishop of Rome, c. 100
24	f	
25	g	
26	A	
27	b	
28	c	
29	d	
30	e	**Saint Andrew the Apostle**

December

1	f	Nicholas Ferrar, Deacon, 1637
2	g	Channing Moore Williams, Missionary Bishop in China and Japan, 1910
3	A	
4	b	John of Damascus, Priest, c. 760
5	c	Clement of Alexandria, Priest, c. 210
6	d	Nicholas, Bishop of Myra, c. 342
7	e	Ambrose, Bishop of Milan, 397
8	f	
9	g	
10	A	
11	b	
12	c	
13	d	
14	e	
15	f	
16	g	
17	A	
18	b	
19	c	
20	d	
21	e	**Saint Thomas the Apostle**
22	f	
23	g	
24	A	
25	b	**The Nativity of Our Lord Jesus Christ**
26	c	**Saint Stephen, Deacon and Martyr**
27	d	**Saint John, Apostle and Evangelist**
28	e	**The Holy Innocents**
29	f	
30	g	
31	A	

The Titles of the Seasons
Sundays and Major Holy Days
observed in this Church throughout the Year

Advent Season

The First Sunday of Advent
The Second Sunday of Advent
The Third Sunday of Advent
The Fourth Sunday of Advent

Christmas Season

The Nativity of Our Lord Jesus Christ: Christmas Day, *December 25*
The First Sunday after Christmas Day
The Holy Name of Our Lord Jesus Christ, *January 1*
The Second Sunday after Christmas Day

Epiphany Season

The Epiphany, or the Manifestation of Christ to the Gentiles, *January 6*
The First Sunday after the Epiphany: The Baptism of Our Lord
    Jesus Christ
The Second Sunday through the Eighth Sunday after the Epiphany
The Last Sunday after the Epiphany

Lenten Season

The First Day of Lent, or Ash Wednesday
The First Sunday in Lent
The Second Sunday in Lent
The Third Sunday in Lent
The Fourth Sunday in Lent
The Fifth Sunday in Lent

Holy Week

The Sunday of the Passion: Palm Sunday
Monday in Holy Week

Tuesday in Holy Week
Wednesday in Holy Week
Maundy Thursday
Good Friday
Holy Saturday

Easter Season

Easter Eve
The Sunday of the Resurrection, or Easter Day
Monday in Easter Week
Tuesday in Easter Week
Wednesday in Easter Week
Thursday in Easter Week
Friday in Easter Week
Saturday in Easter Week
The Second Sunday of Easter
The Third Sunday of Easter
The Fourth Sunday of Easter
The Fifth Sunday of Easter
The Sixth Sunday of Easter
Ascension Day
The Seventh Sunday of Easter: The Sunday after Ascension Day
The Day of Pentecost: Whitsunday

The Season After Pentecost

The First Sunday after Pentecost: Trinity Sunday
The Second Sunday through the Twenty-Seventh Sunday after Pentecost
The Last Sunday after Pentecost

Holy Days

Saint Andrew the Apostle, *November 30*
Saint Thomas the Apostle, *December 21*
Saint Stephen, Deacon and Martyr, *December 26*
Saint John, Apostle and Evangelist, *December 27*
The Holy Innocents, *December 28*
The Confession of Saint Peter the Apostle, *January 18*

The Conversion of Saint Paul the Apostle, *January 25*
The Presentation of Our Lord Jesus Christ in the Temple,
    also called the Purification of Saint Mary the Virgin, *February 2*
Saint Matthias the Apostle, *February 24*
Saint Joseph, *March 19*
The Annunciation of Our Lord Jesus Christ
    to the Blessed Virgin Mary, *March 25*
Saint Mark the Evangelist, *April 25*
Saint Philip and Saint James, Apostles, *May 1*
The Visitation of the Blessed Virgin Mary, *May 31*
Saint Barnabas the Apostle, *June 11*
The Nativity of Saint John the Baptist, *June 24*
Saint Peter and Saint Paul, Apostles, *June 29*
Saint Mary Magdalene, *July 22*
Saint James the Apostle, *July 25*
The Transfiguration of Our Lord Jesus Christ, *August 6*
Saint Mary the Virgin, Mother of Our Lord Jesus Christ, *August 15*
Saint Bartholomew the Apostle, *August 24*
Holy Cross Day, *September 14*
Saint Matthew, Apostle and Evangelist, *September 21*
Saint Michael and All Angels, *September 29*
Saint Luke the Evangelist, *October 18*
Saint James of Jerusalem, Brother of Our Lord Jesus Christ,
    and Martyr, *October 23*
Saint Simon and Saint Jude, Apostles, *October 28*
All Saints' Day, *November 1*

National Days

Independence Day, *July 4*
Thanksgiving Day

The Daily Office

Concerning the Service

In the Daily Office, the term "Officiant" is used to denote the person, clerical or lay, who leads the Office.

It is appropriate that other persons be assigned to read the Lessons, and to lead other parts of the service not assigned to the officiant. The bishop, when present, appropriately concludes the Office with a blessing.

At celebrations of the Holy Eucharist, the Order for Morning or Evening Prayer may be used in place of all that precedes the Offertory.

Additional Directions are on page 141.

Daily Morning Prayer: Rite One

The Officiant begins the service with one or more of these sentences of Scripture, or with the versicle "O Lord, open thou our lips" on page 42.

Advent

Watch ye, for ye know not when the master of the house cometh, at even, or at midnight, or at the cock-crowing, or in the morning; lest coming suddenly he find you sleeping. *Mark 13:35, 36*

Prepare ye the way of the Lord, make straight in the desert a highway for our God. *Isaiah 40:3*

The glory of the Lord shall be revealed, and all flesh shall see it together. *Isaiah 40:5*

Christmas

Behold, I bring you good tidings of great joy, which shall be to all people. For unto you is born this day in the city of David a Savior, which is Christ the Lord. *Luke 2:10, 11*

Behold, the tabernacle of God is with men, and he will dwell with them, and they shall be his people, and God himself shall be with them, and be their God. *Revelation 21:3*

Epiphany

The Gentiles shall come to thy light, and kings to the brightness of thy rising.   *Isaiah 60:3*

I will give thee for a light to the Gentiles, that thou mayest be my salvation unto the end of the earth.   *Isaiah 49:6b*

From the rising of the sun even unto the going down of the same my Name shall be great among the Gentiles, and in every place incense shall be offered unto my Name, and a pure offering: for my Name shall be great among the heathen, saith the Lord of hosts.   *Malachi 1:11*

Lent

If we say that we have no sin, we deceive ourselves, and the truth is not in us; but if we confess our sins, God is faithful and just to forgive us our sins, and to cleanse us from all unrighteousness.   *1 John 1:8, 9*

Rend your heart, and not your garments, and turn unto the Lord your God; for he is gracious and merciful, slow to anger and of great kindness, and repenteth him of the evil.   *Joel 2:13*

I will arise and go to my father, and will say unto him, "Father, I have sinned against heaven, and before thee, and am no more worthy to be called thy son."   *Luke 15:18, 19*

To the Lord our God belong mercies and forgivenesses, though we have rebelled against him; neither have we obeyed the voice of the Lord our God, to walk in his laws which he set before us.   *Daniel 9:9, 10*

Jesus said, "Whosoever will come after me, let him deny himself, and take up his cross, and follow me."   *Mark 8:34*

Holy Week

All we like sheep have gone astray; we have turned every one to his own way; and the Lord hath laid on him the iniquity of us all. *Isaiah 53:6*

Is it nothing to you, all ye that pass by? Behold and see if there be any sorrow like unto my sorrow which is done unto me, wherewith the Lord hath afflicted me. *Lamentations 1:12*

Easter Season, including Ascension Day and the Day of Pentecost

Alleluia! Christ is risen.
The Lord is risen indeed. Alleluia!

This is the day which the Lord hath made; we will rejoice and be glad in it. *Psalm 118:24*

Thanks be to God, which giveth us the victory through our Lord Jesus Christ. *1 Corinthians 15:57*

If ye then be risen with Christ, seek those things which are above, where Christ sitteth on the right hand of God.
Colossians 3:1

Christ is not entered into the holy places made with hands, which are the figures of the true; but into heaven itself, now to appear in the presence of God for us. *Hebrews 9:24*

Ye shall receive power, after that the Holy Ghost is come upon you; and ye shall be witnesses unto me both in Jerusalem, and in all Judaea, and in Samaria, and unto the uttermost part of the earth. *Acts 1:8*

Trinity Sunday

Holy, holy, holy, Lord God Almighty, which was, and is, and is to come. *Revelation 4:8*

All Saints and other Major Saints' Days

We give thanks unto the Father, which hath made us meet to be partakers of the inheritance of the saints in light.
Colossians 1:12

Ye are no more strangers and foreigners, but fellow-citizens with the saints and of the household of God.   *Ephesians 2:19*

Their sound is gone out into all lands; and their words into the ends of the world.   *Psalm 19:4*

Occasions of Thanksgiving

O give thanks unto the Lord, and call upon his Name; tell the people what things he hath done.   *Psalm 105:1*

At any Time

Grace be unto you, and peace, from God our Father, and from the Lord Jesus Christ.   *Philippians 1:2*

I was glad when they said unto me, "We will go into the house of the Lord."   *Psalm 122:1*

Let the words of my mouth, and the meditation of my heart, be alway acceptable in thy sight, O Lord, my strength and my redeemer.   *Psalm 19:14*

O send out thy light and thy truth, that they may lead me, and bring me unto thy holy hill, and to thy dwelling.
Psalm 43:3

The Lord is in his holy temple; let all the earth keep silence before him.   *Habakkuk 2:20*

The hour cometh, and now is, when the true worshipers shall worship the Father in spirit and in truth; for the Father seeketh such to worship him.   *John 4:23*

Thus saith the high and lofty One that inhabiteth eternity,

whose name is Holy," I dwell in the high and holy place, with him also that is of a contrite and humble spirit, to revive the spirit of the humble, and to revive the heart of the contrite ones."   *Isaiah 57:15*

The following Confession of Sin may then be said; or the Office may continue at once with "O Lord, open thou our lips."

Confession of Sin

The Officiant says to the people

Dearly beloved, we have come together in the presence of Almighty God our heavenly Father, to render thanks for the great benefits that we have received at his hands, to set forth his most worthy praise, to hear his holy Word, and to ask, for ourselves and on behalf of others, those things that are necessary for our life and our salvation. And so that we may prepare ourselves in heart and mind to worship him, let us kneel in silence, and with penitent and obedient hearts confess our sins, that we may obtain forgiveness by his infinite goodness and mercy.

or this

Let us humbly confess our sins unto Almighty God.

Silence may be kept.

Officiant and People together, all kneeling

Almighty and most merciful Father,
we have erred and strayed from thy ways like lost sheep,
we have followed too much the devices and desires of our
    own hearts,
we have offended against thy holy laws,
we have left undone those things which we ought to
    have done,

and we have done those things which we ought not to
  have done.
But thou, O Lord, have mercy upon us,
spare thou those who confess their faults,
restore thou those who are penitent,
according to thy promises declared unto mankind
in Christ Jesus our Lord;
and grant, O most merciful Father, for his sake,
that we may hereafter live a godly, righteous, and sober life,
to the glory of thy holy Name. Amen.

The Priest alone stands and says

The Almighty and merciful Lord grant you absolution and
remission of all your sins, true repentance, amendment of
life, and the grace and consolation of his Holy Spirit. *Amen.*

*A deacon or lay person using the preceding form remains kneeling, and
substitutes "us" for "you" and "our" for "your."*

The Invitatory and Psalter

All stand

Officiant	O Lord, open thou our lips.
People	And our mouth shall show forth thy praise.

Officiant and People

Glory to the Father, and to the Son, and to the Holy Spirit: as
it was in the beginning, is now, and will be for ever. Amen.

Except in Lent,   Alleluia   *may be added.*

Then follows one of the Invitatory Psalms, Venite or Jubilate.

One of the following Antiphons may be sung or said with the Invitatory Psalm

In Advent

Our King and Savior draweth nigh: O come, let us adore him.

On the Twelve Days of Christmas

Alleluia. Unto us a child is born: O come, let us adore him. Alleluia.

From the Epiphany through the Baptism of Christ, and on the Feasts of the Transfiguration and Holy Cross

The Lord hath manifested forth his glory: O come, let us adore him.

In Lent

The Lord is full of compassion and mercy: O come, let us adore him.

From Easter Day until the Ascension

Alleluia. The Lord is risen indeed: O come, let us adore him. Alleluia.

From Ascension Day until the Day of Pentecost

Alleluia. Christ the Lord ascendeth into heaven: O come, let us adore him. Alleluia.

On the Day of Pentecost

Alleluia. The Spirit of the Lord filleth the world: O come, let us adore him. Alleluia.

On Trinity Sunday

Father, Son, and Holy Ghost, one God: O come, let us adore him.

On other Sundays and Weekdays

The earth is the Lord's for he made it: O come, let us adore him.

or this

Worship the Lord in the beauty of holiness: O come, let us adore him.

or this

The mercy of the Lord is everlasting: O come, let us adore him.

The Alleluias in the following Antiphons are used only in Easter Season.

On Feasts of the Incarnation

[Alleluia.] The Word was made flesh and dwelt among us: O come, let us adore him. [Alleluia.]

On All Saints and other Major Saints' Days

[Alleluia.] The Lord is glorious in his saints: O come, let us adore him. [Alleluia.]

Venite   *Psalm 95:1-7; 96:9, 13*

O come, let us sing unto the Lord; *
    let us heartily rejoice in the strength of our salvation.
Let us come before his presence with thanksgiving, *
    and show ourselves glad in him with psalms.

For the Lord is a great God, *
    and a great King above all gods.
In his hand are all the corners of the earth, *
    and the strength of the hills is his also.
The sea is his and he made it, *
    and his hands prepared the dry land.

O come, let us worship and fall down *
    and kneel before the Lord our Maker.
For he is the Lord our God, *
    and we are the people of his pasture
    and the sheep of his hand.

O worship the Lord in the beauty of holiness; *
    let the whole earth stand in awe of him.
For he cometh, for he cometh to judge the earth, *
    and with righteousness to judge the world
    and the peoples with his truth.

or Psalm 95, page 146.

Jubilate   *Psalm 100*

O be joyful in the Lord all ye lands; *
    serve the Lord with gladness
    and come before his presence with a song.

Be ye sure that the Lord he is God;
it is he that hath made us and not we ourselves;*
    we are his people and the sheep of his pasture.

O go your way into his gates with thanksgiving
and into his courts with praise; *
    be thankful unto him and speak good of his Name.

For the Lord is gracious;
his mercy is everlasting; *
    and his truth endureth from generation to generation.

*In Easter Week, in place of an Invitatory Psalm, the following is sung or
said. It may also be used daily until the Day of Pentecost.*

Christ our Passover   *Pascha nostrum*

1 Corinthians 5:7-8; Romans 6:9-11; 1 Corinthians 15:20-22

Alleluia.
Christ our Passover is sacrificed for us, *
    therefore let us keep the feast,
Not with old leaven,
neither with the leaven of malice and wickedness, *
    but with the unleavened bread of sincerity and truth. Alleluia.

Christ being raised from the dead dieth no more; *
    death hath no more dominion over him.
For in that he died, he died unto sin once; *
    but in that he liveth, he liveth unto God.
Likewise reckon ye also yourselves to be dead indeed unto sin, *
    but alive unto God through Jesus Christ our Lord. Alleluia.

Christ is risen from the dead, *
    and become the first fruits of them that slept.
For since by man came death, *
    by man came also the resurrection of the dead.
For as in Adam all die, *
    even so in Christ shall all be made alive. Alleluia.

Then follows

The Psalm or Psalms Appointed

At the end of the Psalms is sung or said

Glory to the Father, and to the Son, and to the Holy Spirit: *
    as it was in the beginning, is now, and will be for ever. Amen.

The Lessons

One or two Lessons, as appointed, are read, the Reader first saying

A Reading (Lesson) from _____.

A citation giving chapter and verse may be added.

After each Lesson the Reader may say

The Word of the Lord.
Answer   Thanks be to God.

Or the Reader may say   Here endeth the Lesson (Reading).

Silence may be kept after each Reading. One of the following Canticles, or one of those on pages 85-95 (Canticles 8-21), is sung or said after each Reading. If three Lessons are used, the Lesson from the Gospel is read after the second Canticle.

1 A Song of Creation *Benedicite, omnia opera Domini*
Song of the Three Young Men, 35-65

This Canticle may be shortened by omitting section II or III

I *Invocation*

O all ye works of the Lord, bless ye the Lord; *
  praise him and magnify him for ever.
O ye angels of the Lord, bless ye the Lord; *
  praise him and magnify him for ever.

II *The Cosmic Order*

O ye heavens, bless ye the Lord; *
  O ye waters that be above the firmament, bless ye the Lord;
O all ye powers of the Lord, bless ye the Lord; *
  praise him and magnify him for ever.

O ye sun and moon, bless ye the Lord; *
   O ye stars of heaven, bless ye the Lord;
O ye showers and dew, bless ye the Lord; *
   praise him and magnify him for ever.

O ye winds of God, bless ye the Lord; *
   O ye fire and heat, bless ye the Lord;
O ye winter and summer, bless ye the Lord; *
   praise him and magnify him for ever.

O ye dews and frosts, bless ye the Lord; *
   O ye frost and cold, bless ye the Lord;
O ye ice and snow, bless ye the Lord; *
   praise him and magnify him for ever.

O ye nights and days, bless ye the Lord; *
   O ye light and darkness, bless ye the Lord;
O ye lightnings and clouds, bless ye the Lord; *
   praise him and magnify him for ever.

III   The Earth and its Creatures

O let the earth bless the Lord; *
   O ye mountains and hills, bless ye the Lord;
O all ye green things upon the earth, bless ye the Lord; *
   praise him and magnify him for ever.

O ye wells, bless ye the Lord; *
   O ye seas and floods, bless ye the Lord;
O ye whales and all that move in the waters, bless ye the Lord; *
   praise him and magnify him for ever.

O all ye fowls of the air, bless ye the Lord; *
   O all ye beasts and cattle, bless ye the Lord;
O ye children of men, bless ye the Lord; *
   praise him and magnify him for ever.

IV   The People of God

O ye people of God, bless ye the Lord; *
    O ye priests of the Lord, bless ye the Lord;
O ye servants of the Lord, bless ye the Lord; *
    praise him and magnify him for ever.

O ye spirits and souls of the righteous, bless ye the Lord; *
    O ye holy and humble men of heart, bless ye the Lord.
Let us bless the Father, the Son, and the Holy Spirit; *
    praise him and magnify him for ever.

2   A Song of Praise   *Benedictus es, Domine*

Song of the Three Young Men, 29-34

Blessed art thou, O Lord God of our fathers; *
    praised and exalted above all for ever.
Blessed art thou for the Name of thy Majesty; *
    praised and exalted above all for ever.
Blessed art thou in the temple of thy holiness; *
    praised and exalted above all for ever.
Blessed art thou that beholdest the depths,
and dwellest between the Cherubim; *
    praised and exalted above all for ever.
Blessed art thou on the glorious throne of thy kingdom; *
    praised and exalted above all for ever.
Blessed art thou in the firmament of heaven; *
    praised and exalted above all for ever.
Blessed art thou, O Father, Son, and Holy Spirit; *
    praised and exalted above all for ever.

3 The Song of Mary *Magnificat*
Luke 1:46-55

My soul doth magnify the Lord, *
 and my spirit hath rejoiced in God my Savior.
For he hath regarded *
 the lowliness of his handmaiden.
For behold from henceforth *
 all generations shall call me blessed.
For he that is mighty hath magnified me, *
 and holy is his Name.
And his mercy is on them that fear him *
 throughout all generations.
He hath showed strength with his arm; *
 he hath scattered the proud in the imagination of their hearts.
He hath put down the mighty from their seat, *
 and hath exalted the humble and meek.
He hath filled the hungry with good things, *
 and the rich he hath sent empty away.
He remembering his mercy hath holpen his servant Israel, *
 as he promised to our forefathers,
 Abraham and his seed for ever.

Glory to the Father, and to the Son, and to the Holy Spirit: *
 as it was in the beginning, is now, and will be for ever. Amen.

4 The Song of Zechariah *Benedictus Dominus Deus*
Luke 1:68-79

Blessed be the Lord God of Israel, *
 for he hath visited and redeemed his people;
And hath raised up a mighty salvation for us *
 in the house of his servant David,
As he spake by the mouth of his holy prophets,*
 which have been since the world began:

That we should be saved from our enemies, *
    and from the hand of all that hate us;
To perform the mercy promised to our forefathers, *
    and to remember his holy covenant;
To perform the oath which he sware to our forefather Abraham, *
    that he would give us,
That we being delivered out of the hand of our enemies *
    might serve him without fear,
In holiness and righteousness before him, *
    all the days of our life.

And thou, child, shalt be called the prophet of the Highest, *
    for thou shalt go before the face of the Lord
              to prepare his ways;
To give knowledge of salvation unto his people *
    for the remission of their sins,
Through the tender mercy of our God, *
    whereby the dayspring from on high hath visited us;
To give light to them that sit in darkness
and in the shadow of death, *
    and to guide our feet into the way of peace.

Glory to the Father, and to the Son, and to the Holy Spirit: *
    as it was in the beginning, is now, and will be for ever. Amen.

5   The Song of Simeon   *Nunc dimittis*
Luke 2:29-32

Lord, now lettest thou thy servant depart in peace, *
    according to thy word;
For mine eyes have seen thy salvation, *
    which thou hast prepared before the face of all people,
To be a light to lighten the Gentiles, *
    and to be the glory of thy people Israel.

Glory to the Father, and to the Son, and to the Holy Spirit: *
    as it was in the beginning, is now, and will be for ever. Amen.

6 Glory be to God *Gloria in excelsis*

Glory be to God on high,
    and on earth peace, good will towards men.

We praise thee, we bless thee,
    we worship thee,
    we glorify thee,
    we give thanks to thee for thy great glory,
O Lord God, heavenly King, God the Father Almighty.

O Lord, the only-begotten Son, Jesus Christ;
O Lord God, Lamb of God, Son of the Father,
    that takest away the sins of the world,
    have mercy upon us.
Thou that takest away the sins of the world,
    receive our prayer.
Thou that sittest at the right hand of God the Father,
    have mercy upon us.

For thou only art holy,
thou only art the Lord,
thou only, O Christ,
    with the Holy Ghost,
    art most high in the glory of God the Father. Amen.

7 We Praise Thee *Te Deum laudamus*

We praise thee, O God; we acknowledge thee to be the Lord.
All the earth doth worship thee, the Father everlasting.
To thee all Angels cry aloud,
    the Heavens and all the Powers therein.
To thee Cherubim and Seraphim continually do cry:

Holy, holy, holy, Lord God of Sabaoth;
Heaven and earth are full of the majesty of thy glory.
The glorious company of the apostles praise thee.
The goodly fellowship of the prophets praise thee.
The noble army of martyrs praise thee.
The holy Church throughout all the world
doth acknowledge thee,
the Father, of an infinite majesty,
thine adorable, true, and only Son,
also the Holy Ghost the Comforter.

Thou art the King of glory, O Christ.
Thou art the everlasting Son of the Father.
When thou tookest upon thee to deliver man,
thou didst humble thyself to be born of a Virgin.
When thou hadst overcome the sharpness of death,
thou didst open the kingdom of heaven to all believers.
Thou sittest at the right hand of God, in the glory of the Father.
We believe that thou shalt come to be our judge.
We therefore pray thee, help thy servants,
whom thou hast redeemed with thy precious blood.
Make them to be numbered with thy saints,
in glory everlasting.

The Apostles' Creed

Officiant and People together, all standing

I believe in God, the Father almighty,
maker of heaven and earth;
And in Jesus Christ his only Son our Lord;
who was conceived by the Holy Ghost,
born of the Virgin Mary,
suffered under Pontius Pilate,
was crucified, dead, and buried.
He descended into hell.

The third day he rose again from the dead.
He ascended into heaven,
    and sitteth on the right hand of God the Father almighty.
From thence he shall come to judge the quick and the dead.
I believe in the Holy Ghost,
    the holy catholic Church,
    the communion of saints,
    the forgiveness of sins,
    the resurrection of the body,
    and the life everlasting. Amen.

The text of the Creed on page 96 may be used instead.

The Prayers

The people stand or kneel

Officiant   The Lord be with you.
People   And with thy spirit.
Officiant   Let us pray.

Officiant and People

Our Father, who art in heaven,
    hallowed be thy Name,
    thy kingdom come,
    thy will be done,
        on earth as it is in heaven.
Give us this day our daily bread.
And forgive us our trespasses,
    as we forgive those who trespass against us.
And lead us not into temptation,
    but deliver us from evil.
For thine is the kingdom, and the power, and the glory,
    for ever and ever. Amen.

Then follows one of these sets of Suffrages

A

V.   O Lord, show thy mercy upon us;
R.   And grant us thy salvation.
V.   Endue thy ministers with righteousness;
R.   And make thy chosen people joyful.
V.   Give peace, O Lord, in all the world;
R.   For only in thee can we live in safety.
V.   Lord, keep this nation under thy care;
R.   And guide us in the way of justice and truth.
V.   Let thy way be known upon earth;
R.   Thy saving health among all nations.
V.   Let not the needy, O Lord, be forgotten;
R.   Nor the hope of the poor be taken away.
V.   Create in us clean hearts, O God;
R.   And sustain us with thy Holy Spirit.

B

V.   O Lord, save thy people, and bless thine heritage;
R.   Govern them and lift them up for ever.
V.   Day by day we magnify thee;
R.   And we worship thy Name ever, world without end.
V.   Vouchsafe, O Lord, to keep us this day without sin;
R.   O Lord, have mercy upon us, have mercy upon us.
V.   O Lord, let thy mercy be upon us;
R.   As our trust is in thee.
V.   O Lord, in thee have I trusted;
R.   Let me never be confounded.

The Officiant then says one or more of the following Collects

The Collect of the Day

A Collect for Sundays

O God, who makest us glad with the weekly remembrance of the glorious resurrection of thy Son our Lord: Grant us this day such blessing through our worship of thee, that the days to come may be spent in thy favor; through the same Jesus Christ our Lord. *Amen.*

A Collect for Fridays

Almighty God, whose most dear Son went not up to joy but first he suffered pain, and entered not into glory before he was crucified: Mercifully grant that we, walking in the way of the cross, may find it none other than the way of life and peace; through the same thy Son Jesus Christ our Lord. *Amen.*

A Collect for Saturdays

Almighty God, who after the creation of the world didst rest from all thy works and sanctify a day of rest for all thy creatures: Grant that we, putting away all earthly anxieties, may be duly prepared for the service of thy sanctuary, and that our rest here upon earth may be a preparation for the eternal rest promised to thy people in heaven; through Jesus Christ our Lord. *Amen.*

A Collect for the Renewal of Life

O God, the King eternal, who dividest the day from the night and turnest the shadow of death into the morning: Drive far from us all wrong desires, incline our hearts to keep thy law, and guide our feet into the way of peace; that, having done thy will with cheerfulness while it was day, we may, when the night cometh, rejoice to give thee thanks; through Jesus Christ our Lord. *Amen.*

A Collect for Peace

O God, who art the author of peace and lover of concord, in knowledge of whom standeth our eternal life, whose service is perfect freedom: Defend us, thy humble servants, in all assaults of our enemies; that we, surely trusting in thy defense, may not fear the power of any adversaries; through the might of Jesus Christ our Lord. *Amen.*

A Collect for Grace

O Lord, our heavenly Father, almighty and everlasting God, who hast safely brought us to the beginning of this day: Defend us in the same with thy mighty power; and grant that this day we fall into no sin, neither run into any kind of danger; but that we, being ordered by thy governance, may do always what is righteous in thy sight; through Jesus Christ our Lord. *Amen.*

A Collect for Guidance

O heavenly Father, in whom we live and move and have our being: We humbly pray thee so to guide and govern us by thy Holy Spirit, that in all the cares and occupations of our life we may not forget thee, but may remember that we are ever walking in thy sight; through Jesus Christ our Lord. *Amen.*

Then, unless the Eucharist or a form of general intercession is to follow, one of these prayers for mission is added

Almighty and everlasting God, by whose Spirit the whole body of thy faithful people is governed and sanctified: Receive our supplications and prayers which we offer before thee for all members of thy holy Church, that in their vocation and ministry they may truly and godly serve thee; through our Lord and Savior Jesus Christ. *Amen.*

or the following

O God, who hast made of one blood all the peoples of the earth, and didst send thy blessed Son to preach peace to those who are far off and to those who are near: Grant that people everywhere may seek after thee and find thee; bring the nations into thy fold; pour out thy Spirit upon all flesh; and hasten the coming of thy kingdom; through the same thy Son Jesus Christ our Lord. *Amen.*

or this

Lord Jesus Christ, who didst stretch out thine arms of love on the hard wood of the cross that everyone might come within the reach of thy saving embrace: So clothe us in thy Spirit that we, reaching forth our hands in love, may bring those who do not know thee to the knowledge and love of thee; for the honor of thy Name. *Amen.*

Here may be sung a hymn or anthem.

Authorized intercessions and thanksgivings may follow.

Before the close of the Office one or both of the following may be used

The General Thanksgiving

Officiant and People

Almighty God, Father of all mercies,
we thine unworthy servants
do give thee most humble and hearty thanks
for all thy goodness and loving-kindness
to us and to all men.
We bless thee for our creation, preservation,
and all the blessings of this life;
but above all for thine inestimable love
in the redemption of the world by our Lord Jesus Christ,
for the means of grace, and for the hope of glory.

And, we beseech thee,
give us that due sense of all thy mercies,
that our hearts may be unfeignedly thankful;
and that we show forth thy praise,
not only with our lips, but in our lives,
by giving up our selves to thy service,
and by walking before thee
in holiness and righteousness all our days;
through Jesus Christ our Lord,
to whom, with thee and the Holy Ghost,
be all honor and glory, world without end. Amen.

A Prayer of St. Chrysostom

Almighty God, who hast given us grace at this time with one accord to make our common supplication unto thee, and hast promised through thy well-beloved Son that when two or three are gathered together in his Name thou wilt be in the midst of them: Fulfill now, O Lord, the desires and petitions of thy servants as may be best for us; granting us in this world knowledge of thy truth, and in the world to come life everlasting. *Amen.*

Then may be said

Let us bless the Lord.
Thanks be to God.

From Easter Day through the Day of Pentecost "Alleluia, alleluia" may be added to the preceding versicle and response.

The Officiant may then conclude with one of the following

The grace of our Lord Jesus Christ, and the love of God, and the fellowship of the Holy Ghost, be with us all evermore.
Amen.   *2 Corinthians 13:14*

May the God of hope fill us with all joy and peace in believing through the power of the Holy Spirit. *Amen.*
Romans 15:13

Glory to God whose power, working in us, can do infinitely more than we can ask or imagine: Glory to him from generation to generation in the Church, and in Christ Jesus for ever and ever. *Amen.*   *Ephesians 3:20, 21*

Daily Evening Prayer: Rite One

The Officiant begins the service with one or more of the following sentences of Scripture, or of those on pages 37-40;

or with the Service of Light on pages 109-112, and continuing with the appointed Psalmody;

or with the versicle "O God, make speed to save us" on page 63.

Let my prayer be set forth in thy sight as the incense, and let the lifting up of my hands be an evening sacrifice.
Psalm 141:2

Grace be unto you, and peace, from God our Father, and from the Lord Jesus Christ.   *Philippians 1:2*

O worship the Lord in the beauty of holiness; let the whole earth stand in awe of him.   *Psalm 96:9*

Thine is the day, O God, thine also the night; thou hast established the moon and the sun. Thou hast fixed all the boundaries of the earth; thou hast made summer and winter.
Psalm 74:15, 16

I will bless the Lord who giveth me counsel; my heart teacheth me, night after night. I have set the Lord always before me; because he is at my right hand, I shall not fall.
Psalm 16:7, 8

Seek him that made the Pleiades and Orion, that turneth deep darkness into the morning, and darkeneth the day into night; that calleth for the waters of the sea, and poureth them out upon the face of the earth: The Lord is his Name.   *Amos 5:8*

If I say, "Surely the darkness will cover me, and the light around me turn to night," darkness is not dark to thee, O Lord; the night is as bright as the day; darkness and light to thee are both alike.   *Psalm 139:10, 11*

Jesus said, " I am the light of the world; he that followeth me shall not walk in darkness, but shall have the light of life." *John 8:12*

The following Confession of Sin may then be said; or the Office may continue at once with "O God make speed to save us."

Confession of Sin

The Officiant says to the people

Dear friends in Christ, here in the presence of Almighty God, let us kneel in silence, and with penitent and obedient hearts confess our sins, so that we may obtain forgiveness by his infinite goodness and mercy.

or this

Let us humbly confess our sins unto Almighty God.

Silence may be kept.

Officiant and People together, all kneeling

Almighty and most merciful Father,
we have erred and strayed from thy ways like lost sheep,
we have followed too much the devices and desires of our
    own hearts,

we have offended against thy holy laws,
we have left undone those things which we ought to
     have done,
and we have done those things which we ought not to
     have done.
But thou, O Lord, have mercy upon us,
spare thou those who confess their faults,
restore thou those who are penitent,
according to thy promises declared unto mankind
in Christ Jesus our Lord;
and grant, O most merciful Father, for his sake,
that we may hereafter live a godly, righteous, and sober life,
to the glory of thy holy Name. Amen.

The Priest alone stands and says

The Almighty and merciful Lord grant you absolution and
remission of all your sins, true repentance, amendment of
life, and the grace and consolation of his Holy Spirit. *Amen.*

*A deacon or lay person using the preceding form remains kneeling, and
substitutes "us" for "you" and "our" for "your."*

The Invitatory and Psalter

All stand

Officiant   O God, make speed to save us.
People   O Lord, make haste to help us.

Officiant and People

Glory to the Father, and to the Son, and to the Holy Spirit: as
it was in the beginning, is now, and will be for ever. Amen.

Except in Lent,   Alleluia   *may be added.*

O Gracious Light   *Phos hilaron*

O gracious Light,
pure brightness of the everliving Father in heaven,
O Jesus Christ, holy and blessed!

Now as we come to the setting of the sun,
and our eyes behold the vesper light,
we sing thy praises, O God: Father, Son, and Holy Spirit.

Thou art worthy at all times to be praised by happy voices,
O Son of God, O Giver of life,
and to be glorified through all the worlds.

Then follows

The Psalm or Psalms Appointed

At the end of the Psalms is sung or said

Glory to the Father, and to the Son, and to the Holy Spirit: *
    as it was in the beginning, is now, and will be for ever. Amen.

The Lessons

One or two Lessons, as appointed, are read, the Reader first saying

A Reading (Lesson) from _____.

A citation giving chapter and verse may be added.

After each Lesson the Reader may say

The Word of the Lord.
Answer   Thanks be to God.

Or the Reader may say   Here endeth the Lesson (Reading).

Silence may be kept after each Reading. One of the following Canticles, or one of those on pages 47-52, or 85-95, is sung or said after each Reading. If three Lessons are used, the Lesson from the Gospel is read after the second Canticle.

The Song of Mary   *Magnificat*
Luke 1:46-55

My soul doth magnify the Lord, *
    and my spirit hath rejoiced in God my Savior.
For he hath regarded *
    the lowliness of his handmaiden.
For behold from henceforth *
    all generations shall call me blessed.
For he that is mighty hath magnified me, *
    and holy is his Name.
And his mercy is on them that fear him *
    throughout all generations.
He hath showed strength with his arm; *
    he hath scattered the proud in the imagination of their hearts.
He hath put down the mighty from their seat, *
    and hath exalted the humble and meek.
He hath filled the hungry with good things, *
    and the rich he hath sent empty away.
He remembering his mercy hath holpen his servant Israel, *
    as he promised to our forefathers,
    Abraham and his seed for ever.

Glory to the Father, and to the Son, and to the Holy Spirit: *
    as it was in the beginning, is now, and will be for ever. Amen.

The Song of Simeon *Nunc dimittis*

Luke 2:29-32

Lord, now lettest thou thy servant depart in peace, *
   according to thy word;
For mine eyes have seen thy salvation, *
   which thou hast prepared before the face of all people,
To be a light to lighten the Gentiles, *
   and to be the glory of thy people Israel.

Glory to the Father, and to the Son, and to the Holy Spirit: *
   as it was in the beginning, is now, and will be for ever. Amen.

The Apostles' Creed

Officiant and People together, all standing

I believe in God, the Father almighty,
   maker of heaven and earth;
And in Jesus Christ his only Son our Lord;
   who was conceived by the Holy Ghost,
   born of the Virgin Mary,
   suffered under Pontius Pilate,
   was crucified, dead, and buried.
   He descended into hell.
   The third day he rose again from the dead.
   He ascended into heaven,
   and sitteth on the right hand of God the Father almighty.
   From thence he shall come to judge the quick and the dead.
I believe in the Holy Ghost,
   the holy catholic Church,
   the communion of saints,
   the forgiveness of sins,
   the resurrection of the body,
   and the life everlasting. Amen.

The text of the Creed on page 120 may be used instead.

The Prayers

The people stand or kneel

Officiant	The Lord be with you.
People	And with thy spirit.
Officiant	Let us pray.

Officiant and People

Our Father, who art in heaven,
   hallowed be thy Name,
   thy kingdom come,
   thy will be done,
      on earth as it is in heaven.
Give us this day our daily bread.
And forgive us our trespasses,
   as we forgive those who trespass against us.
And lead us not into temptation,
   but deliver us from evil.
For thine is the kingdom, and the power, and the glory,
   for ever and ever. Amen.

Then follows one of these sets of Suffrages

A

V.   O Lord, show thy mercy upon us;
R.   And grant us thy salvation.
V.   Endue thy ministers with righteousness;
R.   And make thy chosen people joyful.
V.   Give peace, O Lord, in all the world;
R.   For only in thee can we live in safety.
V.   Lord, keep this nation under thy care;
R.   And guide us in the way of justice and truth.

V. Let thy way be known upon earth;
R. Thy saving health among all nations.
V. Let not the needy, O Lord, be forgotten;
R. Nor the hope of the poor be taken away.
V. Create in us clean hearts, O God;
R. And sustain us with thy Holy Spirit.

B

That this evening may be holy, good, and peaceful,
We entreat thee, O Lord.

That thy holy angels may lead us in paths of peace and
goodwill,
We entreat thee, O Lord.

That we may be pardoned and forgiven for our sins
and offenses,
We entreat thee, O Lord.

That there may be peace to thy Church and to the whole
world,
We entreat thee, O Lord.

That we may depart this life in thy faith and fear, and
not be condemned before the great judgment seat
of Christ,
We entreat thee, O Lord.

That we may be bound together by thy Holy Spirit in
the communion of [_____ and] all thy saints,
entrusting one another and all our life to Christ,
We entreat thee, O Lord.

The Officiant then says one or more of the following Collects

The Collect of the Day

A Collect for Sundays

Lord God, whose Son our Savior Jesus Christ triumphed over the powers of death and prepared for us our place in the new Jerusalem: Grant that we, who have this day given thanks for his resurrection, may praise thee in that City of which he is the light; and where he liveth and reigneth for ever and ever. *Amen.*

A Collect for Fridays

O Lord Jesus Christ, who by thy death didst take away the sting of death: Grant unto us thy servants so to follow in faith where thou hast led the way, that we may at length fall asleep peacefully in thee, and awake up after thy likeness; for thy tender mercies' sake. *Amen.*

A Collect for Saturdays

O God, the source of eternal light: Shed forth thine unending day upon us who watch for thee, that our lips may praise thee, our lives may bless thee, and our worship on the morrow may give thee glory; through Jesus Christ our Lord. *Amen.*

A Collect for Peace

O God, from whom all holy desires, all good counsels, and all just works do proceed: Give unto thy servants that peace which the world cannot give, that our hearts may be set to obey thy commandments, and also that by thee, we, being defended from the fear of all enemies, may pass our time in rest and quietness; through the merits of Jesus Christ our Savior. *Amen.*

A Collect for Aid against Perils

Lighten our darkness, we beseech thee, O Lord; and by thy great mercy defend us from all perils and dangers of this night; for the love of thy only Son, our Savior Jesus Christ. *Amen.*

A Collect for Protection

O God, who art the life of all who live, the light of the faithful, the strength of those who labor, and the repose of the dead: We thank thee for the timely blessings of the day, and humbly beseech thy merciful protection all the night. Bring us, we pray thee, in safety to the morning hours; through him who died for us and rose again, thy Son our Savior Jesus Christ. *Amen.*

A Collect for the Presence of Christ

Lord Jesus, stay with us, for evening is at hand and the day is past; be our companion in the way, kindle our hearts, and awaken hope, that we may know thee as thou art revealed in Scripture and the breaking of bread. Grant this for the sake of thy love. *Amen.*

Then, unless the Eucharist or a form of general intercession is to follow, one of these prayers for mission is added

O God and Father of all, whom the whole heavens adore: Let the whole earth also worship thee, all nations obey thee, all tongues confess and bless thee, and men and women everywhere love thee and serve thee in peace; through Jesus Christ our Lord. *Amen.*

or the following

Keep watch, dear Lord, with those who work, or watch, or weep this night, and give thine angels charge over those who sleep. Tend the sick, Lord Christ; give rest to the weary, bless the dying, soothe the suffering, pity the afflicted, shield the joyous; and all for thy love's sake. *Amen.*

or this

O God, who dost manifest in thy servants the signs of thy presence: Send forth upon us the Spirit of love, that in companionship with one another thine abounding grace may increase among us; through Jesus Christ our Lord. *Amen.*

Here may be sung a hymn or anthem.

Authorized intercessions and thanksgivings may follow.

Before the close of the Office one or both of the following may be used

The General Thanksgiving

Officiant and People

Almighty God, Father of all mercies,
we thine unworthy servants
do give thee most humble and hearty thanks
for all thy goodness and loving-kindness
to us and to all men.
We bless thee for our creation, preservation,
and all the blessings of this life;
but above all for thine inestimable love
in the redemption of the world by our Lord Jesus Christ,
for the means of grace, and for the hope of glory.
And, we beseech thee,
give us that due sense of all thy mercies,
that our hearts may be unfeignedly thankful;

and that we show forth thy praise,
not only with our lips, but in our lives,
by giving up our selves to thy service,
and by walking before thee
in holiness and righteousness all our days;
through Jesus Christ our Lord,
to whom, with thee and the Holy Ghost,
be all honor and glory, world without end. Amen.

A Prayer of St. Chrysostom

Almighty God, who hast given us grace at this time with one
accord to make our common supplication unto thee, and
hast promised through thy well-beloved Son that when two
or three are gathered together in his Name thou wilt be in the
midst of them: Fulfill now, O Lord, the desires and petitions
of thy servants as may be best for us; granting us in this
world knowledge of thy truth, and in the world to come life
everlasting. *Amen.*

Then may be said

Let us bless the Lord.
Thanks be to God.

*From Easter Day through the Day of Pentecost "Alleluia, alleluia" may
be added to the preceding versicle and response.*

The Officiant may then conclude with one of the following

The grace of our Lord Jesus Christ, and the love of God, and
the fellowship of the Holy Ghost, be with us all evermore.
Amen.   *2 Corinthians 13:14*

May the God of hope fill us with all joy and peace in believing through the power of the Holy Spirit. *Amen.*
Romans 15:13

Glory to God whose power, working in us, can do infinitely more than we can ask or imagine: Glory to him from generation to generation in the Church, and in Christ Jesus for ever and ever. *Amen.*   *Ephesians 3:20, 21*

Concerning the Service

In the Daily Office, the term "Officiant" is used to denote the person, clerical or lay, who leads the Office.

It is appropriate that other persons be assigned to read the Lessons, and to lead other parts of the service not assigned to the officiant. The bishop, when present, appropriately concludes the Office with a blessing.

At celebrations of the Holy Eucharist, the Order for Morning or Evening Prayer may be used in place of all that precedes the Offertory.

Additional Directions are on page 141.

Daily Morning Prayer:
Rite Two

The Officiant begins the service with one or more of these sentences of Scripture, or with the versicle "Lord, open our lips" on page 80.

Advent

Watch, for you do not know when the master of the house will come, in the evening, or at midnight, or at cockcrow, or in the morning, lest he come suddenly and find you asleep. *Mark 13:35, 36*

In the wilderness prepare the way of the Lord, make straight in the desert a highway for our God. *Isaiah 40:3*

The glory of the Lord shall be revealed, and all flesh shall see it together. *Isaiah 40:5*

Christmas

Behold, I bring you good news of a great joy which will come to all the people; for to you is born this day in the city of David, a Savior, who is Christ the Lord. *Luke 2:10, 11*

Behold, the dwelling of God is with mankind. He will dwell with them, and they shall be his people, and God himself will be with them, and be their God. *Revelation 21:3*

Epiphany

Nations shall come to your light, and kings to the brightness of your rising. *Isaiah 60:3*

I will give you as a light to the nations, that my salvation may reach to the end of the earth. *Isaiah 49:6b*

From the rising of the sun to its setting my Name shall be great among the nations, and in every place incense shall be offered to my Name, and a pure offering; for my Name shall be great among the nations, says the Lord of hosts. *Malachi 1:11*

Lent

If we say we have no sin, we deceive ourselves, and the truth is not in us, but if we confess our sins, God, who is faithful and just, will forgive our sins and cleanse us from all unrighteousness. *1 John 1:8, 9*

Rend your hearts and not your garments. Return to the Lord your God, for he is gracious and merciful, slow to anger and abounding in steadfast love, and repents of evil. *Joel 2:13*

I will arise and go to my father, and I will say to him, "Father, I have sinned against heaven and before you; I am no longer worthy to be called your son." *Luke 15:18, 19*

To the Lord our God belong mercy and forgiveness, because we have rebelled against him and have not obeyed the voice of the Lord our God by following his laws which he set before us. *Daniel 9:9, 10*

Jesus said, "If anyone would come after me, let him deny himself and take up his cross and follow me." *Mark 8:34*

Holy Week

All we like sheep have gone astray; we have turned every one to his own way; and the Lord has laid on him the iniquity of us all.   *Isaiah 53:6*

Is it nothing to you, all you who pass by? Look and see if there is any sorrow like my sorrow which was brought upon me, whom the Lord has afflicted.   *Lamentations 1:12*

Easter Season, including Ascension Day
and the Day of Pentecost

Alleluia! Christ is risen.
The Lord is risen indeed. Alleluia!

On this day the Lord has acted; we will rejoice and be glad in it.   *Psalm 118:24*

Thanks be to God, who gives us the victory through our Lord Jesus Christ.   *1 Corinthians 15:57*

If then you have been raised with Christ, seek the things that are above, where Christ is, seated at the right hand of God.
Colossians 3:1

Christ has entered, not into a sanctuary made with hands, a copy of the true one, but into heaven itself, now to appear in the presence of God on our behalf.   *Hebrews 9:24*

You shall receive power when the Holy Spirit has come upon you; and you shall be my witnesses in Jerusalem, and in all Judea, and Samaria, and to the ends of the earth.   *Acts 1:8*

Trinity Sunday

Holy, holy, holy is the Lord God Almighty, who was, and is, and is to come!   *Revelation 4:8*

All Saints and other Major Saints' Days

We give thanks to the Father, who has made us worthy to share in the inheritance of the saints in light.   *Colossians 1:12*

You are no longer strangers and sojourners, but fellow citizens with the saints and members of the household of God.   *Ephesians 2:19*

Their sound has gone out into all lands, and their message to the ends of the world.   *Psalm 19:4*

Occasions of Thanksgiving

Give thanks to the Lord, and call upon his Name; make known his deeds among the peoples.   *Psalm 105:1*

At any Time

Grace to you and peace from God our Father and the Lord Jesus Christ.   *Philippians 1:2*

I was glad when they said to me, "Let us go to the house of the Lord."   *Psalm 122:1*

Let the words of my mouth and the meditation of my heart be acceptable in your sight, O Lord, my strength and my redeemer.   *Psalm 19:14*

Send out your light and your truth, that they may lead me, and bring me to your holy hill and to your dwelling.
Psalm 43:3

The Lord is in his holy temple; let all the earth keep silence before him.   *Habakkuk 2:20*

The hour is coming, and now is, when the true worshipers will worship the Father in spirit and truth, for such the Father seeks to worship him.   *John 4:23*

Thus says the high and lofty One who inhabits eternity, whose name is Holy, "I dwell in the high and holy place and also with the one who has a contrite and humble spirit, to revive the spirit of the humble and to revive the heart of the contrite."   *Isaiah 57:15*

Confession of Sin

The Officiant says to the people

Dearly beloved, we have come together in the presence of Almighty God our heavenly Father, to set forth his praise, to hear his holy Word, and to ask, for ourselves and on behalf of others, those things that are necessary for our life and our salvation. And so that we may prepare ourselves in heart and mind to worship him, let us kneel in silence, and with penitent and obedient hearts confess our sins, that we may obtain forgiveness by his infinite goodness and mercy.

or this

Let us confess our sins against God and our neighbor.

Silence may be kept.

Officiant and People together, all kneeling

Most merciful God,
we confess that we have sinned against you
in thought, word, and deed,
by what we have done,
and by what we have left undone.
We have not loved you with our whole heart;
we have not loved our neighbors as ourselves.
We are truly sorry and we humbly repent.
For the sake of your Son Jesus Christ,
have mercy on us and forgive us;
that we may delight in your will,
and walk in your ways,
to the glory of your Name. Amen.

Almighty God have mercy on you, forgive you all your sins through our Lord Jesus Christ, strengthen you in all goodness, and by the power of the Holy Spirit keep you in eternal life. *Amen.*

A deacon or lay person using the preceding form remains kneeling, and substitutes "us" for "you" and "our" for "your."

The Invitatory and Psalter

All stand

Officiant　Lord, open our lips.
People　　And our mouth shall proclaim your praise.

Officiant and People

Glory to the Father, and to the Son, and to the Holy Spirit: as it was in the beginning, is now, and will be for ever. Amen.

Except in Lent, add　Alleluia.

Then follows one of the Invitatory Psalms, Venite or Jubilate.

One of the following Antiphons may be sung or said with the Invitatory Psalm

In Advent

Our King and Savior now draws near: Come let us adore him.

On the Twelve Days of Christmas

Alleluia. To us a child is born: Come let us adore him. Alleluia.

From the Epiphany through the Baptism of Christ, and on the Feasts of the Transfiguration and Holy Cross

The Lord has shown forth his glory: Come let us adore him.

In Lent

The Lord is full of compassion and mercy: Come let us adore him.

From Easter Day until the Ascension

Alleluia. The Lord is risen indeed: Come let us adore him. Alleluia.

From Ascension Day until the Day of Pentecost

Alleluia. Christ the Lord has ascended into heaven: Come let us adore him. Alleluia.

On the Day of Pentecost

Alleluia. The Spirit of the Lord renews the face of the earth: Come let us adore him. Alleluia.

On Trinity Sunday

Father, Son, and Holy Spirit, one God: Come let us adore him.

On other Sundays and weekdays

The earth is the Lord's for he made it: Come let us adore him.

or this

Worship the Lord in the beauty of holiness: Come let us adore him.

or this

The mercy of the Lord is everlasting: Come let us adore him.

The Alleluias in the following Antiphons are used only in Easter Season.

On Feasts of the Incarnation

[Alleluia.] The Word was made flesh and dwelt among us:
Come let us adore him. [Alleluia.]

On All Saints and other Major Saints' Days

[Alleluia.] The Lord is glorious in his saints: Come let us
adore him. [Alleluia.]

Venite   *Psalm 95:1-7*

Come, let us sing to the Lord; *
    let us shout for joy to the Rock of our salvation.
Let us come before his presence with thanksgiving *
    and raise a loud shout to him with psalms.

For the Lord is a great God, *
    and a great King above all gods.
In his hand are the caverns of the earth, *
    and the heights of the hills are his also.
The sea is his, for he made it, *
    and his hands have molded the dry land.

Come, let us bow down, and bend the knee, *
    and kneel before the Lord our Maker.
For he is our God,
and we are the people of his pasture and the sheep of his hand. *
    Oh, that today you would hearken to his voice!

or Psalm 95, page 724.

Jubilate   *Psalm 100*

Be joyful in the Lord, all you lands; *
    serve the Lord with gladness
    and come before his presence with a song.

Know this: The Lord himself is God; *
　he himself has made us, and we are his;
　we are his people and the sheep of his pasture.

Enter his gates with thanksgiving;
go into his courts with praise; *
　give thanks to him and call upon his Name.

For the Lord is good;
his mercy is everlasting; *
　and his faithfulness endures from age to age.

In Easter Week, in place of an Invitatory Psalm, the following is sung or said. It may also be used daily until the Day of Pentecost.

Christ our Passover　*Pascha nostrum*

1 Corinthians 5:7-8; Romans 6:9-11; 1 Corinthians 15:20-22

Alleluia.
Christ our Passover has been sacrificed for us; *
　therefore let us keep the feast,
Not with the old leaven, the leaven of malice and evil, *
　but with the unleavened bread of sincerity and truth. Alleluia.

Christ being raised from the dead will never die again; *
　death no longer has dominion over him.
The death that he died, he died to sin, once for all; *
　but the life he lives, he lives to God.
So also consider yourselves dead to sin, *
　and alive to God in Jesus Christ our Lord. Alleluia.

Christ has been raised from the dead, *
　the first fruits of those who have fallen asleep.
For since by a man came death, *
　by a man has come also the resurrection of the dead.
For as in Adam all die, *
　so also in Christ shall all be made alive. Alleluia.

Then follows

The Psalm or Psalms Appointed

At the end of the Psalms is sung or said

Glory to the Father, and to the Son, and to the Holy Spirit: *
   as it was in the beginning, is now, and will be for ever. Amen.

The Lessons

One or two Lessons, as appointed, are read, the Reader first saying

A Reading (Lesson) from _____ .

A citation giving chapter and verse may be added.

After each Lesson the Reader may say

      The Word of the Lord.
Answer   Thanks be to God.

Or the Reader may say   Here ends the Lesson (Reading).

*Silence may be kept after each Reading. One of the following Canticles,
or one of those on pages 47-52 (Canticles 1-7), is sung or said after
each Reading. If three Lessons are used, the Lesson from the Gospel is
read after the second Canticle.*

8   The Song of Moses   *Cantemus Domino*
Exodus 15:1-6, 11-13, 17-18

Especially suitable for use in Easter Season

I will sing to the Lord, for he is lofty and uplifted; *
  the horse and its rider has he hurled into the sea.
The Lord is my strength and my refuge; *
  the Lord has become my Savior.
This is my God and I will praise him, *
  the God of my people and I will exalt him.
The Lord is a mighty warrior; *
  Yahweh is his Name.
The chariots of Pharaoh and his army has he hurled into the sea; *
  the finest of those who bear armor have been
                    drowned in the Red Sea.
The fathomless deep has overwhelmed them; *
  they sank into the depths like a stone.
Your right hand, O Lord, is glorious in might; *
  your right hand, O Lord, has overthrown the enemy.
Who can be compared with you, O Lord, among the gods? *
  who is like you, glorious in holiness,
  awesome in renown, and worker of wonders?
You stretched forth your right hand; *
  the earth swallowed them up.
With your constant love you led the people you redeemed; *
  with your might you brought them in safety to
                    your holy dwelling.
You will bring them in and plant them *
  on the mount of your possession,
The resting-place you have made for yourself, O Lord, *
  the sanctuary, O Lord, that your hand has established.
The Lord shall reign *
  for ever and for ever.

Glory to the Father, and to the Son, and to the Holy Spirit: *
  as it was in the beginning, is now, and will be for ever. Amen.

9 The First Song of Isaiah   *Ecce, Deus*
Isaiah 12:2-6

Surely, it is God who saves me; *
    I will trust in him and not be afraid.
For the Lord is my stronghold and my sure defense, *
    and he will be my Savior.
Therefore you shall draw water with rejoicing *
    from the springs of salvation.
And on that day you shall say, *
    Give thanks to the Lord and call upon his Name;
Make his deeds known among the peoples; *
    see that they remember that his Name is exalted.
Sing the praises of the Lord, for he has done great things, *
    and this is known in all the world.
Cry aloud, inhabitants of Zion, ring out your joy, *
    for the great one in the midst of you is the Holy One of Israel.

Glory to the Father, and to the Son, and to the Holy Spirit: *
    as it was in the beginning, is now, and will be for ever. Amen.

10 The Second Song of Isaiah   *Quærite Dominum*
Isaiah 55:6-11

Seek the Lord while he wills to be found; *
    call upon him when he draws near.
Let the wicked forsake their ways *
    and the evil ones their thoughts;
And let them turn to the Lord, and he will have compassion, *
    and to our God, for he will richly pardon.
For my thoughts are not your thoughts, *
    nor your ways my ways, says the Lord.
For as the heavens are higher than the earth, *
    so are my ways higher than your ways,
    and my thoughts than your thoughts.

For as rain and snow fall from the heavens *
    and return not again, but water the earth,
Bringing forth life and giving growth, *
    seed for sowing and bread for eating,
So is my word that goes forth from my mouth; *
    it will not return to me empty;
But it will accomplish that which I have purposed, *
    and prosper in that for which I sent it.

Glory to the Father, and to the Son, and to the Holy Spirit: *
    as it was in the beginning, is now, and will be for ever. Amen.

11 The Third Song of Isaiah *Surge, illuminare*

Isaiah 60:1-3, 11a, 14c, 18-19

Arise, shine, for your light has come, *
    and the glory of the Lord has dawned upon you.
For behold, darkness covers the land; *
    deep gloom enshrouds the peoples.
But over you the Lord will rise, *
    and his glory will appear upon you.
Nations will stream to your light, *
    and kings to the brightness of your dawning.
Your gates will always be open; *
    by day or night they will never be shut.
They will call you, The City of the Lord, *
    The Zion of the Holy One of Israel.
Violence will no more be heard in your land, *
    ruin or destruction within your borders.
You will call your walls, Salvation, *
    and all your portals, Praise.
The sun will no more be your light by day; *
    by night you will not need the brightness of the moon.

The Lord will be your everlasting light, *
    and your God will be your glory.

Glory to the Father, and to the Son, and to the Holy Spirit: *
    as it was in the beginning, is now, and will be for ever. Amen.

12 A Song of Creation *Benedicite, omnia opera Domini*
Song of the Three Young Men, 35-65

*One or more sections of this Canticle may be used. Whatever the
selection, it begins with the Invocation and concludes with the Doxology.*

Invocation

Glorify the Lord, all you works of the Lord, *
    praise him and highly exalt him for ever.
In the firmament of his power, glorify the Lord, *
    praise him and highly exalt him for ever.

I The Cosmic Order

Glorify the Lord, you angels and all powers of the Lord, *
    O heavens and all waters above the heavens.
Sun and moon and stars of the sky, glorify the Lord, *
    praise him and highly exalt him for ever.

Glorify the Lord, every shower of rain and fall of dew, *
    all winds and fire and heat.
Winter and summer, glorify the Lord, *
    praise him and highly exalt him for ever.

Glorify the Lord, O chill and cold, *
    drops of dew and flakes of snow.
Frost and cold, ice and sleet, glorify the Lord, *
    praise him and highly exalt him for ever.

Glorify the Lord, O nights and days, *
 O shining light and enfolding dark.
Storm clouds and thunderbolts, glorify the Lord, *
 praise him and highly exalt him for ever.

II   The Earth and its Creatures

Let the earth glorify the Lord, *
 praise him and highly exalt him for ever.
Glorify the Lord, O mountains and hills,
and all that grows upon the earth, *
 praise him and highly exalt him for ever.

Glorify the Lord, O springs of water, seas, and streams, *
 O whales and all that move in the waters.
All birds of the air, glorify the Lord, *
 praise him and highly exalt him for ever.

Glorify the Lord, O beasts of the wild, *
 and all you flocks and herds.
O men and women everywhere, glorify the Lord, *
 praise him and highly exalt him for ever.

III   The People of God

Let the people of God glorify the Lord, *
 praise him and highly exalt him for ever.
Glorify the Lord, O priests and servants of the Lord, *
 praise him and highly exalt him for ever.

Glorify the Lord, O spirits and souls of the righteous, *
 praise him and highly exalt him for ever.
You that are holy and humble of heart, glorify the Lord, *
 praise him and highly exalt him for ever.

Doxology

Let us glorify the Lord: Father, Son, and Holy Spirit; *
  praise him and highly exalt him for ever.
In the firmament of his power, glorify the Lord, *
  praise him and highly exalt him for ever.

13 A Song of Praise   *Benedictus es, Domine*
   Song of the Three Young Men, 29-34

Glory to you, Lord God of our fathers; *
  you are worthy of praise; glory to you.
Glory to you for the radiance of your holy Name; *
  we will praise you and highly exalt you for ever.

Glory to you in the splendor of your temple; *
  on the throne of your majesty, glory to you.
Glory to you, seated between the Cherubim; *
  we will praise you and highly exalt you for ever.

Glory to you, beholding the depths; *
  in the high vault of heaven, glory to you.
Glory to you, Father, Son, and Holy Spirit; *
  we will praise you and highly exalt you for ever.

14 A Song of Penitence   *Kyrie Pantokrator*
   Prayer of Manasseh, 1-2, 4, 6-7, 11-15

Especially suitable in Lent, and on other penitential occasions

O Lord and Ruler of the hosts of heaven, *
  God of Abraham, Isaac, and Jacob,
  and of all their righteous offspring:
You made the heavens and the earth, *
  with all their vast array.

All things quake with fear at your presence; *
    they tremble because of your power.
But your merciful promise is beyond all measure; *
    it surpasses all that our minds can fathom.
O Lord, you are full of compassion, *
    long-suffering, and abounding in mercy.
You hold back your hand; *
    you do not punish as we deserve.
In your great goodness, Lord,
you have promised forgiveness to sinners, *
    that they may repent of their sin and be saved.
And now, O Lord, I bend the knee of my heart, *
    and make my appeal, sure of your gracious goodness.
I have sinned, O Lord, I have sinned, *
    and I know my wickedness only too well.
Therefore I make this prayer to you: *
    Forgive me, Lord, forgive me.
Do not let me perish in my sin, *
    nor condemn me to the depths of the earth.
For you, O Lord, are the God of those who repent, *
    and in me you will show forth your goodness.
Unworthy as I am, you will save me,
in accordance with your great mercy, *
    and I will praise you without ceasing all the days of my life.
For all the powers of heaven sing your praises, *
    and yours is the glory to ages of ages. Amen.

15 The Song of Mary *Magnificat*

Luke 1:46-55

My soul proclaims the greatness of the Lord,
my spirit rejoices in God my Savior; *
    for he has looked with favor on his lowly servant.

From this day all generations will call me blessed: *
    the Almighty has done great things for me,
    and holy is his Name.
He has mercy on those who fear him *
    in every generation.
He has shown the strength of his arm, *
    he has scattered the proud in their conceit.
He has cast down the mighty from their thrones, *
    and has lifted up the lowly.
He has filled the hungry with good things, *
    and the rich he has sent away empty.
He has come to the help of his servant Israel, *
    for he has remembered his promise of mercy,
The promise he made to our fathers, *
    to Abraham and his children for ever.

Glory to the Father, and to the Son, and to the Holy Spirit: *
    as it was in the beginning, is now, and will be for ever. Amen.

16 The Song of Zechariah   *Benedictus Dominus Deus*
   Luke 1:68-79

Blessed be the Lord, the God of Israel; *
    he has come to his people and set them free.
He has raised up for us a mighty savior, *
    born of the house of his servant David.
Through his holy prophets he promised of old,
  that he would save us from our enemies, *
    from the hands of all who hate us.
He promised to show mercy to our fathers *
    and to remember his holy covenant.
This was the oath he swore to our father Abraham, *
    to set us free from the hands of our enemies,
Free to worship him without fear, *
    holy and righteous in his sight
    all the days of our life.

You, my child, shall be called the prophet of the Most High, *
 for you will go before the Lord to prepare his way,
To give his people knowledge of salvation *
 by the forgiveness of their sins.
In the tender compassion of our God *
 the dawn from on high shall break upon us,
To shine on those who dwell in darkness and the
 shadow of death, *
 and to guide our feet into the way of peace.

Glory to the Father, and to the Son, and to the Holy Spirit: *
 as it was in the beginning, is now, and will be for ever. Amen.

17 The Song of Simeon *Nunc dimittis*
Luke 2:29-32

Lord, you now have set your servant free *
 to go in peace as you have promised;
For these eyes of mine have seen the Savior, *
 whom you have prepared for all the world to see:
A Light to enlighten the nations, *
 and the glory of your people Israel.

Glory to the Father, and to the Son, and to the Holy Spirit: *
 as it was in the beginning, is now, and will be for ever. Amen.

18 A Song to the Lamb *Dignus es*
Revelation 4:11; 5:9-10, 13

Splendor and honor and kingly power *
 are yours by right, O Lord our God,
For you created everything that is, *
 and by your will they were created and have their being;

And yours by right, O Lamb that was slain, *
    for with your blood you have redeemed for God,
From every family, language, people, and nation, *
    a kingdom of priests to serve our God.

And so, to him who sits upon the throne, *
    and to Christ the Lamb,
Be worship and praise, dominion and splendor, *
    for ever and for evermore.

19   The Song of the Redeemed   *Magna et mirabilia*
Revelation 15:3-4

O ruler of the universe, Lord God,
great deeds are they that you have done, *
    surpassing human understanding.
Your ways are ways of righteousness and truth, *
    O King of all the ages.

Who can fail to do you homage, Lord,
and sing the praises of your Name? *
    for you only are the Holy One.
All nations will draw near and fall down before you, *
    because your just and holy works have been revealed.

Glory to the Father, and to the Son, and to the Holy Spirit: *
    as it was in the beginning, is now, and will be for ever. Amen.

20   Glory to God   *Gloria in excelsis*

Glory to God in the highest,
    and peace to his people on earth.

Lord God, heavenly King,
almighty God and Father,

we worship you, we give you thanks,
we praise you for your glory.

Lord Jesus Christ, only Son of the Father,
Lord God, Lamb of God,
you take away the sin of the world;
   have mercy on us;
you are seated at the right hand of the Father;
   receive our prayer.

For you alone are the Holy One,
you alone are the Lord,
you alone are the Most High,
   Jesus Christ,
   with the Holy Spirit,
   in the glory of God the Father. Amen.

21   You are God   *Te Deum laudamus*

You are God: we praise you;
You are the Lord: we acclaim you;
You are the eternal Father:
All creation worships you.
To you all angels, all the powers of heaven,
Cherubim and Seraphim, sing in endless praise:
   Holy, holy, holy Lord, God of power and might,
   heaven and earth are full of your glory.
The glorious company of apostles praise you.
The noble fellowship of prophets praise you.
The white-robed army of martyrs praise you.
Throughout the world the holy Church acclaims you;
   Father, of majesty unbounded,
   your true and only Son, worthy of all worship,
   and the Holy Spirit, advocate and guide.

You, Christ, are the king of glory,
the eternal Son of the Father.
When you became man to set us free
you did not shun the Virgin's womb.
You overcame the sting of death
and opened the kingdom of heaven to all believers.
You are seated at God's right hand in glory.
We believe that you will come and be our judge.
   Come then, Lord, and help your people,
   bought with the price of your own blood,
   and bring us with your saints
   to glory everlasting.

The Apostles' Creed

Officiant and People together, all standing

I believe in God, the Father almighty,
   creator of heaven and earth.
I believe in Jesus Christ, his only Son, our Lord.
   He was conceived by the power of the Holy Spirit
      and born of the Virgin Mary.
   He suffered under Pontius Pilate,
      was crucified, died, and was buried.
   He descended to the dead.
   On the third day he rose again.
   He ascended into heaven,
      and is seated at the right hand of the Father.
   He will come again to judge the living and the dead.
I believe in the Holy Spirit,
   the holy catholic Church,
   the communion of saints,
   the forgiveness of sins,
   the resurrection of the body,
   and the life everlasting. Amen.

The Prayers

The people stand or kneel

Officiant **The Lord be with you.**
People **And also with you.**
Officiant **Let us pray.**

Officiant and People

Our Father, who art in heaven,	Our Father in heaven,
hallowed be thy Name,	hallowed be your Name,
thy kingdom come,	your kingdom come,
thy will be done,	your will be done,
on earth as it is in heaven.	on earth as in heaven.
Give us this day our daily bread.	Give us today our daily bread.
And forgive us our trespasses,	Forgive us our sins
as we forgive those	as we forgive those
who trespass against us.	who sin against us.
And lead us not into temptation,	Save us from the time of trial,
but deliver us from evil.	and deliver us from evil.
For thine is the kingdom,	For the kingdom, the power,
and the power, and the glory,	and the glory are yours,
for ever and ever. Amen.	now and for ever. Amen.

Then follows one of these sets of Suffrages

A

V. Show us your mercy, O Lord;
R. And grant us your salvation.
V. Clothe your ministers with righteousness;
R. Let your people sing with joy.
V. Give peace, O Lord, in all the world;
R. For only in you can we live in safety.

V. Lord, keep this nation under your care;
R. And guide us in the way of justice and truth.
V. Let your way be known upon earth;
R. Your saving health among all nations.
V. Let not the needy, O Lord, be forgotten;
R. Nor the hope of the poor be taken away.
V. Create in us clean hearts, O God;
R. And sustain us with your Holy Spirit.

B

V. Save your people, Lord, and bless your inheritance;
R. Govern and uphold them, now and always.
V. Day by day we bless you;
R. We praise your Name for ever.
V. Lord, keep us from all sin today;
R. Have mercy on us, Lord, have mercy.
V. Lord, show us your love and mercy;
R. For we put our trust in you.
V. In you, Lord, is our hope;
R. And we shall never hope in vain.

The Officiant then says one or more of the following Collects

The Collect of the Day

A Collect for Sundays

O God, you make us glad with the weekly remembrance of
the glorious resurrection of your Son our Lord: Give us this
day such blessing through our worship of you, that the week
to come may be spent in your favor; through Jesus Christ our
Lord. *Amen.*

A Collect for Fridays

Almighty God, whose most dear Son went not up to joy but first he suffered pain, and entered not into glory before he was crucified: Mercifully grant that we, walking in the way of the cross, may find it none other than the way of life and peace; through Jesus Christ your Son our Lord. *Amen.*

A Collect for Saturdays

Almighty God, who after the creation of the world rested from all your works and sanctified a day of rest for all your creatures: Grant that we, putting away all earthly anxieties, may be duly prepared for the service of your sanctuary, and that our rest here upon earth may be a preparation for the eternal rest promised to your people in heaven; through Jesus Christ our Lord. *Amen.*

A Collect for the Renewal of Life

O God, the King eternal, whose light divides the day from the night and turns the shadow of death into the morning: Drive far from us all wrong desires, incline our hearts to keep your law, and guide our feet into the way of peace; that, having done your will with cheerfulness during the day, we may, when night comes, rejoice to give you thanks; through Jesus Christ our Lord. *Amen.*

A Collect for Peace

O God, the author of peace and lover of concord, to know you is eternal life and to serve you is perfect freedom: Defend us, your humble servants, in all assaults of our enemies; that we, surely trusting in your defense, may not fear the power of any adversaries; through the might of Jesus Christ our Lord. *Amen.*

A Collect for Grace

Lord God, almighty and everlasting Father, you have brought us in safety to this new day: Preserve us with your mighty power, that we may not fall into sin, nor be overcome by adversity; and in all we do, direct us to the fulfilling of your purpose; through Jesus Christ our Lord. *Amen.*

A Collect for Guidance

Heavenly Father, in you we live and move and have our being: We humbly pray you so to guide and govern us by your Holy Spirit, that in all the cares and occupations of our life we may not forget you, but may remember that we are ever walking in your sight; through Jesus Christ our Lord. *Amen.*

Then, unless the Eucharist or a form of general intercession is to follow, one of these prayers for mission is added

Almighty and everlasting God, by whose Spirit the whole body of your faithful people is governed and sanctified: Receive our supplications and prayers which we offer before you for all members of your holy Church, that in their vocation and ministry they may truly and devoutly serve you; through our Lord and Savior Jesus Christ. *Amen.*

or this

O God, you have made of one blood all the peoples of the earth, and sent your blessed Son to preach peace to those who are far off and to those who are near: Grant that people everywhere may seek after you and find you; bring the nations into your fold; pour out your Spirit upon all flesh; and hasten the coming of your kingdom; through Jesus Christ our Lord. *Amen.*

or the following

Lord Jesus Christ, you stretched out your arms of love on the hard wood of the cross that everyone might come within the reach of your saving embrace: So clothe us in your Spirit that we, reaching forth our hands in love, may bring those who do not know you to the knowledge and love of you; for the honor of your Name. *Amen.*

Here may be sung a hymn or anthem.

Authorized intercessions and thanksgivings may follow.

Before the close of the Office one or both of the following may be used

The General Thanksgiving

Officiant and People

Almighty God, Father of all mercies,
we your unworthy servants give you humble thanks
for all your goodness and loving-kindness
to us and to all whom you have made.
We bless you for our creation, preservation,
and all the blessings of this life;
but above all for your immeasurable love
in the redemption of the world by our Lord Jesus Christ;
for the means of grace, and for the hope of glory.
And, we pray, give us such an awareness of your mercies,
that with truly thankful hearts we may show forth your praise,
not only with our lips, but in our lives,
by giving up our selves to your service,
and by walking before you
in holiness and righteousness all our days;
through Jesus Christ our Lord,
to whom, with you and the Holy Spirit,
be honor and glory throughout all ages. Amen.

A Prayer of St. Chrysostom

Almighty God, you have given us grace at this time with one accord to make our common supplication to you; and you have promised through your well-beloved Son that when two or three are gathered together in his Name you will be in the midst of them: Fulfill now, O Lord, our desires and petitions as may be best for us; granting us in this world knowledge of your truth, and in the age to come life everlasting. *Amen.*

Then may be said

Let us bless the Lord.
Thanks be to God.

From Easter Day through the Day of Pentecost "Alleluia, alleluia" may be added to the preceding versicle and response.

The Officiant may then conclude with one of the following

The grace of our Lord Jesus Christ, and the love of God, and the fellowship of the Holy Spirit, be with us all evermore. *Amen.*   *2 Corinthians 13:14*

May the God of hope fill us with all joy and peace in believing through the power of the Holy Spirit. *Amen.*
Romans 15:13

Glory to God whose power, working in us, can do infinitely more than we can ask or imagine: Glory to him from generation to generation in the Church, and in Christ Jesus for ever and ever. *Amen.*   *Ephesians 3:20, 21*

An Order of Service
for Noonday

Officiant   O God, make speed to save us.
People   O Lord, make haste to help us.

Officiant and People

Glory to the Father, and to the Son, and to the Holy Spirit: as it was in the beginning, is now, and will be for ever. Amen.

Except in Lent, add   Alleluia.

A suitable hymn may be sung.

One or more of the following Psalms is sung or said. Other suitable selections include Psalms 19, 67, one or more sections of Psalm 119, or a selection from Psalms 120 through 133.

Psalm 119   *Lucerna pedibus meis*

105 Your word is a lantern to my feet *
        and a light upon my path.

106 I have sworn and am determined *
        to keep your righteous judgments.

107 I am deeply troubled; *
    preserve my life, O LORD, according to your word.

108 Accept, O LORD, the willing tribute of my lips, *
    and teach me your judgments.

109 My life is always in my hand, *
    yet I do not forget your law.

110 The wicked have set a trap for me, *
    but I have not strayed from your commandments.

111 Your decrees are my inheritance for ever; *
    truly, they are the joy of my heart.

112 I have applied my heart to fulfill your statutes *
    for ever and to the end.

Psalm 121 *Levavi oculos*

1 I lift up my eyes to the hills; *
    from where is my help to come?

2 My help comes from the LORD, *
    the maker of heaven and earth.

3 He will not let your foot be moved *
    and he who watches over you will not fall asleep.

4 Behold, he who keeps watch over Israel *
    shall neither slumber nor sleep;

5 The LORD himself watches over you; *
    the LORD is your shade at your right hand,

6 So that the sun shall not strike you by day, *
    nor the moon by night.

7 The LORD shall preserve you from all evil; *
    it is he who shall keep you safe.

8   The LORD shall watch over your going out and
                          your coming in, *
     from this time forth for evermore.

     Psalm 126   *In convertendo*

1   When the LORD restored the fortunes of Zion, *
        then were we like those who dream.

2   Then was our mouth filled with laughter, *
        and our tongue with shouts of joy.

3   Then they said among the nations, *
        "The LORD has done great things for them."

4   The LORD has done great things for us, *
        and we are glad indeed.

5   Restore our fortunes, O LORD, *
        like the watercourses of the Negev.

6   Those who sowed with tears *
        will reap with songs of joy.

7   Those who go out weeping, carrying the seed, *
        will come again with joy, shouldering their sheaves.

At the end of the Psalms is sung or said

Glory to the Father, and to the Son, and to the Holy Spirit: *
   as it was in the beginning, is now, and will be for ever. Amen.

One of the following, or some other suitable passage of Scripture, is read

The love of God has been poured into our hearts through the
Holy Spirit that has been given to us.   *Romans 5:5*

People   Thanks be to God.

or the following

If anyone is in Christ he is a new creation; the old has passed away, behold the new has come. All this is from God, who through Christ reconciled us to himself and gave us the ministry of reconciliation. *2 Corinthians 5:17-18*

People   Thanks be to God.

or this

From the rising of the sun to its setting my Name shall be great among the nations, and in every place incense shall be offered to my Name, and a pure offering; for my Name shall be great among the nations, says the Lord of Hosts. *Malachi 1:11*

People   Thanks be to God.

A meditation, silent or spoken, may follow.

The Officiant then begins the Prayers

Lord, have mercy.
Christ, have mercy.
Lord, have mercy.

Officiant and People

Our Father, who art in heaven,	Our Father in heaven,
hallowed be thy Name,	hallowed be your Name,
thy kingdom come,	your kingdom come,
thy will be done,	your will be done,
on earth as it is in heaven.	on earth as in heaven.
Give us this day our daily bread.	Give us today our daily bread.
And forgive us our trespasses,	Forgive us our sins
as we forgive those	as we forgive those
who trespass against us.	who sin against us.
And lead us not into temptation,	Save us from the time of trial,
but deliver us from evil.	and deliver us from evil.

Officiant	Lord, hear our prayer;
People	And let our cry come to you.
Officiant	Let us pray.

The Officiant then says one of the following Collects. If desired, the Collect of the Day may be used.

Heavenly Father, send your Holy Spirit into our hearts, to direct and rule us according to your will, to comfort us in all our afflictions, to defend us from all error, and to lead us into all truth; through Jesus Christ our Lord. *Amen.*

Blessed Savior, at this hour you hung upon the cross, stretching out your loving arms: Grant that all the peoples of the earth may look to you and be saved; for your tender mercies' sake. *Amen.*

Almighty Savior, who at noonday called your servant Saint Paul to be an apostle to the Gentiles: We pray you to illumine the world with the radiance of your glory, that all nations may come and worship you; for you live and reign for ever and ever. *Amen.*

Lord Jesus Christ, you said to your apostles, "Peace I give to you; my own peace I leave with you:" Regard not our sins, but the faith of your Church, and give to us the peace and unity of that heavenly City, where with the Father and the Holy Spirit you live and reign, now and for ever. *Amen.*

Free intercessions may be offered.

The service concludes as follows

Officiant	Let us bless the Lord.
People	Thanks be to God.

Concerning the Service

This Order provides a form of evening service or vespers for use on suitable occasions in the late afternoon or evening. It may be used as a complete rite in place of Evening Prayer, or as the introduction to Evening Prayer or some other service, or as the prelude to an evening meal or other activity. It is appropriate also for use in private houses.

Any part or parts of this service may be led by lay persons. A priest or deacon, when presiding, should read the Prayer for Light, and the Blessing or Dismissal at the end. The bishop, when present, should give the Blessing.

This order is not appropriate for use on Monday, Tuesday, or Wednesday in Holy Week, or on Good Friday. Easter Eve has its own form for the Lighting of the Paschal Candle.

For the Short Lesson at the beginning of the service, any one of the following is also appropriate, especially for the seasons suggested:

Isaiah 60:19-20 (Advent)	Revelation 21:10, 22-24 (Easter)
Luke 12:35-37 (Advent)	Psalm 36:5-9 (Ascension)
John 1:1-5 (Christmas)	Joel 2:28-30 (Whitsunday)
Isaiah 60:1-3 (Epiphany)	Colossians 1:9, 11-14 (Saints' Days)
1 John 1:5-7 (Lent)	1 Peter 2:9 (Saints' Days)
John 12:35-36 A (Lent)	Revelation 22:1, 4-5 (Saints' Days)

Any of the prayers in contemporary language may be adapted to traditional language by changing the pronouns and the corresponding verbs.

Additional Directions are on page 142.

An Order of Worship
for the Evening

The church is dark, or partially so, when the service is to begin.

All stand, and the Officiant greets the people with these words

               Light and peace, in Jesus Christ our Lord.
People   Thanks be to God.

In place of the above, from Easter Day through the Day of Pentecost

Officiant   Alleluia. Christ is risen.
People   The Lord is risen indeed. Alleluia.

In Lent and on other penitential occasions

Officiant   Bless the Lord who forgives all our sins;
People   His mercy endures for ever.

One of the following, or some other Short Lesson of Scripture appropriate to the occasion or to the season, may then be read

Jesus said, "You are the light of the world. A city built on a hill cannot be hid. No one lights a lamp to put it under a bucket, but on a lamp-stand where it gives light for everyone in the house. And you, like the lamp, must shed light among your fellow men, so that they may see the good you do, and give glory to your Father in heaven." *Matthew 5:14-16*

It is not ourselves that we proclaim; we proclaim Christ
Jesus as Lord, and ourselves as your servants, for Jesus' sake.
For the same God who said, "Out of darkness let light shine,"
has caused his light to shine within us, to give the light of
revelation — the revelation of the glory of God in the face of
Jesus Christ.   *2 Corinthians 4:5-6*

If I say, "Surely the darkness will cover me, and the light
around me turn to night," darkness is not dark to you, O
Lord; the night is as bright as the day; darkness and light to
you are both alike.   *Psalm 139:10-11*

*The Officiant then says the Prayer for Light, using any one of the
following or some other suitable prayer, first saying*

Let us pray.

Almighty God, we give you thanks for surrounding us, as
daylight fades, with the brightness of the vesper light; and we
implore you of your great mercy that, as you enfold us with
the radiance of this light, so you would shine into our hearts
the brightness of your Holy Spirit; through Jesus Christ our
Lord. *Amen.*

Grant us, Lord, the lamp of charity which never fails, that it
may burn in us and shed its light on those around us, and
that by its brightness we may have a vision of that holy City,
where dwells the true and never-failing Light, Jesus Christ
our Lord. *Amen.*

O Lord God Almighty, as you have taught us to call the
evening, the morning, and the noonday one day; and have
made the sun to know its going down: Dispel the darkness of
our hearts, that by your brightness we may know you to be
the true God and eternal light, living and reigning for ever
and ever. *Amen.*

Lighten our darkness, we beseech thee, O Lord; and by thy great mercy defend us from all perils and dangers of this night; for the love of thy only Son, our Savior, Jesus Christ. *Amen.*

Advent

Collect for the First Sunday of Advent

Christmas, Epiphany, and other Feasts of the Incarnation

Collect for the First Sunday after Christmas

Lent and other times of penitence

Almighty and most merciful God, kindle within us the fire of love, that by its cleansing flame we may be purged of all our sins and made worthy to worship you in spirit and in truth; through Jesus Christ our Lord. *Amen.*

Easter Season

Eternal God, who led your ancient people into freedom by a pillar of cloud by day and a pillar of fire by night: Grant that we who walk in the light of your presence may rejoice in the liberty of the children of God; through Jesus Christ our Lord. *Amen.*

Festivals of Saints

Lord Christ, your saints have been the lights of the world in every generation: Grant that we who follow in their footsteps may be made worthy to enter with them into that heavenly country where you live and reign for ever and ever. *Amen.*

The candles at the Altar are now lighted, as are other candles and lamps as may be convenient.

During the candle-lighting, an appropriate anthem or psalm may be sung, or silence kept.

The following hymn, or a metrical version of it, or some other hymn, is then sung

O Gracious Light   *Phos hilaron*

O gracious Light,
pure brightness of the everliving Father in heaven,
O Jesus Christ, holy and blessed!

Now as we come to the setting of the sun,
and our eyes behold the vesper light,
we sing your praises, O God: Father, Son, and Holy Spirit.

You are worthy at all times to be praised by happy voices,
O Son of God, O Giver of life,
and to be glorified through all the worlds.

The service may then continue in any of the following ways:

With Evening Prayer, beginning with the Psalms; or with some other Office or Devotion;

With the celebration of the Holy Eucharist, beginning with the Salutation and Collect of the Day;

Or, it may be followed by a meal or other activity, in which case Phos hilaron may be followed by the Lord's Prayer and a grace or blessing;

Or, it may continue as a complete evening Office with the following elements:

Selection from the Psalter. Silence, or a suitable Collect, or both, may follow the Psalmody.

Bible Reading. A sermon or homily, a passage from Christian literature, or a brief silence, may follow the Reading.

Canticle. The Magnificat or other canticle, or some other hymn of praise.

Prayers. A litany, or other suitable devotions, including the Lord's Prayer.

Blessing or Dismissal, or both. The Peace may then be exchanged.

On feasts or other days of special significance, the Collect of the Day, or one proper to the season, may precede the Blessing or Dismissal. On other days, either of the following, or one of the Collects from Evening Prayer or from Compline, may be so used

Blessed are you, O Lord, the God of our fathers, creator of the changes of day and night, giving rest to the weary, renewing the strength of those who are spent, bestowing upon us occasions of song in the evening. As you have protected us in the day that is past, so be with us in the coming night; keep us from every sin, every evil, and every fear; for you are our light and salvation, and the strength of our life. To you be glory for endless ages. *Amen.*

Almighty, everlasting God, let our prayer in your sight be as incense, the lifting up of our hands as the evening sacrifice. Give us grace to behold you, present in your Word and Sacraments, and to recognize you in the lives of those around us. Stir up in us the flame of that love which burned in the heart of your Son as he bore his passion, and let it burn in us to eternal life and to the ages of ages. *Amen.*

A bishop or priest may use the following or some other blessing or grace

The Lord bless you and keep you. *Amen.*
The Lord make his face to shine upon you
  and be gracious to you. *Amen.*
The Lord lift up his countenance upon you
  and give you peace. *Amen.*

A deacon or lay person using the preceding blessing substitutes "us" for "you."

A Dismissal may be used (adding "Alleluia, alleluia" in Easter Season)

The People respond

Thanks be to God.

In Easter Season the People respond

Thanks be to God. Alleluia, alleluia.

Daily Evening Prayer:
Rite Two

The Officiant begins the service with one or more of the following sentences of Scripture, or of those on pages 75-78;

or with the Service of Light on pages 109-112, and continuing with the appointed Psalmody;

or with the versicle "O God, make speed to save us" on page 117

Let my prayer be set forth in your sight as incense, the lifting up of my hands as the evening sacrifice.   *Psalm 141:2*

Grace to you and peace from God our Father and from the Lord Jesus Christ.   *Philippians 1:2*

Worship the Lord in the beauty of holiness; let the whole earth tremble before him.   *Psalm 96:9*

Yours is the day, O God, yours also the night; you established the moon and the sun. You fixed all the boundaries of the earth; you made both summer and winter.   *Psalm 74:15,16*

I will bless the Lord who gives me counsel; my heart teaches me, night after night. I have set the Lord always before me; because he is at my right hand, I shall not fall.   *Psalm 16:7,8*

Seek him who made the Pleiades and Orion, and turns deep darkness into the morning, and darkens the day into night; who calls for the waters of the sea and pours them out upon the surface of the earth: The Lord is his name.   *Amos 5:8*

If I say, "Surely the darkness will cover me, and the light around me turn to night," darkness is not dark to you, O Lord; the night is as bright as the day; darkness and light to you are both alike.   *Psalm 139:10, 11*

Jesus said, "I am the light of the world; whoever follows me will not walk in darkness, but will have the light of life." *John 8:12*

The following Confession of Sin may then be said; or the Office may continue at once with "O God make speed to save us."

Confession of Sin

The Officiant says to the people

Dear friends in Christ, here in the presence of Almighty God, let us kneel in silence, and with penitent and obedient hearts confess our sins, so that we may obtain forgiveness by his infinite goodness and mercy.

or this

Let us confess our sins against God and our neighbor.

Silence may be kept.

Officiant and People together, all kneeling

Most merciful God,
we confess that we have sinned against you
in thought, word, and deed,
by what we have done,
and by what we have left undone.
We have not loved you with our whole heart;
we have not loved our neighbors as ourselves.
We are truly sorry and we humbly repent.

For the sake of your Son Jesus Christ,
have mercy on us and forgive us;
that we may delight in your will,
and walk in your ways,
to the glory of your Name. Amen.

The Priest alone stands and says

Almighty God have mercy on you, forgive you all your
sins through our Lord Jesus Christ, strengthen you in all
goodness, and by the power of the Holy Spirit keep you in
eternal life. *Amen.*

*A deacon or lay person using the preceding form remains kneeling, and
substitutes "us" for "you" and "our" for "your."*

The Invitatory and Psalter

All stand

Officiant	O God, make speed to save us.
People	O Lord, make haste to help us.

Officiant and People

Glory to the Father, and to the Son, and to the Holy Spirit: as
it was in the beginning, is now, and will be for ever. Amen.

Except in Lent, add   Alleluia.

*The following, or some other suitable hymn, or an Invitatory Psalm, may
be sung or said*

O Gracious Light *Phos hilaron*

O gracious Light,
pure brightness of the everliving Father in heaven,
O Jesus Christ, holy and blessed!

Now as we come to the setting of the sun,
and our eyes behold the vesper light,
we sing your praises, O God: Father, Son, and Holy Spirit.

You are worthy at all times to be praised by happy voices,
O Son of God, O Giver of life,
and to be glorified through all the worlds.

Then follows

The Psalm or Psalms Appointed

At the end of the Psalms is sung or said

Glory to the Father, and to the Son, and to the Holy Spirit: *
as it was in the beginning, is now, and will be for ever. Amen.

The Lessons

One or two Lessons, as appointed, are read, the Reader first saying

A Reading (Lesson) from _____.

A citation giving chapter and verse may be added.

After each Lesson the Reader may say

The Word of the Lord.

Answer   Thanks be to God.

Or the Reader may say   Here ends the Lesson (Reading).

Silence may be kept after each Reading. One of the following Canticles, or one of those on pages 47-52, or 85-95, is sung or said after each Reading. If three Lessons are used, the Lesson from the Gospel is read after the second Canticle.

The Song of Mary *Magnificat*

Luke 1:46-55

My soul proclaims the greatness of the Lord,
my spirit rejoices in God my Savior; *
    for he has looked with favor on his lowly servant.
From this day all generations will call me blessed: *
    the Almighty has done great things for me,
    and holy is his Name.
He has mercy on those who fear him *
    in every generation.
He has shown the strength of his arm, *
    he has scattered the proud in their conceit.
He has cast down the mighty from their thrones, *
    and has lifted up the lowly.
He has filled the hungry with good things, *
    and the rich he has sent away empty.
He has come to the help of his servant Israel, *
    for he has remembered his promise of mercy,
The promise he made to our fathers, *
    to Abraham and his children for ever.

Glory to the Father, and to the Son, and to the Holy Spirit: *
    as it was in the beginning, is now, and will be for ever. Amen.

The Song of Simeon   *Nunc dimittis*

Luke 2:29-32

Lord, you now have set your servant free *
    to go in peace as you have promised;
For these eyes of mine have seen the Savior, *
    whom you have prepared for all the world to see:
A Light to enlighten the nations, *
    and the glory of your people Israel.

Glory to the Father, and to the Son, and to the Holy Spirit: *
    as it was in the beginning, is now, and will be for ever. Amen.

The Apostles' Creed

Officiant and People together, all standing

I believe in God, the Father almighty,
    creator of heaven and earth.
I believe in Jesus Christ, his only Son, our Lord.
    He was conceived by the power of the Holy Spirit
        and born of the Virgin Mary.
    He suffered under Pontius Pilate,
        was crucified, died, and was buried.
    He descended to the dead.
    On the third day he rose again.
    He ascended into heaven,
        and is seated at the right hand of the Father.
    He will come again to judge the living and the dead.
I believe in the Holy Spirit,
    the holy catholic Church,
    the communion of saints,
    the forgiveness of sins,
    the resurrection of the body,
    and the life everlasting. Amen.

The Prayers

The people stand or kneel

Officiant   The Lord be with you.
People   And also with you.
Officiant   Let us pray.

Officiant and People

Our Father, who art in heaven,
  hallowed be thy Name,
  thy kingdom come,
  thy will be done,
    on earth as it is in heaven.
Give us this day our daily bread.
And forgive us our trespasses,
  as we forgive those
    who trespass against us.
And lead us not into temptation,
  but deliver us from evil.
For thine is the kingdom,
  and the power, and the glory,
  for ever and ever. Amen.

Our Father in heaven,
  hallowed be your Name,
  your kingdom come,
  your will be done,
    on earth as in heaven.
Give us today our daily bread.
Forgive us our sins
  as we forgive those
    who sin against us.
Save us from the time of trial,
  and deliver us from evil.
For the kingdom, the power,
  and the glory are yours,
  now and for ever. Amen.

Then follows one of these sets of Suffrages

A

V.   Show us your mercy, O Lord;
R.   And grant us your salvation.
V.   Clothe your ministers with righteousness;
R.   Let your people sing with joy.
V.   Give peace, O Lord, in all the world;
R.   For only in you can we live in safety.

V. Lord, keep this nation under your care;
R. And guide us in the way of justice and truth.
V. Let your way be known upon earth;
R. Your saving health among all nations.
V. Let not the needy, O Lord, be forgotten;
R. Nor the hope of the poor be taken away.
V. Create in us clean hearts, O God;
R. And sustain us with your Holy Spirit.

B

That this evening may be holy, good, and peaceful,
We entreat you, O Lord.

That your holy angels may lead us in paths of peace and
goodwill,
We entreat you, O Lord.

That we may be pardoned and forgiven for our sins
and offenses,
We entreat you, O Lord.

That there may be peace to your Church and to the whole
world,
We entreat you, O Lord.

That we may depart this life in your faith and fear,
and not be condemned before the great judgment seat
of Christ,
We entreat you, O Lord.

That we may be bound together by your Holy Spirit in
the communion of [_____ and] all your saints,
entrusting one another and all our life to Christ,
We entreat you, O Lord.

The Officiant then says one or more of the following Collects

The Collect of the Day

A Collect for Sundays

Lord God, whose Son our Savior Jesus Christ triumphed over the powers of death and prepared for us our place in the new Jerusalem: Grant that we, who have this day given thanks for his resurrection, may praise you in that City of which he is the light, and where he lives and reigns for ever and ever. *Amen.*

A Collect for Fridays

Lord Jesus Christ, by your death you took away the sting of death: Grant to us your servants so to follow in faith where you have led the way, that we may at length fall asleep peacefully in you and wake up in your likeness; for your tender mercies' sake. *Amen.*

A Collect for Saturdays

O God, the source of eternal light: Shed forth your unending day upon us who watch for you, that our lips may praise you, our lives may bless you, and our worship on the morrow give you glory; through Jesus Christ our Lord. *Amen.*

A Collect for Peace

Most holy God, the source of all good desires, all right judgments, and all just works: Give to us, your servants, that peace which the world cannot give, so that our minds may be fixed on the doing of your will, and that we, being delivered from the fear of all enemies, may live in peace and quietness; through the mercies of Christ Jesus our Savior. *Amen.*

A Collect for Aid against Perils

Be our light in the darkness, O Lord, and in your great mercy defend us from all perils and dangers of this night; for the love of your only Son, our Savior Jesus Christ. *Amen.*

A Collect for Protection

O God, the life of all who live, the light of the faithful, the
strength of those who labor, and the repose of the dead: We
thank you for the blessings of the day that is past, and
humbly ask for your protection through the coming night.
Bring us in safety to the morning hours; through him who
died and rose again for us, your Son our Savior Jesus Christ.
Amen.

A Collect for the Presence of Christ

Lord Jesus, stay with us, for evening is at hand and the day
is past; be our companion in the way, kindle our hearts, and
awaken hope, that we may know you as you are revealed in
Scripture and the breaking of bread. Grant this for the sake
of your love. *Amen.*

*Then, unless the Eucharist or a form of general intercession is to follow,
one of these prayers for mission is added*

O God and Father of all, whom the whole heavens adore:
Let the whole earth also worship you, all nations obey you,
all tongues confess and bless you, and men and women
everywhere love you and serve you in peace; through Jesus
Christ our Lord. *Amen.*

or this

Keep watch, dear Lord, with those who work, or watch, or
weep this night, and give your angels charge over those who
sleep. Tend the sick, Lord Christ; give rest to the weary, bless
the dying, soothe the suffering, pity the afflicted, shield the
joyous; and all for your love's sake. *Amen.*

or the following

O God, you manifest in your servants the signs of your
presence: Send forth upon us the Spirit of love, that in
companionship with one another your abounding grace may
increase among us; through Jesus Christ our Lord. *Amen.*

Here may be sung a hymn or anthem.

Authorized intercessions and thanksgivings may follow.

Before the close of the Office one or both of the following may be used

The General Thanksgiving

Officiant and People

Almighty God, Father of all mercies,
we your unworthy servants give you humble thanks
for all your goodness and loving-kindness
to us and to all whom you have made.
We bless you for our creation, preservation,
and all the blessings of this life;
but above all for your immeasurable love
in the redemption of the world by our Lord Jesus Christ;
for the means of grace, and for the hope of glory.
And, we pray, give us such an awareness of your mercies,
that with truly thankful hearts we may show forth your praise,
not only with our lips, but in our lives,
by giving up our selves to your service,
and by walking before you
in holiness and righteousness all our days;
through Jesus Christ our Lord,
to whom, with you and the Holy Spirit,
be honor and glory throughout all ages. Amen.

A Prayer of St. Chrysostom

Almighty God, you have given us grace at this time with one accord to make our common supplication to you; and you have promised through your well-beloved Son that when two or three are gathered together in his Name you will be in the midst of them: Fulfill now, O Lord, our desires and petitions as may be best for us; granting us in this world knowledge of your truth, and in the age to come life everlasting. *Amen.*

Then may be said

Let us bless the Lord.
Thanks be to God.

From Easter Day through the Day of Pentecost "Alleluia, alleluia" may be added to the preceding versicle and response.

The Officiant may then conclude with one of the following

The grace of our Lord Jesus Christ, and the love of God, and the fellowship of the Holy Spirit, be with us all evermore. *Amen.*   *2 Corinthians 13:14*

May the God of hope fill us with all joy and peace in believing through the power of the Holy Spirit. *Amen.*
Romans 15:13

Glory to God whose power, working in us, can do infinitely more than we can ask or imagine: Glory to him from generation to generation in the Church, and in Christ Jesus for ever and ever. *Amen.*   *Ephesians 3:20,21*

An Order for Compline

The Officiant begins

The Lord Almighty grant us a peaceful night and a perfect
end. *Amen.*

Officiant   Our help is in the Name of the Lord;
People   The maker of heaven and earth.

The Officiant may then say

Let us confess our sins to God.

Officiant and People

Almighty God, our heavenly Father:
We have sinned against you,
through our own fault,
in thought, and word, and deed,
and in what we have left undone.
For the sake of your Son our Lord Jesus Christ,
forgive us all our offenses;
and grant that we may serve you
in newness of life,
to the glory of your Name. Amen.

May the Almighty God grant us forgiveness of all our sins, and the grace and comfort of the Holy Spirit. *Amen.*

The Officiant then says

       O God, make speed to save us.
People   O Lord, make haste to help us.

Officiant and People

Glory to the Father, and to the Son, and to the Holy Spirit: as it was in the beginning, is now, and will be for ever. Amen.

Except in Lent, add   Alleluia.

One or more of the following Psalms are sung or said. Other suitable selections may be substituted.

Psalm 4   *Cum invocarem*

1   Answer me when I call, O God, defender of my cause; *
     you set me free when I am hard-pressed;
     have mercy on me and hear my prayer.

2   "You mortals, how long will you dishonor my glory? *
     how long will you worship dumb idols
     and run after false gods?"

3   Know that the LORD does wonders for the faithful; *
     when I call upon the LORD, he will hear me.

4   Tremble, then, and do not sin; *
     speak to your heart in silence upon your bed.

5   Offer the appointed sacrifices *
     and put your trust in the LORD.

6   Many are saying,
    "Oh, that we might see better times!" *
      Lift up the light of your countenance upon us, O LORD.

7   You have put gladness in my heart,*
      more than when grain and wine and oil increase.

8   I lie down in peace; at once I fall asleep; *
      for only you, LORD, make me dwell in safety.

Psalm 31   *In te, Domine, speravi*

1   In you, O LORD, have I taken refuge;
    let me never be put to shame: *
      deliver me in your righteousness.

2   Incline your ear to me; *
      make haste to deliver me.

3   Be my strong rock, a castle to keep me safe,
    for you are my crag and my stronghold; *
      for the sake of your Name, lead me and guide me.

4   Take me out of the net that they have secretly set for me, *
      for you are my tower of strength.

5   Into your hands I commend my spirit, *
    for you have redeemed me,
    O LORD, O God of truth.

Psalm 91   *Qui habitat*

1   He who dwells in the shelter of the Most High *
      abides under the shadow of the Almighty.

2   He shall say to the LORD ,
    "You are my refuge and my stronghold, *
      my God in whom I put my trust."

3 He shall deliver you from the snare of the hunter *
   and from the deadly pestilence.

4 He shall cover you with his pinions,
   and you shall find refuge under his wings; *
      his faithfulness shall be a shield and buckler.

5 You shall not be afraid of any terror by night, *
   nor of the arrow that flies by day;

6 Of the plague that stalks in the darkness, *
   nor of the sickness that lays waste at mid-day.

7 A thousand shall fall at your side
   and ten thousand at your right hand, *
      but it shall not come near you.

8 Your eyes have only to behold *
   to see the reward of the wicked.

9 Because you have made the LORD your refuge, *
   and the Most High your habitation,

10 There shall no evil happen to you, *
   neither shall any plague come near your dwelling.

11 For he shall give his angels charge over you, *
   to keep you in all your ways.

12 They shall bear you in their hands, *
   lest you dash your foot against a stone.

13 You shall tread upon the lion and adder; *
   you shall trample the young lion and the serpent
      under your feet.

14 Because he is bound to me in love,
   therefore will I deliver him; *
      I will protect him, because he knows my Name.

15 He shall call upon me, and I will answer him; *
    I am with him in trouble;
    I will rescue him and bring him to honor.

16 With long life will I satisfy him, *
    and show him my salvation.

Psalm 134 *Ecce nunc*

1 Behold now, bless the LORD, all you servants of the LORD, *
    you that stand by night in the house of the LORD.

2 Lift up your hands in the holy place and bless the LORD; *
    the LORD who made heaven and earth bless you out of Zion.

At the end of the Psalms is sung or said

Glory to the Father, and to the Son, and to the Holy Spirit: *
    as it was in the beginning, is now, and will be for ever. Amen.

One of the following, or some other suitable passage of Scripture, is read

Lord, you are in the midst of us, and we are called by your
Name: Do not forsake us, O Lord our God.   *Jeremiah 14:9, 22*

People   Thanks be to God.

or this

Come to me, all who labor and are heavy-laden, and I will
give you rest. Take my yoke upon you, and learn from me;
for I am gentle and lowly in heart, and you will find rest for
your souls. For my yoke is easy, and my burden is light.
Matthew 11:28-30

People   Thanks be to God.

or the following

May the God of peace, who brought again from the dead our Lord Jesus, the great shepherd of the sheep, by the blood of the eternal covenant, equip you with everything good that you may do his will, working in you that which is pleasing in his sight; through Jesus Christ, to whom be glory for ever and ever.   *Hebrews 13:20-21*

People   Thanks be to God.

or this

Be sober, be watchful. Your adversary the devil prowls around like a roaring lion, seeking someone to devour. Resist him, firm in your faith.   *1 Peter 5:8-9a*

People   Thanks be to God.

A hymn suitable for the evening may be sung.

Then follows

V.   Into your hands, O Lord, I commend my spirit;
R.   For you have redeemed me, O Lord, O God of truth.
V.   Keep us, O Lord, as the apple of your eye;
R.   Hide us under the shadow of your wings.

Lord, have mercy.
Christ, have mercy.
Lord, have mercy.

Officiant and People

Our Father, who art in heaven,
    hallowed be thy Name,
    thy kingdom come,
    thy will be done,
        on earth as it is in heaven.

Our Father in heaven,
    hallowed be your Name,
    your kingdom come,
    your will be done,
        on earth as in heaven.

Give us this day our daily bread.	Give us today our daily bread.

Give us this day our daily bread.
And forgive us our trespasses,
   as we forgive those
      who trespass against us.
And lead us not into temptation,
   but deliver us from evil.

Give us today our daily bread.
Forgive us our sins
   as we forgive those
      who sin against us.
Save us from the time of trial,
   and deliver us from evil.

Officiant   Lord, hear our prayer;
People   And let our cry come to you.
Officiant   Let us pray.

The Officiant then says one of the following Collects

Be our light in the darkness, O Lord, and in your great mercy defend us from all perils and dangers of this night; for the love of your only Son, our Savior Jesus Christ. *Amen.*

Be present, O merciful God, and protect us through the hours of this night, so that we who are wearied by the changes and chances of this life may rest in your eternal changelessness; through Jesus Christ our Lord. *Amen.*

Look down, O Lord, from your heavenly throne, and illumine this night with your celestial brightness; that by night as by day your people may glorify your holy Name; through Jesus Christ our Lord. *Amen.*

Visit this place, O Lord, and drive far from it all snares of the enemy; let your holy angels dwell with us to preserve us in peace; and let your blessing be upon us always; through Jesus Christ our Lord. *Amen.*

A Collect for Saturdays

We give you thanks, O God, for revealing your Son Jesus Christ to us by the light of his resurrection: Grant that as we sing your glory at the close of this day, our joy may abound in the morning as we celebrate the Paschal mystery; through Jesus Christ our Lord. *Amen.*

One of the following prayers may be added

Keep watch, dear Lord, with those who work, or watch, or weep this night, and give your angels charge over those who sleep. Tend the sick, Lord Christ; give rest to the weary, bless the dying, soothe the suffering, pity the afflicted, shield the joyous; and all for your love's sake. *Amen.*

or this

O God, your unfailing providence sustains the world we live in and the life we live: Watch over those, both night and day, who work while others sleep, and grant that we may never forget that our common life depends upon each other's toil; through Jesus Christ our Lord. *Amen.*

Silence may be kept, and free intercessions and thanksgivings may be offered.

The service concludes with the Song of Simeon with this Antiphon, which is sung or said by all

Guide us waking, O Lord, and guard us sleeping; that awake we may watch with Christ, and asleep we may rest in peace.

In Easter Season, add   Alleluia, alleluia, alleluia.

Lord, you now have set your servant free *
   to go in peace as you have promised;

For these eyes of mine have seen the Savior, *
   whom you have prepared for all the world to see:

A Light to enlighten the nations, *
   and the glory of your people Israel.

Glory to the Father, and to the Son, and to the Holy Spirit: *
   as it was in the beginning, is now, and will be for ever. Amen.

All repeat the Antiphon

Guide us waking, O Lord, and guard us sleeping; that awake
we may watch with Christ, and asleep we may rest in peace.

In Easter Season, add   Alleluia, alleluia, alleluia.

Officiant   Let us bless the Lord.
People   Thanks be to God.

The Officiant concludes

The almighty and merciful Lord, Father, Son, and Holy Spirit,
bless us and keep us. *Amen.*

Daily Devotions for Individuals and Families

These devotions follow the basic structure of the Daily Office of the Church.

When more than one person is present, the Reading and the Collect should be read by one person, and the other parts said in unison, or in some other convenient manner. (For suggestions about reading the Psalms, see page 582.)

For convenience, appropriate Psalms, Readings, and Collects are provided in each service. When desired, however, the Collect of the Day, or any of the Collects appointed in the Daily Offices, may be used instead.

The Psalms and Readings may be replaced by those appointed in

a) the Lectionary for Sundays, Holy Days, the Common of Saints, and Various Occasions, page 888

b) the Daily Office Lectionary, page 934

c) some other manual of devotion which provides daily selections for the Church Year.

In the Morning

From Psalm 51

Open my lips, O Lord, *
  and my mouth shall proclaim your praise.
Create in me a clean heart, O God, *
  and renew a right spirit within me.
Cast me not away from your presence *
  and take not your holy Spirit from me.
Give me the joy of your saving help again *
  and sustain me with your bountiful Spirit.
Glory to the Father, and to the Son, and to the Holy Spirit: *
  as it was in the beginning, is now, and will be for ever. Amen.

A Reading

Blessed be the God and Father of our Lord Jesus Christ!
By his great mercy we have been born anew to a living hope
through the resurrection of Jesus Christ from the dead.
1 Peter 1:3

A period of silence may follow.

A hymn or canticle may be used; the Apostles' Creed may be said.

Prayers may be offered for ourselves and others.

The Lord's Prayer

The Collect

Lord God, almighty and everlasting Father, you have brought
us in safety to this new day: Preserve us with your mighty
power, that we may not fall into sin, nor be overcome by
adversity; and in all we do, direct us to the fulfilling of your
purpose; through Jesus Christ our Lord. *Amen.*

At Noon

From Psalm 113

Give praise, you servants of the LORD; *
  praise the Name of the LORD.
Let the Name of the LORD be blessed, *
  from this time forth for evermore.
From the rising of the sun to its going down *
  let the Name of the LORD be praised.
The LORD is high above all nations, *
  and his glory above the heavens.

A Reading

O God, you will keep in perfect peace those whose minds are
fixed on you; for in returning and rest we shall be saved; in
quietness and trust shall be our strength.   *Isaiah 26:3; 30:15*

Prayers may be offered for ourselves and others.

The Lord's Prayer

The Collect

Blessed Savior, at this hour you hung upon the cross,
stretching out your loving arms: Grant that all the peoples of
the earth may look to you and be saved; for your mercies'
sake. *Amen.*

or this

Lord Jesus Christ, you said to your apostles,"Peace I give to
you; my own peace I leave with you:" Regard not our sins,
but the faith of your Church, and give to us the peace and
unity of that heavenly City, where with the Father and the
Holy Spirit you live and reign, now and for ever. *Amen.*

In the Early Evening

This devotion may be used before or after the evening meal.

The Order of Worship for the Evening, page 109, may be used instead.

O gracious Light,
pure brightness of the everliving Father in heaven,
O Jesus Christ, holy and blessed!

Now as we come to the setting of the sun,
and our eyes behold the vesper light,
we sing your praises O God: Father, Son, and Holy Spirit.

You are worthy at all times to be praised by happy voices,
O Son of God, O Giver of life,
and to be glorified through all the worlds.

A Reading

It is not ourselves that we proclaim; we proclaim Christ
Jesus as Lord, and ourselves as your servants, for Jesus' sake.
For the same God who said, "Out of darkness let light
shine," has caused his light to shine within us, to give the
light of revelation—the revelation of the glory of God in the
face of Jesus Christ.   *2 Corinthians 4:5-6*

Prayers may be offered for ourselves and others.

The Lord's Prayer

The Collect

Lord Jesus, stay with us, for evening is at hand and the day is
past; be our companion in the way, kindle our hearts, and
awaken hope, that we may know you as you are revealed in
Scripture and the breaking of bread. Grant this for the sake
of your love. *Amen.*

At the Close of Day

Psalm 134

Behold now, bless the LORD, all you servants of the LORD, *
  you that stand by night in the house of the LORD.
Lift up your hands in the holy place and bless the LORD; *
  the LORD who made heaven and earth bless you out of Zion.

A Reading

Lord, you are in the midst of us and we are called by your
Name: Do not forsake us, O Lord our God.   *Jeremiah 14:9,22*

The following may be said

Lord, you now have set your servant free *
  to go in peace as you have promised;
For these eyes of mine have seen the Savior, *
  whom you have prepared for all the world to see:
A Light to enlighten the nations, *
  and the glory of your people Israel.

*Prayers for ourselves and others may follow. It is appropriate that
prayers of thanksgiving for the blessings of the day, and penitence for our
sins, be included.*

The Lord's Prayer

The Collect

Visit this place, O Lord, and drive far from it all snares of the
enemy; let your holy angels dwell with us to preserve us in
peace; and let your blessing be upon us always; through Jesus
Christ our Lord. *Amen.*

The almighty and merciful Lord, Father, Son, and Holy Spirit,
bless us and keep us. *Amen.*

Additional Directions

Morning and Evening Prayer

Any of the opening sentences of Scripture, including those listed for specific seasons or days, may be used at any time according to the discretion of the officiant.

The proper antiphons on pages 43-44 and 80-82 may be used as refrains with either of the Invitatory Psalms.

Antiphons drawn from the Psalms themselves, or from the opening sentences given in the Offices, or from other passages of Scripture may be used with the Psalms and biblical Canticles.

Gloria Patri is always sung or said at the conclusion of the entire portion of the Psalter; and may be used after the Invitatory Psalm or the Canticle "Christ our Passover," after each Psalm, and after each section of Psalm 119.

The Gloria printed at the conclusion of certain Canticles may be omitted when desired.

The following pointing of the Gloria may be used:

Glory to the Father, and to the Son, *
   and to the Holy Spirit:

As it was in the beginning, is now, *
   and will be for ever. Amen.

In Rite One services of Morning Prayer and Evening Prayer, the following form of the Gloria may be used:

Glory be to the Father, and to the Son, *
   and to the Holy Ghost:

As it was in the beginning, is now, and ever shall be, *
   world without end. Amen.

Metrical versions of the Invitatory Psalms, and of the Canticles after the Readings, may be used.

In special circumstances, in place of a Canticle, a hymn may be sung.

The Apostles' Creed is omitted from the Office when the Eucharist with its own Creed is to follow. It may also be omitted at one of the Offices on weekdays.

The Lord's Prayer may be omitted from the Office when the Litany or the Eucharist is to follow immediately.

In the Intercessions and Thanksgivings, opportunity may be given for the members of the congregation to express intentions or objects of prayer and thanksgiving, either at the bidding, or in the course of the prayer; and opportunity may be given for silent prayer.

A sermon may be preached after the Office; or, within the Office, after the Readings or at the time of the hymn or anthem after the Collects.

On occasion, at the discretion of the Minister, a reading from non-biblical Christian literature may follow the biblical Readings.

An offering may be received and presented at the Office.

When there is a Communion

When Morning or Evening Prayer is used as the Liturgy of the Word at the Eucharist, the Nicene Creed may take the place of the Apostles' Creed, and the officiant may pass at once from the salutation "The Lord be with you," and its response, to the Collect of the Day. A Lesson from the Gospel is always included.

The Intercessions on such occasions are to conform to the directions on page 383.

The service then continues with the [Peace and] Offertory.

Order of Worship for the Evening

Before this service, there should be as little artificial light as possible in the church. A musical prelude or processional is not appropriate.

When the ministers enter, one or two lighted candles may be carried before them, and used to provide light for reading the opening Short Lesson and the Prayer for Light. From Easter Day through the Day of Pentecost, the Paschal Candle, if used, should be burning in its customary place before the people assemble; the officiant then goes to a place close by it to begin the service by its light.

The Short Lessons may be read from any version of the Scriptures authorized for public worship in this Church, and should be read without announcement or conclusion. When one or more Scripture Lessons are to be read later in the service, the Short Lesson may be omitted.

For the lighting of the candles at the Altar and elsewhere, in Easter Season the flame may be taken from the Paschal Candle. At other times, the candle or candles carried in at the beginning of the service may be placed on or near the Altar, and other candles may be lighted from them. During Advent, the lighting of an Advent Wreath may take place after the Prayer for Light. On special occasions, lighted candles may be distributed to members of the congregation.

When this service is used in private houses, candles may be lighted at the dining table, or at some other convenient place.

If incense is to be used, it is appropriate after the candles have been lighted and while the hymn Phos hilaron is being sung.

When this service continues as a complete Office, Psalms and Lessons from the Office Lectionary or the Proper of the Day, or ones suitable to the season or the occasion, may be used. Psalms generally appropriate to the evening include: 8, 23, 27, 36, 84, 93, 113, 114, 117, 121, 134, 139, 141, 143. When desired, more than one Lesson may be read, with silence or singing between them.

If an additional hymn is desired, it may be sung immediately before the Blessing or Dismissal.

When a meal is to follow, a blessing over food may serve as the conclusion of this form of service.

Suggested Canticles at Morning Prayer

	After the *Old Testament Reading*	*After the* *New Testament Reading*
Sun.	4. or 16. Benedictus Dominus *Advent:* 11. Surge, illuminare *Lent:* 14. Kyrie Pantokrator *Easter:* 8. Cantemus Domino	7. or 21. Te Deum laudamus *Advent and Lent:* 4. or 16. Benedictus Dominus
Mon.	9. Ecce, Deus	19. Magna et mirabilia
Tue.	2. or 13. Benedictus es	18. Dignus es
Wed.	11. Surge, illuminare *Lent:* 14. Kyrie Pantokrator	4. or 16. Benedictus Dominus
Thu.	8. Cantemus Domino	6. or 20. Gloria in excelsis *Advent and Lent:* 19. Magna et mirabilia
Fri.	10. Quærite Dominum *Lent:* 14. Kyrie Pantokrator	18. Dignus es
Sat.	1. or 12. Benedicite	19. Magna et mirabilia

On Feasts of our Lord and other Major Feasts

4. or 16. Benedictus Dominus   7. or 21. Te Deum laudamus

Suggested Canticles at Evening Prayer

	After the *Old Testament Reading*	*After the* *New Testament Reading*
Sun.	Magnificat	Nunc dimittis*
Mon.	8. Cantemus Domino *Lent:* 14. Kyrie Pantokrator	Nunc dimittis
Tue.	10. Quærite Dominum	Magnificat
Wed.	1. or 12. Benedicite	Nunc dimittis
Thu.	11. Surge, illuminare	Magnificat
Fri.	2. or 13. Benedictus es	Nunc dimittis
Sat.	9. Ecce, Deus	Magnificat

On Feasts of our Lord and other Major Feasts

Magnificat	Nunc dimittis*

* *If only one Reading is used, the suggested Canticle is the Magnificat.*

Psalm 95: Traditional   *Venite, exultemus*

O come, let us sing unto the Lord; *
   let us heartily rejoice in the strength of our salvation.
Let us come before his presence with thanksgiving, *
   and show ourselves glad in him with psalms.

For the Lord is a great God, *
   and a great King above all gods.
In his hand are all the corners of the eárth, *
   and the strength of the hills is his also.
The sea is his and he made it, *
   and his hands prepared the dry land.

O come, let us worship and fall down *
   and kneel before the Lord our Maker.
For he is the Lord our God, *
   and we are the people of his pasture
   and the sheep of his hand.

Today if ye will hear his voice, harden not your hearts*
   as in the provocation,
   and as in the day of temptation in the wilderness;
When your fathers tempted me, *
   proved me, and saw my works.

Forty years long was I grieved with this generation, and said, *
   It is a people that do err in their hearts,
   for they have not known my ways;
Unto whom I sware in my wrath, *
   that they should not enter into my rest.

The Great Litany

The Great Litany

To be said or sung, kneeling, standing, or in procession; before the Eucharist or after the Collects of Morning or Evening Prayer; or separately; especially in Lent and on Rogation days.

O God the Father, Creator of heaven and earth,
Have mercy upon us.

O God the Son, Redeemer of the world,
Have mercy upon us.

O God the Holy Ghost, Sanctifier of the faithful,
Have mercy upon us.

O holy, blessed, and glorious Trinity, one God,
Have mercy upon us.

Remember not, Lord Christ, our offenses, nor the offenses of our forefathers; neither reward us according to our sins. Spare us, good Lord, spare thy people, whom thou hast redeemed with thy most precious blood, and by thy mercy preserve us for ever.
Spare us, good Lord.

From all evil and wickedness; from sin; from the crafts and assaults of the devil; and from everlasting damnation,
Good Lord, deliver us.

From all blindness of heart; from pride, vainglory, and hypocrisy; from envy, hatred, and malice; and from all want of charity,
Good Lord, deliver us.

From all inordinate and sinful affections; and from all the deceits of the world, the flesh, and the devil,
Good Lord, deliver us.

From all false doctrine, heresy, and schism; from hardness of heart, and contempt of thy Word and commandment,
Good Lord, deliver us.

From lightning and tempest; from earthquake, fire, and flood; from plague, pestilence, and famine,
Good Lord, deliver us.

From all oppression, conspiracy, and rebellion; from violence, battle, and murder; and from dying suddenly and unprepared,
Good Lord, deliver us.

By the mystery of thy holy Incarnation; by thy holy Nativity and submission to the Law; by thy Baptism, Fasting, and Temptation,
Good Lord, deliver us.

By thine Agony and Bloody Sweat; by thy Cross and Passion; by thy precious Death and Burial; by thy glorious Resurrection and Ascension; and by the Coming of the Holy Ghost,
Good Lord, deliver us.

In all time of our tribulation; in all time of our prosperity; in the hour of death, and in the day of judgment,
Good Lord, deliver us.

We sinners do beseech thee to hear us, O Lord God; and that it may please thee to rule and govern thy holy Church Universal in the right way,
We beseech thee to hear us, good Lord.

That it may please thee to illumine all bishops, priests, and deacons, with true knowledge and understanding of thy Word; and that both by their preaching and living, they may set it forth, and show it accordingly,
We beseech thee to hear us, good Lord.

That it may please thee to bless and keep all thy people,
We beseech thee to hear us, good Lord.

That it may please thee to send forth laborers into thy harvest, and to draw all mankind into thy kingdom,
We beseech thee to hear us, good Lord.

That it may please thee to give to all people increase of grace to hear and receive thy Word, and to bring forth the fruits of the Spirit,
We beseech thee to hear us, good Lord.

That it may please thee to bring into the way of truth all such as have erred, and are deceived,
We beseech thee to hear us, good Lord.

That it may please thee to give us a heart to love and fear thee, and diligently to live after thy commandments,
We beseech thee to hear us, good Lord.

That it may please thee so to rule the hearts of thy servants, the President of the United States (*or* of this nation), and all others in authority, that they may do justice, and love mercy, and walk in the ways of truth,
We beseech thee to hear us, good Lord.

That it may please thee to make wars to cease in all the world;
to give to all nations unity, peace, and concord; and to
bestow freedom upon all peoples,
We beseech thee to hear us, good Lord.

That it may please thee to show thy pity upon all prisoners
and captives, the homeless and the hungry, and all who are
desolate and oppressed,
We beseech thee to hear us, good Lord.

That it may please thee to give and preserve to our use the
bountiful fruits of the earth, so that in due time all may enjoy
them,
We beseech thee to hear us, good Lord.

That it may please thee to inspire us, in our several callings,
to do the work which thou givest us to do with singleness of
heart as thy servants, and for the common good,
We beseech thee to hear us, good Lord.

That it may please thee to preserve all who are in danger by
reason of their labor or their travel,
We beseech thee to hear us, good Lord.

That it may please thee to preserve, and provide for, all
women in childbirth, young children and orphans, the
widowed, and all whose homes are broken or torn by strife,
We beseech thee to hear us, good Lord.

That it may please thee to visit the lonely; to strengthen all
who suffer in mind, body, and spirit; and to comfort with thy
presence those who are failing and infirm,
We beseech thee to hear us, good Lord.

That it may please thee to support, help, and comfort all who
are in danger, necessity, and tribulation,
We beseech thee to hear us, good Lord.

That it may please thee to have mercy upon all mankind,
We beseech thee to hear us, good Lord.

That it may please thee to give us true repentance; to forgive us all our sins, negligences, and ignorances; and to endue us with the grace of thy Holy Spirit to amend our lives according to thy holy Word,
We beseech thee to hear us, good Lord.

That it may please thee to forgive our enemies, persecutors, and slanderers, and to turn their hearts,
We beseech thee to hear us, good Lord.

That it may please thee to strengthen such as do stand; to comfort and help the weak-hearted; to raise up those who fall; and finally to beat down Satan under our feet,
We beseech thee to hear us, good Lord.

That it may please thee to grant to all the faithful departed eternal life and peace,
We beseech thee to hear us, good Lord.

That it may please thee to grant that, in the fellowship of [_____ and] all the saints, we may attain to thy heavenly kingdom,
We beseech thee to hear us, good Lord.

Son of God, we beseech thee to hear us.
Son of God, we beseech thee to hear us.

O Lamb of God, that takest away the sins of the world,
Have mercy upon us.

O Lamb of God, that takest away the sins of the world,
Have mercy upon us.

O Lamb of God, that takest away the sins of the world,
Grant us thy peace.

O Christ, hear us.
O Christ, hear us.

Lord, have mercy upon us.   Kyrie eleison.
Christ, have mercy upon us.   *or*   *Christe eleison.*
Lord, have mercy upon us.   Kyrie eleison.

*When the Litany is sung or said immediately before the Eucharist, the
Litany concludes here, and the Eucharist begins with the Salutation and
the Collect of the Day.*

On all other occasions, the Officiant and People say together

Our Father, who art in heaven,
    hallowed be thy Name,
    thy kingdom come,
    thy will be done,
        on earth as it is in heaven.
Give us this day our daily bread.
And forgive us our trespasses,
    as we forgive those who trespass against us.
And lead us not into temptation,
    but deliver us from evil. Amen.

V.   O Lord, let thy mercy be showed upon us;
R.   As we do put our trust in thee.

The Officiant concludes with the following or some other Collect

Let us pray.

Almighty God, who hast promised to hear the petitions of
those who ask in thy Son's Name: We beseech thee mercifully
to incline thine ear to us who have now made our prayers
and supplications unto thee; and grant that those things
which we have asked faithfully according to thy will, may be
obtained effectually, to the relief of our necessity, and to the
setting forth of thy glory; through Jesus Christ our Lord.
Amen.

The grace of our Lord Jesus Christ, and the love of God, and the fellowship of the Holy Ghost, be with us all evermore. *Amen.*

The Supplication

For use in the Litany in place of the Versicle and Collect which follows the Lord's Prayer; or at the end of Morning or Evening Prayer; or as a separate devotion; especially in times of war, or of national anxiety, or of disaster.

O Lord, arise, help us;
And deliver us for thy Name's sake.

O God, we have heard with our ears, and our fathers have declared unto us, the noble works that thou didst in their days, and in the old time before them.

O Lord, arise, help us;
and deliver us for thy Name's sake.

Glory be to the Father, and to the Son, and to the Holy Ghost; as it was in the beginning, is now, and ever shall be, world without end. Amen.

O Lord, arise, help us;
and deliver us for thy Name's sake.

V.   From our enemies defend us, O Christ;
R.   Graciously behold our afflictions.
V.   With pity behold the sorrows of our hearts;
R.   Mercifully forgive the sins of thy people.

V. Favorably with mercy hear our prayers;
R. O Son of David, have mercy upon us.
V. Both now and ever vouchsafe to hear us, O Christ;
R. Graciously hear us, O Christ; graciously hear us, O Lord Christ.

The Officiant concludes

Let us pray.

We humbly beseech thee, O Father, mercifully to look upon our infirmities; and, for the glory of thy Name, turn from us all those evils that we most justly have deserved; and grant that in all our troubles we may put our whole trust and confidence in thy mercy, and evermore serve thee in holiness and pureness of living, to thy honor and glory; through our only Mediator and Advocate, Jesus Christ our Lord. *Amen.*

The Collects
for the
Church Year

Concerning the Proper of the Church Year

The Proper of the Church Year includes the appointed Collects; the Proper Prefaces, directions for which are to be found in the pages following; and the appointed Psalms and Lessons, which appear in tables beginning on page 889.

The Proper appointed for the Sunday is also used at celebrations of the Eucharist on the weekdays following, unless otherwise ordered for Holy Days and Various Occasions.

The Proper to be used on each of the Sundays after Pentecost (except for Trinity Sunday) is determined by the calendar date of that Sunday. Thus, in any year, the Proper for the Sunday after Trinity Sunday (the Second Sunday after Pentecost) is the numbered Proper (number 3 through number 8), the calendar date of which falls on that Sunday, or is closest to it, whether before or after. Thereafter, the Propers are used consecutively. For example, if the Sunday after Trinity Sunday is May 26, the sequence begins with Proper 3 (Propers 1 and 2 being used on the weekdays of Pentecost and Trinity weeks). If the Sunday after Trinity Sunday is June 13, the sequence begins with Proper 6 (Propers 1 through 3 being omitted that year, and Propers 4 and 5 being used in Pentecost and Trinity weeks). See also the Table on pages 884-885.

The Collect appointed for any Sunday or other Feast may be used at the evening service of the day before.

Directions concerning the Common of Saints and services for Various Occasions are on pages 195, 199, 246 and 251.

Collects: Traditional

First Sunday of Advent

Almighty God, give us grace that we may cast away the works of darkness, and put upon us the armor of light, now in the time of this mortal life in which thy Son Jesus Christ came to visit us in great humility; that in the last day, when he shall come again in his glorious majesty to judge both the quick and the dead, we may rise to the life immortal; through him who liveth and reigneth with thee and the Holy Ghost, one God, now and for ever. *Amen.*

Preface of Advent

Second Sunday of Advent

Merciful God, who sent thy messengers the prophets to preach repentance and prepare the way for our salvation: Give us grace to heed their warnings and forsake our sins, that we may greet with joy the coming of Jesus Christ our Redeemer; who liveth and reigneth with thee and the Holy Spirit, one God, now and for ever. *Amen.*

Preface of Advent

Third Sunday of Advent

Stir up thy power, O Lord, and with great might come among us; and, because we are sorely hindered by our sins, let thy bountiful grace and mercy speedily help and deliver us; through Jesus Christ our Lord, to whom, with thee and the Holy Ghost, be honor and glory, world without end. *Amen.*

Preface of Advent

Wednesday, Friday, and Saturday of this week are the traditional winter Ember Days.

Fourth Sunday of Advent

We beseech thee, Almighty God, to purify our consciences by thy daily visitation, that when thy Son our Lord cometh he may find in us a mansion prepared for himself; through the same Jesus Christ our Lord, who liveth and reigneth with thee, in the unity of the Holy Spirit, one God, now and for ever. *Amen.*

Preface of Advent

The Nativity of Our Lord: Christmas Day   *December 25*

O God, who makest us glad with the yearly remembrance of the birth of thy only Son Jesus Christ: Grant that as we joyfully receive him for our Redeemer, so we may with sure confidence behold him when he shall come to be our Judge; who liveth and reigneth with thee and the Holy Ghost, one God, world without end. *Amen.*

or the following

O God, who hast caused this holy night to shine with the illumination of the true Light: Grant us, we beseech thee, that as we have known the mystery of that Light upon earth, so may we also perfectly enjoy him in heaven; where with thee and the Holy Spirit he liveth and reigneth, one God, in glory everlasting. *Amen*.

or this

Almighty God, who hast given us thy only-begotten Son to take our nature upon him and as at this time to be born of a pure virgin: Grant that we, being regenerate and made thy children by adoption and grace, may daily be renewed by thy Holy Spirit; through the same our Lord Jesus Christ, who liveth and reigneth with thee and the same Spirit ever, one God, world without end. *Amen*.

Preface of the Incarnation

The Collect immediately preceding and any of the sets of Proper Lessons for Christmas Day serve for any weekdays between Holy Innocents' Day and the First Sunday after Christmas Day.

First Sunday after Christmas Day

This Sunday takes precedence over the three Holy Days which follow Christmas Day. As necessary, the observance of one, two, or all three of them, is postponed one day.

Almighty God, who hast poured upon us the new light of thine incarnate Word: Grant that the same light, enkindled in our hearts, may shine forth in our lives; through the same Jesus Christ our Lord, who liveth and reigneth with thee, in the unity of the Holy Spirit, one God, now and for ever. *Amen*.

Preface of the Incarnation

The Holy Name *January 1*

Eternal Father, who didst give to thine incarnate Son the holy name of Jesus to be the sign of our salvation: Plant in every heart, we beseech thee, the love of him who is the Savior of the world, even our Lord Jesus Christ; who liveth and reigneth with thee and the Holy Spirit, one God, in glory everlasting. *Amen.*

Preface of the Incarnation

Second Sunday after Christmas Day

O God, who didst wonderfully create, and yet more wonderfully restore, the dignity of human nature: Grant that we may share the divine life of him who humbled himself to share our humanity, thy Son Jesus Christ; who liveth and reigneth with thee, in the unity of the Holy Spirit, one God, for ever and ever. *Amen.*

Preface of the Incarnation

The Epiphany *January 6*

O God, who by the leading of a star didst manifest thy only-begotten Son to the peoples of the earth: Lead us, who know thee now by faith, to thy presence, where we may behold thy glory face to face; through the same Jesus Christ our Lord, who liveth and reigneth with thee and the Holy Spirit, one God, now and for ever. *Amen.*

Preface of the Epiphany

The preceding Collect, with the Psalm and Lessons for the Epiphany, or those for the Second Sunday after Christmas Day, serves for weekdays between the Epiphany and the following Sunday. The Preface of the Epiphany is used.

First Sunday after the Epiphany: The Baptism of our Lord

Father in heaven, who at the baptism of Jesus in the River
Jordan didst proclaim him thy beloved Son and anoint him
with the Holy Spirit: Grant that all who are baptized into his
Name may keep the covenant they have made, and boldly
confess him as Lord and Savior; who with thee and the same
Spirit liveth and reigneth, one God, in glory everlasting.
Amen.

Preface of the Epiphany

Second Sunday after the Epiphany

Almighty God, whose Son our Savior Jesus Christ is the light
of the world: Grant that thy people, illumined by thy Word
and Sacraments, may shine with the radiance of Christ's
glory, that he may be known, worshiped, and obeyed to the
ends of the earth; through the same Jesus Christ our Lord,
who with thee and the Holy Spirit liveth and reigneth, one
God, now and for ever. *Amen.*

Preface of the Epiphany, or of the Lord's Day

Third Sunday after the Epiphany

Give us grace, O Lord, to answer readily the call of our
Savior Jesus Christ and proclaim to all people the Good
News of his salvation, that we and all the whole world may
perceive the glory of his marvelous works; who liveth and
reigneth with thee and the Holy Spirit, one God, for ever and
ever. *Amen.*

Preface of the Epiphany, or of the Lord's Day

Fourth Sunday after the Epiphany

Almighty and everlasting God, who dost govern all things in heaven and earth: Mercifully hear the supplications of thy people, and in our time grant us thy peace; through Jesus Christ our Lord, who liveth and reigneth with thee and the Holy Spirit, one God, for ever and ever. *Amen.*

Preface of the Epiphany, or of the Lord's Day

Fifth Sunday after the Epiphany

Set us free, O God, from the bondage of our sins and give us, we beseech thee, the liberty of that abundant life which thou hast manifested to us in thy Son our Savior Jesus Christ; who liveth and reigneth with thee, in the unity of the Holy Spirit, one God, now and for ever. *Amen.*

Preface of the Epiphany, or of the Lord's Day

Sixth Sunday after the Epiphany

O God, the strength of all those who put their trust in thee: Mercifully accept our prayers; and because, through the weakness of our mortal nature, we can do no good thing without thee, grant us the help of thy grace, that in keeping thy commandments we may please thee both in will and deed; through Jesus Christ our Lord, who liveth and reigneth with thee and the Holy Spirit, one God, for ever and ever. *Amen.*

Preface of the Epiphany, or of the Lord's Day

Seventh Sunday after the Epiphany

O Lord, who hast taught us that all our doings without charity are nothing worth: Send thy Holy Ghost and pour into our hearts that most excellent gift of charity, the very bond of peace and of all virtues, without which whosoever liveth is counted dead before thee. Grant this for thine only Son Jesus Christ's sake, who liveth and reigneth with thee and the same Holy Ghost, one God, now and for ever. *Amen.*

Preface of the Epiphany, or of the Lord's Day

Eighth Sunday after the Epiphany

O most loving Father, who willest us to give thanks for all things, to dread nothing but the loss of thee, and to cast all our care on thee who carest for us: Preserve us from faithless fears and worldly anxieties, and grant that no clouds of this mortal life may hide from us the light of that love which is immortal, and which thou hast manifested unto us in thy Son Jesus Christ our Lord; who liveth and reigneth with thee, in the unity of the Holy Spirit, one God, now and for ever. *Amen.*

Preface of the Epiphany, or of the Lord's Day

Last Sunday after the Epiphany

This Proper is always used on the Sunday before Ash Wednesday.

O God, who before the passion of thy only-begotten Son didst reveal his glory upon the holy mount: Grant unto us that we, beholding by faith the light of his countenance, may be strengthened to bear our cross, and be changed into his likeness from glory to glory; through the same Jesus Christ our Lord, who liveth and reigneth with thee and the Holy Spirit, one God, for ever and ever. *Amen.*

Preface of the Epiphany

Ash Wednesday

The Proper Liturgy for this day is on page 264.

Almighty and everlasting God, who hatest nothing that thou hast made and dost forgive the sins of all those who are penitent: Create and make in us new and contrite hearts, that we, worthily lamenting our sins and acknowledging our wretchedness, may obtain of thee, the God of all mercy, perfect remission and forgiveness; through Jesus Christ our Lord, who liveth and reigneth with thee and the Holy Spirit, one God, for ever and ever. *Amen.*

Preface of Lent

This Collect, with the corresponding Psalm and Lessons, serves for the weekdays which follow, except as otherwise appointed.

First Sunday in Lent

Almighty God, whose blessed Son was led by the Spirit to be tempted of Satan: Make speed to help thy servants who are assaulted by manifold temptations; and, as thou knowest their several infirmities, let each one find thee mighty to save; through Jesus Christ thy Son our Lord, who liveth and reigneth with thee and the Holy Spirit, one God, now and for ever. *Amen.*

Preface of Lent

Wednesday, Friday, and Saturday of this week are the traditional spring Ember Days.

Second Sunday in Lent

O God, whose glory it is always to have mercy: Be gracious to all who have gone astray from thy ways, and bring them again with penitent hearts and steadfast faith to embrace and hold fast the unchangeable truth of thy Word, Jesus Christ thy Son; who with thee and the Holy Spirit liveth and reigneth, one God, for ever and ever. *Amen.*

Preface of Lent

Third Sunday in Lent

Almighty God, who seest that we have no power of ourselves to help ourselves: Keep us both outwardly in our bodies and inwardly in our souls, that we may be defended from all adversities which may happen to the body, and from all evil thoughts which may assault and hurt the soul; through Jesus Christ our Lord, who liveth and reigneth with thee and the Holy Spirit, one God, for ever and ever. *Amen.*

Preface of Lent

Fourth Sunday in Lent

Gracious Father, whose blessed Son Jesus Christ came down from heaven to be the true bread which giveth life to the world: Evermore give us this bread, that he may live in us, and we in him; who liveth and reigneth with thee and the Holy Spirit, one God, now and for ever. *Amen.*

Preface of Lent

Fifth Sunday in Lent

O Almighty God, who alone canst order the unruly wills and affections of sinful men: Grant unto thy people that they may love the thing which thou commandest, and desire that which thou dost promise; that so, among the sundry and manifold changes of the world, our hearts may surely there be fixed where true joys are to be found; through Jesus Christ our Lord, who liveth and reigneth with thee and the Holy Spirit, one God, now and for ever. *Amen.*

Preface of Lent

Sunday of the Passion: Palm Sunday

The Proper Liturgy for this day is on page 270.

Almighty and everlasting God, who, of thy tender love towards mankind, hast sent thy Son our Savior Jesus Christ to take upon him our flesh, and to suffer death upon the cross, that all mankind should follow the example of his great humility: Mercifully grant that we may both follow the example of his patience, and also be made partakers of his resurrection; through the same Jesus Christ our Lord, who liveth and reigneth with thee and the Holy Spirit, one God, for ever and ever. *Amen.*

Preface of Holy Week

Monday in Holy Week

Almighty God, whose most dear Son went not up to joy but first he suffered pain, and entered not into glory before he was crucified: Mercifully grant that we, walking in the way of the cross, may find it none other than the way of life and peace; through the same thy Son Jesus Christ our Lord, who liveth and reigneth with thee and the Holy Spirit, one God, for ever and ever. *Amen.*

Preface of Holy Week

Tuesday in Holy Week

O God, who by the passion of thy blessed Son didst make an instrument of shameful death to be unto us the means of life: Grant us so to glory in the cross of Christ, that we may gladly suffer shame and loss for the sake of thy Son our Savior Jesus Christ; who liveth and reigneth with thee and the Holy Spirit, one God, for ever and ever. *Amen.*

Preface of Holy Week

Wednesday in Holy Week

O Lord God, whose blessed Son our Savior gave his back to the smiters and hid not his face from shame: Grant us grace to take joyfully the sufferings of the present time, in full assurance of the glory that shall be revealed; through the same thy Son Jesus Christ our Lord, who liveth and reigneth with thee and the Holy Spirit, one God, for ever and ever. *Amen.*

Preface of Holy Week

Maundy Thursday

The Proper Liturgy for this day is on page 274.

Almighty Father, whose dear Son, on the night before he suffered, did institute the Sacrament of his Body and Blood: Mercifully grant that we may thankfully receive the same in remembrance of him who in these holy mysteries giveth us a pledge of life eternal, the same thy Son Jesus Christ our Lord; who now liveth and reigneth with thee and the Holy Spirit ever, one God, world without end. *Amen.*

Preface of Holy Week

Good Friday

The Proper Liturgy for this day is on page 276.

Almighty God, we beseech thee graciously to behold this thy family, for which our Lord Jesus Christ was contented to be betrayed, and given up into the hands of sinners, and to suffer death upon the cross; who now liveth and reigneth with thee and the Holy Ghost ever, one God, world without end. *Amen.*

Holy Saturday

The Proper Liturgy for this day is on page 283.

O God, Creator of heaven and earth: Grant that, as the crucified body of thy dear Son was laid in the tomb and rested on this holy Sabbath, so we may await with him the coming of the third day, and rise with him to newness of life; who now liveth and reigneth with thee and the Holy Spirit, one God, for ever and ever. *Amen.*

Easter Day

The Liturgy of the Easter Vigil is on page 285.

O God, who for our redemption didst give thine only-begotten Son to the death of the cross, and by his glorious resurrection hast delivered us from the power of our enemy: Grant us so to die daily to sin, that we may evermore live with him in the joy of his resurrection; through the same thy Son Christ our Lord, who liveth and reigneth with thee and the Holy Spirit, one God, now and for ever. *Amen.*

or this

O God, who didst make this most holy night to shine with the glory of the Lord's resurrection: Stir up in thy Church that Spirit of adoption which is given to us in Baptism, that we, being renewed both in body and mind, may worship thee in sincerity and truth; through the same Jesus Christ our Lord, who liveth and reigneth with thee in the unity of the same Spirit, one God, now and for ever. *Amen.*

or this

Almighty God, who through thine only-begotten Son Jesus Christ hast overcome death and opened unto us the gate of everlasting life: Grant that we, who celebrate with joy the

day of the Lord's resurrection, may be raised from the death
of sin by thy life-giving Spirit; through the same Jesus Christ
our Lord, who liveth and reigneth with thee and the same
Spirit ever, one God, world without end. *Amen.*

Preface of Easter

Monday in Easter Week

Grant, we beseech thee, Almighty God, that we who celebrate
with reverence the Paschal feast may be found worthy to
attain to everlasting joys; through Jesus Christ our Lord,
who liveth and reigneth with thee and the Holy Spirit, one
God, now and for ever. *Amen.*

Preface of Easter

Tuesday in Easter Week

O God, who by the glorious resurrection of thy Son Jesus
Christ destroyed death and brought life and immortality to
light: Grant that we, who have been raised with him, may
abide in his presence and rejoice in the hope of eternal glory;
through the same Jesus Christ our Lord, to whom, with thee
and the Holy Spirit, be dominion and praise for ever and
ever. *Amen.*

Preface of Easter

Wednesday in Easter Week

O God, whose blessed Son did manifest himself to his disciples
in the breaking of bread: Open, we pray thee, the eyes of our
faith, that we may behold him in all his redeeming work;
through the same thy Son Jesus Christ our Lord, who liveth
and reigneth with thee, in the unity of the Holy Spirit, one
God, now and for ever. *Amen.*

Preface of Easter

Thursday in Easter Week

Almighty and everlasting God, who in the Paschal mystery hast established the new covenant of reconciliation: Grant that all who have been reborn into the fellowship of Christ's Body may show forth in their lives what they profess by their faith; through the same Jesus Christ our Lord, who liveth and reigneth with thee and the Holy Spirit, one God, for ever and ever. *Amen.*

Preface of Easter

Friday in Easter Week

Almighty Father, who hast given thine only Son to die for our sins and to rise again for our justification: Grant us so to put away the leaven of malice and wickedness, that we may always serve thee in pureness of living and truth; through the same thy Son Jesus Christ our Lord, who liveth and reigneth with thee and the Holy Spirit, one God, now and for ever. *Amen.*

Preface of Easter

Saturday in Easter Week

We thank thee, heavenly Father, for that thou hast delivered us from the dominion of sin and death and hast brought us into the kingdom of thy Son; and we pray thee that, as by his death he hath recalled us to life, so by his love he may raise us to joys eternal; who liveth and reigneth with thee, in the unity of the Holy Spirit, one God, now and for ever. *Amen.*

Preface of Easter

Second Sunday of Easter

Almighty and everlasting God, who in the Paschal mystery hast established the new covenant of reconciliation: Grant that all who have been reborn into the fellowship of Christ's

Body may show forth in their lives what they profess by their faith; through the same Jesus Christ our Lord, who liveth and reigneth with thee and the Holy Spirit, one God, for ever and ever. *Amen.*

Preface of Easter

Third Sunday of Easter

O God, whose blessed Son did manifest himself to his disciples in the breaking of bread: Open, we pray thee, the eyes of our faith, that we may behold him in all his redeeming work; through the same thy Son Jesus Christ our Lord, who liveth and reigneth with thee, in the unity of the Holy Spirit, one God, now and for ever. *Amen.*

Preface of Easter

Fourth Sunday of Easter

O God, whose Son Jesus is the good shepherd of thy people: Grant that when we hear his voice we may know him who calleth us each by name, and follow where he doth lead; who, with thee and the Holy Spirit, liveth and reigneth, one God, for ever and ever. *Amen.*

Preface of Easter

Fifth Sunday of Easter

O Almighty God, whom truly to know is everlasting life: Grant us so perfectly to know thy Son Jesus Christ to be the way, the truth, and the life, that we may steadfastly follow his steps in the way that leadeth to eternal life; through the same thy Son Jesus Christ our Lord, who liveth and reigneth with thee, in the unity of the Holy Spirit, one God, for ever and ever. *Amen.*

Preface of Easter

Sixth Sunday of Easter

O God, who hast prepared for those who love thee such good things as pass man's understanding: Pour into our hearts such love toward thee, that we, loving thee in all things and above all things, may obtain thy promises, which exceed all that we can desire; through Jesus Christ our Lord, who liveth and reigneth with thee and the Holy Spirit, one God, for ever and ever. *Amen.*

Preface of Easter

Monday, Tuesday, and Wednesday of this week are the traditional Rogation Days.

Ascension Day

O Almighty God, whose blessed Son our Savior Jesus Christ ascended far above all heavens that he might fill all things: Mercifully give us faith to perceive that, according to his promise, he abideth with his Church on earth, even unto the end of the ages; through the same Jesus Christ our Lord, who liveth and reigneth with thee and the Holy Spirit, one God, in glory everlasting. *Amen.*

or this

Grant, we beseech thee, Almighty God, that like as we do believe thy only-begotten Son our Lord Jesus Christ to have ascended into the heavens, so we may also in heart and mind thither ascend, and with him continually dwell; who liveth and reigneth with thee and the Holy Ghost, one God, world without end. *Amen.*

Preface of the Ascension

Either of the preceding Collects, with the proper Psalm and Lessons for Ascension Day, serves for the following weekdays, except as otherwise appointed.

Seventh Sunday of Easter: The Sunday after Ascension Day

O God, the King of glory, who hast exalted thine only Son Jesus Christ with great triumph unto thy kingdom in heaven: We beseech thee, leave us not comfortless, but send to us thine Holy Ghost to comfort us, and exalt us unto the same place whither our Savior Christ is gone before; who liveth and reigneth with thee and the same Holy Ghost, one God, world without end. *Amen.*

Preface of the Ascension

The Day of Pentecost: Whitsunday

When a Vigil of Pentecost is observed, it begins with the Service of Light, page 109 (substituting, if desired, the Gloria in excelsis for the Phos hilaron), and continues with the Salutation and Collect of the Day. Three or more of the appointed Lessons are read before the Gospel, each followed by a Psalm, Canticle, or hymn. Holy Baptism or Confirmation (beginning with the Presentation of the Candidates), or the Renewal of Baptismal Vows, page 292, follows the Sermon.

Almighty God, who on this day didst open the way of eternal life to every race and nation by the promised gift of thy Holy Spirit: Shed abroad this gift throughout the world by the preaching of the Gospel, that it may reach to the ends of the earth; through Jesus Christ our Lord, who liveth and reigneth with thee, in the unity of the same Spirit, one God, for ever and ever. *Amen.*

or this

O God, who on this day didst teach the hearts of thy faithful people by sending to them the light of thy Holy Spirit: Grant us by the same Spirit to have a right judgment in all things, and evermore to rejoice in his holy comfort; through the merits of Christ Jesus our Savior, who liveth and reigneth with thee, in the unity of the same Spirit, one God, world without end. *Amen.*

Preface of Pentecost

On the weekdays which follow, the numbered Proper which corresponds most closely to the date of Pentecost in that year is used. See page 158.

Wednesday, Friday, and Saturday of this week are the traditional summer Ember Days.

First Sunday after Pentecost: Trinity Sunday

Almighty and everlasting God, who hast given unto us thy servants grace, by the confession of a true faith, to acknowledge the glory of the eternal Trinity, and in the power of the Divine Majesty to worship the Unity: We beseech thee that thou wouldest keep us steadfast in this faith and worship, and bring us at last to see thee in thy one and eternal glory, O Father; who with the Son and the Holy Spirit livest and reignest, one God, for ever and ever. *Amen.*

Preface of Trinity Sunday

On the weekdays which follow, the numbered Proper which corresponds most closely to the date of Trinity Sunday in that year is used.

The Season after Pentecost

Directions for the use of the Propers which follow are on page 158.

Proper 1   *Week of the Sunday closest to May 11*

Remember, O Lord, what thou hast wrought in us and not what we deserve; and, as thou hast called us to thy service, make us worthy of our calling; through Jesus Christ our

Lord, who liveth and reigneth with thee and the Holy Spirit, one God, now and for ever. *Amen.*

No Proper Preface is used.

Proper 2   *Week of the Sunday closest to May 18*

O Almighty and most merciful God, of thy bountiful goodness keep us, we beseech thee, from all things that may hurt us, that we, being ready both in body and soul, may with free hearts accomplish those things which belong to thy purpose; through Jesus Christ our Lord, who liveth and reigneth with thee and the Holy Spirit, one God, now and for ever. *Amen.*

No Proper Preface is used.

Proper 3   *The Sunday closest to May 25*

Grant, O Lord, we beseech thee, that the course of this world may be peaceably governed by thy providence, and that thy Church may joyfully serve thee in confidence and serenity; through Jesus Christ our Lord, who liveth and reigneth with thee and the Holy Spirit, one God, for ever and ever. *Amen.*

Preface of the Lord's Day

Proper 4   *The Sunday closest to June 1*

O God, whose never-failing providence ordereth all things both in heaven and earth: We humbly beseech thee to put away from us all hurtful things, and to give us those things which are profitable for us; through Jesus Christ our Lord, who liveth and reigneth with thee and the Holy Spirit, one God, for ever and ever. *Amen.*

Preface of the Lord's Day

Proper 5   *The Sunday closest to June 8*

O God, from whom all good doth come: Grant that by thy inspiration we may think those things that are right, and by thy merciful guiding may perform the same; through Jesus Christ our Lord, who liveth and reigneth with thee and the Holy Spirit, one God, for ever and ever. *Amen.*

Preface of the Lord's Day

Proper 6   *The Sunday closest to June 15*

Keep, O Lord, we beseech thee, thy household the Church in thy steadfast faith and love, that by the help of thy grace we may proclaim thy truth with boldness, and minister thy justice with compassion; for the sake of our Savior Jesus Christ, who liveth and reigneth with thee and the Holy Spirit, one God, now and for ever. *Amen.*

Preface of the Lord's Day

Proper 7   *The Sunday closest to June 22*

O Lord, we beseech thee, make us to have a perpetual fear and love of thy holy Name, for thou never failest to help and govern those whom thou hast set upon the sure foundation of thy loving-kindness; through Jesus Christ our Lord, who liveth and reigneth with thee and the Holy Spirit, one God, for ever and ever. *Amen.*

Preface of the Lord's Day

Proper 8   *The Sunday closest to June 29*

O Almighty God, who hast built thy Church upon the foundation of the apostles and prophets, Jesus Christ himself being the chief cornerstone: Grant us so to be joined together in unity of spirit by their doctrine, that we may be made an holy temple acceptable unto thee; through the same Jesus Christ our Lord, who liveth and reigneth with thee and the Holy Spirit, one God, for ever and ever. *Amen.*

Preface of the Lord's Day

Proper 9 *The Sunday closest to July 6*

O God, who hast taught us to keep all thy commandments by loving thee and our neighbor: Grant us the grace of thy Holy Spirit, that we may be devoted to thee with our whole heart, and united to one another with pure affection; through Jesus Christ our Lord, who liveth and reigneth with thee and the same Spirit, one God, for ever and ever. *Amen.*

Preface of the Lord's Day

Proper 10 *The Sunday closest to July 13*

O Lord, we beseech thee mercifully to receive the prayers of thy people who call upon thee, and grant that they may both perceive and know what things they ought to do, and also may have grace and power faithfully to fulfill the same; through Jesus Christ our Lord, who liveth and reigneth with thee and the Holy Spirit, one God, now and for ever. *Amen.*

Preface of the Lord's Day

Proper 11 *The Sunday closest to July 20*

Almighty God, the fountain of all wisdom, who knowest our necessities before we ask and our ignorance in asking: Have compassion, we beseech thee, upon our infirmities, and those things which for our unworthiness we dare not, and for our blindness we cannot ask, mercifully give us for the worthiness of thy Son Jesus Christ our Lord; who liveth and reigneth with thee and the Holy Spirit, one God, now and for ever. *Amen.*

Preface of the Lord's Day

Proper 12   *The Sunday closest to July 27*

O God, the protector of all that trust in thee, without whom nothing is strong, nothing is holy: Increase and multiply upon us thy mercy, that, thou being our ruler and guide, we may so pass through things temporal, that we finally lose not the things eternal; through Jesus Christ our Lord, who liveth and reigneth with thee and the Holy Spirit, one God, for ever and ever. *Amen.*

Preface of the Lord's Day

Proper 13   *The Sunday closest to August 3*

O Lord, we beseech thee, let thy continual pity cleanse and defend thy Church, and, because it cannot continue in safety without thy succor, preserve it evermore by thy help and goodness; through Jesus Christ our Lord, who liveth and reigneth with thee and the Holy Spirit, one God, for ever and ever. *Amen.*

Preface of the Lord's Day

Proper 14   *The Sunday closest to August 10*

Grant to us, Lord, we beseech thee, the spirit to think and do always such things as are right, that we, who cannot exist without thee, may by thee be enabled to live according to thy will; through Jesus Christ our Lord, who liveth and reigneth with thee and the Holy Spirit, one God, for ever and ever. *Amen.*

Preface of the Lord's Day

Proper 15   *The Sunday closest to August 17*

Almighty God, who hast given thy only Son to be unto us both a sacrifice for sin and also an example of godly life: Give us grace that we may always most thankfully receive that his inestimable benefit, and also daily endeavor ourselves to follow the blessed steps of his most holy life; through the same thy Son Jesus Christ our Lord, who liveth and reigneth with thee and the Holy Spirit, one God, now and for ever. *Amen.*

Preface of the Lord's Day

Proper 16   *The Sunday closest to August 24*

Grant, we beseech thee, merciful God, that thy Church, being gathered together in unity by thy Holy Spirit, may manifest thy power among all peoples, to the glory of thy Name; through Jesus Christ our Lord, who liveth and reigneth with thee and the same Spirit, one God, world without end. *Amen.*

Preface of the Lord's Day

Proper 17   *The Sunday closest to August 31*

Lord of all power and might, who art the author and giver of all good things: Graft in our hearts the love of thy Name, increase in us true religion, nourish us with all goodness, and bring forth in us the fruit of good works; through Jesus Christ our Lord, who liveth and reigneth with thee and the Holy Spirit, one God, for ever and ever. *Amen.*

Preface of the Lord's Day

Proper 18   *The Sunday closest to September 7*

Grant us, O Lord, we pray thee, to trust in thee with all our heart; seeing that, as thou dost alway resist the proud who confide in their own strength, so thou dost not forsake those who make their boast of thy mercy; through Jesus Christ our Lord, who liveth and reigneth with thee and the Holy Spirit, one God, now and for ever. *Amen.*

Preface of the Lord's Day

Proper 19 *The Sunday closest to September 14*

O God, forasmuch as without thee we are not able to please thee, mercifully grant that thy Holy Spirit may in all things direct and rule our hearts; through Jesus Christ our Lord, who with thee and the same Spirit liveth and reigneth, one God, now and for ever. *Amen.*

Preface of the Lord's Day

The Wednesday, Friday, and Saturday after September 14 are the traditional autumnal Ember Days.

Proper 20 *The Sunday closest to September 21*

Grant us, O Lord, not to mind earthly things, but to love things heavenly; and even now, while we are placed among things that are passing away, to cleave to those that shall abide; through Jesus Christ our Lord, who liveth and reigneth with thee and the Holy Spirit, one God, for ever and ever. *Amen.*

Preface of the Lord's Day

Proper 21 *The Sunday closest to September 28*

O God, who declarest thy almighty power chiefly in showing mercy and pity: Mercifully grant unto us such a measure of thy grace, that we, running to obtain thy promises, may be made partakers of thy heavenly treasure; through Jesus Christ our Lord, who liveth and reigneth with thee and the Holy Spirit, one God, for ever and ever. *Amen.*

Preface of the Lord's Day

Proper 22 *The Sunday closest to October 5*

Almighty and everlasting God, who art always more ready to hear than we to pray, and art wont to give more than either we desire or deserve: Pour down upon us the abundance of thy mercy, forgiving us those things whereof our conscience is afraid, and giving us those good things which we are not worthy to ask, but through the merits and mediation of Jesus Christ thy Son our Lord; who liveth and reigneth with thee and the Holy Spirit, one God, for ever and ever. *Amen.*

Preface of the Lord's Day

Proper 23   *The Sunday closest to October 12*

Lord, we pray thee that thy grace may always precede and follow us, and make us continually to be given to all good works; through Jesus Christ our Lord, who liveth and reigneth with thee and the Holy Spirit, one God, now and for ever. *Amen.*

Preface of the Lord's Day

Proper 24   *The Sunday closest to October 19*

Almighty and everlasting God, who in Christ hast revealed thy glory among the nations: Preserve the works of thy mercy, that thy Church throughout the world may persevere with steadfast faith in the confession of thy Name; through the same Jesus Christ our Lord, who liveth and reigneth with thee and the Holy Spirit, one God, for ever and ever. *Amen.*

Preface of the Lord's Day

Proper 25   *The Sunday closest to October 26*

Almighty and everlasting God, give unto us the increase of faith, hope, and charity; and, that we may obtain that which thou dost promise, make us to love that which thou dost command; through Jesus Christ our Lord, who liveth and reigneth with thee and the Holy Spirit, one God, for ever and ever. *Amen.*

Preface of the Lord's Day

Proper 26 *The Sunday closest to November 2*

Almighty and merciful God, of whose only gift it cometh that
thy faithful people do unto thee true and laudable service:
Grant, we beseech thee, that we may run without stumbling
to obtain thy heavenly promises; through Jesus Christ our
Lord, who liveth and reigneth with thee and the Holy Spirit,
one God, now and for ever. *Amen.*

Preface of the Lord's Day

Proper 27 *The Sunday closest to November 9*

O God, whose blessed Son was manifested that he might
destroy the works of the devil and make us the children of
God and heirs of eternal life: Grant us, we beseech thee, that,
having this hope, we may purify ourselves even as he is pure;
that, when he shall appear again with power and great glory,
we may be made like unto him in his eternal and glorious
kingdom; where with thee, O Father, and thee, O Holy Ghost,
he liveth and reigneth ever, one God, world without end.
Amen.

Preface of the Lord's Day

Proper 28 *The Sunday closest to November 16*

Blessed Lord, who hast caused all holy Scriptures to be
written for our learning: Grant that we may in such wise
hear them, read, mark, learn, and inwardly digest them; that,
by patience and comfort of thy holy Word, we may embrace
and ever hold fast the blessed hope of everlasting life, which
thou hast given us in our Savior Jesus Christ; who liveth and
reigneth with thee and the Holy Spirit, one God, for ever and
ever. *Amen.*

Preface of the Lord's Day

Proper 29   *The Sunday closest to November 23*

Almighty and everlasting God, whose will it is to restore all things in thy well-beloved Son, the King of kings and Lord of lords: Mercifully grant that the peoples of the earth, divided and enslaved by sin, may be freed and brought together under his most gracious rule; who liveth and reigneth with thee and the Holy Spirit, one God, now and for ever. *Amen.*

Preface of the Lord's Day, or of Baptism

Holy Days

Saint Andrew   *November 30*

Almighty God, who didst give such grace to thine apostle Andrew that he readily obeyed the call of thy Son Jesus Christ, and brought his brother with him: Give unto us, who are called by thy Word, grace to follow him without delay, and to bring those near to us into his gracious presence; who liveth and reigneth with thee and the Holy Spirit, one God, now and for ever. *Amen.*

Preface of Apostles

Saint Thomas   *December 21*

Everliving God, who didst strengthen thine apostle Thomas with sure and certain faith in thy Son's resurrection: Grant us so perfectly and without doubt to believe in Jesus Christ, our Lord and our God, that our faith may never be found wanting in thy sight; through him who liveth and reigneth with thee and the Holy Spirit, one God, now and for ever. *Amen.*

Preface of Apostles

Saint Stephen   *December 26*

We give thee thanks, O Lord of glory, for the example of the first martyr Stephen, who looked up to heaven and prayed for his persecutors to thy Son Jesus Christ, who standeth at thy right hand; where he liveth and reigneth with thee and the Holy Spirit, one God, in glory everlasting. *Amen.*

Preface of the Incarnation

Saint John   *December 27*

Shed upon thy Church, we beseech thee, O Lord, the brightness of thy light; that we, being illumined by the teaching of thine apostle and evangelist John, may so walk in the light of thy truth, that we may at length attain to the fullness of life everlasting; through Jesus Christ our Lord, who liveth and reigneth with thee and the Holy Spirit, one God, for ever and ever. *Amen.*

Preface of the Incarnation

The Holy Innocents   *December 28*

We remember this day, O God, the slaughter of the holy innocents of Bethlehem by the order of King Herod. Receive, we beseech thee, into the arms of thy mercy all innocent victims; and by thy great might frustrate the designs of evil tyrants and establish thy rule of justice, love, and peace; through Jesus Christ our Lord, who liveth and reigneth with thee, in the unity of the Holy Spirit, one God, for ever and ever. *Amen.*

Preface of the Incarnation

Confession of Saint Peter   *January 18*

Almighty Father, who didst inspire Simon Peter, first among
the apostles, to confess Jesus as Messiah and Son of the living
God: Keep thy Church steadfast upon the rock of this faith,
that in unity and peace we may proclaim the one truth and
follow the one Lord, our Savior Jesus Christ; who liveth and
reigneth with thee and the Holy Spirit, one God, now and for
ever. *Amen.*

Preface of Apostles

Conversion of Saint Paul   *January 25*

O God, who, by the preaching of thine apostle Paul, hast
caused the light of the Gospel to shine throughout the world:
Grant, we beseech thee, that we, having his wonderful
conversion in remembrance, may show forth our thankfulness
unto thee for the same by following the holy doctrine which
he taught; through Jesus Christ our Lord, who liveth and
reigneth with thee, in the unity of the Holy Spirit, one God,
now and for ever. *Amen.*

Preface of Apostles

The Presentation   *February 2*

Almighty and everliving God, we humbly beseech thee that,
as thy only-begotten Son was this day presented in the
temple, so we may be presented unto thee with pure and
clean hearts by the same thy Son Jesus Christ our Lord; who
liveth and reigneth with thee and the Holy Spirit, one God,
now and for ever. *Amen.*

Preface of the Epiphany

Saint Matthias *February 24*

O Almighty God, who into the place of Judas didst choose thy
faithful servant Matthias to be of the number of the Twelve:
Grant that thy Church, being delivered from false apostles,
may always be ordered and guided by faithful and true pastors;
through Jesus Christ our Lord, who liveth and reigneth with
thee, in the unity of the Holy Spirit, one God, now and for
ever. *Amen.*

Preface of Apostles

Saint Joseph *March 19*

O God, who from the family of thy servant David didst raise
up Joseph to be the guardian of thy incarnate Son and the
spouse of his virgin mother: Give us grace to imitate his
uprightness of life and his obedience to thy commands;
through the same thy Son Jesus Christ our Lord, who liveth
and reigneth with thee and the Holy Spirit, one God, for ever
and ever. *Amen.*

Preface of the Epiphany

The Annunciation *March 25*

We beseech thee, O Lord, pour thy grace into our hearts, that
we who have known the incarnation of thy Son Jesus Christ,
announced by an angel to the Virgin Mary, may by his cross
and passion be brought unto the glory of his resurrection;
who liveth and reigneth with thee, in the unity of the Holy
Spirit, one God, now and for ever. *Amen.*

Preface of the Epiphany

Saint Mark *April 25*

Almighty God, who by the hand of Mark the evangelist hast
given to thy Church the Gospel of Jesus Christ the Son of

God: We thank thee for this witness, and pray that we may be firmly grounded in its truth; through the same Jesus Christ our Lord, who liveth and reigneth with thee and the Holy Spirit, one God, for ever and ever. *Amen.*

Preface of All Saints

Saint Philip and Saint James   *May 1*

Almighty God, who didst give to thine apostles Philip and James grace and strength to bear witness to the truth: Grant that we, being mindful of their victory of faith, may glorify in life and death the Name of our Lord Jesus Christ; who liveth and reigneth with thee and the Holy Spirit, one God, now and for ever. *Amen.*

Preface of Apostles

The Visitation   *May 31*

Father in heaven, by whose grace the virgin mother of thy incarnate Son was blessed in bearing him, but still more blessed in keeping thy word: Grant us who honor the exaltation of her lowliness to follow the example of her devotion to thy will; through the same Jesus Christ our Lord, who liveth and reigneth with thee and the Holy Spirit, one God, for ever and ever. *Amen.*

Preface of the Epiphany

Saint Barnabas   *June 11*

Grant, O God, that we may follow the example of thy faithful servant Barnabas, who, seeking not his own renown but the well-being of thy Church, gave generously of his life and substance for the relief of the poor and the spread of the Gospel; through Jesus Christ our Lord, who liveth and reigneth with thee and the Holy Spirit, one God, for ever and ever. *Amen.*

Preface of Apostles

The Nativity of Saint John the Baptist   *June 24*

Almighty God, by whose providence thy servant John the Baptist was wonderfully born, and sent to prepare the way of thy Son our Savior by preaching repentance: Make us so to follow his doctrine and holy life, that we may truly repent according to his preaching; and after his example constantly speak the truth, boldly rebuke vice, and patiently suffer for the truth's sake; through the same thy Son Jesus Christ our Lord, who liveth and reigneth with thee and the Holy Spirit, one God, for ever and ever. *Amen.*

Preface of Advent

Saint Peter and Saint Paul   *June 29*

Almighty God, whose blessed apostles Peter and Paul glorified thee by their martyrdom: Grant that thy Church, instructed by their teaching and example, and knit together in unity by thy Spirit, may ever stand firm upon the one foundation, which is Jesus Christ our Lord; who liveth and reigneth with thee, in the unity of the same Spirit, one God, for ever and ever. *Amen.*

Preface of Apostles

Independence Day   *July 4*

Lord God Almighty, in whose Name the founders of this country won liberty for themselves and for us, and lit the torch of freedom for nations then unborn: Grant, we beseech thee, that we and all the people of this land may have grace to maintain these liberties in righteousness and peace; through Jesus Christ our Lord, who liveth and reigneth with thee and the Holy Spirit, one God, for ever and ever. *Amen.*

The Collect "For the Nation," page 207, may be used instead.

Preface of Trinity Sunday

Saint Mary Magdalene   *July 22*

Almighty God, whose blessed Son restored Mary Magdalene to health of body and mind, and called her to be a witness of his resurrection: Mercifully grant that by thy grace we may be healed of all our infirmities and know thee in the power of his endless life; who with thee and the Holy Spirit liveth and reigneth, one God, now and for ever. *Amen.*

Preface of All Saints

Saint James   *July 25*

O gracious God, we remember before thee this day thy servant and apostle James, first among the Twelve to suffer martyrdom for the Name of Jesus Christ; and we pray that thou wilt pour out upon the leaders of thy Church that spirit of self-denying service by which alone they may have true authority among thy people; through the same Jesus Christ our Lord, who liveth and reigneth with thee and the Holy Spirit, one God, now and for ever. *Amen.*

Preface of Apostles

The Transfiguration   *August 6*

O God, who on the holy mount didst reveal to chosen witnesses thy well-beloved Son, wonderfully transfigured, in raiment white and glistening: Mercifully grant that we, being delivered from the disquietude of this world, may by faith behold the King in his beauty; who with thee, O Father, and thee, O Holy Ghost, liveth and reigneth, one God, world without end. *Amen.*

Preface of the Epiphany

Saint Mary the Virgin   *August 15*

O God, who hast taken to thyself the blessed Virgin Mary, mother of thy incarnate Son: Grant that we, who have been redeemed by his blood, may share with her the glory of thine eternal kingdom; through the same thy Son Jesus Christ our Lord, who liveth and reigneth with thee, in the unity of the Holy Spirit, one God, now and for ever. *Amen.*

Preface of the Incarnation

Saint Bartholomew   *August 24*

O Almighty and everlasting God, who didst give to thine apostle Bartholomew grace truly to believe and to preach thy Word: Grant, we beseech thee, unto thy Church to love what he believed and to preach what he taught; through Jesus Christ our Lord, who liveth and reigneth with thee and the Holy Spirit, one God, for ever and ever. *Amen.*

Preface of Apostles

Holy Cross Day   *September 14*

Almighty God, whose Son our Savior Jesus Christ was lifted high upon the cross that he might draw the whole world unto himself: Mercifully grant that we, who glory in the mystery of our redemption, may have grace to take up our cross and follow him; who liveth and reigneth with thee and the Holy Spirit, one God, in glory everlasting. *Amen.*

Preface of Holy Week

Saint Matthew   *September 21*

We thank thee, heavenly Father, for the witness of thine apostle and evangelist Matthew to the Gospel of thy Son our Savior; and we pray that, after his example, we may with ready wills and hearts obey the calling of our Lord to follow him; through Jesus Christ our Lord, who liveth and reigneth with thee and the Holy Spirit, one God, now and for ever. *Amen.*

Preface of Apostles

Saint Michael and All Angels *September 29*

O everlasting God, who hast ordained and constituted the ministries of angels and men in a wonderful order: Mercifully grant that, as thy holy angels always serve and worship thee in heaven, so by thy appointment they may help and defend us on earth; through Jesus Christ our Lord, who liveth and reigneth with thee and the Holy Spirit, one God, for ever and ever. *Amen.*

Preface of Trinity Sunday

Saint Luke *October 18*

Almighty God, who didst inspire thy servant Luke the physician to set forth in the Gospel the love and healing power of thy Son: Graciously continue in thy Church the like love and power to heal, to the praise and glory of thy Name; through the same thy Son Jesus Christ our Lord, who liveth and reigneth with thee, in the unity of the Holy Spirit, one God, now and for ever. *Amen.*

Preface of All Saints

Saint James of Jerusalem *October 23*

Grant, we beseech thee, O God, that after the example of thy servant James the Just, brother of our Lord, thy Church may give itself continually to prayer and to the reconciliation of all who are at variance and enmity; through the same our Lord Jesus Christ, who liveth and reigneth with thee and the Holy Spirit, one God, now and for ever. *Amen.*

Preface of All Saints

Saint Simon and Saint Jude   *October 28*

O God, we thank thee for the glorious company of the
apostles, and especially on this day for Simon and Jude; and
we pray that, as they were faithful and zealous in their
mission, so we may with ardent devotion make known the
love and mercy of our Lord and Savior Jesus Christ; who
liveth and reigneth with thee and the Holy Spirit, one God,
for ever and ever. *Amen.*

Preface of Apostles

All Saints' Day   *November 1*

O Almighty God, who hast knit together thine elect in one
communion and fellowship in the mystical body of thy Son
Christ our Lord: Grant us grace so to follow thy blessed
saints in all virtuous and godly living, that we may come to
those ineffable joys which thou hast prepared for those who
unfeignedly love thee; through the same Jesus Christ our
Lord, who with thee and the Holy Spirit liveth and reigneth,
one God, in glory everlasting. *Amen.*

Preface of All Saints

Thanksgiving Day

Almighty and gracious Father, we give thee thanks for the
fruits of the earth in their season and for the labors of those
who harvest them. Make us, we beseech thee, faithful stewards
of thy great bounty, for the provision of our necessities and
the relief of all who are in need, to the glory of thy Name;
through Jesus Christ our Lord, who liveth and reigneth with
thee and the Holy Spirit, one God, now and for ever. *Amen.*

*For the Prayers of the People, the Litany of Thanksgiving on page 836
may be used.*

Preface of Trinity Sunday

The Common of Saints

The festival of a saint is observed in accordance with the rules of precedence set forth in the Calendar of the Church Year.

At the discretion of the Celebrant, and as appropriate, any of the following Collects, with one of the corresponding sets of Psalms and Lessons, may be used

a) at the commemoration of a saint listed in the Calendar for which no Proper is provided in this Book

b) at the patronal festival or commemoration of a saint not listed in the Calendar.

Of a Martyr

O Almighty God, who didst give to thy servant N. boldness to confess the Name of our Savior Jesus Christ before the rulers of this world, and courage to die for this faith: Grant that we may always be ready to give a reason for the hope that is in us, and to suffer gladly for the sake of the same our Lord Jesus Christ; who liveth and reigneth with thee and the Holy Spirit, one God, for ever and ever. *Amen.*

or this

O Almighty God, by whose grace and power thy holy martyr N. triumphed over suffering and was faithful even unto death: Grant us, who now remember *him* with thanksgiving, to be so faithful in our witness to thee in this world, that we may receive with *him* the crown of life; through Jesus Christ our Lord, who liveth and reigneth with thee and the Holy Spirit, one God, for ever and ever. *Amen.*

or the following

Almighty and everlasting God, who didst enkindle the flame of thy love in the heart of thy holy martyr *N.*: Grant to us, thy humble servants, a like faith and power of love, that we who rejoice in *her* triumph may profit by *her* example; through Jesus Christ our Lord, who liveth and reigneth with thee and the Holy Spirit, one God, for ever and ever. *Amen.*

Preface of a Saint

Of a Missionary

Almighty and everlasting God, we thank thee for thy servant *N.*, whom thou didst call to preach the Gospel to the people of _____ (*or* to the _____ people). Raise up, we beseech thee, in this and every land evangelists and heralds of thy kingdom, that thy Church may proclaim the unsearchable riches of our Savior Jesus Christ; who liveth and reigneth with thee and the Holy Spirit, one God, now and for ever. *Amen.*

or this

Almighty God, who willest to be glorified in thy saints, and didst raise up thy servant *N.* to be a light in the world: Shine, we pray thee, in our hearts, that we also in our generation may show forth thy praise, who hast called us out of darkness into thy marvelous light; through Jesus Christ our Lord, who liveth and reigneth with thee and the Holy Spirit, one God, now and for ever. *Amen.*

Preface of Pentecost

Of a Pastor

O heavenly Father, Shepherd of thy people, we give thee thanks for thy servant *N.*, who was faithful in the care and nurture of thy flock; and we pray that, following his example and the teaching of his holy life, we may by thy grace grow

into the stature of the fullness of our Lord and Savior Jesus
Christ; who liveth and reigneth with thee and the Holy
Spirit, one God, for ever and ever. *Amen*.

or this

O God, our heavenly Father, who didst raise up thy faithful
servant N. to be a [bishop and] pastor in thy Church and to
feed thy flock: Give abundantly to all pastors the gifts of thy
Holy Spirit, that they may minister in thy household as true
servants of Christ and stewards of thy divine mysteries;
through the same Jesus Christ our Lord, who liveth and
reigneth with thee and the same Spirit, one God, for ever and
ever. *Amen*.

Preface of a Saint

Of a Theologian and Teacher

O God, who by thy Holy Spirit dost give to some the word of
wisdom, to others the word of knowledge, and to others the
word of faith: We praise thy Name for the gifts of grace
manifested in thy servant N., and we pray that thy Church
may never be destitute of such gifts; through Jesus Christ our
Lord, who with thee and the same Spirit liveth and reigneth,
one God, for ever and ever. *Amen*.

or this

O Almighty God, who didst give to thy servant N. special
gifts of grace to understand and teach the truth as it is in
Christ Jesus: Grant, we beseech thee, that by this teaching we
may know thee, the one true God, and Jesus Christ whom
thou hast sent; who liveth and reigneth with thee and the
Holy Spirit, one God, for ever and ever. *Amen*.

Preface of a Saint, or of Trinity Sunday

Of a Monastic

O God, whose blessed Son became poor that we through his
poverty might be rich: Deliver us, we pray thee, from an
inordinate love of this world, that, inspired by the devotion
of thy servant N., we may serve thee with singleness of heart,
and attain to the riches of the age to come; through the same
thy Son Jesus Christ our Lord, who liveth and reigneth with
thee, in the unity of the Holy Spirit, one God, now and for
ever. *Amen.*

or this

O God, by whose grace thy servant N., enkindled with the
fire of thy love, became a burning and a shining light in thy
Church: Grant that we also may be aflame with the spirit
of love and discipline, and may ever walk before thee as
children of light; through Jesus Christ our Lord, who with
thee, in the unity of the Holy Spirit, liveth and reigneth, one
God, now and for ever. *Amen.*

Preface of a Saint

Of a Saint

O Almighty God, who hast compassed us about with so great
a cloud of witnesses: Grant that we, encouraged by the good
example of thy servant N., may persevere in running the race
that is set before us, until at length, through thy mercy, we may
with *him* attain to thine eternal joy; through Jesus Christ, the
author and perfecter of our faith, who liveth and reigneth
with thee and the Holy Spirit, one God, for ever and ever. *Amen.*

or this

O God, who hast brought us near to an innumerable
company of angels and to the spirits of just men made
perfect: Grant us during our earthly pilgrimage to abide in
their fellowship, and in our heavenly country to become

partakers of their joy; through Jesus Christ our Lord, who liveth and reigneth with thee and the Holy Spirit, one God, now and for ever. *Amen*.

or this

O Almighty God, who by thy Holy Spirit hast made us one with thy saints in heaven and on earth: Grant that in our earthly pilgrimage we may ever be supported by this fellowship of love and prayer, and may know ourselves to be surrounded by their witness to thy power and mercy. We ask this for the sake of Jesus Christ, in whom all our intercessions are acceptable through the Spirit, and who liveth and reigneth for ever and ever. *Amen*.

Preface of a Saint

Various Occasions

For optional use, when desired, subject to the rules set forth in the Calendar of the Church Year.

1. Of the Holy Trinity

Almighty God, who hast revealed to thy Church thine eternal Being of glorious majesty and perfect love as one God in Trinity of Persons: Give us grace to continue steadfast in the confession of this faith, and constant in our worship of thee, Father, Son, and Holy Spirit; who livest and reignest, one God, now and for ever. *Amen*.

Preface of Trinity Sunday

2. Of the Holy Spirit

Almighty and most merciful God, grant, we beseech thee, that by the indwelling of thy Holy Spirit we may be enlightened and strengthened for thy service; through Jesus Christ our Lord, who liveth and reigneth with thee, in the unity of the same Spirit ever, one God, world without end. *Amen.*

Preface of Pentecost

3. Of the Holy Angels

O everlasting God, who hast ordained and constituted the ministries of angels and men in a wonderful order: Mercifully grant that, as thy holy angels always serve and worship thee in heaven, so by thy appointment they may help and defend us on earth; through Jesus Christ our Lord, who liveth and reigneth with thee and the Holy Spirit, one God, for ever and ever. *Amen.*

Preface of Trinity Sunday

4. Of the Incarnation

O God, who didst wonderfully create, and yet more wonderfully restore, the dignity of human nature: Grant that we may share the divine life of him who humbled himself to share our humanity, thy Son Jesus Christ; who liveth and reigneth with thee, in the unity of the Holy Spirit, one God, for ever and ever. *Amen.*

Preface of the Epiphany

5. Of the Holy Eucharist

Especially suitable for Thursdays

God our Father, whose Son our Lord Jesus Christ in a wonderful Sacrament hath left unto us a memorial of his passion: Grant us so to venerate the sacred mysteries of his Body and Blood, that we may ever perceive within ourselves the fruit of his redemption; who liveth and reigneth with thee and the Holy Spirit, one God, for ever and ever. *Amen.*

Preface of the Epiphany

6. Of the Holy Cross

Especially suitable for Fridays

Almighty God, whose beloved Son willingly endured the agony and shame of the cross for our redemption: Give us courage, we beseech thee, to take up our cross and follow him; who liveth and reigneth with thee and the Holy Spirit, one God, now and for ever. *Amen.*

Preface of Holy Week

7. For All Baptized Christians

Especially suitable for Saturdays

Grant, O Lord God, to all who have been baptized into the death and resurrection of thy Son Jesus Christ, that, as we have put away the old life of sin, so we may be renewed in the spirit of our minds, and live in righteousness and true holiness; through the same Jesus Christ our Lord, who liveth and reigneth with thee, in the unity of the Holy Spirit, one God, now and for ever. *Amen.*

Preface of Baptism

8. For the Departed

O eternal Lord God, who holdest all souls in life: Give, we beseech thee, to thy whole Church in paradise and on earth thy light and thy peace; and grant that we, following the good examples of those who have served thee here and are now at rest, may at the last enter with them into thine unending joy; through Jesus Christ our Lord, who liveth and reigneth with thee, in the unity of the Holy Spirit, one God, now and for ever. *Amen.*

or this

Almighty God, we remember this day before thee thy faithful servant N.; and we pray that, having opened to *him* the gates of larger life, thou wilt receive *him* more and more into thy joyful service, that, with all who have faithfully served thee in the past, *he* may share in the eternal victory of Jesus Christ our Lord; who liveth and reigneth with thee, in the unity of the Holy Spirit, one God, for ever and ever. *Amen.*

Any of the Collects appointed for use at the Burial of the Dead may be used instead.

For the Prayers of the People, one of the forms appointed for the Burial of the Dead may be used.

Preface of the Commemoration of the Dead

The postcommunion prayer on page 482 may be used.

9. Of the Reign of Christ

Almighty and everlasting God, whose will it is to restore all things in thy well-beloved Son, the King of kings and Lord of lords: Mercifully grant that the peoples of the earth, divided and enslaved by sin, may be freed and brought together under his most gracious rule; who liveth and reigneth with thee and the Holy Spirit, one God, now and for ever. *Amen.*

Preface of the Ascension, or of Baptism

10. At Baptism

Almighty God, who by our baptism into the death and resurrection of thy Son Jesus Christ dost turn us from the old life of sin: Grant that we, being reborn to new life in him, may live in righteousness and holiness all our days; through the same thy Son Jesus Christ our Lord, who liveth and reigneth with thee and the Holy Spirit, one God, now and for ever. *Amen.*

Preface of Baptism

11. At Confirmation

Grant, Almighty God, that we, who have been redeemed from the old life of sin by our baptism into the death and resurrection of thy Son Jesus Christ, may be renewed in thy Holy Spirit, and live in righteousness and true holiness; through the same Jesus Christ our Lord, who liveth and reigneth with thee and the same Spirit, one God, now and for ever. *Amen.*

Preface of Baptism, or of Pentecost

12. On the Anniversary of the Dedication of a Church

O Almighty God, to whose glory we celebrate the dedication of this house of prayer: We give thee thanks for the fellowship of those who have worshiped in this place; and we pray that all who seek thee here may find thee, and be filled with thy joy and peace; through Jesus Christ our Lord, who liveth and reigneth with thee, in the unity of the Holy Spirit, one God, now and for ever. *Amen.*

The Litany of Thanksgiving for a Church, page 578, may be used for the Prayers of the People.

Preface of the Dedication of a Church

13. For a Church Convention

Almighty and everlasting Father, who hast given the Holy Spirit to abide with us for ever: Bless, we beseech thee, with his grace and presence, the bishops and the other clergy and the laity here (*or* now, *or* soon to be) assembled in thy Name, that thy Church, being preserved in true faith and godly discipline, may fulfill all the mind of him who loved it and gave himself for it, thy Son Jesus Christ our Savior; who liveth and reigneth with thee, in the unity of the same Spirit, one God, now and for ever. *Amen.*

Preface of Pentecost, or of the Season

14. For the Unity of the Church

Almighty Father, whose blessed Son before his passion prayed for his disciples that they might be one, even as thou and he are one: Grant that thy Church, being bound together in love and obedience to thee, may be united in one body by the one Spirit, that the world may believe in him whom thou didst send, the same thy Son Jesus Christ our Lord; who liveth and reigneth with thee, in the unity of the same Spirit, one God, now and for ever. *Amen.*

Preface of Baptism, or of Trinity Sunday

15. For the Ministry (Ember Days)

For use on the traditional days or at other times

I. *For those to be ordained*

Almighty God, the giver of all good gifts, who of thy divine providence hast appointed various orders in thy Church: Give thy grace, we humbly beseech thee, to all who are [now] called to any office and ministry for thy people; and so fill them with the truth of thy doctrine and clothe them with holiness of life, that they may faithfully serve before thee, to the glory of thy great Name and for the benefit of thy holy Church; through Jesus Christ our Lord, who liveth and reigneth with thee, in the unity of the Holy Spirit, one God, now and for ever. *Amen.*

Preface of Apostles

II. *For the choice of fit persons for the ministry*

O God, who didst lead thy holy apostles to ordain ministers in every place: Grant that thy Church, under the guidance of the Holy Spirit, may choose suitable persons for the ministry of Word and Sacrament, and may uphold them in their work for the extension of thy kingdom; through him who is the Shepherd and Bishop of our souls, Jesus Christ our Lord, who liveth and reigneth with thee and the same Spirit, one God, for ever and ever. *Amen.*

Preface of the Season

III. For all Christians in their vocation

Almighty and everlasting God, by whose Spirit the whole
body of thy faithful people is governed and sanctified:
Receive our supplications and prayers, which we offer before
thee for all members of thy holy Church, that in their
vocation and ministry they may truly and godly serve thee;
through our Lord and Savior Jesus Christ, who liveth and
reigneth with thee, in the unity of the same Spirit, one God,
now and for ever. *Amen.*

Preface of Baptism, or of the Season

16. For the Mission of the Church

O God, who hast made of one blood all the peoples of the
earth, and didst send thy blessed Son to preach peace to those
who are far off and to those who are near: Grant that people
everywhere may seek after thee and find thee, bring the
nations into thy fold, pour out thy Spirit upon all flesh, and
hasten the coming of thy kingdom; through the same thy
Son Jesus Christ our Lord, who liveth and reigneth with thee
and the same Spirit, one God, now and for ever.
Amen.

or this

O God of all the nations of the earth: Remember the
multitudes who have been created in thine image but have
not known the redeeming work of our Savior Jesus Christ;
and grant that, by the prayers and labors of thy holy Church,
they may be brought to know and worship thee as thou hast
been revealed in thy Son; who liveth and reigneth with thee
and the Holy Spirit, one God, for ever and ever. *Amen.*

Preface of the Season, or of Pentecost

17. For the Nation

Lord God Almighty, who hast made all peoples of the earth for thy glory, to serve thee in freedom and peace: Grant to the people of our country a zeal for justice and the strength of forbearance, that we may use our liberty in accordance with thy gracious will; through Jesus Christ our Lord, who liveth and reigneth with thee and the Holy Spirit, one God, for ever and ever. *Amen*.

The Collect for Independence Day may be used instead.

Preface of Trinity Sunday

18. For Peace

O Almighty God, kindle, we beseech thee, in every heart the true love of peace, and guide with thy wisdom those who take counsel for the nations of the earth, that in tranquillity thy dominion may increase till the earth is filled with the knowledge of thy love; through Jesus Christ our Lord, who liveth and reigneth with thee, in the unity of the Holy Spirit, one God, now and for ever. *Amen*.

Preface of the Season

19. For Rogation Days

For use on the traditional days or at other times

I. For fruitful seasons

Almighty God, Lord of heaven and earth: We humbly pray that thy gracious providence may give and preserve to our use the harvests of the land and of the seas, and may prosper all who labor to gather them, that we, who constantly receive good things from thy hand, may always give thee thanks; through Jesus Christ our Lord, who liveth and reigneth with thee and the Holy Spirit, one God, for ever and ever. *Amen*.

Preface of the Season

II. For commerce and industry

Almighty God, whose Son Jesus Christ in his earthly life
shared our toil and hallowed our labor: Be present with
thy people where they work; make those who carry on
the industries and commerce of this land responsive to thy
will; and give to us all a pride in what we do, and a just
return for our labor; through Jesus Christ our Lord, who
liveth and reigneth with thee, in the unity of the Holy Spirit,
one God, now and for ever. *Amen.*

Preface of the Season

III. For stewardship of creation

O merciful Creator, whose hand is open wide to satisfy the
needs of every living creature: Make us, we beseech thee,
ever thankful for thy loving providence; and grant that we,
remembering the account that we must one day give, may be
faithful stewards of thy bounty; through Jesus Christ our
Lord, who with thee and the Holy Spirit liveth and reigneth,
one God, for ever and ever. *Amen.*

Preface of the Season

20. For the Sick

Heavenly Father, giver of life and health: Comfort and
relieve thy sick servants, and give thy power of healing to
those who minister to their needs, that those (*or N., or NN.*)
for whom our prayers are offered may be strengthened in
their weakness and have confidence in thy loving care;
through Jesus Christ our Lord, who liveth and reigneth with
thee and the Holy Spirit, one God, now and for ever. *Amen.*

Preface of the Season

The postcommunion prayer on page 457 may be used.

21. For Social Justice

Almighty God, who hast created us in thine own image:
Grant us grace fearlessly to contend against evil and to make
no peace with oppression; and, that we may reverently use
our freedom, help us to employ it in the maintenance of
justice in our communities and among the nations, to the
glory of thy holy Name; through Jesus Christ our Lord, who
liveth and reigneth with thee and the Holy Spirit, one God,
now and for ever. *Amen.*

Preface of the Season

22. For Social Service

O Lord our heavenly Father, whose blessed Son came not to
be ministered unto but to minister: Bless, we beseech thee, all
who, following in his steps, give themselves to the service of
others; that with wisdom, patience, and courage, they may
minister in his name to the suffering, the friendless, and the
needy; for the love of him who laid down his life for us, the
same thy Son our Savior Jesus Christ, who liveth and reigneth
with thee and the Holy Spirit, one God, for ever and ever.
Amen.

Preface of the Season

23. For Education

Almighty God, the fountain of all wisdom: Enlighten by thy
Holy Spirit those who teach and those who learn, that,
rejoicing in the knowledge of thy truth, they may worship
thee and serve thee from generation to generation; through
Jesus Christ our Lord, who liveth and reigneth with thee and
the same Spirit, one God, for ever and ever. *Amen.*

Preface of the Season

24. For Vocation in Daily Work

Almighty God our heavenly Father, who declarest thy glory
and showest forth thy handiwork in the heavens and in the
earth: Deliver us, we beseech thee, in our several occupations
from the service of self alone, that we may do the work
which thou givest us to do, in truth and beauty and for the
common good; for the sake of him who came among us as
one that serveth, thy Son Jesus Christ our Lord, who liveth
and reigneth with thee and the Holy Spirit, one God, for ever
and ever. *Amen.*

Preface of the Season

25. For Labor Day

Almighty God, who hast so linked our lives one with another
that all we do affects, for good or ill, all other lives: So guide
us in the work we do, that we may do it not for self alone, but
for the common good; and, as we seek a proper return for
our own labor, make us mindful of the rightful aspirations of
other workers, and arouse our concern for those who are out
of work; through Jesus Christ our Lord, who liveth and
reigneth with thee and the Holy Spirit, one God, for ever and
ever. *Amen.*

Preface of the Season

Collects: Contemporary

First Sunday of Advent

Almighty God, give us grace to cast away the works of darkness, and put on the armor of light, now in the time of this mortal life in which your Son Jesus Christ came to visit us in great humility; that in the last day, when he shall come again in his glorious majesty to judge both the living and the dead, we may rise to the life immortal; through him who lives and reigns with you and the Holy Spirit, one God, now and for ever. *Amen.*

Preface of Advent

Second Sunday of Advent

Merciful God, who sent your messengers the prophets to preach repentance and prepare the way for our salvation: Give us grace to heed their warnings and forsake our sins, that we may greet with joy the coming of Jesus Christ our Redeemer; who lives and reigns with you and the Holy Spirit, one God, now and for ever. *Amen.*

Preface of Advent

Third Sunday of Advent

Stir up your power, O Lord, and with great might come among us; and, because we are sorely hindered by our sins, let your bountiful grace and mercy speedily help and deliver us; through Jesus Christ our Lord, to whom, with you and the Holy Spirit, be honor and glory, now and for ever. *Amen.*

Preface of Advent

Wednesday, Friday, and Saturday of this week are the traditional winter Ember Days.

Fourth Sunday of Advent

Purify our conscience, Almighty God, by your daily visitation, that your Son Jesus Christ, at his coming, may find in us a mansion prepared for himself; who lives and reigns with you, in the unity of the Holy Spirit, one God, now and for ever. *Amen.*

Preface of Advent

The Nativity of Our Lord: Christmas Day   *December 25*

O God, you make us glad by the yearly festival of the birth of your only Son Jesus Christ: Grant that we, who joyfully receive him as our Redeemer, may with sure confidence behold him when he comes to be our Judge; who lives and reigns with you and the Holy Spirit, one God, now and for ever. *Amen.*

or this

O God, you have caused this holy night to shine with the brightness of the true Light: Grant that we, who have known the mystery of that Light on earth, may also enjoy him perfectly in heaven; where with you and the Holy Spirit he lives and reigns, one God, in glory everlasting. *Amen.*

or this

Almighty God, you have given your only-begotten Son to take our nature upon him, and to be born [this day] of a pure virgin: Grant that we, who have been born again and made your children by adoption and grace, may daily be renewed by your Holy Spirit; through our Lord Jesus Christ, to whom with you and the same Spirit be honor and glory, now and for ever. *Amen.*

Preface of the Incarnation

The Collect immediately preceding and any of the sets of Proper Lessons for Christmas Day serve for any weekdays between Holy Innocents' Day and the First Sunday after Christmas Day.

First Sunday after Christmas Day

This Sunday takes precedence over the three Holy Days which follow Christmas Day. As necessary, the observance of one, two, or all three of them, is postponed one day.

Almighty God, you have poured upon us the new light of your incarnate Word: Grant that this light, enkindled in our hearts, may shine forth in our lives; through Jesus Christ our Lord, who lives and reigns with you, in the unity of the Holy Spirit, one God, now and for ever. *Amen.*

Preface of the Incarnation

The Holy Name   *January 1*

Eternal Father, you gave to your incarnate Son the holy name of Jesus to be the sign of our salvation: Plant in every heart, we pray, the love of him who is the Savior of the world, our Lord Jesus Christ; who lives and reigns with you and the Holy Spirit, one God, in glory everlasting. *Amen.*

Preface of the Incarnation

Second Sunday after Christmas Day

O God, who wonderfully created, and yet more wonderfully restored, the dignity of human nature: Grant that we may share the divine life of him who humbled himself to share our humanity, your Son Jesus Christ; who lives and reigns with you, in the unity of the Holy Spirit, one God, for ever and ever. *Amen.*

Preface of the Incarnation

The Epiphany *January 6*

O God, by the leading of a star you manifested your only Son to the peoples of the earth: Lead us, who know you now by faith, to your presence, where we may see your glory face to face; through Jesus Christ our Lord, who lives and reigns with you and the Holy Spirit, one God, now and for ever. *Amen.*

Preface of the Epiphany

The preceding Collect, with the Psalm and Lessons for the Epiphany, or those for the Second Sunday after Christmas, serves for weekdays between the Epiphany and the following Sunday. The Preface of the Epiphany is used.

First Sunday after the Epiphany: The Baptism of our Lord

Father in heaven, who at the baptism of Jesus in the River Jordan proclaimed him your beloved Son and anointed him with the Holy Spirit: Grant that all who are baptized into his Name may keep the covenant they have made, and boldly confess him as Lord and Savior; who with you and the Holy Spirit lives and reigns, one God, in glory everlasting. *Amen.*

Preface of the Epiphany

Second Sunday after the Epiphany

Almighty God, whose Son our Savior Jesus Christ is the light of the world: Grant that your people, illumined by your Word and Sacraments, may shine with the radiance of Christ's glory, that he may be known, worshiped, and obeyed to the ends of the earth; through Jesus Christ our Lord, who with you and the Holy Spirit lives and reigns, one God, now and for ever. *Amen.*

Preface of the Epiphany, or of the Lord's Day

Third Sunday after the Epiphany

Give us grace, O Lord, to answer readily the call of our Savior Jesus Christ and proclaim to all people the Good News of his salvation, that we and the whole world may perceive the glory of his marvelous works; who lives and reigns with you and the Holy Spirit, one God, for ever and ever. *Amen.*

Preface of the Epiphany, or of the Lord's Day

Fourth Sunday after the Epiphany

Almighty and everlasting God, you govern all things both in heaven and on earth: Mercifully hear the supplications of your people, and in our time grant us your peace; through Jesus Christ our Lord, who lives and reigns with you and the Holy Spirit, one God, for ever and ever. *Amen.*

Preface of the Epiphany, or of the Lord's Day

Fifth Sunday after the Epiphany

Set us free, O God, from the bondage of our sins, and give us the liberty of that abundant life which you have made known to us in your Son our Savior Jesus Christ; who lives and reigns with you, in the unity of the Holy Spirit, one God, now and for ever. *Amen.*

Preface of the Epiphany, or of the Lord's Day

Sixth Sunday after the Epiphany

O God, the strength of all who put their trust in you: Mercifully accept our prayers; and because in our weakness we can do nothing good without you, give us the help of your grace, that in keeping your commandments we may please you both in will and deed; through Jesus Christ our Lord, who lives and reigns with you and the Holy Spirit, one God, for ever and ever. *Amen.*

Preface of the Epiphany, or of the Lord's Day

Seventh Sunday after the Epiphany

O Lord, you have taught us that without love whatever we do is worth nothing: Send your Holy Spirit and pour into our hearts your greatest gift, which is love, the true bond of peace and of all virtue, without which whoever lives is accounted dead before you. Grant this for the sake of your only Son Jesus Christ, who lives and reigns with you and the Holy Spirit, one God, now and for ever. *Amen.*

Preface of the Epiphany, or of the Lord's Day

Eighth Sunday after the Epiphany

Most loving Father, whose will it is for us to give thanks for all things, to fear nothing but the loss of you, and to cast all our care on you who care for us: Preserve us from faithless fears and worldly anxieties, that no clouds of this mortal life may hide from us the light of that love which is immortal, and which you have manifested to us in your Son Jesus Christ our Lord; who lives and reigns with you, in the unity of the Holy Spirit, one God, now and for ever. *Amen.*

Preface of the Epiphany, or of the Lord's Day

Last Sunday after the Epiphany

This Proper is always used on the Sunday before Ash Wednesday

O God, who before the passion of your only-begotten Son revealed his glory upon the holy mountain: Grant to us that we, beholding by faith the light of his countenance, may be strengthened to bear our cross, and be changed into his likeness from glory to glory; through Jesus Christ our Lord, who lives and reigns with you and the Holy Spirit, one God, for ever and ever. *Amen.*

Preface of the Epiphany

Ash Wednesday

The Proper Liturgy for this day is on page 264.

Almighty and everlasting God, you hate nothing you have made and forgive the sins of all who are penitent: Create and make in us new and contrite hearts, that we, worthily lamenting our sins and acknowledging our wretchedness, may obtain of you, the God of all mercy, perfect remission and forgiveness; through Jesus Christ our Lord, who lives and reigns with you and the Holy Spirit, one God, for ever and ever. *Amen.*

Preface of Lent

This Collect, with the corresponding Psalm and Lessons, also serves for the weekdays which follow, except as otherwise appointed.

First Sunday in Lent

Almighty God, whose blessed Son was led by the Spirit to be tempted by Satan: Come quickly to help us who are assaulted by many temptations; and, as you know the weaknesses of each of us, let each one find you mighty to save; through Jesus Christ your Son our Lord, who lives and reigns with you and the Holy Spirit, one God, now and for ever. *Amen.*

Preface of Lent

Wednesday, Friday, and Saturday of this week are the traditional spring Ember Days.

Second Sunday in Lent

O God, whose glory it is always to have mercy: Be gracious to all who have gone astray from your ways, and bring them again with penitent hearts and steadfast faith to embrace and hold fast the unchangeable truth of your Word, Jesus Christ your Son; who with you and the Holy Spirit lives and reigns, one God, for ever and ever. *Amen.*

Preface of Lent

Third Sunday in Lent

Almighty God, you know that we have no power in ourselves to help ourselves: Keep us both outwardly in our bodies and inwardly in our souls, that we may be defended from all adversities which may happen to the body, and from all evil thoughts which may assault and hurt the soul; through Jesus Christ our Lord, who lives and reigns with you and the Holy Spirit, one God, for ever and ever. *Amen.*

Preface of Lent

Fourth Sunday in Lent

Gracious Father, whose blessed Son Jesus Christ came down from heaven to be the true bread which gives life to the world: Evermore give us this bread, that he may live in us, and we in him; who lives and reigns with you and the Holy Spirit, one God, now and for ever. *Amen.*

Preface of Lent

Fifth Sunday in Lent

Almighty God, you alone can bring into order the unruly wills and affections of sinners: Grant your people grace to love what you command and desire what you promise; that, among the swift and varied changes of the world, our hearts may surely there be fixed where true joys are to be found; through Jesus Christ our Lord, who lives and reigns with you and the Holy Spirit, one God, now and for ever. *Amen.*

Preface of Lent

Sunday of the Passion: Palm Sunday

The Proper Liturgy for this day is on page 270.

Almighty and everliving God, in your tender love for the human race you sent your Son our Savior Jesus Christ to take upon him our nature, and to suffer death upon the cross, giving us the example of his great humility: Mercifully grant that we may walk in the way of his suffering, and also share in his resurrection; through Jesus Christ our Lord, who lives and reigns with you and the Holy Spirit, one God, for ever and ever. *Amen.*

Preface of Holy Week

Monday in Holy Week

Almighty God, whose most dear Son went not up to joy but first he suffered pain, and entered not into glory before he was crucified: Mercifully grant that we, walking in the way of the cross, may find it none other than the way of life and peace; through Jesus Christ your Son our Lord, who lives and reigns with you and the Holy Spirit, one God, for ever and ever. *Amen.*

Preface of Holy Week

Tuesday in Holy Week

O God, by the passion of your blessed Son you made an instrument of shameful death to be for us the means of life: Grant us so to glory in the cross of Christ, that we may gladly suffer shame and loss for the sake of your Son our Savior Jesus Christ; who lives and reigns with you and the Holy Spirit, one God, for ever and ever. *Amen.*

Preface of Holy Week

Wednesday in Holy Week

Lord God, whose blessed Son our Savior gave his body to be whipped and his face to be spit upon: Give us grace to accept joyfully the sufferings of the present time, confident of the glory that shall be revealed; through Jesus Christ your Son our Lord, who lives and reigns with you and the Holy Spirit, one God, for ever and ever. *Amen.*

Preface of Holy Week

Maundy Thursday

The Proper Liturgy for this day is on page 274.

Almighty Father, whose dear Son, on the night before he suffered, instituted the Sacrament of his Body and Blood: Mercifully grant that we may receive it thankfully in remembrance of Jesus Christ our Lord, who in these holy mysteries gives us a pledge of eternal life; and who now lives and reigns with you and the Holy Spirit, one God, for ever and ever. *Amen.*

Preface of Holy Week

Good Friday

The Proper Liturgy for this day is on page 276.

Almighty God, we pray you graciously to behold this your family, for whom our Lord Jesus Christ was willing to be betrayed, and given into the hands of sinners, and to suffer death upon the cross; who now lives and reigns with you and the Holy Spirit, one God, for ever and ever. *Amen.*

Holy Saturday

The Proper Liturgy for this day is on page 283.

O God, Creator of heaven and earth: Grant that, as the crucified body of your dear Son was laid in the tomb and rested on this holy Sabbath, so we may await with him the coming of the third day, and rise with him to newness of life; who now lives and reigns with you and the Holy Spirit, one God, for ever and ever. *Amen.*

Easter Day

The Liturgy of the Easter Vigil is on page 285.

O God, who for our redemption gave your only-begotten
Son to the death of the cross, and by his glorious resurrection
delivered us from the power of our enemy: Grant us so to die
daily to sin, that we may evermore live with him in the joy of
his resurrection; through Jesus Christ your Son our Lord,
who lives and reigns with you and the Holy Spirit, one God,
now and for ever. *Amen.*

or this

O God, who made this most holy night to shine with the
glory of the Lord's resurrection: Stir up in your Church that
Spirit of adoption which is given to us in Baptism, that we,
being renewed both in body and mind, may worship you in
sincerity and truth; through Jesus Christ our Lord, who lives
and reigns with you, in the unity of the Holy Spirit, one God,
now and for ever. *Amen.*

or this

Almighty God, who through your only-begotten Son Jesus
Christ overcame death and opened to us the gate of
everlasting life: Grant that we, who celebrate with joy the
day of the Lord's resurrection, may be raised from the death
of sin by your life-giving Spirit; through Jesus Christ our
Lord, who lives and reigns with you and the Holy Spirit, one
God, now and for ever. *Amen.*

Preface of Easter

Monday in Easter Week

Grant, we pray, Almighty God, that we who celebrate with
awe the Paschal feast may be found worthy to attain to

everlasting joys; through Jesus Christ our Lord, who lives and reigns with you and the Holy Spirit, one God, now and for ever. *Amen.*

Preface of Easter

Tuesday in Easter Week

O God, who by the glorious resurrection of your Son Jesus Christ destroyed death and brought life and immortality to light: Grant that we, who have been raised with him, may abide in his presence and rejoice in the hope of eternal glory; through Jesus Christ our Lord, to whom, with you and the Holy Spirit, be dominion and praise for ever and ever. *Amen.*

Preface of Easter

Wednesday in Easter Week

O God, whose blessed Son made himself known to his disciples in the breaking of bread: Open the eyes of our faith, that we may behold him in all his redeeming work; who lives and reigns with you, in the unity of the Holy Spirit, one God, now and for ever. *Amen.*

Preface of Easter

Thursday in Easter Week

Almighty and everlasting God, who in the Paschal mystery established the new covenant of reconciliation: Grant that all who have been reborn into the fellowship of Christ's Body may show forth in their lives what they profess by their faith; through Jesus Christ our Lord, who lives and reigns with you and the Holy Spirit, one God, for ever and ever. *Amen.*

Preface of Easter

Friday in Easter Week

Almighty Father, who gave your only Son to die for our sins and to rise for our justification: Give us grace so to put away the leaven of malice and wickedness, that we may always serve you in pureness of living and truth; through Jesus Christ your Son our Lord, who lives and reigns with you and the Holy Spirit, one God, now and for ever. *Amen.*

Preface of Easter

Saturday in Easter Week

We thank you, heavenly Father, that you have delivered us from the dominion of sin and death and brought us into the kingdom of your Son; and we pray that, as by his death he has recalled us to life, so by his love he may raise us to eternal joys; who lives and reigns with you, in the unity of the Holy Spirit, one God, now and for ever. *Amen.*

Preface of Easter

Second Sunday of Easter

Almighty and everlasting God, who in the Paschal mystery established the new covenant of reconciliation: Grant that all who have been reborn into the fellowship of Christ's Body may show forth in their lives what they profess by their faith; through Jesus Christ our Lord, who lives and reigns with you and the Holy Spirit, one God, for ever and ever. *Amen.*

Preface of Easter

Third Sunday of Easter

O God, whose blessed Son made himself known to his disciples in the breaking of bread: Open the eyes of our faith, that we may behold him in all his redeeming work; who lives and reigns with you, in the unity of the Holy Spirit, one God, now and for ever. *Amen.*

Preface of Easter

Fourth Sunday of Easter

O God, whose Son Jesus is the good shepherd of your people: Grant that when we hear his voice we may know him who calls us each by name, and follow where he leads; who, with you and the Holy Spirit, lives and reigns, one God, for ever and ever. *Amen.*

Preface of Easter

Fifth Sunday of Easter

Almighty God, whom truly to know is everlasting life: Grant us so perfectly to know your Son Jesus Christ to be the way, the truth, and the life, that we may steadfastly follow his steps in the way that leads to eternal life; through Jesus Christ your Son our Lord, who lives and reigns with you, in the unity of the Holy Spirit, one God, for ever and ever. *Amen.*

Preface of Easter

Sixth Sunday of Easter

O God, you have prepared for those who love you such good things as surpass our understanding: Pour into our hearts such love towards you, that we, loving you in all things and above all things, may obtain your promises, which exceed all that we can desire; through Jesus Christ our Lord, who lives and reigns with you and the Holy Spirit, one God, for ever and ever. *Amen.*

Preface of Easter

Monday, Tuesday, and Wednesday of this week are the traditional Rogation Days.

Ascension Day

Almighty God, whose blessed Son our Savior Jesus Christ ascended far above all heavens that he might fill all things: Mercifully give us faith to perceive that, according to his promise, he abides with his Church on earth, even to the end of the ages; through Jesus Christ our Lord, who lives and reigns with you and the Holy Spirit, one God, in glory everlasting. *Amen.*

or this

Grant, we pray, Almighty God, that as we believe your only-begotten Son our Lord Jesus Christ to have ascended into heaven, so we may also in heart and mind there ascend, and with him continually dwell; who lives and reigns with you and the Holy Spirit, one God, for ever and ever. *Amen.*

Preface of the Ascension

Either of the preceding Collects, with the proper Psalm and Lessons for Ascension Day, serves for the following weekdays, except as otherwise appointed.

Seventh Sunday of Easter: The Sunday after Ascension Day

O God, the King of glory, you have exalted your only Son Jesus Christ with great triumph to your kingdom in heaven: Do not leave us comfortless, but send us your Holy Spirit to strengthen us, and exalt us to that place where our Savior Christ has gone before; who lives and reigns with you and the Holy Spirit, one God, in glory everlasting. *Amen.*

Preface of the Ascension

The Day of Pentecost: Whitsunday

When a Vigil of Pentecost is observed, it begins with the Service of Light, page 109 (substituting, if desired, the Gloria in excelsis for the Phos hilaron), and continues with the Salutation and Collect of the Day. Three or more of the appointed Lessons are read before the Gospel, each followed by a Psalm, Canticle, or hymn. Holy Baptism or Confirmation (beginning with the Presentation of the Candidates), or the Renewal of Baptismal Vows, page 292, follows the Sermon.

Almighty God, on this day you opened the way of eternal life to every race and nation by the promised gift of your Holy Spirit: Shed abroad this gift throughout the world by the preaching of the Gospel, that it may reach to the ends of the earth; through Jesus Christ our Lord, who lives and reigns with you, in the unity of the Holy Spirit, one God, for ever and ever. *Amen.*

or this

O God, who on this day taught the hearts of your faithful people by sending to them the light of your Holy Spirit: Grant us by the same Spirit to have a right judgment in all things, and evermore to rejoice in his holy comfort; through Jesus Christ your Son our Lord, who lives and reigns with you, in the unity of the Holy Spirit, one God, for ever and ever. *Amen.*

Preface of Pentecost

On the weekdays which follow, the numbered Proper which corresponds most closely to the date of Pentecost in that year is used. See page 158.

Wednesday, Friday, and Saturday of this week are the traditional summer Ember Days.

First Sunday after Pentecost: Trinity Sunday

Almighty and everlasting God, you have given to us
your servants grace, by the confession of a true faith, to
acknowledge the glory of the eternal Trinity, and in the
power of your divine Majesty to worship the Unity: Keep
us steadfast in this faith and worship, and bring us at last to
see you in your one and eternal glory, O Father; who with
the Son and the Holy Spirit live and reign, one God, for ever
and ever. *Amen.*

Preface of Trinity Sunday

*On the weekdays which follow, the numbered Proper which corresponds
most closely to the date of Trinity Sunday in that year is used.*

The Season after Pentecost

Directions for the use of the Propers which follow are on page 158.

Proper 1   *Week of the Sunday closest to May 11*

Remember, O Lord, what you have wrought in us and not
what we deserve; and, as you have called us to your service,
make us worthy of our calling; through Jesus Christ our Lord,
who lives and reigns with you and the Holy Spirit, one God,
now and for ever. *Amen.*

No Proper Preface is used.

Proper 2   *Week of the Sunday closest to May 18*

Almighty and merciful God, in your goodness keep us, we
pray, from all things that may hurt us, that we, being ready

both in mind and body, may accomplish with free hearts those things which belong to your purpose; through Jesus Christ our Lord, who lives and reigns with you and the Holy Spirit, one God, now and for ever. *Amen.*

No Proper Preface is used.

Proper 3   *The Sunday closest to May 25*

Grant, O Lord, that the course of this world may be peaceably governed by your providence; and that your Church may joyfully serve you in confidence and serenity; through Jesus Christ our Lord, who lives and reigns with you and the Holy Spirit, one God, for ever and ever. *Amen.*

Preface of the Lord's Day

Proper 4   *The Sunday closest to June 1*

O God, your never-failing providence sets in order all things both in heaven and earth: Put away from us, we entreat you, all hurtful things, and give us those things which are profitable for us; through Jesus Christ our Lord, who lives and reigns with you and the Holy Spirit, one God, for ever and ever. *Amen.*

Preface of the Lord's Day

Proper 5   *The Sunday closest to June 8*

O God, from whom all good proceeds: Grant that by your inspiration we may think those things that are right, and by your merciful guiding may do them; through Jesus Christ our Lord, who lives and reigns with you and the Holy Spirit, one God, for ever and ever. *Amen.*

Preface of the Lord's Day

Proper 6 *The Sunday closest to June 15*

Keep, O Lord, your household the Church in your steadfast faith and love, that through your grace we may proclaim your truth with boldness, and minister your justice with compassion; for the sake of our Savior Jesus Christ, who lives and reigns with you and the Holy Spirit, one God, now and for ever. *Amen.*

Preface of the Lord's Day

Proper 7 *The Sunday closest to June 22*

O Lord, make us have perpetual love and reverence for your holy Name, for you never fail to help and govern those whom you have set upon the sure foundation of your loving-kindness; through Jesus Christ our Lord, who lives and reigns with you and the Holy Spirit, one God, for ever and ever. *Amen.*

Preface of the Lord's Day

Proper 8 *The Sunday closest to June 29*

Almighty God, you have built your Church upon the foundation of the apostles and prophets, Jesus Christ himself being the chief cornerstone: Grant us so to be joined together in unity of spirit by their teaching, that we may be made a holy temple acceptable to you; through Jesus Christ our Lord, who lives and reigns with you and the Holy Spirit, one God, for ever and ever. *Amen.*

Preface of the Lord's Day

Proper 9 *The Sunday closest to July 6*

O God, you have taught us to keep all your commandments by loving you and our neighbor: Grant us the grace of your Holy Spirit, that we may be devoted to you with our whole heart, and united to one another with pure affection; through Jesus Christ our Lord, who lives and reigns with you and the Holy Spirit, one God, for ever and ever. *Amen.*

Preface of the Lord's Day

Proper 10   *The Sunday closest to July 13*

O Lord, mercifully receive the prayers of your people who call upon you, and grant that they may know and understand what things they ought to do, and also may have grace and power faithfully to accomplish them; through Jesus Christ our Lord, who lives and reigns with you and the Holy Spirit, one God, now and for ever. *Amen.*

Preface of the Lord's Day

Proper 11   *The Sunday closest to July 20*

Almighty God, the fountain of all wisdom, you know our necessities before we ask and our ignorance in asking: Have compassion on our weakness, and mercifully give us those things which for our unworthiness we dare not, and for our blindness we cannot ask; through the worthiness of your Son Jesus Christ our Lord, who lives and reigns with you and the Holy Spirit, one God, now and for ever. *Amen.*

Preface of the Lord's Day

Proper 12   *The Sunday closest to July 27*

O God, the protector of all who trust in you, without whom nothing is strong, nothing is holy: Increase and multiply upon us your mercy; that, with you as our ruler and guide, we may so pass through things temporal, that we lose not the things eternal; through Jesus Christ our Lord, who lives and reigns with you and the Holy Spirit, one God, for ever and ever. *Amen.*

Preface of the Lord's Day

Proper 13   *The Sunday closest to August 3*

Let your continual mercy, O Lord, cleanse and defend your Church; and, because it cannot continue in safety without your help, protect and govern it always by your goodness; through Jesus Christ our Lord, who lives and reigns with you and the Holy Spirit, one God, for ever and ever. *Amen.*

Preface of the Lord's Day

Proper 14   *The Sunday closest to August 10*

Grant to us, Lord, we pray, the spirit to think and do always those things that are right, that we, who cannot exist without you, may by you be enabled to live according to your will; through Jesus Christ our Lord, who lives and reigns with you and the Holy Spirit, one God, for ever and ever. *Amen.*

Preface of the Lord's Day

Proper 15   *The Sunday closest to August 17*

Almighty God, you have given your only Son to be for us a sacrifice for sin, and also an example of godly life: Give us grace to receive thankfully the fruits of his redeeming work, and to follow daily in the blessed steps of his most holy life; through Jesus Christ your Son our Lord, who lives and reigns with you and the Holy Spirit, one God, now and for ever. *Amen.*

Preface of the Lord's Day

Proper 16   *The Sunday closest to August 24*

Grant, O merciful God, that your Church, being gathered together in unity by your Holy Spirit, may show forth your power among all peoples, to the glory of your Name;

through Jesus Christ our Lord, who lives and reigns with you and the Holy Spirit, one God, for ever and ever. *Amen.*

Preface of the Lord's Day

Proper 17   *The Sunday closest to August 31*

Lord of all power and might, the author and giver of all good things: Graft in our hearts the love of your Name; increase in us true religion; nourish us with all goodness; and bring forth in us the fruit of good works; through Jesus Christ our Lord, who lives and reigns with you and the Holy Spirit, one God for ever and ever. *Amen.*

Preface of the Lord's Day

Proper 18   *The Sunday closest to September 7*

Grant us, O Lord, to trust in you with all our hearts; for, as you always resist the proud who confide in their own strength, so you never forsake those who make their boast of your mercy; through Jesus Christ our Lord, who lives and reigns with you and the Holy Spirit, one God, now and for ever. *Amen.*

Preface of the Lord's Day

Proper 19   *The Sunday closest to September 14*

O God, because without you we are not able to please you, mercifully grant that your Holy Spirit may in all things direct and rule our hearts; through Jesus Christ our Lord, who lives and reigns with you and the Holy Spirit, one God, now and for ever. *Amen.*

Preface of the Lord's Day

The Wednesday, Friday, and Saturday after September 14 are the traditional autumnal Ember Days.

Proper 20   *The Sunday closest to September 21*

Grant us, Lord, not to be anxious about earthly things, but to love things heavenly; and even now, while we are placed among things that are passing away, to hold fast to those that shall endure; through Jesus Christ our Lord, who lives and reigns with you and the Holy Spirit, one God, for ever and ever. *Amen.*

Preface of the Lord's Day

Proper 21   *The Sunday closest to September 28*

O God, you declare your almighty power chiefly in showing mercy and pity: Grant us the fullness of your grace, that we, running to obtain your promises, may become partakers of your heavenly treasure; through Jesus Christ our Lord, who lives and reigns with you and the Holy Spirit, one God, for ever and ever. *Amen.*

Preface of the Lord's Day

Proper 22   *The Sunday closest to October 5*

Almighty and everlasting God, you are always more ready to hear than we to pray, and to give more than we either desire or deserve: Pour upon us the abundance of your mercy, forgiving us those things of which our conscience is afraid, and giving us those good things for which we are not worthy to ask, except through the merits and mediation of Jesus Christ our Savior; who lives and reigns with you and the Holy Spirit, one God, for ever and ever. *Amen.*

Preface of the Lord's Day

Proper 23   *The Sunday closest to October 12*

Lord, we pray that your grace may always precede and follow us, that we may continually be given to good works;

through Jesus Christ our Lord, who lives and reigns with you and the Holy Spirit, one God, now and for ever. *Amen.*

Preface of the Lord's Day

Proper 24   *The Sunday closest to October 19*

Almighty and everlasting God, in Christ you have revealed your glory among the nations: Preserve the works of your mercy, that your Church throughout the world may persevere with steadfast faith in the confession of your Name; through Jesus Christ our Lord, who lives and reigns with you and the Holy Spirit, one God, for ever and ever. *Amen.*

Preface of the Lord's Day

Proper 25   *The Sunday closest to October 26*

Almighty and everlasting God, increase in us the gifts of faith, hope, and charity; and, that we may obtain what you promise, make us love what you command; through Jesus Christ our Lord, who lives and reigns with you and the Holy Spirit, one God, for ever and ever. *Amen.*

Preface of the Lord's Day

Proper 26   *The Sunday closest to November 2*

Almighty and merciful God, it is only by your gift that your faithful people offer you true and laudable service: Grant that we may run without stumbling to obtain your heavenly promises; through Jesus Christ our Lord, who lives and reigns with you and the Holy Spirit, one God, now and for ever. *Amen.*

Preface of the Lord's Day

Proper 27 *The Sunday closest to November 9*

O God, whose blessed Son came into the world that he might destroy the works of the devil and make us children of God and heirs of eternal life: Grant that, having this hope, we may purify ourselves as he is pure; that, when he comes again with power and great glory, we may be made like him in his eternal and glorious kingdom; where he lives and reigns with you and the Holy Spirit, one God, for ever and ever. *Amen.*

Preface of the Lord's Day

Proper 28 *The Sunday closest to November 16*

Blessed Lord, who caused all holy Scriptures to be written for our learning: Grant us so to hear them, read, mark, learn, and inwardly digest them, that we may embrace and ever hold fast the blessed hope of everlasting life, which you have given us in our Savior Jesus Christ; who lives and reigns with you and the Holy Spirit, one God, for ever and ever. *Amen.*

Preface of the Lord's Day

Proper 29 *The Sunday closest to November 23*

Almighty and everlasting God, whose will it is to restore all things in your well-beloved Son, the King of kings and Lord of lords: Mercifully grant that the peoples of the earth, divided and enslaved by sin, may be freed and brought together under his most gracious rule; who lives and reigns with you and the Holy Spirit, one God, now and for ever. *Amen.*

Preface of the Lord's Day, or of Baptism

Holy Days

Saint Andrew   *November 30*

Almighty God, who gave such grace to your apostle Andrew
that he readily obeyed the call of your Son Jesus Christ, and
brought his brother with him: Give us, who are called by
your holy Word, grace to follow him without delay, and to
bring those near to us into his gracious presence; who lives
and reigns with you and the Holy Spirit, one God, now and
for ever. *Amen.*

Preface of Apostles

Saint Thomas   *December 21*

Everliving God, who strengthened your apostle Thomas with
firm and certain faith in your Son's resurrection: Grant us so
perfectly and without doubt to believe in Jesus Christ, our
Lord and our God, that our faith may never be found wanting
in your sight; through him who lives and reigns with you and
the Holy Spirit, one God, now and for ever. *Amen.*

Preface of Apostles

Saint Stephen   *December 26*

We give you thanks, O Lord of glory, for the example of the
first martyr Stephen, who looked up to heaven and prayed
for his persecutors to your Son Jesus Christ, who stands at
your right hand; where he lives and reigns with you and the
Holy Spirit, one God, in glory everlasting. *Amen.*

Preface of the Incarnation

Saint John   *December 27*

Shed upon your Church, O Lord, the brightness of your light, that we, being illumined by the teaching of your apostle and evangelist John, may so walk in the light of your truth, that at length we may attain to the fullness of eternal life; through Jesus Christ our Lord, who lives and reigns with you and the Holy Spirit, one God, for ever and ever. *Amen.*

Preface of the Incarnation

The Holy Innocents   *December 28*

We remember today, O God, the slaughter of the holy innocents of Bethlehem by King Herod. Receive, we pray, into the arms of your mercy all innocent victims; and by your great might frustrate the designs of evil tyrants and establish your rule of justice, love, and peace; through Jesus Christ our Lord, who lives and reigns with you, in the unity of the Holy Spirit, one God, for ever and ever. *Amen.*

Preface of the Incarnation

Confession of Saint Peter   *January 18*

Almighty Father, who inspired Simon Peter, first among the apostles, to confess Jesus as Messiah and Son of the living God: Keep your Church steadfast upon the rock of this faith, so that in unity and peace we may proclaim the one truth and follow the one Lord, our Savior Jesus Christ; who lives and reigns with you and the Holy Spirit, one God, now and for ever. *Amen.*

Preface of Apostles

Conversion of Saint Paul   *January 25*

O God, by the preaching of your apostle Paul you have caused the light of the Gospel to shine throughout the world:

Grant, we pray, that we, having his wonderful conversion in remembrance, may show ourselves thankful to you by following his holy teaching; through Jesus Christ our Lord, who lives and reigns with you, in the unity of the Holy Spirit, one God, now and for ever. *Amen.*

Preface of Apostles

The Presentation   *February 2*

Almighty and everliving God, we humbly pray that, as your only-begotten Son was this day presented in the temple, so we may be presented to you with pure and clean hearts by Jesus Christ our Lord; who lives and reigns with you and the Holy Spirit, one God, now and for ever. *Amen.*

Preface of the Epiphany

Saint Matthias   *February 24*

Almighty God, who in the place of Judas chose your faithful servant Matthias to be numbered among the Twelve: Grant that your Church, being delivered from false apostles, may always be guided and governed by faithful and true pastors; through Jesus Christ our Lord, who lives and reigns with you, in the unity of the Holy Spirit, one God, now and for ever. *Amen.*

Preface of Apostles

Saint Joseph   *March 19*

O God, who from the family of your servant David raised up Joseph to be the guardian of your incarnate Son and the spouse of his virgin mother: Give us grace to imitate his uprightness of life and his obedience to your commands; through Jesus Christ our Lord, who lives and reigns with you and the Holy Spirit, one God, for ever and ever. *Amen.*

Preface of the Epiphany

The Annunciation   *March 25*

Pour your grace into our hearts, O Lord, that we who have
known the incarnation of your Son Jesus Christ, announced
by an angel to the Virgin Mary, may by his cross and passion
be brought to the glory of his resurrection; who lives and
reigns with you, in the unity of the Holy Spirit, one God, now
and for ever. *Amen.*

Preface of the Epiphany

Saint Mark   *April 25*

Almighty God, by the hand of Mark the evangelist you have
given to your Church the Gospel of Jesus Christ the Son of
God: We thank you for this witness, and pray that we may be
firmly grounded in its truth; through Jesus Christ our Lord,
who lives and reigns with you and the Holy Spirit, one God,
for ever and ever. *Amen.*

Preface of All Saints

Saint Philip and Saint James   *May 1*

Almighty God, who gave to your apostles Philip and James grace
and strength to bear witness to the truth: Grant that we, being
mindful of their victory of faith, may glorify in life and death the
Name of our Lord Jesus Christ; who lives and reigns with you
and the Holy Spirit, one God, now and for ever. *Amen.*

Preface of Apostles

The Visitation   *May 31*

Father in heaven, by your grace the virgin mother of your
incarnate Son was blessed in bearing him, but still more
blessed in keeping your word: Grant us who honor the
exaltation of her lowliness to follow the example of her
devotion to your will; through Jesus Christ our Lord, who

lives and reigns with you and the Holy Spirit, one God, for ever and ever. *Amen.*

Preface of the Epiphany

Saint Barnabas *June 11*

Grant, O God, that we may follow the example of your faithful servant Barnabas, who, seeking not his own renown but the well-being of your Church, gave generously of his life and substance for the relief of the poor and the spread of the Gospel; through Jesus Christ our Lord, who lives and reigns with you and the Holy Spirit, one God, for ever and ever. *Amen.*

Preface of Apostles

The Nativity of Saint John the Baptist *June 24*

Almighty God, by whose providence your servant John the Baptist was wonderfully born, and sent to prepare the way of your Son our Savior by preaching repentance: Make us so to follow his teaching and holy life, that we may truly repent according to his preaching; and, following his example, constantly speak the truth, boldly rebuke vice, and patiently suffer for the truth's sake; through Jesus Christ your Son our Lord, who lives and reigns with you and the Holy Spirit, one God, for ever and ever. *Amen.*

Preface of Advent

Saint Peter and Saint Paul *June 29*

Almighty God, whose blessed apostles Peter and Paul glorified you by their martyrdom: Grant that your Church, instructed by their teaching and example, and knit together in unity by your Spirit, may ever stand firm upon the one foundation, which is Jesus Christ our Lord; who lives and reigns with you, in the unity of the Holy Spirit, one God, now and for ever. *Amen.*

Preface of Apostles

Independence Day *July 4*

Lord God Almighty, in whose Name the founders of this
country won liberty for themselves and for us, and lit the
torch of freedom for nations then unborn: Grant that we and
all the people of this land may have grace to maintain our
liberties in righteousness and peace; through Jesus Christ our
Lord, who lives and reigns with you and the Holy Spirit, one
God, for ever and ever. *Amen.*

The Collect "For the Nation," page 258, may be used instead.

Preface of Trinity Sunday

Saint Mary Magdalene *July 22*

Almighty God, whose blessed Son restored Mary Magdalene
to health of body and of mind, and called her to be a witness
of his resurrection: Mercifully grant that by your grace we
may be healed from all our infirmities and know you in the
power of his unending life; who with you and the Holy Spirit
lives and reigns, one God, now and for ever. *Amen.*

Preface of All Saints

Saint James *July 25*

O gracious God, we remember before you today your servant
and apostle James, first among the Twelve to suffer martyrdom
for the Name of Jesus Christ; and we pray that you will pour
out upon the leaders of your Church that spirit of self-denying
service by which alone they may have true authority among
your people; through Jesus Christ our Lord, who lives and
reigns with you and the Holy Spirit, one God, now and for
ever. *Amen.*

Preface of Apostles

The Transfiguration   *August 6*

O God, who on the holy mount revealed to chosen witnesses your well-beloved Son, wonderfully transfigured, in raiment white and glistening: Mercifully grant that we, being delivered from the disquietude of this world, may by faith behold the King in his beauty; who with you, O Father, and you, O Holy Spirit, lives and reigns, one God, for ever and ever. *Amen.*

Preface of the Epiphany

Saint Mary the Virgin   *August 15*

O God, you have taken to yourself the blessed Virgin Mary, mother of your incarnate Son: Grant that we, who have been redeemed by his blood, may share with her the glory of your eternal kingdom; through Jesus Christ our Lord, who lives and reigns with you, in the unity of the Holy Spirit, one God, now and for ever. *Amen.*

Preface of the Incarnation

Saint Bartholomew   *August 24*

Almighty and everlasting God, who gave to your apostle Bartholomew grace truly to believe and to preach your Word: Grant that your Church may love what he believed and preach what he taught; through Jesus Christ our Lord, who lives and reigns with you and the Holy Spirit, one God, for ever and ever. *Amen.*

Preface of Apostles

Holy Cross Day *September 14*

Almighty God, whose Son our Savior Jesus Christ was lifted high upon the cross that he might draw the whole world to himself: Mercifully grant that we, who glory in the mystery of our redemption, may have grace to take up our cross and follow him; who lives and reigns with you and the Holy Spirit, one God, in glory everlasting. *Amen.*

Preface of Holy Week

Saint Matthew *September 21*

We thank you, heavenly Father, for the witness of your apostle and evangelist Matthew to the Gospel of your Son our Savior; and we pray that, after his example, we may with ready wills and hearts obey the calling of our Lord to follow him; through Jesus Christ our Lord, who lives and reigns with you and the Holy Spirit, one God, now and for ever. *Amen.*

Preface of Apostles

Saint Michael and All Angels *September 29*

Everlasting God, you have ordained and constituted in a wonderful order the ministries of angels and mortals: Mercifully grant that, as your holy angels always serve and worship you in heaven, so by your appointment they may help and defend us here on earth; through Jesus Christ our Lord, who lives and reigns with you and the Holy Spirit, one God, for ever and ever. *Amen.*

Preface of Trinity Sunday

Saint Luke *October 18*

Almighty God, who inspired your servant Luke the physician to set forth in the Gospel the love and healing power of your Son: Graciously continue in your Church this love and power to heal, to the praise and glory of your Name; through Jesus Christ our Lord, who lives and reigns with you, in the unity of the Holy Spirit, one God, now and for ever. *Amen.*

Preface of All Saints

Saint James of Jerusalem   *October 23*

Grant, O God, that, following the example of your servant James the Just, brother of our Lord, your Church may give itself continually to prayer and to the reconciliation of all who are at variance and enmity; through Jesus Christ our Lord, who lives and reigns with you and the Holy Spirit, one God, now and for ever. *Amen.*

Preface of All Saints

Saint Simon and Saint Jude   *October 28*

O God, we thank you for the glorious company of the apostles, and especially on this day for Simon and Jude; and we pray that, as they were faithful and zealous in their mission, so we may with ardent devotion make known the love and mercy of our Lord and Savior Jesus Christ; who lives and reigns with you and the Holy Spirit, one God, for ever and ever. *Amen.*

Preface of Apostles

All Saints' Day   *November 1*

Almighty God, you have knit together your elect in one communion and fellowship in the mystical body of your Son Christ our Lord: Give us grace so to follow your blessed saints in all virtuous and godly living, that we may come to those ineffable joys that you have prepared for those who truly love you; through Jesus Christ our Lord, who with you and the Holy Spirit lives and reigns, one God, in glory everlasting. *Amen.*

Preface of All Saints

Thanksgiving Day

Almighty and gracious Father, we give you thanks for the fruits of the earth in their season and for the labors of those who harvest them. Make us, we pray, faithful stewards of your great bounty, for the provision of our necessities and the relief of all who are in need, to the glory of your Name; through Jesus Christ our Lord, who lives and reigns with you and the Holy Spirit, one God, now and for ever. *Amen.*

For the Prayers of the People, the Litany of Thanksgiving on page 836 may be used.

Preface of Trinity Sunday

The Common of Saints

The festival of a saint is observed in accordance with the rules of precedence set forth in the Calendar of the Church Year.

At the discretion of the Celebrant, and as appropriate, any of the following Collects, with one of the corresponding sets of Psalms and Lessons, may be used

a) at the commemoration of a saint listed in the Calendar for which no Proper is provided in this Book

b) at the patronal festival or commemoration of a saint not listed in the Calendar.

Of a Martyr

Almighty God, who gave to your servant N. boldness to confess the Name of our Savior Jesus Christ before the rulers of this world, and courage to die for this faith: Grant that we may always be ready to give a reason for the hope that is in us, and to suffer gladly for the sake of our Lord Jesus Christ; who lives and reigns with you and the Holy Spirit, one God, for ever and ever. *Amen.*

or this

Almighty God, by whose grace and power your holy martyr N. triumphed over suffering and was faithful even to death: Grant us, who now remember *him* in thanksgiving, to be so faithful in our witness to you in this world, that we may receive with *him* the crown of life; through Jesus Christ our Lord, who lives and reigns with you and the Holy Spirit, one God, for ever and ever. *Amen.*

or this

Almighty and everlasting God, who kindled the flame of your love in the heart of your holy martyr N.: Grant to us, your humble servants, a like faith and power of love, that we who rejoice in *her* triumph may profit by *her* example; through Jesus Christ our Lord, who lives and reigns with you and the Holy Spirit, one God, for ever and ever. *Amen.*

Preface of a Saint

Of a Missionary

Almighty and everlasting God, we thank you for your servant N., whom you called to preach the Gospel to the people of _____ *(or* to the _____ people). Raise up in this and every land evangelists and heralds of your kingdom, that your Church may proclaim the unsearchable riches of our Savior Jesus Christ; who lives and reigns with you and the Holy Spirit, one God, now and for ever. *Amen.*

or the following

Almighty God, whose will it is to be glorified in your saints, and who raised up your servant N. to be a light in the world: Shine, we pray, in our hearts, that we also in our generation may show forth your praise, who called us out of darkness into your marvelous light; through Jesus Christ our Lord, who lives and reigns with you and the Holy Spirit, one God, now and for ever. *Amen.*

Preface of Pentecost

Of a Pastor

Heavenly Father, Shepherd of your people, we thank you for your servant N., who was faithful in the care and nurture of your flock; and we pray that, following his example and the teaching of his holy life, we may by your grace grow into the stature of the fullness of our Lord and Savior Jesus Christ; who lives and reigns with you and the Holy Spirit, one God, for ever and ever. *Amen.*

or this

O God, our heavenly Father, who raised up your faithful servant N., to be a [bishop and] pastor in your Church and to feed your flock: Give abundantly to all pastors the gifts of your Holy Spirit, that they may minister in your household as true servants of Christ and stewards of your divine mysteries; through Jesus Christ our Lord, who lives and reigns with you and the Holy Spirit, one God, for ever and ever. *Amen.*

Preface of a Saint

Of a Theologian and Teacher

O God, by your Holy Spirit you give to some the word of wisdom, to others the word of knowledge, and to others the word of faith: We praise your Name for the gifts of grace manifested in your servant N., and we pray that your Church may never be destitute of such gifts; through Jesus Christ our Lord, who with you and the Holy Spirit lives and reigns, one God, for ever and ever. *Amen.*

or this

Almighty God, you gave to your servant N. special gifts of grace to understand and teach the truth as it is in Christ Jesus: Grant that by this teaching we may know you, the one true God, and Jesus Christ whom you have sent; who lives and reigns with you and the Holy Spirit, one God, for ever and ever. *Amen.*

Preface of a Saint, or of Trinity Sunday

Of a Monastic

O God, whose blessed Son became poor that we through his poverty might be rich: Deliver us from an inordinate love of this world, that we, inspired by the devotion of your servant N., may serve you with singleness of heart, and attain to the riches of the age to come; through Jesus Christ our Lord, who lives and reigns with you, in the unity of the Holy Spirit, one God, now and for ever. *Amen.*

or this

O God, by whose grace your servant N., kindled with the flame of your love, became a burning and a shining light in your Church: Grant that we also may be aflame with the spirit of love and discipline, and walk before you as children of light; through Jesus Christ our Lord, who lives and reigns with you, in the unity of the Holy Spirit, one God, now and for ever. *Amen.*

Preface of a Saint

Of a Saint

Almighty God, you have surrounded us with a great cloud of witnesses: Grant that we, encouraged by the good example of your servant N., may persevere in running the race that is set before us, until at last we may with *him* attain to your eternal joy; through Jesus Christ, the pioneer and perfecter of our faith, who lives and reigns with you and the Holy Spirit, one God, for ever and ever. *Amen.*

or this

O God, you have brought us near to an innumerable company of angels, and to the spirits of just men made perfect: Grant us during our earthly pilgrimage to abide in their fellowship, and in our heavenly country to become partakers of their joy; through Jesus Christ our Lord, who lives and reigns with you and the Holy Spirit, one God, now and for ever. *Amen.*

or this

Almighty God, by your Holy Spirit you have made us one with your saints in heaven and on earth: Grant that in our earthly pilgrimage we may always be supported by this fellowship of love and prayer, and know ourselves to be surrounded by their witness to your power and mercy. We ask this for the sake of Jesus Christ, in whom all our intercessions are acceptable through the Spirit, and who lives and reigns for ever and ever. *Amen.*

Preface of a Saint

Various Occasions

For optional use, when desired, subject to the rules set forth in the Calendar of the Church Year.

1. Of the Holy Trinity

Almighty God, you have revealed to your Church your eternal Being of glorious majesty and perfect love as one God in Trinity of Persons: Give us grace to continue steadfast in the confession of this faith, and constant in our worship of you, Father, Son, and Holy Spirit; for you live and reign, one God, now and for ever. *Amen.*

Preface of Trinity Sunday

2. Of the Holy Spirit

Almighty and most merciful God, grant that by the indwelling of your Holy Spirit we may be enlightened and strengthened for your service; through Jesus Christ our Lord, who lives and reigns with you, in the unity of the Holy Spirit, one God, now and for ever. *Amen.*

Preface of Pentecost

3. Of the Holy Angels

Everlasting God, you have ordained and constituted in a wonderful order the ministries of angels and mortals: Mercifully grant that, as your holy angels always serve and worship you in heaven, so by your appointment they may help and defend us here on earth; through Jesus Christ our Lord, who lives and reigns with you and the Holy Spirit, one God, for ever and ever. *Amen.*

Preface of Trinity Sunday

4. Of the Incarnation

O God, who wonderfully created, and yet more wonderfully restored, the dignity of human nature: Grant that we may share the divine life of him who humbled himself to share our humanity, your Son Jesus Christ; who lives and reigns with you, in the unity of the Holy Spirit, one God, for ever and ever. *Amen*

Preface of the Epiphany

5. Of the Holy Eucharist

Especially suitable for Thursdays

God our Father, whose Son our Lord Jesus Christ in a wonderful Sacrament has left us a memorial of his passion: Grant us so to venerate the sacred mysteries of his Body and Blood, that we may ever perceive within ourselves the fruit of his redemption; who lives and reigns with you and the Holy Spirit, one God, for ever and ever. *Amen.*

Preface of the Epiphany

6. Of the Holy Cross

Especially suitable for Fridays

Almighty God, whose beloved Son willingly endured the agony and shame of the cross for our redemption: Give us courage to take up our cross and follow him; who lives and reigns with you and the Holy Spirit, one God, now and for ever. *Amen.*

Preface of Holy Week

7. For all Baptized Christians

Especially suitable for Saturdays

Grant, Lord God, to all who have been baptized into the

death and resurrection of your Son Jesus Christ, that, as we
have put away the old life of sin, so we may be renewed in the
spirit of our minds, and live in righteousness and true holiness;
through Jesus Christ our Lord, who lives and reigns with you,
in the unity of the Holy Spirit, one God, now and for ever.
Amen.

Preface of Baptism

8. For the Departed

Eternal Lord God, you hold all souls in life: Give to your
whole Church in paradise and on earth your light and your
peace; and grant that we, following the good examples of
those who have served you here and are now at rest, may at
the last enter with them into your unending joy; through
Jesus Christ our Lord, who lives and reigns with you, in the
unity of the Holy Spirit, one God, now and for ever. *Amen.*

or this

Almighty God, we remember before you today your faithful
servant N.; and we pray that, having opened to *him* the gates
of larger life, you will receive *him* more and more into your
joyful service, that, with all who have faithfully served you in
the past, *he* may share in the eternal victory of Jesus Christ
our Lord; who lives and reigns with you, in the unity of the
Holy Spirit, one God, for ever and ever. *Amen.*

*Any of the Collects appointed for use at the Burial of the Dead may be
used instead.*

*For the Prayers of the People, one of the forms appointed for the
Burial of the Dead may be used.*

Preface of the Commemoration of the Dead

The postcommunion prayer on page 498 may be used.

9. Of the Reign of Christ

Almighty and everlasting God, whose will it is to restore all things in your well-beloved Son, the King of kings and Lord of lords: Mercifully grant that the peoples of the earth, divided and enslaved by sin, may be freed and brought together under his most gracious rule; who lives and reigns with you and the Holy Spirit, one God, now and for ever. *Amen.*

Preface of the Ascension, or of Baptism

10. At Baptism

Almighty God, by our baptism into the death and resurrection of your Son Jesus Christ, you turn us from the old life of sin: Grant that we, being reborn to new life in him, may live in righteousness and holiness all our days; through Jesus Christ our Lord, who lives and reigns with you and the Holy Spirit, one God, now and for ever. *Amen.*

Preface of Baptism

11. At Confirmation

Grant, Almighty God, that we, who have been redeemed from the old life of sin by our baptism into the death and resurrection of your Son Jesus Christ, may be renewed in your Holy Spirit, and live in righteousness and true holiness; through Jesus Christ our Lord, who lives and reigns with you and the Holy Spirit, one God, now and for ever. *Amen.*

Preface of Baptism, or of Pentecost

12. On the Anniversary of the Dedication of a Church

Almighty God, to whose glory we celebrate the dedication of this house of prayer: We give you thanks for the fellowship of those who have worshiped in this place, and we pray that all who seek you here may find you, and be filled with your joy and peace; through Jesus Christ our Lord, who lives and reigns with you, in the unity of the Holy Spirit, one God, now and for ever. *Amen.*

The Litany of Thanksgiving for a Church, page 578, may be used for the Prayers of the People.

Preface of the Dedication of a Church

13. For a Church Convention

Almighty and everlasting Father, you have given the Holy Spirit to abide with us for ever: Bless, we pray, with his grace and presence, the bishops and the other clergy and the laity here (*or* now, *or* soon to be) assembled in your Name, that your Church, being preserved in true faith and godly discipline, may fulfill all the mind of him who loved it and gave himself for it, your Son Jesus Christ our Savior; who lives and reigns with you, in the unity of the Holy Spirit, one God, now and for ever. *Amen.*

Preface of Pentecost, or of the Season

14. For the Unity of the Church

Almighty Father, whose blessed Son before his passion prayed for his disciples that they might be one, as you and he are one: Grant that your Church, being bound together in love and obedience to you, may be united in one body by the one Spirit, that the world may believe in him whom you have sent, your Son Jesus Christ our Lord; who lives and reigns with you, in the unity of the Holy Spirit, one God, now and for ever. *Amen.*

Preface of Baptism, or of Trinity Sunday

15. For the Ministry (Ember Days)

For use on the traditional days or at other times

I. For those to be ordained

Almighty God, the giver of all good gifts, in your divine providence you have appointed various orders in your Church: Give your grace, we humbly pray, to all who are [now] called to any office and ministry for your people; and so fill them with the truth of your doctrine and clothe them with holiness of life, that they may faithfully serve before you, to the glory of your great Name and for the benefit of your holy Church; through Jesus Christ our Lord, who lives and reigns with you, in the unity of the Holy Spirit, one God, now and for ever. *Amen.*

Preface of Apostles

II. For the choice of fit persons for the ministry

O God, you led your holy apostles to ordain ministers in every place: Grant that your Church, under the guidance of the Holy Spirit, may choose suitable persons for the ministry of Word and Sacrament, and may uphold them in their work for the extension of your kingdom; through him who is the Shepherd and Bishop of our souls, Jesus Christ our Lord, who lives and reigns with you and the Holy Spirit, one God, for ever and ever. *Amen.*

Preface of the Season

III. For all Christians in their vocation

Almighty and everlasting God, by whose Spirit the whole body of your faithful people is governed and sanctified: Receive our supplications and prayers, which we offer before

you for all members of your holy Church, that in their vocation
and ministry they may truly and devoutly serve you; through
our Lord and Savior Jesus Christ, who lives and reigns with
you, in the unity of the Holy Spirit, one God, now and for ever.
Amen.

Preface of Baptism, or of the Season

16. For the Mission of the Church

O God, you have made of one blood all the peoples of the
earth, and sent your blessed Son to preach peace to those
who are far off and to those who are near: Grant that people
everywhere may seek after you and find you, bring the nations
into your fold, pour out your Spirit upon all flesh, and hasten
the coming of your kingdom; through Jesus Christ our Lord,
who lives and reigns with you and the Holy Spirit, one God,
now and for ever. *Amen.*

or this

O God of all the nations of the earth: Remember the
multitudes who have been created in your image but have not
known the redeeming work of our Savior Jesus Christ; and
grant that, by the prayers and labors of your holy Church,
they may be brought to know and worship you as you have
been revealed in your Son; who lives and reigns with you and
the Holy Spirit, one God, for ever and ever. *Amen.*

Preface of the Season, or of Pentecost

17. For the Nation

Lord God Almighty, you have made all the peoples of the earth for your glory, to serve you in freedom and in peace: Give to the people of our country a zeal for justice and the strength of forbearance, that we may use our liberty in accordance with your gracious will; through Jesus Christ our Lord, who lives and reigns with you and the Holy Spirit, one God, for ever and ever. *Amen.*

The Collect for Independence Day may be used instead.

Preface of Trinity Sunday

18. For Peace

Almighty God, kindle, we pray, in every heart the true love of peace, and guide with your wisdom those who take counsel for the nations of the earth, that in tranquillity your dominion may increase until the earth is filled with the knowledge of your love; through Jesus Christ our Lord, who lives and reigns with you, in the unity of the Holy Spirit, one God, now and for ever. *Amen.*

Preface of the Season

19. For Rogation Days

For use on the traditional days or at other times

I. For fruitful seasons

Almighty God, Lord of heaven and earth: We humbly pray that your gracious providence may give and preserve to our use the harvests of the land and of the seas, and may prosper all who labor to gather them, that we, who are constantly receiving good things from your hand, may always give you thanks; through Jesus Christ our Lord, who lives and reigns with you and the Holy Spirit, one God, for ever and ever. *Amen.*

Preface of the Season

II. For commerce and industry

Almighty God, whose Son Jesus Christ in his earthly life shared our toil and hallowed our labor: Be present with your people where they work; make those who carry on the industries and commerce of this land responsive to your will; and give to us all a pride in what we do, and a just return for our labor; through Jesus Christ our Lord, who lives and reigns with you, in the unity of the Holy Spirit, one God, now and for ever. *Amen.*

Preface of the Season

III. For stewardship of creation

O merciful Creator, your hand is open wide to satisfy the needs of every living creature: Make us always thankful for your loving providence; and grant that we, remembering the account that we must one day give, may be faithful stewards of your good gifts; through Jesus Christ our Lord, who with you and the Holy Spirit lives and reigns, one God, for ever and ever. *Amen.*

Preface of the Season

20. For the Sick

Heavenly Father, giver of life and health: Comfort and relieve your sick servants, and give your power of healing to those who minister to their needs, that those *(or N., or NN.)* for whom our prayers are offered may be strengthened in *their* weakness and have confidence in your loving care; through Jesus Christ our Lord, who lives and reigns with you and the Holy Spirit, one God, now and for ever. *Amen.*

Preface of the Season

The postcommunion prayer on page 457 may be used.

21. For Social Justice

Almighty God, who created us in your own image: Grant us grace fearlessly to contend against evil and to make no peace with oppression; and, that we may reverently use our freedom, help us to employ it in the maintenance of justice in our communities and among the nations, to the glory of your holy Name; through Jesus Christ our Lord, who lives and reigns with you and the Holy Spirit, one God, now and for ever. *Amen.*

Preface of the Season

22. For Social Service

Heavenly Father, whose blessed Son came not to be served but to serve: Bless all who, following in his steps, give themselves to the service of others; that with wisdom, patience, and courage, they may minister in his Name to the suffering, the friendless, and the needy; for the love of him who laid down his life for us, your Son our Savior Jesus Christ, who lives and reigns with you and the Holy Spirit, one God, for ever and ever. *Amen.*

Preface of the Season

23. For Education

Almighty God, the fountain of all wisdom: Enlighten by your
Holy Spirit those who teach and those who learn, that,
rejoicing in the knowledge of your truth, they may worship
you and serve you from generation to generation; through
Jesus Christ our Lord, who lives and reigns with you and the
Holy Spirit, one God, for ever and ever. *Amen.*

Preface of the Season

24. For Vocation in Daily Work

Almighty God our heavenly Father, you declare your glory
and show forth your handiwork in the heavens and in the
earth: Deliver us in our various occupations from the service
of self alone, that we may do the work you give us to do in
truth and beauty and for the common good; for the sake of
him who came among us as one who serves, your Son Jesus
Christ our Lord, who lives and reigns with you and the Holy
Spirit, one God, for ever and ever. *Amen.*

Preface of the Season

25. For Labor Day

Almighty God, you have so linked our lives one with another
that all we do affects, for good or ill, all other lives: So guide
us in the work we do, that we may do it not for self alone, but
for the common good; and, as we seek a proper return for
our own labor, make us mindful of the rightful aspirations of
other workers, and arouse our concern for those who are out
of work; through Jesus Christ our Lord, who lives and reigns
with you and the Holy Spirit, one God, for ever and ever.
Amen.

Preface of the Season

Proper Liturgies
for Special Days

Ash Wednesday

On this day, the Celebrant begins the liturgy with the Salutation and the Collect of the Day.

Let us pray.

Almighty and everlasting God, you hate nothing you have made and forgive the sins of all who are penitent: Create and make in us new and contrite hearts, that we, worthily lamenting our sins and acknowledging our wretchedness, may obtain of you, the God of all mercy, perfect remission and forgiveness; through Jesus Christ our Lord, who lives and reigns with you and the Holy Spirit, one God, for ever and ever. *Amen.*

Old Testament   Joel 2:1-2, 12-17,   *or* Isaiah 58:1-12
Psalm   103,   *or* 103:8-14
Epistle   2 Corinthians 5:20b—6:10
Gospel   Matthew 6:1-6, 16-21

After the Sermon, all stand, and the Celebrant or Minister appointed invites the people to the observance of a holy Lent, saying

Dear People of God: The first Christians observed with great devotion the days of our Lord's passion and resurrection, and it became the custom of the Church to prepare for them by a season of penitence and fasting. This season of Lent provided a time in which converts to the faith were prepared for Holy Baptism. It was also a time when those who, because of notorious sins, had been separated from the body of the faithful were reconciled by penitence and forgiveness, and restored to the fellowship of the Church. Thereby, the whole congregation was put in mind of the message of pardon and absolution set forth in the Gospel of our Savior, and of the need which all Christians continually have to renew their repentance and faith.

I invite you, therefore, in the name of the Church, to the observance of a holy Lent, by self-examination and repentance; by prayer, fasting, and self-denial; and by reading and meditating on God's holy Word. And, to make a right beginning of repentance, and as a mark of our mortal nature, let us now kneel before the Lord, our maker and redeemer.

Silence is then kept for a time, all kneeling.

If ashes are to be imposed, the Celebrant says the following prayer

Almighty God, you have created us out of the dust of the earth: Grant that these ashes may be to us a sign of our mortality and penitence, that we may remember that it is only by your gracious gift that we are given everlasting life; through Jesus Christ our Savior. *Amen.*

The ashes are imposed with the following words

Remember that you are dust, and to dust you shall return.

The following Psalm is then sung or said

Psalm 51 *Miserere mei, Deus*

1 Have mercy on me, O God, according to your
         loving-kindness; *
   in your great compassion blot out my offenses.

2 Wash me through and through from my wickedness *
   and cleanse me from my sin.

3 For I know my transgressions, *
   and my sin is ever before me.

4 Against you only have I sinned *
   and done what is evil in your sight.

5 And so you are justified when you speak *
   and upright in your judgment.

6 Indeed, I have been wicked from my birth, *
   a sinner from my mother's womb.

7 For behold, you look for truth deep within me, *
   and will make me understand wisdom secretly.

8 Purge me from my sin, and I shall be pure; *
   wash me, and I shall be clean indeed.

9 Make me hear of joy and gladness, *
   that the body you have broken may rejoice.

10 Hide your face from my sins *
   and blot out all my iniquities.

11 Create in me a clean heart, O God, *
   and renew a right spirit within me.

12 Cast me not away from your presence *
   and take not your holy Spirit from me.

13 Give me the joy of your saving help again *
   and sustain me with your bountiful Spirit.

14   I shall teach your ways to the wicked, *
      and sinners shall return to you.

15   Deliver me from death, O God, *
      and my tongue shall sing of your righteousness,
      O God of my salvation.

16   Open my lips, O Lord, *
      and my mouth shall proclaim your praise.

17   Had you desired it, I would have offered sacrifice; *
      but you take no delight in burnt-offerings.

18   The sacrifice of God is a troubled spirit; *
      a broken and contrite heart, O God, you will not despise.

Litany of Penitence

The Celebrant and People together, all kneeling

Most holy and merciful Father:
We confess to you and to one another,
and to the whole communion of saints
in heaven and on earth,
that we have sinned by our own fault
in thought, word, and deed;
by what we have done, and by what we have left undone.

The Celebrant continues

We have not loved you with our whole heart, and mind, and
strength. We have not loved our neighbors as ourselves. We
have not forgiven others, as we have been forgiven.
Have mercy on us, Lord.

We have been deaf to your call to serve, as Christ served us.
We have not been true to the mind of Christ. We have grieved
your Holy Spirit.
Have mercy on us, Lord.

We confess to you, Lord, all our past unfaithfulness: the pride, hypocrisy, and impatience of our lives,
We confess to you, Lord.

Our self-indulgent appetites and ways, and our exploitation of other people,
We confess to you, Lord.

Our anger at our own frustration, and our envy of those more fortunate than ourselves,
We confess to you, Lord.

Our intemperate love of worldly goods and comforts, and our dishonesty in daily life and work,
We confess to you, Lord.

Our negligence in prayer and worship, and our failure to commend the faith that is in us,
We confess to you, Lord.

Accept our repentance, Lord, for the wrongs we have done: for our blindness to human need and suffering, and our indifference to injustice and cruelty,
Accept our repentance, Lord.

For all false judgments, for uncharitable thoughts toward our neighbors, and for our prejudice and contempt toward those who differ from us,
Accept our repentance, Lord.

For our waste and pollution of your creation, and our lack of concern for those who come after us,
Accept our repentance, Lord.

Restore us, good Lord, and let your anger depart from us;
Favorably hear us, for your mercy is great.

Accomplish in us the work of your salvation,
That we may show forth your glory in the world.

By the cross and passion of your Son our Lord,
Bring us with all your saints to the joy of his resurrection.

The Bishop, if present, or the Priest, stands and, facing the people, says

Almighty God, the Father of our Lord Jesus Christ, who desires not the death of sinners, but rather that they may turn from their wickedness and live, has given power and commandment to his ministers to declare and pronounce to his people, being penitent, the absolution and remission of their sins. He pardons and absolves all those who truly repent, and with sincere hearts believe his holy Gospel.

Therefore we beseech him to grant us true repentance and his Holy Spirit, that those things may please him which we do on this day, and that the rest of our life hereafter may be pure and holy, so that at the last we may come to his eternal joy; through Jesus Christ our Lord. *Amen.*

A deacon or lay reader leading the service remains kneeling and substitutes the prayer for forgiveness appointed at Morning Prayer.

The Peace is then exchanged.

In the absence of a bishop or priest, all that precedes may be led by a deacon or lay reader.

The Litany of Penitence may be used at other times, and may be preceded by an appropriate invitation and a penitential psalm.

When Communion follows, the service continues with the Offertory.

Preface of Lent

The Sunday of the Passion: Palm Sunday

The Liturgy of the Palms

When circumstances permit, the congregation may gather at a place apart from the church, so that all may go into the church in procession.

The branches of palm or of other trees or shrubs to be carried in the procession may be distributed to the people before the service, or after the prayer of blessing.

The following or some other suitable anthem is sung or said, the people standing

Blessed is the King who comes in the name of the Lord:
Peace in heaven and glory in the highest.

Celebrant Let us pray.

Assist us mercifully with your help, O Lord God of our salvation, that we may enter with joy upon the contemplation of those mighty acts, whereby you have given us life and immortality; through Jesus Christ our Lord. *Amen.*

Here a Deacon or other person appointed reads one of the following

Year A Matthew 21:1-11
Year B Mark 11:1-11a
Year C Luke 19:29-40

The Celebrant then says the following blessing

The Lord be with you.
People   And also with you.
Celebrant   Let us give thanks to the Lord our God.
People   It is right to give him thanks and praise.

It is right to praise you, Almighty God, for the acts of love by which you have redeemed us through your Son Jesus Christ our Lord. On this day he entered the holy city of Jerusalem in triumph, and was proclaimed as King of kings by those who spread their garments and branches of palm along his way. Let these branches be for us signs of his victory, and grant that we who bear them in his name may ever hail him as our King, and follow him in the way that leads to eternal life; who lives and reigns in glory with you and the Holy Spirit, now and for ever. *Amen.*

The following or some other suitable anthem may then be sung or said

Blessed is he who comes in the name of the Lord.
Hosanna in the highest.

The Procession

Deacon   Let us go forth in peace.
People   In the name of Christ. Amen.

During the procession, all hold branches in their hands, and appropriate hymns, psalms, or anthems are sung, such as the hymn "All glory, laud, and honor" and Psalm 118:19-29.

At a suitable place, the procession may halt while the following or some other appropriate Collect is said

Almighty God, whose most dear Son went not up to joy but
first he suffered pain, and entered not into glory before he
was crucified: Mercifully grant that we, walking in the way
of the cross, may find it none other than the way of life and
peace; through Jesus Christ our Lord. *Amen.*

*In the absence of a bishop or priest, the preceding service may be led by a
deacon or lay reader.*

*At services on this day other than the principal celebration, suitable
portions of the preceding may be used.*

At the Eucharist

*When the Liturgy of the Palms immediately precedes the Eucharist, the
celebration begins with the Salutation and Collect of the Day*

Let us pray.

Almighty and everliving God, in your tender love for the
human race you sent your Son our Savior Jesus Christ to take
upon him our nature, and to suffer death upon the cross,
giving us the example of his great humility: Mercifully grant
that we may walk in the way of his suffering, and also share
in his resurrection; through Jesus Christ our Lord, who lives
and reigns with you and the Holy Spirit, one God, for ever
and ever. *Amen.*

Old Testament   Isaiah 45:21-25,   *or* Isaiah 52:13—53:12
Psalm   22:1-21,   *or* 22:1-11
Epistle   Philippians 2:5-11

The Passion Gospel is announced in the following manner

The Passion of our Lord Jesus Christ according to _____.

The customary responses before and after the Gospel are omitted.

Year A   Matthew 26:36—27:54(55-66)   *or* 27:1-54(55-66)
Year B   Mark 14:32—15:39(40-47)   *or* 15:1-39(40-47)
Year C   Luke 22:39—23:49(50-56)   *or* 23:1-49(50-56)

The Passion Gospel may be read or chanted by lay persons. Specific roles may be assigned to different persons, the congregation taking the part of the crowd.

The congregation may be seated for the first part of the Passion. At the verse which mentions the arrival at Golgotha (Matthew 27:33, Mark 15:22, Luke 23:33) all stand.

When the Liturgy of the Palms has preceded, the Nicene Creed and the Confession of Sin may be omitted at this service.

Preface of Holy Week

Maundy Thursday

The Eucharist begins in the usual manner, using the following Collect, Psalm, and Lessons

Almighty Father, whose dear Son, on the night before he suffered, instituted the Sacrament of his Body and Blood: Mercifully grant that we may receive it thankfully in remembrance of Jesus Christ our Lord, who in these holy mysteries gives us a pledge of eternal life; and who now lives and reigns with you and the Holy Spirit, one God, for ever and ever. *Amen.*

Old Testament   Exodus 12:1-14a
Psalm   78:14-20, 23-25
Epistle   1 Corinthians 11:23-26(27-32)
Gospel   John 13:1-15,   *or* Luke 22:14-30

When observed, the ceremony of the washing of feet appropriately follows the Gospel and homily.

During the ceremony, the following or other suitable anthems may be sung or said

The Lord Jesus, after he had supped with his disciples and had washed their feet, said to them, "Do you know what I, your Lord and Master, have done to you? I have given you an example, that you should do as I have done."

Peace is my last gift to you, my own peace I now leave with you; peace which the world cannot give, I give to you.

I give you a new commandment: Love one another as I have loved you.

Peace is my last gift to you, my own peace I now leave with you; peace which the world cannot give, I give to you.

By this shall the world know that you are my disciples: That you have love for one another.

The service continues with the Prayers of the People.

Where it is desired to administer Holy Communion from the reserved Sacrament on Good Friday, the Sacrament for that purpose is consecrated at this service.

Preface of Holy Week

Good Friday

On this day the ministers enter in silence.

All then kneel for silent prayer, after which the Celebrant stands and begins the liturgy with the Collect of the Day.

Immediately before the Collect, the Celebrant may say

> **Blessed be our God.**

People For ever and ever. Amen.

Let us pray.

Almighty God, we pray you graciously to behold this your family, for whom our Lord Jesus Christ was willing to be betrayed, and given into the hands of sinners, and to suffer death upon the cross; who now lives and reigns with you and the Holy Spirit, one God, for ever and ever. *Amen.*

Old Testament Isaiah 52:13—53:12, *or* Genesis 22:1-18,
or Wisdom 2:1, 12-24
Psalm 22:1-11(12-21), *or* 40:1-14, *or* 69:1-23
Epistle Hebrews 10:1-25

The Passion Gospel is announced in the following manner

The Passion of our Lord Jesus Christ according to John.

The customary responses before and after the Gospel are omitted.

John 18:1—19:37   *or* 19:1-37.

The Passion Gospel may be read or chanted by lay persons. Specific roles may be assigned to different persons, the congregation taking the part of the crowd.

The congregation may be seated for the first part of the Passion. At the verse which mentions the arrival at Golgotha (John 19:17) all stand.

The Sermon follows.

A hymn may then be sung.

The Solemn Collects

All standing, the Deacon, or other person appointed, says to the people

Dear People of God: Our heavenly Father sent his Son into the world, not to condemn the world, but that the world through him might be saved; that all who believe in him might be delivered from the power of sin and death, and become heirs with him of everlasting life.

We pray, therefore, for people everywhere according to their needs.

In the biddings which follow, the indented petitions may be adapted by addition or omission, as appropriate, at the discretion of the Celebrant. The people may be directed to stand or kneel.

The biddings may be read by a Deacon or other person appointed. The Celebrant says the Collects.

Let us pray for the holy Catholic Church of Christ
throughout the world;

> For its unity in witness and service
> For all bishops and other ministers
>   and the people whom they serve
> For N., our Bishop, and all the people of this diocese
> For all Christians in this community
> For those about to be baptized (particularly _____)

That God will confirm his Church in faith, increase it in love,
and preserve it in peace.

Silence

Almighty and everlasting God, by whose Spirit the whole
body of your faithful people is governed and sanctified:
Receive our supplications and prayers which we offer before
you for all members of your holy Church, that in their
vocation and ministry they may truly and devoutly serve you;
through our Lord and Savior Jesus Christ. *Amen.*

Let us pray for all nations and peoples of the earth, and for
those in authority among them;

> For N., the President of the United States
> For the Congress and the Supreme Court
> For the Members and Representatives of the United Nations
> For all who serve the common good

That by God's help they may seek justice and truth, and live
in peace and concord.

Silence

Almighty God, kindle, we pray, in every heart the true love of
peace, and guide with your wisdom those who take counsel for
the nations of the earth; that in tranquillity your dominion may

increase, until the earth is filled with the knowledge of your love; through Jesus Christ our Lord. *Amen.*

Let us pray for all who suffer and are afflicted in body or in mind;

> For the hungry and the homeless, the destitute
>   and the oppressed
> For the sick, the wounded, and the crippled
> For those in loneliness, fear, and anguish
> For those who face temptation, doubt, and despair
> For the sorrowful and bereaved
> For prisoners and captives, and those in mortal danger

That God in his mercy will comfort and relieve them, and grant them the knowledge of his love, and stir up in us the will and patience to minister to their needs.

Silence

Gracious God, the comfort of all who sorrow, the strength of all who suffer: Let the cry of those in misery and need come to you, that they may find your mercy present with them in all their afflictions; and give us, we pray, the strength to serve them for the sake of him who suffered for us, your Son Jesus Christ our Lord. *Amen.*

Let us pray for all who have not received the Gospel of Christ;

> For those who have never heard the word of salvation
> For those who have lost their faith
> For those hardened by sin or indifference
> For the contemptuous and the scornful
> For those who are enemies of the cross of Christ and
>   persecutors of his disciples
> For those who in the name of Christ have persecuted others

That God will open their hearts to the truth, and lead them to faith and obedience.

Silence

Merciful God, Creator of all the peoples of the earth and lover of souls: Have compassion on all who do not know you as you are revealed in your Son Jesus Christ; let your Gospel be preached with grace and power to those who have not heard it; turn the hearts of those who resist it; and bring home to your fold those who have gone astray; that there may be one flock under one shepherd, Jesus Christ our Lord. *Amen.*

Let us commit ourselves to our God, and pray for the grace of a holy life, that, with all who have departed this world and have died in the peace of Christ, and those whose faith is known to God alone, we may be accounted worthy to enter into the fullness of the joy of our Lord, and receive the crown of life in the day of resurrection.

Silence

O God of unchangeable power and eternal light: Look favorably on your whole Church, that wonderful and sacred mystery; by the effectual working of your providence, carry out in tranquillity the plan of salvation; let the whole world see and know that things which were cast down are being raised up, and things which had grown old are being made new, and that all things are being brought to their perfection by him through whom all things were made, your Son Jesus Christ our Lord; who lives and reigns with you, in the unity of the Holy Spirit, one God, for ever and ever. *Amen.*

The service may be concluded here with the singing of a hymn or anthem, the Lord's Prayer, and the final prayer on page 282.

If desired, a wooden cross may now be brought into the church and placed in the sight of the people.

Appropriate devotions may follow, which may include any or all of the following, or other suitable anthems. If the texts are recited rather than sung, the congregation reads the parts in italics.

Anthem 1

We glory in your cross, O Lord,
and praise and glorify your holy resurrection;
for by virtue of your cross
joy has come to the whole world.

May God be merciful to us and bless us,
show us the light of his countenance, and come to us.

Let your ways be known upon earth,
your saving health among all nations.

Let the peoples praise you, O God;
let all the peoples praise you.

We glory in your cross, O Lord,
and praise and glorify your holy resurrection;
for by virtue of your cross
joy has come to the whole world.

Anthem 2

We adore you, O Christ, and we bless you,
because by your holy cross you have redeemed the world.

If we have died with him, we shall also live with him;
if we endure, we shall also reign with him.

We adore you, O Christ, and we bless you,
because by your holy cross you have redeemed the world.

Anthem 3

O Savior of the world,
who by thy cross and precious blood hast redeemed us:
Save us and help us, we humbly beseech thee, O Lord.

The hymn "Sing, my tongue, the glorious battle," or some other hymn
extolling the glory of the cross, is then sung.

The service may be concluded here with the Lord's Prayer and the final
prayer below.

In the absence of a bishop or priest, all that precedes may be led by a
deacon or lay reader.

In places where Holy Communion is to be administered from the
reserved Sacrament, the following order is observed

A Confession of Sin
The Lord's Prayer
The Communion

The service concludes with the following prayer. No blessing or dismissal
is added.

Lord Jesus Christ, Son of the living God, we pray you to set
your passion, cross, and death between your judgment and
our souls, now and in the hour of our death. Give mercy and
grace to the living; pardon and rest to the dead; to your holy
Church peace and concord; and to us sinners everlasting life
and glory; for with the Father and the Holy Spirit you
live and reign, one God, now and for ever. *Amen.*

Holy Saturday

There is no celebration of the Eucharist on this day.

When there is a Liturgy of the Word, the Celebrant begins with the Collect of the Day

O God, Creator of heaven and earth: Grant that, as the crucified body of your dear Son was laid in the tomb and rested on this holy Sabbath, so we may await with him the coming of the third day, and rise with him to newness of life; who now lives and reigns with you and the Holy Spirit, one God, for ever and ever. *Amen.*

Old Testament   Job 14:1-14
Psalm   130,   *or* 31:1-5
Epistle   1 Peter 4:1-8
Gospel   Matthew 27:57-66,   *or* John 19:38-42

After the Gospel (and homily), in place of the Prayers of the People, the Anthem "In the midst of life" (page 484 or 492) is sung or said.

The service then concludes with the Lord's Prayer and the Grace.

Concerning the Vigil

The Great Vigil, when observed, is the first service of Easter Day. It is celebrated at a convenient time between sunset on Holy Saturday and sunrise on Easter Morning.

The service normally consists of four parts:
1. The Service of Light.
2. The Service of Lessons.
3. Christian Initiation, or the Renewal of Baptismal Vows.
4. The Holy Eucharist with the administration of Easter Communion.

It is customary for all the ordained ministers present, together with lay readers, singers, and other persons, to take active parts in the service.

The bishop, when present, is the chief celebrant, presides at Baptism and administers Confirmation, and normally preaches the sermon.

The priests who are present share among them the reading of the Collects which follow each Lesson, and assist at Baptism and the Eucharist. In the absence of a bishop, a priest presides at the service.

It is the prerogative of a deacon to carry the Paschal Candle to its place, and to chant the Exsultet. Deacons likewise assist at Baptism and the Eucharist according to their order.

Lay persons read the Lessons and the Epistle, and assist in other ways. A lay person may be assigned to chant the Exsultet. It is desirable that each Lesson be read by a different reader.

In the absence of a bishop or priest, a deacon or lay reader may lead the first two parts of the service, the Renewal of Baptismal Vows, and the Ministry of the Word of the Vigil Eucharist, concluding with the Prayers of the People, the Lord's Prayer, and the Dismissal.

A deacon may also, when the services of a priest cannot be obtained, and with the authorization of the bishop, officiate at public Baptism; and may administer Easter Communion from the Sacrament previously consecrated.

When the Vigil is not celebrated, the Service of Light may take place at a convenient time before the Liturgy on Easter Day.

The Great Vigil of Easter

The Lighting of the Paschal Candle

In the darkness, fire is kindled; after which the Celebrant may address the people in these or similar words

Dear friends in Christ: On this most holy night, in which our Lord Jesus passed over from death to life, the Church invites her members, dispersed throughout the world, to gather in vigil and prayer. For this is the Passover of the Lord, in which, by hearing his Word and celebrating his Sacraments, we share in his victory over death.

The Celebrant may say the following prayer

Let us pray.

O God, through your Son you have bestowed upon your people the brightness of your light: Sanctify this new fire, and grant that in this Paschal feast we may so burn with heavenly desires, that with pure minds we may attain to the festival of everlasting light; through Jesus Christ our Lord. *Amen.*

The Paschal Candle is then lighted from the newly kindled fire, and the Deacon (the Celebrant if there is no deacon) bearing the Candle, leads the procession to the chancel, pausing three times and singing or saying

       The light of Christ.
People   Thanks be to God.

If candles have been distributed to members of the congregation, they are lighted from the Paschal Candle at this time. Other candles and lamps in the church, except for those at the Altar, may also be lighted.

The Paschal Candle is placed in its stand.

Then the Deacon, or other person appointed, standing near the Candle, sings or says the Exsultet, as follows (the indicated sections may be omitted)

Rejoice now, heavenly hosts and choirs of angels,
and let your trumpets shout Salvation
for the victory of our mighty King.

Rejoice and sing now, all the round earth,
bright with a glorious splendor,
for darkness has been vanquished by our eternal King.

Rejoice and be glad now, Mother Church,
and let your holy courts, in radiant light,
resound with the praises of your people.

All you who stand near this marvelous and holy flame,
pray with me to God the Almighty
for the grace to sing the worthy praise of this great light;
through Jesus Christ his Son our Lord,
who lives and reigns with him,
in the unity of the Holy Spirit,
one God, for ever and ever. *Amen.*

The Lord be with you.

Answer   And also with you.
Deacon   Let us give thanks to the Lord our God.
Answer   It is right to give him thanks and praise.

Deacon

It is truly right and good, always and everywhere, with our

whole heart and mind and voice, to praise you, the invisible, almighty, and eternal God, and your only-begotten Son, Jesus Christ our Lord; for he is the true Paschal Lamb, who at the feast of the Passover paid for us the debt of Adam's sin, and by his blood delivered your faithful people.

This is the night, when you brought our fathers, the children of Israel, out of bondage in Egypt, and led them through the Red Sea on dry land.

This is the night, when all who believe in Christ are delivered from the gloom of sin, and are restored to grace and holiness of life.

This is the night, when Christ broke the bonds of death and hell, and rose victorious from the grave.

How wonderful and beyond our knowing, O God, is your mercy and loving-kindness to us, that to redeem a slave, you gave a Son.

How holy is this night, when wickedness is put to flight, and sin is washed away. It restores innocence to the fallen, and joy to those who mourn. It casts out pride and hatred, and brings peace and concord.

How blessed is this night, when earth and heaven are joined and man is reconciled to God.

Holy Father, accept our evening sacrifice, the offering of this candle in your honor. May it shine continually to drive away all darkness. May Christ, the Morning Star who knows no setting, find it ever burning—he who gives his light to all creation, and who lives and reigns for ever and ever. *Amen.*

It is customary that the Paschal Candle burn at all services from Easter Day through the Day of Pentecost.

The Liturgy of the Word

The Celebrant may introduce the Scripture readings in these or similar words

Let us hear the record of God's saving deeds in history, how he saved his people in ages past; and let us pray that our God will bring each of us to the fullness of redemption.

At least two of the following Lessons are read, of which one is always the Lesson from Exodus. After each Lesson, the Psalm or Canticle listed, or some other suitable psalm, canticle, or hymn may be sung. A period of silence may be kept; and the Collect provided, or some other suitable Collect, may be said.

The story of Creation
Genesis 1:1—2:2

Psalm 33:1-11, *or* Psalm 36:5-10

Let us pray.　*(Silence)*

O God, who wonderfully created, and yet more wonderfully restored, the dignity of human nature: Grant that we may share the divine life of him who humbled himself to share our humanity, your Son Jesus Christ our Lord. *Amen.*

The Flood
Genesis 7:1-5, 11-18; 8:6-18; 9:8-13

Psalm 46

Let us pray.　*(Silence)*

Almighty God, you have placed in the skies the sign of your covenant with all living things: Grant that we, who are saved through water and the Spirit, may worthily offer to you our sacrifice of thanksgiving; through Jesus Christ our Lord. *Amen.*

Abraham's sacrifice of Isaac
Genesis 22:1-18

Psalm 33:12-22, *or* Psalm 16

Let us pray.　*(Silence)*

God and Father of all believers, for the glory of your Name multiply, by the grace of the Paschal sacrament, the number of your children; that your Church may rejoice to see fulfilled your promise to our father Abraham; through Jesus Christ our Lord. *Amen.*

Israel's deliverance at the Red Sea
Exodus 14:10—15:1

Canticle 8, *The Song of Moses*

Let us pray.　*(Silence)*

O God, whose wonderful deeds of old shine forth even to our own day, you once delivered by the power of your mighty arm your chosen people from slavery under Pharaoh, to be a sign for us of the salvation of all nations by the water of Baptism: Grant that all the peoples of the earth may be numbered among the offspring of Abraham, and rejoice in the inheritance of Israel; through Jesus Christ our Lord. *Amen.*

God's Presence in a renewed Israel
Isaiah 4:2-6

Psalm 122

Let us pray.   *(Silence)*

O God, you led your ancient people by a pillar of cloud by day
and a pillar of fire by night: Grant that we, who serve you
now on earth, may come to the joy of that heavenly Jerusalem,
where all tears are wiped away and where your saints for ever
sing your praise; through Jesus Christ our Lord. *Amen.*

Salvation offered freely to all
Isaiah 55:1-11

Canticle 9, *The First Song of Isaiah, or* Psalm 42:1-7

Let us pray.   *(Silence)*

O God, you have created all things by the power of your
Word, and you renew the earth by your Spirit: Give now the
water of life to those who thirst for you, that they may bring
forth abundant fruit in your glorious kingdom; through Jesus
Christ our Lord. *Amen.*

A new heart and a new spirit
Ezekiel 36:24-28

Psalm 42:1-7, *or* Canticle 9, *The First Song of Isaiah*

Let us pray.   *(Silence)*

Almighty and everlasting God, who in the Paschal mystery
established the new covenant of reconciliation: Grant that all

who are reborn into the fellowship of Christ's Body may show
forth in their lives what they profess by their faith; through
Jesus Christ our Lord. *Amen*.

The valley of dry bones
Ezekiel 37:1-14

Psalm 30, *or* Psalm 143

Let us pray. *(Silence)*

Almighty God, by the Passover of your Son you have brought
us out of sin into righteousness and out of death into life:
Grant to those who are sealed by your Holy Spirit the will
and the power to proclaim you to all the world; through Jesus
Christ our Lord. *Amen*.

The gathering of God's people
Zephaniah 3:12-20

Psalm 98, *or* Psalm 126

Let us pray. *(Silence)*

O God of unchangeable power and eternal light: Look
favorably on your whole Church, that wonderful and sacred
mystery; by the effectual working of your providence, carry
out in tranquillity the plan of salvation; let the whole world
see and know that things which were cast down are being
raised up, and things which had grown old are being made
new, and that all things are being brought to their perfection
by him through whom all things were made, your Son Jesus
Christ our Lord. *Amen*.

A homily may be preached after any of the preceding Readings.

Holy Baptism (beginning with the Presentation of the Candidates, page 301, and concluding with the reception of the newly baptized) may be administered here or after the Gospel. Confirmation may also be administered.

In the absence of candidates for Baptism or Confirmation, the Celebrant leads the people in the Renewal of Baptismal Vows, either here or after the Gospel.

The Celebrant may first address the people in these or similar words, all standing

Through the Paschal mystery, dear friends, we are buried with Christ by Baptism into his death, and raised with him to newness of life. I call upon you, therefore, now that our Lenten observance is ended, to renew the solemn promises and vows of Holy Baptism, by which we once renounced Satan and all his works, and promised to serve God faithfully in his holy Catholic Church.

The Renewal of Baptismal Vows

Celebrant Do you reaffirm your renunciation of evil and
             renew your commitment to Jesus Christ?
People   I do.

Celebrant Do you believe in God the Father?
People   I believe in God, the Father almighty,
             creator of heaven and earth.

Celebrant Do you believe in Jesus Christ, the Son of God?
People I believe in Jesus Christ, his only Son, our Lord.
    He was conceived by the power of the Holy Spirit
      and born of the Virgin Mary.
    He suffered under Pontius Pilate,
      was crucified, died, and was buried.
    He descended to the dead.
    On the third day he rose again.
    He ascended into heaven,
      and is seated at the right hand of the Father.
    He will come again to judge the living and the dead.

Celebrant Do you believe in God the Holy Spirit?
People I believe in the Holy Spirit,
    the holy catholic Church,
    the communion of saints,
    the forgiveness of sins,
    the resurrection of the body,
    and the life everlasting.

Celebrant Will you continue in the apostles' teaching and
fellowship, in the breaking of bread, and in the
prayers?
People I will, with God's help.

Celebrant Will you persevere in resisting evil, and, whenever
you fall into sin, repent and return to the Lord?
People I will, with God's help.

Celebrant Will you proclaim by word and example the Good
News of God in Christ?
People I will, with God's help.

Celebrant Will you seek and serve Christ in all persons, loving
your neighbor as yourself?
People I will, with God's help.

Celebrant Will you strive for justice and peace among all people,
          and respect the dignity of every human being?
People   I will, with God's help.

The Celebrant concludes the Renewal of Vows as follows

May Almighty God, the Father of our Lord Jesus Christ, who
has given us a new birth by water and the Holy Spirit, and
bestowed upon us the forgiveness of sins, keep us in eternal
life by his grace, in Christ Jesus our Lord. *Amen.*

At the Eucharist

The candles at the Altar may now be lighted from the Paschal Candle.

*One of the following Canticles is then sung. Immediately before the
Canticle the Celebrant may say to the people*

          Alleluia. Christ is risen.
People   The Lord is risen indeed. Alleluia.

The Canticles

Gloria in excelsis
Te Deum laudamus
Pascha nostrum

The Celebrant then says

          The Lord be with you.
People   And also with you.
Celebrant Let us pray.

Almighty God, who for our redemption gave your only-begotten Son to the death of the cross, and by his glorious resurrection delivered us from the power of our enemy: Grant us so to die daily to sin, that we may evermore live with him in the joy of his resurrection; through Jesus Christ your Son our Lord, who lives and reigns with you and the Holy Spirit, one God, now and for ever. *Amen.*

or this

O God, who made this most holy night to shine with the glory of the Lord's resurrection: Stir up in your Church that Spirit of adoption which is given to us in Baptism, that we, being renewed both in body and mind, may worship you in sincerity and truth; through Jesus Christ our Lord, who lives and reigns with you, in the unity of the Holy Spirit, one God, now and for ever. *Amen.*

Epistle   Romans 6:3-11

"Alleluia" may be sung and repeated.

Psalm 114, or some other suitable psalm or a hymn may be sung.

Gospel   Matthew 28:1-10

If a sermon or homily was not preached earlier, it follows here.

The Nicene Creed is not used at this service.

Holy Baptism, Confirmation, or the Renewal of Baptismal Vows may take place here.

The celebration continues with the Prayers of the People.

Preface of Easter

Holy Baptism

Concerning the Service

Holy Baptism is full initiation by water and the Holy Spirit into Christ's Body the Church. The bond which God establishes in Baptism is indissoluble.

Holy Baptism is appropriately administered within the Eucharist as the chief service on a Sunday or other feast.

The bishop, when present, is the celebrant; and is expected to preach the Word and preside at Baptism and the Eucharist. At Baptism, the bishop officiates at the Presentation and Examination of the Candidates; says the Thanksgiving over the Water; [consecrates the Chrism;] reads the prayer, "Heavenly Father, we thank you that by water and the Holy Spirit;" and officiates at what follows.

In the absence of a bishop, a priest is the celebrant and presides at the service. If a priest uses Chrism in signing the newly baptized, it must have been previously consecrated by the bishop.

Each candidate for Holy Baptism is to be sponsored by one or more baptized persons.

Sponsors of adults and older children present their candidates and thereby signify their endorsement of the candidates and their intention to support them by prayer and example in their Christian life. Sponsors of infants, commonly called godparents, present their candidates, make promises in their own names, and also take vows on behalf of their candidates.

It is fitting that parents be included among the godparents of their own children. Parents and godparents are to be instructed in the meaning of Baptism, in their duties to help the new Christians grow in the knowledge and love of God, and in their responsibilities as members of his Church.

Additional Directions are on page 312.

Holy Baptism

A hymn, psalm, or anthem may be sung.

The people standing, the Celebrant says

        Blessed be God: Father, Son, and Holy Spirit.
People   And blessed be his kingdom, now and for ever. Amen.

In place of the above, from Easter Day through the Day of Pentecost
Celebrant Alleluia. Christ is risen.
People   The Lord is risen indeed. Alleluia.

In Lent and on other penitential occasions

Celebrant Bless the Lord who forgives all our sins;
People   His mercy endures for ever.

The Celebrant then continues

        There is one Body and one Spirit;
People   There is one hope in God's call to us;
Celebrant One Lord, one Faith, one Baptism;
People   One God and Father of all.

Celebrant The Lord be with you.
People   And also with you.
Celebrant Let us pray.

The Collect of the Day

People   Amen.

At the principal service on a Sunday or other feast, the Collect and Lessons are properly those of the Day. On other occasions they are selected from "At Baptism." (See Additional Directions, page 312.)

The Lessons

The people sit. One or two Lessons, as appointed, are read, the Reader first saying

A Reading (Lesson) from _____.

A citation giving chapter and verse may be added.

After each Reading, the Reader may say

The Word of the Lord.
People   Thanks be to God.

or the Reader may say   Here ends the Reading (Epistle).

Silence may follow.

A Psalm, hymn, or anthem may follow each Reading.

Then, all standing, the Deacon or a Priest reads the Gospel, first saying

The Holy Gospel of our Lord Jesus Christ according to _____.
People   Glory to you, Lord Christ.

After the Gospel, the Reader says

The Gospel of the Lord.
People   Praise to you, Lord Christ.

The Sermon

Or the Sermon may be preached after the Peace.

Presentation and Examination of the Candidates

The Celebrant says
The Candidate(s) for Holy Baptism will now be presented.

Adults and Older Children

The candidates who are able to answer for themselves are presented individually by their Sponsors, as follows

Sponsor   I present N. to receive the Sacrament of Baptism.

The Celebrant asks each candidate when presented

Do you desire to be baptized?
Candidate I do.

Infants and Younger Children

Then the candidates unable to answer for themselves are presented individually by their Parents and Godparents, as follows

Parents and Godparents

I present N. to receive the Sacrament of Baptism.

When all have been presented the Celebrant asks the parents and godparents

Will you be responsible for seeing that the child you present is brought up in the Christian faith and life?

Parents and Godparents

I will, with God's help.

Celebrant

Will you by your prayers and witness help this child to grow into the full stature of Christ?

Parents and Godparents

I will, with God's help.

Then the Celebrant asks the following questions of the candidates who can speak for themselves, and of the parents and godparents who speak on behalf of the infants and younger children

Question Do you renounce Satan and all the spiritual forces of wickedness that rebel against God?

Answer I renounce them.

Question Do you renounce the evil powers of this world which corrupt and destroy the creatures of God?

Answer I renounce them.

Question Do you renounce all sinful desires that draw you from the love of God?

Answer I renounce them.

Question Do you turn to Jesus Christ and accept him as your Savior?

Answer I do.

Question Do you put your whole trust in his grace and love?

Answer I do.

| Question | Do you promise to follow and obey him as your Lord? |
| Answer | I do. |

When there are others to be presented, the Bishop says

The other Candidate(s) will now be presented.

Presenters	I present *these persons* for Confirmation.
or	I present *these persons* to be received into this Communion.
or	I present *these persons* who *desire* to reaffirm *their* baptismal vows.

The Bishop asks the candidates

Do you reaffirm your renunciation of evil?

Candidate I do.

Bishop

Do you renew your commitment to Jesus Christ?

Candidate

I do, and with God's grace I will follow him as my Savior and Lord.

After all have been presented, the Celebrant addresses the congregation, saying

Will you who witness these vows do all in your
power to support *these persons* in *their* life in Christ?

People We will.

The Celebrant then says these or similar words

Let us join with *those* who *are* committing *themselves* to Christ
and renew our own baptismal covenant.

The Baptismal Covenant

Celebrant Do you believe in God the Father?
People   I believe in God, the Father almighty,
     creator of heaven and earth.

Celebrant Do you believe in Jesus Christ, the Son of God?
People   I believe in Jesus Christ, his only Son, our Lord.
     He was conceived by the power of the Holy Spirit
      and born of the Virgin Mary.
     He suffered under Pontius Pilate,
      was crucified, died, and was buried.
     He descended to the dead.
     On the third day he rose again.
     He ascended into heaven,
      and is seated at the right hand of the Father.
     He will come again to judge the living and the dead.

Celebrant Do you believe in God the Holy Spirit?
People   I believe in the Holy Spirit,
     the holy catholic Church,
     the communion of saints,
     the forgiveness of sins,
     the resurrection of the body,
     and the life everlasting.

Celebrant Will you continue in the apostles' teaching and
     fellowship, in the breaking of bread, and in the
     prayers?
People   I will, with God's help.

Celebrant Will you persevere in resisting evil, and, whenever
     you fall into sin, repent and return to the Lord?
People   I will, with God's help.

Celebrant	Will you proclaim by word and example the Good News of God in Christ?
People	I will, with God's help.

Celebrant	Will you seek and serve Christ in all persons, loving your neighbor as yourself?
People	I will, with God's help.

Celebrant	Will you strive for justice and peace among all people, and respect the dignity of every human being?
People	I will, with God's help.

Prayers for the Candidates

The Celebrant then says to the congregation

Let us now pray for *these persons* who *are* to receive the Sacrament of new birth [and for those (this person) who *have* renewed *their* commitment to Christ.]

A Person appointed leads the following petitions

Leader	Deliver *them*, O Lord, from the way of sin and death.
People	Lord, hear our prayer.

Leader	Open *their hearts* to your grace and truth.
People	Lord, hear our prayer.

Leader	Fill *them* with your holy and life-giving Spirit.
People	Lord, hear our prayer.

Leader	Keep *them* in the faith and communion of your holy Church.
People	Lord, hear our prayer.

Leader	Teach *them* to love others in the power of the Spirit.
People	Lord, hear our prayer.

Leader	Send *them* into the world in witness to your love.
People	Lord, hear our prayer.
Leader	Bring *them* to the fullness of your peace and glory.
People	Lord, hear our prayer.

The Celebrant says

Grant, O Lord, that all who are baptized into the death
of Jesus Christ your Son may live in the power of his
resurrection and look for him to come again in glory; who
lives and reigns now and for ever. *Amen.*

Thanksgiving over the Water

The Celebrant blesses the water, first saying

	The Lord be with you.
People	And also with you.
Celebrant	Let us give thanks to the Lord our God.
People	It is right to give him thanks and praise.

Celebrant

We thank you, Almighty God, for the gift of water.
Over it the Holy Spirit moved in the beginning of creation.
Through it you led the children of Israel out of their bondage
in Egypt into the land of promise. In it your Son Jesus
received the baptism of John and was anointed by the Holy
Spirit as the Messiah, the Christ, to lead us, through his death
and resurrection, from the bondage of sin into everlasting life.

We thank you, Father, for the water of Baptism. In it we are
buried with Christ in his death. By it we share in his
resurrection. Through it we are reborn by the Holy Spirit.
Therefore in joyful obedience to your Son, we bring into his

fellowship those who come to him in faith, baptizing them in the Name of the Father, and of the Son, and of the Holy Spirit.

At the following words, the Celebrant touches the water

Now sanctify this water, we pray you, by the power of your Holy Spirit, that those who here are cleansed from sin and born again may continue for ever in the risen life of Jesus Christ our Savior.

To him, to you, and to the Holy Spirit, be all honor and glory, now and for ever. *Amen.*

Consecration of the Chrism

The Bishop may then consecrate oil of Chrism, placing a hand on the vessel of oil, and saying

Eternal Father, whose blessed Son was anointed by the Holy Spirit to be the Savior and servant of all, we pray you to consecrate this oil, that those who are sealed with it may share in the royal priesthood of Jesus Christ; who lives and reigns with you and the Holy Spirit, for ever and ever. *Amen.*

The Baptism

Each candidate is presented by name to the Celebrant, or to an assisting priest or deacon, who then immerses, or pours water upon, the candidate, saying

N., I baptize you in the Name of the Father, and of the Son, and of the Holy Spirit. *Amen.*

When this action has been completed for all candidates, the Bishop or Priest, at a place in full sight of the congregation, prays over them, saying

Let us pray.

Heavenly Father, we thank you that by water and the Holy Spirit you have bestowed upon *these* your *servants* the forgiveness of sin, and have raised *them* to the new life of grace. Sustain *them,* O Lord, in your Holy Spirit. Give *them* an inquiring and discerning heart, the courage to will and to persevere, a spirit to know and to love you, and the gift of joy and wonder in all your works. *Amen.*

Then the Bishop or Priest places a hand on the person's head, marking on the forehead the sign of the cross [using Chrism if desired] and saying to each one

N., you are sealed by the Holy Spirit in Baptism and marked as Christ's own for ever. *Amen.*

Or this action may be done immediately after the administration of the water and before the preceding prayer.

When all have been baptized, the Celebrant says

Let us welcome the newly baptized.

Celebrant and People

We receive you into the household of God. Confess the faith of Christ crucified, proclaim his resurrection, and share with us in his eternal priesthood.

If Confirmation, Reception, or the Reaffirmation of Baptismal Vows is not to follow, the Peace is now exchanged

Celebrant   The peace of the Lord be always with you.
People   And also with you.

At Confirmation, Reception, or Reaffirmation

The Bishop says to the congregation

Let us now pray for *these persons* who *have* renewed *their* commitment to Christ.

Silence may be kept.

Then the Bishop says

Almighty God, we thank you that by the death and resurrection of your Son Jesus Christ you have overcome sin and brought us to yourself, and that by the sealing of your Holy Spirit you have bound us to your service. Renew in *these* your *servants* the covenant you made with *them* at *their* Baptism. Send *them* forth in the power of that Spirit to perform the service you set before *them*; through Jesus Christ your Son our Lord, who lives and reigns with you and the Holy Spirit, one God, now and for ever. *Amen.*

For Confirmation

The Bishop lays hands upon each one and says

Strengthen, O Lord, your servant N. with your Holy Spirit; empower *him* for your service; and sustain *him* all the days of *his* life. *Amen.*

or this

Defend, O Lord, your servant N. with your heavenly grace, that *he* may continue yours for ever, and daily increase in your Holy Spirit more and more, until *he* comes to your everlasting kingdom. *Amen.*

For Reception

N., we recognize you as a member of the one holy catholic and apostolic Church, and we receive you into the fellowship of this Communion. God, the Father, Son, and Holy Spirit, bless, preserve, and keep you. *Amen.*

For Reaffirmation

N., may the Holy Spirit, who has begun a good work in you, direct and uphold you in the service of Christ and his kingdom. *Amen.*

Then the Bishop says

Almighty and everliving God, let your fatherly hand ever be over *these* your *servants;* let your Holy Spirit ever be with *them;* and so lead *them* in the knowledge and obedience of your Word, that *they* may serve you in this life, and dwell with you in the life to come; through Jesus Christ our Lord. *Amen.*

The Peace is then exchanged

Bishop	The peace of the Lord be always with you.
People	And also with you.

At the Eucharist

The service then continues with the Prayers of the People or the Offertory of the Eucharist, at which the Bishop, when present, should be the principal Celebrant.

Except on Principal Feasts, the Proper Preface of Baptism may be used.

Alternative Ending

If there is no celebration of the Eucharist, the service continues with the Lord's Prayer

Our Father, who art in heaven,
    hallowed be thy Name,
    thy kingdom come,
    thy will be done,
        on earth as it is in heaven.
Give us this day our daily bread.
And forgive us our trespasses,
    as we forgive those
        who trespass against us.
And lead us not into temptation,
    but deliver us from evil.
For thine is the kingdom,
    and the power, and the glory,
    for ever and ever. Amen.

Our Father in heaven,
    hallowed be your Name,
    your kingdom come,
    your will be done,
        on earth as in heaven.
Give us today our daily bread.
Forgive us our sins
    as we forgive those
        who sin against us.
Save us from the time of trial
    and deliver us from evil.
For the kingdom, the power,
    and the glory are yours,
    now and for ever. Amen.

The Celebrant then says

All praise and thanks to you, most merciful Father, for adopting us as your own children, for incorporating us into your holy Church, and for making us worthy to share in the inheritance of the saints in light; through Jesus Christ your Son our Lord, who lives and reigns with you and the Holy Spirit, one God, for ever and ever. *Amen.*

Alms may be received and presented, and other prayers may be added, concluding with this prayer

Almighty God, the Father of our Lord Jesus Christ, from whom every family in heaven and earth is named, grant you to be strengthened with might by his Holy Spirit, that, Christ dwelling in your hearts by faith, you may be filled with all the fullness of God. *Amen.*

Additional Directions

Holy Baptism is especially appropriate at the Easter Vigil, on the Day of Pentecost, on All Saints' Day or the Sunday after All Saints' Day, and on the Feast of the Baptism of our Lord (the First Sunday after the Epiphany). It is recommended that, as far as possible, Baptisms be reserved for these occasions or when a bishop is present.

If on any one of the above-named days the ministry of a bishop or priest cannot be obtained, the bishop may specially authorize a deacon to preside. In that case, the deacon omits the prayer over the candidates, page 308, and the formula and action which follow.

These omitted portions of the rite may be administered on some subsequent occasion of public baptism at which a bishop or priest presides.

If on the four days listed above there are no candidates for Baptism, the Renewal of Baptismal Vows, page 292, may take the place of the Nicene Creed at the Eucharist.

If desired, the hymn Gloria in excelsis may be sung immediately after the opening versicles and before the salutation "The Lord be with you."

When a bishop is present, or on other occasions for sufficient reason, the Collect (page 203 or 254) and one or more of the Lessons provided for use at Baptism (page 928) may be substituted for the Proper of the Day.

Lay persons may act as readers, and it is appropriate for sponsors to be assigned this function. The petitions (page 305) may also be led by one of the sponsors.

The Nicene Creed is not used at this service.

If the Presentation of the Candidates does not take place at the font, then before or during the petitions (page 305), the ministers, candidates, and sponsors go to the font for the Thanksgiving over the Water.

If the movement to the font is a formal procession, a suitable psalm, such as Psalm 42, or a hymn or anthem, may be sung.

Where practicable, the font is to be filled with clean water immediately before the Thanksgiving over the Water.

At the Thanksgiving over the Water, and at the administration of Baptism, the celebrant, whenever possible, should face the people across the font, and the sponsors should be so grouped that the people may have a clear view of the action.

After the Baptism, a candle (which may be lighted from the Paschal Candle) may be given to each of the newly baptized or to a godparent.

It may be found desirable to return to the front of the church for the prayer, "Heavenly Father, we thank you that by water and the Holy Spirit," and the ceremonies that follow it. A suitable psalm, such as Psalm 23, or a hymn or anthem, may be sung during the procession.

The oblations of bread and wine at the baptismal Eucharist may be presented by the newly baptized or their godparents.

Conditional Baptism

If there is reasonable doubt that a person has been baptized with water, "In the Name of the Father, and of the Son, and of the Holy Spirit" (which are the essential parts of Baptism), the person is baptized in the usual manner, but this form of words is used

If you are not already baptized, N., I baptize you in the Name of the Father, and of the Son, and of the Holy Spirit.

Emergency Baptism

In case of emergency, any baptized person may administer Baptism according to the following form.

Using the given name of the one to be baptized (if known), pour water on him or her, saying

I baptize you in the Name of the Father, and of the Son, and of the Holy Spirit.

The Lord's Prayer is then said.

Other prayers, such as the following, may be added

Heavenly Father, we thank you that by water and the Holy
Spirit you have bestowed upon this your servant the
forgiveness of sin and have raised *him* to the new life of
grace. Strengthen *him,* O Lord, with your presence, enfold
him in the arms of your mercy, and keep *him* safe for ever.

*The person who administers emergency Baptism should inform the priest
of the appropriate parish, so that the fact can be properly registered.*

*If the baptized person recovers, the Baptism should be recognized
at a public celebration of the Sacrament with a bishop or priest
presiding, and the person baptized under emergency conditions,
together with the sponsors or godparents, taking part in everything
except the administration of the water.*

The Holy Eucharist

The Liturgy for the
Proclamation of the Word of God and
Celebration of the Holy Communion

An Exhortation

Beloved in the Lord: Our Savior Christ, on the night before he suffered, instituted the Sacrament of his Body and Blood as a sign and pledge of his love, for the continual remembrance of the sacrifice of his death, and for a spiritual sharing in his risen life. For in these holy Mysteries we are made one with Christ, and Christ with us; we are made one body in him, and members one of another.

Having in mind, therefore, his great love for us, and in obedience to his command, his Church renders to Almighty God our heavenly Father never-ending thanks for the creation of the world, for his continual providence over us, for his love for all mankind, and for the redemption of the world by our Savior Christ, who took upon himself our flesh, and humbled himself even to death on the cross, that he might make us the children of God by the power of the Holy Spirit, and exalt us to everlasting life.

But if we are to share rightly in the celebration of those holy Mysteries, and be nourished by that spiritual Food, we must remember the dignity of that holy Sacrament. I therefore call upon you to consider how Saint Paul exhorts all persons to prepare themselves carefully before eating of that Bread and drinking of that Cup.

For, as the benefit is great, if with penitent hearts and living faith we receive the holy Sacrament, so is the danger great, if we receive it improperly, not recognizing the Lord's Body. Judge yourselves, therefore, lest you be judged by the Lord.

Examine your lives and conduct by the rule of God's commandments, that you may perceive wherein you have offended in what you have done or left undone, whether in thought, word, or deed. And acknowledge your sins before Almighty God, with full purpose of amendment of life, being ready to make restitution for all injuries and wrongs done by you to others; and also being ready to forgive those who have offended you, in order that you yourselves may be forgiven. And then, being reconciled with one another, come to the banquet of that most heavenly Food.

And if, in your preparation, you need help and counsel, then go and open your grief to a discreet and understanding priest, and confess your sins, that you may receive the benefit of absolution, and spiritual counsel and advice; to the removal of scruple and doubt, the assurance of pardon, and the strengthening of your faith.

To Christ our Lord who loves us, and washed us in his own blood, and made us a kingdom of priests to serve his God and Father, to him be glory in the Church evermore. Through him let us offer continually the sacrifice of praise, which is our bounden duty and service, and, with faith in him, come boldly before the throne of grace [and humbly confess our sins to Almighty God].

The Decalogue: Traditional

God spake these words, and said:
I am the Lord thy God who brought thee out of the land of Egypt, out of the house of bondage. Thou shalt have none other gods but me.
Lord, have mercy upon us,
and incline our hearts to keep this law.

Thou shalt not make to thyself any graven image, nor the likeness of any thing that is in heaven above, or in the earth beneath, or in the water under the earth; thou shalt not bow down to them, nor worship them.
Lord, have mercy upon us,
and incline our hearts to keep this law.

Thou shalt not take the Name of the Lord thy God in vain.
Lord, have mercy upon us,
and incline our hearts to keep this law.

Remember that thou keep holy the Sabbath day.
Lord, have mercy upon us,
and incline our hearts to keep this law.

Honor thy father and thy mother.
Lord, have mercy upon us,
and incline our hearts to keep this law.

Thou shalt do no murder.
Lord, have mercy upon us,
and incline our hearts to keep this law.

Thou shalt not commit adultery.
Lord, have mercy upon us,
and incline our hearts to keep this law.

Thou shalt not steal.
Lord, have mercy upon us,
and incline our hearts to keep this law.

Thou shalt not bear false witness against thy neighbor.
Lord, have mercy upon us,
and incline our hearts to keep this law.

Thou shalt not covet.
Lord, have mercy upon us,
and write all these thy laws in our hearts, we beseech thee.

A Penitential Order: Rite One

For use at the beginning of the Liturgy, or as a separate service.

A hymn, psalm, or anthem may be sung.

The people standing, the Celebrant says

Blessed be God: Father, Son, and Holy Spirit.
People   And blessed be his kingdom, now and for ever.
Amen.

In place of the above, from Easter Day through the Day of Pentecost

Celebrant Alleluia. Christ is risen.
People   The Lord is risen indeed. Alleluia.

In Lent and on other penitential occasions

Celebrant Bless the Lord who forgiveth all our sins;
People   His mercy endureth for ever.

When used as a separate service, the Exhortation, page 316, may be read, or a homily preached.

The Decalogue, page 317, may be said, the people kneeling.

The Celebrant may read one of the following sentences

Hear what our Lord Jesus Christ saith:
Thou shalt love the Lord thy God with all thy heart, and with all thy soul, and with all thy mind. This is the first and great commandment. And the second is like unto it: Thou shalt love thy neighbor as thyself. On these two commandments hang all the Law and the Prophets.   *Matthew 22:37-40*

If we say that we have no sin, we deceive ourselves, and the truth is not in us; but if we confess our sins, God is faithful and just to forgive us our sins, and to cleanse us from all unrighteousness.   *1 John 1:8, 9*

Seeing that we have a great high priest, that is passed into the heavens, Jesus the Son of God, let us come boldly unto the throne of grace, that we may obtain mercy, and find grace to help in time of need.   *Hebrews 4:14, 16*

The Deacon or Celebrant then says

Let us humbly confess our sins unto Almighty God.

Silence may be kept.

Minister and People

Most merciful God,
we confess that we have sinned against thee
in thought, word, and deed,
by what we have done,
and by what we have left undone.
We have not loved thee with our whole heart;
we have not loved our neighbors as ourselves.
We are truly sorry and we humbly repent.
For the sake of thy Son Jesus Christ,
have mercy on us and forgive us;
that we may delight in thy will,
and walk in thy ways,
to the glory of thy Name. Amen.

or this

Almighty and most merciful Father,
we have erred and strayed from thy ways like lost sheep,
we have followed too much the devices and desires of our
    own hearts,

we have offended against thy holy laws,
we have left undone those things which we ought to
have done,
and we have done those things which we ought not to
have done.
But thou, O Lord, have mercy upon us,
spare thou those who confess their faults,
restore thou those who are penitent,
according to thy promises declared unto mankind
in Christ Jesus our Lord;
and grant, O most merciful Father, for his sake,
that we may hereafter live a godly, righteous, and sober life,
to the glory of thy holy Name. Amen.

The Bishop when present, or the Priest, stands and says

The Almighty and merciful Lord grant you absolution and
remission of all your sins, true repentance, amendment of
life, and the grace and consolation of his Holy Spirit. *Amen.*

*A deacon or lay person using the preceding form substitutes "us" for
"you" and "our" for "your."*

*When this Order is used at the beginning of the Liturgy, the service
continues with the Kyrie eleison, the Trisagion, or the Gloria in excelsis.*

*When used separately, it concludes with suitable prayers, and the Grace
or a blessing.*

Concerning the Celebration

It is the bishop's prerogative, when present, to be the principal celebrant at the Lord's Table, and to preach the Gospel.

At all celebrations of the Liturgy, it is fitting that the principal celebrant, whether bishop or priest, be assisted by other priests, and by deacons and lay persons.

It is appropriate that the other priests present stand with the celebrant at the Altar, and join in the consecration of the gifts, in breaking the Bread, and in distributing Communion.

A deacon should read the Gospel and may lead the Prayers of the People. Deacons should also serve at the Lord's Table, preparing and placing on it the offerings of bread and wine, and assisting in the ministration of the Sacrament to the people. In the absence of a deacon, these duties may be performed by an assisting priest.

Lay persons appointed by the celebrant should normally be assigned the reading of the Lessons which precede the Gospel, and may lead the Prayers of the People.

Morning or Evening Prayer may be used in place of all that precedes the Peace and the Offertory, provided that a lesson from the Gospel is always included, and that the intercessions conform to the directions given for the Prayers of the People.

Additional Directions are on page 406.

The Holy Eucharist: Rite One

The Word of God

A hymn, psalm, or anthem may be sung.

The people standing, the Celebrant may say

Blessed be God: Father, Son, and Holy Spirit.
People And blessed be his kingdom, now and for ever.
Amen.

In place of the above, from Easter Day through the Day of Pentecost

Celebrant Alleluia. Christ is risen.
People The Lord is risen indeed. Alleluia.

In Lent and on other penitential occasions

Celebrant Bless the Lord who forgiveth all our sins.
People His mercy endureth for ever.

The Celebrant says

Almighty God, unto whom all hearts are open, all desires known, and from whom no secrets are hid: Cleanse the thoughts of our hearts by the inspiration of thy Holy Spirit, that we may perfectly love thee, and worthily magnify thy holy Name; through Christ our Lord. *Amen.*

Then the Ten Commandments (page 317) may be said, or the following

Hear what our Lord Jesus Christ saith:
Thou shalt love the Lord thy God with all thy heart, and with
all thy soul, and with all thy mind. This is the first and great
commandment. And the second is like unto it: Thou shalt
love thy neighbor as thyself. On these two commandments
hang all the Law and the Prophets.

Here is sung or said

Lord, have mercy upon us.		Kyrie eleison.
Christ, have mercy upon us.	*or*	*Christe eleison.*
Lord, have mercy upon us.		Kyrie eleison.

or this

Holy God,
Holy and Mighty,
Holy Immortal One,
Have mercy upon us.

*When appointed, the following hymn or some other song of praise is
sung or said, in addition to, or in place of, the preceding, all standing*

Glory be to God on high,
    and on earth peace, good will towards men.

We praise thee, we bless thee,
    we worship thee,
    we glorify thee,
    we give thanks to thee for thy great glory,
O Lord God, heavenly King, God the Father Almighty.

O Lord, the only-begotten Son, Jesus Christ;
O Lord God, Lamb of God, Son of the Father,
    that takest away the sins of the world,
    have mercy upon us.

Thou that takest away the sins of the world,
 receive our prayer.
Thou that sittest at the right hand of God the Father,
 have mercy upon us.

For thou only art holy;
thou only art the Lord;
thou only, O Christ,
 with the Holy Ghost,
 art most high in the glory of God the Father. Amen.

The Collect of the Day

The Celebrant says to the people

> The Lord be with you.
People   And with thy spirit.
Celebrant Let us pray.

The Celebrant says the Collect.

People   Amen.

The Lessons

*The people sit. One or two Lessons, as appointed, are read, the Reader
first saying*

A Reading (Lesson) from _____.

A citation giving chapter and verse may be added.

After each Reading, the Reader may say

> · The Word of the Lord.
People   Thanks be to God.

or the Reader may say   Here endeth the Reading (Epistle).

Silence may follow.

A Psalm, hymn, or anthem may follow each Reading.

Then, all standing, the Deacon or a Priest reads the Gospel, first saying

> The Holy Gospel of our Lord Jesus Christ
> according to _____.

People Glory be to thee, O Lord.

After the Gospel, the Reader says

> The Gospel of the Lord.

People Praise be to thee, O Christ.

The Sermon

On Sundays and other Major Feasts there follows, all standing

The Nicene Creed

We believe in one God,
    the Father, the Almighty,
    maker of heaven and earth,
    of all that is, seen and unseen.

We believe in one Lord, Jesus Christ,
    the only Son of God,
    eternally begotten of the Father,
    God from God, Light from Light,
    true God from true God,
    begotten, not made,
    of one Being with the Father.
    Through him all things were made.
    For us and for our salvation
        he came down from heaven:

by the power of the Holy Spirit
he became incarnate from the Virgin Mary,
and was made man.
For our sake he was crucified under Pontius Pilate;
he suffered death and was buried.
On the third day he rose again
in accordance with the Scriptures;
he ascended into heaven
and is seated at the right hand of the Father.
He will come again in glory to judge the living and the dead,
and his kingdom will have no end.

We believe in the Holy Spirit, the Lord, the giver of life,
who proceeds from the Father and the Son.
With the Father and the Son he is worshiped and glorified.
He has spoken through the Prophets.
We believe in one holy catholic and apostolic Church.
We acknowledge one baptism for the forgiveness of sins.
We look for the resurrection of the dead,
and the life of the world to come. Amen.

or this

I believe in one God,
the Father Almighty,
maker of heaven and earth,
and of all things visible and invisible;

And in one Lord Jesus Christ,
the only-begotten Son of God,
begotten of his Father before all worlds,
God of God, Light of Light,
very God of very God,
begotten, not made,
being of one substance with the Father;
by whom all things were made;

who for us men and for our salvation
   came down from heaven,
and was incarnate by the Holy Ghost of the Virgin Mary,
   and was made man;
and was crucified also for us under Pontius Pilate;
he suffered and was buried;
and the third day he rose again according to the Scriptures,
and ascended into heaven,
and sitteth on the right hand of the Father;
and he shall come again, with glory,
   to judge both the quick and the dead;
whose kingdom shall have no end.

And I believe in the Holy Ghost the Lord, and Giver of Life,
   who proceedeth from the Father and the Son;
   who with the Father and the Son together is worshiped
      and glorified;
   who spake by the Prophets.
   And I believe one holy Catholic and Apostolic Church;
   I acknowledge one Baptism for the remission of sins;
   and I look for the resurrection of the dead,
      and the life of the world to come. Amen.

The Prayers of the People

*Intercession is offered according to the following form, or in accordance
with the directions on page 383.*

The Deacon or other person appointed says

Let us pray for the whole state of Christ's Church and the
world.

*After each paragraph of this prayer, the People may make an appropriate
response, as directed.*

Almighty and everliving God, who in thy holy Word hast taught us to make prayers, and supplications, and to give thanks for all men: Receive these our prayers which we offer unto thy divine Majesty, beseeching thee to inspire continually the Universal Church with the spirit of truth, unity, and concord; and grant that all those who do confess thy holy Name may agree in the truth of thy holy Word, and live in unity and godly love.

Give grace, O heavenly Father, to all bishops and other ministers [especially _____], that they may, both by their life and doctrine, set forth thy true and lively Word, and rightly and duly administer thy holy Sacraments.

And to all thy people give thy heavenly grace, and especially to this congregation here present; that, with meek heart and due reverence, they may hear and receive thy holy Word, truly serving thee in holiness and righteousness all the days of their life.

We beseech thee also so to rule the hearts of those who bear the authority of government in this and every land [especially _____], that they may be led to wise decisions and right actions for the welfare and peace of the world.

Open, O Lord, the eyes of all people to behold thy gracious hand in all thy works, that, rejoicing in thy whole creation, they may honor thee with their substance, and be faithful stewards of thy bounty.

And we most humbly beseech thee, of thy goodness, O Lord, to comfort and succor [_____ and] all those who, in this transitory life, are in trouble, sorrow, need, sickness, or any other adversity.

Additional petitions and thanksgivings may be included here.

And we also bless thy holy Name for all thy servants
departed this life in thy faith and fear [especially _____],
beseeching thee to grant them continual growth in thy love
and service; and to grant us grace so to follow the good
examples of [_____ and of] all thy saints, that with
them we may be partakers of thy heavenly kingdom.

Grant these our prayers, O Father, for Jesus Christ's sake,
our only Mediator and Advocate. *Amen.*

*If there is no celebration of the Communion, or if a priest is not available,
the service is concluded as directed on page 406.*

Confession of Sin

*A Confession of Sin is said here if it has not been said earlier. On
occasion, the Confession may be omitted.*

*The Deacon or Celebrant says the following, or else the Exhortation
on page 316*

Ye who do truly and earnestly repent you of your sins, and
are in love and charity with your neighbors, and intend to
lead a new life, following the commandments of God, and
walking from henceforth in his holy ways: Draw near with
faith, and make your humble confession to Almighty God,
devoutly kneeling.

or this

Let us humbly confess our sins unto Almighty God.

Silence may be kept.

Almighty God,
Father of our Lord Jesus Christ,
maker of all things, judge of all men:
We acknowledge and bewail our manifold sins
    and wickedness,
which we from time to time most grievously have committed,
by thought, word, and deed, against thy divine Majesty,
provoking most justly thy wrath and indignation against us.
We do earnestly repent,
and are heartily sorry for these our misdoings;
the remembrance of them is grievous unto us,
the burden of them is intolerable.
Have mercy upon us,
have mercy upon us, most merciful Father;
for thy Son our Lord Jesus Christ's sake,
forgive us all that is past;
and grant that we may ever hereafter
serve and please thee in newness of life,
to the honor and glory of thy Name;
through Jesus Christ our Lord. Amen.

or this

Most merciful God,
we confess that we have sinned against thee
in thought, word, and deed,
by what we have done,
and by what we have left undone.
We have not loved thee with our whole heart;
we have not loved our neighbors as ourselves.
We are truly sorry and we humbly repent.
For the sake of thy Son Jesus Christ,
have mercy on us and forgive us;
that we may delight in thy will,
and walk in thy ways,
to the glory of thy Name. Amen.

The Bishop when present, or the Priest, stands and says

Almighty God, our heavenly Father, who of his great mercy hath promised forgiveness of sins to all those who with hearty repentance and true faith turn unto him, have mercy upon you, pardon and deliver you from all your sins, confirm and strengthen you in all goodness, and bring you to everlasting life; through Jesus Christ our Lord. *Amen*.

A Minister may then say one or more of the following sentences, first saying

Hear the Word of God to all who truly turn to him.

Come unto me, all ye that travail and are heavy laden, and I will refresh you. *Matthew 11:28*

God so loved the world, that he gave his only-begotten Son, to the end that all that believe in him should not perish, but have everlasting life. *John 3:16*

This is a true saying, and worthy of all men to be received, that Christ Jesus came into the world to save sinners. *1 Timothy 1:15*

If any man sin, we have an Advocate with the Father, Jesus Christ the righteous; and he is the perfect offering for our sins, and not for ours only, but for the sins of the whole world. *1 John 2:1-2*

The Peace

All stand. The Celebrant says to the people

       The peace of the Lord be always with you.
People   And with thy spirit.

Then the Ministers and People may greet one another in the name of the Lord.

Minister and People

The Holy Communion

The Celebrant may begin the Offertory with one of the sentences on pages 343-344, or with some other sentence of Scripture.

During the Offertory, a hymn, psalm, or anthem may be sung.

Representatives of the congregation bring the people's offerings of bread and wine, and money or other gifts, to the deacon or celebrant. The people stand while the offerings are presented and placed on the Altar.

The Great Thanksgiving

An alternative form will be found on page 340.

Eucharistic Prayer I

The people remain standing. The Celebrant, whether bishop or priest, faces them and sings or says

	The Lord be with you.
People	And with thy spirit.
Celebrant	Lift up your hearts.
People	We lift them up unto the Lord.
Celebrant	Let us give thanks unto our Lord God.
People	It is meet and right so to do.

Then, facing the Holy Table, the Celebrant proceeds

It is very meet, right, and our bounden duty, that we should at all times, and in all places, give thanks unto thee, O Lord, holy Father, almighty, everlasting God.

Here a Proper Preface is sung or said on all Sundays, and on other occasions as appointed.

Therefore with Angels and Archangels, and with all the company of heaven, we laud and magnify thy glorious Name; evermore praising thee, and saying,

Celebrant and People

Holy, holy, holy, Lord God of Hosts:
Heaven and earth are full of thy glory.
Glory be to thee, O Lord Most High.

Here may be added

Blessed is he that cometh in the name of the Lord.
Hosanna in the highest.

The people kneel or stand.

Then the Celebrant continues

All glory be to thee, Almighty God, our heavenly Father, for that thou, of thy tender mercy, didst give thine only Son Jesus Christ to suffer death upon the cross for our redemption; who made there, by his one oblation of himself once offered, a full, perfect, and sufficient sacrifice, oblation, and satisfaction, for the sins of the whole world; and did institute, and in his holy Gospel command us to continue, a perpetual memory of that his precious death and sacrifice, until his coming again.

At the following words concerning the bread, the Celebrant is to hold it, or lay a hand upon it; and at the words concerning the cup, to hold or place a hand upon the cup and any other vessel containing wine to be consecrated.

For in the night in which he was betrayed, he took bread; and when he had given thanks, he brake it, and gave it to his disciples, saying, "Take, eat, this is my Body, which is given for you. Do this in remembrance of me."

Likewise, after supper, he took the cup; and when he had given thanks, he gave it to them, saying, "Drink ye all of this; for this is my Blood of the New Testament, which is shed for you, and for many, for the remission of sins. Do this, as oft as ye shall drink it, in remembrance of me."

Wherefore, O Lord and heavenly Father, according to the institution of thy dearly beloved Son our Savior Jesus Christ, we, thy humble servants, do celebrate and make here before thy divine Majesty, with these thy holy gifts, which we now offer unto thee, the memorial thy Son hath commanded us to make; having in remembrance his blessed passion and precious death, his mighty resurrection and glorious ascension; rendering unto thee most hearty thanks for the innumerable benefits procured unto us by the same.

And we most humbly beseech thee, O merciful Father, to hear us; and, of thy almighty goodness, vouchsafe to bless and sanctify, with thy Word and Holy Spirit, these thy gifts and creatures of bread and wine; that we, receiving them according to thy Son our Savior Jesus Christ's holy institution, in remembrance of his death and passion, may be partakers of his most blessed Body and Blood.

And we earnestly desire thy fatherly goodness mercifully to accept this our sacrifice of praise and thanksgiving; most humbly beseeching thee to grant that, by the merits and death of thy Son Jesus Christ, and through faith in his blood, we, and all thy whole Church, may obtain remission of our sins, and all other benefits of his passion.

And here we offer and present unto thee, O Lord, our selves, our souls and bodies, to be a reasonable, holy, and living sacrifice unto thee; humbly beseeching thee that we, and all others who shall be partakers of this Holy Communion, may worthily receive the most precious Body and Blood of thy Son Jesus Christ, be filled with thy grace and heavenly benediction, and made one body with him, that he may dwell in us, and we in him.

And although we are unworthy, through our manifold sins, to offer unto thee any sacrifice, yet we beseech thee to accept this our bounden duty and service, not weighing our merits, but pardoning our offenses, through Jesus Christ our Lord;

By whom, and with whom, in the unity of the Holy Ghost all honor and glory be unto thee, O Father Almighty, world without end. *AMEN.*

And now, as our Savior Christ hath taught us, we are bold to say,

People and Celebrant

Our Father, who art in heaven,
    hallowed be thy Name,
    thy kingdom come,
    thy will be done,
        on earth as it is in heaven.
Give us this day our daily bread.
And forgive us our trespasses,
    as we forgive those who trespass against us.
And lead us not into temptation,
    but deliver us from evil.
For thine is the kingdom, and the power, and the glory,
    for ever and ever. Amen.

The Breaking of the Bread

The Celebrant breaks the consecrated Bread.

A period of silence is kept.

Then may be sung or said

[Alleluia.] Christ our Passover is sacrificed for us;
Therefore let us keep the feast. [*Alleluia.*]

In Lent, Alleluia is omitted, and may be omitted at other times except during Easter Season.

The following or some other suitable anthem may be sung or said here

O Lamb of God, that takest away the sins of the world,
have mercy upon us.
O Lamb of God, that takest away the sins of the world,
have mercy upon us.
O Lamb of God, that takest away the sins of the world,
grant us thy peace.

*The following prayer may be said. The People may join in saying
this prayer*

We do not presume to come to this thy Table, O merciful
Lord, trusting in our own righteousness, but in thy manifold
and great mercies. We are not worthy so much as to gather
up the crumbs under thy Table. But thou art the same Lord
whose property is always to have mercy. Grant us therefore,
gracious Lord, so to eat the flesh of thy dear Son Jesus Christ,
and to drink his blood, that we may evermore dwell in him,
and he in us. *Amen.*

Facing the people, the Celebrant may say the following Invitation

The Gifts of God for the People of God.

and may add   Take them in remembrance that Christ died for
you, and feed on him in your hearts by faith,
with thanksgiving.

*The ministers receive the Sacrament in both kinds, and then immediately
deliver it to the people.*

The Bread and the Cup are given to the communicants with these words

The Body of our Lord Jesus Christ, which was given for thee,
preserve thy body and soul unto everlasting life. Take and eat
this in remembrance that Christ died for thee, and feed on
him in thy heart by faith, with thanksgiving.

The Blood of our Lord Jesus Christ, which was shed for thee,
preserve thy body and soul unto everlasting life. Drink this in
remembrance that Christ's Blood was shed for thee, and be
thankful.

or with these words

The Body (Blood) of our Lord Jesus Christ keep you in
everlasting life. [*Amen.*]

or with these words

The Body of Christ, the bread of heaven. [*Amen.*]
The Blood of Christ, the cup of salvation. [*Amen.*]

*During the ministration of Communion, hymns, psalms, or anthems may
be sung.*

*When necessary, the Celebrant consecrates additional bread and wine,
using the form on page 408.*

Let us pray.

Almighty and everliving God, we most heartily thank thee
for that thou dost feed us, in these holy mysteries, with the
spiritual food of the most precious Body and Blood of thy
Son our Savior Jesus Christ; and dost assure us thereby of
thy favor and goodness towards us; and that we are very
members incorporate in the mystical body of thy Son, the
blessed company of all faithful people; and are also heirs,
through hope, of thy everlasting kingdom. And we humbly
beseech thee, O heavenly Father, so to assist us with thy
grace, that we may continue in that holy fellowship, and do
all such good works as thou hast prepared for us to walk in;
through Jesus Christ our Lord, to whom, with thee and the
Holy Ghost, be all honor and glory, world without end.
Amen.

The Bishop when present, or the Priest, gives the blessing

The peace of God, which passeth all understanding, keep
your hearts and minds in the knowledge and love of God,
and of his Son Jesus Christ our Lord; and the blessing of
God Almighty, the Father, the Son, and the Holy Ghost, be
amongst you, and remain with you always. *Amen.*

or this

The blessing of God Almighty, the Father, the Son, and the
Holy Spirit, be upon you and remain with you for ever. *Amen.*

The Deacon, or the Celebrant, may dismiss the people with these words

　　　　　Let us go forth in the name of Christ.
People　　Thanks be to God.

or the following

Deacon	Go in peace to love and serve the Lord.
People	Thanks be to God.

or this

Deacon	Let us go forth into the world, rejoicing in the power of the Spirit.
People	Thanks be to God.

or this

Deacon	Let us bless the Lord.
People	Thanks be to God.

From the Easter Vigil through the Day of Pentecost "Alleluia, alleluia" may be added to any of the dismissals.

The People respond   Thanks be to God. Alleluia, alleluia.

Alternative Form of the Great Thanksgiving

Eucharistic Prayer II

The people remain standing. The Celebrant, whether bishop or priest, faces them and sings or says

	The Lord be with you.
People	And with thy spirit.
Celebrant	Lift up your hearts.
People	We lift them up unto the Lord.
Celebrant	Let us give thanks unto our Lord God.
People	It is meet and right so to do.

Then, facing the Holy Table, the Celebrant proceeds

It is very meet, right, and our bounden duty, that we should at all times, and in all places, give thanks unto thee, O Lord, holy Father, almighty, everlasting God.

Here a Proper Preface is sung or said on all Sundays, and on other occasions as appointed.

Therefore with Angels and Archangels, and with all the company of heaven, we laud and magnify thy glorious Name; evermore praising thee, and saying,

Celebrant and people

Holy, holy, holy, Lord God of Hosts:
Heaven and earth are full of thy glory.
Glory be to thee, O Lord Most High.

Here may be added

Blessed is he that cometh in the name of the Lord.
Hosanna in the highest.

The people kneel or stand.

Then the Celebrant continues

All glory be to thee, O Lord our God, for that thou didst create heaven and earth, and didst make us in thine own image; and, of thy tender mercy, didst give thine only Son Jesus Christ to take our nature upon him, and to suffer death upon the cross for our redemption. He made there a full and perfect sacrifice for the whole world; and did institute, and in his holy Gospel command us to continue, a perpetual memory of that his precious death and sacrifice, until his coming again.

At the following words concerning the bread, the Celebrant is to hold it, or lay a hand upon it; and at the words concerning the cup, to hold or place a hand upon the cup and any other vessel containing wine to be consecrated.

For in the night in which he was betrayed, he took bread; and when he had given thanks to thee, he broke it, and gave it to his disciples, saying, "Take, eat, this is my Body, which is given for you. Do this in remembrance of me."

Likewise, after supper, he took the cup; and when he had given thanks, he gave it to them, saying, "Drink this, all of you; for this is my Blood of the New Covenant, which is shed for you, and for many, for the remission of sins. Do this, as oft as ye shall drink it, in remembrance of me."

Wherefore, O Lord and heavenly Father, we thy people do celebrate and make, with these thy holy gifts which we now offer unto thee, the memorial thy Son hath commanded us to make; having in remembrance his blessed passion and precious death, his mighty resurrection and glorious ascension; and looking for his coming again with power and great glory.

And we most humbly beseech thee, O merciful Father, to hear us, and, with thy Word and Holy Spirit, to bless and sanctify these gifts of bread and wine, that they may be unto us the Body and Blood of thy dearly-beloved Son Jesus Christ.

And we earnestly desire thy fatherly goodness to accept this our sacrifice of praise and thanksgiving, whereby we offer and present unto thee, O Lord, our selves, our souls and bodies. Grant, we beseech thee, that all who partake of this Holy Communion may worthily receive the most precious Body and Blood of thy Son Jesus Christ, and be filled with thy grace and heavenly benediction; and also that we and all thy whole Church may be made one body with him, that he

may dwell in us, and we in him; through the same Jesus
Christ our Lord;

By whom, and with whom, and in whom, in the unity of the
Holy Ghost all honor and glory be unto thee, O Father
Almighty, world without end. *AMEN.*

And now, as our Savior Christ hath taught us, we are bold
to say,

Continue with the Lord's Prayer, page 336.

Offertory Sentences

*One of the following, or some other appropriate sentence of Scripture,
may be used*

Offer to God a sacrifice of thanksgiving, and make good thy
vows unto the Most High.   *Psalm 50:14*

Ascribe to the Lord the honor due his Name; bring offerings
and come into his courts.   *Psalm 96:8*

Walk in love, as Christ loved us and gave himself for us, an
offering and sacrifice to God.   *Ephesians 5:2*

I beseech you, brethren, by the mercies of God, to present
yourselves as a living sacrifice, holy and acceptable to God,
which is your spiritual worship.   *Romans 12:1*

If thou bring thy gift to the altar, and there rememberest that
thy brother hath aught against thee, leave there thy gift
before the altar, and go thy way; first be reconciled to thy
brother, and then come and offer thy gift.   *Matthew 5:23,24*

Holy Eucharist I   343

Through Christ let us continually offer to God the sacrifice of praise, that is, the fruit of lips that acknowledge his Name. But to do good and to distribute, forget not; for with such sacrifices God is well pleased.   *Hebrews 13:15,16*

Worthy art thou, O Lord our God, to receive glory and honor and power; for thou hast created all things, and by thy will they were created and have their being.   *Revelation 4:11*

Thine, O Lord, is the greatness, and the power, and the glory, and the victory, and the majesty. For all that is in the heaven and in the earth is thine. Thine is the kingdom, O Lord, and thou art exalted as head above all.   *1 Chronicles 29:11*

or this bidding

Let us with gladness present the offerings and oblations of our life and labor to the Lord.

Proper Prefaces

Preface of the Lord's Day

To be used on Sundays as appointed, but not on the succeeding weekdays

1. Of God the Father

Creator of the light and source of life, who hast made us in thine image, and called us to new life in Jesus Christ our Lord.

or the following

2. Of God the Son

Through Jesus Christ our Lord; who on the first day of the week overcame death and the grave, and by his glorious resurrection opened to us the way of everlasting life.

or this

3. Of God the Holy Spirit

Who by water and the Holy Spirit hast made us a new people in Jesus Christ our Lord, to show forth thy glory in all the world.

Prefaces for Seasons

To be used on Sundays and weekdays alike, except as otherwise appointed for Holy Days and Various Occasions

Advent

Because thou didst send thy beloved Son to redeem us from sin and death, and to make us heirs in him of everlasting life; that when he shall come again in power and great triumph to judge the world, we may without shame or fear rejoice to behold his appearing.

Incarnation

Because thou didst give Jesus Christ, thine only Son, to be born for us; who, by the mighty power of the Holy Ghost, was made very Man of the substance of the Virgin Mary his mother; that we might be delivered from the bondage of sin, and receive power to become thy children.

Epiphany

Because in the mystery of the Word made flesh, thou hast caused a new light to shine in our hearts, to give the knowledge of thy glory in the face of thy Son Jesus Christ our Lord.

Lent

Through Jesus Christ our Lord, who was in every way tempted as we are, yet did not sin; by whose grace we are able to triumph over every evil, and to live no longer unto ourselves, but unto him who died for us and rose again.

or this

Who dost bid thy faithful people cleanse their hearts, and prepare with joy for the Paschal feast; that, fervent in prayer and in works of mercy, and renewed by thy Word and Sacraments, they may come to the fullness of grace which thou hast prepared for those who love thee.

Holy Week

Through Jesus Christ our Lord; who for our sins was lifted high upon the cross, that he might draw the whole world to himself; who by his suffering and death became the author of eternal salvation for all who put their trust in him.

Easter

But chiefly are we bound to praise thee for the glorious resurrection of thy Son Jesus Christ our Lord; for he is the very Paschal Lamb, who was sacrificed for us, and hath taken away the sin of the world; who by his death hath destroyed death, and by his rising to life again hath won for us everlasting life.

Ascension

Through thy dearly beloved Son Jesus Christ our Lord; who after his glorious resurrection manifestly appeared to his disciples; and in their sight ascended into heaven, to prepare a place for us; that where he is, there we might also be, and reign with him in glory.

Pentecost

Through Jesus Christ our Lord; according to whose true promise the Holy Ghost came down [on this day] from heaven, lighting upon the disciples, to teach them and to lead them into all truth; uniting peoples of many tongues in the confession of one faith, and giving to thy Church the power to serve thee as a royal priesthood, and to preach the Gospel to all nations.

Prefaces for Other Occasions

Trinity Sunday

For with thy co-eternal Son and Holy Spirit, thou art one God, one Lord, in Trinity of Persons and in Unity of Substance; and we celebrate the one and equal glory of thee, O Father, and of the Son, and of the Holy Spirit.

All Saints

Who, in the multitude of thy saints, hast compassed us about with so great a cloud of witnesses, that we, rejoicing in their fellowship, may run with patience the race that is set before us; and, together with them, may receive the crown of glory that fadeth not away.

A Saint

For the wonderful grace and virtue declared in all thy saints, who have been the chosen vessels of thy grace, and the lights of the world in their generations.

or this

Who in the obedience of thy saints hast given us an example of righteousness, and in their eternal joy a glorious pledge of the hope of our calling.

or this

Because thou art greatly glorified in the assembly of thy saints. All thy creatures praise thee, and thy faithful servants bless thee, confessing before the rulers of this world the great Name of thine only Son.

Apostles and Ordinations

Through the great shepherd of thy flock, Jesus Christ our Lord; who after his resurrection sent forth his apostles to preach the Gospel and to teach all nations; and promised to be with them always, even unto the end of the ages.

Dedication of a Church

Through Jesus Christ our great High Priest, in whom we are built up as living stones of a holy temple, that we might offer before thee a sacrifice of praise and prayer which is holy and pleasing in thy sight.

Baptism

Because in Jesus Christ our Lord thou hast received us as thy sons and daughters, made us citizens of thy kingdom, and given us the Holy Spirit to guide us into all truth.

Marriage

Because in the love of wife and husband, thou hast given us an image of the heavenly Jerusalem, adorned as a bride for her bridegroom, thy Son Jesus Christ our Lord; who loveth her and gave himself for her, that he might make the whole creation new.

Commemoration of the Dead

Through Jesus Christ our Lord; who rose victorious from the dead, and doth comfort us with the blessed hope of everlasting life; for to thy faithful people, O Lord, life is changed, not ended; and when our mortal body doth lie in death, there is prepared for us a dwelling place eternal in the heavens.

The Decalogue: Contemporary

Hear the commandments of God to his people:
I am the Lord your God who brought you out of bondage.
You shall have no other gods but me.
Amen. Lord have mercy.

You shall not make for yourself any idol.
Amen. Lord have mercy.

You shall not invoke with malice the Name of the Lord your God
Amen. Lord have mercy.

Remember the Sabbath Day and keep it holy.
Amen. Lord have mercy.

Honor your father and your mother.
Amen. Lord have mercy.

You shall not commit murder.
Amen. Lord have mercy.

You shall not commit adultery.
Amen. Lord have mercy.

You shall not steal.
Amen. Lord have mercy.

You shall not be a false witness.
Amen. Lord have mercy.

You shall not covet anything that belongs to your neighbor.
Amen. Lord have mercy.

A Penitential Order: Rite Two

For use at the beginning of the Liturgy, or as a separate service.

A hymn, psalm, or anthem may be sung.

The people standing, the Celebrant says

Blessed be God: Father, Son, and Holy Spirit.
People   And blessed be his kingdom, now and for ever.
Amen.

In place of the above, from Easter Day through the Day of Pentecost

Celebrant Alleluia. Christ is risen.
People   The Lord is risen indeed. Alleluia.

In Lent and on other penitential occasions

Celebrant Bless the Lord who forgives all our sins;
People   His mercy endures for ever.

When used as a separate service, the Exhortation, page 316, may be read, or a homily preached.

The Decalogue may be said, the people kneeling.

The Celebrant may read one of the following sentences

Jesus said, "The first commandment is this: Hear, O Israel: The Lord our God is the only Lord. Love the Lord your God with all your heart, with all your soul, with all your mind, and with all your strength. The second is this: Love your neighbor as yourself. There is no other commandment greater than these."   *Mark 12:29-31*

If we say that we have no sin, we deceive ourselves, and the truth is not in us. But if we confess our sins, God, who is faithful and just, will forgive our sins and cleanse us from all unrighteousness.   *1 John 1:8,9*

Since we have a great high priest who has passed through the heavens, Jesus, the Son of God, let us with confidence draw near to the throne of grace, that we may receive mercy and find grace to help in time of need.   *Hebrews 4:14,16*

The Deacon or Celebrant then says

Let us confess our sins against God and our neighbor.

Silence may be kept.

Minister and People

Most merciful God,
we confess that we have sinned against you
in thought, word, and deed,
by what we have done,
and by what we have left undone.
We have not loved you with our whole heart;
we have not loved our neighbors as ourselves.
We are truly sorry and we humbly repent.
For the sake of your Son Jesus Christ,
have mercy on us and forgive us;
that we may delight in your will,
and walk in your ways,
to the glory of your Name. Amen.

The Bishop when present, or the Priest, stands and says

Almighty God have mercy on you, forgive you all your sins through our Lord Jesus Christ, strengthen you in all goodness, and by the power of the Holy Spirit keep you in eternal life. *Amen.*

A deacon or lay person using the preceding form substitutes "us" for "you" and "our" for "your."

When this Order is used at the beginning of the Liturgy, the service continues with the Gloria in excelsis, the Kyrie eleison, or the Trisagion.

When used separately, it concludes with suitable prayers, and the Grace or a blessing.

Concerning the Celebration

It is the bishop's prerogative, when present, to be the principal celebrant at the Lord's Table, and to preach the Gospel.

At all celebrations of the Liturgy, it is fitting that the principal celebrant, whether bishop or priest, be assisted by other priests, and by deacons and lay persons.

It is appropriate that the other priests present stand with the celebrant at the Altar, and join in the consecration of the gifts, in breaking the Bread, and in distributing Communion.

A deacon should read the Gospel and may lead the Prayers of the People. Deacons should also serve at the Lord's Table, preparing and placing on it the offerings of bread and wine, and assisting in the ministration of the Sacrament to the people. In the absence of a deacon, these duties may be performed by an assisting priest.

Lay persons appointed by the celebrant should normally be assigned the reading of the Lessons which precede the Gospel, and may lead the Prayers of the People.

Morning or Evening Prayer may be used in place of all that precedes the Peace and the Offertory, provided that a lesson from the Gospel is always included, and that the intercessions conform to the directions given for the Prayers of the People.

Additional Directions are on page 406.

The Holy Eucharist: Rite Two

The Word of God

A hymn, psalm, or anthem may be sung.

The people standing, the Celebrant says

Blessed be God: Father, Son, and Holy Spirit.
People   And blessed be his kingdom, now and for ever.
Amen.

In place of the above, from Easter Day through the Day of Pentecost

Celebrant   Alleluia. Christ is risen.
People   The Lord is risen indeed. Alleluia.

In Lent and on other penitential occasions

Celebrant   Bless the Lord who forgives all our sins.
People   His mercy endures for ever.

The Celebrant may say

Almighty God, to you all hearts are open, all desires known,
and from you no secrets are hid: Cleanse the thoughts of our
hearts by the inspiration of your Holy Spirit, that we may
perfectly love you, and worthily magnify your holy Name;
through Christ our Lord. *Amen.*

When appointed, the following hymn or some other song of praise is sung or said, all standing

Glory to God in the highest,
   and peace to his people on earth.

Lord God, heavenly King,
almighty God and Father,
   we worship you, we give you thanks,
   we praise you for your glory.

Lord Jesus Christ, only Son of the Father,
Lord God, Lamb of God,
you take away the sin of the world:
   have mercy on us;
you are seated at the right hand of the Father:
   receive our prayer.

For you alone are the Holy One,
you alone are the Lord,
you alone are the Most High,
   Jesus Christ,
   with the Holy Spirit,
   in the glory of God the Father. Amen.

On other occasions the following is used

Lord, have mercy.		Kyrie eleison.
Christ, have mercy.	*or*	*Christe eleison.*
Lord, have mercy.		Kyrie eleison.

or this

Holy God,
Holy and Mighty,
Holy Immortal One,
Have mercy upon us.

The Collect of the Day

The Celebrant says to the people

>The Lord be with you.
>
>*People*   And also with you.
>*Celebrant* Let us pray.

The Celebrant says the Collect.

People   Amen.

The Lessons

The people sit. One or two Lessons, as appointed, are read, the Reader first saying

A Reading (Lesson) from _____.

A citation giving chapter and verse may be added.

After each Reading, the Reader may say

>The Word of the Lord.
>
>*People*   Thanks be to God.

or the Reader may say   Here ends the Reading (Epistle).

Silence may follow.

A Psalm, hymn, or anthem may follow each Reading.

Then, all standing, the Deacon or a Priest reads the Gospel, first saying

>The Holy Gospel of our Lord Jesus Christ
>according to _____.
>
>*People*   Glory to you, Lord Christ.

After the Gospel, the Reader says

        The Gospel of the Lord.
People   Praise to you, Lord Christ.

The Sermon

On Sundays and other Major Feasts there follows, all standing

The Nicene Creed

We believe in one God,
  the Father, the Almighty,
  maker of heaven and earth,
  of all that is, seen and unseen.

We believe in one Lord, Jesus Christ,
  the only Son of God,
  eternally begotten of the Father,
  God from God, Light from Light,
  true God from true God,
  begotten, not made,
  of one Being with the Father.
  Through him all things were made.
For us and for our salvation
  he came down from heaven:
by the power of the Holy Spirit
  he became incarnate from the Virgin Mary,
  and was made man.
For our sake he was crucified under Pontius Pilate;
  he suffered death and was buried.
  On the third day he rose again
    in accordance with the Scriptures;
  he ascended into heaven
    and is seated at the right hand of the Father.

He will come again in glory to judge the living and the dead,
  and his kingdom will have no end.

We believe in the Holy Spirit, the Lord, the giver of life,
  who proceeds from the Father and the Son.
  With the Father and the Son he is worshiped and glorified.
  He has spoken through the Prophets.
  We believe in one holy catholic and apostolic Church.
  We acknowledge one baptism for the forgiveness of sins.
  We look for the resurrection of the dead,
    and the life of the world to come. Amen.

The Prayers of the People

Prayer is offered with intercession for

The Universal Church, its members, and its mission
The Nation and all in authority
The welfare of the world
The concerns of the local community
Those who suffer and those in any trouble
The departed (with commemoration of a saint when appropriate)

See the forms beginning on page 383.

If there is no celebration of the Communion, or if a priest is not available, the service is concluded as directed on page 406.

Confession of Sin

A Confession of Sin is said here if it has not been said earlier. On occasion, the Confession may be omitted.

One of the sentences from the Penitential Order on page 351 may be said.

Let us confess our sins against God and our neighbor.

Silence may be kept.

Minister and People

Most merciful God,
we confess that we have sinned against you
in thought, word, and deed,
by what we have done,
and by what we have left undone.
We have not loved you with our whole heart;
we have not loved our neighbors as ourselves.
We are truly sorry and we humbly repent.
For the sake of your Son Jesus Christ,
have mercy on us and forgive us;
that we may delight in your will,
and walk in your ways,
to the glory of your Name. Amen.

The Bishop when present, or the Priest, stands and says

Almighty God have mercy on you, forgive you all your sins
through our Lord Jesus Christ, strengthen you in all
goodness, and by the power of the Holy Spirit keep you in
eternal life. *Amen.*

The Peace

All stand. The Celebrant says to the people

      The peace of the Lord be always with you.
People   And also with you.

*Then the Ministers and People may greet one another in the
name of the Lord.*

The Holy Communion

The Celebrant may begin the Offertory with one of the sentences on page 376, or with some other sentence of Scripture.

During the Offertory, a hymn, psalm, or anthem may be sung.

Representatives of the congregation bring the people's offerings of bread and wine, and money or other gifts, to the deacon or celebrant. The people stand while the offerings are presented and placed on the Altar.

The Great Thanksgiving

Alternative forms will be found on page 367 and following.

Eucharistic Prayer A

The people remain standing. The Celebrant, whether bishop or priest, faces them and sings or says

	The Lord be with you.
People	And also with you.
Celebrant	Lift up your hearts.
People	We lift them to the Lord.
Celebrant	Let us give thanks to the Lord our God.
People	It is right to give him thanks and praise.

Then, facing the Holy Table, the Celebrant proceeds

It is right, and a good and joyful thing, always and every-where to give thanks to you, Father Almighty, Creator of heaven and earth.

Here a Proper Preface is sung or said on all Sundays, and on other occasions as appointed.

Therefore we praise you, joining our voices with Angels and Archangels and with all the company of heaven, who for ever sing this hymn to proclaim the glory of your Name:

Celebrant and People

Holy, holy, holy Lord, God of power and might,
heaven and earth are full of your glory.
     Hosanna in the highest.
Blessed is he who comes in the name of the Lord.
     Hosanna in the highest.

The people stand or kneel.

Then the Celebrant continues

Holy and gracious Father: In your infinite love you made us for yourself; and, when we had fallen into sin and become subject to evil and death, you, in your mercy, sent Jesus Christ, your only and eternal Son, to share our human nature, to live and die as one of us, to reconcile us to you, the God and Father of all.

He stretched out his arms upon the cross, and offered himself, in obedience to your will, a perfect sacrifice for the whole world.

At the following words concerning the bread, the Celebrant is to hold it, or lay a hand upon it; and at the words concerning the cup, to hold or place a hand upon the cup and any other vessel containing wine to be consecrated.

On the night he was handed over to suffering and death, our Lord Jesus Christ took bread; and when he had given thanks to you, he broke it, and gave it to his disciples, and said, "Take, eat: This is my Body, which is given for you. Do this for the remembrance of me."

After supper he took the cup of wine; and when he had given thanks, he gave it to them, and said, "Drink this, all of you: This is my Blood of the new Covenant, which is shed for you and for many for the forgiveness of sins. Whenever you drink it, do this for the remembrance of me."

Therefore we proclaim the mystery of faith:

Celebrant and People

Christ has died.
Christ is risen.
Christ will come again.

The Celebrant continues

We celebrate the memorial of our redemption, O Father, in this sacrifice of praise and thanksgiving. Recalling his death, resurrection, and ascension, we offer you these gifts.

Sanctify them by your Holy Spirit to be for your people the Body and Blood of your Son, the holy food and drink of new and unending life in him. Sanctify us also that we may faithfully receive this holy Sacrament, and serve you in unity, constancy, and peace; and at the last day bring us with all your saints into the joy of your eternal kingdom.

All this we ask through your Son Jesus Christ. By him, and with him, and in him, in the unity of the Holy Spirit all honor and glory is yours, Almighty Father, now and for ever. *AMEN.*

And now, as our Savior Christ has taught us, we are bold to say,	As our Savior Christ has taught us, we now pray,

Our Father, who art in heaven,
   hallowed be thy Name,
   thy kingdom come,
   thy will be done,
      on earth as it is in heaven.
Give us this day our daily bread.
And forgive us our trespasses,
   as we forgive those
      who trespass against us.
And lead us not into temptation,
   but deliver us from evil.
For thine is the kingdom,
   and the power, and the glory,
   for ever and ever. Amen.

Our Father in heaven,
   hallowed be your Name,
   your kingdom come,
   your will be done,
      on earth as in heaven.
Give us today our daily bread.
Forgive us our sins
   as we forgive those
      who sin against us.
Save us from the time of trial,
   and deliver us from evil.
For the kingdom, the power,
   and the glory are yours,
   now and for ever. Amen.

The Breaking of the Bread

The Celebrant breaks the consecrated Bread.

A period of silence is kept.

Then may be sung or said

[Alleluia.] Christ our Passover is sacrificed for us;
Therefore let us keep the feast. [*Alleluia.*]

*In Lent, Alleluia is omitted, and may be omitted at other times except
during Easter Season.*

*In place of, or in addition to, the preceding, some other suitable
anthem may be used.*

Facing the people, the Celebrant says the following Invitation
The Gifts of God for the People of God.

and may add Take them in remembrance that Christ died for
you, and feed on him in your hearts by faith,
with thanksgiving.

*The ministers receive the Sacrament in both kinds, and then immediately
deliver it to the people.*

The Bread and the Cup are given to the communicants with these words

The Body (Blood) of our Lord Jesus Christ keep you in
everlasting life. [*Amen.*]

or with these words

The Body of Christ, the bread of heaven. [*Amen.*]
The Blood of Christ, the cup of salvation. [*Amen.*]

*During the ministration of Communion, hymns, psalms, or anthems may
be sung.*

*When necessary, the Celebrant consecrates additional bread and wine,
using the form on page 408.*

After Communion, the Celebrant says

Let us pray.

Celebrant and People

Eternal God, heavenly Father,
you have graciously accepted us as living members
of your Son our Savior Jesus Christ,
and you have fed us with spiritual food
in the Sacrament of his Body and Blood.
Send us now into the world in peace,
and grant us strength and courage
to love and serve you
with gladness and singleness of heart;
through Christ our Lord. Amen.

or the following

Almighty and everliving God,
we thank you for feeding us with the spiritual food
of the most precious Body and Blood
of your Son our Savior Jesus Christ;
and for assuring us in these holy mysteries
that we are living members of the Body of your Son,
and heirs of your eternal kingdom.
And now, Father, send us out
to do the work you have given us to do,
to love and serve you
as faithful witnesses of Christ our Lord.
To him, to you, and to the Holy Spirit,
be honor and glory, now and for ever. Amen.

The Bishop when present, or the Priest, may bless the people.

The Deacon, or the Celebrant, dismisses them with these words

Let us go forth in the name of Christ.
People Thanks be to God.

or this

Deacon Go in peace to love and serve the Lord.
People Thanks be to God.

or this

Deacon Let us go forth into the world,
rejoicing in the power of the Spirit.
People Thanks be to God.

or this

Deacon Let us bless the Lord.
People Thanks be to God.

*From the Easter Vigil through the Day of Pentecost "Alleluia, alleluia"
may be added to any of the dismissals.*

The People respond Thanks be to God. Alleluia, alleluia.

Alternative Forms
of the Great Thanksgiving

Eucharistic Prayer B

The people remain standing. The Celebrant, whether bishop or priest, faces them and sings or says

           The Lord be with you.
People   And also with you.
Celebrant Lift up your hearts.
People   We lift them to the Lord.
Celebrant Let us give thanks to the Lord our God.
People   It is right to give him thanks and praise.

Then, facing the Holy Table, the Celebrant proceeds

It is right, and a good and joyful thing, always and everywhere to give thanks to you, Father Almighty, Creator of heaven and earth.

Here a Proper Preface is sung or said on all Sundays, and on other occasions as appointed.

Therefore we praise you, joining our voices with Angels and Archangels and with all the company of heaven, who for ever sing this hymn to proclaim the glory of your Name:

Celebrant and People

Holy, holy, holy Lord, God of power and might,
heaven and earth are full of your glory.
    Hosanna in the highest.
Blessed is he who comes in the name of the Lord.
    Hosanna in the highest.

The people stand or kneel.

Then the Celebrant continues

We give thanks to you, O God, for the goodness and love which you have made known to us in creation; in the calling of Israel to be your people; in your Word spoken through the prophets; and above all in the Word made flesh, Jesus, your Son. For in these last days you sent him to be incarnate from the Virgin Mary, to be the Savior and Redeemer of the world. In him, you have delivered us from evil, and made us worthy to stand before you. In him, you have brought us out of error into truth, out of sin into righteousness, out of death into life.

At the following words concerning the bread, the Celebrant is to hold it, or lay a hand upon it; and at the words concerning the cup, to hold or place a hand upon the cup and any other vessel containing wine to be consecrated.

On the night before he died for us, our Lord Jesus Christ took bread; and when he had given thanks to you, he broke it, and gave it to his disciples, and said, "Take, eat: This is my Body, which is given for you. Do this for the remembrance of me."

After supper he took the cup of wine; and when he had given thanks, he gave it to them, and said, "Drink this, all of you: This is my Blood of the new Covenant, which is shed for you and for many for the forgiveness of sins. Whenever you drink it, do this for the remembrance of me."

Therefore, according to his command, O Father,

Celebrant and People

We remember his death,
We proclaim his resurrection,
We await his coming in glory;

And we offer our sacrifice of praise and thanksgiving to you,
O Lord of all; presenting to you, from your creation, this
bread and this wine.

We pray you, gracious God, to send your Holy Spirit upon
these gifts that they may be the Sacrament of the Body of
Christ and his Blood of the new Covenant. Unite us to your
Son in his sacrifice, that we may be acceptable through him,
being sanctified by the Holy Spirit. In the fullness of time,
put all things in subjection under your Christ, and bring us to
that heavenly country where, with [_____ and] all your
saints, we may enter the everlasting heritage of your sons and
daughters; through Jesus Christ our Lord, the firstborn of all
creation, the head of the Church, and the author of our
salvation.

By him, and with him, and in him, in the unity of the Holy
Spirit all honor and glory is yours, Almighty Father, now and
for ever. *AMEN.*

And now, as our Savior Christ has taught us, we are bold to say,	As our Savior Christ has taught us, we now pray,

Continue with the Lord's Prayer on page 364.

Eucharistic Prayer C

In this prayer, the lines in italics are spoken by the People.

The Celebrant, whether bishop or priest, faces them and sings or says

The Lord be with you.
And also with you.

Lift up your hearts.
We lift them to the Lord.

Let us give thanks to the Lord our God.
It is right to give him thanks and praise.

Then, facing the Holy Table, the Celebrant proceeds

God of all power, Ruler of the Universe, you are worthy of
glory and praise.
Glory to you for ever and ever.

At your command all things came to be: the vast expanse of
interstellar space, galaxies, suns, the planets in their courses,
and this fragile earth, our island home.
By your will they were created and have their being.

From the primal elements you brought forth the human race,
and blessed us with memory, reason, and skill. You made us
the rulers of creation. But we turned against you, and betrayed
your trust; and we turned against one another.
Have mercy, Lord, for we are sinners in your sight.

Again and again, you called us to return. Through prophets
and sages you revealed your righteous Law. And in the
fullness of time you sent your only Son, born of a woman, to
fulfill your Law, to open for us the way of freedom and peace.
By his blood, he reconciled us.
By his wounds, we are healed.

And therefore we praise you, joining with the heavenly
chorus, with prophets, apostles, and martyrs, and with all
those in every generation who have looked to you in hope, to
proclaim with them your glory, in their unending hymn:

Holy, holy, holy Lord, God of power and might,
heaven and earth are full of your glory.
 Hosanna in the highest.
Blessed is he who comes in the name of the Lord.
 Hosanna in the highest.

The Celebrant continues

And so, Father, we who have been redeemed by him, and
made a new people by water and the Spirit, now bring before
you these gifts. Sanctify them by your Holy Spirit to be the
Body and Blood of Jesus Christ our Lord.

*At the following words concerning the bread, the Celebrant is to hold it,
or lay a hand upon it; and at the words concerning the cup, to hold or
place a hand upon the cup and any other vessel containing wine to be
consecrated.*

On the night he was betrayed he took bread, said the
blessing, broke the bread, and gave it to his friends, and
said,"Take, eat: This is my Body, which is given for you. Do
this for the remembrance of me."

After supper, he took the cup of wine, gave thanks, and
said,"Drink this, all of you: This is my Blood of the new
Covenant, which is shed for you and for many for the
forgiveness of sins. Whenever you drink it, do this for the
remembrance of me."

Remembering now his work of redemption, and offering to
you this sacrifice of thanksgiving,
We celebrate his death and resurrection,
as we await the day of his coming.

Lord God of our Fathers; God of Abraham, Isaac, and Jacob; God and Father of our Lord Jesus Christ: Open our eyes to see your hand at work in the world about us. Deliver us from the presumption of coming to this Table for solace only, and not for strength; for pardon only, and not for renewal. Let the grace of this Holy Communion make us one body, one spirit in Christ, that we may worthily serve the world in his name.

Risen Lord, be known to us in the breaking of the Bread.

Accept these prayers and praises, Father, through Jesus Christ our great High Priest, to whom, with you and the Holy Spirit, your Church gives honor, glory, and worship, from generation to generation. *AMEN.*

And now, as our Savior Christ has taught us, we are bold to say,	As our Savior Christ has taught us, we now pray,

Continue with the Lord's Prayer on page 364.

Eucharistic Prayer D

The people remain standing. The Celebrant, whether bishop or priest, faces them and sings or says

> The Lord be with you.

People   And also with you.

Celebrant   Lift up your hearts.

People   We lift them to the Lord.

Celebrant   Let us give thanks to the Lord our God.

People   It is right to give him thanks and praise.

Then, facing the Holy Table, the Celebrant proceeds

It is truly right to glorify you, Father, and to give you thanks; for you alone are God, living and true, dwelling in light inaccessible from before time and for ever.

Fountain of life and source of all goodness, you made all things and fill them with your blessing; you created them to rejoice in the splendor of your radiance.

Countless throngs of angels stand before you to serve you night and day; and, beholding the glory of your presence, they offer you unceasing praise. Joining with them, and giving voice to every creature under heaven, we acclaim you, and glorify your Name, as we sing (say),

Celebrant and People

Holy, holy, holy Lord, God of power and might,
heaven and earth are full of your glory.
    Hosanna in the highest.
Blessed is he who comes in the name of the Lord.
    Hosanna in the highest.

The people stand or kneel.

Then the Celebrant continues

We acclaim you, holy Lord, glorious in power. Your mighty works reveal your wisdom and love. You formed us in your own image, giving the whole world into our care, so that, in obedience to you, our Creator, we might rule and serve all your creatures. When our disobedience took us far from you, you did not abandon us to the power of death. In your mercy you came to our help, so that in seeking you we might find you. Again and again you called us into covenant with you, and through the prophets you taught us to hope for salvation.

Father, you loved the world so much that in the fullness of time you sent your only Son to be our Savior. Incarnate by the Holy Spirit, born of the Virgin Mary, he lived as one of us, yet without sin. To the poor he proclaimed the good news of salvation; to prisoners, freedom; to the sorrowful, joy. To fulfill your purpose he gave himself up to death; and, rising from the grave, destroyed death, and made the whole creation new.

And, that we might live no longer for ourselves, but for him who died and rose for us, he sent the Holy Spirit, his own first gift for those who believe, to complete his work in the world, and to bring to fulfillment the sanctification of all.

At the following words concerning the bread, the Celebrant is to hold it, or lay a hand upon it; and at the words concerning the cup, to hold or place a hand upon the cup and any other vessel containing wine to be consecrated.

When the hour had come for him to be glorified by you, his heavenly Father, having loved his own who were in the world, he loved them to the end; at supper with them he took bread, and when he had given thanks to you, he broke it, and gave it to his disciples, and said, "Take, eat: This is my Body, which is given for you. Do this for the remembrance of me."

After supper he took the cup of wine; and when he had given thanks, he gave it to them, and said, "Drink this, all of you: This is my Blood of the new Covenant, which is shed for you and for many for the forgiveness of sins. Whenever you drink it, do this for the remembrance of me."

Father, we now celebrate this memorial of our redemption. Recalling Christ's death and his descent among the dead, proclaiming his resurrection and ascension to your right hand, awaiting his coming in glory; and offering to you, from the gifts you have given us, this bread and this cup, we praise you and we bless you.

We praise you, we bless you,
we give thanks to you,
and we pray to you, Lord our God.

The Celebrant continues

Lord, we pray that in your goodness and mercy your Holy
Spirit may descend upon us, and upon these gifts, sanctifying
them and showing them to be holy gifts for your holy people,
the bread of life and the cup of salvation, the Body and Blood
of your Son Jesus Christ.

Grant that all who share this bread and cup may become one
body and one spirit, a living sacrifice in Christ, to the praise
of your Name.

Remember, Lord, your one holy catholic and apostolic
Church, redeemed by the blood of your Christ. Reveal its
unity, guard its faith, and preserve it in peace.

[Remember (*NN*. and) all who minister in your Church.]
[Remember all your people, and those who seek your truth.]
[Remember _____.]
[Remember all who have died in the peace of Christ, and
those whose faith is known to you alone; bring them into
the place of eternal joy and light.]

And grant that we may find our inheritance with [the Blessed
Virgin Mary, with patriarchs, prophets, apostles, and martyrs,
(with_____) and] all the saints who have found favor
with you in ages past. We praise you in union with them
and give you glory through your Son Jesus Christ our Lord.

Through Christ, and with Christ, and in Christ, all honor and
glory are yours, Almighty God and Father, in the unity of the
Holy Spirit, for ever and ever. *AMEN.*

And now, as our Savior	As our Savior Christ
Christ has taught us,	has taught us,
we are bold to say,	we now pray,

Continue with the Lord's Prayer on page 364.

Offertory Sentences

One of the following, or some other appropriate sentence of Scripture, may be used

Offer to God a sacrifice of thanksgiving, and make good your vows to the Most High. *Psalm 50:14*

Ascribe to the Lord the honor due his Name; bring offerings and come into his courts. *Psalm 96:8*

Walk in love, as Christ loved us and gave himself for us, an offering and sacrifice to God. *Ephesians 5:2*

I appeal to you, brethren, by the mercies of God, to present yourselves as a living sacrifice, holy and acceptable to God, which is your spiritual worship. *Romans 12:1*

If you are offering your gift at the altar, and there remember that your brother has something against you, leave your gift there before the altar and go; first be reconciled to your brother, and then come and offer your gift. *Matthew 5:23, 24*

Through Christ let us continually offer to God the sacrifice of praise, that is, the fruit of lips that acknowledge his Name.

But do not neglect to do good and to share what you have, for such sacrifices are pleasing to God.   *Hebrews 13:15,16*

O Lord our God, you are worthy to receive glory and honor and power; because you have created all things, and by your will they were created and have their being.   *Revelation 4:11*

Yours, O Lord, is the greatness, the power, the glory, the victory, and the majesty. For everything in heaven and on earth is yours. Yours, O Lord, is the kingdom, and you are exalted as head over all.   *1 Chronicles 29:11*

or this bidding

Let us with gladness present the offerings and oblations of our life and labor to the Lord.

Proper Prefaces

Preface of the Lord's Day

To be used on Sundays as appointed, but not on the succeeding weekdays

1. Of God the Father

For you are the source of light and life, you made us in your image, and called us to new life in Jesus Christ our Lord.

or this

2. Of God the Son

Through Jesus Christ our Lord; who on the first day of the week overcame death and the grave, and by his glorious resurrection opened to us the way of everlasting life.

or the following

3. Of God the Holy Spirit

For by water and the Holy Spirit you have made us a new people in Jesus Christ our Lord, to show forth your glory in all the world.

Prefaces for Seasons

To be used on Sundays and weekdays alike, except as otherwise appointed for Holy Days and Various Occasions

Advent

Because you sent your beloved Son to redeem us from sin and death, and to make us heirs in him of everlasting life; that when he shall come again in power and great triumph to judge the world, we may without shame or fear rejoice to behold his appearing.

Incarnation

Because you gave Jesus Christ, your only Son, to be born for us; who, by the mighty power of the Holy Spirit, was made perfect Man of the flesh of the Virgin Mary his mother; so that we might be delivered from the bondage of sin, and receive power to become your children.

Epiphany

Because in the mystery of the Word made flesh, you have caused a new light to shine in our hearts, to give the knowledge of your glory in the face of your Son Jesus Christ our Lord.

Lent

Through Jesus Christ our Lord, who was tempted in every
way as we are, yet did not sin. By his grace we are able to
triumph over every evil, and to live no longer for ourselves
alone, but for him who died for us and rose again.

or this

You bid your faithful people cleanse their hearts, and prepare
with joy for the Paschal feast; that, fervent in prayer and in
works of mercy, and renewed by your Word and Sacraments,
they may come to the fullness of grace which you have
prepared for those who love you.

Holy Week

Through Jesus Christ our Lord. For our sins he was lifted
high upon the cross, that he might draw the whole world to
himself; and, by his suffering and death, he became the
source of eternal salvation for all who put their trust in him.

Easter

But chiefly are we bound to praise you for the glorious
resurrection of your Son Jesus Christ our Lord; for he is the
true Paschal Lamb, who was sacrificed for us, and has taken
away the sin of the world. By his death he has destroyed
death, and by his rising to life again he has won for us
everlasting life.

Ascension

Through your dearly beloved Son Jesus Christ our Lord.
After his glorious resurrection he openly appeared to his
disciples, and in their sight ascended into heaven, to prepare
a place for us; that where he is, there we might also be, and
reign with him in glory.

Pentecost

Through Jesus Christ our Lord. In fulfillment of his true
promise, the Holy Spirit came down [on this day] from
heaven, lighting upon the disciples, to teach them and to lead
them into all truth; uniting peoples of many tongues in the
confession of one faith, and giving to your Church the power
to serve you as a royal priesthood, and to preach the Gospel
to all nations.

Prefaces for Other Occasions

Trinity Sunday

For with your co-eternal Son and Holy Spirit, you are one
God, one Lord, in Trinity of Persons and in Unity of Being:
and we celebrate the one and equal glory of you, O Father,
and of the Son, and of the Holy Spirit.

All Saints

For in the multitude of your saints you have surrounded us
with a great cloud of witnesses, that we might rejoice in their
fellowship, and run with endurance the race that is set before
us; and, together with them, receive the crown of glory that
never fades away.

A Saint

For the wonderful grace and virtue declared in all your saints,
who have been the chosen vessels of your grace, and the lights
of the world in their generations.

or this

Because in the obedience of your saints you have given us an
example of righteousness, and in their eternal joy a glorious
pledge of the hope of our calling.

or this

Because you are greatly glorified in the assembly of your saints. All your creatures praise you, and your faithful servants bless you, confessing before the rulers of this world the great Name of your only Son.

Apostles and Ordinations

Through the great shepherd of your flock, Jesus Christ our Lord; who after his resurrection sent forth his apostles to preach the Gospel and to teach all nations; and promised to be with them always, even to the end of the ages.

Dedication of a Church

Through Jesus Christ our great High Priest; in whom we are built up as living stones of a holy temple, that we might offer before you a sacrifice of praise and prayer which is holy and pleasing in your sight.

Baptism

Because in Jesus Christ our Lord you have received us as your sons and daughters, made us citizens of your kingdom, and given us the Holy Spirit to guide us into all truth.

Marriage

Because in the love of wife and husband, you have given us an image of the heavenly Jerusalem, adorned as a bride for her bridegroom, your Son Jesus Christ our Lord; who loves her and gave himself for her, that he might make the whole creation new.

Commemoration of the Dead

Through Jesus Christ our Lord; who rose victorious from the dead, and comforts us with the blessed hope of everlasting life. For to your faithful people, O Lord, life is changed, not ended; and when our mortal body lies in death, there is prepared for us a dwelling place eternal in the heavens.

The Prayers of the People

Prayer is offered with intercession for

The Universal Church, its members, and its mission
The Nation and all in authority
The welfare of the world
The concerns of the local community
Those who suffer and those in any trouble
The departed (with commemoration of a saint when appropriate)

Any of the forms which follow may be used.

Adaptations or insertions suitable to the occasion may be made.

Any of the forms may be conformed to the language of the Rite being used.

A bar in the margin indicates petitions which may be omitted.

The Celebrant may introduce the Prayers with a sentence of invitation related to the occasion, or the season, or the Proper of the Day.

Form I

Deacon or other leader

With all our heart and with all our mind, let us pray to the Lord, saying, "Lord, have mercy."

For the peace from above, for the loving-kindness of God, and for the salvation of our souls, let us pray to the Lord. *Lord, have mercy.*

For the peace of the world, for the welfare of the holy Church of God, and for the unity of all peoples, let us pray to the Lord. *Lord, have mercy.*

For our Bishop, and for all the clergy and people, let us pray to the Lord.
Lord, have mercy.

For our President, for the leaders of the nations, and for all in authority, let us pray to the Lord.
Lord, have mercy.

For this city (town, village, _____), for every city and community, and for those who live in them, let us pray to the Lord.
Lord, have mercy.

For seasonable weather, and for an abundance of the fruits of the earth, let us pray to the Lord.
Lord, have mercy.

For the good earth which God has given us, and for the wisdom and will to conserve it, let us pray to the Lord.
Lord, have mercy.

For those who travel on land, on water, or in the air [or through outer space], let us pray to the Lord.
Lord, have mercy.

For the aged and infirm, for the widowed and orphans, and for the sick and the suffering, let us pray to the Lord.
Lord, have mercy.

For _____ , let us pray to the Lord.
Lord, have mercy.

For the poor and the oppressed, for the unemployed and the destitute, for prisoners and captives, and for all who remember and care for them, let us pray to the Lord.
Lord, have mercy.

For all who have died in the hope of the resurrection, and for all the departed, let us pray to the Lord.
Lord, have mercy.

For deliverance from all danger, violence, oppression, and degradation, let us pray to the Lord.
Lord, have mercy.

For the absolution and remission of our sins and offenses, let us pray to the Lord.
Lord, have mercy.

That we may end our lives in faith and hope, without suffering and without reproach, let us pray to the Lord.
Lord, have mercy.

Defend us, deliver us, and in thy compassion protect us, O Lord, by thy grace.
Lord, have mercy.

In the communion of [_____ and of all the] saints, let us commend ourselves, and one another, and all our life, to Christ our God.
To thee, O Lord our God.

Silence

The Celebrant adds a concluding Collect.

Form II

In the course of the silence after each bidding, the People offer their own prayers, either silently or aloud.

I ask your prayers for God's people throughout the world; for our Bishop(s) _____ ; for this gathering; and for all ministers and people.
Pray for the Church.

Silence

I ask your prayers for peace; for goodwill among nations; and for the well-being of all people.
Pray for justice and peace.

Silence

I ask your prayers for the poor, the sick, the hungry, the oppressed, and those in prison.
Pray for those in any need or trouble.

Silence

I ask your prayers for all who seek God, or a deeper knowledge of him.
Pray that they may find and be found by him.

Silence

I ask your prayers for the departed [especially _____].
Pray for those who have died.

Silence

Members of the congregation may ask the prayers or the thanksgivings of those present

I ask your prayers for _____ .

I ask your thanksgiving for _____ .

Silence

Praise God for those in every generation in whom Christ has been honored [especially _____ whom we remember today].
Pray that we may have grace to glorify Christ in our own day.

Silence

The Celebrant adds a concluding Collect.

Form III

The Leader and People pray responsively

Father, we pray for your holy Catholic Church;
That we all may be one.

Grant that every member of the Church may truly and
humbly serve you;
That your Name may be glorified by all people.

We pray for all bishops, priests, and deacons;
*That they may be faithful ministers of your Word and
Sacraments.*

We pray for all who govern and hold authority in the nations
of the world;
That there may be justice and peace on the earth.

Give us grace to do your will in all that we undertake;
That our works may find favor in your sight.

Have compassion on those who suffer from any grief or
trouble;
That they may be delivered from their distress.

Give to the departed eternal rest;
Let light perpetual shine upon them.

We praise you for your saints who have entered into joy;
May we also come to share in your heavenly kingdom.

Let us pray for our own needs and those of others.

Silence

The People may add their own petitions.

The Celebrant adds a concluding Collect.

Form IV

Deacon or other leader

Let us pray for the Church and for the world.

Grant, Almighty God, that all who confess your Name may be united in your truth, live together in your love, and reveal your glory in the world.

Silence

Lord, in your mercy
Hear our prayer.

Guide the people of this land, and of all the nations, in the ways of justice and peace; that we may honor one another and serve the common good.

Silence

Lord, in your mercy
Hear our prayer.

Give us all a reverence for the earth as your own creation, that we may use its resources rightly in the service of others and to your honor and glory.

Silence

Lord, in your mercy
Hear our prayer.

Bless all whose lives are closely linked with ours, and grant that we may serve Christ in them, and love one another as he loves us.

Silence

Lord, in your mercy
Hear our prayer.

Comfort and heal all those who suffer in body, mind, or
spirit; give them courage and hope in their troubles, and
bring them the joy of your salvation.

Silence

Lord, in your mercy
Hear our prayer.

We commend to your mercy all who have died, that your will
for them may be fulfilled; and we pray that we may share
with all your saints in your eternal kingdom.

Silence

Lord, in your mercy
Hear our prayer.

The Celebrant adds a concluding Collect.

Form V

Deacon or other leader

In peace, let us pray to the Lord, saying, "Lord, have mercy"
(*or* "Kyrie eleison").

For the holy Church of God, that it may be filled with truth
and love, and be found without fault at the day of your
coming, we pray to you, O Lord.

Here and after every petition the People respond

Kyrie eleison.   or   *Lord, have mercy.*

For *N.* our Presiding Bishop, for *N.* (*N.*) our own Bishop(s), for all bishops and other ministers, and for all the holy people of God, we pray to you, O Lord.

For all who fear God and believe in you, Lord Christ, that our divisions may cease, and that all may be one as you and the Father are one, we pray to you, O Lord.

For the mission of the Church, that in faithful witness it may preach the Gospel to the ends of the earth, we pray to you, O Lord.

For those who do not yet believe, and for those who have lost their faith, that they may receive the light of the Gospel, we pray to you, O Lord.

For the peace of the world, that a spirit of respect and forbearance may grow among nations and peoples, we pray to you, O Lord.

For those in positions of public trust [especially _____], that they may serve justice, and promote the dignity and freedom of every person, we pray to you, O Lord.

For all who live and work in this community [especially _____], we pray to you, O Lord.

For a blessing upon all human labor, and for the right use of the riches of creation, that the world may be freed from poverty, famine, and disaster, we pray to you, O Lord.

For the poor, the persecuted, the sick, and all who suffer; for refugees, prisoners, and all who are in danger; that they may be relieved and protected, we pray to you, O Lord.

For this *congregation* [for those who are present, and for those who are absent], that we may be delivered from hardness of heart, and show forth your glory in all that we do, we pray to you, O Lord.

For our enemies and those who wish us harm; and for all whom we have injured or offended, we pray to you, O Lord.

For ourselves; for the forgiveness of our sins, and for the grace of the Holy Spirit to amend our lives, we pray to you, O Lord.

For all who have commended themselves to our prayers; for our families, friends, and neighbors; that being freed from anxiety, they may live in joy, peace, and health, we pray to you, O Lord.

For _____ , we pray to you, O Lord.

For all who have died in the communion of your Church, and those whose faith is known to you alone, that, with all the saints, they may have rest in that place where there is no pain or grief, but life eternal, we pray to you, O Lord.

Rejoicing in the fellowship of [the ever-blessed Virgin Mary, (*blessed N.*) and] all the saints, let us commend ourselves, and one another, and all our life to Christ our God.
To you, O Lord our God.

Silence

The Celebrant adds a concluding Collect, or the following Doxology

For yours is the majesty, O Father, Son, and Holy Spirit; yours is the kingdom and the power and the glory, now and for ever. *Amen.*

Form VI

The Leader and People pray responsively

In peace, we pray to you, Lord God.

Silence

For all people in their daily life and work;
For our families, friends, and neighbors, and for those who are alone.

For this community, the nation, and the world;
For all who work for justice, freedom, and peace.

For the just and proper use of your creation;
For the victims of hunger, fear, injustice, and oppression.

For all who are in danger, sorrow, or any kind of trouble;
For those who minister to the sick, the friendless, and the needy.

For the peace and unity of the Church of God;
For all who proclaim the Gospel, and all who seek the Truth.

For [N. our Presiding Bishop, and N. (N.) our Bishop(s); and for] all bishops and other ministers;
For all who serve God in his Church.

For the special needs and concerns of this congregation.

Silence

The People may add their own petitions

Hear us, Lord;
For your mercy is great.

We thank you, Lord, for all the blessings of this life.

Silence

The People may add their own thanksgivings

We will exalt you, O God our King;
And praise your Name for ever and ever.

We pray for all who have died, that they may have a place in your eternal kingdom.

Silence

The People may add their own petitions

Lord, let your loving-kindness be upon them;
Who put their trust in you.

We pray to you also for the forgiveness of our sins.

Silence may be kept.

Leader and People

Have mercy upon us, most merciful Father;
in your compassion forgive us our sins,
known and unknown,
things done and left undone;
and so uphold us by your Spirit
that we may live and serve you in newness of life,
to the honor and glory of your Name;
through Jesus Christ our Lord. Amen.

The Celebrant concludes with an absolution or a suitable Collect.

The Collect at the Prayers

For the concluding Collect, the Celebrant selects

(a) a Collect appropriate to the season or occasion being celebrated;

(b) a Collect expressive of some special need in the life of the local congregation;

(c) a Collect for the mission of the Church;

(d) a general Collect such as the following:

1

Lord, hear the prayers of *thy* people; and what we have asked faithfully, grant that we may obtain effectually, to the glory of *thy* Name; through Jesus Christ our Lord. *Amen.*

2

Heavenly Father, you have promised to hear what we ask in the Name of your Son: Accept and fulfill our petitions, we pray, not as we ask in our ignorance, nor as we deserve in our sinfulness, but as you know and love us in your Son Jesus Christ our Lord. *Amen.*

3

Almighty and eternal God, ruler of all things in heaven and earth: Mercifully accept the prayers of your people, and strengthen us to do your will; through Jesus Christ our Lord. *Amen.*

4

Almighty God, to whom our needs are known before we ask: Help us to ask only what accords with your will; and those good things which we dare not, or in our blindness cannot ask, grant us for the sake of your Son Jesus Christ our Lord. *Amen.*

5

O Lord our God, accept the fervent prayers of your people; in the multitude of your mercies, look with compassion upon us and all who turn to you for help; for you are gracious, O lover of souls, and to you we give glory, Father, Son, and Holy Spirit, now and for ever. *Amen.*

6

Lord Jesus Christ, you said to your apostles,"Peace I give to you; my own peace I leave with you:" Regard not our sins, but the faith of your Church, and give to us the peace and unity of that heavenly City, where with the Father and the Holy Spirit you live and reign, now and for ever. *Amen.*

7

Hasten, O Father, the coming of *thy* kingdom; and grant that we *thy* servants, who now live by faith, may with joy behold *thy* Son at his coming in glorious majesty; even Jesus Christ, our only Mediator and Advocate. *Amen.*

8

Almighty God, by your Holy Spirit you have made us one with your saints in heaven and on earth: Grant that in our earthly pilgrimage we may always be supported by this fellowship of love and prayer, and know ourselves to be surrounded by their witness to your power and mercy. We ask this for the sake of Jesus Christ, in whom all our intercessions are acceptable through the Spirit, and who lives and reigns for ever and ever. *Amen.*

Communion under
Special Circumstances

This form is intended for use with those who for reasonable cause cannot be present at a public celebration of the Eucharist.

When persons are unable to be present for extended periods, it is desirable that the priest arrange to celebrate the Eucharist with them from time to time on a regular basis, using either the Proper of the Day or one of those appointed for Various Occasions. If it is necessary to shorten the service, the priest may begin the celebration at the Offertory, but it is desirable that a passage from the Gospel first be read.

At other times, or when desired, such persons may be communicated from the reserved Sacrament, using the following form.

It is desirable that fellow parishioners, relatives, and friends be present, when possible, to communicate with them.

The Celebrant, whether priest or deacon, reads a passage of Scripture appropriate to the day or occasion, or else one of the following

God so loved the world that he gave his only Son, that whoever believes in him should not perish, but have eternal life.   *John 3:16*

Jesus said, "I am the bread of life; whoever comes to me shall not hunger, and whoever believes in me shall never thirst." *John 6:35*

Jesus said, "I am the living bread which came down from heaven; if anyone eats of this bread, he will live for ever; and the bread which I shall give for the life of the world is my flesh. For my flesh is food indeed, and my blood is drink indeed. Whoever eats my flesh and drinks my blood abides in me, and I in him." *John 6:51,55-56*

Jesus said, "Abide in me, as I in you. As the branch cannot bear fruit by itself, unless it abides in the vine, neither can you, unless you abide in me. I am the vine, you are the branches. By this my Father is glorified, that you bear much fruit, and so prove to be my disciples. As the Father has loved me, so have I loved you; abide in my love." *John 15:4-5a,8-9*

After the Reading, the Celebrant may comment on it briefly.

Suitable prayers may be offered, concluding with the following or some other Collect

Almighty Father, whose dear Son, on the night before he suffered, instituted the Sacrament of his Body and Blood: Mercifully grant that we may receive it thankfully in remembrance of Jesus Christ our Lord, who in these holy mysteries gives us a pledge of eternal life; and who lives and reigns for ever and ever. *Amen.*

A Confession of Sin may follow. The following or some other form is used

Most merciful God,
we confess that we have sinned against you
in thought, word, and deed,
by what we have done,
and by what we have left undone.
We have not loved you with our whole heart;
we have not loved our neighbors as ourselves.

We are truly sorry and we humbly repent.
For the sake of your Son Jesus Christ,
have mercy on us and forgive us;
that we may delight in your will,
and walk in your ways,
to the glory of your Name. Amen.

The Priest alone says

Almighty God have mercy on you, forgive you all your sins
through our Lord Jesus Christ, strengthen you in all
goodness, and by the power of the Holy Spirit keep you in
eternal life. *Amen.*

*A deacon using the preceding form substitutes "us" for "you" and "our"
for "your."*

The Peace may then be exchanged.

The Lord's Prayer is said, the Celebrant first saying

Let us pray in the words our Savior Christ has taught us.

Our Father, who art in heaven,
    hallowed be thy Name,
    thy kingdom come,
    thy will be done,
        on earth as it is in heaven.
Give us this day our daily bread.
And forgive us our trespasses,
    as we forgive those
        who trespass against us.
And lead us not into temptation,
    but deliver us from evil.
For thine is the kingdom,
    and the power, and the glory,
    for ever and ever. Amen.
	Our Father in heaven,
	    hallowed be your Name,
	    your kingdom come,
	    your will be done,
	        on earth as in heaven.
	Give us today our daily bread.
	Forgive us our sins
	    as we forgive those
	        who sin against us.
	Save us from the time of trial,
	    and deliver us from evil.
	For the kingdom, the power,
	    and the glory are yours,
	    now and for ever. Amen.

The Celebrant may say the following Invitation

The Gifts of God for the People of God.

and may add   Take them in remembrance that Christ died for
you, and feed on him in your hearts by faith,
with thanksgiving.

The Sacrament is administered with the following or other words

The Body (Blood) of our Lord Jesus Christ keep you in
everlasting life. [*Amen.*]

One of the usual postcommunion prayers is then said, or the following

Gracious Father, we give you praise and thanks for this Holy
Communion of the Body and Blood of your beloved Son
Jesus Christ, the pledge of our redemption; and we pray that
it may bring us forgiveness of our sins, strength in our
weakness, and everlasting salvation; through Jesus Christ
our Lord. *Amen.*

The service concludes with a blessing or with a dismissal

Let us bless the Lord.
Thanks be to God.

An Order for Celebrating the Holy Eucharist

This rite requires careful preparation by the Priest and other participants.

It is not intended for use at the principal Sunday or weekly celebration of the Holy Eucharist.

The People and Priest

Gather in the Lord's Name

Proclaim and Respond to the Word of God

The proclamation and response may include readings, song, talk, dance, instrumental music, other art forms, silence. A reading from the Gospel is always included.

Pray for the World and the Church

Exchange the Peace

Either here or elsewhere in the service, all greet one another in the name of the Lord.

Prepare the Table

Some of those present prepare the table; the bread, the cup of wine, and other offerings, are placed upon it.

Make Eucharist

The Great Thanksgiving is said by the Priest in the name of the gathering, using one of the eucharistic prayers provided.

The people respond—Amen!

Break the Bread

Share the Gifts of God

The Body and Blood of the Lord are shared in a reverent manner; after all have received, any of the Sacrament that remains is then consumed.

When a common meal or Agapé is a part of the celebration, it follows here.

At the Great Thanksgiving

*In making Eucharist, the Celebrant uses one of the Eucharistic Prayers
from Rite One or Rite Two, or one of the following forms*

Form 1

Celebrant	The Lord be with you.
People	And also with you.
Celebrant	Lift up your hearts.
People	We lift them to the Lord.
Celebrant	Let us give thanks to the Lord our God.
People	It is right to give him thanks and praise.

*The Celebrant gives thanks to God the Father for his work in creation
and his revelation of himself to his people;*

*Recalls before God, when appropriate, the particular occasion being
celebrated;*

Incorporates or adapts the Proper Preface of the day, if desired.

*If the Sanctus is to be included, it is introduced with these or similar
words*

And so we join the saints and angels in proclaiming your
glory, as we sing (say),

Celebrant and People

Holy, holy, holy Lord, God of power and might,
heaven and earth are full of your glory.
   Hosanna in the highest.
Blessed is he who comes in the name of the Lord.
   Hosanna in the highest.

The Celebrant now praises God for the salvation of the world through Jesus Christ our Lord.

The Prayer continues with these words

And so, Father, we bring you these gifts. Sanctify them by your Holy Spirit to be for your people the Body and Blood of Jesus Christ our Lord.

At the following words concerning the bread, the Celebrant is to hold it, or lay a hand upon it; and at the words concerning the cup, to hold or place a hand upon the cup and any other vessel containing wine to be consecrated.

On the night he was betrayed he took bread, said the blessing, broke the bread, and gave it to his friends, and said,"Take, eat: This is my Body, which is given for you. Do this for the remembrance of me."

After supper, he took the cup of wine, gave thanks, and said, "Drink this, all of you; This is my Blood of the new Covenant, which is shed for you and for many for the forgiveness of sins. Whenever you drink it, do this for the remembrance of me."

Father, we now celebrate the memorial of your Son. By means of this holy bread and cup, we show forth the sacrifice of his death, and proclaim his resurrection, until he comes again.

Gather us by this Holy Communion into one body in your Son Jesus Christ. Make us a living sacrifice of praise.

By him, and with him, and in him, in the unity of the Holy Spirit all honor and glory is yours, Almighty Father, now and for ever. *AMEN.*

Form 2

Celebrant	The grace of our Lord Jesus Christ and the love of God and the fellowship of the Holy Spirit be with you all.
People	And also with you.
Celebrant	Lift up your hearts.
People	We lift them to the Lord.
Celebrant	Let us give thanks to the Lord our God.
People	It is right to give him thanks and praise.

The Celebrant gives thanks to God the Father for his work in creation and his revelation of himself to his people;

Recalls before God, when appropriate, the particular occasion being celebrated;

Incorporates or adapts the Proper Preface of the day, if desired.

If the Sanctus is to be included, it is introduced with these or similar words

And so we join the saints and angels in proclaiming your glory, as we sing (say),

Celebrant and People

Holy, holy, holy Lord, God of power and might,
heaven and earth are full of your glory.
   Hosanna in the highest.
Blessed is he who comes in the name of the Lord.
   Hosanna in the highest.

The Celebrant now praises God for the salvation of the world through Jesus Christ our Lord.

404   *Order for Eucharist*

At the following words concerning the bread, the Celebrant is to hold it, or lay a hand upon it; and at the words concerning the cup, to hold or place a hand upon the cup and any other vessel containing wine to be consecrated.

On the night he was handed over to suffering and death, our Lord Jesus Christ took bread; and when he had given thanks to you, he broke it, and gave it to his disciples, and said, "Take, eat: This is my Body, which is given for you. Do this for the remembrance of me."

After supper he took the cup of wine; and when he had given thanks, he gave it to them, and said, "Drink this, all of you: This is my Blood of the new Covenant, which is shed for you and for many for the forgiveness of sins. Whenever you drink it, do this for the remembrance of me."

Recalling now his suffering and death, and celebrating his resurrection and ascension, we await his coming in glory.

Accept, O Lord, our sacrifice of praise, this memorial of our redemption.

Send your Holy Spirit upon these gifts. Let them be for us the Body and Blood of your Son. And grant that we who eat this bread and drink this cup may be filled with your life and goodness.

The Celebrant then prays that all may receive the benefits of Christ's work, and the renewal of the Holy Spirit.

The Prayer concludes with these or similar words

All this we ask through your Son Jesus Christ. By him, and with him, and in him, in the unity of the Holy Spirit all honor and glory is yours, Almighty Father, now and for ever. *AMEN.*

Additional Directions

The Holy Table is spread with a clean white cloth during the celebration.

When the Great Litany is sung or said immediately before the Eucharist, the Litany concludes with the Kyries, and the Eucharist begins with the Salutation and the Collect of the Day. The Prayers of the People following the Creed may be omitted.

When a psalm is used, it may be concluded with Gloria Patri. In Rite One services, the following form of the Gloria may be used:

Glory be to the Father, and to the Son, *
   and to the Holy Ghost:

As it was in the beginning, is now, and ever shall be, *
   world without end. Amen.

The Kyrie eleison (or "Lord, have mercy") may be sung or said in threefold, sixfold, or ninefold form. The Trisagion, "Holy God," may be sung or said three times, or antiphonally.

Gloria in excelsis, or the hymn used in place of it, is sung or said from Christmas Day through the Feast of the Epiphany; on Sundays from Easter Day through the Day of Pentecost, on all the days of Easter Week, and on Ascension Day; and at other times as desired; but it is not used on the Sundays or ordinary weekdays of Advent or Lent.

It is desirable that the Lessons be read from a lectern or pulpit, and that the Gospel be read from the same lectern, or from the pulpit, or from the midst of the congregation. It is desirable that the Lessons and Gospel be read from a book or books of appropriate size and dignity.

When a portion of the congregation is composed of persons whose native tongue is other than English, a reader appointed by the celebrant may read the Gospel in the language of the people, either in place of, or in addition to, the Gospel in English.

If there is no Communion, all that is appointed through the Prayers of the People may be said. (If it is desired to include a Confession of Sin, the service begins with the Penitential Order.) A hymn or anthem may then be sung, and the offerings of the people received. The service may then conclude with the Lord's Prayer; and with either the Grace or a blessing, or with the exchange of the Peace.

In the absence of a priest, all that is described above, except for the blessing, may be said by a deacon, or, if there is no deacon, by a lay reader.

The greeting, "The peace of the Lord be always with you," is addressed to the entire assembly. In the exchange between individuals which may follow, any appropriate words of greeting may be used. If preferred, the exchange of the Peace may take place at the time of the administration of the Sacrament (before or after the sentence of Invitation).

Necessary announcements may be made before the service, after the Creed, before the Offertory, or at the end of the service, as convenient.

It is the function of a deacon to make ready the Table for the celebration, preparing and placing upon it the bread and cup of wine. It is customary to add a little water to the wine. The deacon may be assisted by other ministers.

During the Great Thanksgiving, it is appropriate that there be only one chalice on the Altar, and, if need be, a flagon of wine from which additional chalices may be filled after the Breaking of the Bread.

The following anthem may be used at the Breaking of the Bread:

Lamb of God, you take away the sins of the world:
      have mercy on us.
Lamb of God, you take away the sins of the world:
      have mercy on us.
Lamb of God, you take away the sins of the world:
      grant us peace.

While the people are coming forward to receive Communion, the celebrant receives the Sacrament in both kinds. The bishops, priests, and deacons at the Holy Table then communicate, and after them the people.

Opportunity is always to be given to every communicant to receive the consecrated Bread and Wine separately. But the Sacrament may be received in both kinds simultaneously, in a manner approved by the bishop.

When the celebrant is assisted by a deacon or another priest, it is customary for the celebrant to administer the consecrated Bread and the assistant the Chalice. When several deacons or priests are present, some may administer the Bread and others the Wine. In the absence of sufficient deacons and priests, lay persons licensed by the bishop according to the canon may administer the Chalice.

If the consecrated Bread or Wine does not suffice for the number of communicants, the celebrant is to return to the Holy Table, and consecrate more of either or both, by saying

Hear us, O heavenly Father, and with thy (your) Word and Holy Spirit bless and sanctify this bread (wine) that it, also, may be the Sacrament of the precious Body (Blood) of thy (your) Son Jesus Christ our Lord, who took bread (the cup) and said, "This is my Body (Blood)." *Amen.*

or else the celebrant may consecrate more of both kinds, saying again the words of the Eucharistic Prayer, beginning with the words which follow the Sanctus, and ending with the Invocation (in the case of Eucharistic Prayer C, ending with the narrative of the Institution).

When the services of a priest cannot be obtained, the bishop may, at discretion, authorize a deacon to distribute Holy Communion to the congregation from the reserved Sacrament in the following manner:

1. After the Liturgy of the Word (and the receiving of the people's offering), the deacon reverently places the consecrated Sacrament on the Altar, during which time a communion hymn may be sung.

2. The Lord's Prayer is then said, the deacon first saying, "Let us pray in the words our Savior Christ hath (has) taught us."

3. And then, omitting the breaking of the Bread, the deacon proceeds with what follows in the liturgy as far as the end of the postcommunion prayer, and then dismisses the people.

If any of the consecrated Bread or Wine remain, apart from any which may be required for the Communion of the sick, or of others who for weighty cause could not be present at the celebration, or for the administration of Communion by a deacon to a congregation when no priest is available, the celebrant or deacon, and other communicants, reverently eat and drink it, either after the Communion of the people or after the Dismissal.

A hymn may be sung before or after the postcommunion prayer.

Disciplinary Rubrics

If the priest knows that a person who is living a notoriously evil life intends to come to Communion, the priest shall speak to that person privately, and tell *him* that *he* may not come to the Holy Table until *he* has given clear proof of repentance and amendment of life.

The priest shall follow the same procedure with those who have done wrong to their neighbors and are a scandal to the other members of the congregation, not allowing such persons to receive Communion until they have made restitution for the wrong they have done, or have at least promised to do so.

When the priest sees that there is hatred between members of the congregation, *he* shall speak privately to each of them, telling them that they may not receive Communion until they have forgiven each other. And if the person or persons on one side truly forgive the others and desire and promise to make up for their faults, but those on the other side refuse to forgive, the priest shall allow those who are penitent to come to Communion, but not those who are stubborn.

In all such cases, the priest is required to notify the bishop, within fourteen days at the most, giving the reasons for refusing Communion.

Pastoral Offices

Concerning the Service

In the course of their Christian development, those baptized at an early age are expected, when they are ready and have been duly prepared, to make a mature public affirmation of their faith and commitment to the responsibilities of their Baptism and to receive the laying on of hands by the bishop.

Those baptized as adults, unless baptized with laying on of hands by a bishop, are also expected to make a public affirmation of their faith and commitment to the responsibilities of their Baptism in the presence of a bishop and to receive the laying on of hands.

When there is no Baptism, the rites of Confirmation, Reception, and the Reaffirmation of Baptismal Vows are administered in the following form.

If desired, the hymn Gloria in excelsis may be sung immediately after the opening versicles and before the salutation "The Lord be with you."

The Nicene Creed is not used at this service.

It is appropriate that the oblations of bread and wine be presented by persons newly confirmed.

Confirmation
with forms for Reception and for
the Reaffirmation of Baptismal Vows

A hymn, psalm, or anthem may be sung.

The people standing, the Bishop says

        Blessed be God: Father, Son, and Holy Spirit.
People   And blessed be his kingdom, now and for ever. Amen.

In place of the above, from Easter Day through the Day of Pentecost

        Alleluia. Christ is risen.
People   The Lord is risen indeed. Alleluia.

In Lent and on other penitential occasions

Bishop   Bless the Lord who forgives all our sins.
People   His mercy endures for ever.

The Bishop then continues

        There is one Body and one Spirit;
People   There is one hope in God's call to us;
Bishop   One Lord, one Faith, one Baptism;
People   One God and Father of all.

Bishop   The Lord be with you.
People   And also with you.
Bishop   Let us pray.

The Collect of the Day

People   **Amen.**

At the principal service on a Sunday or other feast, the Collect and Lessons are properly those of the Day. At the discretion of the bishop, however, the Collect (page 203 or 254) and one or more of the Lessons provided "At Confirmation" (page 929) may be substituted.

The Lessons

The people sit. One or two Lessons, as appointed, are read, the Reader first saying

A Reading (Lesson) from _____.

A citation giving chapter and verse may be added.

After each Reading the Reader may say

    The Word of the Lord.
People   Thanks be to God.

or the Reader may say   Here ends the Reading (Epistle).

Silence may follow.

A Psalm, hymn, or anthem may follow each Reading.

Then, all standing, the Deacon or a Priest reads the Gospel, first saying

    The Holy Gospel of our Lord Jesus Christ
    according to _____.
People   Glory to you, Lord Christ.

         The Gospel of the Lord.

People   Praise to you, Lord Christ.

The Sermon

Presentation and Examination of the Candidates

The Bishop says

The Candidate(s) will now be presented.

Presenters I present *these persons* for Confirmation.

or   I present *these persons* to be received into this Communion.

or   I present *these persons* who *desire* to reaffirm *their* baptismal vows.

The Bishop asks the candidates

Do you reaffirm your renunciation of evil?

Candidate I do.

Bishop

Do you renew your commitment to Jesus Christ?

Candidate

I do, and with God's grace I will follow him as my Savior and Lord.

After all have been presented, the Bishop addresses the congregation, saying

Will you who witness these vows do all in your power to support *these persons* in *their* life in Christ?

People   We will.

The Bishop then says these or similar words

Let us join with *those* who *are* committing *themselves* to Christ and renew our own baptismal covenant.

The Baptismal Covenant

Bishop	Do you believe in God the Father?
People	I believe in God, the Father almighty, creator of heaven and earth.
Bishop	Do you believe in Jesus Christ, the Son of God?

People	I believe in Jesus Christ, his only Son, our Lord.
	     He was conceived by the power of the Holy Spirit
	         and born of the Virgin Mary.
	     He suffered under Pontius Pilate,
	         was crucified, died, and was buried.
	     He descended to the dead.
	     On the third day he rose again.
	     He ascended into heaven,
	         and is seated at the right hand of the Father.
	     He will come again to judge the living and the dead.

Bishop	Do you believe in God the Holy Spirit?

People	I believe in the Holy Spirit,
	     the holy catholic Church,
	     the communion of saints,

the forgiveness of sins,
the resurrection of the body,
and the life everlasting.

Bishop	Will you continue in the apostles' teaching and fellowship, in the breaking of bread, and in the prayers?
People	I will, with God's help.
Bishop	Will you persevere in resisting evil, and, whenever you fall into sin, repent and return to the Lord?
People	I will, with God's help.
Bishop	Will you proclaim by word and example the Good News of God in Christ?
People	I will, with God's help.
Bishop	Will you seek and serve Christ in all persons, loving your neighbor as yourself?
People	I will, with God's help.
Bishop	Will you strive for justice and peace among all people, and respect the dignity of every human being?
People	I will, with God's help.

Prayers for the Candidates

The Bishop then says to the congregation

Let us now pray for *these persons* who *have* renewed *their* commitment to Christ.

The petitions on pages 305-306 may be used.

A period of silence follows.

Then the Bishop says

Almighty God, we thank you that by the death and resurrection of your Son Jesus Christ you have overcome sin and brought us to yourself, and that by the sealing of your Holy Spirit you have bound us to your service. Renew in *these* your *servants* the covenant you made with *them* at *their* Baptism. Send *them* forth in the power of that Spirit to perform the service you set before *them*; through Jesus Christ your Son our Lord, who lives and reigns with you and the Holy Spirit, one God, now and for ever. *Amen.*

For Confirmation

The Bishop lays hands upon each one and says

Strengthen, O Lord, your servant N. with your Holy Spirit; empower *him* for your service; and sustain *him* all the days of *his* life. *Amen.*

or this

Defend, O Lord, your servant N. with your heavenly grace, that *he* may continue yours for ever, and daily increase in your Holy Spirit more and more, until *he* comes to your everlasting kingdom. *Amen.*

For Reception

N., we recognize you as a member of the one holy catholic and apostolic Church, and we receive you into the fellowship of this Communion. God, the Father, Son, and Holy Spirit, bless, preserve, and keep you. *Amen.*

For Reaffirmation

N., may the Holy Spirit, who has begun a good work in you, direct and uphold you in the service of Christ and his kingdom. *Amen.*

The Bishop concludes with this prayer

Almighty and everliving God, let your fatherly hand ever be over *these* your *servants*; let your Holy Spirit ever be with *them*; and so lead *them* in the knowledge and obedience of your Word, that *they* may serve you in this life, and dwell with you in the life to come; through Jesus Christ our Lord. *Amen.*

The Peace is then exchanged

Bishop The peace of the Lord be always with you.
People And also with you.

The service then continues with the Prayers of the People or the Offertory of the Eucharist, at which the bishop should be the principal celebrant.

If there is no celebration of the Eucharist, the service continues with the Lord's Prayer and such other devotions as the bishop may direct.

The bishop may consecrate oil of Chrism for use at Baptism, using the prayer on page 307.

A Form of Commitment
to Christian Service

*This form may be used when a person wishes to make or renew a
commitment to the service of Christ in the world, either in general terms,
or upon undertaking some special responsibility.*

*It is essential that the person seeking to make or renew a commitment
prepare in advance, in consultation with the celebrant, the Act of
Commitment, which may be in the form either of a statement of intention
or of a series of questions and answers, but which should include a
reaffirmation of baptismal promises.*

*Before the Offertory of the Eucharist, the person comes forward at the
invitation of the celebrant, and, standing before the congregation, makes
the Act of Commitment.*

After this, the Celebrant says these or similar words

May the Holy Spirit guide and strengthen you, that in this,
and in all things, you may do God's will in the service of the
kingdom of his Christ. *Amen.*

In the name of this congregation I commend you to this
work, and pledge you our prayers, encouragement, and
support.

The Celebrant then says this or some other appropriate prayer

Let us pray.

Almighty God, look with favor upon *this person* who *has* now reaffirmed *his* commitment to follow Christ and to serve in his name. Give *him* courage, patience, and vision; and strengthen us all in our Christian vocation of witness to the world, and of service to others; through Jesus Christ our Lord. *Amen.*

A prayer for the special work in which the person will be engaged may be added.

The service then continues with the exchange of the Peace and the Offertory.

Concerning the Service

Christian marriage is a solemn and public covenant between a man and a woman in the presence of God. In the Episcopal Church it is required that one, at least, of the parties must be a baptized Christian; that the ceremony be attested by at least two witnesses; and that the marriage conform to the laws of the State and the canons of this Church.

A priest or a bishop normally presides at the Celebration and Blessing of a Marriage, because such ministers alone have the function of pronouncing the nuptial blessing, and of celebrating the Holy Eucharist.

When both a bishop and a priest are present and officiating, the bishop should pronounce the blessing and preside at the Eucharist.

A deacon, or an assisting priest, may deliver the charge, ask for the Declaration of Consent, read the Gospel, and perform other assisting functions at the Eucharist.

Where it is permitted by civil law that deacons may perform marriages, and no priest or bishop is available, a deacon may use the service which follows, omitting the nuptial blessing which follows The Prayers.

It is desirable that the Lessons from the Old Testament and the Epistles be read by lay persons.

In the opening exhortation (at the symbol of *N.N.*), the full names of the persons to be married are declared. Subsequently, only their Christian names are used.

Additional Directions are on page 437.

The Celebration and Blessing of a Marriage

*At the time appointed, the persons to be married, with their witnesses,
assemble in the church or some other appropriate place.*

*During their entrance, a hymn, psalm, or anthem may be sung,
or instrumental music may be played.*

*Then the Celebrant, facing the people and the persons to be married,
with the woman to the right and the man to the left, addresses the
congregation and says*

Dearly beloved: We have come together in the presence of
God to witness and bless the joining together of this man and
this woman in Holy Matrimony. The bond and covenant of
marriage was established by God in creation, and our Lord
Jesus Christ adorned this manner of life by his presence and
first miracle at a wedding in Cana of Galilee. It signifies to us
the mystery of the union between Christ and his Church, and
Holy Scripture commends it to be honored among all people.

The union of husband and wife in heart, body, and mind is
intended by God for their mutual joy; for the help and comfort
given one another in prosperity and adversity; and, when it is
God's will, for the procreation of children and their nurture
in the knowledge and love of the Lord. Therefore marriage is
not to be entered into unadvisedly or lightly, but reverently,
deliberately, and in accordance with the purposes for which it
was instituted by God.

Into this holy union *N.N.* and *N.N.* now come to be joined. If any of you can show just cause why they may not lawfully be married, speak now; or else for ever hold your peace.

Then the Celebrant says to the persons to be married

I require and charge you both, here in the presence of God, that if either of you know any reason why you may not be united in marriage lawfully, and in accordance with God's Word, you do now confess it.

The Declaration of Consent

The Celebrant says to the woman

N., will you have this man to be your husband; to live together in the covenant of marriage? Will you love him, comfort him, honor and keep him, in sickness and in health; and, forsaking all others, be faithful to him as long as you both shall live?

The Woman answers

I will.

The Celebrant says to the man

N., will you have this woman to be your wife; to live together in the covenant of marriage? Will you love her, comfort her, honor and keep her, in sickness and in health; and, forsaking all others, be faithful to her as long as you both shall live?

The Man answers

I will.

The Celebrant then addresses the congregation, saying

Will all of you witnessing these promises do all in your power to uphold these two persons in their marriage?

People   We will.

*If there is to be a presentation or a giving in marriage,
it takes place at this time. See page 437.*

A hymn, psalm, or anthem may follow.

The Ministry of the Word

The Celebrant then says to the people

The Lord be with you.
People   And also with you.

Let us pray.

O gracious and everliving God, you have created us male and female in your image: Look mercifully upon this man and this woman who come to you seeking your blessing, and assist them with your grace, that with true fidelity and steadfast love they may honor and keep the promises and vows they make; through Jesus Christ our Savior, who lives and reigns with you in the unity of the Holy Spirit, one God, for ever and ever. *Amen.*

Then one or more of the following passages from Holy Scripture is read. If there is to be a Communion, a passage from the Gospel always concludes the Readings.

Genesis 1:26-28 (Male and female he created them)
Genesis 2:4-9, 15-24 (A man cleaves to his wife and they become one flesh)
Song of Solomon 2:10-13; 8:6-7 (Many waters cannot quench love)
Tobit 8:5b-8 (*New English Bible*) (That she and I may grow old together)

1 Corinthians 13:1-13 (Love is patient and kind)
Ephesians 3:14-19 (The Father from whom every family is named)
Ephesians 5:1-2, 21-33 (Walk in love, as Christ loved us)
Colossians 3:12-17 (Love which binds everything together in harmony)
1 John 4:7-16 (Let us love one another for love is of God)

Between the Readings, a Psalm, hymn, or anthem may be sung or said. Appropriate Psalms are 67, 127, and 128.

When a passage from the Gospel is to be read, all stand, and the Deacon or Minister appointed says

> The Holy Gospel of our Lord Jesus Christ according to _____.

People Glory to you, Lord Christ.

Matthew 5:1-10 (The Beatitudes)
Matthew 5:13-16 (You are the light . . . Let your light so shine)
Matthew 7:21, 24-29 (Like a wise man who built his house upon the rock)
Mark 10:6-9, 13-16 (They are no longer two but one)
John 15:9-12 (Love one another as I have loved you)

After the Gospel, the Reader says

> The Gospel of the Lord.

People Praise to you, Lord Christ.

A homily or other response to the Readings may follow.

The Marriage

The Man, facing the woman and taking her right hand in his, says

In the Name of God, I, N., take you, N., to be my wife, to have and to hold from this day forward, for better for worse, for richer for poorer, in sickness and in health, to love and to cherish, until we are parted by death. This is my solemn vow.

Then they loose their hands, and the Woman, still facing the man, takes his right hand in hers, and says

In the Name of God, I, N., take you, N., to be my husband, to have and to hold from this day forward, for better for worse, for richer for poorer, in sickness and in health, to love and to cherish, until we are parted by death. This is my solemn vow.

They loose their hands.

The Priest may ask God's blessing on a ring or rings as follows

Bless, O Lord, *this ring* to be *a sign* of the vows by which this man and this woman have bound themselves to each other; through Jesus Christ our Lord. *Amen.*

The giver places the ring on the ring-finger of the other's hand and says

N., I give you this ring as a symbol of my vow, and with all that I am, and all that I have, I honor you, in the Name of the Father, and of the Son, and of the Holy Spirit (*or* in the Name of God).

Then the Celebrant joins the right hands of husband and wife and says

Now that N. and N. have given themselves to each other by solemn vows, with the joining of hands and the giving and receiving of *a ring*, I pronounce that they are husband and wife, in the Name of the Father, and of the Son, and of the Holy Spirit.

Those whom God has joined together let no one put asunder.

People   Amen.

The Prayers

All standing, the Celebrant says

Let us pray together in the words our Savior taught us.

People and Celebrant

Our Father, who art in heaven,
    hallowed be thy Name,
    thy kingdom come,
    thy will be done,
        on earth as it is in heaven.
Give us this day our daily bread.
And forgive us our trespasses,
    as we forgive those
        who trespass against us.
And lead us not into temptation,
    but deliver us from evil.
For thine is the kingdom,
    and the power, and the glory,
    for ever and ever. Amen.
	Our Father in heaven,
	    hallowed be your Name,
	    your kingdom come,
	    your will be done,
	        on earth as in heaven.
	Give us today our daily bread.
	Forgive us our sins
	    as we forgive those
	        who sin against us.
	Save us from the time of trial,
	    and deliver us from evil.
	For the kingdom, the power,
	    and the glory are yours,
	    now and for ever. Amen.

If Communion is to follow, the Lord's Prayer may be omitted here.

The Deacon or other person appointed reads the following prayers, to which the People respond, saying, Amen.

If there is not to be a Communion, one or more of the prayers may be omitted.

Let us pray.

Eternal God, creator and preserver of all life, author of salvation, and giver of all grace: Look with favor upon the world you have made, and for which your Son gave his life, and especially upon this man and this woman whom you make one flesh in Holy Matrimony. *Amen.*

Give them wisdom and devotion in the ordering of their common life, that each may be to the other a strength in need, a counselor in perplexity, a comfort in sorrow, and a companion in joy. *Amen.*

Grant that their wills may be so knit together in your will, and their spirits in your Spirit, that they may grow in love and peace with you and one another all the days of their life. *Amen.*

Give them grace, when they hurt each other, to recognize and acknowledge their fault, and to seek each other's forgiveness and yours. *Amen.*

Make their life together a sign of Christ's love to this sinful and broken world, that unity may overcome estrangement, forgiveness heal guilt, and joy conquer despair. *Amen.*

Bestow on them, if it is your will, the gift and heritage of children, and the grace to bring them up to know you, to love you, and to serve you. *Amen.*

Give them such fulfillment of their mutual affection that they may reach out in love and concern for others. *Amen.*

Grant that all married persons who have witnessed these vows may find their lives strengthened and their loyalties confirmed. *Amen.*

Grant that the bonds of our common humanity, by which all your children are united one to another, and the living to the dead, may be so transformed by your grace, that your will may be done on earth as it is in heaven; where, O Father, with your Son and the Holy Spirit, you live and reign in perfect unity, now and for ever. *Amen.*

The Blessing of the Marriage

The people remain standing. The husband and wife kneel, and the Priest says one of the following prayers

Most gracious God, we give you thanks for your tender love in sending Jesus Christ to come among us, to be born of a human mother, and to make the way of the cross to be the way of life. We thank you, also, for consecrating the union of man and woman in his Name. By the power of your Holy Spirit, pour out the abundance of your blessing upon this man and this woman. Defend them from every enemy. Lead them into all peace. Let their love for each other be a seal upon their hearts, a mantle about their shoulders, and a crown upon their foreheads. Bless them in their work and in their companionship; in their sleeping and in their waking; in their joys and in their sorrows; in their life and in their death. Finally, in your mercy, bring them to that table where your saints feast for ever in your heavenly home; through Jesus Christ our Lord, who with you and the Holy Spirit lives and reigns, one God, for ever and ever. *Amen.*

or this

O God, you have so consecrated the covenant of marriage that in it is represented the spiritual unity between Christ and his Church: Send therefore your blessing upon these your servants, that they may so love, honor, and cherish each other in faithfulness and patience, in wisdom and true godliness, that their home may be a haven of blessing and peace; through Jesus Christ our Lord, who lives and reigns with you and the Holy Spirit, one God, now and for ever. *Amen.*

The husband and wife still kneeling, the Priest adds this blessing

God the Father, God the Son, God the Holy Spirit, bless, preserve, and keep you; the Lord mercifully with his favor look upon you, and fill you with all spiritual benediction and grace; that you may faithfully live together in this life, and in the age to come have life everlasting. *Amen.*

The Peace

The Celebrant may say to the people

The peace of the Lord be always with you.
People   And also with you.

The newly married couple then greet each other, after which greetings may be exchanged throughout the congregation.

When Communion is not to follow, the wedding party leaves the church. A hymn, psalm, or anthem may be sung, or instrumental music may be played.

At the Eucharist

The liturgy continues with the Offertory, at which the newly married couple may present the offerings of bread and wine.

Preface of Marriage

At the Communion, it is appropriate that the newly married couple receive Communion first, after the ministers.

In place of the usual postcommunion prayer, the following is said

O God, the giver of all that is true and lovely and gracious: We give you thanks for binding us together in these holy mysteries of the Body and Blood of your Son Jesus Christ. Grant that by your Holy Spirit, N. and N., now joined in Holy Matrimony, may become one in heart and soul, live in fidelity and peace, and obtain those eternal joys prepared for all who love you; for the sake of Jesus Christ our Lord. *Amen.*

As the wedding party leaves the church, a hymn, psalm, or anthem may be sung; or instrumental music may be played.

The Blessing
of a Civil Marriage

The Rite begins as prescribed for celebrations of the Holy Eucharist, using the Collect and Lessons appointed in the Marriage service.

After the Gospel (and homily), the husband and wife stand before the Celebrant, who addresses them in these or similar words

N. and N., you have come here today to seek the blessing of God and of his Church upon your marriage. I require, therefore, that you promise, with the help of God, to fulfill the obligations which Christian Marriage demands.

The Celebrant then addresses the husband, saying

N., you have taken N. to be your wife. Do you promise to love her, comfort her, honor and keep her, in sickness and in health; and, forsaking all others, to be faithful to her as long as you both shall live?

The Husband answers I do.

The Celebrant then addresses the wife, saying

N., you have taken N. to be your husband. Do you promise to love him, comfort him, honor and keep him, in sickness and in health; and, forsaking all others, to be faithful to him as long as you both shall live?

The Wife answers I do.

The Celebrant then addresses the congregation, saying

Will you who have witnessed these promises do all in your power to uphold these two persons in their marriage?

People   We will.

If a ring or rings are to be blessed, the wife extends her hand (and the husband extends his hand) toward the Priest, who says

Bless, O Lord, *this ring* to be *a sign* of the vows by which this man and this woman have bound themselves to each other; through Jesus Christ our Lord. *Amen.*

The Celebrant joins the right hands of the husband and wife and says

Those whom God has joined together let no one put asunder.

The Congregation responds   Amen.

The service continues with The Prayers on page 428.

An Order for Marriage

If it is desired to celebrate a marriage otherwise than as provided on page 423 of this Book, this Order is used.

Normally, the celebrant is a priest or bishop. Where permitted by civil law, and when no priest or bishop is available, a deacon may function as celebrant, but does not pronounce a nuptial blessing.

The laws of the State and the canons of this Church having been complied with, the man and the woman, together with their witnesses, families, and friends assemble in the church or in some other convenient place.

1. The teaching of the Church concerning Holy Matrimony, as it is declared in the formularies and canons of this Church, is briefly stated.

2. The intention of the man and the woman to enter the state of matrimony, and their free consent, is publicly ascertained.

3. One or more Readings, one of which is always from Holy Scripture, may precede the exchange of vows. If there is to be a Communion, a Reading from the Gospel is always included.

4. The vows of the man and woman are exchanged, using the following form

In the Name of God, I, *N.*, take you, *N.*, to be my
(wife) (husband), to have and to hold from this day forward,
for better for worse, for richer for poorer, in sickness and in
health, to love and to cherish, until we are parted by death.
This is my solemn vow.

or this

I, *N.*, take thee *N.*, to my wedded (wife) (husband), to have
and to hold from this day forward, for better for worse, for
richer for poorer, in sickness and in health, to love and to
cherish, till death us do part, according to God's holy
ordinance; and thereto I (plight) (give) thee my troth.

5. The Celebrant declares the union of the man and woman as husband
and wife, in the Name of the Father, and of the Son, and of the Holy
Spirit.

6. Prayers are offered for the husband and wife, for their life together, for
the Christian community, and for the world.

7. A priest or bishop pronounces a solemn blessing upon the couple.

8. If there is no Communion, the service concludes with the Peace, the
husband and wife first greeting each other. The Peace may be exchanged
throughout the assembly.

9. If there is to be a Communion, the service continues with the Peace and
the Offertory. The Holy Eucharist may be celebrated either according to
Rite One or Rite Two in this Book, or according to the Order on page 401.

Additional Directions

If Banns are to be published, the following form is used

I publish the Banns of Marriage between *N.N.* of _____ and *N.N.* of _____. If any of you know just cause why they may not be joined together in Holy Matrimony, you are bidden to declare it. This is the first (*or* second, *or* third) time of asking.

The Celebration and Blessing of a Marriage may be used with any authorized liturgy for the Holy Eucharist. This service then replaces the Ministry of the Word, and the Eucharist begins with the Offertory.

After the Declaration of Consent, if there is to be a giving in marriage, or presentation, the Celebrant asks,

Who gives (presents) this woman to be married to this man?

or the following

Who presents this woman and this man to be married to each other?

To either question, the appropriate answer is, "I do." If more than one person responds, they do so together.

For the Ministry of the Word it is fitting that the man and woman to be married remain where they may conveniently hear the reading of Scripture. They may approach the Altar, either for the exchange of vows, or for the Blessing of the Marriage.

It is appropriate that all remain standing until the conclusion of the Collect. Seating may be provided for the wedding party, so that all may be seated for the Lessons and the homily.

The Apostles' Creed may be recited after the Lessons, or after the homily, if there is one.

When desired, some other suitable symbol of the vows may be used in place of the ring.

At the Offertory, it is desirable that the bread and wine be presented to the ministers by the newly married persons. They may then remain before the Lord's Table and receive Holy Communion before other members of the congregation.

A Thanksgiving for the Birth or Adoption of a Child

As soon as convenient after the birth of a child, or after receiving a child by adoption, the parents, with other members of the family, should come to the church to be welcomed by the congregation and to give thanks to Almighty God. It is desirable that this take place at a Sunday service. In the Eucharist it may follow the Prayers of the People preceding the Offertory. At Morning or Evening Prayer it may take place before the close of the Office.

When desired, a briefer form of this service may be used, especially in the hospital or at home; in which case the Celebrant may begin with the Act of Thanksgiving, or with the prayer "O God, you have taught us." A passage from Scripture may first be read. Either Luke 2:41-51, or Luke 18:15-17, is appropriate.

During the prayers, some parents may wish to express thanks in their own words.

At the proper time, the Celebrant invites the parents and other members of the family to present themselves before the Altar.

For the Birth of a Child

The Celebrant addresses the congregation in these or similar words

Dear Friends: The birth of a child is a joyous and solemn occasion in the life of a family. It is also an occasion for rejoicing in the Christian community. I bid you, therefore, to join N. [and N.] in giving thanks to Almighty God our heavenly Father, the Lord of all life, for the gift of N. to be their son (daughter) [and with N. (and NN.), for a new brother (sister)]. Let us say together:

The service continues with the Magnificat or one of the Psalms on pages 441-443.

For an Adoption

The Celebrant addresses the congregation in these or similar words

Dear Friends: It has pleased God our heavenly Father to answer the earnest prayers of N. [and N.], member(s) of this Christian family, for the gift of a child. I bid you join with *them* [and with N. (and NN.), who now *has* a new brother (sister)] in offering heartfelt thanks for the joyful and solemn responsibility which is *theirs* by the coming of N. to be a member of *their* family. But first, our friends wish us, here assembled, to witness the inauguration of this new relationship.

The Celebrant asks the parent or parents

N. [and N.], do you take this child for your own?
Parent(s) I do.

Then if the child is old enough to answer, the Celebrant asks

N., do you take this woman as your mother?

Child   I do.

Celebrant   Do you take this man as your father?

Child   I do.

Then the Celebrant, holding or taking the child by the hand, gives the child to the mother or father, saying

As God has made us his children by adoption and grace, may you receive N. as your own son (daughter).

Then one or both parents say these or similar words

May God, the Father of all, bless our child N., and us who have given to *him* our family name, that we may live together in love and affection; through Jesus Christ our Lord. *Amen.*

Act of Thanksgiving

The Celebrant says

Since it has pleased God to bestow upon N. [and N.] the gift of a child, let us now give thanks to him, and say together:

The Song of Mary

My soul proclaims the greatness of the Lord,
my spirit rejoices in God my Savior;*
    for he has looked with favor on his lowly servant.
From this day all generations will call me blessed:*
    the Almighty has done great things for me,
    and holy is his Name.
He has mercy on those who fear him*
    in every generation.

He has shown the strength of his arm, *
   he has scattered the proud in their conceit.
He has cast down the mighty from their thrones, *
   and has lifted up the lowly.
He has filled the hungry with good things, *
   and the rich he has sent away empty.
He has come to the help of his servant Israel, *
   for he has remembered his promise of mercy,
The promise he made to our fathers, *
   to Abraham and his children for ever.
Glory to the Father, and to the Son, and to the Holy Spirit: *
   as it was in the beginning, is now, and will be for ever. Amen.

or this

Psalm 116

I love the LORD, because he has heard the voice of my
                           supplication; *
   because he has inclined his ear to me whenever I called
                           upon him.
Gracious is the LORD and righteous; *
   our God is full of compassion.
How shall I repay the LORD *
   for all the good things he has done for me?
I will lift up the cup of salvation *
   and call upon the Name of the LORD,
I will fulfill my vows to the LORD *
   in the presence of all his people,
In the courts of the LORD's house, *
   in the midst of you, O Jerusalem.
   Hallelujah!
Glory to the Father, and to the Son, and to the Holy Spirit: *
   as it was in the beginning, is now, and will be for ever. Amen.

or this

Psalm 23

The LORD is my shepherd; *
   I shall not be in want.
He makes me lie down in green pastures*
   and leads me beside still waters.
He revives my soul*
   and guides me along right pathways for his Name's sake.
Though I walk through the valley of the shadow of death,
I shall fear no evil;*
   for you are with me;
   your rod and your staff, they comfort me.
You spread a table before me in the presence of those
                who trouble me;*
   you have anointed my head with oil,
   and my cup is running over.
Surely your goodness and mercy shall follow me all the
                days of my life,*
   and I will dwell in the house of the LORD for ever.
Glory to the Father, and to the Son, and to the Holy Spirit:*
   as it was in the beginning, is now, and will be for ever. Amen.

The Celebrant then says this prayer

Let us pray.

O God, you have taught us through your blessed Son that
whoever receives a little child in the name of Christ receives
Christ himself: We give you thanks for the blessing you have
bestowed upon this family in giving them a child. Confirm
their joy by a lively sense of your presence with them, and
give them calm strength and patient wisdom as they seek to
bring this child to love all that is true and noble, just and
pure, lovable and gracious, excellent and admirable,
following the example of our Lord and Savior, Jesus Christ.
Amen.

Prayers

The Celebrant may add one or more of the following prayers

For a safe delivery

O gracious God, we give you humble and hearty thanks that you have preserved through the pain and anxiety of child-birth your servant N., who desires now to offer you her praises and thanksgivings. Grant, most merciful Father, that by your help she may live faithfully according to your will in this life, and finally partake of everlasting glory in the life to come; through Jesus Christ our Lord. *Amen.*

For the parents

Almighty God, giver of life and love, bless N. and N. Grant them wisdom and devotion in the ordering of their common life, that each may be to the other a strength in need, a counselor in perplexity, a comfort in sorrow, and a companion in joy. And so knit their wills together in your will and their spirits in your Spirit, that they may live together in love and peace all the days of their life; through Jesus Christ our Lord. *Amen.*

For a child not yet. baptized

O eternal God, you have promised to be a father to a thousand generations of those who love and fear you: Bless this child and preserve *his* life; receive *him* and enable *him* to receive you, that through the Sacrament of Baptism *he* may become the child of God; through Jesus Christ our Lord. *Amen.*

For a child already baptized

Into your hands, O God, we place your child N. Support *him* in *his* successes and in *his* failures, in *his* joys and in *his* sorrows. As *he* grows in age, may *he* grow in grace, and in the knowledge of *his* Savior Jesus Christ. *Amen.*

The Celebrant may then bless the family

May God the Father, who by Baptism adopts us as his children, grant you grace. *Amen.*

May God the Son, who sanctified a home at Nazareth, fill you with love. *Amen.*

May God the Holy Spirit, who has made the Church one family, keep you in peace. *Amen.*

The Peace may be exchanged.

The Minister of the Congregation is directed to instruct the people, from time to time, about the duty of Christian parents to make prudent provision for the well-being of their families, and of all persons to make wills, while they are in health, arranging for the disposal of their temporal goods, not neglecting, if they are able, to leave bequests for religious and charitable uses.

Concerning the Rite

The ministry of reconciliation, which has been committed by Christ to his Church, is exercised through the care each Christian has for others, through the common prayer of Christians assembled for public worship, and through the priesthood of the Church and its ministers declaring absolution.

The Reconciliation of a Penitent is available for all who desire it. It is not restricted to times of sickness. Confessions may be heard anytime and anywhere.

Two equivalent forms of service are provided here to meet the needs of penitents. The absolution in these services may be pronounced only by a bishop or priest. Another Christian may be asked to hear a confession, but it must be made clear to the penitent that absolution will not be pronounced; instead, a declaration of forgiveness is provided.

When a confession is heard in a church building, the confessor may sit inside the altar rails or in a place set aside to give greater privacy, and the penitent kneels nearby. If preferred, the confessor and penitent may sit face to face for a spiritual conference leading to absolution or a declaration of forgiveness.

When the penitent has confessed all serious sins troubling the conscience and has given evidence of due contrition, the priest gives such counsel and encouragement as are needed and pronounces absolution. Before giving absolution, the priest may assign to the penitent a psalm, prayer, or hymn to be said, or something to be done, as a sign of penitence and act of thanksgiving.

The content of a confession is not normally a matter of subsequent discussion. The secrecy of a confession is morally absolute for the confessor, and must under no circumstances be broken.

The Reconciliation
of a Penitent

Form One

The Penitent begins

Bless me, for I have sinned.

The Priest says

The Lord be in your heart and upon your lips that you may truly and humbly confess your sins: In the Name of the Father, and of the Son, and of the Holy Spirit. *Amen.*

Penitent

I confess to Almighty God, to his Church, and to you, that I have sinned by my own fault in thought, word, and deed, in things done and left undone; especially _____. For these and all other sins which I cannot now remember, I am truly sorry. I pray God to have mercy on me. I firmly intend amendment of life, and I humbly beg forgiveness of God and his Church, and ask you for counsel, direction, and absolution.

Here the Priest may offer counsel, direction, and comfort.

The Priest then pronounces this absolution

Our Lord Jesus Christ, who has left power to his Church to absolve all sinners who truly repent and believe in him, of his great mercy forgive you all your offenses; and by his authority committed to me, I absolve you from all your sins: In the Name of the Father, and of the Son, and of the Holy Spirit. *Amen.*

or this

Our Lord Jesus Christ, who offered himself to be sacrificed for us to the Father, and who conferred power on his Church to forgive sins, absolve you through my ministry by the grace of the Holy Spirit, and restore you in the perfect peace of the Church. *Amen.*

The Priest adds

The Lord has put away all your sins.

Penitent   Thanks be to God.

The Priest concludes

Go (*or* abide) in peace, and pray for me, a sinner.

*Declaration of Forgiveness
to be used by a Deacon or Lay Person*

Our Lord Jesus Christ, who offered himself to be sacrificed for us to the Father, forgives your sins by the grace of the Holy Spirit. *Amen.*

Form Two

The Priest and Penitent begin as follows

Have mercy on me, O God, according to your loving-kindness;
in your great compassion blot out my offenses.
Wash me through and through from my wickedness,
and cleanse me from my sin.
For I know my transgressions only too well,
and my sin is ever before me.

Holy God, Holy and Mighty, Holy Immortal One,
have mercy upon us.

Penitent Pray for me, a sinner.

Priest

May God in his love enlighten your heart, that you may
remember in truth all your sins and his unfailing mercy.
Amen.

*The Priest may then say one or more of these or other appropriate verses
of Scripture, first saying*

Hear the Word of God to all who truly turn to him.

Come unto me, all ye that travail and are heavy laden, and I
will refresh you.   *Matthew 11:28*

God so loved the world, that he gave his only-begotten Son,
to the end that all that believe in him should not perish, but
have everlasting life.   *John 3:16*

This is a true saying, and worthy of all men to be received,
that Christ Jesus came into the world to save sinners.
1 Timothy 1:15

If any man sin, we have an Advocate with the Father, Jesus Christ the righteous; and he is the perfect offering for our sins, and not for ours only, but for the sins of the whole world.   *1 John 2:1-2*

The Priest then continues

Now, in the presence of Christ, and of me, his minister, confess your sins with a humble and obedient heart to Almighty God, our Creator and our Redeemer.

The Penitent says

Holy God, heavenly Father, you formed me from the dust in your image and likeness, and redeemed me from sin and death by the cross of your Son Jesus Christ. Through the water of baptism you clothed me with the shining garment of his righteousness, and established me among your children in your kingdom. But I have squandered the inheritance of your saints, and have wandered far in a land that is waste.

Especially, I confess to you and to the Church . . .

Here the penitent confesses particular sins.

Therefore, O Lord, from these and all other sins I cannot now remember, I turn to you in sorrow and repentance. Receive me again into the arms of your mercy, and restore me to the blessed company of your faithful people; through him in whom you have redeemed the world, your Son our Savior Jesus Christ. Amen.

The Priest may then offer words of comfort and counsel.

Priest

Will you turn again to Christ as your Lord?

Penitent   I will.

Do you, then, forgive those who have sinned against you?

Penitent   I forgive them.

Priest

May Almighty God in mercy receive your confession of sorrow and of faith, strengthen you in all goodness, and by the power of the Holy Spirit keep you in eternal life. *Amen.*

The Priest then lays a hand upon the penitent's head (or extends a hand over the penitent), saying one of the following

Our Lord Jesus Christ, who offered himself to be sacrificed for us to the Father, and who conferred power on his Church to forgive sins, absolve you through my ministry by the grace of the Holy Spirit, and restore you in the perfect peace of the Church. *Amen.*

or this

Our Lord Jesus Christ, who has left power to his Church to absolve all sinners who truly repent and believe in him, of his great mercy forgive you all your offenses; and by his authority committed to me, I absolve you from all your sins: In the Name of the Father, and of the Son, and of the Holy Spirit. *Amen.*

The Priest concludes

Now there is rejoicing in heaven; for you were lost, and are found; you were dead, and are now alive in Christ Jesus our Lord. Go (*or* abide) in peace. The Lord has put away all your sins.

Penitent   Thanks be to God.

Declaration of Forgiveness
to be used by a Deacon or Lay Person

Our Lord Jesus Christ, who offered himself to be sacrificed for us to the Father, forgives your sins by the grace of the Holy Spirit. *Amen.*

Ministration to the Sick

In case of illness, the Minister of the Congregation is to be notified.

At the Ministration, one or more parts of the following service are used, as appropriate; but when two or more are used together, they are used in the order indicated. The Lord's Prayer is always included.

Part One of this service may always be led by a deacon or lay person.

When the Laying on of Hands or Anointing takes place at a public celebration of the Eucharist, it is desirable that it precede the distribution of Holy Communion, and it is recommended that it take place immediately before the exchange of the Peace.

The Celebrant begins the service with the following or some other greeting

Peace be to this house (place), and to all who dwell in it.

Part I.   Ministry of the Word

One or more of the following or other passages of Scripture are read

General

2 Corinthians 1:3-5   (God comforts us in affliction)
Psalm 91   (He will give his angels charge over you)
Luke 17:11-19   (Your faith has made you well)

Penitence

Hebrews 12:1-2   (Looking to Jesus, the perfecter of our faith)
Psalm 103   (He forgives all your sins)
Matthew 9:2-8   (Your sins are forgiven)

When Anointing is to follow

James 5:14-16   (Is any among you sick?)
Psalm 23   (You have anointed my head with oil)
Mark 6:7, 12-13   (They anointed with oil many that were sick)

When Communion is to follow

1 John 5:13-15   (That you may know that you have eternal life)
Psalm 145:14-22   (The eyes of all wait upon you, O Lord)
John 6:47-51   (I am the bread of life)

After any Reading, the Celebrant may comment on it briefly.

Prayers may be offered according to the occasion.

The Priest may suggest the making of a special confession, if the sick person's conscience is troubled, and use the form for the Reconciliation of a Penitent.

Or else the following general confession may be said

Most merciful God,
we confess that we have sinned against you
in thought, word, and deed,
by what we have done,
and by what we have left undone.
We have not loved you with our whole heart;
we have not loved our neighbors as ourselves.
We are truly sorry and we humbly repent.

For the sake of your Son Jesus Christ,
have mercy on us and forgive us;
that we may delight in your will,
and walk in your ways,
to the glory of your Name. Amen.

The Priest alone says

Almighty God have mercy on you, forgive you all your sins
through our Lord Jesus Christ, strengthen you in all goodness,
and by the power of the Holy Spirit keep you in eternal life.
Amen.

*A deacon or lay person using the preceding form substitutes "us" for
"you" and "our" for "your."*

Part II.   Laying on of Hands and Anointing

If oil for the Anointing of the Sick is to be blessed, the Priest says

O Lord, holy Father, giver of health and salvation: Send your
Holy Spirit to sanctify this oil; that, as your holy apostles
anointed many that were sick and healed them, so may those
who in faith and repentance receive this holy unction be
made whole; through Jesus Christ our Lord, who lives and
reigns with you and the Holy Spirit, one God, for ever and
ever. *Amen.*

The following anthem is said

Savior of the world, by your cross and precious blood you
have redeemed us;
Save us, and help us, we humbly beseech you, O Lord.

*The Priest then lays hands upon the sick person, and says one of the
following*

N., I lay my hands upon you in the Name of the Father, and of the Son, and of the Holy Spirit, beseeching our Lord Jesus Christ to sustain you with his presence, to drive away all sickness of body and spirit, and to give you that victory of life and peace which will enable you to serve him both now and evermore. *Amen.*

or this

N., I lay my hands upon you in the Name of our Lord and Savior Jesus Christ, beseeching him to uphold you and fill you with his grace, that you may know the healing power of his love. *Amen.*

If the person is to be anointed, the Priest dips a thumb in the holy oil, and makes the sign of the cross on the sick person's forehead, saying

N., I anoint you with oil in the Name of the Father, and of the Son, and of the Holy Spirit. *Amen.*

The Priest may add

As you are outwardly anointed with this holy oil, so may our heavenly Father grant you the inward anointing of the Holy Spirit. Of his great mercy, may he forgive you your sins, release you from suffering, and restore you to wholeness and strength. May he deliver you from all evil, preserve you in all goodness, and bring you to everlasting life; through Jesus Christ our Lord. *Amen.*

In cases of necessity, a deacon or lay person may perform the anointing, using oil blessed by a bishop or priest.

If Communion is not to follow, the Lord's Prayer is now said.

The Priest concludes

The Almighty Lord, who is a strong tower to all who put their trust in him, to whom all things in heaven, on earth, and under the earth bow and obey: Be now and evermore your defense, and make you know and feel that the only Name under heaven given for health and salvation is the Name of our Lord Jesus Christ. *Amen.*

Part III.   Holy Communion

If the Eucharist is to be celebrated, the Priest begins with the [Peace and] Offertory.

If Communion is to be administered from the reserved Sacrament, the form for Communion under Special Circumstances is used, beginning with the [Peace and] Lord's Prayer on page 398.

If the sick person cannot receive either the consecrated Bread or the Wine, it is suitable to administer the Sacrament in one kind only.

One of the usual postcommunion prayers is said, or the following

Gracious Father, we give you praise and thanks for this Holy Communion of the Body and Blood of your beloved Son Jesus Christ, the pledge of our redemption; and we pray that it may bring us forgiveness of our sins, strength in our weakness, and everlasting salvation; through Jesus Christ our Lord. *Amen.*

The service concludes with a blessing or with a dismissal

Let us bless the Lord.
Thanks be to God.

If a person desires to receive the Sacrament, but, by reason of extreme sickness or physical disability, is unable to eat and drink the Bread and Wine, the Celebrant is to assure that person that all the benefits of Communion are received, even though the Sacrament is not received with the mouth.

Prayers for the Sick

For a Sick Person

O Father of mercies and God of all comfort, our only help in time of need: We humbly beseech thee to behold, visit, and relieve thy sick servant N. for whom our prayers are desired. Look upon *him* with the eyes of thy mercy; comfort *him* with a sense of thy goodness; preserve *him* from the temptations of the enemy; and give *him* patience under *his* affliction. In thy good time, restore *him* to health, and enable *him* to lead the residue of *his* life in thy fear, and to thy glory; and grant that finally *he* may dwell with thee in life everlasting; through Jesus Christ our Lord. *Amen.*

For Recovery from Sickness

O God, the strength of the weak and the comfort of sufferers: Mercifully accept our prayers, and grant to your servant N. the help of your power, that *his* sickness may be turned into health, and our sorrow into joy; through Jesus Christ our Lord. *Amen.*

or this

O God of heavenly powers, by the might of your command you drive away from our bodies all sickness and all infirmity: Be present in your goodness with your servant N., that *his* weakness may be banished and *his* strength restored; and that, *his* health being renewed, *he* may bless your holy Name; through Jesus Christ our Lord. *Amen.*

For a Sick Child

Heavenly Father, watch with us over your child N., and grant that *he* may be restored to that perfect health which it is yours alone to give; through Jesus Christ our Lord. *Amen.*

or this

Lord Jesus Christ, Good Shepherd of the sheep, you gather
the lambs in your arms and carry them in your bosom: We
commend to your loving care this child N. Relieve *his* pain,
guard *him* from all danger, restore to *him* your gifts of
gladness and strength, and raise *him* up to a life of service to
you. Hear us, we pray, for your dear Name's sake. *Amen.*

Before an Operation

Almighty God our heavenly Father, graciously comfort your
servant N. in *his* suffering, and bless the means made use of
for *his* cure. Fill *his* heart with confidence that, though at times
he may be afraid, *he* yet may put *his* trust in you; through Jesus
Christ our Lord. *Amen.*

or this

Strengthen your servant N., O God, to do what *he* has to do
and bear what *he* has to bear; that, accepting your healing
gifts through the skill of surgeons and nurses, *he* may be
restored to usefulness in your world with a thankful heart;
through Jesus Christ our Lord. *Amen.*

For Strength and Confidence

Heavenly Father, giver of life and health: Comfort and
relieve your sick servant N., and give your power of healing to
those who minister to *his* needs, that *he* may be strengthened in
his weakness and have confidence in your loving care; through
Jesus Christ our Lord. *Amen.*

For the Sanctification of Illness

Sanctify, O Lord, the sickness of your servant N., that the sense of *his* weakness may add strength to *his* faith and seriousness to *his* repentance; and grant that *he* may live with you in everlasting life; through Jesus Christ our Lord. *Amen.*

For Health of Body and Soul

May God the Father bless you, God the Son heal you, God the Holy Spirit give you strength. May God the holy and undivided Trinity guard your body, save your soul, and bring you safely to his heavenly country; where he lives and reigns for ever and ever. *Amen.*

For Doctors and Nurses

Sanctify, O Lord, those whom you have called to the study and practice of the arts of healing, and to the prevention of disease and pain. Strengthen them by your life-giving Spirit, that by their ministries the health of the community may be promoted and your creation glorified; through Jesus Christ our Lord. *Amen.*

Thanksgiving for a Beginning of Recovery

O Lord, your compassions never fail and your mercies are new every morning: We give you thanks for giving our brother (sister) N. both relief from pain and hope of health renewed. Continue in *him*, we pray, the good work you have begun; that *he*, daily increasing in bodily strength, and rejoicing in your goodness, may so order *his* life and conduct that *he* may always think and do those things that please you; through Jesus Christ our Lord. *Amen.*

Prayers for use by a Sick Person

For Trust in God

O God, the source of all health: So fill my heart with faith in
your love, that with calm expectancy I may make room for
your power to possess me, and gracefully accept your
healing; through Jesus Christ our Lord. Amen.

In Pain

Lord Jesus Christ, by your patience in suffering you hallowed
earthly pain and gave us the example of obedience to your
Father's will: Be near me in my time of weakness and pain;
sustain me by your grace, that my strength and courage may
not fail; heal me according to your will; and help me always
to believe that what happens to me here is of little account if
you hold me in eternal life, my Lord and my God. Amen.

For Sleep

O heavenly Father, you give your children sleep for the
refreshing of soul and body: Grant me this gift, I pray; keep
me in that perfect peace which you have promised to those
whose minds are fixed on you; and give me such a sense of
your presence, that in the hours of silence I may enjoy the
blessed assurance of your love; through Jesus Christ our
Savior. Amen.

In the Morning

This is another day, O Lord. I know not what it will bring
forth, but make me ready, Lord, for whatever it may be. If I
am to stand up, help me to stand bravely. If I am to sit still,
help me to sit quietly. If I am to lie low, help me to do it
patiently. And if I am to do nothing, let me do it gallantly.
Make these words more than words, and give me the Spirit
of Jesus. Amen.

Ministration at the Time of Death

When a person is near death, the Minister of the Congregation should be notified, in order that the ministrations of the Church may be provided.

A Prayer for a Person near Death

Almighty God, look on this your servant, lying in great weakness, and comfort *him* with the promise of life everlasting, given in the resurrection of your Son Jesus Christ our Lord. *Amen.*

Litany at the Time of Death

When possible, it is desirable that members of the family and friends come together to join in the Litany.

God the Father,
Have mercy on your servant.

God the Son,
Have mercy on your servant.

God the Holy Spirit,
Have mercy on your servant.

Holy Trinity, one God,
Have mercy on your servant.

From all evil, from all sin, from all tribulation,
Good Lord, deliver him.

By your holy Incarnation, by your Cross and Passion, by
your precious Death and Burial,
Good Lord, deliver him.

By your glorious Resurrection and Ascension, and by the
Coming of the Holy Spirit,
Good Lord, deliver him.

We sinners beseech you to hear us, Lord Christ: That it may
please you to deliver the soul of your servant from the power
of evil, and from eternal death,
We beseech you to hear us, good Lord.

That it may please you mercifully to pardon all *his* sins,
We beseech you to hear us, good Lord.

That it may please you to grant *him* a place of refreshment
and everlasting blessedness,
We beseech you to hear us, good Lord.

That it may please you to give *him* joy and gladness in your
kingdom, with your saints in light,
We beseech you to hear us, good Lord.

Jesus, Lamb of God:
Have mercy on him.

Jesus, bearer of our sins:
Have mercy on him.

Jesus, redeemer of the world:
Give him *your peace.*

Lord, have mercy.
Christ, have mercy.
Lord, have mercy.

Our Father, who art in heaven,
   hallowed be thy Name,
   thy kingdom come,
   thy will be done,
     on earth as it is in heaven.
Give us this day our daily bread.
And forgive us our trespasses,
   as we forgive those
     who trespass against us.
And lead us not into temptation,
   but deliver us from evil.

Our Father in heaven,
   hallowed be your Name,
   your kingdom come,
   your will be done,
     on earth as in heaven.
Give us today our daily bread.
Forgive us our sins
   as we forgive those
     who sin against us.
Save us from the time of trial,
   and deliver us from evil.

The Officiant says this Collect

Let us pray.

Deliver your servant, *N.*, O Sovereign Lord Christ, from all
evil, and set *him* free from every bond; that *he* may rest with
all your saints in the eternal habitations; where with the
Father and the Holy Spirit you live and reign, one God, for
ever and ever. *Amen.*

A Commendation at the Time of Death

Depart, O Christian soul, out of this world;
In the Name of God the Father Almighty who created you;
In the Name of Jesus Christ who redeemed you;
In the Name of the Holy Spirit who sanctifies you.
May your rest be this day in peace,
   and your dwelling place in the Paradise of God.

A Commendatory Prayer

Into your hands, O merciful Savior, we commend your
servant N. Acknowledge, we humbly beseech you, a sheep of
your own fold, a lamb of your own flock, a sinner of your
own redeeming. Receive *him* into the arms of your mercy,
into the blessed rest of everlasting peace, and into the
glorious company of the saints in light. *Amen.*

May *his* soul and the souls of all the departed, through the
mercy of God, rest in peace. *Amen.*

Prayers for a Vigil

*It is appropriate that the family and friends come together for prayers
prior to the funeral. Suitable Psalms, Lessons, and Collects (such as those
in the Burial service) may be used. The Litany at the Time of Death may
be said, or the following*

Dear Friends: It was our Lord Jesus himself who said,
"Come to me, all you who labor and are burdened, and I will
give you rest." Let us pray, then, for our brother (sister) N.,
that *he* may rest from *his* labors, and enter into the light of
God's eternal sabbath rest.

Receive, O Lord, your servant, for *he* returns to you.
Into your hands, O Lord,
we commend our brother (sister) N.

Wash *him* in the holy font of everlasting life, and clothe
him in *his* heavenly wedding garment.
Into your hands, O Lord,
we commend our brother (sister) N.

May *he* hear your words of invitation, "Come, you blessed of
my Father."
Into your hands, O Lord,
we commend our brother (sister) N.

May *he* gaze upon you, Lord, face to face, and taste the blessedness of perfect rest.
Into your hands, O Lord,
we commend our brother (sister) N.

May angels surround *him*, and saints welcome *him* in peace.
Into your hands, O Lord,
we commend our brother (sister) N.

The Officiant concludes

Almighty God, our Father in heaven, before whom live all who die in the Lord: Receive our *brother N.* into the courts of your heavenly dwelling place. Let *his* heart and soul now ring out in joy to you, O Lord, the living God, and the God of those who live. This we ask through Christ our Lord. *Amen.*

Reception of the Body

The following form may be used at whatever time the body is brought to the church.

The Celebrant meets the body at the door of the church and says

With faith in Jesus Christ, we receive the body of our brother (sister) N. for burial. Let us pray with confidence to God, the Giver of life, that he will raise *him* to perfection in the company of the saints.

Silence may be kept; after which the Celebrant says

Deliver your servant, N., O Sovereign Lord Christ, from all evil, and set *him* free from every bond; that *he* may rest with all your saints in the eternal habitations; where with the Father and the Holy Spirit you live and reign, one God, for ever and ever. *Amen.*

Let us also pray for all who mourn, that they may cast their care on God, and know the consolation of his love.

Silence may be kept; after which the Celebrant says

Almighty God, look with pity upon the sorrows of your servants for whom we pray. Remember them, Lord, in mercy; nourish them with patience; comfort them with a sense of your goodness; lift up your countenance upon them; and give them peace; through Jesus Christ our Lord. *Amen.*

If the Burial service is not to follow immediately, the body is then brought into the church, during which time a suitable psalm or anthem may be sung or said. Appropriate devotions, such as those appointed for the Vigil on page 465, may follow.

When the order for the Burial of the Dead follows immediately, the service continues on page 469 or 491.

A member of the congregation bearing the lighted Paschal Candle may lead the procession into the church.

Concerning the Service

The death of a member of the Church should be reported as soon as possible to, and arrangements for the funeral should be made in consultation with, the Minister of the Congregation.

Baptized Christians are properly buried from the church. The service should be held at a time when the congregation has opportunity to be present.

The coffin is to be closed before the service, and it remains closed thereafter. It is appropriate that it be covered with a pall or other suitable covering.

If necessary, or if desired, all or part of the service of Committal may be said in the church. If preferred, the Committal service may take place before the service in the church. It may also be used prior to cremation.

A priest normally presides at the service. It is appropriate that the bishop, when present, preside at the Eucharist and pronounce the Commendation.

It is desirable that the Lesson from the Old Testament, and the Epistle, be read by lay persons.

When the services of a priest cannot be obtained, a deacon or lay reader may preside at the service.

At the burial of a child, the passages from Lamentations, 1 John, and John 6, together with Psalm 23, are recommended.

It is customary that the celebrant meet the body and go before it into the church or towards the grave.

The anthems at the beginning of the service are sung or said as the body is borne into the church, or during the entrance of the ministers, or by the celebrant standing in the accustomed place.

The Burial of the Dead: Rite One

All stand while one or more of the following anthems are sung or said

I am the resurrection and the life, saith the Lord;
he that believeth in me, though he were dead, yet shall he live;
and whosoever liveth and believeth in me shall never die.

I know that my Redeemer liveth,
and that he shall stand at the latter day upon the earth;
and though this body be destroyed, yet shall I see God;
whom I shall see for myself and mine eyes shall behold,
and not as a stranger.

For none of us liveth to himself,
and no man dieth to himself.
For if we live, we live unto the Lord;
and if we die, we die unto the Lord.
Whether we live, therefore, or die, we are the Lord's.

Blessed are the dead who die in the Lord;
even so saith the Spirit, for they rest from their labors.

The Celebrant says one of the following Collects, first saying

The Lord be with you.
People   And with thy spirit.
Celebrant Let us pray.

At the Burial of an Adult

O God, whose mercies cannot be numbered: Accept our prayers on behalf of thy servant N., and grant *him* an entrance into the land of light and joy, in the fellowship of thy saints; through Jesus Christ thy Son our Lord, who liveth and reigneth with thee and the Holy Spirit, one God, now and for ever. *Amen.*

At the Burial of a Child

O God, whose beloved Son did take little children into his arms and bless them: Give us grace, we beseech thee, to entrust this child N. to thy never-failing care and love, and bring us all to thy heavenly kingdom; through the same thy Son Jesus Christ our Lord, who liveth and reigneth with thee and the Holy Spirit, one God, now and for ever. *Amen.*

The people sit.

One or more of the following passages from Holy Scripture is read. If there is to be a Communion, a passage from the Gospel always concludes the Readings.

From the Old Testament

Isaiah 25:6-9 (He will swallow up death in victory)
Isaiah 61:1-3 (To comfort all that mourn)
Lamentations 3:22-26, 31-33 (The Lord is good unto them that wait for him)
Wisdom 3:1-5, 9 (The souls of the righteous are in the hand of God)

After the Old Testament Lesson, a suitable canticle or one of the following Psalms may be sung or said

Psalm 42   *Quemadmodum*

Like as the hart desireth the water-brooks, *
  so longeth my soul after thee, O God.

My soul is athirst for God, yea, even for the living God; *
  when shall I come to appear before the presence of God?

My tears have been my meat day and night, *
  while they daily say unto me, Where is now thy God?

Now when I think thereupon, I pour out my heart by myself; *
  for I went with the multitude, and brought them forth into
    the house of God;

In the voice of praise and thanksgiving, *
  among such as keep holy-day.

Why art thou so full of heaviness, O my soul? *
  and why art thou so disquieted within me?

O put thy trust in God; *
  for I will yet thank him, which is the help of my
    countenance, and my God.

Psalm 46   *Deus noster refugium*

God is our hope and strength, *
  a very present help in trouble.

Therefore will we not fear, though the earth be moved, *
  and though the hills be carried into the midst of the sea;

Though the waters thereof rage and swell, *
  and though the mountains shake at the tempest of the same.

There is a river, the streams whereof make glad the city of God, *
  the holy place of the tabernacle of the Most Highest.

God is in the midst of her,
therefore shall she not be removed; *
    God shall help her, and that right early.

Be still then, and know that I am God; *
    I will be exalted among the nations,
    and I will be exalted in the earth.

The LORD of hosts is with us; *
    the God of Jacob is our refuge.

Psalm 90   *Domine, refugium*

LORD, thou hast been our refuge, *
    from one generation to another.

Before the mountains were brought forth,
or ever the earth and the world were made, *
    thou art God from everlasting, and world without end.

Thou turnest man to destruction; *
    again thou sayest, Come again, ye children of men.

For a thousand years in thy sight are but as yesterday
                   when it is past, *
    and as a watch in the night.

As soon as thou scatterest them they are even as a sleep, *
    and fade away suddenly like the grass.

In the morning it is green, and groweth up; *
    but in the evening it is cut down, dried up, and withered.

For we consume away in thy displeasure, *
    and are afraid at thy wrathful indignation.

Thou hast set our misdeeds before thee,*
    and our secret sins in the light of thy countenance.

For when thou art angry all our days are gone; *
    we bring our years to an end, as it were a tale that is told.

The days of our age are threescore years and ten;
and though men be so strong that they come to fourscore years, *
    yet is their strength then but labor and sorrow,
    so soon passeth it away, and we are gone.

So teach us to number our days, *
    that we may apply our hearts unto wisdom.

Psalm 121   *Levavi oculos*

I will lift up mine eyes unto the hills; *
    from whence cometh my help?

My help cometh even from the LORD, *
    who hath made heaven and earth.

He will not suffer thy foot to be moved, *
    and he that keepeth thee will not sleep.

Behold, he that keepeth Israel *
    shall neither slumber nor sleep.

The LORD himself is thy keeper; *
    the LORD is thy defence upon thy right hand;

So that the sun shall not burn thee by day, *
    neither the moon by night.

The LORD shall preserve thee from all evil; *
    yea, it is even he that shall keep thy soul.

The LORD shall preserve thy going out, and thy coming in, *
    from this time forth for evermore.

Psalm 130 *De profundis*

Out of the deep have I called unto thee, O LORD; *
  Lord, hear my voice.

O let thine ears consider well *
  the voice of my complaint.

If thou, LORD, wilt be extreme to mark what is done amiss, *
  O Lord, who may abide it?

For there is mercy with thee, *
  therefore shalt thou be feared.

I look for the LORD; my soul doth wait for him; *
  in his word is my trust.

My soul fleeth unto the Lord before the morning watch; *
  I say, before the morning watch.

O Israel, trust in the LORD,
for with the LORD there is mercy, *
  and with him is plenteous redemption.

And he shall redeem Israel *
  from all his sins.

Psalm 139 *Domine, probasti*

O LORD, thou hast searched me out, and known me. *
  Thou knowest my down-sitting and mine up-rising;
  thou understandest my thoughts long before.

Thou art about my path, and about my bed, *
  and art acquainted with all my ways.

For lo, there is not a word in my tongue, *
  but thou, O LORD, knowest it altogether.

Thou hast beset me behind and before, *
    and laid thine hand upon me.

Such knowledge is too wonderful and excellent for me; *
    I cannot attain unto it.

Whither shall I go then from thy Spirit? *
    or whither shall I go then from thy presence?

If I climb up into heaven, thou art there; *
    if I go down to hell, thou art there also.

If I take the wings of the morning, *
    and remain in the uttermost parts of the sea;

Even there also shall thy hand lead me, *
    and thy right hand shall hold me.

If I say, Peradventure the darkness shall cover me, *
    then shall my night be turned to day.

Yea, the darkness is no darkness with thee,
but the night is as clear as day; *
    the darkness and light to thee are both alike.

From the New Testament

Romans 8:14-19, 34-35, 37-39 (The glory that shall be revealed)
1 Corinthians 15:20-26, 35-38, 42-44, 53-58 (Raised in incorruption)
2 Corinthians 4:16—5:9 (Things which are not seen are eternal)
1 John 3:1-2 (We shall be like him)
Revelation 7:9-17 (God shall wipe away all tears)
Revelation 21:2-7 (Behold, I make all things new)

After the New Testament Lesson, a suitable canticle or hymn, or one of the following Psalms may be sung or said

Psalm 23 *Dominus regit me*

The LORD is my shepherd; *
  therefore can I lack nothing.

He shall feed me in a green pasture, *
  and lead me forth beside the waters of comfort.

He shall convert my soul, *
  and bring me forth in the paths of righteousness for his
    Name's sake.

Yea, though I walk through the valley of the shadow of death,
I will fear no evil; *
  for thou art with me;
  thy rod and thy staff comfort me.

Thou shalt prepare a table before me in the presence of them
    that trouble me; *
  thou hast anointed my head with oil,
  and my cup shall be full.

Surely thy loving-kindness and mercy shall follow me all the
    days of my life; *
  and I will dwell in the house of the LORD for ever.

Psalm 23 *King James Version*

The LORD is my shepherd; *
  I shall not want.

He maketh me to lie down in green pastures; *
  he leadeth me beside the still waters.

He restoreth my soul; *
  he leadeth me in the paths of righteousness for his
    Name's sake.

Yea, though I walk through the valley of the shadow of death,
I will fear no evil; *
    for thou art with me;
    thy rod and thy staff, they comfort me.

Thou preparest a table before me in the presence of
                  mine enemies; *
    thou anointest my head with oil;
    my cup runneth over.

Surely goodness and mercy shall follow me all the days
                  of my life, *
    and I will dwell in the house of the LORD for ever.

Psalm 27   *Dominus illuminatio*

The LORD is my light and my salvation;
whom then shall I fear? *
    the LORD is the strength of my life;
    of whom then shall I be afraid?

One thing have I desired of the LORD, which I will require, *
    even that I may dwell in the house of the LORD all the
                  days of my life,
    to behold the fair beauty of the LORD, and to visit his temple.

For in the time of trouble he shall hide me in his tabernacle; *
    yea, in the secret place of his dwelling shall he hide me,
    and set me up upon a rock of stone.

And now shall he lift up mine head *
    above mine enemies round about me.

Therefore will I offer in his dwelling an oblation with
                  great gladness; *
    I will sing and speak praises unto the LORD.

Hearken unto my voice, O LORD, when I cry unto thee; *
    have mercy upon me, and hear me.

My heart hath talked of thee, Seek ye my face. *
  Thy face, LORD, will I seek.

O hide not thou thy face from me, *
  nor cast thy servant away in displeasure.

I should utterly have fainted, *
  but that I believe verily to see the goodness of the LORD in
      the land of the living.

O tarry thou the LORD's leisure; *
  be strong, and he shall comfort thine heart;
  and put thou thy trust in the LORD.

Psalm 106   *Confitemini Domino*

O give thanks unto the LORD, for he is gracious, *
  and his mercy endureth for ever.

Who can express the noble acts of the LORD, *
  or show forth all his praise?

Blessed are they that alway keep judgment, *
  and do righteousness.

Remember me, O LORD, according to the favor that thou
      bearest unto thy people; *
  O visit me with thy salvation;

That I may see the felicity of thy chosen, *
  and rejoice in the gladness of thy people,
  and give thanks with thine inheritance.

Psalm 116   *Dilexi, quoniam*

My delight is in the LORD, *
  because he hath heard the voice of my prayer;

Because he hath inclined his ear unto me, *
   therefore will I call upon him as long as I live.

The snares of death compassed me round about, *
   and the pains of hell gat hold upon me.

I found trouble and heaviness;
then called I upon the Name of the LORD; *
   O LORD, I beseech thee, deliver my soul.

Gracious is the LORD, and righteous; *
   yea, our God is merciful.

The LORD preserveth the simple; *
   I was in misery, and he helped me.

Turn again then unto thy rest, O my soul, *
   for the LORD hath rewarded thee.

And why? thou hast delivered my soul from death, *
   mine eyes from tears, and my feet from falling.

I will walk before the LORD *
   in the land of the living.

I will pay my vows now in the presence of all his people; *
   right dear in the sight of the LORD is the death of his saints.

The Gospel

Then, all standing, the Deacon or Minister appointed reads the Gospel, first saying

> The Holy Gospel of our Lord Jesus Christ
> according to John.
People   Glory be to thee, O Lord.

John 5:24-27 (He that believeth hath everlasting life)
John 6:37-40 (All that the Father giveth me shall come to me)
John 10:11-16 (I am the good shepherd)
John 11:21-27 (I am the resurrection and the life)
John 14:1-6 (In my Father's house are many mansions)

At the end of the Gospel, the Reader says

> The Gospel of the Lord.
>
> *People* Praise be to thee, O Christ.

A homily may be preached, the people being seated.

The Apostles' Creed may be said, all standing.

If there is not to be a Communion, the Lord's Prayer is said here, and the service continues with the following prayer of intercession, or with one or more suitable prayers (see pages 487-489).

When there is a Communion, the following serves for the Prayers of the People.

The People respond to every petition with Amen.

The Deacon or other leader says

In peace, let us pray to the Lord.

Almighty God, who hast knit together thine elect in one communion and fellowship, in the mystical body of thy Son Christ our Lord: Grant, we beseech thee, to thy whole Church in paradise and on earth, thy light and thy peace. *Amen.*

Grant that all who have been baptized into Christ's death and resurrection may die to sin and rise to newness of life, and that through the grave and gate of death we may pass with him to our joyful resurrection. *Amen.*

Grant to us who are still in our pilgrimage, and who walk as yet by faith, that thy Holy Spirit may lead us in holiness and righteousness all our days. *Amen.*

Grant to thy faithful people pardon and peace, that we may be cleansed from all our sins, and serve thee with a quiet mind. *Amen.*

Grant to all who mourn a sure confidence in thy fatherly care, that, casting all their grief on thee, they may know the consolation of thy love. *Amen.*

Give courage and faith to those who are bereaved, that they may have strength to meet the days ahead in the comfort of a reasonable and holy hope, in the joyful expectation of eternal life with those they love. *Amen.*

Help us, we pray, in the midst of things we cannot understand, to believe and trust in the communion of saints, the forgiveness of sins, and the resurrection to life everlasting. *Amen.*

Grant us grace to entrust N. to thy never-failing love; receive *him* into the arms of thy mercy, and remember *him* according to the favor which thou bearest unto thy people. *Amen.*

Grant that, increasing in knowledge and love of thee, *he* may go from strength to strength in the life of perfect service in thy heavenly kingdom. *Amen.*

Grant us, with all who have died in the hope of the resurrection, to have our consummation and bliss in thy eternal and everlasting glory, and, with [blessed N. and] all thy saints, to receive the crown of life which thou dost promise to all who share in the victory of thy Son Jesus Christ; who liveth and reigneth with thee and the Holy Spirit, one God, for ever and ever. *Amen.*

When there is no Communion, the service continues with the Commendation, or with the Committal.

At the Eucharist

The service continues with the Peace and the Offertory.

Preface of the Commemoration of the Dead

In place of the usual postcommunion prayer, the following is said

Almighty God, we thank thee that in thy great love thou hast fed us with the spiritual food and drink of the Body and Blood of thy Son Jesus Christ, and hast given unto us a foretaste of thy heavenly banquet. Grant that this Sacrament may be unto us a comfort in affliction, and a pledge of our inheritance in that kingdom where there is no death, neither sorrow nor crying, but the fullness of joy with all thy saints; through Jesus Christ our Savior. *Amen.*

If the body is not present, the service continues with the [blessing and] dismissal.

Unless the Committal follows immediately in the church, the following Commendation is used.

The Commendation

The Celebrant and other ministers take their places at the body.

This anthem, or some other suitable anthem, or a hymn, may be sung or said.

Give rest, O Christ, to thy servant(s) with thy saints,
where sorrow and pain are no more,
neither sighing, but life everlasting.

Thou only art immortal, the creator and maker of mankind; and we are mortal, formed of the earth, and unto earth shall we return. For so thou didst ordain when thou createdst me, saying, "Dust thou art, and unto dust shalt thou return." All we go down to the dust; yet even at the grave we make our song: Alleluia, alleluia, alleluia.

Give rest, O Christ, to thy servant(s) with thy saints,
where sorrow and pain are no more,
neither sighing, but life everlasting.

The Celebrant, facing the body, says

Into thy hands, O merciful Savior, we commend thy servant N. Acknowledge, we humbly beseech thee, a sheep of thine own fold, a lamb of thine own flock, a sinner of thine own redeeming. Receive *him* into the arms of thy mercy, into the blessed rest of everlasting peace, and into the glorious company of the saints in light. *Amen.*

The Celebrant, or the Bishop if present, may then bless the people, and a Deacon or other Minister may dismiss them, saying

Let us go forth in the name of Christ.
Thanks be to God.

As the body is borne from the church, a hymn, or one or more of these anthems may be sung or said

Christ is risen from the dead, trampling down death by death, and giving life to those in the tomb.

The Sun of Righteousness is gloriously risen, giving light to those who sat in darkness and in the shadow of death.

The Lord will guide our feet into the way of peace, having taken away the sin of the world.

Christ will open the kingdom of heaven to all who believe in his Name, saying, Come, O blessed of my Father; inherit the kingdom prepared for you.

Into paradise may the angels lead thee; and at thy coming may the martyrs receive thee, and bring thee into the holy city Jerusalem.

or one of these Canticles

The Song of Zechariah, *Benedictus*
The Song of Simeon, *Nunc dimittis*
Christ our Passover, *Pascha nostrum*

The Committal

The following anthem is sung or said

In the midst of life we are in death;
of whom may we seek for succor,
but of thee, O Lord,
who for our sins art justly displeased?

Yet, O Lord God most holy, O Lord most mighty,
O holy and most merciful Savior,
deliver us not into the bitter pains of eternal death.

Thou knowest, Lord, the secrets of our hearts;
shut not thy merciful ears to our prayer;
but spare us, Lord most holy, O God most mighty,
O holy and merciful Savior,
thou most worthy Judge eternal.
Suffer us not, at our last hour,
through any pains of death, to fall from thee.

or this

All that the Father giveth me shall come to me;
and him that cometh to me I will in no wise cast out.

He that raised up Jesus from the dead
will also give life to our mortal bodies,
by his Spirit that dwelleth in us.

Wherefore my heart is glad, and my spirit rejoiceth;
my flesh also shall rest in hope.

Thou shalt show me the path of life;
in thy presence is the fullness of joy,
and at thy right hand there is pleasure for evermore.

Then, while earth is cast upon the coffin, the Celebrant says these words

In sure and certain hope of the resurrection to eternal life
through our Lord Jesus Christ, we commend to Almighty
God our *brother N*; and we commit *his* body to the ground;*
earth to earth, ashes to ashes, dust to dust. The Lord bless
him and keep *him*, the Lord make his face to shine upon *him*
and be gracious unto *him*, the Lord lift up his countenance
upon *him* and give *him* peace. *Amen.*

* *Or* the deep, *or* the elements, *or* its resting place.

The Celebrant says

       The Lord be with you.
People   And with thy spirit.
Celebrant Let us pray.

Celebrant and People

Our Father, who art in heaven,
   hallowed be thy Name,
   thy kingdom come,
   thy will be done,
     on earth as it is in heaven.
Give us this day our daily bread.

And forgive us our trespasses,
    as we forgive those who trespass against us.
And lead us not into temptation,
    but deliver us from evil.
For thine is the kingdom, and the power, and the glory,
    for ever and ever. *Amen.*

Then the Celebrant may say

O Almighty God, the God of the spirits of all flesh, who by a voice from heaven didst proclaim, Blessed are the dead who die in the Lord: Multiply, we beseech thee, to those who rest in Jesus the manifold blessings of thy love, that the good work which thou didst begin in them may be made perfect unto the day of Jesus Christ. And of thy mercy, O heavenly Father, grant that we, who now serve thee on earth, may at last, together with them, be partakers of the inheritance of the saints in light; for the sake of thy Son Jesus Christ our Lord. *Amen.*

In place of this prayer, or in addition to it, the Celebrant may use any of the Additional Prayers.

Then may be said

Rest eternal grant to *him*, O Lord:
And let light perpetual shine upon him.

May *his* soul, and the souls of all the departed, through the mercy of God, rest in peace. *Amen.*

The Celebrant dismisses the people with these words

The God of peace, who brought again from the dead our Lord Jesus Christ, the great Shepherd of the sheep, through the blood of the everlasting covenant: Make you perfect in every good work to do his will, working in you that which is well pleasing in his sight; through Jesus Christ, to whom be glory for ever and ever. *Amen.*

The Consecration of a Grave

If the grave is in a place that has not previously been set apart for Christian burial, the Priest may use the following prayer, either before the service of Committal or at some other convenient time

O God, whose blessed Son was laid in a sepulcher in the garden: Bless, we pray, this grave, and grant that *he* whose body is (is to be) buried here may dwell with Christ in paradise, and may come to thy heavenly kingdom; through thy Son Jesus Christ our Lord. *Amen.*

Additional Prayers

Almighty and everlasting God, we yield unto thee most high praise and hearty thanks for the wonderful grace and virtue declared in all thy saints, who have been the choice vessels of thy grace, and the lights of the world in their several generations; most humbly beseeching thee to give us grace so to follow the example of their steadfastness in thy faith, and obedience to thy holy commandments, that at the day of the general resurrection, we, with all those who are of the mystical body of thy Son, may be set on his right hand, and hear that his most joyful voice: "Come, ye blessed of my Father, inherit the kingdom prepared for you from the foundation of the world." Grant this, O Father, for the sake of the same thy Son Jesus Christ, our only Mediator and Advocate. *Amen.*

Almighty God, with whom do live the spirits of those who depart hence in the Lord, and with whom the souls of the faithful, after they are delivered from the burden of the flesh, are in joy and felicity: We give thee hearty thanks for the good examples of all those thy servants, who, having finished their course in faith, do now rest from their labors. And we beseech thee that we, with all those who are departed in the true faith of thy holy Name, may have our perfect consummation and bliss, both in body and soul, in thy eternal and everlasting glory; through Jesus Christ our Lord. *Amen.*

Into thy hands, O Lord, we commend thy servant *N.,* our dear *brother,* as into the hands of a faithful Creator and most merciful Savior, beseeching thee that *he* may be precious in thy sight. Wash *him,* we pray thee, in the blood of that immaculate Lamb that was slain to take away the sins of the world; that, whatsoever defilements *he* may have contracted in the midst of this earthly life being purged and done away, *he* may be presented pure and without spot before thee; through the merits of Jesus Christ thine only Son our Lord. *Amen.*

Remember thy servant, O Lord, according to the favor which thou bearest unto thy people; and grant that, increasing in knowledge and love of thee, *he* may go from strength to strength in the life of perfect service in thy heavenly kingdom; through Jesus Christ our Lord. *Amen.*

Almighty God, our heavenly Father, in whose hands are the living and the dead: We give thee thanks for all thy servants who have laid down their lives in the service of our country. Grant to them thy mercy and the light of thy presence; and give us such a lively sense of thy righteous will, that the work which thou hast begun in them may be perfected; through Jesus Christ thy Son our Lord. *Amen.*

O God, whose days are without end, and whose mercies cannot be numbered: Make us, we beseech thee, deeply sensible of the shortness and uncertainty of life; and let thy Holy Spirit lead us in holiness and righteousness all our days; that, when we shall have served thee in our generation, we may be gathered unto our fathers, having the testimony of a good conscience; in the communion of the Catholic Church; in the confidence of a certain faith; in the comfort of a reasonable, religious, and holy hope; in favor with thee our God; and in perfect charity with the world. All which we ask through Jesus Christ our Lord. *Amen.*

O God, the King of saints, we praise and magnify thy holy Name for all thy servants who have finished their course in thy faith and fear; for the blessed Virgin Mary; for the holy patriarchs, prophets, apostles, and martyrs; and for all other thy righteous servants, known to us and unknown; and we beseech thee that, encouraged by their examples, aided by their prayers, and strengthened by their fellowship, we also may be partakers of the inheritance of the saints in light; through the merits of thy Son Jesus Christ our Lord. *Amen.*

O Lord Jesus Christ, Son of the living God, we pray thee to set thy passion, cross, and death, between thy judgment and our souls, now and in the hour of our death. Give mercy and grace to the living, pardon and rest to the dead, to thy holy Church peace and concord, and to us sinners everlasting life and glory; who with the Father and the Holy Spirit livest and reignest, one God, now and for ever. *Amen.*

Almighty God, Father of mercies and giver of all comfort: Deal graciously, we pray thee, with all those who mourn, that casting every care on thee, they may know the consolation of thy love; through Jesus Christ our Lord. *Amen.*

Concerning the Service

The death of a member of the Church should be reported as soon as possible to, and arrangements for the funeral should be made in consultation with, the Minister of the Congregation.

Baptized Christians are properly buried from the church. The service should be held at a time when the congregation has opportunity to be present.

The coffin is to be closed before the service, and it remains closed thereafter. It is appropriate that it be covered with a pall or other suitable covering.

If necessary, or if desired, all or part of the service of Committal may be said in the church. If preferred, the Committal service may take place before the service in the church. It may also be used prior to cremation.

A priest normally presides at the service. It is appropriate that the bishop, when present, preside at the Eucharist and pronounce the Commendation.

It is desirable that the Lesson from the Old Testament, and the Epistle, be read by lay persons.

When the services of a priest cannot be obtained, a deacon or lay reader may preside at the service.

At the burial of a child, the passages from Lamentations, 1 John, and John 6, together with Psalm 23, are recommended.

It is customary that the celebrant meet the body and go before it into the church or towards the grave.

The anthems at the beginning of the service are sung or said as the body is borne into the church, or during the entrance of the ministers, or by the celebrant standing in the accustomed place.

The Burial of the Dead: Rite Two

*All stand while one or more of the following anthems are sung or said.
A hymn, psalm, or some other suitable anthem may be sung instead.*

I am Resurrection and I am Life, says the Lord.
Whoever has faith in me shall have life,
even though he die.
And everyone who has life,
and has committed himself to me in faith,
shall not die for ever.

As for me, I know that my Redeemer lives
and that at the last he will stand upon the earth.
After my awaking, he will raise me up;
and in my body I shall see God.
I myself shall see, and my eyes behold him
who is my friend and not a stranger.

For none of us has life in himself,
and none becomes his own master when he dies.
For if we have life, we are alive in the Lord,
and if we die, we die in the Lord.
So, then, whether we live or die,
we are the Lord's possession.

Happy from now on
are those who die in the Lord!
So it is, says the Spirit,
for they rest from their labors.

Or else this anthem

In the midst of life we are in death;
from whom can we seek help?
From you alone, O Lord,
who by our sins are justly angered.

Holy God, Holy and Mighty,
Holy and merciful Savior,
deliver us not into the bitterness of eternal death.

Lord, you know the secrets of our hearts;
shut not your ears to our prayers,
but spare us, O Lord.

Holy God, Holy and Mighty,
Holy and merciful Savior,
deliver us not into the bitterness of eternal death.

O worthy and eternal Judge,
do not let the pains of death
turn us away from you at our last hour.

Holy God, Holy and Mighty,
Holy and merciful Savior,
deliver us not into the bitterness of eternal death.

When all are in place, the Celebrant may address the congregation,
acknowledging briefly the purpose of their gathering, and bidding their
prayers for the deceased and the bereaved.

The Celebrant then says

> The Lord be with you.
> *People*   And also with you.
> *Celebrant*   Let us pray.

Silence may be kept; after which the Celebrant says one of the following Collects

At the Burial of an Adult

O God, who by the glorious resurrection of your Son Jesus Christ destroyed death, and brought life and immortality to light: Grant that your servant N., being raised with him, may know the strength of his presence, and rejoice in his eternal glory; who with you and the Holy Spirit lives and reigns, one God, for ever and ever. *Amen.*

or this

O God, whose mercies cannot be numbered: Accept our prayers on behalf of your servant N., and grant *him* an entrance into the land of light and joy, in the fellowship of your saints; through Jesus Christ our Lord, who lives and reigns with you and the Holy Spirit, one God, now and for ever. *Amen.*

or this

O God of grace and glory, we remember before you this day our brother (sister) N. We thank you for giving *him* to us, *his* family and friends, to know and to love as a companion on our earthly pilgrimage. In your boundless compassion, console us who mourn. Give us faith to see in death the gate of eternal life, so that in quiet confidence we may continue our course on earth, until, by your call, we are reunited with those who have gone before; through Jesus Christ our Lord. *Amen.*

At the Burial of a Child

O God, whose beloved Son took children into his arms and blessed them: Give us grace to entrust *N.* to your never-failing care and love, and bring us all to your heavenly kingdom; through Jesus Christ our Lord, who lives and reigns with you and the Holy Spirit, one God, now and for ever. *Amen.*

The Celebrant may add the following prayer

Most merciful God, whose wisdom is beyond our understanding: Deal graciously with *NN.* in *their* grief. Surround *them* with your love, that *they* may not be overwhelmed by *their* loss, but have confidence in your goodness, and strength to meet the days to come; through Jesus Christ our Lord. *Amen.*

The people sit.

One or more of the following passages from Holy Scripture is read. If there is to be a Communion, a passage from the Gospel always concludes the Readings.

The Liturgy of the Word

From the Old Testament

Isaiah 25:6-9 (He will swallow up death for ever)
Isaiah 61:1-3 (To comfort those who mourn)
Lamentations 3:22-26, 31-33 (The Lord is good to those who wait for him)
Wisdom 3:1-5, 9 (The souls of the righteous are in the hands of God)
Job 19:21-27a (I know that my Redeemer lives)

A suitable psalm, hymn, or canticle may follow. The following Psalms are appropriate: 42:1-7, 46, 90:1-12, 121, 130, 139:1-11.

From the New Testament

Romans 8:14-19, 34-35, 37-39 (The glory that shall be revealed)
1 Corinthians 15:20-26, 35-38, 42-44, 53-58 (The imperishable body)
2 Corinthians 4:16—5:9 (Things that are unseen are eternal)
1 John 3:1-2 (We shall be like him)
Revelation 7:9-17 (God will wipe away every tear)
Revelation 21:2-7 (Behold, I make all things new)

A suitable psalm, hymn, or canticle may follow. The following Psalms are appropriate: 23, 27, 106:1-5, 116.

The Gospel

Then, all standing, the Deacon or Minister appointed reads the Gospel, first saying

> The Holy Gospel of our Lord Jesus Christ
> according to John.

People   Glory to you, Lord Christ.

John 5:24-27 (He who believes has everlasting life)
John 6:37-40 (All that the Father gives me will come to me)
John 10:11-16 (I am the good shepherd)
John 11:21-27 (I am the resurrection and the life)
John 14:1-6 (In my Father's house are many rooms)

At the end of the Gospel, the Reader says

> The Gospel of the Lord.

People   Praise to you, Lord Christ.

Here there may be a homily by the Celebrant, or a member of the family, or a friend.

The Apostles' Creed may then be said, all standing. The Celebrant may introduce the Creed with these or similar words

In the assurance of eternal life given at Baptism, let us proclaim our faith and say,

Celebrant and People

I believe in God, the Father almighty,
    creator of heaven and earth.

I believe in Jesus Christ, his only Son, our Lord.
    He was conceived by the power of the Holy Spirit
        and born of the Virgin Mary.
    He suffered under Pontius Pilate,
        was·crucified, died, and was buried.
    He descended to the dead.
    On the third day he rose again.
    He ascended into heaven,
        and is seated at the right hand of the Father.
    He will come again to judge the living and the dead.

I believe in the Holy Spirit,
    the holy catholic Church,
    the communion of saints,
    the forgiveness of sins,
    the resurrection of the body,
    and the life everlasting. Amen.

If there is not to be a Communion, the Lord's Prayer is said here, and the service continues with the Prayers of the People, or with one or more suitable prayers (see pages 503-505).

When there is a Communion, the following form of the Prayers of the People is used, or else the form on page 465 or 480.

For our brother (sister) N., let us pray to our Lord Jesus Christ who said, "I am Resurrection and I am Life."

Lord, you consoled Martha and Mary in their distress; draw near to us who mourn for N., and dry the tears of those who weep.
Hear us, Lord.

You wept at the grave of Lazarus, your friend; comfort us in our sorrow.
Hear us, Lord.

You raised the dead to life; give to our brother (sister) eternal life.
Hear us, Lord.

You promised paradise to the thief who repented; bring our brother (sister) to the joys of heaven.
Hear us, Lord.

Our brother (sister) was washed in Baptism and anointed with the Holy Spirit; give *him* fellowship with all your saints.
Hear us, Lord.

He was nourished with your Body and Blood; grant *him* a place at the table in your heavenly kingdom.
Hear us, Lord.

Comfort us in our sorrows at the death of our brother (sister); let our faith be our consolation, and eternal life our hope.

Silence may be kept.

The Celebrant concludes with one of the following or some other prayer

Lord Jesus Christ, we commend to you our brother (sister) N., who was reborn by water and the Spirit in Holy Baptism. Grant that *his* death may recall to us your victory over death, and be an occasion for us to renew our trust in your Father's love. Give us, we pray, the faith to follow where you have led the way; and where you live and reign with the Father and the Holy Spirit, to the ages of ages. *Amen.*

or this

Father of all, we pray to you for N., and for all those whom we love but see no longer. Grant to them eternal rest. Let light perpetual shine upon them. May *his* soul and the souls of all the departed, through the mercy of God, rest in peace. *Amen.*

When there is no Communion, the service continues with the Commendation, or with the Committal.

At the Eucharist.

The service continues with the Peace and the Offertory.

Preface of the Commemoration of the Dead

In place of the usual postcommunion prayer, the following is said

Almighty God, we thank you that in your great love you have fed us with the spiritual food and drink of the Body and Blood of your Son Jesus Christ, and have given us a foretaste of your heavenly banquet. Grant that this Sacrament may be to us a comfort in affliction, and a pledge of our inheritance in that kingdom where there is no death, neither sorrow nor crying, but the fullness of joy with all your saints; through Jesus Christ our Savior. *Amen.*

If the body is not present, the service continues with the (blessing and) dismissal.

Unless the Committal follows immediately in the church, the following Commendation is used.

The Commendation

The Celebrant and other ministers take their places at the body.

This anthem, or some other suitable anthem, or a hymn, may be sung or said

Give rest, O Christ, to your servant(s) with your saints,
where sorrow and pain are no more,
neither sighing, but life everlasting.

You only are immortal, the creator and maker of mankind; and we are mortal, formed of the earth, and to earth shall we return. For so did you ordain when you created me, saying, "You are dust, and to dust you shall return." All of us go down to the dust; yet even at the grave we make our song: Alleluia, alleluia, alleluia.

Give rest, O Christ, to your servant(s) with your saints,
where sorrow and pain are no more,
neither sighing, but life everlasting.

The Celebrant, facing the body, says

Into your hands, O merciful Savior, we commend your servant N. Acknowledge, we humbly beseech you, a sheep of your own fold, a lamb of your own flock, a sinner of your own redeeming. Receive *him* into the arms of your mercy, into the blessed rest of everlasting peace, and into the glorious company of the saints in light. *Amen.*

The Celebrant, or the Bishop if present, may then bless the people, and a Deacon or other Minister may dismiss them, saying

Let us go forth in the name of Christ.
Thanks be to God.

As the body is borne from the church, a hymn, or one or more of these anthems may be sung or said

Christ is risen from the dead, trampling down death by death, and giving life to those in the tomb.

The Sun of Righteousness is gloriously risen, giving light to those who sat in darkness and in the shadow of death.

The Lord will guide our feet into the way of peace, having taken away the sin of the world.

Christ will open the kingdom of heaven to all who believe in his Name, saying, Come, O blessed of my Father; inherit the kingdom prepared for you.

Into paradise may the angels lead you. At your coming may the martyrs receive you, and bring you into the holy city Jerusalem.

or one of these Canticles,

The Song of Zechariah, *Benedictus*
The Song of Simeon, *Nunc dimittis*
Christ our Passover, *Pascha nostrum*

The Committal

The following anthem or one of those on pages 491-492 is sung or said

Everyone the Father gives to me will come to me;
I will never turn away anyone who believes in me.

He who raised Jesus Christ from the dead
will also give new life to our mortal bodies
through his indwelling Spirit.

My heart, therefore, is glad, and my spirit rejoices;
my body also shall rest in hope.

You will show me the path of life;
in your presence there is fullness of joy,
and in your right hand are pleasures for evermore.

Then, while earth is cast upon the coffin, the Celebrant says these words

In sure and certain hope of the resurrection to eternal life
through our Lord Jesus Christ, we commend to Almighty
God our *brother N.*, and we commit *his* body to the ground;*
earth to earth, ashes to ashes, dust to dust. The Lord bless
him and keep *him*, the Lord make his face to shine upon *him*
and be gracious to *him*, the Lord lift up his countenance upon
him and give *him* peace. *Amen.*

*Or the deep, or the elements, or its resting place.

The Celebrant says

        The Lord be with you.
People   And also with you.
Celebrant Let us pray.

Our Father, who art in heaven,
  hallowed be thy Name,
  thy kingdom come,
  thy will be done,
    on earth as it is in heaven.
Give us this day our daily bread.
And forgive us our trespasses,
  as we forgive those
    who trespass against us.
And lead us not into temptation,
  but deliver us from evil.
For thine is the kingdom,
  and the power, and the glory,
  for ever and ever. Amen.

Our Father in heaven,
  hallowed be your Name,
  your kingdom come,
  your will be done,
    on earth as in heaven.
Give us today our daily bread.
Forgive us our sins
  as we forgive those
    who sin against us.
Save us from the time of trial,
  and deliver us from evil.
For the kingdom, the power,
  and the glory are yours,
  now and for ever. Amen.

Other prayers may be added.

Then may be said

Rest eternal grant to *him*, O Lord;
And let light perpetual shine upon him.

May *his* soul, and the souls of all the departed,
through the mercy of God, rest in peace. *Amen.*

The Celebrant dismisses the people with these words

        Alleluia. Christ is risen.
People   The Lord is risen indeed. Alleluia.
Celebrant Let us go forth in the name of Christ.
People   Thanks be to God.

or with the following

The God of peace, who brought again from the dead our Lord Jesus Christ, the great Shepherd of the sheep, through the blood of the everlasting covenant: Make you perfect in every good work to do his will, working in you that which is well-pleasing in his sight; through Jesus Christ, to whom be glory for ever and ever. *Amen.*

The Consecration of a Grave

If the grave is in a place that has not previously been set apart for Christian burial, the Priest may use the following prayer, either before the service of Committal or at some other convenient time

O God, whose blessed Son was laid in a sepulcher in the garden: Bless, we pray, this grave, and grant that *he* whose body is (is to be) buried here may dwell with Christ in paradise, and may come to your heavenly kingdom; through your Son Jesus Christ our Lord. *Amen.*

Additional prayers

Almighty God, with whom still live the spirits of those who die in the Lord, and with whom the souls of the faithful are in joy and felicity: We give you heartfelt thanks for the good examples of all your servants, who, having finished their course in faith, now find rest and refreshment. May we, with all who have died in the true faith of your holy Name, have perfect fulfillment and bliss in your eternal and everlasting glory; through Jesus Christ our Lord. *Amen.*

O God, whose days are without end, and whose mercies cannot be numbered: Make us, we pray, deeply aware of the shortness and uncertainty of human life; and let your Holy Spirit lead us in holiness and righteousness all our days; that, when we shall have served you in our generation, we may be gathered to our ancestors, having the testimony of a good conscience, in the communion of the Catholic Church, in the confidence of a certain faith, in the comfort of a religious and holy hope, in favor with you, our God, and in perfect charity with the world. All this we ask through Jesus Christ our Lord. *Amen.*

O God, the King of saints, we praise and glorify your holy Name for all your servants who have finished their course in your faith and fear: for the blessed Virgin Mary; for the holy patriarchs, prophets, apostles, and martyrs; and for all your other righteous servants, known to us and unknown; and we pray that, encouraged by their examples, aided by their prayers, and strengthened by their fellowship, we also may be partakers of the inheritance of the saints in light; through the merits of your Son Jesus Christ our Lord. *Amen.*

Lord Jesus Christ, by your death you took away the sting of death: Grant to us your servants so to follow in faith where you have led the way, that we may at length fall asleep peacefully in you and wake up in your likeness; for your tender mercies' sake. *Amen.*

Father of all, we pray to you for those we love, but see no longer: Grant them your peace; let light perpetual shine upon them; and, in your loving wisdom and almighty power, work in them the good purpose of your perfect will; through Jesus Christ our Lord. *Amen.*

Merciful God, Father of our Lord Jesus Christ who is the Resurrection and the Life: Raise us, we humbly pray, from the death of sin to the life of righteousness; that when we depart this life we may rest in him, and at the resurrection receive that blessing which your well-beloved Son shall then pronounce: "Come, you blessed of my Father, receive the kingdom prepared for you from the beginning of the world." Grant this, O merciful Father, through Jesus Christ, our Mediator and Redeemer. *Amen.*

Grant, O Lord, to all who are bereaved the spirit of faith and courage, that they may have strength to meet the days to come with steadfastness and patience; not sorrowing as those without hope, but in thankful remembrance of your great goodness, and in the joyful expectation of eternal life with those they love. And this we ask in the Name of Jesus Christ our Savior. *Amen.*

Almighty God, Father of mercies and giver of comfort: Deal graciously, we pray, with all who mourn; that, casting all their care on you, they may know the consolation of your love; through Jesus Christ our Lord. *Amen.*

An Order for Burial

When, for pastoral considerations, neither of the burial rites in this Book is deemed appropriate, the following form is used.

1. The body is received. The celebrant may meet the body and conduct it into the church or chapel, or it may be in place before the congregation assembles.

2. Anthems from Holy Scripture or psalms may be sung or said, or a hymn may be sung.

3. Prayer may be offered for the bereaved.

4. One or more passages of Holy Scripture are read. Psalms, hymns, or anthems may follow the readings. If there is to be a Communion, the last Reading is from the Gospel.

5. A homily may follow the Readings, and the Apostles' Creed may be recited.

6. Prayer, including the Lord's Prayer, is offered for the deceased, for those who mourn, and for the Christian community, remembering the promises of God in Christ about eternal life.

7. The deceased is commended to God, and the body is committed to its resting place. The committal may take place either where the preceding service has been held, or at the graveside.

8. If there is a Communion, it precedes the commendation, and begins with the Peace and Offertory of the Eucharist. Any of the authorized eucharistic prayers may be used.

Note:

The liturgy for the dead is an Easter liturgy. It finds all its meaning in the resurrection. Because Jesus was raised from the dead, we, too, shall be raised.

The liturgy, therefore, is characterized by joy, in the certainty that "neither death, nor life, nor angels, nor principalities, nor things present, nor things to come, nor powers, nor height, nor depth, nor anything else in all creation, will be able to separate us from the love of God in Christ Jesus our Lord."

This joy, however, does not make human grief unchristian. The very love we have for each other in Christ brings deep sorrow when we are parted by death. Jesus himself wept at the grave of his friend. So, while we rejoice that one we love has entered into the nearer presence of our Lord, we sorrow in sympathy with those who mourn.

Episcopal Services

Preface to the Ordination Rites

The Holy Scriptures and ancient Christian writers make it clear that from the apostles' time, there have been different ministries within the Church. In particular, since the time of the New Testament, three distinct orders of ordained ministers have been characteristic of Christ's holy catholic Church. First, there is the order of bishops who carry on the apostolic work of leading, supervising, and uniting the Church. Secondly, associated with them are the presbyters, or ordained elders, in subsequent times generally known as priests. Together with the bishops, they take part in the governance of the Church, in the carrying out of its missionary and pastoral work, and in the preaching of the Word of God and administering his holy Sacraments. Thirdly, there are deacons who assist bishops and priests in all of this work. It is also a special responsibility of deacons to minister in Christ's name to the poor, the sick, the suffering, and the helpless.

The persons who are chosen and recognized by the Church as being called by God to the ordained ministry are admitted to these sacred orders by solemn prayer and the laying on of episcopal hands. It has been, and is, the intention and purpose of this Church to maintain and continue these three orders; and for this purpose these services of ordination and consecration are appointed. No persons are allowed to exercise the offices of bishop, priest, or deacon in this Church unless they are so ordained, or have already received such ordination with the laying on of hands by bishops who are themselves duly qualified to confer Holy Orders.

It is also recognized and affirmed that the threefold ministry is not the exclusive property of this portion of Christ's catholic Church, but is a gift from God for the nurture of his people and the proclamation of his Gospel everywhere. Accordingly, the manner of ordaining in this Church is to be such as has been, and is, most generally recognized by Christian people as suitable for the conferring of the sacred orders of bishop, priest, and deacon.

Concerning the
Ordination of a Bishop

In accordance with ancient custom, it is desirable, if possible, that bishops be ordained on Sundays and other feasts of our Lord or on the feasts of apostles or evangelists.

When a bishop is to be ordained, the Presiding Bishop of the Church, or a bishop appointed by the Presiding Bishop, presides and serves as chief consecrator. At least two other bishops serve as co-consecrators. Representatives of the presbyterate, diaconate, and laity of the diocese for which the new bishop is to be consecrated, are assigned appropriate duties in the service.

From the beginning of the service until the Offertory, the chief consecrator presides from a chair placed close to the people, so that all may see and hear what is done. The other bishops, or a convenient number of them, sit to the right and left of the chief consecrator.

The bishop-elect is vested in a rochet or alb, without stole, tippet, or other vesture distinctive of ecclesiastical or academic rank or order.

When the bishop-elect is presented, *his* full name (designated by the symbol *N.N.*) is used. Thereafter, it is appropriate to refer to *him* only by the Christian name by which *he* wishes to be known.

At the Offertory, it is appropriate that the bread and wine be brought to the Altar by the family or friends of the newly ordained.

The family of the newly ordained may receive Communion before other members of the congregation. Opportunity is always given to the people to communicate.

Additional directions are on page 552.

The Ordination of a Bishop

Hymns, psalms, and anthems may be sung during the entrance of the bishops and other ministers.

The people standing, the Bishop appointed says

Blessed be God: Father, Son, and Holy Spirit.

People   And blessed be his kingdom, now and for ever. Amen.

In place of the above, from Easter Day through the Day of Pentecost

Bishop   Alleluia. Christ is risen.
People   The Lord is risen indeed. Alleluia.

In Lent and on other penitential occasions

Bishop   Bless the Lord who forgives all our sins.
People   His mercy endures for ever.

The Bishop then says

Almighty God, to you all hearts are open, all desires known, and from you no secrets are hid: Cleanse the thoughts of our hearts by the inspiration of your Holy Spirit, that we may perfectly love you, and worthily magnify your holy Name; through Christ our Lord. *Amen.*

The Presentation

The bishops and people sit. Representatives of the diocese, both Priests and Lay Persons, standing before the Presiding Bishop, present the bishop-elect, saying

N., Bishop in the Church of God, the clergy and people of the Diocese of N., trusting in the guidance of the Holy Spirit, have chosen N.N. to be a bishop and chief pastor. We therefore ask you to lay your hands upon *him* and in the power of the Holy Spirit to consecrate *him* a bishop in the one, holy, catholic, and apostolic Church.

The Presiding Bishop then directs that testimonials of the election be read.

When the reading of the testimonials is ended, the Presiding Bishop requires the following promise from the Bishop-elect

In the Name of the Father, and of the Son, and of the Holy Spirit, I, N.N., chosen Bishop of the Church in N., solemnly declare that I do believe the Holy Scriptures of the Old and New Testaments to be the Word of God, and to contain all things necessary to salvation; and I do solemnly engage to conform to the doctrine, discipline, and worship of The Episcopal Church.

The Bishop-elect then signs the above Declaration in the sight of all present. The witnesses add their signatures.

All stand.

The Presiding Bishop then says the following, or similar words, and asks the response of the people

Brothers and sisters in Christ Jesus, you have heard testimony given that *N.N.* has been duly and lawfully elected to be a bishop of the Church of God to serve in the Diocese of *N.* You have been assured of *his* suitability and that the Church has approved *him* for this sacred responsibility. Nevertheless, if any of you know any reason why we should not proceed, let it now be made known.

If no objection is made, the Presiding Bishop continues

Is it your will that we ordain *N.* a bishop?

The People respond in these or other words

That is our will.

Presiding Bishop

Will you uphold *N.* as bishop?

The People respond in these or other words

We will.

The Presiding Bishop then says

The Scriptures tell us that our Savior Christ spent the whole night in prayer before he chose and sent forth his twelve apostles. Likewise, the apostles prayed before they appointed Matthias to be one of their number. Let us, therefore, follow their examples, and offer our prayers to Almighty God before we ordain *N.* for the work to which we trust the Holy Spirit has called *him.*

All kneel, and the Person appointed leads the Litany for Ordinations, or some other approved litany. At the end of the litany, after the Kyries, the Presiding Bishop stands and reads the Collect for the Day, or the following Collect, or both, first saying

The Lord be with you
People   And also with you.

Let us pray.

O God of unchangeable power and eternal light: Look favorably on your whole Church, that wonderful and sacred mystery; by the effectual working of your providence, carry out in tranquillity the plan of salvation; let the whole world see and know that things which were cast down are being raised up, and things which had grown old are being made new, and that all things are being brought to their perfection by him through whom all things were made, your Son Jesus Christ our Lord; who lives and reigns with you, in the unity of the Holy Spirit, one God, for ever and ever. *Amen.*

The Ministry of the Word

Three Lessons are read. Lay persons read the Old Testament Lesson and the Epistle.

The Readings are ordinarily selected from the following list and may be lengthened if desired. On a Major Feast or on a Sunday, the Presiding Bishop may select Readings from the Proper of the Day.

Old Testament   Isaiah 61:1-8, *or* Isaiah 42:1-9
Psalm   99, *or* 40:1-14, *or* 100
Epistle   Hebrews 5:1-10, *or* 1 Timothy 3:1-7, *or* 2 Corinthians 3:4-9

The Reader first says

A Reading (Lesson) from _____ .

A citation giving chapter and verse may be added.

After each Reading, the Reader may say

        The Word of the Lord.

People   Thanks be to God.

or the Reader may say   Here ends the Reading (Epistle).

Silence may follow.

A Psalm, canticle, or hymn follows each Reading.

Then, all standing, a Deacon or a Priest reads the Gospel, first saying

        The Holy Gospel of our Lord Jesus Christ
        according to _____ .

People   Glory to you, Lord Christ.

        John 20:19-23,   *or* John 17:1-9, 18-21,   *or* Luke 24:44-49a

After the Gospel, the Reader says

        The Gospel of the Lord.

People   Praise to you, Lord Christ.

The Sermon

After the Sermon, the Congregation sings a hymn.

The Examination

All now sit, except the bishop-elect, who stands facing the bishops. The Presiding Bishop addresses the bishop-elect

My *brother*, the people have chosen you and have affirmed their trust in you by acclaiming your election. A bishop in God's holy Church is called to be one with the apostles in proclaiming Christ's resurrection and interpreting the Gospel, and to testify to Christ's sovereignty as Lord of lords and King of kings.

You are called to guard the faith, unity, and discipline of the Church; to celebrate and to provide for the administration of the sacraments of the New Covenant; to ordain priests and deacons and to join in ordaining bishops; and to be in all things a faithful pastor and wholesome example for the entire flock of Christ.

With your fellow bishops you will share in the leadership of the Church throughout the world. Your heritage is the faith of patriarchs, prophets, apostles, and martyrs, and those of every generation who have looked to God in hope. Your joy will be to follow him who came, not to be served, but to serve, and to give his life a ransom for many.

Are you persuaded that God has called you to the office of bishop?

Answer   I am so persuaded.

The following questions are then addressed to the bishop-elect by one or more of the other bishops

Bishop	Will you accept this call and fulfill this trust in obedience to Christ?
Answer	I will obey Christ, and will serve in his name.
Bishop	Will you be faithful in prayer, and in the study of Holy Scripture, that you may have the mind of Christ?
Answer	I will, for he is my help.
Bishop	Will you boldly proclaim and interpret the Gospel of Christ, enlightening the minds and stirring up the conscience of your people?
Answer	I will, in the power of the Spirit.
Bishop	As a chief priest and pastor, will you encourage and support all baptized people in their gifts and ministries, nourish them from the riches of God's grace, pray for them without ceasing, and celebrate with them the sacraments of our redemption?
Answer	I will, in the name of Christ, the Shepherd and Bishop of our souls.
Bishop	Will you guard the faith, unity, and discipline of the Church?
Answer	I will, for the love of God.
Bishop	Will you share with your fellow bishops in the government of the whole Church; will you sustain your fellow presbyters and take counsel with them; will you guide and strengthen the deacons and all others who minister in the Church?
Answer	I will, by the grace given me.
Bishop	Will you be merciful to all, show compassion to the poor and strangers, and defend those who have no helper?
Answer	I will, for the sake of Christ Jesus.

N., through these promises you have committed yourself to God, to serve his Church in the office of bishop. We therefore call upon you, chosen to be a guardian of the Church's faith, to lead us in confessing that faith.

Bishop-elect
We believe in one God.

Then all sing or say together
We believe in one God,
    the Father, the Almighty,
    maker of heaven and earth,
    of all that is, seen and unseen.

We believe in one Lord, Jesus Christ,
    the only Son of God,
    eternally begotten of the Father,
    God from God, Light from Light,
    true God from true God,
    begotten, not made,
    of one Being with the Father.
    Through him all things were made.
For us and for our salvation
    he came down from heaven:
by the power of the Holy Spirit
    he became incarnate from the Virgin Mary,
    and was made man.
For our sake he was crucified under Pontius Pilate;
    he suffered death and was buried.
    On the third day he rose again
        in accordance with the Scriptures;
    he ascended into heaven
        and is seated at the right hand of the Father.

He will come again in glory to judge the living and the dead,
    and his kingdom will have no end.
We believe in the Holy Spirit, the Lord, the giver of life,
    who proceeds from the Father and the Son.
    With the Father and the Son he is worshiped and glorified.
    He has spoken through the Prophets.
    We believe in one holy catholic and apostolic Church.
    We acknowledge one baptism for the forgiveness of sins.
    We look for the resurrection of the dead,
        and the life of the world to come. Amen.

The Consecration of the Bishop

*All continue to stand, except the bishop-elect, who kneels before the
Presiding Bishop. The other bishops stand to the right and left of the
Presiding Bishop.*

*The hymn, Veni Creator Spiritus, or the hymn, Veni Sancte Spiritus, is
sung.*

A period of silent prayer follows, the people still standing.

The Presiding Bishop then begins this Prayer of Consecration

God and Father of our Lord Jesus Christ, Father of mercies
and God of all comfort, dwelling on high but having regard
for the lowly, knowing all things before they come to pass:
We give you thanks that from the beginning you have
gathered and prepared a people to be heirs of the covenant of
Abraham, and have raised up prophets, kings, and priests,
never leaving your temple untended. We praise you also that
from the creation you have graciously accepted the ministry
of those whom you have chosen.

The Presiding Bishop and other Bishops now lay their hands upon the head of the bishop-elect, and say together

Therefore, Father, make N. a bishop in your Church. Pour out upon *him* the power of your princely Spirit, whom you bestowed upon your beloved Son Jesus Christ, with whom he endowed the apostles, and by whom your Church is built up in every place, to the glory and unceasing praise of your Name.

The Presiding Bishop continues

To you, O Father, all hearts are open; fill, we pray, the heart of this your servant whom you have chosen to be a bishop in your Church, with such love of you and of all the people, that *he* may feed and tend the flock of Christ, and exercise without reproach the high priesthood to which you have called *him*, serving before you day and night in the ministry of reconciliation, declaring pardon in your Name, offering the holy gifts, and wisely overseeing the life and work of the Church. In all things may *he* present before you the acceptable offering of a pure, and gentle, and holy life; through Jesus Christ your Son, to whom, with you and the Holy Spirit, be honor and power and glory in the Church, now and for ever.

The People in a loud voice respond   Amen.

The new bishop is now vested according to the order of bishops.

A Bible is presented with these words

Receive the Holy Scriptures. Feed the flock of Christ committed to your charge, guard and defend them in his truth, and be a faithful steward of his holy Word and Sacraments.

After this other symbols of office may be given.

The Presiding Bishop presents to the people their new bishop.

The Clergy and People offer their acclamation and applause.

The Peace

The new Bishop then says

> The peace of the Lord be always with you.

People   And also with you.

The Presiding Bishop and other Bishops greet the new bishop.

The People greet one another.

The new Bishop also greets other members of the clergy, family members, and the congregation.

The new Bishop, if the Bishop of the Diocese, may now be escorted to the episcopal chair.

At the Celebration of the Eucharist

The liturgy continues with the Offertory.

Deacons prepare the Table.

Then the new Bishop goes to the Lord's Table as chief Celebrant and, joined by other bishops and presbyters, proceeds with the celebration of the Eucharist.

After Communion

In place of the usual postcommunion prayer, one of the bishops leads the people in the following

Almighty Father, we thank you for feeding us with the holy food of the Body and Blood of your Son, and for uniting us through him in the fellowship of your Holy Spirit. We thank you for raising up among us faithful servants for the ministry of your Word and Sacraments. We pray that N. may be to us an effective example in word and action, in love and patience, and in holiness of life. Grant that we, with *him*, may serve you now, and always rejoice in your glory; through Jesus Christ your Son our Lord, who lives and reigns with you and the Holy Spirit, one God, now and for ever. Amen.

The new Bishop blesses the people, first saying

Our help is in the Name of the Lord;
People The maker of heaven and earth.

New Bishop Blessed be the Name of the Lord;
People   From this time forth for evermore.

New Bishop The blessing, mercy, and grace of God Almighty, the Father, the Son, and the Holy Spirit, be upon you, and remain with you for ever. *Amen.*

A Deacon dismisses the people

Let us go forth into the world, rejoicing in the power of the Spirit.
People Thanks be to God.

From Easter Day through the Day of Pentecost "Alleluia, alleluia," may be added to the dismissal and to the response.

Concerning the Service

When a bishop is to confer Holy Orders, at least two presbyters must be present.

From the beginning of the service until the Offertory, the bishop presides from a chair placed close to the people, and facing them, so that all may see and hear what is done.

The ordinand is to be vested in surplice or alb, without stole, tippet, or other vesture distinctive of ecclesiastical or academic rank or order.

When the ordinand is presented, *his* full name (designated by the symbol N.N.) is used. Thereafter, it is appropriate to refer to *him* only by the Christian name by which *he* wishes to be known.

At the Offertory, it is appropriate that the bread and wine be brought to the Altar by the family and friends of the newly ordained.

At the Great Thanksgiving, the new priest and other priests stand at the Altar with the bishop, as associates and fellow ministers of the Sacrament, and communicate with the bishop.

The family of the newly ordained may receive Communion before other members of the congregation. Opportunity is always given to the people to communicate.

Additional Directions are on page 552.

The Ordination of a Priest

A hymn, psalm, or anthem may be sung.

The people standing, the Bishop says

Blessed be God: Father, Son, and Holy Spirit.

People   And blessed be his kingdom, now and for ever. Amen.

In place of the above, from Easter Day through the Day of Pentecost

Bishop   Alleluia. Christ is risen.
People   The Lord is risen indeed. Alleluia.

In Lent and on other penitential occasions

Bishop   Bless the Lord who forgives all our sins.
People   His mercy endures for ever.

Bishop

Almighty God, to you all hearts are open, all desires known, and from you no secrets are hid: Cleanse the thoughts of our hearts by the inspiration of your Holy Spirit, that we may perfectly love you, and worthily magnify your holy Name; through Christ our Lord. *Amen.*

The Presentation

The bishop and people sit. A Priest and a Lay Person, and additional presenters if desired, standing before the bishop, present the ordinand, saying

N., Bishop in the Church of God, on behalf of the clergy and people of the Diocese of N., we present to you N.N. to be ordained a priest in Christ's holy catholic Church.

Bishop

Has *he* been selected in accordance with the canons of this Church? And do you believe *his* manner of life to be suitable to the exercise of this ministry?

Presenters

We certify to you that *he* has satisfied the requirements of the canons, and we believe *him* to be qualified for this order.

The Bishop says to the ordinand

Will you be loyal to the doctrine, discipline, and worship of Christ as this Church has received them? And will you, in accordance with the canons of this Church, obey your bishop and other ministers who may have authority over you and your work?

Answer

I am willing and ready to do so; and I solemnly declare that I do believe the Holy Scriptures of the Old and New Testaments to be the Word of God, and to contain all things necessary to salvation; and I do solemnly engage to conform to the doctrine, discipline, and worship of The Episcopal Church.

The Ordinand then signs the above Declaration in the sight of all present.

All stand. The Bishop says to the people

Dear friends in Christ, you know the importance of this ministry, and the weight of your responsibility in presenting N.N. for ordination to the sacred priesthood. Therefore if any of you know any impediment or crime because of which we should not proceed, come forward now, and make it known.

If no objection is made, the Bishop continues

Is it your will that N. be ordained a priest?

The People respond in these or other words

It is.

Bishop

Will you uphold *him* in this ministry?

The People respond in these or other words

We will.

The Bishop then calls the people to prayer with these or similar words

In peace let us pray to the Lord.

All kneel, and the Person appointed leads the Litany for Ordinations, or some other approved litany. At the end of the litany, after the Kyries, the Bishop stands and reads the Collect for the Day, or the following Collect, or both, first saying

The Lord be with you.
People   And also with you.

Let us pray.

O God of unchangeable power and eternal light: Look
favorably on your whole Church, that wonderful and sacred
mystery; by the effectual working of your providence, carry
out in tranquillity the plan of salvation; let the whole world
see and know that things which were cast down are being
raised up, and things which had grown old are being made
new, and that all things are being brought to their perfection
by him through whom all things were made, your Son Jesus
Christ our Lord; who lives and reigns with you, in the unity
of the Holy Spirit, one God, for ever and ever. *Amen.*

The Ministry of the Word

*Three Lessons are read. Lay persons read the Old Testament Lesson and
the Epistle.*

*The Readings are ordinarily selected from the following list and may be
lengthened if desired. On a Major Feast, or on a Sunday, the Bishop may
select Readings from the Proper of the Day.*

Old Testament   Isaiah 6:1-8,   or Numbers 11:16-17, 24-25
                                      (omitting the final clause)

Psalm   43,   *or* 132:8-19
Epistle   1 Peter 5:1-4,*   *or* Ephesians 4:7, 11-16,   *or* Philippians 4:4-9

*It is to be noted that where the words elder, elders, and fellow elder, appear in
translations of 1 Peter 5:1, the original Greek terms presbyter, presbyters, and
fellow presbyter, are to be substituted.*

The Reader first says

A Reading (Lesson) from _____ .

A citation giving chapter and verse may be added.

After each Reading, the Reader may say

The Word of the Lord.
People   Thanks be to God.

or the Reader may say   Here ends the Reading (Epistle).

Silence may follow.

A Psalm, canticle, or hymn follows each Reading.

Then, all standing, the Deacon or, if no deacon is present, a Priest reads the Gospel, first saying

The Holy Gospel of our Lord Jesus Christ
according to _____.
People   Glory to you, Lord Christ.

Matthew 9:35-38,   *or* John 10:11-18,   *or* John 6:35-38

After the Gospel, the Reader says

The Gospel of the Lord.
People   Praise to you, Lord Christ.

The Sermon

The Congregation then says or sings the Nicene Creed

We believe in one God,
the Father, the Almighty,
maker of heaven and earth,
of all that is, seen and unseen.

We believe in one Lord, Jesus Christ,
   the only Son of God,
   eternally begotten of the Father,
   God from God, Light from Light,
   true God from true God,
   begotten, not made,
   of one Being with the Father.
   Through him all things were made.
   For us and for our salvation
      he came down from heaven:
   by the power of the Holy Spirit
      he became incarnate from the Virgin Mary,
      and was made man.
   For our sake he was crucified under Pontius Pilate;
      he suffered death and was buried.
      On the third day he rose again
         in accordance with the Scriptures;
      he ascended into heaven
         and is seated at the right hand of the Father.
   He will come again in glory to judge the living and the dead,
      and his kingdom will have no end.

We believe in the Holy Spirit, the Lord, the giver of life,
   who proceeds from the Father and the Son.
   With the Father and the Son he is worshiped and glorified.
   He has spoken through the Prophets.
   We believe in one holy catholic and apostolic Church.
   We acknowledge one baptism for the forgiveness of sins.
   We look for the resurrection of the dead,
      and the life of the world to come. Amen.

The Examination

All are seated except the ordinand, who stands before the Bishop.

The Bishop addresses the ordinand as follows

My *brother*, the Church is the family of God, the body of Christ, and the temple of the Holy Spirit. All baptized people are called to make Christ known as Savior and Lord, and to share in the renewing of his world. Now you are called to work as a pastor, priest, and teacher, together with your bishop and fellow presbyters, and to take your share in the councils of the Church.

As a priest, it will be your task to proclaim by word and deed the Gospel of Jesus Christ, and to fashion your life in accordance with its precepts. You are to love and serve the people among whom you work, caring alike for young and old, strong and weak, rich and poor. You are to preach, to declare God's forgiveness to penitent sinners, to pronounce God's blessing, to share in the administration of Holy Baptism and in the celebration of the mysteries of Christ's Body and Blood, and to perform the other ministrations entrusted to you.

In all that you do, you are to nourish Christ's people from the riches of his grace, and strengthen them to glorify God in this life and in the life to come.

My *brother*, do you believe that you are truly called by God and his Church to this priesthood?

Answer I believe I am so called.

Bishop Do you now in the presence of the Church commit yourself to this trust and responsibility?

Answer I do.

Bishop	Will you respect and be guided by the pastoral direction and leadership of your bishop?
Answer	I will.
Bishop	Will you be diligent in the reading and study of the Holy Scriptures, and in seeking the knowledge of such things as may make you a stronger and more able minister of Christ?
Answer	I will.
Bishop	Will you endeavor so to minister the Word of God and the sacraments of the New Covenant, that the reconciling love of Christ may be known and received?
Answer	I will.
Bishop	Will you undertake to be a faithful pastor to all whom you are called to serve, laboring together with them and with your fellow ministers to build up the family of God?
Answer	I will.
Bishop	Will you do your best to pattern your life [and that of your family, *or* household, *or* community] in accordance with the teachings of Christ, so that you may be a wholesome example to your people?
Answer	I will.
Bishop	Will you persevere in prayer, both in public and in private, asking God's grace, both for yourself and for others, offering all your labors to God, through the mediation of Jesus Christ, and in the sanctification of the Holy Spirit?
Answer	I will.
Bishop	May the Lord who has given you the will to do these things give you the grace and power to perform them.
Answer	Amen.

The Consecration of the Priest

All now stand except the ordinand, who kneels facing the Bishop and the presbyters who stand to the right and left of the Bishop.

The hymn, Veni Creator Spiritus, or the hymn, Veni Sancte Spiritus, is sung.

A period of silent prayer follows, the people still standing.

The Bishop then says this Prayer of Consecration

God and Father of all, we praise you for your infinite love in calling us to be a holy people in the kingdom of your Son Jesus our Lord, who is the image of your eternal and invisible glory, the firstborn among many brethren, and the head of the Church. We thank you that by his death he has overcome death, and, having ascended into heaven, has poured his gifts abundantly upon your people, making some apostles, some prophets, some evangelists, some pastors and teachers, to equip the saints for the work of ministry and the building up of his body.

Here the Bishop lays hands upon the head of the ordinand, the Priests who are present also laying on their hands. At the same time the Bishop prays

Therefore, Father, through Jesus Christ your Son, give your Holy Spirit to N.; fill *him* with grace and power, and make *him* a priest in your Church.

The Bishop then continues

May *he* exalt you, O Lord, in the midst of your people; offer spiritual sacrifices acceptable to you; boldly proclaim the gospel of salvation; and rightly administer the sacraments of the New Covenant. Make *him* a faithful pastor, a patient teacher, and a wise councilor. Grant that in all things *he* may serve without reproach, so that your people may be strengthened and your Name glorified in all the world. All this we ask through Jesus Christ our Lord, who with you and the Holy Spirit lives and reigns, one God, for ever and ever.

The People in a loud voice respond   Amen.

The new priest is now vested according to the order of priests.

The Bishop then gives a Bible to the newly ordained, saying

Receive this Bible as a sign of the authority given you to preach the Word of God and to administer his holy Sacraments. Do not forget the trust committed to you as a priest of the Church of God.

The Bishop greets the newly ordained.

The Peace

The new Priest then says to the congregation

The peace of the Lord be always with you.
People   And also with you.

The Presbyters present greet the newly ordained; who then greets family members and others, as may be convenient. The Clergy and People greet one another.

At the Celebration of the Eucharist

The liturgy continues with the Offertory. Deacons prepare the Table.

Standing at the Lord's Table, with the Bishop and other presbyters, the newly ordained Priest joins in the celebration of the Holy Eucharist and in the Breaking of the Bread.

After Communion

In place of the usual postcommunion prayer, the following is said

Almighty Father, we thank you for feeding us with the holy food of the Body and Blood of your Son, and for uniting us through him in the fellowship of your Holy Spirit. We thank you for raising up among us faithful servants for the ministry of your Word and Sacraments. We pray that N. may be to us an effective example in word and action, in love and patience, and in holiness of life. Grant that we, with *him*, may serve you now, and always rejoice in your glory; through Jesus Christ your Son our Lord, who lives and reigns with you and the Holy Spirit, one God, now and for ever. *Amen.*

The Bishop then asks the new priest to bless the people.

The new Priest says

The blessing of God Almighty, the Father, the Son, and the Holy Spirit, be among you, and remain with you always. *Amen.*

A Deacon, or a Priest if no deacon is present, dismisses the people.

> Let us go forth into the world, rejoicing in the power of the Spirit.

People   Thanks be to God.

From Easter Day through the Day of Pentecost "Alleluia, alleluia," may be added to the dismissal and to the response.

Concerning the Service

When a bishop is to confer Holy Orders, at least two presbyters must be present.

From the beginning of the service until the Offertory, the bishop presides from a chair placed close to the people, and facing them, so that all may see and hear what is done.

The ordinand is to be vested in a surplice or alb, without tippet or other vesture distinctive of ecclesiastical or academic rank or office.

When the ordinand is presented, *his* full name (designated by the symbol *N.N.*) is used. Thereafter, it is appropriate to refer to *him* only by the Christian name by which *he* wishes to be known.

At the Offertory, it is appropriate that the bread and wine be brought to the Altar by the family or friends of the newly ordained.

After receiving Holy Communion, the new deacon assists in the distribution of the Sacrament, ministering either the Bread or the Wine, or both.

The family of the newly ordained may receive Communion before other members of the congregation. Opportunity is always given to the people to communicate.

Additional Directions are on page 552.

The Ordination of a Deacon

A hymn, psalm, or anthem may be sung.

The people standing, the Bishop says

> Blessed be God: Father, Son, and Holy Spirit.

People   And blessed be his kingdom, now and for ever. Amen.

In place of the above, from Easter Day through the Day of Pentecost

Bishop   Alleluia. Christ is risen.
People   The Lord is risen indeed. Alleluia.

In Lent and on other penitential occasions

Bishop   Bless the Lord who forgives all our sins.
People   His mercy endures for ever.

Bishop

Almighty God, to you all hearts are open, all desires known, and from you no secrets are hid: Cleanse the thoughts of our hearts by the inspiration of your Holy Spirit, that we may perfectly love you, and worthily magnify your holy Name; through Christ our Lord. *Amen.*

The Presentation

The bishop and people sit. A Priest and a Lay Person, and additional presenters if desired, standing before the bishop, present the ordinand, saying

N., Bishop in the Church of God, on behalf of the clergy and people of the Diocese of N., we present to you N.N. to be ordained a deacon in Christ's holy catholic Church.

Bishop

Has *he* been selected in accordance with the canons of this Church? And do you believe *his* manner of life to be suitable to the exercise of this ministry?

Presenters

We certify to you that *he* has satisfied the requirements of the canons, and we believe *him* qualified for this order.

The Bishop says to the ordinand

Will you be loyal to the doctrine, discipline, and worship of Christ as this Church has received them? And will you, in accordance with the canons of this Church, obey your bishop and other ministers who may have authority over you and your work?

Answer

I am willing and ready to do so; and I solemnly declare that I do believe the Holy Scriptures of the Old and New Testaments to be the Word of God, and to contain all things necessary to salvation; and I do solemnly engage to conform to the doctrine, discipline, and worship of The Episcopal Church.

The Ordinand then signs the above Declaration in the sight of all present.

All stand. The Bishop says to the people

Dear friends in Christ, you know the importance of this ministry, and the weight of your responsibility in presenting N.N. for ordination to the sacred order of deacons. Therefore if any of you know any impediment or crime because of which we should not proceed, come forward now and make it known.

If no objection is made, the Bishop continues

Is it your will that N. be ordained a deacon?

The People respond in these or other words

It is.

Bishop

Will you uphold *him* in this ministry?

The People respond in these or other words

We will.

The Bishop then calls the people to prayer with these or similar words

In peace let us pray to the Lord.

All kneel, and the Person appointed leads the Litany for Ordinations, or some other approved litany. At the end of the litany, after the Kyries, the Bishop stands and reads the Collect for the Day, or the following Collect, or both, first saying

	The Lord be with you.
People	And also with you.

Let us pray.

O God of unchangeable power and eternal light: Look favorably on your whole Church, that wonderful and sacred mystery; by the effectual working of your providence, carry out in tranquillity the plan of salvation; let the whole world see and know that things which were cast down are being raised up, and things which had grown old are being made new, and that all things are being brought to their perfection by him through whom all things were made, your Son Jesus Christ our Lord; who lives and reigns with you, in the unity of the Holy Spirit, one God, for ever and ever. *Amen.*

The Ministry of the Word

Three Lessons are read. Lay persons read the Old Testament Lesson and the Epistle.

The Readings are ordinarily selected from the following list and may be lengthened if desired. On a Major Feast, or on a Sunday, the Bishop may select Readings from the Proper of the Day.

Old Testament   Jeremiah 1:4-9,   *or* Ecclesiasticus 39:1-8
Psalm   84,   *or* 119:33-40
Epistle   2 Corinthians 4:1-6,   *or* 1 Timothy 3:8-13,   *or* Acts 6:2-7

The Reader first says

A Reading (Lesson) from ——————— .

A citation giving chapter and verse may be added.

After each Reading, the Reader may say

The Word of the Lord.
People   Thanks be to God.

or the Reader may say   Here ends the Reading (Epistle).

Silence may follow.

A Psalm, canticle, or hymn follows each Reading.

Then, all standing, the Deacon or, if no deacon is present, a Priest reads the Gospel, first saying

The Holy Gospel of our Lord Jesus Christ according to _____ .

People   Glory to you, Lord Christ.

Luke 12:35-38, *or* Luke 22:24-27

After the Gospel, the Reader says

The Gospel of the Lord.
People   Praise to you, Lord Christ.

The Sermon

The Congregation then says or sings the Nicene Creed

We believe in one God,
    the Father, the Almighty,
    maker of heaven and earth,
    of all that is, seen and unseen.

We believe in one Lord, Jesus Christ,
   the only Son of God,
   eternally begotten of the Father,
   God from God, Light from Light,
   true God from true God,
   begotten, not made,
   of one Being with the Father.
   Through him all things were made.
For us and for our salvation
   he came down from heaven:
by the power of the Holy Spirit
   he became incarnate from the Virgin Mary,
   and was made man.
For our sake he was crucified under Pontius Pilate;
   he suffered death and was buried.
   On the third day he rose again
      in accordance with the Scriptures;
   he ascended into heaven
      and is seated at the right hand of the Father.
He will come again in glory to judge the living and the dead,
   and his kingdom will have no end.

We believe in the Holy Spirit, the Lord, the giver of life,
   who proceeds from the Father and the Son.
   With the Father and the Son he is worshiped and glorified.
   He has spoken through the Prophets.
   We believe in one holy catholic and apostolic Church.
   We acknowledge one baptism for the forgiveness of sins.
   We look for the resurrection of the dead,
      and the life of the world to come. Amen.

The Examination

All are seated except the ordinand, who stands before the Bishop.
The Bishop addresses the ordinand as follows

My *brother*, every Christian is called to follow Jesus Christ, serving God the Father, through the power of the Holy Spirit. God now calls you to a special ministry of servanthood directly under your bishop. In the name of Jesus Christ, you are to serve all people, particularly the poor, the weak, the sick, and the lonely.

As a deacon in the Church, you are to study the Holy Scriptures, to seek nourishment from them, and to model your life upon them. You are to make Christ and his redemptive love known, by your word and example, to those among whom you live, and work, and worship. You are to interpret to the Church the needs, concerns, and hopes of the world. You are to assist the bishop and priests in public worship and in the ministration of God's Word and Sacraments, and you are to carry out other duties assigned to you from time to time. At all times, your life and teaching are to show Christ's people that in serving the helpless they are serving Christ himself.

My *brother*, do you believe that you are truly called by God and his Church to the life and work of a deacon?

Answer	I believe I am so called.
Bishop	Do you now in the presence of the Church commit yourself to this trust and responsibility?
Answer	I do.
Bishop	Will you be guided by the pastoral direction and leadership of your bishop?
Answer	I will.

Bishop	Will you be faithful in prayer, and in the reading and study of the Holy Scriptures?
Answer	I will.
Bishop	Will you look for Christ in all others, being ready to help and serve those in need?
Answer	I will.
Bishop	Will you do your best to pattern your life [and that of your family, *or* household, *or* community] in accordance with the teachings of Christ, so that you may be a wholesome example to all people?
Answer	I will.
Bishop	Will you in all things seek not your glory but the glory of the Lord Christ?
Answer	I will.
Bishop	May the Lord by his grace uphold you in the service he lays upon you.
Answer	Amen.

The Consecration of the Deacon

All now stand except the ordinand, who kneels facing the bishop.

The hymn, Veni Creator Spiritus, or the hymn, Veni Sancte Spiritus, is sung.

A period of silent prayer follows, the people still standing.

O God, most merciful Father, we praise you for sending your Son Jesus Christ, who took on himself the form of a servant, and humbled himself, becoming obedient even to death on the cross. We praise you that you have highly exalted him, and made him Lord of all; and that, through him, we know that whoever would be great must be servant of all. We praise you for the many ministries in your Church, and for calling this your servant to the order of deacons.

Here the Bishop lays hands upon the head of the ordinand, and prays

Therefore, Father, through Jesus Christ your Son, give your Holy Spirit to N.; fill *him* with grace and power, and make *him* a deacon in your Church.

The Bishop then continues

Make *him*, O Lord, modest and humble, strong and constant, to observe the discipline of Christ. Let *his* life and teaching so reflect your commandments, that through *him* many may come to know you and love you. As your Son came not to be served but to serve, may this deacon share in Christ's service, and come to the unending glory of him who, with you and the Holy Spirit, lives and reigns, one God, for ever and ever.

The People in a loud voice respond   Amen.

The new deacon is now vested according to the order of deacons.

The Bishop gives a Bible to the newly ordained, saying

Receive this Bible as the sign of your authority to proclaim God's Word and to assist in the ministration of his holy Sacraments.

The Peace

The Bishop then says to the congregation

>The peace of the Lord be always with you.

People And also with you.

The Bishop and the Clergy present now greet the newly ordained.

The new Deacon then exchanges greetings with family members and others, as may be convenient.

The Clergy and People greet one another.

At the Celebration of the Eucharist

The liturgy continues with the Offertory.

The newly ordained Deacon prepares the bread, pours sufficient wine (and a little water) into the chalice, and places the vessels on the Lord's Table.

The Bishop goes to the Table and begins the Great Thanksgiving.

After Communion

In place of the usual postcommunion prayer, the following is said

Almighty Father, we thank you for feeding us with the holy food of the Body and Blood of your Son, and for uniting us through him in the fellowship of your Holy Spirit. We thank you for raising up among us faithful servants for the ministry of your Word and Sacraments. We pray that N. may be to us an effective example in word and action, in love and patience, and in holiness of life. Grant that we, with *him*, may serve you now, and always rejoice in your glory; through Jesus Christ your Son our Lord, who lives and reigns with you and the Holy Spirit, one God, now and for ever. *Amen.*

The Bishop blesses the people, after which the new Deacon dismisses them

> Let us go forth into the world,
> rejoicing in the power of the Spirit.

People   Thanks be to God.

From Easter Day through the Day of Pentecost, "Alleluia, alleluia" may be added to the dismissal and to the response.

The Litany for Ordinations

For use at Ordinations as directed. On Ember Days or other occasions, if desired, this Litany may be used for the Prayers of the People at the Eucharist or the Daily Office, or it may be used separately.

God the Father,
Have mercy on us.

God the Son,
Have mercy on us.

God the Holy Spirit,
Have mercy on us.

Holy Trinity, one God,
Have mercy on us.

We pray to you, Lord Christ.
Lord, hear our prayer.

For the holy Church of God, that it may be filled with truth and love, and be found without fault at the Day of your Coming,
we pray to you, O Lord.
Lord, hear our prayer.

For all members of your Church in their vocation and ministry, that they may serve you in a true and godly life,
we pray to you, O Lord.
Lord, hear our prayer.

For N., our Presiding Bishop, and for all bishops, priests, and deacons, that they may be filled with your love, may hunger for truth, and may thirst after righteousness,
we pray to you, O Lord.
Lord, hear our prayer.

For N., chosen bishop (priest, deacon) in your Church,
we pray to you, O Lord.
Lord, hear our prayer.

That *he* may faithfully fulfill the duties of this ministry, build
up your Church, and glorify your Name,
we pray to you, O Lord.
Lord, hear our prayer.

That by the indwelling of the Holy Spirit *he* may be sustained
and encouraged to persevere to the end,
we pray to you, O Lord.
Lord, hear our prayer.

For *his* family [the members of *his* household *or* community],
that they may be adorned with all Christian virtues,
we pray to you, O Lord.
Lord, hear our prayer.

For all who fear God and believe in you, Lord Christ, that
our divisions may cease and that all may be one as you
and the Father are one,
we pray to you, O Lord.
Lord, hear our prayer.

For the mission of the Church, that in faithful witness it may
preach the Gospel to the ends of the earth,
we pray to you, O Lord.
Lord, hear our prayer.

For those who do not yet believe, and for those who have lost
their faith, that they may receive the light of the Gospel,
we pray to you, O Lord.
Lord, hear our prayer.

For the peace of the world, that a spirit of respect and
forbearance may grow among nations and peoples,
we pray to you, O Lord.
Lord, hear our prayer.

For those in positions of public trust [especially _____],
that they may serve justice and promote the dignity and
freedom of every person,
we pray to you, O Lord.
Lord, hear our prayer.

For a blessing upon all human labor, and for the right use
of the riches of creation, that the world may be freed from
poverty, famine, and disaster,
we pray to you, O Lord.
Lord, hear our prayer.

For the poor, the persecuted, the sick, and all who suffer; for
refugees, prisoners, and all who are in danger; that they may
be relieved and protected,
we pray to you, O Lord.
Lord, hear our prayer.

For ourselves; for the forgiveness of our sins, and for the
grace of the Holy Spirit to amend our lives,
we pray to you, O Lord.
Lord, hear our prayer.

For all who have died in the communion of your Church, and
those whose faith is known to you alone, that, with all the
saints, they may have rest in that place where there is no pain
or grief, but life eternal,
we pray to you, O Lord.
Lord, hear our prayer.

Rejoicing in the fellowship of [the ever-blessed Virgin Mary,
(*blessed N.*) and] all the saints, let us commend ourselves,
and one another, and all our life to Christ our God.
To you, O Lord our God.

Lord, have mercy.
Christ, have mercy.
Lord, have mercy.

At ordinations, the Bishop who is presiding stands and says

	The Lord be with you.
People	And also with you.
Bishop	Let us pray.

The Bishop says the appointed Collect.

When this Litany is used on other occasions, the Officiant concludes with a suitable Collect.

Additional Directions

At all Ordinations

The celebration of the Holy Eucharist may be according to Rite One or Rite Two. In either case, the rubrics of the service of ordination are followed. The Summary of the Law, the Gloria in excelsis, the Prayers of the People after the Creed, the General Confession, and the usual postcommunion prayer are not used.

At the Presentation of the Ordinand, the Declaration "I do believe the Holy Scriptures . . ." is to be provided as a separate document to be signed, as directed by Article VIII of the Constitution of this Church and by the rubrics in each of the ordination rites. (When there are more ordinands than one, each is to be presented with a separate copy for signature.)

The hymn to the Holy Spirit before the Prayer of Consecration may be sung responsively between a bishop and the congregation, or in some other convenient manner.

If vestments or other symbols of office are to be dedicated, such blessing is to take place at some convenient time prior to the service. The following form may be used

V. Our help is in the Name of the Lord;
R. The maker of heaven and earth.
V. The Lord be with you.
R. And also with you.

Let us pray.

Everliving God, whose power is limitless, we place before you, with our praise and thanks, *these tokens* of your servant's ministry and dignity. Grant that *N.*, who has been called to leadership in your Church, and bears *these signs*, may faithfully serve you and share in the fullness of your life-giving Spirit; through the high priest and good shepherd of us all, Jesus Christ our Lord. *Amen.*

At the Ordination of a Bishop

Following the Consecration Prayer, and while the new bishop is being clothed with the vesture of the episcopate, instrumental music may be played.

Following the presentation of the Bible, and the formula "Receive the Holy Scriptures . . ." a ring, staff, and mitre, or other suitable insignia of office may be presented.

During the Eucharistic Prayer, it is appropriate that some of the consecrating bishops, and representative presbyters of the diocese, stand with the new bishop at the Altar as fellow ministers of the Sacrament.

The newly ordained bishop, assisted by other ministers, distributes Holy Communion to the people. When necessary, the administration may take place at several conveniently separated places in the church.

After the pontifical blessing and the dismissal, a hymn of praise may be sung.

The bishops who are present are not to depart without signing the Letters of Consecration.

At the Ordination of a Priest

Reasonable opportunity is to be given for the priests present to join in the laying on of hands.

The stole worn about the neck, or other insignia of the office of priest, is placed upon the new priest after the entire Prayer of Consecration is completed, and immediately before the Bible is presented. Afterwards, other instruments or symbols of office may be given.

If two or more are ordained together, each is to have *his* own presenters. The ordinands may be presented together, or in succession, as the bishop may direct. Thereafter, references to the ordinand in the singular are changed to the plural where necessary. The ordinands are examined together.

During the Prayer of Consecration, the bishop and priests lay their hands upon the head of each ordinand. During the laying on of hands, the bishop alone says over each ordinand "Father, through Jesus Christ your

Son, give your Holy Spirit to N.; fill *him* with grace and power, and make *him* a priest in your Church." When they have laid their hands upon all the ordinands, the bishop continues "May they exalt you, O Lord, in the midst . . ."

A Bible is to be given to each new priest, and the words "Receive this Bible . . ." are to be said to each one.

All the newly ordained take part in the exchange of the Peace, and join the bishop and other priests at the Altar for the Great Thanksgiving. Similarly, all the new priests break the consecrated Bread and receive Holy Communion.

At the Ordination of a Deacon

The stole worn over the left shoulder, or other insignia of the office of deacon, is placed upon the new deacon after the entire Prayer of Consecration is completed, and immediately before the Bible is given.

If two or more are ordained together, each is to have *his* own presenters. The ordinands may be presented together, or in succession, as the bishop may direct. Thereafter, references to the ordinand in the singular are changed to the plural where necessary. The ordinands are examined together.

During the Prayer of Consecration the Bishop is to lay hands upon the head of each ordinand, and say over each one "Father, through Jesus Christ your Son, give your Holy Spirit to N.; fill *him* with grace and power, and make *him* a deacon in your Church." After laying hands upon all the ordinands, the bishop continues "Make them, O Lord, modest and humble. . ."

A Bible is to be given to each new deacon, and the words "Receive this Bible . . ." are also to be said to each one.

After participating in the Peace, the deacons go to the Altar for the Offertory. If there are many deacons, some assist in the Offertory and others administer Holy Communion. One, appointed by the bishop, is to say the dismissal.

When desired, deacons may be appointed to carry the Sacrament and minister Holy Communion to those communicants who, because of sickness or other grave cause, could not be present at the ordination.

If the remaining Elements are not required for the Communion of the absent, it is appropriate for the deacons to remove the vessels from the Altar, consume the remaining Elements, and cleanse the vessels in some convenient place.

Letter of Institution of a Minister

N.N., Presbyter of the Church of God, you have been called to work together with your Bishop and fellow-Presbyters as a pastor, priest, and teacher, and to take your share in the councils of the Church.

Now, in accordance with the Canons, you have been selected to serve God in _____ Church [of] _____.

This letter is a sign that you are fully empowered and authorized to exercise this ministry, accepting its privileges and responsibilities as a priest of this Diocese, in communion with your Bishop.

Having committed yourself to this work, do not forget the trust of those who have chosen you. Care alike for young and old, strong and weak, rich and poor. By your words, and in your life, proclaim the Gospel. Love and serve Christ's people. Nourish them, and strengthen them to glorify God in this life and in the life to come.

May the Lord, who has given you the will to do these things, give you the grace and power to perform them.

Given under my hand and seal, in the city of _____, on the _____ day of _____, 19 _____, and in the _____ year of my consecration.

(Signed) _____
Bishop of _____.

Concerning the Service

This order is for use when a priest is being instituted and inducted as the rector of a parish. It may also be used for the installation of deans and canons of cathedrals, or the inauguration of other ministries, diocesan or parochial, including vicars of missions and assistant ministers. Alterations in the service are then made according to circumstances.

The chief minister is normally the bishop; but, if necessary, a deputy may be appointed. The bishop, when present, is the chief celebrant of the Eucharist. In the bishop's absence, a priest being inducted is the chief celebrant.

Other priests, if any, who serve in the same congregation also stand with the chief celebrant at the Altar, and deacons assist according to their order.

Lay persons from the congregation read the Old Testament Lesson and the Epistle, and perform other actions as indicated in the rubrics. A deacon or priest reads the Gospel. Other clergy of the diocese participate in this celebration as an expression of the collegiality of the ministry in which they share.

Ministers of other Churches may appropriately be invited to participate.

The new minister, if a deacon, should read the Gospel, prepare the elements at the Offertory, assist the celebrant at the Altar, and dismiss the congregation.

A lay person being instituted should read one of the Lessons and assist where appropriate.

Additional Directions are on page 564.

Celebration of a
New Ministry

A hymn, psalm, or anthem may be sung.

The Institution

The Wardens, standing before the bishop with the new minister, say these or similar words

Bishop N., we have come together today to welcome N.N., who has been chosen to serve as *Rector* of (*name of church*). We believe that *he* is well qualified, and that *he* has been prayerfully and lawfully selected.

The Bishop may read the Letter of Institution, or else may state the purpose of the new ministry.

The Bishop then says

N., do you, in the presence of this congregation, commit yourself to this new trust and responsibility?

New minister   I do.

The Bishop then addresses the congregation

Will you who witness this new beginning support and uphold N. in this ministry?

People   We will.

The Bishop, standing, says

Let us then offer our prayers to God for all his people, for this congregation, and for *N.* their *Rector.*

The Litany for Ordinations, or some other appropriate litany, is led by a person appointed. At the end of the litany, the Bishop, standing, says the following or some other Collect, first saying

	The Lord be with you.
People	And also with you.
Bishop	Let us pray.

Everliving God, strengthen and sustain *N.,* that with patience and understanding *he* may love and care for your people; and grant that together they may follow Jesus Christ, offering to you their gifts and talents; through him who lives and reigns with you and the Holy Spirit, one God, for ever and ever. *Amen.*

At the Liturgy of the Word

The Readings are selected from the following list, or in accordance with the directions on page 565.

Old Testament   Joshua 1:7-9,   *or* Numbers 11:16-17, 24-25a
Psalm   43,   *or* 132:1-9,   *or* 146,   *or* 133 and 134 (especially suitable
for use in the evening)
Epistle   Romans 12:1-18,   *or* Ephesians 4:7, 11-16
Gospel   John 15:9-16,   *or* Luke 10:1-2,   *or* John 14:11-15

The Sermon

After the Sermon, and any responses to it, the congregation sings a hymn.

The Induction

Representatives of the congregation and of the clergy of the diocese stand
before the bishop with the new minister. Any of the presentations that
follow may be added to, omitted, or adapted, as appropriate to the
nature of the new ministry, and to the order of the minister. In
the absence of the bishop, the deputy substitutes the words given
in parentheses.

Representatives of the congregation present a Bible, saying

N., accept this Bible, and be among us (*or* be in this place) as
one who proclaims the Word.

People   Amen.

The Bishop presents a vessel of water, saying

N., take this water, and help me (help the bishop) baptize in
obedience to our Lord.

People   Amen.

Others present a stole or other symbol, saying

N., receive this *stole,* and be among us as a pastor and priest.

People   Amen.

Others present a book of prayers or other symbol, saying

N., receive this *book,* and be among us as a *man* of prayer.

People   Amen.

Others present olive oil or some other symbol, saying

N., use this *oil,* and be among us as a healer and reconciler.

People   Amen.

If the new minister is the rector or vicar of the parish, a Warden may now present the keys of the church, saying

N., receive these keys, and let the doors of this place be open to all people.

People   Amen.

Representative clergy of the diocese present the Constitution and Canons of this Church, saying

N., obey these Canons, and be among us to share in the councils of this diocese.

People   Amen.

Other Representatives of the congregation present bread and wine, saying

N., take this bread and wine, and be among us to break the Bread and bless the Cup.

People   Amen.

The Bishop then says

N., let all these be signs of the ministry which is mine and yours (the Bishop's and yours) in this place.

People   Amen.

The new Minister, if a priest, may then kneel in the midst of the church, and say

O Lord my God, I am not worthy to have you come under my roof; yet you have called your servant to stand in your house, and to serve at your altar. To you and to your service I devote myself, body, soul, and spirit. Fill my memory with the record of your mighty works; enlighten my understanding with the light of your Holy Spirit; and may all the desires of my heart and will center in what you would have me do. Make me an instrument of your salvation for the people entrusted to my care, and grant that I may faithfully administer your holy Sacraments, and by my life and teaching set forth your true and living Word. Be always with me in carrying out the duties of my ministry. In prayer, quicken my devotion; in praises, heighten my love and gratitude; in preaching, give me readiness of thought and expression; and grant that, by the clearness and brightness of your holy Word, all the world may be drawn into your blessed kingdom. All this I ask for the sake of your Son our Savior Jesus Christ. *Amen.*

The Bishop then presents the new minister to the congregation, saying

Greet your new *Rector.*

When appropriate, the family of the new minister may also be presented at this time.

The Congregation expresses its approval. Applause is appropriate.

The Bishop greets the new minister.

The new Minister then says to the people

The peace of the Lord be always with you.
People   And also with you.

The new Minister then greets other members of the clergy, family members, and the congregation. The People greet one another.

At the Eucharist

The service continues with the Offertory.

The Bishop, or in the Bishop's absence a Priest beginning a new ministry, standing at the Lord's Table as chief celebrant, and joined by the other clergy, proceeds with the Great Thanksgiving of the Eucharist.

Except on Major Feasts, the Preface may be that for Apostles and Ordinations.

After Communion

At the Induction of a priest or deacon, in place of the usual post-communion prayer, the Bishop leads the people in the following prayer; but if the new minister is a lay person, the usual postcommunion prayer is used.

Almighty Father, we thank you for feeding us with the holy food of the Body and Blood of your Son, and for uniting us through him in the fellowship of your Holy Spirit. We thank you for raising up among us faithful servants for the ministry of your Word and Sacraments. We pray that *N.* may be to us an effective example in word and action, in love and patience, and in holiness of life. Grant that we, with *him*, may serve you now, and always rejoice in your glory; through Jesus Christ your Son our Lord, who lives and reigns with you and the Holy Spirit, one God, now and for ever. Amen.

A newly inducted Priest may, at the bishop's request, pronounce a blessing.

A Deacon, or a Priest if no deacon is present, dismisses the assembly.

Additional Directions

The Institution, the Ministry of the Word, and the Induction should occur at the entrance of the chancel, or in some other place where the bishop and other ministers may be clearly seen and heard by the people.

The Letter of Institution is appropriate for the induction of a rector of a parish, the dean of a cathedral, and others having similar tenure of office.

Its wording may be altered by the bishop when circumstances require. In other cases, the bishop may state briefly the nature of the person's office and the authority being conferred.

The new minister is normally presented to the bishop by the wardens of the parish, but additional, or other, persons may do this when desired.

The Litany may be sung or said standing or kneeling, but the bishop always stands for the salutation and Collect at the end of it. The Collect of the Day, or a Collect of the season, or another prayer suitable to the occasion, may be used instead.

Before the Gospel, there may be one or two Readings from Scripture. Any of the Readings, including the Gospel, may be selected from the Proper of the Day, or from the passages cited in the service. Other passages suitable to the circumstances may be substituted. Appropriate selections may be found in the service for the Ordination of a Deacon or in the Lectionary for Various Occasions.

The sermon may be preached by the bishop, the new minister, or some other person; or an address about the work of the congregation and of the new minister may be made. Representatives of the congregation or of the community, the bishop, or other persons present, may speak in response to the address or sermon.

The symbols presented should be large enough to be visible to all and should remain in the sight of the congregation during the Induction. The vestments and bread and wine may be used in the Eucharist which follows.

The priest's prayer on page 562 is appropriate only for rectors of parishes, vicars of missions, hospital chaplains, and other priests having similar canonical charge.

For the Great Thanksgiving, any of the authorized eucharistic prayers may be used.

Concerning the Service

This service provides for the dedication and consecration of a church and its furnishings. Portions of the service may be used, or adapted when necessary, for dedicating parts of a building, or furnishings, that have been added, altered, or renovated. Likewise, suitable parts of this rite may be used for dedicating a chapel or an oratory within another building. Provisions for adapting the rite to special circumstances are given on page 576.

This service may be used to dedicate and consecrate a church at any time after the building is ready for regular use as a place of worship.

The service does not preclude the use of the building for educational or social purposes, or for other suitable activities.

The bishop presides. The rector or minister in charge takes part as indicated. Neighboring ministers should be invited to participate, and may be assigned appropriate parts in the service.

It is desirable that all members of the congregation, young and old, have some individual or collective part in the celebration, as well as the architect, builders, musicians, artists, benefactors, and friends.

For a church or chapel long in use, a special order is provided on page 577.

Additional Directions are on page 575.

The Dedication and Consecration of a Church

On the day appointed, the clergy and people gather with the bishop in a place apart from the church or chapel.

When all are ready, the Bishop says the following or similar words

Through the ages, Almighty God has moved his people to build houses of prayer and praise, and to set apart places for the ministry of his holy Word and Sacraments. With gratitude for the building (rebuilding, *or* adornment) of (*name of church*), we are now gathered to dedicate and consecrate it in God's Name.

Let us pray.

Almighty God, we thank you for making us in your image, to share in the ordering of your world. Receive the work of our hands in this place, now to be set apart for your worship, the building up of the living, and the remembrance of the dead, to the praise and glory of your Name; through Jesus Christ our Lord. *Amen.*

Necessary announcements may now be made.

As the procession approaches the door of the church, singing and instrumental music are appropriate.

Standing at the door of the church, the Bishop says

Let the door(s) be opened.

The door is opened. With the pastoral staff the Bishop marks the threshold with the sign of the cross saying

Peace be to this house, and to all who enter here: ✣ In the Name of the Father, and of the Son, and of the Holy Spirit. *Amen.*

As the procession moves into the church, Psalm 122 or some other appropriate psalm is sung. Hymns and anthems may also be sung.

The congregation standing, the Bishop begins the Prayer for the Consecration of the Church

	Our help is in the Name of the Lord;
People	The maker of heaven and earth.
Bishop	Let us pray.

Everliving Father, watchful and caring, our source and our end: All that we are and all that we have is yours. Accept us now, as we dedicate this place to which we come to praise your Name, to ask your forgiveness, to know your healing power, to hear your Word, and to be nourished by the Body and Blood of your Son. Be present always to guide and to judge, to illumine and to bless your people.

A Warden or other representative of the congregation continues

Lord Jesus Christ, make this a temple of your presence and a house of prayer. Be always near us when we seek you in this place. Draw us to you, when we come alone and when we come with others, to find comfort and wisdom, to be supported and strengthened, to rejoice and give thanks. May it be here, Lord Christ, that we are made one with you and with one another, so that our lives are sustained and sanctified for your service.

The Rector or Minister in charge continues

Holy Spirit, open our eyes, our ears, and our hearts, that we may grow closer to you through joy and through suffering. Be with us in the fullness of your power as new members are added to your household, as we grow in grace through the years, when we are joined in marriage, when we turn to you in sickness or special need, and, at the last, when we are committed into the Father's hands.

The Bishop concludes

	Now, O Father, Son, and Holy Spirit, sanctify this place;
People	For everything in heaven and on earth is yours.
Bishop	Yours, O Lord, is the kingdom;
People	And you are exalted as head over all. Amen.

The Bishop moves to the Font, lays a hand upon it, and says

Father, we thank you that through the waters of Baptism we die to sin and are made new in Christ. Grant through your Spirit that those baptized here may enjoy the liberty and splendor of the children of God.

V.   There is one Lord, one Faith, one Baptism;
R.   One God and Father of all.

We dedicate this Font in the Name of the Father, and of the Son, and of the Holy Spirit. *Amen.*

If there are persons to be baptized, water is now poured into the Font, and the service continues as directed on page 575.

If no Baptism is to take place [water may be poured into the Font, and] the Bishop says

	The Lord be with you.
People	And also with you.
Bishop	Let us give thanks to the Lord our God.
People	It is right to give him thanks and praise.

Facing the Font, the Bishop says

We thank you, Almighty God, for the gift of water. Over it the Holy Spirit moved in the beginning of creation. Through it you led the children of Israel out of their bondage in Egypt into the land of promise. In it your Son Jesus received the baptism of John and was anointed by the Holy Spirit as the Messiah, the Christ, to lead us, through his death and resurrection, from the bondage of sin into everlasting life.

We thank you, Father, for the water of Baptism. In it we are buried with Christ in his death. By it we share in his resurrection. Through it we are reborn by the Holy Spirit. Therefore in joyful obedience to your Son, we bring into his fellowship those who come to him in faith, baptizing them in the Name of the Father, and of the Son, and of the Holy Spirit.

Grant, by the power of your Holy Spirit, that those who here are cleansed from sin and born again may continue for ever in the risen life of Jesus Christ our Savior.

To him, to you, and to the Holy Spirit, be all honor and glory, now and for ever. *Amen.*

The Bishop proceeds to the Lectern, lays a hand upon it, and says

Father, your eternal Word speaks to us through the words of Holy Scripture. Here we read about your mighty acts and purposes in history, and about those whom you chose as the agents of your will. Inspired by the revelation of your Son, we seek your present purposes. Give us ears to hear and hearts to obey.

V. May the words of our mouth, and the meditation
of our heart,
R. Be acceptable to you, O Lord our God.

We dedicate this Lectern in the Name of the Father, and of the Son, and of the Holy Spirit. *Amen.*

The Bishop goes to the Pulpit, lays a hand upon it, and says

Father, in every age you have spoken through the voices of prophets, pastors, and teachers. Purify the lives and the lips of those who speak here, that your word only may be proclaimed, and your word only may be heard.

V. Your word is a lantern to our feet,
R. And a light upon our path.

We dedicate this Pulpit in the Name of the Father, and of the Son, and of the Holy Spirit. *Amen.*

At the Liturgy of the Word

Three Lessons are read. Lay persons read the Old Testament Lesson and the Epistle. The Deacon (or a Priest) reads the Gospel. Selections are ordinarily made from the following list; but on a Major Feast, Sunday, or Patronal Feast, selections may be made from the Proper of the Day.

Old Testament   1 Kings 8:22-23, 27b-30,   *or* 2 Samuel 6:12-15, 17-19
Psalm   84,   *or* 48
Epistle   Revelation 21:2-7,   *or* 1 Corinthians 3:1-11, 16-17,
          or 1 Peter 2:1-9

When an instrument of music is to be dedicated, after the Epistle the Bishop proceeds to an appropriate place, and says

Father, your people worship you with many voices and sounds, in times of joy and sorrow. Move us to express the wonder, the power, and the glory of your creation in the music we make and in the songs we sing.

V. Praise him with the sound of the trumpet;
R. Praise him with strings and pipe.

We dedicate this (*name of instrument*) in the Name of the Father, and of the Son, and of the Holy Spirit. *Amen.*

Instrumental music is now played, or a hymn or anthem sung.

All then stand for the Gospel, which may be the following

Matthew 7:13-14, 24-25,   *or* Matthew 21:10-14

Sermon or Address

Other Pastoral Offices may follow.

If the Apostles' Creed has not already been said, the Nicene Creed is now said or sung.

The Deacon or a member of the congregation leads the Prayers of the People.

After a period of silence, the Bishop concludes with the following prayers

Almighty God, all times are your seasons, and all occasions invite your tender mercies: Accept our prayers and intercessions offered in this place today and in the days to come; through Jesus Christ, our Mediator and Advocate. *Amen.*

We give you thanks, O God, for the gifts of your people, and for the work of many hands, which have beautified this place and furnished it for the celebration of your holy mysteries. Accept and bless all we have done, and grant that in these earthly things we may behold the order and beauty of things heavenly; through Jesus Christ our Lord. *Amen.*

The Bishop then says

Let us now pray for the setting apart of the Altar.

The Bishop goes to the Table and, with arms extended, says

We praise you, Almighty and eternal God, that for us and for our salvation, you sent your Son Jesus Christ to be born among us, that through him we might become your sons and daughters.
Blessed be your Name, Lord God.

We praise you for his life on earth, and for his death upon the cross, through which he offered himself as a perfect sacrifice.
Blessed be your Name, Lord God.

We praise you for raising him from the dead, and for exalting him to be our great High Priest.
Blessed be your Name, Lord God.

We praise you for sending your Holy Spirit to make us holy, and to unite us in your holy Church.
Blessed be your Name, Lord God.

The Bishop lays a hand upon the Table, and continues

Lord God, hear us. Sanctify this Table dedicated to you. Let it be to us a sign of the heavenly Altar where your saints and angels praise you for ever. Accept here the continual recalling of the sacrifice of your Son. Grant that all who eat and drink at this holy Table may be fed and refreshed by his flesh and blood, be forgiven for their sins, united with one another, and strengthened for your service.
Blessed be your Name, Father, Son, and Holy Spirit; now and for endless ages. Amen.

Bells may now be rung and music played. Members of the congregation vest the Altar, place the vessels on it, and light the candles.

The Peace

The Bishop says to the people

The peace of the Lord be always with you.

People　　And also with you.

Then the bishop and other clergy and the people greet one another.

At the Eucharist

The service continues with the Offertory.

The bishop, or a priest appointed, is the chief celebrant.

The Preface of the Dedication of a Church may be used.

After the postcommunion prayer, the Bishop blesses the people; and a Deacon or Priest dismisses them.

Additional Directions

The complete form of the service for the Dedication and Consecration of a Church is to be used at the opening of a church or chapel. This service does not require that the premises be debt-free or owned.

When the clergy and people assemble before the service, they may gather out of doors, in the parish house, in a former or neighboring place of worship, or in some other building. When convenient, the procession may go around the building(s) to be dedicated and then go to the principal door. Hymns or psalms may be used in procession. The use of portable musical instruments is suitable. If there is an organ, it is appropriate that it remain silent until dedicated. When the weather is inclement, or other circumstances make it necessary, the congregation may assemble inside the church; but the bishop, other clergy, and attendants will enter in procession through the principal door.

When a new church is being consecrated, it is desirable that sacred vessels, ornaments, and decorations be carried into the building in the procession. Such things as the deed for the property and the blueprint of the building(s), the keys, and tools used in its construction may also be carried by appropriate persons.

The cross signed on the threshold by the bishop may be marked in lasting form (incised, painted, inlaid). In place of a pastoral staff, the foot of a processional cross may be used for the signing.

At the dedication of the font, children or other lay persons are to be assigned the task of pouring the water. If Holy Baptism is not to be administered, in addition to saying the prayer over the font as given, the bishop may consecrate oil of Chrism, as in the service of Holy Baptism, for subsequent use in this church.

If Baptism is to be administered, the following order is used: the Gospel from "At Baptism," page 928; then the service of Holy Baptism, beginning with the Presentation of the Candidates, and concluding with the reception of the newly baptized.

As the furnishings in the church are dedicated, they may be decorated by members of the congregation with flowers, candles, hangings, or other ornaments.

Selected verses of psalms and hymns, or instrumental music may be used as the ministers move from one part of the church to another.

If one reading stand is to serve as both lectern and pulpit, only one of the prayers, and one of the versicles and responses, are used, followed by the words of dedication.

At the dedication of the lectern, the Bible is brought forward and put into place by a donor, or a lay reader, or another suitable person.

If there is an address instead of a sermon, it is suitable that a warden or other lay person outline the plans of the congregation for witness to the Gospel. The bishop may respond, indicating the place of this congregation within the life of the Diocese.

The sermon or address may be followed by an appropriate Pastoral Office, such as Thanksgiving for the Birth or Adoption of a Child, Commitment to Christian Service, or Blessing of Oil for the Sick.

Any of the usual forms of the Prayers of the People may be used; or some other form may be composed for the occasion, having due regard for the distinctive nature of the community, and with commemoration of benefactors, donors, artists, artisans, and others.

For the covering and decoration of the Altar, it is suitable that the donors of these furnishings, or other lay persons, bring them forward and put them in place. If incense is to be used, it is appropriate at this time.

Instead of the Proper Preface suggested, that of the season may be used, or one appropriate to the name of the church.

For the Dedication of Churches and Chapels in Special Cases

If the place of public worship is also to serve as a school or parish hall, or for some other suitable purpose, the service may be adapted to the circumstances.

If the church is also to be used for regular worship by other Christian bodies, it is appropriate that their representatives take part in the service, and that the service be adapted.

Suitable portions of this service may be used by the bishop, or by a priest with the bishop's permission, for dedicating a private chapel or oratory.

For the Dedication of Furnishings, or Parts of a Church or Chapel

Relevant portions of the service for the Dedication and Consecration of a Church may be used by the bishop or a priest for blessing alterations, additions, or new furnishings in a church or chapel. In each such case, the appropriate prayer may be said, or adapted to the circumstances; and prayers and Bible readings related to the particular occasion may be selected. When possible, the areas or furnishings should be put into use at this time.

The blessing of a new font or baptistry should always be done by a bishop, and should be followed, if possible, by the administration of Holy Baptism.

The blessing of an Altar is also reserved for a bishop, and is always to be followed by the celebration of the Holy Eucharist.

For a Church or Chapel Long in Use

When buildings have been used for public worship for an extended period of time without having been consecrated, the following order may provide an opportunity for the congregation to reaffirm its commitment to its mission and ministry, and it will be particularly appropriate when a congregation attains recognition as a parish.

1. Procession
2. Signing of threshold
3. Litany of Thanksgiving for a Church, page 578
4. Te Deum

5. Liturgy of the Word, with sermon or address
6. Renewal of Baptismal Vows
7. Intercessions, including commemoration of benefactors
8. The Peace
9. The Eucharist, beginning with the Offertory

A Litany of Thanksgiving for a Church

Let us thank God whom we worship here in the beauty of holiness.

Eternal God, the heaven of heavens cannot contain you, much less the walls of temples made with hands. Graciously receive our thanks for this place, and accept the work of our hands, offered to your honor and glory.

For the Church universal, of which these visible buildings are the symbol,
We thank you, Lord.

For your presence whenever two or three have gathered together in your Name,
We thank you, Lord.

For this place where we may be still and know that you are God,
We thank you, Lord.

For making us your children by adoption and grace, and refreshing us day by day with the bread of life.
We thank you, Lord.

For the knowledge of your will and the grace to perform it,
We thank you, Lord.

For the fulfilling of our desires and petitions as you see best for us,
We thank you, Lord.

For the pardon of our sins, which restores us to the company of your faithful people,
We thank you, Lord.

For the blessing of our vows and the crowning of our years with your goodness,
We thank you, Lord.

For the faith of those who have gone before us and for our encouragement by their perseverance,
We thank you, Lord.

For the fellowship of [N., our patron, and of] all your Saints,
We thank you, Lord.

After a brief silence, the Celebrant concludes with the following Doxology

Yours, O Lord, is the greatness, the power, the glory, the victory, and the majesty;
People   For everything in heaven and on earth is yours.
Celebrant Yours, O Lord, is the kingdom;
People   And you are exalted as head over all. Amen.

This Litany may also be used on the anniversary of the dedication or consecration of a church, or on other suitable occasions.

The Psalter

Concerning the Psalter

The Psalter is a body of liturgical poetry. It is designed for vocal, congregational use, whether by singing or reading. There are several traditional methods of psalmody. The exclusive use of a single method makes the recitation of the Psalter needlessly monotonous. The traditional methods, each of which can be elaborate or simple, are the following:

Direct recitation denotes the reading or chanting of a whole psalm, or portion of a psalm, in unison. It is particularly appropriate for the psalm verses suggested in the lectionary for use between the Lessons at the Eucharist, when the verses are recited rather than sung, and may often be found a satisfactory method of chanting them.

Antiphonal recitation is the verse-by-verse alternation between groups of singers or readers; *e.g.*, between choir and congregation, or between one side of the congregation and the other. The alternate recitation concludes either with the Gloria Patri, or with a refrain (called the antiphon) recited in unison. This is probably the most satisfying method for reciting the psalms in the Daily Office.

Responsorial recitation is the name given to a method of psalmody in which the verses of a psalm are sung by a solo voice, with the choir and congregation singing a refrain after each verse or group of verses. This was the traditional method of singing the Venite, and the restoration of Invitatory Antiphons for the Venite makes possible a recovery of this form of sacred song in the Daily Office. It was also a traditional manner of chanting the psalms between the Lessons at the Eucharist, and it is increasingly favored by modern composers.

Responsive recitation is the method which has been most frequently used in Episcopal churches, the minister alternating with the congregation, verse by verse.

The version of the Psalms which follows is set out in lines of poetry. The lines correspond to Hebrew versification, which is not based on meter or rhyme, but on parallelism of clauses, a symmetry of form and sense. The parallelism can take the form of similarity (The waters have lifted up, O Lord / the waters have lifted up their voice; / the waters have lifted up their pounding waves. *Psalm 93:4)*, or of contrast (The Lord knows the ways of the righteous; / but the way of the wicked is doomed. *Psalm 1:6)*, or of logical expansion (Our eyes look to the Lord our God, / until he show us his mercy. *Psalm 123:3)*.

The most common verse is a couplet, but triplets are very frequent, and quatrains are not unknown; although quatrains are usually distributed over two verses.

An asterisk divides each verse into two parts for reading or chanting. In reading, a distinct pause should be made at the asterisk.

Three terms are used in the Psalms with reference to God: *Elohim* ("God"), *Adonai* ("Lord") and the personal name *YHWH*. The "Four-letter Name" (Tetragrammaton) is probably to be vocalized Yahweh; but this is by no means certain, because from very ancient times it has been considered too sacred to be pronounced; and, whenever it occurred, *Adonai* was substituted for it. In the oldest manuscripts, the Divine Name was written in antique and obsolete letters; in more recent manuscripts and in printed Bibles, after the invention of vowel points, the Name was provided with the vowels of the word *Adonai*. This produced a hybrid form which has been transliterated "Jehovah."

The Hebrew reverence and reticence with regard to the Name of God has been carried over into the classical English versions, the Prayer Book Psalter and the King James Old Testament, where it is regularly rendered "Lord". In order to distinguish it, however, from "Lord" as a translation of *Adonai, YHWH* is represented in capital and small capital letters: LORD.

From time to time, the Hebrew text has *Adonai* and *YHWH* in conjunction. Then, the Hebrew custom is to substitute *Elohim* for *YHWH,* and our English tradition follows suit, rendering the combined title as "Lord GOD."

In two passages *(Psalm 68:4* and *Psalm 83:18),* the context requires that the Divine Name be spelled out, and it appears as YAHWEH. A similar construction occurs in the Canticle, "The Song of Moses."

The ancient praise-shout, "Hallelujah," has been restored, in place of its English equivalent, "Praise the Lord." The Hebrew form has been used, rather than the Latin form "Alleluia," as being more appropriate to this context; but also to regain for our liturgy a form of the word that is familiar from its use in many well-known anthems. The word may, if desired, be omitted during the season of Lent.

The Psalter

First Day: Morning Prayer

I   *Beatus vir qui non abiit*

1   Happy are they who have not walked in the counsel of
                    the wicked, *
    nor lingered in the way of sinners,
    nor sat in the seats of the scornful!

2   Their delight is in the law of the LORD,*
    and they meditate on his law day and night.

3   They are like trees planted by streams of water,
    bearing fruit in due season, with leaves that do not wither; *
    everything they do shall prosper.

4   It is not so with the wicked; *
    they are like chaff which the wind blows away.

5   Therefore the wicked shall not stand upright when
                    judgment comes, *
    nor the sinner in the council of the righteous.

6   For the LORD knows the way of the righteous, *
    but the way of the wicked is doomed.

2   *Quare fremuerunt gentes?*

1   Why are the nations in an uproar? *
   Why do the peoples mutter empty threats?

2   Why do the kings of the earth rise up in revolt,
   and the princes plot together, *
   against the LORD and against his Anointed?

3   "Let us break their yoke," they say; *
   "let us cast off their bonds from us."

4   He whose throne is in heaven is laughing; *
   the Lord has them in derision.

5   Then he speaks to them in his wrath, *
   and his rage fills them with terror.

6   "I myself have set my king *
   upon my holy hill of Zion."

7   Let me announce the decree of the LORD: *
   he said to me,"You are my Son;
   this day have I begotten you.

8   Ask of me, and I will give you the nations for
                     your inheritance *
   and the ends of the earth for your possession.

9   You shall crush them with an iron rod *
   and shatter them like a piece of pottery."

10   And now, you kings, be wise; *
   be warned, you rulers of the earth.

11   Submit to the LORD with fear, *
   and with trembling bow before him;

12   Lest he be angry and you perish; *
   for his wrath is quickly kindled.

13 Happy are they all *
       who take refuge in him!

3 *Domine, quid multiplicati*

1 LORD, how many adversaries I have! *
       how many there are who rise up against me!

2 How many there are who say of me, *
       "There is no help for him in his God."

3 But you, O LORD, are a shield about me; *
       you are my glory, the one who lifts up my head.

4 I call aloud upon the LORD, *
       and he answers me from his holy hill;

5 I lie down and go to sleep; *
       I wake again, because the LORD sustains me.

6 I do not fear the multitudes of people *
       who set themselves against me all around.

7 Rise up, O LORD; set me free, O my God; *
       surely, you will strike all my enemies across the face,
       you will break the teeth of the wicked.

8 Deliverance belongs to the LORD. *
       Your blessing be upon your people!

4 *Cum invocarem*

1 Answer me when I call, O God, defender of my cause; *
       you set me free when I am hard-pressed;
       have mercy on me and hear my prayer.

2 "You mortals, how long will you dishonor my glory; *
      how long will you worship dumb idols
      and run after false gods?"

3 Know that the LORD does wonders for the faithful; *
      when I call upon the LORD, he will hear me.

4 Tremble, then, and do not sin; *
      speak to your heart in silence upon your bed.

5 Offer the appointed sacrifices *
      and put your trust in the LORD.

6 **Many are saying,**
   "Oh, that we might see better times!" *
      Lift up the light of your countenance upon us, O LORD.

7 You have put gladness in my heart, *
      more than when grain and wine and oil increase.

8 I lie down in peace; at once I fall asleep; *
      for only you, LORD, make me dwell in safety.

5 *Verba mea auribus*

1 Give ear to my words, O LORD; *
      consider my meditation.

2 Hearken to my cry for help, my King and my God, *
      for I make my prayer to you.

3 In the morning, LORD, you hear my voice; *
      early in the morning I make my appeal and watch for you.

4 For you are not a God who takes pleasure in wickedness, *
      and evil cannot dwell with you.

5 Braggarts cannot stand in your sight; *
      you hate all those who work wickedness.

6   You destroy those who speak lies; *
       the bloodthirsty and deceitful, O Lord, you abhor.

7   But as for me, through the greatness of your mercy I will
                        go into your house; *
       I will bow down toward your holy temple in awe of you.

8   Lead me, O Lord, in your righteousness,
     because of those who lie in wait for me; *
       make your way straight before me.

9   For there is no truth in their mouth; *
       there is destruction in their heart;

10   Their throat is an open grave; *
       they flatter with their tongue.

11   Declare them guilty, O God; *
       let them fall, because of their schemes.

12   Because of their many transgressions cast them out, *
       for they have rebelled against you.

13   But all who take refuge in you will be glad; *
       they will sing out their joy for ever.

14   You will shelter them, *
       so that those who love your Name may exult in you.

15   For you, O Lord, will bless the righteous; *
       you will defend them with your favor as with a shield.

First Day: Evening Prayer

6   *Domine, ne in furore*

1   Lord, do not rebuke me in your anger; *
       do not punish me in your wrath.

2   Have pity on me, LORD, for I am weak; *
      heal me, LORD, for my bones are racked.

3   My spirit shakes with terror; *
      how long, O LORD, how long?

4   Turn, O LORD, and deliver me; *
      save me for your mercy's sake.

5   For in death no one remembers you; *
      and who will give you thanks in the grave?

6   I grow weary because of my groaning; *
      every night I drench my bed
      and flood my couch with tears.

7   My eyes are wasted with grief *
      and worn away because of all my enemies.

8   Depart from me, all evildoers, *
      for the LORD has heard the sound of my weeping.

9   The LORD has heard my supplication; *
      the LORD accepts my prayer.

10   All my enemies shall be confounded and quake with fear; *
      they shall turn back and suddenly be put to shame.

7   *Domine, Deus meus*

1   O LORD my God, I take refuge in you; *
      save and deliver me from all who pursue me;

2   Lest like a lion they tear me in pieces *
      and snatch me away with none to deliver me.

3   O LORD my God, if I have done these things: *
      if there is any wickedness in my hands,

4   If I have repaid my friend with evil, *
      or plundered him who without cause is my enemy;

5   Then let my enemy pursue and overtake me, *
      trample my life into the ground,
      and lay my honor in the dust.

6   Stand up, O LORD, in your wrath; *
      rise up against the fury of my enemies.

7   Awake, O my God, decree justice; *
      let the assembly of the peoples gather round you.

8   Be seated on your lofty throne, O Most High; *
      O LORD, judge the nations.

9   Give judgment for me according to my
           righteousness, O LORD, *
      and according to my innocence, O Most High.

10   Let the malice of the wicked come to an end,
      but establish the righteous; *
        for you test the mind and heart, O righteous God.

11   God is my shield and defense; *
      he is the savior of the true in heart.

12   God is a righteous judge; *
      God sits in judgment every day.

13   If they will not repent, God will whet his sword; *
      he will bend his bow and make it ready.

14   He has prepared his weapons of death; *
      he makes his arrows shafts of fire.

15   Look at those who are in labor with wickedness, *
      who conceive evil, and give birth to a lie.

16 They dig a pit and make it deep *
    and fall into the hole that they have made.

17 Their malice turns back upon their own head; *
    their violence falls on their own scalp.

18 I will bear witness that the LORD is righteous; *
    I will praise the Name of the LORD Most High.

8 *Domine, Dominus noster*

1 O LORD our Governor, *
    how exalted is your Name in all the world!

2 Out of the mouths of infants and children *
    your majesty is praised above the heavens.

3 You have set up a stronghold against your adversaries, *
    to quell the enemy and the avenger.

4 When I consider your heavens, the work of your fingers, *
    the moon and the stars you have set in their courses,

5 What is man that you should be mindful of him? *
    the son of man that you should seek him out?

6 You have made him but little lower than the angels; *
    you adorn him with glory and honor;

7 You give him mastery over the works of your hands; *
    you put all things under his feet:

8 All sheep and oxen, *
    even the wild beasts of the field,

9 The birds of the air, the fish of the sea, *
    and whatsoever walks in the paths of the sea.

10 O LORD our Governor, *
    how exalted is your Name in all the world!

9 *Confitebor tibi*

1 I will give thanks to you, O LORD, with my whole heart; *
    I will tell of all your marvelous works.

2 I will be glad and rejoice in you; *
    I will sing to your Name, O Most High.

3 When my enemies are driven back, *
    they will stumble and perish at your presence.

4 For you have maintained my right and my cause; *
    you sit upon your throne judging right.

5 You have rebuked the ungodly and destroyed the wicked; *
    you have blotted out their name for ever and ever.

6 As for the enemy, they are finished, in perpetual ruin, *
    their cities ploughed under, the memory of them perished;

7 But the LORD is enthroned for ever; *
    he has set up his throne for judgment.

8 It is he who rules the world with righteousness; *
    he judges the peoples with equity.

9 The LORD will be a refuge for the oppressed, *
    a refuge in time of trouble.

10 Those who know your Name will put their trust in you, *
    for you never forsake those who seek you, O LORD.

11 Sing praise to the LORD who dwells in Zion; *
    proclaim to the peoples the things he has done.

12 The Avenger of blood will remember them; *
    he will not forget the cry of the afflicted.

13 Have pity on me, O LORD; *
    see the misery I suffer from those who hate me,
    O you who lift me up from the gate of death;

14 So that I may tell of all your praises
and rejoice in your salvation *
    in the gates of the city of Zion.

15 The ungodly have fallen into the pit they dug, *
    and in the snare they set is their own foot caught.

16 The LORD is known by his acts of justice; *
    the wicked are trapped in the works of their own hands.

17 The wicked shall be given over to the grave, *
    and also all the peoples that forget God.

18 For the needy shall not always be forgotten, *
    and the hope of the poor shall not perish for ever.

19 Rise up, O LORD, let not the ungodly have the upper hand; *
    let them be judged before you.

20 Put fear upon them, O LORD; *
    let the ungodly know they are but mortal.

10 *Ut quid, Domine?*

1 Why do you stand so far off, O LORD, *
    and hide yourself in time of trouble?

2 The wicked arrogantly persecute the poor, *
    but they are trapped in the schemes they have devised.

3 The wicked boast of their heart's desire; *
    the covetous curse and revile the LORD.

4 The wicked are so proud that they care not for God; *
    their only thought is, "God does not matter."

5   Their ways are devious at all times;
      your judgments are far above out of their sight; *
         they defy all their enemies.

6   They say in their heart, "I shall not be shaken; *
      no harm shall happen to me ever."

7   Their mouth is full of cursing, deceit, and oppression; *
      under their tongue are mischief and wrong.

8   They lurk in ambush in public squares
      and in secret places they murder the innocent; *
         they spy out the helpless.

9   They lie in wait, like a lion in a covert;
      they lie in wait to seize upon the lowly; *
         they seize the lowly and drag them away in their net.

10   The innocent are broken and humbled before them; *
      the helpless fall before their power.

11   They say in their heart, "God has forgotten; *
      he hides his face; he will never notice."

12   Rise up, O Lord;
      lift up your hand, O God; *
         do not forget the afflicted.

13   Why should the wicked revile God? *
      why should they say in their heart, "You do not care"?

14   Surely, you behold trouble and misery; *
      you see it and take it into your own hand.

15   The helpless commit themselves to you, *
      for you are the helper of orphans.

16   Break the power of the wicked and evil; *
      search out their wickedness until you find none.

17 The LORD is King for ever and ever; *
    the ungodly shall perish from his land.

18 The LORD will hear the desire of the humble; *
    you will strengthen their heart and your ears shall hear;

19 To give justice to the orphan and oppressed, *
    so that mere mortals may strike terror no more.

11   *In Domino confido*

1 In the LORD have I taken refuge; *
    how then can you say to me,
  "Fly away like a bird to the hilltop;

2 For see how the wicked bend the bow
and fit their arrows to the string, *
    to shoot from ambush at the true of heart.

3 When the foundations are being destroyed, *
    what can the righteous do?"

4 The LORD is in his holy temple; *
    the LORD's throne is in heaven.

5 His eyes behold the inhabited world; *
    his piercing eye weighs our worth.

6 The LORD weighs the righteous as well as the wicked, *
    but those who delight in violence he abhors.

7 Upon the wicked he shall rain coals of fire and
                     burning sulphur; *
    a scorching wind shall be their lot.

8 For the LORD is righteous;
he delights in righteous deeds; *
    and the just shall see his face.

I2 *Salvum me fac*

1 Help me, LORD, for there is no godly one left; *
   the faithful have vanished from among us.

2 Everyone speaks falsely with his neighbor; *
   with a smooth tongue they speak from a double heart.

3 Oh, that the LORD would cut off all smooth tongues, *
   and close the lips that utter proud boasts!

4 Those who say,"With our tongue will we prevail; *
   our lips are our own; who is lord over us?"

5 "Because the needy are oppressed,
   and the poor cry out in misery, *
     I will rise up,"says the LORD,
   "and give them the help they long for."

6 The words of the LORD are pure words, *
   like silver refined from ore
   and purified seven times in the fire.

7 O LORD, watch over us *
   and save us from this generation for ever.

8 The wicked prowl on every side, *
   and that which is worthless is highly prized by everyone.

I3 *Usquequo, Domine?*

1 How long, O LORD?
will you forget me for ever? *
   how long will you hide your face from me?

2   How long shall I have perplexity in my mind,
and grief in my heart, day after day? *
    how long shall my enemy triumph over me?

3   Look upon me and answer me, O LORD my God; *
    give light to my eyes, lest I sleep in death;

4   Lest my enemy say, "I have prevailed over him," *
    and my foes rejoice that I have fallen.

5   But I put my trust in your mercy; *
    my heart is joyful because of your saving help.

6   I will sing to the LORD, for he has dealt with me richly; *
    I will praise the Name of the Lord Most High.

14   *Dixit insipiens*

1   The fool has said in his heart, "There is no God." *
    All are corrupt and commit abominable acts;
    there is none who does any good.

2   The LORD looks down from heaven upon us all, *
    to see if there is any who is wise,
    if there is one who seeks after God.

3   Every one has proved faithless;
all alike have turned bad; *
    there is none who does good; no, not one.

4   Have they no knowledge, all those evildoers *
    who eat up my people like bread
    and do not call upon the LORD?

5   See how they tremble with fear, *
    because God is in the company of the righteous.

6   Their aim is to confound the plans of the afflicted, *
    but the LORD is their refuge.

7 Oh, that Israel's deliverance would come out of Zion! *
    when the LORD restores the fortunes of his people,
    Jacob will rejoice and Israel be glad.

Third Day: Morning Prayer

15   *Domine, quis habitabit?*

1 LORD, who may dwell in your tabernacle? *
    who may abide upon your holy hill?

2 Whoever leads a blameless life and does what is right, *
    who speaks the truth from his heart.

3 There is no guile upon his tongue;
    he does no evil to his friend; *
      he does not heap contempt upon his neighbor.

4 In his sight the wicked is rejected, *
    but he honors those who fear the LORD.

5 He has sworn to do no wrong *
    and does not take back his word.

6 He does not give his money in hope of gain, *
    nor does he take a bribe against the innocent.

7 Whoever does these things *
    shall never be overthrown.

16   *Conserva me, Domine*

1 Protect me, O God, for I take refuge in you; *
    I have said to the LORD, "You are my Lord,
    my good above all other."

2   All my delight is upon the godly that are in the land, *
      upon those who are noble among the people.

3   But those who run after other gods *
      shall have their troubles multiplied.

4   Their libations of blood I will not offer, *
      nor take the names of their gods upon my lips.

5   O LORD, you are my portion and my cup; *
      it is you who uphold my lot.

6   My boundaries enclose a pleasant land; *
      indeed, I have a goodly heritage.

7   I will bless the LORD who gives me counsel; *
      my heart teaches me, night after night.

8   I have set the LORD always before me; *
      because he is at my right hand I shall not fall.

9   My heart, therefore, is glad, and my spirit rejoices; *
      my body also shall rest in hope.

10 For you will not abandon me to the grave, *
      nor let your holy one see the Pit.

11 You will show me the path of life; *
      in your presence there is fullness of joy,
      and in your right hand are pleasures for evermore.

17   *Exaudi, Domine*

1   Hear my plea of innocence, O LORD;
    give heed to my cry; *
      listen to my prayer, which does not come from lying lips.

2   Let my vindication come forth from your presence; *
     let your eyes be fixed on justice.

3   Weigh my heart, summon me by night, *
     melt me down; you will find no impurity in me.

4   I give no offense with my mouth as others do; *
     I have heeded the words of your lips.

5   My footsteps hold fast to the ways of your law; *
     in your paths my feet shall not stumble.

6   I call upon you, O God, for you will answer me; *
     incline your ear to me and hear my words.

7   Show me your marvelous loving-kindness, *
     O Savior of those who take refuge at your right hand
     from those who rise up against them.

8   Keep me as the apple of your eye; *
     hide me under the shadow of your wings,

9   From the wicked who assault me, *
     from my deadly enemies who surround me.

10   They have closed their heart to pity, *
     and their mouth speaks proud things.

11   They press me hard,
now they surround me, *
     watching how they may cast me to the ground,

12   Like a lion, greedy for its prey, *
     and like a young lion lurking in secret places.

13   Arise, O LORD; confront them and bring them down; *
     deliver me from the wicked by your sword.

14   Deliver me, O LORD, by your hand *
     from those whose portion in life is this world;

15 Whose bellies you fill with your treasure, *
    who are well supplied with children
    and leave their wealth to their little ones.

16 But at my vindication I shall see your face; *
    when I awake, I shall be satisfied, beholding
        your likeness.

Third Day: Evening Prayer

18

Part I   *Diligam te, Domine.*

1 I love you, O LORD my strength, *
    O LORD my stronghold, my crag, and my haven.

2 My God, my rock in whom I put my trust, *
    my shield, the horn of my salvation, and my refuge;
    you are worthy of praise.

3 I will call upon the LORD, *
    and so shall I be saved from my enemies.

4 The breakers of death rolled over me, *
    and the torrents of oblivion made me afraid.

5 The cords of hell entangled me, *
    and the snares of death were set for me.

6 I called upon the LORD in my distress *
    and cried out to my God for help.

7 He heard my voice from his heavenly dwelling; *
    my cry of anguish came to his ears.

8   The earth reeled and rocked; *
        the roots of the mountains shook;
        they reeled because of his anger.

9   Smoke rose from his nostrils
     and a consuming fire out of his mouth; *
        hot burning coals blazed forth from him.

10   He parted the heavens and came down *
        with a storm cloud under his feet.

11   He mounted on cherubim and flew; *
        he swooped on the wings of the wind.

12   He wrapped darkness about him; *
        he made dark waters and thick clouds his pavilion.

13   From the brightness of his presence, through the clouds, *
        burst hailstones and coals of fire.

14   The LORD thundered out of heaven; *
        the Most High uttered his voice.

15   He loosed his arrows and scattered them; *
        he hurled thunderbolts and routed them.

16   The beds of the seas were uncovered,
     and the foundations of the world laid bare, *
        at your battle cry, O LORD,
        at the blast of the breath of your nostrils.

17   He reached down from on high and grasped me; *
        he drew me out of great waters.

18   He delivered me from my strong enemies
     and from those who hated me; *
        for they were too mighty for me.

19   They confronted me in the day of my disaster; *
        but the LORD was my support.

20 He brought me out into an open place; *
  he rescued me because he delighted in me.

Psalm 18: Part II *Et retribuet mihi*

21 The LORD rewarded me because of my righteous dealing; *
  because my hands were clean he rewarded me;

22 For I have kept the ways of the LORD *
  and have not offended against my God;

23 For all his judgments are before my eyes, *
  and his decrees I have not put away from me;

24 For I have been blameless with him *
  and have kept myself from iniquity;

25 Therefore the LORD rewarded me according to my
      righteous dealing, *
  because of the cleanness of my hands in his sight.

26 With the faithful you show yourself faithful, O God; *
  with the forthright you show yourself forthright.

27 With the pure you show yourself pure, *
  but with the crooked you are wily.

28 You will save a lowly people, *
  but you will humble the haughty eyes.

29 You, O LORD, are my lamp; *
  my God, you make my darkness bright.

30 With you I will break down an enclosure; *
  with the help of my God I will scale any wall.

31 As for God, his ways are perfect;
  the words of the LORD are tried in the fire; *
   he is a shield to all who trust in him.

32   For who is God, but the LORD? *
     who is the Rock, except our God?

33   It is God who girds me about with strength *
     and makes my way secure.

34   He makes me sure-footed like a deer *
     and lets me stand firm on the heights.

35   He trains my hands for battle *
     and my arms for bending even a bow of bronze.

36   You have given me your shield of victory; *
     your right hand also sustains me;
     your loving care makes me great.

37   You lengthen my stride beneath me, *
     and my ankles do not give way.

38   I pursue my enemies and overtake them; *
     I will not turn back till I have destroyed them.

39   I strike them down, and they cannot rise; *
     they fall defeated at my feet.

40   You have girded me with strength for the battle; *
     you have cast down my adversaries beneath me;
     you have put my enemies to flight.

41   I destroy those who hate me;
     they cry out, but there is none to help them; *
     they cry to the LORD, but he does not answer.

42   I beat them small like dust before the wind; *
     I trample them like mud in the streets.

43   You deliver me from the strife of the peoples; *
     you put me at the head of the nations.

44   A people I have not known shall serve me;
     no sooner shall they hear than they shall obey me; *
     strangers will cringe before me.

45   The foreign peoples will lose heart; *
       they shall come trembling out of their strongholds.

46   The LORD lives! Blessed is my Rock! *
       Exalted is the God of my salvation!

47   He is the God who gave me victory *
       and cast down the peoples beneath me.

48   You rescued me from the fury of my enemies;
    you exalted me above those who rose against me; *
       you saved me from my deadly foe.

49   Therefore will I extol you among the nations, O LORD, *
       and sing praises to your Name.

50   He multiplies the victories of his king; *
       he shows loving-kindness to his anointed,
       to David and his descendants for ever.

Fourth Day: Morning Prayer

19   *Cæli enarrant*

1   The heavens declare the glory of God, *
       and the firmament shows his handiwork.

2   One day tells its tale to another, *
       and one night imparts knowledge to another.

3   Although they have no words or language, *
       and their voices are not heard,

4   Their sound has gone out into all lands, *
       and their message to the ends of the world.

5   In the deep has he set a pavilion for the sun; *
       it comes forth like a bridegroom out of his chamber;
       it rejoices like a champion to run its course.

6   It goes forth from the uttermost edge of the heavens
and runs about to the end of it again; *
    nothing is hidden from its burning heat.

7   The law of the LORD is perfect
        and revives the soul; *
    the testimony of the LORD is sure
        and gives wisdom to the innocent.

8   The statutes of the LORD are just
        and rejoice the heart; *
    the commandment of the LORD is clear
        and gives light to the eyes.

9   The fear of the LORD is clean
        and endures for ever; *
    the judgments of the LORD are true
        and righteous altogether.

10   More to be desired are they than gold,
        more than much fine gold, *
    sweeter far than honey,
        than honey in the comb.

11   By them also is your servant enlightened, *
    and in keeping them there is great reward.

12   Who can tell how often he offends? *
    cleanse me from my secret faults.

13   Above all, keep your servant from presumptuous sins;
let them not get dominion over me; *
    then shall I be whole and sound,
    and innocent of a great offense.

14   Let the words of my mouth and the meditation of my
        heart be acceptable in your sight, *
    O LORD, my strength and my redeemer.

20 *Exaudiat te Dominus*

1 May the LORD answer you in the day of trouble, *
    the Name of the God of Jacob defend you;

2 Send you help from his holy place *
    and strengthen you out of Zion;

3 Remember all your offerings *
    and accept your burnt sacrifice;

4 Grant you your heart's desire *
    and prosper all your plans.

5 We will shout for joy at your victory
and triumph in the Name of our God; *
    may the LORD grant all your requests.

6 Now I know that the LORD gives victory to his anointed; *
    he will answer him out of his holy heaven,
    with the victorious strength of his right hand.

7 Some put their trust in chariots and some in horses, *
    but we will call upon the Name of the LORD our God.

8 They collapse and fall down, *
    but we will arise and stand upright.

9 O LORD, give victory to the king *
    and answer us when we call.

21 *Domine, in virtute tua*

1 The king rejoices in your strength, O LORD; *
    how greatly he exults in your victory!

2 You have given him his heart's desire; *
    you have not denied him the request of his lips.

3   For you meet him with blessings of prosperity, *
     and set a crown of fine gold upon his head.

4   He asked you for life, and you gave it to him: *
     length of days, for ever and ever.

5   His honor is great, because of your victory; *
     splendor and majesty have you bestowed upon him.

6   For you will give him everlasting felicity *
     and will make him glad with the joy of your presence.

7   For the king puts his trust in the LORD; *
     because of the loving-kindness of the Most High, he
       will not fall.

8   Your hand will lay hold upon all your enemies; *
     your right hand will seize all those who hate you.

9   You will make them like a fiery furnace *
     at the time of your appearing, O LORD;

10   You will swallow them up in your wrath, *
     and fire shall consume them.

11   You will destroy their offspring from the land *
     and their descendants from among the peoples of the earth.

12   Though they intend evil against you
   and devise wicked schemes, *
     yet they shall not prevail.

13   For you will put them to flight *
     and aim your arrows at them.

14   Be exalted, O LORD, in your might; *
     we will sing and praise your power.

22 *Deus, Deus meus*

1 My God, my God, why have you forsaken me? *
    and are so far from my cry
    and from the words of my distress?

2 O my God, I cry in the daytime, but you do not answer; *
    by night as well, but I find no rest.

3 Yet you are the Holy One, *
    enthroned upon the praises of Israel.

4 Our forefathers put their trust in you; *
    they trusted, and you delivered them.

5 They cried out to you and were delivered; *
    they trusted in you and were not put to shame.

6 But as for me, I am a worm and no man, *
    scorned by all and despised by the people.

7 All who see me laugh me to scorn; *
    they curl their lips and wag their heads, saying,

8 "He trusted in the LORD; let him deliver him; *
    let him rescue him, if he delights in him."

9 Yet you are he who took me out of the womb, *
    and kept me safe upon my mother's breast.

10 I have been entrusted to you ever since I was born; *
    you were my God when I was still in my
            mother's womb.

11 Be not far from me, for trouble is near, *
    and there is none to help.

12 Máwas young bulls encircle me; *
    strong bulls of Bashan surround me.

13 They open wide their jaws at me, *
    like a ravening and a roaring lion.

14 I am poured out like water;
    all my bones are out of joint; *
    my heart within my breast is melting wax.

15 My mouth is dried out like a pot-sherd;
    my tongue sticks to the roof of my mouth; *
    and you have laid me in the dust of the grave.

16 Packs of dogs close me in,
    and gangs of evildoers circle around me; *
    they pierce my hands and my feet;
    I can count all my bones.

17 They stare and gloat over me; *
    they divide my garments among them;
    they cast lots for my clothing.

18 Be not far away, O LORD; *
    you are my strength; hasten to help me.

19 Save me from the sword, *
    my life from the power of the dog.

20 Save me from the lion's mouth, *
    my wretched body from the horns of wild bulls.

21 I will declare your Name to my brethren; *
    in the midst of the congregation I will praise you.

22 Praise the LORD, you that fear him; *
    stand in awe of him, O offspring of Israel;
    all you of Jacob's line, give glory.

23   For he does not despise nor abhor the poor in their poverty;
neither does he hide his face from them; *
    but when they cry to him he hears them.

24   My praise is of him in the great assembly; *
    I will perform my vows in the presence of those who
       worship him.

25   The poor shall eat and be satisfied,
and those who seek the LORD shall praise him: *
    "May your heart live for ever!"

26   All the ends of the earth shall remember and turn to
       the LORD, *
    and all the families of the nations shall bow before him.

27   For kingship belongs to the LORD; *
    he rules over the nations.

28   To him alone all who sleep in the earth bow down
       in worship; *
    all who go down to the dust fall before him.

29   My soul shall live for him;
my descendants shall serve him; *
    they shall be known as the LORD's for ever.

30   They shall come and make known to a people yet unborn *
    the saving deeds that he has done.

23   *Dominus regit me*

1   The LORD is my shepherd; *
    I shall not be in want.

2   He makes me lie down in green pastures *
    and leads me beside still waters.

3   He revives my soul *
      and guides me along right pathways for his Name's sake.

4   Though I walk through the valley of the shadow of death,
   I shall fear no evil; *
      for you are with me;
      your rod and your staff, they comfort me.

5   You spread a table before me in the presence of those
          who trouble me; *
      you have anointed my head with oil,
      and my cup is running over.

6   Surely your goodness and mercy shall follow me all the days
          of my life, *
      and I will dwell in the house of the LORD for ever.

Fifth Day: Morning Prayer

24   *Domini est terra*

1   The earth is the LORD's and all that is in it, *
      the world and all who dwell therein.

2   For it is he who founded it upon the seas *
      and made it firm upon the rivers of the deep.

3   "Who can ascend the hill of the LORD? *
      and who can stand in his holy place?"

4   "Those who have clean hands and a pure heart, *
      who have not pledged themselves to falsehood,
      nor sworn by what is a fraud.

5   They shall receive a blessing from the LORD *
      and a just reward from the God of their salvation."

6   Such is the generation of those who seek him, *
      of those who seek your face, O God of Jacob.

7   Lift up your heads, O gates;
      lift them high, O everlasting doors; *
        and the King of glory shall come in.

8   "Who is this King of glory?" *
      "The LORD, strong and mighty,
        the LORD, mighty in battle."

9   Lift up your heads, O gates;
      lift them high, O everlasting doors; *
        and the King of glory shall come in.

10 "Who is he, this King of glory?" *
      "The LORD of hosts,
        he is the King of glory."

25   *Ad te, Domine, levavi*

1   To you, O LORD, I lift up my soul;
      my God, I put my trust in you; *
        let me not be humiliated,
          nor let my enemies triumph over me.

2   Let none who look to you be put to shame; *
      let the treacherous be disappointed in their schemes.

3   Show me your ways, O LORD, *
      and teach me your paths.

4   Lead me in your truth and teach me, *
      for you are the God of my salvation;
        in you have I trusted all the day long.

5   Remember, O LORD, your compassion and love, *
      for they are from everlasting.

6   Remember not the sins of my youth and my transgressions; *
      remember me according to your love
      and for the sake of your goodness, O LORD.

7   Gracious and upright is the LORD; *
      therefore he teaches sinners in his way.

8   He guides the humble in doing right *
      and teaches his way to the lowly.

9   All the paths of the LORD are love and faithfulness *
      to those who keep his covenant and his testimonies.

10   For your Name's sake, O LORD, *
      forgive my sin, for it is great.

11   Who are they who fear the LORD? *
      he will teach them the way that they should choose.

12   They shall dwell in prosperity, *
      and their offspring shall inherit the land.

13   The LORD is a friend to those who fear him *
      and will show them his covenant.

14   My eyes are ever looking to the LORD, *
      for he shall pluck my feet out of the net.

15   Turn to me and have pity on me, *
      for I am left alone and in misery.

16   The sorrows of my heart have increased; *
      bring me out of my troubles.

17   Look upon my adversity and misery *
      and forgive me all my sin.

18   Look upon my enemies, for they are many, *
      and they bear a violent hatred against me.

19 Protect my life and deliver me; *
    let me not be put to shame, for I have trusted in you.

20 Let integrity and uprightness preserve me, *
    for my hope has been in you.

21 Deliver Israel, O God, *
    out of all his troubles.

26 *Judica me, Domine*

1 Give judgment for me, O LORD,
  for I have lived with integrity; *
    I have trusted in the Lord and have not faltered.

2 Test me, O LORD, and try me; *
    examine my heart and my mind.

3 For your love is before my eyes; *
    I have walked faithfully with you.

4 I have not sat with the worthless, *
    nor do I consort with the deceitful.

5 I have hated the company of evildoers; *
    I will not sit down with the wicked.

6 I will wash my hands in innocence, O LORD, *
    that I may go in procession round your altar,

7 Singing aloud a song of thanksgiving *
    and recounting all your wonderful deeds.

8 LORD, I love the house in which you dwell *
    and the place where your glory abides.

9 Do not sweep me away with sinners, *
    nor my life with those who thirst for blood,

10   Whose hands are full of evil plots, *
           and their right hand full of bribes.

11   As for me, I will live with integrity; *
           redeem me, O LORD, and have pity on me.

12   My foot stands on level ground; *
           in the full assembly I will bless the LORD.

Fifth Day: Evening Prayer

27   *Dominus illuminatio*

1   The LORD is my light and my salvation;
      whom then shall I fear? *
           the LORD is the strength of my life;
           of whom then shall I be afraid?

2   When evildoers came upon me to eat up my flesh, *
           it was they, my foes and my adversaries, who
                   stumbled and fell.

3   Though an army should encamp against me, *
           yet my heart shall not be afraid;

4   And though war should rise up against me, *
           yet will I put my trust in him.

5   One thing have I asked of the LORD;
      one thing I seek; *
           that I may dwell in the house of the LORD all the days
                   of my life;

6   To behold the fair beauty of the LORD *
           and to seek him in his temple.

7   For in the day of trouble he shall keep me safe
                 in his shelter; *
     he shall hide me in the secrecy of his dwelling
     and set me high upon a rock.

8   Even now he lifts up my head *
     above my enemies round about me.

9   Therefore I will offer in his dwelling an oblation
     with sounds of great gladness; *
     I will sing and make music to the LORD.

10   Hearken to my voice, O LORD, when I call; *
     have mercy on me and answer me.

11   You speak in my heart and say, "Seek my face." *
     Your face, LORD, will I seek.

12   Hide not your face from me, *
     nor turn away your servant in displeasure.

13   You have been my helper;
     cast me not away; *
     do not forsake me, O God of my salvation.

14   Though my father and my mother forsake me, *
     the LORD will sustain me.

15   Show me your way, O LORD; *
     lead me on a level path, because of my enemies.

16   Deliver me not into the hand of my adversaries, *
     for false witnesses have risen up against me,
     and also those who speak malice.

17   What if I had not believed
     that I should see the goodness of the LORD *
     in the land of the living!

18 O tarry and await the LORD's pleasure;
be strong, and he shall comfort your heart; *
    wait patiently for the LORD.

28 *Ad te, Domine*

1 O LORD, I call to you;
my Rock, do not be deaf to my cry; *
    lest, if you do not hear me,
    I become like those who go down to the Pit.

2 Hear the voice of my prayer when I cry out to you, *
    when I lift up my hands to your holy of holies.

3 Do not snatch me away with the wicked or with the
        evildoers, *
    who speak peaceably with their neighbors,
    while strife is in their hearts.

4 Repay them according to their deeds, *
    and according to the wickedness of their actions.

5 According to the work of their hands repay them, *
    and give them their just deserts.

6 They have no understanding of the LORD's doings,
nor of the works of his hands; *
    therefore he will break them down and not
            build them up.

7 Blessed is the LORD! *
    for he has heard the voice of my prayer.

8 The LORD is my strength and my shield; *
    my heart trusts in him, and I have been helped;

9 Therefore my heart dances for joy, *
    and in my song will I praise him.

10   The LORD is the strength of his people, *
       a safe refuge for his anointed.

11   Save your people and bless your inheritance; *
       shepherd them and carry them for ever.

29   *Afferte Domino*

1   Ascribe to the LORD, you gods, *
       ascribe to the LORD glory and strength.

2   Ascribe to the LORD the glory due his Name; *
       worship the LORD in the beauty of holiness.

3   The voice of the LORD is upon the waters;
       the God of glory thunders; *
       the LORD is upon the mighty waters.

4   The voice of the LORD is a powerful voice; *
       the voice of the LORD is a voice of splendor.

5   The voice of the LORD breaks the cedar trees; *
       the LORD breaks the cedars of Lebanon;

6   He makes Lebanon skip like a calf, *
       and Mount Hermon like a young wild ox.

7   The voice of the LORD splits the flames of fire;
       the voice of the LORD shakes the wilderness; *
       the LORD shakes the wilderness of Kadesh.

8   The voice of the LORD makes the oak trees writhe *
       and strips the forests bare.

9   And in the temple of the LORD *
       all are crying, "Glory!"

10   The LORD sits enthroned above the flood; *
       the LORD sits enthroned as King for evermore.

11   The Lord shall give strength to his people; *
       the Lord shall give his people the blessing of peace.

Sixth Day: Morning Prayer

30   *Exaltabo te, Domine*

1   I will exalt you, O Lord,
    because you have lifted me up *
       and have not let my enemies triumph over me.

2   O Lord my God, I cried out to you, *
       and you restored me to health.

3   You brought me up, O Lord, from the dead; *
       you restored my life as I was going down to the grave.

4   Sing to the Lord, you servants of his; *
       give thanks for the remembrance of his holiness.

5   For his wrath endures but the twinkling of an eye, *
       his favor for a lifetime.

6   Weeping may spend the night, *
       but joy comes in the morning.

7   While I felt secure, I said,
    "I shall never be disturbed. *
       You, Lord, with your favor, made me as strong as
          the mountains."

8   Then you hid your face, *
       and I was filled with fear.

9   I cried to you, O Lord; *
       I pleaded with the Lord, saying,

10   "What profit is there in my blood, if I go down to the Pit? *
       will the dust praise you or declare your faithfulness?

11   Hear, O Lord, and have mercy upon me; *
       O Lord, be my helper."

12   You have turned my wailing into dancing; *
       you have put off my sack-cloth and clothed me with joy.

13   Therefore my heart sings to you without ceasing; *
       O Lord my God, I will give you thanks for ever.

31 *In te, Domine, speravi*

1   In you, O Lord, have I taken refuge;
let me never be put to shame; *
       deliver me in your righteousness.

2   Incline your ear to me; *
       make haste to deliver me.

3   Be my strong rock, a castle to keep me safe,
for you are my crag and my stronghold; *
       for the sake of your Name, lead me and guide me.

4   Take me out of the net that they have secretly set for me, *
       for you are my tower of strength.

5   Into your hands I commend my spirit, *
       for you have redeemed me,
       O Lord, O God of truth.

6   I hate those who cling to worthless idols, *
       and I put my trust in the Lord.

7   I will rejoice and be glad because of your mercy; *
       for you have seen my affliction;
       you know my distress.

8   You have not shut me up in the power of the enemy; *
      you have set my feet in an open place.

9   Have mercy on me, O LORD, for I am in trouble; *
      my eye is consumed with sorrow,
      and also my throat and my belly.

10   For my life is wasted with grief,
   and my years with sighing; *
      my strength fails me because of affliction,
      and my bones are consumed.

11   I have become a reproach to all my enemies and
          even to my neighbors,
   a dismay to those of my acquaintance; *
      when they see me in the street they avoid me.

12   I am forgotten like a dead man, out of mind; *
      I am as useless as a broken pot.

13   For I have heard the whispering of the crowd;
   fear is all around; *
      they put their heads together against me;
      they plot to take my life.

14   But as for me, I have trusted in you, O LORD. *
      I have said, "You are my God.

15   My times are in your hand; *
      rescue me from the hand of my enemies,
      and from those who persecute me.

16   Make your face to shine upon your servant, *
      and in your loving-kindness save me."

17   LORD, let me not be ashamed for having called upon you; *
      rather, let the wicked be put to shame;
      let them be silent in the grave.

18   Let the lying lips be silenced which speak against
                 the righteous, *
      haughtily, disdainfully, and with contempt.

19   How great is your goodness, O LORD!
      which you have laid up for those who fear you; *
        which you have done in the sight of all
        for those who put their trust in you.

20   You hide them in the covert of your presence from those
                 who slander them; *
      you keep them in your shelter from the strife of tongues.

21   Blessed be the LORD! *
      for he has shown me the wonders of his love in a
                 besieged city.

22   Yet I said in my alarm,
   "I have been cut off from the sight of your eyes." *
      Nevertheless, you heard the sound of my entreaty
      when I cried out to you.

23   Love the LORD, all you who worship him; *
      the LORD protects the faithful,
      but repays to the full those who act haughtily.

24   Be strong and let your heart take courage, *
      all you who wait for the LORD.

Sixth Day: Evening Prayer

32   *Beati quorum*

1   Happy are they whose transgressions are forgiven, *
      and whose sin is put away!

2   Happy are they to whom the LORD imputes no guilt, *
      and in whose spirit there is no guile!

3   While I held my tongue, my bones withered away, *
      because of my groaning all day long.

4   For your hand was heavy upon me day and night; *
      my moisture was dried up as in the heat of summer.

5   Then I acknowledged my sin to you, *
      and did not conceal my guilt.

6   I said, "I will confess my transgressions to the LORD." *
      Then you forgave me the guilt of my sin.

7   Therefore all the faithful will make their prayers to you in
      time of trouble; *
      when the great waters overflow, they shall not reach them.

8   You are my hiding-place;
      you preserve me from trouble; *
      you surround me with shouts of deliverance.

9   "I will instruct you and teach you in the way that you
      should go; *
      I will guide you with my eye.

10   Do not be like horse or mule, which have no understanding; *
      who must be fitted with bit and bridle,
      or else they will not stay near you."

11   Great are the tribulations of the wicked; *
      but mercy embraces those who trust in the LORD.

12   Be glad, you righteous, and rejoice in the LORD; *
      shout for joy, all who are true of heart.

33　*Exultate, justi*

1　Rejoice in the LORD, you righteous; *
　　it is good for the just to sing praises.

2　Praise the LORD with the harp; *
　　play to him upon the psaltery and lyre.

3　Sing for him a new song; *
　　sound a fanfare with all your skill upon the trumpet.

4　For the word of the LORD is right, *
　　and all his works are sure.

5　He loves righteousness and justice; *
　　the loving-kindness of the LORD fills the whole earth.

6　By the word of the LORD were the heavens made, *
　　by the breath of his mouth all the heavenly hosts.

7　He gathers up the waters of the ocean as in a water-skin *
　　and stores up the depths of the sea.

8　Let all the earth fear the LORD; *
　　let all who dwell in the world stand in awe of him.

9　For he spoke, and it came to pass; *
　　he commanded, and it stood fast.

10　The LORD brings the will of the nations to naught; *
　　he thwarts the designs of the peoples.

11　But the LORD's will stands fast for ever, *
　　and the designs of his heart from age to age.

12　Happy is the nation whose God is the LORD! *
　　happy the people he has chosen to be his own!

13   The LORD looks down from heaven, *
     and beholds all the people in the world.

14   From where he sits enthroned he turns his gaze *
     on all who dwell on the earth.

15   He fashions all the hearts of them *
     and understands all their works.

16   There is no king that can be saved by a mighty army; *
     a strong man is not delivered by his great strength.

17   The horse is a vain hope for deliverance; *
     for all its strength it cannot save.

18   Behold, the eye of the LORD is upon those who fear him, *
     on those who wait upon his love,

19   To pluck their lives from death, *
     and to feed them in time of famine.

20   Our soul waits for the LORD; *
     he is our help and our shield.

21   Indeed, our heart rejoices in him, *
     for in his holy Name we put our trust.

22   Let your loving-kindness, O LORD, be upon us, *
     as we have put our trust in you.

34   *Benedicam Dominum*

1   I will bless the LORD at all times; *
     his praise shall ever be in my mouth.

2   I will glory in the LORD; *
     let the humble hear and rejoice.

3   Proclaim with me the greatness of the LORD; *
     let us exalt his Name together.

4 I sought the LORD, and he answered me *
   and delivered me out of all my terror.

5 Look upon him and be radiant, *
   and let not your faces be ashamed.

6 I called in my affliction and the LORD heard me *
   and saved me from all my troubles.

7 The angel of the LORD encompasses those who fear him, *
   and he will deliver them.

8 Taste and see that the LORD is good; *
   happy are they who trust in him!

9 Fear the LORD, you that are his saints, *
   for those who fear him lack nothing.

10 The young lions lack and suffer hunger, *
    but those who seek the LORD lack nothing that is good.

11 Come, children, and listen to me; *
    I will teach you the fear of the LORD.

12 Who among you loves life *
    and desires long life to enjoy prosperity?

13 Keep your tongue from evil-speaking *
    and your lips from lying words.

14 Turn from evil and do good; *
    seek peace and pursue it.

15 The eyes of the LORD are upon the righteous, *
    and his ears are open to their cry.

16 The face of the LORD is against those who do evil, *
    to root out the remembrance of them from the earth.

17   The righteous cry, and the LORD hears them *
     and delivers them from all their troubles.

18   The LORD is near to the brokenhearted *
     and will save those whose spirits are crushed.

19   Many are the troubles of the righteous, *
     but the LORD will deliver him out of them all.

20   He will keep safe all his bones; *
     not one of them shall be broken.

21   Evil shall slay the wicked, *
     and those who hate the righteous will be punished.

22   The LORD ransoms the life of his servants, *
     and none will be punished who trust in him.

Seventh Day: Morning Prayer

35 *Judica, Domine*

1   Fight those who fight me, O LORD; *
     attack those who are attacking me.

2   Take up shield and armor *
     and rise up to help me.

3   Draw the sword and bar the way against those
              who pursue me; *
     say to my soul, "I am your salvation."

4   Let those who seek after my life be shamed and humbled; *
     let those who plot my ruin fall back and be dismayed.

5   Let them be like chaff before the wind, *
     and let the angel of the LORD drive them away.

6   Let their way be dark and slippery, *
         and let the angel of the LORD pursue them.

7   For they have secretly spread a net for me without a cause; *
         without a cause they have dug a pit to take me alive.

8   Let ruin come upon them unawares; *
         let them be caught in the net they hid;
         let them fall into the pit they dug.

9   Then I will be joyful in the LORD; *
         I will glory in his victory.

10   My very bones will say, "LORD, who is like you? *
         You deliver the poor from those who are too strong for them,
         the poor and needy from those who rob them."

11   Malicious witnesses rise up against me; *
         they charge me with matters I know nothing about.

12   They pay me evil in exchange for good; *
         my soul is full of despair.

13   But when they were sick I dressed in sack-cloth *
         and humbled myself by fasting;

14   I prayed with my whole heart,
         as one would for a friend or a brother; *
         I behaved like one who mourns for his mother,
         bowed down and grieving.

15   But when I stumbled, they were glad and gathered together;
         they gathered against me; *
         strangers whom I did not know tore me to pieces and
                 would not stop.

16   They put me to the test and mocked me; *
         they gnashed at me with their teeth.

17 O Lord, how long will you look on? *
        rescue me from the roaring beasts,
        and my life from the young lions.

18 I will give you thanks in the great congregation; *
        I will praise you in the mighty throng.

19 Do not let my treacherous foes rejoice over me, *
        nor let those who hate me without a cause
            wink at each other.

20 For they do not plan for peace, *
        but invent deceitful schemes against the
            quiet in the land.

21 They opened their mouths at me and said, *
        "Aha! we saw it with our own eyes."

22 You saw it, O LORD; do not be silent; *
        O Lord, be not far from me.

23 Awake, arise, to my cause! *
        to my defense, my God and my Lord!

24 Give me justice, O LORD my God,
        according to your righteousness; *
        do not let them triumph over me.

25 Do not let them say in their hearts,
    "Aha! just what we want!" *
        Do not let them say, "We have swallowed him up."

26 Let all who rejoice at my ruin be ashamed and disgraced; *
        let those who boast against me be clothed with
            dismay and shame.

27 Let those who favor my cause sing out with joy and be glad; *
        let them say always, "Great is the LORD,
        who desires the prosperity of his servant."

28   And my tongue shall be talking of your righteousness *
       and of your praise all the day long.

36   *Dixit injustus*

1   There is a voice of rebellion deep in the heart of the wicked; *
       there is no fear of God before his eyes.

2   He flatters himself in his own eyes *
       that his hateful sin will not be found out.

3   The words of his mouth are wicked and deceitful; *
       he has left off acting wisely and doing good.

4   He thinks up wickedness upon his bed
    and has set himself in no good way; *
       he does not abhor that which is evil.

5   Your love, O LORD, reaches to the heavens, *
       and your faithfulness to the clouds.

6   Your righteousness is like the strong mountains,
    your justice like the great deep; *
       you save both man and beast, O LORD.

7   How priceless is your love, O God! *
       your people take refuge under the
                shadow of your wings.

8   They feast upon the abundance of your house; *
       you give them drink from the river of your delights.

9   For with you is the well of life, *
       and in your light we see light.

10   Continue your loving-kindness to those who know you, *
       and your favor to those who are true of heart.

11 Let not the foot of the proud come near me, *
    nor the hand of the wicked push me aside.

12 See how they are fallen, those who work wickedness! *
    they are cast down and shall not be able to rise.

Seventh Day: Evening Prayer

37

Part I   *Noli æmulari*

1 Do not fret yourself because of evildoers; *
    do not be jealous of those who do wrong.

2 For they shall soon wither like the grass, *
    and like the green grass fade away.

3 Put your trust in the LORD and do good; *
    dwell in the land and feed on its riches.

4 Take delight in the LORD, *
    and he shall give you your heart's desire.

5 Commit your way to the LORD and put your trust in him, *
    and he will bring it to pass.

6 He will make your righteousness as clear as the light *
    and your just dealing as the noonday.

7 Be still before the LORD *
    and wait patiently for him.

8 Do not fret yourself over the one who prospers, *
    the one who succeeds in evil schemes.

9 Refrain from anger, leave rage alone; *
    do not fret yourself; it leads only to evil.

10   For evildoers shall be cut off, *
       but those who wait upon the LORD shall possess the land.

11   In a little while the wicked shall be no more; *
       you shall search out their place, but they will not be there.

12   But the lowly shall possess the land; *
       they will delight in abundance of peace.

13   The wicked plot against the righteous *
       and gnash at them with their teeth.

14   The Lord laughs at the wicked, *
       because he sees that their day will come.

15   The wicked draw their sword and bend their bow
     to strike down the poor and needy, *
       to slaughter those who are upright in their ways.

16   Their sword shall go through their own heart, *
       and their bow shall be broken.

17   The little that the righteous has *
       is better than great riches of the wicked.

18   For the power of the wicked shall be broken, *
       but the LORD upholds the righteous.

Psalm 37: Part II   *Novit Dominus*

19   The LORD cares for the lives of the godly, *
       and their inheritance shall last for ever.

20   They shall not be ashamed in bad times, *
       and in days of famine they shall have enough.

21   As for the wicked, they shall perish, *
       and the enemies of the LORD, like the glory of
                           the meadows, shall vanish;
       they shall vanish like smoke.

22   The wicked borrow and do not repay, *
     but the righteous are generous in giving.

23   Those who are blessed by God shall possess the land, *
     but those who are cursed by him shall be destroyed.

24   Our steps are directed by the LORD; *
     he strengthens those in whose way he delights.

25   If they stumble, they shall not fall headlong, *
     for the LORD holds them by the hand.

26   I have been young and now I am old, *
     but never have I seen the righteous forsaken,
     or their children begging bread.

27   The righteous are always generous in their lending, *
     and their children shall be a blessing.

28   Turn from evil, and do good, *
     and dwell in the land for ever.

29   For the LORD loves justice; *
     he does not forsake his faithful ones.

30   They shall be kept safe for ever, *
     but the offspring of the wicked shall be destroyed.

31   The righteous shall possess the land *
     and dwell in it for ever.

32   The mouth of the righteous utters wisdom, *
     and their tongue speaks what is right.

33   The law of their God is in their heart, *
     and their footsteps shall not falter.

34   The wicked spy on the righteous *
     and seek occasion to kill them.

35 The LORD will not abandon them to their hand, *
   nor let them be found guilty when brought to trial.

36 Wait upon the LORD and keep his way; *
   he will raise you up to possess the land,
   and when the wicked are cut off, you will see it.

37 I have seen the wicked in their arrogance, *
   flourishing like a tree in full leaf.

38 I went by, and behold, they were not there; *
   I searched for them, but they could not be found.

39 Mark those who are honest;
   observe the upright; *
   for there is a future for the peaceable.

40 Transgressors shall be destroyed, one and all; *
   the future of the wicked is cut off.

41 But the deliverance of the righteous comes from the LORD; *
   he is their stronghold in time of trouble.

42 The LORD will help them and rescue them; *
   he will rescue them from the wicked and deliver them,
   because they seek refuge in him.

Eighth Day: Morning Prayer

38 *Domine, ne in furore*

1 O LORD, do not rebuke me in your anger; *
   do not punish me in your wrath.

2 For your arrows have already pierced me, *
   and your hand presses hard upon me.

3   There is no health in my flesh,
    because of your indignation; *
        there is no soundness in my body, because of my sin.

4   For my iniquities overwhelm me; *
        like a heavy burden they are too much for me to bear.

5   My wounds stink and fester *
        by reason of my foolishness.

6   I am utterly bowed down and prostrate; *
        I go about in mourning all the day long.

7   My loins are filled with searing pain; *
        there is no health in my body.

8   I am utterly numb and crushed; *
        I wail, because of the groaning of my heart.

9   O Lord, you know all my desires, *
        and my sighing is not hidden from you.

10 My heart is pounding, my strength has failed me, *
        and the brightness of my eyes is gone from me.

11 My friends and companions draw back from my affliction; *
        my neighbors stand afar off.

12 Those who seek after my life lay snares for me; *
        those who strive to hurt me speak of my ruin
        and plot treachery all the day long.

13 But I am like the deaf who do not hear, *
        like those who are mute and do not open their mouth.

14 I have become like one who does not hear *
        and from whose mouth comes no defense.

15 For in you, O Lord, have I fixed my hope; *
        you will answer me, O Lord my God.

16 For I said,"Do not let them rejoice at my expense, *
    those who gloat over me when my foot slips."

17 Truly, I am on the verge of falling, *
    and my pain is always with me.

18 I will confess my iniquity *
    and be sorry for my sin.

19 Those who are my enemies without cause are mighty, *
    and many in number are those who wrongfully hate me.

20 Those who repay evil for good slander me, *
    because I follow the course that is right.

21 O LORD, do not forsake me; *
    be not far from me, O my God.

22 Make haste to help me, *
    O Lord of my salvation.

39 *Dixi, Custodiam*

1   I said,"I will keep watch upon my ways, *
    so that I do not offend with my tongue.

2   I will put a muzzle on my mouth *
    while the wicked are in my presence."

3   So I held my tongue and said nothing; *
    I refrained from rash words;
    but my pain became unbearable.

4   My heart was hot within me;
    while I pondered, the fire burst into flame; *
    I spoke out with my tongue:

5   LORD, let me know my end and the number of my days, *
      so that I may know how short my life is.

6   You have given me a mere handful of days,
      and my lifetime is as nothing in your sight; *
       truly, even those who stand erect are but a puff of wind.

7   We walk about like a shadow,
      and in vain we are in turmoil; *
       we heap up riches and cannot tell who will gather them.

8   And now, what is my hope? *
      O Lord, my hope is in you.

9   Deliver me from all my transgressions *
      and do not make me the taunt of the fool.

10   I fell silent and did not open my mouth, *
      for surely it was you that did it.

11   Take your affliction from me; *
      I am worn down by the blows of your hand.

12   With rebukes for sin you punish us;
      like a moth you eat away all that is dear to us; *
       truly, everyone is but a puff of wind.

13   Hear my prayer, O LORD,
      and give ear to my cry; *
       hold not your peace at my tears.

14   For I am but a sojourner with you, *
      a wayfarer, as all my forebears were.

15   Turn your gaze from me, that I may be glad again, *
      before I go my way and am no more.

40　*Expectans, expectavi*

1　I waited patiently upon the LORD; *
　　he stooped to me and heard my cry.

2　He lifted me out of the desolate pit, out of the mire and clay; *
　　he set my feet upon a high cliff and made my footing sure.

3　He put a new song in my mouth,
　　a song of praise to our God; *
　　　　many shall see, and stand in awe,
　　　　and put their trust in the LORD.

4　Happy are they who trust in the LORD! *
　　they do not resort to evil spirits or turn to false gods.

5　Great things are they that you have done, O LORD my God!
　　how great your wonders and your plans for us! *
　　　　there is none who can be compared with you.

6　Oh, that I could make them known and tell them! *
　　but they are more than I can count.

7　In sacrifice and offering you take no pleasure *
　　(you have given me ears to hear you);

8　Burnt-offering and sin-offering you have not required, *
　　and so I said, "Behold, I come.

9　In the roll of the book it is written concerning me: *
　　'I love to do your will, O my God;
　　your law is deep in my heart.'"

10　I proclaimed righteousness in the great congregation; *
　　　behold, I did not restrain my lips;
　　　and that, O LORD, you know.

11　Your righteousness have I not hidden in my heart;
　　I have spoken of your faithfulness and your deliverance; *
　　　　I have not concealed your love and faithfulness from the
　　　　　　great congregation.

12   You are the LORD;
do not withhold your compassion from me; *
    let your love and your faithfulness keep me safe for ever,

13   For innumerable troubles have crowded upon me;
my sins have overtaken me, and I cannot see; *
    they are more in number than the hairs of my head,
    and my heart fails me.

14   Be pleased, O LORD, to deliver me; *
    O Lord, make haste to help me.

15   Let them be ashamed and altogether dismayed
who seek after my life to destroy it; *
    let them draw back and be disgraced
    who take pleasure in my misfortune.

16   Let those who say "Aha!" and gloat over me be confounded, *
    because they are ashamed.

17   Let all who seek you rejoice in you and be glad; *
    let those who love your salvation continually say,
    "Great is the LORD!"

18   Though I am poor and afflicted, *
    the Lord will have regard for me.

19   You are my helper and my deliverer; *
    do not tarry, O my God.

Eighth Day: Evening Prayer

41   *Beatus qui intelligit*

1   Happy are they who consider the poor and needy! *
    the LORD will deliver them in the time of trouble.

2   The LORD preserves them and keeps them alive,
so that they may be happy in the land; *
     he does not hand them over to the will of their enemies.

3   The LORD sustains them on their sickbed *
     and ministers to them in their illness.

4   I said, "LORD, be merciful to me; *
     heal me, for I have sinned against you."

5   My enemies are saying wicked things about me: *
     "When will he die, and his name perish?"

6   Even if they come to see me, they speak empty words; *
     their heart collects false rumors;
     they go outside and spread them.

7   All my enemies whisper together about me *
     and devise evil against me.

8   "A deadly thing," they say, "has fastened on him; *
     he has taken to his bed and will never get up again."

9   Even my best friend, whom I trusted,
who broke bread with me, *
     has lifted up his heel and turned against me.

10   But you, O LORD, be merciful to me and raise me up, *
     and I shall repay them.

11   By this I know you are pleased with me, *
     that my enemy does not triumph over me.

12   In my integrity you hold me fast, *
     and shall set me before your face for ever.

13   Blessed be the LORD God of Israel, *
     from age to age. Amen. Amen.

Book Two

42 *Quemadmodum*

1 As the deer longs for the water-brooks, *
   so longs my soul for you, O God.

2 My soul is athirst for God, athirst for the living God; *
   when shall I come to appear before the presence of God?

3 My tears have been my food day and night, *
   while all day long they say to me,
  "Where now is your God?"

4 I pour out my soul when I think on these things: *
   how I went with the multitude and led them into the
       house of God,

5 With the voice of praise and thanksgiving, *
   among those who keep holy-day.

6 Why are you so full of heaviness, O my soul? *
   and why are you so disquieted within me?

7 Put your trust in God; *
   for I will yet give thanks to him,
   who is the help of my countenance, and my God.

8 My soul is heavy within me; *
   therefore I will remember you from the land of Jordan,
   and from the peak of Mizar among the heights of Hermon.

9 One deep calls to another in the noise of your cataracts; *
   all your rapids and floods have gone over me.

10 The LORD grants his loving-kindness in the daytime; *
   in the night season his song is with me,
   a prayer to the God of my life.

11 I will say to the God of my strength,
    "Why have you forgotten me? *
        and why do I go so heavily while the enemy
                            oppresses me?"

12 While my bones are being broken, *
        my enemies mock me to my face;

13 All day long they mock me *
        and say to me, "Where now is your God?"

14 Why are you so full of heaviness, O my soul? *
        and why are you so disquieted within me?

15 Put your trust in God; *
        for I will yet give thanks to him,
        who is the help of my countenance, and my God.

43 *Judica me, Deus*

1 Give judgment for me, O God,
    and defend my cause against an ungodly people; *
        deliver me from the deceitful and the wicked.

2 For you are the God of my strength;
    why have you put me from you? *
        and why do I go so heavily while the enemy
                            oppresses me?

3 Send out your light and your truth, that they may lead me, *
        and bring me to your holy hill
        and to your dwelling;

4 That I may go to the altar of God,
    to the God of my joy and gladness; *
        and on the harp I will give thanks to you, O God my God.

5 Why are you so full of heaviness, O my soul? *
    and why are you so disquieted within me?

6 Put your trust in God; *
    for I will yet give thanks to him,
    who is the help of my countenance, and my God.

Ninth Day: Morning Prayer

44 *Deus, auribus*

1 We have heard with our ears, O God,
our forefathers have told us, *
    the deeds you did in their days,
    in the days of old.

2 How with your hand you drove the peoples out
and planted our forefathers in the land; *
    how you destroyed nations and made your people flourish.

3 For they did not take the land by their sword,
nor did their arm win the victory for them; *
    but your right hand, your arm, and the
                        light of your countenance,
    because you favored them.

4 You are my King and my God; *
    you command victories for Jacob.

5 Through you we pushed back our adversaries; *
    through your Name we trampled on those who
                        rose up against us.

6 For I do not rely on my bow, *
    and my sword does not give me the victory.

7 Surely, you gave us victory over our adversaries *
    and put those who hate us to shame.

8 Every day we gloried in God, *
    and we will praise your Name for ever.

9 Nevertheless, you have rejected and humbled us *
    and do not go forth with our armies.

10 You have made us fall back before our adversary, *
    and our enemies have plundered us.

11 You have made us like sheep to be eaten *
    and have scattered us among the nations.

12 You are selling your people for a trifle *
    and are making no profit on the sale of them.

13 You have made us the scorn of our neighbors, *
    a mockery and derision to those around us.

14 You have made us a byword among the nations, *
    a laughing-stock among the peoples.

15 My humiliation is daily before me, *
    and shame has covered my face;

16 Because of the taunts of the mockers and blasphemers, *
    because of the enemy and avenger.

17 All this has come upon us; *
    yet we have not forgotten you,
    nor have we betrayed your covenant.

18 Our heart never turned back, *
    nor did our footsteps stray from your path;

19 Though you thrust us down into a place of misery, *
    and covered us over with deep darkness.

20 If we have forgotten the Name of our God, *
    or stretched out our hands to some strange god,

21 Will not God find it out? *
    for he knows the secrets of the heart.

22 Indeed, for your sake we are killed all the day long; *
   we are accounted as sheep for the slaughter.

23 Awake, O Lord! why are you sleeping? *
   Arise! do not reject us for ever.

24 Why have you hidden your face *
   and forgotten our affliction and oppression?

25 We sink down into the dust; *
   our body cleaves to the ground.

26 Rise up, and help us, *
   and save us, for the sake of your steadfast love.

45 *Eructavit cor meum*

1 My heart is stirring with a noble song;
  let me recite what I have fashioned for the king; *
    my tongue shall be the pen of a skilled writer.

2 You are the fairest of men; *
    grace flows from your lips,
    because God has blessed you for ever.

3 Strap your sword upon your thigh, O mighty warrior, *
    in your pride and in your majesty.

4 Ride out and conquer in the cause of truth *
    and for the sake of justice.

5 Your right hand will show you marvelous things; *
    your arrows are very sharp, O mighty warrior.

6 The peoples are falling at your feet, *
    and the king's enemies are losing heart.

7   Your throne, O God, endures for ever and ever, *
     a scepter of righteousness is the scepter of your kingdom;
     you love righteousness and hate iniquity.

8   Therefore God, your God, has anointed you *
     with the oil of gladness above your fellows.

9   All your garments are fragrant with myrrh, aloes, and cassia, *
     and the music of strings from ivory palaces makes you glad.

10   Kings' daughters stand among the ladies of the court; *
     on your right hand is the queen,
         adorned with the gold of Ophir.

11   "Hear, O daughter; consider and listen closely; *
     forget your people and your father's house.

12   The king will have pleasure in your beauty; *
     he is your master; therefore do him honor.

13   The people of Tyre are here with a gift; *
     the rich among the people seek your favor."

14   All glorious is the princess as she enters; *
     her gown is cloth-of-gold.

15   In embroidered apparel she is brought to the king; *
     after her the bridesmaids follow in procession.

16   With joy and gladness they are brought, *
     and enter into the palace of the king.

17   "In place of fathers, O king, you shall have sons; *
     you shall make them princes over all the earth.

18   I will make your name to be remembered
     from one generation to another; *
         therefore nations will praise you for ever and ever."

46 *Deus noster refugium*

1 God is our refuge and strength, *
  a very present help in trouble.

2 Therefore we will not fear, though the earth be moved, *
  and though the mountains be toppled into the
  depths of the sea;

3 Though its waters rage and foam, *
  and though the mountains tremble at its tumult.

4 The LORD of hosts is with us; *
  the God of Jacob is our stronghold.

5 There is a river whose streams make glad the city of God, *
  the holy habitation of the Most High.

6 God is in the midst of her;
  she shall not be overthrown; *
  God shall help her at the break of day.

7 The nations make much ado, and the kingdoms are shaken; *
  God has spoken, and the earth shall melt away.

8 The LORD of hosts is with us; *
  the God of Jacob is our stronghold.

9 Come now and look upon the works of the LORD, *
  what awesome things he has done on earth.

10 It is he who makes war to cease in all the world; *
  he breaks the bow, and shatters the spear,
  and burns the shields with fire.

11   "Be still, then, and know that I am God; *
      I will be exalted among the nations;
      I will be exalted in the earth."

12   The LORD of hosts is with us; *
      the God of Jacob is our stronghold.

Ninth Day: Evening Prayer

47   *Omnes gentes, plaudite*

1   Clap your hands, all you peoples; *
      shout to God with a cry of joy.

2   For the LORD Most High is to be feared; *
      he is the great King over all the earth.

3   He subdues the peoples under us, *
      and the nations under our feet.

4   He chooses our inheritance for us, *
      the pride of Jacob whom he loves.

5   God has gone up with a shout, *
      the LORD with the sound of the ram's-horn.

6   Sing praises to God, sing praises; *
      sing praises to our King, sing praises.

7   For God is King of all the earth; *
      sing praises with all your skill.

8   God reigns over the nations; *
      God sits upon his holy throne.

9   The nobles of the peoples have gathered together *
      with the people of the God of Abraham.

10   The rulers of the earth belong to God, *
      and he is highly exalted.

48 *Magnus Dominus*

1 Great is the LORD, and highly to be praised; *
   in the city of our God is his holy hill.

2 Beautiful and lofty, the joy of all the earth, is the
                    hill of Zion, *
   the very center of the world and the city of the great King.

3 God is in her citadels; *
   he is known to be her sure refuge.

4 Behold, the kings of the earth assembled *
   and marched forward together.

5 They looked and were astounded; *
   they retreated and fled in terror.

6 Trembling seized them there; *
   they writhed like a woman in childbirth,
   like ships of the sea when the east wind shatters them.

7 As we have heard, so have we seen,
   in the city of the LORD of hosts, in the city of our God; *
   God has established her for ever.

8 We have waited in silence on your loving-kindness, O God, *
   in the midst of your temple.

9 Your praise, like your Name, O God, reaches to
                    the world's end; *
   your right hand is full of justice.

10 Let Mount Zion be glad
   and the cities of Judah rejoice, *
   because of your judgments.

11 Make the circuit of Zion;
   walk round about her; *
   count the number of her towers.

12 Consider well her bulwarks;
 examine her strongholds; *
  that you may tell those who come after.

13 This God is our God for ever and ever; *
 he shall be our guide for evermore.

49 *Audite hæc, omnes*

1 Hear this, all you peoples;
 hearken, all you who dwell in the world, *
  you of high degree and low, rich and poor together.

2 My mouth shall speak of wisdom, *
 and my heart shall meditate on understanding.

3 I will incline my ear to a proverb *
 and set forth my riddle upon the harp.

4 Why should I be afraid in evil days, *
 when the wickedness of those at my heels surrounds me,

5 The wickedness of those who put their trust in their goods, *
 and boast of their great riches?

6 We can never ransom ourselves, *
 or deliver to God the price of our life;

7 For the ransom of our life is so great, *
 that we should never have enough to pay it,

8 In order to live for ever and ever, *
 and never see the grave.

9 For we see that the wise die also;
 like the dull and stupid they perish *
  and leave their wealth to those who come after them.

10 Their graves shall be their homes for ever,
   their dwelling places from generation to generation, *
      though they call the lands after their own names.

11 Even though honored, they cannot live for ever; *
      they are like the beasts that perish.

12 Such is the way of those who foolishly trust in themselves, *
      and the end of those who delight in their own words.

13 Like a flock of sheep they are destined to die;
   Death is their shepherd; *
      they go down straightway to the grave.

14 Their form shall waste away, *
      and the land of the dead shall be their home.

15 But God will ransom my life; *
      he will snatch me from the grasp of death.

16 Do not be envious when some become rich, *
      or when the grandeur of their house increases;

17 For they will carry nothing away at their death, *
      nor will their grandeur follow them.

18 Though they thought highly of themselves while they lived, *
      and were praised for their success,

19 They shall join the company of their forebears, *
      who will never see the light again.

20 Those who are honored, but have no understanding, *
      are like the beasts that perish.

50 *Deus deorum*

1 The LORD, the God of gods, has spoken; *
 he has called the earth from the rising of the sun to
  its setting.

2 Out of Zion, perfect in its beauty, *
 God reveals himself in glory.

3 Our God will come and will not keep silence; *
 before him there is a consuming flame,
 and round about him a raging storm.

4 He calls the heavens and the earth from above *
 to witness the judgment of his people.

5 "Gather before me my loyal followers, *
 those who have made a covenant with me
 and sealed it with sacrifice."

6 Let the heavens declare the rightness of his cause; *
 for God himself is judge.

7 Hear, O my people, and I will speak:
 "O Israel, I will bear witness against you; *
 for I am God, your God.

8 I do not accuse you because of your sacrifices; *
 your offerings are always before me.

9 I will take no bull-calf from your stalls, *
 nor he-goats out of your pens;

10 For all the beasts of the forest are mine, *
 the herds in their thousands upon the hills.

11   I know every bird in the sky, *
      and the creatures of the fields are in my sight.

12   If I were hungry, I would not tell you, *
      for the whole world is mine and all that is in it.

13   Do you think I eat the flesh of bulls, *
      or drink the blood of goats?

14   Offer to God a sacrifice of thanksgiving *
      and make good your vows to the Most High.

15   Call upon me in the day of trouble; *
      I will deliver you, and you shall honor me."

16   But to the wicked God says: *
      "Why do you recite my statutes,
        and take my covenant upon your lips;

17   Since you refuse discipline, *
      and toss my words behind your back?

18   When you see a thief, you make him your friend, *
      and you cast in your lot with adulterers.

19   You have loosed your lips for evil, *
      and harnessed your tongue to a lie.

20   You are always speaking evil of your brother *
      and slandering your own mother's son.

21   These things you have done, and I kept still, *
      and you thought that I am like you."

22   "I have made my accusation; *
      I have put my case in order before your eyes.

23   Consider this well, you who forget God, *
      lest I rend you and there be none to deliver you.

24 Whoever offers me the sacrifice of thanksgiving honors me; *
but to those who keep in my way will I show the salvation of God."

51 *Miserere mei, Deus*

1 Have mercy on me, O God, according to your loving-kindness; *
in your great compassion blot out my offenses.

2 Wash me through and through from my wickedness *
and cleanse me from my sin.

3 For I know my transgressions, *
and my sin is ever before me.

4 Against you only have I sinned *
and done what is evil in your sight.

5 And so you are justified when you speak *
and upright in your judgment.

6 Indeed, I have been wicked from my birth, *
a sinner from my mother's womb.

7 For behold, you look for truth deep within me, *
and will make me understand wisdom secretly.

8 Purge me from my sin, and I shall be pure; *
wash me, and I shall be clean indeed.

9 Make me hear of joy and gladness, *
that the body you have broken may rejoice.

10 Hide your face from my sins *
and blot out all my iniquities.

11   Create in me a clean heart, O God, *
     and renew a right spirit within me.

12   Cast me not away from your presence *
     and take not your holy Spirit from me.

13   Give me the joy of your saving help again *
     and sustain me with your bountiful Spirit.

14   I shall teach your ways to the wicked, *
     and sinners shall return to you.

15   Deliver me from death, O God, *
     and my tongue shall sing of your righteousness,
     O God of my salvation.

16   Open my lips, O Lord, *
     and my mouth shall proclaim your praise.

17   Had you desired it, I would have offered sacrifice, *
     but you take no delight in burnt-offerings.

18   The sacrifice of God is a troubled spirit; *
     a broken and contrite heart, O God, you will not despise.

19   Be favorable and gracious to Zion, *
     and rebuild the walls of Jerusalem.

20   Then you will be pleased with the appointed sacrifices,
     with burnt-offerings and oblations; *
     then shall they offer young bullocks upon your altar.

52   *Quid gloriaris?*

1   You tyrant, why do you boast of wickedness *
     against the godly all day long?

2   You plot ruin;
    your tongue is like a sharpened razor, *
        O worker of deception.

3   You love evil more than good *
        and lying more than speaking the truth.

4   You love all words that hurt, *
        O you deceitful tongue.

5   Oh, that God would demolish you utterly, *
        topple you, and snatch you from your dwelling,
        and root you out of the land of the living!

6   The righteous shall see and tremble, *
        and they shall laugh at him, saying,

7   "This is the one who did not take God for a refuge, *
        but trusted in great wealth
        and relied upon wickedness."

8   But I am like a green olive tree in the house of God; *
        I trust in the mercy of God for ever and ever.

9   I will give you thanks for what you have done *
        and declare the goodness of your Name in the presence
            of the godly.

Tenth Day: Evening Prayer

53   *Dixit insipiens*

1   The fool has said in his heart, "There is no God." *
        All are corrupt and commit abominable acts;
        there is none who does any good.

2   God looks down from heaven upon us all, *
       to see if there is any who is wise,
       if there is one who seeks after God.

3   Every one has proved faithless;
    all alike have turned bad; *
       there is none who does good; no, not one.

4   Have they no knowledge, those evildoers *
       who eat up my people like bread
       and do not call upon God?

5   See how greatly they tremble,
    such trembling as never was; *
       for God has scattered the bones of the enemy;
       they are put to shame, because God has rejected them.

6   Oh, that Israel's deliverance would come out of Zion! *
       when God restores the fortunes of his people
       Jacob will rejoice and Israel be glad.

54   *Deus, in nomine*

1   Save me, O God, by your Name; *
       in your might, defend my cause.

2   Hear my prayer, O God; *
       give ear to the words of my mouth.

3   For the arrogant have risen up against me,
    and the ruthless have sought my life, *
       those who have no regard for God.

4   Behold, God is my helper; *
       it is the Lord who sustains my life.

5   Render evil to those who spy on me; *
       in your faithfulness, destroy them.

6   I will offer you a freewill sacrifice *
      and praise your Name, O LORD, for it is good.

7   For you have rescued me from every trouble, *
      and my eye has seen the ruin of my foes.

55   *Exaudi, Deus*

1   Hear my prayer, O God; *
      do not hide yourself from my petition.

2   Listen to me and answer me; *
      I have no peace, because of my cares.

3   I am shaken by the noise of the enemy *
      and by the pressure of the wicked;

4   For they have cast an evil spell upon me *
      and are set against me in fury.

5   My heart quakes within me, *
      and the terrors of death have fallen upon me.

6   Fear and trembling have come over me, *
      and horror overwhelms me.

7   And I said,"Oh, that I had wings like a dove! *
      I would fly away and be at rest.

8   I would flee to a far-off place *
      and make my lodging in the wilderness.

9   I would hasten to escape *
      from the stormy wind and tempest."

10   Swallow them up, O Lord;
     confound their speech; *
      for I have seen violence and strife in the city.

11 Day and night the watchmen make their rounds
        upon her walls, *
    but trouble and misery are in the midst of her.

12 There is corruption at her heart; *
    her streets are never free of oppression and deceit.

13 For had it been an adversary who taunted me,
    then I could have borne it; *
        or had it been an enemy who vaunted himself against me,
        then I could have hidden from him.

14 But it was you, a man after my own heart, *
    my companion, my own familiar friend.

15 We took sweet counsel together, *
    and walked with the throng in the house of God.

16 Let death come upon them suddenly;
    let them go down alive into the grave; *
        for wickedness is in their dwellings, in their very midst.

17 But I will call upon God, *
    and the LORD will deliver me.

18 In the evening, in the morning, and at noonday,
    I will complain and lament, *
        and he will hear my voice.

19 He will bring me safely back from the battle
        waged against me; *
    for there are many who fight me.

20 God, who is enthroned of old, will hear me and
        bring them down; *
    they never change; they do not fear God.

21 My companion stretched forth his hand against his comrade; *
    he has broken his covenant.

22 His speech is softer than butter, *
    but war is in his heart.

23 His words are smoother than oil, *
    but they are drawn swords.

24 Cast your burden upon the LORD,
   and he will sustain you; *
    he will never let the righteous stumble.

25 For you will bring the bloodthirsty and deceitful *
    down to the pit of destruction, O God.

26 They shall not live out half their days, *
    but I will put my trust in you.

Eleventh Day: Morning Prayer

56 *Miserere mei, Deus*

1 Have mercy on me, O God,
  for my enemies are hounding me; *
    all day long they assault and oppress me.

2 They hound me all the day long; *
    truly there are many who fight against me, O Most High.

3 Whenever I am afraid, *
    I will put my trust in you.

4 In God, whose word I praise,
  in God I trust and will not be afraid, *
    for what can flesh do to me?

5 All day long they damage my cause; *
    their only thought is to do me evil.

6 They band together; they lie in wait; *
    they spy upon my footsteps;
    because they seek my life.

7 Shall they escape despite their wickedness? *
    O God, in your anger, cast down the peoples.

8 You have noted my lamentation;
    put my tears into your bottle; *
    are they not recorded in your book?

9 Whenever I call upon you, my enemies will be put to flight; *
    this I know, for God is on my side.

10 In God the LORD, whose word I praise,
    in God I trust and will not be afraid, *
    for what can mortals do to me?

11 I am bound by the vow I made to you, O God; *
    I will present to you thank-offerings;

12 For you have rescued my soul from death and my feet
               from stumbling, *
    that I may walk before God in the light of the living.

57 *Miserere mei, Deus*

1 Be merciful to me, O God, be merciful,
    for I have taken refuge in you; *
    in the shadow of your wings will I take refuge
    until this time of trouble has gone by.

2 I will call upon the Most High God, *
    the God who maintains my cause.

3 He will send from heaven and save me;
    he will confound those who trample upon me; *
    God will send forth his love and his faithfulness.

4   I lie in the midst of lions that devour the people; *
       their teeth are spears and arrows,
       their tongue a sharp sword.

5   They have laid a net for my feet,
     and I am bowed low; *
       they have dug a pit before me,
       but have fallen into it themselves.

6   Exalt yourself above the heavens, O God, *
       and your glory over all the earth.

7   My heart is firmly fixed, O God, my heart is fixed; *
       I will sing and make melody.

8   Wake up, my spirit;
     awake, lute and harp; *
       I myself will waken the dawn.

9   I will confess you among the peoples, O LORD; *
       I will sing praise to you among the nations.

10   For your loving-kindness is greater than the heavens, *
       and your faithfulness reaches to the clouds.

11   Exalt yourself above the heavens, O God, *
       and your glory over all the earth.

58   *Si vere utique*

1   Do you indeed decree righteousness, you rulers? *
       do you judge the peoples with equity?

2   No; you devise evil in your hearts, *
       and your hands deal out violence in the land.

3   The wicked are perverse from the womb; *
       liars go astray from their birth.

4 They are as venomous as a serpent, *
    they are like the deaf adder which stops its ears,

5 Which does not heed the voice of the charmer, *
    no matter how skillful his charming.

6 O God, break their teeth in their mouths; *
    pull the fangs of the young lions, O LORD.

7 Let them vanish like water that runs off; *
    let them wither like trodden grass.

8 Let them be like the snail that melts away, *
    like a stillborn child that never sees the sun.

9 Before they bear fruit, let them be cut down like a brier; *
    like thorns and thistles let them be swept away.

10 The righteous will be glad when they see the vengeance; *
    they will bathe their feet in the blood of the wicked.

11 And they will say,
    "Surely, there is a reward for the righteous; *
        surely, there is a God who rules in the earth."

Eleventh Day: Evening Prayer

59 *Eripe me de inimicis*

1 Rescue me from my enemies, O God; *
    protect me from those who rise up against me.

2 Rescue me from evildoers *
    and save me from those who thirst for my blood.

3 See how they lie in wait for my life,
    how the mighty gather together against me; *
        not for any offense or fault of mine, O LORD.

4   Not because of any guilt of mine *
      they run and prepare themselves for battle.

5   Rouse yourself, come to my side, and see; *
      for you, LORD God of hosts, are Israel's God.

6   Awake, and punish all the ungodly; *
      show no mercy to those who are faithless and evil.

7   They go to and fro in the evening; *
      they snarl like dogs and run about the city.

8   Behold, they boast with their mouths,
    and taunts are on their lips; *
    "For who," they say, "will hear us?"

9   But you, O LORD, you laugh at them; *
      you laugh all the ungodly to scorn.

10   My eyes are fixed on you, O my Strength; *
      for you, O God, are my stronghold.

11   My merciful God comes to meet me; *
      God will let me look in triumph on my enemies.

12   Slay them, O God, lest my people forget; *
      send them reeling by your might
      and put them down, O Lord our shield.

13   For the sins of their mouths, for the words of their lips,
    for the cursing and lies that they utter, *
      let them be caught in their pride.

14   Make an end of them in your wrath; *
      make an end of them, and they shall be no more.

15   Let everyone know that God rules in Jacob, *
      and to the ends of the earth.

16   They go to and fro in the evening; *
      they snarl like dogs and run about the city.

17 They forage for food, *
 and if they are not filled, they howl.

18 For my part, I will sing of your strength; *
 I will celebrate your love in the morning;

19 For you have become my stronghold, *
 a refuge in the day of my trouble.

20 To you, O my Strength, will I sing; *
 for you, O God, are my stronghold and my merciful God.

60 *Deus, repulisti nos*

1 O God, you have cast us off and broken us; *
 you have been angry;
 oh, take us back to you again.

2 You have shaken the earth and split it open; *
 repair the cracks in it, for it totters.

3 You have made your people know hardship; *
 you have given us wine that makes us stagger.

4 You have set up a banner for those who fear you, *
 to be a refuge from the power of the bow.

5 Save us by your right hand and answer us, *
 that those who are dear to you may be delivered.

6 God spoke from his holy place and said: *
 "I will exult and parcel out Shechem;
 I will divide the valley of Succoth.

7 Gilead is mine and Manasseh is mine; *
 Ephraim is my helmet and Judah my scepter.

8   Moab is my wash-basin,
        on Edom I throw down my sandal to claim it, *
        and over Philistia will I shout in triumph."

9   Who will lead me into the strong city? *
        who will bring me into Edom?

10 Have you not cast us off, O God? *
        you no longer go out, O God, with our armies.

11 Grant us your help against the enemy, *
        for vain is the help of man.

12 With God we will do valiant deeds, *
        and he shall tread our enemies under foot.

61   *Exaudi, Deus*

1   Hear my cry, O God, *
        and listen to my prayer.

2   I call upon you from the ends of the earth
    with heaviness in my heart; *
        set me upon the rock that is higher than I.

3   For you have been my refuge, *
        a strong tower against the enemy.

4   I will dwell in your house for ever; *
        I will take refuge under the cover of your wings.

5   For you, O God, have heard my vows; *
        you have granted me the heritage of those
                            who fear your Name.

6   Add length of days to the king's life; *
        let his years extend over many generations.

7　Let him sit enthroned before God for ever; *
　　bid love and faithfulness watch over him.

8　So will I always sing the praise of your Name, *
　　and day by day I will fulfill my vows.

Twelfth Day: Morning Prayer

62 *Nonne Deo?*

1　For God alone my soul in silence waits; *
　　from him comes my salvation.

2　He alone is my rock and my salvation, *
　　my stronghold, so that I shall not be greatly shaken.

3　How long will you assail me to crush me,
　　all of you together, *
　　as if you were a leaning fence, a toppling wall?

4　They seek only to bring me down from my place of honor; *
　　lies are their chief delight.

5　They bless with their lips, *
　　but in their hearts they curse.

6　For God alone my soul in silence waits; *
　　truly, my hope is in him.

7　He alone is my rock and my salvation, *
　　my stronghold, so that I shall not be shaken.

8　In God is my safety and my honor; *
　　God is my strong rock and my refuge.

9　Put your trust in him always, O people, *
　　pour out your hearts before him, for God is our refuge.

10   Those of high degree are but a fleeting breath, *
        even those of low estate cannot be trusted.

11   On the scales they are lighter than a breath, *
        all of them together.

12   Put no trust in extortion;
     in robbery take no empty pride; *
        though wealth increase, set not your heart upon it.

13   God has spoken once, twice have I heard it, *
        that power belongs to God.

14   Steadfast love is yours, O Lord, *
        for you repay everyone according to his deeds.

63   *Deus, Deus meus*

1   O God, you are my God; eagerly I seek you; *
        my soul thirsts for you, my flesh faints for you,
        as in a barren and dry land where there is no water.

2   Therefore I have gazed upon you in your holy place, *
        that I might behold your power and your glory.

3   For your loving-kindness is better than life itself; *
        my lips shall give you praise.

4   So will I bless you as long as I live *
        and lift up my hands in your Name.

5   My soul is content, as with marrow and fatness, *
        and my mouth praises you with joyful lips,

6   When I remember you upon my bed, *
        and meditate on you in the night watches.

7   For you have been my helper, *
        and under the shadow of your wings I will rejoice.

8   My soul clings to you; *
         your right hand holds me fast.

9   May those who seek my life to destroy it *
         go down into the depths of the earth;

10   Let them fall upon the edge of the sword, *
         and let them be food for jackals.

11   But the king will rejoice in God;
     all those who swear by him will be glad; *
         for the mouth of those who speak lies shall be stopped.

64   *Exaudi, Deus*

1   Hear my voice, O God, when I complain; *
         protect my life from fear of the enemy.

2   Hide me from the conspiracy of the wicked, *
         from the mob of evildoers.

3   They sharpen their tongue like a sword, *
         and aim their bitter words like arrows,

4   That they may shoot down the blameless from ambush; *
         they shoot without warning and are not afraid.

5   They hold fast to their evil course; *
         they plan how they may hide their snares.

6   They say, "Who will see us?
     who will find out our crimes? *
         we have thought out a perfect plot."

7   The human mind and heart are a mystery; *
         but God will loose an arrow at them,
         and suddenly they will be wounded.

8   He will make them trip over their tongues, *
     and all who see them will shake their heads.

9   Everyone will stand in awe and declare God's deeds; *
     they will recognize his works.

10   The righteous will rejoice in the LORD and put their trust in him, *
     and all who are true of heart will glory.

Twelfth Day: Evening Prayer

65   *Te decet hymnus*

1   You are to be praised, O God, in Zion; *
     to you shall vows be performed in Jerusalem.

2   To you that hear prayer shall all flesh come, *
     because of their transgressions.

3   Our sins are stronger than we are, *
     but you will blot them out.

4   Happy are they whom you choose
     and draw to your courts to dwell there! *
          they will be satisfied by the beauty of your house,
          by the holiness of your temple.

5   Awesome things will you show us in your righteousness,
     O God of our salvation, *
          O Hope of all the ends of the earth
          and of the seas that are far away.

6   You make fast the mountains by your power; *
     they are girded about with might.

7   You still the roaring of the seas, *
     the roaring of their waves,
     and the clamor of the peoples.

8   Those who dwell at the ends of the earth will tremble at your
              marvelous signs; *
         you make the dawn and the dusk to sing for joy.

9   You visit the earth and water it abundantly;
         you make it very plenteous; *
              the river of God is full of water.

10   You prepare the grain, *
         for so you provide for the earth.

11   You drench the furrows and smooth out the ridges; *
         with heavy rain you soften the ground and bless its increase.

12   You crown the year with your goodness, *
         and your paths overflow with plenty.

13   May the fields of the wilderness be rich for grazing, *
         and the hills be clothed with joy.

14   May the meadows cover themselves with flocks,
         and the valleys cloak themselves with grain; *
              let them shout for joy and sing.

66   *Jubilate Deo*

1   Be joyful in God, all you lands; *
         sing the glory of his Name;
         sing the glory of his praise.

2   Say to God, "How awesome are your deeds! *
         because of your great strength your enemies
              cringe before you.

3   All the earth bows down before you, *
         sings to you, sings out your Name."

4   Come now and see the works of God, *
       how wonderful he is in his doing toward all people.

5   He turned the sea into dry land,
     so that they went through the water on foot, *
       and there we rejoiced in him.

6   In his might he rules for ever;
     his eyes keep watch over the nations; *
       let no rebel rise up against him.

7   Bless our God, you peoples; *
       make the voice of his praise to be heard;

8   Who holds our souls in life, *
       and will not allow our feet to slip.

9   For you, O God, have proved us; *
       you have tried us just as silver is tried.

10   You brought us into the snare; *
       you laid heavy burdens upon our backs.

11   You let enemies ride over our heads;
     we went through fire and water; *
       but you brought us out into a place of refreshment.

12   I will enter your house with burnt-offerings
     and will pay you my vows, *
       which I promised with my lips
       and spoke with my mouth when I was in trouble.

13   I will offer you sacrifices of fat beasts
     with the smoke of rams; *
       I will give you oxen and goats.

14   Come and listen, all you who fear God, *
       and I will tell you what he has done for me.

15 I called out to him with my mouth, *
       and his praise was on my tongue.

16 If I had found evil in my heart, *
       the Lord would not have heard me;

17 But in truth God has heard me; *
       he has attended to the voice of my prayer.

18 Blessed be God, who has not rejected my prayer, *
       nor withheld his love from me.

67 *Deus misereatur*

1 May God be merciful to us and bless us, *
      show us the light of his countenance and come to us.

2 Let your ways be known upon earth, *
      your saving health among all nations.

3 Let the peoples praise you, O God; *
      let all the peoples praise you.

4 Let the nations be glad and sing for joy, *
      for you judge the peoples with equity
      and guide all the nations upon earth.

5 Let the peoples praise you, O God; *
      let all the peoples praise you.

6 The earth has brought forth her increase; *
      may God, our own God, give us his blessing.

7 May God give us his blessing, *
      and may all the ends of the earth stand in awe of him.

68 *Exsurgat Deus*

1 Let God arise, and let his enemies be scattered; *
   let those who hate him flee before him.

2 Let them vanish like smoke when the wind drives it away; *
   as the wax melts at the fire, so let the wicked perish at
        the presence of God.

3 But let the righteous be glad and rejoice before God; *
   let them also be merry and joyful.

4 Sing to God, sing praises to his Name;
   exalt him who rides upon the heavens; *
        YAHWEH is his Name, rejoice before him!

5 Father of orphans, defender of widows, *
   God in his holy habitation!

6 God gives the solitary a home and brings forth prisoners
        into freedom; *
   but the rebels shall live in dry places.

7 O God, when you went forth before your people, *
   when you marched through the wilderness,

8 The earth shook, and the skies poured down rain,
   at the presence of God, the God of Sinai, *
        at the presence of God, the God of Israel.

9 You sent a gracious rain, O God, upon your inheritance; *
   you refreshed the land when it was weary.

10 Your people found their home in it; *
    in your goodness, O God, you have made provision
        for the poor.

11   The Lord gave the word; *
        great was the company of women who bore the tidings:

12   "Kings with their armies are fleeing away; *
        the women at home are dividing the spoils."

13   Though you lingered among the sheepfolds, *
        you shall be like a dove whose wings are covered with silver,
        whose feathers are like green gold.

14   When the Almighty scattered kings, *
        it was like snow falling in Zalmon.

15   O mighty mountain, O hill of Bashan! *
        O rugged mountain, O hill of Bashan!

16   Why do you look with envy, O rugged mountain,
        at the hill which God chose for his resting place? *
        truly, the LORD will dwell there for ever.

17   The chariots of God are twenty thousand,
        even thousands of thousands; *
        the Lord comes in holiness from Sinai.

18   You have gone up on high and led captivity captive;
        you have received gifts even from your enemies, *
        that the LORD God might dwell among them.

19   Blessed be the Lord day by day, *
        the God of our salvation, who bears our burdens.

20   He is our God, the God of our salvation; *
        God is the LORD, by whom we escape death.

21   God shall crush the heads of his enemies, *
        and the hairy scalp of those who go on still in their
              wickedness.

22 The Lord has said, " I will bring them back from Bashan; *
   I will bring them back from the depths of the sea;

23 That your foot may be dipped in blood, *
   the tongues of your dogs in the blood of your enemies."

24 They see your procession, O God, *
   your procession into the sanctuary, my God and my King.

25 The singers go before, musicians follow after, *
   in the midst of maidens playing upon the hand-drums.

26 Bless God in the congregation; *
   bless the LORD, you that are of the fountain of Israel.

27 There is Benjamin, least of the tribes, at the head;
   the princes of Judah in a company; *
   and the princes of Zebulon and Naphtali.

28 Send forth your strength, O God; *
   establish, O God, what you have wrought for us.

29 Kings shall bring gifts to you, *
   for your temple's sake at Jerusalem.

30 Rebuke the wild beast of the reeds, *
   and the peoples, a herd of wild bulls with its calves.

31 Trample down those who lust after silver; *
   scatter the peoples that delight in war.

32 Let tribute be brought out of Egypt; *
   let Ethiopia stretch out her hands to God.

33 Sing to God, O kingdoms of the earth; *
   sing praises to the Lord.

34 He rides in the heavens, the ancient heavens; *
   he sends forth his voice, his mighty voice.

35 Ascribe power to God; *
        his majesty is over Israel;
        his strength is in the skies.

36 How wonderful is God in his holy places! *
        the God of Israel giving strength and power to his people!
        Blessed be God!

Thirteenth Day: Evening Prayer

69 *Salvum me fac*

1 Save me, O God, *
        for the waters have risen up to my neck.

2 I am sinking in deep mire, *
        and there is no firm ground for my feet.

3 I have come into deep waters, *
        and the torrent washes over me.

4 I have grown weary with my crying;
    my throat is inflamed; *
        my eyes have failed from looking for my God.

5 Those who hate me without a cause are more than the hairs
                                    of my head;
    my lying foes who would destroy me are mighty. *
        Must I then give back what I never stole?

6 O God, you know my foolishness, *
        and my faults are not hidden from you.

7 Let not those who hope in you be put to shame through me,
                        Lord GOD of hosts; *
    let not those who seek you be disgraced because of me,
                        O God of Israel.

8   Surely, for your sake have I suffered reproach, *
        and shame has covered my face.

9   I have become a stranger to my own kindred, *
        an alien to my mother's children.

10 Zeal for your house has eaten me up; *
        the scorn of those who scorn you has fallen upon me.

11 I humbled myself with fasting, *
        but that was turned to my reproach.

12 I put on sack-cloth also, *
        and became a byword among them.

13 Those who sit at the gate murmur against me, *
        and the drunkards make songs about me.

14 But as for me, this is my prayer to you, *
        at the time you have set, O LORD:

15 "In your great mercy, O God, *
        answer me with your unfailing help.

16 Save me from the mire; do not let me sink; *
        let me be rescued from those who hate me
        and out of the deep waters.

17 Let not the torrent of waters wash over me,
    neither let the deep swallow me up; *
        do not let the Pit shut its mouth upon me.

18 Answer me, O LORD, for your love is kind; *
        in your great compassion, turn to me."

19 "Hide not your face from your servant; *
        be swift and answer me, for I am in distress.

20 Draw near to me and redeem me; *
        because of my enemies deliver me.

21   You know my reproach, my shame, and my dishonor; *
       my adversaries are all in your sight."

22   Reproach has broken my heart, and it cannot be healed; *
       I looked for sympathy, but there was none,
       for comforters, but I could find no one.

23   They gave me gall to eat, *
       and when I was thirsty, they gave me vinegar to drink.

24   Let the table before them be a trap *
       and their sacred feasts a snare.

25   Let their eyes be darkened, that they may not see, *
       and give them continual trembling in their loins.

26   Pour out your indignation upon them, *
       and let the fierceness of your anger overtake them.

27   Let their camp be desolate, *
       and let there be none to dwell in their tents.

28   For they persecute him whom you have stricken *
       and add to the pain of those whom you have pierced.

29   Lay to their charge guilt upon guilt, *
       and let them not receive your vindication.

30   Let them be wiped out of the book of the living *
       and not be written among the righteous.

31   As for me, I am afflicted and in pain; *
       your help, O God, will lift me up on high.

32   I will praise the Name of God in song; *
       I will proclaim his greatness with thanksgiving.

33   This will please the LORD more than an offering of oxen, *
       more than bullocks with horns and hoofs.

34 The afflicted shall see and be glad; *
   you who seek God, your heart shall live.

35 For the LORD listens to the needy, *
   and his prisoners he does not despise.

36 Let the heavens and the earth praise him, *
   the seas and all that moves in them;

37 For God will save Zion and rebuild the cities of Judah; *
   they shall live there and have it in possession.

38 The children of his servants will inherit it, *
   and those who love his Name will dwell therein.

70 *Deus, in adjutorium*

1 Be pleased, O God, to deliver me; *
   O LORD, make haste to help me.

2 Let those who seek my life be ashamed
  and altogether dismayed; *
   let those who take pleasure in my misfortune
   draw back and be disgraced.

3 Let those who say to me "Aha!" and gloat over me turn back, *
   because they are ashamed.

4 Let all who seek you rejoice and be glad in you; *
   let those who love your salvation say for ever,
   "Great is the LORD!"

5 But as for me, I am poor and needy; *
   come to me speedily, O God.

6 You are my helper and my deliverer; *
   O LORD, do not tarry.

7 1   *In te, Domine, speravi*

1   In you, O LORD, have I taken refuge; *
    let me never be ashamed.

2   In your righteousness, deliver me and set me free; *
    incline your ear to me and save me.

3   Be my strong rock, a castle to keep me safe; *
    you are my crag and my stronghold.

4   Deliver me, my God, from the hand of the wicked, *
    from the clutches of the evildoer and the oppressor.

5   For you are my hope, O Lord GOD, *
    my confidence since I was young.

6   I have been sustained by you ever since I was born;
    from my mother's womb you have been my strength; *
    my praise shall be always of you.

7   I have become a portent to many; *
    but you are my refuge and my strength.

8   Let my mouth be full of your praise *
    and your glory all the day long.

9   Do not cast me off in my old age; *
    forsake me not when my strength fails.

10 For my enemies are talking against me, *
    and those who lie in wait for my life take counsel together.

11 They say, "God has forsaken him;
    go after him and seize him; *
    because there is none who will save."

12 O God, be not far from me; *
     come quickly to help me, O my God.

13 Let those who set themselves against me be put to shame and
          be disgraced; *
     let those who seek to do me evil be covered with scorn
          and reproach.

14 But I shall always wait in patience, *
     and shall praise you more and more.

15 My mouth shall recount your mighty acts
     and saving deeds all day long; *
     though I cannot know the number of them.

16 I will begin with the mighty works of the Lord GOD; *
     I will recall your righteousness, yours alone.

17 O God, you have taught me since I was young, *
     and to this day I tell of your wonderful works.

18 And now that I am old and gray-headed, O God, do not
          forsake me, *
     till I make known your strength to this generation
     and your power to all who are to come.

19 Your righteousness, O God, reaches to the heavens; *
     you have done great things;
     who is like you, O God?

20 You have showed me great troubles and adversities, *
     but you will restore my life
     and bring me up again from the deep places of the earth.

21 You strengthen me more and more; *
     you enfold and comfort me,

22 Therefore I will praise you upon the lyre for your
            faithfulness, O my God; *
    I will sing to you with the harp, O Holy One of Israel.

23 My lips will sing with joy when I play to you, *
    and so will my soul, which you have redeemed.

24 My tongue will proclaim your righteousness all day long, *
    for they are ashamed and disgraced who sought
            to do me harm.

72 *Deus, judicium*

1 Give the King your justice, O God, *
    and your righteousness to the King's Son;

2 That he may rule your people righteously *
    and the poor with justice;

3 That the mountains may bring prosperity to the people, *
    and the little hills bring righteousness.

4 He shall defend the needy among the people; *
    he shall rescue the poor and crush the oppressor.

5 He shall live as long as the sun and moon endure, *
    from one generation to another.

6 He shall come down like rain upon the mown field, *
    like showers that water the earth.

7 In his time shall the righteous flourish; *
    there shall be abundance of peace till the moon shall
            be no more.

8 He shall rule from sea to sea, *
    and from the River to the ends of the earth.

9 His foes shall bow down before him, *
   and his enemies lick the dust.

10 The kings of Tarshish and of the isles shall pay tribute, *
   and the kings of Arabia and Saba offer gifts.

11 All kings shall bow down before him, *
   and all the nations do him service.

12 For he shall deliver the poor who cries out in distress, *
   and the oppressed who has no helper.

13 He shall have pity on the lowly and poor; *
   he shall preserve the lives of the needy.

14 He shall redeem their lives from oppression and violence, *
   and dear shall their blood be in his sight.

15 Long may he live!
   and may there be given to him gold from Arabia; *
      may prayer be made for him always,
      and may they bless him all the day long.

16 May there be abundance of grain on the earth,
   growing thick even on the hilltops; *
      may its fruit flourish like Lebanon,
      and its grain like grass upon the earth.

17 May his Name remain for ever
   and be established as long as the sun endures; *
      may all the nations bless themselves in him and
         call him blessed.

18 Blessed be the Lord GOD, the God of Israel, *
   who alone does wondrous deeds!

19 And blessed be his glorious Name for ever! *
   and may all the earth be filled with his glory.
   Amen. Amen.

Book Three

73 *Quam bonus Israel!*

1 Truly, God is good to Israel, *
    to those who are pure in heart.

2 But as for me, my feet had nearly slipped; *
    I had almost tripped and fallen;

3 Because I envied the proud *
    and saw the prosperity of the wicked:

4 For they suffer no pain, *
    and their bodies are sleek and sound;

5 In the misfortunes of others they have no share; *
    they are not afflicted as others are;

6 Therefore they wear their pride like a necklace *
    and wrap their violence about them like a cloak.

7 Their iniquity comes from gross minds, *
    and their hearts overflow with wicked thoughts.

8 They scoff and speak maliciously; *
    out of their haughtiness they plan oppression.

9 They set their mouths against the heavens, *
    and their evil speech runs through the world.

10 And so the people turn to them *
    and find in them no fault.

11 They say, "How should God know? *
    is there knowledge in the Most High?"

12 So then, these are the wicked; *
   always at ease, they increase their wealth.

13 In vain have I kept my heart clean, *
   and washed my hands in innocence.

14 I have been afflicted all day long, *
   and punished every morning.

15 Had I gone on speaking this way, *
   I should have betrayed the generation of your children.

16 When I tried to understand these things, *
   it was too hard for me;

17 Until I entered the sanctuary of God *
   and discerned the end of the wicked.

18 Surely, you set them in slippery places; *
   you cast them down in ruin.

19 Oh, how suddenly do they come to destruction, *
   come to an end, and perish from terror!

20 Like a dream when one awakens, O Lord, *
   when you arise you will make their image vanish.

21 When my mind became embittered, *
   I was sorely wounded in my heart.

22 I was stupid and had no understanding; *
   I was like a brute beast in your presence.

23 Yet I am always with you; *
   you hold me by my right hand.

24 You will guide me by your counsel, *
   and afterwards receive me with glory.

25 Whom have I in heaven but you? *
   and having you I desire nothing upon earth.

26 Though my flesh and my heart should waste away, *
    God is the strength of my heart and my portion for ever.

27 Truly, those who forsake you will perish; *
    you destroy all who are unfaithful.

28 But it is good for me to be near God; *
    I have made the Lord GOD my refuge.

29 I will speak of all your works *
    in the gates of the city of Zion.

74 *Ut quid, Deus?*

1 O God, why have you utterly cast us off? *
    why is your wrath so hot against the sheep of your pasture?

2 Remember your congregation that you purchased long ago, *
    the tribe you redeemed to be your inheritance,
    and Mount Zion where you dwell.

3 Turn your steps toward the endless ruins; *
    the enemy has laid waste everything in your sanctuary.

4 Your adversaries roared in your holy place; *
    they set up their banners as tokens of victory.

5 They were like men coming up with axes to a grove of trees; *
    they broke down all your carved work with hatchets
        and hammers.

6 They set fire to your holy place; *
    they defiled the dwelling-place of your Name
    and razed it to the ground.

7 They said to themselves, "Let us destroy them altogether." *
    They burned down all the meeting-places of God
        in the land.

8   There are no signs for us to see;
    there is no prophet left; *
        there is not one among us who knows how long.

9   How long, O God, will the adversary scoff? *
    will the enemy blaspheme your Name for ever?

10 Why do you draw back your hand? *
    why is your right hand hidden in your bosom?

11 Yet God is my King from ancient times, *
    victorious in the midst of the earth.

12 You divided the sea by your might *
    and shattered the heads of the dragons upon the waters;

13 You crushed the heads of Leviathan *
    and gave him to the people of the desert for food.

14 You split open spring and torrent; *
    you dried up ever-flowing rivers.

15 Yours is the day, yours also the night; *
    you established the moon and the sun.

16 You fixed all the boundaries of the earth; *
    you made both summer and winter.

17 Remember, O LORD, how the enemy scoffed, *
    how a foolish people despised your Name.

18 Do not hand over the life of your dove to wild beasts; *
    never forget the lives of your poor.

19 Look upon your covenant; *
    the dark places of the earth are haunts of violence.

20 Let not the oppressed turn away ashamed; *
    let the poor and needy praise your Name.

21 Arise, O God, maintain your cause; *
    remember how fools revile you all day long.

22 Forget not the clamor of your adversaries, *
    the unending tumult of those who rise up against you.

Fifteenth Day: Morning Prayer

75 *Confitebimur tibi*

1 We give you thanks, O God, we give you thanks, *
    calling upon your Name and declaring all your
        wonderful deeds.

2 "I will appoint a time," says God; *
    "I will judge with equity.

3 Though the earth and all its inhabitants are quaking, *
    I will make its pillars fast.

4 I will say to the boasters,'Boast no more,' *
    and to the wicked,'Do not toss your horns;

5 Do not toss your horns so high, *
    nor speak with a proud neck.' "

6 For judgment is neither from the east nor from the west, *
    nor yet from the wilderness or the mountains.

7 It is God who judges; *
    he puts down one and lifts up another.

8 For in the LORD's hand there is a cup,
    full of spiced and foaming wine, which he pours out, *
    and all the wicked of the earth shall drink and
        drain the dregs.

9 But I will rejoice for ever; *
    I will sing praises to the God of Jacob.

10 He shall break off all the horns of the wicked; *
    but the horns of the righteous shall be exalted.

76 *Notus in Judæa*

1   In Judah is God known; *
       his Name is great in Israel.

2   At Salem is his tabernacle, *
       and his dwelling is in Zion.

3   There he broke the flashing arrows, *
       the shield, the sword, and the weapons of battle.

4   How glorious you are! *
       more splendid than the everlasting mountains!

5   The strong of heart have been despoiled;
       they sink into sleep; *
         none of the warriors can lift a hand.

6   At your rebuke, O God of Jacob, *
       both horse and rider lie stunned.

7   What terror you inspire! *
       who can stand before you when you are angry?

8   From heaven you pronounced judgment; *
       the earth was afraid and was still;

9   When God rose up to judgment *
       and to save all the oppressed of the earth.

10   Truly, wrathful Edom will give you thanks, *
       and the remnant of Hamath will keep your feasts.

11   Make a vow to the Lord your God and keep it; *
       let all around him bring gifts to him who is worthy
               to be feared.

12   He breaks the spirit of princes, *
       and strikes terror in the kings of the earth.

77 *Voce mea ad Dominum*

1   I will cry aloud to God; *
    I will cry aloud, and he will hear me.

2   In the day of my trouble I sought the Lord; *
    my hands were stretched out by night and did not tire;
    I refused to be comforted.

3   I think of God, I am restless, *
    I ponder, and my spirit faints.

4   You will not let my eyelids close; *
    I am troubled and I cannot speak.

5   I consider the days of old; *
    I remember the years long past;

6   I commune with my heart in the night; *
    I ponder and search my mind.

7   Will the Lord cast me off for ever? *
    will he no more show his favor?

8   Has his loving-kindness come to an end for ever? *
    has his promise failed for evermore?

9   Has God forgotten to be gracious? *
    has he, in his anger, withheld his compassion?

10 And I said, "My grief is this: *
    the right hand of the Most High has lost its power."

11 I will remember the works of the LORD, *
    and call to mind your wonders of old time.

12 I will meditate on all your acts *
    and ponder your mighty deeds.

13 Your way, O God, is holy; *
    who is so great a god as our God?

14   You are the God who works wonders *
        and have declared your power among the peoples.

15   By your strength you have redeemed your people, *
        the children of Jacob and Joseph.

16   The waters saw you, O God;
        the waters saw you and trembled; *
        the very depths were shaken.

17   The clouds poured out water;
        the skies thundered; *
        your arrows flashed to and fro;

18   The sound of your thunder was in the whirlwind;
        your lightnings lit up the world; *
        the earth trembled and shook.

19   Your way was in the sea,
        and your paths in the great waters, *
        yet your footsteps were not seen.

20   You led your people like a flock *
        by the hand of Moses and Aaron.

Fifteenth Day: Evening Prayer

78

Part I   *Attendite, popule*

1   Hear my teaching, O my people; *
        incline your ears to the words of my mouth.

2   I will open my mouth in a parable; *
        I will declare the mysteries of ancient times.

3   That which we have heard and known,
       and what our forefathers have told us, *
         we will not hide from their children.

4   We will recount to generations to come
       the praiseworthy deeds and the power of the LORD, *
       and the wonderful works he has done.

5   He gave his decrees to Jacob
       and established a law for Israel, *
         which he commanded them to teach their children;

6   That the generations to come might know,
       and the children yet unborn; *
         that they in their turn might tell it to their children;

7   So that they might put their trust in God, *
       and not forget the deeds of God,
       but keep his commandments;

8   And not be like their forefathers,
       a stubborn and rebellious generation, *
         a generation whose heart was not steadfast,
         and whose spirit was not faithful to God.

9   The people of Ephraim, armed with the bow, *
       turned back in the day of battle;

10   They did not keep the covenant of God, *
       and refused to walk in his law;

11   They forgot what he had done, *
       and the wonders he had shown them.

12   He worked marvels in the sight of their forefathers, *
       in the land of Egypt, in the field of Zoan.

13   He split open the sea and let them pass through; *
       he made the waters stand up like walls.

14   He led them with a cloud by day, *
       and all the night through with a glow of fire.

15   He split the hard rocks in the wilderness *
       and gave them drink as from the great deep.

16   He brought streams out of the cliff, *
       and the waters gushed out like rivers.

17   But they went on sinning against him, *
       rebelling in the desert against the Most High.

18   They tested God in their hearts, *
       demanding food for their craving.

19   They railed against God and said, *
       "Can God set a table in the wilderness?

20   True, he struck the rock, the waters gushed out, and the
               gullies overflowed; *
       but is he able to give bread
       or to provide meat for his people?"

21   When the LORD heard this, he was full of wrath; *
       a fire was kindled against Jacob,
       and his anger mounted against Israel;

22   For they had no faith in God, *
       nor did they put their trust in his saving power.

23   So he commanded the clouds above *
       and opened the doors of heaven.

24   He rained down manna upon them to eat *
       and gave them grain from heaven.

25   So mortals ate the bread of angels; *
       he provided for them food enough.

26 He caused the east wind to blow in the heavens *
      and led out the south wind by his might.

27 He rained down flesh upon them like dust *
      and wingèd birds like the sand of the sea.

28 He let it fall in the midst of their camp *
      and round about their dwellings.

29 So they ate and were well filled, *
      for he gave them what they craved.

30 But they did not stop their craving, *
      though the food was still in their mouths.

31 So God's anger mounted against them; *
      he slew their strongest men
      and laid low the youth of Israel.

32 In spite of all this, they went on sinning *
      and had no faith in his wonderful works.

33 So he brought their days to an end like a breath *
      and their years in sudden terror.

34 Whenever he slew them, they would seek him, *
      and repent, and diligently search for God.

35 They would remember that God was their rock, *
      and the Most High God their redeemer.

36 But they flattered him with their mouths *
      and lied to him with their tongues.

37 Their heart was not steadfast toward him, *
      and they were not faithful to his covenant.

38 But he was so merciful that he forgave their sins
and did not destroy them; *
  many times he held back his anger
  and did not permit his wrath to be roused.

39 For he remembered that they were but flesh, *
  a breath that goes forth and does not return.

Psalm 78: Part II   *Quoties exacerbaverunt*

40 How often the people disobeyed him in the wilderness *
  and offended him in the desert!

41 Again and again they tempted God *
  and provoked the Holy One of Israel.

42 They did not remember his power *
  in the day when he ransomed them from the enemy;

43 How he wrought his signs in Egypt *
  and his omens in the field of Zoan.

44 He turned their rivers into blood, *
  so that they could not drink of their streams.

45 He sent swarms of flies among them, which ate them up, *
  and frogs, which destroyed them.

46 He gave their crops to the caterpillar, *
  the fruit of their toil to the locust.

47 He killed their vines with hail *
  and their sycamores with frost.

48 He delivered their cattle to hailstones *
  and their livestock to hot thunderbolts.

49 He poured out upon them his blazing anger: *
    fury, indignation, and distress,
    a troop of destroying angels.

50 He gave full rein to his anger;
    he did not spare their souls from death; *
    but delivered their lives to the plague.

51 He struck down all the firstborn of Egypt, *
    the flower of manhood in the dwellings of Ham.

52 He led out his people like sheep *
    and guided them in the wilderness like a flock.

53 He led them to safety, and they were not afraid; *
    but the sea overwhelmed their enemies.

54 He brought them to his holy land, *
    the mountain his right hand had won.

55 He drove out the Canaanites before them
    and apportioned an inheritance to them by lot; *
    he made the tribes of Israel to dwell in their tents.

56 But they tested the Most High God, and defied him, *
    and did not keep his commandments.

57 They turned away and were disloyal like their fathers; *
    they were undependable like a warped bow.

58 They grieved him with their hill-altars *
    and provoked his displeasure with their idols.

59 When God heard this, he was angry *
    and utterly rejected Israel.

60 He forsook the shrine at Shiloh, *
    the tabernacle where he had lived among his people.

61 He delivered the ark into captivity, *
   his glory into the adversary's hand.

62 He gave his people to the sword *
   and was angered against his inheritance.

63 The fire consumed their young men; *
   there were no wedding songs for their maidens.

64 Their priests fell by the sword, *
   and their widows made no lamentation.

65 Then the LORD woke as though from sleep, *
   like a warrior refreshed with wine.

66 He struck his enemies on the backside *
   and put them to perpetual shame.

67 He rejected the tent of Joseph *
   and did not choose the tribe of Ephraim;

68 He chose instead the tribe of Judah *
   and Mount Zion, which he loved.

69 He built his sanctuary like the heights of heaven, *
   like the earth which he founded for ever.

70 He chose David his servant, *
   and took him away from the sheepfolds.

71 He brought him from following the ewes, *
   to be a shepherd over Jacob his people
   and over Israel his inheritance.

72 So he shepherded them with a faithful and true heart *
   and guided them with the skillfulness of his hands.

79 *Deus, venerunt*

1 O God, the heathen have come into your inheritance;
they have profaned your holy temple; *
    they have made Jerusalem a heap of rubble.

2 They have given the bodies of your servants as food for the
    birds of the air, *
    and the flesh of your faithful ones to the beasts
        of the field.

3 They have shed their blood like water on every side
        of Jerusalem, *
    and there was no one to bury them.

4 We have become a reproach to our neighbors, *
    an object of scorn and derision to those around us.

5 How long will you be angry, O LORD? *
    will your fury blaze like fire for ever?

6 Pour out your wrath upon the heathen who have not
        known you *
    and upon the kingdoms that have not called upon
        your Name.

7 For they have devoured Jacob *
    and made his dwelling a ruin.

8 Remember not our past sins;
let your compassion be swift to meet us; *
    for we have been brought very low.

9 Help us, O God our Savior, for the glory of your Name; *
    deliver us and forgive us our sins, for your Name's sake.

10   Why should the heathen say, "Where is their God?" *
       Let it be known among the heathen and in our sight
       that you avenge the shedding of your servants' blood.

11   Let the sorrowful sighing of the prisoners come before you, *
       and by your great might spare those who are
            condemned to die.

12   May the revilings with which they reviled you, O Lord, *
       return seven-fold into their bosoms.

13   For we are your people and the sheep of your pasture; *
       we will give you thanks for ever
       and show forth your praise from age to age.

80   *Qui regis Israel*

1   Hear, O Shepherd of Israel, leading Joseph like a flock; *
       shine forth, you that are enthroned upon the cherubim.

2   In the presence of Ephraim, Benjamin, and Manasseh, *
       stir up your strength and come to help us.

3   Restore us, O God of hosts; *
       show the light of your countenance, and we shall be saved.

4   O LORD God of hosts, *
       how long will you be angered
       despite the prayers of your people?

5   You have fed them with the bread of tears; *
       you have given them bowls of tears to drink.

6   You have made us the derision of our neighbors, *
       and our enemies laugh us to scorn.

7 Restore us, O God of hosts; *
    show the light of your countenance, and we shall be saved.

8 You have brought a vine out of Egypt; *
    you cast out the nations and planted it.

9 You prepared the ground for it; *
    it took root and filled the land.

10 The mountains were covered by its shadow *
    and the towering cedar trees by its boughs.

11 You stretched out its tendrils to the Sea *
    and its branches to the River.

12 Why have you broken down its wall, *
    so that all who pass by pluck off its grapes?

13 The wild boar of the forest has ravaged it, *
    and the beasts of the field have grazed upon it.

14 Turn now, O God of hosts, look down from heaven;
behold and tend this vine; *
    preserve what your right hand has planted.

15 They burn it with fire like rubbish; *
    at the rebuke of your countenance let them perish.

16 Let your hand be upon the man of your right hand, *
    the son of man you have made so strong for yourself.

17 And so will we never turn away from you; *
    give us life, that we may call upon your Name.

18 Restore us, O LORD God of hosts; *
    show the light of your countenance, and we shall be saved.

81 *Exultate Deo*

1 Sing with joy to God our strength *
   and raise a loud shout to the God of Jacob.

2 Raise a song and sound the timbrel, *
   the merry harp, and the lyre.

3 Blow the ram's-horn at the new moon, *
   and at the full moon, the day of our feast.

4 For this is a statute for Israel, *
   a law of the God of Jacob.

5 He laid it as a solemn charge upon Joseph, *
   when he came out of the land of Egypt.

6 I heard an unfamiliar voice saying, *
   "I eased his shoulder from the burden;
   his hands were set free from bearing the load."

7 You called on me in trouble, and I saved you; *
   I answered you from the secret place of thunder
   and tested you at the waters of Meribah.

8 Hear, O my people, and I will admonish you: *
   O Israel, if you would but listen to me!

9 There shall be no strange god among you; *
   you shall not worship a foreign god.

10 I am the LORD your God,
   who brought you out of the land of Egypt and said, *
   "Open your mouth wide, and I will fill it."

11 And yet my people did not hear my voice, *
   and Israel would not obey me.

12 So I gave them over to the stubbornness of their hearts, *
   to follow their own devices.

13   Oh, that my people would listen to me! *
       that Israel would walk in my ways!

14   I should soon subdue their enemies *
       and turn my hand against their foes.

15   Those who hate the LORD would cringe before him, *
       and their punishment would last for ever.

16   But Israel would I feed with the finest wheat *
       and satisfy him with honey from the rock.

Sixteenth Day: Evening Prayer

82 *Deus stetit*

1   God takes his stand in the council of heaven; *
       he gives judgment in the midst of the gods:

2   "How long will you judge unjustly, *
       and show favor to the wicked?

3   Save the weak and the orphan; *
       defend the humble and needy;

4   Rescue the weak and the poor; *
       deliver them from the power of the wicked.

5   They do not know, neither do they understand;
they go about in darkness; *
       all the foundations of the earth are shaken.

6   Now I say to you, 'You are gods, *
       and all of you children of the Most High;

7   Nevertheless, you shall die like mortals, *
       and fall like any prince.'"

8   Arise, O God, and rule the earth, *
       for you shall take all nations for your own.

83   *Deus, quis similis?*

1   O God, do not be silent; *
       do not keep still nor hold your peace, O God;

2   For your enemies are in tumult, *
       and those who hate you have lifted up their heads.

3   They take secret counsel against your people *
       and plot against those whom you protect.

4   They have said, "Come, let us wipe them out from among
       the nations; *
       let the name of Israel be remembered no more."

5   They have conspired together; *
       they have made an alliance against you:

6   The tents of Edom and the Ishmaelites; *
       the Moabites and the Hagarenes;

7   Gebal, and Ammon, and Amalek; *
       the Philistines and those who dwell in Tyre.

8   The Assyrians also have joined them, *
       and have come to help the people of Lot.

9   Do to them as you did to Midian, *
       to Sisera, and to Jabin at the river of Kishon:

10   They were destroyed at Endor; *
       they became like dung upon the ground.

11   Make their leaders like Oreb and Zeëb, *
       and all their commanders like Zebah and Zalmunna,

12 Who said, "Let us take for ourselves *
 the fields of God as our possession."

13 O my God, make them like whirling dust *
 and like chaff before the wind;

14 Like fire that burns down a forest, *
 like the flame that sets mountains ablaze.

15 Drive them with your tempest *
 and terrify them with your storm;

16 Cover their faces with shame, O LORD, *
 that they may seek your Name.

17 Let them be disgraced and terrified for ever; *
 let them be put to confusion and perish.

18 Let them know that you, whose Name is YAHWEH, *
 you alone are the Most High over all the earth.

84 *Quam dilecta!*

1 How dear to me is your dwelling, O LORD of hosts! *
 My soul has a desire and longing for the courts of
  the LORD;
 my heart and my flesh rejoice in the living God.

2 The sparrow has found her a house
 and the swallow a nest where she may lay her young; *
 by the side of your altars, O LORD of hosts,
 my King and my God.

3 Happy are they who dwell in your house! *
 they will always be praising you.

4 Happy are the people whose strength is in you! *
 whose hearts are set on the pilgrims' way.

5   Those who go through the desolate valley will find
                 it a place of springs, *
       for the early rains have covered it with pools of water.

6   They will climb from height to height, *
       and the God of gods will reveal himself in Zion.

7   LORD God of hosts, hear my prayer; *
       hearken, O God of Jacob.

8   Behold our defender, O God; *
       and look upon the face of your Anointed.

9   For one day in your courts is better than
                 a thousand in my own room, *
       and to stand at the threshold of the house of my God
       than to dwell in the tents of the wicked.

10   For the LORD God is both sun and shield; *
       he will give grace and glory;

11   No good thing will the LORD withhold *
       from those who walk with integrity.

12   O LORD of hosts, *
       happy are they who put their trust in you!

85   *Benedixisti, Domine*

1   You have been gracious to your land, O LORD, *
       you have restored the good fortune of Jacob.

2   You have forgiven the iniquity of your people *
       and blotted out all their sins.

3   You have withdrawn all your fury *
       and turned yourself from your wrathful indignation.

4 Restore us then, O God our Savior; *
    let your anger depart from us.

5 Will you be displeased with us for ever? *
    will you prolong your anger from age to age?

6 Will you not give us life again, *
    that your people may rejoice in you?

7 Show us your mercy, O LORD, *
    and grant us your salvation.

8 I will listen to what the LORD God is saying, *
    for he is speaking peace to his faithful people
    and to those who turn their hearts to him.

9 Truly, his salvation is very near to those who fear him, *
    that his glory may dwell in our land.

10 Mercy and truth have met together; *
    righteousness and peace have kissed each other.

11 Truth shall spring up from the earth, *
    and righteousness shall look down from heaven.

12 The LORD will indeed grant prosperity, *
    and our land will yield its increase.

13 Righteousness shall go before him, *
    and peace shall be a pathway for his feet.

Seventeenth Day: Morning Prayer

86 *Inclina, Domine*

1 Bow down your ear, O LORD, and answer me, *
    for I am poor and in misery.

2   Keep watch over my life, for I am faithful; *
     save your servant who puts his trust in you.

3   Be merciful to me, O LORD, for you are my God; *
     I call upon you all the day long.

4   Gladden the soul of your servant, *
     for to you, O LORD, I lift up my soul.

5   For you, O LORD, are good and forgiving, *
     and great is your love toward all who call upon you.

6   Give ear, O LORD, to my prayer, *
     and attend to the voice of my supplications.

7   In the time of my trouble I will call upon you, *
     for you will answer me.

8   Among the gods there is none like you, O LORD, *
     nor anything like your works.

9   All nations you have made will come and
                     worship you, O LORD, *
     and glorify your Name.

10   For you are great;
     you do wondrous things; *
     and you alone are God.

11   Teach me your way, O LORD,
     and I will walk in your truth; *
     knit my heart to you that I may fear your Name.

12   I will thank you, O LORD my God, with all my heart, *
     and glorify your Name for evermore.

13   For great is your love toward me; *
     you have delivered me from the nethermost Pit.

14 The arrogant rise up against me, O God,
     and a band of violent men seeks my life; *
          they have not set you before their eyes.

15 But you, O LORD, are gracious and full of compassion, *
          slow to anger, and full of kindness and truth.

16 Turn to me and have mercy upon me; *
          give your strength to your servant;
          and save the child of your handmaid.

17 Show me a sign of your favor,
     so that those who hate me may see it and be ashamed; *
          because you, O LORD, have helped me and comforted me.

87 *Fundamenta ejus*

1 On the holy mountain stands the city he has founded; *
          the LORD loves the gates of Zion
          more than all the dwellings of Jacob.

2 Glorious things are spoken of you, *
          O city of our God.

3 I count Egypt and Babylon among those who know me; *
          behold Philistia, Tyre, and Ethiopia:
          in Zion were they born.

4 Of Zion it shall be said,"Everyone was born in her, *
          and the Most High himself shall sustain her."

5 The LORD will record as he enrolls the peoples, *
          "These also were born there."

6 The singers and the dancers will say, *
          "All my fresh springs are in you."

88 *Domine, Deus*

1 O LORD, my God, my Savior, *
   by day and night I cry to you.

2 Let my prayer enter into your presence; *
   incline your ear to my lamentation.

3 For I am full of trouble; *
   my life is at the brink of the grave.

4 I am counted among those who go down to the Pit; *
   I have become like one who has no strength;

5 Lost among the dead, *
   like the slain who lie in the grave,

6 Whom you remember no more, *
   for they are cut off from your hand.

7 You have laid me in the depths of the Pit, *
   in dark places, and in the abyss.

8 Your anger weighs upon me heavily, *
   and all your great waves overwhelm me.

9 You have put my friends far from me;
   you have made me to be abhorred by them; *
   I am in prison and cannot get free.

10 My sight has failed me because of trouble; *
   LORD, I have called upon you daily;
   I have stretched out my hands to you.

11 Do you work wonders for the dead? *
   will those who have died stand up and give you thanks?

12 Will your loving-kindness be declared in the grave? *
   your faithfulness in the land of destruction?

13 Will your wonders be known in the dark? *
   or your righteousness in the country where all
            is forgotten?

14 But as for me, O LORD, I cry to you for help; *
   in the morning my prayer comes before you.

15 LORD, why have you rejected me? *
   why have you hidden your face from me?

16 Ever since my youth, I have been wretched and at the
            point of death; *
   I have borne your terrors with a troubled mind.

17 Your blazing anger has swept over me; *
   your terrors have destroyed me;

18 They surround me all day long like a flood; *
   they encompass me on every side.

19 My friend and my neighbor you have put away from me, *
   and darkness is my only companion.

Seventeenth Day: Evening Prayer

89

Part I   *Misericordias Domini*

1 Your love, O LORD, for ever will I sing; *
   from age to age my mouth will proclaim your faithfulness.

2 For I am persuaded that your love is established for ever; *
   you have set your faithfulness firmly in the heavens.

3 "I have made a covenant with my chosen one; *
   I have sworn an oath to David my servant:

4   'I will establish your line for ever, *
     and preserve your throne for all generations.' "

5   The heavens bear witness to your wonders, O LORD, *
     and to your faithfulness in the assembly of the holy ones;

6   For who in the skies can be compared to the LORD? *
     who is like the LORD among the gods?

7   God is much to be feared in the council of the holy ones, *
     great and terrible to all those round about him.

8   Who is like you, LORD God of hosts? *
     O mighty LORD, your faithfulness is all around you.

9   You rule the raging of the sea *
     and still the surging of its waves.

10   You have crushed Rahab of the deep with a deadly wound; *
     you have scattered your enemies with your mighty arm.

11   Yours are the heavens; the earth also is yours; *
     you laid the foundations of the world and all that is in it.

12   You have made the north and the south; *
     Tabor and Hermon rejoice in your Name.

13   You have a mighty arm; *
     strong is your hand and high is your right hand.

14   Righteousness and justice are the foundations of your throne; *
     love and truth go before your face.

15   Happy are the people who know the festal shout! *
     they walk, O LORD, in the light of your presence.

16   They rejoice daily in your Name; *
     they are jubilant in your righteousness.

17   For you are the glory of their strength, *
     and by your favor our might is exalted.

18   Truly, the LORD is our ruler; *
        the Holy One of Israel is our King.

Psalm 89: Part II   *Tunc locutus es*

19   You spoke once in a vision and said to your faithful people: *
        "I have set the crown upon a warrior
        and have exalted one chosen out of the people.

20   I have found David my servant; *
        with my holy oil have I anointed him.

21   My hand will hold him fast *
        and my arm will make him strong.

22   No enemy shall deceive him, *
        nor any wicked man bring him down.

23   I will crush his foes before him *
        and strike down those who hate him.

24   My faithfulness and love shall be with him, *
        and he shall be victorious through my Name.

25   I shall make his dominion extend *
        from the Great Sea to the River.

26   He will say to me,'You are my Father, *
        my God, and the rock of my salvation.'

27   I will make him my firstborn *
        and higher than the kings of the earth.

28   I will keep my love for him for ever, *
        and my covenant will stand firm for him.

29   I will establish his line for ever *
        and his throne as the days of heaven."

30 "If his children forsake my law *
and do not walk according to my judgments;

31 If they break my statutes *
and do not keep my commandments;

32 I will punish their transgressions with a rod *
and their iniquities with the lash;

33 But I will not take my love from him, *
nor let my faithfulness prove false.

34 I will not break my covenant, *
nor change what has gone out of my lips.

35 Once for all I have sworn by my holiness: *
'I will not lie to David.

36 His line shall endure for ever *
and his throne as the sun before me;

37 It shall stand fast for evermore like the moon, *
the abiding witness in the sky.'"

38 But you have cast off and rejected your anointed; *
you have become enraged at him.

39 You have broken your covenant with your servant, *
defiled his crown, and hurled it to the ground.

40 You have breached all his walls *
and laid his strongholds in ruins.

41 All who pass by despoil him; *
he has become the scorn of his neighbors.

42 You have exalted the right hand of his foes *
and made all his enemies rejoice.

43 You have turned back the edge of his sword *
and have not sustained him in battle.

44   You have put an end to his splendor *
      and cast his throne to the ground.

45   You have cut short the days of his youth *
      and have covered him with shame.

46   How long will you hide yourself, O LORD?
      will you hide yourself for ever? *
      how long will your anger burn like fire?

47   Remember, LORD, how short life is, *
      how frail you have made all flesh.

48   Who can live and not see death? *
      who can save himself from the power of the grave?

49   Where, Lord, are your loving-kindnesses of old, *
      which you promised David in your faithfulness?

50   Remember, Lord, how your servant is mocked, *
      how I carry in my bosom the taunts of many peoples,

51   The taunts your enemies have hurled, O LORD, *
      which they hurled at the heels of your anointed.

52   Blessed be the LORD for evermore! *
      Amen, I say, Amen.

Book Four

Eighteenth Day: Morning Prayer

90   *Domine, refugium*

1   Lord, you have been our refuge *
      from one generation to another.

2   Before the mountains were brought forth,
or the land and the earth were born, *
    from age to age you are God.

3   You turn us back to the dust and say, *
"Go back, O child of earth."

4   For a thousand years in your sight are like yesterday
when it is past *
    and like a watch in the night.

5   You sweep us away like a dream; *
we fade away suddenly like the grass.

6   In the morning it is green and flourishes; *
in the evening it is dried up and withered.

7   For we consume away in your displeasure; *
we are afraid because of your wrathful indignation.

8   Our iniquities you have set before you, *
and our secret sins in the light of your countenance.

9   When you are angry, all our days are gone; *
we bring our years to an end like a sigh.

10   The span of our life is seventy years,
perhaps in strength even eighty; *
    yet the sum of them is but labor and sorrow,
for they pass away quickly and we are gone.

11   Who regards the power of your wrath? *
who rightly fears your indignation?

12   So teach us to number our days *
that we may apply our hearts to wisdom.

13   Return, O LORD; how long will you tarry? *
be gracious to your servants.

14 Satisfy us by your loving-kindness in the morning; *
   so shall we rejoice and be glad all the days of our life.

15 Make us glad by the measure of the days that you afflicted us *
   and the years in which we suffered adversity.

16 Show your servants your works *
   and your splendor to their children.

17 May the graciousness of the LORD our God be upon us; *
   prosper the work of our hands;
   prosper our handiwork.

91 *Qui habitat*

1 He who dwells in the shelter of the Most High, *
   abides under the shadow of the Almighty.

2 He shall say to the LORD,
   "You are my refuge and my stronghold, *
   my God in whom I put my trust."

3 He shall deliver you from the snare of the hunter *
   and from the deadly pestilence.

4 He shall cover you with his pinions,
   and you shall find refuge under his wings; *
   his faithfulness shall be a shield and buckler.

5 You shall not be afraid of any terror by night, *
   nor of the arrow that flies by day;

6 Of the plague that stalks in the darkness, *
   nor of the sickness that lays waste at mid-day.

7 A thousand shall fall at your side
   and ten thousand at your right hand, *
   but it shall not come near you.

8   Your eyes have only to behold *
     to see the reward of the wicked.

9   Because you have made the LORD your refuge, *
     and the Most High your habitation,

10   There shall no evil happen to you, *
     neither shall any plague come near your dwelling.

11   For he shall give his angels charge over you, *
     to keep you in all your ways.

12   They shall bear you in their hands, *
     lest you dash your foot against a stone.

13   You shall tread upon the lion and adder; *
     you shall trample the young lion and the serpent
          under your feet.

14   Because he is bound to me in love,
     therefore will I deliver him; *
      I will protect him, because he knows my Name.

15   He shall call upon me, and I will answer him; *
     I am with him in trouble;
     I will rescue him and bring him to honor.

16   With long life will I satisfy him, *
     and show him my salvation.

92   *Bonum est confiteri*

1   It is a good thing to give thanks to the LORD, *
     and to sing praises to your Name, O Most High;

2   To tell of your loving-kindness early in the morning *
     and of your faithfulness in the night season;

3   On the psaltery, and on the lyre, *
     and to the melody of the harp.

4   For you have made me glad by your acts, O LORD; *
     and I shout for joy because of the works of your hands.

5   LORD, how great are your works! *
     your thoughts are very deep.

6   The dullard does not know,
   nor does the fool understand, *
     that though the wicked grow like weeds,
     and all the workers of iniquity flourish,

7   They flourish only to be destroyed for ever; *
     but you, O LORD, are exalted for evermore.

8   For lo, your enemies, O LORD,
   lo, your enemies shall perish, *
     and all the workers of iniquity shall be scattered.

9   But my horn you have exalted like the horns of wild bulls; *
     I am anointed with fresh oil.

10   My eyes also gloat over my enemies, *
     and my ears rejoice to hear the doom of the wicked who
       rise up against me.

11   The righteous shall flourish like a palm tree, *
     and shall spread abroad like a cedar of Lebanon.

12   Those who are planted in the house of the LORD *
     shall flourish in the courts of our God;

13   They shall still bear fruit in old age; *
     they shall be green and succulent;

14   That they may show how upright the LORD is, *
     my Rock, in whom there is no fault.

93 *Dominus regnavit*

1 The LORD is King;
he has put on splendid apparel; *
   the LORD has put on his apparel
   and girded himself with strength.

2 He has made the whole world so sure *
   that it cannot be moved;

3 Ever since the world began, your throne has been established; *
   you are from everlasting.

4 The waters have lifted up, O LORD,
the waters have lifted up their voice; *
   the waters have lifted up their pounding waves.

5 Mightier than the sound of many waters,
mightier than the breakers of the sea, *
   mightier is the LORD who dwells on high.

6 Your testimonies are very sure, *
   and holiness adorns your house, O LORD,
   for ever and for evermore.

94 *Deus ultionum*

1 O LORD God of vengeance, *
   O God of vengeance, show yourself.

2 Rise up, O Judge of the world; *
   give the arrogant their just deserts.

3 How long shall the wicked, O LORD, *
   how long shall the wicked triumph?

4 They bluster in their insolence; *
   all evildoers are full of boasting.

5 They crush your people, O LORD, *
   and afflict your chosen nation.

6 They murder the widow and the stranger *
   and put the orphans to death.

7 Yet they say, "The LORD does not see, *
   the God of Jacob takes no notice."

8 Consider well, you dullards among the people; *
   when will you fools understand?

9 He that planted the ear, does he not hear? *
   he that formed the eye, does he not see?

10 He who admonishes the nations, will he not punish? *
   he who teaches all the world, has he no knowledge?

11 The LORD knows our human thoughts; *
   how like a puff of wind they are.

12 Happy are they whom you instruct, O Lord! *
   whom you teach out of your law;

13 To give them rest in evil days, *
   until a pit is dug for the wicked.

14 For the LORD will not abandon his people, *
   nor will he forsake his own.

15 For judgment will again be just, *
   and all the true of heart will follow it.

16 Who rose up for me against the wicked? *
   who took my part against the evildoers?

17 If the LORD had not come to my help, *
   I should soon have dwelt in the land of silence.

18 As often as I said, "My foot has slipped," *
    your love, O LORD, upheld me.

19 When many cares fill my mind, *
    your consolations cheer my soul.

20 Can a corrupt tribunal have any part with you, *
    one which frames evil into law?

21 They conspire against the life of the just *
    and condemn the innocent to death.

22 But the LORD has become my stronghold, *
    and my God the rock of my trust.

23 He will turn their wickedness back upon them
    and destroy them in their own malice; *
      the LORD our God will destroy them.

Nineteenth Day: Morning Prayer

95 *Venite, exultemus*

1 Come, let us sing to the LORD; *
    let us shout for joy to the Rock of our salvation.

2 Let us come before his presence with thanksgiving *
    and raise a loud shout to him with psalms.

3 For the LORD is a great God, *
    and a great King above all gods.

4 In his hand are the caverns of the earth, *
    and the heights of the hills are his also.

5 The sea is his, for he made it, *
    and his hands have molded the dry land.

6   Come, let us bow down, and bend the knee, *
      and kneel before the LORD our Maker.

7   For he is our God,
      and we are the people of his pasture and the sheep of his hand. *
        Oh, that today you would hearken to his voice!

8   Harden not your hearts,
      as your forebears did in the wilderness, *
        at Meribah, and on that day at Massah,
        when they tempted me.

9   They put me to the test, *
      though they had seen my works.

10   Forty years long I detested that generation and said, *
      "This people are wayward in their hearts;
        they do not know my ways."

11   So I swore in my wrath, *
      "They shall not enter into my rest."

96   *Cantate Domino*

1   Sing to the LORD a new song; *
      sing to the LORD, all the whole earth.

2   Sing to the LORD and bless his Name; *
      proclaim the good news of his salvation from day to day.

3   Declare his glory among the nations *
      and his wonders among all peoples.

4   For great is the LORD and greatly to be praised; *
      he is more to be feared than all gods.

5   As for all the gods of the nations, they are but idols; *
       but it is the LORD who made the heavens.

6   Oh, the majesty and magnificence of his presence! *
       Oh, the power and the splendor of his sanctuary!

7   Ascribe to the LORD, you families of the peoples; *
       ascribe to the LORD honor and power.

8   Ascribe to the LORD the honor due his Name; *
       bring offerings and come into his courts.

9   Worship the LORD in the beauty of holiness; *
       let the whole earth tremble before him.

10   Tell it out among the nations: "The LORD is King! *
       he has made the world so firm that it cannot be moved;
       he will judge the peoples with equity."

11   Let the heavens rejoice, and let the earth be glad;
       let the sea thunder and all that is in it; *
       let the field be joyful and all that is therein.

12   Then shall all the trees of the wood shout for joy
       before the LORD when he comes, *
       when he comes to judge the earth.

13   He will judge the world with righteousness *
       and the peoples with his truth.

97 *Dominus regnavit*

1   The LORD is King;
       let the earth rejoice; *
       let the multitude of the isles be glad.

2   Clouds and darkness are round about him, *
       righteousness and justice are the foundations of his throne.

3   A fire goes before him *
        and burns up his enemies on every side.

4   His lightnings light up the world; *
        the earth sees it and is afraid.

5   The mountains melt like wax at the presence of the LORD, *
        at the presence of the Lord of the whole earth.

6   The heavens declare his righteousness, *
        and all the peoples see his glory.

7   Confounded be all who worship carved images
    and delight in false gods! *
        Bow down before him, all you gods.

8   Zion hears and is glad, and the cities of Judah rejoice, *
        because of your judgments, O LORD.

9   For you are the LORD,
    most high over all the earth; *
        you are exalted far above all gods.

10 The LORD loves those who hate evil; *
        he preserves the lives of his saints
        and delivers them from the hand of the wicked.

11 Light has sprung up for the righteous, *
        and joyful gladness for those who are truehearted.

12 Rejoice in the LORD, you righteous, *
        and give thanks to his holy Name.

Nineteenth Day: Evening Prayer

98   *Cantate Domino*

1   Sing to the LORD a new song, *
        for he has done marvelous things.

2   With his right hand and his holy arm *
        has he won for himself the victory.

3   The LORD has made known his victory; *
        his righteousness has he openly shown in
                the sight of the nations.

4   He remembers his mercy and faithfulness to
                the house of Israel, *
        and all the ends of the earth have seen the
                victory of our God.

5   Shout with joy to the LORD, all you lands; *
        lift up your voice, rejoice, and sing.

6   Sing to the LORD with the harp, *
        with the harp and the voice of song.

7   With trumpets and the sound of the horn *
        shout with joy before the King, the LORD.

8   Let the sea make a noise and all that is in it, *
        the lands and those who dwell therein.

9   Let the rivers clap their hands, *
        and let the hills ring out with joy before the LORD,
        when he comes to judge the earth.

10 In righteousness shall he judge the world *
        and the peoples with equity.

99   *Dominus regnavit*

1   The LORD is King;
        let the people tremble; *
            he is enthroned upon the cherubim;
            let the earth shake.

2   The LORD is great in Zion; *
      he is high above all peoples.

3   Let them confess his Name, which is great and awesome; *
      he is the Holy One.

4   "O mighty King, lover of justice,
      you have established equity; *
        you have executed justice and righteousness in Jacob."

5   Proclaim the greatness of the LORD our God
      and fall down before his footstool; *
      he is the Holy One.

6   Moses and Aaron among his priests,
      and Samuel among those who call upon his Name, *
        they called upon the LORD, and he answered them.

7   He spoke to them out of the pillar of cloud; *
      they kept his testimonies and the decree that he gave them.

8   "O LORD our God, you answered them indeed; *
      you were a God who forgave them,
        yet punished them for their evil deeds."

9   Proclaim the greatness of the LORD our God
      and worship him upon his holy hill; *
      for the LORD our God is the Holy One.

100   *Jubilate Deo*

1   Be joyful in the LORD, all you lands; *
      serve the LORD with gladness
      and come before his presence with a song.

2   Know this: The LORD himself is God; *
      he himself has made us, and we are his;
      we are his people and the sheep of his pasture.

3   Enter his gates with thanksgiving;
go into his courts with praise; *
    give thanks to him and call upon his Name.

4   For the LORD is good;
his mercy is everlasting; *
    and his faithfulness endures from age to age.

101   *Misericordiam et judicium*

1   I will sing of mercy and justice; *
    to you, O LORD, will I sing praises.

2   I will strive to follow a blameless course;
oh, when will you come to me? *
    I will walk with sincerity of heart within my house.

3   I will set no worthless thing before my eyes; *
    I hate the doers of evil deeds;
    they shall not remain with me.

4   A crooked heart shall be far from me; *
    I will not know evil.

5   Those who in secret slander their neighbors I will destroy; *
    those who have a haughty look and a proud
        heart I cannot abide.

6   My eyes are upon the faithful in the land, that they may
        dwell with me, *
    and only those who lead a blameless life shall
        be my servants.

7   Those who act deceitfully shall not dwell in my house, *
    and those who tell lies shall not continue in my sight.

8   I will soon destroy all the wicked in the land, *
    that I may root out all evildoers from the city of the LORD.

102 *Domine, exaudi*

1 LORD, hear my prayer, and let my cry come before you; *
   hide not your face from me in the day of my trouble.

2 Incline your ear to me; *
   when I call, make haste to answer me,

3 For my days drift away like smoke, *
   and my bones are hot as burning coals.

4 My heart is smitten like grass and withered, *
   so that I forget to eat my bread.

5 Because of the voice of my groaning *
   I am but skin and bones.

6 I have become like a vulture in the wilderness, *
   like an owl among the ruins.

7 I lie awake and groan; *
   I am like a sparrow, lonely on a house-top.

8 My enemies revile me all day long, *
   and those who scoff at me have taken an oath against me.

9 For I have eaten ashes for bread *
   and mingled my drink with weeping.

10 Because of your indignation and wrath *
   you have lifted me up and thrown me away.

11 My days pass away like a shadow, *
   and I wither like the grass.

12 But you, O LORD, endure for ever, *
   and your Name from age to age.

13 You will arise and have compassion on Zion,
for it is time to have mercy upon her; *
indeed, the appointed time has come.

14 For your servants love her very rubble, *
and are moved to pity even for her dust.

15 The nations shall fear your Name, O LORD, *
and all the kings of the earth your glory.

16 For the LORD will build up Zion, *
and his glory will appear.

17 He will look with favor on the prayer of the homeless; *
he will not despise their plea.

18 Let this be written for a future generation, *
so that a people yet unborn may praise the LORD.

19 For the LORD looked down from his holy place on high; *
from the heavens he beheld the earth;

20 That he might hear the groan of the captive *
and set free those condemned to die;

21 That they may declare in Zion the Name of the LORD, *
and his praise in Jerusalem;

22 When the peoples are gathered together, *
and the kingdoms also, to serve the LORD.

23 He has brought down my strength before my time; *
he has shortened the number of my days;

24 And I said, "O my God,
do not take me away in the midst of my days; *
your years endure throughout all generations.

25 In the beginning, O LORD, you laid the foundations
of the earth, *
and the heavens are the work of your hands;

26 They shall perish, but you will endure;
   they all shall wear out like a garment; *
      as clothing you will change them,
      and they shall be changed;

27 But you are always the same, *
      and your years will never end.

28 The children of your servants shall continue, *
      and their offspring shall stand fast in your sight."

103 *Benedic, anima mea*

1 Bless the LORD, O my soul, *
      and all that is within me, bless his holy Name.

2 Bless the LORD, O my soul, *
      and forget not all his benefits.

3 He forgives all your sins *
      and heals all your infirmities;

4 He redeems your life from the grave *
      and crowns you with mercy and loving-kindness;

5 He satisfies you with good things, *
      and your youth is renewed like an eagle's.

6 The LORD executes righteousness *
      and judgment for all who are oppressed.

7 He made his ways known to Moses *
      and his works to the children of Israel.

8 The LORD is full of compassion and mercy, *
      slow to anger and of great kindness.

9 He will not always accuse us, *
      nor will he keep his anger for ever.

10　He has not dealt with us according to our sins, *
　　　nor rewarded us according to our wickedness.

11　For as the heavens are high above the earth, *
　　　so is his mercy great upon those who fear him.

12　As far as the east is from the west, *
　　　so far has he removed our sins from us.

13　As a father cares for his children, *
　　　so does the LORD care for those who fear him.

14　For he himself knows whereof we are made; *
　　　he remembers that we are but dust.

15　Our days are like the grass; *
　　　we flourish like a flower of the field;

16　When the wind goes over it, it is gone, *
　　　and its place shall know it no more.

17　But the merciful goodness of the LORD endures for ever
　　　　　　　on those who fear him, *
　　　and his righteousness on children's children;

18　On those who keep his covenant *
　　　and remember his commandments and do them.

19　The LORD has set his throne in heaven, *
　　　and his kingship has dominion over all.

20　Bless the LORD, you angels of his,
　　you mighty ones who do his bidding, *
　　　and hearken to the voice of his word.

21　Bless the LORD, all you his hosts, *
　　　you ministers of his who do his will.

22　Bless the LORD, all you works of his,
　　in all places of his dominion; *
　　　bless the LORD, O my soul.

104 *Benedic, anima mea*

1 Bless the LORD, O my soul; *
   O LORD my God, how excellent is your greatness!
   you are clothed with majesty and splendor.

2 You wrap yourself with light as with a cloak *
   and spread out the heavens like a curtain.

3 You lay the beams of your chambers in the waters above; *
   you make the clouds your chariot;
   you ride on the wings of the wind.

4 You make the winds your messengers *
   and flames of fire your servants.

5 You have set the earth upon its foundations, *
   so that it never shall move at any time.

6 You covered it with the Deep as with a mantle; *
   the waters stood higher than the mountains.

7 At your rebuke they fled; *
   at the voice of your thunder they hastened away.

8 They went up into the hills and down to the valleys beneath, *
   to the places you had appointed for them.

9 You set the limits that they should not pass; *
   they shall not again cover the earth.

10 You send the springs into the valleys; *
   they flow between the mountains.

11 All the beasts of the field drink their fill from them, *
   and the wild asses quench their thirst.

12 Beside them the birds of the air make their nests *
   and sing among the branches.

13   You water the mountains from your dwelling on high; *
     the earth is fully satisfied by the fruit of your works.

14   You make grass grow for flocks and herds *
     and plants to serve mankind;

15   That they may bring forth food from the earth, *
     and wine to gladden our hearts,

16   Oil to make a cheerful countenance, *
     and bread to strengthen the heart.

17   The trees of the LORD are full of sap, *
     the cedars of Lebanon which he planted,

18   In which the birds build their nests, *
     and in whose tops the stork makes his dwelling.

19   The high hills are a refuge for the mountain goats, *
     and the stony cliffs for the rock badgers.

20   You appointed the moon to mark the seasons, *
     and the sun knows the time of its setting.

21   You make darkness that it may be night, *
     in which all the beasts of the forest prowl.

22   The lions roar after their prey *
     and seek their food from God.

23   The sun rises, and they slip away *
     and lay themselves down in their dens.

24   Man goes forth to his work *
     and to his labor until the evening.

25   O LORD, how manifold are your works! *
     in wisdom you have made them all;
     the earth is full of your creatures.

26   Yonder is the great and wide sea
        with its living things too many to number, *
        creatures both small and great.

27   There move the ships,
        and there is that Leviathan, *
        which you have made for the sport of it.

28   All of them look to you *
        to give them their food in due season.

29   You give it to them; they gather it; *
        you open your hand, and they are filled with good things.

30   You hide your face, and they are terrified; *
        you take away their breath,
        and they die and return to their dust.

31   You send forth your Spirit, and they are created; *
        and so you renew the face of the earth.

32   May the glory of the LORD endure for ever; *
        may the LORD rejoice in all his works.

33   He looks at the earth and it trembles; *
        he touches the mountains and they smoke.

34   I will sing to the LORD as long as I live; *
        I will praise my God while I have my being.

35   May these words of mine please him; *
        I will rejoice in the LORD.

36   Let sinners be consumed out of the earth, *
        and the wicked be no more.

37   Bless the LORD, O my soul. *
        Hallelujah!

105

Part I *Confitemini Domino*

1 Give thanks to the L ORD and call upon his Name; *
 make known his deeds among the peoples.

2 Sing to him, sing praises to him, *
 and speak of all his marvelous works.

3 Glory in his holy Name; *
 let the hearts of those who seek the L ORD rejoice.

4 Search for the L ORD and his strength; *
 continually seek his face.

5 Remember the marvels he has done, *
 his wonders and the judgments of his mouth,

6 O offspring of Abraham his servant, *
 O children of Jacob his chosen.

7 He is the L ORD our God; *
 his judgments prevail in all the world.

8 He has always been mindful of his covenant, *
 the promise he made for a thousand generations:

9 The covenant he made with Abraham, *
 the oath that he swore to Isaac,

10 Which he established as a statute for Jacob, *
 an everlasting covenant for Israel,

11 Saying, "To you will I give the land of Canaan *
 to be your allotted inheritance."

12 When they were few in number, *
    of little account, and sojourners in the land,

13 Wandering from nation to nation *
    and from one kingdom to another,

14 He let no one oppress them *
    and rebuked kings for their sake,

15 Saying, "Do not touch my anointed *
    and do my prophets no harm."

16 Then he called for a famine in the land *
    and destroyed the supply of bread.

17 He sent a man before them, *
    Joseph, who was sold as a slave.

18 They bruised his feet in fetters; *
    his neck they put in an iron collar.

19 Until his prediction came to pass, *
    the word of the LORD tested him.

20 The king sent and released him; *
    the ruler of the peoples set him free.

21 He set him as a master over his household, *
    as a ruler over all his possessions,

22 To instruct his princes according to his will *
    and to teach his elders wisdom.

Psalm 105: Part II *Et intravit Israel*

23 Israel came into Egypt, *
    and Jacob became a sojourner in the land of Ham.

24 The LORD made his people exceedingly fruitful; *
    he made them stronger than their enemies;

25 Whose heart he turned, so that they hated his people, *
    and dealt unjustly with his servants.

26 He sent Moses his servant, *
    and Aaron whom he had chosen.

27 They worked his signs among them, *
    and portents in the land of Ham.

28 He sent darkness, and it grew dark; *
    but the Egyptians rebelled against his words.

29 He turned their waters into blood *
    and caused their fish to die.

30 Their land was overrun by frogs, *
    in the very chambers of their kings.

31 He spoke, and there came swarms of insects *
    and gnats within all their borders.

32 He gave them hailstones instead of rain, *
    and flames of fire throughout their land.

33 He blasted their vines and their fig trees *
    and shattered every tree in their country.

34 He spoke, and the locust came, *
    and young locusts without number,

35 Which ate up all the green plants in their land *
    and devoured the fruit of their soil.

36 He struck down the firstborn of their land, *
    the firstfruits of all their strength.

37 He led out his people with silver and gold; *
    in all their tribes there was not one that stumbled.

38 Egypt was glad of their going, *
    because they were afraid of them.

39 He spread out a cloud for a covering *
    and a fire to give light in the night season.

40 They asked, and quails appeared, *
    and he satisfied them with bread from heaven.

41 He opened the rock, and water flowed, *
    so the river ran in the dry places.

42 For God remembered his holy word *
    and Abraham his servant.

43 So he led forth his people with gladness, *
    his chosen with shouts of joy.

44 He gave his people the lands of the nations, *
    and they took the fruit of others' toil,

45 That they might keep his statutes *
    and observe his laws.
    Hallelujah!

Twenty-first Day: Evening Prayer

106

Part I *Confitemini Domino*

1 Hallelujah!
    Give thanks to the LORD, for he is good, *
    for his mercy endures for ever.

2 Who can declare the mighty acts of the LORD *
    or show forth all his praise?

3   Happy are those who act with justice *
         and always do what is right!

4   Remember me, O LORD, with the favor you have
                        for your people, *
         and visit me with your saving help;

5   That I may see the prosperity of your elect
         and be glad with the gladness of your people, *
         that I may glory with your inheritance.

6   We have sinned as our forebears did; *
         we have done wrong and dealt wickedly.

7   In Egypt they did not consider your marvelous works,
     nor remember the abundance of your love; *
         they defied the Most High at the Red Sea.

8   But he saved them for his Name's sake, *
         to make his power known.

9   He rebuked the Red Sea, and it dried up, *
         and he led them through the deep as through a desert.

10   He saved them from the hand of those who hated them *
         and redeemed them from the hand of the enemy.

11   The waters covered their oppressors; *
         not one of them was left.

12   Then they believed his words *
         and sang him songs of praise.

13   But they soon forgot his deeds *
         and did not wait for his counsel.

14   A craving seized them in the wilderness, *
         and they put God to the test in the desert.

15　He gave them what they asked, *
　　　but sent leanness into their soul.

16　They envied Moses in the camp, *
　　　and Aaron, the holy one of the LORD.

17　The earth opened and swallowed Dathan *
　　　and covered the company of Abiram.

18　Fire blazed up against their company, *
　　　and flames devoured the wicked.

Psalm 106: Part II　*Et fecerunt vitulum*

19　Israel made a bull-calf at Horeb *
　　　and worshiped a molten image;

20　And so they exchanged their Glory *
　　　for the image of an ox that feeds on grass.

21　They forgot God their Savior, *
　　　who had done great things in Egypt,

22　Wonderful deeds in the land of Ham, *
　　　and fearful things at the Red Sea.

23　So he would have destroyed them,
　　　had not Moses his chosen stood before him in the breach, *
　　　to turn away his wrath from consuming them.

24　They refused the pleasant land *
　　　and would not believe his promise.

25　They grumbled in their tents *
　　　and would not listen to the voice of the LORD.

26　So he lifted his hand against them, *
　　　to overthrow them in the wilderness,

27 To cast out their seed among the nations, *
and to scatter them throughout the lands.

28 They joined themselves to Baal-Peor *
and ate sacrifices offered to the dead.

29 They provoked him to anger with their actions, *
and a plague broke out among them.

30 Then Phinehas stood up and interceded, *
and the plague came to an end.

31 This was reckoned to him as righteousness *
throughout all generations for ever.

32 Again they provoked his anger at the waters of Meribah, *
so that he punished Moses because of them;

33 For they so embittered his spirit *
that he spoke rash words with his lips.

34 They did not destroy the peoples *
as the LORD had commanded them.

35 They intermingled with the heathen *
and learned their pagan ways,

36 So that they worshiped their idols, *
which became a snare to them.

37 They sacrificed their sons *
and their daughters to evil spirits.

38 They shed innocent blood,
the blood of their sons and daughters, *
which they offered to the idols of Canaan,
and the land was defiled with blood.

39 Thus they were polluted by their actions *
and went whoring in their evil deeds.

40 Therefore the wrath of the LORD was kindled against
his people *
and he abhorred his inheritance.

41 He gave them over to the hand of the heathen, *
and those who hated them ruled over them.

42 Their enemies oppressed them, *
and they were humbled under their hand.

43 Many a time did he deliver them,
but they rebelled through their own devices, *
and were brought down in their iniquity.

44 Nevertheless, he saw their distress, *
when he heard their lamentation.

45 He remembered his covenant with them *
and relented in accordance with his great mercy.

46 He caused them to be pitied *
by those who held them captive.

47 Save us, O LORD our God,
and gather us from among the nations, *
that we may give thanks to your holy Name
and glory in your praise.

48 Blessed be the LORD, the God of Israel,
from everlasting and to everlasting; *
and let all the people say, "Amen!"
Hallelujah!

Book Five

Twenty-second Day: Morning Prayer

107

Part I *Confitemini Domino*

1   Give thanks to the LORD, for he is good, *
      and his mercy endures for ever.

2   Let all those whom the LORD has redeemed proclaim *
      that he redeemed them from the hand of the foe.

3   He gathered them out of the lands; *
      from the east and from the west,
      from the north and from the south.

4   Some wandered in desert wastes; *
      they found no way to a city where they might dwell.

5   They were hungry and thirsty; *
      their spirits languished within them.

6   Then they cried to the LORD in their trouble, *
      and he delivered them from their distress.

7   He put their feet on a straight path *
      to go to a city where they might dwell.

8   Let them give thanks to the LORD for his mercy *
      and the wonders he does for his children.

9   For he satisfies the thirsty *
      and fills the hungry with good things.

10   Some sat in darkness and deep gloom, *
      bound fast in misery and iron;

11   Because they rebelled against the words of God *
      and despised the counsel of the Most High.

12   So he humbled their spirits with hard labor; *
      they stumbled, and there was none to help.

13   Then they cried to the LORD in their trouble, *
      and he delivered them from their distress.

14   He led them out of darkness and deep gloom *
      and broke their bonds asunder.

15   Let them give thanks to the LORD for his mercy *
      and the wonders he does for his children.

16   For he shatters the doors of bronze *
      and breaks in two the iron bars.

17   Some were fools and took to rebellious ways; *
      they were afflicted because of their sins.

18   They abhorred all manner of food *
      and drew near to death's door.

19   Then they cried to the LORD in their trouble, *
      and he delivered them from their distress.

20   He sent forth his word and healed them *
      and saved them from the grave.

21   Let them give thanks to the LORD for his mercy *
      and the wonders he does for his children.

22   Let them offer a sacrifice of thanksgiving *
      and tell of his acts with shouts of joy.

23 Some went down to the sea in ships *
    and plied their trade in deep waters;

24 They beheld the works of the LORD *
    and his wonders in the deep.

25 Then he spoke, and a stormy wind arose, *
    which tossed high the waves of the sea.

26 They mounted up to the heavens and fell back to the depths; *
    their hearts melted because of their peril.

27 They reeled and staggered like drunkards *
    and were at their wits' end.

28 Then they cried to the LORD in their trouble, *
    and he delivered them from their distress.

29 He stilled the storm to a whisper *
    and quieted the waves of the sea.

30 Then were they glad because of the calm, *
    and he brought them to the harbor they were bound for.

31 Let them give thanks to the LORD for his mercy *
    and the wonders he does for his children.

32 Let them exalt him in the congregation of the people *
    and praise him in the council of the elders.

Psalm 107: Part II   *Posuit flumina*

33 The LORD changed rivers into deserts, *
    and water-springs into thirsty ground,

34 A fruitful land into salt flats, *
    because of the wickedness of those who dwell there.

35 He changed deserts into pools of water *
    and dry land into water-springs.

36 He settled the hungry there, *
   and they founded a city to dwell in.

37 They sowed fields, and planted vineyards, *
   and brought in a fruitful harvest.

38 He blessed them, so that they increased greatly; *
   he did not let their herds decrease.

39 Yet when they were diminished and brought low, *
   through stress of adversity and sorrow,

40 (He pours contempt on princes *
   and makes them wander in trackless wastes)

41 He lifted up the poor out of misery *
   and multiplied their families like flocks of sheep.

42 The upright will see this and rejoice, *
   but all wickedness will shut its mouth.

43 Whoever is wise will ponder these things, *
   and consider well the mercies of the LORD.

Twenty-second Day: Evening Prayer

108 *Paratum cor meum*

1 My heart is firmly fixed, O God, my heart is fixed; *
   I will sing and make melody.

2 Wake up, my spirit;
   awake, lute and harp; *
   I myself will waken the dawn.

3 I will confess you among the peoples, O LORD; *
   I will sing praises to you among the nations.

4   For your loving-kindness is greater than the heavens, *
        and your faithfulness reaches to the clouds.

5   Exalt yourself above the heavens, O God, *
        and your glory over all the earth.

6   So that those who are dear to you may be delivered, *
        save with your right hand and answer me.

7   God spoke from his holy place and said, *
        "I will exult and parcel out Shechem;
        I will divide the valley of Succoth.

8   Gilead is mine and Manasseh is mine; *
        Ephraim is my helmet and Judah my scepter.

9   Moab is my washbasin,
        on Edom I throw down my sandal to claim it, *
        and over Philistia will I shout in triumph."

10 Who will lead me into the strong city? *
        who will bring me into Edom?

11 Have you not cast us off, O God? *
        you no longer go out, O God, with our armies.

12 Grant us your help against the enemy, *
        for vain is the help of man.

13 With God we will do valiant deeds, *
        and he shall tread our enemies under foot.

109   *Deus, laudem*

1   Hold not your tongue, O God of my praise; *
        for the mouth of the wicked,
        the mouth of the deceitful, is opened against me.

2 They speak to me with a lying tongue; *
  they encompass me with hateful words
  and fight against me without a cause.

3 Despite my love, they accuse me; *
  but as for me, I pray for them.

4 They repay evil for good, *
  and hatred for my love.

5 Set a wicked man against him, *
  and let an accuser stand at his right hand.

6 When he is judged, let him be found guilty, *
  and let his appeal be in vain.

7 Let his days be few, *
  and let another take his office.

8 Let his children be fatherless, *
  and his wife become a widow.

9 Let his children be waifs and beggars; *
  let them be driven from the ruins of their homes.

10 Let the creditor seize everything he has; *
  let strangers plunder his gains.

11 Let there be no one to show him kindness, *
  and none to pity his fatherless children.

12 Let his descendants be destroyed, *
  and his name be blotted out in the next generation.

13 Let the wickedness of his fathers be remembered before
   the Lord, *
  and his mother's sin not be blotted out;

14 Let their sin be always before the Lord; *
  but let him root out their names from the earth;

15 Because he did not remember to show mercy, *
    but persecuted the poor and needy
    and sought to kill the brokenhearted.

16 He loved cursing,
  let it come upon him; *
    he took no delight in blessing,
    let it depart from him.

17 He put on cursing like a garment, *
    let it soak into his body like water
    and into his bones like oil;

18 Let it be to him like the cloak which he
                  wraps around himself, *
    and like the belt that he wears continually.

19 Let this be the recompense from the LORD to my accusers, *
    and to those who speak evil against me.

20 But you, O Lord my GOD,
  oh, deal with me according to your Name; *
    for your tender mercy's sake, deliver me.

21 For I am poor and needy, *
    and my heart is wounded within me.

22 I have faded away like a shadow when it lengthens; *
    I am shaken off like a locust.

23 My knees are weak through fasting, *
    and my flesh is wasted and gaunt.

24 I have become a reproach to them; *
    they see and shake their heads.

25 Help me, O LORD my God; *
    save me for your mercy's sake.

26   Let them know that this is your hand, *
        that you, O LORD, have done it.

27   They may curse, but you will bless; *
        let those who rise up against me be put to shame,
        and your servant will rejoice.

28   Let my accusers be clothed with disgrace *
        and wrap themselves in their shame as in a cloak.

29   I will give great thanks to the LORD with my mouth; *
        in the midst of the multitude will I praise him;

30   Because he stands at the right hand of the needy, *
        to save his life from those who would condemn him.

Twenty-third Day: Morning Prayer

110   *Dixit Dominus*

1   The LORD said to my Lord, "Sit at my right hand, *
        until I make your enemies your footstool."

2   The LORD will send the scepter of your power out of Zion, *
        saying, "Rule over your enemies round about you.

3   Princely state has been yours from the day of your birth; *
        in the beauty of holiness have I begotten you,
        like dew from the womb of the morning."

4   The LORD has sworn and he will not recant: *
        "You are a priest for ever after the order of Melchizedek."

5   The Lord who is at your right hand
    will smite kings in the day of his wrath; *
        he will rule over the nations.

6   He will heap high the corpses; *
      he will smash heads over the wide earth.

7   He will drink from the brook beside the road; *
      therefore he will lift high his head.

III   *Confitebor tibi*

1   Hallelujah!
      I will give thanks to the LORD with my whole heart, *
       in the assembly of the upright, in the congregation.

2   Great are the deeds of the LORD! *
      they are studied by all who delight in them.

3   His work is full of majesty and splendor, *
      and his righteousness endures for ever.

4   He makes his marvelous works to be remembered; *
      the LORD is gracious and full of compassion.

5   He gives food to those who fear him; *
      he is ever mindful of his covenant.

6   He has shown his people the power of his works *
      in giving them the lands of the nations.

7   The works of his hands are faithfulness and justice; *
      all his commandments are sure.

8   They stand fast for ever and ever, *
      because they are done in truth and equity.

9   He sent redemption to his people;
      he commanded his covenant for ever; *
       holy and awesome is his Name.

10 The fear of the LORD is the beginning of wisdom; *
     those who act accordingly have a good understanding;
     his praise endures for ever.

112 *Beatus vir*

1 Hallelujah!
   Happy are they who fear the Lord *
     and have great delight in his commandments!

2 Their descendants will be mighty in the land; *
     the generation of the upright will be blessed.

3 Wealth and riches will be in their house, *
     and their righteousness will last for ever.

4 Light shines in the darkness for the upright; *
     the righteous are merciful and full of compassion.

5 It is good for them to be generous in lending *
     and to manage their affairs with justice.

6 For they will never be shaken; *
     the righteous will be kept in everlasting remembrance.

7 They will not be afraid of any evil rumors; *
     their heart is right;
     they put their trust in the Lord.

8 Their heart is established and will not shrink, *
     until they see their desire upon their enemies.

9 They have given freely to the poor, *
     and their righteousness stands fast for ever;
     they will hold up their head with honor.

10 The wicked will see it and be angry;
     they will gnash their teeth and pine away; *
     the desires of the wicked will perish.

I I 3 *Laudate, pueri*

1   Hallelujah!
    Give praise, you servants of the LORD; *
      praise the Name of the LORD.

2   Let the Name of the LORD be blessed, *
      from this time forth for evermore.

3   From the rising of the sun to its going down *
      let the Name of the LORD be praised.

4   The LORD is high above all nations, *
      and his glory above the heavens.

5   Who is like the LORD our God, who sits enthroned on high, *
      but stoops to behold the heavens and the earth?

6   He takes up the weak out of the dust *
      and lifts up the poor from the ashes.

7   He sets them with the princes, *
      with the princes of his people.

8   He makes the woman of a childless house *
      to be a joyful mother of children.

Twenty-third Day: Evening Prayer

I I 4 *In exitu Israel*

1   Hallelujah!
    When Israel came out of Egypt, *
      the house of Jacob from a people of strange speech,

2   Judah became God's sanctuary *
      and Israel his dominion.

3   The sea beheld it and fled; *
      Jordan turned and went back.

4   The mountains skipped like rams, *
      and the little hills like young sheep.

5   What ailed you, O sea, that you fled? *
      O Jordan, that you turned back?

6   You mountains, that you skipped like rams? *
      you little hills like young sheep?

7   Tremble, O earth, at the presence of the Lord, *
      at the presence of the God of Jacob,

8   Who turned the hard rock into a pool of water *
      and flint-stone into a flowing spring.

115   *Non nobis, Domine*

1   Not to us, O LORD, not to us,
    but to your Name give glory; *
      because of your love and because of your faithfulness.

2   Why should the heathen say, *
      "Where then is their God?"

3   Our God is in heaven; *
      whatever he wills to do he does.

4   Their idols are silver and gold, *
      the work of human hands.

5   They have mouths, but they cannot speak; *
      eyes have they, but they cannot see;

6   They have ears, but they cannot hear; *
      noses, but they cannot smell;

7   They have hands, but they cannot feel;
    feet, but they cannot walk; *
        they make no sound with their throat.

8   Those who make them are like them, *
        and so are all who put their trust in them.

9   O Israel, trust in the LORD; *
        he is their help and their shield.

10 O house of Aaron, trust in the LORD; *
        he is their help and their shield.

11 You who fear the LORD, trust in the LORD; *
        he is their help and their shield.

12 The LORD has been mindful of us, and he will bless us; *
        he will bless the house of Israel;
        he will bless the house of Aaron;

13 He will bless those who fear the LORD, *
        both small and great together.

14 May the LORD increase you more and more, *
        you and your children after you.

15 May you be blessed by the LORD, *
        the maker of heaven and earth.

16 The heaven of heavens is the LORD's, *
        but he entrusted the earth to its peoples.

17 The dead do not praise the LORD, *
        nor all those who go down into silence;

18 But we will bless the LORD, *
        from this time forth for evermore.
        Hallelujah!

116 *Dilexi, quoniam*

1 I love the LORD, because he has heard the voice of
       my supplication, *
  because he has inclined his ear to me whenever
       I called upon him.

2 The cords of death entangled me;
  the grip of the grave took hold of me; *
    I came to grief and sorrow.

3 Then I called upon the Name of the LORD: *
  "O LORD, I pray you, save my life."

4 Gracious is the LORD and righteous; *
  our God is full of compassion.

5 The LORD watches over the innocent; *
  I was brought very low, and he helped me.

6 Turn again to your rest, O my soul, *
  for the LORD has treated you well.

7 For you have rescued my life from death, *
  my eyes from tears, and my feet from stumbling.

8 I will walk in the presence of the LORD *
  in the land of the living.

9 I believed, even when I said,
  "I have been brought very low." *
    In my distress I said, "No one can be trusted."

10 How shall I repay the LORD *
  for all the good things he has done for me?

11 I will lift up the cup of salvation *
  and call upon the Name of the LORD.

12 I will fulfill my vows to the LORD *
      in the presence of all his people.

13 Precious in the sight of the LORD *
      is the death of his servants.

14 O LORD, I am your servant; *
      I am your servant and the child of your handmaid;
      you have freed me from my bonds.

15 I will offer you the sacrifice of thanksgiving *
      and call upon the Name of the LORD.

16 I will fulfill my vows to the LORD *
      in the presence of all his people,

17 In the courts of the LORD's house, *
      in the midst of you, O Jerusalem.
      Hallelujah!

117 *Laudate Dominum*

1 Praise the LORD, all you nations; *
      laud him, all you peoples.

2 For his loving-kindness toward us is great, *
      and the faithfulness of the LORD endures for ever.
      Hallelujah!

118 *Confitemini Domino*

1 Give thanks to the LORD, for he is good; *
      his mercy endures for ever.

2 Let Israel now proclaim, *
      "His mercy endures for ever."

3 Let the house of Aaron now proclaim, *
    "His mercy endures for ever."

4 Let those who fear the LORD now proclaim, *
    "His mercy endures for ever."

5 I called to the LORD in my distress; *
    the LORD answered by setting me free.

6 The LORD is at my side, therefore I will not fear; *
    what can anyone do to me?

7 The LORD is at my side to help me; *
    I will triumph over those who hate me.

8 It is better to rely on the LORD *
    than to put any trust in flesh.

9 It is better to rely on the LORD *
    than to put any trust in rulers.

10 All the ungodly encompass me; *
    in the name of the LORD I will repel them.

11 They hem me in, they hem me in on every side; *
    in the name of the LORD I will repel them.

12 They swarm about me like bees;
    they blaze like a fire of thorns; *
    in the name of the LORD I will repel them.

13 I was pressed so hard that I almost fell, *
    but the LORD came to my help.

14 The LORD is my strength and my song, *
    and he has become my salvation.

15 There is a sound of exultation and victory *
    in the tents of the righteous:

16   "The right hand of the LORD has triumphed! *
        the right hand of the LORD is exalted!
        the right hand of the LORD has triumphed!"

17   I shall not die, but live, *
        and declare the works of the LORD.

18   The LORD has punished me sorely, *
        but he did not hand me over to death.

19   Open for me the gates of righteousness; *
        I will enter them;
        I will offer thanks to the LORD.

20   "This is the gate of the LORD; *
        he who is righteous may enter."

21   I will give thanks to you, for you answered me *
        and have become my salvation.

22   The same stone which the builders rejected *
        has become the chief cornerstone.

23   This is the LORD's doing, *
        and it is marvelous in our eyes.

24   On this day the LORD has acted; *
        we will rejoice and be glad in it.

25   Hosannah, LORD, hosannah! *
        LORD, send us now success.

26   Blessed is he who comes in the name of the Lord; *
        we bless you from the house of the LORD.

27   God is the LORD; he has shined upon us; *
        form a procession with branches up to the horns of the altar.

28 "You are my God, and I will thank you; *
    you are my God, and I will exalt you."

29 Give thanks to the LORD, for he is good; *
    his mercy endures for ever.

Twenty-fourth Day: Evening Prayer

119

Aleph   *Beati immaculati*

1 Happy are they whose way is blameless, *
    who walk in the law of the LORD!

2 Happy are they who observe his decrees *
    and seek him with all their hearts!

3 Who never do any wrong, *
    but always walk in his ways.

4 You laid down your commandments, *
    that we should fully keep them.

5 Oh, that my ways were made so direct *
    that I might keep your statutes!

6 Then I should not be put to shame, *
    when I regard all your commandments.

7 I will thank you with an unfeigned heart, *
    when I have learned your righteous judgments.

8 I will keep your statutes; *
    do not utterly forsake me.

Beth *In quo corrigit?*

9   How shall a young man cleanse his way? *
       By keeping to your words.

10   With my whole heart I seek you; *
       let me not stray from your commandments.

11   I treasure your promise in my heart, *
       that I may not sin against you.

12   Blessed are you, O LORD; *
       instruct me in your statutes.

13   With my lips will I recite *
       all the judgments of your mouth.

14   I have taken greater delight in the way of your decrees *
       than in all manner of riches.

15   I will meditate on your commandments *
       and give attention to your ways.

16   My delight is in your statutes; *
       I will not forget your word.

Gimel *Retribue servo tuo*

17   Deal bountifully with your servant, *
       that I may live and keep your word.

18   Open my eyes, that I may see *
       the wonders of your law.

19   I am a stranger here on earth; *
       do not hide your commandments from me.

20   My soul is consumed at all times *
       with longing for your judgments.

21   You have rebuked the insolent; *
      cursed are they who stray from your commandments!

22   Turn from me shame and rebuke, *
      for I have kept your decrees.

23   Even though rulers sit and plot against me, *
      I will meditate on your statutes.

24   For your decrees are my delight, *
      and they are my counselors.

Daleth   *Adhæsit pavimento*

25   My soul cleaves to the dust; *
      give me life according to your word.

26   I have confessed my ways, and you answered me; *
      instruct me in your statutes.

27   Make me understand the way of your commandments, *
      that I may meditate on your marvelous works.

28   My soul melts away for sorrow; *
      strengthen me according to your word.

29   Take from me the way of lying; *
      let me find grace through your law.

30   I have chosen the way of faithfulness; *
      I have set your judgments before me.

31   I hold fast to your decrees; *
      O LORD, let me not be put to shame.

32   I will run the way of your commandments, *
      for you have set my heart at liberty.

He   *Legem pone*

33   Teach me, O LORD, the way of your statutes, *
       and I shall keep it to the end.

34   Give me understanding, and I shall keep your law; *
       I shall keep it with all my heart.

35   Make me go in the path of your commandments, *
       for that is my desire.

36   Incline my heart to your decrees *
       and not to unjust gain.

37   Turn my eyes from watching what is worthless; *
       give me life in your ways.

38   Fulfill your promise to your servant, *
       which you make to those who fear you.

39   Turn away the reproach which I dread, *
       because your judgments are good.

40   Behold, I long for your commandments; *
       in your righteousness preserve my life.

Waw   *Et veniat super me*

41   Let your loving-kindness come to me, O LORD, *
       and your salvation, according to your promise.

42   Then shall I have a word for those who taunt me, *
       because I trust in your words.

43   Do not take the word of truth out of my mouth, *
       for my hope is in your judgments.

44 I shall continue to keep your law; *
    I shall keep it for ever and ever.

45 I will walk at liberty, *
    because I study your commandments.

46 I will tell of your decrees before kings *
    and will not be ashamed.

47 I delight in your commandments, *
    which I have always loved.

48 I will lift up my hands to your commandments, *
    and I will meditate on your statutes.

Zayin *Memor esto verbi tui*

49 Remember your word to your servant, *
    because you have given me hope.

50 This is my comfort in my trouble, *
    that your promise gives me life.

51 The proud have derided me cruelly, *
    but I have not turned from your law.

52 When I remember your judgments of old, *
    O Lord, I take great comfort.

53 I am filled with a burning rage, *
    because of the wicked who forsake your law.

54 Your statutes have been like songs to me *
    wherever I have lived as a stranger.

55 I remember your Name in the night, O Lord, *
    and dwell upon your law.

56 This is how it has been with me, *
    because I have kept your commandments.

Heth *Portio mea, Domine*

57 You only are my portion, O LORD; *
   I have promised to keep your words.

58 I entreat you with all my heart, *
   be merciful to me according to your promise.

59 I have considered my ways *
   and turned my feet toward your decrees.

60 I hasten and do not tarry *
   to keep your commandments.

61 Though the cords of the wicked entangle me, *
   I do not forget your law.

62 At midnight I will rise to give you thanks, *
   because of your righteous judgments.

63 I am a companion of all who fear you *
   and of those who keep your commandments.

64 The earth, O LORD, is full of your love; *
   instruct me in your statutes.

Teth *Bonitatem fecisti*

65 O LORD, you have dealt graciously with your servant, *
   according to your word.

66 Teach me discernment and knowledge, *
   for I have believed in your commandments.

67 Before I was afflicted I went astray, *
   but now I keep your word.

68 You are good and you bring forth good; *
   instruct me in your statutes.

69 The proud have smeared me with lies, *
but I will keep your commandments with my whole heart.

70 Their heart is gross and fat, *
but my delight is in your law.

71 It is good for me that I have been afflicted, *
that I might learn your statutes.

72 The law of your mouth is dearer to me *
than thousands in gold and silver.

Twenty-fifth Day: Evening Prayer

Yodh *Manus tuæ fecerunt me*

73 Your hands have made me and fashioned me; *
give me understanding, that I may learn your
commandments.

74 Those who fear you will be glad when they see me, *
because I trust in your word.

75 I know, O LORD, that your judgments are right *
and that in faithfulness you have afflicted me.

76 Let your loving-kindness be my comfort, *
as you have promised to your servant.

77 Let your compassion come to me, that I may live, *
for your law is my delight.

78 Let the arrogant be put to shame, for they wrong me
with lies; *
but I will meditate on your commandments.

79 Let those who fear you turn to me, *
and also those who know your decrees.

80   Let my heart be sound in your statutes, *
       that I may not be put to shame.

Kaph   *Defecit in salutare*

81   My soul has longed for your salvation; *
       I have put my hope in your word.

82   My eyes have failed from watching for your promise, *
       and I say, "When will you comfort me?"

83   I have become like a leather flask in the smoke, *
       but I have not forgotten your statutes.

84   How much longer must I wait? *
       when will you give judgment against those who
          persecute me?

85   The proud have dug pits for me; *
       they do not keep your law.

86   All your commandments are true; *
       help me, for they persecute me with lies.

87   They had almost made an end of me on earth, *
       but I have not forsaken your commandments.

88   In your loving-kindness, revive me, *
       that I may keep the decrees of your mouth.

Lamedh   *In æternum, Domine*

89   O LORD, your word is everlasting; *
       it stands firm in the heavens.

90   Your faithfulness remains from one generation to another; *
       you established the earth, and it abides.

91   By your decree these continue to this day, *
       for all things are your servants.

92   If my delight had not been in your law, *
       I should have perished in my affliction.

93   I will never forget your commandments, *
       because by them you give me life.

94   I am yours; oh, that you would save me! *
       for I study your commandments.

95   Though the wicked lie in wait for me to destroy me, *
       I will apply my mind to your decrees.

96   I see that all things come to an end, *
       but your commandment has no bounds.

Mem   *Quomodo dilexi!*

97   Oh, how I love your law! *
       all the day long it is in my mind.

98   Your commandment has made me wiser than my enemies, *
       and it is always with me.

99   I have more understanding than all my teachers, *
       for your decrees are my study.

100 I am wiser than the elders, *
       because I observe your commandments.

101 I restrain my feet from every evil way, *
       that I may keep your word.

102 I do not shrink from your judgments, *
       because you yourself have taught me.

103 How sweet are your words to my taste! *
       they are sweeter than honey to my mouth.

104 Through your commandments I gain understanding; *
    therefore I hate every lying way.

Nun   *Lucerna pedibus meis*

105 Your word is a lantern to my feet *
    and a light upon my path.

106 I have sworn and am determined *
    to keep your righteous judgments.

107 I am deeply troubled; *
    preserve my life, O LORD, according to your word.

108 Accept, O LORD, the willing tribute of my lips, *
    and teach me your judgments.

109 My life is always in my hand, *
    yet I do not forget your law.

110 The wicked have set a trap for me, *
    but I have not strayed from your commandments.

111 Your decrees are my inheritance for ever; *
    truly, they are the joy of my heart.

112 I have applied my heart to fulfill your statutes *
    for ever and to the end.

Samekh   *Iniquos odio habui*

113 I hate those who have a divided heart, *
    but your law do I love.

114   You are my refuge and shield; *
      my hope is in your word.

115   Away from me, you wicked! *
      I will keep the commandments of my God.

116   Sustain me according to your promise, that I may live, *
      and let me not be disappointed in my hope.

117   Hold me up, and I shall be safe, *
      and my delight shall be ever in your statutes.

118   You spurn all who stray from your statutes; *
      their deceitfulness is in vain.

119   In your sight all the wicked of the earth are but dross; *
      therefore I love your decrees.

120   My flesh trembles with dread of you; *
      I am afraid of your judgments.

Ayin   *Feci judicium*

121   I have done what is just and right; *
      do not deliver me to my oppressors.

122   Be surety for your servant's good; *
      let not the proud oppress me.

123   My eyes have failed from watching for your salvation *
      and for your righteous promise.

124   Deal with your servant according to your loving-kindness *
      and teach me your statutes.

125   I am your servant; grant me understanding, *
      that I may know your decrees.

126   It is time for you to act, O LORD, *
      for they have broken your law.

127 Truly, I love your commandments *
        more than gold and precious stones.

128 I hold all your commandments to be right for me; *
        all paths of falsehood I abhor.

        Pe   *Mirabilia*

129 Your decrees are wonderful; *
        therefore I obey them with all my heart.

130 When your word goes forth it gives light; *
        it gives understanding to the simple.

131 I open my mouth and pant; *
        I long for your commandments.

132 Turn to me in mercy, *
        as you always do to those who love your Name.

133 Steady my footsteps in your word; *
        let no iniquity have dominion over me.

134 Rescue me from those who oppress me, *
        and I will keep your commandments.

135 Let your countenance shine upon your servant *
        and teach me your statutes.

136 My eyes shed streams of tears, *
        because people do not keep your law.

        Sadhe   *Justus es, Domine*

137 You are righteous, O LORD, *
        and upright are your judgments.

138 You have issued your decrees *
     with justice and in perfect faithfulness.

139 My indignation has consumed me, *
     because my enemies forget your words.

140 Your word has been tested to the uttermost, *
     and your servant holds it dear.

141 I am small and of little account, *
     yet I do not forget your commandments.

142 Your justice is an everlasting justice *
     and your law is the truth.

143 Trouble and distress have come upon me, *
     yet your commandments are my delight.

144 The righteousness of your decrees is everlasting; *
     grant me understanding, that I may live.

Twenty-sixth Day: Evening Prayer

Qoph *Clamavi in toto corde meo*

145 I call with my whole heart; *
     answer me, O LORD, that I may keep your statutes.

146 I call to you;
     oh, that you would save me! *
          I will keep your decrees.

147 Early in the morning I cry out to you, *
     for in your word is my trust.

148 My eyes are open in the night watches, *
     that I may meditate upon your promise.

149　Hear my voice, O LORD, according to your loving-kindness; *
　　　according to your judgments, give me life.

150　They draw near who in malice persecute me; *
　　　they are very far from your law.

151　You, O LORD, are near at hand, *
　　　and all your commandments are true.

152　Long have I known from your decrees *
　　　that you have established them for ever.

Resh　*Vide humilitatem*

153　Behold my affliction and deliver me, *
　　　for I do not forget your law.

154　Plead my cause and redeem me; *
　　　according to your promise, give me life.

155　Deliverance is far from the wicked, *
　　　for they do not study your statutes.

156　Great is your compassion, O LORD; *
　　　preserve my life, according to your judgments.

157　There are many who persecute and oppress me, *
　　　yet I have not swerved from your decrees.

158　I look with loathing at the faithless, *
　　　for they have not kept your word.

159　See how I love your commandments! *
　　　O LORD, in your mercy, preserve me.

160　The heart of your word is truth; *
　　　all your righteous judgments endure for evermore.

Shin *Principes persecuti sunt*

161　Rulers have persecuted me without a cause, *
　　　 but my heart stands in awe of your word.

162　I am as glad because of your promise *
　　　 as one who finds great spoils.

163　As for lies, I hate and abhor them, *
　　　 but your law is my love.

164　Seven times a day do I praise you, *
　　　 because of your righteous judgments.

165　Great peace have they who love your law; *
　　　 for them there is no stumbling block.

166　I have hoped for your salvation, O LORD, *
　　　 and I have fulfilled your commandments.

167　I have kept your decrees *
　　　 and I have loved them deeply.

168　I have kept your commandments and decrees, *
　　　 for all my ways are before you.

Taw *Appropinquet deprecatio*

169　Let my cry come before you, O LORD; *
　　　 give me understanding, according to your word.

170　Let my supplication come before you; *
　　　 deliver me, according to your promise.

171　My lips shall pour forth your praise, *
　　　 when you teach me your statutes.

172　My tongue shall sing of your promise, *
　　　 for all your commandments are righteous.

173   Let your hand be ready to help me, *
       for I have chosen your commandments.

174   I long for your salvation, O LORD, *
       and your law is my delight.

175   Let me live, and I will praise you, *
       and let your judgments help me.

176   I have gone astray like a sheep that is lost; *
       search for your servant,
       for I do not forget your commandments.

Twenty-seventh Day: Morning Prayer

120   *Ad Dominum*

1   When I was in trouble, I called to the LORD; *
       I called to the LORD, and he answered me.

2   Deliver me, O LORD, from lying lips *
       and from the deceitful tongue.

3   What shall be done to you, and what more besides, *
       O you deceitful tongue?

4   The sharpened arrows of a warrior, *
       along with hot glowing coals.

5   How hateful it is that I must lodge in Meshech *
       and dwell among the tents of Kedar!

6   Too long have I had to live *
       among the enemies of peace.

7   I am on the side of peace, *
       but when I speak of it, they are for war.

121 *Levavi oculos*

1 I lift up my eyes to the hills; *
    from where is my help to come?

2 My help comes from the LORD, *
    the maker of heaven and earth.

3 He will not let your foot be moved *
    and he who watches over you will not fall asleep.

4 Behold, he who keeps watch over Israel *
    shall neither slumber nor sleep;

5 The LORD himself watches over you; *
    the LORD is your shade at your right hand,

6 So that the sun shall not strike you by day, *
    nor the moon by night.

7 The LORD shall preserve you from all evil; *
    it is he who shall keep you safe.

8 The LORD shall watch over your going out and
                    your coming in, *
    from this time forth for evermore.

122 *Lætatus sum*

1 I was glad when they said to me, *
    "Let us go to the house of the LORD."

2 Now our feet are standing *
    within your gates, O Jerusalem.

3 Jerusalem is built as a city *
    that is at unity with itself;

4   To which the tribes go up,
       the tribes of the Lord, *
          the assembly of Israel,
          to praise the Name of the Lord.

5   For there are the thrones of judgment, *
       the thrones of the house of David.

6   Pray for the peace of Jerusalem: *
       "May they prosper who love you.

7   Peace be within your walls *
       ˉand quietness within your towers.

8   For my brethren and companions' sake, *
       I pray for your prosperity.

9   Because of the house of the Lord our God, *
       I will seek to do you good."

123   *Ad te levavi oculos meos*

1   To you I lift up my eyes, *
       to you enthroned in the heavens.

2   As the eyes of servants look to the hand of their masters, *
       and the eyes of a maid to the hand of her mistress,

3   So our eyes look to the Lord our God, *
       until he show us his mercy.

4   Have mercy upon us, O Lord, have mercy, *
       for we have had more than enough of contempt,

5   Too much of the scorn of the indolent rich, *
       and of the derision of the proud.

124 *Nisi quia Dominus*

1   If the LORD had not been on our side, *
   let Israel now say;

2   If the LORD had not been on our side, *
   when enemies rose up against us;

3   Then would they have swallowed us up alive *
   in their fierce anger toward us;

4   Then would the waters have overwhelmed us *
   and the torrent gone over us;

5   Then would the raging waters *
   have gone right over us.

6   Blessed be the LORD! *
   he has not given us over to be a prey for their teeth.

7   We have escaped like a bird from the snare of the fowler; *
   the snare is broken, and we have escaped.

8   Our help is in the Name of the LORD, *
   the maker of heaven and earth.

125 *Qui confidunt*

1   Those who trust in the LORD are like Mount Zion, *
   which cannot be moved, but stands fast for ever.

2   The hills stand about Jerusalem; *
   so does the LORD stand round about his people,
   from this time forth for evermore.

3   The scepter of the wicked shall not hold sway over the
                land alloted to the just, *
   so that the just shall not put their hands to evil.

4   Show your goodness, O LORD, to those who are good *
     and to those who are true of heart.

5   As for those who turn aside to crooked ways,
     the LORD will lead them away with the evildoers; *
     but peace be upon Israel.

Twenty-seventh Day: Evening Prayer

126   *In convertendo*

1   When the LORD restored the fortunes of Zion, *
     then were we like those who dream.

2   Then was our mouth filled with laughter, *
     and our tongue with shouts of joy.

3   Then they said among the nations, *
     "The LORD has done great things for them."

4   The LORD has done great things for us, *
     and we are glad indeed.

5   Restore our fortunes, O LORD, *
     like the watercourses of the Negev.

6   Those who sowed with tears *
     will reap with songs of joy.

7   Those who go out weeping, carrying the seed, *
     will come again with joy, shouldering their sheaves.

127   *Nisi Dominus*

1   Unless the LORD builds the house, *
     their labor is in vain who build it.

2   Unless the LORD watches over the city, *
        in vain the watchman keeps his vigil.

3   It is in vain that you rise so early and go to bed so late; *
        vain, too, to eat the bread of toil,
        for he gives to his beloved sleep.

4   Children are a heritage from the LORD, *
        and the fruit of the womb is a gift.

5   Like arrows in the hand of a warrior *
        are the children of one's youth.

6   Happy is the man who has his quiver full of them! *
        he shall not be put to shame
        when he contends with his enemies in the gate.

128   *Beati omnes*

1   Happy are they all who fear the LORD, *
        and who follow in his ways!

2   You shall eat the fruit of your labor; *
        happiness and prosperity shall be yours.

3   Your wife shall be like a fruitful vine within your house, *
        your children like olive shoots round about your table.

4   The man who fears the LORD *
        shall thus indeed be blessed.

5   The LORD bless you from Zion, *
        and may you see the prosperity of Jerusalem all the days
            of your life.

6   May you live to see your children's children; *
        may peace be upon Israel.

129 *Sæpe expugnaverunt*

1 "Greatly have they oppressed me since my youth," *
    let Israel now say;

2 "Greatly have they oppressed me since my youth, *
    but they have not prevailed against me."

3 The plowmen plowed upon my back *
    and made their furrows long.

4 The LORD, the Righteous One, *
    has cut the cords of the wicked.

5 Let them be put to shame and thrown back, *
    all those who are enemies of Zion.

6 Let them be like grass upon the housetops, *
    which withers before it can be plucked;

7 Which does not fill the hand of the reaper, *
    nor the bosom of him who binds the sheaves;

8 So that those who go by say not so much as,
"The LORD prosper you. *
    We wish you well in the Name of the LORD."

130 *De profundis*

1 Out of the depths have I called to you, O LORD;
LORD, hear my voice; *
    let your ears consider well the voice of my supplication.

2 If you, LORD, were to note what is done amiss, *
    O Lord, who could stand?

3 For there is forgiveness with you; *
    therefore you shall be feared.

4   I wait for the LORD; my soul waits for him; *
         in his word is my hope.

5   My soul waits for the LORD,
     more than watchmen for the morning, *
         more than watchmen for the morning.

6   O Israel, wait for the LORD, *
         for with the LORD there is mercy;

7   With him there is plenteous redemption, *
         and he shall redeem Israel from all their sins.

131   *Domine, non est*

1   O LORD, I am not proud; *
         I have no haughty looks.

2   I do not occupy myself with great matters, *
         or with things that are too hard for me.

3   But I still my soul and make it quiet,
     like a child upon its mother's breast; *
         my soul is quieted within me.

4   O Israel, wait upon the LORD, *
         from this time forth for evermore.

Twenty-eighth Day: Morning Prayer

132   *Memento, Domine*

1   LORD, remember David, *
         and all the hardships he endured;

2   How he swore an oath to the LORD *
    and vowed a vow to the Mighty One of Jacob:

3   "I will not come under the roof of my house, *
    nor climb up into my bed;

4   I will not allow my eyes to sleep, *
    nor let my eyelids slumber;

5   Until I find a place for the LORD, *
    a dwelling for the Mighty One of Jacob."

6   "The ark! We heard it was in Ephratah; *
    we found it in the fields of Jearim.

7   Let us go to God's dwelling place; *
    let us fall upon our knees before his footstool."

8   Arise, O LORD, into your resting-place, *
    you and the ark of your strength.

9   Let your priests be clothed with righteousness; *
    let your faithful people sing with joy.

10   For your servant David's sake, *
    do not turn away the face of your Anointed.

11   The LORD has sworn an oath to David; *
    in truth, he will not break it:

12   "A son, the fruit of your body *
    will I set upon your throne.

13   If your children keep my covenant
    and my testimonies that I shall teach them, *
    their children will sit upon your throne for evermore."

14   For the LORD has chosen Zion; *
    he has desired her for his habitation:

15   "This shall be my resting-place for ever; *
    here will I dwell, for I delight in her.

16 I will surely bless her provisions, *
   and satisfy her poor with bread.

17 I will clothe her priests with salvation, *
   and her faithful people will rejoice and sing.

18 There will I make the horn of David flourish; *
   I have prepared a lamp for my Anointed.

19 As for his enemies, I will clothe them with shame; *
   but as for him, his crown will shine."

133 *Ecce, quam bonum!*

1 Oh, how good and pleasant it is, *
   when brethren live together in unity!

2 It is like fine oil upon the head *
   that runs down upon the beard,

3 Upon the beard of Aaron, *
   and runs down upon the collar of his robe.

4 It is like the dew of Hermon *
   that falls upon the hills of Zion.

5 For there the LORD has ordained the blessing: *
   life for evermore.

134 *Ecce nunc*

1 Behold now, bless the LORD, all you servants of the LORD, *
   you that stand by night in the house of the LORD.

2 Lift up your hands in the holy place and bless the LORD; *
   the LORD who made heaven and earth bless
                         you out of Zion.

135 *Laudate nomen*

1 Hallelujah!
   Praise the Name of the LORD; *
      give praise, you servants of the LORD,

2 You who stand in the house of the LORD, *
      in the courts of the house of our God.

3 Praise the LORD, for the LORD is good; *
      sing praises to his Name, for it is lovely.

4 For the LORD has chosen Jacob for himself *
      and Israel for his own possession.

5 For I know that the LORD is great, *
      and that our Lord is above all gods.

6 The LORD does whatever pleases him, in heaven and on earth, *
      in the seas and all the deeps.

7 He brings up rain clouds from the ends of the earth; *
      he sends out lightning with the rain,
      and brings the winds out of his storehouse.

8 It was he who struck down the firstborn of Egypt, *
      the firstborn both of man and beast.

9 He sent signs and wonders into the midst of you, O Egypt, *
      against Pharaoh and all his servants.

10 He overthrew many nations *
      and put mighty kings to death:

11 Sihon, king of the Amorites,
   and Og, the king of Bashan, *
      and all the kingdoms of Canaan.

12 He gave their land to be an inheritance, *
      an inheritance for Israel his people.

13 O LORD, your Name is everlasting; *
   your renown, O LORD, endures from age to age.

14 For the LORD gives his people justice *
   and shows compassion to his servants.

15 The idols of the heathen are silver and gold, *
   the work of human hands.

16 They have mouths, but they cannot speak; *
   eyes have they, but they cannot see.

17 They have ears, but they cannot hear; *
   neither is there any breath in their mouth.

18 Those who make them are like them, *
   and so are all who put their trust in them.

19 Bless the LORD, O house of Israel; *
   O house of Aaron, bless the LORD.

20 Bless the LORD, O house of Levi; *
   you who fear the LORD, bless the LORD.

21 Blessed be the LORD out of Zion, *
   who dwells in Jerusalem.
   Hallelujah!

Twenty-eighth Day: Evening Prayer

136 *Confitemini*

1 Give thanks to the LORD, for he is good, *
   for his mercy endures for ever.

2 Give thanks to the God of gods, *
   for his mercy endures for ever.

3   Give thanks to the Lord of lords, *
     for his mercy endures for ever.

4   Who only does great wonders, *
     for his mercy endures for ever;

5   Who by wisdom made the heavens, *
     for his mercy endures for ever;

6   Who spread out the earth upon the waters, *
     for his mercy endures for ever;

7   Who created great lights, *
     for his mercy endures for ever;

8   The sun to rule the day, *
     for his mercy endures for ever;

9   The moon and the stars to govern the night, *
     for his mercy endures for ever.

10   Who struck down the firstborn of Egypt, *
     for his mercy endures for ever;

11   And brought out Israel from among them, *
     for his mercy endures for ever;

12   With a mighty hand and a stretched-out arm, *
     for his mercy endures for ever;

13   Who divided the Red Sea in two, *
     for his mercy endures for ever;

14   And made Israel to pass through the midst of it, *
     for his mercy endures for ever;

15   But swept Pharaoh and his army into the Red Sea, *
     for his mercy endures for ever;

16   Who led his people through the wilderness, *
         for his mercy endures for ever.

17   Who struck down great kings, *
         for his mercy endures for ever;

18   And slew mighty kings, *
         for his mercy endures for ever;

19   Sihon, king of the Amorites, *
         for his mercy endures for ever;

20   And Og, the king of Bashan, *
         for his mercy endures for ever;

21   And gave away their lands for an inheritance, *
         for his mercy endures for ever;

22   An inheritance for Israel his servant, *
         for his mercy endures for ever.

23   Who remembered us in our low estate, *
         for his mercy endures for ever;

24   And delivered us from our enemies, *
         for his mercy endures for ever;

25   Who gives food to all creatures, *
         for his mercy endures for ever.

26   Give thanks to the God of heaven, *
         for his mercy endures for ever.

137 *Super flumina*

1 By the waters of Babylon we sat down and wept, *
   when we remembered you, O Zion.

2 As for our harps, we hung them up *
   on the trees in the midst of that land.

3 For those who led us away captive asked us for a song,
   and our oppressors called for mirth: *
   "Sing us one of the songs of Zion."

4 How shall we sing the LORD's song *
   upon an alien soil?

5 If I forget you, O Jerusalem, *
   let my right hand forget its skill.

6 Let my tongue cleave to the roof of my mouth
   if I do not remember you, *
   if I do not set Jerusalem above my highest joy.

7 Remember the day of Jerusalem, O LORD,
   against the people of Edom, *
   who said, "Down with it! down with it!
   even to the ground!"

8 O Daughter of Babylon, doomed to destruction, *
   happy the one who pays you back
   for what you have done to us!

9 Happy shall he be who takes your little ones, *
   and dashes them against the rock!

138 *Confitebor tibi*

1   I will give thanks to you, O LORD, with my whole heart; *
     before the gods I will sing your praise.

2   I will bow down toward your holy temple
  and praise your Name, *
     because of your love and faithfulness;

3   For you have glorified your Name *
     and your word above all things.

4   When I called, you answered me; *
     you increased my strength within me.

5   All the kings of the earth will praise you, O LORD, *
     when they have heard the words of your mouth.

6   They will sing of the ways of the LORD, *
     that great is the glory of the LORD.

7   Though the LORD be high, he cares for the lowly; *
     he perceives the haughty from afar.

8   Though I walk in the midst of trouble, you keep me safe; *
     you stretch forth your hand against the fury of my enemies;
     your right hand shall save me.

9   The LORD will make good his purpose for me; *
     O LORD, your love endures for ever;
     do not abandon the works of your hands.

139 *Domine, probasti*

1 LORD, you have searched me out and known me; *
      you know my sitting down and my rising up;
      you discern my thoughts from afar.

2 You trace my journeys and my resting-places *
      and are acquainted with all my ways.

3 Indeed, there is not a word on my lips, *
      but you, O LORD, know it altogether.

4 You press upon me behind and before *
      and lay your hand upon me.

5 Such knowledge is too wonderful for me; *
      it is so high that I cannot attain to it.

6 Where can I go then from your Spirit? *
      where can I flee from your presence?

7 If I climb up to heaven, you are there; *
      if I make the grave my bed, you are there also.

8 If I take the wings of the morning *
      and dwell in the uttermost parts of the sea,

9 Even there your hand will lead me *
      and your right hand hold me fast.

10 If I say, "Surely the darkness will cover me, *
      and the light around me turn to night,"

11 Darkness is not dark to you;
   the night is as bright as the day; *
      darkness and light to you are both alike.

12 For you yourself created my inmost parts; *
      you knit me together in my mother's womb.

13   I will thank you because I am marvelously made; *
      your works are wonderful, and I know it well.

14   My body was not hidden from you, *
      while I was being made in secret
      and woven in the depths of the earth.

15   Your eyes beheld my limbs, yet unfinished in the womb;
      all of them were written in your book; *
      they were fashioned day by day,
      when as yet there was none of them.

16   How deep I find your thoughts, O God! *
      how great is the sum of them!

17   If I were to count them, they would be more in number
      than the sand; *
      to count them all, my life span would need to
      be like yours.

18   Oh, that you would slay the wicked, O God! *
      You that thirst for blood, depart from me.

19   They speak despitefully against you; *
      your enemies take your Name in vain.

20   Do I not hate those, O LORD, who hate you? *
      and do I not loathe those who rise up against you?

21   I hate them with a perfect hatred; *
      they have become my own enemies.

22   Search me out, O God, and know my heart; *
      try me and know my restless thoughts.

23   Look well whether there be any wickedness in me *
      and lead me in the way that is everlasting.

140 *Eripe me, Domine*

1 Deliver me, O LORD, from evildoers; *
   protect me from the violent,

2 Who devise evil in their hearts *
   and stir up strife all day long.

3 They have sharpened their tongues like a serpent; *
   adder's poison is under their lips.

4 Keep me, O LORD, from the hands of the wicked; *
   protect me from the violent,
   who are determined to trip me up.

5 The proud have hidden a snare for me
   and stretched out a net of cords; *
   they have set traps for me along the path.

6 I have said to the LORD, "You are my God; *
   listen, O LORD, to my supplication.

7 O Lord GOD, the strength of my salvation, *
   you have covered my head in the day of battle.

8 Do not grant the desires of the wicked, O LORD, *
   nor let their evil plans prosper.

9 Let not those who surround me lift up their heads; *
   let the evil of their lips overwhelm them.

10 Let hot burning coals fall upon them; *
    let them be cast into the mire, never to rise up again."

11 A slanderer shall not be established on the earth, *
    and evil shall hunt down the lawless.

12 I know that the LORD will maintain the cause of the poor *
    and render justice to the needy.

13 Surely, the righteous will give thanks to your Name, *
    and the upright shall continue in your sight.

Twenty-ninth Day: Evening Prayer

141 *Domine, clamavi*

1 O LORD, I call to you; come to me quickly; *
    hear my voice when I cry to you.

2 Let my prayer be set forth in your sight as incense, *
    the lifting up of my hands as the evening sacrifice.

3 Set a watch before my mouth, O LORD,
   and guard the door of my lips; *
    let not my heart incline to any evil thing.

4 Let me not be occupied in wickedness with evildoers, *
    nor eat of their choice foods.

5 Let the righteous smite me in friendly rebuke;
   let not the oil of the unrighteous anoint my head; *
    for my prayer is continually against their wicked deeds.

6 Let their rulers be overthrown in stony places, *
    that they may know my words are true.

7 As when a plowman turns over the earth in furrows, *
    let their bones be scattered at the mouth of the grave.

8 But my eyes are turned to you, Lord GOD; *
    in you I take refuge;
    do not strip me of my life.

9 Protect me from the snare which they have laid for me *
    and from the traps of the evildoers.

10 Let the wicked fall into their own nets, *
    while I myself escape.

142 *Voce mea ad Dominum*

1 I cry to the LORD with my voice; *
    to the LORD I make loud supplication.

2 I pour out my complaint before him *
    and tell him all my trouble.

3 When my spirit languishes within me, you know my path; *
    in the way wherein I walk they have hidden a trap for me.

4 I look to my right hand and find no one who knows me; *
    I have no place to flee to, and no one cares for me.

5 I cry out to you, O LORD; *
    I say, "You are my refuge,
       my portion in the land of the living."

6 Listen to my cry for help, for I have been brought very low; *
    save me from those who pursue me,
       for they are too strong for me.

7 Bring me out of prison, that I may give thanks to your Name; *
    when you have dealt bountifully with me,
       the righteous will gather around me.

143 *Domine, exaudi*

1 LORD, hear my prayer,
    and in your faithfulness heed my supplications; *
       answer me in your righteousness.

2 Enter not into judgment with your servant, *
    for in your sight shall no one living be justified.

3 For my enemy has sought my life;
he has crushed me to the ground; *
    he has made me live in dark places like those who
        are long dead.

4 My spirit faints within me; *
    my heart within me is desolate.

5 I remember the time past;
I muse upon all your deeds; *
    I consider the works of your hands.

6 I spread out my hands to you; *
    my soul gasps to you like a thirsty land.

7 O Lord, make haste to answer me; my spirit fails me; *
do not hide your face from me
    or I shall be like those who go down to the Pit.

8 Let me hear of your loving-kindness in the morning,
for I put my trust in you; *
    show me the road that I must walk,
        for I lift up my soul to you.

9 Deliver me from my enemies, O Lord, *
    for I flee to you for refuge.

10 Teach me to do what pleases you, for you are my God; *
    let your good Spirit lead me on level ground.

11 Revive me, O Lord, for your Name's sake; *
    for your righteousness' sake, bring me out of trouble.

12 Of your goodness, destroy my enemies
and bring all my foes to naught, *
    for truly I am your servant.

144 *Benedictus Dominus*

1   Blessed be the LORD my rock! *
   who trains my hands to fight and my fingers to battle;

2   My help and my fortress, my stronghold and my deliverer, *
   my shield in whom I trust,
   who subdues the peoples under me.

3   O LORD, what are we that you should care for us? *
   mere mortals that you should think of us?

4   We are like a puff of wind; *
   our days are like a passing shadow.

5   Bow your heavens, O LORD, and come down; *
   touch the mountains, and they shall smoke.

6   Hurl the lightning and scatter them; *
   shoot out your arrows and rout them.

7   Stretch out your hand from on high; *
   rescue me and deliver me from the great waters,
   from the hand of foreign peoples,

8   Whose mouths speak deceitfully *
   and whose right hand is raised in falsehood.

9   O God, I will sing to you a new song; *
   I will play to you on a ten-stringed lyre.

10 You give victory to kings *
   and have rescued David your servant.

11 Rescue me from the hurtful sword *
   and deliver me from the hand of foreign peoples,

12 Whose mouths speak deceitfully *
   and whose right hand is raised in falsehood.

13 May our sons be like plants well nurtured from their youth, *
    and our daughters like sculptured corners of a palace.

14 May our barns be filled to overflowing with all manner
        of crops; *
    may the flocks in our pastures increase by thousands
            and tens of thousands;
    may our cattle be fat and sleek.

15 May there be no breaching of the walls, no going into exile, *
    no wailing in the public squares.

16 Happy are the people of whom this is so! *
    happy are the people whose God is the LORD!

145 *Exaltabo te, Deus*

1 I will exalt you, O God my King, *
    and bless your Name for ever and ever.

2 Every day will I bless you *
    and praise your Name for ever and ever.

3 Great is the LORD and greatly to be praised; *
    there is no end to his greatness.

4 One generation shall praise your works to another *
    and shall declare your power.

5 I will ponder the glorious splendor of your majesty *
    and all your marvelous works.

6 They shall speak of the might of your wondrous acts, *
    and I will tell of your greatness.

7 They shall publish the remembrance of your great goodness; *
    they shall sing of your righteous deeds.

8   The LORD is gracious and full of compassion, *
     slow to anger and of great kindness.

9   The LORD is loving to everyone *
     and his compassion is over all his works.

10   All your works praise you, O LORD, *
     and your faithful servants bless you.

11   They make known the glory of your kingdom *
     and speak of your power;

12   That the peoples may know of your power *
     and the glorious splendor of your kingdom.

13   Your kingdom is an everlasting kingdom; *
     your dominion endures throughout all ages.

14   The LORD is faithful in all his words *
     and merciful in all his deeds.

15   The LORD upholds all those who fall; *
     he lifts up those who are bowed down.

16   The eyes of all wait upon you, O LORD, *
     and you give them their food in due season.

17   You open wide your hand *
     and satisfy the needs of every living creature.

18   The LORD is righteous in all his ways *
     and loving in all his works.

19   The LORD is near to those who call upon him, *
     to all who call upon him faithfully.

20   He fulfills the desire of those who fear him; *
     he hears their cry and helps them.

21   The LORD preserves all those who love him, *
     but he destroys all the wicked.

22   My mouth shall speak the praise of the LORD; *
      let all flesh bless his holy Name for ever and ever.

146   *Lauda, anima mea*

1   Hallelujah!
      Praise the LORD, O my soul! *
        I will praise the LORD as long as I live;
        I will sing praises to my God while I have my being.

2   Put not your trust in rulers, nor in any child of earth, *
      for there is no help in them.

3   When they breathe their last, they return to earth, *
      and in that day their thoughts perish.

4   Happy are they who have the God of Jacob for their help! *
      whose hope is in the LORD their God;

5   Who made heaven and earth, the seas, and all that is in them; *
      who keeps his promise for ever;

6   Who gives justice to those who are oppressed, *
      and food to those who hunger.

7   The LORD sets the prisoners free;
      the LORD opens the eyes of the blind; *
        the LORD lifts up those who are bowed down;

8   The LORD loves the righteous;
      the LORD cares for the stranger; *
        he sustains the orphan and widow,
        but frustrates the way of the wicked.

9   The LORD shall reign for ever, *
      your God, O Zion, throughout all generations.
      Hallelujah!

147 *Laudate Dominum*

1 Hallelujah!
How good it is to sing praises to our God! *
   how pleasant it is to honor him with praise!

2 The LORD rebuilds Jerusalem; *
   he gathers the exiles of Israel.

3 He heals the brokenhearted *
   and binds up their wounds.

4 He counts the number of the stars *
   and calls them all by their names.

5 Great is our LORD and mighty in power; *
   there is no limit to his wisdom.

6 The LORD lifts up the lowly, *
   but casts the wicked to the ground.

7 Sing to the LORD with thanksgiving; *
   make music to our God upon the harp.

8 He covers the heavens with clouds *
   and prepares rain for the earth;

9 He makes grass to grow upon the mountains *
   and green plants to serve mankind.

10 He provides food for flocks and herds *
   and for the young ravens when they cry.

11 He is not impressed by the might of a horse; *
   he has no pleasure in the strength of a man;

12 But the LORD has pleasure in those who fear him, *
   in those who await his gracious favor.

13 Worship the LORD, O Jerusalem; *
    praise your God, O Zion;

14 For he has strengthened the bars of your gates; *
    he has blessed your children within you.

15 He has established peace on your borders; *
    he satisfies you with the finest wheat.

16 He sends out his command to the earth, *
    and his word runs very swiftly.

17 He gives snow like wool; *
    he scatters hoarfrost like ashes.

18 He scatters his hail like bread crumbs; *
    who can stand against his cold?

19 He sends forth his word and melts them; *
    he blows with his wind, and the waters flow.

20 He declares his word to Jacob, *
    his statutes and his judgments to Israel.

21 He has not done so to any other nation; *
    to them he has not revealed his judgments.
    Hallelujah!

148 *Laudate Dominum*

1 Hallelujah!
    Praise the LORD from the heavens; *
    praise him in the heights.

2 Praise him, all you angels of his; *
    praise him, all his host.

3 Praise him, sun and moon; *
    praise him, all you shining stars.

4   Praise him, heaven of heavens, *
        and you waters above the heavens.

5   Let them praise the Name of the LORD; *
        for he commanded, and they were created.

6   He made them stand fast for ever and ever; *
        he gave them a law which shall not pass away.

7   Praise the LORD from the earth, *
        you sea-monsters and all deeps;

8   Fire and hail, snow and fog, *
        tempestuous wind, doing his will;

9   Mountains and all hills, *
        fruit trees and all cedars;

10   Wild beasts and all cattle, *
        creeping things and wingèd birds;

11   Kings of the earth and all peoples, *
        princes and all rulers of the world;

12   Young men and maidens, *
        old and young together.

13   Let them praise the Name of the LORD, *
        for his Name only is exalted,
        his splendor is over earth and heaven.

14   He has raised up strength for his people
     and praise for all his loyal servants, *
        the children of Israel, a people who are near him.
        Hallelujah!

149 *Cantate Domino*

1 Hallelujah!
Sing to the LORD a new song; *
  sing his praise in the congregation of the faithful.

2 Let Israel rejoice in his Maker; *
  let the children of Zion be joyful in their King.

3 Let them praise his Name in the dance; *
  let them sing praise to him with timbrel and harp.

4 For the LORD takes pleasure in his people *
  and adorns the poor with victory.

5 Let the faithful rejoice in triumph; *
  let them be joyful on their beds.

6 Let the praises of God be in their throat *
  and a two-edged sword in their hand;

7 To wreak vengeance on the nations *
  and punishment on the peoples;

8 To bind their kings in chains *
  and their nobles with links of iron;

9 To inflict on them the judgment decreed; *
  this is glory for all his faithful people.
  Hallelujah!

150 *Laudate Dominum*

1 Hallelujah!
Praise God in his holy temple; *
  praise him in the firmament of his power.

2   Praise him for his mighty acts; *
     praise him for his excellent greatness.

3   Praise him with the blast of the ram's-horn; *
     praise him with lyre and harp.

4   Praise him with timbrel and dance; *
     praise him with strings and pipe.

5   Praise him with resounding cymbals; *
     praise him with loud-clanging cymbals.

6   Let everything that has breath *
     praise the LORD.
     Hallelujah!

Prayers and Thanksgivings

Prayers and Thanksgivings

Prayers

Prayers for the World

1. For Joy in God's Creation
2. For all Sorts and Conditions of Men
3. For the Human Family
4. For Peace
5. For Peace among the Nations
6. For our Enemies

Prayers for the Church

7. For the Church
8. For the Mission of the Church
9. For Clergy and People
10. For the Diocese
11. For the Parish
12. For a Church Convention or Meeting
13. For the Election of a Bishop or other Minister
14. For the Unity of the Church
15. For those about to be Baptized or to renew their Baptismal Covenant
16. For Monastic Orders and Vocations
17. For Church Musicians and Artists

Prayers for the Ordained Ministry are on pages 205 and 256.

Prayers for National Life

18. For our Country
19. For the President of the United States and all in Civil Authority
20. For Congress or a State Legislature
21. For Courts of Justice
22. For Sound Government

Other Prayers

Thanksgivings

General Thanksgivings

The General Thanksgiving is on pages 58 and 101.

Thanksgivings for the Church

Thanksgivings for National Life

Thanksgiving for the Social Order

Thanksgivings for the Natural Order

Thanksgivings for Family and Personal Life

Thanksgivings for the departed are on pages 487-489 and 503-504.

The term "Various Occasions" in the following pages refers to the numbered Collects beginning on pages 199 and 251.

Prayers and Thanksgivings

Prayers

For use after the Collects of Morning or Evening Prayer or separately.

Prayers originally composed in traditional idiom have not been modernized; but, except in certain classical prayers which do not lend themselves to modernization, pronouns and verbs have been put in italics to assist in rendering them into contemporary speech.

Prayers for the World

1. *For Joy in God's Creation*

O heavenly Father, *who hast* filled the world with beauty: Open our eyes to behold *thy* gracious hand in all *thy* works; that, rejoicing in *thy* whole creation, we may learn to serve *thee* with gladness; for the sake of him through whom all things were made, *thy* Son Jesus Christ our Lord. *Amen.*

2. *For All Sorts and Conditions of Men*

O God, the creator and preserver of all mankind, we humbly beseech thee for all sorts and conditions of men; that thou wouldest be pleased to make thy ways known unto them, thy saving health unto all nations. More especially we pray for thy holy Church universal; that it may be so guided and governed by thy good Spirit, that all who profess and call themselves Christians may be led into the way of truth, and hold the faith in unity of spirit, in the bond of peace, and in righteousness of life. Finally, we commend to thy fatherly goodness all those who are in any ways afflicted or distressed, in mind, body, or estate; [especially those for whom our prayers are desired]; that it may please thee to comfort and relieve them according to their several necessities, giving them patience under their sufferings, and a happy issue out of all their afflictions. And this we beg for Jesus Christ's sake. *Amen.*

3. *For the Human Family*

O God, you made us in your own image and redeemed us through Jesus your Son: Look with compassion on the whole human family; take away the arrogance and hatred which infect our hearts; break down the walls that separate us; unite us in bonds of love; and work through our struggle and confusion to accomplish your purposes on earth; that, in your good time, all nations and races may serve you in harmony around your heavenly throne; through Jesus Christ our Lord. *Amen.*

4. *For Peace*

See also Various Occasions no. 18.

Eternal God, in whose perfect kingdom no sword is drawn but the sword of righteousness, no strength known but the strength of love: So mightily spread abroad your Spirit, that all peoples may be gathered under the banner of the Prince of Peace, as children of one Father; to whom be dominion and glory, now and for ever. *Amen.*

5. For Peace Among the Nations

Almighty God our heavenly Father, guide the nations of the world into the way of justice and truth, and establish among them that peace which is the fruit of righteousness, that they may become the kingdom of our Lord and Savior Jesus Christ. *Amen.*

6. For our Enemies

O God, the Father of all, whose Son commanded us to love our enemies: Lead them and us from prejudice to truth; deliver them and us from hatred, cruelty, and revenge; and in your good time enable us all to stand reconciled before you; through Jesus Christ our Lord. *Amen.*

Prayers for the Church

7. For the Church

Gracious Father, we pray for thy holy Catholic Church. Fill it with all truth, in all truth with all peace. Where it is corrupt, purify it; where it is in error, direct it; where in any thing it is amiss, reform it. Where it is right, strengthen it; where it is in want, provide for it; where it is divided, reunite it; for the sake of Jesus Christ thy Son our Savior. *Amen.*

8. For the Mission of the Church

See also the prayers for the Mission of the Church on pages 58, 100 and 101, and Various Occasions no. 16.

Everliving God, whose will it is that all should come to you through your Son Jesus Christ: Inspire our witness to him, that all may know the power of his forgiveness and the hope of his resurrection; who lives and reigns with you and the Holy Spirit, one God, now and for ever. *Amen.*

9. *For Clergy and People*

Almighty and everlasting God, from whom cometh every good and perfect gift: Send down upon our bishops, and other clergy, and upon the congregations committed to their charge, the healthful Spirit of thy grace; and, that they may truly please thee, pour upon them the continual dew of thy blessing. Grant this, O Lord, for the honor of our Advocate and Mediator, Jesus Christ. *Amen.*

10. *For the Diocese*

O God, by your grace you have called us in this Diocese to a goodly fellowship of faith. Bless our Bishop(s) N. [and N.], and other clergy, and all our people. Grant that your Word may be truly preached and truly heard, your Sacraments faithfully administered and faithfully received. By your Spirit, fashion our lives according to the example of your Son, and grant that we may show the power of your love to all among whom we live; through Jesus Christ our Lord. *Amen.*

11. *For the Parish*

Almighty and everliving God, ruler of all things in heaven and earth, hear our prayers for this parish family. Strengthen the faithful, arouse the careless, and restore the penitent. Grant us all things necessary for our common life, and bring us all to be of one heart and mind within your holy Church; through Jesus Christ our Lord. *Amen.*

12. For a Church Convention or Meeting

See also Various Occasions no. 13.

Almighty and everliving God, source of all wisdom and understanding, be present with those who take counsel [in _____] for the renewal and mission of your Church. Teach us in all things to seek first your honor and glory. Guide us to perceive what is right, and grant us both the courage to pursue it and the grace to accomplish it; through Jesus Christ our Lord. *Amen.*

13. For the Election of a Bishop or other Minister

Almighty God, giver of every good gift: Look graciously on your Church, and so guide the minds of those who shall choose a bishop for this Diocese (*or*, rector for this parish), that we may receive a faithful pastor, who will care for your people and equip us for our ministries; through Jesus Christ our Lord. *Amen.*

14. For the Unity of the Church

See also Various Occasions no. 14, and Collect no. 6 (page 395).

O God the Father of our Lord Jesus Christ, our only Savior, the Prince of Peace: Give us grace seriously to lay to heart the great dangers we are in by our unhappy divisions; take away all hatred and prejudice, and whatever else may hinder us from godly union and concord; that, as there is but one Body and one Spirit, one hope of our calling, one Lord, one Faith, one Baptism, one God and Father of us all, so we may be all of one heart and of one soul, united in one holy bond of truth and peace, of faith and charity, and may with one mind and one mouth glorify *thee*; through Jesus Christ our Lord. *Amen.*

15. For those about to be Baptized or
to renew their Baptismal Covenant

O God, you prepared your disciples for the coming of the
Spirit through the teaching of your Son Jesus Christ: Make
the hearts and minds of your servants ready to receive the
blessing of the Holy Spirit, that they may be filled with the
strength of his presence; through Jesus Christ our Lord.
Amen.

For those to be ordained, see Various Occasions no. 15.

16. For Monastic Orders and Vocations

O Lord Jesus Christ, you became poor for our sake, that we
might be made rich through your poverty: Guide and sanctify,
we pray, those whom you call to follow you under the vows
of poverty, chastity, and obedience, that by their prayer and
service they may enrich your Church, and by their life and
worship may glorify your Name; for you reign with the Father
and the Holy Spirit, one God, now and for ever. *Amen.*

17. For Church Musicians and Artists

O God, whom saints and angels delight to worship in
heaven: Be ever present with your servants who seek through
art and music to perfect the praises offered by your people on
earth; and grant to them even now glimpses of your beauty,
and make them worthy at length to behold it unveiled for
evermore; through Jesus Christ our Lord. *Amen.*

Prayers for National Life

18. *For our Country*

See also Various Occasions no. 17.

Almighty God, who hast given us this good land for our
heritage: We humbly beseech thee that we may always prove
ourselves a people mindful of thy favor and glad to do thy will.
Bless our land with honorable industry, sound learning, and
pure manners. Save us from violence, discord, and confusion;
from pride and arrogance, and from every evil way. Defend
our liberties, and fashion into one united people the multitudes
brought hither out of many kindreds and tongues. Endue
with the spirit of wisdom those to whom in thy Name we entrust
the authority of government, that there may be justice and
peace at home, and that, through obedience to thy law, we
may show forth thy praise among the nations of the earth.
In the time of prosperity, fill our hearts with thankfulness,
and in the day of trouble, suffer not our trust in thee to fail;
all which we ask through Jesus Christ our Lord. *Amen.*

19. *For the President of the United States and all in Civil Authority*

O Lord our Governor, whose glory is in all the world: We
commend this nation to *thy* merciful care, that, being guided
by *thy* Providence, we may dwell secure in *thy* peace. Grant
to the President of the United States, the Governor of this
State (*or* Commonwealth), and to all in authority, wisdom
and strength to know and to do *thy* will. Fill them with the
love of truth and righteousness, and make them ever mindful
of their calling to serve this people in *thy* fear; through Jesus
Christ our Lord, who *liveth* and *reigneth* with *thee* and the
Holy Spirit, one God, world without end. *Amen.*

20. For Congress or a State Legislature

O God, the fountain of wisdom, whose will is good and gracious, and whose law is truth: We beseech *thee* so to guide and bless our Senators and Representatives in Congress assembled (*or* in the Legislature of this State, *or* Commonwealth), that they may enact such laws as shall please *thee*, to the glory of *thy* Name and the welfare of this people; through Jesus Christ our Lord. *Amen.*

21. For Courts of Justice

Almighty God, *who sittest* in the throne judging right: We humbly beseech *thee* to bless the courts of justice and the magistrates in all this land; and give *unto* them the spirit of wisdom and understanding, that they may discern the truth, and impartially administer the law in the fear of *thee* alone; through him who shall come to be our Judge, *thy* Son our Savior Jesus Christ. *Amen.*

22. For Sound Government

The responses in italics may be omitted.

O Lord our Governor, bless the leaders of our land, that we may be a people at peace among ourselves and a blessing to other nations of the earth.
Lord, keep this nation under your care.

To the President and members of the Cabinet, to Governors of States, Mayors of Cities, and to all in administrative authority, grant wisdom and grace in the exercise of their duties.
Give grace to your servants, O Lord.

To Senators and Representatives, and those who make our laws in States, Cities, and Towns, give courage, wisdom, and foresight to provide for the needs of all our people, and to fulfill our obligations in the community of nations.
Give grace to your servants, O Lord.

To the Judges and officers of our Courts give understanding and integrity, that human rights may be safeguarded and justice served.
Give grace to your servants, O Lord.

And finally, teach our people to rely on your strength and to accept their responsibilities to their fellow citizens, that they may elect trustworthy leaders and make wise decisions for the well-being of our society; that we may serve you faithfully in our generation and honor your holy Name.
For yours is the kingdom, O Lord, and you are exalted as head above all. Amen.

23. *For Local Government*

Almighty God our heavenly Father, send down upon those who hold office in this State (Commonwealth, City, County, Town, _____) the spirit of wisdom, charity, and justice; that with steadfast purpose they may faithfully serve in their offices to promote the well-being of all people; through Jesus Christ our Lord. *Amen.*

24. *For an Election*

Almighty God, to whom we must account for all our powers and privileges: Guide the people of the United States (*or* of this community) in the election of officials and representatives; that, by faithful administration and wise laws, the rights of all may be protected and our nation be enabled to fulfill your purposes; through Jesus Christ our Lord. *Amen.*

25. *For those in the Armed Forces of our Country*

Almighty God, we commend to your gracious care and keeping all the men and women of our armed forces at home and abroad. Defend them day by day with your heavenly grace; strengthen them in their trials and temptations; give them courage to face the perils which beset them; and grant them a sense of your abiding presence wherever they may be; through Jesus Christ our Lord. *Amen.*

26. *For those who suffer for the sake of Conscience*

O God our Father, whose Son forgave his enemies while he was suffering shame and death: Strengthen those who suffer for the sake of conscience; when they are accused, save them from speaking in hate; when they are rejected, save them from bitterness; when they are imprisoned, save them from despair; and to us your servants, give grace to respect their witness and to discern the truth, that our society may be cleansed and strengthened. This we ask for the sake of Jesus Christ, our merciful and righteous Judge. *Amen.*

Prayers for the Social Order

27. *For Social Justice*

See also Various Occasions no. 21.

Grant, O God, that your holy and life-giving Spirit may so move every human heart [and especially the hearts of the people of this land], that barriers which divide us may crumble, suspicions disappear, and hatreds cease; that our divisions being healed, we may live in justice and peace; through Jesus Christ our Lord. *Amen.*

28. In Times of Conflict

O God, you have bound us together in a common life. Help us, in the midst of our struggles for justice and truth, to confront one another without hatred or bitterness, and to work together with mutual forbearance and respect; through Jesus Christ our Lord. *Amen.*

29. For Agriculture

See also Various Occasions no. 19.

Almighty God, we thank you for making the earth fruitful, so that it might produce what is needed for life: Bless those who work in the fields; give us seasonable weather; and grant that we may all share the fruits of the earth, rejoicing in your goodness; through Jesus Christ our Lord. *Amen.*

For prayers for Industry and Labor, see Various Occasions no. 19, no. 24, and no. 25.

30. For the Unemployed

Heavenly Father, we remember before you those who suffer want and anxiety from lack of work. Guide the people of this land so to use our public and private wealth that all may find suitable and fulfilling employment, and receive just payment for their labor; through Jesus Christ our Lord. *Amen.*

31. For Schools and Colleges

O Eternal God, bless all schools, colleges, and universities [and especially ⎯⎯⎯⎯], that they may be lively centers for sound learning, new discovery, and the pursuit of wisdom; and grant that those who teach and those who learn may find you to be the source of all truth; through Jesus Christ our Lord. *Amen.*

For Education, see Various Occasions no. 23.

32. For the Good Use of Leisure

O God, in the course of this busy life, give us times of
refreshment and peace; and grant that we may so use our
leisure to rebuild our bodies and renew our minds, that our
spirits may be opened to the goodness of your creation;
through Jesus Christ our Lord. *Amen.*

33. For Cities

Heavenly Father, in your Word you have given us a vision of
that holy City to which the nations of the world bring their
glory: Behold and visit, we pray, the cities of the earth.
Renew the ties of mutual regard which form our civic life.
Send us honest and able leaders. Enable us to eliminate
poverty, prejudice, and oppression, that peace may prevail
with righteousness, and justice with order, and that men and
women from different cultures and with differing talents may
find with one another the fulfillment of their humanity;
through Jesus Christ our Lord. *Amen.*

34. For Towns and Rural Areas

Lord Christ, when you came among us, you proclaimed the
kingdom of God in villages, towns, and lonely places: Grant
that your presence and power may be known throughout this
land. Have mercy upon all of us who live and work in rural
areas [especially _____]; and grant that all the people
of our nation may give thanks to you for food and drink and
all other bodily necessities of life, respect those who labor to
produce them, and honor the land and the water from which
these good things come. All this we ask in your holy Name.
Amen.

35. For the Poor and the Neglected

Almighty and most merciful God, we remember before you all poor and neglected persons whom it would be easy for us to forget: the homeless and the destitute, the old and the sick, and all who have none to care for them. Help us to heal those who are broken in body or spirit, and to turn their sorrow into joy. Grant this, Father, for the love of your Son, who for our sake became poor, Jesus Christ our Lord. *Amen.*

36. For the Oppressed

Look with pity, O heavenly Father, upon the people in this land who live with injustice, terror, disease, and death as their constant companions. Have mercy upon us. Help us to eliminate our cruelty to these our neighbors. Strengthen those who spend their lives establishing equal protection of the law and equal opportunities for all. And grant that every one of us may enjoy a fair portion of the riches of this land; through Jesus Christ our Lord. *Amen.*

37. For Prisons and Correctional Institutions

Lord Jesus, for our sake you were condemned as a criminal: Visit our jails and prisons with your pity and judgment. Remember all prisoners, and bring the guilty to repentance and amendment of life according to your will, and give them hope for their future. When any are held unjustly, bring them release; forgive us, and teach us to improve our justice. Remember those who work in these institutions; keep them humane and compassionate; and save them from becoming brutal or callous. And since what we do for those in prison, O Lord, we do for you, constrain us to improve their lot. All this we ask for your mercy's sake. *Amen.*

38. *For the Right Use of God's Gifts*

Almighty God, whose loving hand *hath* given us all that we possess: Grant us grace that we may honor *thee* with our substance, and, remembering the account which we must one day give, may be faithful stewards of *thy* bounty, through Jesus Christ our Lord. *Amen.*

39. *For those who Influence Public Opinion*

Almighty God, you proclaim your truth in every age by many voices: Direct, in our time, we pray, those who speak where many listen and write what many read; that they may do their part in making the heart of this people wise, its mind sound, and its will righteous; to the honor of Jesus Christ our Lord. *Amen.*

For Social Service, see Various Occasions no.22.

Prayers for the Natural Order

40. *For Knowledge of God's Creation*

Almighty and everlasting God, you made the universe with all its marvelous order, its atoms, worlds, and galaxies, and the infinite complexity of living creatures: Grant that, as we probe the mysteries of your creation, we may come to know you more truly, and more surely fulfill our role in your eternal purpose; in the name of Jesus Christ our Lord. *Amen.*

41. *For the Conservation of Natural Resources*

See also Various Occasions no. 19.

Almighty God, in giving us dominion over things on earth, you made us fellow workers in your creation: Give us wisdom and reverence so to use the resources of nature, that no one may suffer from our abuse of them, and that generations yet to come may continue to praise you for your bounty; through Jesus Christ our Lord. *Amen.*

42. *For the Harvest of Lands and Waters*

O gracious Father, *who openest thine* hand and *fillest* all things living with plenteousness: Bless the lands and waters, and multiply the harvests of the world; let *thy* Spirit go forth, that it may renew the face of the earth; show *thy* loving-kindness, that our land may give her increase; and save us from selfish use of what *thou givest*, that men and women everywhere may give *thee* thanks; through Christ our Lord. *Amen.*

43. *For Rain*

O God, heavenly Father, who by *thy* Son Jesus Christ *hast* promised to all those who seek *thy* kingdom and its righteousness all things necessary to sustain their life: Send us, we entreat *thee*, in this time of need, such moderate rain and showers, that we may receive the fruits of the earth, to our comfort and to *thy* honor; through Jesus Christ our Lord. *Amen.*

44. *For the Future of the Human Race*

O God our heavenly Father, you have blessed us and given us dominion over all the earth: Increase our reverence before the mystery of life; and give us new insight into your purposes for the human race, and new wisdom and determination in making provision for its future in accordance with your will; through Jesus Christ our Lord. *Amen.*

Prayers for Family and Personal Life

45. *For Families*

Almighty God, our heavenly Father, who settest the solitary in families: We commend to thy continual care the homes in which thy people dwell. Put far from them, we beseech thee, every root of bitterness, the desire of vainglory, and the pride of life. Fill them with faith, virtue, knowledge, temperance, patience, godliness. Knit together in constant affection those who, in holy wedlock, have been made one flesh. Turn the hearts of the parents to the children, and the hearts of the children to the parents; and so enkindle fervent charity among us all, that we may evermore be kindly affectioned one to another; through Jesus Christ our Lord. *Amen.*

A prayer for parents is on page 444.

46. *For the Care of Children*

Almighty God, heavenly Father, you have blessed us with the joy and care of children: Give us calm strength and patient wisdom as we bring them up, that we may teach them to love whatever is just and true and good, following the example of our Savior Jesus Christ. *Amen.*

47. *For Young Persons*

God our Father, you see your children growing up in an unsteady and confusing world: Show them that your ways give more life than the ways of the world, and that following you is better than chasing after selfish goals. Help them to take failure, not as a measure of their worth, but as a chance for a new start. Give them strength to hold their faith in you, and to keep alive their joy in your creation; through Jesus Christ our Lord. *Amen.*

48. *For Those Who Live Alone*

Almighty God, whose Son had nowhere to lay his head: Grant that those who live alone may not be lonely in their solitude, but that, following in his steps, they may find fulfillment in loving you and their neighbors; through Jesus Christ our Lord. *Amen.*

49. *For the Aged*

Look with mercy, O God our Father, on all whose increasing years bring them weakness, distress, or isolation. Provide for them homes of dignity and peace; give them understanding helpers, and the willingness to accept help; and, as their strength diminishes, increase their faith and their assurance of your love. This we ask in the name of Jesus Christ our Lord. *Amen.*

50. *For a Birthday*

O God, our times are in your hand: Look with favor, we pray, on your servant N. as *he* begins another year. Grant that *he* may grow in wisdom and grace, and strengthen *his* trust in your goodness all the days of *his* life; through Jesus Christ our Lord. *Amen.*

51. *For a Birthday*

Watch over thy child, O Lord, as *his* days increase; bless and guide *him* wherever *he* may be. Strengthen *him* when *he* stands; comfort *him* when discouraged or sorrowful; raise *him* up if *he* fall; and in *his* heart may thy peace which passeth understanding abide all the days of *his* life; through Jesus Christ our Lord. *Amen.*

52. *For the Absent*

O God, whose fatherly care *reacheth* to the uttermost parts of the earth: We humbly beseech *thee* graciously to behold and bless those whom we love, now absent from us. Defend them from all dangers of soul and body; and grant that both they and we, drawing nearer to *thee*, may be bound together by *thy* love in the communion of *thy* Holy Spirit, and in the fellowship of *thy* saints; through Jesus Christ our Lord. *Amen.*

53. For Travelers

O God, our heavenly Father, whose glory fills the whole creation, and whose presence we find wherever we go: Preserve those who travel [in particular _____]; surround them with your loving care; protect them from every danger; and bring them in safety to their journey's end; through Jesus Christ our Lord. *Amen.*

54. For those we Love

Almighty God, we entrust all who are dear to us to *thy* never-failing care and love, for this life and the life to come, knowing that *thou art* doing for them better things than we can desire or pray for; through Jesus Christ our Lord. *Amen.*

55. For a Person in Trouble or Bereavement

O merciful Father, who hast taught us in thy holy Word that thou dost not willingly afflict or grieve the children of men: Look with pity upon the sorrows of thy servant for whom our prayers are offered. Remember *him*, O Lord, in mercy, nourish *his* soul with patience, comfort *him* with a sense of thy goodness, lift up thy countenance upon *him*, and give *him* peace; through Jesus Christ our Lord. *Amen.*

Prayers for the sick are on pages 458-461. See also Various Occasions no. 20.

56. For the Victims of Addiction

O blessed Lord, you ministered to all who came to you: Look with compassion upon all who through addiction have lost their health and freedom. Restore to them the assurance of your unfailing mercy; remove from them the fears that beset them; strengthen them in the work of their recovery; and to those who care for them, give patient understanding and persevering love. *Amen.*

57. For Guidance

Direct us, O Lord, in all our doings with *thy* most gracious favor, and further us with *thy* continual help; that in all our works begun, continued, and ended in *thee*, we may glorify *thy* holy Name, and finally, by *thy* mercy, obtain everlasting life; through Jesus Christ our Lord. *Amen.*

58. For Guidance

O God, by whom the meek are guided in judgment, and light *riseth* up in darkness for the godly: Grant us, in all our doubts and uncertainties, the grace to ask what *thou wouldest* have us to do, that the Spirit of wisdom may save us from all false choices, and that in *thy* light we may see light, and in *thy* straight path may not stumble; through Jesus Christ our Lord. *Amen.*

59. For Quiet Confidence

O God of peace, *who hast* taught us that in returning and rest we shall be saved, in quietness and in confidence shall be our strength: By the might of *thy* Spirit lift us, we pray *thee*, to *thy* presence, where we may be still and know that *thou art* God; through Jesus Christ our Lord. *Amen.*

60. For Protection

Assist us mercifully, O Lord, in these our supplications and prayers, and dispose the way of *thy* servants towards the attainment of everlasting salvation; that, among all the changes and chances of this mortal life, they may ever be defended by *thy* gracious and ready help; through Jesus Christ our Lord. *Amen.*

61. A Prayer of Self-Dedication

Almighty and eternal God, so draw our hearts to *thee*, so guide our minds, so fill our imaginations, so control our wills, that we may be wholly *thine*, utterly dedicated *unto thee*; and then use us, we pray *thee*, as *thou wilt*, and always to *thy* glory and the welfare of *thy* people; through our Lord and Savior Jesus Christ. *Amen.*

62. *A Prayer attributed to St. Francis*

Lord, make us instruments of your peace. Where there is hatred, let us sow love; where there is injury, pardon; where there is discord, union; where there is doubt, faith; where there is despair, hope; where there is darkness, light; where there is sadness, joy. Grant that we may not so much seek to be consoled as to console; to be understood as to understand; to be loved as to love. For it is in giving that we receive; it is in pardoning that we are pardoned; and it is in dying that we are born to eternal life. *Amen.*

Other Prayers

Prayers for Friday, Saturday, and Sunday, and for morning and evening, are on pages 56, 69, 98, and 123.

63. *In the Evening*

O Lord, support us all the day long, until the shadows lengthen, and the evening comes, and the busy world is hushed, and the fever of life is over, and our work is done. Then in *thy* mercy, grant us a safe lodging, and a holy rest, and peace at the last. *Amen.*

64. *Before Worship*

O Almighty God, *who pourest* out on all who desire it the spirit of grace and of supplication: Deliver us, when we draw near to *thee*, from coldness of heart and wanderings of mind, that with steadfast thoughts and kindled affections we may worship *thee* in spirit and in truth; through Jesus Christ our Lord. *Amen.*

65. *For the Answering of Prayer*

Almighty God, who hast promised to hear the petitions of those who ask in thy Son's Name: We beseech thee mercifully to incline thine ear to us who have now made our prayers and supplications unto thee; and grant that those things which we have faithfully asked according to thy will, may effectually be obtained, to the relief of our necessity, and to the setting forth of thy glory; through Jesus Christ our Lord. *Amen.*

66. *Before Receiving Communion*

See also the Prayer of Humble Access on page 337.

Be present, be present, O Jesus, our great High Priest, as you were present with your disciples, and be known to us in the breaking of bread; who live and reign with the Father and the Holy Spirit, now and for ever. *Amen.*

67. *After Receiving Communion*

O Lord Jesus Christ, who in a wonderful Sacrament hast left unto us a memorial of thy passion: Grant us, we beseech thee, so to venerate the sacred mysteries of thy Body and Blood, that we may ever perceive within ourselves the fruit of thy redemption; who livest and reignest with the Father and the Holy Spirit, one God, for ever and ever. *Amen.*

68. *After Worship*

Grant, we beseech *thee*, Almighty God, that the words which we have heard this day with our outward ears, may, through *thy* grace, be so grafted inwardly in our hearts, that they may bring forth in us the fruit of good living, to the honor and praise of *thy* Name; through Jesus Christ our Lord. *Amen.*

69. *On Sunday*

O God our King, by the resurrection of your Son Jesus Christ on the first day of the week, you conquered sin, put death to flight, and gave us the hope of everlasting life: Redeem all our days by this victory; forgive our sins, banish our fears, make us bold to praise you and to do your will; and steel us to wait for the consummation of your kingdom on the last great Day; through the same Jesus Christ our Lord. *Amen.*

70. *Grace at Meals*

Give us grateful hearts, our Father, for all *thy* mercies, and make us mindful of the needs of others; through Jesus Christ our Lord. *Amen.*

or this

Bless, O Lord, *thy* gifts to our use and us to *thy* service; for Christ's sake. *Amen.*

or this

Blessed are you, O Lord God, King of the Universe, for you give us food to sustain our lives and make our hearts glad; through Jesus Christ our Lord. *Amen.*

or this

For these and all his mercies, God's holy Name be blessed and praised; through Jesus Christ our Lord. *Amen.*

Thanksgivings

General Thanksgivings

1. *A General Thanksgiving*

Accept, O Lord, our thanks and praise for all that you have done for us. We thank you for the splendor of the whole creation, for the beauty of this world, for the wonder of life, and for the mystery of love.

We thank you for the blessing of family and friends, and for the loving care which surrounds us on every side.

We thank you for setting us at tasks which demand our best efforts, and for leading us to accomplishments which satisfy and delight us.

We thank you also for those disappointments and failures that lead us to acknowledge our dependence on you alone.

Above all, we thank you for your Son Jesus Christ; for the truth of his Word and the example of his life; for his steadfast obedience, by which he overcame temptation; for his dying, through which he overcame death; and for his rising to life again, in which we are raised to the life of your kingdom.

Grant us the gift of your Spirit, that we may know him and make him known; and through him, at all times and in all places, may give thanks to you in all things. *Amen.*

2. *A Litany of Thanksgiving*

For optional use on Thanksgiving Day, in place of the Prayers of the People at the Eucharist, or at any time after the Collects at Morning or Evening Prayer, or separately.

Let us give thanks to God our Father for all his gifts so freely bestowed upon us.

For the beauty and wonder of your creation, in earth and sky and sea,
We thank you, Lord.

For all that is gracious in the lives of men and women, revealing the image of Christ,
We thank you, Lord.

For our daily food and drink, our homes and families, and our friends,
We thank you, Lord.

For minds to think, and hearts to love, and hands to serve,
We thank you, Lord.

For health and strength to work, and leisure to rest and play,
We thank you, Lord.

For the brave and courageous, who are patient in suffering and faithful in adversity,
We thank you, Lord.

For all valiant seekers after truth, liberty, and justice,
We thank you, Lord.

For the communion of saints, in all times and places,
We thank you, Lord.

Above all, we give you thanks for the great mercies and promises given to us in Christ Jesus our Lord;
To him be praise and glory, with you, O Father, and the Holy Spirit, now and for ever. Amen.

See also The General Thanksgiving on pages 58 and 101.

Thanksgivings for the Church

3. For the Mission of the Church

Almighty God, you sent your Son Jesus Christ to reconcile the world to yourself: We praise and bless you for those whom you have sent in the power of the Spirit to preach the Gospel to all nations. We thank you that in all parts of the earth a community of love has been gathered together by their prayers and labors, and that in every place your servants call upon your Name; for the kingdom and the power and the glory are yours for ever. *Amen.*

4. For the Saints and Faithful Departed

See also the prayer "O God, the King of Saints," page 489 and 504.

We give thanks to you, O Lord our God, for all your servants and witnesses of time past: for Abraham, the father of believers and Sarah his wife; for Moses, the lawgiver, and Aaron, the priest; for Miriam and Joshua, Deborah and Gideon, and Samuel with Hannah his mother; for Isaiah and all the prophets; for Mary, the mother of our Lord; for Peter and Paul and all the apostles; for Mary and Martha, and Mary Magdalene; for Stephen, the first martyr, and all the martyrs and saints in every age and in every land. In your mercy, O Lord our God, give us, as you gave to them, the hope of salvation and the promise of eternal life; through Jesus Christ our Lord, the first-born of many from the dead. *Amen.*

Thanksgivings for National Life

5. For the Nation

Almighty God, giver of all good things:
We thank you for the natural majesty and beauty of this land.
They restore us, though we often destroy them.
Heal us.

We thank you for the great resources of this nation. They make us rich, though we often exploit them.
Forgive us.

We thank you for the men and women who have made this country strong. They are models for us, though we often fall short of them.
Inspire us.

We thank you for the torch of liberty which has been lit in this land. It has drawn people from every nation, though we have often hidden from its light.
Enlighten us.

We thank you for the faith we have inherited in all its rich variety. It sustains our life, though we have been faithless again and again.
Renew us.

Help us, O Lord, to finish the good work here begun. Strengthen our efforts to blot out ignorance and prejudice, and to abolish poverty and crime. And hasten the day when all our people, with many voices in one united chorus, will glorify your holy Name. *Amen.*

6. *For Heroic Service*

O Judge of the nations, we remember before you with grateful hearts the men and women of our country who in the day of decision ventured much for the liberties we now enjoy. Grant that we may not rest until all the people of this land share the benefits of true freedom and gladly accept its disciplines. This we ask in the Name of Jesus Christ our Lord. *Amen.*

Thanksgiving for the Social Order

7. *For the Diversity of Races and Cultures*

O God, who created all peoples in your image, we thank you for the wonderful diversity of races and cultures in this world. Enrich our lives by ever-widening circles of fellowship, and show us your presence in those who differ most from us, until our knowledge of your love is made perfect in our love for all your children; through Jesus Christ our Lord. *Amen.*

Thanksgivings for the Natural Order

8. *For the Beauty of the Earth*

We give you thanks, most gracious God, for the beauty of earth and sky and sea; for the richness of mountains, plains, and rivers; for the songs of birds and the loveliness of flowers. We praise you for these good gifts, and pray that we may safeguard them for our posterity. Grant that we may continue to grow in our grateful enjoyment of your abundant creation, to the honor and glory of your Name, now and for ever. *Amen.*

9. *For the Harvest*

Most gracious God, by whose knowledge the depths are broken up and the clouds drop down the dew: We yield thee hearty thanks and praise for the return of seedtime and harvest, for the increase of the ground and the gathering in of its fruits, and for all the other blessings of thy merciful providence bestowed upon this nation and people. And, we beseech thee, give us a just sense of these great mercies, such as may appear in our lives by a humble, holy, and obedient walking before thee all our days; through Jesus Christ our Lord, to whom, with thee and the Holy Ghost be all glory and honor, world without end. *Amen.*

Thanksgivings for Family and Personal Life

10. *For the Gift of a Child*

See also the Thanksgiving for a Child on page 439.

Heavenly Father, you sent your own Son into this world. We thank you for the life of this child, N., entrusted to our care. Help us to remember that we are all your children, and so to love and nurture *him*, that *he* may attain to that full stature intended for *him* in your eternal kingdom; for the sake of your dear Son, Jesus Christ our Lord. *Amen.*

11. *For the Restoration of Health*

Almighty God and heavenly Father, we give *thee* humble thanks because *thou hast* been graciously pleased to deliver from *his* sickness *thy* servant N., in whose behalf we bless and praise *thy* Name. Grant, O gracious Father, that *he*, through *thy* help, may live in this world according to *thy* will, and also be partaker of everlasting glory in the life to come; through Jesus Christ our Lord. *Amen.*

Thanksgivings for the departed are on pages 487-489 and 503-504.

An Outline of the Faith

Concerning the Catechism

This catechism is primarily intended for use by parish priests, deacons, and lay catechists, to give an outline for instruction. It is a commentary on the creeds, but is not meant to be a complete statement of belief and practice; rather, it is a point of departure for the teacher, and it is cast in the traditional question and answer form for ease of reference.

The second use of this catechism is to provide a brief summary of the Church's teaching for an inquiring stranger who picks up a Prayer Book.

It may also be used to form a simple service; since the matter is arranged under headings, it is suitable for selective use, and the leader may introduce prayers and hymns as needed.

An Outline of the Faith

commonly called the Catechism

Human Nature

Q. What are we by nature?

A. We are part of God's creation, made in the image of God.

Q. What does it mean to be created in the image of God?

A. It means that we are free to make choices: to love, to create, to reason, and to live in harmony with creation and with God.

Q. Why then do we live apart from God and out of harmony with creation?

A. From the beginning, human beings have misused their freedom and made wrong choices.

Q. Why do we not use our freedom as we should?

A. Because we rebel against God, and we put ourselves in the place of God.

Q. What help is there for us?

A. Our help is in God.

Q. How did God first help us?

A. God first helped us by revealing himself and his will, through nature and history, through many seers and saints, and especially through the prophets of Israel.

God the Father

Q. What do we learn about God as creator from the revelation to Israel?

A. We learn that there is one God, the Father Almighty, creator of heaven and earth, of all that is, seen and unseen.

Q. What does this mean?

A. This means that the universe is good, that it is the work of a single loving God who creates, sustains, and directs it.

Q. What does this mean about our place in the universe?

A. It means that the world belongs to its creator; and that we are called to enjoy it and to care for it in accordance with God's purposes.

Q. What does this mean about human life?

A. It means that all people are worthy of respect and honor, because all are created in the image of God, and all can respond to the love of God.

Q. How was this revelation handed down to us?

A. This revelation was handed down to us through a community created by a covenant with God.

The Old Covenant

Q. What is meant by a covenant with God?

A. A covenant is a relationship initiated by God, to which a body of people responds in faith.

Q. What is the Old Covenant?

A. The Old Covenant is the one given by God to the Hebrew people.

Q. What did God promise them?

A. God promised that they would be his people to bring all the nations of the world to him.

Q. What response did God require from the chosen people?
A. God required the chosen people to be faithful; to love justice, to do mercy, and to walk humbly with their God.

Q. Where is this Old Covenant to be found?
A. The covenant with the Hebrew people is to be found in the books which we call the Old Testament.

Q. Where in the Old Testament is God's will for us shown most clearly?
A. God's will for us is shown most clearly in the Ten Commandments.

The Ten Commandments

See pages 317 and 350.

Q. What are the Ten Commandments?
A. The Ten Commandments are the laws given to Moses and the people of Israel.

Q. What do we learn from these commandments?
A. We learn two things: our duty to God, and our duty to our neighbors.

Q. What is our duty to God?
A. Our duty is to believe and trust in God;
    I To love and obey God and to bring others to know him;
    II To put nothing in the place of God;
    III To show God respect in thought, word, and deed;
    IV And to set aside regular times for worship, prayer, and the study of God's ways.

Q. What is our duty to our neighbors?
A. Our duty to our neighbors is to love them as ourselves, and to do to other people as we wish them to do to us;

    V To love, honor, and help our parents and family; to honor those in authority, and to meet their just demands;

    VI To show respect for the life God has given us; to work and pray for peace; to bear no malice, prejudice, or hatred in our hearts; and to be kind to all the creatures of God;

    VII To use all our bodily desires as God intended;

    VIII To be honest and fair in our dealings; to seek justice, freedom, and the necessities of life for all people; and to use our talents and possessions as ones who must answer for them to God;

    IX To speak the truth, and not to mislead others by our silence;

    X To resist temptations to envy, greed, and jealousy; to rejoice in other people's gifts and graces; and to do our duty for the love of God, who has called us into fellowship with him.

Q. What is the purpose of the Ten Commandments?
A. The Ten Commandments were given to define our relationship with God and our neighbors.

Q. Since we do not fully obey them, are they useful at all?
A. Since we do not fully obey them, we see more clearly our sin and our need for redemption.

Sin and Redemption

Q. What is sin?
A. Sin is the seeking of our own will instead of the will of God, thus distorting our relationship with God, with other people, and with all creation.

Q. How does sin have power over us?

A. Sin has power over us because we lose our liberty when our relationship with God is distorted.

Q. What is redemption?

A. Redemption is the act of God which sets us free from the power of evil, sin, and death.

Q. How did God prepare us for redemption?

A. God sent the prophets to call us back to himself, to show us our need for redemption, and to announce the coming of the Messiah.

Q. What is meant by the Messiah?

A. The Messiah is one sent by God to free us from the power of sin, so that with the help of God we may live in harmony with God, within ourselves, with our neighbors, and with all creation.

Q. Who do we believe is the Messiah?

A. The Messiah, or Christ, is Jesus of Nazareth, the only Son of God.

God the Son

Q. What do we mean when we say that Jesus is the only Son of God?

A. We mean that Jesus is the only perfect image of the Father, and shows us the nature of God.

Q. What is the nature of God revealed in Jesus?

A. God is love.

Q. What do we mean when we say that Jesus was conceived by the power of the Holy Spirit and became incarnate from the Virgin Mary?

A. We mean that by God's own act, his divine Son received our human nature from the Virgin Mary, his mother.

Q. Why did he take our human nature?

A. The divine Son became human, so that in him human beings might be adopted as children of God, and be made heirs of God's kingdom.

Q. What is the great importance of Jesus' suffering and death?

A. By his obedience, even to suffering and death, Jesus made the offering which we could not make; in him we are freed from the power of sin and reconciled to God.

Q. What is the significance of Jesus' resurrection?

A. By his resurrection, Jesus overcame death and opened for us the way of eternal life.

Q. What do we mean when we say that he descended to the dead?

A. We mean that he went to the departed and offered them also the benefits of redemption.

Q. What do we mean when we say that he ascended into heaven and is seated at the right hand of the Father?

A. We mean that Jesus took our human nature into heaven where he now reigns with the Father and intercedes for us.

Q. How can we share in his victory over sin, suffering, and death?

A. We share in his victory when we are baptized into the New Covenant and become living members of Christ.

The New Covenant

Q. What is the New Covenant?

A. The New Covenant is the new relationship with God given by Jesus Christ, the Messiah, to the apostles; and, through them, to all who believe in him.

Q. What did the Messiah promise in the New Covenant?
A. Christ promised to bring us into the kingdom of God and give us life in all its fullness.

Q. What response did Christ require?
A. Christ commanded us to believe in him and to keep his commandments.

Q. What are the commandments taught by Christ?
A. Christ taught us the Summary of the Law and gave us the New Commandment.

Q. What is the Summary of the Law?
A. You shall love the Lord your God with all your heart, with all your soul, and with all your mind. This is the first and the great commandment. And the second is like it: You shall love your neighbor as yourself.

Q. What is the New Commandment?
A. The New Commandment is that we love one another as Christ loved us.

Q. Where may we find what Christians believe about Christ?
A. What Christians believe about Christ is found in the Scriptures and summed up in the creeds.

The Creeds

See pages 53, 96, 326, 327, and 864.

Q. What are the creeds?
A. The creeds are statements of our basic beliefs about God.

Q. How many creeds does this Church use in its worship?
A. This Church uses two creeds: The Apostles' Creed and the Nicene Creed.

Q. What is the Apostles' Creed?
A. The Apostles' Creed is the ancient creed of Baptism; it is used in the Church's daily worship to recall our Baptismal Covenant.

Q. What is the Nicene Creed?
A. The Nicene Creed is the creed of the universal Church and is used at the Eucharist.

Q. What, then, is the Athanasian Creed?
A. The Athanasian Creed is an ancient document proclaiming the nature of the Incarnation and of God as Trinity.

Q. What is the Trinity?
A. The Trinity is one God: Father, Son, and Holy Spirit.

The Holy Spirit

Q. Who is the Holy Spirit?
A. The Holy Spirit is the Third Person of the Trinity, God at work in the world and in the Church even now.

Q. How is the Holy Spirit revealed in the Old Covenant?
A. The Holy Spirit is revealed in the Old Covenant as the giver of life, the One who spoke through the prophets.

Q. How is the Holy Spirit revealed in the New Covenant?
A. The Holy Spirit is revealed as the Lord who leads us into all truth and enables us to grow in the likeness of Christ.

Q. How do we recognize the presence of the Holy Spirit in our lives?
A. We recognize the presence of the Holy Spirit when we confess Jesus Christ as Lord and are brought into love and harmony with God, with ourselves, with our neighbors, and with all creation.

Q. How do we recognize the truths taught by the Holy
    Spirit?
A. We recognize truths to be taught by the Holy Spirit
    when they are in accord with the Scriptures.

The Holy Scriptures

Q. What are the Holy Scriptures?
A. The Holy Scriptures, commonly called the Bible, are the
    books of the Old and New Testaments; other books,
    called the Apocrypha, are often included in the Bible.

Q. What is the Old Testament?
A. The Old Testament consists of books written by the
    people of the Old Covenant, under the inspiration of the
    Holy Spirit, to show God at work in nature and history.

Q. What is the New Testament?
A. The New Testament consists of books written by the
    people of the New Covenant, under the inspiration of
    the Holy Spirit, to set forth the life and teachings of
    Jesus and to proclaim the Good News of the Kingdom
    for all people.

Q. What is the Apocrypha?
A. The Apocrypha is a collection of additional books
    written by people of the Old Covenant, and used in
    the Christian Church.

Q. Why do we call the Holy Scriptures the Word of God?
A. We call them the Word of God because God inspired
    their human authors and because God still speaks to us
    through the Bible.

Q. How do we understand the meaning of the Bible?
A. We understand the meaning of the Bible by the help of

the Holy Spirit, who guides the Church in the true interpretation of the Scriptures.

The Church

Q. What is the Church?
A. The Church is the community of the New Covenant.

Q. How is the Church described in the Bible?
A. The Church is described as the Body of which Jesus Christ is the Head and of which all baptized persons are members. It is called the People of God, the New Israel, a holy nation, a royal priesthood, and the pillar and ground of truth.

Q. How is the Church described in the creeds?
A. The Church is described as one, holy, catholic, and apostolic.

Q. Why is the Church described as one?
A. The Church is one, because it is one Body, under one Head, our Lord Jesus Christ.

Q. Why is the Church described as holy?
A. The Church is holy, because the Holy Spirit dwells in it, consecrates its members, and guides them to do God's work.

Q. Why is the Church described as catholic?
A. The Church is catholic, because it proclaims the whole Faith to all people, to the end of time.

Q. Why is the Church described as apostolic?
A. The Church is apostolic, because it continues in the teaching and fellowship of the apostles and is sent to carry out Christ's mission to all people.

Q. What is the mission of the Church?
A. The mission of the Church is to restore all people to unity with God and each other in Christ.

Q. How does the Church pursue its mission?
A. The Church pursues its mission as it prays and worships, proclaims the Gospel, and promotes justice, peace, and love.

Q. Through whom does the Church carry out its mission?
A. The Church carries out its mission through the ministry of all its members.

The Ministry

Q. Who are the ministers of the Church?
A. The ministers of the Church are lay persons, bishops, priests, and deacons.

Q. What is the ministry of the laity?
A. The ministry of lay persons is to represent Christ and his Church; to bear witness to him wherever they may be; and, according to the gifts given them, to carry on Christ's work of reconciliation in the world; and to take their place in the life, worship, and governance of the Church.

Q. What is the ministry of a bishop?
A. The ministry of a bishop is to represent Christ and his Church, particularly as apostle, chief priest, and pastor of a diocese; to guard the faith, unity, and discipline of the whole Church; to proclaim the Word of God; to act in Christ's name for the reconciliation of the world and the building up of the Church; and to ordain others to continue Christ's ministry.

Q. What is the ministry of a priest or presbyter?
A. The ministry of a priest is to represent Christ and his Church, particularly as pastor to the people; to share with the bishop in the overseeing of the Church; to proclaim the Gospel; to administer the sacraments; and to bless and declare pardon in the name of God.

Q. What is the ministry of a deacon?
A. The ministry of a deacon is to represent Christ and his Church, particularly as a servant of those in need; and to assist bishops and priests in the proclamation of the Gospel and the administration of the sacraments.

Q. What is the duty of all Christians?
A. The duty of all Christians is to follow Christ; to come together week by week for corporate worship; and to work, pray, and give for the spread of the kingdom of God.

Prayer and Worship

Q. What is prayer?
A. Prayer is responding to God, by thought and by deeds, with or without words.

Q. What is Christian Prayer?
A. Christian prayer is response to God the Father, through Jesus Christ, in the power of the Holy Spirit.

Q. What prayer did Christ teach us?
A. Our Lord gave us the example of prayer known as the Lord's Prayer. *See page 364.*

Q. What are the principal kinds of prayer?
A. The principal kinds of prayer are adoration, praise, thanksgiving, penitence, oblation, intercession, and petition.

Q. What is adoration?
A. Adoration is the lifting up of the heart and mind to God, asking nothing but to enjoy God's presence.

Q. Why do we praise God?
A. We praise God, not to obtain anything, but because God's Being draws praise from us.

Q. For what do we offer thanksgiving?
A. Thanksgiving is offered to God for all the blessings of this life, for our redemption, and for whatever draws us closer to God.

Q. What is penitence?
A. In penitence, we confess our sins and make restitution where possible, with the intention to amend our lives.

Q. What is prayer of oblation?
A. Oblation is an offering of ourselves, our lives and labors, in union with Christ, for the purposes of God.

Q. What are intercession and petition?
A. Intercession brings before God the needs of others; in petition, we present our own needs, that God's will may be done.

Q. What is corporate worship?
A. In corporate worship, we unite ourselves with others to acknowledge the holiness of God, to hear God's Word, to offer prayer, and to celebrate the sacraments.

The Sacraments

Q. What are the sacraments?
A. The sacraments are outward and visible signs of inward and spiritual grace, given by Christ as sure and certain means by which we receive that grace.

Q. What is grace?
A. Grace is God's favor towards us, unearned and undeserved; by grace God forgives our sins, enlightens our minds, stirs our hearts, and strengthens our wills.

Q. What are the two great sacraments of the Gospel?
A. The two great sacraments given by Christ to his Church are Holy Baptism and the Holy Eucharist.

Holy Baptism

Q. What is Holy Baptism?
A. Holy Baptism is the sacrament by which God adopts us as his children and makes us members of Christ's Body, the Church, and inheritors of the kingdom of God.

Q. What is the outward and visible sign in Baptism?
A. The outward and visible sign in Baptism is water, in which the person is baptized in the Name of the Father, and of the Son, and of the Holy Spirit.

Q. What is the inward and spiritual grace in Baptism?
A. The inward and spiritual grace in Baptism is union with Christ in his death and resurrection, birth into God's family the Church, forgiveness of sins, and new life in the Holy Spirit.

Q. What is required of us at Baptism?
A. It is required that we renounce Satan, repent of our sins, and accept Jesus as our Lord and Savior.

Q. Why then are infants baptized?
A. Infants are baptized so that they can share citizenship in the Covenant, membership in Christ, and redemption by God.

Q. How are the promises for infants made and carried out?

A.   Promises are made for them by their parents and sponsors, who guarantee that the infants will be brought up within the Church, to know Christ and be able to follow him.

The Holy Eucharist

Q.   What is the Holy Eucharist?
A.   The Holy Eucharist is the sacrament commanded by Christ for the continual remembrance of his life, death, and resurrection, until his coming again.

Q.   Why is the Eucharist called a sacrifice?
A.   Because the Eucharist, the Church's sacrifice of praise and thanksgiving, is the way by which the sacrifice of Christ is made present, and in which he unites us to his one offering of himself.

Q.   By what other names is this service known?
A.   The Holy Eucharist is called the Lord's Supper, and Holy Communion; it is also known as the Divine Liturgy, the Mass, and the Great Offering.

Q.   What is the outward and visible sign in the Eucharist?
A.   The outward and visible sign in the Eucharist is bread and wine, given and received according to Christ's command.

Q.   What is the inward and spiritual grace given in the Eucharist?
A.   The inward and spiritual grace in the Holy Communion is the Body and Blood of Christ given to his people, and received by faith.

Q.   What are the benefits which we receive in the Lord's Supper?
A.   The benefits we receive are the forgiveness of our sins,

the strengthening of our union with Christ and one
another, and the foretaste of the heavenly banquet which
is our nourishment in eternal life.

Q. What is required of us when we come to the Eucharist?
A. It is required that we should examine our lives, repent
of our sins, and be in love and charity with all people.

Other Sacramental Rites

Q. What other sacramental rites evolved in the Church
under the guidance of the Holy Spirit?
A. Other sacramental rites which evolved in the Church
include confirmation, ordination, holy matrimony,
reconciliation of a penitent, and unction.

Q. How do they differ from the two sacraments of the
Gospel?
A. Although they are means of grace, they are not
necessary for all persons in the same way that Baptism
and the Eucharist are.

Q. What is Confirmation?
A. Confirmation is the rite in which we express a mature
commitment to Christ, and receive strength from the
Holy Spirit through prayer and the laying on of hands
by a bishop.

Q. What is required of those to be confirmed?
A. It is required of those to be confirmed that they have
been baptized, are sufficiently instructed in the Christian
Faith, are penitent for their sins, and are ready to affirm
their confession of Jesus Christ as Savior and Lord.

Q. What is Ordination?
A. Ordination is the rite in which God gives authority and
the grace of the Holy Spirit to those being made bishops,

priests, and deacons, through prayer and the laying on of hands by bishops.

Q. What is Holy Matrimony?

A. Holy Matrimony is Christian marriage, in which the woman and man enter into a life-long union, make their vows before God and the Church, and receive the grace and blessing of God to help them fulfill their vows.

Q. What is Reconciliation of a Penitent?

A. Reconciliation of a Penitent, or Penance, is the rite in which those who repent of their sins may confess them to God in the presence of a priest, and receive the assurance of pardon and the grace of absolution.

Q. What is Unction of the Sick?

A. Unction is the rite of anointing the sick with oil, or the laying on of hands, by which God's grace is given for the healing of spirit, mind, and body.

Q. Is God's activity limited to these rites?

A. God does not limit himself to these rites; they are patterns of countless ways by which God uses material things to reach out to us.

Q. How are the sacraments related to our Christian hope?

A. Sacraments sustain our present hope and anticipate its future fulfillment.

The Christian Hope

Q. What is the Christian hope?

A. The Christian hope is to live with confidence in newness and fullness of life, and to await the coming of Christ in glory, and the completion of God's purpose for the world.

Q. What do we mean by the coming of Christ in glory?
A. By the coming of Christ in glory, we mean that Christ will come, not in weakness but in power, and will make all things new.

Q. What do we mean by heaven and hell?
A. By heaven, we mean eternal life in our enjoyment of God; by hell, we mean eternal death in our rejection of God.

Q. Why do we pray for the dead?
A. We pray for them, because we still hold them in our love, and because we trust that in God's presence those who have chosen to serve him will grow in his love, until they see him as he is.

Q. What do we mean by the last judgment?
A. We believe that Christ will come in glory and judge the living and the dead.

Q. What do we mean by the resurrection of the body?
A. We mean that God will raise us from death in the fullness of our being, that we may live with Christ in the communion of the saints.

Q. What is the communion of saints?
A. The communion of saints is the whole family of God, the living and the dead, those whom we love and those whom we hurt, bound together in Christ by sacrament, prayer, and praise.

Q. What do we mean by everlasting life?
A. By everlasting life, we mean a new existence, in which we are united with all the people of God, in the joy of fully knowing and loving God and each other.

Q. What, then, is our assurance as Christians?
A. Our assurance as Christians is that nothing, not even death, shall separate us from the love of God which is in Christ Jesus our Lord. Amen.

Historical
Documents
of the Church

Definition of the Union of the Divine and Human Natures in the Person of Christ

Council of Chalcedon, 451 A.D., Act V

Therefore, following the holy fathers, we all with one accord teach men to acknowledge one and the same Son, our Lord Jesus Christ, at once complete in Godhead and complete in manhood, truly God and truly man, consisting also of a reasonable soul and body; of one substance (homoousios) with the Father as regards his Godhead, and at the same time of one substance with us as regards his manhood; like us in all respects, apart from sin; as regards his Godhead, begotten of the Father before the ages, but yet as regards his manhood begotten, for us men and for our salvation, of Mary the Virgin, the God-bearer (Theotokos); one and the same Christ, Son, Lord, Only-begotten, recognized in two natures, without confusion, without change, without division, without separation; the distinction of natures being in no way annulled by the union, but rather the characteristics of each nature being preserved and coming together to form one person and subsistence, not as parted or separated into two persons, but one and the same Son and Only-begotten God the Word, Lord Jesus Christ; even as the prophets from earliest times spoke of him, and our Lord Jesus Christ himself taught us, and the creed of the Fathers has handed down to us.

Quicunque Vult

commonly called

The Creed of Saint Athanasius

Whosoever will be saved, before all things it is necessary that he hold the Catholic Faith.
Which Faith except everyone do keep whole and undefiled, without doubt he shall perish everlastingly.
And the Catholic Faith is this: That we worship one God in Trinity, and Trinity in Unity, neither confounding the Persons, nor dividing the Substance.
For there is one Person of the Father, another of the Son, and another of the Holy Ghost.
But the Godhead of the Father, of the Son, and of the Holy Ghost, is all one, the Glory equal, the Majesty co-eternal.
Such as the Father is, such is the Son, and such is the Holy Ghost.
The Father uncreate, the Son uncreate, and the Holy Ghost uncreate.
The Father incomprehensible, the Son incomprehensible, and the Holy Ghost incomprehensible.
The Father eternal, the Son eternal, and the Holy Ghost eternal.
And yet they are not three eternals, but one eternal.
As also there are not three incomprehensibles, nor three uncreated, but one uncreated, and one incomprehensible.
So likewise the Father is Almighty, the Son Almighty, and the Holy Ghost Almighty.
And yet they are not three Almighties, but one Almighty.

So the Father is God, the Son is God, and the Holy Ghost is God.

And yet they are not three Gods, but one God.

So likewise the Father is Lord, the Son Lord, and the Holy Ghost Lord.

And yet not three Lords, but one Lord.

For like as we are compelled by the Christian verity to acknowledge every Person by
himself to be both God and Lord,

So are we forbidden by the Catholic Religion, to say, There be three Gods, or three Lords.

The Father is made of none, neither created, nor begotten.

The Son is of the Father alone, not made, nor created, but begotten.

The Holy Ghost is of the Father and of the Son, neither made, nor created, nor begotten,
but proceeding.

So there is one Father, not three Fathers; one Son, not three Sons; one Holy Ghost, not three
Holy Ghosts.

And in this Trinity none is afore, or after other; none is greater, or less than another;

But the whole three Persons are co-eternal together and co-equal.

So that in all things, as is aforesaid, the Unity in Trinity and the Trinity in Unity is to be
worshipped.

He therefore that will be saved must thus think of the Trinity.

Furthermore, it is necessary to everlasting salvation that he also believe rightly the
Incarnation of our Lord Jesus Christ.

For the right Faith is, that we believe and confess, that our Lord Jesus Christ, the Son of
God, is God and Man;

God, of the Substance of the Father, begotten before the worlds; and Man, of the Substance
of his Mother, born in the world;

Perfect God and perfect Man, of a reasonable soul and human flesh subsisting;

Equal to the Father, as touching his Godhead; and inferior to the Father, as touching his
Manhood.

Who although he be God and Man, yet he is not two, but one Christ;

One, not by conversion of the Godhead into flesh, but by taking of the Manhood into God;

One altogether; not by confusion of Substance, but by unity of Person.

For as the reasonable soul and flesh is one man, so God and Man is one Christ;

Who suffered for our salvation, descended into hell, rose again the third day from the dead.

He ascended into heaven, he sitteth on the right hand of the Father, God Almighty, from
whence he shall come to judge the quick and the dead.

At whose coming all men shall rise again with their bodies and shall give account for their
own works.

And they that have done good shall go into life everlasting; and they that have done evil into
everlasting fire.

This is the Catholic Faith, which except a man believe faithfully, he cannot be saved.

Preface

The First Book of Common Prayer (1549)

There was never any thing by the wit of man so well devised, or so sure established, which in continuance of time hath not been corrupted: as, among other things, it may plainly appear by the common prayers in the Church, commonly called Divine Service: the first original and ground whereof, if a man would search out by the ancient fathers, he shall find, that the same was not ordained, but of a good purpose, and for a great advancement of godliness: For they so ordered the matter, that all the whole Bible (or the greatest part thereof) should be read over once in the year, intending thereby, that the Clergy, and especially such as were Ministers of the congregation, should (by often reading, and meditation of God's word) be stirred up to godliness themselves, and be more able to exhort others by wholesome doctrine, and to confute them that were adversaries to the truth. And further, that the people (by daily hearing of holy Scripture read in the Church) should continually profit more and more in the knowledge of God, and be the more inflamed with the love of his true religion.

But these many years passed, this godly and decent order of the ancient fathers hath been so altered, broken, and neglected, by planting in uncertain stories, Legends, Responds, Verses, vain repetitions, Commemorations, and Synodals, that commonly when any book of the Bible was begun, before three or four Chapters were read out, all the rest were unread. And in this sort the book of Isaiah was begun in Advent, and the book of Genesis in Septuagesima; but they were only begun, and never read through. After a like sort were other books of holy Scripture used. And moreover, whereas St. Paul would have such language spoken to the people in the Church, as they might understand, and have profit by hearing the same, the Service in the Church of England (these many years) hath been read in Latin to the people, which they understood not; so that they have heard with their ears only; and their hearts, spirit, and mind, have not been edified thereby. And furthermore, notwithstanding that the ancient fathers had divided the Psalms into seven portions, whereof every one was called a nocturn, now of late time a few of them have been daily said (and oft repeated), and the rest utterly omitted. Moreover, the number and hardness of the Rules called the Pie, and the manifold changings of the service, was the cause, that to turn the Book only, was so hard and intricate a matter, that many times, there was more business to find out what should be read, than to read it when it was found out.

These inconveniences therefore considered, here is set forth such an order, whereby the same shall be redressed. And for a readiness in this matter, here is drawn out a Kalendar for that purpose, which is plain and easy to be understood, wherein (so much as may be) the reading of holy Scripture is so set forth, that all things shall be done in order, without breaking one piece thereof from another. For this cause be cut off Anthems, Responds, Invitatories, and such like things, as did break the continual course of the reading of the Scripture.

Yet because there is no remedy, but that of necessity there must be some rules: therefore certain rules are here set forth, which, as they be few in number; so they be plain and easy to be understood. So that here you have an order for prayer (as touching the reading of the holy Scripture), much agreeable to the mind and purpose of the old fathers, and a great deal more profitable and commodious, than that which of late was used. It is more profitable, because here are left out many things, whereof some be untrue, some uncertain, some vain and superstitious: and is ordained nothing to be read, but the very pure word of God, the holy Scriptures, or that which is evidently grounded upon the same; and that in such a language and order as is most easy and plain for the understanding, both of the readers and hearers. It is also more commodious, both for the shortness thereof, and for the plainness of the order, and for that the rules be few and easy. Furthermore, by this order the curates shall need none other books for their public service, but this book and the Bible: by the means whereof, the people shall not be at so great charge for books, as in time past they have been.

And where heretofore, there hath been great diversity in saying and singing in churches within this realm: some following Salisbury use, some Hereford use, some the use of Bangor, some of York, and some of Lincoln: now from henceforth, all the whole realm shall have but one use. And if any would judge this way more painful, because that all things must be read upon the book, whereas before, by reason of so often repetition, they could say many things by heart: if those men will weigh their labor with the profit in knowledge, which daily they shall obtain by reading upon the book, they will not refuse the pain, in consideration of the great profit that shall ensue thereof.

And forasmuch as nothing can, almost, be so plainly set forth, but doubts may arise in the use and practicing of the same: to appease all such diversity (if any arise), and for the resolution of all doubts, concerning the manner how to understand, do, and execute, the things contained in this book: the parties that so doubt, or diversely take any thing, shall always resort to the Bishop of the Diocese, who by his discretion shall take order for the quieting and appeasing of the same; so that the same order be not contrary to any thing contained in this book.

Though it be appointed in the afore written preface, that all things shall be read and sung in the church in the English tongue, to the end that the congregation may be thereby edified: yet it is not meant, but when men say Matins and Evensong privately, they may say the same in any language that they themselves do understand. Neither that any man shall be bound to the saying of them, but such as from time to time, in Cathedral and Collegiate Churches, parish Churches, and Chapels to the same annexed, shall serve the congregation.

Articles of Religion

As established by the Bishops, the Clergy, and the Laity
of the Protestant Episcopal Church in the United States
of America, in Convention, on the twelfth
day of September, in the Year of our Lord, 1801.

I. Of Faith in the Holy Trinity.

There is but one living and true God, everlasting, without body, parts, or passions; of infinite power, wisdom, and goodness; the Maker, and Preserver of all things both visible and invisible. And in unity of this Godhead there be three Persons, of one substance, power, and eternity; the Father, the Son, and the Holy Ghost.

II. Of the Word or Son of God, which was made very Man.

The Son, which is the Word of the Father, begotten from everlasting of the Father, the very and eternal God, and of one substance with the Father, took Man's nature in the womb of the blessed Virgin, of her substance: so that two whole and perfect Natures, that is to say, the Godhead and Manhood, were joined together in one Person, never to be divided, whereof is one Christ, very God, and very Man; who truly suffered, was crucified, dead, and buried, to reconcile his Father to us, and to be a sacrifice, not only for original guilt, but also for actual sins of men.

III. Of the going down of Christ into Hell.

As Christ died for us, and was buried; so also is it to be believed, that he went down into Hell.

IV. Of the Resurrection of Christ.

Christ did truly rise again from death, and took again his body, with flesh, bones, and all things appertaining to the perfection of Man's nature; wherewith he ascended into Heaven, and there sitteth, until he return to judge all Men at the last day.

V. Of the Holy Ghost.

The Holy Ghost, proceeding from the Father and the Son, is of one substance, majesty, and glory, with the Father and the Son, very and eternal God.

VI. Of the Sufficiency of the Holy Scriptures for Salvation.

Holy Scripture containeth all things necessary to salvation: so that whatsoever is not read therein, nor may be proved thereby, is not to be required of any man, that it should be believed as an article of the Faith, or be thought requisite or necessary to salvation. In the name of the Holy Scripture we do understand those canonical Books of the Old and New Testament, of whose authority was never any doubt in the Church.

Of the Names and Number of the Canonical Books.

Genesis,	The First Book of Samuel,	The Book of Esther,
Exodus,	The Second Book of Samuel,	The Book of Job,
Leviticus,	The First Book of Kings,	The Psalms,
Numbers,	The Second Book of Kings,	The Proverbs,
Deuteronomy,	The First Book of Chronicles,	Ecclesiastes or Preacher,
Joshua,	The Second Book of Chronicles,	Cantica, or Songs of Solomon,
Judges,	The First Book of Esdras,	Four Prophets the greater,
Ruth,	The Second Book of Esdras,	Twelve Prophets the less.

And the other Books (as Hierome saith) the Church doth read for example of life and instruction of manners; but yet doth it not apply them to establish any doctrine; such are these following:

The Third Book of Esdras,	The rest of the Book of Esther,
The Fourth Book of Esdras,	The Book of Wisdom,
The Book of Tobias,	Jesus the Son of Sirach,
The Book of Judith,	Baruch the Prophet,

The Song of the Three Children,	The Prayer of Manasses,
The Story of Susanna,	The First Book of Maccabees,
Of Bel and the Dragon,	The Second Book of Maccabees.

All the Books of the New Testament, as they are commonly received, we do receive, and account them Canonical.

VII. Of the Old Testament.

The Old Testament is not contrary to the New: for both in the Old and New Testament everlasting life is offered to Mankind by Christ, who is the only Mediator between God and Man, being both God and Man. Wherefore they are not to be heard, which feign that the old Fathers did look only for transitory promises. Although the Law given from God by Moses, as touching Ceremonies and Rites, do not bind Christian men, nor the Civil precepts thereof ought of necessity to be received in any commonwealth; yet notwithstanding, no Christian man whatsoever is free from the obedience of the Commandments which are called Moral.

VIII. Of the Creeds.

The Nicene Creed, and that which is commonly called the Apostles' Creed, ought thoroughly to be received and believed: for they may be proved by most certain warrants of Holy Scripture.

The original Article given Royal assent in 1571 and reaffirmed in 1662, was entitled "Of the Three Creeds; and began as follows,"The Three Creeds, Nicene Creed, Athanasius's Creed, and that which is commonly called the Apostles' Creed . . ."

IX. Of Original or Birth-Sin.

Original sin standeth not in the following of Adam, (as the Pelagians do vainly talk;) but it is the fault and corruption of the Nature of every man, that naturally is engendered of the offspring of Adam; whereby man is very far gone from original righteousness, and is of his own nature inclined to evil, so that the flesh lusteth always contrary to the Spirit; and therefore in every person born into this world, it deserveth God's wrath and damnation. And this infection of nature doth remain, yea in them that are regenerated; whereby the lust of the flesh, called in Greek, $\phi\rho\acute{o}\nu\eta\mu\alpha$ $\sigma\alpha\rho\kappa\acute{o}\varsigma$, (which some do expound the wisdom, some sensuality, some the affection, some the desire, of the flesh), is not subject to the Law of God. And although there is no condemnation for them that believe and are baptized; yet the Apostle doth confess, that concupiscence and lust hath of itself the nature of sin.

X. Of Free-Will.

The condition of Man after the fall of Adam is such, that he cannot turn and prepare himself, by his own natural strength and good works, to faith, and calling upon God. Wherefore we have no power to do good works pleasant and acceptable to God, without the grace of God by Christ preventing us, that we may have a good will, and working with us, when we have that good will.

XI. Of the Justification of Man.

We are accounted righteous before God, only for the merit of our Lord and Saviour Jesus Christ by Faith, and not for our own works or deservings. Wherefore, that we are justified by Faith only, is a most wholesome Doctrine, and very full of comfort, as more largely is expressed in the Homily of Justification.

XII. Of Good Works.

Albeit that Good Works, which are the fruits of Faith, and follow after Justification, cannot put away our sins, and endure the severity of God's judgment; yet are they pleasing and acceptable to God in Christ, and do spring out necessarily of a true and lively Faith; insomuch that by them a lively Faith may be as evidently known as a tree discerned by the fruit.

XIII. Of Works before Justification.

Works done before the grace of Christ, and the Inspiration of his Spirit, are not pleasant to God, forasmuch as they spring not of faith in Jesus Christ; neither do they make men meet to receive grace, or (as the School-authors say) deserve grace of congruity: yea rather, for that they are not done as God hath willed and commanded them to be done, we doubt not but they have the nature of sin.

XIV. Of Works of Supererogation.

Voluntary Works besides, over and above, God's Commandments, which they call Works of Supererogation, cannot be taught without arrogancy and impiety: for by them men do declare, that they do not only render unto God as much as they are bound to do, but that they do more for his sake, than of bounden duty is required: whereas Christ saith plainly, When ye have done all that are commanded to you, say, We are unprofitable servants.

XV. Of Christ alone without Sin.

Christ in the truth of our nature was made like unto us in all things, sin only except, from which he was clearly void, both in his flesh, and in his spirit. He came to be the Lamb without spot, who, by sacrifice of himself once made, should take away the sins of the world; and sin (as Saint John saith) was not in him. But all we the rest, although baptized, and born again in Christ, yet offend in many things; and if we say we have no sin, we deceive ourselves, and the truth is not in us.

XVI. Of Sin after Baptism.

Not every deadly sin willingly committed after Baptism is sin against the Holy Ghost, and unpardonable. Wherefore the grant of repentance is not to be denied to such as fall into sin after Baptism. After we have received the Holy Ghost, we may depart from grace given, and fall into sin, and by the grace of God we may arise again, and amend our lives. And therefore they are to be condemned, which say, they can no more sin as long as they live here, or deny the place of forgiveness to such as truly repent.

XVII. Of Predestination and Election.

Predestination to Life is the everlasting purpose of God, whereby (before the foundations of the world were laid) he hath constantly decreed by his counsel secret to us, to deliver from curse and damnation those whom he hath chosen in Christ out of mankind, and to bring them by Christ to everlasting salvation, as vessels made to honour. Wherefore, they which be endued with so excellent a benefit of God, be called according to God's purpose by his Spirit working in due season: they through Grace obey the calling: they be justified freely: they be made sons of God by adoption: they be made like the image of his only-begotten Son Jesus Christ: they walk religiously in good works, and at length, by God's mercy, they attain to everlasting felicity.

As the godly consideration of Predestination, and our Election in Christ, is full of sweet, pleasant, and unspeakable comfort to godly persons, and such as feel in themselves the working of the Spirit of Christ, mortifying the works of the flesh, and their earthly members, and drawing up their mind to high and heavenly things, as well because it doth greatly establish and confirm their faith of eternal Salvation to be enjoyed through Christ, as because it doth fervently kindle their love towards God: So, for curious and carnal persons, lacking the Spirit of Christ, to have continually before their eyes the sentence of God's Predestination, is a most dangerous downfall, whereby the Devil doth thrust them either into desperation, or into wretchlessness of most unclean living, no less perilous than desperation.

Furthermore, we must receive God's promises in such wise, as they be generally set forth to us in Holy Scripture: and, in our doings, that Will of God is to be followed, which we have expressly declared unto us in the Word of God.

XVIII. Of obtaining eternal Salvation only by the Name of Christ.

They also are to be had accursed that presume to say, That every man shall be saved by the Law or Sect which he professeth, so that he be diligent to frame his life according to that Law, and the light of Nature. For Holy Scripture doth set out unto us only the Name of Jesus Christ, whereby men must be saved.

XIX. Of the Church.

The visible Church of Christ is a congregation of faithful men, in which the pure Word of God is preached, and the Sacraments be duly ministered according to Christ's ordinance, in all those things that of necessity are requisite to the same.

As the Church of Jerusalem, Alexandria, and Antioch, have erred; so also the Church of Rome hath erred, not only in their living and manner of Ceremonies, but also in matters of Faith.

XX. Of the Authority of the Church.

The Church hath power to decree Rites or Ceremonies, and authority in Controversies of Faith: and yet it is not lawful for the Church to ordain any thing that is contrary to God's Word written, neither may it so expound one place of Scripture, that it be repugnant to another. Wherefore, although the Church be a witness and a keeper of Holy Writ, yet, as it ought not to decree any thing against the same, so besides the same ought it not to enforce any thing to be believed for necessity of Salvation.

XXI. Of the Authority of General Councils.

[The Twenty-first of the former Articles is omitted; because it is partly of a local and civil nature, and is provided for, as to the remaining parts of it, in other Articles.]

The original 1571, 1662 text of this Article, omitted in the version of 1801, reads as follows:"General Councils may not be gathered together without the commandment and will of Princes. And when they be gathered together, (forasmuch as they be an assembly of men, whereof all be not governed with the Spirit and Word of God,) they may err, and sometimes have erred, even in things pertaining unto God. Wherefore things ordained by them as necessary to salvation have neither strength nor authority, unless it may be declared that they be taken out of holy Scripture."

XXII. Of Purgatory.

The Romish Doctrine concerning Purgatory, Pardons, Worshipping and Adoration, as well of Images as of Relics, and also Invocation of Saints, is a fond thing, vainly invented, and grounded upon no warranty of Scripture, but rather repugnant to the Word of God.

XXIII. Of Ministering in the Congregation.

It is not lawful for any man to take upon him the office of public preaching, or ministering the Sacraments in the Congregation, before he be lawfully called, and sent to execute the same. And those we ought to judge lawfully called and sent, which be chosen and called to this work by men who have public authority given unto them in the Congregation, to call and send Ministers into the Lord's vineyard.

XXIV. Of Speaking in the Congregation in such a Tongue as the people understandeth.

It is a thing plainly repugnant to the Word of God, and the custom of the Primitive Church, to have public Prayer in the Church, or to minister the Sacraments, in a tongue not understanded of the people.

XXV. Of the Sacraments.

Sacraments ordained of Christ be not only badges or tokens of Christian men's profession, but rather they be certain sure witnesses, and effectual signs of grace, and God's good will towards us, by the which he doth work invisibly in us, and doth not only quicken, but also strengthen and confirm our Faith in him.

There are two Sacraments ordained of Christ our Lord in the Gospel, that is to say, Baptism, and the Supper of the Lord.

Those five commonly called Sacraments, that is to say, Confirmation, Penance, Orders, Matrimony, and Extreme Unction, are not to be counted for Sacraments of the Gospel, being such as have grown partly of the corrupt following of the Apostles, partly are states of life allowed in the Scriptures; but yet have not like nature of Sacraments with Baptism, and the Lord's Supper, for that they have not any visible sign or ceremony ordained of God.

The Sacraments were not ordained of Christ to be gazed upon, or to be carried about, but that we should duly use them. And in such only as worthily receive the same, they have a wholesome effect or operation: but they that receive them unworthily, purchase to themselves damnation, as Saint Paul saith.

XXVI. Of the Unworthiness of the Ministers, which hinders not the effect of the Sacraments.

Although in the visible Church the evil be ever mingled with the good, and sometimes the evil have chief authority in the Ministration of the Word and Sacraments, yet forasmuch as they do not the same in their own name, but in Christ's, and do minister by his commission and authority, we may use their Ministry, both in hearing the Word of God, and in receiving the Sacraments. Neither is the effect of Christ's ordinance taken away by their wickedness, nor the grace of God's gifts diminished from such as by faith, and rightly, do receive the Sacraments ministered unto them; which be effectual, because of Christ's institution and promise, although they be ministered by evil men.

Nevertheless, it appertaineth to the discipline of the Church, that inquiry be made of evil Ministers, and that they be accused by those that have knowledge of their offences; and finally, being found guilty, by just judgment be deposed.

XXVII. Of Baptism.

Baptism is not only a sign of profession, and mark of difference, whereby Christian men are discerned from others that be not christened, but it is also a sign of Regeneration or New-Birth, whereby, as by an instrument, they that receive Baptism rightly are grafted into the Church; the promises of the forgiveness of sin, and of our adoption to be the sons of God by the Holy Ghost, are visibly signed and sealed; Faith is confirmed, and Grace increased by virtue of prayer unto God.

The Baptism of young Children is in any wise to be retained in the Church, as most agreeable with the institution of Christ.

XXVIII. Of the Lord's Supper.

The Supper of the Lord is not only a sign of the love that Christians ought to have among themselves one to another; but rather it is a Sacrament of our Redemption by Christ's death: insomuch that to such as rightly, worthily, and with faith, receive the same, the Bread which we break is a partaking of the Body of Christ; and likewise the Cup of Blessing is a partaking of the Blood of Christ.

Transubstantiation (or the change of the substance of Bread and Wine) in the Supper of the Lord, cannot be proved by Holy Writ; but is repugnant to the plain words of Scripture, overthroweth the nature of a Sacrament, and hath given occasion to many superstitions.

The Body of Christ is given, taken, and eaten, in the Supper, only after an heavenly and spiritual manner. And the mean whereby the Body of Christ is received and eaten in the Supper, is Faith.

The Sacrament of the Lord's Supper was not by Christ's ordinance reserved, carried about, lifted up, or worshipped.

XXIX. Of the Wicked, which eat not the Body of Christ in the use of the Lord's Supper.

The Wicked, and such as be void of a lively faith, although they do carnally and visibly press with their teeth (as Saint Augustine saith) the Sacrament of the Body and Blood of Christ; yet in no wise are they partakers of Christ: but rather, to their condemnation, do eat and drink the sign or Sacrament of so great a thing.

XXX. Of both Kinds.

The Cup of the Lord is not to be denied to the Lay-people: for both the parts of the Lord's Sacrament, by Christ's ordinance and commandment, ought to be ministered to all Christian men alike.

XXXI. Of the one Oblation of Christ finished upon the Cross.

The Offering of Christ once made is that perfect redemption, propitiation, and satisfaction, for all the sins of the whole world, both original and actual; and there is none other satisfaction for sin, but that alone. Wherefore the sacrifices of Masses, in the which it was commonly said, that the Priest did offer Christ for the quick and the dead, to have remission of pain or guilt, were blasphemous fables, and dangerous deceits.

XXXII. Of the Marriage of Priests.

Bishops, Priests, and Deacons, are not commanded by God's Law, either to vow the estate of single life, or to abstain from marriage: therefore it is lawful for them, as for all other Christian men, to marry at their own discretion, as they shall judge the same to serve better to godliness.

XXXIII. Of excommunicate Persons, how they are to be avoided.

That person which by open denunciation of the Church is rightly cut off from the unity of the Church, and excommunicated, ought to be taken of the whole multitude of the faithful, as an Heathen and Publican, until he be openly reconciled by penance, and received into the Church by a Judge that hath authority thereunto.

XXXIV. Of the Traditions of the Church.

It is not necessary that Traditions and Ceremonies be in all places one, or utterly like; for at all times they have been divers, and may be changed according to the diversity of countries, times, and men's manners, so that nothing be ordained against God's Word. Whosoever, through his private judgment, willingly and purposely, doth openly break the Traditions and Ceremonies of the Church, which be not repugnant to the Word of God, and be ordained and approved by common authority, ought to be rebuked openly, (that others may fear to do the like,) as he that offendeth against the common order of the Church, and hurteth the authority of the Magistrate, and woundeth the consciences of the weak brethren.

Every particular or national Church hath authority to ordain, change, and abolish, Ceremonies or Rites of the Church ordained only by man's authority, so that all things be done to edifying.

XXXV. Of the Homilies.

The Second Book of Homilies, the several titles whereof we have joined under this Article, doth contain a godly and wholesome Doctrine, and necessary for these times, as doth the former Book of Homilies, which were set forth in the time of Edward the Sixth; and therefore we judge them to be read in Churches by the Ministers, diligently and distinctly, that they may be understanded of the people.

Of the Names of the Homilies.

[This Article is received in this Church, so far as it declares the Books of Homilies to be an explication of Christian doctrine, and instructive in piety and morals. But all references to the constitution and laws of England are considered as inapplicable to the circumstances of this Church; which also suspends the order for the reading of said Homilies in churches, until a revision of them may be conveniently made, for the clearing of them, as well from obsolete words and phrases, as from the local references.]

XXXVI. Of Consecration of Bishops and Ministers.

The Book of Consecration of Bishops, and Ordering of Priests and Deacons, as set forth by the General Convention of this Church in 1792, doth contain all things necessary to such Consecration and Ordering; neither hath it any thing that, of itself, is superstitious and ungodly. And, therefore, whosoever are consecrated or ordered according to said Form, we decree all such to be rightly, orderly, and lawfully consecrated and ordered.

The original 1571, 1662 text of this Article reads as follows: "The Book of Consecration of Archbishops and Bishops, and Ordering of Priests and Deacons, lately set forth in the time of Edward the Sixth, and confirmed at the same time by authority of Parliament, doth contain all things necessary to such Consecration and Ordering: neither hath it any thing, that of itself is superstitious and ungodly. And therefore whosoever are consecrated or ordered according to the Rites of that Book, since the second year of the forenamed King Edward unto this time, or hereafter shall be consecrated or ordered according to the same Rites; we decree all such to be rightly, orderly, and lawfully consecrated and ordered."

XXXVII. Of the Power of the Civil Magistrates.

The Power of the Civil Magistrate extendeth to all men, as well Clergy as Laity, in all things temporal; but hath no authority in things purely spiritual. And we hold it to be the duty of all men who are professors of the Gospel, to pay respectful obedience to the Civil Authority, regularly and legitimately constituted.

The original 1571, 1662 text of this Article reads as follows: "The King's Majesty hath the chief power in this Realm of England, and other his Dominions, unto whom the chief Government of all Estates of this Realm, whether they be Ecclesiastical or Civil, in all causes doth appertain, and is not, nor ought to be, subject to any foreign Jurisdiction. Where we attribute to the King's Majesty the chief government, by which Titles we understand the minds of some slanderous folks to be offended; we give not our Princes the ministering either of God's Word, or of the Sacraments, the which thing the Injunctions also lately set forth by Elizabeth our Queen do most plainly testify; but that only prerogative, which we see to have been given always to all godly Princes in holy Scriptures by God himself; that is, that they should rule all estates and degrees committed to their charge by God, whether they be Ecclesiastical or Temporal, and restrain with the civil sword the stubborn and evil-doers.

The Bishop of Rome hath no jurisdiction in this Realm of England.

The Laws of the Realm may punish Christian men with death, for heinous and grievous offences.

It is lawful for Christian men, at the commandment of the Magistrate, to wear weapons, and serve in the wars."

XXXVIII. Of Christian Men's Goods, which are not common.

The Riches and Goods of Christians are not common, as touching the right, title, and possession of the same; as certain Anabaptists do falsely boast. Notwithstanding, every man ought, of such things as he possesseth, liberally to give alms to the poor, according to his ability.

XXXIX. Of a Christian Man's Oath.

As we confess that vain and rash Swearing is forbidden Christian men by our Lord Jesus Christ, and James his Apostle, so we judge, that Christian Religion doth not prohibit, but that a man may swear when the Magistrate requireth, in a cause of faith and charity, so it be done according to the Prophet's teaching in justice, judgment, and truth.

The Chicago-Lambeth Quadrilateral 1886, 1888

Adopted by the House of Bishops Chicago, 1886

We, Bishops of the Protestant Episcopal Church in the United States of America, in Council assembled as Bishops in the Church of God, do hereby solemnly declare to all whom it may concern, and especially to our fellow-Christians of the different Communions in this land, who, in their several spheres, have contended for the religion of Christ:

1.   Our earnest desire that the Saviour's prayer,"That we all may be one," may, in its deepest and truest sense, be speedily fulfilled;

2.   That we believe that all who have been duly baptized with water, in the name of the Father, and of the Son, and of the Holy Ghost, are members of the Holy Catholic Church;

3.   That in all things of human ordering or human choice, relating to modes of worship and discipline, or to traditional customs, this Church is ready in the spirit of love and humility to forego all preferences of her own;

4. That this Church does not seek to absorb other Communions, but rather, co-operating with them on the basis of a common Faith and Order, to discountenance schism, to heal the wounds of the Body of Christ, and to promote the charity which is the chief of Christian graces and the visible manifestation of Christ to the world;

But furthermore, we do hereby affirm that the Christian unity . . . can be restored only by the return of all Christian communions to the principles of unity exemplified by the undivided Catholic Church during the first ages of its existence; which principles we believe to be the substantial deposit of Christian Faith and Order committed by Christ and his Apostles to the Church unto the end of the world, and therefore incapable of compromise or surrender by those who have been ordained to be its stewards and trustees for the common and equal benefit of all men.

As inherent parts of this sacred deposit, and therefore as essential to the restoration of unity among the divided branches of Christendom, we account the following, to wit:

1. The Holy Scriptures of the Old and New Testament as the revealed Word of God.

2. The Nicene Creed as the sufficient statement of the Christian Faith.

3. The two Sacraments, — Baptism and the Supper of the Lord, — ministered with unfailing use of Christ's words of institution and of the elements ordained by Him.

4. The Historic Episcopate, locally adapted in the methods of its administration to the varying needs of the nations and peoples called of God into the unity of His Church.

Furthermore, Deeply grieved by the sad divisions which affect the Christian Church in our own land, we hereby declare our desire and readiness, so soon as there shall be any authorized response to this Declaration, to enter into brotherly conference with all or any Christian Bodies seeking the restoration of the organic unity of the Church, with a view to the earnest study of the conditions under which so priceless a blessing might happily be brought to pass.

Note: *While the above form of the Quadrilateral was adopted by the House of Bishops, it was not enacted by the House of Deputies, but rather incorporated in a general plan referred for study and action to a newly created Joint Commission on Christian Reunion.*

Lambeth Conference of 1888
Resolution 11

That, in the opinion of this Conference, the following Articles supply a basis on which approach may be by God's blessing made towards Home Reunion:

(a) The Holy Scriptures of the Old and New Testaments, as "containing all things necessary to salvation," and as being the rule and ultimate standard of faith.

(b) The Apostles' Creed, as the Baptismal Symbol; and the Nicene Creed, as the sufficient statement of the Christian faith.

(c) The two Sacraments ordained by Christ Himself — Baptism and the Supper of the Lord — ministered with unfailing use of Christ's words of Institution, and of the elements ordained by Him.

(d) The Historic Episcopate, locally adapted in the methods of its administration to the varying needs of the nations and peoples called of God into the Unity of His Church.

Tables for Finding Holy Days

Tables and Rules for Finding the Date of Easter Day

Rules for Finding the Date of Easter Day

Easter Day is always the Sunday after the full moon that occurs on or after the spring equinox on March 21. This full moon may happen on any date between March 21 and April 18 inclusive. If the full moon falls on a Sunday, Easter Day is the Sunday following. But Easter Day cannot be earlier than March 22 or later than April 25.

To find the date of Easter Day in any particular year, it is necessary to have two points of reference—the Golden Number and the Sunday Letter for that year.

1. The Golden Number indicates the date of the full moon on or after the spring equinox of March 21, according to a nineteen-year cycle. These Numbers are prefixed in the Calendar to the days of the month from March 22 to April 18 inclusive. In the present Calendar they are applicable from A.D. 1900 to A.D. 2099, after which they will change.

2. The Sunday Letter identifies the days of the year when Sundays occur. After every date in the Calendar a letter appears—from A to g. Thus, if January 1 is a Sunday, the Sunday Letter for the year is A, and every date in the Calendar marked by A is a Sunday. If January 2 is a Sunday, then every date marked with b is a Sunday, and so on through the seven letters.

In Leap Years, however, the Sunday Letter changes on the first day of March. In such years, when A is the Sunday Letter, this applies only to Sundays in January and February, and g is the Sunday Letter for the rest of the year. Or if d is the Sunday Letter, then c is the Sunday Letter on and after March 1.

To Find the Golden Number

The Golden Number of any year is calculated as follows: Take the number of the year, add 1, and then divide the sum by 19. The remainder, if any, is the Golden Number. If nothing remains, then 19 is the Golden Number.

To Find the Sunday Letter

The following Table provides ready reference to the Sunday Letter of any year between A.D. 1900 and A.D. 2099. It will be found on the line of the hundredth year above the column that contains the remaining digits of the year. But in Leap Years the Letter above the number marked with an asterisk is the Sunday Letter for January and February, and the Letter over the number not so marked is the Sunday Letter for the rest of the year.

Hundred Years: 1900		g	f	e	d	c	b	A
2000	b	A	g	f	e	d	c	b
Years in	00*	00	01	02	03	04*	04	05
Excess of		06	07	08*	08	09	10	11
Hundreds		12*	12	13	14	15	16*	16
		17	18	19	20*	20	21	22
		23	24*	24	25	26	27	28*
		28	29	30	31	32*	32	33
		34	35	36*	36	37	38	39
		40*	40	41	42	43	44*	44
		45	46	47	48*	48	49	50
		51	52*	52	53	54	55	56*
		56	57	58	59	60*	60	61
		62	63	64*	64	65	66	67
		68*	68	69	70	71	72*	72
		73	74	75	76*	76	77	78
		79	80*	80	81	82	83	84*
		84	85	86	87	88*	88	89
		90	91	92*	92	93	94	95
		96*	96	97	98	99		

To Find Easter Day

When one has both the Golden Number and the Sunday Letter for any particular year, then the date of Easter Day may be found in the Calendar, pages 21 and 22, as follows:

1. The Golden Number prefixed to a day in the month of March or of April in the Calendar marks the date of the full moon in that year.

2. Easter Day will be the next date bearing the Sunday Letter of that year. But when the Golden Number of a given year and the Sunday Letter of that year occur on the same date, then Easter day is one week later. (For example, if the Golden Number is 19—which appears in the Calendar prefixed to March 27—and the Sunday Letter is d, then Easter Day in that year will fall on March 29. If the Golden Number is 10 and the Sunday Letter is A, then Easter Day will fall on April 9. But if the Golden Number is 19 and the Sunday Letter is b, then Easter Day will be one week later, namely April 3.)

A Table to Find Easter Day

Golden Number	Year	Easter Day	Year	Easter Day	Year	Easter Day
1	1900	April 15	1938	April 17	1976*	April 18
2	1901	April 7	1939	April 9	1977	April 10
3	1902	March 30	1940*	March 24	1978	March 26
4	1903	April 12	1941	April 13	1979	April 15
5	1904*	April 3	1942	April 5	1980*	April 6
6	1905	April 23	1943	April 25	1981	April 19
7	1906	April 15	1944*	April 9	1982	April 11
8	1907	March 31	1945	April 1	1983	April 3
9	1908*	April 19	1946	April 21	1984*	April 22
10	1909	April 11	1947	April 6	1985	April 7
11	1910	March 27	1948*	March 28	1986	March 30
12	1911	April 16	1949	April 17	1987	April 19
13	1912*	April 7	1950	April 9	1988*	April 3
14	1913	March 23	1951	March 25	1989	March 26
15	1914	April 12	1952*	April 13	1990	April 15
16	1915	April 4	1953	April 5	1991	March 31
17	1916*	April 23	1954	April 18	1992*	April 19
18	1917	April 8	1955	April 10	1993	April 11
19	1918	March 31	1956*	April 1	1994	April 3
1	1919	April 20	1957	April 21	1995	April 16
2	1920*	April 4	1958	April 6	1996*	April 7
3	1921	March 27	1959	March 29	1997	March 30
4	1922	April 16	1960*	April 17	1998	April 12
5	1923	April 1	1961	April 2	1999	April 4
6	1924*	April 20	1962	April 22	2000*	April 23
7	1925	April 12	1963	April 14	2001	April 15
8	1926	April 4	1964*	March 29	2002	March 31
9	1927	April 17	1965	April 18	2003	April 20
10	1928*	April 8	1966	April 10	2004*	April 11
11	1929	March 31	1967	March 26	2005	March 27
12	1930	April 20	1968*	April 14	2006	April 16
13	1931	April 5	1969	April 6	2007	April 8
14	1932*	March 27	1970	March 29	2008*	March 23
15	1933	April 16	1971	April 11	2009	April 12
16	1934	April 1	1972*	April 2	2010	April 4
17	1935	April 21	1973	April 22	2011	April 24
18	1936*	April 12	1974	April 14	2012*	April 8
19	1937	March 28	1975	March 30	2013	March 31

A Table to Find Easter Day

Golden Number	Year	Easter Day	Year	Easter Day
1	2014	April 20	2052*	April 21
2	2015	April 5	2053	April 6
3	2016*	March 27	2054	March 29
4	2017	April 16	2055	April 18
5	2018	April 1	2056*	April 2
6	2019	April 21	2057	April 22
7	2020*	April 12	2058	April 14
8	2021	April 4	2059	March 30
9	2022	April 17	2060*	April 18
10	2023	April 9	2061	April 10
11	2024*	March 31	2062	March 26
12	2025	April 20	2063	April 15
13	2026	April 5	2064*	April 6
14	2027	March 28	2065	March 29
15	2028*	April 16	2066	April 11
16	2029	April 1	2067	April 3
17	2030	April 21	2068*	April 22
18	2031	April 13	2069	April 14
19	2032*	March 28	2070	March 30
1	2033	April 17	2071	April 19
2	2034	April 9	2072*	April 10
3	2035	March 25	2073	March 26
4	2036*	April 13	2074	April 15
5	2037	April 5	2075	April 7
6	2038	April 25	2076*	April 19
7	2039	April 10	2077	April 11
8	2040*	April 1	2078	April 3
9	2041	April 21	2079	April 23
10	2042	April 6	2080*	April 7
11	2043	March 29	2081	March 30
12	2044*	April 17	2082	April 19
13	2045	April 9	2083	April 4
14	2046	March 25	2084*	March 26
15	2047	April 14	2085	April 15
16	2048*	April 5	2086	March 31
17	2049	April 18	2087	April 20
18	2050	April 10	2088*	April 11
19	2051	April 2	2089	April 3

*The years marked with an asterisk are Leap Years.

A Table to Find Movable Feasts and Holy Days

Easter Day	Sundays after Epiphany*	Ash Wednesday†	Ascension Day	Pentecost	Numbered Proper of 2 Pentecost‡	Advent Sunday
March 22	4	Feb. 4	April 30	May 10	#3	November 29
March 23	4	Feb. 5	May 1	May 11	#3	November 30
March 24	4	Feb. 6	May 2	May 12	#3	December 1
March 25	5	Feb. 7	May 3	May 13	#3	December 2
March 26	5	Feb. 8	May 4	May 14	#3	December 3
March 27	5	Feb. 9	May 5	May 15	#4	November 27
March 28	5	Feb. 10	May 6	May 16	#4	November 28
March 29	5	Feb. 11	May 7	May 17	#4	November 29
March 30	5	Feb. 12	May 8	May 18	#4	November 30
March 31	5	Feb. 13	May 9	May 19	#4	December 1
April 1	6	Feb. 14	May 10	May 20	#4	December 2
April 2	6	Feb. 15	May 11	May 21	#4	December 3
April 3	6	Feb. 16	May 12	May 22	#5	November 27
April 4	6	Feb. 17	May 13	May 23	#5	November 28
April 5	6	Feb. 18	May 14	May 24	#5	November 29
April 6	6	Feb. 19	May 15	May 25	#5	November 30
April 7	6	Feb. 20	May 16	May 26	#5	December 1

* In Leap Years, the number of Sundays after the Epiphany will be the same as if Easter Day were one day later than in the above Table.

† In Leap Years, the date of Ash Wednesday will be one day later in the month of February than in the above Table.

‡ Indicates the numbered Proper to be used on the Sunday after Trinity Sunday. Subsequently, the Propers are used consecutively.

Easter Day	Sundays after Epiphany*	Ash Wednesday†	Ascension Day	Pentecost	Numbered Proper of 2 Pentecost‡	Advent Sunday
April 8	7	Feb. 21	May 17	May 27	#5	December 2
April 9	7	Feb. 22	May 18	May 28	#5	December 3
April 10	7	Feb. 23	May 19	May 29	#6	November 27
April 11	7	Feb. 24	May 20	May 30	#6	November 28
April 12	7	Feb. 25	May 21	May 31	#6	November 29
April 13	7	Feb. 26	May 22	June 1	#6	November 30
April 14	7	Feb. 27	May 23	June 2	#6	December 1
April 15	8	Feb. 28	May 24	June 3	#6	December 2
April 16	8	March 1	May 25	June 4	#6	December 3
April 17	8	March 2	May 26	June 5	#7	November 27
April 18	8	March 3	May 27	June 6	#7	November 28
April 19	8	March 4	May 28	June 7	#7	November 29
April 20	8	March 5	May 29	June 8	#7	November 30
April 21	8	March 6	May 30	June 9	#7	December 1
April 22	9	March 7	May 31	June 10	#7	December 2
April 23	9	March 8	June 1	June 11	#7	December 3
April 24	9	March 9	June 2	June 12	#8	November 27
April 25	9	March 10	June 3	June 13	#8	November 28

* In Leap Years, the number of Sundays after the Epiphany will be the same as if Easter Day were one day later than in the above Table.

† In Leap Years, the date of Ash Wednesday will be one day later in the month of February than in the above Table.

‡ Indicates the numbered Proper to be used on the Sunday after Trinity Sunday. Subsequently, the Propers are used consecutively.

The Lectionary

Concerning the Lectionary

The Lectionary for Sundays is arranged in a three-year cycle, in which Year A always begins on the First Sunday of Advent in years evenly divisible by three. (For example, 1977 divided by 3 is 659 with no remainder. Year A, therefore, begins on Advent Sunday of that year.)

The Psalms and Lessons appointed for the Sundays and for other major Holy Days are intended for use at all public services on such days, except when the same congregation attends two or more services. Thus, the same Lessons are to be read at the principal morning service, whether the Liturgy of the Word takes the form given in the Holy Eucharist, or that of the Daily Office.

When the same congregation is present for Morning or Evening Prayer, in addition to the Eucharist, the Lessons at the Office may be selected from one of the other years of the three-year Sunday cycle, or from the Lectionary for the Daily Office. The Psalms at such Offices are normally those appointed in the Office Lectionary; but, when desired, the Psalm cited in the selected Sunday Proper may be used instead.

In this Lectionary, the selections from the Psalter are frequently cited in a longer and shorter version, usually from the same Psalm. The longer version is particularly appropriate for use at the Office, the shorter version when the Psalm is sung between the Lessons at the Eucharist. The selections may be further lengthened or shortened at discretion.

When an alternative Lesson is cited, it is sometimes identical with a Lesson appointed for the same day in the Daily Office Lectionary.

In the opening verses of Lessons, the Reader should omit initial conjunctions which refer only to what has preceded, substitute nouns for pronouns when the referent is not otherwise clear, or else prefix to the Reading some such introduction as, "N. said (to N.)."

Any Reading may be lengthened at discretion. Suggested lengthenings are shown in parentheses.

The Lectionary

Year A

	Psalm	Lessons
First Sunday of Advent	122	Isaiah 2:1-5 Romans 13:8-14 Matthew 24:37-44
Second Sunday of Advent	72 or 72:1-8	Isaiah 11:1-10 Romans 15:4-13 Matthew 3:1-12
Third Sunday of Advent	146 or 146:4-9	Isaiah 35:1-10 James 5:7-10 Matthew 11:2-11
Fourth Sunday of Advent	24 or 24:1-7	Isaiah 7:10-17 Romans 1:1-7 Matthew 1:18-25
Christmas Day I	96 or 96:1-4,11-12	Isaiah 9:2-4,6-7 Titus 2:11-14 Luke 2:1-14(15-20)
Christmas Day II	97 or 97:1-4,11-12	Isaiah 62:6-7,10-12 Titus 3:4-7 Luke 2:(1-14)15-20

	Psalm	Lessons
Christmas Day III	98 *or* 98:1-6	Isaiah 52:7-10 Hebrews 1:1-12 John 1:1-14
First Sunday after Christmas	147 *or* 147:13-21	Isaiah 61:10—62:3 Galatians 3:23-25; 4:4-7 John 1:1-18
Holy Name *January 1*	8	Exodus 34:1-8 Romans 1:1-7 *or* Philippians 2:9-13 Luke 2:15-21
Second Sunday after Christmas	84 *or* 84:1-8	Jeremiah 31:7-14 Ephesians 1:3-6,15-19a Matthew 2:13-15,19-23 *or* Luke 2:41-52 *or* Matthew 2:1-12
The Epiphany *January 6*	72 *or* 72:1-2,10-17	Isaiah 60:1-6,9 Ephesians 3:1-12 Matthew 2:1-12
First Sunday after Epiphany	89:1-29 *or* 89:20-29	Isaiah 42:1-9 Acts 10:34-38 Matthew 3:13-17
Second Sunday after Epiphany	40:1-10	Isaiah 49:1-7 1 Corinthians 1:1-9 John 1:29-41
Third Sunday after Epiphany	139:1-17 *or* 139:1-11	Amos 3:1-8 1 Corinthians 1:10-17 Matthew 4:12-23

	Psalm	Lessons
Fourth Sunday **after Epiphany**	37:1-18 *or* 37:1-6	Micah 6:1-8 1 Corinthians 1:(18-25)26-31 Matthew 5:1-12
Fifth Sunday **after Epiphany**	27 *or* 27:1-7	Habakkuk 3:2-6,17-19 1 Corinthians 2:1-11 Matthew 5:13-20
Sixth Sunday **after Epiphany**	119:1-16 *or* 119:9-16	Ecclesiasticus 15:11-20 1 Corinthians 3:1-9 Matthew 5:21-24,27-30,33-37
Seventh Sunday **after Epiphany**	71 *or* 71:16-24	Leviticus 19:1-2,9-18 1 Corinthians 3:10-11,16-23 Matthew 5:38-48
Eighth Sunday **after Epiphany**	62 *or* 62:6-14	Isaiah 49:8-18 1 Corinthians 4:1-5(6-7)8-13 Matthew 6:24-34
Last Sunday **after Epiphany**	99	Exodus 24:12(13-14)15-18 Philippians 3:7-14 Matthew 17:1-9
Ash Wednesday	103 *or* 103:8-14	Joel 2:1-2,12-17 *or* Isaiah 58:1-12 2 Corinthians 5:20b—6:10 Matthew 6:1-6,16-21
First Sunday **in Lent**	51 *or* 51:1-13	Genesis 2:4b-9,15-17,25—3:7 Romans 5:12-19(20-21) Matthew 4:1-11
Second Sunday **in Lent**	33:12-22	Genesis 12:1-8 Romans 4:1-5(6-12)13-17 John 3:1-17

	Psalm	Lessons
Third Sunday in Lent	95 *or* 95:6-11	Exodus 17:1-7 Romans 5:1-11 John 4:5-26(27-38)39-42
Fourth Sunday in Lent	23	1 Samuel 16:1-13 Ephesians 5:(1-7)8-14 John 9:1-13(14-27)28-38
Fifth Sunday in Lent	130	Ezekiel 37:1-3(4-10)11-14 Romans 6:16-23 John 11:(1-16)17-44
Palm Sunday		
Liturgy of the Palms	118:19-29	Matthew 21:1-11
Liturgy of the Word	22:1-21 *or* 22:1-11	Isaiah 45:21-25 *or* Isaiah 52:13—53:12 Philippians 2:5-11 Matthew (26:36-75) 27:1-54(55-66)
Monday in Holy Week	36:5-10	Isaiah 42:1-9 Hebrews 11:39—12:3 John 12:1-11 *or* Mark 14:3-9
Tuesday in Holy Week	71:1-12	Isaiah 49:1-6 1 Corinthians 1:18-31 John 12:37-38,42-50 *or* Mark 11:15-19
Wednesday in Holy Week	69:7-15, 22-23	Isaiah 50:4-9a Hebrews 9:11-15,24-28 John 13:21-35 *or* Matthew 26:1-5,14-25

	Psalm	Lessons

Maundy Thursday   78:14-20,23-25

Exodus 12:1-14a
1 Corinthians 11:23-26(27-32)
John 13:1-15
or Luke 22:14-30

Good Friday   22:1-21
or 22:1-11
or 40:1-14
or 69:1-23

Isaiah 52:13—53:12
or Genesis 22:1-18
or Wisdom 2:1,12-24
Hebrews 10:1-25
John (18:1-40)
19:1-37

Holy Saturday   130
or 31:1-5

Job 14:1-14
1 Peter 4:1-8
Matthew 27:57-66
or John 19:38-42

Easter Day

The Great Vigil   *See pages 288-291.*

Early Service   *Use one of the Old Testament Lessons
from the Vigil with*

114

Romans 6:3-11
Matthew 28:1-10

Principal Service   118:14-29
or 118:14-17,22-24

Acts 10:34-43
or Exodus 14:10-14,21-25;
15:20-21
Colossians 3:1-4
or Acts 10:34-43
John 20:1-10(11-18)
or Matthew 28:1-10

Evening Service   114
or 136
or 118:14-17,22-24

Acts 5:29a,30-32
or Daniel 12:1-3
1 Corinthians 5:6b-8
or Acts 5:29a,30-32
Luke 24:13-35

	Psalm	Lessons
Monday in Easter Week	16:8-11 *or* 118:19-24	Acts 2:14,22b-32 Matthew 28:9-15
Tuesday in Easter Week	33:18-22 *or* 118:19-24	Acts 2:36-41 John 20:11-18
Wednesday in Easter Week	105:1-8 *or* 118:19-24	Acts 3:1-10 Luke 24:13-35
Thursday in Easter Week	8 *or* 114 *or* 118:19-24	Acts 3:11-26 Luke 24:36b-48
Friday in Easter Week	116:1-8 *or* 118:19-24	Acts 4:1-12 John 21:1-14
Saturday in Easter Week	118:14-18 *or* 118:19-24	Acts 4:13-21 Mark 16:9-15,20
Second Sunday of Easter	111 *or* 118:19-24	Acts 2:14a,22-32 *or* Genesis 8:6-16; 9:8-16 1 Peter 1:3-9 *or* Acts 2:14a,22-32 John 20:19-31
Third Sunday of Easter	116 *or* 116:10-17	Acts 2:14a,36-47 *or* Isaiah 43:1-12 1 Peter 1:17-23 *or* Acts 2:14a,36-47 Luke 24:13-35

	Psalm	Lessons
Fourth Sunday of Easter	23	Acts 6:1-9; 7:2a,51-60 *or* Nehemiah 9:6-15 1 Peter 2:19-25 *or* Acts 6:1-9; 7:2a,51-60 John 10:1-10
Fifth Sunday of Easter	66:1-11 *or* 66:1-8	Acts 17:1-15 *or* Deuteronomy 6:20-25 1 Peter 2:1-10 *or* Acts 17:1-15 John 14:1-14
Sixth Sunday of Easter	148 *or* 148:7-14	Acts 17:22-31 *or* Isaiah 41:17-20 1 Peter 3:8-18 *or* Acts 17:22-31 John 15:1-8
Ascension Day	47 *or* 110:1-5	Acts 1:1-11 *or* Daniel 7:9-14 Ephesians 1:15-23 *or* Acts 1:1-11 Luke 24:49-53 *or* Mark 16:9-15,19-20
Seventh Sunday of Easter	68:1-20 *or* 47	Acts 1:(1-7)8-14 *or* Ezekiel 39:21-29 1 Peter 4:12-19 *or* Acts 1:(1-7)8-14 John 17:1-11

	Psalm	Lessons

Day of Pentecost

Early or	33:12-22	Genesis 11:1-9
Vigil Service	Canticle 2 or 13	*or* Exodus 19:1-9a,16-20a; 20:18-20
	130	*or* Ezekiel 37:1-14
	Canticle 9	*or* Joel 2:28-32
	104:25-32	Acts 2:1-11
		or Romans 8:14-17,22-27
		John 7:37-39a

Principal Service	104:25-37	Acts 2:1-11
	or 104:25-32	*or* Ezekiel 11:17-20
	or 33:12-15,18-22	1 Corinthians 12:4-13
		or Acts 2:1-11
		John 20:19-23
		or John 14:8-17

On the weekdays which follow, the numbered Proper which corresponds most closely to the date of Pentecost in that year is used. See page 158.

Trinity Sunday	150	Genesis 1:1—2:3
	or Canticle 2	2 Corinthians 13:(5-10)11-14
	or 13	Matthew 28:16-20

On the weekdays which follow, the numbered Proper which corresponds most closely to the date of Trinity Sunday in that year is used.

The Season after Pentecost

Directions for the use of the Propers which follow are on page 158.

Proper 1	119:1-16	Ecclesiasticus 15:11-20
Closest to	*or* 119:9-16	1 Corinthians 3:1-9
May 11		Matthew 5:21-24,27-30,33-37

	Psalm	Lessons
Proper 2 *Closest to* *May 18*	71 *or* 71:16-24	Leviticus 19:1-2,9-18 1 Corinthians 3:10-11,16-23 Matthew 5:38-48
Proper 3 *Closest to* *May 25*	62 *or* 62:6-14	Isaiah 49:8-18 1 Corinthians 4:1-5(6-7)8-13 Matthew 6:24-34
Proper 4 *Closest to* *June 1*	31 *or* 31:1-5,19-24	Deuteronomy 11:18-21,26-28 Romans 3:21-25a,28 Matthew 7:21-27
Proper 5 *Closest to* *June 8*	50 *or* 50:7-15	Hosea 5:15—6:6 Romans 4:13-18 Matthew 9:9-13
Proper 6 *Closest to* *June 15*	100	Exodus 19:2-8a Romans 5:6-11 Matthew 9:35—10:8(9-15)
Proper 7 *Closest to* *June 22*	69:1-18 *or* 69:7-10,16-18	Jeremiah 20:7-13 Romans 5:15b-19 Matthew 10:(16-23)24-33
Proper 8 *Closest to* *June 29*	89:1-18 *or* 89:1-4,15-18	Isaiah 2:10-17 Romans 6:3-11 Matthew 10:34-42
Proper 9 *Closest to* *July 6*	145 *or* 145:8-14	Zechariah 9:9-12 Romans 7:21—8:6 Matthew 11:25-30
Proper 10 *Closest to* *July 13*	65 *or* 65:9-14	Isaiah 55:1-5,10-13 Romans 8:9-17 Matthew 13:1-9,18-23

	Psalm	**Lessons**
Proper 11 *Closest to* *July 20*	86 *or* 86:11-17	Wisdom 12:13,16-19 Romans 8:18-25 Matthew 13:24-30,36-43
Proper 12 *Closest to* *July 27*	119:121-136 *or* 119:129-136	1 Kings 3:5-12 Romans 8:26-34 Matthew 13:31-33,44-49a
Proper 13 *Closest to* *August 3*	78:1-29 *or* 78:14-20,23-25	Nehemiah 9:16-20 Romans 8:35-39 Matthew 14:13-21
Proper 14 *Closest to* *August 10*	29	Jonah 2:1-9 Romans 9:1-5 Matthew 14:22-33
Proper 15 *Closest to* *August 17*	67	Isaiah 56:1(2-5)6-7 Romans 11:13-15,29-32 Matthew 15:21-28
Proper 16 *Closest to* *August 24*	138	Isaiah 51:1-6 Romans 11:33-36 Matthew 16:13-20
Proper 17 *Closest to* *August 31*	26 *or* 26:1-8	Jeremiah 15:15-21 Romans 12:1-8 Matthew 16:21-27
Proper 18 *Closest to* *September 7*	119:33-48 *or* 119:33-40	Ezekiel 33:(1-6)7-11 Romans 12:9-21 Matthew 18:15-20
Proper 19 *Closest to* *September 14*	103 *or* 103:8-13	Ecclesiasticus 27:30—28:7 Romans 14:5-12 Matthew 18:21-35

	Psalm	**Lessons**
Proper 20 *Closest to* *September 21*	145 *or* 145:1-8	Jonah 3:10—4:11 Philippians 1:21-27 Matthew 20:1-16
Proper 21 *Closest to* *September 28*	25:1-14 *or* 25:3-9	Ezekiel 18:1-4,25-32 Philippians 2:1-13 Matthew 21:28-32
Proper 22 *Closest to* *October 5*	80 *or* 80:7-14	Isaiah 5:1-7 Philippians 3:14-21 Matthew 21:33-43
Proper 23 *Closest to* *October 12*	23	Isaiah 25:1-9 Philippians 4:4-13 Matthew 22:1-14
Proper 24 *Closest to* *October 19*	96 *or* 96:1-9	Isaiah 45:1-7 1 Thessalonians 1:1-10 Matthew 22:15-22
Proper 25 *Closest to* *October 26*	1	Exodus 22:21-27 1 Thessalonians 2:1-8 Matthew 22:34-46
Proper 26 *Closest to* *November 2*	43	Micah 3:5-12 1 Thessalonians 2:9-13,17-20 Matthew 23:1-12
Proper 27 *Closest to* *November 9*	70	Amos 5:18-24 1 Thessalonians 4:13-18 Matthew 25:1-13
Proper 28 *Closest to* *November 16*	90 *or* 90:1-8,12	Zephaniah 1:7,12-18 1 Thessalonians 5:1-10 Matthew 25:14-15,19-29

	Psalm	Lessons
Proper 29 *Closest to* *November 23*	95:1-7	Ezekiel 34:11-17 1 Corinthians 15:20-28 Matthew 25:31-46

Year B

First Sunday **of Advent**	80 *or* 80:1-7	Isaiah 64:1-9a 1 Corinthians 1:1-9 Mark 13:(24-32)33-37
Second Sunday **of Advent**	85 *or* 85:7-13	Isaiah 40:1-11 2 Peter 3:8-15a,18 Mark 1:1-8
Third Sunday **of Advent**	126 *or* Canticle 3 or 15	Isaiah 65:17-25 1 Thessalonians 5:(12-15)16-28 John 1:6-8,19-28 *or* John 3:23-30
Fourth Sunday **of Advent**	132 *or* 132:8-15	2 Samuel 7:4,8-16 Romans 16:25-27 Luke 1:26-38
Christmas Day I	96 *or* 96:1-4,11-12	Isaiah 9:2-4,6-7 Titus 2:11-14 Luke 2:1-14(15-20)

	Psalm	Lessons
Christmas Day II	97 *or* 97:1-4,11-12	Isaiah 62:6-7,10-12 Titus 3:4-7 Luke 2:(1-14)15-20
Christmas Day III	98 *or* 98:1-6	Isaiah 52:7-10 Hebrews 1:1-12 John 1:1-14
First Sunday **after Christmas**	147 *or* 147:13-21	Isaiah 61:10—62:3 Galatians 3:23-25; 4:4-7 John 1:1-18
Holy Name *January 1*	8	Exodus 34:1-8 Romans 1:1-7 Luke 2:15-21
Second Sunday **after Christmas**	84 *or* 84:1-8	Jeremiah 31:7-14 Ephesians 1:3-6,15-19a Matthew 2:13-15,19-23 *or* Luke 2:41-52 *or* Matthew 2:1-12
The Epiphany *January 6*	72 *or* 72:1-2,10-17	Isaiah 60:1-6,9 Ephesians 3:1-12 Matthew 2:1-12
First Sunday **after Epiphany**	89:1-29 *or* 89:20-29	Isaiah 42:1-9 Acts 10:34-38 Mark 1:7-11
Second Sunday **after Epiphany**	63:1-8	1 Samuel 3:1-10(11-20) 1 Corinthians 6:11b-20 John 1:43-51
Third Sunday **after Epiphany**	130	Jeremiah 3:21—4:2 1 Corinthians 7:17-23 Mark 1:14-20

	Psalm	Lessons
Fourth Sunday after Epiphany	111	Deuteronomy 18:15-20 1 Corinthians 8:1b-13 Mark 1:21-28
Fifth Sunday after Epiphany	142	2 Kings 4:(8-17)18-21(22-31) 32-37 1 Corinthians 9:16-23 Mark 1:29-39
Sixth Sunday after Epiphany	42 or 42:1-7	2 Kings 5:1-15ab 1 Corinthians 9:24-27 Mark 1:40-45
Seventh Sunday after Epiphany	32 or 32:1-8	Isaiah 43:18-25 2 Corinthians 1:18-22 Mark 2:1-12
Eighth Sunday after Epiphany	103 or 103:1-6	Hosea 2:14-23 2 Corinthians 3:(4-11)17—4:2 Mark 2:18-22
Last Sunday after Epiphany	27 or 27:5-11	1 Kings 19:9-18 2 Peter 1:16-19(20-21) Mark 9:2-9
Ash Wednesday	103 or 103:8-14	Joel 2:1-2,12-17 or Isaiah 58:1-12 2 Corinthians 5:20b—6:10 Matthew 6:1-6,16-21
First Sunday in Lent	25 or 25:3-9	Genesis 9:8-17 1 Peter 3:18-22 Mark 1:9-13
Second Sunday in Lent	16 or 16:5-11	Genesis 22:1-14 Romans 8:31-39 Mark 8:31-38

	Psalm	Lessons
Third Sunday **in Lent**	19:7-14	Exodus 20:1-17 Romans 7:13-25 John 2:13-22
Fourth Sunday **in Lent**	122	2 Chronicles 36:14-23 Ephesians 2:4-10 John 6:4-15
Fifth Sunday **in Lent**	51 *or* 51:11-16	Jeremiah 31:31-34 Hebrews 5:(1-4)5-10 John 12:20-33

Palm Sunday

Liturgy of the Palms	118:19-29	Mark 11:1-11a
Liturgy of the Word	22:1-21 *or* 22:1-11	Isaiah 45:21-25 *or* Isaiah 52:13—53:12 Philippians 2:5-11 Mark (14:32-72) 15:1-39(40-47)
Monday in **Holy Week**	36:5-10	Isaiah 42:1-9 Hebrews 11:39—12:3 John 12:1-11 *or* Mark 14:3-9
Tuesday in **Holy Week**	71:1-12	Isaiah 49:1-6 1 Corinthians 1:18-31 John 12:37-38,42-50 *or* Mark 11:15-19
Wednesday in **Holy Week**	69:7-15,22-23	Isaiah 50:4-9a Hebrews 9:11-15,24-28 John 13:21-35 *or* Matthew 26:1-5,14-25

	Psalm	Lessons
Maundy Thursday	78:14-20,23-25	Exodus 12:1-14a
		1 Corinthians 11:23-26(27-32)
		John 13:1-15
		or Luke 22:14-30
Good Friday	22:1-21	Isaiah 52:13—53:12
	or 22:1-11	*or* Genesis 22:1-18
	or 40:1-14	*or* Wisdom 2:1,12-24
	or 69:1-23	Hebrews 10:1-25
		John (18:1-40)
		19:1-37
Holy Saturday	130	Job 14:1-14
	or 31:1-5	1 Peter 4:1-8
		Matthew 27:57-66
		or John 19:38-42
Easter Day		
The Great Vigil	*See pages 288-291.*	
Early Service	*Use one of the Old Testament Lessons from the Vigil with*	
	114	Romans 6:3-11
		Matthew 28:1-10
Principal Service	118:14-29	Acts 10:34-43
	or 118:14-17,22-24	*or* Isaiah 25:6-9
		Colossians 3:1-4
		or Acts 10:34-43
		Mark 16:1-8
Evening Service	114	Acts 5:29a,30-32
	or 136	*or* Daniel 12:1-3
	or 118:14-17,22-24	1 Corinthians 5:6b-8
		or Acts 5:29a,30-32
		Luke 24:13-35

	Psalm	Lessons
Monday in Easter Week	16:8-11 or 118:19-24	Acts 2:14,22b-32 Matthew 28:9-15
Tuesday in Easter Week	33:18-22 or 118:19-24	Acts 2:36-41 John 20:11-18
Wednesday in Easter Week	105:1-8 or 118:19-24	Acts 3:1-10 Luke 24:13-35
Thursday in Easter Week	8 or 114 or 118:19-24	Acts 3:11-26 Luke 24:36b-48
Friday in Easter Week	116:1-8 or 118:19-24	Acts 4:1-12 John 21:1-14
Saturday in Easter Week	118:14-18 or 118:19-24	Acts 4:13-21 Mark 16:9-15,20
Second Sunday of Easter	111 or 118:19-24	Acts 3:12a,13-15,17-26 or Isaiah 26:2-9,19 1 John 5:1-6 or Acts 3:12a,13-15,17-26 John 20:19-31
Third Sunday of Easter	98 or 98:1-5	Acts 4:5-12 or Micah 4:1-5 1 John 1:1—2:2 or Acts 4:5-12 Luke 24:36b-48
Fourth Sunday of Easter	23 or 100	Acts 4:(23-31)32-37 or Ezekiel 34:1-10 1 John 3:1-8 or Acts 4:(23-31)32-37 John 10:11-16

	Psalm	Lessons
Fifth Sunday **of Easter**	66:1-11 *or* 66:1-8	Acts 8:26-40 *or* Deuteronomy 4:32-40 1 John 3:(14-17)18-24 *or* Acts 8:26-40 John 14:15-21
Sixth Sunday **of Easter**	33 *or* 33:1-8,18-22	Acts 11:19-30 *or* Isaiah 45:11-13,18-19 1 John 4:7-21 *or* Acts 11:19-30 John 15:9-17
Ascension Day	47 *or* 110:1-5	Acts 1:1-11 *or* Ezekiel 1:3-5a,15-22,26-28 Ephesians 1:15-23 *or* Acts 1:1-11 Luke 24:49-53 *or* Mark 16:9-15,19-20
Seventh Sunday **of Easter**	68:1-20 *or* 47	Acts 1:15-26 *or* Exodus 28:1-4,9-10,29-30 1 John 5:9-15 *or* Acts 1:15-26 John 17:11b-19
Day of Pentecost		
Early or Vigil Service	33:12-22 Canticle 2 or 13 130 Canticle 9 104:25-32	Genesis 11:1-9 *or* Exodus 19:1-9a,16-20a; 20:18-20 *or* Ezekiel 37:1-14 *or* Joel 2:28-32 Acts 2:1-11 *or* Romans 8:14-17,22-27 John 7:37-39a

	Psalm	Lessons
Principal Service	104:25-37	Acts 2:1-11
	or 104:25-32	or Isaiah 44:1-8
	or 33:12-15,18-22	1 Corinthians 12:4-13
		or Acts 2:1-11
		John 20:19-23
		or John 14:8-17

On the weekdays which follow, the numbered Proper which corresponds most closely to the date of Pentecost in that year is used. See page 158.

Trinity Sunday	93	Exodus 3:1-6
	or Canticle 2	Romans 8:12-17
	or 13	John 3:1-16

On the weekdays which follow, the numbered Proper which corresponds most closely to the date of Trinity Sunday in that year is used.

The Season after Pentecost

Directions for the use of the Propers which follow are on page 158.

Proper 1	42	2 Kings 5:1-15ab
Closest to	or 42:1-7	1 Corinthians 9:24-27
May 11		Mark 1:40-45

Proper 2	32	Isaiah 43:18-25
Closest to	or 32:1-8	2 Corinthians 1:18-22
May 18		Mark 2:1-12

Proper 3	103	Hosea 2:14-23
Closest to	or 103:1-6	2 Corinthians 3:(4-11)17—4:2
May 25		Mark 2:18-22

	Psalm	Lessons
Proper 4 *Closest to* *June 1*	81 *or* 81:1-10	Deuteronomy 5:6-21 2 Corinthians 4:5-12 Mark 2:23-28
Proper 5 *Closest to* *June 8*	130	Genesis 3:(1-7)8-21 2 Corinthians 4:13-18 Mark 3:20-35
Proper 6 *Closest to* *June 15*	92 *or* 92:1-4,11-14	Ezekiel 31:1-6,10-14 2 Corinthians 5:1-10 Mark 4:26-34
Proper 7 *Closest to* *June 22*	107:1-32 *or* 107:1-3,23-32	Job 38:1-11,16-18 2 Corinthians 5:14-21 Mark 4:35-41; (5:1-20)
Proper 8 *Closest to* *June 29*	112	Deuteronomy 15:7-11 2 Corinthians 8:1-9,13-15 Mark 5:22-24,35b-43
Proper 9 *Closest to* *July 6*	123	Ezekiel 2:1-7 2 Corinthians 12:2-10 Mark 6:1-6
Proper 10 *Closest to* *July 13*	85 *or* 85:7-13	Amos 7:7-15 Ephesians 1:1-14 Mark 6:7-13
Proper 11 *Closest to* *July 20*	22:22-30	Isaiah 57:14b-21 Ephesians 2:11-22 Mark 6:30-44
Proper 12 *Closest to* *July 27*	114	2 Kings 2:1-15 Ephesians 4:1-7,11-16 Mark 6:45-52

	Psalm	**Lessons**
Proper 13 *Closest to* *August 3*	78:1-25 *or* 78:14-20,23-25	Exodus 16:2-4,9-15 Ephesians 4:17-25 John 6:24-35
Proper 14 *Closest to* *August 10*	34 *or* 34:1-8	Deuteronomy 8:1-10 Ephesians 4:(25-29)30—5:2 John 6:37-51
Proper 15 *Closest to* *August 17*	147 *or* 34:9-14	Proverbs 9:1-6 Ephesians 5:15-20 John 6:53-59
Proper 16 *Closest to* *August 24*	16 *or* 34:15-22	Joshua 24:1-2a,14-25 Ephesians 5:21-33 John 6:60-69
Proper 17 *Closest to* *August 31*	15	Deuteronomy 4:1-9 Ephesians 6:10-20 Mark 7:1-8,14-15,21-23
Proper 18 *Closest to* *September 7*	146 *or* 146:4-9	Isaiah 35:4-7a James 1:17-27 Mark 7:31-37
Proper 19 *Closest to* *September 14*	116 *or* 116:1-8	Isaiah 50:4-9 James 2:1-5,8-10,14-18 Mark 8:27-38 *or* Mark 9:14-29
Proper 20 *Closest to* *September 21*	54	Wisdom 1:16—2:1(6-11)12-22 James 3:16—4:6 Mark 9:30-37
Proper 21 *Closest to* *September 28*	19 *or* 19:7-14	Numbers 11:4-6,10-16,24-29 James 4:7-12(13—5:6) Mark 9:38-43,45,47-48

	Psalm	Lessons
Proper 22 *Closest to* *October 5*	8 *or* 128	Genesis 2:18-24 Hebrews 2:(1-8)9-18 Mark 10:2-9
Proper 23 *Closest to* *October 12*	90 *or* 90:1-8,12	Amos 5:6-7,10-15 Hebrews 3:1-6 Mark 10:17-27(28-31)
Proper 24 *Closest to* *October 19*	91 *or* 91:9-16	Isaiah 53:4-12 Hebrews 4:12-16 Mark 10:35-45
Proper 25 *Closest to* *October 26*	13	Isaiah 59:(1-4)9-19 Hebrews 5:12—6:1,9-12 Mark 10:46-52
Proper 26 *Closest to* *November 2*	119:1-16 *or* 119:1-8	Deuteronomy 6:1-9 Hebrews 7:23-28 Mark 12:28-34
Proper 27 *Closest to* *November 9*	146 *or* 146:4-9	1 Kings 17:8-16 Hebrews 9:24-28 Mark 12:38-44
Proper 28 *Closest to* *November 16*	16 *or* 16:5-11	Daniel 12:1-4a(5-13) Hebrews 10:31-39 Mark 13:14-23
Proper 29 *Closest to* *November 23*	93	Daniel 7:9-14 Revelation 1:1-8 John 18:33-37 *or* Mark 11:1-11

Year C

	Psalm	Lessons
First Sunday of Advent	50 or 50:1-6	Zechariah 14:4-9 1 Thessalonians 3:9-13 Luke 21:25-31
Second Sunday of Advent	126	Baruch 5:1-9 Philippians 1:1-11 Luke 3:1-6
Third Sunday of Advent	85 or 85:7-13 or Canticle 9	Zephaniah 3:14-20 Philippians 4:4-7(8-9) Luke 3:7-18
Fourth Sunday of Advent	80 or 80:1-7	Micah 5:2-4 Hebrews 10:5-10 Luke 1:39-49(50-56)
Christmas Day I	96 or 96:1-4,11-12	Isaiah 9:2-4,6-7 Titus 2:11-14 Luke 2:1-14(15-20)
Christmas Day II	97 or 97:1-4,11-12	Isaiah 62:6-7,10-12 Titus 3:4-7 Luke 2:(1-14)15-20
Christmas Day III	98 or 98:1-6	Isaiah 52:7-10 Hebrews 1:1-12 John 1:1-14
First Sunday after Christmas	147 or 147:13-21	Isaiah 61:10—62:3 Galatians 3:23-25; 4:4-7 John 1:1-18

	Psalm	Lessons
Holy Name *January 1*	8	Exodus 34:1-8 Romans 1:1-7 Luke 2:15-21
Second Sunday **after Christmas**	84 *or* 84:1-8	Jeremiah 31:7-14 Ephesians 1:3-6,15-19a Matthew 2:13-15,19-23 *or* Luke 2:41-52 *or* Matthew 2:1-12
The Epiphany *January 6*	72 *or* 72:1-2,10-17	Isaiah 60:1-6,9 Ephesians 3:1-12 Matthew 2:1-12
First Sunday **after Epiphany**	89:1-29 *or* 89:20-29	Isaiah 42:1-9 Acts 10:34-38 Luke 3:15-16,21-22
Second Sunday **after Epiphany**	96 *or* 96:1-10	Isaiah 62:1-5 1 Corinthians 12:1-11 John 2:1-11
Third Sunday **after Epiphany**	113	Nehemiah 8:2-10 1 Corinthians 12:12-27 Luke 4:14-21
Fourth Sunday **after Epiphany**	71:1-17 *or* 71:1-6,15-17	Jeremiah 1:4-10 1 Corinthians 14:12b-20 Luke 4:21-32
Fifth Sunday **after Epiphany**	85 *or* 85:7-13	Judges 6:11-24a 1 Corinthians 15:1-11 Luke 5:1-11
Sixth Sunday **after Epiphany**	1	Jeremiah 17:5-10 1 Corinthians 15:12-20 Luke 6:17-26

	Psalm	**Lessons**
Seventh Sunday after Epiphany	37:1-18 *or* 37:3-10	Genesis 45:3-11,21-28 1 Corinthians 15:35-38,42-50 Luke 6:27-38
Eighth Sunday after Epiphany	92 *or* 92:1-5,11-14	Jeremiah 7:1-7(8-15) 1 Corinthians 15:50-58 Luke 6:39-49
Last Sunday after Epiphany	99	Exodus 34:29-35 1 Corinthians 12:27—13:13 Luke 9:28-36
Ash Wednesday	103 *or* 103:8-14	Joel 2:1-2,12-17 *or* Isaiah 58:1-12 2 Corinthians 5:20b—6:10 Matthew 6:1-6,16-21
First Sunday in Lent	91 or 91:9-15	Deuteronomy 26:(1-4)5-11 Romans 10:(5-8a)8b-13 Luke 4:1-13
Second Sunday in Lent	27 *or* 27:10-18	Genesis 15:1-12,17-18 Philippians 3:17—4:1 Luke 13:(22-30)31-35
Third Sunday in Lent	103 *or* 103:1-11	Exodus 3:1-15 1 Corinthians 10:1-13 Luke 13:1-9
Fourth Sunday in Lent	34 *or* 34:1-8	Joshua (4:19-24); 5:9-12 2 Corinthians 5:17-21 Luke 15:11-32
Fifth Sunday in Lent	126	Isaiah 43:16-21 Philippians 3:8-14 Luke 20:9-19

	Psalm	Lessons
Palm Sunday		
Liturgy of the Palms	118:19-29	Luke 19:29-40
Liturgy of the Word	22:1-21 or 22:1-11	Isaiah 45:21-25 or Isaiah 52:13—53:12 Philippians 2:5-11 Luke (22:39-71) 23:1-49(50-56)
Monday in Holy Week	36:5-10	Isaiah 42:1-9 Hebrews 11:39—12:3 John 12:1-11 or Mark 14:3-9
Tuesday in Holy Week	71:1-12	Isaiah 49:1-6 1 Corinthians 1:18-31 John 12:37-38,42-50 or Mark 11:15-19
Wednesday in Holy Week	69:7-15,22-23	Isaiah 50:4-9a Hebrews 9:11-15,24-28 John 13:21-35 or Matthew 26:1-5,14-25
Maundy Thursday	78:14-20,23-25	Exodus 12:1-14a 1 Corinthians 11:23-26(27-32) John 13:1-15 or Luke 22:14-30
Good Friday	22:1-21 or 22:1-11 or 40:1-14 or 69:1-23	Isaiah 52:13—53:12 or Genesis 22:1-18 or Wisdom 2:1,12-24 Hebrews 10:1-25 John (18:1-40) 19:1-37

	Psalm	**Lessons**
Holy Saturday	130 *or* 31:1-5	Job 14:1-14 1 Peter 4:1-8 Matthew 27:57-66 *or* John 19:38-42

Easter Day

The Great Vigil	*See pages 288-291.*

Early Service	*Use one of the Old Testament Lessons* *from the Vigil with*	
	114	Romans 6:3-11 Matthew 28:1-10

Principal Service	118:14-29 *or* 118:14-17,22-24	Acts 10:34-43 *or* Isaiah 51:9-11 Colossians 3:1-4 *or* Acts 10:34-43 Luke 24:1-10

Evening Service	114 *or* 136 *or* 118:14-17,22-24	Acts 5:29a,30-32 *or* Daniel 12:1-3 1 Corinthians 5:6b-8 *or* Acts 5:29a,30-32 Luke 24:13-35

Monday in **Easter Week**	16:8-11 *or* 118:19-24	Acts 2:14,22b-32 Matthew 28:9-15

Tuesday in **Easter Week**	33:18-22 *or* 118:19-24	Acts 2:36-41 John 20:11-18

Wednesday in **Easter Week**	105:1-8 *or* 118:19-24	Acts 3:1-10 Luke 24:13-35

Thursday in **Easter Week**	8 *or* 114 *or* 118:19-24	Acts 3:11-26 Luke 24:36b-48

	Psalm	Lessons
Friday in **Easter Week**	116:1-8 *or* 118:19-24	Acts 4:1-12 John 21:1-14
Saturday in **Easter Week**	118:14-18 *or* 118:19-24	Acts 4:13-21 Mark 16:9-15,20
Second Sunday **of Easter**	111 *or* 118:19-24	Acts 5:12a,17-22,25-29 *or* Job 42:1-6 Revelation 1:(1-8)9-19 *or* Acts 5:12a,17-22,25-29 John 20:19-31
Third Sunday **of Easter**	33 *or* 33:1-11	Acts 9:1-19a *or* Jeremiah 32:36-41 Revelation 5:6-14 *or* Acts 9:1-19a John 21:1-14
Fourth Sunday **of Easter**	100	Acts 13:15-16,26-33(34-39) *or* Numbers 27:12-23 Revelation 7:9-17 *or* Acts 13:15-16,26-33(34-39) John 10:22-30
Fifth Sunday **of Easter**	145 *or* 145:1-9	Acts 13:44-52 *or* Leviticus 19:1-2,9-18 Revelation 19:1,4-9 *or* Acts 13:44-52 John 13:31-35
Sixth Sunday **of Easter**	67	Acts 14:8-18 *or* Joel 2:21-27 Revelation 21:22—22:5 *or* Acts 14:8-18 John 14:23-29

	Psalm	Lessons
Ascension Day	47 *or* 110:1-5	Acts 1:1-11 *or* 2 Kings 2:1-15 Ephesians 1:15-23 *or* Acts 1:1-11 Luke 24:49-53 *or* Mark 16:9-15,19-20
Seventh Sunday **of Easter**	68:1-20 *or* 47	Acts 16:16-34 *or* 1 Samuel 12:19-24 Revelation 22:12-14,16-17,20 *or* Acts 16:16-34 John 17:20-26

Day of Pentecost

Early or Vigil Service	33:12-22 Canticle 2 or 13 130 Canticle 9 104:25-32	Genesis 11:1-9 *or* Exodus 19:1-9a,16-20a; 20:18-20 *or* Ezekiel 37:1-14 *or* Joel 2:28-32 Acts 2:1-11 *or* Romans 8:14-17,22-27 John 7:37-39a
Principal Service	104:25-37 *or* 104:25-32 *or* 33:12-15,18-22	Acts 2:1-11 *or* Joel 2:28-32 1 Corinthians 12:4-13 *or* Acts 2:1-11 John 20:19-23 *or* John 14:8-17

On the weekdays which follow, the numbered Proper which corresponds most closely to the date of Pentecost in that year is used. See page 158.

Lectionary C 917

	Psalms	Lessons
Trinity Sunday	29	Isaiah 6:1-8
	or Canticle 2	Revelation 4:1-11
	or 13	John 16:(5-11)12-15

On the weekdays which follow, the numbered Proper which corresponds most closely to the date of Trinity Sunday in that year is used.

The Season after Pentecost

Directions for the use of the Propers which follow are on page 158.

Proper 1 *Closest to* *May 11*	1	Jeremiah 17:5-10 1 Corinthians 15:12-20 Luke 6:17-26
Proper 2 *Closest to* *May 18*	37:1-18 *or* 37:3-10	Genesis 45:3-11,21-28 1 Corinthians 15:35-38,42-50 Luke 6:27-38
Proper 3 *Closest to* *May 25*	92 *or* 92:1-5,11-14	Jeremiah 7:1-7(8-15) 1 Corinthians 15:50-58 Luke 6:39-49
Proper 4 *Closest to* *June 1*	96 *or* 96:1-9	1 Kings 8:22-23,27-30,41-43 Galatians 1:1-10 Luke 7:1-10
Proper 5 *Closest to* *June 8*	30 *or* 30:1-6,12-13	1 Kings 17:17-24 Galatians 1:11-24 Luke 7:11-17
Proper 6 *Closest to* *June 15*	32 *or* 32:1-8	2 Samuel 11:26—12:10,13-15 Galatians 2:11-21 Luke 7:36-50

	Psalm	Lessons
Proper 7 *Closest to* *June 22*	63:1-8	Zechariah 12:8-10; 13:1 Galatians 3:23-29 Luke 9:18-24
Proper 8 *Closest to* *June 29*	16 *or* 16:5-11	1 Kings 19:15-16,19-21 Galatians 5:1,13-25 Luke 9:51-62
Proper 9 *Closest to* *July 6*	66 *or* 66:1-8	Isaiah 66:10-16 Galatians 6:(1-10)14-18 Luke 10:1-12,16-20
Proper 10 *Closest to* *July 13*	25 *or* 25:3-9	Deuteronomy 30:9-14 Colossians 1:1-14 Luke 10:25-37
Proper 11 *Closest to* *July 20*	15	Genesis 18:1-10a(10b-14) Colossians 1:21-29 Luke 10:38-42
Proper 12 *Closest to* *July 27*	138	Genesis 18:20-33 Colossians 2:6-15 Luke 11:1-13
Proper 13 *Closest to* *August 3*	49 *or* 49:1-11	Ecclesiastes 1:12-14; 2:(1-7,11)18-23 Colossians 3:(5-11)12-17 Luke 12:13-21
Proper 14 *Closest to* *August 10*	33 *or* 33:12-15,18-22	Genesis 15:1-6 Hebrews 11:1-3(4-7)8-16 Luke 12:32-40
Proper 15 *Closest to* *August 17*	82	Jeremiah 23:23-29 Hebrews 12:1-7(8-10)11-14 Luke 12:49-56

	Psalm	**Lessons**
Proper 16 *Closest to* *August 24*	46	Isaiah 28:14-22 Hebrews 12:18-19,22-29 Luke 13:22-30
Proper 17 *Closest to* *August 31*	112	Ecclesiasticus 10:(7-11)12-18 Hebrews 13:1-8 Luke 14:1,7-14
Proper 18 *Closest to* *September 7*	1	Deuteronomy 30:15-20 Philemon 1-20 Luke 14:25-33
Proper 19 *Closest to* *September 14*	51:1-18 *or* 51:1-11	Exodus 32:1,7-14 1 Timothy 1:12-17 Luke 15:1-10
Proper 20 *Closest to* *September 21*	138	Amos 8:4-7(8-12) 1 Timothy 2:1-8 Luke 16:1-13
Proper 21 *Closest to* *September 28*	146 *or* 146:4-9	Amos 6:1-7 1 Timothy 6:11-19 Luke 16:19-31
Proper 22 *Closest to* *October 5*	37:1-18 *or* 37:3-10	Habakkuk 1:1-6(7-11)12-13; 2:1-4 2 Timothy 1:(1-5)6-14 Luke 17:5-10
Proper 23 *Closest to* *October 12*	113	Ruth 1:(1-7)8-19a 2 Timothy 2:(3-7)8-15 Luke 17:11-19
Proper 24 *Closest to* *October 19*	121	Genesis 32:3-8,22-30 2 Timothy 3:14—4:5 Luke 18:1-8a

	Psalm	Lessons
Proper 25 *Closest to* *October 26*	84 *or* 84:1-6	Jeremiah 14:(1-6)7-10,19-22 2 Timothy 4:6-8,16-18 Luke 18:9-14
Proper 26 *Closest to* *November 2*	32 *or* 32:1-8	Isaiah 1:10-20 2 Thessalonians 1:1-5(6-10)11-12 Luke 19:1-10
Proper 27 *Closest to* *November 9*	17 *or* 17:1-8	Job 19:23-27a 2 Thessalonians 2:13—3:5 Luke 20:27(28-33)34-38
Proper 28 *Closest to* *November 16*	98 *or* 98:5-10	Malachi 3:13—4:2a,5-6 2 Thessalonians 3:6-13 Luke 21:5-19
Proper 29 *Closest to* *November 23*	46	Jeremiah 23:1-6 Colossians 1:11-20 Luke 23:35-43 *or* Luke 19:29-38

Holy Days

	Psalm	Lessons
St. Andrew *November 30*	19 *or* 19:1-6	Deuteronomy 30:11-14 Romans 10:8b-18 Matthew 4:18-22
St. Thomas *December 21*	126	Habakkuk 2:1-4 Hebrews 10:35—11:1 John 20:24-29

	Psalm	Lessons
St. Stephen *December 26*	31 *or* 31:1-5	Jeremiah 26:1-9,12-15 Acts 6:8—7:2a,51c-60 Matthew 23:34-39
St. John *December 27*	92 *or* 92:1-4,11-14	Exodus 33:18-23 1 John 1:1-9 John 21:19b-24
Holy Innocents *December 28*	124	Jeremiah 31:15-17 Revelation 21:1-7 Matthew 2:13-18
Confession of St. Peter *January 18*	23	Acts 4:8-13 1 Peter 5:1-4 Matthew 16:13-19
Conversion of St. Paul *January 25*	67	Acts 26:9-21 Galatians 1:11-24 Matthew 10:16-22
The Presentation *February 2*	84 *or* 84:1-6	Malachi 3:1-4 Hebrews 2:14-18 Luke 2:22-40
St. Matthias *February 24*	15	Acts 1:15-26 Philippians 3:13b-22 John 15:1,6-16
St. Joseph *March 19*	89:1-29 *or* 89:1-4,26-29	2 Samuel 7:4,8-16 Romans 4:13-18 Luke 2:41-52
The Annunciation *March 25*	40:1-11 *or* 40:5-10 *or* Canticle 3 or 15	Isaiah 7:10-14 Hebrews 10:5-10 Luke 1:26-38

	Psalm	Lessons
St. Mark *April 25*	2 *or* 2:7-10	Isaiah 52:7-10 Ephesians 4:7-8,11-16 Mark 1:1-15 *or* Mark 16:15-20
St. Philip & **St. James** *May 1*	119:33-40	Isaiah 30:18-21 2 Corinthians 4:1-6 John 14:6-14
The Visitation *May 31*	113 *or* Canticle 9	Zephaniah 3:14-18a Colossians 3:12-17 Luke 1:39-49
St. Barnabas *June 11*	112	Isaiah 42:5-12 Acts 11:19-30; 13:1-3 Matthew 10:7-16
Nativity of **St. John** **the Baptist** *June 24*	85 *or* 85:7-13	Isaiah 40:1-11 Acts 13:14b-26 Luke 1:57-80
St. Peter & **St. Paul** *June 29*	87	Ezekiel 34:11-16 2 Timothy 4:1-8 John 21:15-19
Independence Day July 4	145 *or* 145:1-9	Deuteronomy 10:17-21 Hebrews 11:8-16 Matthew 5:43-48

The Psalm and Lessons "For the Nation," page 930, may be used instead.

St. Mary **Magdalene** *July 22*	42:1-7	Judith 9:1,11-14 2 Corinthians 5:14-18 John 20:11-18

	Psalm	Lessons
St. James *July 25*	7:1-10	Jeremiah 45:1-5 Acts 11:27—12:3 Matthew 20:20-28
The Transfiguration *August 6*	99 *or* 99:5-9	Exodus 34:29-35 2 Peter 1:13-21 Luke 9:28-36
St. Mary **the Virgin** *August 15*	34 *or* 34:1-9	Isaiah 61:10-11 Galatians 4:4-7 Luke 1:46-55
St. Bartholomew *August 24*	91 *or* 91:1-4	Deuteronomy 18:15-18 1 Corinthians 4:9-15 Luke 22:24-30
Holy Cross Day *September 14*	98 *or* 98:1-4	Isaiah 45:21-25 Philippians 2:5-11 *or* Galatians 6:14-18 John 12:31-36a
St. Matthew *September 21*	119:33-40	Proverbs 3:1-6 2 Timothy 3:14-17 Matthew 9:9-13
St. Michael & **All Angels** *September 29*	103 *or* 103:19-22	Genesis 28:10-17 Revelation 12:7-12 John 1:47-51
St. Luke *October 18*	147 *or* 147:1-7	Ecclesiasticus 38:1-4,6-10,12-14 2 Timothy 4:5-13 Luke 4:14-21
St. James **of Jerusalem** *October 23*	1	Acts 15:12-22a 1 Corinthians 15:1-11 Matthew 13:54-58

	Psalm	Lessons
St. Simon & **St. Jude** *October 28*	119:89-96	Deuteronomy 32:1-4 Ephesians 2:13-22 John 15:17-27
All Saints' Day *November 1*	149	Ecclesiasticus 44:1-10,13-14 Revelation 7:2-4,9-17 Matthew 5:1-12
or this	149	Ecclesiasticus 2:(1-6)7-11 Ephesians 1:(11-14)15-23 Luke 6:20-26(27-36)
Thanksgiving Day	65 *or* 65:9-14	Deuteronomy 8:1-3,6-10(17-20) James 1:17-18,21-27 Matthew 6:25-33

The Common of Saints

Of a Martyr I	126 *or* 121	2 Esdras 2:42-48 1 Peter 3:14-18,22 Matthew 10:16-22
Of a Martyr II	116 *or* 116:1-8	Ecclesiasticus 51:1-12 Revelation 7:13-17 Luke 12:2-12
Of a Martyr III	124 *or* 31:1-5	Jeremiah 15:15-21 1 Peter 4:12-19 Mark 8:34-38
Of a Missionary I	96 *or* 96:1-7	Isaiah 52:7-10 Acts 1:1-9 Luke 10:1-9

	Psalm	Lessons
Of a Missionary II	98 *or* 98:1-4	Isaiah 49:1-6 Acts 17:22-31 Matthew 28:16-20
Of a Pastor I	23	Ezekiel 34:11-16 1 Peter 5:1-4 John 21:15-17
Of a Pastor II	84 *or* 84:7-12	Acts 20:17-35 Ephesians 3:14-21 Matthew 24:42-47
Of a Theologian and Teacher I	119:97-104	Wisdom 7:7-14 1 Corinthians 2:6-10,13-16 John 17:18-23
Of a Theologian and Teacher II	119:89-96	Proverbs 3:1-7 1 Corinthians 3:5-11 Matthew 13:47-52
Of a Monastic I	34 *or* 34:1-8	Song of Songs 8:6-7 Philippians 3:7-15 Luke 12:33-37 *or* Luke 9:57-62
Of a Monastic II	133 *or* 119:161-168	Acts 2:42-47a 2 Corinthians 6:1-10 Matthew 6:24-33
Of a Saint I	15	Micah 6:6-8 Hebrews 12:1-2 Matthew 25:31-40
Of a Saint II	34 *or* 34:15-22	Wisdom 3:1-9 Philippians 4:4-9 Luke 6:17-23

	Psalm	Lessons
Of a Saint III	1	Ecclesiasticus 2:7-11
		1 Corinthians 1:26-31
		Matthew 25:1-13

Various Occasions

	Psalm	Lessons
1. Of the Holy Trinity	29	Exodus 3:11-15
		Romans 11:33-36
		Matthew 28:18-20
2. Of the Holy Spirit	139:1-17 *or* 139:1-9	Isaiah 61:1-3
		1 Corinthians 12:4-14
		Luke 11:9-13
3. Of the Holy Angels	148 *or* 103:19-22	Daniel 7:9-10a *or* 2 Kings 6:8-17
		Revelation 5:11-14
		John 1:47-51
4. Of the Incarnation	111 *or* 132:11-19	Isaiah 11:1-10 *or* Genesis 17:1-8
		1 John 4:1-11 *or* 1 Timothy 3:14-16
		Luke 1:26-33(34-38) *or* Luke 11:27-28
5. Of the Holy Eucharist	34 *or* 116:10-17	Deuteronomy 8:2-3
		Revelation 19:1-2a,4-9 *or* 1 Corinthians 10:1-4,16-17 *or* 1 Corinthians 11:23-29
		John 6:47-58

	Psalm	Lessons
6. Of the Holy Cross	40:1-11 *or* 40:5-11	Isaiah 52:13-15; 53:10-12 1 Corinthians 1:18-24 John 12:23-33
7. For All Baptized Christians	16:5-11	Jeremiah 17:7-8 *or* Ezekiel 36:24-28 Romans 6:3-11 Mark 10:35-45
8. For the Departed	116 *or* 103:13-22 *or* 130	Isaiah 25:6-9 *or* Wisdom 3:1-9 1 Corinthians 15:50-58 John 5:24-27 *or* John 6:37-40 *or* John 11:21-27

Any of the Psalms and Lessons appointed at the Burial of the Dead may be used instead.

	Psalm	Lessons
9. Of the Reign of Christ	93 *or* Canticle 18	Daniel 7:9-14 Colossians 1:11-20 John 18:33-37

Any of the Psalms and Lessons appointed in Proper 29 may be used instead.

	Psalm	Lessons
10. At Baptism	15 *or* 23 *or* 27 *or* 42:1-7 *or* 84 *or* Canticle 9	Ezekiel 36:24-28* Romans 6:3-5 *or* Romans 8:14-17 *or* 2 Corinthians 5:17-20 Mark 1:9-11 *or* Mark 10:13-16 *or* John 3:1-6

* Any of the other Old Testament Lessons for the Easter Vigil may be substituted.

	Psalm	Lessons
11. At Confirmation	1 *or* 139:1-9	Isaiah 61:1-9 *or* Jeremiah 31:31-34 *or* Ezekiel 37:1-10 Romans 8:18-27 *or* Romans 12:1-8 *or* Galatians 5:16-25 *or* Ephesians 4:7,11-16 Matthew 5:1-12 *or* Matthew 16:24-27 *or* Luke 4:16-22 *or* John 14:15-21
12. Anniversary of the Dedication of a Church	84 *or* 84:1-6	1 Kings 8:22-30 *or* Genesis 28:10-17 1 Peter 2:1-5,9-10 Matthew 21:12-16
13. For a Church Convention	19:7-14	Isaiah 55:1-13 2 Corinthians 4:1-10 John 15:1-11
14. For the Unity of the Church	122	Isaiah 35:1-10 Ephesians 4:1-6 John 17:6a,15-23
15. For the Ministry I	99 *or* 27:1-9	Numbers 11:16-17,24-29 1 Corinthians 3:5-11 John 4:31-38
15. For the Ministry II	63:1-8	1 Samuel 3:1-10 Ephesians 4:11-16 Matthew 9:35-38
15. For the Ministry III	15	Exodus 19:3-8 1 Peter 4:7-11 Matthew 16:24-27

	Psalm	Lessons
16. For the Mission of the Church I	96 or 96:1-7	Isaiah 2:2-4 Ephesians 2:13-22 Luke 10:1-9
16. For the Mission of the Church II	67	Isaiah 49:5-13 Ephesians 3:1-12 Matthew 28:16-20
17. For the Nation	47	Isaiah 26:1-8 Romans 13:1-10 Mark 12:13-17

The Psalm and any of the Lessons appointed for Independence Day may be used instead.

18. For Peace	85:7-13	Micah 4:1-5 Ephesians 2:13-18 *or* Colossians 3:12-15 John 16:23-33 *or* Matthew 5:43-48
19. For Rogation Days I	147 *or* 147:1-13	Deuteronomy 11:10-15 *or* Ezekiel 47:6-12 *or* Jeremiah 14:1-9 Romans 8:18-25 Mark 4:26-32
19. For Rogation Days II	107:1-9	Ecclesiasticus 38:27-32 1 Corinthians 3:10-14 Matthew 6:19-24
19. For Rogation Days III	104:25-37 *or* 104:1,13-15, 25-32	Job 38:1-11,16-18 1 Timothy 6:7-10,17-19 Luke 12:13-21

	Psalm	Lessons
20. For the Sick	13 *or* 86:1-7	2 Kings 20:1-5 James 5:13-16 Mark 2:1-12

Any of the Psalms and Lessons appointed at the Ministration to the Sick may be used instead.

	Psalm	Lessons
21. For Social Justice	72 *or* 72:1-4,12-14	Isaiah 42:1-7 James 2:5-9,12-17 Matthew 10:32-42
22. For Social Service	146 *or* 22:22-27	Zechariah 8:3-12,16-17 1 Peter 4:7-11 Mark 10:42-52
23. For Education	78:1-7	Deuteronomy 6:4-9,20-25 2 Timothy 3:14—4:5 Matthew 11:25-30
24. For Vocation in Daily Work	8	Ecclesiastes 3:1,9-13 1 Peter 2:11-17 Matthew 6:19-24
25. For Labor Day	107:1-9 *or* 90:1-2,16-17	Ecclesiasticus 38:27-32 1 Corinthians 3:10-14 Matthew 6:19-24

Daily Office
Lectionary

Concerning the Daily Office Lectionary

The Daily Office Lectionary is arranged in a two-year cycle. Year One begins on the First Sunday of Advent preceding odd-numbered years, and Year Two begins on the First Sunday of Advent preceding even-numbered years. (Thus, on the First Sunday of Advent, 1976, the Lectionary for Year One is begun.)

Three Readings are provided for each Sunday and weekday in each of the two years. Two of the Readings may be used in the morning and one in the evening; or, if the Office is read only once in the day, all three Readings may be used. When the Office is read twice in the day, it is suggested that the Gospel Reading be used in the evening in Year One, and in the morning in Year Two. If two Readings are desired at both Offices, the Old Testament Reading for the alternate year is used as the First Reading at Evening Prayer.

When more than one Reading is used at an Office, the first is always from the Old Testament (or the Apocrypha).

When a Major Feast interrupts the sequence of Readings, they may be re-ordered by lengthening, combining, or omitting some of them, to secure continuity or avoid repetition.

Any Reading may be lengthened at discretion. Suggested lengthenings are shown in parentheses.

In this Lectionary (except in the weeks from 4 Advent to 1 Epiphany, and Palm Sunday to 2 Easter), the Psalms are arranged in a seven-week pattern which recurs throughout the year, except for appropriate variations in Lent and Easter Season.

In the citation of the Psalms, those for the morning are given first, and then those for the evening. At the discretion of the officiant, however, any of the Psalms appointed for a given day may be used in the morning or in the evening. Likewise, Psalms appointed for any day may be used on any other day in the same week, except on major Holy Days.

Brackets and parentheses are used (brackets in the case of whole Psalms, parentheses in the case of verses) to indicate Psalms and verses of Psalms which may be omitted. In some instances, the entire portion of the Psalter assigned to a given Office has been bracketed, and alternative Psalmody provided. Those who desire to recite the Psalter in its entirety should, in each instance, use the bracketed Psalms rather than the alternatives.

Antiphons drawn from the Psalms themselves, or from the opening sentences given in the Offices, or from other passages of Scripture, may be used with the Psalms and biblical Canticles. The antiphons may be sung or said at the beginning and end of each Psalm or Canticle, or may be used as refrains after each verse or group of verses.

On Special Occasions, the officiant may select suitable Psalms and Readings.

Week of 1 Advent

Sunday   146, 147   ❖   111, 112, 113
              Isa. 1:1-9   2 Pet. 3:1-10   Matt. 25:1-13

Monday   1, 2, 3   ❖   4, 7
              Isa. 1:10-20   1 Thess. 1:1-10   Luke 20:1-8

Tuesday   5, 6   ❖   10, 11
              Isa. 1:21-31   1 Thess. 2:1-12   Luke 20:9-18

Wednesday   119:1-24   ❖   12, 13, 14
              Isa. 2:1-11   1 Thess. 2:13-20   Luke 20:19-26

Thursday   18:1-20   ❖   18:21-50
              Isa. 2:12-22   1 Thess. 3:1-13   Luke 20:27-40

Friday   16, 17   ❖   22
              Isa. 3:8-15   1 Thess. 4:1-12   Luke 20:41—21:4

Saturday   20, 21:1-7(8-14)   ❖   110:1-5(6-7), 116, 117
              Isa. 4:2-6   1 Thess. 4:13-18   Luke 21:5-19

Week of 2 Advent

Sunday   148, 149, 150   ❖   114, 115
              Isa. 5:1-7   2 Pet. 3:11-18   Luke 7:28-35

Monday   25   ❖   9, 15
              Isa. 5:8-12, 18-23   1 Thess. 5:1-11   Luke 21:20-28

Tuesday   26, 28   ❖   36, 39
              Isa. 5:13-17, 24-25   1 Thess. 5:12-28   Luke 21:29-38

Wednesday   38   ❖   119:25-48
              Isa. 6:1-13   2 Thess. 1:1-12   John 7:53—8:11

Thursday   37:1-18   ❖   37:19-42
              Isa. 7:1-9   2 Thess. 2:1-12   Luke 22:1-13

Friday   31   ❖   35
              Isa. 7:10-25   2 Thess. 2:13—3:5   Luke 22:14-30

Saturday   30, 32   ❖   42, 43
              Isa. 8:1-15   2 Thess. 3:6-18   Luke 22:31-38

Week of 1 Advent

Sunday 146, 147 ∴ 111, 112, 113
Amos 1:1-5, 13—2:8   1 Thess. 5:1-11   Luke 21:5-19

Monday 1, 2, 3 ∴ 4, 7
Amos 2:6-16   2 Pet. 1:1-11   Matt. 21:1-11

Tuesday 5, 6 ∴ 10, 11
Amos 3:1-11   2 Pet. 1:12-21   Matt. 21:12-22

Wednesday 119:1-24 ∴ 12, 13, 14
Amos 3:12—4:5   2 Pet. 3:1-10   Matt. 21:23-32

Thursday 18:1-20 ∴ 18:21-50
Amos 4:6-13   2 Pet. 3:11-18   Matt. 21:33-46

Friday 16, 17 ∴ 22
Amos 5:1-17   Jude 1-16   Matt. 22:1-14

Saturday 20, 21:1-7(8-14) ∴ 110:1-5(6-7), 116, 117
Amos 5:18-27   Jude 17-25   Matt. 22:15-22

Week of 2 Advent

Sunday 148, 149, 150 ∴ 114, 115
Amos 6:1-14   2 Thess. 1:5-12   Luke 1:57-68

Monday 25 ∴ 9, 15
Amos 7:1-9   Rev. 1:1-8   Matt. 22:23-33

Tuesday 26, 28 ∴ 36, 39
Amos 7:10-17   Rev. 1:9-16   Matt. 22:34-46

Wednesday 38 ∴ 119:25-48
Amos 8:1-14   Rev. 1:17—2:7   Matt. 23:1-12

Thursday 37:1-18 ∴ 37:19-42
Amos 9:1-10   Rev. 2:8-17   Matt. 23:13-26

Friday 31 ∴ 35
Haggai 1:1-15   Rev. 2:18-29   Matt. 23:27-39

Saturday 30, 32 ∴ 42, 43
Haggai 2:1-9   Rev. 3:1-6   Matt. 24:1-14

Week of 3 Advent

Sunday　　63:1-8(9-11), 98　❖　103
　　　　　Isa. 13:6-13　　Heb. 12:18-29　　John 3:22-30

Monday　　41, 52　❖　44
　　　　　Isa. 8:16—9:1　　2 Pet. 1:1-11　　Luke 22:39-53

Tuesday　　45　❖　47, 48
　　　　　Isa. 9:1-7　　2 Pet. 1:12-21　　Luke 22:54-69

Wednesday　119:49-72　❖　49, [53]
　　　　　Isa. 9:8-17　　2 Pet. 2:1-10a　　Mark 1:1-8

Thursday　　50　❖　[59, 60] *or* 33
　　　　　Isa. 9:18—10:4　　2 Pet. 2:10b-16　　Matt. 3:1-12

Friday　　40, 54　❖　51
　　　　　Isa. 10:5-19　　2 Pet. 2:17-22　　Matt. 11:2-15

Saturday　　55　❖　138, 139:1-17(18-23)
　　　　　Isa. 10:20-27　　Jude 17-25　　Luke 3:1-9

Week of 4 Advent

Sunday　　24, 29　❖　8, 84
　　　　　Isa. 42:1-12　　Eph. 6:10-20　　John 3:16-21

Monday　　61, 62　❖　112, 115
　　　　　Isa. 11:1-9　　Rev. 20:1-10　　John 5:30-47

Tuesday　　66, 67　❖　116, 117
　　　　　Isa. 11:10-16　　Rev. 20:11—21:8　　Luke 1:5-25

Wednesday　72　❖　111, 113
　　　　　Isa. 28:9-22　　Rev. 21:9-21　　Luke 1:26-38

Thursday　　80　❖　146, 147
　　　　　Isa. 29:13-24　　Rev. 21:22—22:5　　Luke 1:39-48a(48b-56)

Friday　　93, 96　❖　148, 150
　　　　　Isa. 33:17-22　　Rev. 22:6-11, 18-20　　Luke 1:57-66

Dec. 24　　45, 46　❖　——
　　　　　Isa. 35:1-10　　Rev. 22:12-17, 21　　Luke 1:67-80

Christmas Eve　——　❖　89:1-29
　　　　　Isa. 59:15b-21　　Phil. 2:5-11

Week of 3 Advent

Sunday   63:1-8(9-11), 98 ❖ 103
Amos 9:11-15   2 Thess. 2:1-3, 13-17   John 5:30-47

Monday   41, 52 ❖ 44
Zech. 1:7-17   Rev. 3:7-13   Matt. 24:15-31

Tuesday   45 ❖ 47, 48
Zech. 2:1-13   Rev. 3:14-22   Matt. 24:32-44

Wednesday   119:49-72 ❖ 49, [53]
Zech. 3:1-10   Rev. 4:1-8   Matt. 24:45-51

Thursday   50 ❖ [59, 60] *or* 33
Zech. 4:1-14   Rev. 4:9—5:5   Matt. 25:1-13

Friday   40, 54 ❖ 51
Zech. 7:8—8:8   Rev. 5:6-14   Matt. 25:14-30

Saturday   55 ❖ 138, 139:1-17(18-23)
Zech. 8:9-17   Rev. 6:1-17   Matt. 25:31-46

Week of 4 Advent

Sunday   24, 29 ❖ 8, 84
Gen. 3:8-15   Rev. 12:1-10   John 3:16-21

Monday   61, 62 ❖ 112, 115
Zeph. 3:14-20   Titus 1:1-16   Luke 1:1-25

Tuesday   66, 67 ❖ 116, 117
1 Samuel 2:1b-10   Titus 2:1-10   Luke 1:26-38

Wednesday   72 ❖ 111, 113
2 Samuel 7:1-17   Titus 2:11—3:8a   Luke 1:39-48a(48b-56)

Thursday   80 ❖ 146, 147
2 Samuel 7:18-29   Gal. 3:1-14   Luke 1:57-66

Friday   93, 96 ❖ 148, 150
Baruch 4:21-29   Gal. 3:15-22   Luke 1:67-80 *or* Matt. 1:1-17

Dec. 24   45, 46 ❖ ——
Baruch 4:36—5:9   Gal. 3:23—4:7   Matt. 1:18-25

Christmas Eve   —— ❖ 89:1-29
Isa. 59:15b-21   Phil. 2:5-11

Christmas Day and Following

Christmas Day   2, 85   ❖   110:1-5(6-7), 132
    Zech. 2:10-13   1 John 4:7-16   John 3:31-36

First Sunday after Christmas   93, 96   ❖   34
    Isa. 62:6-7, 10-12   Heb. 2:10-18   Matt. 1:18-25

Dec. 29   18:1-20   ❖   18:21-50*
    Isa. 12:1-6   Rev. 1:1-8   John 7:37-52

Dec. 30   20, 21:1-7(8-14)   ❖   23, 27
    Isa. 25:1-9   Rev. 1:9-20   John 7:53—8:11

Dec. 31   46, 48   ❖   ——
    Isa. 26:1-9   2 Cor. 5:16—6:2   John 8:12-19

Eve of Holy Name   ——   ❖   90
    Isa. 65:15b-25   Rev. 21:1-6

Holy Name   103   ❖   148
    Gen. 17:1-12a, 15-16   Col. 2:6-12   John 16:23b-30

Second Sunday after Christmas   66, 67   ❖   145
    Ecclus. 3:3-9, 14-17   1 John 2:12-17   John 6:41-47

Jan. 2   34   ❖   33
    Gen. 12:1-7   Heb. 11:1-12   John 6:35-42, 48-51

Jan. 3   68   ❖   72**
    Gen. 28:10-22   Heb. 11:13-22   John 10:7-17

Jan. 4   85, 87   ❖   89:1-29**
    Exod. 3:1-12   Heb. 11:23-31   John 14:6-14

Jan. 5   2, 110:1-5(6-7)   ❖   ——
    Joshua 1:1-9   Heb. 11:32—12:2   John 15:1-16

Eve of Epiphany   ——   ❖   29, 98
    Isa. 66:18-23   Rom. 15:7-13

*If today is Saturday, use Psalms 23 and 27 at Evening Prayer.
**If today is Saturday, use Psalm 136 at Evening Prayer.

Christmas Day and Following

Christmas Day   2, 85   ∻   110:1-5(6-7), 132
Micah 4:1-5; 5:2-4   1 John 4:7-16   John 3:31-36

First Sunday after Christmas   93, 96   ∻   34
1 Samuel 1:1-2, 7b-28   Col. 1:9-20   Luke 2:22-40

Dec. 29   18:1-20   ∻   18:21-50*
2 Samuel 23:13-17b   2 John 1-13   John 2:1-11

Dec. 30   20, 21:1-7(8-14)   ∻   23, 27
1 Kings 17:17-24   3 John 1-15   John 4:46-54

Dec. 31   46, 48   ∻   ——
1 Kings 3:5-14   James 4:13-17; 5:7-11   John 5:1-15

Eve of Holy Name   ——   ∻   90
Isa. 65:15b-25   Rev. 21:1-6

Holy Name   103   ∻   148
Isa. 62:1-5, 10-12   Rev. 19:11-16   Matt. 1:18-25

Second Sunday after Christmas   66, 67   ∻   145
Wisdom 7:3-14   Col. 3:12-17   John 6:41-47

Jan. 2   34   ∻   33
1 Kings 19:1-8   Eph. 4:1-16   John 6:1-14

Jan. 3   68   ∻   72**
1 Kings 19:9-18   Eph. 4:17-32   John 6:15-27

Jan. 4   85, 87   ∻   89:1-29**
Joshua 3:14—4:7   Eph. 5:1-20   John 9:1-12, 35-38

Jan. 5   2, 110:1-5(6-7)   ∻   ——
Jonah 2:2-9   Eph. 6:10-20   John 11:17-27, 38-44

Eve of Epiphany   —   ∻   29, 98
Isa. 66:18-23   Rom. 15:7-13

*If today is Saturday, use Psalms 23 and 27 at Evening Prayer.
**If today is Saturday, use Psalm 136 at Evening Prayer.

The Epiphany and Following

Epiphany	46, 97 ∴	96, 100	
	Isa. 52:7-10	Rev. 21:22-27	Matt. 12:14-21
Jan. 7*	103 ∴	114, 115	
	Isa. 52:3-6	Rev. 2:1-7	John 2:1-11
Jan. 8	117, 118 ∴	112, 113	
	Isa. 59:15-21	Rev. 2:8-17	John 4:46-54
Jan. 9	121, 122, 123 ∴	131, 132	
	Isa. 63:1-5	Rev. 2:18-29	John 5:1-15
Jan. 10	138, 139:1-17(18-23) ∴	147	
	Isa. 65:1-9	Rev. 3:1-6	John 6:1-14
Jan. 11	148, 150 ∴	91, 92	
	Isa. 65:13-16	Rev. 3:7-13	John 6:15-27
Jan. 12	98, 99, [100] ∴	——	
	Isa. 66:1-2, 22-23	Rev. 3:14-22	John 9:1-12, 35-38
Eve of 1 Epiphany	—— ∴	104	
	Isa. 61:1-9	Gal. 3:23-29; 4:4-7	

Week of 1 Epiphany

Sunday	146, 147 ∴	111, 112, 113	
	Isa. 40:1-11	Heb. 1:1-12	John 1:1-7, 19-20, 29-34
Monday	1, 2, 3 ∴	4, 7	
	Isa. 40:12-23	Eph. 1:1-14	Mark 1:1-13
Tuesday	5, 6 ∴	10, 11	
	Isa. 40:25-31	Eph. 1:15-23	Mark 1:14-28
Wednesday	119:1-24 ∴	12, 13, 14	
	Isa. 41:1-16	Eph. 2:1-10	Mark 1:29-45
Thursday	18:1-20 ∴	18:21-50	
	Isa. 41:17-29	Eph. 2:11-22	Mark 2:1-12
Friday	16, 17 ∴	22	
	Isa. 42:(1-9)10-17	Eph. 3:1-13	Mark 2:13-22
Saturday	20, 21:1-7(8-14) ∴	110:1-5(6-7), 116, 117	
	Isa. 43:1-13	Eph. 3:14-21	Mark 2:23—3:6

*The Psalms and Readings for the dated days after the Epiphany are used only until the following Saturday evening.

The Epiphany and Following

Epiphany	46, 97 ❖	96, 100	
	Isa. 49:1-7	Rev. 21:22-27	Matt. 12:14-21
Jan. 7*	103 ❖	114, 115	
	Deut. 8:1-3	Col. 1:1-14	John 6:30-33, 48-51
Jan. 8	117, 118 ❖	112, 113	
	Exod. 17:1-7	Col. 1:15-23	John 7:37-52
Jan. 9	121, 122, 123 ❖	131, 132	
	Isa. 45:14-19	Col. 1:24—2:7	John 8:12-19
Jan. 10	138, 139:1-17(18-23) ❖	147	
	Jer. 23:1-8	Col. 2:8-23	John 10:7-17
Jan. 11	148, 150 ❖	91, 92	
	Isa. 55:3-9	Col. 3:1-17	John 14:6-14
Jan. 12	98, 99, [100] ❖	——	
	Gen. 49:1-2, 8-12	Col. 3:18—4:6	John 15:1-16
Eve of 1 Epiphany	—— ❖	104	
	Isa. 61:1-9	Gal. 3:23-29; 4:4-7	

Week of 1 Epiphany

Sunday	146, 147 ❖	111, 112, 113	
	Gen. 1:1—2:3	Eph. 1:3-14	John 1:29-34
Monday	1, 2, 3 ❖	4, 7	
	Gen. 2:4-9(10-15)16-25	Heb. 1:1-14	John 1:1-18
Tuesday	5, 6 ❖	10, 11	
	Gen. 3:1-24	Heb. 2:1-10	John 1:19-28
Wednesday	119:1-24 ❖	12, 13, 14	
	Gen. 4:1-16	Heb. 2:11-18	John 1:(29-34)35-42
Thursday	18:1-20 ❖	18:21-50	
	Gen. 4:17-26	Heb. 3:1-11	John 1:43-51
Friday	16, 17 ❖	22	
	Gen. 6:1-8	Heb. 3:12-19	John 2:1-12
Saturday	20, 21:1-7(8-14) ❖	110:1-5(6-7), 116, 117	
	Gen. 6:9-22	Heb. 4:1-13	John 2:13-22

**The Psalms and Readings for the dated days after the Epiphany are used only until the following Saturday evening.*

Week of 2 Epiphany

| Sunday | 148, 149, 150 ∴ 114, 115 |
| Isa. 43:14—44:5 | Heb. 6:17—7:10 | John 4:27-42 |

Sunday 148, 149, 150 ∴ 114, 115
Isa. 43:14—44:5   Heb. 6:17—7:10   John 4:27-42

Monday 25 ∴ 9, 15
Isa. 44:6-8, 21-23   Eph. 4:1-16   Mark 3:7-19a

Tuesday 26, 28 ∴ 36, 39
Isa. 44:9-20   Eph. 4:17-32   Mark 3:19b-35

Wednesday 38 ∴ 119:25-48
Isa. 44:24—45:7   Eph. 5:1-14   Mark 4:1-20

Thursday 37:1-18 ∴ 37:19-42
Isa. 45:5-17   Eph. 5:15-33   Mark 4:21-34

Friday 31 ∴ 35
Isa. 45:18-25   Eph. 6:1-9   Mark 4:35-41

Saturday 30, 32 ∴ 42, 43
Isa. 46:1-13   Eph. 6:10-24   Mark 5:1-20

Week of 3 Epiphany

Sunday 63:1-8(9-11), 98 ∴ 103
Isa. 47:1-15   Heb. 10:19-31   John 5:2-18

Monday 41, 52 ∴ 44
Isa. 48:1-11   Gal. 1:1-17   Mark 5:21-43

Tuesday 45 ∴ 47, 48
Isa. 48:12-21   Gal. 1:18—2:10   Mark 6:1-13

Wednesday 119:49-72 ∴ 49, [53]
Isa. 49:1-12   Gal. 2:11-21   Mark 6:13-29

Thursday 50 ∴ [59, 60] or 118
Isa. 49:13-23   Gal. 3:1-14   Mark 6:30-46

Friday 40, 54 ∴ 51
Isa. 50:1-11   Gal. 3:15-22   Mark 6:47-56

Saturday 55 ∴ 138, 139:1-17(18-23)
Isa. 51:1-8   Gal. 3:23-29   Mark 7:1-23

Week of 2 Epiphany

Sunday   148, 149, 150   ∻   114, 115
Gen. 7:1-10, 17-23   Eph. 4:1-16   Mark 3:7-19

Monday   25   ∻   9, 15
Gen. 8:6-22   Heb. 4:14—5:6   John 2:23—3:15

Tuesday   26, 28   ∻   36, 39
Gen. 9:1-17   Heb. 5:7-14   John 3:16-21

Wednesday   38   ∻   119:25-48
Gen. 9:18-29   Heb. 6:1-12   John 3:22-36

Thursday   37:1-18   ∻   37:19-42
Gen. 11:1-9   Heb. 6:13-20   John 4:1-15

Friday   31   ∻   35
Gen. 11:27—12:8   Heb. 7:1-17   John 4:16-26

Saturday   30, 32   ∻   42, 43
Gen. 12:9—13:1   Heb. 7:18-28   John 4:27-42

Week of 3 Epiphany

Sunday   63:1-8(9-11), 98   ∻   103
Gen. 13:2-18   Gal. 2:1-10   Mark 7:31-37

Monday   41, 52   ∻   44
Gen. 14:(1-7)8-24   Heb. 8:1-13   John 4:43-54

Tuesday   45   ∻   47, 48
Gen. 15:1-11, 17-21   Heb. 9:1-14   John 5:1-18

Wednesday   119:49-72   ∻   49, [53]
Gen. 16:1-14   Heb. 9:15-28   John 5:19-29

Thursday   50   ∻   [59, 60] or 118
Gen. 16:15—17:14   Heb. 10:1-10   John 5:30-47

Friday   40, 54   ∻   51
Gen. 17:15-27   Heb. 10:11-25   John 6:1-15

Saturday   55   ∻   138, 139:1-17(18-23)
Gen. 18:1-16   Heb. 10:26-39   John 6:16-27

Week of 4 Epiphany

Sunday	24, 29 ∴	8, 84	
	Isa. 51:9-16	Heb. 11:8-16	John 7:14-31
Monday	56, 57, [58] ∴	64, 65	
	Isa. 51:17-23	Gal. 4:1-11	Mark 7:24-37
Tuesday	61, 62 ∴	68:1-20(21-23)24-36	
	Isa. 52:1-12	Gal. 4:12-20	Mark 8:1-10
Wednesday	72 ∴	119:73-96	
	Isa. 54:1-10(11-17)	Gal. 4:21-31	Mark 8:11-26
Thursday	[70], 71 ∴	74	
	Isa. 55:1-13	Gal. 5:1-15	Mark 8:27—9:1
Friday	69:1-23(24-30)31-38 ∴	73	
	Isa. 56:1-8	Gal. 5:16-24	Mark 9:2-13
Saturday	75, 76 ∴	23, 27	
	Isa. 57:3-13	Gal. 5:25—6:10	Mark 9:14-29

Week of 5 Epiphany

Sunday	93, 96 ∴	34	
	Isa. 57:14-21	Heb. 12:1-6	John 7:37-46
Monday	80 ∴	77, [79]	
	Isa. 58:1-12	Gal. 6:11-18	Mark 9:30-41
Tuesday	78:1-39 ∴	78:40-72	
	Isa. 59:1-15a	2 Tim. 1:1-14	Mark 9:42-50
Wednesday	119:97-120 ∴	81, 82	
	Isa. 59:15b-21	2 Tim. 1:15—2:13	Mark 10:1-16
Thursday	[83] *or* 146, 147 ∴	85, 86	
	Isa. 60:1-17	2 Tim. 2:14-26	Mark 10:17-31
Friday	88 ∴	91, 92	
	Isa. 61:1-9	2 Tim. 3:1-17	Mark 10:32-45
Saturday	87, 90 ∴	136	
	Isa. 61:10—62:5	2 Tim. 4:1-8	Mark 10:46-52

Week of 4 Epiphany

Sunday	24, 29 ∴ 8, 84		
	Gen. 18:16-33	Gal. 5:13-25	Mark 8:22-30
Monday	56, 57, [58] ∴ 64, 65		
	Gen. 19:1-17(18-23)24-29	Heb. 11:1-12	John 6:27-40
Tuesday	61, 62 ∴ 68:1-20(21-23)24-36		
	Gen. 21:1-21	Heb. 11:13-22	John 6:41-51
Wednesday	72 ∴ 119:73-96		
	Gen. 22:1-18	Heb. 11:23-31	John 6:52-59
Thursday	[70], 71 ∴ 74		
	Gen. 23:1-20	Heb. 11:32—12:2	John 6:60-71
Friday	69:1-23(24-30)31-38 ∴ 73		
	Gen. 24:1-27	Heb. 12:3-11	John 7:1-13
Saturday	75, 76 ∴ 23, 27		
	Gen. 24:28-38, 49-51	Heb. 12:12-29	John 7:14-36

Week of 5 Epiphany

Sunday	93, 96 ∴ 34		
	Gen. 24:50-67	2 Tim. 2:14-21	Mark 10:13-22
Monday	80 ∴ 77, [79]		
	Gen. 25:19-34	Heb. 13:1-16	John 7:37-52
Tuesday	78:1-39 ∴ 78:40-72		
	Gen. 26:1-6, 12-33	Heb. 13:17-25	John 7:53—8:11
Wednesday	119:97-120 ∴ 81, 82		
	Gen. 27:1-29	Rom. 12:1-8	John 8:12-20
Thursday	[83] *or* 146, 147 ∴ 85, 86		
	Gen. 27:30-45	Rom. 12:9-21	John 8:21-32
Friday	88 ∴ 91, 92		
	Gen. 27:46—28:4, 10-22	Rom. 13:1-14	John 8:33-47
Saturday	87, 90 ∴ 136		
	Gen. 29:1-20	Rom. 14:1-23	John 8:47-59

Week of 6 Epiphany

Sunday	66, 67 ∴	19, 46	
	Isa. 62:6-12	1 John 2:3-11	John 8:12-19
Monday	89:1-18 ∴	89:19-52	
	Isa. 63:1-6	1 Tim. 1:1-17	Mark 11:1-11
Tuesday	97, 99, [100] ∴	94, [95]	
	Isa. 63:7-14	1 Tim. 1:18—2:8	Mark 11:12-26
Wednesday	101, 109:1-4(5-19)20-30 ∴	119:121-144	
	Isa. 63:15—64:9	1 Tim. 3:1-16	Mark 11:27—12:12
Thursday	105:1-22 ∴	105:23-45	
	Isa. 65:1-12	1 Tim. 4:1-16	Mark 12:13-27
Friday	102 ∴	107:1-32	
	Isa. 65:17-25	1 Tim 5:17-22(23-25)	Mark 12:28-34
Saturday	107:33-43, 108:1-6(7-13) ∴	33	
	Isa. 66:1-6	1 Tim. 6:6-21	Mark 12:35-44

Week of 7 Epiphany

Sunday	118 ∴	145	
	Isa. 66:7-14	1 John 3:4-10	John 10:7-16
Monday	106:1-18 ∴	106:19-48	
	Ruth 1:1-14	2 Cor. 1:1-11	Matt. 5:1-12
Tuesday	[120], 121, 122, 123 ∴	124, 125, 126, [127]	
	Ruth 1:15-22	2 Cor. 1:12-22	Matt. 5:13-20
Wednesday	119:145-176 ∴	128, 129, 130	
	Ruth 2:1-13	2 Cor. 1:23—2:17	Matt. 5:21-26
Thursday	131, 132, [133] ∴	134, 135	
	Ruth 2:14-23	2 Cor. 3:1-18	Matt. 5:27-37
Friday	140, 142 ∴	141, 143:1-11(12)	
	Ruth 3:1-18	2 Cor. 4:1-12	Matt. 5:38-48
Saturday	137:1-6(7-9), 144 ∴	104	
	Ruth 4:1-17	2 Cor. 4:13—5:10	Matt. 6:1-6

Week of 6 Epiphany

Sunday	66, 67 ∴ 19, 46		
	Gen. 29:20-35	1 Tim. 3:14—4:10	Mark 10:23-31
Monday	89:1-18 ∴ 89:19-52		
	Gen. 30:1-24	1 John 1:1-10	John 9:1-17
Tuesday	97, 99, [100] ∴ 94, [95]		
	Gen. 31:1-24	1 John 2:1-11	John 9:18-41
Wednesday	101, 109:1-4(5-19)20-30 ∴ 119:121-144		
	Gen. 31:25-50	1 John 2:12-17	John 10:1-18
Thursday	105:1-22 ∴ 105:23-45		
	Gen. 32:3-21	1 John 2:18-29	John 10:19-30
Friday	102 ∴ 107:1-32		
	Gen. 32:22—33:17	1 John 3:1-10	John 10:31-42
Saturday	107:33-43, 108:1-6(7-13) ∴ 33		
	Gen. 35:1-20	1 John 3:11-18	John 11:1-16

Week of 7 Epiphany

Sunday	118 ∴ 145		
	Prov. 1:20-33	2 Cor. 5:11-21	Mark 10:35-45
Monday	106:1-18 ∴ 106:19-48		
	Prov. 3:11-20	1 John 3:18—4:6	John 11:17-29
Tuesday	[120], 121, 122, 123 ∴ 124, 125, 126, [127]		
	Prov. 4:1-27	1 John 4:7-21	John 11:30-44
Wednesday	119:145-176 ∴ 128, 129, 130		
	Prov. 6:1-19	1 John 5:1-12	John 11:45-54
Thursday	131, 132, [133] ∴ 134, 135		
	Prov. 7:1-27	1 John 5:13-21	John 11:55—12:8
Friday	140, 142 ∴ 141, 143:1-11(12)		
	Prov. 8:1-21	Philemon 1-25	John 12:9-19
Saturday	137:1-6(7-9), 144 ∴ 104		
	Prov. 8:22-36	2 Tim. 1:1-14	John 12:20-26

Week of 8 Epiphany

| Sunday | 146, 147 ∴ 111, 112, 113 |
| | Deut. 4:1-9   2 Tim. 4:1-8   John 12:1-8 |

Sunday 146, 147 ∴ 111, 112, 113
Deut. 4:1-9   2 Tim. 4:1-8   John 12:1-8

Monday 1, 2, 3 ∴ 4, 7
Deut. 4:9-14   2 Cor. 10:1-18   Matt. 6:7-15

Tuesday 5, 6 ∴ 10, 11
Deut. 4:15-24   2 Cor. 11:1-21a   Matt. 6:16-23

Wednesday 119:1-24 ∴ 12, 13, 14
Deut. 4:25-31   2 Cor. 11:21b-33   Matt. 6:24-34

Thursday 18:1-20 ∴ 18:21-50
Deut. 4:32-40   2 Cor. 12:1-10   Matt. 7:1-12

Friday 16, 17 ∴ 22
Deut. 5:1-22   2 Cor. 12:11-21   Matt. 7:13-21

Saturday 20, 21:1-7(8-14) ∴ 110:1-5(6-7), 116, 117
Deut. 5:22-33   2 Cor. 13:1-14   Matt. 7:22-29

Week of Last Epiphany

Sunday 148, 149, 150 ∴ 114, 115
Deut. 6:1-9   Heb. 12:18-29   John 12:24-32

Monday 25 ∴ 9, 15
Deut. 6:10-15   Heb. 1:1-14   John 1:1-18

Tuesday 26, 28 ∴ 36, 39
Deut. 6:16-25   Heb. 2:1-10   John 1:19-28

Ash Wednesday 95* & 32, 143 ∴ 102, 130
Jonah 3:1—4:11   Heb. 12:1-14   Luke 18:9-14

Thursday 37:1-18 ∴ 37:19-42
Deut. 7:6-11   Titus 1:1-16   John 1:29-34

Friday 95* & 31 ∴ 35
Deut. 7:12-16   Titus 2:1-15   John 1:35-42

Saturday 30, 32 ∴ 42, 43
Deut. 7:17-26   Titus 3:1-15   John 1:43-51

*For the Invitatory

Week of 8 Epiphany

Sunday   146, 147   ∴   111, 112, 113
              Prov. 9:1-12   2 Cor. 9:6b-15   Mark 10:46-52

Monday   1, 2, 3   ∴   4, 7
              Prov. 10:1-12   2 Tim. 1:15—2:13   John 12:27-36a

Tuesday   5, 6   ∴   10, 11
              Prov. 15:16-33   2 Tim. 2:14-26   John 12:36b-50

Wednesday   119:1-24   ∴   12, 13, 14
              Prov. 17:1-20   2 Tim 3:1-17   John 13:1-20

Thursday   18:1-20   ∴   18:21-50
              Prov. 21:30—22:6   2 Tim. 4:1-8   John 13:21-30

Friday   16, 17   ∴   22
              Prov. 23:19-21, 29—24:2   2 Tim. 4:9-22   John 13:31-38

Saturday   20, 21:1-7(8-14)   ∴   110:1-5(6-7), 116, 117
              Prov. 25:15-28   Phil. 1:1-11   John 18:1-14

Week of Last Epiphany

Sunday   148, 149, 150   ∴   114, 115
              Ecclus. 48:1-11   2 Cor. 3:7-18   Luke 9:18-27

Monday   25   ∴   9, 15
              Prov. 27:1-6, 10-12   Phil. 2:1-13   John 18:15-18, 25-27

Tuesday   26, 28   ∴   36, 39
              Prov. 30:1-4, 24-33   Phil. 3:1-11   John 18:28-38

Ash Wednesday   95* & 32, 143   ∴   102, 130
              Amos 5:6-15   Heb. 12:1-14   Luke 18:9-14

Thursday   37:1-18   ∴   37:19-42
              Hab. 3:1-10(11-15)16-18   Phil. 3:12-21   John 17:1-8

Friday   95* & 31   ∴   35
              Ezek. 18:1-4, 25-32   Phil. 4:1-9   John 17:9-19

Saturday   30, 32   ∴   42, 43
              Ezek. 39:21-29   Phil. 4:10-20   John 17:20-26

*For the Invitatory

Week of 1 Lent

| Sunday | 63:1-8(9-11), 98 ∴ 103 |
| | Deut. 8:1-10 1 Cor. 1:17-31 Mark 2:18-22 |

| Monday | 41, 52 ∴ 44 |
| | Deut. 8:11-20 Heb. 2:11-18 John 2:1-12 |

| Tuesday | 45 ∴ 47, 48 |
| | Deut. 9:4-12 Heb. 3:1-11 John 2:13-22 |

| Wednesday | 119:49-72 ∴ 49, [53] |
| | Deut. 9:13-21 Heb. 3:12-19 John 2:23—3:15 |

| Thursday | 50 ∴ [59, 60] or 19, 46 |
| | Deut. 9:23—10:5 Heb. 4:1-10 John 3:16-21 |

| Friday | 95* & 40, 54 ∴ 51 |
| | Deut. 10:12-22 Heb. 4:11-16 John 3:22-36 |

| Saturday | 55 ∴ 138, 139:1-17(18-23) |
| | Deut. 11:18-28 Heb. 5:1-10 John 4:1-26 |

Week of 2 Lent

| Sunday | 24, 29 ∴ 8, 84 |
| | Jer. 1:1-10 1 Cor. 3:11-23 Mark 3:31—4:9 |

| Monday | 56, 57, [58] ∴ 64, 65 |
| | Jer. 1:11-19 Rom. 1:1-15 John 4:27-42 |

| Tuesday | 61, 62 ∴ 68:1-20(21-23)24-36 |
| | Jer. 2:1-13 Rom. 1:16-25 John 4:43-54 |

| Wednesday | 72 ∴ 119:73-96 |
| | Jer. 3:6-18 Rom. 1:28—2:11 John 5:1-18 |

| Thursday | [70], 71 ∴ 74 |
| | Jer. 4:9-10, 19-28 Rom. 2:12-24 John 5:19-29 |

| Friday | 95* & 69:1-23(24-30)31-38 ∴ 73 |
| | Jer. 5:1-9 Rom. 2:25—3:18 John 5:30-47 |

| Saturday | 75, 76 ∴ 23, 27 |
| | Jer. 5:20-31 Rom. 3:19-31 John 7:1-13 |

*For the Invitatory

Week of 1 Lent

Sunday	63:1-8(9-11), 98 ∻ 103	
	Dan. 9:3-10	Heb. 2:10-18	John 12:44-50
Monday	41, 52 ∻ 44	
	Gen. 37:1-11	1 Cor. 1:1-19	Mark 1:1-13
Tuesday	45 ∻ 47, 48	
	Gen. 37:12-24	1 Cor. 1:20-31	Mark 1:14-28
Wednesday	119:49-72 ∻ 49, [53]	
	Gen. 37:25-36	1 Cor. 2:1-13	Mark 1:29-45
Thursday	50 ∻ [59, 60] *or* 19, 46	
	Gen. 39:1-23	1 Cor. 2:14—3:15	Mark 2:1-12
Friday	95* & 40, 54 ∻ 51	
	Gen. 40:1-23	1 Cor. 3:16-23	Mark 2:13-22
Saturday	55 ∻ 138, 139:1-17(18-23)	
	Gen. 41:1-13	1 Cor. 4:1-7	Mark 2:23—3:6

Week of 2 Lent

Sunday	24, 29 ∻ 8, 84	
	Gen. 41:14-45	Rom. 6:3-14	John 5:19-24
Monday	56, 57, [58] ∻ 64, 65	
	Gen. 41:46-57	1 Cor. 4:8-20(21)	Mark 3:7-19a
Tuesday	61, 62 ∻ 68:1-20(21-23)24-36	
	Gen. 42:1-17	1 Cor. 5:1-8	Mark 3:19b-35
Wednesday	72 ∻ 119:73-96	
	Gen. 42:18-28	1 Cor. 5:9—6:8	Mark 4:1-20
Thursday	[70], 71 ∻ 74	
	Gen. 42:29-38	1 Cor. 6:12-20	Mark 4:21-34
Friday	95* & 69:1-23(24-30)31-38 ∻ 73	
	Gen. 43:1-15	1 Cor. 7:1-9	Mark 4:35-41
Saturday	75, 76 ∻ 23, 27	
	Gen. 43:16-34	1 Cor. 7:10-24	Mark 5:1-20

*For the Invitatory

Week of 3 Lent

Sunday	93, 96 ∴ 34		
	Jer. 6:9-15	1 Cor. 6:12-20	Mark 5:1-20
Monday	80 ∴ 77, [79]		
	Jer. 7:1-15	Rom. 4:1-12	John 7:14-36
Tuesday	78:1-39 ∴ 78:40-72		
	Jer. 7:21-34	Rom. 4:13-25	John 7:37-52
Wednesday	119:97-120 ∴ 81, 82		
	Jer. 8:18—9:6	Rom. 5:1-11	John 8:12-20
Thursday	[83] *or* 42, 43 ∴ 85, 86		
	Jer. 10:11-24	Rom. 5:12-21	John 8:21-32
Friday	95* & 88 ∴ 91, 92		
	Jer. 11:1-8, 14-20	Rom. 6:1-11	John 8:33-47
Saturday	87, 90 ∴ 136		
	Jer. 13:1-11	Rom. 6:12-23	John 8:47-59

Week of 4 Lent

Sunday	66, 67 ∴ 19, 46		
	Jer. 14:1-9, 17-22	Gal. 4:21—5:1	Mark 8:11-21
Monday	89:1-18 ∴ 89:19-52		
	Jer. 16:10-21	Rom. 7:1-12	John 6:1-15
Tuesday	97, 99, [100] ∴ 94, [95]		
	Jer. 17:19-27	Rom. 7:13-25	John 6:16-27
Wednesday	101, 109:1-4(5-19)20-30 ∴ 119:121-144		
	Jer. 18:1-11	Rom. 8:1-11	John 6:27-40
Thursday	69:1-23(24-30)31-38 ∴ 73		
	Jer. 22:13-23	Rom. 8:12-27	John 6:41-51
Friday	95* & 102 ∴ 107:1-32		
	Jer. 23:1-8	Rom. 8:28-39	John 6:52-59
Saturday	107:33-43, 108:1-6(7-13) ∴ 33		
	Jer. 23:9-15	Rom. 9:1-18	John 6:60-71

*For the Invitatory

Week of 3 Lent

Sunday	93, 96 ❖ 34
	Gen. 44:1-17 Rom. 8:1-10 John 5:25-29

Monday	80 ❖ 77, [79]
	Gen. 44:18-34 1 Cor. 7:25-31 Mark 5:21-43

Tuesday	78:1-39 ❖ 78:40-72
	Gen. 45:1-15 1 Cor. 7:32-40 Mark 6:1-13

Wednesday	119:97-120 ❖ 81, 82
	Gen. 45:16-28 1 Cor. 8:1-13 Mark 6:13-29

Thursday	[83] or 42, 43 ❖ 85, 86
	Gen. 46:1-7, 28-34 1 Cor. 9:1-15 Mark 6:30-46

Friday	95* & 88 ❖ 91, 92
	Gen. 47:1-26 1 Cor. 9:16-27 Mark 6:47-56

Saturday	87, 90 ❖ 136
	Gen. 47:27—48:7 1 Cor. 10:1-13 Mark 7:1-23

Week of 4 Lent

Sunday	66, 67 ❖ 19, 46
	Gen. 48:8-22 Rom. 8:11-25 John 6:27-40

Monday	89:1-18 ❖ 89:19-52
	Gen. 49:1-28 1 Cor. 10:14—11:1 Mark 7:24-37

Tuesday	97, 99, [100] ❖ 94, [95]
	Gen. 49:29—50:14 1 Cor. 11:17-34 Mark 8:1-10

Wednesday	101, 109:1-4(5-19)20-30 ❖ 119:121-144
	Gen. 50:15-26 1 Cor. 12:1-11 Mark 8:11-26

Thursday	69:1-23(24-30)31-38 ❖ 73
	Exod. 1:6-22 1 Cor. 12:12-26 Mark 8:27—9:1

Friday	95* & 102 ❖ 107:1-32
	Exod. 2:1-22 1 Cor. 12:27—13:3 Mark 9:2-13

Saturday	107:33-43, 108:1-6(7-13) ❖ 33
	Exod. 2:23—3:15 1 Cor. 13:1-13 Mark 9:14-29

*For the Invitatory

Week of 5 Lent

Sunday 118 ❖ 145
Jer. 23:16-32   1 Cor. 9:19-27   Mark 8:31—9:1

Monday 31 ❖ 35
Jer. 24:1-10   Rom. 9:19-33   John 9:1-17

Tuesday [120], 121, 122, 123 ❖ 124, 125, 126, [127]
Jer. 25:8-17   Rom. 10:1-13   John 9:18-41

Wednesday 119:145-176 ❖ 128, 129, 130
Jer. 25:30-38   Rom. 10:14-21   John 10:1-18

Thursday 131, 132, [133] ❖ 140, 142
Jer. 26:1-16   Rom. 11:1-12   John 10:19-42

Friday 95* & 22 ❖ 141, 143:1-11(12)
Jer. 29:1, 4-13   Rom. 11:13-24   John 11:1-27, or 12:1-10

Saturday 137:1-6(7-9), 144 ❖ 42, 43
Jer. 31:27-34   Rom. 11:25-36   John 11:28-44, or 12:37-50

Holy Week

Palm Sunday 24, 29 ❖ 103
Zech. 9:9-12**   1 Tim. 6:12-16**
Zech. 12:9-11, 13:1, 7-9***   Matt. 21:12-17***

Monday 51:1-18(19-20) ❖ 69:1-23
Jer. 12:1-16   Phil. 3:1-14   John 12:9-19

Tuesday 6, 12 ❖ 94
Jer. 15:10-21   Phil. 3:15-21   John 12:20-26

Wednesday 55 ❖ 74
Jer. 17:5-10, 14-17   Phil. 4:1-13   John 12:27-36

Maundy Thursday 102 ❖ 142, 143
Jer. 20:7-11   1 Cor. 10:14-17; 11:27-32   John 17:1-11(12-26)

Good Friday 95* & 22 ❖ 40:1-14(15-19), 54
Wisdom 1:16—2:1, 12-22   1 Peter 1:10-20   John 13:36-38**
or Gen. 22:1-14   John 19:38-42***

Holy Saturday 95* & 88 ❖ 27
Job 19:21-27a   Heb. 4:1-16**   Rom. 8:1-11***

---

*For the Invitatory   **Intended for use in the morning   ***Intended for use in the evening

Week of 5 Lent

Sunday 118 ∴ 145
Exod. 3:16—4:12　　Rom. 12:1-21　　John 8:46-59

Monday 31 ∴ 35
Exod. 4:10-20(21-26)27-31　　1 Cor. 14:1-19　　Mark 9:30-41

Tuesday [120], 121, 122, 123 ∴ 124, 125, 126, [127]
Exod. 5:1—6:1　　1 Cor. 14:20-33a, 39-40　　Mark 9:42-50

Wednesday 119:145-176 ∴ 128, 129, 130
Exod. 7:8-24　　2 Cor. 2:14—3:6　　Mark 10:1-16

Thursday 131, 132, [133] ∴ 140, 142
Exod. 7:25—8:19　　2 Cor. 3:7-18　　Mark 10:17-31

Friday 95* & 22 ∴ 141, 143:1-11(12)
Exod. 9:13-35　　2 Cor. 4:1-12　　Mark 10:32-45

Saturday 137:1-6(7-9), 144 ∴ 42, 43
Exod. 10:21—11:8　　2 Cor. 4:13-18　　Mark 10:46-52

Holy Week

Palm Sunday 24, 29 ∴ 103
Zech. 9:9-12**　　1 Tim. 6:12-16**
Zech. 12:9-11; 13:1, 7-9***　　Luke 19:41-48***

Monday 51:1-18(19-20) ∴ 69:1-23
Lam. 1:1-2, 6-12　　2 Cor. 1:1-7　　Mark 11:12-25

Tuesday 6, 12 ∴ 94
Lam. 1:17-22　　2 Cor. 1:8-22　　Mark 11:27-33

Wednesday 55 ∴ 74
Lam. 2:1-9　　2 Cor. 1:23—2:11　　Mark 12:1-11

Maundy Thursday 102 ∴ 142, 143
Lam. 2:10-18　　1 Cor. 10:14-17; 11:27-32　　Mark 14:12-25

Good Friday 95* & 22 ∴ 40:1-14(15-19), 54
Lam. 3:1-9, 19-33　　1 Pet. 1:10-20　　John 13:36-38**
　　　　　　　　　　　　　　　　　　　　John 19:38-42***

Holy Saturday 95* & 88 ∴ 27
Lam. 3:37-58　　Heb. 4:1-16**　　Rom. 8:1-11***

*For the Invitatory　　**Intended for use in the morning　　***Intended for use in the evening*

Daily Office Year Two 957

Easter Week

Easter Day   148, 149, 150   ❖   113, 114, *or* 118
               Exod. 12:1-14**   ——   John 1:1-18**
               Isa. 51:9-11***   Luke 24:13-35, *or* John 20:19-23***

Monday   93, 98   ❖   66
               Jonah 2:1-9   Acts 2:14, 22-32*   John 14:1-14

Tuesday   103   ❖   111, 114
               Isa. 30:18-21   Acts 2:36-41(42-47)*   John 14:15-31

Wednesday   97, 99   ❖   115
               Micah 7:7-15   Acts 3:1-10*   John 15:1-11

Thursday   146, 147   ❖   148, 149
               Ezek. 37:1-14   Acts 3:11-26*   John 15:12-27

Friday   136   ❖   118
               Dan. 12:1-4, 13   Acts 4:1-12*   John 16:1-15

Saturday   145   ❖   104
               Isa. 25:1-9   Acts 4:13-21(22-31)*   John 16:16-33

Week of 2 Easter

Sunday   146, 147   ❖   111, 112, 113
               Isa. 43:8-13   1 Pet. 2:2-10   John 14:1-7

Monday   1, 2, 3   ❖   4, 7
               Dan. 1:1-21   1 John 1:1-10   John 17:1-11

Tuesday   5, 6   ❖   10, 11
               Dan. 2:1-16   1 John 2:1-11   John 17:12-19

Wednesday   119:1-24   ❖   12, 13, 14
               Dan. 2:17-30   1 John 2:12-17   John 17:20-26

Thursday   18:1-20   ❖   18:21-50
               Dan. 2:31-49   1 John 2:18-29   Luke 3:1-14

Friday   16, 17   ❖   134, 135
               Dan. 3:1-18   1 John 3:1-10   Luke 3:15-22

Saturday   20, 21:1-7(8-14)   ❖   110:1-5(6-7), 116, 117
               Dan. 3:19-30   1 John 3:11-18   Luke 4:1-13

**Intended for use in the morning   *Duplicates the First Lesson at the Eucharist.
***Intended for use in the evening   Readings from Year Two may be substituted.*

Easter Week

Easter Day	148, 149, 150 ∴ 113, 114, *or* 118		
	Exod. 12:1-14** —— John 1:1-18**		
	Isa. 51:9-11*** Luke 24:13-35, *or* John 20:19-23***		
Monday	93, 98 ∴ 66		
	Exod. 12:14-27	1 Cor. 15:1-11	Mark 16:1-8
Tuesday	103 ∴ 111, 114		
	Exod. 12:28-39	1 Cor. 15:12-28	Mark 16:9-20
Wednesday	97, 99 ∴ 115		
	Exod. 12:40-51	1 Cor. 15:(29)30-41	Matt. 28:1-16
Thursday	146, 147 ∴ 148, 149		
	Exod. 13:3-10	1 Cor. 15:41-50	Matt. 28:16-20
Friday	136 ∴ 118		
	Exod. 13:1-2, 11-16	1 Cor. 15:51-58	Luke 24:1-12
Saturday	145 —∴ 104		
	Exod. 13:17—14:4	2 Cor. 4:16—5:10	Mark 12:18-27

Week of 2 Easter

Sunday	146, 147 ∴ 111, 112, 113		
	Exod. 14:5-22	1 John 1:1-7	John 14:1-7
Monday	1, 2, 3 ∴ 4, 7		
	Exod. 14:21-31	1 Pet. 1:1-12	John 14:(1-7)8-17
Tuesday	5, 6 ∴ 10, 11		
	Exod. 15:1-21	1 Pet. 1:13-25	John 14:18-31
Wednesday	119:1-24 ∴ 12, 13, 14		
	Exod. 15:22—16:10	1 Pet. 2:1-10	John 15:1-11
Thursday	18:1-20 ∴ 18:21-50		
	Exod. 16:10-22	1 Pet. 2:11-25	John 15:12-27
Friday	16, 17 ∴ 134, 135		
	Exod. 16:23-36	1 Pet. 3:13—4:6	John 16:1-15
Saturday	20, 21:1-7(8-14) ∴ 110:1-5(6-7), 116, 117		
	Exod. 17:1-16	1 Pet. 4:7-19	John 16:16-33

***Intended for use in the morning*   ********Intended for use in the evening*

Week of 3 Easter

Sunday
148, 149, 150   ∴   114, 115
Dan. 4:1-18   1 Pet. 4:7-11   John 21:15-25

Monday
25   ∴   9, 15
Dan. 4:19-27   1 John 3:19—4:6   Luke 4:14-30

Tuesday
26, 28   ∴   36, 39
Dan. 4:28-37   1 John 4:7-21   Luke 4:31-37

Wednesday
38   ∴   119:25-48
Dan. 5:1-12   1 John 5:1-12   Luke 4:38-44

Thursday
37:1-18   ∴   37:19-42
Dan. 5:13-30   1 John 5:13-20(21)   Luke 5:1-11

Friday
105:1-22   ∴   105:23-45
Dan. 6:1-15   2 John 1-13   Luke 5:12-26

Saturday
30, 32   ∴   42, 43
Dan. 6:16-28   3 John 1-15   Luke 5:27-39

Week of 4 Easter

Sunday
63:1-8(9-11), 98   ∴   103
Wisdom 1:1-15   1 Pet. 5:1-11   Matt. 7:15-29

Monday
41, 52   ∴   44
Wisdom 1:16—2:11, 21-24   Col. 1:1-14   Luke 6:1-11

Tuesday
45   ∴   47, 48
Wisdom 3:1-9   Col. 1:15-23   Luke 6:12-26

Wednesday
119:49-72   ∴   49, [53]
Wisdom 4:16—5:8   Col. 1:24—2:7   Luke 6:27-38

Thursday
50   ∴   [59, 60] *or* 114, 115
Wisdom 5:9-23   Col. 2:8-23   Luke 6:39-49

Friday
40, 54   ∴   51
Wisdom 6:12-23   Col. 3:1-11   Luke 7:1-17

Saturday
55   ∴   138, 139:1-17(18-23)
Wisdom 7:1-14   Col. 3:12-17   Luke 7:18-28(29-30)31-35

Week of 3 Easter

Sunday	148, 149, 150 ∴ 114, 115		
	Exod. 18:1-12	1 John 2:7-17	Mark 16:9-20
Monday	25 ∴ 9, 15		
	Exod. 18:13-27	1 Pet. 5:1-14	Matt. (1:1-17); 3:1-6
Tuesday	26, 28 ∴ 36, 39		
	Exod. 19:1-16	Col. 1:1-14	Matt. 3:7-12
Wednesday	38 ∴ 119:25-48		
	Exod. 19:16-25	Col. 1:15-23	Matt. 3:13-17
Thursday	37:1-18 ∴ 37:19-42		
	Exod. 20:1-21	Col. 1:24—2:7	Matt. 4:1-11
Friday	105:1-22 ∴ 105:23-45		
	Exod. 24:1-18	Col. 2:8-23	Matt. 4:12-17
Saturday	30, 32 ∴ 42, 43		
	Exod. 25:1-22	Col. 3:1-17	Matt. 4:18-25

Week of 4 Easter

Sunday	63:1-8(9-11), 98 ∴ 103		
	Exod. 28:1-4, 30-38	1 John 2:18-29	Mark 6:30-44
Monday	41, 52 ∴ 44		
	Exod. 32:1-20	Col. 3:18—4:6(7-18)	Matt. 5:1-10
Tuesday	45 ∴ 47, 48		
	Exod. 32:21-34	1 Thess. 1:1-10	Matt. 5:11-16
Wednesday	119:49-72 ∴ 49, [53]		
	Exod. 33:1-23	1 Thess. 2:1-12	Matt. 5:17-20
Thursday	50 ∴ [59, 60] *or* 114, 115		
	Exod. 34:1-17	1 Thess. 2:13-20	Matt. 5:21-26
Friday	40, 54 ∴ 51		
	Exod. 34:18-35	1 Thess. 3:1-13	Matt. 5:27-37
Saturday	55 ∴ 138, 139:1-17(18-23)		
	Exod. 40:18-38	1 Thess. 4:1-12	Matt. 5:38-48

Week of 5 Easter

Sunday   24, 29   ∴   8, 84
              Wisdom 7:22—8:1   2 Thess. 2:13-17   Matt. 7:7-14

Monday   56, 57, [58]   ∴   64, 65
              Wisdom 9:1, 7-18   Col. (3:18—4:1)2-18   Luke 7:36-50

Tuesday   61, 62   ∴   68:1-20(21-23)24-36
              Wisdom 10:1-4(5-12)13-21   Rom. 12:1-21   Luke 8:1-15

Wednesday   72   ∴   119:73-96
              Wisdom 13:1-9   Rom. 13:1-14   Luke 8:16-25

Thursday   [70], 71   ∴   74
              Wisdom 14:27—15:3   Rom. 14:1-12   Luke 8:26-39

Friday   106:1-18   ∴   106:19-48
              Wisdom 16:15—17:1   Rom. 14:13-23   Luke 8:40-56

Saturday   75, 76   ∴   23, 27
              Wisdom 19:1-8, 18-22   Rom. 15:1-13   Luke 9:1-17

Week of 6 Easter

Sunday   93, 96   ∴   34
              Ecclus. 43:1-12, 27-32   1 Tim. 3:14—4:5   Matt. 13:24-34a

Monday   80   ∴   77, [79]
              Deut. 8:1-10   James 1:1-15   Luke 9:18-27

Tuesday   78:1-39   ∴   78:40-72
              Deut. 8:11-20   James 1:16-27   Luke 11:1-13

Wednesday   119:97-120   ∴   ——
              Baruch 3:24-37   James 5:13-18   Luke 12:22-31

Eve of Ascension   ——   ∴   68:1-20
              2 Kings 2:1-15   Rev. 5:1-14

Ascension Day   8, 47   ∴   24, 96
              Ezek. 1:1-14, 24-28b   Heb. 2:5-18   Matt. 28:16-20

Friday   85, 86   ∴   91, 92
              Ezek. 1:28—3:3   Heb. 4:14—5:6   Luke 9:28-36

Saturday   87, 90   ∴   136
              Ezek. 3:4-17   Heb. 5:7-14   Luke 9:37-50

Week of 5 Easter

Sunday	24, 29 ∴ 8, 84		
	Lev. 8:1-13, 30-36	Heb. 12:1-14	Luke 4:16-30
Monday	56, 57, [58] ∴ 64, 65		
	Lev. 16:1-19	1 Thess. 4:13-18	Matt. 6:1-6, 16-18
Tuesday	61, 62 ∴ 68:1-20(21-23)24-36		
	Lev. 16:20-34	1 Thess. 5:1-11	Matt. 6:7-15
Wednesday	72 ∴ 119:73-96		
	Lev. 19:1-18	1 Thess. 5:12-28	Matt. 6:19-24
Thursday	[70], 71 ∴ 74		
	Lev. 19:26-37	2 Thess. 1:1-12	Matt. 6:25-34
Friday	106:1-18 ∴ 106:19-48		
	Lev. 23:1-22	2 Thess. 2:1-17	Matt. 7:1-12
Saturday	75, 76 ∴ 23, 27		
	Lev. 23:23-44	2 Thess. 3:1-18	Matt. 7:13-21

Week of 6 Easter

Sunday	93, 96 ∴ 34		
	Lev. 25:1-17	James 1:2-8, 16-18	Luke 12:13-21
Monday	80 ∴ 77, [79]		
	Lev. 25:35-55	Col. 1:9-14	Matt. 13:1-16
Tuesday	78:1-39 ∴ 78:40-72		
	Lev. 26:1-20	1 Tim. 2:1-6	Matt. 13:18-23
Wednesday	119:97-120 ∴ ——		
	Lev. 26:27-42	Eph. 1:1-10	Matt. 22:41-46
Eve of Ascension	—— ∴ 68:1-20		
	2 Kings 2:1-15	Rev. 5:1-14	
Ascension Day	8, 47 ∴ 24, 96		
	Dan. 7:9-14	Heb. 2:5-18	Matt. 28:16-20
Friday	85, 86 ∴ 91, 92		
	1 Sam. 2:1-10	Eph. 2:1-10	Matt. 7:22-27
Saturday	87, 90 ∴ 136		
	Num. 11:16-17, 24-29	Eph. 2:11-22	Matt. 7:28—8:4

Week of 7 Easter

Sunday	66, 67 ∴	19, 46	
	Ezek. 3:16-27	Eph. 2:1-10	Matt. 10:24-33, 40-42
Monday	89:1-18 ∴	89:19-52	
	Ezek. 4:1-17	Heb. 6:1-12	Luke 9:51-62
Tuesday	97, 99, [100] ∴	94, [95]	
	Ezek. 7:10-15, 23b-27	Heb. 6:13-20	Luke 10:1-17
Wednesday	101, 109:1-4(5-19)20-30 ∴	119:121-144	
	Ezek. 11:14-25	Heb. 7:1-17	Luke 10:17-24
Thursday	105:1-22 ∴	105:23-45	
	Ezek. 18:1-4, 19-32	Heb. 7:18-28	Luke 10:25-37
Friday	102 ∴	107:1-32	
	Ezek. 34:17-31	Heb. 8:1-13	Luke 10:38-42
Saturday	107:33-43, 108:1-6(7-13) ∴	———	
	Ezek. 43:1-12	Heb. 9:1-14	Luke 11:14-23
Eve of Pentecost	——— ∴	33	
	Exod. 19:3-8a, 16-20	1 Pet. 2:4-10	
The Day of Pentecost	118 ∴	145	
	Isa. 11:1-9	1 Cor. 2:1-13	John 14:21-29

*On the weekdays which follow, the Readings are taken from
the numbered Proper (one through six) which corresponds
most closely to the date of Pentecost.*

Eve of Trinity Sunday	——— ∴	104	
	Ecclus. 42:15-25	Eph. 3:14-21	
Trinity Sunday	146, 147 ∴	111, 112, 113	
	Ecclus. 43:1-12(27-33)	Eph. 4:1-16	John 1:1-18

*On the weekdays which follow, the Readings are taken from
the numbered Proper (two through seven) which corresponds
most closely to the date of Trinity Sunday.*

Week of 7 Easter

Sunday	66, 67 ∴	19, 46	
	Exod. 3:1-12	Heb. 12:18-29	Luke 10:17-24
Monday	89:1-18 ∴	89:19-52	
	Joshua 1:1-9	Eph. 3:1-13	Matt. 8:5-17
Tuesday	97, 99, [100] ∴	94, [95]	
	1 Sam. 16:1-13a	Eph. 3:14-21	Matt. 8:18-27
Wednesday	101, 109:1-4(5-19)20-30 ∴	119:121-144	
	Isa. 4:2-6	Eph. 4:1-16	Matt. 8:28-34
Thursday	105:1-22 ∴	105:23-45	
	Zech. 4:1-14	Eph. 4:17-32	Matt. 9:1-8
Friday	102 ∴	107:1-32	
	Jer. 31:27-34	Eph. 5:1-20	Matt. 9:9-17
Saturday	107:33-43, 108:1-6(7-13) ∴	——	
	Ezek. 36:22-27	Eph. 6:10-24	Matt. 9:18-26
Eve of Pentecost	—— ∴	33	
	Exod. 19:3-8a, 16-20	1 Pet. 2:4-10	
The Day of Pentecost	118 ∴	145	
	Deut. 16:9-12	Acts 4:18-21, 23-33	John 4:19-26

> On the weekdays which follow, the Readings are taken from
> the numbered Proper (one through six) which corresponds
> most closely to the date of Pentecost.

Eve of Trinity Sunday	—— ∴	104	
	Ecclus. 42:15-25	Eph. 3:14-21	
Trinity Sunday	146, 147 ∴	111, 112, 113	
	Job 38:1-11; 42:1-5	Rev. 19:4-16	John 1:29-34

> On the weekdays which follow, the Readings are taken from
> the numbered Proper (two through seven) which corresponds
> most closely to the date of Trinity Sunday.

The Season after Pentecost

Directions for the use of the Propers which follow are on page 158.

Proper 1   *Week of the Sunday closest to May 11*

Monday
106:1-18   ❖   106:19-48
Isa. 63:7-14   2 Tim. 1:1-14   Luke 11:24-36

Tuesday
[120], 121, 122, 123   ❖   124, 125, 126, [127]
Isa. 63:15—64:9   2 Tim. 1:15—2:13   Luke 11:37-52

Wednesday
119:145-176   ❖   128, 129, 130
Isa. 65:1-12   2 Tim. 2:14-26   Luke 11:53—12:12

Thursday
131, 132, [133]   ❖   134, 135
Isa. 65:17-25   2 Tim. 3:1-17   Luke 12:13-31

Friday
140, 142   ❖   141, 143:1-11(12)
Isa. 66:1-6   2 Tim. 4:1-8   Luke 12:32-48

Saturday
137:1-6(7-9), 144   ❖   104
Isa. 66:7-14   2 Tim. 4:9-22   Luke 12:49-59

Proper 2   *Week of the Sunday closest to May 18*

Monday
1, 2, 3   ❖   4, 7
Ruth 1:1-18   1 Tim. 1:1-17   Luke 13:1-9

Tuesday
5, 6   ❖   10, 11
Ruth 1:19—2:13   1 Tim. 1:18—2:8   Luke 13:10-17

Wednesday
119:1-24   ❖   12, 13, 14
Ruth 2:14-23   1 Tim. 3:1-16   Luke 13:18-30

Thursday
18:1-20   ❖   18:21-50
Ruth 3:1-18   1 Tim. 4:1-16   Luke 13:31-35

Friday
16, 17   ❖   22
Ruth 4:1-17   1 Tim. 5:17-22(23-25)   Luke 14:1-11

Saturday
20, 21:1-7(8-14)   ❖   110:1-5(6-7), 116, 117
Deut. 1:1-8   1 Tim. 6:6-21   Luke 14:12-24

The Season after Pentecost

Directions for the use of the Propers which follow are on page 158.

Proper 1   *Week of the Sunday closest to May 11*

Monday   106:1-18   ∻   106:19-48
               Ezek. 33:1-11   1 John 1:1-10   Matt. 9:27-34

Tuesday   [120], 121, 122, 123   ∻   124, 125, 126, [127]
               Ezek. 33:21-33   1 John 2:1-11   Matt. 9:35—10:4

Wednesday   119:145-176   ∻   128, 129, 130
               Ezek. 34:1-16   1 John 2:12-17   Matt. 10:5-15

Thursday   131, 132, [133]   ∻   134, 135
               Ezek. 37:21b-28   1 John 2:18-29   Matt. 10:16-23

Friday   140, 142   ∻   141, 143:1-11(12)
               Ezek. 39:21-29   1 John 3:1-10   Matt. 10:24-33

Saturday   137:1-6(7-9); 144   ∻   104
               Ezek. 47:1-12   1 John 3:11-18   Matt. 10:34-42

Proper 2   *Week of the Sunday closest to May 18*

Monday   1, 2, 3   ∻   4, 7
               Prov. 3:11-20   1 John 3:18—4:6   Matt. 11:1-6

Tuesday   5, 6   ∻   10, 11
               Prov. 4:1-27   1 John 4:7-21   Matt. 11:7-15

Wednesday   119:1-24   ∻   12, 13, 14
               Prov. 6:1-19   1 John 5:1-12   Matt. 11:16-24

Thursday   18:1-20   ∻   18:21-50
               Prov. 7:1-27   1 John 5:13-21   Matt. 11:25-30

Friday   16, 17   ∻   22
               Prov. 8:1-21   2 John 1-13   Matt. 12:1-14

Saturday   20, 21:1-7(8-14)   ∻   110:1-5(6-7), 116, 117
               Prov. 8:22-36   3 John 1-15   Matt. 12:15-21

Proper 3   *Week of the Sunday closest to May 25*

Sunday   148, 149, 150   ❖   114, 115
               Deut. 4:1-9   Rev. 7:1-4, 9-17   Matt. 12:33-45

Monday   25   ❖   9, 15
               Deut. 4:9-14   2 Cor. 1:1-11   Luke 14:25-35

Tuesday   26, 28   ❖   36, 39
               Deut. 4:15-24   2 Cor. 1:12-22   Luke 15:1-10

Wednesday   38   ❖   119:25-48
               Deut. 4:25-31   2 Cor. 1:23—2:17   Luke 15:1-2, 11-32

Thursday   37:1-18   ❖   37:19-42
               Deut. 4:32-40   2 Cor. 3:1-18   Luke 16:1-9

Friday   31   ❖   35
               Deut. 5:1-22   2 Cor. 4:1-12   Luke 16:10-17(18)

Saturday   30, 32   ❖   42, 43
               Deut. 5:22-33   2 Cor. 4:13—5:10   Luke 16:19-31

Proper 4   *Week of the Sunday closest to June 1*

Sunday   63:1-8(9-11), 98   ❖   103
               Deut. 11:1-12   Rev. 10:1-11   Matt. 13:44-58

Monday   41, 52   ❖   44
               Deut. 11:13-19   2 Cor. 5:11—6:2   Luke 17:1-10

Tuesday   45   ❖   47, 48
               Deut. 12:1-12   2 Cor. 6:3-13 (14—7:1)   Luke 17:11-19

Wednesday   119:49-72   ❖   49, [53]
               Deut. 13:1-11   2 Cor. 7:2-16   Luke 17:20-37

Thursday   50   ❖   [59, 60] *or* 8, 84
               Deut. 16:18-20; 17:14-20   2 Cor. 8:1-16   Luke 18:1-8

Friday   40, 54   ❖   51
               Deut. 26:1-11   2 Cor. 8:16-24   Luke 18:9-14

Saturday   55   ❖   138, 139:1-17(18-23)
               Deut. 29:2-15   2 Cor. 9:1-15   Luke 18:15-30

Proper 3   *Week of the Sunday closest to May 25*

Sunday   148, 149, 150   ∴   114, 115
           Prov. 9:1-12   Acts 8:14-25   Luke 10:25-28, 38-42

Monday   25   ∴   9, 15
           Prov. 10:1-12   1 Tim. 1:1-17   Matt. 12:22-32

Tuesday   26, 28   ∴   36, 39
           Prov. 15:16-33   1 Tim. 1:18—2:8   Matt. 12:33-42

Wednesday 38   ∴   119:25-48
           Prov. 17:1-20   1 Tim. 3:1-16   Matt. 12:43-50

Thursday   37:1-18   ∴   37:19-42
           Prov. 21:30—22:6   1 Tim. 4:1-16   Matt. 13:24-30

Friday   31   ∴   35
           Prov. 23:19-21, 29—24:2   1 Tim. 5:17-22(23-25)   Matt. 13:31-35

Saturday   30, 32   ∴   42, 43
           Prov. 25:15-28   1 Tim. 6:6-21   Matt. 13:36-43

Proper 4   *Week of the Sunday closest to June 1*

Sunday   63:1-8(9-11), 98   ∴   103
           Eccles. 1:1-11   Acts 8:26-40   Luke 11:1-13

Monday   41, 52   ∴   44
           Eccles. 2:1-15   Gal. 1:1-17   Matt. 13:44-52

Tuesday   45   ∴   47, 48
           Eccles. 2:16-26   Gal. 1:18—2:10   Matt. 13:53-58

Wednesday 119:49-72   ∴   49, [53]
           Eccles. 3:1-15   Gal. 2:11-21   Matt. 14:1-12

Thursday   50   ∴   [59, 60] *or* 8, 84
           Eccles. 3:16—4:3   Gal. 3:1-14   Matt. 14:13-21

Friday   40, 54   ∴   51
           Eccles. 5:1-7   Gal. 3:15-22   Matt. 14:22-36

Saturday   55   ∴   138, 139:1-17(18-23)
           Eccles. 5:8-20   Gal. 3:23—4:11   Matt. 15:1-20

Proper 5   *Week of the Sunday closest to June 8*

Sunday   24, 29   ❖   8, 84
                Deut. 29:16-29   Rev. 12:1-12   Matt. 15:29-39

Monday   56, 57, [58]   ❖   64, 65
                Deut. 30:1-10   2 Cor. 10:1-18   Luke 18:31-43

Tuesday   61, 62   ❖   68:1-20(21-23)24-36
                Deut. 30:11-20   2 Cor. 11:1-21a   Luke 19:1-10

Wednesday   72   ❖   119:73-96
                Deut. 31:30—32:14   2 Cor. 11:21b-33   Luke 19:11-27

Thursday   [70], 71   ❖   74
                Ecclus. 44:19—45:5   2 Cor. 12:1-10   Luke 19:28-40

Friday   69:1-23(24-30)31-38   ❖   73
                Ecclus. 45:6-16   2 Cor. 12:11-21   Luke 19:41-48

Saturday   75, 76   ❖   23, 27
                Ecclus. 46:1-10   2 Cor. 13:1-14   Luke 20:1-8

Proper 6   *Week of the Sunday closest to June 15*

Sunday   93, 96   ❖   34
                Ecclus. 46:11-20   Rev. 15:1-8   Matt. 18:1-14

Monday   80   ❖   77, [79]
                1 Samuel 1:1-20   Acts 1:1-14   Luke 20:9-19

Tuesday   78:1-39   ❖   78:40-72
                1 Samuel 1:21—2:11   Acts 1:15-26   Luke 20:19-26

Wednesday   119:97-120   ❖   81, 82
                1 Samuel 2:12-26   Acts 2:1-21   Luke 20:27-40

Thursday   [83] *or* 34   ❖   85, 86
                1 Samuel 2:27-36   Acts 2:22-36   Luke 20:41—21:4

Friday   88   ❖   91, 92
                1 Samuel 3:1-21   Acts 2:37-47   Luke 21:5-19

Saturday   87, 90   ❖   136
                1 Samuel 4:1b-11   Acts 4:32—5:11   Luke 21:20-28

Proper 5   *Week of the Sunday closest to June 8*

Sunday   24, 29   ❖   8, 84
Eccles. 6:1-12   Acts 10:9-23   Luke 12:32-40

Monday   56, 57, [58]   ❖   64, 65
Eccles. 7:1-14   Gal. 4:12-20   Matt. 15:21-28

Tuesday   61, 62   ❖   68:1-20(21-23)24-36
Eccles. 8:14—9:10   Gal. 4:21-31   Matt. 15:29-39

Wednesday   72   ❖   119:73-96
Eccles. 9:11-18   Gal. 5:1-15   Matt. 16:1-12

Thursday   [70], 71   ❖   74
Eccles. 11:1-8   Gal. 5:16-24   Matt. 16:13-20

Friday   69:1-23(24-30)31-38   ❖   73
Eccles. 11:9—12:14   Gal. 5:25—6:10   Matt. 16:21-28

Saturday   75, 76   ❖   23, 27
Num. 3:1-13   Gal. 6:11-18   Matt. 17:1-13

Proper 6   *Week of the Sunday closest to June 15*

Sunday   93, 96   ❖   34
Num. 6:22-27   Acts 13:1-12   Luke 12:41-48

Monday   80   ❖   77, [79]
Num. 9:15-23; 10:29-36   Rom. 1:1-15   Matt. 17:14-21

Tuesday   78:1-39   ❖   78:40-72
Num. 11:1-23   Rom. 1:16-25   Matt. 17:22-27

Wednesday   119:97-120   ❖   81, 82
Num. 11:24-33(34-35)   Rom. 1:28—2:11   Matt. 18:1-9

Thursday   [83] *or* 34   ❖   85, 86
Num. 12:1-16   Rom. 2:12-24   Matt. 18:10-20

Friday   88   ❖   91, 92
Num. 13:1-3, 21-30   Rom. 2:25—3:8   Matt. 18:21-35

Saturday   87, 90   ❖   136
Num. 13:31—14:25   Rom. 3:9-20   Matt. 19:1-12

Proper 7   *Week of the Sunday closest to June 22*

Sunday	66, 67 ∴ 19, 46		
	1 Samuel 4:12-22	James 1:1-18	Matt. 19:23-30
Monday	89:1-18 ∴ 89:19-52		
	1 Samuel 5:1-12	Acts 5:12-26	Luke 21:29-36
Tuesday	97, 99, [100] ∴ 94, [95]		
	1 Samuel 6:1-16	Acts 5:27-42	Luke 21:37—22:13
Wednesday	101, 109:1-4(5-19) 20-30 ∴ 119:121-144		
	1 Samuel 7:2-17	Acts 6:1-15	Luke 22:14-23
Thursday	105:1-22 ∴ 105:23-45		
	1 Samuel 8:1-22	Acts 6:15—7:16	Luke 22:24-30
Friday	102 ∴ 107:1-32		
	1 Samuel 9:1-14	Acts 7:17-29	Luke 22:31-38
Saturday	107:33-43, 108:1-6(7-13) ∴ 33		
	1 Samuel 9:15—10:1	Acts 7:30-43	Luke 22:39-51

Proper 8   *Week of the Sunday closest to June 29*

Sunday	118 ∴ 145		
	1 Samuel 10:1-16	Rom. 4:13-25	Matt. 21:23-32
Monday	106:1-18 ∴ 106:19-48		
	1 Samuel 10:17-27	Acts 7:44—8:1a	Luke 22:52-62
Tuesday	[120], 121, 122, 123 ∴ 124, 125, 126, [127]		
	1 Samuel 11:1-15	Acts 8:1-13	Luke 22:63-71
Wednesday	119:145-176 ∴ 128, 129, 130		
	1 Samuel 12:1-6, 16-25	Acts 8:14-25	Luke 23:1-12
Thursday	131, 132, [133] ∴ 134, 135		
	1 Samuel 13:5-18	Acts 8:26-40	Luke 23:13-25
Friday	140, 142 ∴ 141, 143:1-11(12)		
	1 Samuel 13:19—14:15	Acts 9:1-9	Luke 23:26-31
Saturday	137:1-6(7-9), 144 ∴ 104		
	1 Samuel 14:16-30	Acts 9:10-19a	Luke 23:32-43

Proper 7   *Week of the Sunday closest to June 22*

Sunday   66, 67   ∴   19, 46
Num. 14:26-45   Acts 15:1-12   Luke 12:49-56

Monday   89:1-18   ∴   89:19-52
Num. 16:1-19   Rom. 3:21-31   Matt. 19:13-22

Tuesday   97, 99, [100]   ∴   94, [95]
Num. 16:20-35   Rom. 4:1-12   Matt. 19:23-30

Wednesday   101, 109:1-4(5-19)20-30   ∴   119:121-144
Num. 16:36-50   Rom. 4:13-25   Matt. 20:1-16

Thursday   105:1-22   ∴   105:23-45
Num. 17:1-11   Rom. 5:1-11   Matt. 20:17-28

Friday   102   ∴   107:1-32
Num. 20:1-13   Rom. 5:12-21   Matt. 20:29-34

Saturday   107:33-43, 108:1-6(7-13)   ∴   33
Num. 20:14-29   Rom. 6:1-11   Matt. 21:1-11

Proper 8   *Week of the Sunday closest to June 29*

Sunday   118   ∴   145
Num. 21:4-9, 21-35   Acts 17:(12-21)22-34   Luke 13:10-17

Monday   106:1-18   ∴   106:19-48
Num. 22:1-21   Rom. 6:12-23   Matt. 21:12-22

Tuesday   [120], 121, 122, 123   ∴   124, 125, 126, [127]
Num. 22:21-38   Rom. 7:1-12   Matt. 21:23-32

Wednesday   119:145-176   ∴   128, 129, 130
Num. 22:41—23:12   ∴   Rom. 7:13-25   Matt. 21:33-46

Thursday   131, 132, [133]   ∴   134, 135
Num. 23:11-26   Rom. 8:1-11   Matt. 22:1-14

Friday   140, 142   ∴   141, 143:1-11(12)
Num. 24:1-13   Rom. 8:12-17   Matt. 22:15-22

Saturday   137:1-6(7-9), 144   ∴   104
Num. 24:12-25   Rom. 8:18-25   Matt. 22:23-40

Proper 9   *Week of the Sunday closest to July 6*

| Sunday | 146, 147   ❖   111, 112, 113 |
| | 1 Samuel 14:36-45   Rom. 5:1-11   Matt. 22:1-14 |

Sunday   146, 147   ❖   111, 112, 113
            1 Samuel 14:36-45   Rom. 5:1-11   Matt. 22:1-14

Monday   1, 2, 3   ❖   4, 7
            1 Samuel 15:1-3, 7-23   Acts 9:19b-31   Luke 23:44-56a

Tuesday   5, 6   ❖   10, 11
            1 Samuel 15:24-35   Acts 9:32-43   Luke 23:56b—24:11

Wednesday   119:1-24   ❖   12, 13, 14
            1 Samuel 16:1-13   Acts 10:1-16   Luke 24:13-35

Thursday   18:1-20   ❖   18:21-50
            1 Samuel 16:14—17:11   Acts 10:17-33   Luke 24:36-53

Friday   16, 17   ❖   22
            1 Samuel 17:17-30   Acts 10:34-48   Mark 1:1-13

Saturday   20, 21:1-7(8-14)   ❖   110:1-5(6-7), 116, 117
            1 Samuel 17:31-49   Acts 11:1-18   Mark 1:14-28

Proper 10   *Week of the Sunday closest to July 13*

Sunday   148, 149, 150   ❖   114, 115
            1 Samuel 17:50—18:4   Rom. 10:4-17   Matt. 23:29-39

Monday   25   ❖   9, 15
            1 Samuel 18:5-16, 27b-30   Acts 11:19-30   Mark 1:29-45

Tuesday   26, 28   ❖   36, 39
            1 Samuel 19:1-18   Acts 12:1-17   Mark 2:1-12

Wednesday   38   ❖   119:25-48
            1 Samuel 20:1-23   Acts 12:18-25   Mark 2:13-22

Thursday   37:1-18   ❖   37:19-42
            1 Samuel 20:24-42   Acts 13:1-12   Mark 2:23—3:6

Friday   31   ❖   35
            1 Samuel 21:1-15   Acts 13:13-25   Mark 3:7-19a

Saturday   30, 32   ❖   42, 43
            1 Samuel 22:1-23   Acts 13:26-43   Mark 3:19b-35

Proper 9   *Week of the Sunday closest to July 6*

| Sunday | 146, 147 ❖ 111, 112, 113 |
| | Num. 27:12-23   Acts 19:11-20   Mark 1:14-20 |

Monday   1, 2, 3 ❖ 4, 7
Num. 32:1-6, 16-27   Rom. 8:26-30   Matt. 23:1-12

Tuesday   5, 6 ❖ 10, 11
Num. 35:1-3, 9-15, 30-34   Rom. 8:31-39   Matt. 23:13-26

Wednesday   119:1-24 ❖ 12, 13, 14
Deut. 1:1-18   Rom. 9:1-18   Matt. 23:27-39

Thursday   18:1-20 ❖ 18:21-50
Deut. 3:18-28   Rom. 9:19-33   Matt. 24:1-14

Friday   16, 17 ❖ 22
Deut. 31:7-13, 24—32:4   Rom. 10:1-13   Matt. 24:15-31

Saturday   20, 21:1-7(8-14) ❖ 110:1-5(6-7), 116, 117
Deut. 34:1-12   Rom. 10:14-21   Matt. 24:32-51

Proper 10   *Week of the Sunday closest to July 13*

Sunday   148, 149, 150 ❖ 114, 115
Joshua 1:1-18   Acts 21:3-15   Mark 1:21-27

Monday   25 ❖ 9, 15
Joshua 2:1-14   Rom. 11:1-12   Matt. 25:1-13

Tuesday   26, 28 ❖ 36, 39
Joshua 2:15-24   Rom. 11:13-24   Matt. 25:14-30

Wednesday   38 ❖ 119:25-48
Joshua 3:1-13   Rom. 11:25-36   Matt. 25:31-46

Thursday   37:1-18 ❖ 37:19-42
Joshua 3:14—4:7   Rom. 12:1-8   Matt. 26:1-16

Friday   31 ❖ 35
Joshua 4:19—5:1, 10-15   Rom. 12:9-21   Matt. 26:17-25

Saturday   30, 32 ❖ 42, 43
Joshua 6:1-14   Rom. 13:1-7   Matt. 26:26-35

Proper 11   *Week of the Sunday closest to July 20*

| *Sunday* | 63:1-8(9-11), 98   ❖   103 |
| | 1 Samuel 23:7-18   Rom. 11:33—12:2   Matt. 25:14-30 |

| *Monday* | 41, 52   ❖   44 |
| | 1 Samuel 24:1-22   Acts 13:44-52   Mark 4:1-20 |

| *Tuesday* | 45   ❖   47, 48 |
| | 1 Samuel 25:1-22   Acts 14:1-18   Mark 4:21-34 |

| *Wednesday* | 119:49-72   ❖   49, [53] |
| | 1 Samuel 25:23-44   Acts 14:19-28   Mark 4:35-41 |

| *Thursday* | 50   ❖   [59, 60] *or* 66, 67 |
| | 1 Samuel 28:3-20   Acts 15:1-11   Mark 5:1-20 |

| *Friday* | 40, 54   ❖   51 |
| | 1 Samuel 31:1-13   Acts 15:12-21   Mark 5:21-43 |

| *Saturday* | 55   ❖   138, 139:1-17(18-23) |
| | 2 Samuel 1:1-16   Acts 15:22-35   Mark 6:1-13 |

Proper 12   *Week of the Sunday closest to July 27*

| *Sunday* | 24, 29   ❖   8, 84 |
| | 2 Samuel 1:17-27   Rom. 12:9-21   Matt. 25:31-46 |

| *Monday* | 56, 57, [58]   ❖   64, 65 |
| | 2 Samuel 2:1-11   Acts 15:36—16:5   Mark 6:14-29 |

| *Tuesday* | 61, 62   ❖   68:1-20(21-23)24-36 |
| | 2 Samuel 3:6-21   Acts 16:6-15   Mark 6:30-46 |

| *Wednesday* | 72   ❖   119:73-96 |
| | 2 Samuel 3:22-39   Acts 16:16-24   Mark 6:47-56 |

| *Thursday* | [70], 71   ❖   74 |
| | 2 Samuel 4:1-12   Acts 16:25-40   Mark 7:1-23 |

| *Friday* | 69:1-23(24-30)31-38   ❖   73 |
| | 2 Samuel 5:1-12   Acts 17:1-15   Mark 7:24-37 |

| *Saturday* | 75, 76   ❖   23, 27 |
| | 2 Samuel 5:22—6:11   Acts 17:16-34   Mark 8:1-10 |

Proper 11   *Week of the Sunday closest to July 20*

Sunday	63:1-8(9-11), 98 ∴ 103		
	Joshua 6:15-27	Acts 22:30—23:11	Mark 2:1-12
Monday	41, 52 ∴ 44		
	Joshua 7:1-13	Rom. 13:8-14	Matt. 26:36-46
Tuesday	45 ∴ 47, 48		
	Joshua 8:1-22	Rom. 14:1-12	Matt. 26:47-56
Wednesday	119:49-72 ∴ 49, [53]		
	Joshua 8:30-35	Rom. 14:13-23	Matt. 26:57-68
Thursday	50 ∴ [59, 60] or 66, 67		
	Joshua 9:3-21	Rom. 15:1-13	Matt. 26:69-75
Friday	40, 54 ∴ 51		
	Joshua 9:22—10:15	Rom. 15:14-24	Matt. 27:1-10
Saturday	55 ∴ 138, 139:1-17(18-23)		
	Joshua 23:1-16	Rom. 15:25-33	Matt. 27:11-23

Proper 12   *Week of the Sunday closest to July 27*

Sunday	24, 29 ∴ 8, 84		
	Joshua 24:1-15	Acts 28:23-31	Mark 2:23-28
Monday	56, 57, [58] ∴ 64, 65		
	Joshua 24:16-33	Rom. 16:1-16	Matt. 27:24-31
Tuesday	61, 62 ∴ 68:1-20(21-23)24-36		
	Judges 2:1-5, 11-23	Rom. 16:17-27	Matt. 27:32-44
Wednesday	72 ∴ 119:73-96		
	Judges 3:12-30	Acts 1:1-14	Matt. 27:45-54
Thursday	[70], 71 ∴ 74		
	Judges 4:4-23	Acts 1:15-26	Matt. 27:55-66
Friday	69:1-23(24-30)31-38 ∴ 73		
	Judges 5:1-18	Acts 2:1-21	Matt. 28:1-10
Saturday	75, 76 ∴ 23, 27		
	Judges 5:19-31	Acts 2:22-36	Matt. 28:11-20

Proper 13   *Week of the Sunday closest to August 3*

Sunday   93, 96   ❖   34
              2 Samuel 6:12-23   Rom. 14:7-12   John 1:43-51

Monday   80   ❖   77, [79]
              2 Samuel 7:1-17   Acts 18:1-11   Mark 8:11-21

Tuesday   78:1-39   ❖   78:40-72
              2 Samuel 7:18-29   Acts 18:12-28   Mark. 8:22-33

Wednesday   119:97-120   ❖   81, 82
              2 Samuel 9:1-13   Acts 19:1-10   Mark 8:34—9:1

Thursday   [83] or 145   ❖   85, 86
              2 Samuel 11:1-27   Acts 19:11-20   Mark 9:2-13

Friday   88   ❖   91, 92
              2 Samuel 12:1-14   Acts 19:21-41   Mark 9:14-29

Saturday   87, 90   ❖   136
              2 Samuel 12:15-31   Acts 20:1-16   Mark 9:30-41

Proper 14   *Week of the Sunday closest to August 10*

Sunday   66, 67   ❖   19, 46
              2 Samuel 13:1-22   Rom. 15:1-13   John 3:22-36

Monday   89:1-18   ❖   89:19-52
              2 Samuel 13:23-39   Acts 20:17-38   Mark 9:42-50

Tuesday   97, 99, [100]   ❖   94, [95]
              2 Samuel 14:1-20   Acts 21:1-14   Mark 10:1-16

Wednesday   101, 109:1-4(5-19)20-30   ❖   119:121-144
              2 Samuel 14:21-33   Acts 21:15-26   Mark 10:17-31

Thursday   105:1-22   ❖   105:23-45
              2 Samuel 15:1-18   Acts 21:27-36   Mark 10:32-45

Friday   102   ❖   107:1-32
              2 Samuel 15:19-37   Acts 21:37—22:16   Mark 10:46-52

Saturday   107:33-43, 108:1-6(7-13)   ❖   33
              2 Samuel 16:1-23   Acts 22:17-29   Mark 11:1-11

Proper 13   *Week of the Sunday closest to August 3*

Sunday	93, 96 ∴ 34		
	Judges 6:1-24	2 Cor. 9:6-15	Mark 3:20-30
Monday	80 ∴ 77, [79]		
	Judges 6:25-40	Acts 2:37-47	John 1:1-18
Tuesday	78:1-39 ∴ 78:40-72		
	Judges 7:1-18	Acts 3:1-11	John 1:19-28
Wednesday	119:97-120 ∴ 81, 82		
	Judges 7:19—8:12	Acts 3:12-26	John 1:29-42
Thursday	[83] *or* 145 ∴ 85, 86		
	Judges 8:22-35	Acts 4:1-12	John 1:43-51
Friday	88 ∴ 91, 92		
	Judges 9:1-16, 19-21	Acts 4:13-31	John 2:1-12
Saturday	87, 90 ∴ 136		
	Judges 9:22-25, 50-57	Acts 4:32—5:11	John 2:13-25

Proper 14   *Week of the Sunday closest to August 10*

Sunday	66, 67 ∴ 19, 46		
	Judges 11:1-11, 29-40	2 Cor. 11:21b-31	Mark 4:35-41
Monday	89:1-18 ∴ 89:19-52		
	Judges 12:1-7	Acts 5:12-26	John 3:1-21
Tuesday	97, 99, [100] ∴ 94, [95]		
	Judges 13:1-15	Acts 5:27-42	John 3:22-36
Wednesday	101, 109:1-4(5-19)20-30 ∴ 119:121-144		
	Judges 13:15-24	Acts 6:1-15	John 4:1-26
Thursday	105:1-22 ∴ 105:23-45		
	Judges 14:1-19	Acts 6:15—7:16	John 4:27-42
Friday	102 ∴ 107:1-32		
	Judges 14:20—15:20	Acts 7:17-29	John 4:43-54
Saturday	107:33-43, 108:1-6(7-13) ∴ 33		
	Judges 16:1-14	Acts 7:30-43	John 5:1-18

Proper 15 *Week of the Sunday closest to August 17*

Sunday   118   ⫶   145
2 Samuel 17:1-23   Gal. 3:6-14   John 5:30-47

Monday   106:1-18   ⫶   106:19-48
2 Samuel 17:24—18:8   Acts 22:30—23:11   Mark 11:12-26

Tuesday   [120], 121, 122, 123   ⫶   124, 125, 126, [127]
2 Samuel 18:9-18   Acts 23:12-24   Mark 11:27—12:12

Wednesday   119:145-176   ⫶   128, 129, 130
2 Samuel 18:19-33   Acts 23:23-35   Mark 12:13-27

Thursday   131, 132, [133]   ⫶   134, 135
2 Samuel 19:1-23   Acts 24:1-23   Mark 12:28-34

Friday   140, 142   ⫶   141, 143:1-11(12)
2 Samuel 19:24-43   Acts 24:24—25:12   Mark 12:35-44

Saturday   137:1-6(7-9), 144   ⫶   104
2 Samuel 23:1-7, 13-17   Acts 25:13-27   Mark 13:1-13

Proper 16 *Week of the Sunday closest to August 24*

Sunday   146, 147   ⫶   111, 112, 113
2 Samuel 24:1-2, 10-25   Gal. 3:23—4:7   John 8:12-20

Monday   1, 2, 3   ⫶   4, 7
1 Kings 1:5-31   Acts 26:1-23   Mark 13:14-27

Tuesday   5, 6   ⫶   10, 11
1 Kings 1:38—2:4   Acts 26:24—27:8   Mark 13:28-37

Wednesday   119:1-24   ⫶   12, 13, 14
1 Kings 3:1-15   Acts 27:9-26   Mark 14:1-11

Thursday   18:1-20   ⫶   18:21-50
1 Kings 3:16-28   Acts 27:27-44   Mark 14:12-26

Friday   16, 17   ⫶   22
1 Kings 5:1—6:1, 7   Acts 28:1-16   Mark 14:27-42

Saturday   20, 21:1-7(8-14)   ⫶   110:1-5(6-7), 116, 117
1 Kings 7:51—8:21   Acts 28:17-31   Mark 14:43-52

Proper 15   *Week of the Sunday closest to August 17*

Sunday   118   ∴   145
             Judges 16:15-31   2 Cor. 13:1-11   Mark 5:25-34

Monday   106:1-18   ∴   106:19-48
             Judges 17:1-13   Acts 7:44—8:1a   John 5:19-29

Tuesday   [120], 121, 122, 123   ∴   124, 125, 126, [127]
             Judges 18:1-15   Acts 8:1-13   John 5:30-47

Wednesday   119:145-176   ∴   128, 129, 130
             Judges 18:16-31   Acts 8:14-25   John 6:1-15

Thursday   131, 132, [133]   ∴   134, 135
             Job 1:1-22   Acts 8:26-40   John 6:16-27

Friday   140, 142   ∴   141, 143:1-11(12)
             Job 2:1-13   Acts 9:1-9   John 6:27-40

Saturday   137:1-6(7-9), 144   ∴   104
             Job 3:1-26   Acts 9:10-19a   John 6:41-51

Proper 16   *Week of the Sunday closest to August 24*

Sunday   146, 147   ∴   111, 112, 113
             Job 4:1-6, 12-21   Rev. 4:1-11   Mark 6:1-6a

Monday   1, 2, 3   ∴   4, 7
             Job 4:1; 5:1-11, 17-21, 26-27   Acts 9:19b-31   John 6:52-59

Tuesday   5, 6   ∴   10, 11
             Job 6:1-4, 8-15, 21   Acts 9:32-43   John 6:60-71

Wednesday   119:1-24   ∴   12, 13, 14
             Job 6:1; 7:1-21   Acts 10:1-16   John 7:1-13

Thursday   18:1-20   ∴   18:21-50
             Job 8:1-10, 20-22   Acts 10:17-33   John 7:14-36

Friday   16, 17   ∴   22
             Job 9:1-15, 32-35   Acts 10:34-48   John 7:37-52

Saturday   20, 21:1-7(8-14)   ∴   110:1-5(6-7), 116, 117
             Job 9:1; 10:1-9, 16-22   Acts 11:1-18   John 8:12-20

Proper 17   *Week of the Sunday closest to August 31*

Sunday   148, 149, 150   ∴   114, 115
                1 Kings 8:22-30(31-40)   1 Tim. 4:7b-16   John 8:47-59

Monday   25   ∴   9, 15
                2 Chron. 6:32—7:7   James 2:1-13   Mark 14:53-65

Tuesday   26, 28   ∴   36, 39
                1 Kings 8:65—9:9   James 2:14-26   Mark 14:66-72

Wednesday   38   ∴   119:25-48
                1 Kings 9:24—10:13   James 3:1-12   Mark 15:1-11

Thursday   37:1-18   ∴   37:19-42
                1 Kings 11:1-13   James 3:13—4:12   Mark 15:12-21

Friday   31   ∴   35
                1 Kings 11:26-43   James 4:13—5:6   Mark 15:22-32

Saturday   30, 32   ∴   42, 43
                1 Kings 12:1-20   James 5:7-12, 19-20   Mark 15:33-39

Proper 18   *Week of the Sunday closest to September 7*

Sunday   63:1-8(9-11), 98   ∴   103
                1 Kings 12:21-33   Acts 4:18-31   John 10:31-42

Monday   41, 52   ∴   44
                1 Kings 13:1-10   Phil. 1:1-11   Mark 15:40-47

Tuesday   45   ∴   47, 48
                1 Kings 16:23-34   Phil. 1:12-30   Mark 16:1-8(9-20)

Wednesday   119:49-72   ∴   49, [53]
                1 Kings 17:1-24   Phil. 2:1-11   Matt. 2:1-12

Thursday   50   ∴   [59, 60] *or* 93, 96
                1 Kings 18:1-19   Phil. 2:12-30   Matt. 2:13-23

Friday   40, 54   ∴   51
                1 Kings 18:20-40   Phil. 3:1-16   Matt. 3:1-12

Saturday   55   ∴   138, 139:1-17(18-23)
                1 Kings 18:41—19:8   Phil. 3:17—4:7   Matt. 3:13-17

Proper 17   *Week of the Sunday closest to August 31*

Sunday   148, 149, 150   ∴   114, 115
Job 11:1-9, 13-20   Rev. 5:1-14   Matt. 5:1-12

Monday   25   ∴   9, 15
Job 12:1-6, 13-25   Acts 11:19-30   John 8:21-32

Tuesday   26, 28   ∴   36, 39
Job 12:1; 13:3-17, 21-27   Acts 12:1-17   John 8:33-47

Wednesday   38   ∴   119:25-48
Job 12:1; 14:1-22   Acts 12:18-25   John 8:47-59

Thursday   37:1-18   ∴   37:19-42
Job 16:16-22; 17:1, 13-16   Acts 13:1-12   John 9:1-17

Friday   31   ∴   35
Job 19:1-7, 14-27   Acts 13:13-25   John 9:18-41

Saturday   30, 32   ∴   42, 43
Job 22:1-4, 21—23:7   Acts 13:26-43   John 10:1-18

Proper 18   *Week of the Sunday closest to September 7*

Sunday   63:1-8(9-11), 98   ∴   103
Job 25:1-6; 27:1-6   Rev. 14:1-7, 13   Matt. 5:13-20

Monday   41, 52   ∴   44
Job 32:1-10, 19—33:1, 19-28   Acts 13:44-52   John 10:19-30

Tuesday   45   ∴   47, 48
Job 29:1-20   Acts 14:1-18   John 10:31-42

Wednesday   119:49-72   ∴   49, [53]
Job 29:1; 30:1-2, 16-31   Acts 14:19-28   John 11:1-16

Thursday   50   ∴   [59, 60] *or* 93, 96
Job 29:1; 31:1-23   Acts 15:1-11   John 11:17-29

Friday   40, 54   ∴   51
Job 29:1; 31:24-40   Acts 15:12-21   John 11:30-44

Saturday   55   ∴   138, 139:1-17(18-23)
Job 38:1-17   Acts 15:22-35   John 11:45-54

Proper 19   *Week of the Sunday closest to September 14*

Sunday   24, 29   ∴   8, 84
              1 Kings 19:8-21   Acts 5:34-42   John 11:45-57

Monday   56, 57, [58]   ∴   64, 65
              1 Kings 21:1-16   1 Cor. 1:1-19   Matt. 4:1-11

Tuesday   61, 62   ∴   68:1-20(21-23)24-36
              1 Kings 21:17-29   1 Cor. 1:20-31   Matt. 4:12-17

Wednesday   72   ∴   119:73-96
              1 Kings 22:1-28   1 Cor. 2:1-13   Matt. 4:18-25

Thursday   [70], 71   ∴   74
              1 Kings 22:29-45   1 Cor. 2:14—3:15   Matt. 5:1-10

Friday   69:1-23(24-30)31-38   ∴   73
              2 Kings 1:2-17   1 Cor. 3:16-23   Matt. 5:11-16

Saturday   75, 76   ∴   23, 27
              2 Kings 2:1-18   1 Cor. 4:1-7   Matt. 5:17-20

Proper 20   *Week of the Sunday closest to September 21*

Sunday   93, 96   ∴   34
              2 Kings 4:8-37   Acts 9:10-32   Luke 3:7-18

Monday   80   ∴   77, [79]
              2 Kings 5:1-19   1 Cor. 4:8-21   Matt. 5:21-26

Tuesday   78:1-39   ∴   78:40-72
              2 Kings 5:19-27   1 Cor. 5:1-8   Matt. 5:27-37

Wednesday   119:97-120   ∴   81, 82
              2 Kings 6:1-23   1 Cor. 5:9—6:8   Matt. 5:38-48

Thursday   [83] *or* 116, 117   ∴   85, 86
              2 Kings 9:1-16   1 Cor. 6:12-20   Matt. 6:1-6, 16-18

Friday   88   ∴   91, 92
              2 Kings 9:17-37   1 Cor. 7:1-9   Matt. 6:7-15

Saturday   87, 90   ∴   136
              2 Kings 11:1-20a   1 Cor. 7:10-24   Matt. 6:19-24

Proper 19   *Week of the Sunday closest to September 14*

| Sunday | 24, 29   ∴   8, 84 |
| | Job 38:1, 18-41   Rev. 18:1-8   Matt. 5:21-26 |

Monday   56, 57, [58]   ∴   64, 65
Job 40:1-24   Acts 15:36—16:5   John 11:55—12:8

Tuesday   61, 62   ∴   68:1-20(21-23)24-36
Job 40:1; 41:1-11   Acts 16:6-15   John 12:9-19

Wednesday   72   ∴   119:73-96
Job 42:1-17   Acts 16:16-24   John 12:20-26

Thursday   [70], 71   ∴   74
Job 28:1-28   Acts 16:25-40   John 12:27-36a

Friday   69:1-23(24-30)31-38   ∴   73
Esther 1:1-4, 10-19*   Acts 17:1-15   John 12:36b-43

Saturday   75, 76   ∴   23, 27
Esther 2:5-8, 15-23*   Acts 17:16-34   John 12:44-50

Proper 20   *Week of the Sunday closest to September 21*

Sunday   93, 96   ∴   34
Esther 3:1—4:3*   James 1:19-27   Matt. 6:1-6, 16-18

Monday   80   ∴   77, [79]
Esther 4:4-17*   Acts 18:1-11   Luke (1:1-4); 3:1-14

Tuesday   78:1-39   ∴   78:40-72
Esther 5:1-14*   Acts 18:12-28   Luke 3:15-22

Wednesday   119:97-120   ∴   81, 82
Esther 6:1-14*   Acts 19:1-10   Luke 4:1-13

Thursday   [83] *or* 116, 117   ∴   85, 86
Esther 7:1-10*   Acts 19:11-20   Luke 4:14-30

Friday   88   ∴   91, 92
Esther 8:1-8, 15-17*   Acts 19:21-41   Luke 4:31-37

Saturday   87, 90   ∴   136
Hosea 1:1—2:1   Acts 20:1-16   Luke 4:38-44

In place of Esther may be read Judith:

| F   4:1-15 | Su 5:22–6:4, 10-21 | Tu 8:9-17; 9:1, 7-10 | Th 12:1-20 |
| Sa 5:1-21 | M 7:1-7, 19-32 | W 10:1-23 | F   13:1-20 |

Proper 21   *Week of the Sunday closest to September 28*

Sunday   66, 67   ∴   19, 46
              2 Kings 17:1-18   Acts 9:36-43   Luke 5:1-11

Monday   89:1-18   ∴   89:19-52
              2 Kings 17:24-41   1 Cor. 7:25-31   Matt. 6:25-34

Tuesday   97, 99, [100]   ∴   94, [95]
              2 Chron. 29: 1-3;   1 Cor. 7:32-40   Matt. 7:1-12
                  30:1(2-9) 10-27

Wednesday   101, 109:1-4(5-19)20-30   ∴   119:121-144
              2 Kings 18:9-25   1 Cor. 8:1-13   Matt. 7:13-21

Thursday   105:1-22   ∴   105:23-45
              2 Kings 18:28-37   1 Cor. 9:1-15   Matt. 7:22-29

Friday   102   ∴   107:1-32
              2 Kings 19:1-20   1 Cor. 9:16-27   Matt. 8:1-17

Saturday   107:33-43, 108:1-6(7-13)   ∴   33
              2 Kings 19:21-36   1 Cor. 10:1-13   Matt. 8:18-27

Proper 22   *Week of the Sunday closest to October 5*

Sunday   118   ∴   145
              2 Kings 20:1-21   Acts 12:1-17   Luke 7:11-17

Monday   106:1-18   ∴   106:19-48
              2 Kings 21:1-18   1 Cor. 10:14—11:1   Matt. 8:28-34

Tuesday   [120], 121, 122, 123   ∴   124, 125, 126, [127]
              2 Kings 22:1-13   1 Cor. 11:2, 17-22   Matt. 9:1-8

Wednesday   119:145-176   ∴   128, 129, 130
              2 Kings 22:14—23:3   1 Cor. 11:23-34   Matt. 9:9-17

Thursday   131, 132, [133]   ∴   134, 135
              2 Kings 23:4-25   1 Cor. 12:1-11   Matt. 9:18-26

Friday   140, 142   ∴   141, 143:1-11(12)
              2 Kings 23:36—24:17   1 Cor. 12:12-26   Matt. 9:27-34

Saturday   137:1-6(7-9), 144   ∴   104
              Jer. 35:1-19   1 Cor. 12:27—13:3   Matt. 9:35—10:4

Proper 21 *Week of the Sunday closest to September 28*

Sunday	66, 67 ∴	19, 46	
	Hosea 2:2-14	James 3:1-13	Matt. 13:44-52
Monday	89:1-18 ∴	89:19-52	
	Hosea 2:14-23	Acts 20:17-38	Luke 5:1-11
Tuesday	97, 99, [100] ∴	94, [95]	
	Hosea 4:1-10	Acts 21:1-14	Luke 5:12-26
Wednesday	101, 109:1-4(5-19)20-30 ∴	119:121-144	
	Hosea 4:11-19	Acts 21:15-26	Luke 5:27-39
Thursday	105:1-22 ∴	105:23-45	
	Hosea 5:8—6:6	Acts 21:27-36	Luke 6:1-11
Friday	102 ∴	107:1-32	
	Hosea 10:1-15	Acts 21:37—22:16	Luke 6:12-26
Saturday	107:33-43, 108:1-6(7-13) ∴	33	
	Hosea 11:1-9	Acts 22:17-29	Luke 6:27-38

Proper 22 *Week of the Sunday closest to October 5*

Sunday	118 ∴	145	
	Hosea 13:4-14	1 Cor. 2:6-16	Matt. 14:1-12
Monday	106:1-18 ∴	106:19-48	
	Hosea 14:1-9	Acts 22:30—23:11	Luke 6:39-49
Tuesday	[120], 121, 122, 123 ∴	124, 125, 126, [127]	
	Micah 1:1-9	Acts 23:12-24	Luke 7:1-17
Wednesday	119:145-176 ∴	128, 129, 130	
	Micah 2:1-13	Acts 23:23-35	Luke 7:18-35
Thursday	131, 132, [133] ∴	134, 135	
	Micah 3:1-8	Acts 24:1-23	Luke 7:36-50
Friday	140, 142 ∴	141, 143:1-11(12)	
	Micah 3:9—4:5	Acts 24:24—25:12	Luke 8:1-15
Saturday	137:1-6(7-9), 144 ∴	104	
	Micah 5:1-4, 10-15	Acts 25:13-27	Luke 8:16-25

Proper 23   *Week of the Sunday closest to October 12*

Sunday	146, 147 ∴ 111, 112, 113	
	Jer. 36:1-10 Acts 14:8-18 Luke 7:36-50	

Monday   1, 2, 3   ∴   4, 7
Jer. 36:11-26   1 Cor. 13:(1-3)4-13   Matt. 10:5-15

Tuesday   5, 6   ∴   10, 11
Jer. 36:27—37:2   1 Cor. 14:1-12   Matt. 10:16-23

Wednesday   119:1-24   ∴   12, 13, 14
Jer. 37:3-21   1 Cor. 14:13-25   Matt. 10:24-33

Thursday   18:1-20   ∴   18:21-50
Jer. 38:1-13   1 Cor. 14:26-33a, 37-40   Matt. 10:34-42

Friday   16, 17   ∴   22
Jer. 38:14-28   1 Cor. 15:1-11   Matt. 11:1-6

Saturday   20, 21:1-7(8-14)   ∴   110:1-5(6-7), 116, 117
2 Kings 25:8-12, 22-26   1 Cor. 15:12-29   Matt. 11:7-15

Proper 24   *Week of the Sunday closest to October 19*

Sunday   148, 149, 150   ∴   114, 115
Jer. 29:1, 4-14   Acts 16:6-15   Luke 10:1-12, 17-20

Monday   25   ∴   9, 15
Jer. 44:1-14   1 Cor. 15:30-41   Matt. 11:16-24

Tuesday   26, 28   ∴   36, 39
Lam. 1:1-5(6-9)10-12   1 Cor. 15:41-50   Matt. 11:25-30

Wednesday   38   ∴   119:25-48
Lam. 2:8-15   1 Cor. 15:51-58   Matt. 12:1-14

Thursday   37:1-18   ∴   37:19-42
Ezra 1:1-11   1 Cor. 16:1-9   Matt. 12:15-21

Friday   31   ∴   35
Ezra 3:1-13   1 Cor. 16:10-24   Matt. 12:22-32

Saturday   30, 32   ∴   42, 43
Ezra 4:7, 11-24   Philemon 1-25   Matt. 12:33-42

Proper 23   *Week of the Sunday closest to October 12*

Sunday   146, 147   ∴   111, 112, 113
              Micah 6:1-8   1 Cor. 4:9-16   Matt. 15:21-28

Monday   1, 2, 3   ∴   4, 7
              Micah 7:1-7   Acts 26:1-23   Luke 8:26-39

Tuesday   5, 6   ∴   10, 11
              Jonah 1:1-17a   Acts 26:24—27:8   Luke 8:40-56

Wednesday   119:1-24   ∴   12, 13, 14
              Jonah 1:17—2:10   Acts 27:9-26   Luke 9:1-17

Thursday   18:1-20   ∴   18:21-50
              Jonah 3:1—4:11   Acts 27:27-44   Luke 9:18-27

Friday   16, 17   ∴   22
              Ecclus. 1:1-10, 18-27   Acts 28:1-16   Luke 9:28-36

Saturday   20, 21:1-7(8-14)   ∴   110:1-5(6-7), 116, 117
              Ecclus. 3:17-31   Acts 28:17-31   Luke 9:37-50

Proper 24   *Week of the Sunday closest to October 19*

Sunday   148, 149, 150   ∴   114, 115
              Ecclus. 4:1-10   1 Cor. 10:1-13   Matt. 16:13-20

Monday   25   ∴   9, 15
              Ecclus. 4:20—5:7   Rev. 7:1-8   Luke 9:51-62

Tuesday   26, 28   ∴   36, 39
              Ecclus. 6:5-17   Rev. 7:9-17   Luke 10:1-16

Wednesday   38   ∴   119:25-48
              Ecclus. 7:4-14   Rev. 8:1-13   Luke 10:17-24

Thursday   37:1-18   ∴   37:19-42
              Ecclus. 10:1-18   Rev. 9:1-12   Luke 10:25-37

Friday   31   ∴   35
              Ecclus. 11:2-20   Rev. 9:13-21   Luke 10:38-42

Saturday   30, 32   ∴   42, 43
              Ecclus. 15:9-20   Rev. 10:1-11   Luke 11:1-13

Proper 25   *Week of the Sunday closest to October 26*

Sunday   63:1-8(9-11), 98   ∴   103
               Haggai 1:1—2:9   Acts 18:24—19:7   Luke 10:25-37

Monday   41, 52   ∴   44
               Zech. 1:7-17   Rev. 1:4-20   Matt. 12:43-50

Tuesday   45   ∴   47, 48
               Ezra 5:1-17   Rev. 4:1-11   Matt. 13:1-9

Wednesday   119:49-72   ∴   49, [53]
               Ezra 6:1-22   Rev. 5:1-10   Matt. 13:10-17

Thursday   50   ∴   [59, 60] *or* 103
               Neh. 1:1-11   Rev. 5:11—6:11   Matt. 13:18-23

Friday   40, 54   ∴   51
               Neh. 2:1-20   Rev. 6:12—7:4   Matt. 13:24-30

Saturday   55   ∴   138, 139:1-17(18-23)
               Neh. 4:1-23   Rev. 7:(4-8)9-17   Matt. 13:31-35

Proper 26   *Week of the Sunday closest to November 2*

Sunday   24, 29   ∴   8, 84
               Neh. 5:1-19   Acts 20:7-12   Luke 12:22-31

Monday   56, 57, [58]   ∴   64, 65
               Neh. 6:1-19   Rev. 10:1-11   Matt. 13:36-43

Tuesday   61, 62   ∴   68:1-20(21-23)24-36
               Neh. 12:27-31a, 42b-47   Rev. 11:1-19   Matt. 13:44-52

Wednesday   72   ∴   119:73-96
               Neh. 13:4-22   Rev. 12:1-12   Matt. 13:53-58

Thursday   [70], 71   ∴   74
               Ezra 7:(1-10)11-26   Rev. 14:1-13   Matt. 14:1-12

Friday   69:1-23(24-30)31-38   ∴   73
               Ezra 7:27-28; 8:21-36   Rev. 15:1-8   Matt. 14:13-21

Saturday   75, 76   ∴   23, 27
               Ezra 9:1-15   Rev. 17:1-14   Matt. 14:22-36

Proper 25   *Week of the Sunday closest to October 26*

Sunday   63:1-8(9-11), 98   ∴   103
            Ecclus. 18:19-33   1 Cor. 10:15-24   Matt. 18:15-20

Monday   41, 52   ∴   44
            Ecclus. 19:4-17   Rev. 11:1-14   Luke 11:14-26

Tuesday   45   ∴   47, 48
            Ecclus. 24:1-12   Rev. 11:14-19   Luke 11:27-36

Wednesday   119:49-72   ∴   49, [53]
            Ecclus. 28:14-26   Rev. 12:1-6   Luke 11:37-52

Thursday   50   ∴   [59, 60] *or* 103
            Ecclus. 31:12-18, 25—32:2   Rev. 12:7-17   Luke 11:53—12:12

Friday   40, 54   ∴   51
            Ecclus. 34:1-8, 18-22   Rev. 13:1-10   Luke 12:13-31

Saturday   55   ∴   138, 139:1-17(18-23)
            Ecclus. 35:1-17   Rev. 13:11-18   Luke 12:32-48

Proper 26   *Week of the Sunday closest to November 2*

Sunday   24, 29   ∴   8, 84
            Ecclus. 36:1-17   1 Cor. 12:27—13:13   Matt. 18:21-35

Monday   56, 57, [58]   ∴   64, 65
            Ecclus. 38:24-34   Rev. 14:1-13   Luke 12:49-59

Tuesday   61, 62   ∴   68:1-20(21-23)24-36
            Ecclus. 43:1-22   Rev. 14:14—15:8   Luke 13:1-9

Wednesday   72   ∴   119:73-96
            Ecclus. 43:23-33   Rev. 16:1-11   Luke 13:10-17

Thursday   [70], 71   ∴   74
            Ecclus. 44:1-15   Rev. 16:12-21   Luke 13:18-30

Friday   69:1-23(24-30)31-38   ∴   73
            Ecclus. 50:1, 11-24   Rev. 17:1-18   Luke 13:31-35

Saturday   75, 76   ∴   23, 27
            Ecclus. 51:1-12   Rev. 18:1-14   Luke 14:1-11

Proper 27   *Week of the Sunday closest to November 9*

Sunday   93, 96   ∴   34
               Ezra 10:1-17   Acts 24:10-21   Luke 14:12-24

Monday   80   ∴   77, [79]
               Neh. 9:1-15(16-25)   Rev. 18:1-8   Matt. 15:1-20

Tuesday   78:1-39   ∴   78:40-72
               Neh. 9:26-38   Rev. 18:9-20   Matt. 15:21-28

Wednesday   119:97-120   ∴   81, 82
               Neh. 7:73b—8:3, 5-18   Rev. 18:21-24   Matt. 15:29-39

Thursday   [83] *or* 23, 27   ∴   85, 86
               1 Macc. 1:1-28   Rev. 19:1-10   Matt. 16:1-12

Friday   88   ∴   91, 92
               1 Macc. 1:41-63   Rev. 19:11-16   Matt. 16:13-20

Saturday   87, 90   ∴   136
               1 Macc. 2:1-28   Rev. 20:1-6   Matt. 16:21-28

Proper 28   *Week of the Sunday closest to November 16*

Sunday   66, 67   ∴   19, 46
               1 Macc. 2:29-43, 49-50   Acts 28:14b-23   Luke 16:1-13

Monday   89:1-18   ∴   89:19-52
               1 Macc. 3:1-24   Rev. 20:7-15   Matt. 17:1-13

Tuesday   97, 99, [100]   ∴   94, [95]
               1 Macc. 3:25-41   Rev. 21:1-8   Matt. 17:14-21

Wednesday   101, 109:1-4(5-19)20-30   ∴   119:121-144
               1 Macc. 3:42-60   Rev. 21:9-21   Matt. 17:22-27

Thursday   105:1-22   ∴   105:23-45
               1 Macc. 4:1-25   Rev. 21:22—22:5   Matt. 18:1-9

Friday   102   ∴   107:1-32
               1 Macc. 4:36-59   Rev. 22:6-13   Matt. 18:10-20

Saturday   107:33-43, 108:1-6(7-13)   ∴   33
               Isa. 65:17-25   Rev. 22:14-21   Matt. 18:21-35

Proper 27   *Week of the Sunday closest to November 9*

Sunday   93, 96   ∴   34
             Ecclus. 51:13-22   1 Cor. 14:1-12   Matt. 20:1-16

Monday   80   ∴   77, [79]
             Joel 1:1-13   Rev. 18:15-24   Luke 14:12-24

Tuesday   78:1-39   ∴   78:40-72
             Joel 1:15—2:2(3-11)   Rev. 19:1-10   Luke 14:25-35

Wednesday   119:97-120   ∴   81, 82
             Joel 2:12-19   Rev. 19:11-21   Luke 15:1-10

Thursday   [83] *or* 23, 27   ∴   85, 86
             Joel 2:21-27   James 1:1-15   Luke 15:1-2, 11-32

Friday   88   ∴   91, 92
             Joel 2:28—3:8   James 1:16-27   Luke 16:1-9

Saturday   87, 90   ∴   136
             Joel 3:9-17   James 2:1-13   Luke 16:10-17(18)

Proper 28   *Week of the Sunday closest to November 16*

Sunday   66, 67   ∴   19, 46
             Hab. 1:1-4(5-11)12—2:1   Phil. 3:13—4:1   Matt. 23:13-24

Monday   89:1-18   ∴   89:19-52
             Hab. 2:1-4, 9-20   James 2:14-26   Luke 16:19-31

Tuesday   97, 99, [100]   ∴   94, [95]
             Hab. 3:1-10(11-15)16-18   James 3:1-12   Luke 17:1-10

Wednesday   101, 109:1-4(5-19)20-30   ∴   119:121-144
             Mal. 1:1, 6-14   James 3:13—4:12   Luke 17:11-19

Thursday   105:1-22   ∴   105:23-45
             Mal. 2:1-16   James 4:13—5:6   Luke 17:20-37

Friday   102   ∴   107:1-32
             Mal. 3:1-12   James 5:7-12   Luke 18:1-8

Saturday   107:33-43, 108:1-6(7-13)   ∴   33
             Mal. 3:13—4:6   James 5:13-20   Luke 18:9-14

Proper 29   *Week of the Sunday closest to November 23*

Sunday	118 ∴ 145		
	Isa. 19:19-25	Rom. 15:5-13	Luke 19:11-27
Monday	106:1-18 ∴ 106:19-48		
	Joel 3:1-2, 9-17	1 Pet. 1:1-12	Matt. 19:1-12
Tuesday	[120], 121, 122, 123 ∴ 124, 125, 126, [127]		
	Nahum 1:1-13	1 Pet. 1:13-25	Matt. 19:13-22
Wednesday	119:145-176 ∴ 128, 129, 130		
	Obadiah 15-21	1 Pet. 2:1-10	Matt. 19:23-30
Thursday	131, 132, [133] ∴ 134, 135		
	Zeph. 3:1-13	1 Pet. 2:11-25	Matt. 20:1-16
Friday	140, 142 ∴ 141, 143:1-11(12)		
	Isa. 24:14-23	1 Pet. 3:13—4:6	Matt. 20:17-28
Saturday	137:1-6(7-9), 144 ∴ 104		
	Micah 7:11-20	1 Pet. 4:7-19	Matt. 20:29-34

Proper 29 *Week of the Sunday closest to November 23*

Sunday
118 ∴ 145
Zech. 9:9-16 1 Pet. 3:13-22 Matt. 21:1-13

Monday
106:1-18 ∴ 106:19-48
Zech. 10:1-12 Gal. 6:1-10 Luke 18:15-30

Tuesday
[120], 121, 122, 123 ∴ 124, 125, 126, [127]
Zech. 11:4-17 1 Cor. 3:10-23 Luke 18:31-43

Wednesday
119:145-176 ∴ 128, 129, 130
Zech. 12:1-10 Eph. 1:3-14 Luke 19:1-10

Thursday
131, 132, [133] ∴ 134, 135
Zech. 13:1-9 Eph. 1:15-23 Luke 19:11-27

Friday
140, 142 ∴ 141, 143:1-11(12)
Zech. 14:1-11 Rom. 15:7-13 Luke 19:28-40

Saturday
137:1-6(7-9), 144 ∴ 104
Zech. 14:12-21 Phil. 2:1-11 Luke 19:41-48

Holy Days

	Morning Prayer	Evening Prayer
St. Andrew *November 30*	34 Isaiah 49:1-6 1 Corinthians 4:1-16	96,100 Isaiah 55:1-5 John 1:35-42
St. Thomas *December 21*	23,121 Job 42:1-6 1 Peter 1:3-9	27 Isaiah 43:8-13 John 14:1-7
St. Stephen *December 26*	28,30 2 Chronicles 24:17-22 Acts 6:1-7	118 Wisdom 4:7-15 Acts 7:59—8:8
St. John *December 27*	97,98 Proverbs 8:22-30 John 13:20-35	145 Isaiah 44:1-8 1 John 5:1-12
Holy Innocents *December 28*	2,26 Isaiah 49:13-23 Matthew 18:1-14	19,126 Isaiah 54:1-13 Mark 10:13-16
Confession of **St. Peter** *January 18*	66,67 Ezekiel 3:4-11 Acts 10:34-44	118 Ezekiel 34:11-16 John 21:15-22
Conversion of **St. Paul** *January 25*	19 Isaiah 45:18-25 Philippians 3:4b-11	119:89-112 Ecclesiasticus 39:1-10 Acts 9:1-22
Eve of the **Presentation**		113,122 1 Samuel 1:20-28a Romans 8:14-21

	Morning Prayer	Evening Prayer
The Presentation *February 2*	42, 43 1 Samuel 2:1-10 John 8:31-36	48, 87 Haggai 2:1-9 1 John 3:1-8
St. Matthias *February 24*	80 1 Samuel 16:1-13 1 John 2:18-25	33 1 Samuel 12:1-5 Acts 20:17-35
St. Joseph *March 19*	132 Isaiah 63:7-16 Matthew 1:18-25	34 2 Chronicles 6:12-17 Ephesians 3:14-21
Eve of the **Annunciation**		8, 138 Genesis 3:1-15 Romans 5:12-21 or Galatians 4:1-7
Annunciation *March 25*	85, 87 Isaiah 52:7-12 Hebrews 2:5-10	110:1-5(6-7), 132 Wisdom 9:1-12 John 1:9-14
St. Mark *April 25*	145 Ecclesiasticus 2:1-11 Acts 12:25—13:3	67, 96 Isaiah 62:6-12 2 Timothy 4:1-11
SS. Philip & James *May 1*	119:137-160 Job 23:1-12 John 1:43-51	139 Proverbs 4:7-18 John 12:20-26
Eve of the **Visitation**		132 Isaiah 11:1-10 Hebrews 2:11-18
The Visitation *May 31*	72 1 Samuel 1:1-20 Hebrews 3:1-6	146, 147 Zechariah 2:10-13 John 3:25-30

	Morning Prayer	Evening Prayer
St. Barnabas *June 11*	15,67 Ecclesiasticus 31:3-11 Acts 4:32-37	19,146 Job 29:1-16 Acts 9:26-31
Eve of St. John the Baptist		103 Ecclesiasticus 48:1-11 Luke 1:5-23
Nativity of St. John the Baptist *June 24*	82,98 Malachi 3:1-5 John 3:22-30	80 Malachi 4:1-6 Matthew 11:2-19
SS. Peter & Paul *June 29*	66 Ezekiel 2:1-7 Acts 11:1-18	97,138 Isaiah 49:1-6 Galatians 2:1-9
Independence Day *July 4*	33 Ecclesiasticus 10:1-8,12-18 James 5:7-10	107:1-32 Micah 4:1-5 Revelation 21:1-7
St. Mary Magdalene *July 22*	116 Zephaniah 3:14-20 **Mark** 15:47—16:7	30,149 Exodus 15:19-21 2 Corinthians 1:3-7
St. James *July 25*	34 Jeremiah 16:14-21 Mark 1:14-20	33 Jeremiah 26:1-15 Matthew 10:16-32
Eve of the Transfiguration		84 1 Kings 19:1-12 2 Corinthians 3:1-9,18
The Transfiguration *August 6*	2,24 Exodus 24:12-18 2 Corinthians 4:1-6	72 Daniel 7:9-10,13-14 John 12:27-36a

	Morning Prayer	Evening Prayer

St. Mary
the Virgin
August 15
	113,115
	1 Samuel 2:1-10
	John 2:1-12
		45, *or* 138, 149
		Jeremiah 31:1-14
		  or Zechariah 2:10-13
		John 19:23-27
		  or Acts 1:6-14

St. Bartholomew *August 24*	86 Genesis 28:10-17 John 1:43-51	15,67 Isaiah 66:1-2,18-23 1 Peter 5:1-11
Eve of Holy Cross		46,87 1 Kings 8:22-30 Ephesians 2:11-22
Holy Cross Day *September 14*	66 Numbers 21:4-9 John 3:11-17	118 Genesis 3:1-15 1 Peter 3:17-22
St. Matthew *September 21*	119:41-64 Isaiah 8:11-20 Romans 10:1-15	19,112 Job 28:12-28 Matthew 13:44-52

St. Michael &
All Angels
September 29
	8,148
	Job 38:1-7
	Hebrews 1:1-14
		34, 150, *or* 104
		Daniel 12:1-3
		  or 2 Kings 6:8-17
		Mark 13:21-27
		  or Revelation 5:1-14

St. Luke *October 18*	103 Ezekiel 47:1-12 Luke 1:1-4	67,96 Isaiah 52:7-10 Acts 1:1-8
St. James **of Jerusalem** *October 23*	119:145-168 Jeremiah 11:18-23 Matthew 10:16-22	122,125 Isaiah 65:17-25 Hebrews 12:12-24

	Morning Prayer	Evening Prayer
SS. Simon & Jude *October 28*	66 Isaiah 28:9-16 Ephesians 4:1-16	116,117 Isaiah 4:2-6 John 14:15-31
Eve of All Saints		34 Wisdom 3:1-9 Revelation 19:1,4-10
All Saints' Day *November 1*	111,112 2 Esdras 2:42-47 Hebrews 11:32—12:2	148,150 Wisdom 5:1-5,14-16 Revelation 21:1-4,22—22:5
Thanksgiving Day	147 Deuteronomy 26:1-11 John 6:26-35	145 Joel 2:21-27 1 Thessalonians 5:12-24

Special Occasions

Eve of the **Dedication**		48,122 Haggai 2:1-9 1 Corinthians 3:9-17
Anniversary **of the** **Dedication** **of a Church**	132 1 Kings 8:1-13 John 10:22-30	29,46 1 Kings 8:54-62 Hebrews 10:19-25
Eve of the **Patronal Feast**		27, *or* 116,117 Isaiah 49:1-13 *or* Ecclesiasticus 51:6b-12 Ephesians 4:1-13 *or* Revelation 7:9-17 *or* Luke 10:38-42

	Morning Prayer	Evening Prayer
The Patronal Feast	92,93, *or* 148,149 Isaiah 52:7-10 *or* Job 5:8-21 Acts 4:5-13 *or* Luke 12:1-12	96,97, *or* 111,112 Jeremiah 31:10-14 *or* Ecclesiasticus 2:7-18 Romans 12:1-21 *or* Luke 21:10-19
Eves of Apostles and Evangelists		48, 122, *or* 84, 150 Isaiah 43:10-15* *or* Isaiah 52:7-10** Revelation 21:1-4,9-14 *or* Matthew 9:35—10:4

*Except on the Eve of St. Thomas
**Except on the Eves of St. Mark and St. Luke

NOVELS BY ROBERT MOSS

The Spike
(with Arnaud de Borchgrave)

Death Beam

Monimbó
(with Arnaud de Borchgrave)

Moscow Rules

Carnival of Spies

CARNIVAL OF
SPIES

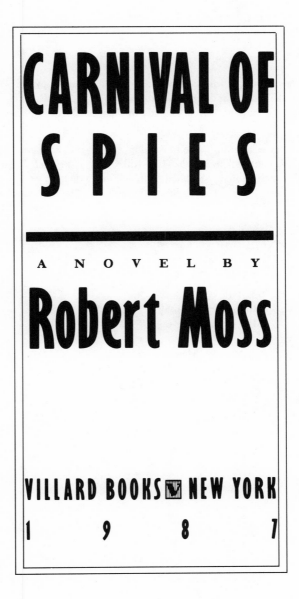

CARNIVAL OF SPIES

A NOVEL BY

Robert Moss

VILLARD BOOKS 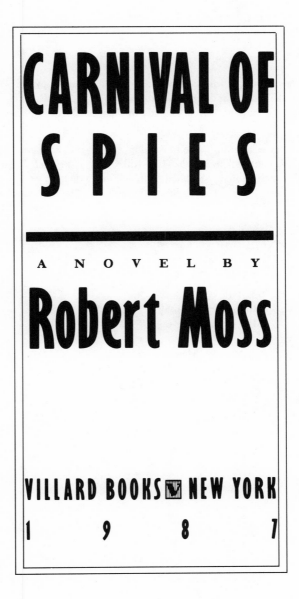 NEW YORK
1 9 8 7

Grateful acknowledgment is made to Random House, Inc., to reprint excerpts from the poem "The Panther," by Rainer Maria Rilke, from *The Selected Poetry of Rainer Maria Rilke*, translated by Stephen Mitchell. Introduction copyright © 1982 by Robert Hass. Copyright © 1980, 1981, 1982 by Stephen Mitchell. Used by permission.

Library of Congress Cataloging-in-Publication Data

Moss, Robert, 1946–
    Carnival of Spies.

    I. Title.
PR6063.083C37 1987   823'.914   86-40292
ISBN 0-394-54971-6

Manufactured in the
United States of America
9 8 7 6 5 4 3 2
First Edition

For Marcia,
who has Bahia in her soul,
com saudade.

The most important thing in life
is love, duty. The most important thing in work
is beauty, discipline.

—MARLENE DIETRICH*

*One of Dietrich's directors, Rouben Mamoulien, kept a book in which he invited his guests to write their "innermost thoughts." This was Dietrich's contribution.

Contents

Part III
THE PATH OF THE DEAD 411
(1936)

CARNIVAL OF
SPIES

Prologue:
Ash Wednesday
(1936)

What is done out of love is beyond good and evil.

—Nietzsche

She rode in a chariot drawn by sea horses. A sickle moon and a shower of stars glittered above her crown. Ropes of make-believe jewels cupped her breasts and snaked around her belly. But her body was burning gold, brighter than these. She moved tirelessly, hypnotically, to the voluptuous rhythm of the samba. Around her, across the width of the avenue, the dancers darted and flashed like fireflies and birds of paradise. Tomorrow she might be back in a tumbledown shack on a muddy hilltop in the Northern Zone or trudging off to work with a broom and a mop in the houses of the rich. But tonight she was Queen of the Nile, goddess of the waters, empress of desire. She arched her back, and the dream-ruby at her navel turned little circles. She danced so Ash Wednesday would never dawn, so that Carnival would never end.

In front of the Copacabana Palace Hotel, a crowd of young swells got up as harlequins and Arabian princes paraded in an open car and squirted the girls with cheap cologne. "Cocococococoró, Coco-coco-cocoró!" They crowed the chorus of one of the new songs that had caught the pulse of Rio. It carried all the laughter and all the sadness of the last night of Carnival:

The cock of the night is singing,
Everyone wants to see
What he has to tell.
When the little rooster replies
Cocococococoró
Cocococococoró
The little hen dies.

On the streetcar bound for Botafogo they were chanting the March of the Little Rooster too, and the tram swayed from side to side under their pounding feet. Along the mosaic sidewalk, a man in a black cassock and flat black hat picked his way through the throng. The words of the song seemed to trouble him, or perhaps it was merely the moist tropical heat that rose from the ground and opened every pore, and the sight of so much naked flesh. He looked unnaturally pale, and his eyes were searching for something beyond the streamers and the traveling hips of the mulatto girls. He trod on a mass of gold paper without noticing that it was the crown of a King of Angola. People didn't want to look at him. It was not the night for priests and Portuguese saints. Their season would come soon enough.

But a dark, pretty girl who was resting at the corner of one of the narrow streets that wound into Lapa, a quarter that lived for the night in all the seasons of the year, stretched out her hand and offered something to him. He paused to look down. It was half a lemon, from the stock she had brought with her in a little string bag so she wouldn't have to pay for *guaraná* from the street vendors. Caught off guard, he took the fruit and sank his teeth into it, watching the girl warily with his intent grey eyes as if she might pose some danger to him. She had been crying. Perhaps she had lost something precious in the riot of Carnival.

She whispered, "Bless me, Father."

He frowned, mumbled a few words and waved his hand over her upturned face.

She couldn't make out what he said. Perhaps he was one of those Dutch fathers who came to Brazil. She watched him with a puzzled expression, and he stumbled on up the street, into a neighborhood where the services of priests were rarely required. He was such a big man, with powerful shoulders and fists like a prizefighter's. The cassock looked silly on him. And there was something wrong with the way he walked. His right leg swung stiff from the hip. She saw him limp past half-shuttered windows from behind which women's voices lapped out, softly propositioning, at the passersby. Then he stood out in bold profile, listing noticeably to starboard, against the illuminated sign of the Babylônia Club.

Zé Pimenta, the keeper of the door to the Babylônia, didn't like being on duty on the last Tuesday of Carnival, even if the tips were good. By the time the patrons inside were done, it would be too late to show off his finery —he was decked out as a Turkish pasha, complete with turban and baggy pants and pasteboard scimitar—to his girlfriends in the Mangue. They would all be sleeping it off. Zé had been consoling himself with a few fingers of *cachaça*. He could sneak imported hooch from the bar, but he preferred the raw, potent cane alcohol of his own country. Its effect, after a while, was as hallucinating and enervating as the steamy heat and the relentless beat of the samba drums. He was half asleep when he saw the man in black rise up in front of him like a monstrous crow.

"*Dá licença,* Zé," the priest addressed him, pleasantly enough.

"Excuse me, Father." Zé hastily adjusted his sash. "You wouldn't want to go in there. It's dreadful what goes on. Human nature, I'm afraid."

But something in the priest's face—was it the strange, set smile or the strong, almost brutal, features?—made Zé step aside. "We don't see a lot of cassocks in the Babylônia," he mumbled as the priest walked into the club.

They didn't play sambas inside the Babylônia. Half the clientele was foreign, and the band alternated between tangos and German and American favorites. As the priest entered, a singer with a powder-white face and vocal chords that had been gutted by chain-smoking was attempting a rendition of Lola-Lola's song from *The Blue Angel*. A few of the German syllables got transposed, but nobody in this crowd seemed to mind. Girls in bright satin with plunging necklines were trying to prise drinks from the regulars who hung along the bar like vampire bats. Few of the couples who revolved on the dance floor had arrived together. The fancy dress on display was mostly compliments of the house—party hats and clowns' red bubble noses. But there were a few men in formal evening dress with stiff collars, looking for company that was certified hygienic. The management of the Babylônia discreetly advertised the claim that its girls were inspected by a qualified doctor once a day.

The whirring propeller fans overhead did not dispel the haze of cigar and cigarette smoke; they distributed it evenly to every corner of the room. The walls were adorned with baroque mirrors and a mural depicting an ancient orgy among hanging gardens. One of the women, dancing with a drink in her hand, shuddered when the reflection of the man in black loomed up suddenly behind her shoulder. Another tittered and called out mockingly, "Coco-coco-coco-cocoró!"

In the mirror he saw the girl he had come for. The candlelight caught the silvery whorls of her butterfly mask and the long white curve of her throat. She was at a corner table with her back to the wall. The two men with her were both wearing dinner jackets. The one he could see in profile was lean and equine and looked mildly bored. The other, squeezed up against the girl, was heavy and flushed and bellowed snatches of Lola-Lola's song in between gulps from his tankard.

Ich bin von Kopf bis Fuss
Auf Liebe eingestellt . . .

A waiter swooped around them, pouring champagne. Before he replaced the bottle in its silver bucket, he flipped it upside down, and a few inches of champagne disappeared into the ice. It was one of the management's little tricks to speed up consumption. Nobody noticed except the man who was glued to the mirror.

The girl looked up, and their eyes met in the glass. She pulled away from her admirer, as if to leave the table. The priest made a motion with his hand for her to stay.

He completed a half circle of the dance floor, trying not to let his right foot drag, and came up behind the men at her table.

"Alms for the poor," he suggested in a wheedling voice.

"Ach, it's unbelievable," the ruddy-faced German complained, shifting his bulk to stare at the source of the petition.

The one who looked like a racehorse turned his mouth down and busied himself by screwing a cigarette into a tortoiseshell holder.

"Have you no charity, mein Herr?"

The heavy one turned a deeper shade of red and said, "Piss off."

"Oh, give him something," the other German said wearily. "It's a country of beggars."

The first German made a disgusted face and threw some money on the table. "Now piss off," he repeated. His speech was thick and slurred, and he had pulled out his top stud so his collar flapped loose. He swore more violently when he saw that the priest was still perched at the table like a bird of ill omen.

"Do you have something for me, Fraulein?" the man in black said to the girl.

"Of course." But instead of reaching for her purse she extended her hand to the priest, who took it and raised it to his lips.

"It's unbelievable!" the first German spluttered. He pawed at the girl's shoulder and said, "Do you know this holy-water man?"

"He's my favorite confessor," she replied with a little smile that dimpled her cheek. She had clear, translucent skin and an oval face framed by waves of fine-spun coppery hair.

"Wait a minute!" the first German slurred. "I know you!" He dragged back his chair and got up to get a better look at the priest. "It's Johnny, isn't it? Johnny Gruber! I thought you'd left Rio."

"It's a hard city to leave. Engineer Hossbach and I used to live in the same guesthouse in Copacabana," the priest explained to the girl, as if he were rounding out introductions at a garden party.

"So I've found out your little secret!" Hossbach roared at Johnny. "You like to fuck in a priest's skirts!"

"I'm afraid our friend Hossbach has had too much to drink," Johnny said to the table.

"Yes," the other German intervened curtly. "Sit down, Hossbach, and apologize to the lady for your language." He had a metallic, rather high-pitched voice that reminded Johnny of a blade being sharpened.

Hossbach did as he was told.

"Wolfgang Trott," the second German introduced himself. "From the embassy. I take it you are living in Rio, Herr Gruber?"

Johnny nodded.

"I'm surprised we haven't met." Trott paused, inspecting Johnny's costume more closely. The cassock was several sizes too small. "I must say, Hossbach has a point," the attaché went on. "Do you often go about dressed like that?"

"It's Carnival." Johnny shrugged as if this explained everything.

"Sit down and have a drink, Johnny," Hossbach interjected, brandishing a bottle.

"I'm afraid I've kept Sigrid waiting too long already. She has to be home before her husband." Johnny winked.

Hossbach snorted and returned to mauling the girl. He got one of his meaty fists on her thigh, but she wriggled free.

"It's become quite a ritual in Rio," Sigrid said coolly, on her feet and smoothing her dress. "Husbands and wives go to different parties during Carnival. But there are still certain courtesies that must be observed."

"Of course," Trott agreed, rising to kiss her hand. "I've been told that it is no crime in Rio for a man to blow out the brains of his wife's lover. Is that so, Herr Gruber?"

"I've heard something about it," Johnny mumbled. There was menace in Trott's icy poise.

"I'm sure we'll have the pleasure of meeting again," Trott said as they shook hands. He wore the Nazi party emblem under his lapel, Johnny noted. The stem showed through.

Johnny took the girl's arm and squired her around the dancers, towards the exit behind the piano.

"It's not right to keep so much woman to yourself!" Hossbach bawled after them.

When they had reached the stairs, she clutched his arm tighter. "In God's name, Johnny," she said in an urgent whisper, "What held you up? And who are those men?"

"Later," he responded sharply. Her voice was still steady enough, but he could feel the trembling in her arm. She was frightened and angry and probably half dead with fatigue, and it was taking all her reserves to keep up a mask of composure.

There were half a dozen rooms above the Babylônia Club that could be rented by the hour or the night. The toll collector was a blowsy woman with dyed red hair who sat in a booth at the top of the stairs eating chocolates. She dealt matter-of-factly with the priest and the girl in the butterfly mask. After all, she had seen strange goings-on at the Babylônia. Just the same, she crossed herself after taking their money and giving them the key to a room at the end of the hall—a room where a federal deputy, no less, had gasped his last while pleasuring two lively brown girls from Bahia.

Johnny locked the door behind them, flung his hat on the bed and took her in his arms. Her mouth tasted of wine and wild strawberries. The edges of her mask chafed his skin, so he pulled it off. In the murky orange light of the bedside sconces he could see the dark rings of worry and fatigue around her eyes. The irises were a pale sea green, the green of pebbles at the bottom of the water. There was a small red scratch mark in one of her eyes, close to the cornea, as if a tiny blood vessel had burst. All the same, she was painfully beautiful.

He pulled her closer, till the contours of their bodies were locked tight together. He was breathing heavily. He did not conceal his quickening desire.

"Johnny—"

He was half waltzing, half shoving her backwards onto the bed. Her body moved in rhythm with his, straining to meet him, as if there was no world, no terror, but this. By an effort of will, she wrenched herself free. The sudden motion caught Johnny off balance. His right leg collided with the brass bed frame, and he winced in pain.

"What's the matter? Are you hurt?"

He shook his head. "Just an old wound," he grunted. He sat down heavily on the bed, nursing his leg.

She folded her arms under her breasts and studied him. "You're lying," she said. "Let me see."

Without waiting for his approval, she hitched up his cassock until she found a rough strip of bandage, crudely knotted above the knee. It was caked with blood.

He did not resist when she stripped away the bandage and probed the blackened trench the bullet had dug across his thigh. But the faint flush that had returned to his cheeks drained away when she started dabbing at the wound with a handkerchief soaked in perfume from her bag. She pulled the covers off the bed and made a new bandage with a strip of linen torn from the sheet. She knotted it tight and said, "It may have chipped a bone. I'll take you to Eusebio. He'll be home by now."

Eusebio was a socialist and a doctor, one of the few who had eluded the police over the last few months.

Johnny tested the bandage and shook his head. "It's not worth the risk. I've found us a boat. It sails in the morning. We can go direct from here to the docks."

"But Johnny, we can't. We have orders—"

"Forget the orders," he snapped. "All orders are canceled. Don't you understand? We're finished in Brazil. The revolution is defeated. *Kaput.* Our only duty now is to save our skins."

She stared at him, and the unspoken question was clear from her expression, a compound of fear and suspicion.

"The police were waiting for me," he said quietly. "They waited for me to walk right inside the sack. There were men all round the block. I got away over the rooftops. There was a church—a priest who was ready to help."

"A priest?" Her surprise was understandable. In that year of revolution, few men of the cloth were on the side of the rebels.

"A man of God," he said impatiently. "It doesn't matter for now."

"What about the others?"

"Max is safe enough," he said bitterly. "We can be sure of that. His kind know how to look out for themselves. By now he'll be drinking at the bar of the Crillón in Buenos Aires. What I want to know is who told the police about the safe house."

She thought about this for a moment. With her dress disarranged, hanging partway off her shoulder, and the fabric stretched tight to reveal the upward tilt of her breasts, she looked wickedly—discordantly—sensual.

She said, "It could have been Emil," and instantly bit her lip, as if to choke back the words. Emil was the chief of the conspiracy, and he had been in jail since Christmas, two full months. What they had done to him in the barracks of the Special Police was almost beyond imagining.

"No," Johnny said flatly. "It wasn't Emil. He never knew the address."

She mentioned the names of other prisoners, the handful of men and women who had been privy to the secrets of the envoys of the Comintern in Rio—the "Grey Cardinals," as one of the Brazilians jeeringly described them—and Johnny dismissed them one after another.

"Only three people knew that house," he said curtly.

He watched the cloud pass across her face. What it left behind was a deeper layer of fear.

"Johnny, you don't think—" she faltered. "You don't think it was *me*?"

"If I believed that," he said carefully, "I think I'd go out in the street and shoot myself. Or possibly both of us."

He covered her hands with his own. "We'll leave it for now," he said softly. *"Das wird auch abgerechnet.* The account will be settled later."

It had been this way since the failure of the rising, since the mutineers in the army barracks on the pretty beach of Praia Vermelha, at the foot of the Sugarloaf, had been bombed and strafed into submission. The surviving conspirators—"Communist bandits," according to the government-controlled press—had been stalking each other, hunting for police spies. Now he was bone tired and wounded and fighting back the blackest doubts about his own mission. For an hour or two at least, he wanted a truce, a sanctuary.

"Sigrid," he said, coaxingly. "I'll never doubt you. I hope you believe me. You must never doubt me either. Promise me that."

"Johnny, you'll never have to ask for that." Her eyes were full of pain and bewilderment.

"Promise me," he insisted.

"All right, I promise. But I don't know what you're saying."

"Whatever I have done—whatever I may have to do—is for love of you." He seemed on the point of making some larger statement. Instead, he nestled his head on her breast. When he plucked at the fastenings of her clothes and tossed them across the room like whirling leaves, she did not resist. There was a great wind in the room whose deliberate violence gathered them together and shut out all the commotion from the dance floor below and the Carnival that was spending its last energies outside.

Afterwards, she fell into a deep sleep and he smoked and listened to the thud of insects beating against the screen in the window and the twang of a single-stringed instrument someone was playing in the street below. Sexual arousal is the last reflex of a hanged man. The thought flicked maliciously, repetitively at the edge of his consciousness, so that sleep, when it came, was shallow and haunted by fearful images.

He dozed until a hammering at the door shook the dresser he had pushed against it to reinforce the simple lock. Still half asleep, with the girl clutching the sheet to her throat while he grabbed for the ten-shot Mauser he had hidden under a pillow, he imagined he was in another city and called out in German, "Who's there?"

In the babble of words from beyond the door he recognized the voice of the woman who collected the rent.

"Forgive me, Father," she was saying. "But the police are downstairs. A raid during Carnival! Whoever heard of such a thing?"

He rushed to the window. There was a truck blocking off one end of the street and men in red kepis, carbines at the ready. Special Police. So it wasn't a matter of checking that the tarts' medical papers were in order.

He tucked the gun back into the waistband of his shorts and slipped the cassock over his head.

"Listen," he said to Sigrid. "They're after me, I'm sure of it. I may have been followed. I want you to stay here till the search is over."

She started to protest, but he put a finger over her lips and went on, "You'll be all right. They'll think you're one of the working girls. I'll fix it with the woman outside."

"But what about you?"

"I'll find a way. Whatever happens, you must be at this place at six o'clock." He made her memorize the address on a street near the Praça Maua. "There'll be a man waiting. You must do whatever he says."

"How will I know him?"

"He'll know you. Whatever happens," he repeated, "you must be on that boat."

"Johnny—"

"You promised you would trust me."

"It's not that. I just want you to kiss me."

He had words with the woman in the booth, and money changed hands. She made sympathetic clucking noises over the plight of a married lady discovered by chance under such circumstances and pointed the way to the fire escape. Leaning from the window over the iron steps, Johnny saw more red caps along the alleyway behind the Babylônia Club. The police seemed to be checking everyone who came and went—but only the men, he noted, were asked for their papers.

The music was still blaring from the dance floor, which suggested that the police were not being over-assertive on the premises of the club itself, and a plan began to shape itself in Johnny's mind. It was insane, just insane enough to work.

He went back down the stairs into the Babylônia Club. He could spot the policemen at once, from their hats and the way their double-breasted jackets were buttoned tight across their midriffs. One had taken off his hat, and his hair was stiff and shiny with cream. They were moving from table to table.

He marched over to the table where the Germans were sitting. The wine waiter, or the intrusion of the police, must have dissatisfied them, because they had sent for their bill. A heavily rouged woman hung on Trott's arm but was clearly getting nowhere.

"I didn't expect to see you again tonight, Herr Gruber," Trott greeted him, shaking off his female companion.

Johnny sat down without waiting to be invited.

Hossbach, who had been sunk in torpor, rallied himself to make a coarse remark about sexual staying power. "I'll go and finish the job," he announced. "Show her what a real German is made of." He launched into a graphic description of what he had in mind.

"By the way," Trott interjected, "what have you done with the lady?" The man from the German Embassy had screwed an eyeglass into his face, and it stayed there as effortlessly as if it were grafted to the skin.

"She went out the back way," Johnny lied. "She was terrified that her husband would find out."

Trott did not comment. He tossed a thick pile of Brazilian banknotes onto the saucer on top of the bill.

"I see you're bored with the Babylônia," Johnny remarked. "I know a superior establishment that is quite diverting, on the Rua Alici."

"Hah!" Hossbach chimed in. "I bet I know the one. You can get anything you want." He dug Trott in the ribs. The attaché looked pained but also mildly inquisitive.

"It's not far," Johnny prodded. "I'll show you the way if you like."

Trott gave a little nod and stood up, indicating the decision was made.

The police stopped them only at the door, and their profuse apologies were amplified when Trott showed his embassy credentials. The inspector peered at the man in the priest's cassock curiously.

"This is our embassy chaplain," Trott announced without the shadow of a smile. Johnny was not asked for his papers.

"These people lack formation," Trott said, when they were outside, waiting for Zé Pimenta to summon the embassy driver. "I'm sure that if I had declined to show my papers they would never have insisted. They can't conceive that a subversive could be dressed in a dinner jacket. We Germans know better, don't we, Herr Gruber? We have a great deal to teach them. But they're a weak race," he added reflectively, "a mongrel race, leached by the climate of the tropics. Hossbach was telling me just now that the reason that half the Brazilian men hold the cup with their left hand when they're drinking their eternal *cafezinhos* is that they are terrified of syphilis. They think that by holding the cup in the wrong hand, they'll avoid sipping from the same spot where a syphilitic might have pressed his lips. Have you seen that?"

"Yes, I've seen it," Johnny acknowledged. He watched the red caps patrolling the street from the corner of his eye.

"But since so many of them do it, they defeat the whole object of the exercise!" Trott observed triumphantly. "And they don't even see their own absurdity! They're worse than Italians. It will take an iron man to change them."

Hossbach puffed himself up as if he thought he were a candidate for this role.

Trott's powerful black Mercedes was waved through the roadblock and purred to a stop in front of them, with Zé Pimenta on the running board. Zé excelled himself, holding his pasteboard scimitar in front of his nose with one hand while the other fished for tips.

To Trott's surprise, Johnny did not accompany them into the house on the Rua Alici, pleading sudden fatigue.

"I'm sorry," he said. "I think I've overdone it."

"My man will drive you home," Trott suggested solicitously. "What's your address?"

"No, but thank you. I'll walk for a while to clear my head."

Trott squinted at him through the eyeglass, which gave him the aspect of a man inspecting an unidentified organism through a microscope.

Johnny set off in search of a taxi. There were always a few on the prowl in this neighborhood, which was home to the most exclusive bordellos in the city. His head was light, but the sky had clouded over. He could no longer see moon or stars, only the great statue of the Redeemer, arms outstretched, lit up on top of the hunched peak of Corcovado. The cobbled street he was following sloped down the hill into a well of darkness where the street lamps were sparse. He must have mistaken his direction. He wheeled around to retrace his steps.

At the same instant a car on the slope above him turned on its headlights. For a moment he stood blinded by the high beams. It occurred to him that Trott might have sent his chauffeur after him.

But it was a Brazilian voice that called out, "Good morning, Senhor Gruber."

He hurled himself into the shadows, out of the headlights, tearing at his useless priest's disguise to find his Mauser. Before he could get it loose, several men came running at him. One of them dealt him a blow to the chest with his rifle butt that sent him toppling backward into the street.

Laid out on his back, he summoned enough strength to send one of his assailants flying with a hard left kick. He got the gun out and fired wildly. He heard the tinkle of glass as one of the car headlights blew out. Then they were all over him. They wrestled the Mauser away from him and one of them rammed it up against his closed teeth so he could taste the steel of the muzzle.

The one in charge sauntered down the hill and stood over him. Behind his captor, beyond the vast bay of Guanabara, a narrow slash of pink had appeared in the eastern sky.

Captain Honorio Schmidt, the chief of the Special Police, studied his prize with satisfaction and decided to allow himself one of his slim Bahian cigars. One of his assistants sprang forward to strike a match.

Captain Honorio huffed life into the cheroot and remarked, "It's Ash Wednesday, Father."

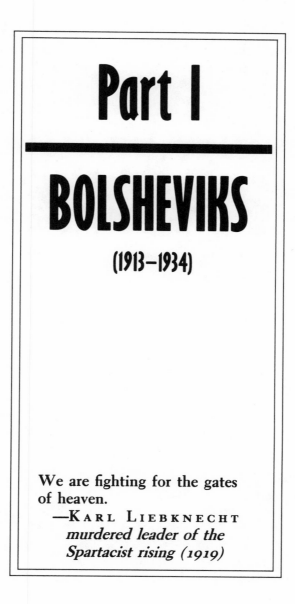

Part I

BOLSHEVIKS

(1913–1934)

We are fighting for the gates
of heaven.
   —Karl Liebknecht
*murdered leader of the
Spartacist rising (1919)*

1

The Call

Man is the only animal who
refuses to be what he is.
—ALBERT CAMUS

1

WHEN he stood by the window, he could hear the sirens from the harbor, calling him. At times they were women's voices, keening on the wind. The siren voices came from places with magical names, across shining oceans, from Ceylon and Madagascar and Manaus. It was all he could do not to drop everything and run out the door, out of that overheated room with its fat-bellied stove and the dark, heavy furniture that seemed to close in on him, squeezing out the air and the life, like someone forcing a pillow down over his face.

"Johann!" his mother barked at him. "Be careful with those!"

It was a few days before Christmas, and he had been conscripted for women's work, helping his mother and his sister Bertha to trim and decorate the *Tannenbaum* that occupied the middle of the front parlor. It was a grey, cheerless day outside, and the light was nearly spent, but that wouldn't have stopped him rushing down to the docks. He liked to hang around the ferry landing and watch the seamen going back and forth to the giant wharves across the river where the ships of the Hamburg-Amerika Line came in. He played games of pirates around the godowns, which smelled of tea and spice. He loved the bustle of the fish market at St. Pauli. More daring, he and his friends would range the streets above it, past tattoo shops with pictures of big-hipped tropical girls in the window, down alleys where the naked girls in the windows were real and where pimps and policemen came running to shoo the boys away.

But here he was, fussing over Christmas decorations. It was part of his punishment. He had been sent home from school early with a note from the headmaster after giving Willi Rausch, the school bully, a black eye. Willi Rausch was a swaggering lout who was suffered by the masters because his father was a boss of the Shipowners' Association. That morning, he had pushed Johnny too far. He started by crowing that Johnny's pants were too short. Then he put two fingers above his head, like horns, and cackled that Herr Lentz was a capon who didn't know who was doing it with his wife. When Johnny went for him, he got out his penknife, but it didn't help him a bit. Johnny knew how to use his fists, and he knew when to ignore the rules. He had learned all about that in the back alleys behind the harbor.

His mother had ordered him to stay inside until his father got home. There would be a reckoning, she promised. And tomorrow Johnny would have to make a formal apology to Willi Rausch and his parents. The Rausch family were important people, and Hermann Rausch was his father's employer.

Herr Lentz was unusually late coming home from the office that night. Johnny did not fear his anger. In that household the mother was the angry one. She seemed to tower over her husband, a big-boned woman who twisted her thick blonde hair into a coronet. She never tired of telling him that she had married beneath her, that he was dragging her down in the world. Johnny often thought of his father as a wounded bird. He wasn't made to walk on the ground, but his wings wouldn't work. He was a shy, unassuming man who went about in a dove-grey tie and striped trousers like a government functionary. His stoop and his pince-nez made him look smaller than he was. He could sometimes be heard tinkling on the harpsichord in the music room. This expensive instrument—as Johnny's mother frequently recalled during family squabbles—had been purchased with *her* money.

The Lentz family, like the street in Hamburg where they lived, had come down sharply in the world. Only Frau Lentz's inheritance kept the bailiffs away. When she had married Gottfried, Johnny's father, he had been thought to be a fine young musician with a brilliant career. But he had wasted years writing experimental pieces that no orchestra wanted to perform, and his brilliant career had receded further and further into the future. By day, he was reduced to toiling as a clerk in the great gloomy hall of the Shipowners' Association down by the docks. By night, he gave himself over to his secret world. Johnny would sometimes wake in the early hours to hear him working on some strange, discordant composition with plunging gaps in the scales, as somber and unsettling as the black well under the trapdoor leading to the coal cellar. Then he would hear his mother's angry tread, her voice raised shrill in anger and, as often as not, the thud of blows rained on his father's unresisting back. She would fly at the failed composer with anything that fell to hand, even a poker. He never fought back. Herr Lentz was a pacifist.

"We're going for a walk," he had announced to his wife one Sunday afternoon, clutching Johnny's hand. They had walked as far as a coffeehouse, where six or seven men were assembled in a back room. Johnny recognized the family doctor and the director of a funeral parlor. They greeted Gottfried Lentz warmly, and Johnny was proud that, here at least, his father commanded respect.

A plump fellow with a Polish accent gave a talk on how technical progress had made war obsolete. In the age of the telegraph and steam shipping, he asserted, the countries of the world were all interdependent; for one to make war on another would be like setting out to burgle your own home. Furthermore, the instruments of slaughter had become so lethally effective—witness the invention of the magazine rifle—that soldiers would never consent to fight each other.

There was a good deal of applause, and Johnny's father got up and made a short speech on the brotherhood of man, garnished with quotations from Fourier in the original French.

"Well, what do you have to say?" Gottfried Lentz asked his son on the way home.

"You can't remake men overnight. Men are made to fight."

"That's not so! We only fight because of the kind of society we live in. When we change the social order, when we abolish class tyranny, everything will be different."

"And do you think that can happen without a fight?" A small troop of hussars came clattering past, splendid in their blue dolmans. "They think your Fourier is just another Frenchman to be put to the sword."

"They're dinosaurs," Gottfried Lentz murmured with quiet contempt. "We have to kill the Prussian in all of us." This was a backhand swipe at his wife, whose family came from East Prussia. "I'll give you some books to read, so you can begin to understand. But Johnny—" Their corner had come into view. "Not a word about this to your mother, do you hear?"

Dutifully and secretly, Johnny had struggled with the tracts of the utopian socialists, but they were too bloodless for his taste. He preferred the mythic romances of his own country—Wolfram's *Parzifal* in particular, with its tale of heroism in a magical quest to rescue a dying kingdom. He liked the Wild West adventures of Karl May, but above all he loved stories of the sea. His imagination was filled with the exploits of Raleigh and Klaus Störtebecker, the buccaneer from Hamburg. He thrilled with pride when he went with a school party to watch the launching of one of Germany's splendid new battle cruisers. His father detested the Kaiser, with his bristling moustaches, as a noisy warmonger, but Johnny could picture himself in the smart uniform of a German naval officer. In his imagination the sea meant release from the drab taboos of family life, from his father's albino abstractions, his mother's petty tyranny and his sister Bertha's tireless pursuit of a comfortable bourgeois marriage.

He was thinking of the sea now, as he worked his way through his mother's box of Christmas ornaments. At fourteen, he was tall enough to reach the topmost branches of the tree without use of the stepladder. His rope-colored hair, wide, chiseled mouth and candid blue-grey eyes came from his mother's side of the family. So did the fussy set of lead crystal angels, trumpets and wings outstretched, that he was disentangling from the shrouds of crepe paper.

He yawned and wondered whether there would be time left before dinner to visit one of their neighbors on the Valentinskamp, a young man called Heinz Kordt, who wore a seaman's cap and had sailed on the ships of the North German Lloyd. Frau Lentz disapproved of Heinz Kordt. She called him a "ruffian" and (on one occasion) a "desperado" and had forbidden Johnny to visit his lodgings—a prohibition Johnny cheerfully ignored. With his bold gaze, his ruddy cheeks and his flourishing jet-black beard, Heinz Kordt was, in Johnny's eyes, a very fair imitation of a pirate. Johnny could picture him storming the walls of Cartagena and getting royally drunk on Spanish wine with a pair of black-eyed girls as the flames leaped from the rooftops. Kordt wove wondrous tales of lost islands in the Pacific, mutiny on the high seas and knife fights in the Boca—the red-light district —of Buenos Aires. He fed the boy's fascination by opening up the huge metal trunk that occupied most of his room and showing him souvenirs from his voyages. One night he pulled out a tiny shrunken head, not much bigger than a walnut, with matted dark hair festooned with shells and parrot's feathers. Kordt said he had bought it from headhunters along the banks of the River of Death, somewhere in the jungles of Brazil.

Johnny was thinking about the shrunken head and the way it felt like baked clay to the touch, when he heard the jangle of the front door.

"Gottfried?" his mother called. "Is that you?"

The man who staggered into the living room was barely recognizable as the prim little clerk of the Shipowners' Association or even the Sunday *philosophe*. His starched collar flapped wide. He was hatless, and his lank, thinning hair hung down to his eyebrows. His pince-nez was precariously suspended above the bulging tip of his nose, which was suspiciously empurpled. His overcoat trailed daringly from his shoulders.

"Gottfried?" Frau Lentz sniffed the air. "Have you been *drinking?*"

Between a belch and a cough Johnny's father mumbled something that might have been, "It's that time of year."

"*Gottfried!* Have you no decency?"

"That's not all," Herr Lentz piped up. "I am no longer in the employ of the Swindlers'—that is, the Shipowners'—Association."

"Have you taken leave of your senses?"

Pink, bouncy Bertha came in from the kitchen and goggled at her father.

"How will you fend for poor Bertha, who is all but engaged?" Frau Lentz pursued. "How will we pay for Johann's school, where he spends all his time brawling? Do you want to disgrace us? Do you want to live in the gutter? You must wash out your mouth and go to Herr Rausch at once—"

Johnny pictured Willi Rausch's father, a bloated version of the son, a walrus with thick moustaches who fancied himself a ladies' man and had flirted with Frau Lentz at office parties.

"Herr Rausch is a fair man," Frau Lentz insisted.

"I did not resign." Gottfried Lentz drew himself up to his full height, till he seemed in danger of toppling backwards.

"What are you saying?" Frau Lentz's eyes widened. Then her arm shot out, pointing straight at Johnny. "It's because of him, isn't it? Because he was picking on the Rausch boy, the godless savage. We must go to them at once and apologize. Bertha, get my shawl—"

"It won't do any good." Johnny's father's lips were curled in a blissfully vacant grin. "I was sacked for expressing dangerous political ideas."

"That can't be true. It's because of the boy. Bertha—"

"Not only true, my dear, but to emphasize my point I told Rausch he could stick my miserable pittance up his backside. Then I stuck *this* in his fat mug." He winked at Johnny and displayed a row of shiny knuckles.

"You're drunk! You're insane!" Heidi Lentz looked ready to faint. An extraordinary mewling sound came from Bertha, whose heart was set on snaring the eldest of the Rausch boys.

Johnny became so excited that he let slip the lead crystal angel he had been trying to fasten to the Christmas tree. It flew to the stone apron of the fireplace and shattered into a dozen shards.

This diversion revived Frau Lentz and provided a momentary reprieve for her husband.

"Johann!" Frau Lentz shrieked.

"I'm sorry—I didn't mean it—" Johnny stammered, but the awesome force of his mother's wrath was now trained on him.

She lashed out with the first object that came to hand—the pair of shears they had used earlier to trim the tree. Johnny dodged the blow, seized hold of his mother's wrist and wrenched until the metal tool fell from her hand.

For a moment she seemed bolted to the ground, stunned by this new rebellion. Then the blood rushed into her cheeks, and she yelled at her husband, "Deal with your son, you miserable excuse for a man!"

Johnny didn't wait to see what response this would bring. Without saying a word he ran to the kitchen, grabbed his ulster from its hook and banged out the side door.

Oblivious to his mother's screams and his sister's wails, he raced down the steps and then west along the Valentinskamp in the direction of St. Pauli, through a fine mist of rain. It was already dark, and the street lamps cast sulfurous pools of light on the wet pavement. He paused half a block away from the house, until he saw his father come out onto the porch.

"I wish I'd been there to see it," Johnny said when his father had caught up.

Gottfried Lentz smiled. For the first time Johnny could remember, his father looked like a free man.

"But it *was* because of my fight with Willi, wasn't it?" Johnny went on.

His father's face clouded. "It would have come to the same thing. So long as the bosses can treat people like replaceable parts. Someday we'll change all of that. But for now—" he sighed. "Life goes on. We'd better go inside."

"I can't go back."

"Don't be silly. It's not the end of the world. It's not your fault. I'll find another job."

"I've been thinking about this for a while, father. I'm old enough to take care of myself—"

"You're fourteen! What can you do without a school certificate? Work as a navvy down at the docks? There are worse bosses than Rausch, I can tell you."

"I've got friends. I'll be all right. Please go inside, father. You'll catch cold."

They heard Frau Lentz's harsh voice raised from the porch. Involuntarily Johnny's father shuddered.

"Don't be too hard on her," he said to his son. "She's not a bad woman, you know. She just can't help herself."

"I know. I have to go, that's all."

Johnny waited for his father's response. He couldn't go back into that house, where he felt his lungs were bursting. He couldn't go back to that expensive school, where the teachers sided with Willi Rausch because his father had money and rode around in a fancy carriage, puffing his cigar. Besides, he knew the school fees had been crippling for his father. Now it would be worse. By leaving he would be doing all of them a favor.

He refused to live as his father had lived, a man with a dream that was broken daily on the wheel. His father had had his moment of glorious revolt, and in that moment Johnny had felt closer to him than ever before. But his father's words suggested that the moment had already passed. "Life goes on . . ."

I'm not going to wait until I'm past forty to punch the Rausches of this world in the nose, Johnny told himself.

"But where will you go?" his father repeated.

"I've got friends. I'll manage. Don't worry yourself."

"You'll write? At least you'll write?"

"Of course I will."

Gottfried made no effort to invoke parental authority. Perhaps he felt his own actions earlier that day had made a mockery of all that. Perhaps he felt it would be more than mildly ridiculous for him to tell this strapping youth, a head taller than himself, that he would not be able to fend for himself. Perhaps he even felt a tinge of envy.

Johnny tried not to recognize the pain in his father's face. I'm doing them a favor, he reminded himself.

Gottfried blinked myopically through his spectacles, which were beaded with rain. Then he rummaged in his vest pocket and pressed something into Johnny's hand. A bank note. He moved as if to hug his son, then stiffened in embarrassment and stuck out his hand instead. This friend of abstract humanity had always shied away from physical contact.

"If only I were younger—" he began, then cleared his throat.

The boy swallowed and walked quickly away.

"Proudhon!" his father's reedy voice wafted after him. "Don't forget to read Proudhon!"

Two blocks farther on, Johnny crossed the street and ran up the steps into the building where Heinz Kordt had his lodgings. Once the mansion of some Hanseatic burgomaster, it was now a disreputable apartment house, only a cut above a tenement.

In the lobby he nearly bowled over a sallow, furtive man in a fedora and an oversized overcoat that billowed around his ankles. The stranger thrust his hand into his pocket, and Johnny imagined that he saw the bulge of a revolver. For an instant their eyes met. The stranger's quick stare was feral, the gaze of a hunted animal ready to round on its pursuers and tear. A low rumble came from the man's throat. Then he was gone.

Johnny's imagination was fired up by this brief encounter. He saw the roof of the Shipowners' Association blown off by an anarchist bomb. He had spotted other wary, vaguely foreign men coming and going at all hours from an office at the back that was rented by a socialist group. These socialists did not look much like his father's circle of henpecked philosophers. Maybe they were Russians. In one of his father's tracts he had come across a reference to "the propaganda of the deed"—the method of the Russian revolutionaries who had blown up a Tsar and a grand duke. The world called these Russians terrorists, yet Johnny thought they were the reverse of cowards. They gladly put their own lives at risk, believing that by offering to sacrifice themselves they would demonstrate the purity of their cause.

The boy who had pictured himself in the uniform of a naval officer (not much chance of that now) could also daydream of joining a party of bomb throwers. He was of an age, and a temperament, in which the call of adventure, not flags or philosophies, was supreme. He wanted to live each day as if it were his last.

He climbed the stairs, and found that the lightbulb on Kordt's landing had burned out. He stood in darkness and tapped gently on the door. There was no response. But he could see, from the chink along the bottom, that the light was on inside the sailor's room, and he could hear gusts of music from a gramophone. He rapped louder on Kordt's door. There was a scuffling sound and a groan that might have been bedsprings.

A sleepy voice called out, "Go away!"

The boy knocked again. "Heinz! It's me. Johnny."

There was an odd smell on the landing, like burning rope. He leaned his ear up against Kordt's door. He heard low whispers, a ripple of laughter and another creak from the bedsprings.

The door was flung open without warning, so abruptly that Johnny went spinning headlong into the room and landed on a heap of pillows that had been dumped providentially on the floor. Kordt's lodgings were suffused with pink light, the effect of the makeshift shade the sailor had constructed by tossing the top of an old pair of red pajamas over his bedside lamp.

The first thing Johnny saw, as he tried to reorient himself, was a narrow, sloping calf in a black fishnet stocking. He raised his eyes higher. All the girl was wearing apart from the stockings was a garter belt and a tart's brassiere with holes snipped out to show off her nipples. Her straight blond hair was cut tight around her head, like a helmet. Despite her outfit, he guessed she was not much older than he—fifteen or sixteen at most. Her breasts were barely formed, and her slender body, straight as a boy's, was almost hairless. He stared at her, open-mouthed.

She burst out laughing and puffed smoke in his face as he tried to scramble to his feet. She was smoking a knobbly pipe, one of Kordt's. Again there was that odd aroma of burning rope.

Heinz Kordt was laughing too. He clapped Johnny on the shoulder and said, "What's the matter, boy? Haven't you seen a girl's backside before?"

Johnny blushed to the roots of his hair, and the seaman laughed louder. He was wearing only his red pajama bottoms. He had various tattoos on his arms, among them a sea monster inscribed in marvelous detail and a cruder design of a South Seas girl in a grass skirt.

Kordt flung his arm around Johnny's neck. "You like the look of her? Her name's Helene. You can play with her, if she lets you."

The girl made a face like a cat preparing to spit.

"She's a little spitfire, all right," Kordt said indulgently. "But she's clean, I'll warrant you that. She's from Berlin. I found her at the station. A runaway, just asking for trouble. I'd thought I'd better bring her up here before she ran into somebody worse."

Helene marched up to Johnny and tweaked his nose. "How old are you?" she demanded. Her voice was surprisingly deep; it might have been a ventriloquist's trick. There was a disturbing vacancy about her ice-blue eyes.

Johnny swallowed and said, "Seventeen."

"Liar," she hissed.

"It's true," he protested.

"Then let me see you smoke this." She offered him the pipe, and he wasn't scared to take it. He had tasted tobacco before in Kordt's room and in secret corners of the schoolyard and down at the fish market. But he had never tasted tobacco like this. After a few puffs, inhaling the way she did to show he was every bit as grown up, the room started to blur and he thought he saw Kordt's red pajama tops burst into flame above the lamp.

"Indian hemp," Kordt remarked mysteriously and confidentially. "Never touch it myself." He confiscated the pipe and added, "You'd better be running back to your own folks. I've met your mother and that's one lady I wouldn't care to cross."

"I'm not going home," Johnny said flatly.

"One drink," Kordt responded with mock severity. "Then it's off with you. Helene and I have unfinished business."

"I mean I've left. For good."

While Kordt stared at Johnny, the girl waggled her finger and chortled, "He's a runaway!"

"Let's see if I've got this straight," Kordt said to Johnny. "You've left home for good?"

Johnny nodded.

"Why? You've got a decent home, you go to a decent school. The whole world is ahead of you. But not if you drop out."

"You told me when you left home, you were younger than me," Johnny countered accusingly.

"I didn't have any choice. I didn't even know my father's name, and my mother was generally too drunk to remember mine. What's your excuse?"

Johnny tried, haltingly at first, then with passion, to explain. Heinz growled when Rausch's name was mentioned.

"I know that bastard," the sailor grunted. "He had me on a blacklist once. For tossing a couple of scabs overboard. If the workers ever get their way, he'll be one of the first to go." He rubbed his chin. "All right. So what's your next step?"

"I'm going to sea."

"Just like that, huh?"

"I thought you might help me find a boat." He stared at the floor, partly to avoid the spectacle of Helene, who had stretched out on the bed and was kicking her legs in the air.

"Listen." Kordt—who had given the boy a couple of boxing lessons— feinted a right jab at his face. "You'll find shits like Rausch on board ship as well as onshore. It's no romance, working a merchant steamer. The officers treat you like dogs, and the men aren't much better. You mustn't go by my stories. You'll learn that whatever you're running away from has a habit of catching up with you."

"I have to go, Heinz."

"What do you expect to find?"

"Myself."

He looked Kordt in the eyes then, and the seaman must have read something he approved of, because after a while he nodded. Then he was on his feet, grabbing for his clothes. He gave the girl on the bed, who had rolled over on her belly, a smack on the rump.

"Put something on, will you? I've a mind to show the boy the town."

THEY went to a dive where Heinz seemed to be well known, on the border of St. Pauli and the workers' district of Altona. An exotic name was picked out in multicolored lights at the top of a rickety flight of steps. From the street Johnny thought the sign read "Ali's Bar." Closer up, he saw that the bulbs in the frame of the first letter had been smashed. The place was the Kali-Bar, named for a Hindu deity.

"There's the old girl herself," Kordt remarked as they entered a dark, cavernous loft, pointing at a weird statue of beaten tin and silver paper daubed with gaudy enamels. It was a female figure with pointed dugs that hung to its waist, a lolling, pointed tongue and a necklace of death's heads. "Time the devourer. Chews her men up, that one. Pretty, isn't she? Some of the black-asses who come here think she's their patron saint."

He shot a sidelong glance at Johnny, to see if the boy was shocked.

Johnny was drinking up the whole scene. Under the smudged light of blue lanterns filtered by hessian sacking, scores of men and women groped and gyrated to a scratchy recording. There were seamen from every port, with a high proportion of lascars and Chinamen. Some of them danced together, others with heavily rouged tarts or pale, overgrown girls who were bussed in at the end of their shifts from the big cement works at Altona. A sinuous creature of indeterminate sex wafted towards them. A pale arm flashed out and, before Johnny realized what was happening, the apparition was trying to shake hands with his private parts.

He pushed the thing away, revolted.

"Pretty, pretty," it hissed at him.

"Go away," Helene said, draping her arm around Johnny's shoulder. "He's taken."

Johnny felt the warmth as his cheeks flushed red. Helene was laughing at him again, and he was furious that his embarrassment showed. He wanted to prove to Heinz that he was the equal of any experience life might throw in his path, not some callow boy who belonged back in school.

Heinz found them an empty corner at a huge trestle table, and an Indian waiter brought foaming steins of Bremen beer.

"You dance with Helene for a bit." Heinz nudged Johnny. "There are some men I have to talk to."

The girl looked older in her red dress. It was real silk, one of Heinz's trophies from the Orient. As they danced, she ground herself against his body. The insistent, repetitive pressure against his thigh became unbearable. He looked into her face, into those eyes like drowning pools. There was no hint there that she was remotely conscious of the physical effect she was having on him.

Dammit, he thought. Is she trying to make me look a complete fool?

He was rescued by Kordt, who got up from the table where he had been playing dice with a rough-looking crowd and signaled to him.

"Johnny, this is Ernst." Kordt introduced a man who was built like a beer keg. His head bulged out of his trunk with only the faintest suggestion of a neck. His stubby legs seemed to have been tacked on as an afterthought. His eyes were dark, narrow slits; the whites didn't show at all.

"There's a Norwegian ship at the Kaiser Quai leaving for Frisco Bay tomorrow," Kordt reported. "Ernst is chief stoker. He can get you signed on if he likes the look of you."

Ernst sized Johnny up and spat a wad of tobacco on to the floor. "Too soft," he muttered, turning away.

Johnny was outraged. He clutched at the stoker's shoulder. "What do you mean, too soft?"

Ernst grabbed his wrist, twisted it round, and pointed at the soft skin of the palm.

"Smooth as a baby's bottom," he complained, addressing himself to Kordt. "He's never done a day's work in his life. You should know better than to bring me spoiled puppies like this."

"He'll learn," Kordt said. "Let's have another beer."

The stoker rubbed the coarse stubble on his chin. "Pretty boys don't last out the first watch on my tub," he said, staring rudely at Johnny. Without warning, he struck out with his fist, aiming straight at Johnny's face. He flattened the palm at the last moment so that he merely patted the boy's cheek. "You know what I'm talking about?" he said mockingly.

Johnny put his fists up straight away and delivered a quick jab to the stoker's belly before he had got his guard up. Ernst swore and took a swing that would have laid the boy out had he not leaped nimbly aside. Johnny feinted with his right and landed two hard left punches. The stoker was winded and angry and came after Johnny with his arms outstretched. For a moment he had the boy caught in a bear hug, and Johnny felt his breath being squeezed out of him. But he wriggled free and a moment later landed a blow to the stoker's jaw that sent him reeling backwards. He crashed into a table, sent the beer mugs flying and landed on his back, bellowing and flailing his stocky legs. His friends came running over, one of them armed with a bottle.

Kordt pushed between them and Johnny.

"I said the boy would learn," he reminded Ernst as the stoker struggled to his feet, puffing, and began to dust himself off.

"All right, he'll do," the stoker agreed grudgingly and shook Johnny's hand.

"And what do you say?" Kordt asked Helene, who had watched the scrap as if it were part of the routine entertainment at the Kali-Bar. She was tapping her foot in time to the music and munching at a big salted horseradish that had been served with the beer.

She moved over to Johnny, light and surefooted as a cat, put her hands on his shoulders and purred, *"Du bist eine Kanone."* Her voice sounded remote, and her hands were unnaturally cool. Her teeth were slightly irregular, and this gave her a primeval, almost animal, look. She opened her mouth so wide he could see its pink roof. Then she pounced on him, biting the side of his neck. It was a real bite, not a love graze, for when he put his hand to the spot he found a bead of blood on the tip of his finger.

2

HEINZ saw him off at the docks after making him swallow a raw egg and a nip of brandy. "It's the best antidote for a night like that," the sailor assured him. Helene came too, and when Johnny, bundled up in the old peajacket Heinz had given him as a going-away present, hugged both of them, he felt, more keenly than the night before, that he was leaving his family.

The squat figure of the chief stoker appeared at the top of the gangway, yelling at Johnny to get on board. He waved to his friends and patted the pocket where he had concealed another gift, a little tattered book with a red cover.

"It's about sharing," Heinz had said.

It had been a night of initiations, a night when everything was more important than sleep. The scent of the girl still traveled with him, so he imagined, in the folds of his skin. Heinz had left them alone for a few hours, to return before dawn with a couple of bottles and an immense thirst for strong liquor and stronger conversation.

"Hey, give a man some room!" Heinz had boomed at them, lunging for the bed so unexpectedly that Johnny had had to hurl himself to one side to avoid his bulk. The sailor squeezed both of them and pulled the cork out of one of the bottles with his teeth. As he passed it back and forth, he studied each of them with an amused, assessing stare.

"She likes you," he pronounced at last. "Are you still set on going to sea?"

"Yes."

But when the girl shrugged and said, "It's all the same to me" between gusts of acrid smoke from a Turkish cigarette, Johnny felt bitterly disappointed. She was Heinz's girl, but even so . . .

"Let's talk!" Heinz roared. "Let's talk of what is and what ought to be!"

For the rest of that magical night, he left no corner of silence where the sadness of parting could take root. He talked of things Johnny had never heard before, of organizing a seamen's strike, of rum running across the Baltic, of staging a jailbreak in Batavia to get a comrade out of the hands of the Dutch colonial authorities. Johnny realized now that if his friend was a pirate, he was a pirate in the mold of the new century—a revolutionary ready to make war on the flags and totems of every nation in the old, decaying world. Heinz spoke with real passion, even eloquence, about a coming world upheaval that would sweep away all the doddering crowned heads of Europe, the monocles and the chimney barons, the paunchy capitalists of the Hamburg Shipowners' Association. Seamen would be in the vanguard, according to Heinz, because their travels freed them from the narrow life of the tribe.

But before revolution came, Heinz predicted, there would have to be war.

"That's where your father's wrong," the sailor pursued. "The system won't collapse under its own weight. But the kings and the capitalists are lighting a bomb under their own backsides. Wait and see. Europe is a heap of loaded rifles. Move one, and all the rest will go off. *Then* it will be our turn."

Johnny was drunk on the words, even more than on the brandy Heinz kept pouring down his throat. Bright yet indistinct, like a flash of sheet lightning over the brow of a hill, he could see a mission shaping itself for him.

"And you?" he questioned Heinz. "What will you do?"

"Oh, I'll make myself useful somewhere or other. Now drink up! Any sailor knows it's terrible luck to put the cork back in a bottle."

Before they left for the harbor Heinz pressed the dog-eared pamphlet into Johnny's hand.

"Here. Stick this in your pocket. But don't let the officers see you, or they'll turn you off the boat."

Johnny saw the title. *The Communist Manifesto.*

"It's about sharing," Heinz went on. "But handle it gently. It's not a book. It's a bomb. A case of dynamite wrapped in forty pages. If you want to talk to someone about it, talk to Ernst. He's a son of a bitch, but he's on our side."

ON BOARD the Norwegian freighter *Ula* Johnny studied Marx and Engels in the breaks from heaving coal into a glowering furnace until his muscles ached and the sweat poured into his eyes. He found a sheltered spot in the lee of a lifeboat and read and reread the *Communist Manifesto.* He was excited by its coiled power. In a handful of pages the authors had compressed an arching theory of world history, a devastating indictment of a society made for the Rausches—a society founded on selfish calculation—and a program for revolutionary action. "Let the ruling classes tremble . . ."

Johnny began to think of himself as a communist. When the *Ula* docked at San Francisco, Ernst took him to a meeting in a smoky hall where twenty men disputed in half a dozen languages. Johnny could follow some of the Yiddish; it was close enough to German. The rest was lost on him. A Javanese seaman got up and jabbered in a tongue that nobody else could understand. But when it was explained that he was pledging the support of the peoples of the Dutch East Indies for the anti-imperialist struggle, he was hailed with rapturous applause.

They gave him leaflets to hand out to the men on the docks. Usually he was rebuffed, sometimes with blows and oaths. The harbor police came to chase him away, but each time he went back. He enjoyed the game of hide and seek. He told himself he was striking a blow for the cause.

But when war came, the call of the tribe—as Heinz had called it disparagingly—was stronger than the canons of Karl Marx.

He was in a honkytonk in Panama drinking with Ernst, who had picked up a pair of olive-skinned girls. They had had to get off their last boat in a hurry after Ernst had led a mutiny against the first officer, a strutting martinet who would flog a man because he didn't like the shine on the deck. The captain had broken out the rifles and threatened to shoot the troublemakers.

Now they were looking for another boat and talking about the carnage in Europe that was reported in the American papers. Johnny felt edgy sitting in foreign bars, sailing under foreign flags, while his own people were fighting and dying in tens of thousands—whether or not the war was just. The Royal Navy was the most powerful on earth, and its arrogant admirals were trying to impose a blockade to starve the Germans into submission. His own family might go hungry. Germany needed sailors, needed them desperately, and a small voice inside him argued that he belonged there, not in a cheap bordello in Panama.

There were French seamen at the next table, six or seven of them, all several sheets to the wind. Johnny heard muttering about *les sales Boches,* obviously directed at them. One of the Frenchmen got up and started bellowing the *Marseillaise,* beating out the rhythm on the table with his fist. The others joined in a ragged chorus.

"Hey, you!" the first Frenchman called over. "Sausage-face! Stand up when we're singing our anthem."

"Go fuck yourself," Ernst spat.

Another French sailor jumped up and made a grab for Rosita, the girl sitting next to Johnny.

"Get away from her!" Johnny snapped.

The Frenchman pushed a paper into the girl's hands.

"Are you going to sit with these *saligauds*? See what they do?"

Johnny snatched the paper away. It was a crude piece of war propaganda. The cartoon showed hoggish German soldiers in pickelhaube helmets skewering French babies on their bayonets.

"They lie to you," he appealed to the Frenchman in broken English. "Don't believe this shit."

The Frenchman either did not understand or did not care. He looked like a real Marseilles harbor rat, spoiling for a fight. He clamped his paws round Rosita's waist and started dragging her away. Johnny jumped to his feet, fists clenched. The sailor dropped the girl like a used rag and peeled a knife out of his sock.

Johnny ducked the first lunge and got his hand around the sailor's wrist, struggling for the knife. Other men's shadows fell over him, closing in.

Ernst did not waste any time. He seized the rum bottle in front of him by its neck, knocked off the bottom against the table edge, and advanced on the Frenchman behind a ring of jagged glass. The shadows started to recede.

"Come on," Ernst hissed. "Let's beat it."

That might have been the end of it, but the barroom patriot wasn't ready to call it a night.

He hurled himself at Ernst as the stoker turned his back to go out the door.

"Ernst!"

Before Johnny's warning had left his lips, the stoker, warned by some sixth sense, had wheeled round with an agility surprising in a man of his girth to meet the Frenchman with the broken bottle. Johnny saw the man's face explode like a ripe watermelon hurled off a cart.

"*Klugscheisser,*" Ernst swore. "Smart-shitter." Then, to Johnny: "What are you gaping at? Run, before the cops arrive."

Johnny found himself running the way he had always run, towards the sea, sickened by the criminal waste of what had happened inside the bawdy house. Those men had been ready to cut out his liver for no better reason than that he spoke German. Now one of them had lost his face. This was the madness that was convulsing Europe. The war had followed him here.

He now knew what he had to do.

There was a German ship in port, bound for Hamburg.

"Go your own way, then," Ernst growled when Johnny announced his intentions.

The stoker shook his head, but he lingered on the wharf, watching the boy clambering along the hawser, hand over hand. In the bright moonlight, Johnny should have been spotted at once; the lookout must have been snoring drunk.

They were three days out into the Atlantic before he was discovered, living off bananas in a forward cargo hold crawling with spiders and cockroaches the size of his thumb.

The captain was all for putting Johnny in the brig. But when the boy announced that he had stowed away because he wanted to get home to enlist in the Kaiser's navy, the captain's long brown face softened.

"How old are you?"

"Eighteen," Johnny lied, promoting himself three years.

"All right. You can work your passage. Germany needs lads with your spirit."

3

THE war changed Johnny and everything else.

He sailed on the battleship *Thüringen* into a night of black horror off the coast of Jutland. Blinded by the North Sea fogs and the smoke blown back from their own stacks by the howling headwinds, the German navy battled the full might of the British Grand Fleet.

"We're on the devil's anvil," one of his shipmates muttered under the thunder of bursting shells.

They were on deck trying to rescue the drowning men from a battle cruiser the British had sent to the bottom.

The next instant, the sailor was silenced by a piece of flying shrapnel. Johnny caught the falling body and clasped his hands around his friend's chest, trying to prop him up. The sailor was curiously light. He stumbled with him towards shelter, oblivious to the warm stickiness that was seeping through his trousers.

"Idiot!" one of the officers snapped at him. It was Lieutenant von Arnim, a wasp-waisted dandy who thought he was a ringer for Prince Rupprecht and who made the men's life a hell. "Throw him over the side!"

Dazed, Johnny staggered on with his burden.

Klaus Behring, another Hamburg man, came hopping over the rolling deck and said gently to Johnny, "I'll take him."

Only then did Johnny realize that he was carrying a detached trunk. The shrapnel had sawed his friend in two, just below the waist.

The German battle fleet made its escape to its boltholes at Kiel and Wilhelmshaven, and the admirals came with boxloads of medals. The men were paraded in their bonnets, the ribbons flapping in the breeze, and told they had won a famous victory for the Fatherland.

Johnny got an Iron Cross for bravery under fire.

What kind of victory? he thought sourly—with thousands of good men dead, a dozen ships sunk and the British in command of the seas, while at home German families gnawed on scraps of leather, waiting for shipments of food that will never come?

Idleness was more subversive than action. Johnny had come home to fight, but after Jutland there was precious little fighting to be done in the

German navy. Only the U-boats slunk out through the British patrols to prey on Allied shipping. The battle fleet stayed cooped up like a set of toy boats in a bathtub. The days passed in mindless, mechanical routine, drilling and scrubbing, with von Arnim lying in wait to reward the tiniest slip with a vicious flogging. In their free hours, denied home leave, the men were left to stew in fetid metal boxes. They were fed on slops while the officers dined on foie gras and fine wines. There was a contest to see who could count the largest number of maggots in his meat. Klaus Behring claimed the prize with a count of thirty-seven, but his record was soon broken.

Johnny came to live with hunger, a dull ache that never went away.

But he did not yet know real hunger. He saw it in the street the day the peace marchers came to the docks. He was lounging near the gates with Klaus when he heard a low buzzing in the distance, more purposeful than angry, like a swarm of borer bees at a crack in the timbers of a house.

The first civilians to appear in the street were women, haggard and shapeless, the loose skin of their faces hanging off the bones, some clutching their suckling infants. Men too old to be called up shuffled along behind them. Some of these granddaddies' faces, grey and set as if they had been rough-etched into stone, terrified Johnny. A red flag trailed from a pole, lifeless as the men's faces. There were a few younger fellows, Johnny noticed, keeping well to the back, one in a sailor's uniform, but hatless— perhaps a deserter. They started singing the *Internationale.*

"Give us bread!" the women croaked.

Johnny went closer to get a better look at the crowd, and one of the women shoved her baby in front of his nose. He saw the unnatural, distended belly, the puny limbs, limp and pale as cold macaroni.

"Give us bread," the mother implored.

"Down with the Kaiser!" men's voices chimed in. "Stop the war!"

The sentries formed a line bristling with bayonets.

"I've got an idea," Johnny said to Klaus. "Quick! Before the officers come!"

Klaus grumbled but trotted along at his heels. As he ran, Johnny scribbled on a card.

Klaus clutched at his arm when he realized they were headed for the storeroom where the officers' provisions were kept.

"We can't go in there," he objected. Indeed, there were armed guards posted outside. At Kiel, in the third year of the war, food was more valuable than artillery shells.

But when Johnny announced "Orders" to the guards, they let him through. One even winked at him. They had been on the *Thüringen* together and had met once or twice in the shipyard latrines, where some of the sailors held secret meetings with socialist activists who slipped into the base from the outside.

A civilian clerk was inside, checking his inventory. He looked like a thoughtful hamster.

Johnny came smartly to attention and presented the card. On the front, embossed in gothic lettering, were the words

ERICH VON ARNIM
Oberleutnant zur See

The clerk frowned over the scrawl on the back.

"Two smoked hams?" he sniffed. "Six tins of paté?" He inspected Johnny over the rims of his spectacles. "This is highly irregular. Why didn't your lieutenant fill out the necessary forms?"

"His apologies, sir. Oberleutnant von Arnim has a pressing social engagement."

The clerk squinted more closely at Johnny. "I remember you. You fetched him a case of champagne only a few days ago. Also without the proper requisition order. Perhaps your Oberleutnant should be reminded that this is a war station, not a catering establishment."

"I believe—" Johnny lowered his voice "—that a royal personage is involved."

This phrase had an immediate effect. The clerk rapped out orders to his assistant, who rushed up and down the aisles with a trolley.

"I can let you have only two bottles of champagne." The clerk jabbed his finger against the last items on the list. "And the schnapps you must order from the mess."

"Very good, sir."

"Naturally, Oberleutnant von Arnim will be personally liable for the expense."

"Naturally, sir. Thank you very much, sir."

As they pushed the trolley back towards the gates, Klaus whispered, "Have you gone out of your mind? Von Arnim will have your guts for garters. And how did you get his card?"

"He had a spare one on his desk. I thought it might come in handy."

"You'll get both of us court-martialed," Klaus muttered unhappily.

At the main gate things had come to a standstill. The crowd was singing revolutionary songs but had no forward momentum. A young lieutenant had taken charge of the guard. He had a frank, open face and ginger hair. Johnny recognized him. His name was Knorr, and he was assigned to their flagship, the *Baden*. His men said he was not a bad sort. Knorr's sailors looked unhappy, hoisting their bayonets against women and children.

"What the devil do you want?" Lieutenant Knorr snapped at the two men with the trolley of provisions.

"Oberleutnant von Arnim's compliments, sir. These are for the people."

"For them?" Knorr looked at the crowd with misgivings. It had swelled in Johnny's absence. Some of the women were drumming on empty cooking pots.

"Yes, sir. Sort of a goodwill gesture, sir."

"A bayonet charge would be more like Erich von Arnim's idea of a goodwill gesture," Knorr remarked.

Johnny's eyes remained level with the ribbon of the Pour le Mérite, Germany's highest military decoration, on the lieutenant's tunic.

"Very well." Knorr opened his cigarette case. There was a faint smile of understanding at the corners of his mouth as he added, "Get on with it, then."

Johnny advanced into a warm tide of human flesh. The smell of the crowd as it washed over him was sweet and stale. It reminded him of the odor of a dead mouse behind the wainscot of his bedroom on the Valentinskamp, multiplied twentyfold. The sentries goggled and grumbled when they saw the hams, the cheese, the tins of sardines and foie gras—things that never graced their common tables. A girl threw her arms around Johnny's neck. Hands plucked at his bonnet, his scarf. But when the supplies ran out, an angry, hollow roar rose from the body of the crowd.

It's the voice of Germany, he thought.

ERICH VON ARNIM assembled the crew of the *Thüringen* on deck to witness a public flogging. He stood off to one side, tapping the palm of his left hand with his riding crop in rhythm with the blows of the cat-o'-nine-tails. Of course, it was a notable breach of decorum for a naval officer to go about with a riding crop, but the captain of the *Thüringen*, impressed by von Arnim's aristocratic connections, interfered with him as little as possible.

When Johnny blacked out, they sloshed salt water over him until he revived. Von Arnim did not call off the flogging until his back had been skinned as neatly as a rabbit's.

"Some of us are fixing to get even," a sailor whispered through the barred porthole of the ship's brig that night.

Johnny, lying belly down, could only grunt.

"It won't be long now. They say Lenin's taken power in Russia."

Despite the pain, Johnny pushed himself up from the bench with the palms of his hands and propped himself against the door.

"Lenin?" he croaked. "Is it true?"

"It's soldiers and sailors who put him in. He's going to stop the war. Liebknecht says we can do the same here."

There was a heavy footfall on deck, and the sailor scuttled away.

In the gloom of his confinement Johnny felt as if a candle had just been lit. There had been wild rumors from Russia early that year, when Kerensky had taken over. But Kerensky, like Ebert and his gang in Germany, was a war socialist, ready to fight the battles of the ruling class for them. Lenin! Now that was different. Johnny had read some of his articles in underground papers put out by Liebknecht's followers that passed from hand to hand inside the shipyards. The Russian looked like a schoolmaster, with his pasty face and his little pointed beard. But he had a mind like a razor. He dissected the crisis of civilization that was killing and starving millions for the sake of profiteers like Rausch and predators like von Arnim. He offered cures for the plagues that were ravaging Johnny's generation: war, hunger and spiritual exhaustion. Above all, he offered hope. In Russia, fighting against impossible odds, he had just proved his own dictum: "There are absolutely no impossible situations."

Johnny thought, We have found our compass.

THE GERMAN revolution came almost a year after Lenin's, and Johnny was in its front ranks.

He made no more quixotic gestures. To all appearances he had learned his lesson and become a dutiful German sailor, suitably deferential to his superiors. But in secret he joined the Spartakus Bund, named for the hero of the celebrated slave revolt against the Roman republic, and plotted mutiny with handpicked socialists from other ships. Soon the conspirators had organized cells on every warship in the harbor.

A champagne party gave them their signal.

Germany was defeated, everyone knew that. There was talk that Kaiser Wilhelm had abdicated and run away to Holland. But that night, Admiral Hipper and his officers sat up in their wardrooms, clinking champagne flutes and toasting the Death Ride of the Fleet.

"*What* did they call it?" Johnny asked the orderly who brought word to the men crowded below on the *Thüringen.*

"The Death Ride of the Fleet," he repeated. "They say the British will seize all our ships when the surrender is signed. They want to take on the British and go down with all guns blazing, if that's what it comes to. For the honor of the navy."

"Honor!" Johnny echoed the word with contempt. "*Their* honor. Not ours. Not one ship leaves harbor. Right?" He stared around the circle of worried, intent faces. "Klaus, you go to the *Baden.* Make sure the men are with us." He gave similar instructions to the others. They accepted his orders without question, without resentment. He was the youngest among them, yet he had already acquired a natural authority that had nothing to with age or epaulettes.

In the morning the sailors doused the furnaces and downed anchors. On the flagship *Baden*, mutineers barricaded themselves in the forward hatches and sang the *Internationale*. On the *Thüringen*, Johnny and a dozen others broke into the armory and passed out rifles.

"Back to your posts," a voice rang out. The voice was confident and superior, the eternal voice of command.

Johnny turned and saw Lieutenant von Arnim in full dress uniform with his monocle and his riding crop. He had to admire the man's coolness. The sailors hesitated.

"You! Lentz! Stand to attention!"

Even Johnny, drilled for months to obey that voice without hesitation, started instinctively to respond. But instead, he leveled his carbine.

"Oberleutnant, you are under arrest. The ship is in the hands of the revolutionary committee."

Von Arnim laughed. In the face of a mutiny, he seemed to be utterly without fear.

"You goddamned little Red," he said softly. "I knew I should have had you shot."

He flicked the riding crop and drove a diagonal welt across Johnny's cheek. The men murmured but started to back off. Erich von Arnim, with his total self-confidence and his riding crop, personified the power that had regimented their lives better than a company of marines with fixed bayonets.

Johnny knew the illusion had to be shattered, or the revolt on the *Thüringen* would end at that moment. If only his hands would stop shaking . . . He tried to recall the pain of his flogging, the haunted faces of the grey women with their empty cooking pots.

He held the carbine in front of him, steadying the barrel with his left hand. When he pulled the trigger, the butt slammed back into his stomach.

Von Arnim pressed his hand to his chest between the collar bones, where a scarlet patch, vivid against his dress white, flowered like a new decoration. His eyeglass dropped from his face and rolled on its edge across the deck. He flailed at the air with his riding crop, but his body crumpled under him.

"Come on!" Klaus Behring rallied the men. "We're in this together! We're going to Hamburg!"

"And then to Berlin!" someone else bellowed.

All along the harborfront women were waiting to garland them with red sashes and red cockades. One of them tied a paper flower into the ribbon of Johnny's hat. The sailors reversed their hatbands and slung their rifles butt upwards. What better symbol that the world was turning upside down?

They commandeered every car and truck they saw, piling on to the running boards, the hoods, even the roofs.

"To Hamburg!" Klaus yelled in Johnny's ear.

Johnny nodded his agreement.

There's no turning back now, he told himself. We win or we die.

4

THE rebel sailors called themselves the *Volksmarine,* the People's Navy, and the world belonged to them in those autumn days of 1918. Johnny went home to Hamburg with them. An elderly general at the head of a column of reservists and policemen marched out, revolver in hand, to order them back to their ships. Klaus Behring, warming to his new role, kicked the revolver out of the general's hand, and the Volksmarine paraded through the port city in triumph. Girls fought for the privilege of bedding a sailor with a red cockade in his hat, and Johnny was not ashamed to take advantage of their liberated spirits. The sailors decked their girls out in silks and furs plundered from the fashionable stores. Johnny was nervous about this orgy of looting. Surely this was not the way to win the people; and the time would come when the middle class, however lethargic and cowardly, would fight for its property. Still, they had announced the formation of a Workers' and Soldiers' Council; perhaps that would impose revolutionary discipline.

For all his scruples, he was not above taking a hamper of "liberated" delicacies with him when he went back to the Valentinskamp to visit his family. From the intermittent letters from his father that had reached him at Kiel, he gathered that the family was living close to the edge, scraping by on the pickings of a lowly clerical job Herr Lentz had found at the cement factory at Altona.

Johnny was shocked to see how they were living. They had all lost weight, even Bertha. The music room and his old bedroom had both been given over to lodgers. The living room was dominated by an ancient Singer sewing machine, which his mother and Bertha took turns operating, stitching party dresses for neighbors who could still afford to pay.

Heidi Lentz scowled at her son's muddied uniform and the sailor's hat with the band reversed, and averted her face when he tried to kiss her cheek. Bertha gave him the briefest squeeze.

"They don't approve," his father whispered when they were alone together in the kitchen. It smelled of lard and boiled cabbage. Herr Lentz's face was the color of old ivory, with two bright, unnatural points of color in the cheeks. He was sweating, despite the chill in the room. Each breath seemed to cause him an intolerable effort.

"Father, you're not well. You must go to a doctor. I have some money—"

"No time for all that," Herr Lentz barked. "I need your advice. You've seen something of what's going on. Will it last?"

"I can't say."

"It's too soon, Johnny. You and your sailors—what have you been up against so far? A few tired reservists. Wait till the frontline troops get home and the General Staff takes over. The Social Democrats won't shed any tears for you. They'll lead the slaughter. They're good Germans, after all. Good Germans believe in order."

"We've got Russia behind us."

"Russia!" Gottfried Lentz snorted. "Lenin is on top because the German General Staff put him there. He won't last much longer than your friend Liebknecht, not with the British and the White generals against him. Tell me I'm wrong."

"You're wrong, father." Johnny talked about the war that had chased three dynasties from their thrones and turned Europe into a gigantic graveyard. The old order was smashed beyond repair. Old conventions—even the old religions—were dying. History belonged to those with the courage to seize the reins, as the Bolsheviks had done in Russia.

"Well, it's no good arguing with a believer. I see that's what you've become."

"Is it wrong to have a cause?"

"Only if it becomes an ersatz religion. That's what Proudhon thought was wrong with Marx, that he wanted to found a new religion, a religion of the state."

"You said you wanted my advice."

"Oh, yes. Our local Lenins—the Workers' and Soldiers' Council, they call themselves—summoned me to see them. I suppose somebody must have it in for me. I found a lot of drunks carousing in a grand salon. They even had a fire going in the middle of the floor. They scared me more than General Ludendorff."

"What did they want?"

"They wanted me to take charge of popular education. I gather I might be paid if they stay in for more than a week. Should I do it?"

Johnny suddenly felt cold. He could gamble with his own life, but not with his father's.

"Father, it's not for me to say—" he began lamely.

"I mean, do you think I might do any good?"

"You might be a restraining influence," Johnny admitted, thinking of the looters running amok in the stores. "They need educated men."

"Then I'll do it!" Herr Lentz announced with a grin. "That will give old Rausch something to worry about. Let's have a beer to celebrate!"

"What about Mother?"

For an instant, his father's head seemed to withdraw between his shoulders. Then he bounced back.

"I am the master of this house," he announced defiantly.

To prove his point, he called to his wife, "Heidi! Bring us two beers!"

Johnny watched in some trepidation as his mother walked heavily into the kitchen. Her expression was thunderous, but, to Johnny's amazement, she brought the beer.

The revolution had entered the house on the Valentinskamp.

5

IN BERLIN, Johnny saw the red blanket draped over the Kaiser's balcony at the imperial *Schloss*, which the rebel sailors had turned into their barracks. He saw the crowds rip the epaulettes off any regular officer who dared to present himself in uniform in the streets. The girls were as welcoming as they had been in Hamburg.

But the carnival did not last long. Soon the streets rang under the boots of endless columns of stern-faced men in steel helmets and field grey, troops coming home from the front. When the crowds sang "Death to hangmen, kings and tyrants!" these soldiers did not join in.

Former cavalry officers caught Karl Liebknecht and Rosa Luxemburg, the two shining names of the German revolution, shot them in the back of the neck, dumped their bodies in the canal and made a marching song out of their exploit.

The Social Democrats in power, Ebert and Noske, turned to the monocles of the General Staff, just as Johnny's father had foreseen. They even appealed to the ultranationalists and out-and-out monarchists of the *Freikorps*—the volunteer detachments—who hated their new rulers as much as they did the Bolsheviks, and possibly more. Together they shelled the rebel sailors out of the Schloss and marched from city to city, liquidating Workers' Councils. Bremen, a Red fortress, was assaulted with heavy artillery.

Johnny returned to Hamburg as a hunted man, disguised in the cloth cap and drab overcoat of a worker.

He approached the family house cautiously. Instead of police agents, he saw a movers' truck outside. Bertha puffed down the steps, carrying the lamp from his old room.

He whistled to her.

"You—" she gaped at him. "You must go away at once!"

"Have you been evicted? Where's father?"

"Go away! Mama mustn't see you!"

"Answer me, Bertha!"

"We're going to Mama's family in East Prussia," she said nervously, looking over her shoulder.

"What about Father?"

"He's gone." She looked ready to burst into tears.

"Tell me!"

"They came for him. They had a list."

"Who?"

"Freikorps. General Maercker's detachment, I think. Willi Rausch was with them. They shot him at the front door." Her chest heaved, and she could hardly get out the last words. "They put him down like a dog. Now go. Please. Before she comes."

It was too late. Johnny's mother was already hurrying down the steps.

"Bertha!"

"It's Johnny, Mama."

She turned her face away. "I have no son."

"Mother—" Johnny appealed to her.

She faced him then, for an instant, and he saw that she had grown terribly old.

"*You* pulled the trigger," she said.

HE DRANK into the night at a whores' bar off the Reeperbahn, where the lights of the honky-tonks burned brighter than ever, despite the misery outside. In that dead port you could buy any kind of sex for money or chocolates or cigarettes, or merely a bed and a chance of breakfast.

I have lost everything, he told himself. My family. God. (Nietzsche, before Marx, had persuaded him that God was dead, and even if he had never read either, the war might have had the same effect.) Country. Profession. Everything except my comrades and that will-o'-the-wisp—the revolution. All the more reason to cling tight to them.

It was past midnight when he went to the Rausch residence, on an elegant boulevard near the Binnen-Alster. He still had his pistol, confiscated from an unlucky member of the Berlin police. At least he could settle one score.

He banged on the door knocker until Herr Rausch leaned out of an upstairs window in his nightcap.

"What do you want?" he shouted down. "Go away or I'll call the police." The sight of the big man in a cloth cap made him nervous.

"Willi told me to come!" Johnny called back.

"Willi?" Herr Rausch's flabby features creased in puzzlement. Then he added with pride, "Willi's on the eastern border, fighting the Reds!"

One more stupidity, Johnny thought. He had heard that some of the Freikorps had gone east, dreaming of the Teutonic knights. That account would have to be settled later.

Trudging back to his bolthole, Klaus Behring's dingy room in the Gängeviertel, he was accosted by a trembling woman with a daughter about his own age. The woman had a decent, homely face.

"We have nowhere to go," she said. "You have a kind face. Will you help us?"

"I wish I could." He thought of the rising damp on the walls of Klaus's room.

"My husband was killed in the war. My daughter could warm your bed," the woman implored. "Or I could, if you prefer." The girl kept her face hidden.

"Here—take this—" he blurted out, handing them his last pack of cigarettes. He rushed on into the dark.

My God, he thought, has it come to this? His head was pounding. There must be tens of thousands of such women all over Germany. He had seen the packs of orphans by the docks, fighting over scraps of rotting fish. He had to help change all of that. But he would need to be part of an organization of professionals. The mutiny in the fleet, the risings in Hamburg and Berlin, had been a glorious amateur stunt and had captured the imagination of the country—for about as long as a traveling circus. Next time, it would be different.

WHEN THE Communist party of Germany was formed as the German section of a world movement, the Communist International, Johnny was one of the first to join. They gave him a membership card in his own name, and a pocket calendar with a questionnaire on the first page headed, "Important: To Be Filled in Immediately." He gnawed on his pencil as he studied the page. "This book belongs to . . . (space for name). Address . . . Membership number . . . Union . . ."

He tore the calendar into strips, lit a match and watched it burn. Then he chopped the membership card into tiny pieces with his pocketknife and tossed them into the toilet. They were still amateurs—or worse, good Germans, sticklers for form. How could he, a man on the run with blood on his hands, go about with these lethal documents on his person?

Since the party was unable, or unwilling, to support him, he survived by doing odd jobs, first around the waterfront in Hamburg and later in the steel mills of the Ruhr. He made himself useful to the cause in little ways. He organized self-help groups, flying squads of men on bicycles who could be called in to save tenants from being evicted. Even the police were scared of them. He went on a gun-running assignment in the Baltic in a leaky old forty-footer, the *Lisl*. They met a disguised Soviet freighter in the middle of the night and collected a pile of antique tsarist rifles bundled up in tarpaulins and cartridges buried in barrels of flour.

The party gave him the sense of security that comes from belonging to a large family, and the women were easy. Many of them thought him handsome, now that the lines of his face had sharpened. More compelling than mere looks was the sense of danger that traveled with him. "When I kiss you," one of his girls said, "I smell gunpowder."

Committee meetings bored him with the endless quibbling over petty points of doctrine, and as the months passed his impatience grew. He felt that for some reason he had been marooned in the outer circle. He wanted to be *inside*. And he needed action.

6

He found lodgings nearer the harbor, above a curio shop. When he came home that night, the gas lamps were sputtering. The wail of a ship's siren floated in from the sea, lonely and plaintive like a cat begging to be let in from the cold. He clenched his fists inside his pockets. He was restless and angry; as winter came on, he felt the days slipping through his hands. He had been out on recruiting work, trying to persuade the men coming off a freighter of the North German Lloyd to come to a party meeting. The sailors were nervous; they wanted to get home to their wives or girlfriends. Johnny recognized one of them, an old shipmate from the *Thüringen*. In the winter of 1918 the man had been ready for anything. Now all he could do was to mumble that he had mouths to feed and couldn't risk getting his name on the blacklists. He fled from Johnny as he might have fled from a mugger.

They'll become mules without action, Johnny told himself. We must have *movement*.

Greta, the landlord's daughter, came out into the hall as soon as she heard the latch and fluttered her eyelashes at him.

She was round as a pumpkin and had no waist at all, but she was soft and giving and good to hold on a raw night when the harbor mists rose above the windows.

"How are you, Lovie?" He gave her a quick kiss on the lips, turning his hips as she slipped her arms around him so she would not feel the angular bulge of the pistol that lay flat against the small of his back, hidden in the waistband of his trousers.

"Father's out," Greta announced, looking suggestively at the open door behind her. "And I've got some cherry brandy."

"Later. I have work to do."

"Those stuffy old books can wait." She hung on his neck.

How could he explain to her that he was ravenous for the stack of dog-eared, broken-backed books that formed a barricade beside his bed? Books were weapons, no less than the gun he had carried since the mutiny. He had to master so many, with so little time. He had to make up for the schooling he had lost and prepare himself for the next stage of the fight. He had already worked his way through the two volumes of a selected edition of Marx. He reveled in the Promethean defiance of the early writings, the sense of stealing fire from heaven. From Marx he had learned to see history as a process of constant struggle. From Engels, from the *Anti-Dühring,* he obtained the answer to the moral question. Nothing was final, absolute or sacred; everything was relative. History, only history, would decide whether a man's actions were good or evil. The murder of a thousand Erich von Arnims was justified if it accelerated the march of history.

From Lenin, Johnny learned what revolution required: an elite corps of legionnaires, secret and disciplined, utterly divorced from the sticky web of comforts and constraints that made lesser men slaves of the social order. He believed his own destiny belonged with that secret order.

But here was little Greta, grazing on his neck.

"Later," he repeated.

"I know what's on your mind," she pouted. "You've got a new one, haven't you? Your taste's gone off a bit. Black as a witch and flat as an ironing board. Four eyes to boot. My poor mother used to say men will make love to the back of a bus."

Johnny was mystified. "What the hell are you talking about?"

"She came round here looking for you, didn't she?"

Johnny's alarm showed in his face. Nobody knew his address except Klaus and Harold Beer, the district party chief.

"What did she want?"

"Don't look at me like that, Johnny." His expression scared the girl. She dipped into her bodice and pulled out a folded square of paper. "Here. She left you this."

Johnny snatched it from her.

Nothing more than a place and a time. He knew the place, a hall in a workers' district just outside Altona.

"What did she say?"

"Nothing—just her name."

"What name?"

"Ula. She said you'd remember. Silly kind of a monicker, if you ask me."

Johnny remembered. The *Ula* had been his first boat. He consulted the paper again. Eight o'clock. That gave him less than an hour.

THERE WERE guards outside the hall, and one of them wanted to frisk Johnny before letting him in. He was rescued by a girl in wire-rimmed glasses and a short leather coat, with kinky black hair that flew off in all directions from under her beret.

"You're late," she greeted him.

"And you must be Ula."

She didn't return his smile. "I'm Magda," she said curtly, and wrung his hand like a man trying to prove something.

She might be pretty, he thought as he followed her past the guards, if she were ever prepared to let on she's a woman.

He sat next to her, on the aisle. The faces around him were those of workers and seamen like himself, people living on the waterline. It would take little to sink them, but then again they had nothing much to lose. The man on the platform, however, looked different. He wore a decent suit and a watch chain across his vest and talked through his nose about the theory of surplus value.

There was some whispering behind the rostrum. Then the chairman got up, tugged at the speaker's coattails to signal that his time was up and announced, "The comrade from Russia is here!"

This revived the audience. While the pianist banged out a few bars of the *Internationale,* people craned to get a good look at the new arrival. A burly figure in a brown leather coat like Magda's, his cap rakishly askew, he marched across the stage and vaulted right onto the table at which the party leaders were seated, sending pencils and ashtrays flying.

"We sit talking while Germany starves!" he roared at his audience. "But every one of us knows what's required! The rich must die so the poor can live!"

The previous speaker fidgeted and rubbed his nose, but several men jumped up and chorused their approval. Johnny got on his feet too, trying to get a better look at the speaker. The beard was gone, except for a bluish shadow. The face was leaner and harder, with deep lines scored between nose and chin. But there was no mistaking the man. The comrade from Russia was Heinz Kordt.

"You know my voice!" Kordt went on. "It's the voice inside every one of you. A man can take so much before he breaks—or breaks out. I've been in Petrograd, and in Moscow. I've seen the future. I've seen a country without monocles or profiteers, where men are equal and earn the fruits of their labor. I've seen a place where children don't go hungry while their mothers hawk their bodies for bread.

"Comrades, the revolution in Russia is still imperiled. The capitalist world, terrified of the future, has conspired to strangle it. The Russian people need our help. Their final victory, which is inevitable, will bring ours closer—until a Soviet Russia and a Soviet Germany stand together as the mightiest power on earth! Then no cabal will be able to stand against us. Together we shall ignite the world! It's not a dream of the next century, it's a dream of tomorrow!

"But the monocles and the profiteers and their lapdogs in Weimar won't give up without a fight. We must arm! We must build a Red Army in every German city! Each man among you, every woman, has to make your choice. *Es geht im die Wurst.* The sausage depends on it."

The old man sitting in front of Johnny nodded his head at this. But at the end of Kordt's speech, which returned to the theme of a new man in a new society, he tugged at his beard and muttered, "And ye shall be as gods."

Curious, Johnny tapped his shoulder. "What did you say?"

The old man turned in his seat. His eyes were watery. He sucked on his pipe and said, "It's what the serpent said to Eve. It's what they always promise. You'll see what comes of it."

"Fool!" Magda snapped at him. "You don't belong here." She jogged Johnny's elbow, coaxing him into the aisle.

She took his arm and steered him around the crowd, through a side door. The old man's words left a sour taste.

It was my father's warning too, Johnny thought. Beware of building a false church. But they're wrong. Of course they're wrong. If only my father had lived to see Russia . . .

"You must call him Viktor," Magda was saying.

She escorted him across a courtyard, up a treacherous flight of steps. The biblical gloom evaporated the moment Heinz Kordt erupted from a circle of admirers and seized Johnny in a bear hug.

"Let me get a good look at you." He thrust Johnny back, still hanging on to his arms. "By God, you're a man. Isn't he, Magda?"

"There's no contrary evidence," she shrugged, and sidled off to the table where tea and whiskey were laid out.

"She's from Cracow." Kordt watched her trim backside as she moved away. "A cold-assed bitch, but very reliable."

"Heinz—I mean Viktor—"

"Listen. We drink. Then we get rid of the others and we talk, you and me. I've got plans for you."

THE NIGHT was as long as the last one they had spent together almost six years before, in the world before the war. Sometime before dawn, Kordt dragged out a Victrola and put on a recording of the mercenary marching songs of the Thirty Years' War. He hooked one arm around Magda's, the other around Johnny's, and turned a little jig, as he boomed out the chorus of the famous song of *Der verlone Haufen*, the Lost Band:

> Let the flags blow wide,
> We are going into battle . . .

This was the Heinz Johnny remembered.

"I got your address from Harold Beer," Kordt announced at one point.

"I guessed as much."

"Harold says you're a good man, but impatient."

"Beer's an old woman. He spends all his time bitching about his rivals. He's scared to move. He won't understand that this business is like riding a bicycle. If you stop pedaling, you'll fall off."

"I see you've learned a thing or two." Kordt stared at the younger man for a moment, appraising. He seemed to like what he saw. He turned up the volume on the Victrola and leaned close to Johnny. "I've been sent here on a special job," he confided. "We're going to build a Red Army here in Germany. A hundred thousand armed men, enough to sweep the monocles into the Baltic. The Russians are sending their best instructors. Trotsky promised me personally that he will arrange shipment of all the rifles we need. I'm in charge in Hamburg. Within a year—two years at the outside —we'll be ready to seize power, with twenty times the resources the Bolsheviks had when they took St. Petersburg. We can't fail. What do you say?"

Johnny was on his feet, his eyes shining. "Tell me what I can do."

FOR THE next two years he worked for Kordt in the underground party— the *Apparat*—building a revolutionary army. In the woods outside Hamburg he helped train recruits for the Red Hundreds, the workers' militia, under the scrutiny of a tall, imposing Russian Jew who called himself Waldemar. It was rumored that Waldemar had seized the telegraph office in St. Petersburg in 1917 and routed the cossacks in the civil war. Under his direction each clump of trees became a barracks, a police station, a government office.

Again and again Waldemar hammered on the theme that political struggle was different from conventional war.

"Psychology is the key," he told Johnny. "A military setback can be a psychological victory, if it mobilizes support for our side. When you take on the police, make sure there are lots of people around. Get them in the middle if you can. If innocents are killed, the workers will be outraged and join us in their thousands."

When the French sent their troops into the Ruhr—Germany's industrial heartland—on the pretext that the Weimar government had not kept up with the schedule of tribute imposed at Versailles, Johnny went too, at the head of a combat squad, to organize armed resistance. The sight of giant smelters shut down, of swollen, sullen breadlines, told him the revolution could not be long delayed. What he saw on his return to Hamburg made him sure of it.

By late October 1923 the daily wage of a worker on the Hamburg docks was seventeen billion marks. Hungry mobs broke into bakeries and food stores. Near midnight, on his way to an emergency meeting called by Kordt, Johnny passed a crazy old woman who was burning currency in a rust-eaten gasoline drum to warm herself. Everyone knew the French were to blame. When they had marched into the Ruhr, they had starved the German government of money, and the government had turned to the printing presses. Day and night the presses spewed out paper money, with more zeroes on every bill every time you looked. It was the death of the currency and the death of the middle class. A man who had spent his life salting away his savings in bonds and bank deposits was now worth less than his drunken brother who had saved the bottles his booze came out of. It was a good season for speculators—and for the Communist party.

The meeting room, a pistol shot away from the Kali-Bar, was crowded and overheated. They had three or four trestle tables pulled together. Heinz and Waldemar presided together at one end. The men who squeezed in along the sides were not ordinary party members. They were chiefs of Red Hundreds and cadres from the M-group, the party's professional combat organization. They whispered to each other as they waited for the meeting to come to order. It had been a week of wild rumors and false alarms. The political bosses of the German Communist Party were meeting in Chemnitz, on the other side of the country. As far as Johnny was concerned, the only item on their agenda that mattered a damn was whether to order an armed insurrection. The German leaders were said to be divided; so were the observers from the Comintern. So, it was rumored, were the Russians. While telegrams were fired back and forth to Moscow, the men in this room worried at their leash.

Heinz looked drawn and tired. As Johnny watched, Magda crossed the room and whispered something in Kordt's ear. Immediately his face seemed to regain color and life.

He got to his feet and banged his fist on the table.

"Comrades! A courier has just arrived from Chemnitz by train. They've made their decision! By God, I believe it's the right one! We move at first light!"

He made the clenched-fist salute. The next instant, every man in the room was on his feet.

"Red Front!" a dozen voices chorused.

Heinz and Waldemar rehearsed the targets assigned to each group.

There was at least one doubter in the room, a shoemaker from Barmbek who sat across the table from Johnny.

"We can't fight with broomsticks," he pointed out. "My group has only got three revolvers and a few hand grenades."

There were sympathetic murmurs from some of the others. Despite Trotsky's promise, weapons were in short supply.

"If you need a gun, Georg—" Kordt wagged a finger at him "—you catch a policeman. We'll take what we need from the enemy. All right?"

"What if the government sends troops?"

"The honorable Minister for War will be busy saving his own rear end," Kordt said contemptuously. "There will be simultaneous risings in Berlin, Leipzig, Frankfurt, Bremen—where are reinforcements going to come from?"

The shoemaker sucked on his pipe, apparently pacified.

But a young seaman spoke up with a different complaint.

"We can't count on anyone around the docks except our own men," he said. "Not since the strike."

This touched a raw nerve. The communists had called for a total shutdown of the port early in the summer. The strike had been a success to begin with. Then hunger had started to wear down the strikers' resistance. Finally the communists themselves had decided to break the strike. Secret orders had gone out: party members should go down to the docks at first light and get themselves signed up for any job that was going. By this cynical device, the communists had hoped to turn half the ships in the harbor into floating fortresses. But in the eyes of a lot of angry, unemployed men around the waterfront, they were blacklegs. Johnny had heard the ugly word hurled at him. He didn't like the way it sounded. In their ignorance, in their misery, those angry men could not be expected to understand that what looked to them like a sordid maneuver would help them in the long run—by building workers' power.

Heinz might have made a speech along these lines, but it was not a night for speeches. He simply growled at the young sailor, "The Hamburg docks belong to *me!* Let any man try to prove otherwise."

Then Waldemar got up, and a deep hush grew around him. They were all in awe of him, this man who had fought with Lenin and Trotsky.

"I know a bit about revolution." His voice was warm and protective. "On the eve of revolution, there are always voices that say, 'The masses aren't ready.' On the night before, they are probably right. It doesn't matter a damn. Once we strike, the masses will follow."

With that, all hesitation seemed to leave the room.

THE FIRST target for Johnny's group, in the early dawn, was a police station within sound and smell of the harbor. He had twenty men, including Klaus Behring. Only a few were armed with rifles. The rest had to make do with revolvers, bottle bombs, kitchen knives and spiked clubs. Inspecting his ragtag army, Johnny wondered again what had happened to Trotsky's shipments.

By the time they converged on the station, they had two more guns. With knives at their throats, the policemen they ambushed weren't reluctant to part with their Sam Browne belts. But one of them was less cooperative when Johnny ordered him to strip. Johnny knocked him out cold with a blow to the back of the neck. The uniform was a reasonable fit.

He stopped at an all-night café a few blocks from the station, to use the telephone.

"Police? I want to report a rape. Yes. It's still going on. The screams are terrible. Please hurry." He gave a made-up address and hung up.

In the cold morning light he watched two more policemen pedaling off in the direction of the reported crime. The odds were narrowing by the minute. But the men at the station weren't asleep. They had turned their post into a blockhouse, with rolls of barbed wire and a machine gunner up on the roof.

Johnny deployed sentries at the street corners and massed the rest of his men in an alley in the lee of a boarded-up dress shop.

"Can you throw straight?" he asked a muscular young stevedore with a brace of hand grenades in his belt.

"Straight as an arrow."

"Very well. As soon as you hear shooting inside, aim for the machine gun. And don't forget to take out the pin."

Johnny strolled into the police station as if he lived on the premises. He and his companion were wearing the green tunics and shakos of the Hamburg police.

Inside the building, several men were dozing on camp beds. The others were hunched around a table, playing poker.

"Who the hell are you?" the duty sergeant addressed Johnny, turning his attention from a busted straight.

"You've been expropriated, friend." Johnny flourished a pistol in one hand and a grenade in the other. "This station belongs to the people."

"Leck' mich am Arsch," said the sergeant, unimpressed. He grabbed for a rifle from the rack.

He had his hand on it when Johnny shot him behind the ear. The somnolent forms at the back of the room began to stir. Johnny yanked the pin from the grenade with his teeth and lobbed it towards them. Everyone rolled for cover. The building rocked with a double explosion, from inside and overhead. Streaked white with plaster dust, the surviving policemen gave up meekly enough. One of them, cooler than the rest, plucked the scattered playing cards off the floor and said, "Do you mind if we play another hand, Your Excellency?"

Johnny let them go on with their game in the cells. He left the station with enough rifles for all his men and a few to spare for the volunteers who started bobbing up out of nowhere. He did not spare a thought for the sergeant he had killed; history would justify him. All the same, he avoided looking at the man's clumsy body. It was easier to kill when the enemy was impersonal.

By MIDDAY it was obvious that things were going badly wrong. In some areas—especially in the working-class citadel of Barmbek—the people joined the rising in great numbers. But they fled from the armored cars that shoved their ugly snouts over the barricades, spitting machine-gun bullets.

Johnny saw Kordt, riding on the running board of a truck, shouting orders.

"Heinz! Any news from Berlin?"

"Nothing."

Heinz let himself drop from the running board.

"What about the fleet?"

He shook his head. "Listen. To fight the armored cars, we must have explosives. You know the dynamite factory?"

Johnny remembered. It was west of the city and heavily guarded.

"Can you take it?"

"I'll try."

"Good luck." Heinz clapped him on the shoulder and ran after the truck.

The navy got to the factory first. Johnny and his men were pinned down by a hail of fire from blue-uniformed German sailors. These were not the sailors of 1918. The rumor spread that a battle flotilla was steaming up the Elbe, ready to shell the rebels into submission if they captured the port or the business quarter.

Klaus Behring made a mad dash for the blockhouse commanding the gates and was caught in a murderous crossfire. Johnny saw his old shipmate fumble forward and lie still in a pool of his own blood.

Someone will pay, he promised himself, emptying his magazine at the line of sailors that was inching steadily, relentlessly forward.

Finally Magda came on a bicycle with a message from Heinz.

He saw her beside the road, her mouth opening and closing. He couldn't make out the words. He ran towards her, ducking and weaving.

"Give it up!" she yelled. "We've been stabbed in the back!" Before he could reach her she was speeding away, her head bent low over the handlebars.

He was reduced to running to save his skin. The old instinct drove him back towards the harbor. He found the waterfront swarming with police. They were checking anyone who tried to cross to the Free Port by bridge or tunnel. He slipped behind a warehouse and found a dinghy that had been hauled up for repair. It had sprung a leak, but it might hold out long enough to serve his purpose.

Paddling and bailing by turns, he crossed the inner harbor and spotted a passenger boat that was just getting up steam. It was flying the Dutch flag. In the chaos of departure, he was able to haul himself up on deck without being spotted. But almost at once he saw one of the ship's officers strolling his way. Where could he hide? If he were discovered here, they would turn him over to the police. He saw only one chance—the manhole cover a few yards away, in the bow of the boat. He sprang at it and hauled it open. Even as he jumped inside, he realized his mistake.

He was inside the chain locker. Once he had pulled the cover back over his head, he was left squatting uncomfortably on a great iron anaconda— the coiled anchor chain, hundreds of feet long. Still, he would be safe enough until they got out to sea, when he might be able to find a softer berth.

He had not slept for two days and he soon dozed off, lulled by the familiar reek of bilge water and the vibration of the hull against his side. It was an uneasy sleep. In his dream he was being prodded up a cattle run behind Heinz Kordt and a dozen other men he knew from the *Thüringen* and the Hamburg underground. They were all bent over, running on all fours like brutes. At the head of the cattle run stood a masked man with

an iron mallet, waiting to brain them one by one. *Stabbed in the back,*
Magda's words came into the dream. *Stabbed in the back . . .* Now the feet
were thudding harder, faster, threatening to trample him unless he hurried.
A tremendous howl burst against his eardrums—and he snapped awake.

Above, the foghorns wailed. He heard the creak of a windlass. Disoriented, still half in the grip of the dream, he stared at the vertical length
of chain beside him, trailing from the hole in the hull. Suddenly he was
on his feet, wrestling with the manhole cover.

For some reason—the fog on the river?—the ship was going to drop
anchor. When the crushing metal weight was loosed, the coils of chain that
had made his bed would lash up at him and batter him to pieces. The cover
wouldn't shift. He pounded and clawed, but he couldn't move it an inch.
Someone must have secured it from above.

Desperate, he hammered on the metal with both fists.

"For the love of God—"

"For the love of God, is it?" The cover was pulled back and Johnny
found himself looking up into a ruddy face embellished with thick white
eyebrows.

At the same instant, he heard the splash of the anchor. The chain kicked
and sawed, and he clutched at the edges of the manhole, swinging his legs
up under him.

His rescuer seized his forearm and dragged him up on deck.

A white-jacketed purser came running. "Need any help, sir?"

"No, I reckon he'll be docile for a bit."

Johnny realized he was dealing with the skipper himself.

"You'll be one of them Reds, I venture? Well, come along with me. I
want to hear all about it."

For once luck was on Johnny's side. Captain Jan Gallagher, Irish on his
father's side, took a liberal view of human foibles and didn't mind other
men's politics—even the Bolshevist sort—as long as they didn't try to
spread them on his boat. He also had a liberal hand with his *genever.* He
poured both of them a few glasses in his cabin, eager to hear a firsthand
account of the Hamburg rising.

"What happened in Berlin?" Johnny asked him. "Did you hear any
news?"

"None of your comrades lifted a finger, in Berlin or anywhere else. They
left you lot in Hamburg to swing by yourselves."

Johnny was stunned by this information. This must have been what
Magda had meant. They had been stabbed in the back. Even if they had
won in Hamburg, the government would have been free to throttle them
with fresh troops from all over the country. They had been led on a dance

of death. But why? Had the party leaders changed their minds? Were they cowards? Had the groups in other cities been betrayed?

He thought of Klaus Behring, facedown in his own blood. Someone would have to atone for that and all the other wasted lives.

Captain Gallagher looked at him with a sort of pity.

"Here. Have another drop of gin. I'll take you to Rotterdam if you're willing to work your passage. But I won't have any politics on my ship. Agreed?"

It was not a hard promise to keep. On that voyage Johnny was in no mood to play the apostle.

1

"IT WAS a fuck-up." Heinz delivered his postmortem six months later. "The orders were changed at the last minute. The rising was called off. The couriers had already left the party congress in Chemnitz. They sent men to stop them. But when they got to the station the messenger for Hamburg had left. They could still see the lights of his train."

"Wait a minute." Johnny leaned across the table. "What are you telling me? That we spilled our guts because nobody bothered to tell us the operation was canceled? Couldn't they have sent another messenger by car? Don't they even know how to drive?"

He sat back, furious and mildy nauseous. They were in a booth at a restaurant on the Hedermanstrasse in Berlin, shielded by panels of frosted glass. The place served excellent bratwurst and latkes, but it hadn't been chosen for its cuisine. The owner was a member of the N-group, one of the most secret components of the underground party *Apparat.* The "N" stood for *Nachrichten,* or intelligence. He was said to have an unerring nose for police spies.

"It was a fuck-up," Heinz repeated, fanning his hands. "It's not the end of the world. There'll be plenty more battles to fight."

"Not for Klaus Behring," Johnny said savagely. "Or a lot of other good men." By the end of the rising one in three Communists in Hamburg had been killed or captured. "It was Thälmann who lost his nerve, wasn't it?" he pressed on. Thälmann was emerging as the biggest of the *Bonzen,* as the party leaders were unflatteringly described by the rank and file.

"It was the Bonzen," Heinz half confirmed.

Johnny had spent half a year on the run from Rotterdam to Marseilles, where he had washed up at the Comintern liaison office, which operated under the cover of a seamen's club down at the docks. They had given him

odd jobs to do, running around as a messenger boy with an envelope glued
to the skin of his back. Then the telegram ordering him to meet Heinz in
Berlin had come. He hadn't hesitated. Whatever he might think of the
Thälmanns, he would cross oceans for Heinz.

"Have you got something for me?" Johnny asked.

"That depends on the man you're going to meet."

"Do I know him?"

"You may have imagined him," Heinz replied oddly.

"Is he German?"

"No. Though he speaks better German than Thälmann."

"Russian, then."

"He speaks that, too. Someone told me once that he was born in Riga.
Also that he went to school with the Jesuits. I don't know if it's true. I know
he was with Dzerzhinsky, when he defeated the plot against Lenin."

"So he's a chekist." The word was widely used in party circles, as in
Russia, to describe a member of Soviet intelligence. It derived from the
original name Lenin had given to his secret police.

"He is a man who lives in shadow country," Heinz responded. "He has
his own network in the West. He told me once that it extends from Iceland
to the Cape. In Germany, he controls the N-group. Also the T-groups."
The "T" stood for "Terror." "Max is the most extraordinary man I have
ever met. A man like that breeds myths wherever he goes. But let me tell
you one story about him I can vouch for. He had a Polish girl once, called
Zinka. She was a poetess, quite beautiful. She fought with him in Russia.
When the Bolsheviks won the civil war, she insisted on going home to
Lvov, to make the revolution for her own people. But there was a spy in
her circle, and he warned the police. They were waiting for her at the
railway station. She was a Jew, and you know the Poles are not always subtle
with Jews. They invaded her body with a hot iron. I imagine she talked.
Inevitably she died. When word reached Max, he went to Lvov dressed as
a Polish priest, traveling alone. He stalked the police torturer to his home
and shot him on his own doorstep. He traced the spy and gave him the same
rites that Zinka had received. In other words, he rammed a red-hot poker
up his backside. This is the man you are going to deal with."

"Why does he want to meet me?"

"I recommended you."

A girl squeezed into their booth. She was a svelte brunette, elegantly
dressed.

She said to Heinz, "He's coming now." She was attractive and conscious
of it. She flirted with Johnny by affecting to ignore his existence.

"What's the matter, Johnny?" Heinz teased him, noting his interest in
the girl. "Why don't you say hello to Magda?"

"Magda? It's not possible—" But it was. Take away the clothes and the makeup, add wire-rimmed glasses, and he was looking at the mannish guerrilla he had briefly encountered in Hamburg. "I like you better this way," he said, laughing at his own confusion. "Can I buy you a drink?"

"A glass of red wine." Even the voice was softer.

"Heinz?"

But Heinz was sliding out of the booth. "I'll see you later." An ironic salute, and he was gone.

"Well," Johnny turned back to the girl. "I see Berlin has had an agreeable effect."

"For you, too, I trust." This new voice startled Johnny. It was identifiably foreign, but only because of the perfect weight that it gave to every vowel. It had a metallic timbre. The effect was not harsh, but it suggested —at least to Johnny—a distance between what was said and what was intended.

The newcomer slid into Heinz's place before Johnny realized he was there. It was the eyes Johnny saw first. They reached out and touched him with such force that he felt, for an instant, that he had been physically struck. He had to will himself not to look away. Under that violent stare, he felt completely exposed.

He thought, I've got to control myself. He tried to make a rational inventory of the stranger's appearance. The man was of medium height, compact and strongly built. His clothes were dark and conservative, discreetly well cut. The index and second fingers of his right hand were tawny from nicotine. He was already lighting another cigarette. Black tobacco, the kind that smells like camel dung. A commanding forehead. Straight black hair, worn rather long, slicked back from a widow's peak. The slant of the cheekbones, above cavernous hollows, gave the whole face a vaguely oriental cast. The eyes were black—or brown. No. They were violet.

I'm losing my balance. No man has violet eyes.

"I've been looking forward to this meeting," said Max.

The mutual inspection had taken something less than twenty seconds.

MAX wanted the story of his whole life. He acted as if he had no other concern in the world, on that bright spring afternoon, than to listen to the hopes and disappointments of a man twenty years his junior. He interrupted Johnny only to order brandy and cigarettes. When Johnny paused, it was "Go on" or "What happened then?"—so that after a time the younger man forgot all about his initial, inexplicable panic and talked more freely than he had talked to anyone, even Heinz. When he got to Klaus Behring's death and his own flight from Hamburg, he stopped.

Max nodded and said, through a blue haze, "The problem is, some of your countrymen mistook the second month of pregnancy for the ninth. But a good deal was gained, all the same. Don't overlook that just because you lost a friend. Any revolt, any uprising, is *ein Fanal*. A beacon. It helps to show the people that the order of society can be changed. It's a training for the revolution we shall win. And it helps us to know our own.

"You read, don't you?" he suddenly changed tack. "What do you read?"

"Marx. Lenin—"

"Marx. Very well, then. Do you remember what Marx wrote to the French workers in 1850, when all his prophecies for a proletarian revolution next week had gone up the spout? No? He told them they would have to go through fifteen or twenty or fifty years of civil war in order to change themselves, to render themselves fit for political domination. Do you understand?"

"I hope we don't have to wait fifty years."

"Ah, we've learned how to hurry things up. I'm saying, be thankful for Hamburg, Johnny. Yes, I'm serious. Be thankful for anything that tests you. That's how we know our own," he repeated. "The fire that melts the butter tempers the steel. Now I've got a special question for you."

"Anything."

"Who is the greatest enemy of the German revolution?"

Johnny considered for a moment. Not square, ponderous Stresemann, with his face like a side of beef. The chancellor was just a front for the financiers and the industrial barons and the Prussians on the General Staff.

"Seeckt," he decided, picturing the confident, monocled face of the chief of the General Staff, the face of an Erich von Arnim with ten times the brains and a thousand times more low cunning. "General von Seeckt."

"Let's suppose you are right," Max went on. "What effect do you think General Seeckt's assassination would have on the correlation of forces in Germany?"

"It would increase the contradictions within the ruling class." Johnny thought rapidly. "It would disrupt the secret rearmament program. It would lead to reprisals—probably indiscriminate reprisals. More people would be forced to choose between us or the reactionaries."

"Agreed. So. If I sat General von Seeckt down in front of you, at this table—would you be man enough to blow his brains out?"

Johnny was conscious of Magda watching him closely. Her lips were slightly curled. Was she mocking or encouraging?

He met Max's eyes and said, "Yes."

"Why?"

"Because I have nothing to lose."

*   *   *

MAGDA took Johnny back to a lavish apartment with a view of the Tiergarten. Her lovemaking, that night, was like the furniture: elaborate and impersonal. Afterwards she scrubbed herself all over, repeatedly, with a deodorant soap, as if she wanted no trace of another individual on her body.

It occurred to Johnny that this was the second of Heinz's hand-me-downs he had enjoyed. He felt a wave of nostalgia for the first. He wondered what had happened to Helene, with her lust for life. He must find out from Heinz, when he came.

But this time, Heinz did not come.

In the morning Magda shook him awake.

"Get dressed."

"What's happening?"

"You must go to the Anhalter station before eleven. Seeckt is returning from Weimar by train."

She gave him an Ortgies pistol. He had used one before, and it had jammed. He wanted to take his own gun, the Mauser, but she refused.

"There must be nothing that can be traced."

She checked his pockets, removing anything that could be identified. Then she gave him some odd bits and pieces—a death's-head badge to wear under his lapel, a membership card with a false name and the crest of a Fascist secret society.

"What's all this?"

"In case you're shot," she replied blandly. "You're ready for that, aren't you?"

"Of course."

He loitered at the Anhalter station near the entrance to platform four. Seeckt's train was late. No, it was merely his nerves.

There he was now. For a moment he saw the general's head beyond a press of military aides and station guards. In a minute he would be coming this way. But wait. Seeckt had stopped. He stared around, then spun on his heel and marched back to his Pullman. What had happened? The stationmaster, flustered, ran puffing towards his office.

Ten minutes later, a troop of regular soldiers tramped through the station and joined their general. When Seeckt descended from his carriage, he vanished behind a ring of steel. There was no chance of getting a clear shot at him.

Johnny hesitated, his hand toying with the flap of the satchel in which his pistol lay concealed. If only they'd given him a bomb . . .

He heard a low whistle from nearby. He turned, and saw a man with his hands in his pockets. The stranger cocked his head and said, "Leave off. The bastard's got a sixth sense."

Johnny realized then that for every second since he had left the Hedermanstrasse Max had had him watched.

UNDER the full moon, Felseneck was beautiful. It was just a huddle of modest cottages with communal plots in the midst of the wasteland between Berlin and the neighboring town of Reinickedorf. But tonight even the scruffy rows of onions and radishes had a kind of dignity, and the sweltering garbage dumps to the north glowed with unearthly fire.

By day or by night, appearances here were deceiving. Felseneck was a virtual military colony of the Communist party, complete with armed lookouts and concealed machine-gun posts. Max, it seemed, liked to be very sure of his ground. Or perhaps he had other business.

Magda waited with the car at the house of the district organizer while the two men walked side by side past cabbage patches and compost heaps.

"Do you think Seeckt was warned?" Johnny asked.

"It's possible."

"Your watchdog said he's got a sixth sense."

Max ignored the spin Johnny put on his words. "Seeckt has got luck," he commented. "Napoleon said that's the most important quality in a general. We tried before, you know. It was an excellent plan. Seeckt goes riding in the morning, in the Tiergarten, flanked by his spruce young ruffians with dueling scars. We got a girl to make a pass at one of these cavaliers. It looked very promising. She agreed to help us smuggle an assassin into the stables. Do you know what we forgot? No? A handsome young man like you should get to know women better. We forgot about a biological compulsion called love. Women, one gathers, are unusually vulnerable. The girl fell in love with her Prussian hussar and betrayed her contacts to the police. Naturally, we had to get rid of her."

Max struck a match.

Remembering the story of Max's Polish woman and the risks he had taken to avenge her, Johnny wondered how much of his cynicism was feigned.

"By the way," Max turned back to him. "Do you have a woman of your own?"

"No attachments."

"You should keep it that way. Revolutionaries can't afford the luxury of emotional entanglements. Piatnitsky will tell you the same thing."

"Piatnitsky?"

"Yes. You'll see him in Moscow. You'll take him some little presents from me."

Johnny stared at him. Russia! It was what he had dreamed about since he had first heard the news that the Bolsheviks had seized power. But war of one kind or another had always kept him away.

"I made up my mind about you the day we met," Max announced. "The rest was merely a test. I've learned caution, these last years." His eyes were intense, but the violence was no longer directed at Johnny. "You've experienced more than many men go through in their whole lives, and learned more from it, too. But in some ways you're still unformed. In Moscow we have special schools. You'll be joining a very unusual elite recruited from all over the world. You belong on a bigger stage than this—this German cabbage patch." He swung his foot at the vegetables.

"You'll learn we have worse enemies than Seeckt."

Max was silent for a time, apparently lost in his own thoughts.

"Can you be more specific?" Johnny pursued.

"What? Oh, yes. The British are the worst. The British are reactionaries without complexes, but not without subtlety. The *Intelligence Service*—" he pronounced this phrase in English—"is our most fanatical opponent, and the most deadly. You'll learn."

8

JOHNNY'S road to Moscow began in a cigar store in the Wedding district of Berlin.

"You know what they say in Russia," said the little man behind the counter. "We don't go by the passport, we go by the face."

Alfred's business seemed to be languishing. His shelves were half empty. He was coatless but bustled around with his hat on the back of his head. He produced a cigar box and pushed it across the counter.

Johnny inspected the contents. The passport looked real enough. It made him out to be a Dutch commercial traveler born in Eindhoven. There was bric-a-brac to support his cover: letters addressed to him under his assumed name, Dutch guilders, a snapshot of a girl with plump cheeks he had never seen.

The railway tickets were first class. "Always travel first class if you can," Alfred counseled. "The police give you an easier time, and you get a better dinner. There's one thing more." He went into the back room and returned with two handsome cowhide suitcases, secured by straps.

"Your samples," he explained. "Whoever heard of a commercial traveler without samples?"

"What am I selling?"

"Douches." Alfred's round face was positively cherubic.

"To the Russians?"

"You're crossing Poland," Alfred said wickedly. "The Poles are in dire need. Have a cigar, my dear fellow."

THE SUITCASES had false bottoms. Johnny was sure of it. But they were expertly constructed, like his passport. The only way you could tell for certain was to cut open the lining. Neither German nor Polish customs officials would dream of doing that to a first-class passenger's luggage, not without a tip from a very good source.

He boarded the train at the Friedrichstrasse station and had a sleeper to himself. The amenities were even better than Alfred had promised, starting with morning tea on a silver salver and ending with a casual flirtation over champagne with a Baltic countess of violently anti-Bolshevik opinions. There was a two-hour stopover at Warsaw Central. Johnny got off the train and breakfasted in the station buffet. Elegant painted ladies were bidding farewell to paramours in uniforms with lots of gold braid.

He had fallen into a half sleep when he was roused by a faint rattle at the door. Someone was trying the handle. Then there was the scrape of a passkey being inserted in the lock, and the door opened. Two men in broad-brimmed hats and mufflers that concealed part of their faces rushed in. One of them flung himself on top of Johnny, who glimpsed the flash of a steel blade. The other reached for the luggage rack, making a grab for the suitcases.

Johnny wrestled with the first assailant, trying to turn the knife back against its user. Flat on his back, with his attacker's knee on his chest, he was at a serious disadvantage. The knife point ratcheted down until it was inches from his face. He suddenly jerked his attacker's hand closer, twisting so the knife missed his cheek, and sank his teeth into the man's wrist. The man yelped and let the blade fall. In the next instant Johnny had his thumbs on his assailant's throat under the square-cut beard, pressing until the oxygen was cut off and the man fell back inert.

The second intruder was halfway out the door with Johnny's bags. Johnny seized his revolver—he had always gone armed since he had started working for Kordt—and gave pursuit. The thief dropped the suitcases and ran. Johnny let him go. He hauled his bags back into his compartment and secured the door. His first assailant was still laid out, shoulders on the bunk, legs on the floor. Johnny opened the window, got a grip under the man's armpits, and hoisted the body up until the head was lolling over the sill. It was going to be a tight squeeze. The man began to revive as Johnny forced his torso through the window. Johnny's last sight of him was of a pair of thick, flailing legs. An obscure oath was swallowed up in the rush of wind outside the carriage, and Johnny was left holding a patent leather boot. He tossed it after the body. Breathing hard, he flung himself back into his seat. Who were his assailants? Common criminals, or agents—possibly British agents—who knew that he was carrying secret material for the Comintern? He would report the episode as soon as he got to Moscow. He promised himself one thing: nothing would come between him and his mission.

Several hours later, they reached the border. Johnny stayed in his compartment until the train was nearing the Soviet customs post at Niegore-lodzhe. They passed under an arch with a Cyrillic inscription: "The Revolution breaks down all barriers." Ahead was a giant's cabin, a large building of rough-hewn logs rearing up against the grey sky. He saw a sentry with a greatcoat down to his ankles and a star on his tall, peaked cap. There were bright murals depicting stalwart workers and peasants wielding their tools. They had odd, tubular physiques. Tin men, Johnny thought.

"We're in Russia," the attendant announced. He pocketed his tip and added, *"L'Europe est finie."*

9

"WHAT language did they speak?"

The man asking the questions was short, stubby and grizzled, like a small, energetic bear. He scribbled constantly as he talked. He wore a military tunic, unbuttoned, without badges of rank, and worked at a rough wooden table littered with files that was utterly out of place in that enormous, echoing room. With its marble floors and tapestries, its gold leaf and ormolu, it might have served as a ballroom for the Tsars, and no doubt had.

"I only heard a couple of words. Curses," Johnny specified, trying to summon up the dying gasp of the man he had pushed out the window. "It could have been Polish."

"Or Russian," Osip Piatnitsky suggested. "Poland is full of Whites who are still fighting the civil war. They hire out themselves out to Western special services and gun down our agents for fun. Many have sold themselves to the British secret service. There's only one answer for these retrogrades. Shooting."

The little light bulb on the desk beside the telephone flashed red. Piatnitsky picked up the receiver, listened for a moment, and hung up without speaking. He scrawled a note. "I expect you had a brush with the *Intelligence Service.*" Like Max, he pronounced the last phrase in English.

"The first of many, perhaps. Great Britain remains the most fanatically anti-Bolshevik power in Europe."

He refilled their glasses with scalding tea from the samovar bubbling beside his table.

"You delivered your packages," he said. "That's what counts. And you did whatever was required to protect them. I don't forget these things. Max Fabrikant wasn't wrong about you."

It was the first time anyone had mentioned Max's surname. Johnny had no means of knowing whether it was merely another cover. Max had hinted that Osip Piatnitsky was his ultimate boss and the man he most respected in the headquarters of the Communist International. Johnny had gleaned a few crumbs of information about the elusive Comintern chief from the other foreign guests at the Hotel Bristol.

Piatnitsky was the chief of the Orgbureau and the man most feared by party officials in other countries. He was the man who paid their salaries, and who decided when to dump them. Piatnitsky's domain included the OMS, which was talked about in hushed tones. "OMS" stood for *Otdel Meshdunarodnoi Svyasi,* the "International Communications Department." The title was a masterpiece of understatement. The OMS was the heart and lungs of the Comintern. It provided the means for agents to operate all over the world. Its assets included diamond dealers in Antwerp and London, a forgery factory on the Lindenstrasse in Berlin, a smuggling ring based in Copenhagen, a battalion of radio operators and a liaison man in every major port. Beyond all this, Piatnitsky's men kept watch over the others.

"We've learned the lesson of Hamburg," Piatnitsky said. "One of our mistakes was that we failed completely to infiltrate the armed forces and the police. The revolution cannot succeed unless the so-called forces of order are demoralized and divided. We have to undermine the foundations before we can bring the fortress down. Insurrection is a science; there are rules that must be followed. We are opening a new school to teach those rules. You're one of the lucky ones. You'll attend the first course."

Listening to Piatnitsky then and later, in seminars for all the students from the M-school, Johnny began to realize the vastness of the enterprise on which he and his comrades were embarked. Piatnitsky talked of Shanghai and Bucharest, Java and Capetown, as if they were suburbs of Moscow —or vegetable plots in the garden of his dacha. Events separated by thousands of miles, societies made even more remote from each other by differences of language, color and religion, all proved to be intimately connected.

A Chinese student told him about preparations for an armed revolt in the Dutch East Indies. This, he learned, was the opening gambit in a complicated game plan. The Comintern hoped that risings in Java and Sumatra would tempt the voracious Japanese to intervene. This, in turn, would stir the British to assert themselves to defend their own stake in the Far East. If the exercise succeeded, two imperialist powers opposed to Russia would be locked in conflict with each other. With Britain and Japan diverted, Russia would have a free hand to pursue its main objective in the Orient: revolution in China.

"We are at war with the whole of the capitalist world," Piatnitsky declared in the course of a three-hour speech at the M-school. "The war can end only with the triumph of the world revolution."

Viewed from such commanding heights, setbacks like the collapse of the Hamburg rising were parochial and unimportant. Today Russia was the besieged citadel of the world revolution. But it would not be alone for long.

The M-school occupied a Red Army barracks on Pokrovskaya Street. The "M" stood for "military," and the courses included bomb making, marksmanship and street-fighting tactics, as well as all the techniques of clandestine operations: codes and ciphers, secret inks, dead-letter boxes and so on.

One of the instructors was a Russian general, Petrenko-Lunev. He had fantastically detailed knowledge of bridges, telephone exchanges and armaments plants in Germany and Great Britain. He talked as if he had personally reconnoitered each one to see where best to lay the charges. When the general talked, he had a curious habit of rubbing his right thumb and forefinger close to his ear.

"It comes from checking fuses in the dark," Petrenko-Lunev explained sheepishly one day, when he caught Johnny watching him closely.

He referred to Germany with affectionate insolence as Wurstland, and his German pupils didn't seem to mind. Some of them even picked up the habit.

The Russian general wasn't much older than his students, and his heart was set on going to Shanghai, where the next revolution was expected to start.

The dream exploded the day he took a bottle bomb from a Czech student in Johnny's class, the German-speaking group. Petrenko-Lunev wanted to demonstrate how the bomb should be thrown to make certain of blowing up a tank. The flustered Czech had gotten confused about what type of fuse he had attached to the bomb, the slow-burning or fast-burning type. It cost the Russian instructor his right arm to set him straight. The bomb went off as he reached down to pick it up. He gave a terrible scream and fainted dead away, while Johnny and one of the girls in the group tried to stanch the torrent of blood from the socket of his arm. The Czech doubled over and retched for a very long time, making a sound like a cistern that wouldn't shut off. To Johnny's amazement, Petrenko-Lunev reappeared before he finished his course, brandishing his pointer with his left arm instead of the right, paler but still enthusing about a mission to Shanghai. The Russian general, with his right sleeve pinned across the breast, seemed living proof of what all of them felt: they were indestructible. Destiny had joined the party.

Another intriguing instructor was the German who called himself Emil. He was a big, hearty man with vivid blue eyes set deeply under his bulging forehead. One of Emil's driving themes was that there was no room in the movement for narrow nationalistic feelings—for *Lokalpatriotismus.* Theirs was an international cause. They were members of a World Party, of which all the individual Communist parties were merely "sections." They had no homeland, no loyalties, except the world revolution.

But when Emil got together with the German students over a few beers, his line was somewhat different. "It will all be decided in Germany," he would say. He was scornful of most of the German party leaders, especially Thälmann, the dubious figurehead of the Hamburg rising who had emerged from the rubble stronger than before. "A top sergeant," Emil dismissed him. "A wooden-headed, strutting little zealot." Emil was impatient with those in Moscow and Berlin who insisted that the Social Democrats, not the Fascists, were the party's main enemy. "One day," he prophesied, "we're going to have to join ranks to stop the Fascists. You have to forget about family feuds when the whole damn house is on fire."

Emil left for the United States before Johnny's course was over. He had lived in New York before and after the war, and it was rumored that he had been the virtual dictator of the Communist Party, U.S.A. Tired of the endless wrangling inside the American party, the Comintern was sending Emil to crack heads together.

"We go where we're sent," Emil said to Johnny in the midst of a farewell party. "*Moskauer Fremdenlegion.* That's what they call us, isn't it? Moscow's Foreign Legion. But don't forget Wurstland, Johnny. One of two things is going to start there: the next revolution or the next world war. Maybe both."

By DAY they memorized the basic commandments of conspiratorial work. You confided in no one who did not have a clear need to know. You tried to be invisible, to fade into the background. You lived like a bird of passage, constantly changing lodgings and meeting places and always checking on the neighbors. You shared nothing with outsiders, including ordinary Com-the Dutch East Indies. This, he learned, was the opening gambit in a complicated game plan. The Comintern hoped that risings in Java and Sumatra would tempt the voracious Japanese to intervene. This, in turn, would stir the British to assert themselves to defend their own stake in the Far East. If the exercise succeeded, two imperialist powers opposed to Russia would be locked in conflict with each other. With Britain and Japan diverted, Russia would have a free hand to pursue its main objective in the Orient: revolution in China.

"We are at war with the whole of the capitalist world," Piatnitsky declared in the course of a three-hour speech at the M-school. "The war can end only with the triumph of the world revolution."

Viewed from such commanding heights, setbacks like the collapse of the Hamburg rising were parochial and unimportant. Today Russia was the besieged citadel of the world revolution. But it would not be alone for long.

The M-school occupied a Red Army barracks on Pokrovskaya Street. The "M" stood for "military," and the courses included bomb making, marksmanship and street-fighting tactics, as well as all the techniques of clandestine operations: codes and ciphers, secret inks, dead-letter boxes and so on.

One of the instructors was a Russian general, Petrenko-Lunev. He had fantastically detailed knowledge of bridges, telephone exchanges and armaments plants in Germany and Great Britain. He talked as if he had personally reconnoitered each one to see where best to lay the charges. When the general talked, he had a curious habit of rubbing his right thumb and forefinger close to his ear.

"It comes from checking fuses in the dark," Petrenko-Lunev explained sheepishly one day, when he caught Johnny watching him closely.

He referred to Germany with affectionate insolence as Wurstland, and his German pupils didn't seem to mind. Some of them even picked up the habit.

The Russian general wasn't much older than his students, and his heart was set on going to Shanghai, where the next revolution was expected to start.

The dream exploded the day he took a bottle bomb from a Czech student in Johnny's class, the German-speaking group. Petrenko-Lunev wanted to demonstrate how the bomb should be thrown to make certain of blowing up a tank. The flustered Czech had gotten confused about what type of fuse he had attached to the bomb, the slow-burning or fast-burning type. It cost the Russian instructor his right arm to set him straight. The bomb went off as he reached down to pick it up. He gave a terrible scream and fainted dead away, while Johnny and one of the girls in the group tried to stanch the torrent of blood from the socket of his arm. The Czech doubled over and retched for a very long time, making a sound like a cistern that wouldn't shut off. To Johnny's amazement, Petrenko-Lunev reappeared before he finished his course, brandishing his pointer with his left arm instead of the right, paler but still enthusing about a mission to Shanghai. The Russian general, with his right sleeve pinned across the breast, seemed living proof of what all of them felt: they were indestructible. Destiny had joined the party.

Another intriguing instructor was the German who called himself Emil. He was a big, hearty man with vivid blue eyes set deeply under his bulging forehead. One of Emil's driving themes was that there was no room in the movement for narrow nationalistic feelings—for *Lokalpatriotismus.* Theirs was an international cause. They were members of a World Party, of which all the individual Communist parties were merely "sections." They had no homeland, no loyalties, except the world revolution.

But when Emil got together with the German students over a few beers, his line was somewhat different. "It will all be decided in Germany," he would say. He was scornful of most of the German party leaders, especially Thälmann, the dubious figurehead of the Hamburg rising who had emerged from the rubble stronger than before. "A top sergeant," Emil dismissed him. "A wooden-headed, strutting little zealot." Emil was impatient with those in Moscow and Berlin who insisted that the Social Democrats, not the Fascists, were the party's main enemy. "One day," he prophesied, "we're going to have to join ranks to stop the Fascists. You have to forget about family feuds when the whole damn house is on fire."

Emil left for the United States before Johnny's course was over. He had lived in New York before and after the war, and it was rumored that he had been the virtual dictator of the Communist Party, U.S.A. Tired of the endless wrangling inside the American party, the Comintern was sending Emil to crack heads together.

"We go where we're sent," Emil said to Johnny in the midst of a farewell party. *"Moskauer Fremdenlegion.* That's what they call us, isn't it? Moscow's Foreign Legion. But don't forget Wurstland, Johnny. One of two things is going to start there: the next revolution or the next world war. Maybe both."

BY DAY they memorized the basic commandments of conspiratorial work. You confided in no one who did not have a clear need to know. You tried to be invisible, to fade into the background. You lived like a bird of passage, constantly changing lodgings and meeting places and always checking on the neighbors. You shared nothing with outsiders, including ordinary Communist party members, because you belonged to an elite, exacting underground: the *Apparat.* You trusted no one entirely.

By night the rules were abandoned, and they flocked together for wild parties at the Bristol and the other Comintern dosshouses, with girls and vodka and impromptu entertainments. One of the favorite games had been dubbed "The Jumble Sale." As many men and girls as could fit crowded into a room and started swapping clothes—sometimes in the course of a few hands of strip poker, often at random, as the mood took them. The men would wriggle into skirts and stockings, the girls into baggy pants and soldiers' tunics or peasant-style blouses. Then, at a piercing whistle, the lights were turned off. You had until the lights came on again to retrieve your own clothes—wherever they happened to be. This resulted in much groping and whooping and some unexpected anatomical combinations.

At one of these parties, Johnny was still scrambling about on the floor, squeezing various legs in search of his trousers, when the lights snapped on. At eye level he found a young Red Army instructor called Jacob happily grazing at the ample bosom of a large pink Danish girl.

"We have a better name for this sport in Russian," Jacob hissed.

"What's that?"

"Kogo zgreb, togo yevyob. You fuck the one you grab."

Johnny was still looking for his trousers. He was sure he had lost them to the dark girl with frizzy hair who tried to hide her looks behind wire-rimmed glasses. She made a face at him and showed her empty palms.

"The people's tribunal will now convene," announced another young German, one of the few men in the room who had recovered his clothes.

"Citizen Fritz!" he barked. This was addressed to Johnny. Like all the other Comintern recruits, he had been required to adopt a cover name. He had picked the name of a sailor he had known on the *Thüringen*, Fritz Mattern. This was the name on his new party card and the name under which he was registered at the M-school. Members of the *Apparat* changed their names more often than some people changed their shirts, but this one would stay with him; it was reserved for contacts inside the party.

Johnny got off his hands and knees and stood bare-legged with his shirttails hanging out. Some of the girls started giggling.

"The charge is bourgeois indecency!" the self-appointed prosecutor continued. "The case is proven! Citizen Fritz is indecent, but not obscene! That, by definition, is bourgeois. The people's court will now deliberate the sentence."

"Hit him!" a woman's voice rang out. It was deep and strident, like the first bar of a gypsy song. It was also oddly familiar. It brought back something of the past, as the sound of foghorns in the Moskva river brought back boyhood memories of the great ocean steamers on the Elbe.

"So decided!" Johnny's judge pronounced, and they set a tumbler of vodka to his lips and made him drink it down. He spluttered and coughed, and a rivulet of alcohol coursed down from the side of his mouth to his chin.

"Hit him again!" the same woman called out. He was craning around to find her among the press of bodies, but already they were making him tip his head back to swallow another four fingers of vodka.

"*Budem zdorovy!*" Jacob said encouragingly. "Cheers!"

The second tumbler of vodka went down more smoothly than the first.

"Again!" the woman urged. Now he spotted her, bouncing up and down on one of the iron-frame beds so the springs twanged beneath her. Her white-gold hair fell to her shoulders. She was wearing a high-necked, tight-fitting sweater and rumpled grey trousers that were unmistakably his. She seemed much taller, and her body was fuller, her features sharper and more defined. But he knew her at once from her ice-blue eyes and her mocking, infuriating self-confidence.

"Give it to *her*," he said to the boy who was pressing the third tumbler on him. "She's wearing bourgeois pants!"

She laughed, slipped out of his trousers and tossed them across the room. "No, I'm not!" she sang out, with no more embarrassment than she had displayed the night they had met in Heinz Kordt's room in Hamburg.

"I'm going to spend the night with this one," Helene announced to the room, draping herself around Johnny's neck.

10

ROMANTIC attachments were frowned upon in their circle in Moscow. Sex, on the other hand, was accepted as a necessity, and there were only two regulations that had to be observed: proletarian frankness and the higher interest of the party. If you wanted to go to bed with someone you said so, just as Helene had done. If the two of you found you were compatible and wanted to stay together, you didn't talk about marriage; that was a relic of a defunct bourgeois morality, like religion. The correct procedure was to say, "I want you to be with me as long as the party permits," or words to that effect.

This wasn't exactly what Johnny said to Helene, but by the time he had finished his course, it was clear to everyone that they were a couple. Not an orthodox couple, since their lives were pledged to a cause that transcended personal loyalties; and also because spending time with Helene was like standing under a shower with a broken faucet: you never knew whether the water was going to run hot or cold.

In matters of sex she continued to take literally the party's prescription that there were no taboos. She would vanish for days, and each time he suspected a different man. One was Jacob, who, she told him, was being promoted to the British section of the Fourth Department—Soviet military intelligence. Once he went to her room, opened the door without knocking, and found her cuddling with the dark, frizzy-haired girl from the Lenin School. He found the spectacle both disgusting and disturbingly erotic.

"What's the matter with you?" Helene asked coolly. "Girls are human, too."

In these ways, Helene was still inhabited by the same demon he had encountered in Hamburg. In bed she was insatiable. After a wild night of lovemaking she would hurl herself on top of his spent body at dawn, clawing him awake, demanding to ride him. When they fought, which was often, her words flicked at him like a whip. And she used more than words. When she bit or scratched, she drew blood.

Yet there was a stronger force that was driving Helene, and it was this that held him to her. He was astonished to discover a depth of intelligence and commitment that he would never have suspected in the runaway Kordt had picked up at the railroad station, a more natural candidate—it seemed then—for the whorehouses of the Reeperbahn than the Communist underground.

She talked eagerly about what she learned at the Lenin School and had mastered more of Marx than he had even attempted. Once, when she left off grappling on the bed, she launched into a dissertation on the theory of imperialism.

Another time he arrived at her room unannounced and saw a painting leaning against the wall on top of the dresser. It showed street musicians performing with a fiddle and an accordion in a dark, almost medieval courtyard. People were hanging out of their windows to listen, while an old woman crouched by a fire in an open drum. It was a scene of poverty, yet it was suffused with tremendous warmth and life. The dominant colors were rich, earthy shades of russet and green.

"That's very good!" he exclaimed. "Who is the artist?"

But already she was hiding the picture away in a drawer.

"It's nothing," she said curtly.

"But I think it's wonderful. Why don't you hang it on the wall, where it belongs?"

"Because there are things I don't want to be reminded of."

So she had personal secrets after all. It was only after several months that she confided that the artist was her sister.

"You never mentioned your family before," he pointed out.

"There's nothing to be said about them." Her face contorted, and she was a child again, on the brink of a temper tantrum. "My mother's a bitch."

They were both strays, Johnny thought. But he no longer felt this force of animus against his own mother, even though she had rejected him so totally. The hatred that remained was directed at Willi Rausch, the man who had broken up the family and murdered his father. When he thought of his father, it was to remember his moment of heroism, the fleeting, precious moment when Gottfried Lentz had found wings.

"And your father?" he asked Helene.

"I don't have a father!" Her eyes glistened. "I don't want to talk about it."

He let it go. Let her tell him in her own time. Oddly, she chose to return to the subject on an outing to Leningrad, as they were strolling through the splendid halls of the Hermitage museum.

"You know, my father was a Prussian officer," she remarked. "He didn't wait to see the baby. My mother says she got married so I wouldn't be born a bastard. But I was, all the same, wasn't I?"

She said the bit about the Prussian officer with a kind of pride. Johnny pictured the type he had suffered under in the Kaiser's navy, the type that recognized only three kinds of people—officers, women and civilians, the last an inferior breed whose wives and daughters were fair game. Perhaps there was something of the father in the daughter.

What was most dangerous in her was something he recognized in himself, though in him it was less voracious, less indiscriminate. She needed to plumb the depths of experience, both physical and mental. The same drive, the *Drang nach Absoluten,* propelled her in sex, in rehearsals for violence—she was proud of her prowess in unarmed combat—and in ideological debate.

"Man is a process of overcoming," she said to him one afternoon, when they were sitting in the Alexander Gardens. "And the end of that process is communism."

She gave form to his own deepest instinct.

Despite all they had lived through—or perhaps because of it—they really believed they were invincible.

2

Homecoming

Of course, the Fascists are not
asleep, but it is to our advantage
to let them attack first; they will
rally the entire working class
around the movement . . .
Besides, all our information
indicates that in Germany,
fascism is weak.
——JOSEPH STALIN(1923)

1

FOR the next seven years Johnny's homeland was the world revolution.

He was sent to Romania as military adviser to the communist underground. Helene was invaluable to his cover. They posed as a pair of fashionable idlers dripping with money. They hired a yacht and sailed up and down the Black Sea coast south of Costanza. Helene mixed cocktails and sunbathed half nude—which scandalized the Romanians—while Johnny coached underground leaders in the organizational techniques he had mastered in Moscow. His best student was Saul, a Bessarabian Jew and a wool spinner by trade. Within a few weeks Saul had set up a network of cells inside the army and Johnny was schooling civilian recruits in bomb making and marksmanship at a firing range within sight of King Carol's summer palace. For a time the revolt prospered, and in Moscow the Fourth Department was delighted with the intelligence windfalls. One of Saul's men, an employee of the government printing office, supplied them with copies of secret orders and manuals of the Romanian General Staff before they came off the press.

But suspicion fell on one of Johnny's couriers, an itinerant vendor of soybeans and sunflower seeds. The Romanian secret police operated on the old-fashioned principle that a man is put in jail in order to confess. After the unhurried removal of several of his fingernails, the greengrocer confessed everything. Saul was shot. Johnny owed his escape to Helene, who flirted with a lieutenant at the border while he crouched in the trunk of the car, holding his nose in order not to sneeze.

"You make perfect working partners," Max Fabrikant congratulated them afterwards.

In theory Max had no direct authority over Johnny. Max belonged to the OGPU, or Unified State Political Administration—in short, the Russian secret police. Johnny was an agent of the Comintern, the general staff of a world movement that was supposed to be independent of the Soviet government.

But if the frontiers were clear on the map, they were invisible on the ground. Most of the Comintern's military experts were seconded from the Red Army, and General Berzin, the head of the Fourth Department, took a close interest in their activities. Since Stalin had driven out Trotsky and his supporters, the number of chekists in the corridors of the Comintern had increased; often they seemed to be the ones giving the orders. In practice Johnny found himself carrying out assignments for all three agencies—the Comintern, the OGPU and the Fourth Department.

To complicate matters further, the power struggle that was raging in the heart of the Kremlin spilled over into the vast, ramshackle headquarters of the Comintern in Ozhod-Niriat, in the suburbs of Moscow. At one level it was a fight over tactics: whether to pursue the dangerous, solitary road of armed insurrection or, instead, to form fronts and alliances with rival political groups. At another level it was a conflict between old guard Bolsheviks and a new generation of apparatchiks who owed everything to Joseph Stalin.

The most decisive of these shadow battles was played out in 1927, soon after Johnny's return from Romania. There was tragic news from China, where Borodin—one of the most daring of the Old Bolshevik adventurers—had been sent to make a revolution in alliance with the nationalist forces of Chiang Kai-shek and the Kuomintang. The omens were against him from the beginning. Borodin arrived (so Johnny heard in Moscow) in a cattle boat full of stinking carcasses. The ship had been caught up in a terrible storm, and most of the animals, hurled back and forth against the slats of their wooden pens, had perished during the night. Now it was the turn of the Chinese Communists. Chiang took them by surprise. Paid off by the Shanghai financiers and their Western friends, he betrayed his

Communist allies. Striking without warning, soldiers and squads of killers toured the streets of Shanghai in the dead of night, machine-gunning Reds.

Someone had to take the blame for the costly mistake of trusting Chiang Kai-shek. From Moscow directives went out denouncing "conciliators" wherever they might be found. At the end of November Bukharin, the President of the Executive Committee of the Comintern and a senior member of the Soviet Politburo, was abruptly removed, and his fall crushed hundreds of lesser men who had hitched their wagons to his star. The party line was struggle without compromise, no deals with class enemies or "class traitors" like the Social Democrats in Germany. Within the Comintern, power came to rest in the hands of a curious Balkan duo: Georgi Dimitrov, a Bulgarian, and Dmitri Manuilsky, the son of a Greek Orthodox priest from Tarnopol.

In these treacherous times, Max counseled Johnny, the secret of survival was "Bolshevist elasticity"—and, it seemed, a willingness to inform on your friends. When their paths crossed in Moscow or a foreign capital, Max frequently asked Johnny to report his impressions of fellow agents, including their sexual proclivities, their drinking habits and other pecadilloes. Johnny usually complied. He knew that foreign secret services, especially the British, would try to exploit a man's weakness to induce him to betray his comrades. Still secure in his own revolutionary faith, he was genuinely outraged when he discovered that some of those he was ordered to work with were cynical parasites, not above pilfering from operational funds or fabricating reports. When he told Max about them, he did not feel like a sneak; *they* were the ones who were betraying the cause.

But Johnny's sense of rectitude did not survive an encounter with a moon-faced man in a fur hat who collared him at the Hotel Lux in Moscow and introduced himself as "Drozhdov, a friend of Max." The year was 1930, and the first snows were falling outside. Although it was only mid-morning, Drozhdov insisted on squiring him to the best table in the restaurant and plying him with vodka and caviar and salty river crabs.

"I heard from another friend," Drozhdov said confidentially, "that you spent an evening with Emil Brandt."

"Why, yes. I had dinner with him last night. He was my ideological instructor when I was at the M-school."

"Yes, yes. We know all that. What was the content of your conversation?"

"It was personal." He had decided immediately that he did not care for Drozhdov. The Russian's tone was prurient, like that of a man asking to see dirty photographs in the back room of a shop. And Johnny was worried about Emil. He remembered his fellow German as a big, rollicking fellow, quick with a joke, brimming with life—a man who was said to have a

tremendous future ahead of him. It was even whispered that he might oust
Thälmann's crowd and take over the leadership of the German Communist
Party. They had met quite by chance when Johnny had been strolling with
Helene in the Arbat. Emil had called out to them. But for that, they might
have walked on without seeing him. The man had not only aged enormously; he seemed to have shrunk. In the Azerbaijani restaurant where they
had gone for dinner, he had insisted on sitting with his back to the wall,
and his face was contorted by a tic Johnny had never noticed before. Each
day, Emil confided, he had to present himself at the Central Committee.
He was the subject of an investigation.

"Did Emil Brandt discuss the state of affairs in Germany?" Drozhdov
pursued.

"We may have talked about Germany," Johnny conceded. "After all, we
were both born there."

"Naturally, naturally." Drozhdov sucked on his teeth. "And of course,
you must have discussed party policy in relation to the Social Fascists and
the Hitler movement."

"We may have. I really don't remember the details."

"I am sure you would not forget any references to Comrade Manuilsky,"
the chekist purred.

"We did not discuss Comrade Manuilsky," Johnny said flatly. "It was
an innocent reunion of old friends. I don't see that it can be of any interest
to the Organs—" this was one of the euphemisms for the secret police in
circulation in Moscow.

"Our interests are quite catholic, I can assure you, Comrade Lentz."

Johnny wanted to ask Drozhdov what charges were pending against
Emil. But he was worried that by asking he might provide the Russian with
a lever he could use to prise out details of the previous night's conversation
that might do harm to Emil.

Johnny made a show of consulting his watch. "I have an appointment
at Ozhod-Niriat."

"Of course." Drozhdov was positively ingratiating. "It's been a pleasure.
I do look forward to meeting you again." He sucked his teeth. "And please
give my regards to the lovely Helene."

"You don't know when to be afraid," Max Fabrikant reproached him two
months later in Berlin.

"I didn't like him."

"Dear me! And Drozhdov prides himself on being the most cultivated
man in Moscow."

"What are they doing to Emil?"

"Oh, that! It's all been settled." Max rubbed his hands and went hunting for a fresh pack of cigarettes. "Emil has recanted. He has written a full letter of apology. I believe it's in the current issue of *Imprecor.*" This was the news bulletin of the Comintern. "He admits that the Social Democrats —excuse me, the Social Fascists—are the main enemies of the working class in Germany and that it was a grave tactical error to call for a popular front with class traitors. He quotes the Greek three or four times. *Where* are those damn cigarettes? Ah." He found a reserve carton on the bookshelf, wedged between copies of Gide and Malraux. "So you see, all is forgiven. You made an enemy out of Drozhdov for no reason."

"I thought—"

"*What* did you think? Really, Johnny, I'm disappointed. I didn't think you were so naive. Do you actually imagine that Drozhdov needed *you* to tell him what Emil said to you at that idiotic dinner? That story about the Greek, for example—"

For an instant Johnny saw Emil again at the table, regaining his old *élan* as the wine flowed. He saw Emil telling a hilarious story of how the Greek, Manuilsky, had tried to lay down the law at a gathering of German Communists. Several of the Germans, street fighters spoiling to take on the Brownshirts, had yelled out "Go back to Moscow!" Then a gnarled old man, a Bremen delegate, had gotten up and bawled, "He's no good for anything except shish kebab!" Manuilsky had left swearing he was going to break heads in the German party . . .

The implications of what Max had said suddenly dawned on him. They had picked the restaurant at random. It was frequented by Russians, not foreigners. It was hard to believe their table had been bugged—unless there were microphones at every table. That was possible, but there was a more likely explanation. Johnny remembered Drozhdov's parting remark.

It was Helene, he realized. Helene had told Drozhdov everything. Even though she was exposing me at the same time. I mustn't take it personally, he told himself. I mustn't let Max see me look bitter. She's a professional, doing her job. That's the beginning and the end of it. And of our relationship. I'm a fool if I ever forget that.

"Emil was a good man," Johnny said to Max, turning his emotion into a different channel.

"He's a better man now. He forgot about *Parteibefehl.* Party orders. What kind of army allows every man to question orders? Be sure you never make the same mistake, Johnny."

"But Emil may have been *right,* dammit. The Popular Front—"

"—is not for discussion by you and me." Max cut him off. "Don't overreach yourself, my friend. We're Marxists, aren't we? Then we know that history cannot be understood from surface events. There's a deeper level of meaning, accessible to only a few, with the science and the knowledge required. Don't you imagine that Stalin may know things that are concealed from you?"

"Of course."

"Well, then."

1

MARLENE DIETRICH swirled off the screen in the leather coveralls of an aviatrix, her goggles pushed back on top of her head. She reappeared in sequins and satins, the brazen finery of a *poule de luxe*. She was a spy, a mantrap employed by the Austrian secret service. One of her victims appeared on the screen, a man who had sold his country to be betrayed, in turn, by love. He had a revolver; he was preparing to shoot himself. "What a charming evening we might have had," he whispered, "if you had not been a spy and I a traitor."

"Then," she observed calmly, "we might never have met."

A woman in the row behind Johnny started sniffing.

A man slipped into the empty seat on his left and murmured without looking at him, "The Hollywood idea of espionage."

Johnny didn't respond. He stared up at the screen. It was impossible not to think of Helene. There were the visual echoes: the wide, hooded eyes, the tartar cheekbones, the legs that scissored across a room. The character Marlene Dietrich played in *Dishonored* was a prostitute, recruited by her Austrian spymaster because of her allure and her remarkable sangfroid. "I'm not afraid of life, though I'm not afraid of death, either." It wasn't hard to imagine Helene in the role, despite the vagaries of the unlikely plot. This mental association deepened his sense of unease, which encompassed the mission that lay ahead of him, the unknown courier who was sitting at his left hand smelling of onions, the homecoming to Berlin, a place of lengthening shadows, and the woman who resembled Dietrich and was described on three separate passports—Swiss, Belgian and American—as his wife.

The courier belched quietly and whispered a time and an address in the Moabit district. Then he was gone, leaving Johnny with the fleeting impression of a round-shouldered figure in a soft hat.

Johnny stayed in the cinema until the end of the film. In the last scene, the Dietrich character, faced with a firing squad, insisted on dying in her streetwalker's clothes. She was shown going to meet her maker with the same eagerness—or indifference—with which she might encounter a new lover.

The theater was hushed, apart from the woman in the row behind, who started snuffling again, and Johnny himself, who made a stifled sound between a sneeze and a snort. The next instant, he was laughing uncontrollably. He was as surprised as the sentimentalist behind him, who muttered, "Shame." He pressed his hand across his mouth and rushed for the theater exit.

THE WHITE October light gave everything sharper edges: the ominous young men wearing lipstick and rouge who patrolled the Ku'damm, the crowd of Brownshirts daubing swastikas on the windows of a Jewish-owned furniture store, the block-long red banners that festooned the Communist party headquarters on the Bülowplatz. But the scant light that leaked down to the inner courtyard of the peeling workers' tenement in Moabit seemed to have got there by mistake, like water through rotted sacking.

Heinz was true to old habits, Johnny thought as he made his way through a series of low arches. He picked boltholes in places where the neighbors looked after their own kind and had no great love for the police. Nobody challenged him on his way to Kordt's hideout, on the third floor at the back. But a dozen pairs of eyes marked every step, and he was received at the door by a young tough with a pistol in the waistband of his trousers.

Kordt pounced on Johnny, grinning from ear to ear. "I'm glad I found you," he exclaimed. "It's been a long time. I wonder if you can still speak German."

"Only with a Hamburg accent."

"Hamburg!" Kordt's eyes lit up for a moment, but then his smile vanished. "We'll never see times like those again."

Johnny was shocked by how much his friend had aged. Deep lines were gouged across his forehead and down his cheeks, as if the flesh had been sucked back into the bone. His cropped hair was like steel wool.

"You're older too," Kordt said, reading his thoughts. "You look like a man who's found out what the world is about. Let me see. You'll be thirty now. Am I right?"

"Thirty-one," Johnny corrected him.

"Oh yes, that's right. Born with the century, isn't it? Look at Karl here." He aimed his jaw at the boy with the gun. "All of eighteen, and ready to shoot Hitler and take both our jobs. Aren't you, Karl?"

Karl looked at the floor and shuffled his feet.

"Come along, old man." Kordt threw his arm around Johnny's shoulder and steered him into the kitchen. "We've got a lot to catch up on."

They sat across the kitchen table from each other with the blind drawn, and Kordt poured beer. They lolled and drank and nodded at each other for a bit, in a comfortable silence.

"You've filled out," Kordt said.

"You're thinner. Our average weight must be the same."

"Tell me about Helene. I heard you two got hitched."

"We're partners," Johnny said hastily and tried to change the subject.

Kordt jabbed him with the stem of his pipe. "Johnny, this is *me*. Remember? I know you're fond of the girl. I could see you were right for each other that first night at my place in Hamburg. I sent her to Russia, and in a roundabout way I did the same for you. Like it or not, I've got a lot invested in both you kids. So talk to me."

"She's very good at her job. She's a brave girl."

"But you're not happy with her, are you? What's the matter? Is she sleeping around?"

"It's not that." Johnny looked at the tangle of dark hair on the back of his friend's hands and remembered that first night in Kordt's room on the Valentinskamp. No, he wasn't jealous. The capacity for jealousy had been drilled out of him, he thought, in his years with Helene. Perhaps that meant the capacity for love had been burned out of him too. In Helene's presence he felt something more subversive than jealousy. He felt vulnerable.

The night after his last conversation with Max, she had come into his bed, scented from her bath. He had taken her roughly, selfishly, trying to punish her without telling her why. Later, he lay awake for a long time, his head propped up against the heaped pillows, smoking and staring at the sullen panorama of barracklike brick walls beyond the window. In the dark they seemed hostile, pressing forward into the room. He looked at Helene's face, composed in sleep, and thought, even now, even behind closed eyelids, you are watching me.

Kordt waited.

Johnny finally said, "I've had a few problems."

He described his Moscow encounter with Emil Brandt and his reasons for believing that Helene had been reporting on him to the OGPU.

"I heard about Emil," Heinz growled. "They put the poor bastard on the grill. Luckily, there are a few of us left who don't broil so easily."

He rattled around, fetching more bottles.

"We're having a few problems here, too," he went on. "I expect you've got the picture by now."

"I've been in Berlin barely a week," Johnny said. "But I've learned one thing. It's easier to get in to see Stalin than to find Heinz Kordt."

The first signal from Heinz had been a message on a piece of rice paper inside a box of matches Johnny hadn't wanted to buy from a legless street vendor who pursued him on his trolley and pushed it into his hands anyway. Then came a rendezvous with a courier in Neukölln; a last-minute change of address; and finally the assignation in the UFA cinema.

"I have to watch my back these days," Heinz grinned. "So, it would seem, do you."

"The police?"

Kordt's pipe wheezed asthmatically. He blew into it vigorously, scattering ash and live cinders. "The police aren't my worry. Not here in Berlin, anyway. We've got friends on the inside. I can usually count on a tip-off if a big raid is being planned."

"The Nazis?"

"They want my head, all right," Kordt agreed. "But that's not the whole story. Some of our comrades would like to give it to them."

"Thälmann?"

"Him for one. He's the one who denounced Emil. Wollweber's no better. We've got a civil war going on now, inside the party. What it comes down to is that some of us want to fight Hitler and others haven't got the balls or the brains to do it. Thälmann and his cronies think everything is just fine. They think Hitler's a bag of hot air, a help to us because he's helping to drive people one way or the other. They think if Hitler gets too rowdy the monocles and the financiers will sit on him until all the air goes out, *phttt!* They're completely out of touch. You ought to go to a Hitler rally, Johnny. The whole thing grabs you by the throat. You want to tear yourself away, but you can't. It's like witnessing a sex murder. There's the whole crowd, made delirious by the lights and the music and the tramping feet, suddenly sunk in a deathly hush as the great man makes his entry between a forest of standards. He plays with them, ravishes them, lashes them to an orgiastic frenzy, until he stands with the body of the crowd at his feet."

"Hypnosis was a German invention," Johnny commented.

"It has found its master. That's why Hitler could take the country. The monocles are starting to realize it, too. You heard what just happened? Hindenburg invited the Bohemian corporal—that's what he calls him—to tea. He turned up like a bandy-legged penguin with his tails flapping over his bum, and people thought it was funny. Well, it doesn't matter whether the Bohemian corporal knows how to knot his bow tie. He's a master of mass psychology and a master of organized terror. That's why he's going to win—if we let him. There are over a hundred Nazi deputies sitting in the Reichstag, and there could be twice as many after the next elections. He's getting all the money he wants from Hugenberg and Thyssen and other chimney barons. And what are we doing about it? We spend most of our time smashing up Social Democrat rallies. You know the theology. The Nazis aren't a threat to us. The Social Democrats are the main enemy of the working class. I believed that when we were fighting in Hamburg and the Social Democrats were attacking us with armored cars. I don't believe it any more. If we don't stop Hitler, he'll drink our blood."

On another occasion, the expression would have seemed ludicrous to Johnny. But he sat silent, hanging on Heinz's words.

"If we are going to stop Hitler," Kordt went on, "we have to do two things. We have to meet terror with terror. Every time they kill one of our boys, we knock off two of theirs. And we've got to swallow some of the theology and do a deal with the Socialists. I don't even rule out a pact with the center parties. What matters is beating Hitler."

He paused to drain his glass.

"I tried to make Thälmann see sense, but he wouldn't listen. He talks as if Hitler is the best recruitment agent the party ever had."

"I heard that party membership *is* growing fast," Johnny observed.

"Granted. But we're not growing as fast as the Hitler movement, and we're not putting down proper roots. We're just spreading like a ground creeper. We're losing the veterans, the union men, the sailors who were with you at Kiel. We're getting trigger-happy kids off the streets like Karl Vogel out there. And I'll be frank with you about that. It's just accidental that a tearaway like Karl comes to us instead of the Brownshirts. He's not like you, Johnny. He doesn't read. He doesn't question the reasons for his actions. He was down and out, jobless. He wanted a few kicks. I know other kids like Karl who got bored with us and went off and signed up with the jackboots. But they're not our problem. Our problem is *die Bonzen.* The bosses."

"Who else have you talked to?" Johnny asked.

"I talked to Emil. He said he was going to talk to Stalin in Moscow. We saw what came of that." Angry, Kordt knocked his pipe out against the edge of the table, and hot ashes flew about the room.

"Did you talk to Dimitrov?"

"I'm afraid we move in different social circles," Heinz responded with heavy sarcasm. "You know he's the boss of bosses here in Berlin. Have you met him? Are you going to see him?"

Johnny hesitated. He had an appointment with Georgi Dimitrov the following day in the headquarters the Comintern chief maintained behind the urbane facade of a conservative publishing house in the embassy district. Indeed, this appointment was the principal reason for his visit to Berlin. They had told him in Moscow that Dimitrov would give him specific instructions for his next foreign assignment. What harm could there be in revealing this to his friend? But he did not tell Heinz. His recent experience with Emil and the habits entrenched by years of operating under legends and cover names on hostile territory had made him cautious.

Heinz must have smelled this out, because he rushed on. "Don't tell me if you don't want to. No hard feelings, eh? But if you *do* stop in to see the Bulgarian, be sure to hold your nose. He smells worse than a Turkish bathhouse."

He raised another bottle of beer to his lips and sloshed half the contents down his throat. He belched noisily and rubbed his stomach.

He's putting on a show, Johnny thought. I've offended him.

"I got a letter from old Georgi the other day," Heinz sailed on. "A copy went to all the party organizers. I used it for toilet paper. I wish I'd held on to it now. Do you know what Dimitrov said?"

"I have no idea."

"Dimitrov ordered united action—those are the exact words, Johnny— *united action* between the Communist party and the Hitler movement. The aim of this united action—" he half closed his eyes, summoning up the words neatly typed on the page "—is to accelerate the disintegration of the crumbling democratic bloc that governs Germany." He blinked and fixed Johnny with his stare. "What do you make of that?"

"I don't know." Johnny was bewildered. It was hard to believe that Dimitrov, who knew conditions in Germany and was also privy to Stalin's thinking, could have issued such a directive. But why would Heinz make the story up? "Perhaps there was some misunderstanding," he suggested hopefully.

"No misunderstanding," Kordt was flushed. "I've got a story I've been saving up for you, Johnny. It concerns an old pal of yours. Do you remember Willi Rausch?"

Johnny sucked in his breath. The name conjured up the bulging, oily face of the schoolyard bully Johnny had trounced in the winter before the war. He had often pictured Willi Rausch since then, not in school uniform but in the helmet and brassard of a Freikorps officer, stinking of booze as he climbed the steps to the front door of the Lentz family house, crowing as he pumped bullets into a defenseless old man—Johnny's father.

"What about Willi Rausch?"

"I saw him last month. Not here. In Bremen. I was sent there on a Z job. The Bonzen may not like me, but they know that's one thing my group does better than anyone."

Johnny was familiar with the shorthand. The "Z" stood for *Zersetzung,* or "Disruption." The Z-groups, which specialized in terrorizing and sowing confusion among rival political parties and trade unions, were one of the most lethal elements in the underground organization of the German Communist Party.

"The transport workers were having their national congress in Bremen," Heinz went on. "It was supposed to be a really big production. The Social Democrats were running everything, so naturally we had to bust it up. Now wait for this, Johnny. The night before the official opening, I got orders to go to a secret meeting with—who do you think? The area Nazi high command. Shut your mouth, Johnny, you're making a draught. There's better to come.

"I thought it could be a trap, so I went with Karl and some of my kids. We all had automatics and machine guns. The Brownshirts weren't taking any risks either. They picked the right locale—a brewery outside town. The Nazi in charge was a great ugly brute about your age. An Untersturmführer, I think they said. I don't pay much attention to their comic opera ranks. His name didn't click straight away either. But I worked it out later when we'd had a couple of beers and he told me he was from Hamburg.

"I'll give Willi Rausch credit for one thing. He said he didn't like his orders any better than me. We pretty much agreed that if we ever saw each other again, one of us was going to end up a dead man."

"I don't understand," Johnny interjected. "What were the orders?"

"I'm getting to that. Try to picture this, Johnny. We're all inside the hall the next day, Rausch and his goons on one side of the gangway, our lot on the other. We're sprinkled around in groups of four and five, minding our manners, because the stewards have got their eyes on us. The band strikes up, everybody starts singing, and then the chairman is at the rostrum talking about the rights of labor. Then they bring on one of the bigwigs from the Social Democratic party, and I get up on my hind legs and start blowing my lungs out. Soon all my boys are doing the same. The stewards start moving in, and my lads bring out their coshes and iron bars. Someone runs to fetch the police. Things are really livening up, when all hell breaks loose on the other side of the gangway. Rausch jumps up and calls the people on the platform a bunch of ass-lickers, and the Brownshirts go charging at the rostrum. They collared the speaker and threw him out the window. He broke both arms and dislocated his shoulder. They brought the cops in by the truckload, but by that time the congress was wrecked. I got a thank you note from Wollweber later. A job well done, he said. I didn't feel much like looking at myself in the shaving mirror, though."

Johnny sat immobile through most of this, suspended between rage and disbelief.

"You're telling me you had Party orders—"

"*Parteibefehl*," Kordt agreed.

"It's obscene—it's criminal—"

I'll tell Dimitrov, he thought. Obviously he has not been informed of what is happening. Stalin must be told. He's been preoccupied with other things—with famine in the Ukraine, with the Japanese invaders in Manchuria who are threatening Russia itself. Stalin and Dimitrov will put things right. Mistakes have been made in Germany. No, worse than mistakes.

He remembered the Hamburg massacres.

There are traitors in the German party, he told himself. Stalin must be told.

"Tell me, Johnny." His friend had his feet up on the table. "If you'd been me, in that congress hall, what would you have done?"

For an instant Johnny's caution abandoned him. "I would have shot Willi Rausch."

"You know what? I'd sleep better if I'd done just that."

3

JOHNNY walked back to the rooms his Comintern contact had arranged. Shaken by his conversation with Kordt, he lost his way twice, and it was past midnight when he found the building, a few blocks east of police headquarters on the Alexanderplatz. The place had the solid, satisfied look of a strongbox. The manager, Frau Hügel, matched the building in appearance, but she was in the pay of the OMS.

She startled Johnny in the entrance hall.

"I've been waiting up for you, Herr Stoltz." This was the cover name Johnny had been assigned for his trip to Berlin.

"Is something wrong, Frau Hügel?"

"Come inside."

He followed her into her kitchen. Copper pots and cast iron skillets marched along the walls in orderly files.

"The police were here," his landlady whispered.

"Looking for me?"

"No." She took off her spectacles and rubbed them nervously against her quilted robe. Naked, her eyes were bright and never still, like a magpie's. "There was a robbery in the house," she reported. "The widow Teller, on the second floor. The police are questioning everyone in the house. They wanted to search your room."

"What did you tell them?"

"I said I couldn't permit them unless you were present. They said they'll be back."

"Thanks, Hilde." Johnny abandoned formality. "We'll leave tonight."

Frau Hügel hooked her glasses over her nose and said, "Perhaps you will take a small glass of schnapps with me, Herr Stoltz. Frau Stoltz is not yet home."

"I see." He glanced up at the cuckoo clock. He had no idea where Helene was or when to expect her back. It was possible she was doing a job for Max. He knew she had seen Max at least once in his absence. It was equally possible she was warming another man's bed.

"Just a small one," he said to Frau Hügel. But he borrowed what was left in the bottle and took it up to his room.

Afterwards he packed all their possessions into three small suitcases—one for him, two for Helene. It was strange to think that at thirty-one all his property in the world, apart from the books he had left in a steamer trunk in Moscow, could fit into one bag.

When he had finished packing, he finished Frau Hügel's schnapps.

Nearly 3:00 A.M. Helene might not be coming back at all. How long should he give her? Until dawn?

He was getting angrier with her by the minute. He told himself it was only because her nocturnal habits were exposing them both to unnecessary danger.

But there was something else. His friend's story about Willi Rausch had shaken the certainties Johnny had lived and fought by since the war. How could he reconcile his revolutionary faith with the appalling reality of what the party was doing in Germany?

In that moment of doubt, he felt very alone. He wanted Helene with him. She had never been fully his and never could be. She was her own creature, beautiful but inconstant, shining and remote like a distant star. But their lives had raced close together on parallel tracks. They had shared danger and good times, too. She—and Heinz Kordt—were all the family he had.

When she slipped in at 3:20, he said mildly, "Nice of you to drop in."

"Are you still up?" she responded coolly. "God. It smells like an ashtray in here." She opened a window and started picking cigarette stubs off the rug.

"Did you do anything interesting today?"

"I saw my sister. It's her birthday this week."

This might be a half truth, Johnny decided. Better than an outright lie.

Helene walked toward the bedroom. She looked as fresh as she had done the previous morning.

"We're both invited to dinner," she called back.

"You told your sister about me?"

"I said you were a traveling salesman. That's true, in a way, isn't it?"

She turned on the bedroom light. "Johnny! What have you done with our clothes—"

"I was going to mention that. Do you think your family would mind if we made it breakfast instead?"

THEY COULD have gone to Alex, Johnny's Comintern contact, or simply to a hotel. But Alex would be less than overjoyed at being rousted out of bed before dawn, and checking into a hotel at an odd hour increased the risk of attracting the attentions of the police. Besides, Johnny was curious to take a look at Helene's family.

Their apartment building was on a pleasant street in Charlottenburg with lime trees dotted along the pavement. They arrived shortly after five, after stopping for coffee and the morning papers at the Friedrichstrasse station, where no one except a panhandler swilling wine out of a paper cup appeared to take the slightest interest in them.

Helene rang the bell. A dog in a neighboring house started snarling and snapping.

Johnny rapped on one of the frosted glass panes in the door.

A light came on inside, and the door opened a crack.

"Who is it?"

"Sigi?"

The girl inside peered through the crack, disbelieving. Then she pulled the door shut. There was a rattle of chains, the door flew open, and she flung herself into Helene's arms.

Over Helene's shoulder, Johnny glimpsed a face with the soft, smudged beauty of a child just roused from sleep. The sisters moved apart, and the tawny light from the hall lamp played on the bold contours of the girl's body under the filmy nightgown. She looked up, and the color rose in her cheeks when she saw how freely the stranger's eyes ranged over her. She pulled the flaps of her flowered robe together.

"This is Johnny," Helene announced.

Sigrid let him take her hand. Her touch was raw silk. He could see her face more clearly now. It was almost heart shaped, framed by a wild mane of red-gold hair. Her lips were fuller, softer than Helene's. Her eyes were a magical green flecked with hazel and gold.

She looked at the suitcases.

"Sigi, we're in trouble," Helene said. "Can we stay?"

They heard a man's hoarse voice raised from an inner room. "Sigrid? What is it? Who's there?"

"It's all right, Father," she called back. Suddenly brisk and practical, she snatched up their bags, dragged them inside, and relocked the door. "The lodger's got your old room. You can have mine."

"No, Sigi. What about the room at the back? The sewing room?"

"There's just a sofa. And it's such a mess—"

"It doesn't matter."

Sigrid ran lightly ahead of them down the corridor, gloomy in the half light with its suffocating, wine-red wallpaper. They found her gathering up canvases, turning an easel to the wall.

"This is your studio," Johnny said. The room was small and bright and smelled of oils and turpentine. The blend was not unpleasant. Johnny wanted to look at the pictures, but Sigrid hoarded them shyly under her arm.

"Helene." The new voice was husky, even deeper than Helene's.

Johnny turned and saw an extraordinary apparition. The woman's body seemed slender and supple as either of her daughters, but her hair was completely white. The face was Helene's, seen in a cracked mirror.

A stocky man with a red, jowly face barrelled into the doorway beside her.

"So she's back, is she, the little slut?"

"Shut up, Hermann."

"She's not staying here with her fancy man."

Johnny looked anything but fancy, in his hat and shapeless overcoat.

"He's my husband," Helene said.

Johnny saw no reason to amend this statement.

"Probably a fucking Red, like you."

"It's my room," Sigrid interjected. "I told them they could stay."

Hermann Eckhardt appealed to his wife. "For all we know, they've got the cops on their tails. I'm not having them under this roof."

"Shut your face," Helene's mother said. She looked at him like something that ought to be trodden underfoot. "I'll decide."

"It's just for a few nights," Johnny spoke up. "I'm sorry for the inconvenience. Of course, we'll pay for your trouble."

"Bloody right you'll pay."

"Go to bed, Hermann." The mother's voice was oddly compelling. It wasn't the anger or disgust it might have conveyed; it was the absence of emotion.

Hermann grunted and shuffled off along the corridor, muttering to himself.

Clara Eckhardt looked from Helene to Johnny. "You've come from Russia," she said. It was not a question. "You mustn't bring any of that into this house. There are no Communists here."

"We won't," Johnny promised.

"Sigrid," she instructed her daughter, "bring sheets and towels."

As soon as the girl was gone, she said to Helene, with sudden ferocity, "And you leave her alone, do you hear me? Don't go putting anything in her head. Things are hard enough for her as it is."

There wasn't room for both on the sofa, so Johnny lay on the floor, his head resting on his bundled overcoat, and watched the moonlight slanting through the window. He started rehearsing what he would say to Dimitrov when he kept his appointment later that morning. But he found that Sigrid kept drifting in and out of his thoughts. She had something of her sister, but it was softer, unstudied. Something a man could hold on to. Helene reached down and snapped her finger against his cheek.

"What my mother said was meant for you, too," she said quietly.

"What?"

"About Sigi. I saw how you looked at her."

"Well?"

"She's not like us. She can be hurt. I want you to leave her alone."

It was the first time Johnny had ever seen Helene play the big sister, the protectress. He liked this human side, this confession of weakness, and instead of sleeping he made love to her eagerly in the early light. But when he let his eyelids fall, the face he saw was Sigrid's.

4

THE OFFICES of the Führer-Verlag were on the Wilhelmstrasse. Civil servants and foreign diplomats from nearby chanceries would pause on their way to lunch to peer into the windows of the ground-floor bookshop. Johnny would not be mistaken for one of them in his tweed coat, soft collar and comfortable gabardine trousers. But he might very well pass for a writer on his way to discuss a contract. He walked through the bookshop, nodded at the man in a cubbyhole at the back and went up by the service stairs.

There was an atmosphere of frenzied activity on every floor—couriers and copyboys coming and going, typewriters clacking, telephones jangling. There were armed men posted on every landing, because this building housed the headquarters of the Westbureau, the nerve center of Comintern operations in Europe.

Georgi Dimitrov's sanctum smelled and looked more like a cigar humidor—a very expensive one, with sides of dark, polished wood—than a Turkish bath. A portrait of Bismarck in a funereal black frame hung over the immense mahogany desk. The Iron Chancellor looked like a petulant bulldog. There was a glass-fronted bookcase filled with rich leather bindings, the kind of volumes that are ordered by the meter.

The figure that blossomed from behind the desk was sleek and olive skinned, dandyish in a silk smoking jacket. Dimitrov advanced in a haze of tobacco and attar of roses and extended a plump hand garnished with an enormous ruby ring. His eyes were moist. His whole body moved with the rhythms of his speech.

He waved Johnny into a studded leather chair and dipped into a plain manila file.

"You've traveled a good deal, Johann Lentz," he addressed Johnny. "Romania. Scandinavia. France. South America. The Far East. You've never been to Great Britain?"

"No."

"Britain is a special hobby of mine. I asked Moscow to find me a man who has no record with the British authorities. I asked for a military expert, the best available expert in the area of AM measures. They sent me a list of candidates, and I picked you. Did I make the right choice?"

"I'm honored, of course."

"AM" stood for "Anti-Military." Under the statutes of the Comintern, every Communist party was required to maintain its own AM *Apparat.* These secret networks were responsible for recruiting sympathizers and inciting mutiny inside the armed forces, under guidance from Moscow. In his years as a Comintern military adviser Johnny had directed AM operations against the Romanians, the Belgians and the French.

"Do you know why I picked you?" Dimitrov went on. "Not because of that Romanian mess. No, don't say a word. I know it wasn't your fault. I picked you because you're a sailor and because your record doesn't start with Costanza, or even with Hamburg. It starts with the mutiny in the Kaiser's fleet. I want you to go to England and do the same thing in the Royal Navy."

"That's quite an undertaking."

"It's quite an opportunity," Dimitrov corrected him. "Do you read the newspapers? Do you know what's going on in England?"

"I know there was a mutiny in the British fleet. At a base in Scotland."

"At Invergordon. The government tried to cut the sailors' pay, and a strike was called. For several hours, the battle fleet was paralyzed. The British lion was changed into a helpless pussycat. Then the government panicked. It restored full pay and tried to hush everything up. The ringleaders were removed without publicity. And do you know when I received the first report from our comrades in the Communist Party of Great Britain? Four days afterwards!"

Dimitrov got up and waved his cigar like a baton.

"Think of it, Lentz!" he went on. "We had a historic opportunity! What holds the British Empire together? The navy! For a few hours the empire lost its sword and shield. The situation demanded strong, ruthless leadership, the shooting of officers, action to bring things to a boil. And what did our British comrades do? They sat in their semidetached cottages swilling their tea. I know Comrade Pollitt and the rest of that crowd. The British Communists are sluggish and complacent. They run their party like a grocery store. They think that revolution is good business.

"I want you to go and light a fire under them. Don't be scared to throw your weight around. Your credentials are being prepared now. I want you to examine them closely. You are going to Britain as an inspector of the Comintern. Do you know what that means? It means that *you*, Johann Lentz, have the power to issue any orders you like. If you tell Pollitt to shine your boots, he's obliged to do it. If they give you any trouble, hit them where their hearts are—in their hip pockets! Tell them you'll chop off their subsidies. That will bring them around in short order! Every letter they send to Moscow ends with a chiseling demand for money. Tell Harry Pollitt we want value for money, and if he won't give it we'll find someone who will!"

Dimitrov threw himself down on the sofa and inspected his audience. "Well? What have you got to say?"

"I'd rather be doing the same job in Germany," Johnny said quietly.

"You needn't concern yourself with Germany," Dimitrov responded, with faint annoyance. "The German party has a quarter of a million members, and this department is not exactly idle."

"That doesn't seem to be bothering Hitler," Johnny ventured. The remark bordered on open insolence, but he was determined to test what Kordt had told him about the party line on the Hitler movement. He recounted Kordt's story about the Bremen congress, trying to keep his emotion in check.

The Bulgarian's eyelids narrowed. "Where did you hear these things?"

"Friends."

"You should be more cautious who you talk to," Dimitrov warned him. "The German party is a snake pit." He made an effort to revive his earlier bonhomie. "Look, I know you're German. And you've been away from home for a long time. Naturally you're concerned about certain things. But you're really in no position to pass judgment. A foot soldier doesn't see what a general can see."

But the general's mistakes are much deadlier, Johnny thought. Didn't the war teach us that?

"I'll tell you something in confidence," the Bulgarian pressed on. "Just in case you imagine we're asleep at the wheel. I have it from an irrefutable source, a man high up in the General Staff. If Hitler is ever in a position to attempt to seize power, the Reichswehr will prevent him by force. You see? Hitler is a marionette. He can be broken like that." He snapped his fingers and looked triumphantly at Johnny.

Johnny knew at that moment that it was useless appealing to this man. Dimitrov was part of the problem.

I mustn't push it any further, Johnny told himself. Not here. That was Emil's mistake.

Perhaps, after all, he would be better off in England.

HE WALKED north up the Wilhelmstrasse in the perfect afternoon light. It played on the decorations of bankers and high officials and the jewels of their expensive women as they streamed from their phaetons to a grand reception at the Adlon. In the shadow of the great hotel, on the side next to the kitchens where there was an inescapable aroma of cooking oil, the British flag flapped on its staff in front of the former mansion of a railroad millionaire.

A man came out of the side entrance of the embassy and walked briskly towards a waiting sedan. Johnny glanced at him through the wrought-iron gate. Tall, straight-backed, he wore his civilian clothes like a military uniform: homburg, dark chesterfield with a velvet tab on the collar, scrolled umbrella. He moved with utter self-assurance, the model of a defender of the Raj. This is the enemy, Johnny thought, as he watched the Englishman swing into his car. He had had it drilled into him in countless briefings and study sessions in Moscow: Great Britain was the main enemy. His Majesty's Intelligence Service, which had tried to overthrow Lenin, was still the most ferocious of the secret opponents of the revolution. The Englishman was speaking to his chauffeur. There was something enviable about the man's total composure.

Johnny quickened his stride as he turned up the wide boulevard Unter den Linden. He barely registered the romantic triumph of the Brandenburg Gate, flung up against the sky. He needed time and space to sort out his emotions. He had instructions to go to a house in Grünewald, where the Westbureau hid its British section, to start his detailed briefings. That could wait till tomorrow. He rambled on into the Tiergarten without fixed purpose.

5

HE STOPPED at the zoo on his way back to the family flat in Charlottenburg. He found something relaxing in the presence of wild animals; possibly it had to do with their simplicity, their lack of a moral sense. He spent some time inspecting a small herd of blackbucks from southern Africa. The dominant male was distinguished by his black face and neck. As he grew older and weaker, one of the younger bucks would start to acquire this distinctive coloring as he rose in status. One young buck in this herd was well advanced; his head and neck were almost completely black. The old leader watched him warily, waiting to lock horns with his own death.

Johnny rambled on toward the cages of the big cats. There was a girl bent over a sketchbook on one of the benches. She wore a loose beret over her fine-spun red-gold hair. Her ankles were neatly crossed under the calf-length skirt. He knew her before he even saw her face. She looked up from her stub of charcoal to the animal that was padding silently around the narrow ambit of its cage, its shoulders rising and falling rhythmically. It was a panther, black as diamond dust.

He walked quietly along the slope of the path till he was standing just behind her. He stared at the white curve of her neck, at the hunted eyes of the panther, and recited

> Sein Blick ist vom Vorübergehn der Stäbe
> so müd geworden, dass er nichts mehr hält.
> Ihm ist, als ob es tausend Stäbe gäbe
> und hinter tausend Stäben keine Welt.
>
> His vision, from the constantly passing bars,
> has grown so weary that it cannot hold
> anything else. It seems to him there are
> a thousand bars; and behind the bars, no world.

She turned without haste, without fear, and studied him as if she were considering him for one of her sketches. He felt awkward with his big hands dangling at his sides.

"You don't look like someone who would know Rilke," Sigrid said.

"And you look like a woman who does."

One of his yawning afternoons in the schoolroom in Hamburg had been brought alive by a young teacher who had introduced his class to Rilke, reciting from the *Neue Gedichte* with the fire of a convert. The terrifying image of the panther behind bars had lived with Johnny ever since.

He sat down beside her on the bench, so close he could feel the warmth of her thigh. She did not draw away, but he felt her body tense, her legs press together.

"May I?"

He seized the sketchbook before she could close it.

The drawing of the panther was arresting; you could see the muscles rippling beneath the hide.

"You know what it's like to be caged," he said. He looked at her with such intensity that she turned away from him. She didn't exactly blush, but he could sense the heat in her face. It excited him.

"Yes," she murmured.

"You have a gift. Have you been to art school?"

She shook her head. "Father's been out of work for so long," she said by way of explanation. "And now I have to work in the restaurant. When I get a half day off, I come here or go to the exhibitions."

"Will you show me your paintings?"

"If you like."

"I don't know much about art. But I met Grosz once."

"Georg Grosz? His work is wonderful but—so brutal."

"He's an educator. He trains us to see things as they are. And to see why things have to be changed."

"I couldn't draw that way. Not to pass judgment."

"The artist can't be neutral. Neutrality is an illusion. To be neutral means to be on the side of the powers that be." He instantly regretted this statement. It sounded clumsy and pontifical.

She weighed this for a moment. "Is it true what Father says—that you're a Red?"

"I'm a member of the Communist party." He smiled. "Does that offend you?"

"I'm not political. I don't find it easy to take sides. Father votes for the Social Democrats, though I don't know whether he will next time. He says Stalin's worse than Hitler."

"He doesn't know what he's talking about."

"You met Helene in Russia?"

"Yes." He saw no reason to tell Sigrid about her sister's early life in Hamburg.

"You know, she ran away from home."

"You must have been very small."

"I remember her bending over my bed, late at night. She left me with something of hers, something that was close to her. A teddy bear with one eye missing. I still have it. She sent letters, sometimes, from all over the world. She never mentioned you. How long have you been married?"

Johnny hesitated. "We're not married."

"But Helene said—oh. I see." She dropped her eyes, embarrassed.

"It's not quite what you think. We're partners, workmates if you like. You see, the party is our family."

Sigrid's face brightened. "You're involved in secret work, is that it?"

"I'd rather not talk about it."

"Let me see your hands."

"I beg your pardon?"

"Let me see your hands."

He held them out obediently. She bent over them, studying the ridges and raised veins. She turned them over and traced the lifeline with her finger. Her hand looked small and soft as a child's inside his broad, calloused palm.

She said, "I'd like to paint you."

"Really? Like your models in the zoo? I'm flattered. Tell me, which of your animals do I resemble?"

"Oh, that's easy," she replied. "That one." She pointed at the panther. "Strong, very dangerous—but caged."

Startled by her own boldness, she slammed her sketchbook shut. A loose page flew out, and she darted after it. Johnny moved faster.

As he handed it to her, he let his arm graze her waist, as if by accident.

He said, "Are you sure the bars will hold?" and she started to blush as though she felt he was comparing her, not himself, to the animal in the cage.

6

"Kipling's books are decorated with swastikas," Max Fabrikant remarked. "They spin the other way from Hitler's, anticlockwise. The swastika is a very ancient symbol of the oriental mystics. I am told it is also a symbol of the Freemasons—hence, perhaps, Kipling. There are even those who maintain that the Christian cross is a sawn-off swastika."

They were strolling along the Ku'damm into the cabaret district. Johnny glanced back at the swaggering crowd of Nazis who had blocked the pavement on the other side. Max led the way into a street where lone men drifted among lurid signs advertising sex shows and porno films.

"Hitler is plumbing something atavistic in the human psyche," Max went on. "That is the secret of his appeal. He can't be defeated on the level of reason, because he draws directly from the unconscious, from the reptile brain that is older than thought." In the blue light that fell from the neon sign above, Fabrikant's mouth seemed to be molded into a leer. "But you discussed all of that with Heinz Kordt, didn't you?"

"How did you know?"

Max shrugged. "I know what Heinz thinks. And I knew you were bound to seek him out. You're loyal to your friends. That's not always a failing."

Johnny had asked for this meeting. He had also suggested that Helene should not be present. But the choice of locale belonged to Max.

The spymaster glanced up at the sign above their heads. The neon lights picked out the exaggerated profile of a naked woman lowering herself into a tub. *Die Badewanne,* flashed the words underneath. The Bathtub.

"In here."

A person in a blonde wig with breasts like hunting horns led them to a table. Johnny was struck by the legs that showed through the slits in the dress; they were as sturdy as his own, with knobbly knees. He was reminded, for a moment, of a night at the Kali-Bar in Hamburg. The night he had met Helene.

The floor show had already begun. There was a real bathtub on stage, surrounded by people of both sexes in varying stages of nudity. The centerpiece was a young man wearing only a black hood and a studded collar, who was being led around on a chain like a dog.

Max ordered Dom Perignon. He seemed determined to enjoy himself.

"Why here?" Johnny shouted above the din.

"Why not? It's so uplifting, don't you think? The Decline of the West in two acts, with live sex." As if on cue, a masked man with impossible pectorals came onstage and started cracking a whip. He seemed to be a great hit with this crowd.

"About Heinz—" Johnny leaned closer, so as not to shout.

"Well?"

"He thinks we're not doing enough to stop Hitler. I think he's right. I talked to Dimitrov. He seems to be living in some imaginary country."

"Drop it, Johnny. You're talking like a German."

"I *am* a German."

'Don't give me that crap, that *Lokalpatriotismus.* You know better than that. You belong to a world movement. That's your only loyalty."

"I'm worried about Heinz."

"I'm fond of Heinz. You know that. He's a good man to have with you in the trenches. But you should tell him not to make so much noise. The wind carries it further than he imagines."

The wine waiter came up and fussed over them. Max tested the champagne and indicated his approval.

"To London!" he proposed, clinking glasses. "To the girls along the Serpentine!"

"How long have you known?" Johnny asked.

"Longer than you, I expect. I have a piece of advice for you. When you get to England, buy yourself a decent suit. Never mind what it costs."

"Is there something wrong with my clothes?" Johnny glanced down at his grey flannel suit, bought off the peg in Bucharest years before.

"Not from my point of view. But you must come to terms with the English psyche. In the eyes of an Englishman, a man who goes to the right tailor is above suspicion."

"I'll try to keep that in mind." His eyes flitted up to the seminude dancer who was gyrating onstage with her pet boa constrictor around her belly.

"You asked for this meeting," Max reminded him. "It's always a pleasure to see you, of course. But was there something in particular you wanted to say?"

"It's about Helene."

"Yes?"

"I'd rather she didn't come to England with me."

"That's not my province."

"But she works for you—"

Max silenced Johnny with a subtle but sudden flick of his wrist. The young man followed his gaze and saw a newcomer, smartly attired in a broad pinstripe and a bow tie, with a red rose in his buttonhole. The stranger murmured something to the transvestite waiter and was rewarded with giggles. His manner was languid, but his eyes flicked warily from side to side as he crossed the room to join a poised, very fair young man at a corner table. As Max and Johnny watched, the snake-dancer, minus the boa constrictor, threaded her way through the drinkers and sat down at the same table.

Max allowed himself a small sigh of satisfaction.

"A friend of yours?" Johnny tried to provoke him.

"That, my dear fellow, is the head of British Intelligence in Berlin."

Johnny took another look at the Englishman, trying to memorize the face.

Max reached for the champagne bottle, found it empty, and pushed it back nosedown into the bucket.

"About Helene," he remarked, studying the chemistry between the British spy and the colorful crowd at his table, "I may have a solution for you. A temporary one, at any rate."

"Yes?"

"It occurs to me that I may need to borrow her for a few weeks."

1

SIGRID waited on tables in the Palace Café Mondays through Saturdays from eleven until eight, with Wednesday afternoons off. There was a brisk trade at lunchtime (secretaries and clerks from nearby government offices) and in the early evenings (cinemagoers dining out on their way to the UFA theater up the street). In the slack times, in the middle of the afternoon, she would sketch the faces around her. Some of the customers, discovering her hidden talent, would slip her an extra mark for their portraits. It was in those lazy hours that Johnny took to drinking coffee at the Palace Café. Once he brought her a leaflet about the conditions of German workers. It was illustrated with a drawing of a street sweeper, his face corrugated by a lifetime of toil, trudging off to work.

She refused to speak to Johnny for the rest of the day. The sketch was hers, something he had asked for. He had no right to have it printed without her consent, least of all in such a publication. At the bottom of the leaflet was the long-winded title of some organization she had never heard of. She presumed it was something to do with the Communists, and when she questioned Johnny later, he didn't bother with denials.

"Did you read it?" he demanded. "Is there anything you disagree with?"

She had to shake her head.

"Well, then, be proud you're part of something that *matters*. Publications like this are important. People have to be made aware of how the workers are forced to live, of what the Fascists are doing. They have to be made to *see*. Your picture says more than all of the text. They'd like to use more of your work, Sigi. You don't need to worry. Your name won't be used. And they'll pay you, not much, but enough to pay for the best materials you can buy. It's a start, isn't it?"

She had the use of her studio again. The lodger had moved on, and Johnny and Helene had taken over his room. Her father had said he wouldn't stand for it. When drunk, he even threatened to go to the police. But he was scared of his wife, and his grumbling subsided when Johnny handed him twice the usual rent, for a whole month to boot. With the additional allowance Johnny had received from Dimitrov's people, he had no shortage of funds. Now there was meat on the table every night and money for Hermann to loaf all day in his *Lokal.* And morning and evening, Johnny was there, under the same roof. In fact, he was at home far more often than Helene, who would vanish without explanation for days at a time.

His presence disturbed Sigrid. When he entered a room, he seemed to fill it. She could feel his nearness on her skin, like a physical caress. His eyes were changeable as the sea, sometimes calm and gentle, sometimes a violent tide that threatened to envelop her. She wished he would leave. She promised herself to speak to her mother, to make them go. She had the ominous sensation that he was about to tear open the padlocks that secured a sealed room deep inside her, where some nameless, terrible thing thrashed in its chains, striving to break loose. Yet at the Palace Café, when the afternoon wore on and he had still not appeared with his battered hat and his puckish grin, she began to feel empty, almost desolate. And when he suggested little outings, she did not refuse.

These excursions were harmless enough, considered singly: a visit to the UFA cinema after work or to a rehearsal of the new play by Bert Brecht, or a Wednesday afternoon on the Wannsee. That day he hired a boat, and they sculled to the farther shore, where he scrambled onto a rock and squatted, his arms dangling over his knees, his face turned up to the sun.

"You look like a seal, with your nose pointing up like that," she laughed at him. She turned the sketch she had begun into a caricature, with a feminine hand dangling a fish over Johnny's nose.

"It's not the fish I'm pointing at," Johnny said, snatching the drawing away from her.

She made out that she hadn't heard. But rowing back across the Wannsee, half blinded by the late sun that burned on the waters, she was frightened, less of him than of herself.

He had flung off his jacket and rolled up his sleeves. The light traced the flex of his arms, which were strong but not brawny. He leaned forward to point something out, and he smelled like the sun. He bent over her, and all of her body rushed to meet him. He found her lips. His touch scalded, but it took all of her strength to wrench herself away. She sat in the prow of the boat, quivering, her head erect, poised for flight.

"Why?" His tone wasn't entreating or accusing. Slowly she turned back to him. He cocked his head and she wanted to laugh, because now he looked like a dog trying to puzzle out the strange speech of humans.

She said, "Because of Helene," and tried to smooth her dress. It felt unnaturally constricting, pressing so tightly against her bosom she could hardly breathe.

"I told you already," he said gently. "I'm not married to Helene."

"But you sleep together."

"Sometimes." He held her gaze. "But there are no commitments. Except for the mission we share. And that is something I hope one day to share with you."

The boat drifted closer to the home shore, and a copse of fir trees on a rise swallowed the sun. She felt a sudden chill.

"I'm not Helene," she said. "I couldn't live like that."

"You're saving yourself for the man you'll marry?"

This was treacherous ground. She wasn't sure she believed in marriage, not after what she had seen between her parents.

She moved onto safer slopes. "Helene is my sister," she pointed out.

A maddening smile plucked at his lips. "You're not accountable for an accident of birth."

"It's not proper," she said. "It's *unanständig.*"

She made this last remark with such a determined imposture of bourgeois rectitude that he burst out laughing, and it horrified her to find that she wanted to join in. The mood was so convulsive that she had to turn her back on him, so he would mistake the spasms for a different sentiment and not take them as an invitation to return to the attack. What was the matter with her?

She knew, of course, that the situation was hopeless. Johnny was a man on the run, a dangerous agitator likely to spend the rest of his life—which might not be long—behind bars. Further, he was married (well, if not exactly married, then at least pledged) to her sister. In any case, he might be leaving Berlin at any moment for God-knows-where. To cap it all, he was a sailor by trade, and everyone knew how far you could trust sailors with women.

Yet when he reached for her again, she didn't move quickly enough to avoid him (did she move at all?) and when he crushed her against him, her body betrayed her. She should have been stiff and unyielding, wooden as a plank, but every part of her hastened to receive him. She could feel his breath on her neck, his circling hands invading her secret places. With an effort of will she grabbed the side of the dinghy—which rolled dangerously, so that water sloshed over their feet—and dragged herself away.

SHE MOVED through the rest of that week like a sleepwalker. Forms had lost their usual weight and density. In bed, she fell into a shallow, restless sleep. It was like lying on shifting sands, with a gauzy curtain blowing over her face. Waking, she went about her chores like an automaton. At the restaurant she got orders mixed up and dropped a tray, and the manager threatened to fire her.

"There are thousands of girls in Berlin!" he screamed. "Don't think you're anything special."

Johnny turned up at her side one morning at the Ethnological Museum —had he followed her or come with her?—and they wandered among the displays of primitive art. Johnny was fascinated by some of the masks. He stopped in front of a Kwakiutl mask from British Columbia. It showed a frontal view of a face with an enormous, tragic eye, sheared off along the ridge of the nose so that it was suddenly transformed into a dark profile.

They looked at Yoruba initiation masks, at a towering Senufo headdress that was a whole alphabet of hieratic signs, at the abstract Oceanic figures she told him had influenced Giacometti.

"The mask is not just decoration," she told him. "The man who puts on the mask is no longer himself. He dies to the old life to become the god, or the ancestral spirit. The mask belongs to a higher order of reality than the man who wears it."

He considered this without comment, but his face darkened. He strolled away with his hands in his pockets to stare at some shrunken trophy heads from South America. Sigrid shuddered at the sight of one of them, a nut-brown face with black oblong stones for eyes, draped with plaits of dried flowers and blue-and-red feathers. It had a coil of string in its mouth, with a length left dangling underneath like a hangman's noose.

"I saw something like this once before."

"Come away," she said, taking his arm.

"All primitive art is for use," he remarked, when they were standing on the museum steps. "Superstitious use, it's true, but the service of something greater than the individual artist."

"Are you preaching at me again?"

He smiled and patted her hand. "No, but they'd like some more of your drawings for a new magazine. What would a trophy head of Goebbels look like?"

Then a couple of days passed when she didn't see him. Helene flew in and out of the flat to fetch some clothes. She was in a filthy temper and wouldn't exchange more than half a dozen words. Hitler made a violent speech promising revenge for the assassination of a storm troop commander by the Communists. In her free time Sigrid busied herself with the Nazi caricatures Johnny had requested for the magazine. The likenesses weren't bad. Some of them—especially the sketch of Himmler, the poultry farmer, as a turkey with wattles drooping over the collar of his SS uniform—were quite funny.

Wednesday came around, and Johnny still hadn't reappeared. His absence made a wasteland of her afternoon off. Keep away, she had told herself, knowing that she could be only a passing diversion in the life of a man like him. She was bound to lose him soon enough, inevitably and irrevocably. But now she was terrified by the fear that he had been snatched away even sooner than she had calculated, before she had had time to make up her mind about everything. Had she been right to refuse him, that afternoon on the lake? Was it right to spurn something your whole being cried out for because you couldn't have it for keeps? She didn't know the answers, not for sure.

That Wednesday night, long after her parents had gone to bed, she went to the lodger's room. The door was locked, but she opened it with the key to her own room; all the locks inside the apartment were the same.

She examined the familiar furnishings of the room—the ponderous armoire against the wall, the china jug in its bowl on the washstand, the painting of a stag with a pack of dogs at its heels, the double bed with its massive headboard. Nothing was out of place. There was no personal touch to suggest the room was even occupied. The bed cover lay flat and smooth, the ashtray on its brass stand had been wiped clean. Overcome by a kind of panic, she rushed to the cupboard and flung the doors open. His clothes were still there: a couple of suits, the tweed coat he had worn that day on the lake.

A measure of calm returned, and with it insuperable weariness. She lay on the bed, *his* bed, and let sleep take her.

His breath was hot against her face. She smelled raw alcohol and wood smoke. The mattress sagged under the double weight.

He murmured, "Oh, my love."

Coming out of the dream, she realized he had pulled up her nightgown. The fabric lay bunched beneath her armpits while his lips moved to her breasts.

She clawed at him, and there was a dull thud as his shoulder hit the wall.

Then his full weight was on her, pinning her. She opened her mouth and formed words, but no sound escaped.

She stopped wrestling and listened to the rasp of his breathing. When he forced his way between her legs, she stayed the same, not yielding, not resisting. She bit her lip at the first stab of pain and tasted her own blood.

He was bucking and sawing, but then his movements became slower, coaxing and circling as he tried to lead her like a dance partner. She relaxed a little, and began to enter into the rhythm.

But before she had learned it, he was lunging inside her. She saw his face lifted over her, flushed and triumphant, gleaming with sweat.

He whispered, "My love." The rough stubble pricked her skin as he rested his head against her neck.

She slid away from him and went to the washbasin.

In the moonlight he could see the dark patches on the sheet.

"Sigrid," he said hoarsely. "I didn't know. You're a woman made for love. I thought—"

He broke off at the sight of her calmly hoisting her nightgown over her head and shoulders. Without shame, she walked back to the bed and stood over him, examining his body as if she wanted to see how each part worked.

"*Noch einmal,*" she said. "Do it again."

He stared at her. The light showed the thrust of her breasts, the long, voluptuous slope of her belly.

"You took something from me," she said. "Something I dreamed of sharing. You owe me something now. I want to know what it feels like to be a woman."

8

THE Austrian passport was two years old. It was dated October 1929, the year and month of the Great Crash. The name of the holder was entered in a confident copperplate hand: Ludwig Dinkelmeyer. According to the information entered on the second page, his profession was *Kaufmann*— "Merchant"—and he had been born in Vienna in 1894. Oval face, blue eyes, dark blond hair, no visible distinguishing marks.

Johnny's face looked out of the photograph on page three. He was respectably dressed in a dark suit, his tie perfectly in place, his hair slicked back, the image of a successful tradesman. A matching photograph of Helene, described as his wife, Erna, had been inserted next to his. She wore her hair in tight waves and a dress with a broad collar and fashionably padded shoulders. They shared the imprint of the same rubber stamp.

"The shoes are a nice fit, wouldn't you say?" the man in the tailor shop remarked to Johnny. "Scotland Yard has a nose for for dummy passports. But they're not magicians. They'll never fault this."

They were in a back room equipped with a pair of ancient Singer sewing machines and piled high with bolts and remnants of cloth.

"Your credentials," the tailor said, showing Johnny a linen square bearing a dozen lines of black type. "Give me your jacket."

Johnny handed over his coat, and the tailor inspected the lining. He took a pair of scissors and made a brisk incision around the left armpit. He plied his needle, and in a couple of minutes the job was done. Unless the British customs men decided to tear Johnny's clothing apart, they would never find his secret credentials from the Comintern.

"What am I selling this time?" Johnny asked.

"You're in luck, my friend. You're a wine merchant. I'm only sorry I won't have the chance to inspect your samples. You'll pick them up in Hamburg."

* * *

"You're a woman for life," he had told her.

And Sigrid had replied, "But you—you're the man of Sesenheim."

He had not understood the allusion, so she had had to remind him. Goethe had had a tempestuous affair with an innocent country parson's daughter, Friedericke Brion. He had made no effort to guard her reputation, flaunting her as his mistress. But when the poet had decided to leave Sesenheim, he had dropped the girl like a plaything he had outgrown. He had met her on horseback and hadn't even dismounted to say good-bye. He had just leaned over from the saddle and shaken hands. The girl had never looked at another man.

"It's not true," Johnny protested. "I'll come back for you. I'll find a way for us to be together."

"Don't make me any promises," she said, shaking her head. "You're a soldier under orders. Isn't that what you told me? Let's just live in the time we're allowed."

It was stolen time. He had known that all along. So far he had contrived to keep the affair secret from Helene. But in time she was bound to find out. He didn't feel guilty in relation to Helene; on the contrary, he was ready to stand his ground with her. But he could only guess at what Helene would say to her sister, at the weapons she might use to turn Sigrid against him.

He had found excuses to prolong his stay in Berlin, but the excuses had run out. When the signal to leave for England finally came, it was peremptory. His instructions were to take the express from the Lehrter station—less than two hours away—to keep a rendezvous in Hamburg that same night.

He rushed to the Palace Café. Sigrid's face lit up when she saw him.

"Can you come outside for a minute?" he asked.

She saw his expression, and her face went blank. She asked one of the other girls to take over her post, took off her apron and followed him outside. The bite of winter was in the air.

"It's now, isn't it?" she said in a whisper.

"I'm not on horseback." His attempt at a joke fell like a stone. "I'll write. And I'll be back. But I don't know when. I can't possibly ask you to wait for me."

"I won't wait," she said. "I won't even know if you're alive or dead. But I'll be here, just the same."

3

The Lost Band

Out of the ruins of the
Communist revolution we built in
Germany for Soviet Russia a
brilliant intelligence service, the
envy of every other nation.
—WALTER KRIVITSKY,
In Stalin's Secret Service (1939)

1

IT WAS raining when Johnny's plane from Hamburg bumped down onto
the runway at East Croydon. It rained steadily over Greater London for the
next sixteen consecutive days, out of a sky that closed over the rooftops like
a saucepan lid.

His passport raised no questions. The customs inspector waived duty on
his case of wine samples. A police constable whose muttonchop whiskers
gave him the benign aspect of an Old English sheepdog showed Johnny
the way to the train station and asked if he was South African. Everything
but the weather was accommodating.

Following instructions, he took the train to Victoria and checked into
a small, sooty hotel frequented by traveling salesmen and illicit lunchtime
lovers. He bought himself an umbrella, dined on warm beer and cottage
pie in a pub up the road and wrote his first letter to Sigrid before he turned
in for the night. Two days away from her, he felt her absence as an aching
hollow, demanding to be filled.

In the morning he went to the post office to mail his letter. It did not
include a return address. He would look for a safe mailing address when
he found more permanent lodgings.

When he returned to the hotel, a young man in a rather loud plaid suit was chatting up the girl receptionist. Johnny checked his watch against the clock above the desk—9:27 A.M. He was two minutes fast.

The young man followed Johnny into the elevator, whistling an old music-hall song. He pulled the gate shut behind them and unfolded a copy of the *Sporting Guide.* It increased his resemblance to a racetrack tout. Then Johnny noticed the date on the paper. It was a week old.

The stranger's nose popped over the top of his paper.

"You wouldn't have the time, would you, squire?"

"Certainly." Johnny did not consult his pocket watch. "It is precisely quarter to five."

"George Mikes," the young man grinned and stuck out his hand. "At your service."

GEORGE MIKES was as good as his word. For the next two weeks he played guide, chauffeur, drinking crony, racing tipster, amateur pimp and general aide-de-camp. He was the London organizer of the party's AM *Apparat*— a word he pronounced to rhyme with "plate." He had a bedsit in Hampstead, where he brewed Irish coffee over a single gas ring, but he drove Johnny in his little green Austin to new digs on the other side of the river, in Shepherds Bush.

Johnny's hosts were the Roses—Norma and Ernie. Norma was a big, blowsy, warm-hearted girl, the daughter of a Polish baker in Stoke Newington. Every morning, she cooked huge fry-ups for the two men before boarding her bus to the city, where she had some kind of secretarial job. When it wasn't raining, Ernie spent much of the day pottering round his pocket-handkerchief garden. On Saturdays, religiously, he went bowling. He told Johnny that he had once worked as a piano player at the cinema down the road, interpreting the moments of passion on the big screen. But his job had vanished with the demise of the silent movies. Now he did part-time work as a glassblower—a job that seemed to Johnny to have an equally precarious future.

Norma and Ernie were both party members, which made Johnny uneasy, since he had been warned in Berlin that the British Communist Party was crawling with police spies. He became even more nervous when Norma had a couple of sherries too many and let slip that she knew Johnny was in England on a secret Soviet mission.

The second Saturday, he came back to Shepherds Bush in midafternoon in a blazing fury. George had taken him to Paddington to inspect the secret printing press that was used to crank out *Soldier's Voice,* a party publication aimed at enlisted men. Johnny approved of the location in the basement below a shoe-repair shop, where the rumble of the press was camou-flaged by the hammers and the sewing machines overhead. But he was unhappy about an unexpected discovery. He had found a door, half hidden by piles of newsprint. George hadn't wanted him to look inside. It was just a storage closet, according to George. He looked inside anyway—and found a good-sized room, filled from floor to ceiling with bundles of *Soldier's Voice.* The issues dated back more than twelve months. Moscow paid for every copy that was printed—and the British Communists left them to gather dust. They were lazy and corrupt, just as Dimitrov had said. This wasn't the first evidence he had stumbled across, despite George's assiduous efforts to divert his attention to pubs and pliable female sympathizers. Johnny demanded a meeting with Pollitt and was reminded that it was the weekend.

"What are you? Shopkeepers?" Johnny exploded. "You get word to Pollitt I want to see him tomorrow, even if it is bloody Sunday. Do you think the revolution has licensing hours?"

He declined George's offer of a lift and walked to a nearby bus stop. There was a long line and only a few seats on the first bus that came. But nobody jostled or tried to jump the queue. A second bus came, and Johnny climbed on top. The people around him chatted about soccer teams and Christmas shopping.

He remembered a line he had read in Engels. "Even the British proletar-iat is bourgeois." He wanted to yell at them, to make a scene.

He changed buses twice and walked the last half mile to the Roses' terrace house, to make sure he wasn't being followed. Rounding the corner of Holly Street, he stopped short.

A sleek, powerful car was double-parked in front of the house. It looked like a Bristol. It didn't belong in that modest street. As Johnny watched, Norma Rose slid out of the passenger seat and blew a kiss to the driver, who pushed his foot down on the gas pedal so hard that the tires com-plained as he sped off down the street.

Johnny walked round the block, trying to make sense of what he had just seen. A boyfriend Norma had picked up at a cinema or a tea dance? She was a very physical woman, and available—she had suggested that, without much subtlety, to him. Her marriage to Ernie seemed to be fairly sexless. There were no children, and Ernie complained of having to go in for a hernia operation.

The other possibility was the police. But the English police, by Johnny's observation, did not drive around in Bristol motorcars. And they would hardly be so inept as to show themselves at the front door of an agent of the Communist party.

Johnny decided to confront Norma. He was in the mood for a confrontation with someone.

He let himself in with his key and found her in the bedroom, half out of her dress. She had her back to him. As she bent over, he could see the tops of her breasts, swollen and milky white, in the cheval glass on the far side of the room.

She glanced up, gave a stifled squeal, and clapped her hand to her chest. "You gave me quite a turn."

"Have you been out?"

"I had to go in to the office. There's a bit of a panic on." She was smiling, but her eyes looked puffy and sore, as if she had been crying.

"Is something the matter?"

"No. 'Course there isn't." She went to the dresser and blew her nose.

"I see you got a lift home."

For the first time, she looked scared. "You won't tell Ernie, will you?"

"Why should I?" He paused. "Your friend drives a very fancy car."

"It's not his. It's an export model. He's trying it out. No harm in that, is there?"

"I couldn't say."

"Arkady said—"

At the mention of the Russian name, Johnny froze. *"Arkady?"*

"Oh, Jeez. I thought you knew."

"Who is Arkady?"

"He's my boss. I work for Arcos. Jeez. You're not having me on, are you? I mean, I thought you'd know, you two being Russians and all—"

Johnny swore in German and stormed out of the room.

His ANGER was not allayed by the knowledge that it was partly his fault. He had never bothered to inquire where Norma worked; he had counted on George Mikes and his organization to be able to take care of *something*. As a result, he had been living for nearly two weeks at the home of a woman who was not only a party member but an employee of the Soviet trading company, Arcos, which had been the target for a famous police raid a few years before and was publicly identified by Scotland Yard as one of the centers of Russian espionage in Britain. To cap it all, Norma was evidently having an affair with her Russian boss, whose sense of security was clearly as exiguous as her own.

It would be little short of a miracle, he realized, if the police had not had him under observation since he first lugged his suitcase up the Roses' front steps.

He decided to move house immediately. And this time he would find his own lodgings.

HE FOUND them in the Sunday classifieds—a pair of good-sized rooms in a boarding house in Richmond that seemed to be largely patronized by theatrical gentlemen who wafted around in dressing gowns at all hours of the day. The bohemian atmosphere appealed to him; a man with a foreign accent and unusual hours was unlikely to draw comment. He paid a month's deposit in cash and moved in with a newly bought suitcase stuffed with newspapers the same day. He told George to collect his bags from Shepherds Bush and meet him on neutral ground. He did not wish to set foot in the Roses' house again.

GEORGE MIKES was nervous and full of apologies that night, as they drove —interminably, it seemed—across south London. Walworth was the name on the last sign Johnny noticed. George parked the Austin in front of a neat semidetached cottage behind a picket fence. There was a doctor's shingle above the door.

"What is this place?" Johnny demanded.

"It's all right. The doctor's a Socialist. He was our candidate in the last general elections."

Johnny swore copiously. "Haven't you idiots ever heard of a *yafka?*" In his agitation, he slipped into the jargon of his training courses in Moscow.

George blinked at him.

"A safe house!" Johnny translated. "Don't you know what a safe house is? You'll get all of us arrested!"

"You'll be safe enough here," George assured him. The man looked totally bewildered. "Doctor Pratt is a good friend of Harry's."

Johnny sighed and went inside the house. He found Harry Pollitt in the sitting room, warming his backside in front of a gas fire. The leader of the Communist Party of Great Britain was smooth and freshly barbered, soberly but smartly turned out in a dark suit that minimized his girth. His greeting was unctuous. He pressed Johnny's hand for too long.

Pollitt was a former boilermaker, Johnny had read in the files.

Johnny thought, He looks like a minor evangelist getting ready to pass the collection plate.

Pollitt settled himself in an armchair and wasted twenty minutes reminiscing about his visits to the Soviet Union. He waxed eloquent about a holiday at Stalin's private villa on the Black Sea and dropped the names of a dozen other Moscow officials. The message was crude, but impossible to miss; he wanted Johnny to know he had powerful protectors.

A pretty, dark-haired girl brought tea and biscuits.

As she left, Pollitt winked at Johnny and said, "Good-looking bint, isn't she? If there's anything you're missing to make your stay comfortable, you needn't be shy with us. Brother George here is just the man to fix you up."

Johnny said nothing, and Pollitt looked at the teapot with mock dismay. "I think our guest must be in need of something stronger, Georgie."

George Mikes dashed out and returned with a bottle of Dimple Haig. Johnny accepted a glass but let it sit.

You smug bastard, he thought, watching Pollitt. You'd love to get something on me, wouldn't you? Something you could use with your big friends in Moscow. I won't give you that satisfaction.

He resolved to seize the initiative.

"Comrade Pollitt. You know my authority—"

"We don't stand on ceremony here, brother."

"—and you know the urgency of my mission. It is possible that Russia will be at war with Japan in a matter of weeks. It is equally possible that the Western Powers will exploit the opportunity to intervene on the Japanese side while the Soviet Union is isolated. It is imperative that we should have a network in Britain that is capable of paralyzing any war mobilization."

"We know our duty. Our AM *Apparat*—"

"—Exists only on paper."

Pollitt appealed mutely to George, who shuffled his feet.

"I've seen what you're doing in the London area," Johnny pursued. "You're printing appeals to soldiers and sailors that are never distributed. You haven't begun to capitalize on the Invergordon mutiny. You don't have a single party cell inside the barracks.'

"London's tricky," George spoke up. "Wait until you see what we're doing in the provinces."

"I've seen your lists," Johnny glowered at him. "I've also noted you've found one excuse after another to delay my visits to Portsmouth and the north."

"There are always security considerations," Pollitt observed piously.

"Security!" Johnny snorted. "None of you seem to know what the word means! Since I've been here, your people have done everything to blow my cover short of delivering me to Scotland Yard."

Pollitt professed to be shocked.

"I took a day trip to Portsmouth on my own," Johnny announced.

It was George's turn to look shocked. His reaction, at least, was genuine.

"I went to the address of your AM organizer in Portsmouth," Johnny continued. "Billy Shar. Wasn't that the name, George? They'd never heard of him. But it was an interesting establishment. I believe some of your countrymen would refer to it as a knocking shop.'

George Mikes squirmed.

"Surely there's some mistake," Pollitt interceded. "George?"

"Er—I'll look into it."

"It gave me an idea, all the same," Johnny said, relaxing a bit now he had scored a point. "When I was in Belgium, we ran a bordello that was popular with army officers. We developed some useful friends. It's one of the ideas I want to work on here."

"Well, you're the expert, of course." Pollitt cleared his throat. "I'm not qualified to discuss these—ah—technical matters."

"It's going to require money. Like some other ideas I've got."

"Now, that could be a problem." Pollitt was back on home territory. "We're not a wealthy party, you know. Times are hard, and a lot of our lads are on the dole. We scrape by as best we can."

"We gave you more than eighty thousand pounds last year."

"Steady on, now. The figure was nothing like that."

"I've seen the paperwork," Johnny pressed on, implacable. "Thirty thousand in direct grants, the rest fudged in one way or another. Like subscriptions to all those copies of the *Daily Worker* and *Soldier's Voice* that nobody ever reads. And how much of this cash goes on AM work? Sixty bloody quid a month."

He paused to see if either would contradict him. Neither did.

Pollitt poured another drink and said, "I'm not used to being talked to like this."

"I apologize for being direct. I'm impatient to get my job done and get back to where my friends risk getting shot simply because they are Communists. I'm sure that would suit both of us."

Pollitt seemed to like this better. "What do you need?"

"I want to pick new men to run the AM network. And I'll need money. Two thousand to start with."

Pollitt opened his mouth to protest, but Johnny said curtly, "It's already been authorized. You can check if you like."

Pollitt's expression finally resolved itself into a smile. "I'll see what we can do."

Johnny thought, I'll have to watch my back with this bastard.

2

JOHNNY had his own channels of communication, and naturally they had nothing to do with the British party. His regular post office was a rare bookshop near the British Museum, a location that suited him because he could steal an hour or two, upon occasion, in the reading room that—or so he indulged himself—still harbored the ghosts of the authors of the *Communist Manifesto*. Sitting there leafing through old editions of the forerunners—Saint-Just, Buonarroti's strange account of the Conspiracy of the Equals—he sought to renew his revolutionary faith. He had memorized two telephone numbers. One belonged to "Smollett," the resident director of Red Army intelligence; the other was to be used only if he needed to arrange sudden flight. But the post office that meant most to him, as his lonely weeks in England turned into months, was a corner newsagent five minutes away from his bolthole in Richmond. It was the sort of place that had grubby filing cards in the window advertising secondhand bicycles and models who gave French lessons. He got on friendly terms with the owner, stopping in to buy his cigarettes and his copies of the Manchester *Guardian* and the Tory press. He told the man he had to travel a lot in his job and would be glad of someone to receive his mail while he was away. Whether or not the newsagent saw through this excuse, he was happy to oblige.

From then on, intermittently, Johnny received envelopes from Germany addressed to "D. Green." The tone of Sigrid's first letters was cheerful, if forced. She thanked him for the small gifts he had sent—a book of Elizabethan poetry, a poster from the Tate—and told him she had been able to increase her earnings as a commercial artist and would soon be moving to a place of her own. He interpreted this to mean that she was doing regular work for Willi Münzenberg's agitprop organization in Berlin.

In the later letters Sigrid's tone turned sombre, even desperate. She chronicled the daily signals of Hitler's ascent, small things she witnessed in the streets, beatings of Jews, the defection of neighbors—even, it seemed, her father—to the Hitler movement. In the shadow falling over Germany, she seemed to read the death of love, of any hope of private fulfillment.

"Now I begin to understand you," she wrote. "In the world as it is, there is no room for individuals, that is to say, neutrals. I will give up my art and work only as a draughtsman for the cause." Then she added, in anguish, "But isn't this another small triumph for the destroyers? I see Germany at the mercy of terrible legions that will trample everything human in the name of an abstract, impossible humanity. Some of them are singing the

Internationale. On the day I join the party, I will destroy my canvases. Even the ones of you."

He wrote back across the aching distance, begging her not to lose hope. "I'm coming for you," he promised.

Sigrid's letters never mentioned Helene. He found this vaguely ominous, though he tried not to brood on it. He had enough to worry about, trying to lick the British network into shape. He found an energetic man called Jim Straw, a carpenter by trade who had fought on the Somme and knew what wars were about, to take over from George. Together they located some of the sailors discharged after the Invergordon mutiny and put them to work in pubs near the docks at Southampton and Portsmouth. They recruited a sergeant at Catterick camp who had already formed an active cell. With help from Communists in the railwaymen's and transport workers' unions, Johnny roughed out plans for lightning strikes to prevent troops and war materiel from reaching the docks. But less than three hundred pounds of the money he had demanded from Pollitt had been forthcoming, and he was reduced to running to "Smollett," the lugubrious Fourth Department man in London, for funds to pay his own rent.

He sent report after report to Berlin, describing his progress while excoriating Pollitt and the leadership of the British Communist Party. He half hoped that Pollitt was complaining loudly enough to get him recalled. Though he threw himself into his assignment, he felt on the sidelines in Britain. He belonged in Berlin, in the thick of the battle, with Heinz—and with Sigrid.

Besides, the more he saw of the British, the more his conviction grew that Engels was right. Here even the proletariat was bourgeois. The trade unions remained resolutely reformist, and the police and armed forces— for all his efforts—seemed almost impervious to Communist teachings. Even in the sour, smoky slums of the industrial north, in human slagheaps cast off by factories whose machines were half a century out of date, the workers weren't signing up for any revolution. The British Empire was doomed—wasn't the writing on the wall, for all to see?—yet the working class, more than any other social group, seemed to be lulled by the romance of the Raj. Throughout the nation the birthday of the dead Queen-Empress Victoria, May 24, was still celebrated as Empire Day.

On Empire Day 1932, Johnny watched hundreds of schoolchildren dutifully chanting Kipling's hymn of dedication,

> Land of our birth, we pledge to thee
> Our love and toil in years to be

and found that in part of himself he envied them for their uncomplicated faith, their primitive sense of belonging.

Unlike Germans or Russians, the Englishman was allergic to abstract causes. Johnny remembered Max Fabrikant's grudging admiration for the British as "reactionaries without complexes." It would take more than his efforts or those of a thousand like him to bring down the foundations of the British Empire. Only the British themselves could do that, if they ever lost their nerve.

3

In a larger plan the British Communists had their uses. Their seamen's organization smuggled Comintern agents to India and all of the garrison colonies—Malta, Gibraltar, Aden, Hong Kong. Johnny saw it at work when Smollett called on him for a professional favor.

They sat side by side on a bench on Hampstead Heath. Beyond the trees men were hammering tent pegs and setting up booths, getting ready for a summer fair. Englishmen who had escaped from their offices to catch a few precious rays lay prone on the grass or lounged in deck chairs, jackets and ties discarded.

"We're having trouble with Ved Gupta." The Russian wiped his long, pendulous nose. He was getting a summer cold, the most maddening kind. "Do you know him?"

"Only by reputation. He runs the East Indian Seamen's Association, doesn't he?"

"He's a greasy Hindu from Bengal," Smollett said charitably. "Round and dumpy as a piece of *nan.*"

"What's the problem?"

"We ordered him to move his headquarters to Calcutta. The bloody babu won't go—"

Smollett broke off to stifle a sneeze.

"Perhaps he's afraid his ex-wives will catch up with him," Johnny suggested.

"I think he's been lining his nest. He's got his nose into some nice little rackets he doesn't want to give up. Look, I know this isn't really your parish, but I could do with some help."

"What do you want me to do?"

"Pay him a visit. Find out what the score is. Then remind him who's paying for his lifestyle and put some fear of God into him."

"And if he won't be persuaded?"

The Fourth Department man considered this. "Then we'll have to get rid of him," he concluded. "I wouldn't put it past him to go crying to the police. Let me know what happens. Do you need any help?"

"I'll manage with my own boys."

Johnny's personal network was expanding fast. He had rented rooms in Poplar, near the town hall, where he held training sessions for his best recruits. He had found a wiry Tasmanian, Barry Flynn, who had been to the Lenin School in Moscow, to take charge of the docks. He had promoted a thrusting young British Communist, John Gollan, to help run the national *Apparat.*

He told Flynn to pick a couple of sturdy young men who weren't scared to use their fists and to meet him near the entrance to the Blackwall Tunnel the following night. The babu lived and worked above the seamen's club on the East India Dock Road.

Under the uncertain glow of the streetlamps, the street had the grainy, sepia look of an old photograph. There was a stir outside the club. A crowd of lascar seamen, some incoherently drunk, were apparently in the midst of a party.

Johnny led the way around the back and up a fire escape. He had already reconnoitered his ground.

He shouldered his way past the male secretary who tried to stop them at the door and found Ved Gupta in the midst of a business transaction. The Indian's comfortable bulk overflowed a splendid mahogany desk as he scrabbled to sweep several wads of banknotes—American dollars—into the top drawer. There were two other men in the room: a turbaned Sikh, impassive and watchful, and a Cockney with a pinched, nervous face, who clutched a leather satchel and looked ready to jump out the window.

"Relax," Johnny said to him. "We're not the police."

"I've seen this one before," Barry Flynn remarked, pointing his thumb at the Cockney.

"Nice place you've got here," Johnny said to Gupta, examining the lavish appointments of the room. He pulled back a louvered folding door and found a row of steel cabinets. "Are these your files?"

"I say, you can't go in there! This is not at all seemly!" The babu's voice trembled.

"I quite agree. I think we ought to talk privately, don't you?"

Flynn was puzzling over the Cockney.

"I've got it!" he suddenly announced. "It's the Ferret, isn't it? Ferret Friedman! They had you up for dope running!"

Friedman ran for the inside door.

"She'll be apples!" Flynn whooped at Johnny. He sprinted after Friedman and brought him down with a rugby tackle.

In a moment Flynn had the briefcase open. It was packed full of little oilcloth packets. He opened one, took a pinch of the powder inside, sniffed, then dabbed it on his tongue to make sure.

"Opium," he pronounced.

"Did you get it from him?" Johnny demanded, pointing to Gupta.

The Ferret's response was not very helpful. Flynn kicked him just once, in the kidneys.

"Yes," Friedman grunted.

"How many of these deals have you done?"

"This is the first, I swear—blimey!"

A second, more vicious kick, brought the confession that the Ferret had done business with Gupta over a period of more than a year.

"All right," Johnny said to him. *"Out!"*

The Ferret did not need a second invitation. Once he was gone, Johnny identified himself, and the babu's trembling became more violent.

"I'm curious to see how much you've been making," Johnny went to the desk, pushed Gupta aside and wrenched open the drawer. It was full of currency—at least four thousand dollars in American bills plus smaller amounts in British, German and Japanese notes.

"I can see now why you weren't keen on moving to Calcutta," Johnny said.

"Upon my word, sir, those are party funds. I can account for every penny."

"Then you won't object if we examine your financial records."

"I am entirely at your disposal, sir. But my records are kept in Sanskrit. Perhaps you have studied the language?" The Babu displayed a gleaming row of teeth.

"Barry—" Johnny turned to Flynn. "Start clearing out those files, will you?"

"What'll we put them in?"

"That will do for a start." Johnny indicated the most expensive of the oriental rugs.

"You're making a very great mistake," Gupta protested, in high agitation. "Such behavior is not tolerated in London. All my activities have the approval of the very highest authority."

"Indeed? And who might that be?"

"I have had tea with Mr. Pollitt," Gupta said triumphantly.

"I don't doubt it." Johnny called Smollett's private number.

"Yes?"

"You were right. He's turned the place into an opium den. I'd say he's been pocketing five thousand a year."

Smollett didn't waste any time. He issued instructions that wound up

the affair the same night. Gupta was bound and gagged and driven to Harwich by Flynn in the back of a van. Smollett's agents were waiting at the harbor. They chloroformed the Indian, nailed him inside a packing crate and stowed him on board a freighter bound for Leningrad, via Antwerp.

"I'd like to see his face when he gets to the other end," Smollett remarked to Johnny afterwards.

The episode deepened Johnny's skepticism about his assignment. Everywhere he turned, he found the British Communist movement suppurating with corruption and betrayal. Activists like Flynn, willing to take risks without thought of personal gain, were exceptions. There might be few men as venal as Ved Gupta in Pollitt's crowd, but there were even fewer revolutionaries.

4

"I'M GLAD to be able to repay a favor," Smollett told him. "I've got good news for you."

"You mean I've been recalled?"

"What are you thinking of? No, your woman's coming."

It was Sigrid's face that leaped into his mind, so vivid that his own features lit up. The light was gone the next instant.

It's Helene who is coming, he realized. Max is passing her back to me —and his OGPU friends in London.

He said, "When?"

"Thursday. She's coming on the night-boat from Antwerp. You don't look exactly overjoyed. Found a new one, did you?"

Johnny's eyelids narrowed.

"It's none of my business, I know," the Russian backed off. "Good luck all the same."

CECIL HITCHCOCK, the elderly thespian who presided over the boarding house in Richmond, expressed mild dismay at the news that his foreign lodger was about to acquire a roommate whom Johnny described evasively as "his fiancée from the Continent." It was not clear whether Mr. Hitchcock disapproved because the couple were unmarried or simply because the new lodger was to be a woman. Whatever its source, his disapprobation evaporated within an hour of Helene's arrival. He waxed rhapsodic over her accent and her clothes—she appeared in a close-fitted suit with puff shoulders and a hat that dipped low across her forehead—and made her promise to take part in the musical soirees he held in his own apartment "for the pleasure of a few very discriminating friends."

They walked in the park that afternoon. Across the greensward a herd of royal deer kept pace with them.

Helene stretched out her hand to him, and he took it. Her skin was cool and dry.

"Sigrid told me everything," she said, not looking at him. "I expect you know that."

"As a matter of fact, I didn't."

"You might have told me first."

"I was going to—"

"I would have thought you owed me that much. We've shared a few things together, you and I."

"I never asked you about your lovers."

"This is different."

He did not contradict her. He watched her throat move as she swallowed. She was trying to bring herself to some kind of resolution.

After a long silence, she said, "We'll go on as before. We both have work to do, responsibilities. But you must promise me that it's over with Sigrid."

"It's not over. I'm in love with her."

"Then you're making a fool of yourself!" she burst out. She turned her face to the deer and he thought that she might be on the edge of tears. It struck him that he had never seen her cry.

He felt a surge of consuming tenderness towards this woman who had always seemed so utterly in command.

"Sweetheart—" he put his arms around her. "I've never meant to hurt you."

"It's not *me* who'll be hurt!" she flew at him.

He steeled himself for the rest—the impassioned, protective speech about the child sister he had seduced and exposed to danger. He was not prepared for what she said next.

"*You're* the one who will suffer!"

She had the sun behind her, and he had to squint to look at her. Her eyes were very deep, but clouded.

"You can't mean what you're saying," he said gently. "Sigrid feels for me the way I feel for her."

"What do you know about her? That she's a pretty girl who came alive in bed with you like a night flower? That she has dreams? You don't know her, Johnny. She doesn't know herself yet. Neither of you can possess what you imagine you see. Bring her into your life, and you'll find you're living with a different woman—one you never wanted, one who doesn't belong to you at all."

She stopped to pick a late foxglove and crushed it between her fingers.

When Johnny tried to argue with her, she smiled bravely and took his arm.

"You'll choose your own course," she said. "I knew that in Berlin. I wanted to warn you, all the same. But I promise not to repeat myself. Now I'd like you to show me the inside of an English pub."

ANOTHER warning from Helene—a warning of a different kind—brought an end to Johnny's stay in England.

Mr. Hitchcock had given them tickets to the Richmond Theatre for a performance of Bernard Shaw's *Candida.*

"You absolutely *have* to go," Mr. Hitchcock said. "My friend is in the third act. No excuses, now!"

They agreed to meet at the theater. Helene was coming back from Cambridge, where Johnny suspected she was servicing an agent for Kagan, the chief of the OGPU in London. She was as tight-lipped as ever about her own work, but Johnny was intrigued by the idea that Soviet intelligence had found an entrée to the privileged world of Oxbridge.

When they dimmed the lights, Johnny was still waiting. He took his seat and tried to concentrate on the play. Halfway through, one of the characters quoted La Rochefoucauld: "There are convenient marriages but no delightful ones."

It was a fair summation of the years they had spent together, Johnny thought. But perhaps not entirely fair. He had known passion with Helene and later the steady warmth of comradeship. But never full trust, and never the dizzying fusion of spirits he had discovered with Sigrid, when all senses were joined in a single shaft of light.

His mind returned to the conversation he had had with Barry Flynn earlier in the day. If Flynn was right, they were about to make a major breakthrough. Flynn had struck up acquaintance with a Royal Navy lieutenant in a Portsmouth pub. The man expressed socialist leanings and lusted after women and racehorses—and was chronically short of cash because of both these fixations. According to Flynn, the lieutenant was willing to talent spot and to provide information, which could be valuable, since he was an expert on torpedoes. In return for a small advance he had supplied a specimen blueprint that excited Smollett. The lieutenant had already been awarded a code name: "Fisher."

There was one catch. Though Flynn claimed he had played it all close to his chest, never letting on who Fisher would be working for, the lieutenant had come right out and said he wanted to "deal directly with the Russians."

It's a trap, said one voice in Johnny's head.

Let's run with it, said another.

He had more or less decided to take the gamble. He had authorized Flynn to set up a meeting with Fisher in Portsmouth in the morning. He would take the early train.

When the curtain came down for the interval, Johnny lingered inside the theater. He stood up to let a couple pass. Then he felt a light tug on his sleeve.

"Have you given up smoking?" Helene teased him.

He rose and followed her out. She skirted the crush at the bar and went out into the night air.

"Are you enjoying the play?"

"So-so. I haven't seen Hitchcock's friend yet."

"Fine. Then let's go and find something to eat. My tummy's rumbling and we need to talk."

They found a chophouse, and Helene ordered the biggest steak on the menu.

"You're going to Portsmouth. Am I right?"

"How did you know?" The meeting had only been set up that morning. "Or should I ask, how did Kagan find out?"

"Doesn't matter." She tore into her steak and went on talking with her mouth full. "You mustn't go. You've been set up."

"You mean the man in Portsmouth is a plant."

"No, that's not it. One of your friends in the party tipped off the police. You've made powerful enemies."

"Who are you talking about? Not Flynn? George Mikes? Pollitt?"

She shook her head. "I don't know any names. Someone high up. Someone who's out to destroy you."

It could be Pollitt, Johnny thought. The last report I sent stripped the son of a bitch naked. Or someone who's got his nose out of joint because of the Gupta affair. Hell, I wouldn't put it past any of them.

Helene's plate was clean. She speared some potatoes from his and tossed off a glass of claret. Danger always enlarged her appetites.

THEY COLLECTED their bags and moved to the flat in Poplar that Johnny used for his training courses. Fortunately, Mr. Hitchcock was engrossed in one of his cultural evenings. By the time he emerged in his caftan, they were already boarding a taxi.

Johnny tried repeatedly to reach Flynn from a public telephone box down the street. There was no answer. He called Smollett, who said he would try to get a message through and told him to phone again in the morning.

The pubs had just opened the following day, when Johnny heard Smollett say, "Your information was correct."

"What happened?"

"The police got both of them. You know the procedure."

They followed Ved Gupta's path to Leningrad, minus the chloroform and the packing crate. Three days later, they stood in the bow of the steamer, as the storied battlements of the Fortress of Peter and Paul hove into view.

Helene raised her glass and said, "Home!"

5

THERE were beggars on the slow train from Leningrad and droves of them at the station. Even in Moscow people looked grey and half starved, shuffling to work under giant images of Stalin and triumphal banners proclaiming the successes of the Five-Year Plan. There were disturbing rumors from outlying areas—stories that in the fertile Ukraine, the peasants' seed grain was being stolen from them by security troops so it could be sold abroad, that millions had been condemned to die of starvation in the midst of plenty.

"Is it true?" Johnny asked Jacob, his friend from the Fourth Department, when they met for lunch at the Hotel Lux.

"It's all been blown out of proportion by Western propaganda," Jacob responded. "Besides, you don't see anyone going hungry here, do you?"

Johnny glanced around at the crowded tables. The Lux had become a miniature League of Nations, packed with Comintern guests from Peru to Indochina and delegations of favored trade unionists and literati from the West. There were no shortages at the Lux—and no mention of famine on the radio or in the newspapers, which were full of breathless accounts of the horrendous plans for economic sabotage concocted by six British contract engineers who had been arrested as spies.

Johnny had other things to preoccupy him. He had completed his final report to the Comintern on his activities in Britain, and he had not pulled any punches. He accused a member of the national executive of the British Communist Party of betraying him to the police. He had even speculated that Pollitt may have personally authorized this treachery in return for Johnny's attacks on his leadership.

Johnny did not have to wait long for the Comintern's response. He received the summons from Piatnitsky two days later.

He found the chief of the Orgbureau in a new office, smaller and untidier than before. Bulging folders tied up with string rose from the floor on all sides of his desk. Piatnitsky's skin was as pink as a child's under the mane of white hair.

He pumped Johnny's hand.

"This is one of the best reports I've ever read," he announced, waving a copy of Johnny's memorandum. "I sent a copy to the boss." He half turned his head to the full-length portrait of Stalin hanging on the wall behind him.

"Of course, we will make a full investigation," Piatnitsky pursued. "But I can't guarantee what will come of it. Britain, as you observed, is difficult territory for us. And whatever might be said against Comrade Pollitt, you can't fault him in one respect."

"Sir?"

"He has an unerring sense for which ass to lick." His eyes glided to the door, leather-padded like an old chesterfield sofa to foil possible eavesdroppers. "I think you've earned a vacation," he went on briskly. "I've given instructions that you are to be permitted to use one our villas near Livadia. The climate is perfect at this time of year."

"I'm grateful, of course, but—"

"Don't tell me. You're the kind that doesn't take holidays."

"I'd like to make a request."

"I'm listening."

"I request to be reassigned to Germany."

"Personal reasons?"

"In the sense that I'm a German." He tried to express his fears about the rise of the Hitler movement, his conviction that he could serve the party best by working to rebuild a fighting organization in his own country. He did not mention the women.

Piatnitsky heard him out and said, "I won't make any promises, except to mention this to Starik." Starik was a familiar sobriquet for General Jan Berzin, the head of the Fourth Department. "He may have something for you. But you must make me one promise."

Johnny waited.

"You'd better not go shooting your mouth off to Thälmann—or Dimitrov—the way you did to Pollitt. The boss takes a special interest in Germany."

From inside his gilded frame, Stalin smiled down on them enigmatically. The snowcapped mountains in the background seemed to elevate him to a heroic height. The pockmarks that disfigured his face had been tactfully airbrushed out.

* * *

PIATNITSKY was as good as his word. Within the week Johnny was summoned to Starik's headquarters and briefed on his new mission. The job was the one he knew best: he would serve as an adviser to the underground military arm of the German Communist Party, which had been reorganized as the Red Front Fighters' Federation, or RFKB. He was informed that he now held the rank of major in the Red Army. He noted that the man who gave him his orders wore four little diamond-studded stars on his collar. The days when Bolshevik commanders wore no badge of rank except the red star of the revolution had long passed.

"You be careful," Helene said to him through the train window, as the conductors ran along the platform, slamming doors. "I won't be there to look out for you this time. Here—" she reached up and passed him a coat with a fur collar, something of her own. "Give this to Sigi. You won't always be there to keep her warm."

As the great wheels of the locomotive started to turn, he tried not to let Helene see what he felt: a sudden lifting of the heart, the marvelous beating of wings.

6

SIGRID carried out her threat. On the day she joined the Communist party she destroyed her paintings, all the ones that were personal to her. The slashes across the canvas were self-inflicted wounds.

They had been living together for almost a month. They had an apartment to themselves in the Neukölln district—two rooms and a kitchen, which Johnny paid for out of operational funds.

He had had to renew his courtship. The first time she had set eyes on him, she had seemed to glow. But she had held back. Why? And why hadn't she replied to his last letters? Was there another man?

"You'll leave me again," she told him. "You'll always be leaving. Helene warned me of that. It would be death by a thousand cuts, each one deeper."

He made promises, argued, implored. When she consented to make love in the cold hollow of the morning, an hour before dawn, she held her body in check, forcing him to use her like a mannequin.

They reached a watershed on Yom Kippur, the Jewish Day of Atonement. He had gone round to see her at the Palace Café, where she continued to work, and found Sigrid and most of the customers out in the middle of the street.

"It's Herr Silbermann's shop," Sigrid said to him, pointing. "We have to do something, Johnny. The family is upstairs."

Half a dozen Brownshirts were gathered outside a secondhand furniture store. They had smashed in the windows and were allowing casual looters to climb in and out, taking what they pleased. They had daubed swastikas and anti-Jewish slogans on the door. There was not a policeman to be seen, and the large crowd of spectators was impassive.

"Come out of your rats' nest!" the Brownshirt leader bellowed up at the windows above the street. "Come down before we burn you out!"

Johnny saw scared faces peeking out from behind the curtains—faces of children and a man with a heavy beard. The Silbermanns had spent the holy day fasting and in prayers and were assembled for the solemn meal that would be served when the sun went down.

Johnny thought quickly. He could use the telephone in the restaurant to summon help, but there was no telling what would transpire before it arrived. If he tried to step in by himself, he risked being beaten and searched. But he had no compromising documents on his person, except for the scrap of rice paper in the ticket pocket of his trousers that contained several clandestine addresses. And he was armed. He also had one useful item of camouflage: the badge of the Stahlhelm, the militia of the right-wing National Party, under his lapel. It had proved useful in one unexpected encounter with the Berlin police. Perhaps it would help him here.

He moved closer to the back of the crowd around the furniture store. One of the Brownshirts had a bottle bomb. He waved it aloft, with matches in the other hand, threatening to light the wick. Johnny could feel Sigrid's eyes burning into his face.

He stepped forward and said to the SA leader, "Haven't you taught those Yids enough of a lesson?"

"What's it to you?" The tough rounded on him suspiciously.

Johnny flipped back his lapel to show the Stahlhelm badge.

"Just like you shitheads," the Brownshirt spat. "Not man enough to show your colors." He slapped his armband and puffed out his chest.

Johnny moved closer and said in a confidential tone, "Why don't you take care of that shyster Lifshitz, the pawnbroker? I owe him money." He added a fictitious address to the made-up name.

The SA leader roared with laughter and thwacked his rubber truncheon against his leg.

"We'll see about Lifsheiss later," he promised. "I want to finish with these ones first. They've got plenty to atone for. Go on, Fritz!"

Johnny saw the flash as the match was struck and raised to the fuse, the Brownshirt's arm sloping upwards and back. He reached for his Mauser.

"Look out, he's got a gun!" someone yelled.

As Johnny squeezed the trigger, the troop leader's truncheon crashed down on his forearm. The shot went wide, and the gun tumbled from his limp fingers onto the road. At the same instant, the bottle bomb exploded inside Silbermann's store. A sheet of flame swallowed the looters' debris like dry kindling. A child's high, plaintive scream carried from the floor above.

Johnny drove his foot into the troop leader's groin. The man shrieked and was lost from sight as the others flung themselves at Johnny. He dived for the gun, rolling sideways to avoid the first rabbit punch angled at his neck. A jackbooted foot swung at his kidneys, and the pain lanced through his body.

Through the tumult he heard Sigrid's voice, keen and accusing: "Are you men? Are any of you Germans? Are you going to let those poor people burn to death?"

They were hammering at his back with fists and feet, but he kept rolling and weaving. He got one of them by the leg and pulled him down. Then his hand closed on the butt of his pistol. One of the Brownshirts took a running jump and came down hard on top of Johnny, flattening him under his weight. Gasping for air, Johnny tried to wriggle free. But someone had got his head in a vise. They had him.

"Johnny!" It was her voice again. It seemed very distant. He couldn't breathe. Everything around him was shaded red and black, pulsing like the coals of a ship's furnace.

She came whirling into the mass of human flesh that bore down on him, raking with her nails and a kitchen knife that must have come from the café. Taken off guard, the Brownshirt who was trying to break Johnny's neck released his grip.

In that moment of grace, Johnny rallied his last reserves. He lashed out with the snout of his gun. He heard a hoarse yelp, and the weight on his back was gone. In the next instant he was on his feet, ready to open fire.

But something almost miraculous was happening. Shamed by the girl's courage, men were coming out of the crowd in twos and threes and attacking the Brownshirts with their fists. The SA men were already outnumbered by better than two to one. Johnny looked at the Brownshirt leader. He had a gun, too. He had also weighed the odds, and found them unsatisfactory.

"I'll remember you," he promised Johnny. "You better not show your mug round here any more."

He and his toughs straggled away. Half a block on, they launched into a marching song.

"Thank you," Johnny took Sigrid by the shoulders and kissed her cheek. Her blouse was in shreds, and she had a welt along the side of her neck.

He handed her the Mauser. "Here. You stand watch. Remember, the safety is off."

"With you, the safety is never on," she said, with a brave attempt at humor.

He covered his nose and mouth with a handkerchief and rushed into Silbermann's store.

The smoke was worse than the fire. He fought it all the way up the stairs, groping at the bannister until the railing collapsed under his touch.

He found the Silbermann family in a prayer circle in the sitting room.

He announced, "I'm going to take you out of this."

"THE UNEXPECTED things decide your fate," Sigrid said afterwards. "Or perhaps the unexpected *is* fate. Like shooting over a crossroads at night in a car traveling at high speed, without knowing it was possible to go a different way until the chance is gone."

She moved into Johnny's apartment in Neukölln the same night. The choice was made for her by events. The Brownshirts knew her face, and the manager of the Palace Café, who was not to be relied on, could give them her name. Out of concern for the Silbermanns, who meant nothing to her except a kindly old man who occasionally bade her good morning and a brace of children who were never allowed to play in the street—and the sense of shared humanity—she had committed herself. Not yet to the party, but to a life in hiding. *His* life.

Johnny refused to let her go back to the restaurant or her previous lodgings. He sent a messenger to collect her things and settle up with the landlady. She found she had to adjust to the routine of a nocturnal animal. Johnny came and went at all hours, and house guests appeared without warning to camp out on the twin mattresses in the spare room. Their faces sometimes frightened her: the faces of men who had burned their bridges. She sketched them in secret, until she had a collection worthy of Hieronymous Bosch.

The central figure was missing. She realized that only when he arrived at their doorstep.

Johnny was away. He had told her not to wait up; he would not be back until morning, perhaps not for another day. This was what she had expected, and she knew it had nothing to do with other women. His overnight absences, and the night callers, were already familiar.

But this caller was different. In the half light from above, the face was a death mask, with great hollows of darkness under the eyebrows and the flaring cheekbones. Unlike the others, he didn't bother with a *Parole,* a password; Johnny made her memorize a new one every few days.

He merely said, "You are Sigrid. You do not resemble your sister." The words, oddly grammatical, were delivered in a voice she judged to be foreign not because of any identifiable accent, but because of the utter absence of one.

"What are you looking at? Are you going to let me in?"

"Wh-who are you?" she stammered.

"I am a friend of your sister. Also of Johnny. My name is Max. Perhaps he mentioned me?"

"No—I don't think so." Johnny had said little about his secret work for the party, but he had talked a great deal about a boyhood friend, a sailor from Hamburg with a lust for life who had fought with him on the barricades. She remembered Johnny's disappointment when he had found that his friend was not in Berlin and could not be reached immediately. She was sure this vaguely menacing stranger could not be the same man. She said, "Is Johnny expecting you?"

"I wanted to surprise him."

He moved forward into the light, and she saw his eyes. They seemed to reach out and touch her.

She wanted to close the door in his face. She couldn't do it. She was frightened, but fascinated too. She sensed she was in the presence of a tremendous power, a concentrated force of will.

"Johnny's not here," she said, too sharply. "I'll give him a message if you like."

"I don't wish to trouble you. I'll wait for him."

The security chain was still in place. She touched it with her hand, making sure. She felt he was watching her fingers, mocking her caution, though his eyes never traveled from her face.

"It would be pleasant to talk about Helene," Max suggested. "I saw her only a few days ago. In fact, she gave me a letter for you."

He plucked it from the folds of his coat and held it up, so she could see the handwriting on the envelope. It was Helene's.

Sigrid released the chain and drew back the door.

MAX LAY on the sofa, chain-smoking and drinking Johnny's whisky. Sigrid perched on the edge of the armchair, putting records on the Victrola when he asked for them. She had brought a boxful with her when she moved in. They were mostly classical, which suited Max. His tastes were operatic. Their conversation was now accompanied by the third act of *Aida*.

It was less a conversation, she realized, than an interrogation.

The style of the questioning was casual, even languid. But the flow was unremitting.

Which of Johnny's friends did she know?

Did Johnny talk about his work for the party?

Had he ever mentioned Heinz Kordt?

Did she take an interest in politics? What about her parents?

Helene's letter said that Max should be treated as one of the family and that his instructions were to be obeyed without question. Max must therefore be a general in the shadow army in which her lover and her sister were enrolled.

She tried to carry out Helene's wishes. She answered Max's questions, played him records and, when he said he was hungry, went out to the kitchen and cooked eggs and sausage.

The first time she rebelled was when he asked if she would show him her pictures.

She said, "I'd rather not."

She had been working on a portrait of Johnny, a surprise for his birthday. It showed him in a sailor's blue jacket with the sea behind him.

"Why not? I've heard you have an exceptional talent."

"I'd rather not, that's all." How could she explain? There was something of the artist in this man, who understood music and quoted Goethe and Heine in between the questions. Yet her whole spirit revolted at the idea of admitting him to the private world of her art, as if she would be letting in something that would blot out the sun.

"I'll relent on one condition," Max announced.

"Which is?"

"That you draw *me.*"

The eyes were the hardest part. The pencil could not translate the intensity of that stare. But she persevered until she had a certain likeness. She puzzled over it for a time. It reminded her of someone else. Who was it?

Of course.

She scribbled a couplet from Goethe across the bottom and handed him the sketch.

"You've caught something—" He paused over the words, then recited them out loud with his eyes closed:

> When I shall introduce you at this revel,
> Will you appear as sorcerer—or devil?

Max threw back his head and laughed. "Faust to Mephistopheles!" he exclaimed.

"My dear Sigrid, I'm flattered!"

* * *

By 2:00 A.M., she could hardly keep her eyes open.

"Do you mind if I go to bed?"

"Not at all. Would you like some company?" His tongue flicked lightly at the corner of his mouth.

"I'm afraid I'm a reactionary," she responded, making light of it. "My natural proclivity is towards monogamy. Anyway, I'm too tired."

It was another little test, she realized. He was probing her, not pursuing something he particularly wanted.

When he bent to kiss her hand before she retired, his lips never grazed the skin.

She woke to the murmur of voices from the living room.

She threw back the shutters. The sun had not yet risen, though the sky to the east, where it was visible between the squat workers' tenements, was salmon pink.

She slipped out of bed and crouched by the door, trying to make out what the two men were saying.

"I would trust her with my life." That was Johnny. He sounded wounded and angry.

"You are a fool. You are risking everything."

"For God's sake, Max. She's Helene's sister."

"But you're not with Helene. And I am not asking you why. That is immaterial. What matters is the girl is not even a party member."

"She's been doing work for Münzenberg's operation. She did the art-work for that new poster that's all over Berlin."

"You are evading the issue," Max went on, implacable. "You are putting men's lives in danger."

"What men?"

"You and me. The others who have been here. Who knows the whole list? Who knows how much you let slip in the course of this—infatuation?"

"You don't understand."

"On the contrary. I understand only too well."

Sigrid wrapped herself in the fur-trimmed coat Helene had sent from Russia and burst into the front room.

"If you have something to say about me—" she challenged Max Fabri-kant "—then say it to my face."

"You see?" Max turned to Johnny. "She's spirited. Too spirited to run without guiding reins."

"Sigrid—darling—" Johnny moved to hold her, but she stepped around him and pushed up against Max. There was barely a wrinkle in his suit, though he had been lying on the sofa all night long. But a blue-black shadow rose from his jawline all the way to the cheekbones.

"What do you want of us?" she demanded.

"I'm sorry we disturbed your rest," Max responded. "That was thoughtless."

"What do you want?" she repeated.

"You must ask Johnny. He knows well enough." Max ground a cigarette into the ashtray. "For the moment, you will please get dressed and leave. There are private matters we have to discuss."

She was stunned by this sudden brutality. What right did this intruder have to order her out of her own home?

"It's not necessary," Johnny said to Max. "We can go to Müller's place. It's safe enough, and they'll make you a decent breakfast. Sweetheart, why don't you go back to bed and get some sleep?"

"I'm up," she said coldly. "And I want some fresh air."

WHEN SHE came back, Johnny was alone, and he was so gentle and so patient with her that she knew something terrible had happened.

He let her exhaust her complaints about Max's behavior before he said, "They want you to join the party. It's not at all a complicated business, if you agree to do it. You'll be interviewed, of course, but that's just a formality."

He said this matter-of-factly, as if it was a question of catching the right bus. But she could see the anxiety in his face.

She said, "He gave you an order, didn't he?"

"A very direct order," Johnny said quietly.

"For God's sake, what right does that man have to come into our home and tell us how to live? How can he order you to tell *me* what to do? Does he think I'm your property? What right—"

"He has every right," Johnny interrupted her. His tone was soft yet firm. "Listen to me, Sigrid. Max is an extraordinary man, perhaps the most extraordinary man I know."

"He's a spy, isn't he?"

"He is a Soviet officer. It is his duty to guard our secrets. From traitors and from—carelessness. The lives of hundreds, perhaps thousands, of men and women depend on him. In the pursuit of his duty, he is totally honest and absolutely ruthless. In all the years I have known him, I have never known him to do anything for trivial or selfish reasons."

"Am I under suspicion? Does he think I'm a police informer?"

"No, of course not. He knows you belong on our side. But you're not fully committed. Suppose I told you that I am a major in the Red Army?

Suppose I told you that the men who were here the night before last have been smuggling Belgian rifles into Germany so we can fight the Fascists?"

"Do you think I'd betray you?" she came back fiercely. "Do you think I'd love you any less?"

"I know you wouldn't. But to be involved in secret work requires training and discipline. If you are going to share my life, you will have to share the discipline that makes it possible. That's why Max is right. I suppose I recognized that from the day I fell in love with you. I just wanted to postpone the day when you would have to make your choice. I've been ordered to bring you into the party—"

"And if I refuse?"

She sat clutching her knees. He lay his hands over hers, covering them. He said, "Then I am ordered to leave you." He bent and kissed both her hands. "It is your choice," he pursued. "I can't make it for you. I love you more than my life. But if you refuse, I *will* leave you, because I am fighting for a cause that matters more than you or me or the happiness of any individual."

She shook herself like someone in a restless dream.

He did not try to comfort her when she got up and went padding barefoot into the kitchen, her hair tousled and wild.

There was a constant pounding above his eyes, and his tongue was swollen. It hurt him to swallow. He had spent hours wrangling with the organizers of the Red Front Fighters' Federation before he came home to face Max. A rapid inspection of the party's combat units in Berlin and the south had persuaded him that the sanguine reports Willi Leov, the front's burly president, had been sending to Moscow were lies—more deadly lies than Pollitt's. Leov told Moscow what he thought would reflect credit on himself, leaving Johnny with the task of trying to turn a paper army into a real one.

The burden that weighed on his shoulders seemed crushing. But he must not—would not—stumble under it. There were a few of them, only a few, who had the courage and the stamina to overcome the morass of cynical accommodation and appeasement that threatened to engulf the party and deliver Germany to Hitler. Max was one of them. Heinz was another— God, how he yearned to see Heinz, to be with a man who had never run from a battle! Heinz would have known what to say to Sigrid.

Because they were so few in number, they had to demand vastly more of themselves than other men. That was the penalty for belonging to their order—and the reward. That was why Max was right.

If only Sigi could understand . . .

He leaned back against the arm of the sofa, resting his eyes.

*   *   *

HE WOKE with a start and had no idea whether he had been asleep for two minutes or twenty. In his dream Putzi, the cat he had played with as a boy, was raking its claws up and down the arm of his mother's prize sofa, lacerating the crewel upholstery.

The sound of scratching was coming from the bedroom.

Then he remembered the letter and rushed to the door.

She was standing in the middle of the room. In her hand was the chopping knife she had used on the Brownshirts outside Silbermann's store. At her feet were her paintings, hacked to shreds. His own left eye stared back at him from a flapping strip of canvas. At one side he recognized a fragment of Sigrid's portrait of her sister, rigged out in a silk hat and a man's tailcoat like the heroine of a Dietrich film.

Sigrid's face was flushed, her hair spilling over her eyes.

Her chest heaved as she turned to confront him.

She said, "I'm ready now."

1

SHE joined more than the party, and did so with her eyes open. Already the keeper of a safe house, she became a courier for the underground, ferrying messages around the city on a bicycle, servicing dead-drops. She took to wearing a knife on these missions—not a kitchen utensil now but a switchblade, something worthy of a backstreet hoodlum—taped to her leg under her long skirt. Three nights a week, she went to a special school for members of the *Apparat*. They taught her ideology, and they taught her how to kill with her bare hands. The rare nights she and Johnny were at home alone together, she immersed herself in the same books he had struggled with years before, when he was still a novice burning to unlock the secret of history.

Johnny was proud of her; yet the cold frenzy that began to possess her troubled him. He recalled the strange words of warning Helene had used in England. The night she spurned his advances in favor of an unfinished chapter of Lenin, he asked himself whether in winning her to his cause he had not already begun to lose her.

That's nonsense, he thought. I can't be jealous of what I have made her.

And a hour later, when she crept into his arms, sleepy but loving, he told himself Helene was wrong. Sigrid was his, more completely than before. They had lost nothing; they had added a new dimension.

*   *   *

JOHNNY went to Hamburg to report on the reorganization of the party's combat units and found the man he most needed to see.

The newspapers were full of the results of the latest elections. Hitler had stumbled. The Nazis had lost two million votes, compared with the last elections. The Communists had gained ground. Thälmann and the party's propaganda machine trumpeted the news that six million Germans had voted Communist. They boomed out a new slogan: "Hitler's ship is sinking!" They did not dwell on the fact that while the party's strength had increased, it had still attracted only half as many votes as the Nazis.

"Some victory!" Kordt snorted.

They walked by the Alster Pavilion in the tawny afternoon light. It was the perfect hour for discreet liaisons. Courting couples twittered along the railings, their conversations masked by the Viennese waltzes that echoed from the bandstand inside the pavilion.

Heinz had suggested this meeting place. They strolled along the smart promenade to the Binnen-Alster and stood side by side watching the swans and the little screw steamers bobbing on the water. Twenty paces behind, Karl Vogel, the young tough Johnny remembered from Berlin, slouched along with his hands in his pockets.

"Do you always go around with a bodyguard?" Johnny asked.

"Always. And I never spend two nights in the same bed. Lucky for me, there are plenty of friendly beds in Hamburg."

He slapped Johnny on the shoulder. "You needn't look like a dog just pissed on your foot. I still know how to look after myself. You're the one who should worry. It's not smart to be seen with me."

"Don't be silly."

"Haven't they told you?" Heinz looked at him quizzically. "They called a special leadership meeting to discuss my conduct."

"Why?"

"I'm a fighter, Johnny. You know that. I judge men by whether I can count on them if I get cornered, not by the smell of their aftershave. I've built the best anti-Nazi fighting group in the country. You know what the others are like. Tell me I'm wrong. What the bosses don't like is, I'll give a lad a gun even if he can't tell Uncle Joe Stalin from a boiled potato— as long as he's ready to use it on a Nazi."

"What happened?"

"I wasn't supposed to be at the meeting, but I got wind of it and went along anyway. I reckoned nobody else would say much on my behalf. Emil Brandt was leading the pack. He was halfway through his spiel when I got there—and the sight of my mug fairly took the wind out of him, I can tell you. But he pulled himself together again. He called my boys adventurists, terrorists and provocateurs—and half a dozen other things I can't remember. Claimed I was consorting with anarchists and known Trotskyites. I think they were fixing to throw me out of the party, but they didn't dare, not with me staring them in the face. They said there's going to be an inquiry."

"Emil Brandt. I can't believe it. He used to be my instructor."

"They gave him a pretty good working-over in Moscow. Weren't you the one who told me about it? Now he sings whatever music they're handing out."

"Are you saying that Emil was speaking for Moscow?"

"Oh, I used to tell myself the problem was Thälmann and all our pocket Stalins in Berlin. I didn't understand very much in those days, Johnny. You now, you've become a world traveler. You must know all about it. Did you ever meet Neumann?"

Johnny remembered an arrogant, opinionated party leader, the son of a grain millionaire, who treated girl secretaries as if he had the droit du seigneur. He had instantly disliked Neumann as a man but knew that, like Heinz, he believed in fighting the Nazis with any weapon that came to hand.

"Neumann thought everything would be put right if he explained the situation to Stalin. He said it was all a problem of Stalin getting the wrong advice from Berlin. So Neumann went to Moscow. He told Stalin we have to join up with the Social Democrats—the devil if necessary—and break Hitler before he breaks us. Stalin knew better. You know what he told Neumann? He said he doesn't believe Hitler will take power but, if he does, it won't matter because Hitler will spend all his time fighting with Britain and France. The way I look at it, if Stalin *wanted* Hitler in power, he couldn't do much more to help him get in."

It's not possible, Johnny told himself.

But looking out across the water, he felt momentarily dizzy. The solid row of buildings on the far side seemed to sway like a pasteboard facade. His surroundings seemed utterly insubstantial.

If Heinz is right, he thought, my whole life has been wasted.

The cynicism and corruption he had found among local party leaders from London to Berlin; the waste of lives in failed insurrections from Hamburg to Shanghai; the famine in the Ukraine; the flight of Trotsky from Russia—all of that could be explained and subsumed in a larger perspective. None of it touched the core of his revolutionary faith. But the idea that Stalin, the leader of world communism, might *knowingly* collaborate with Hitler . . .

"It's monstrous," he said. "It's a lie."

What he might have said—but was unwilling to face—was that if it were true, he had been living for a lie. And had just committed the woman he loved to the same lie.

He wrestled with his friend for a while, until Kordt squeezed his arm and said, "Don't let's waste all our time arguing. You and I have got serious drinking to do. You'll come to see it my way, I'll bet on it. We can't trust the Russians. Whatever chance we've got depends on fellows like you and me, punch-drunk fighters who care about Germany and don't give a shit about the odds. *Die verlorenen Haufen.* The Lost Band. If some smartass had said this to me ten years ago, even five, I would have punched him in the throat. But we'll have to choose whether we're German Communists or Russian Communists. And if we wait too long, the Austrian corporal will choose for us—whether we go to the headsman or the hangman."

8

"JOHNNY!" Sigrid shook him again. "There's someone at the door."

He snapped awake, sprang from the bed and groped for his trousers and the Mauser under his pillow. He prised open the window and peered down over the fire escape. As far as he could see down into the well of shadow, that way was clear.

"Get dressed," he told her. "If there's any trouble, don't hesitate. Take the fire escape."

He went to the door.

"Who's there?"

"Heinrich Himmler."

He knew that voice, edged with irony, vaguely foreign but without any identifiable accent.

He opened the door, and Max Fabrikant swept into the room. He looked as if he had just come from a job, with his collar turned up and his hat rammed down over his eyes. He had a bodyguard with him, who was told to wait outside.

Max inspected the flat. He went into the bedroom and stared at Sigrid, who was buttoning her blouse. He said, "You wait outside, too."

"For God's sake, Max." Johnny protested. "It's past three in the morning."

But Sigrid said, "I'm used to it," and wrapped herself in her camel-hair coat.

"I'm sorry to disturb your love nest again," Max said, when she was gone. He flung himself full length on the sofa without bothering to take off his hat or coat. He lit up a cigarette while Johnny poured whisky.

"They don't care what time it is in Berlin," Max went on, leaving Johnny

to guess that he was referring to his controllers at the center. "I've got instructions that have to be acted on immediately. They involve you."

Johnny's eyes moved to the door, and Max followed them. "Don't worry," Fabrikant said. "You can leave her out of this. It's about our friend Heinz."

"What about him?"

"The center has received information that he is a police spy, a provocateur."

"That's a lie!" Johnny erupted. "Heinz risks his life every night, fighting the Hitler movement."

"Also that Kordt is associating with known Trotskyites and other enemies of the party." Max had adopted the impersonal manner of a court official reading from a charge sheet. "Also that he was responsible for the arrest of two of our most valuable agents."

"Who's putting out this crap? You know what it's worth."

Max exhaled and watched the smoke circles waft toward the ceiling. "Perhaps you should ask Emil Brandt."

"Emil? What has he got to say about it?" Johnny resolved not to say anything that would reflect his conversation with Heinz, barely a week before.

"It's my understanding that Brandt made the denunciation."

The sniveling bastard, Johnny swore inwardly. The irony of the fact that he had once tried to shield Emil from Max's colleagues in Moscow chafed at him. Emil had sacrificed his beliefs and become a sideshow performer, ready with a song-and-dance routine for any occasion.

"Did *you* put Emil up to this?" Johnny suddenly challenged Max.

The spymaster remained unruffled. He said, "I'm sorry to disappoint you. I had nothing to do with it."

"Then why is Emil spreading these lies?"

"Perhaps he is still trying to prove his own loyalty. I seem to recall that the most vigorous members of the Spanish Inquisition had Jewish blood in their veins."

"It's indecent!" Johnny exploded.

"Do you understand the nature of belief? I wonder." Max closed his eyes, and in the long pause that followed Johnny started to wonder whether he had dropped off to sleep. The ash on his cigarette reached his fingertips, and he let the burning stub fall to the floor.

Johnny got up and stamped it out. There was a sour odor of combustion as Max went on. "The medieval inquisitors had a manual called the *Malleus Maleficarum,* the Hammer of Witches. Perhaps you have heard of it? No? Well, it is written there that some of the crimes attributed to witches are real and many are illusions. However, the illusions are created by the devil at the behest of the witches. So even if the witch's crimes are illusions, the witch is guilty nonetheless."

"Is that what chekists are taught?" Johnny asked, shocked and astonished. He remembered the rumor that Max, like Stalin, had once studied in a religious seminary.

"I warned you once before that Heinz makes too much commotion. Emil isn't the only one who has reported against him. Heinz insults Thälmann and Ulbricht to their faces and bitches all the time about the party line. Someone was bound to report sooner or later that he is attacking Stalin. Stalin *is* the party line. Furthermore, Kordt has gone on the rampage. He launches madcap forays and gets good men shot. He's got waterfront scum, petty criminals, anarchists, even Trotsky sympathizers in his organization. He's set himself up in Hamburg like a gangster in an American movie. Something has to be done. I stand corrected. Something *is* to be done."

"Yes?"

"He's been summoned to Moscow to account for his actions."

"You mean, to answer the witch finders?"

Max shrugged. "Perhaps. If he can only stop playing the fool, he'll be safe enough. He may even return stronger. He's still got friends in Moscow. Piatnitsky's one of them. There are some in my organization, too. I want you to go to Hamburg and give him his marching orders."

"Why me?"

"You're friends. He trusts you."

"He won't agree to leave Germany. Not in the middle of the fight."

"Remind him about *Parteibefehl.* Party orders. This isn't a matter for discussion."

"What if he refuses?"

"You'll report to me."

Johnny was on the morning train.

"IF I go to Moscow," Kordt said to him that night. "I know I won't be coming back."

They were in a room above the Bunte Kuh, a whores' dive in St. Pauli. Kordt was paring his nails with a long hunting knife.

"You don't have any choice," Johnny reminded him.

"I used this last night," Kordt said. He held up the knife so the reflected light from the naked bulb overhead shone in Johnny's face. "On a snitch we caught visiting the Nazis."

"They'll expel you from the party," Johnny warned.

"So let them."

"Heinz, that's only the beginning. You know people like us can't just walk away."

"What are you trying to tell me, Johnny?" He drew the tip of the knife lightly across his throat. "Is that what you mean?"

Johnny said nothing.

Kordt burst out laughing, rocking back and forth in his chair. "I know death too well," he said. "He's as close to me as you are. I can't be scared off that way. But tell Max he's welcome to try. This is my town. My people will protect me."

"People like the Baron?" Johnny had seen the man they called the Baron, a notorious pimp and dope peddler, at the bar downstairs.

"Why not? At least he's not siding with Hitler."

"If you won't follow orders," Johnny said deliberately, "then get out. Get out tonight."

"And go where? My duty is here."

Johnny gave up trying to argue with him. "At least say you'll sleep on it," he suggested.

"I have better things to do at night than sleep."

"I'll come tomorrow."

"Come if you like. My answer will be the same."

He overtook Johnny on his way to the door and embraced him. "You're still my friend," he said. "But they always send someone you trust, don't they?"

THEY WERE waiting for him at the safe house, a comfortable apartment on the Johanniswall kept by a not-so-old widow called Magda whose hospitality was legendary in certain circles. They were eating Magda's pastries, washed down with kirsch, while she flustered over them like a mother hen, apparently unconcerned that one of them, a fellow with a nose like white sausage and a neck that bulged over his collar, had his feet up on the polished rosewood dining table.

"Krichbaum," he introduced himself. He extended a hand without bothering to rearrange his feet. "This is Hirsch."

The one called Hirsch was wiry and compact. There was an unpleasant sheen about his face and clothes.

A real river rat, Johnny thought.

Hirsch contributed nothing to the conversation. Either he had nothing to say, or he didn't understand German. His hands tended to stray towards the middle button of his jacket.

Krichbaum produced his credentials. *Osobiy Otdel,* "Special Department." These two were specialists, all right; the kind of chekists who were hired to shoot men in the back of the neck.

"From Berlin?" Johnny inquired.

Krichbaum wiped the crumbs off his cheek with his thumb. "We've been sent to speed things up," he reported. "You saw Kordt?"

"Yes."

"What did he say?"

Johnny hesitated for only a second. "He said he'd give me an answer tomorrow."

"Why not tonight?" Krichbaum swung his feet off the table. "You know where he is, don't you?"

"I—I'm not sure."

"What do you mean? You were just with him."

"He moves around a lot. He never spends two nights in the same place."

If I can just hold them off for tonight, Johnny was thinking. For long enough to warn Heinz.

"Don't play games with me, smart-shitter," Krichbaum snarled at him. "You were at a whorehouse called the Bunte Kuh. You're going to take us there now."

"He just uses it for meetings. He's probably left by now."

"We'll just have to make sure, then, won't we? How many guards does he have?"

"I don't know. Three or four, maybe more."

"Well, you'll make it simple for us. They trust you. They shit at the Bunte Kuh, don't they?"

"I suppose so," Johnny replied, startled.

"Where's the john?"

He described the layout. The lavatory was on the ground floor, at the back of the stairwell.

"So we'll play it this way," Krichbaum said. "Hirsch and me, we'll take a look at the meat downstairs while you speak to Kordt. Find a reason to get him into the bathroom—tell him you've got a message, anything you like. We'll do the rest."

As Johnny stared at them, the silent one pulled out a straightedged razor, opened it and tested the edge with his thumb.

"It's a piece of cake," Krichbaum said. "Hirsch used to be a barber."

JOHNNY prayed that Kordt had left the Bunte Kuh and gone to another of his haunts. But Heinz was still there, holding court upstairs with some of the complaisant ladies of the house.

Johnny went in first. Krichbaum and Hirsch followed after a few minutes' interval, making a reasonable impersonation of drunken patrons.

Karl Vogel was squatting on the landing, his bony legs straddling the
steps. He made Johnny wait until he had checked with Kordt.

"You again?" Kordt greeted him, less friendly than before. The color in
his cheeks had come straight out of a bottle. "I told you not to waste your
breath. What is it this time?"

"Not here." He looked at the half-naked girls, one angular, the other rosy
and plump, like a pile of heaped pillows. Heinz had become omnivorous.

"Tell him to fuck off," the thin one suggested to Kordt.

But Kordt was already on his feet. "I'll come in a minute," he told the
girls, and gave the fat one a a resounding smack on the rump. *"Zuversich-
tlichst.* Most confidently."

Johnny's heart was thumping so hard that he felt sure Kordt must hear
it. He had put off considering the choice that confronted him—to betray
his friend or his superiors—in the hope that something would simply turn
up. Now that the choice was unavoidable, he chose his friend—although
he knew he might be inviting the same kind of retribution the OGPU had
planned for Heinz.

"There are two men downstairs," he told Kordt. "Chekists. I've seen
their credentials."

Kordt's eyes narrowed. "You brought them here?"

"I had no alternative. I'm supposed to get you into the men's room."

Kordt gave a dry chuckle. "This isn't that type of establishment."

"They're armed. One of them likes to use a razor."

"He does, does he?" Kordt's face brightened. He called to Karl and gave
him some whispered instructions.

"How's your bladder?" he said to Johnny. "I feel a terrible need to water
my horse."

AFTERWARDS, Johnny's mind turned on what Sigrid had said: that you
passed the major crossroads in life before you were aware of them.

He went downstairs with Kordt and made a little signal to Krichbaum,
who was quaffing beer while a tart groped around inside his fly.

There was a man in the washroom taking a long time to rinse his hands.
"Out!" Kordt ordered.

The man blinked myopically. Johnny had the fleeting impression of a
moon-round face, a watch chain stretched across a copious paunch, a pair
of gold-framed spectacles glittering on the edge of the sink.

Then the door banged open.

Hirsch came through first. Kordt saw the light on the open blade and
flung himself clear, leaving the stranger at the washbasin in the line of

attack. The man stood frozen in bewilderment or terror. At the last instant he put up his hands to protect his face.

Hirsch was unable to arrest his forward momentum. His arm came down like a javelin. The razor slipped between the fat man's fingers and sliced deep into the palm. He screamed as blood spurted in all directions, spotting Johnny's shirt.

Hirsch was cursing in Russian, ducking and circling, looking for Kordt, who had slipped behind the stalls.

Krichbaum rushed in, a silencer attached to his pistol. "He squeals like a stuck pig," he said with disgust. "Hurry up—" he addressed this to Johnny as well as Hirsch "—somebody may come."

He had his mouth open to add something, but no more words issued. His face darkened, and as he clutched at his throat, only hoarse gargling sounds came out. His eyes bulged, and his tongue swelled out between his teeth.

As Karl twisted the piano wire tighter, beads of blood erupted from Krichbaum's coarse neck, and his weapon fell to the floor.

Hirsch saw nothing of this because, as he circled the stalls, Kordt lashed out with a short length of iron bar and broke his arm. Johnny didn't turn away when he saw his friend pick up the cutthroat razor and begin to do the barber's job for him. He felt unnaturally warm but also oddly detached.

When Heinz stabbed a finger towards the weeping man at the washbasin and said, "Take care of him," Johnny didn't ask what kind of care he had in mind.

"We'll pin it on the Nazis," Kordt announced over cognac in his room. "It won't be the first time. You'll be covered."

Johnny put off thinking about whether this was true. "You're burned," he told Kordt. "Even if they never prove what happened, they'll blame it on you. And those two won't be the last ones they'll send for you."

Kordt considered this for a while. "I must admit your friend the barber has done a lot to convince me," he conceded at last.

"I'll have to report to Max tomorrow," Johnny said. "I can only delay for a few hours. You've got friends in the port. Get on a boat—any boat —and leave with the first tide."

"All right." Kordt jumped up. He stretched out a hand and then, thinking better of it, clasped Johnny in a bear hug. "But I'll be back. We'll make quite a team, you and I."

"Where will you go?"

Kordt shrugged. "Any port is home to a sailor, isn't that so? But some- where warm, I think. Maybe I'll call on Trotsky. He might be able to explain what insanity spawns people like Barber Hirsch."

9

ALL foreign legions have the same motto: March or Die, *Marschier oder Krapier.* The man who asks questions is lost. Johnny had done more than question. He had saved a life that had been claimed by the party. If his role were discovered, he would face the same fate that had been dictated for Kordt. Yet he boarded his train back to Berlin—and Max Fabrikant—without the slightest hesitation. Because of Sigrid, but not only because of her. Whatever he had done, whatever retribution might lie in store for him, he still belonged to the party. For the whole of his adult life it had been his church, his profession, his family. It was his compass. He had no direction, no purpose, without it.

In Berlin things were both better and worse than he expected. He did not have to face an immediate inquisition over Kordt's escape, because Max had left the capital on one of his mysterious errands. When Max reappeared a few days later, he seemed oddly unconcerned about the whole affair. He asked a few perfunctory questions and seemed content to accept Johnny's answers at face value. It was difficult to understand why Max was so indifferent to a case that had been a consuming obsession earlier that week. Perhaps, lacking evidence of Johnny's part in the escape, he was laying a trap. Perhaps he had larger matters on his mind.

Johnny's own mission in Germany had become impossible. He was supposed to build a fighting underground, but his local chief, Willi Leov, refused to supply him with guns or money. Young activists—the kind who had rallied to Kordt—complained that their orders were always the same: to wait. Instead of trying to mobilize the working class against Hitler, the party instructed Communist railroad workers to join with the Nazis in a strike designed to discredit the Social Democrat union bosses. The strike fizzled out after a few days, leaving a yawning chasm between the Communists and the rest of the anti-Hitler movement. Any militant who presumed to criticize these policies was reminded that he could not see "the big picture"—only Stalin knew what it was—and threatened with expulsion.

By the end of January 1933, Johnny had concluded that if the Communists had set out to install Hitler in power, they could hardly have done a better job.

"GRANDMOTHER is dead!"

In the early hours of January 30 the phrase was flashed across the country, and convoys of Brownshirts from Hamburg and Dresden, Munich and Leipzig, joined the march on Berlin. Count Helldorff, the leader of the storm troops in Berlin, rushed in and out of the Kaiserhof issuing orders. Goering waddled about in his gorgeous sky-blue uniform, his wide-cut trousers flapping like wings.

"Grandmother is dead" was the prearranged Nazi code for the seizure of power. But Hitler did not have to take power by force. He was handed it on a silver salver by the archintriguers around the president. At 11:10 A.M., Hindenburg named the man he had once reviled as "the Bohemian corporal" Chancellor of Germany. Twenty thousand storm troops turned out to ensure that nobody had second thoughts. They set the proper Wagnerian mode with a night of flaming torches.

Johnny listened to the thud of their jackboots as they marched up the Wilhelmstrasse, past the Reich Chancellery, where Hitler, flushed in triumph, took the salute. Anonymous in the crowd, borne along by its tide, he saw the torches licking at the columns of the Brandenburg Gate.

"Everything will be different!" a woman shrilled. She was pleasingly plump with a clear open face, the model German housewife.

Within twenty-four hours the phrase was blazoned in neon lights across the grand façade of the Gloria Palast, the flagship of the UFA cinema chain: EVERYTHING WILL BE DIFFERENT—ADOLF HITLER.

Johnny reeled home that night with the sinking sensation that all of Kordt's fears had taken flesh. He had a bottle with him. Sigrid said nothing when he proceeded to pour glass after glass, but he could read something beyond reproach in her eyes. Her father had used the same crutch until it had become his supporting limb. At the thought, he felt revulsion for himself but drank long after Sigrid had gone to bed, until the bottle was empty.

When he lurched into the bedroom, she lay with her eyes closed, pretending to be asleep. He rolled onto the bed and started fumbling with the straps of her nightgown.

"Stop," she said calmly, quietly, sadly. "You'll tear it." She sat up and eased the garment over her head.

In the light from the street lamp across the road, her body was ivory, lovingly, exquisitely hewn.

But what followed was squalid.

He thrust himself on her, reeking of booze and stale sweat, his breathing harsh and constricted. His desire ebbed away as soon as he entered her. Soon he was panting apologies.

"It won't happen again," he promised. His tongue felt thick and furry.

"Nothing's the way it used to be," she murmured, running her hand through his hair. "Oh, Johnny. What's to become of us?"

"We'll survive." He swallowed. "We're going to survive."

She pursed her lips and said, "Is that all?"

THE SURVIVAL instinct was not highly developed in Karl Liebknecht House, the headquarters of the German Communist Party. The following day, Johnny received orders to prepare for an armed insurrection in Berlin. It would be timed to coincide with a general strike. The instructions came from Willi Leov, his nominal boss—the same man who had refused him the guns and the money he had demanded to prepare an effective underground army.

"You'll be sending men to their deaths," Johnny protested. "We have two thousand trained fighters in Berlin. Only half that number are armed. And the general strike will never take place."

Willi Leov glowered at him over his spectacles. "Are you refusing a party order?"

"I'm telling you how things are." He looked with contempt at Leov's red, puffy face. It was criminal, he thought, that parasites like this sat back and gave orders while Heinz was on the run from OGPU killers.

"You're sailing close to the wind, let me tell you."

"I'll do what you say," he said, in order to get out of the room.

He did nothing of the kind. When the general strike was called, the fighting cells under his command stayed at home. He had no intention of delivering them up to an act of blood sacrifice.

The German people did not respond to the party's belated call. The general strike stirred hardly a ripple. Rank-and-file trade unionists were not disposed to risk their necks for the party now. Who could blame them? Johnny asked himself.

Sigrid came home on her bicycle and announced, "They stormed the Bülowplatz." She described the scene of hundreds of grey-uniformed police and booted storm troopers attacking party headquarters. "They caught a man who was trying to destroy party documents," she reported. "The idiot was throwing the pieces out the window. They threw him out after them. I saw the Nazis carrying out whole cabinets of files."

The fools, Johnny thought. They must have known this was coming on the day Hitler took power, even if they were blind before. Couldn't they even salvage the party records?

"The fight isn't over," he promised Sigrid. But he expressed more confidence than he felt. The party had failed. To build a true resistance to Hitler, he would have to find an alternative—even if it meant fighting Stalin, too. But when he tried to work out the next step, his mind veered away.

It was hard, in any event, to plan for the future when everything revolved around surviving the next twenty-four hours. Soon terror reigned in Berlin. All over the city suspected Communists were dragged from their beds in predawn raids. Presses were wrecked, offices gutted. Some of those arrested informed on their friends and their families in the hope of saving their skins. Others, out of fear or disgust, volunteered their services to the new regime. The Gestapo's net widened.

Johnny and Sigrid abandoned the Neukölln apartment—it was known to too many night callers whose fate was unknown—and lived like vagrants, dossing down in dank, airless rooms in the "rental barracks" of Moabit and Wedding. When they left their places of hiding, often in the late mornings, after working through the night, their partings were tender. They never knew whether that day's farewell would be the last.

He wanted to tell her about Heinz and the larger doubts that wracked him. In the precious few hours they spent together, he did not have the heart. Her courage, her confidence—in defiance of everything—was immense. How could he deprive her of that, when all he could offer were questions without answers?

THE WHIPLASH of winter was in the air as he trudged back to Moabit, his chin buried in a wool muffler. The jail over to his left was a landmark, a great Victorian pile whose barred windows were dressed up with wrought iron as if they were trying to stop burglars from breaking in rather than prisoners from getting out. He crossed the street to dodge a troop of beery SA men, out looking for girls to squeeze or Jews to beat up. Between the street lamps, the darkness was almost impenetrable.

He turned into a quieter street and sensed, rather than saw, a shadow move with him. He ducked up the first alley and pressed himself flat against the wall, waiting and listening, his hand searching for the butt of his Mauser. To begin with, he could hear only the scream of police sirens and, closer, a warm-blooded scream—hard to say if it was a woman or a cat.

There.

It was a light, scurrying sound.

A rat poked its snout out of a mound of garbage and scuttled across his foot. He stayed motionless, listening.

There.

A shadow flitted across the mouth of the alley. A man was coming after him, a slight figure in workman's clothes, advancing almost noiselessly on crepe-soled shoes. Perhaps he was only a common pickpocket. Johnny willed himself invisible.

The stranger let out a low whistle—a signal to confederates? But he was almost abreast of Johnny before he spotted his quarry. He jumped, but Johnny was faster and heavier. He got hold of his pursuer's arm and screwed it up behind his back until the man yelped in pain.

"What do you want?" Johnny let him see the gun.

"Alfred, it's me—"

Johnny was startled to hear himself addressed by a work name he had used in Hamburg. The fellow could be a police spy after all.

"Don't you recognize me?" the stranger pleaded.

Johnny hauled him back into the light. The face was narrow, almost vulpine.

Johnny remembered the young tough on the stairs at the Bunte Kuh. Heinz Kordt's bodyguard.

"It's Karl, isn't it?"

The boy nodded and Johnny let him go.

"What are you doing here?"

"Party orders, what would you expect? We're screwed, wherever we are."

"Why did you follow me?"

"I saw you at the station. I've got some stuff for you."

"What stuff?"

"From Heinz." The boy pulled up his sweater and brought out two small packages he had tucked under his belt. "He made me promise to bring these to you if anything happened to him."

"If anything happened—" An icy hand closed over Johnny's heart. "What is it? What have you heard?"

Karl stood there mute, holding out the brown paper parcels. One of them had the shape and heft of a book.

Johnny reached out and gripped the boy's wrists instead of the packages.

"Please. You have to tell me. He's my friend, too."

"You know someone called Max, don't you? You ought to ask him."

They were moving in a macabre dance, Johnny following as Karl backed away towards the street.

"*Tell me.*"

Johnny squeezed tighter. Karl looked at his hands as if they didn't belong to him.

"I'm cold," the boy said. "And I haven't eaten all day."

"We can go to my place."

"Not there." Karl shivered and glanced furtively at the street. The boy was running scared.

They went to Müller's. It hadn't been raided yet, even though it was popular with factory militants in the area. The bar had been shut for several hours, but Müller could always produce a drink and a sandwich for an old comrade. Karl wolfed down everything that was put before him, cramming the food into his mouth with both hands. Muller set an open bottle of wine on the table and said, "I'm turning in. Lock up after you."

Johnny watched Karl guzzle some of the wine and said, "I'm waiting."

"It's like this." Karl wiped his mouth with the back of his hand. "Heinz got away from Hamburg, all right, on a tub bound for Rotterdam. But there was trouble at the other end. The police nearly nabbed him on the docks. I guess that's when Max's people got on to him, though I can't say for sure. Anyway, Heinz stowed away on a French cargo boat, the *Antoinette.* It was bound for Algiers. Heinz figured he'd be able to find a berth on another ship and get to South America. He hid under a lifeboat. But they caught him out. The captain was a real son of a bitch. He locked Heinz up in a cabin and said he'd have him deported to Germany once they got to Algiers."

"How do you know all this?" Johnny interrupted.

"One of the seamen from the *Antoinette.*"

"Go on."

"Max beat him to Algiers."

"Max? There's some mistake." But even as he spoke, Johnny recalled Max's sudden disappearance after his trip to Hamburg and his curious loss of interest in the topic of Heinz Kordt.

"Listen, the name I heard was Max," Karl insisted. "If you don't want to hear the rest of it, that's fine by me."

Johnny picked at details, hoping the boy's story would fall apart before he reached its conclusion. Not knowing exactly where it would lead, he was already besieged by a creeping horror, colder than the night outside. Colder than any night there had ever been.

"How could Max have beaten the *Antoinette* into port?"

Karl shrugged. "Maybe he took a faster boat. Maybe the French tub had to stop for repairs. Maybe he found a plane. What the hell does it matter?"

Johnny reached for the wine, but his hand was shaking. His glass tipped over, and a pool of red spread across the bare wooden table.

Karl stared at it balefully and went on, "When the *Antoinette* came in, Max was waiting on the dock. He'd hired a gang of layabouts and armed them with axes and sledgehammers. They muscled their way straight up the gangplank. Only a few of the sailors put up any fight. Once he found out he wasn't being hijacked, the captain was only too pleased to show them where Heinz was being held. They didn't wait for someone to fetch the key. They broke down the door right away."

Karl paused. His eyes were damp. His lips barely moved, and Johnny had to strain to make out every word as he said, "From what I was told, Max finished the job himself. With a sledgehammer. Myself, I've only seen a sledgehammer used on wood or cement. I don't reckon a man's skull would hold up for very long."

Johnny sat without speaking for a long time. The spilled wine, unattended, had spread to the edge of the table. The drops made a plopping sound as they hit the linoleum.

Karl's brittle mask of cynicism had cracked. His shoulders were heaving, and he turned his face away to hide the tears.

After a while, he asked, "Why did they do it?"

Johnny felt numb. "It's a time of madness," he whispered.

"He was the best man we had."

"I know."

Heinz and one other, he amplified this inside his head. The one who had murdered him.

Karl's expression was a mixture of disgust and disappointment. He looked at Johnny the way a child might look at a clockwork toy with a broken spring.

"I'm off," he announced, scraping back his chair.

"Where will you go?"

"It's all the same," Karl said, his mask again in place. "We're screwed wherever we are."

The boy's parting shot, Johnny understood later, was the demotic version of the line Heinz Kordt had inscribed on the first page of his diary. The diary was inside the larger of the two packages Karl had brought from Hamburg. It had been recorded in an old ship's logbook. The cover was mottled and warped, and some of the pages had been torn out in haste or anger, leaving jagged rows of paper teeth. Kordt wrote in an oversized, awkward script, like a schoolboy. Johnny leafed through the later sections. The diary was the chronicle of a mind being pushed over the edge, a prolonged howl of rage and pain. "What is the difference between communism under Stalin and national socialism in Germany?" one passage read. "Answer: only that Stalin has yet to settle 'the Jewish problem.' Once he does that, he will be indistinguishable from Hitler."

Johnny turned back to the epigraph. It was a phrase from Leviné: "We Communists are all dead men on leave."

4
The Walk-in

It is not Germany that will turn bolshevist, but Bolshevism that will become a sort of national socialism . . . Besides, there is more that binds us to bolshevism than separates us from it. There is, above all, genuine revolutionary feeling, which is alive everywhere in Russia except where there are Jewish Marxists. I have made allowance for this circumstance and given orders that former Communists are to be admitted to the party at once. The *petit bourgeois* Social Democrat and the trade union boss will never make a National Socialist, but the Communist always will.

—ADOLF HITLER(1934)

1

ADAM DE SALIS strolled up the Wilhemstrasse towards the British Embassy. It was a warmish afternoon, and he had draped his topcoat nonchalantly over his shoulders. This, together with the brown trilby and, above all, the brown suede shoes, gave him a somewhat louche air, despite the perfectly pressed Savile Row suit and the monocle that swung on its cord above the third button of his waistcoat. Louche was the appropriate style for a foreign correspondent, de Salis thought. But while the nameplate on his door, a short canter south on the same avenue, blazoned the title of Fleet Street's noisiest patriotic tabloid, journalism was only his part-time vocation. Adam de Salis, formerly Lieutenant Commander de Salis, R.N., was the chief of British Intelligence in Berlin.

The ambassador's Rolls was waiting at the main entrance to the embassy.

Here comes the old fart now, de Salis thought as a peevish-looking man in a homburg hurried towards the car.

"Good afternoon, sir," said de Salis, touching the brim of his hat.

The ambassador returned his greeting with the most distant of nods. He was the quintessential Foreign Office type, in de Salis' estimation. In his impossibly grammatical missives to London, the ambassador frequently protested the use of his embassy as a postbox for messages sent in codes that he couldn't read by people whose methods, he opined, were unworthy of gentlemen.

The cable de Salis had in his pocket was flagged "CX," which meant that it was for the personal attention of the chief of the Secret Service. De Salis had served under C.—a former admiral—on a dreadnought in the North Sea during the Great War, and he made use of the direct channel when he wanted to make a point.

"How are you, Sandy?" he greeted the cipher clerk. "Still keeping the Fraüleins happy?"

He handed over his text, which he had encrypted himself, and watched while Sandy transcribed it into another numerical code.

He had taken some pains with this report.

The main part dealt with the terrible fire that had gutted the Reichstag in the early hours of the morning. The Nazis had bagged a deranged Dutchman and were blaming the act of arson on the Communists. On that pretext they were rounding up thousands of their critics. In de Salis's opinion, the whole business was a transparent hoax. He cited a curious piece of evidence. One of his sources, an elegant young ex-cavalryman who had ingratiated himself with Himmler, had been to a big party the night before, hosted by Hanussen, the Führer's court astrologer. At the witching hour, the stargazer had gone into an apparent trance and announced to the throng, in a melodramatic basso: "I see a blood-curdling crime committed by the Communists. I see blazing flames! I see a terrible firebrand that lights up the world!"

The Reichstag fire was a fraud, but in terms of British interests—so de Salis maintained—it had already had some useful effects. For years the Comintern had used Berlin as its forward command post. Now the Soviet cause in Germany was a busted flush. The Gestapo had hunted down that Bulgarian trickster, Georgi Dimitrov, and put away scores of his best agents. Some of the Westbureau's secret files had fallen into Nazi hands, and de Salis was hoping to get a look at them through the good offices of the same friend who had told him about Hanussen.

But the best thing about the whole episode, de Salis reported, was that it brought an end to a whole era of secret German-Soviet collaboration. The German General Staff had helped to install the Bolsheviks. The Soviets had returned the favor later on by assisting the Germans to rebuild their army illegally on Russian soil. In de Salis's view, the greatest threat to the status quo was an alliance between Germany and Russia. Herr Hitler had put paid to that.

De Salis knew that some of his colleagues at Broadway Buildings were less sanguine about developments in Germany. Colin Bailey, for one, talked as if Hitler were as much of a menace as the Communists. Hitler was a vulgar upstart surrounded by beerhall louts, no argument on that score. Not the sort of chap you asked to dinner. But de Salis had long contended that Hitler's bad manners and his silly obsession with the Jews were no reason to neglect his usefulness in dealing with the main enemy. He felt completely vindicated.

De Salis appended a shorter message, requesting the transfer of a new man to work in the Passport Control Office. Until recently, the passport office—a mile away from the embassy, at the other end of the Wilhelmstrasse—had provided satisfactory cover for British secret operations. Staff duties were relatively light, and the visa fees collected were a useful supplement to the niggardly budget from headquarters. Herr Hitler and his well-publicized views on the Jewish question had changed all of that. Every day, the passport office was mobbed by would-be emigrants, mostly Jews. A lot of them were Poles who had come to Germany because they thought they would be safe from pogroms. Some were bound to be Comintern agents. Normal business had been hopelessly disrupted. The passport office had been forced to hire local clerks, and who knew where that would lead? Some of the Jews were willing to pay almost any amount to get a visa for Palestine. The Firm operated on trust, not routine bookkeeping, and that trust was being subjected to new strains.

De Salis dallied for a couple of gins with the naval attaché and walked out of the embassy into a powdery dusk. His flat was only a few blocks away. He had plenty of time for a bath before he dined with his latest conquest, an aristocratic lady who made up with experience for what she lacked in youth and enjoyed the most remarkable entrée into Berlin society. De Salis was separated from his wife, which allowed him an agreeable latitude in his extracurricular activities. He found it amusing that both the Russians and the Gestapo had drawn certain conclusions from his bachelor status and had sent young women—and occasionally young men—to try to take advantage of his presumed vulnerability. He had fallen for the oldest trick in the world once, just once. The girl was a stunner. When she did her hair a certain way, you might have mistaken her for Marlene Dietrich. In the act of love, she had shown him things even he had never imagined, and he had discovered reserves of stamina he had never known were there. He was horny for her at breakfast, in the middle of the day, at teatime, like a randy teenager.

She had come to him in the most banal way, looking for a job as a stringer with his newspaper. She was too perfect, in bed and everywhere else. He must have realized what she was, but he did not admit it to himself till he woke in the middle of the night after hours of lovemaking and found her rifling his safe. She got away, and though he put traces out for her he never found her. Her last name was phony, of course. But perhaps not the first name. Helene.

He was thinking of her now, as he turned off the Wilhelmstrasse, heading east, when he sensed that he was being watched. He made a few detours and reversed direction abruptly in front of a department store. He failed to spot anyone. All the same, he decided to turn down the steps of a Bierkeller. Frequented by minor officials from the government offices along the Wilhelmstrasse, it was almost deserted at this time of day.

De Salis settled himself in a booth by the far wall and ordered Berliner-weisse. In his first years in Berlin, he had found the taste of the raspberry syrup in the pale lager offensively sweet. It had grown, like the city, to suit his palate.

A big man in a raincoat came in and surveyed the rows of trestle tables. His eyes fastened on de Salis's table. Then he moved off to the right, slowly circumnavigating the room.

De Salis marked him discreetly. Fair hair. Six-two, maybe six-three. Built like a prize fighter, though the face was alert and intelligent. He was good looking in a primitive sort of way, de Salis thought. The type Lady Chatter-ley would go for. Not the sort you would want on your tail in a dark alley. Not a Slav. Almost certainly a Hun, or perhaps a Scandinavian. He might be from Himmler's mob—they had put a tail on de Salis once or twice.

The Englishman raised his newspaper like a rampart.

He expected the stranger to seat himself at a strategic remove, some-where between his table and the door. There were plenty of empty seats.

To his surprise, the man walked up to his booth.

Bloody cheek, de Salis thought. He *must* be Gestapo. Russian agents tend to show a bit more form.

"May I?" The stranger gestured to the bench opposite.

"Be my guest," de Salis said smoothly. He did not look up from his paper.

"Do you know Richmond-on-Thames?"

De Salis put aside his paper and gave the stranger a closer inspection. The man spoke passable English. There was a touch of the East End in his voice, on top of that Germanic rumble. There was nothing shifty about those eyes.

De Salis thought, he looks at me as if he knows me.

"I've been to Richmond," de Salis conceded. "But how did you know I was English?"

"Your clothes." The stranger's glance encompassed de Salis's bold pin-stripe, the watch chain across his vest, the violet silk handkerchief exploding from his breast pocket. "Only an Englishman dresses like that. Do you know the Richmond Theatre? I have friends there. Actor friends."

"Really?" The Englishman's tone was neutral.

What is this? he asked himself. Another provocation? Perhaps the bugger was merely rough trade, the kind that thought that anyone who went to a public school was a pederast.

"I saw a first-rate production of *Candida,* by George Bernard Shaw, in Richmond last summer."

The fellow was getting tedious.

"Look here," said de Salis, "this is all frightfully interesting, but I'm afraid I have a date." He folded his newspaper.

"I do wish you'd stay, Commander. I promise not to detain you for long."

De Salis raised an eyebrow at the use of his old navy rank.

"You are Commander Adam de Salis, M.B.E., D.S.O."

"You seem to have me at a disadvantage, my dear chap. But since you mention it, it's a C.B.E."

"Our records must be out of date. I congratulate you."

"Perhaps you'd care to introduce yourself."

"I am a major in the Red Army, currently assigned to the Comintern in Germany," Johnny said in an undertone.

"I thought your lot had all scarpered after the Reichstag fire."

"Not quite all. As you see."

"What can I do for you?"

"I am in a position to supply you with certain information. Extremely valuable information."

"You intrigue me, Mister—er—"

Johnny did not fill in the name.

"But perhaps I should warn you," de Salis resumed, "the rag I write for is pretty stingy about paying for stories."

"Can we stop playing games? I've seen your dossier."

"Might I ask where?"

"At the British section of the Westbureau, here in Berlin. You were also pointed out to me once at a nightclub, by a friend of mine called Max. I imagine you have a file on him somewhere. You probably know him as André, or André Bloch."

The mention of this alias excited de Salis. He knew that a man code-named André was one of the most dangerous Russian agents in Europe, responsible for the murder of several British operatives. He had tried repeatedly to run André to ground. Instead, the Russian—or so de Salis suspected—had planted a female spy in his own bed.

De Salis tried to keep up a mask of indifference. This could be another of André's tricks.

"Could you be more specific about this information you are willing to part with?"

"I can give you the names and whereabouts of the principal Russian agents in Britain. I can give you a complete description of Communist sabotage units and the underground organization that is working to incite a mutiny in the Royal Navy. I created them myself."

To de Salis, a former navy man, this was pure gold. He knew that C. would feel the same way. But he kept his guard up.

"What about André? Can you give me André?"

"That, too."

The German spoke quietly, but something flashed in his eyes. Pure hatred, de Salis thought.

Dammit, the Englishman told himself, I'm going to push my luck.

"Do you happen to know a woman called Helene?" He described her quite vividly.

"No." The German touched his collar, as if it were too tight for him.

Is he holding something back? de Salis asked himself. Of course he was. He'd be an idiot not to. But perhaps the girl was too much to hope for.

"I don't suppose you're doing this for love," de Salis suggested.

"I have made a list of conditions," Johnny said. "They are not for negotiation." He brought a copy of a German paper out of his raincoat. It was the *Völkischer Beobachter,* the most vicious of the Nazi hate rags. He slipped it under the table, onto de Salis's lap.

"You realize I'll have to consult on this."

"Of course. Your people will need to check my credentials. You will find something in there—" he angled his chin toward the paper he had slipped to de Salis. "You may also tell them that when I landed in England in 1931 I used a passport in the name of Ludwig Dinkelmeyer."

"That may help."

He's a professional, de Salis told himself. No doubt on that score.

The German was rising from the table.

"Wait a bit, won't you?" de Salis appealed to him. "How can I contact you?"

"You can't. I'll contact you."

"What do I call you, for God's sake?"

"Call me Johnny."

"Is that German?"

The big man smiled. "As German as possible."

1

"THANK GOD."

As Johnny closed the door behind him, Sigrid threw herself into his arms. He caressed her hair and felt her tremble against him. Her face was burning.

"You're running a fever," he said gently. "I'll put you to bed."

"I was scared for you, Johnny. I had a premonition—"

"I'm here."

"They took Müller," she told him, shivering. "I saw them from across the street. There was a police informer, in a hood so I couldn't see his face, jabbing his dirty finger at the people they dragged out of the bar. They took nearly everyone."

"What were you doing there?"

"I was told to meet a man."

"What man?"

"Someone from Max."

Always Max, lying in wait at every turning. My nemesis. You took Helene, he addressed Max mentally. You won't take this one.

"Was the man there?"

"I can't say. I didn't see him. I went to Münzenberg's place, but the police were there too. I didn't know where to turn. So I came back here."

It was his turn to say, "Thank God."

I'm not going to lose you now, he promised himself.

She sat on the window seat, swaying lightly as she talked, as if she were trying to keep her balance in a driving wind. The amber light from outside made a soft aura around her head and shoulders. In the penumbra of the room, her lips were purple, almost black, dark as the plums he'd so often stolen from an orchard on boyhood outings to the country. This mental association tugged at his heart, because it brought with it images of a parallel life they had never shared, a life that had room for children's laughter, and the smell of new-mown hay in the sun, and the heart's leap at the sight of a wisp of smoke from their own chimney as dusk settled over the fields. It was the life he had denied her, the life she might have had with a different man. It was the ordinary life of ordinary people, and at that moment, in that occupied city, he yearned for it with every fiber of his being.

"Listen to me," he said to her. "I think I've found a way to get us out. It may take a few days. You must stay here. Don't go out, not even for groceries. I'll take care of everything."

She tried to argue, talked of duty and responsibility.

"Half the people we know are under arrest," he reminder her. "Most of the others have fled or turned into snitches for the Gestapo." This was reasonably accurate. Gurevitch, the Fourth Department chief, had gotten out the same morning. He had told Johnny that Max Fabrikant had slipped away to Copenhagen on the eve of the Reichstag fire, alerted by a sixth sense or, more likely, by information from his own spies which he did not choose to share with those who depended on him. "It's all falling apart," Johnny went on. "Trust me. I'll get us out of this."

He carried her into the bedroom and tucked her under the covers.

"I'll make you a toddy," he announced.

"There's only one medicine I need." She opened her arms to him, and he made love to her slowly, tenderly, till a warm tide swallowed both of them.

When she fell asleep, he sat up in a chair beside the bed, watching her.

Helene was wrong, he told himself again. We are still the same.

Later, in another country—in England, perhaps, or France—he would be able to explain everything to Sigrid. It would not be easy, he had no delusions about that. It would take time for the wounds to heal, time for understanding to grow. He imagined the conversation they might have if he simply announced, "I'm working for the British." She would spurn him as a traitor, and until two weeks ago—until he learned how Heinz had died —he would have agreed with her.

He would have to begin by explaining, painstakingly, everything along the road that had led to this tremendous watershed in his life. He would have to describe the macabre dance of death he had helped to lead, of revolutionaries betrayed by the corruption and stupidity of their commanders. He would have to show her the proof that men who paraded as paladins of the anti-Fascist cause were secret collaborators with the Nazis. He would tell her why Heinz had died—because he cared more about fighting Hitler than about licking Stalin's backside—and who had killed him.

It would take time, nonetheless. Faith was stronger than facts, and he had watched her faith in the Communist cause grow stronger in these weeks of playing hide-and-seek with the Nazis. It had been reinforced by Max, who had asked her to perform some minor chores—which she had accepted over Johnny's protests. It had disturbed him to see the repulsion she had at first expressed for Max give way to a kind of fascination with the spymaster and his deadly games. Johnny had intimate experience of how that fascination grew, and where it led.

I want Max dead, he had told himself over and over, after Karl had come to him with the story of Heinz's end. Even now, in the silence of the bedroom, beyond Sigrid's shallow breathing, he seemed to hear the sickening crunch of bone under the executioner's iron mallet.

Emil, too, the same voice said inside his head. Emil Brandt was more guilty than Max. He was the one who had denounced Heinz for crimes he had once been charged with himself. And I lied to Max's people to protect that bastard.

Before he had walked in on Adam de Salis, he had deliberated how much he would offer the British. He had been ready to give them Max and Emil —those two had earned anything that might be coming to them—and the British network, which was riddled with cynicism and corruption. But there were large areas of his life that he would not betray, comrades who had fought with him and had given him their trust. And he would let nothing touch the two women who meant most to him. It troubled him that de Salis had asked about Helene.

He had chosen the British because the Intelligence Service—so his briefers in Moscow had never tired of repeating—was the most professional and most dedicated opponent of the Soviet cause. Also because, in his time in England, he had come to admire the unflappability of the English and their visceral distaste for the abstract reasoning that cloaked the crimes of a Stalin or a Max Fabrikant. Most of all because, if he and Sigrid were going to start over, they would need help—a place on which to stand.

Sigrid rolled over in her sleep, uncovering her back, and he pulled the sheet up to her shoulder.

He thought, I'll give de Salis three days.

3

COLIN BAILEY liked to walk to the office. From his Mayfair pied-à-terre, three rooms above a French bistro, he would stroll down Curzon Street past Trumper's—his barber's—duck through Shepherd's Market, deserted at that hour, into Piccadilly, and proceed down St. James's Street to his club, where he would sometimes stop for bacon and eggs. Diana didn't care for breakfast and, in any case, had taken to spending most of the week in Devon. Bailey's club, the Senior, was largely patronized by retired army officers and colonial officials, to both of which castes he belonged. It stood across Waterloo Place from the Atheneum, much loved by Anglican bishops, and the Travellers, which most of his colleagues preferred.

The best part of the walk was across St. James's Park. Following the winding path across the footbridge, he had a choice of views—the palace to the right, Whitehall to the left—and stood about equidistant from both, which was precisely where he placed himself in the invisible order of things. On the far side of the park, he waited for a troop of Life Guards to canter past. They were in full dress, horsehair plumes tossing, early light glinting on steel. It was a sight for the camera-toting Americans who descended on London in larger numbers every year, but Bailey was old-fashioned enough to find it comforting.

When he climbed Cockpit Steps and emerged into Queen Anne's Gate, he found the street empty, apart from the milk cart making its stops. It was really absurdly early, and it was quite unlike C. to issue a dawn summons. But Bailey was not given to idle speculation; the cause would reveal itself soon enough. His mind turned on the party that had kept him up much too late. Over the port he had allowed himself to get into an argument with a languid viscount, one of Diana's endless cousins, who was a prop of the Anglo-German Fellowship. The man refused to believe, of all things, that white men could possibly be descended from the ape. Bailey knew something of ethnology and had followed the debate over Raymond Dart's discoveries in South Africa. He ventured to suggest that Herr Hitler and his admirers were proof positive that man not only had evolved from the killer ape Dart had dug up but was in imminent danger of reverting to his former condition. This remark was not well received.

From his homburg and his starched collar to the mirrorlike polish of his shoes, Bailey looked the model of the army officer in mufti; he had swapped one uniform for another. But inside him was something that could never be regimented—a wild Celtic streak from his mother's side of the family, mad Irish through and through. Try as he might, he could never keep it buttoned down for long. It had caused a minor scandal in Calcutta. It popped out at dinner parties after a bottle of claret. It delighted Diana, who called it his leprechaun, and his daughters, for whom he wrote nonsense rhymes.

The ferrule of his scrolled umbrella rang against the paving stones as he marched briskly past the weathered statue of Anne Regina and up the steps of number twenty-one. It was one of a row of elegant five-story townhouses, with gargoyle heads along the facade and carved foliage over the portico.

Bailey tapped the brass knocker, and a nuggety little man in a black coat opened it at once.

"Morning, Spooner."

"Morning, Major Bailey. Bit early for you, is it?"

Spooner had been the chief's orderly during the war and had stuck to him ever since. He treated all C.'s subordinates with the same cheerful insolence.

He helped Bailey off with his chesterfield and said, "They've just sat down to breakfast."

"They?"

"Mr. de Salis is here from Berlin. Took the boat train, I believe."

Bailey was mildly annoyed that he had not been forewarned. De Salis presumed too much on his personal relationship with the chief. But then, the head of station from Berlin never had been one of Bailey's favorites. There was an element of professional jealousy. For too many years de Salis had been allowed to run the most important SIS station as his own fiefdom. Predictably, he had started to go native. His Germanophilia seemed more pronounced since Hitler had taken power. His latest report provided arguments to sustain what, on the part of upper-class twits like the one at Diana's party, was merely uninformed prejudice. Bailey was second to none in his detestation of Bolshevists. He had helped to frame the plot to sink Lenin and had accompanied the British expeditionary force that had landed at Murmansk. But he viewed the Hitler movement with equal suspicion and contempt, not solely because of the Nazis' bad manners. Hitler, he was convinced, was no less of a revolutionary than Stalin and would prove to be no more of a dictator. Britain and the Empire must be ready to take on both. There were few men in England who understood this, fewer still in North America. Churchill was one of the few, and his reward was to find himself blacklisted by the BBC. De Salis's reports did not help.

Bailey followed Spooner into the dining room and found C. sprinkling sea salt into his porridge.

"Ah, there you are, Colin. Good of you to come."

C. made a habit of addressing men who were acting under orders as if they were doing him a personal favor. His diplomacy, like his comfortable, bluff exterior, could be misleading, as a Labour prime minister had discovered. C. had once called on Ramsay MacDonald and informed him that, unless he had his way, he would draw on the resources of friends in the City and set up an independent intelligence network, answerable only to the King. His bluff—if it was a bluff—had never been called.

De Salis made as if to rise from the table.

"Please don't trouble yourself, Adam," Bailey said. "How are you?"

They shook hands.

"Adam's been traveling all night," C. explained. "He washed up on my doorstep like a shipwreck."

"I thought it best not to wait," de Salis said, quite unruffled. "In view of the prime minister's request."

"Quite so," C. agreed. "Colin, do have something to eat, will you?"

Obediently, Bailey set about slathering Gentleman's Relish onto a piece of toast.

"Might I ask what request that would be?" he said, without looking up.

"It came up in December. You know what I'm talking about, don't you?" C. looked mildly embarrassed, and Bailey immediately knew why.

The prime minister had asked the Secret Service to put together a paper on Comintern activities in Britain. The job had been assigned to Bailey's department, and he had only just completed the draft report. The whole affair was hypersensitive because, in theory, the Firm was not permitted to embroil itself in domestic matters. Communist subversion in England was the preserve of its sister service, MI5. The government was looking for political ammunition, and C.—for reasons of his own—had decided to be accommodating. But the whole investigation was supposed to be kept under wraps. De Salis could only have heard about it from the chief.

Bailey felt his blood pressure rising. He set down his knife and played with the crumbs on his plate.

C. recovered briskly. "Adam, why don't you bring Colin up to date?"

"I have a potential defector," de Salis reported. "A walk-in, as it happens. He is a military specialist for the Comintern and was previously stationed in Britain. He knows all the Communist bosses here—Pollitt, Gollan, the lot. He has given me a digest of his activities in England. I don't think I'm overegging it if I say it will enable us to destroy the most dangerous fifth column that is operating in this country. This is the best catch we've had in years." He glanced at C., who did not contradict him.

"I've had a quick look at the material," C. observed casually. "I think they'll be quite interested at the Admiralty."

"I take it this chap's a Russian," Bailey interjected.

"German. But he's done the Red Army intelligence course in Moscow."

"I assume you've checked his bona fides."

"That's one of the reasons I'm here."

De Salis reported the traces that Johnny had given him—the cover name he had used to travel to Britain, the dates of his various postings, the identities of other agents and operatives he had mentioned.

Bailey made a few notes inside the cover of his checkbook.

"We'll need to check some of this with the Sisters," he remarked.

"You won't give them any inkling what it's about, I hope," de Salis said, in some agitation.

Bailey gave him a basilisk stare.

"Well, he *is* our property," de Salis subsided.

"I'll try to keep that in mind," Bailey said drily. As the man who handled day-to-day liaison with the Security Service, Bailey was well aware that there was no love lost among siblings. "I'll go down to Cromwell Road myself." He directed his words to C. "Max Knight owes me a favor."

Bailey decided to indulge in a poached egg.

"Perhaps I could ask one or two questions, Adam," he said, when he had deployed the egg to his satisfaction on top of a piece of toast.

"Of course."

"What's your chap like?"

"A rough diamond. Self-educated, but bright."

"What does he want?"

"He wants out. I expect he's in a bit of a funk, though he doesn't show it. The Reds have been blown out of the water in Germany. There's also some question of a girl. He wants a British passport for her."

"Oh, he does, does he? I expect he also wants money."

"He mentioned the figure of ten thousand pounds."

Bailey snorted. This was more than a tenth of the budget for the whole Secret Service. "Did your chap also mention a knighthood and an audience with the King?"

"It's not inconceivable something could be arranged," de Salis suggested. "This man's information could be worth a damn sight more than that to the government and certain sections of Fleet Street. I could talk to Bunny," he added, using the family nickname of one of the most powerful and jingoistic of the press barons.

Only now did Bailey begin to appreciate the extravagance of de Salis's ambitions. He wanted to ingratiate himself with the government by creating a tremendous splash—a red scare of the proportions of the Zinoviev Letter that would guarantee a Tory victory in snap elections. Perhaps de Salis even had his eye on C.'s job.

Bailey was by no means allergic to the use of propaganda, black, grey or even white. But his first instinct was operational. If the Berlin walk-in was genuine and not a fabricator or an agent provocateur, then he would be more valuable in place than fulminating against the Comintern in the pages of the Tory press.

"I'll need a little time," he said, looking at C. "I'll want to examine all of Adam's material. And of course Adam will want to put in an appearance at his newspaper."

De Salis looked distinctly peeved.

"Very well." C. drew back his chair, signaling that breakfast was over. "Why don't we regroup next door later on. Shall we say eighteen hundred? I'll have the lift waiting."

*   *   *

BAILEY's designation on interoffice memos looked like the name of an old school form: Va. It meant that he was chief of Section V, the counterintelligence department. Some of his juniors called him the Fakir, a jocular sobriquet that could not be explained by his appearance; he was of middling height, wiry and compact, his wide, domed forehead capped by tight waves of dark brown hair that was just starting to grey. He had acquired his nickname because of his time in India in the intelligence branch of the police. His first experience of Russian intrigues, in those years before the war, had involved Tsarist plotters on the northwest frontier. On his first undercover mission, he had blackened his face and donned the flat turban and loose trousers of a Pathan tribesman to ride through the mountain passes to Kandahar, and found it was harder for an Englishman to pass for a native than it had been in the pages of his favorite story, *Kim*. His sojourn in Kipling country had ended when his family had learned of his romantic involvement with an Indian girl and brought pressure on his superiors to send him home. It had taken him the whole summer to recover from that love affair and a serious bout of malaria. By the end of that summer, there was no time for convalescence: Europe was hurtling over the terrible watershed of the Great War.

The colonial police was an odd career choice for a Scholar of Winchester; there were other oddities in Bailey's makeup. His friend John Buchan, with whom he lunched occasionally at an obscure writer's club that convened on alternate Tuesdays, described him as a model for the "practical mystics" who peopled his tales of adventure. His library, which had outgrown his country house on the borders of Dartmoor as well as the flat in town, ranged from ornithology to the occult.

If Bailey lived in a certain degree of comfort, it was thanks to Diana's inheritance. Secret Service salaries were paid in cash and mercifully free of tax, but nobody could live on one without independent means, a military pension or an aptitude for embezzlement. Bailey had met Diana—Lady Diana Vavassour, as she then was, in the first spring after the war, on the day Mansfield Cumming, the original C., informed him that he had been accepted for the service. He was roaming the corridors of Broadway Buildings, looking for his section. It was lunchtime, and most of the rooms were deserted. He threw open a frosted glass door, hoping it was the right one —and found a tall, generously proportioned girl sprawled full-length on the rug.

"Good God!" Bailey exclaimed.

He had rushed to the girl and knelt over her. Her pulse was still beating. He tried to remember his first aid as he started to undo the top buttons on her high collar.

Suddenly he found himself looking down into two wide, china-blue eyes.

"Do you generally molest women, or just the ones you haven't been introduced to?"

The girl sprang up. She was nearly as tall as Bailey.

"I'm sorry," Bailey stammered. "I thought you'd fainted. Or something. Are you sure you're all right?"

"Oh spiffing, thank you." She straightened her dress and smiled at his red face. "I like to take a catnap when I've been burning the candle at both ends."

That was his introduction to Diana. At that time she was the secretary to one of the directors of the Firm, the kind it favored then and since: a girl with good legs and equally good social connections. It didn't take long for her to cure him of his lingering oriental infatuation. Within a year they were married, and she left the Firm to bear the first of their daughters. It was a pretty good marriage, as marriages went. They made space for each other. Diana spent a good deal of her time in the country, charging over the moors on her favorite hunter, tearing up the roads in the cheeky red Austin roadster he hadn't wanted her to buy. That was no bad thing, Bailey thought. If she were in London more, she would exhaust the social scene and then be demanding to be sent off to overthrow some foreign potentate.

Bailey himself had tried his hand at overthrowing more than one such potentate. But he did not think of himself as "political." Adam de Salis was political, and that was a defect in an intelligence officer; it corrupted his judgment. Bailey believed instinctively in a natural order of things that included the rule of law, civility, and the absolute right of Great Britain, as the principal custodian of both, to defend her interests, wherever threatened, by whatever means fell to hand.

What he most detested were political abstractions. Ideologies, people had taken to calling them—no doubt thanks to the Germans, who had invented the worst of them.

At the same dinner party where he had had to suffer the fool from the Anglo-German Fellowship, he had encountered another typical specimen of the times: the Trinity College Bolshevist. The boy had just come down from Cambridge, full of theories, and had proceeded to thrill his hostess with lurid accounts of what would happen to the ruling class when the inevitable revolution dawned.

"Perhaps you could intercede for our dear hostess," Bailey had suggested.

The Cambridge revolutionist had glowered at the Turner over the mantel. "In Russia," he declaimed, "this house would be expropriated by the people and used to accommodate eight needy families."

He had spoken with such utter lack of humor that Bailey had burst out laughing.

"It's all very well for you to make fun," the young man had said huffily. "The Establishment can afford a sense of humor."

"My dear boy, it's our last line of defense."

"It's obvious you're a Tory."

"I find politics rather a bore. But I'm against the revolution."

"You mean the Russian Revolution?"

"Absolutely."

"Then I suppose you're against the French Revolution too." The Trinity man's tone had been that of a prosecutor marshaling the points of an indictment.

"No question," Bailey had countered blandly. "I don't know if people still read Burke at Cambridge, but I think he polished off the French Revolution rather well." He had been about to cite one of his favorite passages from Burke about the presumption of those "who think of their country as carte blanche, on which they may scribble as they please"— when Diana had decided to head him off at the pass.

"Actually," she'd purred, "Colin doesn't see the point of the agricultural revolution of four thousand B.C."

On the way home, he protested, "I was just starting to enjoy myself."

"Honestly, darling, one can't take you anywhere."

"I thought I was on my best behavior."

Diana started giggling. "You'll cross swords with anyone, from Freddie the Fascist to the Trinity Terrorist."

"They sounded pretty much the same to me."

"Oh, Colin, be serious."

"But that's the point, my love. As I get older, I find there are only two parties worth a damn—the one that's got a sense of humor, and the one that hasn't."

BAILEY returned to the office shortly before six. The temperature had dropped, and the rain that had started coming down in midafternoon, as he left the club, was turning to sleet. Bailey crossed the road from the underground station and hurried up the steps of a greyish, undistinguished office block called Broadway Buildings. He had to squeeze through a crowd of shoppers and commuters taking shelter from the weather under the eye of a uniformed commissionaire on the other side of the glass doors.

The commissionaire opened the door for Bailey.

"Lift's waiting, Major."

Bailey took the reserved elevator that went direct to the fourth floor. According to the directory on the wall in the lobby, the tenant on that floor was the Minimax Fire Extinguisher Company. Bailey had always thought this a rather apt cover name for the Intelligence Service.

He found de Salis smoking a cigarette in C.'s outer office.

They had barely exchanged greetings when the red light above the padded door went off and the green light came on.

C. was engaged in mixing his staple draught: gin and bitters, diluted with soda rather than plain water. Bailey couldn't stand the stuff. He asked for scotch, and C. produced a bottle from among the dummy bindings on the lowest shelf of his bookcase.

The office would have passed for a well-to-do, but quite unexceptional, Edwardian sitting room, except for the model warships in glass cases and the imposing iron safe in the corner. Bailey liked to fancy that inside that quarter ton of metal were things that could make the empire tremble, blood secrets from the time of Elizabeth and Anne and every monarch since.

"Well, Colin," said the owner of the safe. "Do we have a verdict?"

"It's not conclusive." Bailey laid a hand on the tattered file, secured by ribbons, that he had brought with him. "We can't match Adam's chap up with anyone in our records. I did find a reference to a Comintern bomb-thrower identified only as 'Alfred' in the material we got from the French after that nasty business in Brussels. It may fit this chap. Or again, it may not."

"What about the wireless traffic?"

"Nothing of interest."

"What did the Sisters have to say?"

"On this occasion, the Sisters were quite helpful. It seems a Herr Dinkel-meyer did visit this country on the dates Adam's man suggested. The Home Office still had the landing and departure cards. Special Branch reported a meeting between Jim Straw of the CPGB and an unidentified foreigner at King's Cross Station. The foreigner gave them the slip. But he seems to match our man's description. I gave Max Knight a few of the highlights from our man's report on subversion in the armed services—edited of course—and he got quite excited. The names and addresses are right, and it all seems to fit the m.o."

Bailey paused for a sip of whisky.

"Frankly, sir," he went on, "it's the connection with André Bloch that interests me. Or perhaps we'd better call him Max, since he seems to be running with that monicker now. What exactly did your chap say again, Adam?"

"He said he'd give André to us. Or words to that effect."

"Only that?"

"I didn't have time for a leisurely chat, Colin."

"What do you suppose your fellow—Johnny—had in mind?"

De Salis thought about this for a bit. "There's bad blood there," he suggested. "I had the sense Johnny might be ready to have Max killed, even to do the job himself. I must say, I wouldn't mind having a potshot at the bugger myself. At the least, I think Johnny can tell us where to find him."

"I know where Max is," Bailey said mildly. "He's in Copenhagen, rebuilding his organization. And the last thing I think we should do is to have him killed."

C. waggled his tufted eyebrows.

"What did you have in mind, Colin?"

"If we can play Johnny back against Max—and whoever else he reports to—we're home and dry. With luck, we'll know everything their lot is cooking up against us before they do any damage. Needless to say, Adam, I'm speaking on the assumption that your chap is genuine. The best way to find out for sure is to run with him and see how he performs."

"In other words, you want to play him long," C. suggested.

"I want to run him as an agent in place."

"You don't look happy, Adam," C. remarked.

"I'm not at all sure Johnny will go for it. He's suggested a one-time business arrangement. He gives us specified information, we give him enough money to retire somewhere in the sun. He says his terms are nonnegotiable."

"I find that most things in life are negotiable," Bailey commented. "We'll make him a counteroffer. He's not likely to go shopping around for other bids, is he?"

De Salis was still reluctant to let slip his vision of a spectacular defection, complete with banner headlines and a roundup of Russian agents, bringing personal encomiums from a grateful prime minister.

"You realize that Johnny may back off completely." He appealed to C. with his eyes, but the chief was playing silent umpire now and seemed to think Bailey was winning on points.

"It's a risk," Bailey said. "I admit that. But my hunch is that your chap likes the smell of cordite, and might like a chance to get back at his own bunch if he thinks they've let him down badly. That's what we can play with."

"What are we going to pay him?" C. intervened.

"A hundred to start him off, and fifty a month if he produces," Bailey said briskly.

C. noted the figures on a desk pad.

"Bit cheesy, isn't it?" de Salis sniffed.

"It's more than some of our chaps in the field are getting," Bailey observed.

"There's also the matter of the girl."

"I hadn't forgotten the girl. How much does she know about this?"

"All I know is, he wants us to help get her out of the country."

"Can't he use his own network?"

"You don't seem to understand, Colin. His network has collapsed, and the Gestapo could pick both of them up any day of the week. That's one of the reasons he's come to us."

Bailey smoothed the hair at the back of his neck. "We mustn't do anything to show our hand. Do you know what passport Johnny is using?"

"It's Czech, I believe."

"That makes things simpler. At a pinch, we'll find a Czech passport for the woman."

Bailey's mind turned to a rustic inn near the Czech border, where he had lunched during a shooting holiday in Saxony.

"If necessary, we'll point Johnny in the right direction. Once he's out, I want to set up a meet. I'd like to take a look at this chap myself."

4

JOHNNY decided to run on the day his photograph appeared on a wanted poster at the post office. It was an ancient picture; it showed a boy of seventeen in the uniform of a naval rating. He wondered where the police had dredged it up. The youthful face was hardly recognizable as that of a man now prematurely grey, weathered and scored by the life he had lived, and the caption identified him as "Johann Heinrich Lentz," a name that few people in Berlin had ever heard. All the same, the photo told him that their time in Germany was up.

He had met twice with de Salis since the Englishman returned from London, full of promises but little hard cash. De Salis told him he would receive the bulk of his money when he was safely out of Germany and could be thoroughly debriefed. Nonetheless, de Salis tried to squeeze him for more and more information, especially about Max. The Englishman showed him a list of Russian names and asked him to talk about each one. He recognized most of them—OGPU and Fourth Department men—but he made the conscious decision to hold back. The British might be playing games with him, trying to suck him dry before they paid up.

At their last meeting, de Salis brought a passport for Sigrid. It was Czech —not British, as Johnny had specified—and this was a source of new suspicion. But at any rate the passport matched his own. De Salis advised him that if he wanted to slip out of Germany without attracting unnecessary attention, he should make his way to an inn south of Chemnitz, near the Czech border. The mention of Chemnitz filled Johnny with black foreboding. It was at Chemnitz, ten years earlier, that the Communist Party leaders royally screwed up the Hamburg revolt.

"Is that all?" Johnny asked. "Just the name of a country inn?"

"Bailey says it will work," de Salis said defensively.

"Well, I'm glad I haven't put you to excessive trouble," Johnny parodied de Salis's own style.

"We're not babysitters," the Englishman said huffily.

De Salis gave him a telegraphic address to memorize. It belonged to a Savile Row tailor.

"When you're out," de Salis instructed, "order a hacking jacket. Size forty-two if you're in contact with the opposition, forty-four if you're not."

Back in the apartment, Johnny spent more than an hour getting his own passport ready for the trip. He had altered his appearance in minor ways, by dying his hair and putting on spectacles. He pasted a new photograph in the Czech passport to reflect these changes. To transfer the rubber stamp of the Czech police from one to the other, he used a hard-boiled egg. He peeled the egg while it was still hot from the pan and rolled it carefully over the original stamp until the imprint was transferred to the egg white. When he rolled the egg over the corner of the new picture, the stamp reappeared, only slightly paler. He then ate the egg for his breakfast. His job was clumsy compared with the work of the old forgery factory on the Lindenstrasse, but the Gestapo owned those premises now. It would do.

He showed both the passports to Sigrid.

"Brigitte Jelinek." She tested the foreign syllables of the last name. "Yours is easier. Alfred Wittling. But it doesn't sound Czech."

"It sounds Sudeten Czech."

"Aren't all of them Hitlerites?"

"Not all. But I'll practice being one for a day or two, if you don't mind."

He had explained the escape plan to Sigrid in some detail, letting her believe that he had got his directions from the Fourth Department. She approved the general idea and came up with a refinement that he liked. The forced inactivity of the past days had made her listless and depressed. The apartment had become a prison cell. Now, at the prospect of breaking out, she was as chirpy as a bird. She was actually singing when they boarded the train.

They had to change trains at Dresden. As the passengers came out of the cars, they were herded into line by black-uniformed guards. The nails of their boots clacked against the concrete. Johnny glanced along the platform. At the head of the line, a self-important SS officer was installed at a makeshift desk. A roll of fat hung over his collar like a dewlap.

Johnny squeezed Sigrid's arm lightly, nudging her forward. He fell back a few paces. He doubted that his passport would stand up to close inspection. If he was taken, at least they would not be taken together.

She glanced back, doubtful and afraid, and a small vertical crease appeared between her eyebrows. He looked away.

The SS guards worried at the flank of the column, like sheepdogs.

He saw Sigrid shuffle to the head of the line, heard her laugh at the officer's jokes. The SS man returned her passport without even opening it. Her looks were her safe-conduct.

The line shunted forward, then stopped.

The man in front of him was becoming agitated. He put his suitcase down, picked it up immediately, then dropped it again.

"What's going on?" he appealed to Johnny. His accent might have been Polish. "Are they going to arrest us?"

The man was swarthy, with tufts of black hair on the back of his hands. The SS officer wasn't going to give him the nod, not with that hooked nose.

"Will you carry this for me?" he mumbled, indicating the suitcase. It was the cheapest sort, cardboard, with a strap around the middle.

Johnny shook his head.

"I can pay you."

"Keep moving!" an SS guard bellowed.

That instant, the Jew lost his sanity. He dropped his suitcase and dived over the edge of the platform. It looked like a bad fall, but he picked himself up and started scuttling across the tracks, toward the shelter of some freight cars on a siding.

The guard released the safety catch on his rifle and took aim. Two more SS men shouldered their way through the line and brought up their submachine guns.

"Not yet!" the SS officer bellowed. He strutted over to the edge of the platform, gauging the distance between the runaway Jew and the freight cars. When the Jew stumbled and fell across the tracks, the officer waited patiently as he struggled to get up.

Still on his hands and knees, the Jew looked back at the platform, puzzlement written all over his face. All was still, as if the whole scene had been captured under glass.

Then the guard nearest Johnny spoke. "Look at his fat rump. I could hit him with my eyes shut."

"But we're sportsmen, Frick," the commandant said pleasantly.

He waited until his quarry was almost out of danger, until he had his hand on the railing at the back of the caboose, before he drew a bead along the barrel of his Luger and squeezed off a couple of rounds. His aim was excellent. The first bullet found its mark at the midpoint between the victim's shoulder blades. As it crumpled, the body seemed weightless and insubstantial, an emptied sack.

The SS officer stuck his gun back into his holster and returned to business.

"Next!"

Several suspects had already been herded to the far end of the platform. Johnny lit a cigarette. It pleased him that it took only one match.

"Next!"

He walked up to the desk.

"Papers!"

"Jawohl, Obersturmführer," he responded, promoting the SS officer by at least two ranks as he offered his fake passport.

"A shithead Czech," the officer said with disgust, leafing through the passport. "You don't look like a Czech."

"I'm no shithead Czech," Johnny replied in the same tone. "I'm as good a German as any. Heil Hitler!"

Reflexively, the SS man returned the salute.

"Sudeten. Well now, that's different." He returned Johnny's passport. "You'll be joining the Reich soon enough, *Kamarad.* Come see us again before we come to see you!"

The final stage of the train journey was uneventful. At Chemnitz they hired bicycles and pedaled south with backpacks and picnic lunches, like any number of ramblers in those first days of spring. The crocuses were out, and you could smell the sap rising in the forest.

They were close to the border when they found the rutted dirt road Colin Bailey had remembered. The inn at the end of the road hadn't been discovered by tourists. They ate their lunch among local people, both Czechs and Germans. They didn't hurry the meal. Johnny ordered dessert and liqueurs, although Sigrid only toyed with her main course.

Johnny finally paid the bill, and they slipped out the back way, through the owner's private apartments. A schnauzer trotted out and snapped at their heels, but nobody came to stop them. When they walked out the back door, Sigrid froze. There, clearly visible above the pines, was the pointed roof of a watchtower.

"It's all right," Johnny said, clasping her by the waist. "We just crossed the border. Half the inn is in Czechoslovakia."

He tried to give the words a ring of triumph, and she let him press her to his chest. But the warmth of the spring afternoon was not inside him. They were out of Germany, but they had not stopped running.

5

AT THE end of that week a messenger from Colin Bailey's tailors arrived at his flat with a box of detachable collars and a telegram, confirming his belief that the long-established firm of Plunkett & Rice was one of the most reliable institutions in England. The telegram contained an order for a hacking jacket and specified a forty-four chest measurement. It announced that forwarding instructions would be sent from Paris.

The second telegram relayed the information, in suitably disguised language, that Johnny had arrived safely in Paris and was installed in a small hotel in the fourteenth arrondissement. While Bailey consulted a boat train schedule, Diana started laying out clothes. He noticed she had picked one of their larger suitcases.

"I really think an overnight bag will be quite sufficient," he called out to her.

"Not on your life," she rejoined. "You don't imagine I'm going to let you go to Paris by yourself, do you?"

With the children away at school and a fortnight to go before the Easter break, he could not think of a convincing excuse to leave her at home. It meant they would have to stay at the Lancaster. Her family had *always* stayed at the Lancaster. Caught in Paris at the start of the war, her mother had arranged with the management to have her Rolls-Royce driven to Calais, from whence it had been ferried across the Channel on a Royal Navy destroyer.

IN THE room up under the eaves of the Hotel Fouché that looked out over a choppy sea of blue rooftops, a bottle of Moët sat untouched in an ice bucket. Johnny had ordered it—and the white and yellow roses he had strewn everywhere, even across the bed—to celebrate Sigrid's birthday. He was suddenly in no mood for a celebration. He was trying to keep his voice low and calm, to betray none of the fear and anger that was in him.

She had told him she was going shopping, that she wanted to go alone so she could surprise him. She had come back empty-handed, but with news that had floored him.

"Slow down," he said. "Tell me the whole thing again from the beginning."

Sigrid frowned with impatience. She was excited and happy and couldn't understand why he was being difficult.

"I went to Editions du Carrefour," she repeated. That was one Paris address everyone in Berlin knew. The vast publishing house was the hub of Münzenberg's operation. It had scored a resounding success with the publication of the *Brown Book* on the Hitler terror. "I asked for Willi Münzenberg."

"Just like that?"

"I didn't see anything wrong, Johnny. We know he's in Paris. I want to get back to work."

"Aren't you enjoying yourself?"

"Do you expect me to go on holiday while the Fascists are devouring Europe?" she rounded on him.

"All right. What name did you give them?"

"The old one. Firelei. Willi would remember that. But he wasn't there. At least, the receptionist wouldn't say. They made me wait more than an hour in an empty office."

"Didn't you think of leaving?"

"They didn't want me to leave. You can understand that, can't you? They've every right to distrust strangers. I could have been an assassin."

The solemnity with which she said this made him want to laugh, more at himself than at her. He was reminded of the lecture on revolutionary discipline he had given her when she had complained about Max.

"What happened then?"

"Max arrived with his bodyguards. He was charming, Johnny, absolutely charming. He said he's been looking for us for two weeks. He sent men to the flat in Berlin to help get us away, but we had already gone."

"Very thoughtful of him. Did he say when he arrived in Paris?"

"No."

"But you told him when we arrived."

"Why shouldn't I?"

Thank God I sent the cable to Smollett in London, Johnny thought. If Max found out I'd been in Paris for four days without making contact with my controllers, I'd be as good as dead. There'll be enough to explain as things are.

He resolved to put a bold face on things, opened the champagne, whirled her around the room and took her out for a late supper at a bistro near the Pont Neuf. He considered laying it all on the table that night but held back because of the doubts that kept flooding in. Had her visit to Carrefour been as naive as she said? Why hadn't she told him where she was going? How deeply was she under Max's spell?

Max had sent an invitation with Sigrid for both of them to dine with him the following night. The tone of the message was friendly. It was a summons, all the same.

I'll have to keep up appearances, Johnny thought. If it's a trap—he pressed his elbow against his side, feeling the bulk of the Mauser under his armpit—I'll take Max with me.

But first he had to meet an important Englishman from London. He hoped the man had better answers than de Salis.

In the morning he slipped out and sent a telegram to the tailoring firm of Plunkett & Rice, explaining that he had gone on a diet and therefore required to have his jacket taken in two inches.

COLIN BAILEY chose the Île St.-Louis, his favorite corner of Paris, for his first meeting with Johnny. Across the street from the bistro was a splendid apparition: a burnished horse's head, nostrils flaring, glowing in the dozy afternoon sun like an idol. Bailey noted that it was the sign of a butcher's shop dealing in horsemeat. This observation deepened his suspicion that the French were not altogether to be trusted. How could one vest complete confidence in a people whose better classes, it seemed, were given over to practices Diana regarded as lower than cannibalism? He resolved not to mention the incident to her. Diana much preferred horses to people.

Bailey was excited about the interview that lay ahead of him but edgy as well. Hennessy, a tall, gangling young man from the embassy who bore an unfortunate resemblance to a praying mantis, had reached him at the Lancaster just before he'd left, with the news of Johnny's eleventh-hour telegram to his tailors. To Bailey, the message that Johnny was back in contact with the Russians was reassuring. The man was unlikely to have sent the cable if he were playing a double game, and it seemed he was now in place to perform the role that Bailey had scripted for him. There remained the task of making sure of the man, of winning him completely to a job that would be not only dangerous but devastatingly lonely. If Bailey had read his man right, the danger might be more of a lure than a deterrent. But to cope with the loneliness of a double life, Johnny would need a sense of purpose as strong as the faith that had sustained him through his years in the revolutionary underground. Bailey knew he could not supply that; but he might help to mold it from the materials he found.

He knew his man as soon as he entered the restaurant—back to the wall, corner table, eyes on the door. The face was strong but troubled, Bailey thought, capable of—no, prone to—excesses of passion.

They drank the new Beaujolais, and since Johnny had no interest in the menu, Bailey ordered each of them a dozen *belons* and the steak *au poivre* to follow.

"I got your message," Bailey said, when the waiter was out of earshot. "Are you being followed?"

"I don't think so. But I spent all morning getting here, just in case."

Bailey nodded his approval.

He looks bloody miserable, Bailey thought. Better start on the upbeat.

"I wanted to tell you that the prime minister is deeply grateful for the information you have given us. He asked me to send you his personal thanks."

"The prime minister? Oh." Johnny frowned and leaned forward. "Have there been any arrests?"

"There won't be for a good while yet," Bailey assured him. "And when there are, we'll make damn sure there's nothing to tie them to you."

At this, Johnny seemed to relax a little, and he consumed his oysters with relish.

I mustn't push him, Bailey reminded himself. Let him open up in his own sweet time.

"I'm going to see Max tonight," Johnny suddenly announced. "André, if you like."

"I know who you mean. Tell me about him."

"He is the most brilliant man I know. There was a time when I think I would have died for him. He killed my best friend."

De Salis was right about this, at least, thought Bailey. Here was something to build on. Little by little, Johnny told him most of the story.

Then Johnny interrupted himself and said, oddly, "In a way, I don't blame Max."

"I'm not sure that I follow."

"He pulls the trigger. He doesn't aim the gun. It's the party that does that."

"You're saying that your quarrel is not with the individual, but with the cause."

"Not with the cause," Johnny came back fiercely. "With those who have stolen it."

Careful, Bailey cautioned himself. In part of himself, Johnny still believes.

"With the system, then," he suggested.

Johnny didn't dissent from this.

"What are you planning to do about it?" Bailey challenged him.

"Heinz said he was going to Trotsky—" the German went off at a tangent "—before they killed him."

"Did you consider that yourself?"

"No."

"May I ask why not?"

"Because you can't fight Stalin with speeches."

Closer, Bailey thought. We're halfway there.

But a few minutes later, Johnny cut across his questioning. "Did you bring my money?"

"Well, yes. I have something for you."

"Ten thousand pounds?" The corners of Johnny's mouth twitched.

"Not quite, I'm afraid. I can let you have a hundred for now. Actually, I wanted to suggest a more permanent arrangement."

"Meaning?"

"Fifty a month."

"This is not what I discussed with your man in Berlin."

"But is that what you really want? So you can run a pub by the sea or grow cabbages? Forgive me if I'm presumptuous, but you don't strike me as the kind of man who'd be happy in early retirement."

"What exactly are you suggesting?"

"I'm suggesting we join forces for the long haul."

"You mean you want me to spy for you."

"Put it that way if you like. The way I view it, you have a score to settle, and we are in a position to help you do it. Isn't that why you came to us in the first place?"

The waiter came with the steaks, and Bailey held his breath. Had he pushed it too far?

The waiter left and Johnny said, "I'll let you know after tonight."

IN PARIS, Max behaved like a millionaire on holiday. At least he did that night.

His driver called for them at the Hotel Fouché and whisked them off to the Café de la Paix. They ended up at a White Russian nightclub complete with gypsy singers and Cossack dancers, and Max insisted on ordering caviar with the vodka. He seemed entirely unperturbed about the risk of being identified as the wrong sort of Russian.

He expressed no suspicions about their escape from Germany. On the contrary, he toasted Johnny's imagination. But Johnny's stomach tightened as he watched all this show of hilarity, trying to keep his head clear while the bottle swung back and forth like a pendulum.

When the thunderbolt came, it was not what he most expected, but worse than anything he had feared.

"I talked to Marlowe today," Max announced, looking at Sigrid. Johnny knew the name from the cable traffic he had seen in Berlin. It was a code name for the resident director of the OGPU in Paris, who operated from behind the cover of an architect's studio decorated in futuristic style on the Rue de Seine. It was curious, this Russian penchant for literary code names

—novelists for military intelligence, playwrights for the chekists. "It's all been cleared," Max went on.

"Wait a minute!" Johnny exclaimed. Sigrid's face was shining. "Did I miss something?"

"No need for secrets in the family," Max beamed. "Sigrid is going to work for us. Shall we drink her health?"

Oh, no, Johnny thought. You can't do this a second time. Not with Sigrid.

"This is something Sigi and I have to talk over in private," he said.

He got to his feet a trifle unsteadily and took her arm. "Come on. We're going now."

HE CAME perilously close to baring his soul to Sigrid that night. He told her that Max was a killer, that Stalin and his people had betrayed the cause they both believed in, that because of them, the mightiest Communist movement in the world outside Russia had stood frozen like a rabbit in the headlights of an oncoming car, in the face of the Nazi jackboots. She wouldn't hear him.

"You're jealous," she informed him. "You're jealous because I'll be working for Max instead of you. Didn't you teach me that these things are not for us to decide? That the party decides?"

I taught you too well, Johnny told himself. Now I shall have to wait until you hear the same screams that I hear and wake from this dream.

Helene had been right after all.

OVER THE next week he met Bailey several times. They spent the best part of a day in a flat in Neuilly loaned by a retired colleague of Bailey's who had decided to live abroad because, as he put it, the English were best admired from a distance. The apartment was adorned with mildly pornographic sketches of *grisettes* and spiky, inhospitable plants that belonged in a different climate.

Bailey didn't like the way Johnny was drinking. He was drinking like a Russian, drinking himself towards oblivion. Something had evidently happened involving Max and the girl, but Johnny refused to talk about it. On other subjects, however—from the order of battle in Moscow to Fourth Department operations in Oslo—he talked freely, with a wealth of detail. He pulled back abruptly only when Bailey asked about the woman who had lived with him at the Richmond address.

"Some things I'll never give you," he said angrily.

"Yes. I respect that."

Communications became the biggest worry. Johnny had been in touch with the Fourth Department man in Paris and had been told he would probably be recalled to Moscow. Though the Russians saw British spies under every bed, the Intelligence Service did not maintain a station in Moscow—a dereliction about which Bailey had often complained to C. British agents inside Russia were handled by officers stationed in neighboring capitals: Reval, Helsinki, Prague. Bailey undertook to send a special courier to Moscow in the event Johnny was recalled. They discussed possible meeting places and settled on two: the bathroom of an Armenian restaurant and the Arbat metro station. Johnny would send a postcard to a cover address, setting the time and place for the initial contact by means of a simple code.

"If there's any sign of trouble," Bailey promised, "we'll get you out. You have my word on that."

Pray God they don't keep him in Moscow for long, Bailey thought. We need to keep a good man alongside him. Otherwise isolation will start wearing him down, and the bottle will make him careless. Pity about this woman trouble. Although it's helping to bind him to us.

Gingerly, Bailey broached one last item of business.

"You mentioned that a few of your colleagues feel as you do about Stalin."

"More than a few. We German Communists are all displaced persons."

"Would you be willing to talk to any of them on our behalf?"

Johnny did not reject this out of hand. He thought for a bit before saying, "Too risky. They wouldn't trust me. The way things are, everyone goes around looking over his shoulder. They would think I was a provocateur, a second Emil."

"Perhaps there's someone we should talk to directly."

"I'll think about it."

6

THE first requirement for a case handler, in Bailey's estimation, was the same as for a bird-watcher or a fly fisherman: the capacity to wait. He wanted to enlist Johnny's help in recruiting a second agent from inside the ranks of the Comintern, not only to increase his sources but to silence the whispering demon—the soul of Section V—that lived on his left shoulder and was still cackling in his ear that despite all the evidence, despite his gut instincts, there was an outside chance that his new agent was a plant, a phantasm created by Comrade Max. But Bailey did not push his suggestion, and his patience was rewarded.

He was taking a morning glass of champagne with Diana in the elegant courtyard of the Lancaster when a boy materialized with a note on a silver salver. From it Bailey learned that Johnny was waiting for him in a church on the Rue des Augustins.

Half an hour later, he was kneeling beside the German.

"I met someone from Germany," Johnny whispered. "His name is Karl Vogel. I told you about him. Do you remember?"

"Karl—you mean the boy who worked for Heinz Kordt?"

"He came for help," Johnny went on. "All Kordt's people are under suspicion, but he's a useful man. He's a good shot, he can handle himself. He told me he is on probation. He's in France illegally, living from hand to mouth, no better than an Algerian. But one of Marlowe's people came to him and said they're considering him for a job. I think it involves a Russian defector, the one who used to work in Stalin's office. He asked me what he should do."

"What did you tell him?"

"I told him to act according to his conscience. I can't be involved. If you want to try something, that's your affair. I just thought you would like to know."

"Where can I find this Karl?"

Johnny told him.

BAILEY could think of more appetizing sights before breakfast than a row of gutted steers slung from steel hooks. At five in the morning, Les Halles was crowded and bustling. Bailey lengthened his stride to avoid a thin rivulet of blood and followed an opulent pear-shaped figure, embellished with a boutonniere and a waxed moustache—evidently the buyer for one of the fashionable restaurants—between the stands of butchered meat. Bailey was dressed in his civilian uniform, complete with umbrella and homburg hat, as if he were on his way to his club.

He spotted Karl fairly quickly. He was wearing a bloodied apron and was engaged in hoisting a carcass out of the back of a truck. This struck Bailey as suitable employment for a man who, by Johnny's account, had spent a good part of his life disposing of other types of bodies.

Bailey would not, under normal circumstances, have involved himself personally in an approach to a meat porter. However one looked at it, Karl Vogel was a very small fish. Yet he could provide useful bait. There was a chance of catching the Russians red-handed in an assassination attempt. But Bailey's main interest was in quelling that little devil on his left shoulder. If there were any indication that Karl had been forewarned about his approach, he would have to accept that as proof that his instinct about Johnny was wrong. By informing Johnny of the exact time he would attempt the approach, he had invited the other side to arrange a trap—if

Johnny were reporting to them. Bailey had taken certain precautions against that contingency.

"Slumming a bit, aren't we, darling?" Diana squeezed his arm and leaned over to inspect a heap of blood sausage.

It was perhaps unorthodox to take his wife along, but after all she had been in the game and was much handier with a revolver than he. Furthermore, the expedition was a diversion from the little shops set like jewel boxes along the Rue St.-Honoré. Diana had already replaced her entire spring wardrobe and was working her way through the summer collections. In any event, Hennessy from the embassy was loping along on his stiltlike legs beyond the sides of beef. All height and no width, Hennessy in profile looked like a stick insect.

"Is that him?" Diana said, watching the flex of Karl's muscles as he swung the carcass onto his back.

"That's him."

"He's not bad looking, in a caveman sort of way. But he could do with some care and feeding."

Karl swung his burden up onto a hook and wiped his hands on his apron.

"Excuse me," Bailey addressed him in faulty French. "Do you have a few minutes?"

Karl growled something and headed back for the truck.

"There's money in it for you."

Karl paused and looked at Bailey with cold suspicion.

"We could use a healthy young man."

This was too much for Diana, who started giggling.

"That is to say," Bailey went on, "we have a proposal for you. Perhaps we could have breakfast and talk it over."

Karl shrugged and gestured towards the truck.

"Do you think he understands French?" Diana whispered.

"Karl," she addressed him in German, somewhat better than Bailey's French. "I do think you ought to stay and talk with us."

"Why do you call me Karl?" He glowered at her.

"I think it suits you," she smiled beatifically. "Do come and talk to us."

There was something utterly disarming about Diana's smile. Karl hesitated. It was his foreman who settled things by bawling at him to get back to work. He tore off his apron and hurled it at the man in disgust. The apron snagged on the hat of the portly restaurant buyer, who sailed on, oblivious.

Karl's eyes darted back and forth between Bailey and Diana as they ate in an all-night café across the road. It was one of those magical places where people who have not yet gone to bed rub shoulders with those who have just finished half the day's work. What passed for breakfast was not, inevitably, what one would expect at the common table in the dining room at the Senior. Karl devoured an entrecôte steak, more raw than cooked, and washed down with copious draughts of red wine. To Bailey's alarm, Diana joined in the wine and ordered a crock of onion soup. Bowing to circumstance, Bailey called for coffee and a glass of calvados.

Karl's table manners were disappointing, but he was no fool. He guessed they were English and—once assured they were not seeking to hire a gigolo —he guessed the rest.

Bailey concluded there was nothing to be lost by bluntness. He made his proposal, and reinforced it with a fat envelope that he placed next to Karl's wineglass. The boy affected not to see it. A few minutes later, he announced he would need to think things over. He agreed to a second meeting at a couscous dive on the Left Bank, and at a more civilized hour. They let him leave the café first.

"What do you think?" he asked Diana.

"He's hungry," she observed, contemplating the plate Karl had scraped clean.

"Yes," Bailey agreed, noting that the envelope was gone. "I wonder if he's hungry enough."

HE HAD his answer the next morning, when he received a distress signal from Johnny. They met in Notre-Dame cathedral, which was jammed with tourists.

"You seem to be developing a penchant for churches," Bailey remarked. "Are you planning to convert to Catholicism?"

Johnny explained that Karl had called on him again, highly agitated, and divulged everything that had happened at Les Halles. Once again, Karl had wanted to know what to do.

"So what did you say?"

"I told him to go to Marlowe at once," Johnny reported. "He was nervous, so I made the arrangements myself."

"You did the right thing," Bailey assured him.

The next step was to see whether Karl would keep his appointment at the Algerian restaurant, and whether the Russians would try to play him as a double. Bailey, of course, would attend the rendezvous, to ensure that no suspicion fell on Johnny. Naturally he would take his babysitters. But not Diana. She would be left to make another blitzkrieg assault on the Rue St.-Honoré.

AFTERWARDS Bailey told himself he ought to be grateful that the Russians, in the main, were not overly subtle. He suspected that if Max Fabrikant had had charge of the operation things might have worked out rather differently. But Max had apparently left Paris.

Karl kept his appointment at the Casbah restaurant, and they consumed a lunch that later sat in Bailey's stomach like a slab of cement. Karl was nervous and showed it by talking and drinking far more than seemed natural. He even made an attempt to tell a joke. Bailey was convinced that this, in a German, was a sign that a man was acting out of character.

As before, Karl left first.

Bailey lingered for a bit, drinking coffee in the hope that it might dissolve the weight in his stomach.

When he strolled out into the spring sunshine, they came at him—two heavies in long coats, a third at the wheel of a car with the engine running. He didn't see the fourth until he backed into him and the man clamped an arm around his throat, blocking off the windpipe, while letting him feel the hardness of the gun jammed up against his ribs.

Hennessy and his men had the drop on the Russians, and they moved fast. But it might not have been fast enough to save Bailey had he not managed to swing his fist back between his attacker's legs, hard enough for the man's hammerlock to loosen. Bailey doubled over, wrenching at the arm with the gun, and his assailant toppled over in a clumsy arc and was left wriggling on the pavement like a beetle on its back. The pistol went off in the course of the struggle, and an ear-piercing whine went up from an old Moorish lady, invoking the Prophet.

Bailey surveyed the damage. No serious injuries. His men had their guns on the Russians; but the Russians had their guns out, too. There were police whistles from beyond the Boulevard St.-Michel, and klaxons that were getting louder.

"It's a standoff," he announced to Hennessy. "Let's get out of this quietly while we can."

In the car, nursing a bruised elbow, he said to Hennessy, "It's quite fantastic. I believe they intended to abduct me. In the heart of Paris."

"It's happened here before," Hennessy said drily. "Quite often, in fact. I'm afraid they're simply not house-trained."

Bailey briefed his Paris man on how to deal with Johnny and on what to say if the striped-pants brigade chose to make waves. Though the approach to Karl had ended in a fiasco, Bailey had the satisfaction of knowing that Johnny had proved his sincerity. The devil at his left ear had stopped clucking. He decided it would be best to leave on the early train, to avoid any embarrassing questions. His mind turned to Diana's hatboxes. Making room for them on the train might be even more difficult than communicating with Johnny in Moscow.

5

The Long March

Insurrection is a calculus with
very indefinite magnitudes, the
value of which may change every
day.

—KARL MARX

1

WHEN Johnny was ordered to return to Moscow alone, he obeyed, though he felt his heart was breaking. He said goodbye to Sigrid at the hotel, so as not to prolong the leave-taking.

"I'll go to General Berzin," he told her. "I'll get you assigned to work with me. You're not going to refuse, are you?"

"Don't be silly."

The tears came then, and he felt her heart flutter as he held her to his chest, so he knew she wasn't lost to him completely.

"I'll be back before you know it," he said with more conviction than he felt.

In Moscow, General Berzin kept him waiting for a week. When he was finally received at the Fourth Department, he requested to be assigned to Paris. Berzin shook his head. "It's already been decided," he said. "We need you in China."

"Then I request to be accompanied by my companion, Sigrid Eckhardt."

Berzin made a note of the name. "I won't promise anything," he said curtly. "And frankly, you'll be better off on your own. This isn't a job for a woman."

Bitterly disappointed, Johnny listened as the chief of the Fourth Department outlined the urgency of his mission.

The Japanese were in Manchuria, threatening Russia's back door. A Communist insurrection in China would force the Japanese to turn their attentions south. If the Communists won, they would treble the population under Soviet rule, adding four hundred million Chinese to two hundred million Russians. Then the revolution would be unstoppable.

The Chinese rebels had made themselves a fortress up in the mountains of Kiangsi, where they were running things like the first Bolsheviks. They had shot the landlords, closed the temples, abolished marriage and private property. But their enemies were gathering strength. With money from the financiers and gang lords of Shanghai, Chiang Kai-shek was mustering troops and planes for an extermination campaign against the Kiangsi Soviet. Hitler had sent General von Seeckt—the man Johnny had once been ordered to kill—as the head of a German military mission that was advising Chiang's forces. The Communists were desperately in need of weapons, training, organization—and a viable military plan.

"Your first stop is Shanghai," Berzin told Johnny. "That's the gun sight through which we take aim at China." The brains of the insurrection, the Comintern advisers assigned to the Far Eastern Bureau, were in Shanghai. "It'll be like old times for you," Berzin added cheerfully. "You'll be fighting von Seeckt, and you'll find a lot of your old German comrades in China. The German civil war, ass-deep in the rice paddies. By the way, a particular friend of yours is in charge. Emil Brandt."

Johnny stared at him.

"It should be quite a reunion," Berzin suggested.

"It certainly will."

The mention of Emil revived his spirits a little.

Maybe I'll find a way to pay the bastard back, he told himself. I'll have that satisfaction, at least.

"I want you to be completely candid in your reports," Berzin said, as if he had read Johnny's thoughts. "Let me know whether I can believe what Shanghai is telling us."

"Oh, yes," Johnny said, "I'll be candid."

Wherever they send me, he thought, it's the same play. Only the backdrops change.

HE WROTE to Sigrid and found a carrier pigeon to take the letter to Paris. His messenger was a voluble Argentinian revolutionist. Like most of the Argentinians who turned up in Moscow, he had an Italian name; everyone called him Verdi because, with his shaggy mane of grey hair and his staring eyes, he looked like a distracted composer. He was en route to Rio and São Paulo. Brazil, he told Johnny with amazing confidence, would be the next Communist power. But like other Latin Americans Johnny had met in Moscow, Verdi spent so much energy winding himself up verbally that it was doubtful whether there would be any left when the time came for action. Johnny ventured to say as much. Instead of taking offense, the Argentine said, "You don't understand the Latin temperament. It's hard for you wurst eaters, because you come from such a cold climate. You get men to risk their lives by imposing an iron discipline. What do you call it? Cadaver horseshit?"

"Kadavergerhorsam," Johnny corrected him. "The obedience of corpses."

"In South America, to get men to risk their lives, to make a revolution, we have to talk a lot. That's how we attain that fever pitch of excitement in which nobody cares what it costs. In that way talk makes action inescapable."

He makes revolution sound like a crime of passion, Johnny thought. He decided not to prolong the argument, in case something that was said should lose him his carrier pigeon.

His words to Sigrid were tender and full of longing. He asked her not to give up her painting.

It's the artist in her that will bring her back, he told himself. Her conscious mind might be able to rationalize the things she would see in her work for Max into neat, bloodless categories; the artist in her couldn't.

FOR MORE than a week he sat on the Trans-Siberian Express. He rarely stirred from his berth except to go to the lavatory or to visit the dining car, where the tables were embellished with disheveled bouquets of paper flowers and dusty black bottles of wine that never seemed to be opened. The piles of birch logs along the rail bed were black at the core, silvered along the trunks, as if coated with frost.

Vladivostok looked like a city at war. There were submarines in the harbor and flotillas of radio-controlled motorboats, stuffed with explosives, that could be used like monster torpedoes. In the rail yards he saw freight trains with tanks and howitzers and more submarines lashed to their flatcars. He was subjected to repeated identity checks and practiced, on Soviet soil, the role he would play when he stepped off the steamer to Shanghai.

His papers identified him as one Arne Paulsen, born in Minneapolis, Minnesota. The experts at the OMS had assured him that the passport was real enough, the property of an American citizen of Finnish extraction who had decided to migrate to Russia for the sake of socialism and world peace. From Johnny's viewpoint, it had one flaw. He discovered it only on the voyage south from Vladivostok, when he started trying to forge Paulsen's signature. Try as he might, the man's handwriting was almost impossible to reproduce. It seemed as tangled and twisted as a blackberry patch. He did not give up. He needed to be able to toss off a plausible version of Paulsen's signature, because the OMS had arranged to wire ten thousand dollars in the American's name to the Hong Kong and Shanghai Bank. He was still scratching away when he saw the skyscrapers of Shanghai rise out of a flat horizon of yellow mud and flooded paddy fields.

HE HAD been instructed to check into the Palace Hotel. Its Victorian facade looked homely amongst the white palaces of the Bund, overlooking the warships and sampans on the muddy river. He discovered a second defect in his passport when he made his leisurely progress, some hours later, along the Bund to the confident domed tower of the Hong Kong Bank. Brass lions guarded its portals, their features rubbed smooth by the hands of numberless Chinamen anxious to absorb the predator spirit they embodied.

A British clerk, impervious to the heat in his starched collar, dark coat and striped trousers, received Johnny with all proper decorum and begged him to take tea while he verified that the sum in question had indeed been transferred for Mr. Paulsen's benefit. He was gone for less than five minutes and showed no emotion when Johnny informed him that he wanted to have the entire amount in cash.

"Perhaps I might just have your signature, sir. And your passport. I won't keep you a moment, sir."

This time, the delay was appreciably longer, and Johnny thought he saw someone—an authoritative-looking individual with muttonchop whiskers and half-moon spectacles—peer at him from a discreet remove beyond a glass partition. He became uneasy as the minutes ticked by. He was half resolved to get up and leave when the clerk came back, polite and impersonal as before.

"I see that your passport has expired, sir."

"Why, yes. I've been traveling quite a bit. But I had it renewed." Johnny was prepared for this. The passport had indeed expired, but the Comintern's experts had doctored it. It bore the stamp of the American consul in Tokyo, extending it for one year.

"Would you mind very much if I asked why it has been extended for only twelve months, sir?"

Johnny could only guess at the point of this question. "Well, I'll be going back to the States before it runs out again," he said lamely.

"I see."

The clerk rang a bell on his desk. Johnny tensed, but it was only the signal for a cashier to come in with the money, sorted into packets of crisp new bills.

He signed a receipt for the total, minus the bank's commission, and the clerk returned his passport.

"A pleasure to do business with you, sir."

"Likewise."

"Would you like an escort to your hotel, sir? I must warn you, the streets can be quite dangerous for a newcomer."

"I'm sure I'll survive."

1

SHANGHAI was the perfect setting for intrigue. It was many cities, not one, and in all of them allegiances could be bought and sold as cheaply as a man's life or the body of a nine-year-old girl. There was the colonial dream of number three, the Bund, home of the Shanghai Club, where the taipans gulped their *stengahs* at the longest bar in the world. There were the cabarets and stylish villas of Frenchtown. There were the glittering lights and the streetcars of the Nanking Road, with its famed emporiums—the Sun Sun, the Wing On—where the mistresses of Chinese generals and Green Gang mobsters came to shop. There was the stifling, noisy round of the cotton mills, the shoe factories, the silk filatures, where children were worked for fifteen hours a day, or until they dropped. There were the Americanized millionaires who raced around in their big cars with armed bodyguards on the running boards. There were twenty-five thousand women who hawked their bodies. There were followers of every flag in the world—nine flew over the International Settlement, guarded by its fierce, bearded Sikhs—and plenty willing to sell themselves to any or all.

The Communists, though, were not so easily bought. That made them different from the other political factions and elicited grudging admiration from Hugh McIvor of the municipal police. Inspector McIvor, a young man prematurely aged by the Orient—and, no doubt, by the quantities of gin and quinine water he infused as a prophylactic against malaria and misanthropy—was something of a specialist on Communism.

McIvor had no fixed opinions about Chinese politics. One warlord looked much like another. Only their prices varied. His job was to keep

Shanghai open to European commerce. The Communists, who appealed to the misery of the slums and to popular hatred of the "foreign devils," were therefore his main opponents.

McIvor's Chinese detectives kept watch on a list of houses and flats whose tenants were thought to be associated with the Communist International. More than a few of these addresses belonged to Americans. There was that foul-mouthed woman writer on the Avenue Dubail in Frenchtown, stocky as a lumberjack, who looked as if she cut her hair with a lawn mower. She had spent time in Russia and seemed to be the first port of call for every transient radical. McIvor suspected her of running a message center for the Russians, but her passport was genuine and he could not have her deported without further evidence. One of her visitors was a fellow from Seattle who called himself Walsh and had no visible means of employment. McIvor had heard rumors that Walsh was high up in the Communist Party U.S.A. Perhaps they imagined in Moscow that Americans had some special affinity with the Chinese—or that possession of a U.S. passport conveyed some kind of immunity.

McIvor was intrigued by what he had learned about another American recently arrived in the settlement. He called himself Arne Paulsen and had collected a large sum in cash from the Hong Kong Bank. There was an oddity in his passport, which one of McIvor's contacts at the bank had been shrewd enough to spot. The passport had expired, and Paulsen had it renewed at the American Consulate in Tokyo. It was not unusual for an American consulate to extend an out-of-date passport with a rubber stamp, to save its bearer the delay of waiting in a foreign city for delivery of a new travel document. But the standard extension was for two years, not one. McIvor had checked this with the American consulate in Shanghai. Furthermore—he had since received word—though the passport number matched the records, the American consul in Tokyo had never heard of a man called Arne Paulsen.

McIvor ordered two of his Chinese detectives to maintain close surveillance. The results, though disappointing, confirmed his suspicions.

The man calling himself Paulsen was tailed to the Avenue Dubail, where he paused outside the woman writer's apartment building but did not go in. The detectives lost him when he paid a visit to a small shipping agency off the Bund. They watched for him outside, but he did not reemerge. McIvor assumed that he must have found his way out through the partners' entrance and warned his men to be more alert. Paulsen did not return to his hotel that night. One of McIvor's men spotted him in the street, quite by chance, two days later. He was followed to a Szechuan restaurant on the Nanking Road, where he took lunch but was not seen to speak to anyone except the waiter. In the afternoon, the suspect was observed loitering on the Bubbling Well Road near the Buddhist Temple.

When he entered the temple, the policemen followed, determined not to be cheated a second time. But to their consternation, they found their quarry was gone. A white man, a stranger to Shanghai, had become as invisible as a native pickpocket.

This satisfied McIvor that the man was a professional and knew his job. He decided to visit the hotel in person and elicited the fact that the American had paid for a week in advance. The assistant manager agreed to show McIvor the room. All he found was a forlorn suit on a hanger and a pile of laundry waiting for the maid. No personal papers, and the money from the bank had gone.

He assured the assistant manager that there was no cause for alarm, but he wished to be informed as soon as Mr. Arne Paulsen returned. He had no confidence that this event would take place.

The Chinese girl who pressed up against Johnny in the temple said, "Did you see the five T'ang horses?"

"No," he responded without looking at her. "There were two, not five." Then, quickly, "I'm being followed."

"Come with me now, please."

Within two minutes he was running behind her through a warren of narrow streets, crouched low to escape the awnings of the street peddlers. Two minutes more and he was lying in the back of a pushcart under coarse hessian sacking and, above it, a load of hot peppers, holding his nose to avoid sneezing. Within two hours he was in the hold of a junk, heading lazily south from the frantic docks of Hongchew towards the southern port of Swiatow.

From Swiatow, he traveled west by riverboat, pony and finally on foot, up stony mountain trails no wider than a man's body, into liberated China: the Soviet Republic of Kiangsi.

3

Johnny had been in south China for nearly five months when C. asked Colin Bailey to lunch at White's. Bailey kept the appointment with some misgivings. In his experience, C. invited his subordinates onto private territory when he wanted to mount a sudden flank attack. He wondered whether the chief wanted to pursue that awkward business in Brussels, where a member of the service had been caught with his fingers in the till, filching some of the visa money collected from Jews en route to Palestine.

They drank gin and french at the bar, where the appearance of the Prince of Wales caused not the slightest commotion. C. made a point of introducing Bailey.

"Perfectly decent chap," C. remarked after the Prince had moved on. "Rather underrated. It's a pity about that American woman."

"A bit soft on the Germans," Bailey ventured to suggest.

C. affected not to hear.

He delayed his attack until port and cigars had been served in the smoking room.

"You know Adam de Salis is in town," C. suddenly remarked. "He asked to see Johnny's file. Since Johnny was, in a manner of speaking, his discovery, I couldn't actually refuse, could I?"

"Of course not," Bailey said automatically, trying to conceal his annoyance that de Salis had been poaching on his territory.

"Adam thought that some of this China stuff smells a bit high."

"Oh, really? What precisely does he object to?"

Johnny's reports from Manchuria had been spotty, and there had been a lapse in communications when he was up in the mountains in Kiangsi. But since he had come back to Shanghai and settled into a flat on the Avenue Molière, in Frenchtown, his reports had been regular and, to Bailey, a source of mounting fascination.

Johnny described a powerful revolutionary movement that was being led to certain destruction by its foreign controllers. The Communists had scored their biggest military successes by hit-and-run tactics, striking the enemy where he was weakest, melting away whenever they were outnumbered, giving up territory to save lives. Now, under the strategy laid down by Emil Brandt, they were painting themselves into a corner.

Emil—who had never set eyes on the province of Kiangsi—had convinced himself that the rebels' mountain fortress was impregnable. Under the gun and the lash, forced labor battalions were sweating to throw up earthen walls to make it stronger still. In his own reports to Moscow, Emil boasted that the Red Army mustered more than half a million men and could withstand any force the government hurled against it. According to Johnny, there were only half that number, and many of them were armed with sticks and knives. True, the forests of Kiangsi, laced with narrow paths where soldiers could advance only in single file, would be costly to storm in a frontal attack. But the defenders were vulnerable to a protracted siege. Their food supplies were low. All their salt had to be supplied from the outside. If they were squeezed for long enough, their own followers would rise up against them.

Von Seeckt understood this. Steadily, stealthily, he was moving on Kiangsi. His weapon was a garrote. Johnny had seen the chain of concrete blockhouses and tidy forts, joined up by new military roads and bristling coils of barbed wire, that von Seeckt was building all around the Communist base area. Week by week, the lines were being tightened. Week by week, it was harder to smuggle food and weapons through. In Kiangsi they began to feel the bite of the wire against their throats.

The Comintern advisers who had been there had given Emil the same advice: break out of the trap; open escape routes; give up as much land as necessary, but save the Red Army. Some argued that in order to survive the Communists must be ready to seal an alliance with anyone who was ready to fight the Nanking government. Overnight, a powerful ally became available. Its appearance was almost miraculous, a gift of the gods. In the province of Fukien, next door to the soviet republic, the Nineteenth Route Army raised the standard of revolt. Its leaders were nationalists, not Communists, but they were opposed to the landowners, the warlords and the Japanese. Join forces with them, some of the Communists urged. Then we can break out of von Seeckt's ring of steel and open a road to the sea. The Russians will send guns to us from Vladivostok.

Emil was deaf to all these entreaties. The soviet republic is secure, he insisted. The rebels in Fukien are bourgeois opportunists. Those in our camp who promote their cause are Trotskyite adventurers. Until we have overthrown the chiefs of the Nineteenth Route Army and replaced them with Communists, we can have nothing to do with them. Emil had ordered an American journalist on his payroll—whose Shanghai-based publication, *China Forum,* was financed with secret Comintern funds—to write an article quoting fictitious interviews with rebel leaders in Fukien province to make these points. He had later denounced the same journalist as a Trotskyite, forcing him to flee from Shanghai.

So, while Emil hunted Trotskyite adventurers, the military rebels in Fukien were left to face the onslaught of Generalissimo Chiang's brandnew tanks and warplanes. Von Seeckt's influence had begun to tell. For once the government soldiers did not turn and flee at the sound of battle. The Fukien rebels were crushed, and the Communists were left in utter isolation to face the next extermination campaign. The generalissimo bragged that he had marshaled nine hundred thousand men to wipe them off the map of China.

In Johnny's account, Emil Brandt had set himself up as absolute dictator of the Communist party in China. He enforced his authority with bullying and threats of denunciation to Moscow. At the same time he lived in abject terror of incurring Stalin's disfavor. His mind moved in a parallel reality.

By repeating and inflating his fabrications over and over, he had convinced himself that they were truer than the evidence of his own eyes.

Bailey knew the depth of Johnny's hatred and contempt for Emil Brandt and made allowances for this in assessing his material. Even so, he found the head of the Far Eastern Bureau an intriguing psychological study. A man addicted to his own illusions. What would become of him when his illusions—as Johnny predicted with such assurance—exploded in his face?

"De Salis's point," the chief of the Secret Service was saying, "is that Johnny's reports from Shanghai are too good to be true. He's telling us that without anyone's help the Communists are going to blow themselves up. Wouldn't you agree that's the gist of it?"

"More or less," Bailey concurred. "He says the Kiangsi soviet can't hold out for more than six months."

"Which is, of course, what we would wish to hear."

"I'm not sure I follow."

"De Salis believes it possible that Johnny has been turned, and that these reports from China are part of a deception plan."

"With what motive?"

"To keep us smug and inert while the Communists make another grab for Shanghai. It's the richest prize in the East. There's more silver in the Shanghai banks than anywhere else on earth."

"I don't see it," Bailey objected. "An insurrection in Shanghai would be doomed unless they got help from outside. There's no help in sight."

C. reflected on this before asking, "Do we have any independent confirmation of what Johnny is telling us?"

"Well, Killen thinks he's on the right track."

Killen was their man in Shanghai. Only recently arrived in China, he had a job as a griffin—a junior assistant—at the offices of the British Cigarette Company.

"Killen hasn't had much experience though, has he?" C. observed. "Against his opinion, we have to weigh the wireless intercepts."

Recently deciphered traffic had included a message from Emil to Moscow, restating his confident prospectus for the Communists in south China. His figures, of course, had been wildly at variance with Johnny's.

"I suppose it boils down to whether we trust our man or not," Bailey remarked. "For my money, he's proved himself several times over."

"Adam suggested we put it to the test."

De Salis believes . . . Adam suggested . . . one of C.'s more irritating habits was to attribute his own doubts to a third party. It saved him from having to go into the firing line before he had made up his mind.

"May I ask in what way?"

"By using Johnny to stop some of the Red leaders in Shanghai. Emil Brandt, for one. The fellow who poses as a music teacher. And that other military expert, what's-his-name—"

"Otto Braun."

"Just so. I understand we've already had an inquiry from the Shanghai police."

A Scot called McIvor, a police inspector, had indeed paid a call on James Killen. It seemed his detectives had followed Johnny to Killen's home— evidence of a lapse of security on the part of both the Russians and Bailey's own service.

"I expect the locals are jittery," C. went on. "The government didn't do much last time the city was under attack. If we break the back of this conspiracy now, we can do them and ourselves a favor."

"I don't agree," Bailey said mildly.

"Let me be sure I understand you. You're worried that Johnny will be blown. Is that it?"

"He might be blown. But there is something else to consider."

"Well?"

"If Johnny's reports are reliable, the last man in Shanghai we would wish to see behind bars is Emil Brandt. He'll wreck the whole Communist enterprise in China without any assistance from us. The policy called for is masterly inertia."

"Are you serious, Colin?"

"Yes. But I admit the situation does have its humorous side."

When C. failed to respond immediately, Bailey knew he had won his argument. His approach was not quite as passive as he had indicated to his chief. He had culled from Johnny's reports the names of the most effective Communist organizers. Feeding Emil's—and the Russians'—paranoia about Trotsky's influence, Bailey had arranged to have Trotskyite materials mailed to some of them anonymously. He had resolved to deliver the Chinamen on the list to the police when the appropriate occasion presented itself. They included the man code-named "Slavein," who was the main link between the Far Eastern Bureau and the Chinese party. But for the moment, as he had advised Killen in Shanghai, they must be content to watch and wait.

4

FOR Johnny, living in the Shanghai underground under a new identity, waiting was impossible. He found relief in action, as always, in flouting the rules of all his employers by involving himself personally in risky operations. He staged holdups, smuggled guns off a freighter on the Whangpoo river under the noses of the police, planted explosives in a car belonging to the Blue Shirts, Chiang's dreaded secret police. The younger Chinese Communists he helped to train—the ones who had a vocation for death—admired him for it.

He, in turn, admired them. They gave freely of themselves, asking nothing in return, with a generosity of spirit that was totally alien to the carping, conspiring party bigwigs in Berlin and Moscow. These young Chinese reminded Johnny of his own youth, and of Heinz—and then of the men who had murdered him. He had a mournful suspicion that his Chinese commandos would end the same way. He did not feel he was betraying them when he smuggled his reports to Killen, Bailey's man in Shanghai. It was the men in charge of the Chinese revolt who were the betrayers: carping graduates of the Lenin School, less Chinese than Russian; lost souls like Emil Brandt, who toadied to Moscow to cover up his terror and lack of conviction.

Johnny had toyed with the idea of shooting Emil one night, when rumors of a police raid had sent the members of the Far Eastern bureau scuttling out of a meeting and he found himself alone with Brandt on a blacked-out street, silent except for the distant thunder of an angry crowd and the howl of police klaxons. What saved Emil then, and helped to sustain Johnny now, was his realization that Brandt was doing the job himself. All Emil's groveling to Stalin would not save him, surely, when his mistakes in China resulted in another rout. Johnny was scrupulous in relating the full magnitude of those mistakes in his private correspondence with General Berzin.

When he needed women, they were never far. Within Emil's organization, as in Moscow in the old days, it was as natural to go to bed with any consenting partner as to go to the bathroom. It was accepted, too, that for people who lived with the daily prospect of violent death, the urge was stronger than in others. It was not necessary to confine the appetite to party members. In the city of Shanghai, one house in twelve was a bordello. The women were of every age, shape, color and nationality. Some of them, inevitably, were "swallows" in the service of the party, or the police.

Now Johnny was on his back in a room above the Cockatoo Club, a cabaret on the Avenue Joffre, hands folded behind his head, eyes closed, a cigarette dangling from his lower lip. The girl who was working to arouse him with her lips and fingers was patient and skillful. May had the wide cheekbones and blue eyes of her Russian father, the simian grace of her Japanese mother. He had been with her before. He liked her because she was beautiful and clever and never shammed pleasure she did not experience. At least not with him. She had confessed to him that she was utterly indifferent to what took place on her bed.

He found her a useful source because of her other lovers. One of them was a banker who was sending millions abroad in Shanghai silver dollars that could be resold for ten or twenty percent more than their face value in London or New York because the American treasury had decided it needed to hoard silver as well as gold. May had promised to find out what ship would carry the next consignment. One act of piracy could pay for a hundred machine guns, five thousand rifles. But the bags of silver coins would be heavy. And he would need a friendly captain.

"Have you been drinking?" May asked.

"Not enough. Let's have some cognac."

"As you like." The boy was waiting outside the door. She gave him his instructions and said, "You're sad tonight. Are you thinking about your wife?"

"No." The ash spilled from his cigarette. May brushed it off his bare chest and kissed his nipples, the way he might have kissed hers. He began to feel mildly aroused. But he said, "Let's talk. Who else have you been seeing?"

"You'll be jealous."

"On the contrary. You know it excites me."

"Very well. But give me a cigarette." He helped her light it, and she went on, "I saw Tu Yu-seng. Do you believe me?"

"Of course. He's your protector, isn't he?"

Tu Yu-seng—Big-Eared Tu, they called him, because his ears stuck out like bat's wings—was the boss of the Green Gang. It was said that nobody could run a bar or a cabaret or a gambling den in Frenchtown without paying him. It was also said that he controlled the detective section of the police in the French Concession. The taipans sipping whisky at the Long Bar or tea at the Astor House might never admit his existence, but they, too, paid their dues. Nor did Tu's influence end there. The generalissimo, Chiang Kai-shek himself, had taken the vows of the Greens as a young man —terrifying vows that bound a man to give his life to the society, if demanded, and guaranteed that the society, in exchange, would always protect him. The Greens had carried out their part of the bargain in 1927, when their gunmen and axemen went through the streets killing Communists. The generalissimo would be paying his dues to the end of his days.

May held her cigarette between thumb and forefinger, like a Russian. "Where did you see him? Here?"

"I went to his house."

"What's it like?"

"Like an emperor's palace. There were mechanical birds, singing in a tree with gold and silver leaves."

"I don't care about the birds. Why did he send for you?"

"You don't think I have talent?"

She lay back with her legs apart and blew smoke at him.

"Of course."

"There was a party," she explained. "There were generals from Nanking, even the finance minister. A German, too."

"A German? What German?"

"An officer from the front. I don't remember the name."

"Von Seeckt?" He screwed an imaginary monocle into his face. "A man in his fifties? Very arrogant, very Prussian?"

"All of that, but not in his fifties. His name was similar, though."

Johnny thought hard. He had made a personal hobby out of studying the members of of the German military mission that was planning the destruction of the Reds in Kiangsi. He had drawn up a plan to assassinate von Seeckt. It had been approved. But he had been forbidden to take part himself, and one of the Chinese involved had lost his nerve at the last moment and thrown his grenades too soon, missing the general's car and turning a dozen nameless civilians into chopped meat.

He had not reported the episode to James Killen, his well-intentioned but rather insular British contact. One day, given the chance, he might mention it to Colin Bailey. He thought Bailey would understand. Von Seeckt and Emil Brandt were two sides of a German evil. But one of them was going to self-destruct. It was best to focus his hatred, for now, on the one that might not.

He mentally rehearsed the names of other members of the German advisory team, which Hitler had recently doubled in size: Falkenhausen, Zorn . . .

"Steinitz," he suggested. "Colonel Martin Steinitz. Is that the one?"

"It might be—" May yawned. "Why are you so interested? You ask too many questions. What are you? A policeman?"

"I don't pay you to ask questions. And I pay you well enough, don't I?"

"Not as well as Tu."

"Did you sleep with him?"

She crossed her legs and hugged herself as if she felt a chill. "Not him. One of his lieutenants. He carries the marks of the smallpox—everywhere."

"Who went with Steinitz?"

"Some girl—a Russian, I think. You know what they are. The latest fashions, furs, and not two bits of *cash* to scrape together. She looked like a model from Chanel. But hard, very hard. I think your Colonel Steinitz likes that. He really fell for her."

"What is her name?"

"They called her Lena. I never saw her before."

"But you can find out, can't you?" He took a handful of Mexican silver dollars—still the preferred currency in Shanghai—and shaped them into a neat stack on the bedside table.

The boy came with a bottle of Martell. Johnny paid him off, too.

"Is that all you want?" May asked, after draining her glass. She straddled him, letting her breasts swing over his face.

"No," he said, closing his eyes again. He was no longer in Shanghai. He was with Sigrid, in a room in Paris where the afternoon light spilled through the shutters and dropped to the floor like ripe sheaves of wheat.

MAY loved to be taken out. That satisfied her that she moved in a different dimension from the taxi dancers downstairs at the Cockatoo Club or the varnished Chinese whores who paraded two abreast down the Nanking Road, with their amahs at their heels. Like all the denizens of Shanghai, she also loved to gamble. So Johnny took her to the Canidrome. The greyhound she picked in the third race was so heavily drugged that it collapsed on all fours in the home straight. May was outraged. He consoled her with champagne, but she was still fuming when he broached the reason for their meeting.

"What did you find out about Lena?"

"She's too skinny for you," May snickered.

"Did you find out where she lives?" Johnny persisted.

"I can go one better. Colonel Steinitz found out, too."

"You mean he visits her?"

"I gather he is infatuated."

"Give me the woman's address."

May told him, and he made a mental note. The apartment was on the wrong side of Soochow Creek. He knew the area slightly. Some affluent Chinese lived there, but no Europeans, except for a few White Russians.

"We could go to a dinner dance," May suggested. "We could go to the Cathay."

The woman would have made the perfect wife for one of the English taipans, Johnny thought. Indifferent to sex but in love with appearances. The Cathay produced one of the starchier evening entertainments on offer in the settlement. Members of May's profession got in as long as they were suitably attired and not obviously oriental.

"Not tonight," he said.

"Are you going to see Lena?"

"Perhaps. I don't know."

"Why do you care so much about this German officer?" May looked angry. "I bet I know. I bet you're a Communist."

"What do you have against Communists?"

"They pretend that sex doesn't have a price."

"If I were a Communist, would you betray me?"

"It would depend on what I was paid."

5

JOHNNY watched the sweat gleam on the lean, dark back of his rickshaw driver. The man's leathery feet in their straw sandals drummed noiselessly on the pavement. The night smelled of camphor and oil. On sampans pushed nose to tail on the muddy bank of Soochow Creek, families were eating and swapping tales, their laundry hung out on oars that made some of the boats look like wounded flying fish.

They were still in the settlement, but they had left the wide boulevards of the European city. There was no sign of the shells and bombs that had gutted whole streets in Hongkew only two years before, when the Japanese had landed troops at Shanghai. The singsong houses and restaurants, the pawnbrokers and silver shops had sprung back, rank and prolific as tropical weeds. A brass band thumped out a tune from an upstairs window above a department store, primitive but effective advertising. The people in the street were a sea of blue.

He touched the shoulder of the rickshaw puller with the toe of his shoe. *"Man, man!"*

He dismounted at the end of Lena's street. There was an herbalist's shop near the corner with ginseng and dried frogs on display in the window. There was also a black car blocking half the narrow street. Two Chinese toughs loitered on the driver's side, smoking cheap cigars. Opposite was a dress shop with a copy of a Molyneux evening gown in the window. On the second floor, Lena's apartment.

Johnny had come with no fixed plan except to watch and to open his lungs. The hot season was on its way; in the night the humid exhalations of the mud flats rose up through the cement and tar.

Lena and her colonel interested him. He had heard something from Otto Braun about this Steinitz. He was a passionate Hitlerite, according to Braun, but also a soldier who knew his business. He had helped to draw up the plans for Chiang's extermination campaign. If he was dallying in

Shanghai for reasons other than personal pleasure, it was no doubt to arrange the delivery of a new shipload of arms or to squeeze more money out of the Chinese bankers who paid for the generalissimo's campaigns.

Steinitz was a promising target. If the girl could be bought—or persuaded—they could find out the colonel's secrets through her.

The idea was seductive. It might even be a way to strike at two enemies at once and drive the last nail into Emil's coffin. Moscow trusted conspiracy more than common sense. Anyone with his eyes open could see that the Communists in the south were lost unless they changed their strategy. Otto Braun could see it; he had actually asked the center to recall Emil to Moscow on the grounds that his policy was suicidal. Braun had the Kiangsi leaders on his side, including the big, flat-faced peasant philosopher, Mao Tse-tung. But the Central Committee was in Shanghai, and it was run by recent graduates of the Lenin School whose dogmatism made Torquemada look like a freethinker. They would back Emil as long as Moscow did. In the fights that broke out between Emil and Braun, Johnny tried to avoid taking sides. When forced to state his position, he deferred to Emil. But his secret reports to Starik were a damning cumulative indictment. Firsthand evidence, through Steinitz, of the plan to crush the Kiangsi soviet— the plan Emil had done everything to advance—would surely settle Emil's hash when the accounts were drawn up in Moscow.

Failing that, Johnny thought he would quite enjoy putting a bullet into Colonel Steinitz.

He went into the corner pawnshop. There seemed to be a great many samurai swords. He went out the door on the other side, leading into a street the Chinese called Iron Road. He saw it was possible, by climbing over fire escapes and pocket gardens, to get to the back of Lena's building.

He retraced his steps and saw Steinitz march briskly towards his car. He had a handsome, haughty face, marred by the jagged white seam of an old scar that must have been stitched up in haste. He was carrying a leather satchel.

Johnny waited for several minutes after the car moved off. Then he went through the entrance next to the dress shop. On his left, there was an open door: Chinese in black pajamas playing mah-jongg. They watched him pull back the metal grille and step into the lift, but nobody questioned a European.

He tapped on Lena's door.

"Who's there?" The girl called out in English.

"I have a message from Colonel Steinitz," he responded in German.

For what seemed like a long time there was no response. He wondered if she was inspecting him through a concealed peephole. He pressed his ear up against the door. He could hear Mozart on a scratchy recording.

He knocked again and was rewarded with the scrape of metal as she released the bolts inside the door.

But she didn't open it. She merely called out, "Come in."

Even as he turned the handle, he knew it was a trap. The room was a black hole. In the first instants he could see nothing. He only sensed her movements as she slipped behind him, too late to fling himself out of range. The touch of the silk rope against his throat was exquisitely smooth and cool. But he clawed and grabbed at her hands, trying to prise them loose. There was amazing strength in the woman's arms. The garrote is not a weapon for women—at least, not for many. The room was a pattern of purplish blotches in front of his eyes when he managed to grab a fistful of hair and wrench her head over to one side. Instantly, the vise around his windpipe was relaxed. He could hear the light rhythm of her panting as she darted across the room.

He made a leap at her, caught hold of a leg and went crashing on top of her. Glass and porcelain exploded across the floor. She wrestled and bit. She broke something over his head—a bottle or a vase—and went gouging for his eyes, two fingers extended like the talons of a bird of prey.

"You're a fighter. I have to give you that," he said when he finally had her pinioned, her arms twisted up behind her back.

He heard a sharp intake of breath. Perhaps he was holding her too tight. But he had no intention of starting another round.

He found a light switch. She was wearing black silk pajamas. Her skin glowed against them like ivory. Her eyes were pale and bright, ice-blue. One of them would be very black by morning.

"Good God." He released her arms. He was too shocked for a moment to say anything more. Finally he said, "Is this how you receive all your former lovers?"

"Only the ones who deserve it," Helene replied, and laughed till her ribs hurt.

In the little ways, at least, Helene was the same. After sex, or after a fight, she demanded to eat. Johnny took her to a place where Europeans rarely went. The restaurant advertised its cuisine with a newly fried chicken, varnished to a bright vermilion and suspended above the door. Most of the Chinese customers ate standing up at a counter, but there were a few tables at the back.

"I didn't know you at the door. But I knew you weren't from Steinitz," Helene explained, pausing in her demolition of a plate of fried dumplings.

"What did you think I was?"

"Police. Or Gestapo."

"Gestapo? Here? But why?"

Her chopsticks moved from the dumplings to a bowl of saffron-colored rice.

"Because Steinitz is one of us." She took a mouthful and said, "We have been very careful. He is closely watched. The Greens have people everywhere. But who can object to a kept woman? It's only human, isn't it? Besides, they think I'm a White Russian. Who else would live in this part of Hongkew? And they saw Steinitz meet me in the house of the grand vizier, no less. You know that's what he likes to be called, don't you? Big-Eared Tu." She wiped her mouth. "The man is disgusting. But he truly is the grand vizier of Shanghai.'

"How did you manage the introductions?"

"I met Steinitz before, of course. In Berlin. But none of his people know that. They saw him falling in love with me in Tu's house. What do you think of that?"

"Not bad. How did you get invited?"

"An acquaintance. One of those gentleman who likes Chekiang silk and dainty feet and doesn't care where he finds his money."

Johnny realized that a powerful Chinese, a member of the Green Gang, perhaps even a relative of Big-Eared Tu, had been recruited by Helene's network.

"It's dangerous work," Johnny observed. In Shanghai, by his observations, a bribe worked only until a bigger bribe was available.

"More dangerous since you decided to drop in on me," she countered. "You stumbled in like a pathetic amateur. You could have got all our heads cut off."

"Believe me, I had no idea of the relationship. I thought it was a stupid affair of a bar girl, someone who could be bought. Nobody warned me about Steinitz. They didn't even tell me you were in Shanghai."

"Emil Brandt isn't the only game in town," Helene sniffed. "And it's just as well."

HE GOT into the habit of visiting Helene when Steinitz was out of Shanghai, in Nanking or at the front. They drank together and talked about the old days, and about Sigrid.

"Poor Johnny," Helene said to him. "Don't say I didn't warn you. It was the same when Sigi and I were kids. Everybody wanted to give her the treats, she looked so sweet and innocent. Besides which, she was the littlest one. Whenever we had a fight, I'd get belted for it. I was the tomboy, the bad girl, the one who was always running away from home. But guess who won most of the fights? She did."

For Johnny, talk about Sigrid, however banal, was better than nothing.

He had received only a few short letters from her, not much better than postcards. One was postmarked Brussels, another Copenhagen. She made no reference to the long letters he had written her, painting word pictures of the city that he thought might please her. He wondered if she had even received them.

If there had ever been jealousy or hostility between him and Helene, it had been leached away by the passage of time. Sitting with her, completely at his ease, he thought at times they were almost like an old married couple. But there remained an unbridgeable gap defined by professional caution. They could talk about Heinz and laugh at the games the three of them had once played together, and Johnny could express his contempt for Emil for denouncing Heinz to the party. This much was common ground. But Johnny did not dare to go further. He could not attack Max, not to a woman who, by all appearances, remained one of Max's most devoted protégées. He must let nothing slip that would tell her what he had become, nothing to hint at the driving purpose that had supplanted his lost faith in the party: the determination to put a bomb under the little Stalins, and the big one in Moscow too, with the help of British Intelligence.

On her side, too, Helene was reticent. Johnny became certain that they shared a common contact in the Shanghai underground, the shadowy Latvian who posed as a music teacher and represented the OMS. This was the man to whom Johnny delivered his money from the Hong Kong Bank. But Helene never mentioned him. And though she talked about Steinitz's courage and conditions of life at the front, she did not share his reports. Once, though, she asked him to deliver a coded message to the radio man who operated from a room above a sewing shop on Sad Donkey Road. The text was incomprehensible to him, but he made a copy and passed it on to Colin Bailey's man.

Helene was available; she made that plain enough. She changed her clothes in front of him in a matter-of-fact way that said, take it or leave it. He left it. They carried too much baggage.

He slept with May when the mood took him but stopped frequenting the Cockatoo Club. He arranged to meet her at her own studio, a few blocks from the Quai. May liked the new arrangement, because it meant she could pocket the money she would normally have to pay out to the pimps. She forgot that in Frenchtown the pimps were scrupulous about collecting their dues.

On a night of fireworks and whirling dragons—a festival for red-faced Kuan Ti, god of war and peace—Johnny went to the apartment near the quai. The left pocket of his jacket sagged with silver dollars, the bonus he intended to give May. With her information, he had arranged the hijacking of a cargo of silver bound for San Francisco and the American commodity markets.

The success of this operation was not the only reason for his high spirits. Emil and his dour Polish wife had finally been recalled to Moscow. This followed a blazing session at the Far Eastern bureau at which Emil was outvoted seven to two and Otto Braun came close to calling him a traitor. The Kiangsi soviet was finished. The Red Army had suffered a bloody defeat. The population under Communist control had shrunk to one third the original number. Cut off from the outside world, denied even salt, the peasants were turning against their commissars. All of Emil's creative bookkeeping could no longer disguise the real state of affairs. Without salt the Red Republic of Kiangsi would go under. The remnants of Mao's guerrilla army would have to flee for their lives or be ground under the treads of the generalissimo's tanks. Though the official version had it that Emil was returning to help organize the next world congress of the Communist International, Johnny was certain that in Moscow he would be presented with the bill for one of Moscow's most costly failures. Best of all, he had confirmation that his own departure from China was imminent. Emil had suggested that they leave on the same boat. The poor dreamer apparently saw Johnny as a witness for the defense.

He climbed to May's landing and rapped twice on the door. There was no answer. He tried his key but found that the door was already unlocked. When he threw it open, he was assailed by a stench so overpowering that he took a step backward involuntarily. The ceiling light was on. The bulb was weak, but it showed him more than he wanted to see. May was sprawled on the bed, the knuckles of her left hand grazing the floor. From her nostrils and mouth, thick rivulets of slime oozed down, fouling the bright satin of her dress. It might have been vomit, but the smell was a compound of shit and gasoline. He knew what it meant. In China a favorite method of interrogation was to force a mixture of petrol and excrement through a hose into the suspect's nostrils, until his belly swelled up. The next step was to jump on the victim's stomach so the filth erupted from his nose and face. He was unlikely to hold much back after that—if he could still talk.

May had nothing to add to whatever she had told her questioners. From her navel to her vagina, her stomach had been laid open. The butchery was precise: the gash was deep but almost perfectly straight. It must have been made in one or two strokes from an axe or a cleaver. The flies had begun their work. Her spilled intestines were black with them.

May was wearing red, the color that brought good luck.

Johnny supported himself against the door frame, trying not to gag. He could not help himself. The waves of nausea reached his gorge, and he spat bile.

People were moving about on the floor above. He wiped his mouth clean and half ran, half fell down the steps into the cascading lights of the festival.

He tried to stop the singing terror behind his eyes, to force his thoughts into order. An ordinary pimp, angry that May was making money on the side, would have contented himself with giving her a beating and threatening to cut her face; no pimp lightly discarded a source of income. Interrogation with liquid shit was a favorite method of the generalissimo's secret police. Murder with an axe was a specialty of the Greens. They worked hand in glove anyway. Perhaps they had connected May to the theft of the silver consignment. What had she told them under torture? Were they out looking for him?

The singing in his head grew louder, drowning out the fireworks and the bands. May knew Helene's address, and that he had gone to see her.

The mounted Sikhs along the Bund cradled their short carbines, indifferent to all the Chinese exuberance. They showed mild interest in the white man who was hurrying along on foot, deaf to the entreaties of the rickshaw drivers. Privileged servants of the Raj—whose attitudes were faithfully mirrored in the Shanghai Municipal Council—the Sikhs had an exquisite sense of protocol. Only orientals and Russians walked in Shanghai, and weren't the Russians half-Asiatic anyway?

6

HELENE wasn't at home. He jimmied the lock and found that her flat had been ransacked. In the bedroom, even the pillow and the mattress had been ripped open, leaving duck feathers all over the floor.

He decided to go to the radio man in the huddled quarter of Chapai, outside the settlement. But the huge wrought-iron gates of the settlement were closed, and the police were checking identity papers. It was a bad omen. On the night of his festival, Kuan Li, the spirit of a mighty general of the Three Kingdoms, had decreed war.

Johnny took a rickshaw to the Metropole and telephoned James Killen.

"I was starting to worry about you," the Englishman said. "I'm afraid the balloon's gone up."

"What balloon?" Johnny's English was serviceable but far from idiomatic.

"The natives are restless." Killen sounded much too relaxed. Too many whiskeys at the Shanghai Club? "The Greens found out one of their people has been doing favors for your lot. Or he decided to sell you out. Things are a bit muddled, I'm afraid."

"Who are you talking about?"

"The name is Tu Hsiao-lin, or some noise like that. They call him Little Tu, because he's related to the other one, or One-Leg Tu, because he's got a gimpy leg. The family sounds like a collection of missing parts, what? The fellow seems to know rather a lot. The police are trying to take things in hand, but the Greens have a way of settling their own affairs."

So Johnny's instinct had been right. Helene's contact in the Green Gang had sold her out. And God knew who else. He thought of May, and the singing in his ears deadened him to Killen's languid voice on the end of the line.

"Hello? Are you there?"

"You'd better make yourself scarce. You can come here if you like."

"No. I'll call you later."

HE WENT to Frenchtown, to the Latvian with a little card on his door that announced that he was a graduate of the Paris Conservatoire and offered lessons in violin. There were sentries in the street—a boy with a shoebox, a rickshaw-puller who wasn't begging for customers. Johnny made a sign to them as he turned to enter the building, and they signaled "all clear."

The Latvian received him with an outsize revolver in open view on top of his piano. The man was skin and bone; his round Polish wife carried enough weight for both of them. She was busy packing.

"As you see, we're leaving tonight," the Latvian announced. "The Greens are running amok with the right addresses. They have killed a hundred Chinese, maybe more. That's not the worst of it. The municipal police have got Slavein."

Johnny was stunned by this new information.

Jui Tsien-pa, code-named "Slavein," was the top Chinese Communist organizer in Shanghai and the vital link between the Comintern team and the local networks. He was in a position to identify every member of Emil's group—except, perhaps, for the music teacher.

The music teacher continued: "There is a ship in the harbor, out beyond Hongkew. The *Chungking.* The captain and the crew are party members. It is on charter to Sovexport. It will sail for Vladivostok at first light, or whenever we say. Emil and his wife will be on it. So will we." He glanced at his wife. "You knew Slavein as well as anyone. You'd better come too."

"Did the police get anyone else? Any of our own people?"

The Latvian squinted at him through glasses as thick as Coke bottles.

"Nothing is certain. At least one person is missing."

"Who?"

"The one you know best."

"Helene?"

The Latvian nodded. "She told me you had met. You know it was a breach of security."

"It wasn't intentional."

"She told me that, too. All the same, you should have reported it."

"Do you know where she is?"

"The Greens have her. They are going to make a present of her to the generalissimo and the German mission."

"Can't we stop it?"

The Latvian unhooked his glasses and rubbed the bridge of his nose.

"I don't think you know chess," he said wearily. "You must learn to give up a pawn to capture a knight. You give up a bishop to save your own queen. Helene is gone. It's not your fault, so accept it. And be on the *Chungking* before first light."

PERHAPS the madness that took possession of him had to do with the gunpowder quality of the night. The popping of rockets and the clamor of noisemakers were interspersed with the rattle of automatic fire, mostly from the far side of Soochow Creek; it all seemed part of the celebration. Or perhaps what spurred him was Killen's languor and the Latvian's checkerboard abstraction, and the frustration of leaving only another set of cicatrices on the suffering body of China. Or May, the taxi girl who had come so close to the oriental ideal of detachment in life, only to lose it in her unspeakable death. Or perhaps it was that Helene was not merely Sigrid's sister but a part of his life, something he could love or hate, resent or revere, but not cut out without major surgery. Whatever the reason—though he did not doubt that Helene would kill him with her own hands if she ever discovered what he was—he had no intention of leaving her in the hands of the men who had butchered May.

He went to Teng, a cell leader he had trained to blow up ships, and found the quickest and most independent of his Chinese recruits. Teng had led one of the combat squads that had taken part in the seizure of the silver ship. Johnny also knew that he had risked his life in Frenchtown in an attempt to assassinate the finance minister, the brother-in-law of the generalissimo.

Teng undertook to find out where Helene was being held. It took him more than two hours to return with the answer. Johnny passed the time swatting mosquitoes in a fetid room in the Old City. The street lamp was directly opposite the window. Each time someone passed by, a shadow was thrown against the wall behind him—a shadow with pointed ears when an alleycat jumped up on the sill.

"She's in Frenchtown," Teng reported. "Not at Tu's house, but nearby.

The place is a fortress. We would have to use bombs or grenades. Even if we got through, we would probably find her dead. It would be safer to try an ambush. They are taking her to Nanking in the morning."

Johnny pictured the route their cars would take to the North Station. They would have to pass through the International Settlement. That gave him an idea. Perhaps he could make use of the languid Mr. Killen after all.

McIvor, of the municipal police, dealt with the Greens at arm's length. He regarded them as hoodlums who would be put away in any civilized country but were much too powerful to be broken—or ignored—in Shanghai. They virtually ran the police in Frenchtown. Even in the settlement, his own domain, he knew that many of his Chinese agents had taken the vows of the society. He turned a blind eye to this, as long as the Greens did not attempt to prey on the European community. It was not his job to reform native customs. But a report that the Greens were abducting a respectable white woman to put her in a warlord's harem—that was enough to make his blood boil. The Frenchies might turn a blind eye to that sort of thing, but not the settlement, not so long as McIvor had any say in the matter.

The tip came from an unlikely source: James Killen. They had met a number of times on business matters, never socially. Despite his lowly official position at the British Cigarette Company, Killen gave himself the airs of a nabob, playing polo, running a racehorse, dining out with members of the Municipal Council. McIvor, of course, was aware of Killen's *sub rosa* functions but had found him generally unhelpful in responding to inquiries about Comintern activities in Shanghai. However, Killen had done him a singularly good turn within the last forty-eight hours by providing a lead to the top Communist organizer in the city. The fellow's arrest was a feather in McIvor's cap. So the Inspector was more receptive than he might otherwise have been to Killen's rather unorthodox plan of action.

LITTLE Tu rode in person with his prize in the second of the three black limousines. He was sure that when he arrived with her in Nanking and presented Chiang and General von Seeckt with the head of a German spy, rich rewards would be heaped on him and the rest of his clan.

He lit up a fat, stubby Havana, the type they called a Rothschild. The woman wore a veil, as if she were in mourning. It partly camouflaged the marks his men had left on her face the previous night, when she had been repeatedly beaten and raped. There was a swelling the size of a pigeon's egg next to her right eye. A bodyguard sat on the other side of her with his Thompson on his lap.

There was a traffic jam at the bridge over the Soochow Creek, some altercation between a chauffeur in a sedan and some pushcart owners whose load had been spilled in the road. Tu leaned out his window, yelling for them to clear the way. This part of the riverbank, next to the bridge, smelled of raw sewage.

There were more Sikh policemen in evidence than usual. One of them came over to the other side of the car and peered through the window at the Thompson and the girl.

Tu told his driver to honk the horn. Soon all three cars were blaring in unison. The crush of pedestrians—workers in blue denims, women in black pants and blue tunics, half-naked beggars—pressed in on the cars. A British officer in tropical kit strolled up with a swagger stick in the crook of his arm. His ginger moustache extended the narrow line of his upper lip.

"Good morning," McIvor addressed Little Tu, leaning into the car. "It's Mr. Tu, if I'm not mistaken."

The bodyguard made no effort to conceal his Thompson.

Little Tu was not perturbed. Perhaps this Englishman, like the French, wanted his squeeze.

"What is the delay?" he asked McIvor.

"Too many people in a hurry, that's all. We'll have it cleared for you in a moment. Excuse me—" he looked at Helene's face "—is the lady feeling quite well?"

"Quite well," Little Tu chorused.

"She looks to me as if she might be suffering from heatstroke."

"We're on our way to the family doctor now."

How long must this fool go on? Tu asked himself.

As it happened, McIvor did not have the opportunity to pursue his questioning, because another, larger European with a lock of fair hair falling over his forehead came shoving through the crowd and yelled, "Stop them! They've got my wife!"

"Will you please step this way, Madam?" McIvor said to Helene as he opened the car door, though it was Tu who had to get out first.

"Would you please be so kind, Mr. Tu?"

There was the rattle of safety catches being released. Tu looked at his bodyguards, and they at him. Were even the Greens bold enough to risk a shoot-out with the settlement police in broad daylight? Since nobody was quite sure, the Sikhs had their carbines ready. Looming over the cars, they looked as if they were out to shoot rabbits.

Reluctantly Tu moved his bulk. Helene sat still for a long moment, so that McIvor started to wonder if she had been drugged.

Johnny came forward and took her arm, half guiding, half lifting her out of the car. She seemed to need his support as they moved to the pavement. McIvor had the odd impression that part of the crowd opened to receive them and wrapped itself round them like a blanket. Or a shield.

Little Tu's eyes looked ready to burst from their sockets. He screamed and pulled out a heavy pistol, taking aim at the heads of the Europeans, which bobbed up above the crowd.

McIvor cracked him smartly on the funny bone with his baton. Tu yelped and dropped the gun. His bodyguard was less fortunate. Seeing his boss in trouble, he brought up his Thompson. The bearded Sikh by his window shot him just above the ear. The bullet tore through his cranium and settled in the rich leather of the back seat.

McIvor watched the woman in the veil and the unexplained man go down the embankment. Among the thousands of sampans in the mud, there was one that seemed to be waiting just for them.

WHEN Colin Bailey received Killen's report on Johnny's last days in Shanghai, he fired back a very chilly reprimand. Killen might very well have blown Johnny's cover, and for what? To smuggle out a dedicated Communist agent whom Johnny had every reason to fear! Poor McIvor would have a thrombosis if he ever learned who he had helped to safety. And how would Johnny explain himself in Moscow?

The episode had quite conceivably ruined an otherwise highly successful monitoring job. Johnny's predictions had all been on target: the Communist rebellion in south China was growing fainter day by day. Bailey had seen no harm in delivering up the most effective Chinese Communist in the Shanghai underground, fingered by Johnny months before, at this stage of the game. He only wished he could have laid hands on Mao. By Johnny's account, he was one of the few men in China who actually knew how to win a revolutionary war.

Johnny's effort to play the Scarlet Pimpernel and his involvement with some barroom floozie who had been dissected by mobsters confirmed Bailey in his view that women would be the fellow's downfall. For his own sake and that of the Firm, he had to be kept on a tight rein. If Johnny survived whatever lay in store for him in Moscow, Bailey promised himself to see to this in person.

1

FOR much of the journey back to Moscow from Vladivostok, Helene was dazed and disoriented. She couldn't keep food down or look in a mirror. When the questioning began in Moscow, she could remember nothing of her last forty-eight hours in Shanghai. They didn't believe her at first. But finally they brought in a doctor who diagnosed partial amnesia. Her sanity was not impaired. The doctor prescribed a prolonged vacation at one of the spas in the Crimean peninsula.

"You ought to go with her," the doctor told Johnny. "You look as if you've had a touch of yellow fever."

But Johnny had something else to do. He found out that Sigrid had returned to Moscow and had stayed for a time at the Lux Hotel. But she had left two months before, leaving no messages. At the Fourth Department and at Comintern headquarters, people denied all knowledge of what had happened to her. He went to Starik, who had promised to look out for her.

"You've come to the wrong department," General Berzin told him.

He telephoned to the Lubyanka and asked for Max. He had to explain himself to three men in succession before they told him that Max was not in Moscow, but that someone would be coming to see him. He had expected that.

It was after midnight when the chekist came to his hotel room. He introduced himself only as Genrikh. He was slim and well tailored and trailed a faint odor of expensive cologne.

"I have a letter for you," Genrikh announced.

He watched while Johnny scanned it.

It was in Sigrid's hand, but the feel was all wrong. It read as if she were taking dictation. She had been posted to Copenhagen. She hoped he was well. It was a polite note to a stranger.

There was a sentence he read and reread. She had had a miscarriage. His child. And she had never told him.

He glowered at smooth, polished Genrikh. "Why wasn't I told? What happened to her letters? She must have written to me before."

"Don't shoot the messenger boy." Genrikh smiled beatifically.

Copenhagen. It might just as well have been the South Pole.

"Why is she in Denmark?"

"It's livelier than Moscow. It's not something to be sneezed at, a posting abroad."

Johnny calculated that his hands could just about circle Genrikh's thin, perfectly barbered neck.

The chekist may have read that thought in his eyes, because he said, more seriously, "She is working for Max. Copenhagen is his new base."

HE WAS made to write the chronicle of his time in China, then to write it again. Then they questioned him at Ozhod-Niriat and the Fourth Department. He wasn't called to the Lubyanka, but OGPU men sat in on some of these sessions. They hovered silently, like vultures. He told as much of the truth as he could, and in every version the villain was Emil Brandt. He wondered whether Emil was experiencing equally gentle treatment. Come October, Johnny's prophecies were proven right. The Chinese Communists—those that were left—abandoned their base in Kiangsi. Mao squeezed the shattered remnants of the Red Army through a gap that he found in von Seeckt's iron ring and led them off into the wilderness. Nobody knew where the trek would end. Like a psychotic mother, the Comintern smothered its babies and promptly got pregnant again. Johnny had attended enough crib deaths to recognize the pattern. If he had experienced doubts about his double role in the presence of the brave young guerrillas of Shanghai and the peasant fighters of Kiangsi, the behavior of the men from the Big House—as the Latin Americans in Moscow called the Comintern—satisfied him that he had chosen the right course.

Piatnitsky asked Johnny to come and see him. "You've done all right," Piatnitsky told him. "You seem to have a way with people. Both Emil and Otto Braun speak highly about you, and they don't have much time for each other. You can pick your own assignment." Piatnitsky held up a finger. "With certain limitations."

"Yes."

"You can go back to China. We have to get guns to Mao's forces overland. You'd be reporting to Berzin and the Fourth Department."

"What's the alternative?" Johnny asked. He did not think he had anything new to learn about China.

"You can go to Brazil."

His mind flashed back to what Verdi, the Argentinian, had said about how South Americans talked themselves into making revolutions.

"What is the nature of the operation?"

"Armed insurrection. You're going to kick out the government and put in our man. He's here in Moscow. You'll find him quite unusual."

"What resources are available?"

"Do your own homework. There is a young officers' movement opposed to the government. There is only a small urban proletariat, but millions of hungry peasants who can be organized. The requirement is that the revolution should take place by January 1936."

Piatnitsky said all this in a deadpan manner, and Johnny began to realize that the head of the Orgbureau was no enthusiast for the project. Johnny was bemused by the idea. The two most powerful Communist movements outside Russia had just been dealt crushing defeats. What had persuaded the Comintern that it could succeed in a country of sambas and sugar cane when it had failed in Germany and China?

Piatnitsky's tone encouraged Johnny to risk a provocative question. "Isn't this a sideshow?"

"No!" the Comintern chief said sharply. He got up and started pacing, his hands clasped behind his back. "I haven't explained very well. This project has the personal interest of someone very high up. The orders come from the top, the very top. Do you understand?"

"Yes." So the plan for Brazil had Stalin's personal backing.

"We are prepared to spend whatever it costs—millions of dollars, if necessary. Our best operatives are to be made available. So I wouldn't call it a sideshow." Piatnitsky's tone had turned from indifference to almost open disgust. "Well? Are you going or not?"

"I'm going. Who will be in charge? Guralsky?"

Guralsky was the veteran chief of the South American bureau of the Comintern. He had personally recruited many of the local Communist leaders.

"The South American bureau is getting a new boss. Emil Brandt. As a matter of fact, he asked to have you on his team."

Piatnitsky saw Johnny's expression and added, "I read your reports from China. They were accurate. Not a word—" he stopped Johnny from speaking. "I would prefer that you didn't say it. Emil was chosen for this mission by someone very close to the top. Are you still with me? End of story. The man must be given credit for recognizing his deficiencies. Why else would he ask for you?"

EMIL's promotion was emblematic of what was happening in Moscow— how much so became obvious to Johnny in December, when the whole vast organization of the Comintern was shaken by the news that Kirov, the second most powerful man in Russia, had been shot dead in his office in Leningrad. How the assassin had managed to smuggle himself and his revolver past all the security guards was a mystery. It was said that the killer had previously been seen in the company of OGPU men who reported directly to Dzerzhinsky Square. In any event, Kirov's slaying was blamed on Trotskyites in high places and the "Zinoviev clique" in the Communist International. Old Bolsheviks were rounded up. Overnight, Piatnitsky and his files vanished from his office. It was rumored that the head of the Orgbureau was being grilled in the cellars of the Lubyanka. Closed sessions of the Comintern were interrupted by pistol-toting chekists in black coats who hurled accusations at platform speakers in full view of the foreign delegates. "Less literature!" they bellowed when their victims tried to explain themselves. A man's record was worthless unless it demonstrated undeviating loyalty to Stalin. It was plain that the only men Stalin trusted completely were those he had created out of the muck. The city stank of fear.

But Emil took all this in his stride. Emil, Johnny discovered, had a protector, and Dmitri Manuilsky was the right man to have on your side in Moscow at the close of 1934. Manuilsky was Stalin's creature in the Comintern. From Shanghai, Emil had fed him a string of poisonous back-chat, reporting—or inventing—the anti-Stalin gossip of his rivals and even his superiors at the Big House. In Stalin's Moscow, Emil's willingness to betray his comrades counted for infinitely more than success or failure in China.

When they met, Emil was so effusively cordial that Johnny became convinced that the new chief of the South American bureau had ratted on him too. As more and more old faces disappeared from the Big House, it struck Johnny that maybe he and Emil had survived for the same reason: in a climate of generalized distrust, the plausible liar has a better chance of saving his skin than anyone who presumes to speak his mind.

Emil introduced Johnny to the others who would lead the rising in Brazil.

Chief among them was a tiny, taciturn man with delicate features. Indrawn and mystical, he carried a faint aroma of the cloisters. He had been living in a house in Moscow with his mother and sisters for several years. In Brazil they called him the Knight of Hope. It seemed that, a decade before Mao, he had led a Long March of his own through the interior of Brazil, from the parched backlands of the northeast to the great falls of Iguaçu. The revolutionary lieutenants who had marched in his column were scattered all over Brazil. Some had become colonels or governors. They were expected to rise and join the revolution when this little man gave the word. His name was Luis Carlos Prestes. It was hard for Johnny to imagine him on horseback, waving a sword.

Yet Prestes' quiet fanaticism was not unimpressive. The army would rise. He could vouch for it. He had letters from his comrades in all the major garrisons. He even had supporters in the police and on the general staff. Several state governments would turn against the president once they saw that the movement was serious. The peasants would take up arms and chase the landowners into the sea.

After meeting Prestes for the first time, Johnny asked Emil, "Do you like the Brazilians?"

A vacant look, the same one Johnny had observed when he had come back from Kiangsi and reported facts that Emil found inconvenient, took possession of the other man's face.

Emil said, "I haven't given the matter the slightest thought."

* * *

JOHNNY spent time with the files. Just six months before, in June, the South American bureau, under its former management, had drawn up an exhaustive report on the prospects for Communist takeovers in the various countries of the hemisphere. The prospectus for Brazil was discouraging. "In Brazil," Johnny read, "the Communist party is only weakly connected with the masses, and in this respect it is on a downward grade." The authors of the secret report found "great objective possibilities for the development of the revolutionary movement" in the radicalism of junior army officers, popular hatred of the foreign banks and the misery of the peasants, especially in the north. But nothing in their findings suggested that the revolution was at hand.

A summons came from Manuilsky. Perhaps's Stalin's man had the answers.

Manuilsky fingered a moustache that seemed to be made of cotton wool. He might look like a favorite uncle, but he cultivated the manners of a boorish petty official. He kept Johnny standing while he went through a sheaf of papers.

"Another bloody German," he finally greeted Johnny. "Moscow is full of you people."

And whose fault is that? Johnny thought.

"So what do you think of the Popular Front?" Manuilsky challenged him.

"I think it requires study."

"That's a sensible answer. I see you're a strawberry from our patch after all." Manuilsky gave him a shrewd look. "Sit over there, on the sofa. Let's have some brandy."

The stuff he poured was good French cognac, not the Armenian product.

"What do you think of our Knight of Hope?"

"He has a certain quality. It's hard for me to picture him in uniform."

"You know what they say about the Portuguese. They don't kill the bull. It's the same with Brazilians. Prestes spent three years marching up and down the country, with hardly a shot fired in anger. But he's their hero. We work with what we've got. At least he's no Chiang Kai-shek. He's a good party member, and he'll do what he's told."

"But in Brazil the party is insignificant."

"It doesn't matter. Prestes will give us the army. We can buy up half the state governors with money or promises. What you have to do is kill the bull."

Manuilsky embarked on a speech about what a Communist victory in

Brazil would mean. It would be the decisive step toward creating a federation of soviet republics in all of South America. It would knock the stuffing out of the British and American banks. Faced with a knife at its soft underbelly, the United States would be powerless to act outside its own hemisphere. And with Brazil in its pocket, the Soviet Union would control the one raw material it lacked: rubber.

Manuilsky replenished their glasses and said, "It will also show Hitler we mean business."

He paused to assess Johnny's reaction.

Johnny raised his glass. "I'll drink to that."

They clinked glasses.

Manuilsky looked at him approvingly and said, "I'm going to do you a favor you won't forget. I'm going to take you to see the boss."

8

THE NEXT day Johnny received orders to meet Manuilsky at his office at midnight. Since Stalin didn't sleep at night, official Moscow was obliged to be insomniac too.

They took the road along the embankment to the Moskva gate. The river gleamed dully, like pewter, under the thin ice.

Militiamen stopped them under the arch. Their officer snapped smartly to attention at the sight of Manuilsky's papers. There were soldiers with heavy machine guns at the entrance to the vast palace courtyard.

The Kremlin guards in the lobby were a head taller than Johnny. They dwarfed the man who was hopping down the wide staircase. He was birdlike with his narrow, slightly hunched shoulders and hard, bright little eyes.

Manuilsky went up and pumped his hand. He mumbled a joke, and they both laughed. The chekist was looking at Johnny.

"Comrade Yezhov," Manuilsky said, "This is Johann Lentz, one of our Germans."

"A pleasure," Yezhov said. His stare was like a slap across the face. He nodded, and hurried out of the building.

"Yezhov is one of the most powerful men in Moscow," Manuilsky whispered as they crossed an echoing reception room at the top of the stairs. "He may get Yagoda's job. Of course," he added, so softly that Johnny had to strain to make out the words, "Yagoda is Jewish."

Stalin's secretary slid out from behind the padded door.

"The *Vozhd* is waiting."

The Vozhd. It was a curious form of address, just starting to creep into newspaper editorials and official speeches. It was stronger than the English word "leader." Its resonance was the same as that of "Führer" in German.

The Vozhd did not look much like his statues. Stalin was short and squat. His skin was yellowish and deeply pitted. His eyes were puffy and narrowed into slits, so that the whites hardly showed. He wore brown boots and a cotton *rubashka,* and his pipe wheezed like an asthmatic as he sucked at it.

Manuilsky made the introductions. Stalin motioned for Johnny to sit in a low-slung chair and returned to his own desk, which was set high up on a specially built platform so that Johnny had to tilt his head back to see the leader's face.

He expected to be quizzed about the Brazil mission or perhaps about China. Stalin's opening shot caught him completely off guard.

"You're a German. Do you believe that Hitler has the support of the German people?"

"Many of them," Johnny conceded.

"Thousands of former Communists have joined him."

"I'm afraid that's true."

"And he rules with a rod of iron. All opposition has been ruthlessly crushed."

"There is still opposition. But of course it is forced deeper and deeper underground. The Gestapo is a very effective organization."

Stalin grunted.

"If the Japanese strike us," he went on, "will Hitler make war on us, too?"

"I'm in no position to judge. But I think Germany is still weak. Hitler will wait till he has built up his war machine."

"And you think a conflict with Hitler is inevitable?"

"It's in his book—" Johnny began.

"I've read his book, fuck your mother!" Stalin burst out. "All the sermon mongers in that *lavotchka,* that clip-joint you work for spout it at me. I think I know Hitler better than any of you. It's not our system that he hates. It's the Jews. When he wrote *Mein Kampf,* he believed that the Jews were running the Soviet Union. Am I right?"

Johnny said nothing.

"If we show him that we know how to deal with the Jewish problem, what do we have left to fight about?"

Johnny was shaken by this but remained perfectly still.

"We have more in common than either of us has with any of the bourgeois democracies. Germany and Russia are both victims of Versailles. We have been allies since the war, regardless of who sat in the Berlin

Chancellery, united against the Western capitalists. We have no quarrel over territory. Hitler has designs on Poland. Well, there is enough of Poland for both of us. Hitler and I understand the nature of power. As for Britain and France, they are rotting, pustular invalids. They are too feeble to hold on to their empires. Their colonies are waiting to be shared out among those who are not scared to act. The United States is too busy making money to fight."

The words rushed out in Stalin's thick Georgian accent, so that Johnny missed a few, but not the terrifying thrust of the argument.

"Hitler must see this!" The Vozhd shouted. "He must be made to see it!"

Manuilsky nodded, his hands folded piously in his lap.

"We'll show him who's running Russia," Stalin went on. "And we'll make him respect us. There is a big German community in Brazil. If we succeed in Brazil, he'll take notice. What do you think?"

"There's no question about it," Johnny agreed.

Everything he had learned since he had first turned the stiff, water-stained pages of Heinz Kordt's diary should have prepared him for this revelation. But when it came, the raw cynicism and power lust of Stalin's statements left him breathless. Stalin lampooned the most famous advocates of the Popular Front—he called the French writers "shit-eaters"—and heaped contempt on the democratic leaders in the West. He saw enemies on all sides. He quizzed Johnny for material to add to the prosecutor's dossier on Piatnitsky and other "deviationists" in the Comintern. Johnny obliged, so far as memory and imagination would serve him. He was sure that Stalin would not have bared his deepest instincts unless he had been informed by Manuilsky that Johnny was 100 percent reliable. Johnny made every effort to live up to that reputation. One false note after Stalin's revelations, and he would join Piatnitsky in the bowels of the Lubyanka.

The conversation ended after three in the morning.

Johnny came away convinced that the Brazil operation was different in kind from the Comintern's previous revolutionary adventures. The South American bureau wasn't being sent to make a revolution. It was being sent to Rio to stage a coup d'état—to impress Hitler and to cut the ground from under the feet of those who argued that, in a world that contained Hitler and Mussolini, the Communists must make common cause with all the forces opposed to Fascism.

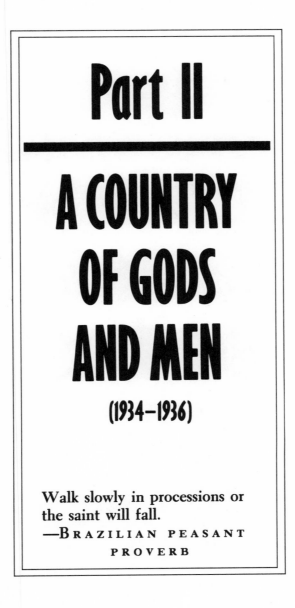

Part II

A COUNTRY OF GODS AND MEN

(1934–1936)

Walk slowly in processions or
the saint will fall.
—BRAZILIAN PEASANT
PROVERB

Our Man in Rio

We of the Game are beyond
protection. If we die, we die.
Our names are blotted from the
book.
—RUDYARD KIPLING,
Kim

1

THERE was a mournful sameness about railroad hotels, Johnny thought.
The same sense of transience, of imminent loss. The beds always looked
as if someone had just got out of them. The whores in the street were brisk
and businesslike, seeking out clients who had time to kill, but not enough
to start living. In the Grand Hotel in Copenhagen—railroad hotels always
had names like that—Johnny's room had a pitch pine dresser, a two-bar
radiator that crackled as if it were frying insects, a mud-colored portrait of
an unknown burgher and twin beds. The bed nearer the window had the
lumpier mattress, but he picked it for the view of the great gabled roof of
the central station, mottled and grey. On top was a spire out of Grimm's
fairy tales and a clock that had stopped at the precise hour they had left
Moscow.

"Hurry up!" Helene rattled the door handle from outside. "I'm starved!"

"Coming!" Johnny called back. He closed his suitcase and shoved it into
the closet. There was no point in unpacking. They had been given forty-
eight hours in Copenhagen—just enough time to call at the Westbureau
and collect travel papers and final instructions—before the onward journey
to Genoa and a "spaghetti boat" full of Italian emigrants bound for Rio.

When Manuilsky had told him that Helene would accompany him to Brazil, Johnny had protested that she wasn't well enough to do the job. Manuilsky had pointed out that she had made a remarkable recovery after her return from Shanghai, which was true. Johnny had explained that there were personal problems. When he had requested point-blank that Sigrid should be sent in her sister's place, Manuilsky had lost his temper.

"Do you think we're sending you to Brazil to screw in the sand dunes?" Manuilsky yelled at him.

"I think I've earned the right to choose my own assistant."

"The choice has been made. What's the matter with you? You know we don't tolerate romantic attachments. Get a new woman. If you don't like it, give me your papers. There are plenty of others who would give their left ball to go."

That had silenced Johnny.

I have to get to Copenhagen, he had told himself. At least that far. Colin Bailey would be waiting for him; Johnny had mailed the postcard, and a courier from Bailey had met him at the Arbat metro station. But there was something more urgent. Sigrid was in Copenhagen. He had to find her. He must try to get her away from Max—if she would still have him.

That first night in Copenhagen, he sat with Helene at a restaurant table in front of an open fire. The wood smoke carried the smell of sour apples. The food was wonderful—a soup made from morels, ham in puff pastry, little delicacies of the sea—but Johnny didn't notice.

Helene looked up and said, "I'm sorry it's me. I didn't ask to go to Brazil. You know that, don't you?"

"I know."

She pushed the crumbs on her plate into little stepped pyramids. "You're still in love with Sigi, aren't you?" she challenged him.

"I haven't changed," he conceded. "I don't know about her. There was a letter—not a good letter."

"You went looking for her today, didn't you?"

He hesitated. He had spent nearly three hours after they'd arrived trying to find Sigrid. He had asked about her at the Vesterport, a big, blocky construction in the center of town. The Westbureau of the Comintern had its secret headquarters on the third floor, behind the brass plate of an obscure engineering firm. Johnny's contacts had professed never to have heard of Sigrid. He had gone to Smollett, the Fourth Department man, who had been transferred from London. Smollett knew nothing about Max's operations but had volunteered to ask about the girl. He had warned that it might take some time. In his frustration Johnny had even gone to

Wollweber, the German boss of the Westbureau, a vulgar bully with eyes like slits in a bulging gourd. He had gone even though Smollett had warned him that there were nasty rumors about Wollweber—specifically, that the German had been trading information with Gestapo agents, ratting on comrades who had presumed to criticize his leadership. Johnny had found Wollweber cordial to begin with, and liberal with his akvavit. But when Johnny had asked about Sigi and Max, the Comintern chief had jabbed a finger at his chest and cautioned him not to go sticking his nose into business that didn't concern him.

Johnny met Helene's eyes.

Can I trust her?

There was a bond between them. In Shanghai it had saved her life. In London it had saved him from arrest. Helene felt something for him—not love, perhaps, but loyalty and affection. But surely that was a reason for her to stand between him and Sigi, not bring them together, especially if she could sense the force of the temptation that had been tugging at him since he arrived in Copenhagen: the temptation to abandon a life of loneliness and lies, to sweep Sigrid up and take her somewhere they could be simply man and woman, without counting the cost to others. And beyond all of that, she still belonged to Max.

"Did you find her?" Helene prodded.

He thought, what have I got to lose? If I leave Copenhagen without seeing Sigrid, God knows if I'll see her again.

"Nobody admits to knowing her," he reported. "Wollweber told me to piss off."

"That sounds like him." She took a slim panatella out of her bag and held it over the candle. "Would you like me to find Sigi for you?" she asked coolly.

"Are you serious?"

"Perfectly serious. If you're sure it's what you want."

"But why?"

"You've lived for thirty-five years," she said through the white haze, "and you've managed to learn absolutely nothing about women."

"That's not fair."

"It's accurate."

"Not quite. I've learned that you'll never cease to surprise me."

1

TINY lights winked on and off in the trees like swarms of darting fireflies. Colin Bailey paused to inspect the strings of lights that were threaded through the drooping branches of a blue spruce.

"The Danes say every bulb in the Tivoli Gardens works," he remarked to Johnny. "Do you suppose it's true? I can't find a dead one on this tree. Good Lord, there must be millions of them—" his glance took in the copses of illuminated trees, a blazing Persian palace, a Chinese theater where the light shimmered on a curtain shaped like a peacock's tail, the bright pavilions and peep-show arcades. "They're a meticulous people, the Danes. Something German in that, I suppose. And yet not like the Germans at all. What about over there?"

Bailey pointed with his umbrella to a beer garden by the lake. The water looked very black, the swans inanimate—decoys sliding on glass.

"Whatever you say," Johnny responded.

They sat at a table in the open air. On the other side of the beer garden a troop of husky young Germans were booming out drinking songs in their own language, making their trestle tables rock like rowing boats on the swell. They looked like a group advertisement for the Hitler Youth, but they were probably harmless, Johnny thought. Tourists looking for beer and girls. He was grateful for the uproar. It would make it very hard for anyone to tune in to his conversation with Bailey.

A bouncing waitress came with their beer. She wore a plunging bodice despite the nip of winter in the air, and Johnny smiled at her.

Habit or nervousness? Bailey asked himself. Johnny was the reverse of relaxed. Bailey sensed that his nerves were stretched taut.

"I'm sorry I couldn't give you more notice," Johnny said when they were alone.

"I've been waiting for your message since we got confirmation you were safely out of Shanghai. That went all right, did it?"

"No complaints."

That's two borders we've helped you across, Bailey thought. We'll have to watch it the third time.

"Your reports from China were flawless," Bailey told him. "If Uncle Joe had read them, he might have learned something."

"They weren't exclusive. I sent almost identical reports to Moscow. They changed nothing, as you know. In Moscow, there are two categories of facts—convenient facts and inconvenient ones. My assessments came under the second heading." He took a pull on his beer. "By the way, I met Stalin last week. He's not very tall."

Bailey sat riveted while Johnny recounted the story of his nocturnal call on the Vozhd.

I'll go to Winston with this, Bailey promised himself when Johnny described the depths of Stalin's longing to impress Hitler. The London clubs—including the cabinet room—were full of comfortable chaps who held that the Nazis and the Russians could never make a deal, almost as many as believed that Hitler meant no real harm. That same week, he had listened to a Tory peer who had insisted that Hitler's territorial appetites could be satisfied with a nice little slice of Portuguese Africa.

Johnny started to explain his new mission.

"Brazil?" Bailey echoed him. "What the devil do the Russians want with that?"

Bailey's knowledge of Brazil was—to put it charitably—sketchy. He knew that Brazil was a very large and very green chunk on the map of South America, that it spoke Portuguese instead of Spanish because of a fifteenth-century Pope, and that slavery had been legal until long after the American Civil War, when a homegrown Brazilian emperor had abolished it just before the slaveowners kicked him out. He dimly remembered one or more articles on Brazil that Kipling had published in the *Telegraph* before the Great Crash. They were about jolly native festivals and thundering hydroelectric turbines; Kipling was rather good on man-made thunder. Then there was that planter fellow Bailey had once met in Kuala Lumpur, a man grown fat and florid and whiskery in the tropics, who clapped his hands to summon the servants. This Malayan planter had spun a long-winded tale about how he had struck a tremendous blow for Britain—not to mention his own pocket—by smuggling rubber plants down the Amazon in the teeth of crocodiles, piranhas and manhunters with rifles and machetes who had orders to kill anyone who tried to break the rubber monopoly. The man had complained bitterly, a quarter of a century after the event, that he deserved a peerage, or a knighthood at least, and had implored Bailey to intercede with the King.

Oh, yes, there was that polo player. Carlos something. Pal of Diana's. Goes about reeking of pomade and making eyes at girls. No. On second thought, he was an Argentinian.

This, then, was the sum of Bailey's knowledge of Brazil. The store was not increased by service reports he might have forgotten or overlooked. In 1935 British Intelligence did not have one single case officer *en poste* anywhere in South America. Bailey thought it would be injudicious to divulge this inconvenient fact to Johnny.

The way Johnny explained things, Stalin had set his sights on Brazil for two reasons: to blow his critics in the Comintern out of the water and to show Hitler that he was no slouch when it came to grabbing *Lebensraum.*

"How much of a chance do you suppose the Russians have got?"

"They've got a front man called Prestes. He doesn't look like anything much, but he talks a lot less than most South Americans, and to better effect. He's something of a national hero. As long as he doesn't go about draped in the red flag, he could pull in quite a following."

Johnny explained the master plan for the revolt, as it had ripened in Moscow. Geography was important. The country was vast, the rivers ran the wrong way and the mountain ranges were in the wrong places; over huge areas, land communications were nonexistent or agonizingly slow. It would probably be impossible to seize the whole country with a single blow. At the same time, if the revolution succeeded in several regions—above all the north, where the peasants were starving and ready to risk everything —it would take months for the government to organize a counterattack. If a rising in the north were combined with lightning coups in the capital and major cities like São Paulo, the counterattack might never come at all. The Russians were confident that Prestes had enough friends who wore epaulettes—even generals at the Ministry of War—to make that happen. The Brazilians weren't fighters. To be sure, they were not averse to killing each other in knife fights in the slums, or in land wars between peasants and the hired guns of the backlands "colonels," or in pursuit of bizarre millenarian visions. But when it came to deciding who was going to sit in the presidential palace, the rival factions would line up their forces in fierce military array and set to frantically counting noses. Then the weaker side would discreetly abandon the field.

"I begin to see," Bailey remarked. "They say the Portuguese don't kill the bull. Your people are ready to kill the bull, and that makes everything different. So you'll be the military adviser?"

"The military specialist," Johnny modified this. "I have been appointed to the South American bureau. It means that with Emil and Prestes—and the Argentinian—I would take part in the strategic decisions."

"Excellent!" Bailey steepled his fingers, trying to calculate the effects of a wrecking job on the Soviet gang in Rio. It would give a definite boost to British influence in South America. It would be a stinging humiliation for Manuilsky and all of Stalin's cronies in the Comintern. It would probably help the Reds like Willi Münzenberg and the French lot, who were campaigning for a Popular Front against the Nazis and had been getting kicked in the teeth up till now. Bailey's mind ranged over the reverse scenario. If Stalin succeeded in turning Brazil into the second Communist power, a whole continent would be in jeopardy. The Americans could probably be counted out as allies in a future war; they would be too busy having kittens over what was going on south of their border. There was also the chance that Stalin would do a cynical swap with Hitler. You take Brazil, with its million-odd Germans. We'll take the Baltic states and a nice chunk of Poland . . .

It dawned on Bailey that there might, just might, be something even bigger at stake.

"For God's sake," he burst out. "This is Uncle Joe's private hobbyhorse. If it all blows up in his face, on top of the way he's treating all the Old Bolsheviks in Moscow—"

He cut himself off just as he was about to add: we might be able to put the skids under the bugger.

He kept the completion of the thought to himself, not because of the jumbling of metaphors, though that was scarcely pardonable in a Wykehamist, but because these were very early days and it simply wouldn't do to get overexcited. He hadn't even worked out how he was going to service his agent on the other side of Rio.

He said merely, "It's splendid. You'll hold all the strands in your two fists. You can make or break this revolt whenever we choose."

"I could," Johnny remarked.

Bailey did not like this repeated use of the subjunctive.

"Something's worrying you, Johnny. Let's have it."

"I'm not going to Rio."

Bailey stared at him. "Would you care to amplify that?"

"I've decided to get out."

Bailey sat very still. "Is this a—sudden decision?"

"You could say so. I decided today. Will you help me?"

Bailey hesitated.

Steady, he cautioned himself. The man is close to breaking. I mustn't put on the screws, mustn't scare him worse than he's scared already. Not unless I have to.

"I might help if I knew the circumstances," Bailey suggested mildly. "Are you under suspicion?"

"No more than all of us are."

"It's the girl, then. The painter."

Johnny did not dissent.

"Is she in Copenhagen?"

"She's in Oslo."

"How did you find out?"

"Her sister told me. She works for the same people." Johnny rubbed the corners of his eyes between thumb and forefinger. He added, "Helene and I are supposed to be traveling to Rio together."

"And this is the same Helene who went after de Salis in Berlin."

"We don't talk about that."

Bailey let the Berlin episode ride. He asked, "Did Helene tell you why the other one went to Oslo?"

"She's doing a job with Max."

"Did Helene tell you the nature of the job?"

"I don't think she knows."

"But you're planning to run off to Oslo and look for the girl, just like that—without knowing where she lives or what she's doing."

"Oslo isn't London or Paris," Johnny countered with stubborn determination. "I have some friends. I'll find her. With or without your help." He was tired of the grilling. "All I need from you is the money that belongs to me. Thirteen hundred pounds."

"A bit more than that, with the interest accrued." Bailey endeavored to sound like a helpful bank manager. Johnny's salary was deposited in an escrow account at Coutts' in the City.

Softly, softly, the Englishman told himself. In his hurry to get to his girl, Johnny may be starting to see *me* as the enemy.

"You can have your money whenever you like," Bailey announced. "But there's something I ought to ask you. If your girl is in Oslo with Max, there's obviously a sensitive job involved. Why would Helene court suspicion by running around asking all sorts of indiscreet questions on your behalf? Why would she tell you even if she knew before?"

"I've asked myself the same things," Johnny said. "Helene is an unusual woman."

"She is also a Russian spy," Bailey responded, letting the steel show. "I don't want to appear insensitive, but it must surely have occurred to you that Helene is putting you through some kind of test. Do you think she'd pack you off to Norway without telling Max?"

"It's possible," Johnny conceded, remembering the episode in Moscow, when Helene had told the secret police about his talk with Emil.

"It's more than possible, in view of what's going on in Oslo."

Johnny was startled. "Do you know something about it?"

"We've had Max under observation for some time. He's made several trips to Norway, sniffing after a well-known compatriot of his. A certain Lev Davidovich Bronstein. Am I making myself clear?"

The shock of recognition showed in Johnny's face.

Of course, he told himself. The Norwegians had given Trotsky asylum. Everyone knew that Stalin would stop at nothing to see Trotsky dead—and

Max was an expert at what the chekists tactfully described as *mokrie dela,* "wet operations."

"What sort of impression do you think it will make if you walk in on Max and your girl unannounced in the middle of a plot to kill Trotsky?"

"I can't imagine that Sigrid is involved."

"Why else would Max take her along?"

Johnny said nothing.

"If you go to Oslo," Bailey pressed on, "they'll nail you as a Trotskyite agent, or worse. You can see that, can't you? What good would you be to Sigrid then?"

"I'll take her away," Johnny countered defiantly.

"Are you sure she'd go?" the Englishman said softly. "Have you done anything to prepare her? If you'll forgive me for saying this, you have a way of picking women with minds of their own."

"It's my neck," Johnny said fiercely, clenching his fists. But a voice inside him said, Bailey is right.

LATER they walked by the lakes, accompanied by the scudding of oars and stifled giggles from lovers who were out there in dinghies. It reminded Johnny of an afternoon on the Wannsee, when Sigrid had blotted out the sun.

He said, "I've thought it over. I'll go to Rio."

"I think you've made the right decision."

Bailey heaved a sigh of relief. The stuff about Trotsky was a stab in the dark. His agents had lost sight of Max several weeks before. It was plausible enough, though, and had worked like a charm with Johnny, who was nobody's fool. Now it would be interesting to check with the Oslo station whether his hunch about Trotsky was correct.

Johnny stopped at the water's edge. The wind had picked up, driving ripples across the lake. "I want you to understand this is the last job I'll do for you," he announced. "Afterwards, I want out. And I want Sigrid with me. You have to promise you'll make that possible."

"Agreed."

"How are we going to stay in contact?"

"That's an easy one," Bailey said decisively. "I'm coming out myself." Now that he had convinced Johnny to carry on—not through deception, he told himself, so much as informed speculation—Bailey had no intention of leaving his man in the lurch. "By the way," he went on, "what cover have the OMS chaps given you this time?"

"I'm supposed to be an Austrian cigar importer, on a busman's holiday with my sister."

"What name?"

"Franz Gruber."

A smile flickered across Bailey's face. He murmured, " 'Silent Night.' "

"I beg your pardon?"

"Franz Gruber is the composer of 'Silent Night.' "

"I doubt whether the man who fixed my passport has much time for Christmas carols."

3

THERE was nothing to compare with Christmas in England, Bailey thought. There were snowmen in the park, while Snow White and the Seven Dwarves revolved in Selfridge's windows. He took the girls to see Father Christmas in the grotto behind the toy department, before he drove down to Odiham to see C. in his country retreat.

He found the chief stomping around in plus fours and muddy boots in his tack room. The place smelled of leather and wet dogs. Three of the latter—a mastiff and two black Labradors—greeted Bailey with a show of teeth and voice projection that would have driven away all but the most determined visitor.

C. announced that he had been shooting with the King. He congratulated himself that he had shot a dozen more birds than H.M. but had managed to fudge the count so as not to commit the sin of lèse-majesté.

C. was startled when Bailey informed him that Johnny was en route to Rio. He wanted to know what Stalin hoped to accomplish.

Bailey explained. He had done some homework and dwelled on the fact that sizable British interests were at stake. British companies owned the railroads and had a stake in other utilities.

"Of course, we can't rely on the Americans to do anything. Roosevelt doesn't see that Communism is a danger. His ambassador in Moscow is hooked on Stalin. There's really nobody we can deal with on this in Washington. Hoover is quite impossible. They don't have anything that resembles a secret service. Their attitude is even worse than the Foreign Office's."

This argument seemed to impress C. more than anything else.

He agreed to sign a chit.

ON NEW YEAR's Eve, Bailey was on platform eleven under the sooty arches of Waterloo station, boarding the train for Southampton. For two hours, ensconced in a cozy, cream-painted Pullman, he watched the home counties flash by, chartreuse watercolors under the rain. The steward brought madeira and cherry cake.

At the docks the revels were in full swing. Young hearties whirled their noisemakers and kissed their girls while a band thumped out songs of farewell; "Good Night, Sweetheart" was the favorite. Nobody had eyes for the trim military figure proceeding up the gangway onto the deck of the R.M.S. *Arthurian*. The crowd was given over to the cheerful chaos of leavetaking, to last-minute packages and flowers and smuggled embraces, and champagne parties that spilled over from the staterooms onto the boat deck.

As Bailey followed a steward below, a girl hopped, giggling, out of a nearby cabin, champagne flute in hand. He had a brief impression of dramatic violet eye shadow and a flying feather boa before she skated along the floor and landed in his arms. He caught her by the elbows, at the cost of getting the contents of her glass all down his shirt front.

"Whoops!" the girl laughed up at him.

"Rather a waste of champagne," Bailey observed.

"Perhaps you'll let us make amends."

Bailey looked for the source of the new voice and found a young man brandishing a bottle of Veuve Cliquot. The stranger was tallish, strong-boned, not stocky, with the supple, wide-legged gate of a man who is equally at ease on a horse or a rolling deck. His hair was chestnut brown, his moustache a touch lighter. His face was flushed with good health, but his skin was the kind that freckles rather than tans. He was well dressed in an offhanded way, in country tweeds and a soft collar, above which a smudge of lipstick burned against the side of his neck.

"Happy New Year!"

"I hope it will be," Bailey said, accepting the proffered glass of champagne. "In the meantime, I've always found this a rather good prophylactic—"

The girl burst into another fit of giggles.

"—against mal de mer."

"Harry Maitland," the young man introduced himself. His handshake was firm, not bone-crushing. He was confident of his place in the world.

"Colin Bailey. Maitland—" the older man brooded on the name. "I knew a Maitland at Winchester. Rather a keen batsman."

"That would have been my father, sir."

"Really?"

"We're having a little farewell party," Maitland said, gesturing towards his door. "You'd be very welcome to join us."

"I think not," Bailey said, peering in at a crowd of bright young things.

"But thank you for this." He returned the empty glass. "How far are you going?"

"To Rio."

"Then we'll have plenty of time to talk."

In his own cabin, Bailey indulged himself for a few minutes in cozy memories of going up to Scholars' Hall at Winchester at six of a winter's evening to toast thick slices of bread on the end of a bamboo pole over the blast furnace of the hulking double stove the boys called the Simon and Jude.

In the distance he heard the cabin boy pattering down the corridors, banging a gong and piping, "All ashore that's going ashore!"

He could summon up only a blurred image of Maitland senior, a bluff sportsman who hated bullies, one of life's spenders. His face darkened as he reflected that Maitland senior was one of England's missing generation, his name inscribed in stone along the cloisters that served as the school's war memorial, on the roll call of those who had fallen in Flanders fields.

Bailey stayed below until the ship's siren howled, the last visitors were shooed onshore and the *Arthurian*, with the pilot's tug at her bow, had completed her tricky passage round the bar and was steaming south across open water to Cherbourg on the green coast of Normandy. Then he made a leisurely ascent to the saloon, ordered whisky and soda and decided that he did not care for the public rooms. The designer had copied the grandiose style of the Cunard liners, but the chairs were jammed in together so that someone's ear was at your neck, while the inevitable skylight, under the sodden curtain of clouds, submerged the whole scene in the cold penumbra of a fish tank.

SEVEN times around the promenade deck, by Bailey's calculation, made a mile. He shifted a florin from one pocket of his flannels to the other at the completion of each circuit. After three miles he returned to the deck chair he had reserved on the port side to take his morning bouillon.

He was soon engrossed in a folder of cuttings from the *Telegraph;* his girl had dug out the old Kipling articles. Bailey was reading about the Brazilians' passion for gambling when Harry Maitland loomed up.

"May I join you?"

"Please." The deck chair next to Bailey was unoccupied. "You know Brazil, do you?"

"I've lived there for four years, on and off."

"Do you know this game called—" he consulted the clipping "—The Beasts?"

"Oh yes," Bailey laughed. "The *jogo do bicho*. Everyone plays it. You bet on an animal—a lion, say, or an elephant. Each animal controls four numbers. If they come up in the daily lottery drawing, you've won. It started as the bright idea of a man who wanted to induce people to visit the zoo. It sprouted up all over the place. Everybody plays. It's illegal, of course, but in my office the locals buy and sell tickets in full view of their supervisors."

"And what kind of office would that be?"

"I work for Rio Light. That's the power company."

"You're an engineer, then?"

"My job is public relations, mostly. Not awfully important, I'm afraid. But it gives me an excuse to live in Rio."

Bailey started to draw him out. Maitland had the endearing self-efface-ment of the sort of Englishman who sails the Atlantic single-handed and talks about it as if he were describing Sunday lunch at a pub. All that Maitland *père* had bequeathed was a mountain of debt, so, when he came down from Bailliol, Harry had been urged to pay court to his senior aunt, a formidable dowager who controlled the family purse strings. Her most beloved possession had been a vicious Pekingese called Harold.

"Things were going pretty well," Harry reported, "until she asked me to tea to discuss her will. Naturally, this was an exciting occasion. I sat down on the blue sofa a bit too quickly. I heard something crunch, but I didn't dare look to see what it was until Aunt Hermanie had gone off in search of the dog. I stood up and found I had squashed poor Harold flat. She was calling and calling in the other rooms. Inspiration seized me. There was a rubber plant by the windows. I pulled it out of its pot and popped Harold underneath. I left as soon as was decent, without being detected. But I am afraid my aunt's suspicions fell on me in the end. I received a note from her lawyers, informing me that she had cut me out of her will. That was the end of my inheritance. And I must say, I feel I owe a debt to old Harold."

"How so?"

"He drove me to Brazil, in a roundabout way. I was faced with the imminent prospect of joining the salaried class."

Maitland made this sound like a sentence to prison.

"You could have taken a rich wife," Bailey observed.

"I gave it some thought. Then I picked up the *Times* and found an advertisement in the agony columns. They wanted an extra gun for an expedition to Brazil, to look for an explorer who had disappeared in the territory of the Xingu Indians."

"Major Fawcett."

"You read about it, then."

"You never found Fawcett," Bailey pointed out.

"No, but I found Brazil. It's—well, it's extraordinary. A country of gods and men."

"And Rio?"

"Rio is simply the most beautiful place in God's creation. The Cariocas say that when God took seven days to create the world, he spent six of them on Rio de Janeiro."

Bailey cocked an eyebrow at this gush of enthusiasm.

"Not very Wykehamist," he said with mock rectitude, alluding to their old school's reputation for turning out dry logicians. "I believe you're a romantic, Mr. Maitland."

Harry grinned and swept the hair off his forehead.

"I'm told revolutions are as common in South America as elections in England," Bailey remarked.

"A revolution is their version of an election. That's why they're usually kind to the losers. The other party may get in next time."

"What about the Communists?"

"There are Communists, of course. They don't play by those rules. But I don't think there's much room for communism in a country where, if you're hungry, you can pluck a banana off a tree."

"I do hope you're right."

Bailey had decided that he liked Harry Maitland. Some of the boy's opinions were naive and superficial; that was to be expected. But he had a quality that appealed to Bailey. More than mere youthfulness, it was his air of constant, delighted expectation. While so many of his class and generation in England—the young men Bailey met at Diana's dinner parties—were suppurating with world-weary cynicism or spouting half-digested nonsense from an unreadable dialectician, Harry gave the impression that he was one of those who would ride over the edge of the world for a dare, or just for the joy of the riding.

Maitland began telling him about a Communist effort to spark a labor dispute at the power company. The Communists had tried to make a big issue out of the fact that foreign employees were paid much better than the Brazilians. Bailey was impressed with Harry's account of how he had personally contributed to the failure of the strike by paying a left-wing journalist to write articles that had set the organizers at each other's throats.

But Bailey's attention strayed with the appearance of a new face at the far end of the deck. He caught only a brief glimpse because the man whipped round immediately, giving them a fine view of his back. But Bailey was sure he knew him. He was young, even younger than Maitland, but his ravaged face was that of a much older man, leached and striated by what life had dumped on him. Bailey was sure that he, too, had been recognized. Neither he nor Karl Vogel would be likely to forget their last encounter at an Algerian dive in Paris.

"Excuse me—" Bailey took Maitland's arm, interrupting his narrative. "Have you seen that fellow before?"

Maitland shook his head. "Perhaps he wandered up from below." Harry inspected the object of Bailey's curiosity more closely. The stranger certainly didn't appear to belong on the first-class deck. "He may have boarded at Cherbourg, of course."

"We dock at Lisbon, don't we?"

"Why, yes. We're due in a couple of hours." Maitland was struck by the change in the older man's manner. All his ease was gone; he had the aspect of a pointer that senses a bird is about to break cover. "Are you going ashore?"

"I think I will," Bailey said. He watched Karl's back until he had ducked out of sight behind the *Arthurian's* funnels. "I can do without the salted codfish," Bailey went on, regaining his aplomb. "But Lisbon's a splendid city. Shall we take in the sights together?"

THE *Arthurian* dropped anchor at Lisbon, dwarfing a school of sardine boats, and the passengers who were going onshore started to assemble along the railings. Bailey had changed into a lightweight suit and a panama hat. It wasn't quite as warm here as he had expected, and there was a brisk wind coming in from the Atlantic.

With mounting nervousness he watched Karl boarding one of the ship's boats among a crowd of second-class passengers. Bailey knew, from Johnny and other sources, that there would be a Comintern liaison office near the docks, as in all major European ports, probably disguised as a seamen's club. He did not know whether Karl was still a member of the *Apparat.* It was conceivable that the young German had finally burned his boats with the party and was running off in search of a new life in the New World. But Bailey didn't much believe in coincidence. It seemed more likely that Karl was on the *Arthurian* for reasons related to his own: that Karl, too, had an assignment in Rio. If Karl headed for the Comintern bureau on shore, that would settle the matter.

It might also blow Bailey and his mission out of the water. There were more sophisticated minds in Stalin's secret service than the ones Bailey had had to contend with outside the Casbah restaurant in Paris, and they were unlikely to set any more store by coincidence than he. If Karl reported that he had sighted the same British Intelligence officer who had approached him in Paris en route to Rio, an inquisitive chekist—perhaps Max Fabrikant—would start making connections. Almost inevitably, the inquiry would lead to Johnny. Bailey realized that more than his own mission was at risk. Johnny's life was at stake.

Maitland appeared at his elbow.

"Ready?" the younger man asked nonchalantly, nodding towards the boat that was filling up with first-class passengers.

"Oh, yes, of course." But he detained Maitland for a moment before they climbed down into the boat. "I may have a spot of bother," he began.

Maitland heard him out and seemed to take it in his stride, even though the sum of his knowledge of Colin Bailey up to this point was that he had been at school with his father, held a presumably boring civilian job in the War Ministry and was an amateur naturalist who was spending his holiday in Brazil to look at birds and animals.

KARL HAD a long head start, and, when they reached the docks, Bailey feared they had lost him. The steep, narrow streets leading away from the harbor were crowded with people. A horse-drawn cart lumbered past, blocking the view and spattering a fresh load of dung over the toes of Bailey's brogues. He swore softly and jumped up on a packing crate to get a better look around.

There. He spotted the German's sandy, close-cropped hair and navy-blue coat. Karl was ambling along a street lined with shops and honky-tonks like a man without a care in the world.

"Give me a good start," Bailey told Maitland. "There's no need for you to get involved. I just want you to watch my back. All right?"

"All right." Maitland grinned at the prospect of an adventure.

Bailey trailed Karl as the German followed a circuitous course through snaky side streets. At one point Karl turned left towards the harbor, then rounded a corner and walked back parallel to the way he had come. He was either lost, or enjoying a simple outing—or checking whether he was being followed.

Bailey hung back, hugging the doorways and trying to stay out of sight.

Then Karl broke into a half run and dashed around another corner. Bailey quickened his stride, anxious not to lose him.

He rounded the same corner. Karl was nowhere to be seen. But two blocks away, in the direction of the port was a down-at-the-heel seamen's club, a likely cover for the Comintern office. Could Karl have reached it already? Even taken at a sprint, the distance seemed too great.

Bailey hesitated. There were alleys off to both sides of the street. He peered down one of them. There was a smell of rotting fish. He heard a faint scuffle and the clang of metal and advanced a few steps. Probably nothing more than an alley cat scavenging the rubbish bins.

He turned on his heel and saw Karl, face tensed and pale, lunging at his belly with a knife.

Bailey flung himself to one side, twisted his ankle and came down in a sprawling heap.

Bailey rarely carried a gun and had not deemed it necessary to go armed on board a cruise ship. As he rolled to avoid Karl's plunging knife, he realized that the omission was likely to prove fatal.

He managed to seize hold of the German's wrist and wrestled with him for control of the knife. It was a losing battle. The point of the blade nicked his ear.

Then another figure irrupted into the alley. Harry Maitland charged at the German like a bull, knocked him to one side and twisted the knife out of his hand.

But Karl wasn't easily dispatched. Bailey had felt his strength; his sinews were tempered steel. He lashed out at Maitland, dealt him a terrific blow on the chest and went gouging for the eyes, his fingers spread like claws.

Maitland was breathing hard, and Bailey saw him go down as he scrambled to his feet, ready to take on the German again.

But before Bailey could make his move, Maitland struck out with his feet, one after the other. He made an amazing sight, suspended above the ground on the palms of his hands, his legs driving high into the air. His right foot connected with the side of Karl's jaw, and the German dropped like an ox under the slaughterer's mallet.

"Are you all right?" Maitland inquired, dusting himself off.

"Thanks to you."

Bailey limped over to where Karl was lying.

"My God," Maitland said. "I haven't killed him, have I?"

"I'm not sure," Bailey said mildly, pressing his ear to the German's chest. He heard an irregular flutter.

He squatted on his haunches, took Karl's head between his hands and wrenched until he heard a distinct crack.

"I'm afraid there's no hope for him," Bailey said blandly.

Maitland stared at him.

"I saw what you did," Maitland said.

"You saw nothing."

"We have to do something."

"I agree. I think we have both earned a stiff drink."

"Look, I don't want to be boring, but we have to go to the police."

Bailey was still crouched over the dead man's body, rummaging through his pockets, inspecting the lining of his coat. He picked up Karl's knife, slit a seam, and extracted a small square of linen that had been stitched inside. He gave no sign of having heard Maitland's last statement.

"I said, we must go to the police," Maitland repeated.

"Listen to me, Harry." Bailey got to his feet and looked the younger man squarely in the eyes. "I am engaged in a secret mission for the War Office. Do you understand what that means?"

"I—I think so."

"That man—" Bailey jabbed his foot at the body "—was a Russian agent. These are his credentials." He held up the linen square covered with minute characters. "*Aut disce, aut discede.* Have you forgotten the last bit?"

"*Manet sors tertium caedi,*" Maitland recited dutifully.

It was the Latin tag that was framed on the wall of the ancient hall at Winchester College that was known simply as "school." The translation was even more awkward than the original: "Either learn or leave. There remains a third lot, to be beaten."

"Exactly," Bailey said.

Maitland still appeared unconvinced.

Bailey put his hand on his shoulder and said quietly, "Harry, are you ready to serve your King?"

Maitland stiffened. "Of course."

"Good. Then help me get this fellow out of the light."

4

BAILEY had seen enough of killing on the battlefields of France to detest the idea of taking life. Karl's death weighed on his conscience. He told himself that what had been begun in self-defense had ended with the plain acknowledgment of necessity; it was Karl's life or Johnny's. He had no means of holding Karl as a prisoner. He could imagine the prunefaces that would have greeted him at the embassy in Lisbon had he turned up with a wounded Bolshevik and asked them to lock him up. He could not afford complications with the Portuguese authorities. And of course there was no question of releasing Karl, once he had shown his colors.

His reasoning was flawless. But it couldn't screen out the image of the downy hair on the German's face, the remembered pulse of his failing heart, the echo of the sickening crack as his neck was broken. It is hardest to kill when the enemy has a human face.

Back on board the *Arthurian,* he set to encrypting a telegram to London. He preferred the easy-to-remember Playfair system to book codes or any of the more elaborate ciphers. It was based on a single word. He selected one that he liked—"phantasmagoria"—from the short list he had committed to memory. He took a sheet of paper and wrote it out as two sides of a square with the initial P in the top left-hand corner, omitting duplicate letters as he went along. This gave him the following construction:

```
P  H  A  N  T  S  M  G  O  R  I
H
A
N
T
S
M
G
O
R
I
```

He proceeded to fill in the letters of the alphabet, as follows:

```
P  H  A  N  T  S  M  G  O  R  I
H  A  B  C  D  E  F  G  H  I  J
A  K  L  M  N  O  P  Q  R  S  T
N  U  V  W  X  Y  Z  A  B  C  D
T  E  F  G  H  I  J  K  L  M  N
S  O  P  Q  R  S  T  U  V  W  X
M  Y  Z  A  B  C  D  E  F  G  H
G  I  J  K  L  M  N  O  P  Q  R
O  S  T  U  V  W  X  Y  Z  A  B
R  C  D  E  F  G  H  I  J  K  L
I  M  N  O  P  Q  R  S  T  U  V
```

Using this table, he could turn each letter of his cable into one of several grid references. The letter A, for example, appearing several times inside the box, could be cross-referenced as HH, or NG, or OR. He translated the words of his message directly into the code, without making an original. When he had finished, he tore the sheet of paper bearing the table into tiny pieces and tossed them out to sea on his way to the ship's radio room. As the cable would be presented to C., it began: "I have to inform you that an unfortunate incident at the start of the voyage set the operation at risk. It has been happily resolved."

When he had satisfied himself that the telegram had been safely transmitted to a cover address in London, he went looking for Harry Maitland and found him in the saloon.

"I gather that Veuve Cliquot is your blood group," Bailey said, signaling the bartender. "Now I want you to tell me where you learned kick boxing. I saw something similar in the Orient. But you're the first white man I ever saw fight like that."

"In Brazil they call it *capoeira*. I'm not really very good. You should see the *moleques*—the street kids—foot fight in Bahia. It's a ballet."

As he listened to Maitland talk, Bailey reflected that the two of them were now committed to each other. It struck him that Johnny would probably like Harry too.

5

"You smell the land before you see it," Maitland remarked.

They had spent nearly two weeks crossing the Atlantic. Now the sea breeze had dropped away, and in place of the tang of salt water, Bailey breathed in the ripe, heavy scent of the tropics. It was intimate and overpowering, like a moist palm pressed over his face. It carried the sweet-sour odor of the jungle, the whole relentless cycle of germination and decay.

The blue haze ahead of them slowly resolved itself into the profile of islands and mountains. On the port side Bailey could make out red-roofed villas and royal palms along a white crescent of sand overhung by the riotous greens of virgin forest.

"Your hotel is over there." Maitland pointed at a palatial building facing the sea. "It's extraordinary to think that Copacabana was almost undiscovered ten years ago. It's hard to conceive of a city so rich in natural beauty that it could turn its back on a glorious beach like that."

Frigate birds escorted them through the mouth of the vast Guanabara Bay, guarded by the twin forts of São João and Santa Cruz, where antique cannon poked their muzzles through the sturdy sea walls. Maitland drew Bailey's attention to the changing colors around them. As the water grew deeper, it turned coppery, like a river.

"That may explain why the discoverers called the place River of January," Maitland observed, enjoying his new role as guide. "They thought they had entered the mouth of a great river."

Bailey was fascinated by the mountains that framed the city and its circling beaches. They rushed down at the water like horses reined in at the last moment, before toppling in. Each had a personality of its own. Maitland pointed out some of the landmarks: the smooth, steep peak of the Sugarloaf; Gavea, flattened and windswept like the mainsail of a caravel; the hunched back of Corcovado, where the giant statue of Christ the Redeemer, arms outstretched, kept vigil over the city; the ominous Fingers of God stabbing the sky away to the north, ragged cloud streamers trailing from their tips.

Nothing in that skyline stayed constant for long. Bailey watched the coastline open and close and open again like a fan, as the *Arthurian* steamed on past the tributary bays of Botafogo and Flamengo and the baroque green filigree of the old customs house towards the docks.

"From one corner to the next, from one day to the next," Maitland said, "Rio is never the same. She's a beautiful woman you can never own. Or predict."

Bailey looked back the way they had come and saw the horizon changing contours again, until the promontory of Niteroi looked like the head of a crocodile lazily basking in the sun.

Harry's a romantic fool, he thought. But perhaps Maitland was right, all the same. This city was a woman, and its welcome was a dance of the veils, both tempting and deceiving.

BAILEY'S hotel was a marbled palace facing the bright sweep of Copacabana, beyond an avenue lined with palms and a mosaic forecourt that looked like a Miró canvas in black and white. A maharaja and his retinue were in the lobby. When Bailey threw back the French doors to his balcony, he had the Sugarloaf to his left, a white fortress to his right, the shining blue of the Atlantic in between. He luxuriated for a while in a bathtub as deep as a well. Then he put on his white dinner jacket and descended to the hotel terrace to wait for Maitland, who had insisted on showing him the town. The colors were all impossibly vivid. The water of the pool was turquoise. The mountains that reared up above the palms and rubber trees turned from chartreuse to curação as the light fell. A grand old man in a pinstriped waistcoat with a long white apron below that fell to his ankles brought mineral water in a silver bucket and a local cocktail, a *caipirinha*, which proved to be a glass of fierce cane alcohol caressed, not weakened, by the pulp of a lime. The liquor seared its way to Bailey's stomach, leaving a heady warmth and a sweet, slightly oily taste on the tongue.

"You can taste the Amazon," Harry Maitland remarked, taking another seat at the table. "Do you like it?"

"I'd rather taste Loch Lomond," Bailey smiled. "But I'm sure I will soon be acclimatized."

There was no dusk. The sun died in a burst of flame, and the sky hung down in folds of purple velvet.

Bailey felt the throbbing before his ears became attuned to it, a steady, insistent pulse that stirred the heavy fronds of the shade trees and the slender, supple women on the terrace in their shimmering Paris gowns. It came from all directions.

"The rhythm of Africa," Maitland said softly. "The samba schools are practicing for Carnival. Every neighborhood, however poor—especially the poorest—has its own school of samba. We can go to one, if you like. Later the drummers will play for the *candomblé.*"

"The *candomblé?*"

"For the spirits of Africa. They came with the slaves and became the masters."

"But this is a Catholic country."

"Oh, yes. But go to any church, and behind the plaster saint you will find a Yoruba god with his axe or his sword."

Bailey listened to the drums and to the voices that came skirling over them down the hillsides from the shantytowns. He had hardly noticed the heat before. Now he found he was mopping his face with his handkerchief.

"Well," he said to Maitland, "what local customs were you planning to initiate me into tonight?"

"We have a dinner invitation."

"We?"

"Well, I do, if you wish to be precise. But you will be more than welcome. Of course, we need only go if you think it would amuse you."

"May I ask who is the host?"

"Doctor Alcibiades."

"I beg your pardon?"

"I suppose we would call him Doctor Guimaraes in England. But in Rio everybody is known by his first name, even the President."

"I imagine that if we had first names like Alcibiades, nobody would bother with our surnames either. At least it suggests an acquaintance with the classics. As I recall, the original Alcibiades was an Athenian drunk who tried to conquer Sicily. What is your one?"

"He's the mayor of Rio. Which means a damn sight more than Lord Mayor of London. In terms of power, if not respect."

"Do you know who else is invited?"

"His parties are unpredictable. There are people who dare not refuse an invitation, and people who dare not accept. You see, before Alcibiades entered politics, he was the city's leading authority on—" Harry cleared his throat "—social diseases.'

"I can see why he's an influential man."

"He speaks excellent English. He went to medical school in Boston."

"I see. Well, I suppose that's as close as one comes to the King's English in these longitudes."

"Shall we go, then?"

"Why not? But do me one favor, will you, Harry? Just say I'm a friend of your father's. If anybody asks, you might say I'm on holiday, looking at tropical wildlife."

"Then you'll have a lot to talk about to Alcibiades. He's one of Brazil's leading naturalists."

He said this straight-faced, and Bailey was pleased to note, once again, that the younger man was quick. He had confided in Harry, to a degree, after the affair in Lisbon, without specifying either the exact nature of his employment or the reason he had come to Rio. He was confident that Maitland would do nothing to cause an embarrassment.

6

DOCTOR ALCIBIADES' house was a red-tiled villa in Flamengo, about equidistant from the British embassy and the presidential palace. They drove there in the open car Harry called the Beast. It was a Hispano-Suiza touring car. When Harry had to brake for a streetcar, there was a low growl from under the hood, as if the Beast were trying to slip the leash.

The streetcar was jammed. The conductor clambered over the passengers contending for space on the running board like a referee trying to pull apart a rugby scrum.

"See the tram?" Maitland said to Bailey. "The trams give you the key to what Rio society is like. Everybody uses them, even the millionaire who built your hotel. So naturally, they reflect every nuance of the class structure. On the first-class trams, a male passenger is admitted only if he is wearing a jacket and tie—preferably, of course, a linen suit worn only once before it is laundered and pressed—and perhaps a boater. A man of humble means will give up his seat on the tram to a man of a higher station, regardless of age. The English colony over in Niteroi has its own tram. Naturally, Brazilians—your old-style Englishman still calls them Portuguese—are not allowed on, any more than they are admitted to the British Club."

The streetcar jangled past, and the Beast leaped over the intersection.

"By and large," Bailey observed, "the great talent of the English abroad is for *not* going native."

They were received at Doctor Alcibiades' house by a black butler with enough fruit salad on his splendid white uniform to equip an admiral. The party spilled out of the house, across a wide terrace and gardens bordered with bougainvillea. All the Brazilians seemed to be drinking scotch whisky. Their host was sleekly handsome. His shining black hair capped his skull like moleskin. He had the longest eyelashes Bailey had ever seen on a man.

Maitland squired Bailey around the terrace, making introductions—a newspaper publisher, a popular artist, a very anglicized Canadian with a monocle who had something to do with the power company. Bailey's eye fell on a woman who was by herself in a circle of men. She was dressed conservatively in comparison to the other beauties at the party, who were flaunting the most daring of the Paris fashions. Her jewels were discreet. Her dress was basic black, and the neckline was high, though it failed to conceal the boldness of her figure.

Bailey thought she looked the way Emma Bovary ought to have looked, just after the fall.

"She's quite a knockout, isn't she?" Maitland murmured, following Harry's glance. "She's the publisher's mistress. I believe her name is Ariana. I expect her presence is causing quite a stir. All the wealthy Brazilians keep mistresses, but they're not supposed to show them at affairs like this."

Bailey noted that a very fair-skinned woman in red—presumably the wife of one of Ariana's admirers—kept glaring menacingly in her direction. A small, lively figure detached itself from the circle around the woman in black.

"Good evening, Harry," he greeted Maitland. "Do you suppose Rio Light could arrange a blackout tonight? It might spare some of our friends the wrath of their wives."

"I wonder if that's all that would happen. Colin, I am honored to present Colonel Plinio Nogueira. Colonel Plinio is the man who makes it possible for us to sleep safe in our beds."

"Or someone else's," the colonel said pleasantly.

Colin Bailey inspected him more closely. Plinio was immaculately turned out in a dark, tailored suit whose quality was discreetly advertised by the fact that the last button on each cuff was left unfastened. The arch of the eyebrows and the silky moustache curling up slightly at either end suggested a capacity for humor. His high color indicated not only a pleasing variety of ancestors but that—in one of the biblical tags he liked to recall from his Catholic education—the colonel had looked at the wine-cup when it was red.

"Colonel Plinio is the chief of the Department of Political and Social Order," Harry explained.

The colonel clicked his heels and made a little bow.

"You are also English, Mr. Bailey?"

"Very much so, I'm afraid."

"I have always liked the English," Colonel Plinio announced. "Even if they do not invite us to their club. I was in London some years ago, and I visited a haberdashery on Savile Row. I have a penchant for ties, you know. It is one of my *serious* vices."

Bailey examined his neckwear, a burgundy silk foulard with a subdued equestrian pattern.

"I had selected half a dozen ties—my collection fills a whole wardrobe —and when the time came to pay the bill, I found, to my embarrassment, that I had no money on me. The sales attendant, one of that superior breed that can pass for housemasters at Eton, was perfectly charming. He asked if I had some means of identification. I had not so much as a visiting card. You see, I had changed my clothes and left my hotel in rather a hurry to keep a rendezvous—a somewhat delicate story I mustn't bore you with here. I told the attendant that I would return to collect the ties later. Still unperturbed, he said, 'That's perfectly all right, sir. May I examine the label in your suit?' I was too astonished to refuse.

"Can you guess what happened? The attendant glanced at the label on my inside breast pocket. Fortunately, it was the label of a well-known tailor, also on Savile Row. The attendant said, 'That will do admirably, sir.' They wrapped up my purchases and let me walk out with them, just like that."

"A man with the right tailor could never belong to the criminal classes," Bailey remarked.

"There it is!" Colonel Plinio exclaimed in triumph. "The quintessence of English social philosophy. To the Raj!"

"I SEE that your Colonel Plinio is something of a humorist," Bailey remarked to Maitland after the policeman moved on. "And something of a ladies' man to boot," he added, noting that Plinio had returned to the assault on the tantalizing woman in black.

"I'm rather surprised to find him here," Maitland observed. "His chief and Doctor Alcibiades can't stand each other."

"And what are Plinio's relations with his chief?"

"Ambiguous. Like Plinio's relations with most people."

"I see that you've brought me into the middle of some intrigue."

"I thought it might be the kind of entertainment that agreed with you."

Bailey's eyes twinkled. He was sure now he was going to enjoy Brazil.

"What can you tell me about Plinio's chief?"

"Well, of course Plinio heads the political police. Filinto Müller, the chief of police for the federal district, is his boss."

"Müller? Is he German?"

"Of German descent. There's quite a large German community here. I'm sure the German embassy must be cultivating Müller. So are the Greenshirts, our local storm troopers. They turned out an honor guard to help him celebrate his birthday. But Müller is an ambiguous character, too. He was one of the *tenentes,* the revolutionary lieutenants. He even marched with the Prestes Column, though when he bailed out they started calling him a coward and a traitor. Things are never black and white in Brazil."

Bailey nodded, surveying the two or three brown faces among the guests.

"You seem to be remarkably well informed," he told Maitland.

"Well, it's a small society here. Much like anywhere else, I expect. If you can sit a horse properly, you're already halfway there."

Dinner included some of the heady delicacies of Bahia—*vatapá, acarajé*—washed down with Chilean wines. The wife of the Canadian monocle was seated on Bailey's left. She was called Stella, and she talked about life with a robust vulgarity that didn't go with her husband's aroma of mothballs.

"Oh, there's no color problem in Brazil," she announced, in response to a question. She leaned closer and whispered in Bailey's ear, "Because the Portuguese will do it with anything on two legs." Then, in a more normal voice, "You don't see many blacks here, of course. You won't see them in the Jockey Club enclosure either. But the Brazilians don't exclude people because they're black. They exclude them because they're poor. If you've got money, you're as white as alabaster, whatever your grannie happened to be."

A BAND played tangoes on the terrace after dinner. When the band paused after its first set, Bailey could hear the drums talking again from the hillsides. Doctor Alcibiades made the round of his guests, puffing on his cigar.

"I am told you are something of a naturalist, Mister Bailey," the mayor addressed him.

"Just an amateur."

"I'm sure you're too modest. Would it amuse you to see my collection?"

"I'd be delighted. Does it have any special focus?"

"Oh, yes." Alcibiades smiled. "I am especially interested in reptiles." His liquid brown eyes shifted to Colonel Plinio. "Perhaps this might amuse you, too, my dear Colonel?"

"I wouldn't miss it for anything."

Doctor Alcibiades led them down a dimly lit corridor that made a right angle bend and along a covered walk smelling of palm oil, where servant boys were sleeping in hammocks. Bailey calculated that the villa must contain at least thirty rooms.

A guard dog rushed out of the shadows, teeth bared, pawing at the air when it reached the end of its tether. A man rose out of the darkness behind it with a rifle under his arm. He spoke to the dog, and it lay down.

"I see you are well protected, Doctor," Bailey remarked to his host.

"More than is necessary, I think. We Brazilians are a pacifistic people. But my friends in the police insist."

They came to a large greenhouse, and Alcibiades unlocked the door with a key that was fastened to his watch fob. Bailey noticed that some kind of talisman was also attached, a small gold fist with the tip of the thumb pushing up between the index and middle fingers.

The mayor turned on the lights, and Bailey saw that both sides of the greenhouse were occupied by large glass cases with wooden hutches and miniature rock gardens inside. In one of the nearer cases, a jet-black reptile advanced on the glass in a series of sudden, whiplike movements and raised up, flicking its tongue. The thing was as long as Bailey.

Doctor Alcibiades picked up an odd implement—a pole with a piece of thick, bent wire on the end, like one tine of a fork—unlatched the case, caught the black snake under its middle, and tossed it straight at Harry Maitland.

"Just hold that for a minute, will you?"

Bailey looked round for something heavy and picked up a rock. Colonel Plinio, who had been hovering at Maitland's right elbow, staged a lightning retreat. He was now by the door, clutching a Smith & Wesson. Harry had managed to catch the heavy, squirming reptile. Its tail thwacked against his thigh. Sweating lightly, he maneuvered till he had a hand round its neck, just below the head. Its jaws opened and closed. It was as cold as a tombstone.

Doctor Alcibiades surveyed the disruption he had caused and burst out laughing.

"I see you really are a novice, Mister Bailey. Otherwise you would have been able to reassure our young friend Harry. That little beauty is a mussurama, a cousin of the North American king snake. He's harmless to men. He even enjoys human company. Here, put him on the table."

Harry dropped the snake onto a surface the size of a billiard table, with a slightly curved, glassy rim.

"Snakes are highly specialized," Alcibiades went on. "Especially in their eating habits. There are some that live exclusively on birds, others on frogs or lizards or even spiders. A very few species are cannibals. This fellow is one of them. He dines exclusively on his fellow snakes. In your honor, gentlemen, I will provide a demonstration."

He opened another of the glass cases and fished around with his hook among a pile of rocks and dead branches. A smaller snake lunged out of its hiding place towards the open door. Alcibiades caught it at the last instant, pinned its head and dropped it on to the table at the opposite end from the mussurama.

It reared up, threw back its pointed head, and opened its jaw to reveal huge fangs dripping with yellow venom.

"The ace of spades, to perfection," Bailey said. "She's a pit viper, isn't she?"

"Very good, Mr. Bailey. We call her a *jararaca*. She is related to the fer-de-lance. Men can sometimes survive her bite for many hours, even a whole day. But not pleasurably. Now watch, please."

The bigger snake was not intimidated by the viper's display. It rippled gently across the table, till it was brushing the viper's side, as if seeking to make friends. For a moment the viper was perfectly still. Then it struck with such speed that it was merely a blur before Bailey's eyes, until he saw its fangs drive deep into the back of the larger snake.

The mussurama seemed utterly oblivious to what had just happened. In a slower but decisive movement, it rounded on its assailant, prisoning the viper's lower jaw inside its mouth. It swung the viper aloft, then brought its body slamming down against the hard surface. After several minutes, the viper seemed to have been thrashed into insensibility.

The bigger snake opened its jaws to their fullest extent. In a series of prodigious gulps, it began to swallow its victim whole.

When its meal was over, its body was unevenly distended, like a string of sausages.

Alcibiades contemplated his cannibal snake with proprietorial affection.

"Doesn't that remind you of our distinguished colonel of police?" the doctor addressed his English guests. "Courtly, a friend to all mankind—and especially, to all womankind—and yet capable of consuming any of us. My dear Plinio. I do hope I haven't offended you."

"On the contrary. I am flattered, of course." Plinio rose to the occasion with a smile and a little bow. "But, being a simple policeman, I lack the subtlety to grasp your analogy completely. If I am not mistaken, this little pet of yours—the mussurama—devours only snakes that are dangerous to other species, such as man."

"That is so."

"Then tell me, my good Alcibiades—" Plinio patted the cold skin of the mussurama, stretched taut over the undigested body of its victim "—would you compare yourself to this useful animal—or his supper?"

1

JOHNNY's Rio was very different from the city of lights that Harry Maitland was showing off to Colin Bailey.

At the hour when the R.M.S. *Arthurian* was steaming into the Bay of Guanabara, Johnny was at a deserted beach, hidden in a fork of the mountains a few miles west along the coast. He was teaching four skinny Brazilian boys, and a skinnier Basque who was old enough to be their father, how to make bombs.

The scene looked more like a cooking lesson. Each man had an empty jam tin and a supply of phosphorus and other chemicals.

Johnny's simplest instructions took time to convey. His Portuguese was still rudimentary, although he had been going twice a week to the home of a language teacher on a shady street in Botafogo. The man was a positivist who made Johnny practice excerpts from the writings of the master, Auguste Comte. This was less than adequate for explaining street fighting tactics or the handling of explosives.

Vasco, the Spaniard, knew some English. So Johnny would call out orders to him, and he would translate for the others.

"The proportions must be exact," Johnny lectured. "Once you have prepared the bomb—"

"Las proporciones deveran ser exactas." Vasco piped across him. In his excitement, he was using his native Spanish instead of Portuguese.

"—don't sit around twiddling your thumbs. Lose it fast. It's like a grenade without a pin, so don't go knocking it over by accident. The mixture will detonate on impact. Does everybody understand?"

After the pause for translation, the response was five sets of grinning teeth.

"All right. Go to it!"

Johnny walked up and down the white sand, watching them. They were one of the cells selected for special training by Nilo, the party organizer in Rio. Two of them had been in the army, though you wouldn't guess it from the way they handled explosives. At the end of Johnny's week-long course —which ranged from the Leninist theory of imperialism to secret communications and homemade bombs—each man was supposed to be ready to teach others.

It was going to take a damn sight longer than a week, Johnny thought.

Still, he could not fault their enthusiasm, even if it was slightly unorthodox. In the midst of one of his minitutorials on scientific Marxism-Leninism, the Spaniard—a painter and a former anarchist—had gotten carried away and started spouting Bakunin. "I suffer because I am a man and wish to be a god!" Vasco quoted with trembling passion. The Brazilians had applauded, not knowing exactly who Bakunin was. The Brazilians seemed to have been nurtured on *Les Misérables* rather than *Das Kapital*. Some of their notions came from even less scientific places. Zé Sampaio, the slim mulatto at the end of the beach, had brought Johnny photographs of his friends. Johnny was surprised to learn that all of them were dead. "They are my spirit friends," Zé amplified. "They visit me every week."

Johnny found that all of this made it easier for him to play the role of ideological mentor.

I teach them one mythology, he told himself, and they blend it into their own, the way the Roman army borrowed Mithra from the East.

There were moments when he actually enjoyed himself.

He noticed that Vasco was shoveling phosphorus into his jam tin.

"Go easy on that!" he called out to his interpreter.

Vasco nodded and grinned and threw in an extra scoop of saltpeter.

All of the bombs were ready. They were primitive devices, but they could be produced quickly, cheaply and in bulk, and Nilo claimed that in Rio alone there would be five thousand civilians willing to use them.

"One at a time!" Johnny shouted. "Zé! You go first! The rest of you— on your bellies!"

Vasco had not finished translating when Zé hurled his bomb, which brought down a royal palm and left a smoking crater where it had stood.

When the Spaniard's turn came, he whooped, "That's the Special Police barracks!" and flung his bomb at a conical rock fifty feet away. The bomb fell short and rolled on its side. The only sound was the crash of the breakers.

"*Coño,*" Vasco swore in Spanish. He started loping along the beach towards the unexploded bomb.

"Vasco!" Johnny yelled, propping himself up on his elbows. "Don't touch it!"

It was too late. Vasco already had his fingers round the can. The moment he lifted it off the sand, the bomb went off.

Vasco howled. His face was blackened, and most of his moustache had been burned off. He was squeezing his hands. From between the fingers, blood spurted high into the air in narrow jets.

Johnny ran to him and prised his hands apart. The right one was normal. On the left hand, the thumb was intact. But above the knuckles, there was only a charred, bloody stump.

Johnny started tearing strips off his shirt, to make a tourniquet.

"Zé! Get your car!" he shouted to the young mulatto, who worked as a taxi driver and acted as chauffeur to the group.

Vasco was sobbing and mumbling incoherently. Something about a wedding ring. Johnny scoured around in the burned grass and found it, a simple gold band with two sets of initials inside. Gently, he pushed it onto the third finger of the Spaniard's right hand.

Johnny had memorized the address of a doctor, one of the ones who would not report a gunshot wound—or bomb damage—to the police. He ran a clinic on the Rua Chile that Johnny had used for secret meetings with Nilo. On their way there in Zé's taxi, Johnny said, in an effort to buck Vasco up, "You're bloody lucky to be alive. And it wasn't your right hand. You'll still be able to paint."

"I'm left-handed," the Spaniard said, and spat out a broken tooth.

JOHNNY and Helene had disembarked in Rio three weeks before, the advance guard of the South American bureau. Their landing was choppier than Bailey's. They had to fight their way through a crush of Sicilian and Neopolitan peasants who were being bullied by petty officials. The customs inspectors behaved as if they had all week to examine each bag, until Johnny slipped one of them a handsome tip. Instantly a dozen small boys sprang into action, and they saw their suitcases being hustled away in different directions. Johnny went racing after the one that contained the books he needed to encipher and decode messages—innocuous-seeming editions of Victor Hugo and a guide for commercial travelers.

Outside the customs hall Johnny paid off the unwanted porters and deposited their bags in a locker. They walked to the contact address they had been given, a hole in the wall off the Praça Maua. It was full of sailors. Whores of every shape, age and color leaned over the gallery above, cooing to attract the men. There was a mulatta in a yellow dress, beautiful except for the gap in her front teeth, who was munching on roasted peanuts. She tossed some of the shells at Johnny and called down in a voice that ended in a screech, like a parrot's.

"I think she said I'm too old for you." Helene winked at him.

They found a table by the wall, half inside, half out. They sipped sweet, strong *cafezinhos* and waited. The scene in the street was a riot of color, almost a carnival. Strolling musicians stopped to serenade them. A shifty-eyed man sidled up and thrust out a forearm festooned with a half-dozen watches. When Johnny turned away, he uncurled his fist and showed Helene a palm full of dull reddish stones that might have been rubies. The women moved by on dancing hips.

A boy wandered along with a cart, selling hot roasted peanuts in little twists of paper. He had made a brazier out of a rusty can; the coals were glowing at the bottom. He tossed a few nuts onto each of the café tables, then retraced his steps, trying to make a sale.

Absentmindedly, Helene started cracking the shells and popping the nuts into her mouth.

"They're good," she said to Johnny when the boy came back. "Let's buy two bags."

The smallest Brazilian banknote Johnny had on him was worth more than the boy's entire stock.

The boy plucked it from his hand and started trotting off round the corner.

"Hey!" Johnny called after him. "Where's my change?"

The boy looked back over his shoulder, grinned, and crooked his finger.

"Come on," Johnny said to Helene. He threw some money on the table and hurried after the boy.

There was a taxi double-parked in the next street, with its engine idling.

A man with slicked-down hair leaned out the back and said, in the voice of an announcer on the World Service of the BBC, "I do hope you had a good trip."

THIS WAS Johnny's first introduction to the man who was known in the underground as Nilo.

Nilo was the head of the Communist network in Rio and number two in the party's national organization. Like Prestes, he owed his advancement to the Russians. Guralsky had picked him up in Buenos Aires, years before. Nilo had little else in common with Prestes—or any of his other comrades in the Brazilian Communist Party.

Behind Nilo's back, Johnny learned, they joked about him as *O Milionário*, The Millionaire, because he received a handsome annuity from his mother. While he was still in short pants, she had taken him to Europe to do the Grand Tour and left him at boarding school in England—and not just any boarding school. Nilo was the first Communist of Johnny's acquaintance who had gone to Eton. In his present milieu, that made him as exotic as a stuffed toucan in a cage might have seemed in a London drawing room.

Nilo became Johnny's constant companion in those first weeks. As he studied the Brazilian, Johnny wondered whether his conversion to the revolutionary cause was bound up with the playing fields of Eton, with some slight he had resented and remembered. Though he talked like an English toff and affected English tailoring, Nilo had a settled hatred for the masters of the Raj. Beyond this, it was hard for Johnny to fathom his motivation.

Nilo was widely read and would shoot off ideas—usually lifted from French and English literary reviews—like fireworks displays. But there seemed to be no fixed anchorage for his beliefs. Certainly he did not allow them to interfere with his pleasures, and he felt no obligation to share his annuity for the sake of the brotherhood of man. Perhaps he was in it simply for the game, playing at revolution the way he had played at other things—at being an army officer (he had been discharged after getting his commandant's daughter pregnant and declining to marry her) or an entrepreneur (he had tried to make a fortune selling orange juice to the Americans, but the bottom had fallen out of the market).

Johnny discovered another side of Nilo the night Colin Bailey was dining with Doctor Alcibiades.

On previous days, when Johnny was not busy with the training sessions on the beach, Nilo had helped him to scout out the enemy dispositions in the capital. They had inspected the guard posts around the Catete and Guanabara palaces, the layout of the Special Police barracks on the hill of San Antonio, the airfields and the military garrisons. Johnny had found a gap several hundred yards long in the security fence around the main air base. He had made sketch maps showing where the roads and the railway lines must be cut to prevent government reinforcements from reaching the capital. Using information from Nilo and other contacts in the party, he had started making lists of which military units in the capital district could be counted on to join the revolt, which would stay neutral, which would have to be beaten into submission.

That night, Nilo picked him up at the clinic on the Rua Chile, where the doctor was stitching up Vasco's wounds.

"You've been working too hard," Nilo announced. "I'm going to take you out on the town."

"Then I'll fetch Helene. I told her I'd meet her for dinner."

"Leave her at home tonight." Nilo winked. "I want to show you the city's other weak points."

Johnny nearly cried off. But on the other hand, why not accept Nilo's invitation? The man was too self-indulgent to be threatening. It wouldn't hurt to get drunk with him, if that was what Nilo had in mind. In a few weeks more, when Emil and Prestes and other members of the bureau arrived, Johnny knew that his life would be far more taxing, much more closely confined.

Besides, he did not particularly relish the prospect of another long evening alone with Helene. A frost had crept into their relationship since Copenhagen. He felt, once again, that she was watching him. He had no proof that Bailey was right—that she had played the role of a provocateur for Max—but there were times when he thought she was acting as if she felt guilty. They had not talked about Sigrid since Denmark, and the fact that Helene did not ask about the decision he had made deepened his suspicions. On the steamy nights when he couldn't sleep, Johnny would walk the beach and stare across the ocean that divided him from Sigrid. Back in his room, he bared his soul to her in long, impassioned letters. He had written one about Trotsky and the crime Stalin had done him, and the greater crime that might already have been committed—though there was no news of that in the papers. He wrote a twelve-page confession, a desperate plea for understanding and forgiveness. He mailed none of these letters. Night after night, with the ink still wet on the last sheet, he would hold a candle to the pages and watch them turn yellow, then black.

NILO's tour started off with dinner in the Rua Ouvidor, washed down with quantities of whisky and soda and a superior red wine—a Macul—from Chile. Nilo gossiped about other members of the party leadership. He joked about Miranda, the party's secretary-general, and his illiterate mistress, making them sound like a pair of country bumpkins.

Nilo's a snob, Johnny thought. And he wants Miranda's job. He's a fool to show me his hand after a couple of drinks.

Nilo and Miranda were polar opposites. Miranda was a bantam rooster, cocky, dedicated and energetic. Johnny liked him immediately. Unlike Nilo, Miranda actually belonged to the working class in whose name the revolution was being waged, the first man in his family to go to school. His strength came from his roots. When he talked about class oppression, you could tell that he knew what he was talking about from the callouses on his hands. His woman—the one Nilo poked fun at because she couldn't read—was a slender beauty from Bahia who had been raped at the age of ten by the owner of the great villa where her mother scrubbed floors.

Miranda is worth twenty of you, Johnny thought, watching his guide. If there were more like Miranda in other countries, I might still belong to the party.

After the meal Nilo lit up a cigar and proposed a stroll before the *digestivos*. They rambled down into Cinelandia. Along both sides of the boulevard men and women were strolling with their own sex, in twos and threes. Some of the girls were escorted by older women. They were all dressed to the nines. They exchanged languorous looks and blown kisses. From time to time one of the boys would let out a complicated wolf whistle that reminded Johnny of an animal in pain.

"Romantic love," Nilo said mockingly. "In Brazil, if you find that your bride is not a virgin, you can call the police and have the marriage annulled on the spot. So if you're courting a girl from a bourgeois family and she's willing, she'll probably tell you to use the back door. Some of our native duchesses develop rather a taste for that."

He smirked at Johnny, who tried to conceal his mounting contempt.

"If she's not willing," Nilo went on, "when you're finished with mooning about down here, relief is just a few blocks away."

He led Johnny into the winding streets of the Lapa district. They moved in a river of pastel lights. Girls called down to them from the balconies. Johnny saw the pink sign of a club, the Babylônia.

"I have a fondness for this area," Nilo announced. "One of my father's friends brought me here, at his request. To make me a man, as he put it. That's still the way with the old families. I'll be eternally grateful. It made me one up on those buggers at Eton."

"Would you describe that as a socialist attitude?" Johnny sniped at him.

"Oh, I don't know. It's certainly fraternal, wouldn't you say? I know that it goes on in Moscow. They sent me a couple of little numbers who did wonders for my socialist orientation."

Yes, Johnny thought. They would have.

A girl came out of the Babylônia Club wearing a strapless red dress. Her skin was wild honey. The tight satin of her dress defined the rhythmic lilt of her hips. She was followed by an American with a panama hat tilted back on his head and a linen suit in need of pressing. A doorman in a turban rushed to help them into a taxi.

"She'll squeeze him for five dollars," Nilo commented. The going rate in the shuttered houses along the streets of Lapa was ten or twenty *milreis*, the equivalent of fifty cents or a dollar.

"What about the police?" Johnny asked.

"The police are paid off. We're safer from the police here than in any other part of the city."

They stopped for a drink at a street café and instantly drew a small crowd. Street hawkers offered beads and curios, even a live parrot. A musician serenaded them on a strange, echoing instrument that resembled a zither. Another twanged at a long, single-stringed *berimboim*. Urchins rushed up, palms outstretched, fingers slyly groping at Johnny's trouser pockets. The waiter shooed them away, flapping his napkin.

"Para manjar," one of them pleaded.

Nilo threw him a coin. He sat there, the tip of his tongue flicking the side of his mouth, like a lizard's, as the girls sauntered by, and Johnny wondered why he had been brought on this outing. If Nilo were interested in hired sex, why take a witness? More probably, Nilo was trying to elicit his own weakness. Beneath the Old Etonian veneer, this unlikely Brazilian was evidently that crude, and that stupid.

"This is the middle circle," Nilo announced. "You must see the others too."

The tour of the *zonas* took them past elegant townhouses in Santa Teresa, where the most recondite sexual passions were catered for discreetly behind the wrought iron filigree, to a corner of Leme where pederasts congregated, and finally to the roughest, most colorful of the red-light districts, the Mangue. It was near the docks and reminded Johnny of furtive boyhood visits to the Reeperbahn, except that here the girls in the bright-lit windows were darker and the busy streets opened off an avenue lined with royal palms. There was a canal beside the palms. Under soft moonlight, the scene looked as timeless and beautiful as a vision of ancient Egypt. The smell spoiled the illusion; the canal was an open sewer. The whores of the Mangue were of all ages and stages of decay. In front of a swaggering group of sailors—Johnny saw from their hatbands that they were off an Italian ship—a huge, toothless *mulata* hoisted her skirts up above her waist and danced a little jig.

Johnny felt faintly queasy. Nilo laughed and steered him in a different direction.

"I have another confession to make," Nilo announced. "I have a weakness for working-class girls. There is nothing more erotic to me than the sight of a well-endowed woman on her hands and knees, scrubbing the floor. Do you believe me? It's also a matter of breeding. We had a housemaid on the plantation, quite a pretty one. My father didn't need to send me to Lapa. So you see, my instincts are truly with the people."

He laughed at his remark and clapped Johnny on the shoulder.

"I picked up a girl here once," he went on. "Coffee colored, wonderful teeth, hips made for child bearing. I paid her well. You know, you can buy it here for the price of a bottle of soda. But you know what she most wanted? She wanted to sit in a bathtub, a real bathtub. She had never used one. Of course, that was all before I saw the light."

Johnny decided then that if anything unpleasant should happen to this Brazilian because of him, he wouldn't lose much sleep over it. Nilo seemed as self-serving, as indifferent to the plight of individuals, as any coffee baron, any backlands *coronel*. Johnny's mission in Rio would be easier—he thought—if the men he met under assumed names were all cynical adventurers like Nilo or toadies and fabricators like Emil. That would have made Johnny's task of betrayal a positive pleasure. The hard thing was, there were real revolutionaries too, men and women in whom he recognized something of himself. There was Miranda, and Prestes, and Verdi, the romantic

Argentine, and Livia, the stunning Communist poetess who had become Helene's special friend in Rio. There was Helene. Lost soldiers, all of them, as Heinz had said—whether they knew it or not.

8

JOHNNY and Helene were living in a white frame building a rifle shot away from Colin Bailey's hotel, facing the beach at Copacabana. The establishment styled itself the Valhalla Guest House. As this improbable name implied, the pension—run by a bosomy widow from the state of Paraná called Hildegard Kapp—catered almost exclusively to visitors with Teutonic bloodlines.

The Valhalla was one of Nilo's discoveries. He insisted that Johnny and Helene would attract less attention at a place where everyone spoke German. Frau Kapp, for her part, was delighted with her new guests, rapturous after Johnny expressed a fervent admiration for the Führer. She plied them with tortes and implored them not to spend too much time on the beach, because the sun's rays were ruinous for the kidneys. The better class of Brazilians, according to Frau Kapp, went bathing before breakfast and were never seen on the beach after eight in the morning.

While Johnny trained saboteurs and scouted government defenses, Helene was fully employed in preparing the ground for the senior members of the South American bureau who would soon be arriving in Rio. She scoured the classified pages, looking for apartments for rent, and found a luxurious flat for Emil in Ipanema, on the Rua Paulo Redfern. She took a lease on a more modest apartment, a few blocks away, that would be convenient for meetings. She bought a Baby Ford with operational funds —she would act as Emil's driver and bodyguard when he arrived—and drove it into the Rio traffic as if she were opening a billiard game.

THE MORNING after Doctor Alcibiades' party, Colin Bailey strolled the Avenida Atlântica and took a seat at a sidewalk cafe facing the water, half a block away from the Valhalla Guest House. He downed two *cafezinhos*, while several boys hopped about, offering to shine his shoes or arrange an assignation with one of their sisters. Bailey contemplated hiring one of them to carry a note to Johnny. Then he saw a tall, striking blonde come out of the *pension* and climb into a little black Ford. He knew Helene immediately from the photographs. She was superbly turned out in a suit with high, padded shoulders and a tailored jacket that drew attention to her narrow waist. She wore a wide-brimmed hat and dark glasses. Bailey wondered who she was setting off to meet. The Ford lurched out into the traffic.

With Helene safely out of the way, Bailey decided to risk a frontal assault on Valhalla. A Negro boy answered the bell. He became nervous and flustered when Bailey asked for Senhor Gruber, and apparently spoke no English. He ended by slamming the screen door in the Englishman's face.

Bemused by this reception, Bailey walked round the block and found that the guest house had a service entrance at the back. He was testing the door when a lace curtain was pulled back and the snout of a long-barreled pistol poked through the window.

"Johnny?" Bailey called out.

"Hold on."

When Johnny unlatched the door, his gun tucked away beneath his jacket, he was apologetic.

"I wasn't expecting you so soon," he told Bailey. "I told the boy to tell anyone who asked for me that I was out."

"Is there some problem?"

"I was worried about the police. These Brazilians aren't very security conscious."

They took a walk on the beach, and Johnny told Bailey about his excursion with Nilo. He made the Brazilian sound like the type who had become a radical because he'd failed to get into the First Eleven at Eton. Bailey resolved that when he got back, he must get Diana to ask her brother, another old Etonian, whether he remembered anything of this Brazilian. Apart from his nervousness about the police, Johnny seemed in good form. But the meeting did not end well for Bailey. He took off his shoes to walk on the sand, and, distracted by a ravishing Carioca in a scandalously skimpy swimsuit, he managed to step on a jellyfish. He hardly noticed it at the time, but he ended up spending much of the night soaking his foot in cold water, until the drums from the *favelas* started pounding inside his head.

BAILEY's subsequent meetings with Johnny took place on safer ground. The Englishman came to favor the warren of gaming rooms at the back of his hotel, which habitués called the Necrópolis. There was a grand casino on the second level of the hotel, with an endless supply of free champagne for the fashionable clientele who turned out to play roulette and blackjack. But Bailey ruled this out as a suitable place for a meet after his first brush with the *physionomiste* who had a perch in the lobby. *Physionomistes* had a photographic memory for faces. Casinos employed them to screen out professional cardsharps and other undesirables. Bailey also had found uses for them. This one, unfortunately, was worthy of his keep. He told Bailey that he remembered him from Divonne, though Bailey had visited the casino there only once in his life, and that had been a decade before, at the least.

In the Necrôpolis, evening dress was not a requisite, and the management did not bother with complimentary champagne or canapés. The *physionomiste* was replaced by a couple of obvious heavies in lounge suits. The rooms were packed with compulsive losers, mostly Brazilians.

The Necrôpolis struck Bailey as an ideal place for a brief meeting or a brush contact, and he taught Johnny the old roulette ruse. To decide the date and place of the next meeting, he would place his chips on red or black —meaning the Necrôpolis itself, or a beachfront cafe—and then on two separate numbers, for the day and hour.

Bailey learned from Johnny's reports that the principal conspirators would not arrive until after Carnival, traveling by steamer via Montevideo. A radio man was en route from California. There were plans to arm peasant leagues in the north. Nilo and Miranda were confident of their support in the armed forces and expected it to grow dramatically once a front movement, in which the Communist involvement would be disguised, was launched.

Two problems still confronted Bailey: how to communicate with his agent once he had returned to Europe and what, if anything, to tell the Brazilian authorities.

AT THE end of his first week in Rio, Bailey went around to the embassy to send his mail and pay his respects to His Majesty's Ambassador Plenipotentiary, Sir Evelyn Paine. The British Mission was pleasantly situated on a leafy boulevard in Flamengo, fronting the sea. The window behind Sir Evelyn's desk was a picture postcard, with the Sugarloaf in the right-hand corner. Summerhayes, the Head of Chancery, had counseled Bailey to seek a morning interview. Sir Evelyn was apparently in the habit of taking a siesta in the afternoons, leaving the business of the embassy in charge of his wife, who treated the striped-pants contingent as an extension of her domestic staff.

Bailey found Sir Evelyn preoccupied with arranging his seasonal escape to Petrôpolis, where the president had his summer palace, before the start of Carnival.

"Damned lot of noise and African mumbo jumbo," was Sir Evelyn's description of the latter. "A poor excuse for an orgy."

"Kipling enjoyed Carnival here."

"I can't think why," Sir Evelyn said stuffily. "You'd be well advised to get away before it begins."

Sir Evelyn made it plain that, from his point of view, Bailey's departure could not come too soon. He presumed to inform the head of Section V that he belonged to the "old school." In other words, Sir Evelyn thought that diplomatists should not be required to dirty their hands by consorting with spies. Bailey refrained from pointing out that his own "school" was rather more ancient than the ambassador's; it could trace its genealogy at least to Moses' spies in the land of Canaan.

"I've been instructed to assist you," Sir Evelyn said, rattling through the small phalanx of medicine bottles arrayed on his desk. "But I do hope you're not going to cause any fuss."

BAILEY accepted Summerhayes' invitation to lunch at the British Club, near the racetrack. The club was full of the types he had used to avoid at Simla. Summerhayes told him in a conspiratorial whisper that the members were engaged in a last-ditch effort to keep up standards; they were trying to keep Americans out.

Summerhayes resembled a melancholy greyhound, but he had a dry sense of humor that appealed to Bailey and seemed well informed on the Brazilian scene.

"I'd like to pick your brains for a bit," Bailey announced after the second gin.

"How can I help?"

"Tell me about President Vargas."

"Getulio? That's what they all call him in the street, you know. Let's see. He's five feet four, goes about in white suits and black cigars and has sons named Luther and Calvin—which is quite a feat in a Catholic country, you know. He's also a fanatic about golf, although he plays so badly I'm afraid even Sir Evelyn has trouble losing to him graciously. He's a very mild-mannered dictator, as dictators go. He got in because of a revolution, one of those typical Brazilian affairs in which almost nobody gets shot.

"Some of the coffee planters backed him because the old government wouldn't do anything for them when coffee prices fell through the floor after the crash on Wall Street. A lot of the *tenentes*—the young nationalists in the military—sided with him too. And of course the cowboys. He's from the south, from gaucho country. He's a reformer, in his way. He's brought in a new constitution and is moving in a more liberal direction. He's doing a lot for the middle class and for the cities. The people who hate him are the old establishment, especially in São Paulo, and various regional warlords who are used to running their own show and don't like the fact that he's increased the power of the federal government. And some members of this club," he added, cocking an eyebrow. "They think he's an upstart, especially since word got around that he received Sir Evelyn at his summer palace wearing his pajamas."

"Is it true?"

"It was a Sunday morning, one gathers. Brazilian men think it's perfectly proper to be seen in pajamas on Sundays, provided they are freshly pressed."

"What is the president's attitude toward Britain?"

"Relations are correct. Getulio plays golf with H.E., as I mentioned. We have some useful connections in the government. But of course the Americans and the Germans are gaining a great deal of influence. They both have vigorous partisans in the government."

"What do you see as the biggest threat to our interests?"

"Well, there is tremendous pressure to cancel the foreign debt. I don't know whether you heard about Souza Dantas. The head of the Bank of Brazil, you know. He went to the United States on a mission and horrified the bankers by announcing that Brazil couldn't afford to pay its debts. Vargas showed some common sense; he promptly reassured everyone that Brazil would go on meeting its obligations. When Souza Dantas got off his boat at Rio, he was met by an honor guard of local Fascists—they call themselves *Integralistas*—in their jackboots and green shirts. I happened to be meeting the same boat, so I saw the whole thing. It was quite uncanny. The Greenshirts let out Red Indian war whoops—"

"Did you say Red Indian?"

"Yes. Brazilian Fascists are frightfully keen on being indigenous."

"What an extraordinary country!"

"The Greenshirts borrowed their war cry from the Tupi Indians. It goes something like this. *Anauê!*"

A florid gentleman at the next table turned and gave Summerhayes a withering glare.

Summerhayes blushed and lowered his voice. "The long and short of it," he pursued, "is that both the Fascists and the Communists stand to gain from the financial crisis, and the place is full of woolly-headed subalterns who will join any revolt as long as it's sufficiently picturesque."

"We may be able to offer some assistance," Bailey said quietly.

When they went in to lunch, Summerhayes was visibly excited.

"I take it you told H.E. about this," the Head of Chancery said over the roast veal.

"Not in any detail. I think it's best not to involve the embassy any more than is strictly necessary, don't you?"

Bailey explained what he had in mind. He would need a friend at the embassy to pass on cables that could not be entrusted to the commercial services, and to help in an emergency.

Summerhayes would be useful, but as a catcher, not a bowler. Bailey had no intention of entrusting Johnny to anyone from the embassy. Sir Evelyn's languour might be contagious and was almost certainly terminal. Besides, Bailey had already found the man for the job.

HARRY MAITLAND lived on the fringe of the Tijuca rain forest, in a Gothic Victorian house with a high, pointed gables and a wide verandah where hammocks were slung under mosquito nets. The forest smelled of rain. All along the winding road, the bright coral reds of impatiens—the Brazilians called them Shameless Maries—blazed among the green.

As Bailey mounted the steps, he was greeted by a low barking sound from close at hand, followed by a series of piercing whistles. He looked around for the dog and found a bird in a cage.

"It's a *curupião*," Harry told him. "A natural impressionist. Actually, it was a present from our friend the mayor. I imagine he keeps birds to feed to his snakes. Come in and have a drink."

The drinks were served by a girl with smiling eyes who moved at a gently rolling gait, more a dance than a walk, that made her whole body quiver. Her skin was cinnamon; her billowing white skirts were trimmed with gold. Her assurance and the way Harry looked at her told Bailey she was more than a housekeeper.

"Her name is Luisa," Maitland said. "She is from Bahia."

The smells of *dendê* and coconut oil wafted through from the kitchen as Luisa prepared some of the favorite dishes of her native city—little crabcakes, sizzling in the dish, *ximxim de galinha* and a sugary dessert, made with beaten eggs, that looked like a mass of fine yellow hair.

It was a farewell dinner, and Bailey was glad that Harry had decided to share another part of his life with him.

Bailey had made his proposition the day after his lunch with the man from the embassy.

"There's no money in it to speak of, I'm afraid," Bailey had warned. "Although of course we'll see that you're not left out of pocket. No glory either. And you'll be pretty much out on a limb. If you get into trouble, the embassy will deny all knowledge. You'll be working for a service that doesn't officially exist."

"No thanks if I succeed and no help if I fail?" Maitland grinned, paraphrasing Buchan.

"That's about it. But you'll be helping both your own country and your adopted one—and a chap I think you are going to like enormously."

Bailey didn't need to dress up the offer to feel confident that it was one that Harry couldn't refuse. How could a man who would sail up the Amazon in search of a lost explorer turn down another adventure? Besides, Harry was perfect for the job. He had proved that both in Lisbon and at dinner with the mayor. He had both spunk and connections, as well as the ability to think on his feet. He was going to need all of them.

Bailey was not disappointed.

Harry's questions were all practical, to do with how to arrange safe meetings and how to send secure messages. Bailey was able to give him all of a day's instruction in basic tradecraft. They went to inspect some possible dead drops. Bailey was pleased that Harry had some ideas of his own, including a church collection box, though he had to rule out a few of them as impractical.

Bailey stressed again, as they smoked cigars after dinner, that Johnny must be protected at any price. If it became necessary to alert the Brazilian authorities, it must be done in such a way as to hide the source. Perhaps, if the occasion arose, Maitland would be able to build on his relationship with Colonel Plinio.

"I'll be sorry to miss Carnival," Bailey said. He did not mention the cable that had persuaded him to return on the next boat. Things were coming to a head in Copenhagen where—acting on Johnny's information—he had set in motion an operation involving a certain Captain Werner of Russian military intelligence.

It seemed hotter and stuffier outside, as if the rain forest were swallowing the air, and Bailey began to perspire under his light jacket.

He shook hands with Luisa. Her touch was warm but dry.

He said, "It was a magical dinner. And you're very beautiful."

"I'm afraid Luisa doesn't speak English," Maitland said.

But Bailey felt that she answered him with her eyes.

As they strolled towards Harry's car, a circle of dancing lights by the roadside drew Bailey's attention.

They were candles, surrounding a curious arrangement of objects—a bottle, a cloth, cigars laid over each other to form a cross, a clay figurine or doll.

Bailey bent down to take a closer look. He reached for the doll.

He felt the restraining pressure of Luisa's hand, light yet firm, against his arm.

She murmured something in Portuguese.

He felt the warmth of her skin. She carried the faint, bewitching aroma of burnt cloves he had smelled before, borne in by the breeze across the Bay of All Saints, when his cruise ship had laid anchor at Bahia, en route to Rio.

"What is she saying?" he appealed to Harry.

"You musn't touch that. It's a *despacho,* an offering to one of the spirits. Those who ask favors must bring gifts."

In the car, Bailey said, "Luisa believes that stuff, doesn't she?"

"She's a daughter of Yemanjá." Harry did not volunteer any further explanation.

Bailey remembered the gold talisman he had seen on Doctor Alcibiades' watch chain and asked about it.

"It's just a *figa,* " Harry explained. "A good luck charm. Many Brazilians wear them."

"So this—voodoo—is widespread?" Bailey had begun to notice other *despachos,* scores of little candles flickering in crevices along the road.

"Call it voodoo if you like. It works for some. There are spiritists in the government. Even among Prestes' followers."

"Do you believe in it?" Bailey suddenly asked him.

"I believe in the power of all faiths," Harry said. "I've seen things—no, let that pass. I believe what Unamuno wrote. To believe is to create. We create gods out of our need, and they are nonetheless real." Harry smiled at his own solemnity. "I told you this was a country of gods and men."

Back at the hotel, folding shirts for the journey ahead, Bailey thought about Harry and Luisa, and then about Kipling. On the face of it, Sir Evelyn was right. It seemed out of character for Kipling to have fallen in love with the land of Carnival. It was hard to imagine a greater contrast than that between the life and attitudes of an Englishman under the Raj and those of the Brazilians. But then again, not *entirely* out of character. The part of Kipling that was Kim would revel in Brazil and its freedom from the taboos of his tribe.

7

The Art of Insurrection

For a cornered mind, salvation
lies in action.

—JAN VALTIN,*
Out of the Night

*Pseudonym of Richard Krebs,
former Comintern operative.

1

As THE Baby Ford crested the rise above the docks, Johnny had a view of
two elderly Brazilian warships. They looked as immobile as the stone fort
at the mouth of the harbor. On the other side, above the baroque cathedral,
shanties clung like mussels to the side of a granite mountain. Scores of them
had been washed away during the rains, but they had sprouted up again
as fast as the xuxu weeds and the Shameless Maries. Soon they left the city
behind and were traveling across swampy flats towards another mountain
range, smoky in the distance. From the passenger seat, Johnny looked out
at the brown faces of women and children at wayside stalls selling manioc
root and *caldo de cana,* sugarcane juice. Then they were climbing. Two
small boys waved at the car and held up an enormous bunch of ladyfinger
bananas. As Johnny looked back, one of them tore off a piece of the fruit
and squeezed from the bottom, gulping down the mashed banana that
came out like toothpaste. The road tilted up a steeper incline, and at last
they left the soggy heat of the Rio summer below.

Strange flowers blazed like jewels among the rocks; the *gravatá* plants
were torches, tongues of yellow fire above the vivid orange stalks. Johnny
wondered what Sigrid would make of this carnival of color. He could see

261

her now, her eyes bright, her lips pursed, capturing with her brush the things he couldn't name. With the image came the hollow pain of absence, so that the rockslide on the road to Petrópolis was almost a welcome diversion.

As a driver, Helene lacked experience, not confidence. Johnny gripped the doorframe to steady himself as she hurled the Baby Ford round a succession of hairpin bends, claiming the whole road as her property.

"Easy!" Johnny cautioned her after she flung the car back into her own lane to avoid a collision with an oncoming bus. The bus driver leaned out his window, shaking his fist.

Helene was flushed and happy, her hair mussed by the wind. His nervousness only seemed to heighten her pleasure. She slammed her foot down on the gas pedal again.

They screeched around a blind corner. On Johnny's right was a jagged wall of rock. To the left, beyond the narrow shoulder, the land fell away abruptly. Thousands of feet below, he could see the silver tracery of a stream at the foot of the gorge. He thought, We're traveling on the rim of a glass.

He heard the sound—like a distant drumroll—before either of them saw the first boulder that came tumbling across the road.

Helene hit the brakes, too hard. The Ford went into a skid. She clutched at the wheel, wrenching it the wrong way. They missed the fallen rock and went lurching straight for the cliff. Johnny grabbed the wheel, fighting for control of the car. By the time he had brought it shuddering to a halt, the left front wheel was suspended over the gorge.

"Get in the back," he ordered Helene.

"You're heavier," she snapped back, determined not to show fear at the vertiginous drop below her. "You get in the back."

It was not the place to argue. Gingerly, he hoisted himself over the back of his seat and maneuvered into the space behind. With the weight in the car more dispersed, Helene tried to start the engine.

On the first two attempts, it sputtered and died. She had the choke full out, and was pumping the accelerator.

"You're flooding the carburetor," he warned her.

Quietly but firmly, he told her what to do.

She let him drive the rest of the way to the summer capital. The smell from the high grass on the outskirts of Petrópolis was pleasurable and oddly familiar to him. It brought back something of his boyhood. It was like the smell inside the tea chests he had used for games of hide-and-seek.

He said, "If we take that road again, you'd better bring your parachute. And one for me, too."

Helene laughed. She was proud of the fact that she was one of the handful of foreign women who had completed parachute training with the Soviet Air Force.

They parked just off the main square, by the canal that divided the avenue in front of the summer palace of the last emperor of Brazil. Johnny could glimpse its pink facade through the exuberant foliage of a tropical garden.

They walked to the café. There was an L-shaped counter in the front section where stand-up customers chose pastries and hot dishes from a large selection under glass. Sit-down customers were served in the back, where every wall presented a reassuring view of the range of alcohol on offer; backed by mirrors, the bottles on display were multiplied into infinity.

At that hour of the morning the back room was deserted, except for the flies and a young man drinking coffee. Johnny recognized him; he had attended one of the bomb-making courses at the beach. In the underground, they called him Escoteiro, or Boy Scout. He was very dark, with lustrous, curly hair, most of which was hidden by the broad-brimmed straw hat he had jammed down over his forehead.

Boy Scout smiled at Johnny and made a thumbs-up sign. "They're all in there," he said, pointing to a door with a handwritten sign that read *Privado.*

Boy Scout did not get up. As they passed him, Johnny saw the snout of the sawn-off shotgun under the table.

Six men and a woman were already assembled in the private room. Emil jumped up to greet the last arrivals. His face was bright with sweat, although he had torn off his jacket and tie. Under the great bulge of his forehead, his eyes shone with excitement.

"It's on the boil!" Emil exclaimed happily. "There's no stopping it, absolutely no stopping it!"

"Hear, hear," said Nilo, in his plummiest BBC voice.

His rival, Miranda, pumped Johnny's hand and kissed Helene on both cheeks.

The proximate cause of Emil's elation was sitting on a humpbacked sofa under a swooning portrait of the Virgin Mary, the kind that was sold outside churches. This conjunction made Prestes look distinctly like a seminarist, Johnny thought, even though the Communist chief was dressed like any modestly successful shopkeeper, in a white suit with black shoes. Dangling from the sofa, his feet barely touched the ground.

"Welcome home," Johnny said to the man Stalin had picked to lend a face to the revolt. "When did you arrive?"

"Not long ago," Prestes said evasively. "We had some passport difficulties. Nothing serious."

Johnny was intrigued by the woman sitting next to Prestes. She looked a real Amazon, tall and big-boned. Her head was curiously elongated, ending in a massive, square-cut jaw. She seemed the least likely person in the room to be doing crochet. At the sight of Helene, she dropped her crochet hook and swept her into a powerful embrace.

"This is Olga," Prestes introduced her to Johnny. Her grip was as strong as his own. "My bride of the Comintern. That's what we used to call the ladies in Moscow, isn't it?"

I don't remember that you ever had much time for the ladies, Johnny addressed him mentally. Except for your mother, whom you worshiped.

"Helene, you're enchanting, as always," Prestes turned to her. "I can see that you and my Olga are old friends."

"We jumped out of a few planes together in Russia," Helene remarked.

"Parachute training," Olga amplified this. "We're like sisters."

That might be very true, Johnny thought. What was this strapping girl to Prestes? A surrogate mother? A baby-sitter from Max's organization? Johnny was certain that there were deadlier weapons in Olga's satchel-sized handbag than a crochet hook.

"Olga goes with me everywhere," Prestes said, patting her back. "Our friends in the Big House think I need looking after."

They made an odd couple, standing side by side. Olga was a foot taller than Prestes and at least sixty pounds heavier. Johnny could not help speculating about what might happen if she rolled on top of him in bed. Olga was attractive in her way, and he sensed a raw sexuality close to the surface. She returned his visual inspection boldly, with a smile on her lips, and he had the distinct sensation that she was mentally undressing him from top to bottom.

Prestes made the last introductions.

"You know Verdi, of course."

Johnny was genuinely glad to see the voluble Argentinian, who made a great fuss over kissing Helene's hand, while his shaggy grey hair tumbled down over his eyes.

The last man in the room was introduced as Tatu, which meant "Armadillo." It seemed to fit. Tatu was one of the regional organizers from the north. His face was cracked and blackened like worn-out saddle leather. Every excess ounce had been stripped from his frame under the northern sun.

Johnny took a chair by the wall and glanced around the circle of faces, some eager or elated, others watchful and appraising.

The high command of the Brazilian revolution was assembled, for the first time, on Brazilian soil.

Emil banged his fist on the coffee table. "We begin!"

* * *

THE REVOLUTION Stalin had planned for Brazil was supposed to move along two parallel tracks.

Track one was a front operation, of the kind Willi Münzenberg was constantly promoting in Europe. The guiding principle was simple: thousands, perhaps millions, of people who would never knowingly support the Communists could easily be recruited to a front organization secretly controlled by the party that campaigned in the name of such admirable causes as world peace, social justice and anti-Fascism. Lenin had called the people who were duped in this way "useful idiots"; Johnny had heard them described by his superiors in Moscow as "shit-eaters."

The creation of the National Liberation Alliance—the ANL for short —was announced before an excited crowd at the João Caetano Theater on March 30, 1935. The guiding slogan was "Bread, Land and Liberty!" The speakers called for the seizure and breakup of the big estates, for the repudiation of foreign debts and the expropriation of the foreign-owned monopolies. The ANL's executive included three retired naval officers; this was calculated to enlist navy support for a revolt. Only one of these ex-mariners, Roberto Sisson, had any clear conception of the strategy behind the new movement. The audience was swelled by trade unionists from the Federation of Seamen and the National Federation of Railwaymen, both of which—Johnny learned—were largely controlled by the party. The taxi drivers', bank clerks' and textile workers' unions were also represented in force.

One of the youngest speakers was a fiery orator called Carlos Lacerda. Just before he took the rostrum, he was approached by Major Costa Leite, a veteran of the Prestes Column and a member of Prestes' intimate circle.

"We think it would be a good idea," said Costa Leite, "if you nominate Luis Carlos Prestes as honorary president of the ANL."

The tone was that of a military command.

When Lacerda mentioned Prestes' name on the platform, he was received with a resounding ovation. Huge banners bearing Prestes' name that had been smuggled into the hall by party members were instantly unfurled.

Soon hundreds of voices were raised in the new marching song of the ANL, sung to the tune of the national anthem:

> Crimson are our Brazilian souls,
> Erect, brave and handsome youth
> Of clear minds and strong physique
> We fight for bread, land and liberty.

It was no competition for the *Internationale,* Johnny thought, when he heard this ballad for the first time. Still, the ANL rapidly gained strength, attracting swarms of new adherents every time its activists clashed with the police or the Fascist Greenshirts. In Rio, ANL organizers backed demonstrations by workers and bank clerks demanding an eight-hour day and a minimum wage. In Minas, they helped tenant farmers fight eviction by the rapacious landlords. Through two dozen newspapers and bulletins, they appealed to liberals to join them as the first line of defense against fascism. The name of Prestes was a magnet, just as the Brazilian leader had promised. To most of those who rallied to his name, Prestes was seen not as a Moscow-line Communist, but as the Cavalier of Hope, the idealistic hero of a revolt that still evoked *saudade*—romantic yearning—because its objectives had never been clearly defined.

The ANL did not flaunt the red star or the hammer and sickle. The fact that it was under the fist of the Communist party—and therefore the South American bureau—was carefully concealed. What was the point of having a front if everybody knew what was in the back room?

Track two was the secret effort to trigger an armed insurrection. The Comintern vested its hopes in Prestes' old comrades, some of whom were now colonels and state governors and police captains, and in the underground work of spreading sedition and training military cells in which Johnny was playing a leading role. At Johnny's suggestion, party and ANL sympathizers in the various garrisons organized new social clubs where soldiers who came along to play Ping-Pong or enjoy a few beers could be drawn into social discussion. In his lectures to his five-man cells, Johnny stressed the need to focus on issues of immediate concern to the sergeants and corporals—living conditions, terms of service, the behavior of unpopular officers, the use of troops to suppress strikes by workers who came from the same social background.

Only a handful of men in the Brazilian Communist Party were told the true nature of the plot. Only Nilo and Miranda knew about the deadline set in Moscow: the revolution was supposed to be unleashed no later than January 1936.

It soon became clear to Johnny that the Brazilian party was riddled with jealousy and suspicion. Veteran party members resented the fact that Prestes—once denounced by the Communists as a "petit bourgeois adventurer"—had been parachuted in by Moscow as their new leader. At the same time Emil and his team were wary of anarchist and Trotskyite heresies among the party faithful, and perhaps with some reason, since in its original incarnation the Brazilian Communist party had been in large part a creation of anarchists.

It was plain to Johnny, at that first gathering of the general staff in

Petrópolis, that jealousy and suspicion reigned even within the South American bureau. It was a matter of temperament as well as tactics. Nilo and Miranda vied with each other in offering more and more optimistic accounts of the progress that had been made.

"Five thousand officers have joined the ANL!"

"The governors of Ceará and Amazonas have sworn to join us!"

"Great news from Recife—they're ready to set up a soviet republic in the interior!"

Tatu, the northerner, would sit silent through most of this, scratching his nose. Verdi, the Argentinian, was openly skeptical, harping on inconvenient facts: the party was small, the class struggle in Brazil was at a primitive stage, President Vargas was popular even on the left. At one of the meetings, when tempers flared, Verdi accused Nilo of being a "victim of passion."

Emil was desperate for success but wary of being deceived again, as he had deceived himself in China. Sometimes, when the others had vented their opinions, he would turn to Johnny for advice, as if Johnny were some kind of referee. Johnny distrusted this excess of deference. Whenever he was obliged to give his views, he sided with Nilo, who was positively baying for blood, or with Prestes, who talked as if he wanted to launch the revolution the next day.

Let's hurry it along, Johnny told himself. The sooner it blows up, the sooner I'll be out of here.

This proved to be almost a terminal miscalculation.

2

It was a soft day in early June, and the sky hung down between the mountaintops like a sodden towel. Harry Maitland was waiting for Johnny at the very center of the Jardim Botánico, at the end of an avenue of royal palms. A rococo fountain bubbled gaily where the paths crossed, but it was overshadowed by an enormous silk-cotton tree beyond. The massive trunk reared up for a hundred feet before dividing into branches, crooked like the brackets of ritual candelabra. There was a sense of brooding power about that solitary giant, made ominous by the dark of the sky and the pendulous deformity of one of the limbs. What hung from the tree might have been a wasp's nest, but it was hard for Johnny to conceive of a wasp's nest twice the length of a man. Everything in nature seemed exaggerated in Brazil, and anything would grow. Perhaps that was why the botanical gardens were so often deserted. They were silent now, except for the low thrum of the insects in the tract that had been turned into a corner of the Amazon Jungle.

The two men broke their walk at a curious stone table, set on a hummock in front of a gazebo. In one direction the eye fell to a yellow lagoon, almost completely covered by giant Victoria Regina lilies; in the other, it rose above waves of green foliage to the slopes of Corcovado. The Redeemer was lost in the mists.

"I've got some messages for you from Colin," Maitland reported. "He wonders if you can verify an address in Paris."

"What is it?"

"74, Rue du Rocher."

"That's easy. It's an OMS apartment, rented in the name of a Portuguese who is a secret party member. Alfonso Figueiredo. I was given his name once in case I needed help with travel documents and visas."

"Thank you. I think that will be very helpful." Since their first meeting, Harry Maitland had been impressed by Johnny's exact memory for dates, cover names and addresses, even after downing a liter of brandy in a late-night drinking session. But there was something that fascinated Harry far more than the mnemonic skill or the boozing capacity; it was the sense that he was in the presence of a man who had taken the world on his shoulders. More often than not, there had been tension between them. When Johnny's judgment was questioned—sometimes simply in order to elucidate a point—he would flare up, ready to lacerate Harry as a rank amateur, fumbling under the weight of the preconceptions of an amateur of his social class. Maitland had to practice being patient. It was an unfamiliar exercise, but he was helped along by the sense that he was learning all the time, not merely as Colin Bailey's proxy in Rio, but as a man.

Johnny said, "What else?"

"The other bit's personal, I think. Colin asked me to let you know that Max and Sigrid are in Paris."

"I see. Thank you."

So they didn't get Trotsky. Not this time. At least Sigi was safe, and in a place that she loved. But still Max's captive. Perhaps his willing captive . . . *No.* Johnny tried to shut off the jeering rush of thoughts and images. He could not allow himself to dwell on any of that.

He reported to Harry, "They're sending me to the north."

"Where?"

"Bahia. Recife. Then the backlands."

"To train the party underground?"

"To assess our military capacities," Johnny specified. "But there's something more. Emil has made me his ambassador to Lampião." He saw the surprise in the young Englishman's face and added with a grin, "I'm afraid I talked myself into it."

Lampião was the most notorious bandit in Brazil. At the mention of his name, a picture flitted through Harry's mind, something he had seen in a Rio newspaper: a blurred daguerrotype of a man in funny pebble glasses, dressed all in leather, with crossed bandoliers over his chest and a rifle in his fist. The wide brim of his hat, studded with silver coins or amulets, was turned up at the front, lending him an oddly Napoleonic aspect. The toe of his boot rested on the corpse of a fallen enemy. Lampião had been credited with killing hundreds of men. He had earned his strange-sounding nickname by squeezing off rounds from his Winchester so fast (it was said) that the rifle barrel glowed like a street lamp.

"I don't understand this at all," Harry said. "Lampião is no Robin Hood, and he's certainly no revolutionary. His men tried to attack the Prestes Column when it marched through the north eight years ago."

"That's what Tatu said to Emil," Johnny responded. "But Emil is convinced that the bandits—the *cangaceiros*—are our natural allies. In his head he's still in China. The bandits made up about half of Mao's forces. You see, revolutionaries are always trying to fight the last revolution. Just as generals are forever trying to fight the last war."

"But why did Emil pick you to send to Lampião?"

"He asked what I thought of the plan, and I said it was inspired. You know that's the game I've been playing, Harry. Egging them on. You didn't find fault with it before now, did you?"

"No," Maitland agreed. He had discussed all of this in general terms with Colin Bailey. The spymaster's instinct was the same as Johnny's: that the agent's role should not be merely to pass on information but to act as agent provocateur, goading or luring the conspirators into overreaching themselves.

"But I don't like the smell of this," Harry went on. "By all accounts, Lampião isn't the most hospitable host to uninvited guests. Has it occurred to you that Emil may be trying to get you killed?"

"It's occurred to me," Johnny agreed. "But I'll manage. Tatu is coming too. He doesn't like the idea any better than I do, so I think I can trust him. And he knows the lie of the land."

"But how does Emil propose to win over Lampião?"

"With money. He's got lots of it."

"Where is it coming from?"

"I brought ten thousand U.S. Emil arrived with fifty thousand more. I've heard that a man from the OMS flew in to São Paulo this week with still more. And there are local contributors."

"Who?"

"Businessmen paying protection money, out-of-work politicos hoping to get their jobs back—I can't tell you for sure. But I ran into something interesting the day after I last saw you. I was running a little seminar on anti-military techniques, specifically aimed at sergeants. You know the kind of pitch. Why are your officers treated better than you? Why can't you pay for a decent house for your family, or your mistress at least? The usual stuff. I had a minor brainwave. The people I'm working with aren't long on theory. Most of them are functional illiterates. Pictures work better than any number of speeches. It struck me that it might be very effective to hand out photographs showing the rich at play—mansions with sixteen gardeners and three swimming pools, that sort of thing—so the sergeants can take a good look at how the top dogs live. I got a camera for one of our boys and told him to go around the city taking pictures. He came back with a good selection. Well, Nilo happened to drop in when we were discussing which photographs to use. He loved the whole idea. Of course, he comes from a wealthy family himself. He was keen to see which of his family friends were going to have their villas expropriated. He looked through the pictures and started laughing as if his sides would split. Then all the wind went out of his sails."

"What happened?"

"He didn't like one of the photographs. In fact, he pulled it out of the batch and put it in his wallet. He said it wasn't appropriate. He wouldn't give any further explanation."

"Can you describe the house in the picture?"

"I can do better than that. I got the negative from Escoteiro. I didn't have time to have it developed."

He took an envelope from his pocket and handed it to Harry, who extracted the negative and held it up to the light.

Even with the image reversed, Maitland recognized the high walls, the wrought-iron gates, the ornamental pond among the shade trees.

He was looking at the house of Doctor Alcibiades, snake collector, mayor of Rio—and the man in charge of the police.

Why would Nilo seek to protect Alcibiades? It was not inconceivable that the doctor had a hold over Nilo; given the millionaire Communist's sexual proclivities, he may well have had occasion to consult a venerealogist. The alternative explanation was that the doctor was in on the plot. Perhaps he was even one of the anonymous local paymasters. That possibility was unsettling. If the man who controlled the capital was part of the conspiracy, then its chances of success were far greater than the British—or Johnny— had anticipated.

3

JOHNNY dined with Helene at Gladstone's, a lively bistro just off the Avenida Atlántica. The little marble tables were jammed tight together, but they had no trouble finding a quiet nook at this hour of the evening; Gladstone's crowded up after midnight and stayed open until its last patrons left for work—or their beds.

"What did you do today?" Johnny asked casually.

"I was typing reports for Emil all morning," she said, lighting a slim black cigarillo. "Then I met Proust."

"Who the hell is Proust?"

"Your radio man, of course! You mean you don't know about him?"

"Are you talking about Harvey?" Johnny had been informed on his return to Rio that a wireless specialist, a Californian called Harvey Prince, would accompany him on the first leg of his trip to the north. As far as Johnny could make out, the job of the radio man was to set up a communications link between Emil's general staff and the local command in Recife.

"I've decided to call him Proust," Helene said mischievously. "I think he's one of the boys. You'd better watch your back, dearest. He's awfully pretty."

She glanced at the menu.

"Then I had to fix Emil's toilet," she went on. "Honestly, the man is as helpless as a child. The bowl overflowed, and when I went back, the filth was seeping out over the living room floor. So I struck my blow for the cause with a plumber's devil. Then I made some deliveries. Then I went home and lay in the bath until the hot water stopped running. Quite a heroic day, wouldn't you say?"

She yawned ostentatiously.

"Oh, but I mustn't forget," she added. "We have a new lodger at the Valhalla. And I have a new admirer. He's asked me to go to the new Ginger Rogers movie with him. You don't object, do you, brother dear?"

"Who is he?" Johnny asked suspiciously.

"His name is Hossbach. Our landlady and everyone else calls him Engineer Hossbach. I don't know whether he has a first name."

"German?"

"As Bavarian as a beerhall."

"What's he doing in Rio?"

"That's the best part, Johnny. Can you imagine a pig looking devious? That is the picture of Hossbach, when I asked. He muttered something about a contract with one of the government departments. But you must ask him yourself. He says he's very anxious to meet you."

JOHNNY resolved to take a look at the new lodger before he left for the north. But on their return to the boarding house he was told that Engineer Hossbach had not yet come back from dinner. Johnny fell asleep with a Portuguese dictionary in one hand and a copy of *Os Sertões*, Euclides da Cunha's haunting account of millenarian revolt in the backlands of the north, open across his chest. His dreams were filled with ragged bands of flagellants fired with a vision of an imminent Kingdom of God. He was wakened by Helene banging on the thin wall between their rooms. He responded by pounding with the heel of his shoe.

"You're lying on your back!" she called out to him. "Roll over before your snoring wakes up the whole of Copacabana!"

"Is that any way to talk to your brother?"

It was strange how such banal, domestic intimacies could still forge a bond between them, as the thinnest fibers, wound tightly together, make the strongest rope. For a moment, lying wide awake on his lumpy mattress, he considered going to her, sharing her bed for a few hours.

Instead, he pulled out an old pipe and filled it with his favorite navy cut tobacco. Then he put on his bush jacket, khaki pants and a pair of light boots and hiked along the beach, wondering which was more real—the images from da Cunha that had taken life in his dreams or the abstract dreams of Emil, for whom Brazil, like China, was a country of the mind. There were candles by the water and what looked like an entire steak dinner. Even the dogs, it seemed, would not touch an offering to the old gods. How did that fit into Emil's schema?

The sky had lightened by the time he recrossed the avenue and approached the Valhalla Guest House, so he had a clear sight of the grey hulk that rose up from the verandah like a whale surfacing for air.

"Good morning! It's Herr Gruber, isn't it?" The words came out in two bursts. The grey hulk could now be identified as a large German in a striped bathing costume. He had his arms folded behind his neck. He threw himself back on the deck, then raised up, as he continued his sit-ups.

"You must be Engineer Hossbach. My sister mentioned you."

Hossbach abandoned his sit-ups and pumped Johnny's hand. Running on the spot, he said, "Delighted, delighted. Come on, I'll race you to the water."

"Perhaps later—"

"Nonsense. One must keep up a regime." He slapped Johnny on the shoulder and went bounding down the steps. On the pavement he wheeled around and marked time, shunting his knees up and down with such fanatical dedication that Johnny couldn't help himself; he grinned and went loping after Hossbach.

"Have to keep *fit!*" Hossbach roared as they jogged between the palms. "The Latin races are *soft!* The mongrel races—just look around!"

Johnny let Hossbach beat him to the water's edge. Or perhaps he merely flattered himself that he had conceded the race because, despite his bulk, the German was surprisingly fleet.

"Did I tell you there is a forfeit?" Hossbach asked, standing in the surf with his hands on his hips, swaying his head from side to side.

"What forfeit?"

"I would like your permission to take your sister out."

"I understand she's already accepted. Besides, I can't remember when she asked me for permission to do anything."

"But that's not right," Hossbach said, with apparent earnestness. "A fine Aryan girl like that. It is the duty of the head of her family to protect her."

"I think you'd better explain that to her yourself."

Helene was going to have a merry time with her suitor, he thought.

"Then perhaps I may ask for another forfeit."

"I suppose you can ask."

"I would like to invite you to have dinner with me. I have found an excellent place. Fine Bavarian cooking. Only Germans go there."

"You forget I'm not German."

Hossbach laughed and patted his arm. "German, Austrian, what's the difference? Wasn't the Führer born in Austria? We are all the same *Volk.*" He winked at Johnny. "Besides, your lovely sister told me about your sympathies," he added conspiratorially. "We may be able to do one another some good."

"Naturally, I'll be pleased to assist you in any way possible. Helene didn't tell me what line of business you're in."

"I'm trying to land a certain contract for German business."

"Then you're dealing with the Brazilian government?"

"With some officials, yes. But business here isn't easy. These people have no sense of punctuality. I could do with the benefit of your experience. What do you say to that dinner?"

"It would give me great pleasure. But I'm afraid I have to go away on business."

"I believe your sister said you deal in cigars."

Johnny inclined his head.

"What an agreeable profession. You'll be going to Bahia, I suppose? Isn't that where they make the best Brazilian cigars?"

Johnny nodded again. "Do you know Bahia?"

"Niggertown," Hossbach spat, with sudden violence. "My boat docked there overnight. The Negroes are entirely given over to sex and superstition. If you want to know why this country is weak, look there."

"You seem to have learned a lot about Brazil in a short time," Johnny remarked in a neutral tone.

"I was in Bahia, and I was in Blumenau," Hossbach said. "Two different poles, one indicating the problem, the other the solution. Do you know Blumenau? You don't? But you must go. I can even arrange it for you. It's in Santa Catarina, in the south. A German community, true to its race, with German newspapers and German schools. There are a million *Volksdeutsche* in Brazil. Think what they would accomplish if they were shaped into a single fist!"

"I see that we have a lot to talk about," Johnny said. "But for now, I'm afraid I have a boat to catch."

"Don't worry about your sister. I'll look after her while you're away."

"I'm quite sure you will."

He left Hossbach on the beach, engaged in a new bout of calisthenics. His large, heaving figure seemed to hold magnetic fascination for a small tribe of brown-skinned boys, who had squatted nearby to watch. Hossbach talked and looked like a coarse buffoon, with his pink, bulging face and his yellow hair, cropped so close that the skin showed through. But Johnny had glimpsed raw cunning behind those piggy eyes, and he was persuaded that the engineer was no more engaged in legitimate import-export business than he. Hossbach's visit to Blumenau suggested that he might be an envoy from the foreign section of the Nazi party, which was reaching out aggressively to mobilize German communities all over the world in the Führer's cause. Equally, Hossbach could be a Gestapo agent, sent to hunt down the anti-Nazis who were seeking exile in South America in ever-increasing numbers, and to make friends in the local police.

Either way, Hossbach's arrival at the guest house was an unwelcome complication. They would need to take soundings, to find out what Hossbach was really up to. Johnny was confident that whatever a woman could wheedle out of a man, Helene would get.

4

THE great city of Recife sprawled across two muddy rivers behind a reef, like a giant crab. Up in the hills, in the leafy quarters of Dos Irmãos and Madalena, were the mansions built on sugar, patrolled day and night by police and private guards. Down in the muck were the *mocambos,* squalid encampments of wooden shacks that were slowly sinking into the swamp. Infants and yellow dogs fought over scraps among rotting heaps of garbage. Adults and older children went digging for crabs in the mud.

"It is the perfect cycle," Tatu explained. "There is a type of crab peculiar to this coast. It feeds on decomposing flesh—human flesh. These unfortunates live on the crabs. When they die, the crabs live on them."

Johnny looked back. The American, the radio man, was only halfway up the slope, even though Johnny was lugging the heaviest part of his equipment. Harvey Prince had acquired a following. Bare brown children with saucer eyes, their stomachs distended by malnutrition, hobbled along beside him on stilt legs. Harvey kept coughing into a handkerchief. The American had dressed like a big game hunter, down to the leopard-skin band around his hat. Now the trousers of his very new, very expensive safari suit were caked with mud and more dubious substances, and he looked ready to throw up his breakfast.

Though Johnny had taken an instant dislike to the young Californian, he could feel passing sympathy with his reactions. In the *favelas* of Rio and the *barracos* of Bahia, where the steamer had docked, there was beauty even in the most abject poverty. Johnny remembered the broken streets around the Terreiro de Jesus, in the old upper city of Bahia, where black chickens ran across the cobblestones and wildflowers grew out of the crumbling walls. What man in his right mind would swap that for gas cooking and running water in a sooty industrial suburb in Liverpool or Chicago or Berlin? But in the *mocambos* of Recife, poverty was terror. It reduced a man, body and soul, to an alimentary canal that was never filled.

Johnny puffed steadily on his pipe. The smoke helped to obscure the stench of ordure and advanced decay. At the top of the rise was a circle of one-room huts, only a small step up from the shanties below, and a larger building with a pitched roof and, rising from it, a wooden cross. This house of God had little in common with the hundred baroque churches and cathedrals that raised their glories above the city. With their Italian saints and their altars of gold and silver, they did not speak to the *mocambos;* they were rich men's apologies to God for lives spent without concern for his laws, eleventh-hour payment for indulgences by people who despised the judgment of others but were terrified, on their deathbeds, of a final reckoning. This church was different.

The man who came to greet them wore rope sandals under his cassock. He walked stoop-shouldered as if to conceal his height.

He gave Tatu the briefest embrace and asked, "Did you bring the morphine?"

Tatu handed him a parcel, and the priest vanished into the nearest hut through a crowd that was waiting in line, three abreast.

"He's everything to these people," Tatu explained. "Doctor, teacher, miracle worker. They call him Father Badó."

"Badó? But that's an insult, isn't it? Doesn't it mean simpleton, or half-wit?"

Tatu smiled. "His name is Baudouin. But the children couldn't say it. Now he makes everyone call him Father Badó. He says it fits."

They sat in the priest's own quarters to wait for him. He cooked, slept and studied between the same four walls, his bed a rough hammock, his table an upturned packing case.

"They say he was to become professor of theology at Louvain," Tatu remarked. "But he came to Recife. Father Badó says that a man with a heart who sees the *mocambos* has no choice except to become a revolutionary."

"So he belongs to the party?" Harvey asked eagerly.

"No," Tatu shook his head impatiently. "Though the archbishop talks about him as if he does. He's a friend, a man of trust. His communism is from the heart."

Tatu explained that since Father Badó had become active in the interests of the poor, he had been threatened with one ecclesiastical sanction after another and finally forbidden to celebrate Mass. The Archbishop had asked the superior of his order to send him back to Belgium. Deaf to all the complaints of the hierarchy, Father Badó went on with his self-appointed mission, losing patience only when grateful families brought him ex-votos—little tin replicas of limbs or organs he had supposedly cured—as if he were a saint in one of those gilded churches in town.

The priest rushed in and plunged his hands into a bowl of water. He rinsed them vigorously, then rubbed at his face with a wet towel.

"I'm a terrible host," he apologized, shaking hands with the newcomers. "No soda, no tea, not even coffee—imagine, to be in Brazil without coffee! But—" he wagged a finger triumphantly "—I do have *cachaça*, and when a poor man has *cachaça*, he can live without a great many lesser things."

They all accepted, except for Harvey, who mumbled something about an upset stomach.

The Belgian priest threw a shot glass of the fiery spirit down his throat, snapped his jaws shut, then opened them again in a gasp of pleasure or pain, perhaps both.

"I have a friend—a Jesuit—who warned me that if I drink too much *cachaça*, I will start to hallucinate. I told him I hallucinate already!"

Johnny was refilling his pipe. The priest followed his motions with visible interest.

"Do you mind?" Johnny asked politely.

"Let me smell before I tell you."

Johnny lit the pipe and Father Badó sniffed ostentatiously.

"That's good!" he enthused. "Latakia?"

"It's a London blend. It has some Turkish in it."

"I knew it. Once I understood something about smoking. But here, I am content with my little *mulatas*. Ah, thank you—"

Apparently on cue, Tatu presented him with a box of black cheroots.

"I will share these with Floriano," he announced. "He is the local witch doctor. We never argue about matters of theology."

"Only about cigars?" Johnny suggested.

"You have it!" Father Badó laughed. "Only about matters of substance."

Behind all his surface jollity, the priest looked utterly exhausted, ready to drop.

"My friend Tatu doesn't come bearing gifts for no reason," Father Badó prompted.

"Father, we are going to the interior. We need to make contact with certain men."

"Which men?"

"With Lampião and other captains."

The priest's face darkened. "You're making a mistake," he said curtly. "It is not the way, even if you could persuade them to join you."

"You have always told us that to see what men are reduced to here is to become a revolutionary," Tatu appealed to him. "Can we make a revolution without guns and men who are trained to use them?"

"You were away for the rally," Father Badó answered him obliquely. The priest was active in the National Liberation Alliance, the party's front movement. The movement had organized a big demonstration in front of the governor's palace, to call for the breakup of the big estates and the expropriation of the foreign monopolies. Thousands had turned out.

"The authorities were terrified," Father Badó told them. "They met us with machine guns and cavalry. As the crowd advanced towards the palace, the order came for the cavalry to charge. There they were—three hundred men on horseback, sabers flashing. They broke into a trot. The hooves shuddered against the cobblestones. We could see the horses snorting and steaming, the moist upper lips of the troopers. Everyone was scared, but the soldiers were more scared than the demonstrators. There was a girl from Rio with us, a dramatic speaker. To listen to her was like listening to opera. She squeezed through the ranks and ran out in front of the horses. I thought she would be trampled to death. She had her arms outstretched. Her voice rose, wild and terrible, above the shouts and the thunder of hooves. 'Soldiers, shoot your lieutenant!' And again, 'Soldiers, you belong to the people! Shoot your lieutenant!'

"We could see the officer, leading from behind, as you would expect. Some of the soldiers in the front rank faltered and reined back their mounts. They weren't going to ride over a girl. The officer pulled out his revolver and yelled out threats, ordering them on. Then one of the troopers wheeled his horse around and rode back. Others followed. The line broke and the crowd surged forward. We could see the officer, bellowing and shooting his pistol into the air. Finally, his fear got the better of him. He galloped off, calling over his shoulder to his men to follow. The soldiers were not ready to fire on the people. For three days, the movement owned the streets. It was like a fiesta."

As the priest talked, Johnny watched a cockroach the size of his big toe scuttle out of a crack in the wall and drop to the floor.

"You see what can be done without violence," Father Badó said.

"It's from Gorky," Johnny remarked.

"I beg your pardon?"

"The girl from Rio must have read Gorky's *Mother*. The trick may not work the next time. Sometimes violence is necessary."

"Are you a Russian?"

"No. But I've traveled in Russia."

"Is it true that they have closed the churches?"

"Many of them."

Father Badó sighed deeply. "That will happen here, too," he said, "unless the church takes the side of the people."

"So you'll help us?" Tatu intervened.

"I will give you a letter to a father at Juazeiro." The priest's tone was one of resignation. "He is like a chaplain to these people. But you must be careful. His vision is not the same as ours."

"May we ask one more favor?"

"What is it?"

"May we use your chapel? To store a few things?"

The canvas sack with Harvey's radio equipment had been left near the open door.

Father Badó frowned. "You know I am forbidden to give Holy Communion. But my church is still consecrated ground."

"That's why the police will never search it."

The priest studied the two foreigners. "Is either of you Catholic?"

"My father was Episcopalian," Harvey said brightly.

Father Badó snorted and looked at Johnny.

"I'm a seeker," Johnny said.

"That's not such a bad answer," the priest responded. "When I came to Brazil, I lost my faith. I'm still searching for it. But as long as you are searching, your soul is alive. You may use my church," he said, getting up. "But you must promise to do nothing to endanger my mission. There are many families that depend on me."

"You have our word," Johnny said, warming to this *cachaça* priest in rope sandals.

5

THE wood-burning locomotive huffed around a great bend in the line where soldiers stood guard over the tracks. The railroad workers had been fighting a running battle with the British-owned company for months. The soldiers were there to stop the strikers' families from blocking the tracks. They were not happy poking their bayonets at women who rocked their babies in their arms and waved little green-and-yellow Brazilian flags. In the daytime, party organizers slipped in and out of the Great Western railyards, singling out foremen and scabs for attack, sowing the seeds of more disruption. At night some of the same organizers gathered in the bars and honky-tonks where the troops from the nearby barracks at Socorro passed their free time. The soldiers were happy to accept a few free drinks, and many of them listened to the talk that accompanied the beers. Most of them had been sent down from Natal, because the state government did not trust its own enlisted men. They wanted to be back with their own families, not bullying those of other men.

Father Badó was not the only priest who had joined the movement. Captains and lieutenants, as well as sergeants and other ranks, had formed cells inside the barracks and met in secret with the party's regional directorate. In the huge railyards of the Great Western Company, the largest concentration of industrial workers in the north would be in the vanguard of the rising. And on the way to the train, Tatu showed Johnny the blackened skeletons of mansions that had been razed five years before, in the revolution that had brought President Vargas to power but had done nothing to change the condition of the poor; they were proof that the passivity of the *mocambos* had its limits.

Tatu, so reticent and retiring in Petrópolis, took on new life now he was back among his own people. But he was obviously nervous about the trip to the interior. He kept finding excuses to put it off, until Johnny and the Californian—who had acquired a Colt .45 and an appetite for adventure —announced that they were ready to leave by themselves.

Beyond the narrow belt of green coastal plain, the land for miles on either side of the tracks had been stripped bare. Every tree had been cut down to feed the furnaces of the locomotives. Beyond this man-made desolation they entered a desolation that escaped man's control, a tormented landscape of thorn trees and dried-up gullies that was worse than open desert, because it narrowed the horizons.

They completed the journey to the down-at-heel river port of Juazeiro on a truck without springs. Father Badó's friend glared at them through the one clear lens of his spectacles; the other had been blacked out. He wore a heavy silver crucifix, but the stains on his cassock could probably have revealed his eating habits for the past three months. His long beard was matted and rank. His manner did not improve after he had scanned the letter from the Belgian priest. But he allowed that he might know where to find Lampião. Of course, his church was poor; the roof was falling in. With the famous Father Cicero gone, fewer people made the pilgrimage to Juazeiro.

"The tears of the Blessed Virgin no longer flow."

This mystified Johnny. He looked at his companions and volunteered to make a modest contribution to the Lord's work in Juazeiro. All three of the travelers were weighted down with padded money belts stuffed with gold and silver coins with which they hoped to buy the bandits' support. The holy man of Juazeiro undertook to provide them with a guide to an isolated ranch two days' ride into the backlands, where Lampião had last been heard from.

More of their money went on the horses, lean, miserable beasts that hardly looked strong enough to support Johnny's weight. Alceu, the guide appointed by the priest, supervised the purchase, and it was obvious he was getting a commission from the sellers. Alceu was walleyed with a stubbly chin, pointed like a fox.

The priest came to see them off.

"You're Communists, aren't you?" he said.

"What if we are?"

The priest merely shook his head. Johnny pressed his heels against his horse's narrow flanks. As they moved off, kicking up a little cloud of dust, he heard the priest humming.

"*E tempo de muricy,*" Tatu sang along to the tune. "*Cada um cuida de si.*"

"What are you singing?" the Californian asked.

"It's an old ballad of these parts," Tatu said.

"How do the words go?"

"It's time to die," Johnny translated. "Every man for himself."

Harvey swallowed and adjusted his bandanna. "That's quite a send-off."

THE guide stood in his stirrups and pointed. "There!"

It was odd to see the man straight-backed. For hours he had seemed more asleep than awake, lolling forward against the neck of his scrawny mare.

Johnny peered into the distance. He could see nothing except the eternal *catinga*, the forest of thorn trees that clawed and cut deep, like a frightened, squirming cat. He was glad Tatu had made him buy leather chaps and a leather jacket, though it was hard to breathe inside them in the brilliant, diamond-sharp light of day. Now the forest of thorns was ghostly in the dusk. Land and sky seemed to meld under a fine shower of ash. The earth, baked hard by the sun, could hold warmth no better than moisture. He felt the chill coming down, seeping into his bones.

Without warning, the guide yanked at the bit, forcing his mount to turn in a narrow circle. He jabbed with his spurs and the little mare carried him past the other riders in a surprising burst of speed.

"Alceu, wait! Where are you going?" Tatu shouted at him.

"I did my part!" the guide yelled back. "No further!"

Tatu looked ready to ride after him.

"Let him go," Johnny ordered. "We must be almost there."

He could make out something now—a wisp of smoke, perhaps from a cooking fire.

"But how will we find our way back?" Tatu protested.

"We have a compass."

Whatever lay ahead, Johnny was anxious to get to it. He was beginning to savor the anticipated pleasure of very ordinary things, like drinking from a rainwater barrel instead of a sour, brackish hole in the clay, of getting out of the saddle and out of the boots that pinched his ankles, of sitting within four walls with company—however unpalatable—that he could see.

Crossing that wilderness on unmarked trails, they had never been truly alone. People loomed up out of nowhere and vanished again like wraiths: cowboys slouched in their saddles like Alceu, at the tail of a sorry herd of half-starved cattle; families of *retirantes*, broken by the drought, fleeing on foot toward a death by salt water; ragged bands trooping the other way, deeper into the backlands, with a mystic fire in their eyes, on their way to the miracle priest who had made real blood flow from the host in the mouth of a poor woman taking Holy Communion. Once their path had crossed that of a gang of bearded, sun-blackened *jagunços*, quick with a gun or a knife, who escorted them in utter silence for a mile or so. Johnny kept his hand on the butt of the Winchester slung behind his saddle till they melted away into the scrub.

"They'd as soon kill you as look you in the eye," the guide had laughed. "They'll wait till you're asleep, or your back is turned."

Now Johnny could see a house in a clearing, a modest place built of rough-hewn logs, with a barn behind and a fenced-in enclosure where a few horses were loose.

A sound unlike anything he had heard before carried across the thorn trees. It reminded Johnny of the pieces of an old tin roof, sawing against each other in a driving gale. He realized he was listening to a harmonica.

Tatu turned very pale.

"Mulher Rendeira," he said. "It's the song of Lampião."

"It's what we came for, then," Johnny responded, kicking his horse on.

"I don't like it," Tatu protested, keeping pace a head behind. "Where is everybody? They must see us coming."

The mouth organ stopped playing in the middle of a bar.

"There's someone now," Harvey called out. "He's waving to us!"

Johnny could make out a silhouette at the very edge of the clearing, among the thorn trees, indistinct in the gloom, except that the man seemed impossibly tall. His arms were spread, but not in greeting. Perhaps it was only a scarecrow.

No. Johnny was close enough now to see the man's eyes, which were dark and alive. The man's shirttails hung loose and flapped against a branch like washing on a line. His outstretched arms were rigid, nailed to the thorn tree in a grim parody of the crucifixion. His boots and his trousers were gone. All that lived in that body were the ants, which had occupied the sockets of the eyes and the bloody refuse that hung between the legs.

"Jesus," the American gasped. His immediate reflex was to reach for his Colt.

"Put that away!" Johnny growled at him.

Tatu's instinct was swifter, and possibly surer. He threw himself over the neck of his horse and galloped off in the direction the guide had taken.

A bullet whistled after him.

At the same instant, someone in the shadows threw a rope around Harvey's neck and dragged him off his horse. The big revolver went off, kicked and fell from his hand.

Johnny found himself looking down into twin shotgun barrels.

"Get down," the man behind the shotgun ordered. "It's the same to me whether you die now or later."

Johnny obeyed. More bandits loomed up out of the scrub. There must have been twenty of them, several of them sporting bits and pieces of army or police uniforms.

They searched Johnny, removing his belt, his pistol and his watch.

There were whoops of elation when they found the money belt.

They made him take off all his clothes down to his undershorts, trussed his hands behind his back and hauled him inside the house.

They flung him on the floor in the kitchen, where a wood stove was burning. The one who appeared to be their chief hacked at a slab of charred beef with his knife while he asked questions. His face was knotted and seamed like old wood, and he wore a silver earring and silver bracelets on his wrist.

"We heard about you before you even got to Juazeiro," the bandit announced. "They call me Captain Elétrico. Even the bushes talk to me."

"You're making a mistake, Captain. We have come in friendship. There are letters to prove it."

"What letters?"

One of Elétrico's men extracted the packet from Johnny's saddlebag. The bandit chief stared at them, obviously baffled.

"Shall I read them to you?"

"You? You can't even speak Portuguese like a man. *You* read—" he threw the bundle at a man wearing eyeglasses.

The first letter was addressed to Captain Virgulino Ferreira, better known as Lampião.

"You are lucky you met me instead of Lampião," Captain Elétrico declared. "He is not such a patient man."

The letter had been drafted by Emil with advice from the chief of the party's regional directorate for the north, a man code-named Cato who was known to Johnny only through his reports. This Cato shared none of Tatu's caution, perhaps because he did not share the same risks. He burned with the same fever as Emil and the leadership in Rio. He had even advised that conditions were ripe for creating soviets among the peasants of the north —the China trap all over again.

The bandit in spectacles stumbled through the letter to Lampião, missing syllables and punctuation marks, and succeeded it making it sound like exactly what it was: an awkward translation from a foreign language and, behind it, a foreign thought process. The letter began with flattery, hailing Lampião's heroic exploits and anointing the most notorious of the *cangaceiros* "the legendary champion of the oppressed." A lengthy passage followed which described the development of class struggle in Brazil and the need for an anti-imperialist revolution.

The Electric Captain grunted and yawned and scratched his private parts through most of this. He blinked at a reference to "the latifundist class." He muttered something to the reader, who paused.

"Hey," he addressed Johnny. "You saw that piece of dogmeat outside?"

"I saw it," Johnny said, thinking of the corpse impaled on the thorn tree.

"He used to farm this place. Does that mean he's a latifundist?"

"How many acres did he own?"

"Who can say? There aren't any fences in the *caatinga*. He had three women to himself, though. And he was ass-buddy with the colonel."

"Then he was a latifundist."

"Good. Go on reading," he ordered his man.

The next section was about the need to carve up the big estates and give the land to the tiller.

"Chickenshit," Captain Elétrico interrupted. "What do you think this land is worth? It's cattle and water holes that matter, and horses and women. You think Lampião cares who owns this godforsaken wilderness? You think I give a shit? You think any lousy cowboy will fight over that?"

"There's more," Johnny said.

The reader squinted and stumbled on. The last part of the letter was all that mattered. Emil made the proposal he believed the bandit chief couldn't refuse. The revolutionaries would help him to take vengeance on his enemies. They would provide him with money, thousands of American dollars, to buy guns. In return, the *cangaceiros* would place themselves at the disposal of the revolutionary high command as a mobile guerrilla force.

"You see," Johnny commented. "The gold you took from us was just a down payment."

Captain Elétrico was plainly intrigued by this promised fortune, but puzzled.

"You are here, showing me these things," he said. "What have you got to do with any of us? Where do you come from? You talk as if your mouth is full of rocks."

"From Germany. From the other side of the ocean."

"From Germany." The Electric Captain rocked with laughter. "Most of us here haven't been further away than Piancó. Recife, Olinda, those are already foreign countries. And that fancy boy you brought with you. Where is he from?"

"He's from California. From the United States."

"Ah, these gringos like to use the back door. Isn't that right?" He nudged one of his companions, who was whittling away at a stick with a wickedly curved knife, and all the bandits started to snigger. Captain Elétrico's assessment of Harvey was evidently the same as Helene's.

"High command—revolution—all these fat words," the bandit chief went on. "They mean nothing without a man. Who is your man?"

"Prestes," Johnny replied quietly.

"What?" The Electric Captain looked thunderous.

"Carlos Prestes."

"Is he here?" The bandit erupted from his seat and squeezed Johnny's throat with his thumbs. "Tell me where."

"Not here," Johnny gasped. "Not—in—Brazil."

The bandit released him abruptly, dropping him so the back of his head thudded against the bare floor.

"You know Piancó?"

Johnny shook his head.

"Four days' ride north of here. That's where I'm from. My brother was there when Prestes' men came to Piancó, eight years ago. They're good Catholics in Piancó, they don't want anything to do with the Reds. There was a priest called Padre Aristides. He decided to make a stand against the Prestes Column. He barricaded himself inside a church with some of the townsfolk. My brother was one. Prestes' men had them outnumbered. They were gauchos, throat slitters from the south. When they captured the church, they cut the throat of every man inside and dumped the bodies in a mass grave, without honor. My brother is in that grave."

The Electric Captain was flushed, and breathing hard.

"So you see," he went on, "I won't be joining *Capitão* Prestes. You're a very brave man to come here and use his name. Or a very stupid one. Chain him to the stove," he ordered his men. One of them produced a leg iron that looked like a relic of the slave trade. The metal was rusted but solid.

The heat of the fire scorched Johnny's bare skin.

"What are you going to do with us?"

"I could sell you to the state police. But this is something personal. Because of Piancó. You're a man, and I'll treat you like one. In the morning, you'll see why they call me Captain Elétrico.'

The night was lacerated by the American's screams from another part of the house. It was only too easy to picture what they were doing to him. Johnny struggled with his ropes and singed his wrists trying to burn through them by pushing up against the hot iron of the stove. He had almost succeeded when one of the bandits came in and slouched down in a chair. The manacle bit into the flesh of his leg; he couldn't shift it.

Between the screams and his efforts to wriggle out of his bonds, Johnny brooded on the web of folly and likely betrayal that had dragged him into this hell. If the massacre at Piancó had really happened, how could Emil and the others have deluded themselves that a revolt bearing the name of Prestes would be welcomed with open arms in this wilderness of thorns? The one-eyed priest at Juazeiro must have known what their reception would be. Perhaps Emil knew, too. It occurred to Johnny that the priest was not the only one who might have been happy to see them riding off to their deaths.

Not here, a voice tolled inside Johnny's skull. I'm not ready.

The sense of waste rose up in his gorge.

It was absurd. He had survived the Gestapo and the OGPU only to find his life in the hands of a scruffy Brazilian bandit with a ridiculous name.

He started laughing. It became uncontrollable, rocking his whole body, until a bandit came and kicked him in the ribs to shut him up.

HE WOKE at first light. The stove was dead, and his hands were numb. There was movement outside, the sound of horses whinnying and stamping their hooves in the dust. The bandits were preparing to move out. There was a strong smell of petrol or kerosene.

Captain Elétrico swaggered in, wearing Harvey's safari jacket under his leather vest. He was sporting his full regalia, complete with crossed bandoliers and a brace of pistols in his belt. He had a rifle slung from his shoulder and, on his head, his high leather hat, hung with amulets and silver stars. "I'm a tidy man," he announced to Johnny. "I always clean up after myself."

He proceeded to sprinkle kerosene from a rusty can along the outer wall.

"Nobody can say I'm not a fair man, too."

He bent down and inspected the solid links of the chain that bound Johnny's foot to one of the thick iron legs of the stove, which was bolted to the floor. Satisfied that the chain would not give, he sawed through the ropes around Johnny's wrists. Johnny felt prickling pains as the blood began to flow back into his hands.

"An old place like this shouldn't take too long to burn," the bandit said. "But I'm giving you a chance." He set his knife down on the floor. Johnny calculated that it was just within his reach, but the captain had his boot on the blade.

"Maybe you'll roast. Or maybe you'll cut yourself loose. It's possible. Of course, you won't walk so good." Elétrico's lips curled back to display a row of ruined yellow teeth.

Johnny stared at the knife and the leg iron, and the bandit's meaning dawned on him in a sudden, sickening perception. He would never be able to saw through the chain before the fire consumed the house. But he might just have time to hack off his own foot, there above the ankle.

The bandit played with a box of matches. He struck one, but merely to light his cigar. He struck another, and blew it out.

He started backing away towards the door.

"Goodbye, gringo," he said, striking a third match.

Johnny grabbed for the knife, got up onto his knees and hurled it at the man with the hat full of stars.

I won't die alone, he promised himself.

He aimed for the face, but his fingers were stiff. The knife flew low, missing its target.

Any soldier knows that the third light is unlucky. The dagger tore into the bandit's abdomen, just below the belt.

He howled and clutched at the wound.

The lighted match, loosed from his hand, fell to the floor, and the room exploded into blue and yellow flame. Blinded by fire and smoke, the bandit reeled backwards. Something clattered to the floor. Johnny leaped at Elétrico, but the gap between them was too great. The leg iron stopped him in midflight, and his face hit the ground too fast for him to cushion the fall. Choking on the acrid smoke, blood streaming from his nose, he writhed and clawed helplessly, like a tethered animal. Then his hand closed on something that hadn't been there before—the barrel of the bandit's rifle. He yanked at it, hoisted it up under his arm, pushed the muzzle against the chain and fired. Slivers of metal like tiny razor blades sliced at his face and chest. But he was free.

Elétrico had managed to hobble to the door.

Johnny hurled himself at the bandit and brought him down in a rugby tackle. They landed in a flailing heap on the verandah. Johnny rolled to keep the captain's body between himself and the *cangaceiros* who were gathered in the clearing, leveling their rifles and shotguns over the necks of their horses. The Californian was with them. They had dressed him in a cotton shift like a girl and roped him to the saddle tree of a heavy, black-bearded ruffian who was sporting Harvey's hand-tooled San Antonio boots.

Elétrico was grappling for one of his pistols, but Johnny was stronger. He wrenched the gun out of the captain's hand and jammed it up behind his ear.

"Tell them to back off," Johnny ordered.

The bandit hesitated. His breath came in short, fetid bursts.

"Tell them to back off," Johnny repeated, "or I'll blow the back of your head off."

Elétrico gave the command. The horses backed off a few paces.

"Now tell them to sling their rifles and dismount. Very slowly."

Grudgingly the *cangaceiros* obeyed. Johnny was nervous of pushing them too far. It was hard to tell how far Captain Elétrico's authority carried.

Johnny could feel the heat of the fire at his back. The timbers of the porch creaked and swayed.

Painfully, he got onto his feet and used Elétrico as a human shield as he inched his way down the steps away from the burning house.

"Now tell them to cut the gringo loose."

Harvey's captor laughed as he slit the young Californian's bonds and gave him a pat on the rump.

Harvey shrieked like a madman and snatched the fat man's rifle from its harness. He fired wildly. The bullets vanished among the thorn trees. Some of the horses panicked and ran off. The *cangaceiros* went diving for cover, drawing their pistols.

"Harvey, *no!*" Johnny bellowed.

"They're going to pay," the Californian sobbed. His whole body was shaking. "Those cocksuckers."

He fired at Blackbeard, who was rolling over on the ground. The bullet went wide again.

"Stop it *now!*" Johnny yelled again. "You'll only get yourself killed!"

He said to Elétrico, "Tell them there'll be no more shooting. Tell them to lay down their guns."

The spell would not last much longer, Johnny thought. He could see some of the bandits widening the circle, edging away to the right and left, so that he would not be able to watch all of them at once.

He fired a single warning shot that made one of them dance.

"Stay in your places!" he roared. "Harvey! Get two—no, three—of the horses. And for God's sake, take some of their clothes."

FIVE MILES from the railroad terminus, Johnny told Prince he could have the honor of disposing of the hostage. The Californian shot Captain Elétrico once in the chest and once, for good measure, in the balls. Then he threw up. There was blood amid the bile.

Johnny made no comment then or during the three hours they had to wait for the train back to Recife.

6

COLIN BAILEY had precious little time in those days to worry about Brazil. He made a second trip to Copenhagen to follow up on Johnny's leads. Working with an old friend in the Danish security police, he was able to roll up a whole Soviet illegals network. To deflect suspicion from Johnny, they tried to make it look like a lucky strike. The police, supposedly on the trail of a gang of counterfeiters, conducted a house-to-house search in the street where the illegal was living.

Bailey went on to Berlin. De Salis had removed the clerk in the passport office whom Johnny had identified as a Russian agent, but there was deep concern about leaks to the Germans.

"The Gestapo has no need to crack our ciphers," de Salis had cabled, "so long as it can listen to His Majesty's Ambassador on the telephone."

For once, Bailey found himself in complete agreement with Adam de Salis. For nights at a time, the residency was left in the sole charge of a German porter who could be presumed to be working for the Gestapo. The ambassador, a fervent believer in the idea of a natural alliance between Britain and Germany, shared all the secrets of the embassy with his telephone.

Two years of firsthand experience of the Hitler regime had worked changes in de Salis. He had developed a network of anti-Nazi sources in business and the German military. From them, and from some of the would-be refugees who streamed daily into the passport office, de Salis chronicled the German race to rearm. He had become convinced that Hitler was hell-bent on a war of aggression and could no longer be contained by his generals. He was disgusted by the foreign secretary's efforts to curry favor with Hitler on the dictator's terms. The British government and the British press seemed determined to give Herr Hitler the benefit of the doubt. De Salis's newspaper had suppressed an article he had written on the growth of the Luftwaffe, on the grounds that it would offend the German government and cause children in London to have nightmares of being bombed in their beds.

"The government must be made to see the writing on the wall," de Salis insisted.

This was a new Adam, a bit alarmist, perhaps, but a welcome change from the vain intriguer Bailey had sparred with in the past. Bailey was pleased to acknowledge a new ally. In the summer of 1935 there were few enough men of influence in London who had taken Hitler's measure. Churchill was one and Vansittart another. But theirs were isolated voices in the House of Commons and the Foreign Office. Even that silly peacock Ribbentrop had not quite managed to rupture the British establishment's love affair with the Nazi dictator by greeting the King, at a diplomatic reception, with a stiff-armed salute and a cry of "Heil Hitler!"

One of Bailey's own colleagues dismissed a report on Hitler's designs on Austria and Czechoslovakia as a plant, the probable work of "Jews and Bolshevists." Like all establishments, Whitehall was hostile to intelligence that contradicted its fixed opinions.

Johnny's account of his night call on Stalin had caused a passing stir but was too exotic to take root. Nobody in Whitehall believed in the possibility of a deal between the German and Soviet dictators. The general view was that Hitler's ambitions lay to the east, not to the west, and that it was clearly in Britain's interest to keep him pointed that way. Bailey, too, was convinced that the moment when an understanding might have been possible between Moscow and Berlin had passed. Reviled by the Nazis, Soviet Russia was becoming a popular cause amongst the people who were most alarmed about the rising tide of fascism. After long hesitation, Stalin had decided to break out of isolation. He had signed pacts with the French and the Czechs. According to an interesting tidbit from Johnny, apparently gleaned from Emil Brandt, the much-delayed Seventh Congress of the Comintern would definitely take place in July; the Popular Front against fascism would be the order of the day.

When Bailey got back from Berlin, he found several cables and letters from Rio waiting for him. Harry Maitland had been scrupulous about filing his weekly reports. It was plain that he was enjoying his work and had established a good rapport with Johnny. If his style was at times exuberant, his judgment was shrewd enough. The longest of the telegrams described a disastrous expedition Johnny had made to the northeast. It seemed he had been lucky to save his skin. An American who had accompanied him had suffered a complete nervous breakdown. The whole thing had the flavor of a bad horse opera. Harry suggested that Emil must have read too many of those Wild West adventure stories that had been all the rage in Germany a few years ago.

Failure to sign up the bandits for the revolt had not slowed the momentum of the Comintern operation. Emil and his associates had drawn up a list of cabinet ministers who would be appointed to a "national revolutionary government." The men selected were not openly Communist. They could be relied on to take party orders because they were secret members or because, through greed or ambition, they had placed themselves in the party's debt.

In another message Maitland described a curious complication in Johnny's life. There was a new lodger at his guest house, a German called Hossbach, who was paying court both to Johnny and his "sister." At their last encounter, Hossbach had boasted of his prowess as an aviator. He claimed to have served under Göring and to be on intimate terms with the former air ace who was now the second most powerful man in the Reich. He had told Johnny that he was holding himself in readiness for "the call." He was taking a keen interest in German refugees who were coming to South America and had sought to enlist Johnny's help in spying on a Jewish research scientist who had once worked for I.G. Farben. Johnny had played along, affecting sympathy for the Nazi cause.

One detail fascinated Bailey. Engineer Hossbach boasted that Göring had told him that Germany would soon have the most powerful air force on earth, able to bomb Paris or London into the stone age. According to Hossbach, Germany now had more than two thousand combat planes and eight thousand trained pilots.

Bailey snatched up the report and rushed down the corridor to C.'s office.

"I'm afraid it will have to wait till this afternoon, Major," the chief's secretary said, glancing up at the clock on the wall. "He's running late for a meeting at the War Office."

"It's about that."

C. was about to slip out the back way through his private apartment. He was dressed up in his admiral's uniform with all the decorations. He had a habit of reverting to naval garb when he was going to do battle.

"Johnny's come up trumps again," Bailey announced.

"Colin, I've no doubt your man can walk on the waters, but Brazil is a very long taxi ride from the Air Parity Committee, and they're waiting for me now."

"I think you'll want to see this first," Bailey insisted.

C. squinted at the cable, then reread the section that mentioned the number of German pilots.

"Good lord," he said softly. Then, in his familiar bark, "You didn't plant this, did you, Colin?"

"I've only just opened my mail."

"Have you seen Winterbotham's report?"

"I'm not privy to the details, of course."

But he knew the gist of it. He could hardly fail to. Since Hitler had boasted to the foreign secretary, at their last meeting in Berlin, that the Luftwaffe had reached "parity" with the Royal Air Force, the top priority for every department of British Intelligence had been to find out exactly what this meant and whether the Führer was bluffing. Group Captain Winterbotham was the head of the firm's air intelligence section. He had been fighting a running battle with Whitehall—and, in particular, with the Air Ministry—over the official estimates of German air power. The conventional wisdom was that Hitler was talking through his hat and that the Luftwaffe was years behind the Royal Air Force. The marshals and mandarins at the Air Ministry insisted that Germany had no more than four thousand trained pilots at its disposal. Cobbling together information from various sources, including members of de Salis' network, Winterbotham had calculated that the true figure might be twice as high. C. had defended his estimate at the often testy sessions of the Air Parity Committee, set up to adjudicate on this single issue. But the voice of C.'s service remained in a minority. For the most part the august members of the committee believed what they wanted to believe: that Germany was weak, that German industry was as inefficient as British industry, that it would take Hitler many years to rebuild. Now, it seemed, an agent in Brazil, half a world away, had supplied what it required to win the argument—proof from the horse's mouth.

C. had reason to be excited. The stakes were high. The country's whole defense program now hung on the agreed estimates of German strength. But a Secret Service victory in a battle with the other arms of the bureaucracy would bring more immediate gains.

"This could be worth another hundred thousand to us in the Secret Vote," C. remarked, with satisfaction.

"I trust we can afford to give Johnny a bonus."

"Oh, I should think so. Now I have to run. I can't wait to see the expression on a certain air vice-marshal's face."

1

HARRY MAITLAND parked the Beast under the palms and strolled under the long colonnaded portico of the member's entrance to the Jockey Club, a white marbled palace worthy of a viceroy of India.

A reporter from the English-language paper was lounging near the betting counters, studying the racing form and the well-heeled patrons of the club. Spotting Maitland, he drifted across the tessclated floor. He was sporting a straw boater, a beard in the style of George V which was obviously dyed, and an Old Harrovian tie to which Harry was perfectly sure he was not entitled.

"They think they're at bloody Royal Ascot, don't they?" He greeted Harry with a blast of whisky and stale tobacco, wagging his finger at a group of men in silk hats and women decked out in furs, despite the heat.

"How are you, Monty? Filling up the gossip column?"

Desmond Wild gave him a sly look. Maitland suspected that Wild supplemented his journalistic earnings by charging prominent members of the Anglo-Brazilian community a fee *not* to publish what he found out about their extramarital affairs. Monty was certainly not averse to writing a puff piece or to passing on a tip when the price was right. Maitland himself had made use of him on occasion, though he preferred, by and large, to deal with Brazilian reporters; they had better access to local politicians, drank less and came cheaper, by and large, than Desmond Wild.

"I just saw His Imperial Majesty's Ambassador Extraordinary," Wild reported. "He was fairly *seething*. They've given his usual table to a bloody Yank."

"Who is it?"

"That oil man from Houston. Don't say you don't read my paper, dear boy. He gave a bash that was the talk of the town. He took over the Golden Room at the Copacabana Palace. The place was *drowning* in champagne."

"I suppose you helped bail them out."

"I did my bit," Desmond Wild allowed. "Speaking of which, what would you say to a stirrup cup?"

They went up the wide marble stairs to the terrace, which commanded a sweeping view of the track and the mountains beyond. Corcovado reared up to the left. It was the start of the season, and the terrace was crowded. Every table was marked out as private turf by a bottle of Chivas or Johnny Walker Black with a tape measure along the side. Wild's eyes glinted at the lineup.

A white-jacketed headwaiter bobbed up, apologizing that the restaurant was completely full. His soft, pale features and half-closed eyes made him look like a calculating grouper. Casually Harry displayed a wad of thousand-cruzeiro banknotes, and a free table miraculously appeared.

"There's the Yank," Wild announced, once he had armed himself with a stiff single malt. "Mister Courtland Bull. I gather he lives up to his monicker. And just look who he's asked to lunch. Our pinko mayor. Now *that's* an interesting conjunction."

Maitland turned without haste. The Texas oil man was in his early sixties and ruggedly handsome, his deep tan set off by a mane of white hair. He was laughing around a big cigar, flanked by two young, exceedingly well-developed women who laughed with him. Doctor Alcibiades' attention flitted back and forth from his host to the neighboring tables, where a number of wealthy Brazilian men affected not to see him. It was not clear whether their objections were personal or political. Some members of the Jockey Club regarded the mayor as a dangerous demagogue who stirred up trouble by flirting with the unions and making speeches on the plight of the poor. Some might have more private reasons for avoiding Doctor Alcibiades, at least while in the company of their wives; Maitland guessed that more than a few had had occasion to visit his VD clinic in previous years.

Their eyes met briefly. Doctor Alcibiades nodded and smiled.

Wild had a point, Johnny thought. It *was* an odd conjunction: the "progressive" mayor and the Texas oil baron. Especially since Doctor Alcibiades had landed himself in hot water with the established oil companies by imposing a freeze on gasoline prices in Rio.

"I'll take the Sugarloaf on the left," Wild said, admiring the blonde who was seated between the American and the mayor, making an inviting show of cleavage. "What do you say? Oh, I forgot. You like them darker, don't you?"

To avoid rising to the bait, Harry called a boy to place a bet for him on the second race, on horse number six.

"*Vencedor,*" he specified. "To win."

Wild was impressed by the sum Maitland was betting.

"Pretty sure of yourself, aren't you?" He consulted his form sheet and shook his head. "She doesn't stand a chance. Melpomene. Bloody silly name for a filly, anyway."

He took another look at the form sheet. The horse was owned by a São Paulo syndicate. A thought struggled to the surface of his consciousness like a fish rising up out of a murky aquarium.

"You own a piece of a horse syndicate, don't you?" he said to Maitland, almost accusingly. "Do you own a piece of this nag?"

"I might," Harry conceded.

"Fuck. I put a bundle on number three. Carlota."

When the boy came back with the betting slips, Wild asked him to put some money on Melpomene for him. He then made a great show of having mislaid his wallet.

"You wouldn't mind, would you, old man—"

Harry cut short the entreaties by loaning him the equivalent of about ten dollars.

"I'll pay you back if I win," Wild said generously. "I can't wait to see the look on Sir Evelyn's face if I do. I told him Carlota was a sure thing."

"Let's hope he doesn't listen to you."

The British Ambassador was sitting at a table a few steps above them on the other side of the terrace, his view of the track obscured by the constant coming and going of waiters and patrons on the level below. Sir Evelyn was looking distinctly peeved. Lady Maude was drinking a good deal of champagne and lecturing in a high, nasal voice. Summerhayes was at their table, trying to make himself invisible. Harry assumed the mousy woman in a chintzy frock who made up the party must be Summerhayes' wife.

The horses were at the starting gate. The jockeys' garb was confusingly similar. Most of them wore tunics in varying shades of red, and St. Andrew's cross, in gold or bright orange, was in great demand as an embellishment.

Lady Maude watched the race through opera glasses, barracking for Carlota, the favorite, as stridently as any of the punters who lined the railing below the members' stand. Harry noticed that Courtland Bull paid no attention to the race. He had swapped seats with one of the women and was talking animatedly to Doctor Alcibiades, punctuating his points with his cigar.

Melpomene led from the beginning and won the race by nearly five lengths.

"Bloody hell!" Wild yelled in high excitement. "It's a good thing I ran into you. How big a piece of that filly do you own?"

"Oh, about two per cent, I should think."

"Well, if she repeats that showing at the Derby" —like other Anglos, Wild persisted in calling the Grande Prémio do Brasil, the biggest event in the local racing calendar, the Derby "—Courtland Bull will be taking *you* to lunch. Excuse me." He got up so hastily he dropped cigarette ash down the front of his jacket. "I must go and pick up my winnings."

Across the terrace Sir Evelyn tore up his betting slips and strewed them over the tablecloth in disgust. The blonde at the American's table clapped her hands and kissed everybody within reach. Harry was intrigued by the relationship between Doctor Alcibiades and his host. Was Bull Petroleum trying to undercut the other oil companies and grab the Brazilian market for itself? Or was Courtland Bull planning to move some of his oil rigs south? There had been speculation—little better than rumor—about some big offshore oil deposits along the coast of Bahia. But those were not in the gift of the mayor of Rio de Janeiro. However, Doctor Alcibiades had the ear of the president, and of other people besides.

It struck Harry that Desmond Wild had been gone for rather a long time. Still, Wild could never be accused of hurrying to settle his debts. No doubt he had repaired to the other bar or the betting counters below.

"Maitland?" The voice was querulous.

Harry looked up to find the British Ambassador hovering over his table, puffed up so that it seemed he was about to pop his collar stud.

"Good afternoon, Sir Evelyn. May I offer you a drink?"

"I've got a bone to pick with you, young man. What the devil do you think you're up to, using my embassy as a postbox? Summerhayes tells me you've been coming in every week, sending off cables none of us can read."

The ambassador was talking loudly enough to be overheard at any of the neighboring tables.

"Sir Evelyn, I hardly think this is the appropriate place—"

"I won't tolerate my embassy being used for any of this shady business!"

"Sir Evelyn—"

"I want to see you in my office first thing on Monday morning, and I shall want some satisfactory answers. Otherwise, I shan't hesitate to speak to your employers. I'm sure Rio Light will take a responsible view."

"Shall we say nine?" Harry responded, as calmly as possible.

Sir Evelyn looked at him as if he had gone quite mad.

"I shall receive you at ten," he said frostily.

THE interview did not go well. In the course of the weekend Harry had prevailed on an acquaintance at Cable & Wireless to open up the shop and send a coded telegram to London, asking Colin Bailey for instructions on how to proceed. When Maitland arrived at the embassy on Monday morning, he was made to cool his heels for nearly half an hour before he was admitted to the ambassador's presence. Sir Evelyn had the transcript of Colin Bailey's reply on his desk.

"Perhaps you would start by translating this," he said, handing the message to Harry.

"It will take me a little time, sir."

"I am prepared to wait."

"I'm afraid I also need special equipment. If you'll give me an hour—"

"Oh, very well," the ambassador acquiesced grudgingly.

Harry drove home to decipher the cable. Its twelve-letter key was based on a parallel-text edition of Xenophon's *Anabasis*, which Maitland and Bailey had both studied in the original at school. The choice of the book on which the simple code was based had less to do with fond memories of Winchester than with Bailey's sense of whimsy. The *Anabasis* was the story of a long march. Prestes, the Communist figurehead, had conducted a long march of his own; Emil, the controller, had been responsible for another.

Harry drove back to the embassy with his notes.

To his discomfiture, Lady Maude was present at the second interview. She offered him tea and settled herself, stiff-backed, in the leather chair in front of the bookcase.

Harry remembered one of Bailey's remarks about the ambassador, an allusion to a Russian novel about a man who was incapable either of getting out of bed or doing anything worthwhile when in it.

"Use your own judgment," Bailey had cabled, "but protect our source at any cost."

Maitland quoted this to Sir Evelyn, along with a few other selected passages.

"Well, I'm waiting," the ambassador rejoined.

Harry gave a brief summary of the facts he had assembled from Johnny's reports. The Communists' hopes centered on the movement in the north, where there was talk of rallying an insurrectionary force of a hundred thousand men, and on Prestes' old comrades in the military, some of whom now held strategic positions in the armed forces and the government. The Communists were strong in a number of trade unions, especially the railroad workers and the taxi drivers, but their popular base in the cities was still weak. They had been training paramilitary cells to carry out acts of sabotage against key buildings and communications. Their front organization, the National Liberation Alliance, was gathering support by advertising a few simple slogans attacking the Anglo-American banks, the big landowners and the Fascist Greenshirts. The aim was a violent revolution under the banners of nationalism and social justice that would be handed over to the Communist party once Vargas was overthrown. The operation was well funded and was under the supervision of a team of veteran revolutionists from Moscow. It was gaining momentum now that Prestes had returned to Brazil and was in personal touch with his admirers.

"You must tell Getulio at once," Lady Maude interrupted, addressing her husband.

Sir Evelyn nodded. "I was hoping to play nine holes with him on Saturday," he reported.

"No, dear. You must go to him today."

Maitland cleared his throat. "If I may say so, I think it would be premature to go to the Brazilian authorities."

"Nonsense," Sir Evelyn admonished him. "We are dealing with a grave conspiracy. The government must be alerted, so it can take appropriate measures. I know the president well. He remembers his friends. This will do no harm to British interests. On the contrary, we can expect a more sympathetic hearing at Guanabara Palace."

"There are some operational matters to be considered."

"Operational matters?" Sir Evelyn's expression implied that Harry had just broken wind in his presence.

"The conspiracy is still in its formative phase, and we do not yet have sufficient information to identify all the ringleaders. If we are patient, we have the chance to bag all of them."

Harry thought that his appeal to masterly inertia might reach Sir Evelyn. But his formidable wife intervened once more.

"If we merely wait," she pointed out, "the balloon may go up while we're all in our beds. Before we know it, we'll have a Bolshevik mob storming the embassy."

"That is most unlikely," Maitland countered, with as much patience as he could muster. "You see, we have an excellent source. A source that must be protected."

"Who is this source?" Sir Evelyn challenged him.

"I'm afraid I'm not at liberty to say, sir. But he is a remarkable man who has already rendered immense service to Britain."

"That's all very well, but Maude has an excellent point. We can't just sit on this type of information. I've made up my mind. I shall seek an audience with the president."

"Might I make one suggestion?"

"Well?"

"If you do talk to Vargas, you might tell him our information comes from sources in Europe—a wireless intercept, something of that kind."

"What are you suggesting? That the president can't keep a secret?"

"He is bound to discuss the matter with his cabinet and his police chiefs. We can't tell which of them may have been compromised. In any event, you know the Brazilians. They're a talkative lot."

Sir Evelyn did not dissent from this.

He was in a markedly better humor when he rose from his desk to indicate that the interview was over.

"I know your family," he said to Harry. "I can't imagine how you got in so deep with Bailey and his gang of eavesdroppers."

"I'm afraid I was always the black sheep."

PRESIDENT VARGAS agreed to see His Majesty's Ambassador on the morning of June 20. Sir Evelyn put on his morning coat and his full decorations and drove to the Palace of Guanabara in the embassy Rolls. The Union Jack stood up stiff and correct on its little mast above the fender. The ambassador was welcomed by an honor guard in white uniforms and helmets with horsehair plumes. The uniforms were in need of pressing, Sir Evelyn noted with a jaundiced eye, and the headgear could have done with more than a touch of brass polish. The honor guard presented arms in a fashion that would have made a British drill sergeant swoon.

Sir Evelyn was received by the president in the grand salon. For part of the time, the president's daughter, a lively, pretty young thing whom he called Alzarinha, was present. She seemed to have almost as much influence in the palace as Lady Maude exercised at the British Embassy, though Sir Evelyn would not have welcomed the analogy.

Vargas smiled and listened and smoked his long cheroots. He was small and dumpy and would have gone totally unremarked in any crowd but for the fact that his portrait hung on the wall of every school and post office and government office in the country, always smiling. The Brazilians said he had the ability to be silent in twelve different languages. He was an anomaly in a continent of shouting, swaggering caudillos. He had come to power through a revolution made by politicians and military men against the old oligarchy of the São Paulo coffee barons. He had held on to power not by force of arms but by a balancing act. His supporters ranged from Greenshirt sympathizers and regional bosses to near Socialists like Doctor Alcibiades and *tenentes* who had marched with the Prestes Column. Getulio Vargas himself seemed to defy definition. Perhaps that was why he had survived numerous plots and an armed revolt by the Paulistas. Certainly he was avoiding showing himself in this interview. His inscrutability was such, Sir Evelyn thought, that he might be practicing to be a Chinaman.

The president's manner changed abruptly when the ambassador mentioned that Prestes was in Brazil.

"How is it possible?" Vargas said, puffing faster on his cheroot. "We have proof that Prestes is in Moscow. Here—" he scrabbled around among the papers on his desk and produced a newspaper. The characters were Cyrillic, Sir Evelyn noticed; it was a Russian paper. It was folded to an inside page.

Vargas showed Sir Evelyn the blurred photograph. Prestes was clearly recognizable among other foreign Communists, and there was no doubt about the locale. They were posing in front of Lenin's tomb.

"This newspaper appeared less than a week ago," Vargas commented. "One of our diplomats arranged to send this copy on the *Graf Zepelin.* How is it possible that Prestes could arrive here before the airship?"

"I don't know," Sir Evelyn replied. "Perhaps the photograph is a hoax. We have positive information from sources in Europe that Prestes has been here for more than a month."

From that moment Vargas was all attention. To Sir Evelyn's satisfaction, he put off an appointment with the German Ambassador to prolong the conversation.

"We will take the most energetic action," Vargas announced.

"If I may say so, *Senhor Presidente,* the appropriate course would seem to be energetic *watching.* "

Sir Evelyn was rather proud of this formulation.

At the end of the audience the president invited the ambassador and his wife to join the First Family in their box for a performance at the Teatro Municipal. Lady Maude would be pleased.

Two DAYS later, President Vargas held a cabinet meeting at which he discussed the plan for a Communist revolution in Brazil. Secret Comintern documents supplied by the British Embassy were passed around the table.

The conservative defense minister expressed the view that it was necessary to "break the backs" of the plotters without delay. The National Liberation Alliance should be banned immediately. Others preferred a waiting game.

Four days after that, on the morning of June 26, *O Globo* ran a scream headline on its front page: THE COMMUNIST PLAN FOR BRAZIL. What followed was a bloodcurdling report drawing extensively on an unidentified Communist document. It contained directives for a "preparatory phase" in which nationalism would be made the "spinal cord of the movement"; any hint of "internationalism" would be "eliminated." At the given time, a swift and furious coup d'état would be launched simultaneously in the north, in the vital Rio-São Paulo-Belo Horizonte triangle, the country's economic hub, and in the south. Trained cells would seize the electricity centers, the telegraph stations and the radio transmitters. Anti-Communist officers would be shot without mercy, "preferably at their own doors or inside their houses," and special forces would range the streets in trucks, using machine guns to cow any attempted resistance.

Harry Maitland read the newspaper over breakfast and flung it down in fury. Someone inside the government had cooked up his own version of the Zinoviev Letter. The "Communist document" cited in the newspaper was a forgery, but a forgery based on the facts. Whole paragraphs had been lifted from the Comintern documents Harry had been ordered to supply to the embassy. *O Globo*'s account conformed very closely to Johnny's description of the plan Emil Brandt was trying to execute. Emil and the others in the South American bureau were bound to suspect a leak.

He arrived at the office in a black mood, which was not relieved by the spectacle of Desmond Wild lolling behind his desk. Wild, with his unerring nose for a liquor source, had found the bottle of scotch Harry kept in a desk drawer and had helped himself to a double. He had also helped himself to one of Harry's favorite cigars, the private stock he had had shipped direct from Havana.

"Make yourself at home, why don't you?"

"Now, don't be a prune, old boy. I come bearing gifts."

"I'm surprised they let you up here. Have you paid your light bill recently?"

Wild treated this as beneath his dignity. Harry noticed he had acquired a monocle, which hung uselessly from a silk cord around his neck.

"I thought you might like a scoop," Wild pursued. "One of my native bearers moonlights as a typesetter for the Commie paper."

"*A Manhã?*"

"And the same to you."

"So?"

"Well, he tells me they're all rather het up about this stuff in *O Globo*. The Reds are going to put out a counterblast, a special edition. They've got a front-page story that claims that old Getulio was fed a lot of info on the Reds by none other than our intrepid ambassador. Perfidious Albion meddling again, trying to squash the glorious workers' movement. That kind of thing."

"It's a red herring," Harry said flatly. "The usual propaganda lies. Would it inconvenience you terribly if I used my desk?"

"I think there's more to it." Wild moved languidly in the direction of the sofa, whisky in hand. "My chappie says the other lot have really got the wind up. You wouldn't know anything about it, I suppose?"

"Why should I?"

"Well, you really ought to, my dear. Aren't the Bolshies supposed to be planning to black out Rio Light so they can cut our throats in the dark?"

"You should ask Sir Evelyn."

"I tried. He won't take my calls. I expect he's still hopping mad about that horse in the second. I tried Summerhayes, too, actually collared him on his way to the embassy. He scuttled off like a frightened rabbit."

A messenger tapped on the door and entered immediately with a note for Maitland. He recognized Johnny's handwriting on the envelope. He glanced at the contents quickly and tucked the note away in his pocket.

The fact that Johnny had taken the risk of sending a message to him here—even though the language was suitably camouflaged—confirmed Maitland's worst fears. His man was in danger.

"You'll have to excuse me," he said to the journalist.

HE MET Johnny at noon in the little museum of mechanical toys on top of the Sugarloaf, fifty yards from where the cable cars stopped.

"You might have warned me," Johnny said.

"I didn't know it would be blown up all over the press," Harry responded lamely.

"I only heard about it last night," Johnny pursued. "Emil received a full report from someone who has access at the highest level of the government. He has seen copies of all the papers your ambassador gave to Vargas. You should never have trusted these people."

"And?"

"Emil told me he thinks the Secret Service got its information in Europe, by deciphering radio signals or intercepting the mail to one of the letter drops in Paris. He may have been testing me."

"Have you been watched?"

"With Helene in town, I'm always under surveillance," Johnny said grimly. "But it will get worse. I'm sure they'll send an investigator from Moscow."

"What can I do to help?"

"Stage a diversion."

Maitland thought for a moment. Johnny had supplied the addresses of several safe houses in Paris that were used for Comintern traffic from South America.

"I could ask Bailey to fix something in Paris," he suggested. If the Russians knew that one of their letter drops had been blown, that might deflect suspicion from Johnny.

"Better to do it here," Johnny said.

Maitland understood. If the Comintern was looking for a traitor, it was his task to deliver one.

8

"WE GO forward!" Emil boomed over the hubbub around the Spaniard's dining room table. "Then all these nervous Nellies will have to choose. They either shit or get off the pot."

The sensational press coverage of the Communist plot had not resulted in any damage to the underground. The police had attacked left-wing speakers in the Praça Maua with their truncheons and beaten up a few union leaders, but that was nothing out of the ordinary. However, inside the National Liberation Alliance and even the Communist party itself, the publicity had sparked off a heated debate. Some people said the leadership was forcing the pace, moving before it had created a solid base of support. The old charge leveled at Prestes by the Communists before Moscow had taken the Cavalier of Hope under its wing was being revived: that Prestes and those around him were romantic militarists, closer in spirit to Blanqui and Bonaparte than to Marx and Lenin. There were doubters even within the ranks of the South American bureau itself. In his cups, Verdi, the Argentinian, was heard to describe Emil as a "comical Chinese warlord, surrounded by sleepwalkers." Emil demanded—and received—a formal apology for the remark.

Emil decided to shunt the skeptics out of the way by packing them off to the north to make speeches. Seven chiefs of the National Liberation Alliance were shoved on board a steamer headed up the coast. The fact that they were accompanied by twice as many police agents was of no consequence to the chief of the South American bureau.

Emil was a man in a fever dream. With the critics neutralized, he was free to rush ahead with the next stage of the operation. Johnny encouraged him. Johnny even helped to draft the new manifesto that Emil insisted must be issued in the name of the ANL.

The ANL had a big rally planned for July 5, the anniversary of previous armed risings. There was quite a turnout. The crowd did not look very revolutionary; the men all wore hats and their best Sunday suits, as if they were going to church.

A nervous young man in a bow tie was on the platform, looking over his notes. Carlos was a fine orator, but prone to stage fright. Before leaving his home, he had played "The March of the Toreadors" over and over on his Victrola, to prime himself for his performance. On his way into the theater, a squad of Integralistas in their green shirts and their stupid Sigma armbands had jeered at him and threatened to rough him up. He knew their leader; they had been at law school together. It anguished him to think that more of the intellectuals of his own generation were gravitating to the Fascists than to the left. Even at the Academy of Letters, the country's literary establishment applauded politely when the leading anti-Semitic ideologue of the Greenshirt movement delivered long harangues, decked out in a pith helmet and his full regalia. Of course, it was the lure of action, strongest of all for men who lived sedentary lives filled with abstractions.

The band struck up a tune; the meeting was under way. Carlos was scheduled to speak second. He hardly listened to the opening address, delivered by a former navy officer who was hopelessly adrift in his own syntax. Another military figure appeared from the wings and glided swiftly behind the speaker's podium. Carlos knew the man. He was a former army captain who had marched with Prestes and held a vague position on the organizing committee of the ANL.

"You're to read this," the captain whispered in his ear, thrusting a script into his hands.

"I don't understand. I've already prepared my speech."

Carlos glanced at the first lines. They read like a cannon roll, like a barrage from the old guns at the Copacabana Fort. Never having met Johnny, Carlos could hardly know that some of the most inflammatory sentences had come from his pen. The whole thing amounted to an open declaration of war on the government.

"I can't read this," the young Brazilian protested.

"Look at the signature."

Carlos turned to the last page. The manifesto was signed by Prestes. It ended with a battle cry: "All power to the ANL!" It was an open appeal for the overthrow of the government.

"This is madness." Carlos began to shake violently. "You'll get us all arrested."

"The orders come from the top. Do as you're told, or I'll read it myself and denounce you as a coward."

The opening speaker had reached his final peroration. The applause was punctuated by catcalls from the Greenshirt supporters and undercover cops in the crowd.

Carlos was being introduced.

"It's suicide," he said unhappily.

"Stop pissing in your pants and get up there."

A FEW days later, Harry Maitland joined the crowd that had gathered outside the ANL headquarters. Most of the windows on the upper floors had been smashed. Policemen were engaged in throwing file cabinets, furniture and typewriters down onto the pavement below. Thousands of copies of *A Manhã* and other left-wing publications were blowing along the street.

The government had answered Prestes' declaration of war—edited and inspired by Emil and Johnny—by banning the ANL and ordering a roundup of leftist union organizers. The Communists had thrown away their legal facade.

Their critics on the left—especially the anarchists and Trotskyites—denounced the party's tactics and claimed that its followers had been deceived by police spies and agents provocateurs. Harry wondered if they realized how much substance there was to their charges. In the decisive meeting of the Communist leaders before the big rally, Johnny had helped to fuel Emil's passion. Verdi predicted that the government might shut down the ANL if its spokesmen made an open appeal for revolt. Johnny countered that the government probably wouldn't dare go so far but that, if it did, it would be doing the revolution a favor. The country would become polarized; the president's reformist pose would be exploded; liberals would move to the left. Above all, many more people would recognize that an armed uprising was the only way forward and be drawn into the party underground. This was the argument that won out.

As Harry watched the police completing their demolition job at the ANL building, Colonel Plinio strolled out the front door, his panama hat tilted rakishly across his forehead.

He greeted Harry in high good spirits.

"They shot themselves in the foot this time, didn't they? Let's have a drink to celebrate."

They went to the Confiteiria Colombo, where a string quartet was playing among the potted palms in the depths of a bustling hall lined with mirrors and mahogany. Above Plinio's head, painted schooners under full sail plowed a sea of glass.

His day's hunting over, the colonel was in a philosophical mood.

"We are a gentle people," he remarked, surveying the powdered ladies in white gloves who were sampling the Colombo's famous pastries and "Petrôpolis bread," toast prepared with butter and Parmesan cheese. "We are also too much addicted to the French and their endless talk about *liberté*. Voltaire, Victor Hugo, Romain Rolland. They—and the anarchists, of course—are far more seductive to us than Marx. But what is freedom? In the real world, freedom can be comprehended only by the boundaries that contain it." He sipped his drink. "Like pure alcohol," he went on, "liberty can be enjoyed only in dilution, and there are few men with the stomach—or the table manners—to withstand the higher proofs."

8

Prince of Shadows

Faust:
When you will introduce us at
this revel,
Will you appear as sorcerer—or devil?

Mephistopheles:
I generally travel without showing
my station,
But on a gala day one shows one's decoration.
—GOETHE

1

"THERE are times I don't know you at all," Verdi remarked to Johnny. "You're an intelligent man. You know that Emil is wrong. Yet you go along with him. You even encourage him."

"Mine wasn't the only voice," Johnny said quietly. "The Brazilians took the same line."

"They're victims of passion." The Argentinian swept his hair off his forehead. "Nilo, Prestes—they can't always help themselves. But you—you're a professional. You've been with Emil, you've seen him make the same mistakes in China. Then he nearly got you killed in the north. That's why I can't fathom you."

"Put a sock in it," Helene cut in rudely. "The decision was made. There's an end of it. If you want to do postmortems, go and work for a coroner."

"Sometimes I think I do—" the Argentinian began daringly, but Helene silenced him with a look.

He knows what I know, Johnny thought, feeling a closer sympathy for Verdi, who looked and smelled as if he had started drinking even earlier than usual that day.

He's heard the screams too.

Helene was steering the Ford with one hand, nursing one of her baby cheroots in the other. She spotted a gap in the traffic and whipped over to the left.

"This is close enough," she announced, pulling up in front of a bank. The Pan Air office was just round the corner.

"Will you wait for me?" Verdi said. "I won't be two minutes."

Helene shrugged and glanced at Johnny.

"Two minutes," Johnny said.

They watched the Argentinian circumnavigate the little crowd that had gathered round a *bicheiro,* to bet on the elephant or the rooster.

"I'm surprised he didn't ask one of us to come in and hold his hand," Helene said with quiet contempt. She glanced at her reflection in the plate glass windows of the bank. "We look like bank robbers in a getaway car."

Verdi came back, visibly agitated.

"They say I must get an exit visa from the police," he reported. "The Pan Air agent says he will go with me to the station. Do you think it's safe?"

He appealed to Helene with moist spaniel eyes. He met that ice-blue stare. "It's your decision," she said curtly. "You can swim to Buenos Aires, if you'd rather."

Verdi looked miserable.

"I'm sure it will be all right," Johnny tried to encourage him. "There's nothing wrong with your passport, is there?"

"We can't sit here all day," Helene announced, revving the engine.

"All right. I'm going."

Helene rammed the Ford into gear and left Verdi standing on the sidewalk.

"You were a bit brutal with him, weren't you?" Johnny said.

"He's just another Hamlet. We can't afford them. He ought to be sitting at home writing clever little philosophical essays that nobody reads. Emil is right to send him away."

Verdi had been instructed to go to Buenos Aires to meet the leaders of the other South American Communist parties and report on their attitudes. Emil had not forgiven the Argentinian for comparing him to a Chinese warlord.

"It is also possible that Verdi is right," Johnny remarked.

"That wasn't what you said at the meeting."

"A man is allowed to change his mind."

"Not about some things, Johnny." The unexpected choice of phrase, and the savage wrench at the wheel that sent the car hurtling towards a group of passengers alighting from a streetcar made Johnny wonder if he had pushed his luck too far.

A WEEK before Sir Evelyn had called on the president, Johnny and Helene had moved from the boarding house to a small apartment in Botafogo. The front windows overlooked the cemetery of John the Baptist. This was a graveyard for the rich. The marble busts were stern images of bourgeois rectitude, complete with pince-nez, wing collars and imperials. Sculpted maidens wept over them soundlessly, their Grecian robes in calculated disarray. In the foreground, just inside the cemetery wall, a wounded lion with an arrow sticking out of its back howled its last from the top of a marble plinth.

It was almost nightfall when Verdi appeared on Johnny's doorstep together with a small suitcase and a wife to match, a nervous, dark-eyed girl called Rosario.

"You must help us," said Verdi breathlessly. "We have nowhere to go—"

"Come in, come in." Johnny took his arm and half pulled him into the sitting room, which opened directly off the landing.

Rosario perched on a corner of the sofa, her hands folded in her lap.

"Who is it?" Helene called from the bathroom.

"It's okay!" Johnny shouted back.

Before he had finished pouring Verdi's brandy, she came padding out, still dripping from the bath and swathed in a huge apricot towel. Helene could subsist on a handful of rice, but not without perfumed soap and soft towels.

"Shit." She glowered at Verdi. "What do you think you're doing here?"

"I'm sorry," the Argentinian apologized, not daring to meet her eyes. "I had to get Rosario away. I think the police are onto me."

Johnny handed him his drink. "Tell us everything that happened. Take it slowly."

"I went to the police station," Verdi began. They had insisted on taking his fingerprints and told him they would have to retain his passport for a few hours, to complete the necessary formalities. He had been instructed to come back at the end of the day.

"I sensed something was wrong," Verdi continued. "So I paid the Pan Air man a few dollars to go back for my passport. The police wouldn't give it to him. They claimed it was a forgery. They said they had checked my fingerprints and believed I was a dangerous man, a man on the run. They told him to tell me I was required to call for my travel documents in person. The man in the airline office is *muy simpático,* no friend of the police. But you know what he said to me? He said, 'Are you really a dynamiter?' What would you have done in my place? Naturally, I got away as fast as I could."

"So you led the cops here," Helene commented, peering around the edge of the curtains.

"I wasn't followed!" Verdi jumped up, his voice rising to a falsetto. "I swear it!"

Johnny went to the window. "There's no one," he pronounced.

Verdi crumpled into the sofa.

"What are we going to do with them?" Helene demanded. In her anger she had let the towel ride up to the tops of her thighs. Verdi was watching as if this, too, were part of his ordeal. His wife blushed and stared at the floor.

"Why don't you get dressed and get us all something to eat?" Johnny suggested calmly. "I'll go and alert the others."

"Johnny—" she followed him into the bedroom. She watched him from behind as he checked the magazine of his pistol and slipped it back into the shoulder holster under his jacket.

"Johnny—" her lower lip trembled.

He saw this in the mirror as he combed his hair. The instant of weakness —was it fear or suppressed fury?—softened her, as did the nakedness of her shoulders, rosy and moist from the bath.

"Yes?"

As he turned to her, her lips made a little bow, and he thought she was going to kiss him.

Instead she said, "Those two are dead weight. It's stupid to risk ourselves for them."

"Maybe. But take care of them, all the same."

"I worry about you, Johnny." She traced the line of his jaw with her finger. She smelled of sandalwood.

"You needn't."

"But I do. You're too patient with the bleeding hearts. You never used to be this way."

"Are you trying to tell me something?"

"Just take care they don't start bleeding over *our* floor."

The threat was not specific, but it was there in her tone and in the cool indifference with which she swung out to the bathroom and pulled off the towel. Naked, with the door open, she proceeded to shave her armpits, as if he had ceased to exist. Her long, firm body was as white as one of those statues in the cemetery.

VERDI did not leave for Buenos Aires, but he got his passport back. Prestes, whom Johnny found dining with Emil at the German's luxurious apartment in Ipanema, undertook to fix everything. Even Emil seemed nervous about the method he proposed.

"Don't worry about it," the Brazilian reassured him. "I know my people."

Prestes wrote a letter to the police, asking them to return the travel papers of a special friend, and signed it with his own name. The letter was hand carried to the central station by a reserve army officer wearing his captain's uniform.

The next morning, Johnny waited for the messenger on a bench in the Praça Maua, next to a stand where they sold watermelons and sweet *caqui* fruit, which looked like fat, overripe tomatoes. He did not expect his man to arrive.

When the captain appeared, beaming from ear to ear, Johnny got up and strolled about, affecting not to see him. He also unbuttoned his jacket, so he could get at his gun quickly.

The captain took the cue. He breezed past Johnny and paused to inspect a mound of papayas. As Johnny came abreast of him, he slipped Verdi's passport into his hand.

He could not refrain from whispering, "Piece of cake."

Johnny fully expected detectives to seize him at any moment. He spent more than three hours before he satisfied himself that he was not under surveillance, even taking a ride out into the harbor with a boatload of sightseers.

When Prestes was told what had happened, he was jubilant.

"You see," he enthused, "the revolution has allies everywhere! We even have friends in the police!"

When Harry Maitland heard the story, two days later, he found himself trapped in a state between sleeping and waking for much of the night, as his mind groped for a satisfactory explanation. The easiest to accept was that Colonel Plinio's men were more subtle than Johnny had counted on and had succeeded in staying out of sight when they tailed Prestes' messenger. For why would the police release the passport of a known subversive —let alone a courier from the most wanted man in the country—if not in the hope of following them to bigger game? No doubt there were a few Communist sympathizers in the police, but it would be madness for them to risk exposing themselves in such an obvious way. Anyway, the orders must have come from high up, perhaps from Colonel Plinio himself.

Harry pictured the faint smile on Colonel Plinio's face as he had watched the duel between the viper and the boa in the mayor's snake house. What game was he playing now? Was he confident to the point of carelessness because he had a spy of his own inside the conspiracy? Did he want the conspiracy to run its course so as to crush it more completely—or because he wanted it to succeed?

"Piece of cake," Prestes' courier had murmured to Johnny.

Colin Bailey had said something similar to Harry when he had asked him to work for the Secret Service.

The memory of the Christmas pudding he had been made to eat at home, as a boy, rose up out of Harry's subconscious—a pudding so heavy they used to joke that if they dropped it, it would make a crater in the floor. He had been induced to eat it only by the promise of silver threepenny bits hidden among the raisins. He remembered the sense of being cheated when he worked his way through a whole piece and found no threepenny bits.

2

JOHNNY met Maitland at the Necrôpolis. It was a simple brush contact by the roulette table. Johnny put his chips on red, and then, as everyone watched the ball, he slipped his report into the pocket of Harry's dinner jacket. The ball landed on a red number. He did not forget to pick up his winnings.

He was standing in line in front of the cashier's grille when a thick, rather guttural voice called out, "Gruber! Johnny Gruber!"

Johnny stiffened as if someone had poked a gun between his shoulder blades.

Very slowly, he turned and saw a large Germanic figure barreling at him through the crush of players.

"You fuckhead!" Engineer Hossbach greeted him. "Did you think you'd given me the slip? Where've you been hiding? Where's that cold-assed sister of yours?"

Hossbach had a hand on his shoulder and wouldn't hear of parting company until they had inspected some of his favorite night spots and killed a bottle or two. Johnny was so relieved Hossbach had failed to notice Maitland that he went along with the German's proposals.

It proved to be quite a productive evening. Hossbach was in a talkative mood, boasting that he had been promised a big job in Berlin and dropping the names of connections at the German Embassy as well as the anatomical details of various women he claimed had enjoyed his favors.

"It was a stroke of luck, running into you like that," Hossbach said. He leaned his face nearer to Johnny's. "I might have a job for you. The money's good. Enough to pay for every floozie in this dump." He waved his arms expansively over the crowded floor of the Babylônia Club.

"Tell me more."

"One of our best men is coming from Germany. He'll be needing some local help. Nothing to do with the embassy, mind. I've been told to find a few men who can keep their mouths shut."

That would rule *you* out, Johnny thought.

He said, "What's it about?"

"It's a spot of debt collecting, that's the size of it."

"What sort of debt?"

"The kind you have to pay." Hossbach smirked. "A blood debt. We got a tip that a big Red is coming to Rio. He killed some of our boys in Germany. The idea is to settle the account."

Johnny thought, he could be talking about *me.*

"How will you find this Red?"

"Our man is bringing a photograph. And we know the kike started in Antwerp, so he's probably got diamonds to hock. That's how those bastards pay their way," he added with assumed authority. "So we've got lots to play with."

Johnny realized he had impersonated a Nazi lover too well in his previous conversations with Hossbach. There was no chance of backing out easily now the German had put this many cards on the table.

"Why don't you go to the police?" he suggested.

"The Brazilians are soft." Hossbach curled his lip. "We know how to take care of these things. Well, are you in?"

"You know you can count on me,' Johnny agreed. 'But I don't know much about guns."

"No need to start pissing on the floor!" Hossbach guffawed. "We'll handle the serious business. You're a salesman, aren't you? We'll find out where the Yid is hiding out, and you can make him an offer he won't be able to resist."

A whore Hossbach couldn't resist, in a dress slit to the waist, saved Johnny from spending the rest of the evening at the Babylônia Club. He even managed to slip away without giving an address.

"I've got a girl waiting for me, too," he announced, as the whore jiggled her bust under Hossbach's nose. "I'll call you tomorrow."

ON THE streetcar back to Botafogo, he went over the conversation in his mind. There was no longer any doubt who Hossbach worked for—or that the Gestapo had a source close to the Comintern operation in Europe. *The kike* . . . was the Gestapo on the trail of Emil, or somebody else?

I'll talk about it with Helene, he decided. It struck him that he had just been handed a chance to do something highly pleasurable—to give the

Gestapo a kick in the balls—and improve his standing with the South American bureau at the same time.

He was in excellent spirits as he turned into the street near the cemetery. There was a light on in their apartment. Helene must have finished earlier than expected or brought some of the typing home. She did that sometimes, and he was then able to steal a look at the secret directives Emil was sending out.

Johnny turned his key in the door. There was an odor of tobacco from light Virginia cigarettes, like the Argentinian smoked. But Verdi and his wife had left several days before, and Helene still favored her black cigarillos.

Johnny reached for his gun as he swung the door open. He saw the battered soles of the man's shoes, stretched out across the ottoman. A record was playing on the Victrola, one he did not recognize. It sounded like a funeral dirge. He ducked down and burst into the room behind the gun.

"I see you've started the revolution already," said the man who was lolling in the armchair, smoking American cigarettes. There was a big revolver in front of him, on the coffee table. He made no move for it. Instead he turned up the volume on the victrola. The voices were reaching a crescendo.

> Dies irae, dies illa
> Solvet saeclum in favilla
> Teste David cum Sybilla.

"Beautiful, isn't it?" said the man in the chair. He began to translate: "On that day of wrath, the world dissolves into ashes . . ."

Johnny put his gun away. He shut the door and stood beside it as if waiting for permission to sit down.

"What is the music?" he asked.

"Verdi's *Requiem*. Do you suppose our Argentinian deserves one?'

Johnny slumped onto the sofa without responding.

"Not much of a welcome, Johnny," said Max Fabrikant. "Are you so sorry to see me?"

"Surprised, that's all. Nobody told me *you* were coming, Max."

"Leon. You have to call me Leon. I'm supposed to be a Belgian."

"What are you doing here?"

"What do you suppose? Land reclamation." Max added with seeming anger, "You're living in a swamp! All of you! I wouldn't expect too much from some of the others, least of all from your Brazilian half-breeds, who can't tell black from white. But *you*, Johnny! You disappoint me."

"What have I done?"

"Come closer to me." Max patted the edge of the sofa closest to his chair. "I want to look into your eyes so I can tell when you're lying. Then you can explain to me why."

Johnny experienced the same sense of panic he had felt at school, when the headmaster had summoned all the boys to assembly and announced that he knew that one of them had been smoking in the toilets. The headmaster had called for the guilty boy to step forward. Johnny had had to wrestle with himself not to confess. In the end it was an innocent boy, a boy who had started shaking and burst into tears, who had been held responsible and suspended from school. That was the way it went. Johnny was no more—and no less—frightened now than then. But he looked steadily into the inquisitor's eyes.

"There's a spy inside your circle," Max announced. "Is it you?"

Johnny tried to see only his own reflection in Max's eyes.

"No."

"You've been in contact with a Gestapo agent, a man called Hossbach."

"Yes." He felt slightly dizzy. It could hardly be coincidence that Max was asking about the man he had just left.

"Why didn't you report your meetings with this man?"

"Helene knew everything," he defended himself. "What more do you want?"

"You should have written your own reports. How can you tell what Helene puts in hers?"

The angle of this attack was so bizarre that Johnny found it impossible to take it seriously. The pressure in his chest lifted; he wanted to laugh in Max's face.

He couldn't restrain himself. He was spluttering as he said, "Max, dear Max. Have you come here to accuse me of working for the Gestapo?"

"This isn't a joking matter."

"Very well, let's talk about the Gestapo. I saw Hossbach tonight. It was a chance meeting—there's room for chance in life sometimes, isn't there? He thinks I'm a good little Nazi, so he asked for my help. They're hunting one of ours."

"Who?"

"I haven't quite worked it out. Perhaps you'll be able to. Hossbach described the target as a big Red and a kike."

Max did not flinch at the coarse epithets. "Emil?" he suggested. "Olga?"

"I couldn't know at the time," Johnny said, "but it seems to me now that Hossbach was talking about *you.*"

"What are you saying?"

For the first time Johnny had the satisfaction of seeing Max on the defensive.

"Well, I don't know if you're Jewish," Johnny went on, milking the situation for all the pleasure he could derive. "But you're certainly a Belgian now, aren't you?"

"Stop farting around and get to the point!"

"*Kamarad* Hossbach says the target started his travels in Antwerp. Also that he's carrying diamonds."

Max did not respond immediately, which was why Johnny was certain he had found his mark.

It was Johnny's moment to attack, and he seized it. "I ask myself," he said, "whether Hossbach is working for you—or you are working for him."

"You bastard!" Max was on his feet, with his fist clenched.

"You try it," Johnny said, not stirring from his place. "I've got a few years on you and a good few pounds as well, and I haven't had a decent fight since Emil tried to get me killed in the north."

Max's fury slowly subsided.

"We need to work this out," he declared, after Johnny had poured them both a stiff brandy.

IT WAS a very long night, as long as any Johnny had spent with Heinz in the days when his world was merrily on fire.

Max ordered him to maintain contact with Hossbach and offered to increase his expenses so he could keep a safe house, an address to supply the Gestapo man when he—inevitably—would ask. Johnny agreed. At the start of the conversation, he had been convinced that Max had somehow contrived the whole episode with Hossbach in order to frame him. Max's emotional response to his accusation had persuaded him he was wrong. There *were* coincidences in life, he told himself. The roulette ball sometimes landed on the same number twice.

When Max returned to the main purpose of his mission, he talked to Johnny as a trusted comrade, not a man under suspicion.

"There is a British spy in the organization," Max announced. "Who would you nominate?"

I mustn't jump into this, Johnny cautioned himself. It would be smarter to condemn by faint praise.

"What about Nilo?" Max prodded him. "He went to school at Eton, didn't he?"

"I don't think he was very popular at school. He doesn't love the British."

"He doesn't love his mother," Max observed. "But I am informed that he still takes an allowance from her. The call him the Millionaire, don't they? He could be bought."

"Only with girls."

If he wants to waste his time watching Nilo, Johnny thought, that's perfect. But let it be his own choice.

There was only one bad moment, when Max remarked, "In my experience the man who calls loudest for blood is usually the provocateur. Wouldn't you agree?"

"Sometimes."

"So why have you been hurrying everything along? You sided with Emil over that idiotic manifesto that got the ANL banned, didn't you?"

He's already talked to Helene, Johnny realized. That was probably why she seemed to be staying out all night.

"I have my orders," Johnny said. "They come from Manuilsky—" he paused "—and from Stalin. If you intend to question my judgment, you should take it up with them."

Max stared at him for a long time before he permitted himself to smile.

"You've learned a few tricks, Johnny Lentz."

"I've had the very best instructors."

"I have one piece of advice for you. Don't forget who your friends are."

"I'll never do that," Johnny promised, thinking of the friend Max had murdered. "Speaking of friends," he went on, "I want you to tell me about Sigrid."

"I admire your restraint in waiting all this time to ask."

"Is she safe?"

"Perfectly safe, except from mosquitoes."

Johnny blinked at him. It was too much to hope for.

"I brought her to Rio," Max confirmed. "I know she wants to see you. Johnny, I don't know quite what you think of me. But I'll promise you this. I won't stand in your way." He took a swallow of brandy and added, "Unless there are compelling professional reasons."

The qualification did not diminish what Johnny felt: a soaring sense of elation, of flying without wings. Here, in this magical country that shattered every prejudice and preconception of the Old World, she would at last be his. Whatever Max had done to her, whatever he had tried to make of her, would not matter a damn in Brazil.

3

A VIOLET-BLUE sail flapped across the windshield, so close, so vivid that Sigrid raised her palm to protect her face.

"It's a butterfly," she said in wonder, as it dipped, caught an updraft and glided off into the highest canopy of the rain forest. "I've never seen one so big."

"That's how it is here," Johnny said, slowing the car to negotiate a hairpin bend. "The country knows no limits."

Guavas grew wild along the road. The forest blazed with flamboyants and mimosas, the yellows and purples of the *ipe* blossoms, the hot, rowdy pinks of the impatiens that sprang up everywhere. Johnny stopped the car at a bend that hung over the green gorge like a balcony. When he turned off the engine, the silence seemed complete, until Sigrid began to listen properly. Then she heard bird song, the whir of insects, the bubble of water in secret springs, the scuffle of unseen monkeys or squirrels among the foliage.

"I saved this place for you," he said. He took her hand and led her along a low stone parapet to a clearing that opened out like a piazza. In the middle was a stone table with narrow stone benches on either side.

He drew her with him to the very edge of the cliff.

"Look."

She followed his pointing hand. The sensation was giddying. The ground fell away at her feet. She felt she was leaning over the neck of a horse as it hurled itself down the mountainside, charging at the sea miles below. She shut her eyes and clutched at Johnny's arm, and felt his hand close over hers.

When she looked again, the sensation was different. A curious sense of calm and completion began to steal over her. What opened out below her appeared as a vast natural amphitheater. There, at the very center, was the circling bay of Botafogo, turned to mother-of-pearl by the distance and the harbor mists. The peaks around it were islands in the haze. There were no sharp edges. Everything was rounded and opaque. The forest enclosed the whole panorama like a pair of broad, cupped hands.

"It's perfect," Sigrid whispered. "It's the landscape of dreams."

He led her back to the stone table. "It's called the Emperor's Table."

"Why?"

"The last emperor of Brazil—Dom Pedro—picked the most breathtaking view in Rio and set his picnic table to command it. Now it belongs to us."

Her face was shaded by a wide-brimmed straw hat. Her dress was foamy white and reached to midcalf. She was even more beautiful than his dreams, her body fuller, her movements more confident. But when he looked directly into her eyes, a shutter seemed to fall.

"You're different," he said to her.

"Did you think it would be the same?"

"I don't know. But I waited for you, all the same."

"You shouldn't have waited."

"What are you saying?" Johnny wanted to shake her. But there was a stronger longing. He took her by the waist and tried to kiss her. She kept her mouth closed and slipped away from him.

"Is it Max?" He couldn't contain himself. He rushed on, "Are you in love with Max?"

"Does it matter?"

"Of course it matters."

"You haven't learned very much, Johnny."

She said it with such weariness, such resignation, that he fell silent.

"Max didn't take me to Copenhagen to sleep with me," she went on. "You know him. You know that's true. He came to me once, just once. He didn't force me."

"Then why?"

"He had been ordered to kill a man."

"He's used to that."

"Yes. But he talked about how much harder it is to kill when you have time to take a good look at your victim, to notice the little, ordinary things that make him human—the way he lies in his sleep, the hairs on the back of his hands, the sound of his breathing. It wasn't an easy assignment. I think Max was scared. He certainly had reason to be. There was a very good chance he would not return alive."

"And you made love to him because of that?"

"Because it was my duty." She folded her arms across her chest. "*You* should know. That's what you taught me, isn't it? That we're all soldiers under orders?"

He turned his head, to look out over the glorious view of Rio with sightless eyes.

"Were there others?" he pursued.

"What makes you think you have the right to ask me these things?" she erupted. "Did you take monastic orders? Are you telling me you never went with another woman?"

"No more than was necessary."

"Hah! And you think you're entitled to ask me what *I* did in bed!"

"Sigrid, I waited for you. In every way that counts, I waited for you."

"What about Helene? Did you sleep with her too?"

"No."

She stared at him, ungiving.

"Have you seen Helene?" he asked quickly.

"Yes, of course."

"What did she say?" He was suddenly terrified that Helene had invented something to try to turn Sigrid against him.

"Nothing that matters. But I think she's still in love with you."

"You're wrong. We're not together by choice. The situation doesn't amuse her any more than it does me."

"Yet you made a choice in Shanghai."

"She told you about that?"

"She told me you saved her life."

"I would have done it for any comrade. It doesn't change anything. If you want to know, I think Helene hates me."

"Love and hate are closely related."

"Like sisters?"

"Like sisters," she agreed, and pursed her lips.

He tried to touch her again, but she twisted away. Why did she keep this distance between them? Surely she wasn't jealous of Helene?

He felt slighted, and because of that, he chose words that would wound her.

"They told me you were going to have a baby."

"What business is it of theirs?" she rounded on him. "Whoever 'they' are?"

"It was ours, wasn't it?"

"How could anyone tell?" she struck back at him.

"*Was it ours?*" he shouted. He shook her so violently that her hat tumbled off and rolled away into the forest.

"You're hurting me."

He relaxed his grip. The tears welled up in her eyes. She tried to turn her face away, so he would not see, but he forced her to look at him.

"Sigrid—"

"Of course it was ours."

The wind blew threads of red-gold hair across her face. He smoothed them gently back into place.

"Why?"

"I heard nothing from you."

"But I wrote to you every week!" Even as he said that, he knew what had happened. The secret police had intercepted the letters. How had Max put it? There was no such thing as a personal conversation.

"How could I keep a child in Russia?" she went on. "By working in a factory? I don't even speak Russian."

"Our people would have looked after you. General Berzin promised me."

"Oh, yes?" she said bitterly. "How? By taking the baby and putting it in a communal crèche?"

"Who told you that? Max?"

"He ought to know."

"That bastard."

"Don't blame Max. He's the only one who helped me. He even found the doctor, a man from the Kremlin clinic, not one of your backyard butchers. The doctor says I might still be able to have children. It's the Russian way, isn't it? The average woman in Russia has six point five abortions in her lifetime." She tried to make herself sound like a statistical yearbook, but her voice was breaking.

"Fuck the average woman in Russia!"

"I imagine you did."

With the tears running down her cheeks, she started laughing. He felt giddy. Suddenly he was laughing and crying, too. He caught her in his arms and pressed her tight against his body, and this time she did not pull away. Their lips met. He tasted salt and wild honey. He struggled with the hooks of her dress.

"Wait." She pushed her palm against his chest. "We have to find my hat."

They held hands and walked into the rain forest. The air was heavy with the scent of bougainvillea. They came to a little clearing where orchids grew wild among the undergrowth. He picked one for her. She smelled it and tucked it behind her ear, smiling and frowning at the same time.

"I can never remember which ear is the right one."

"They're both perfect."

She made him wait while she took off the lacy white dress and hung it from a bough. She flirted with each button as she stripped him of his clothes. The light filtered through the branches dappled her skin. He spread his shirt over a bed of dry leaves. Then he swept her up into his arms and laid her tenderly on it, as if he were taking her for the first time. A shaft of light plunged down from above his head.

She looked up at him and said, "You're wearing the sun in your hair."

Above him she saw a pair of *pássaros de sangue,* the blood-red birds of the jungle, flash past.

He touched her breasts, her thighs, and each time she started giggling.

He ran his fingers along the inside of her leg, and she was convulsed. He grazed her neck, and she reared away, panting with laughter. Her skin was a mass of nerve endings.

He lay still, propped up on his elbows, smiling but puzzled.

"I'm sorry," she said, trying to stifle a new fit of giggles. "I'm ticklish everywhere."

She took him by the upper arms and drew him down on to her.

"Come to me."

She shivered as he entered her. His face under the sunburst was that of a dark lord.

THEY lay silent for a long time afterwards, holding each other and listening to birdcalls like bells and wind chimes.

He said, "I was wrong. It is the same. Each of us may be different, but *we* are the same." He sat up and looked at her. "I won't let anything take you away from me again."

"You can't say that."

His words had broken the magic circle. She started picking up her clothes.

"You're the only thing real I've had to hold on to," he persisted. "I won't give you up now that I've found you again."

"Isn't there a character in Dostoyevsky whose only hold on reality is a toothache?" she countered, trying to make light of it.

"I'm serious."

"Not now, Johnny. Let's not be serious now."

ON THE drive back to the city he asked about Copenhagen.

"What was it like there, working with Max?"

"It wasn't an easy time. You know Max was ordered to kill Trotsky?"

"I didn't know," Johnny lied. "But I guessed as much when I heard you were both in Norway. Evidently he didn't succeed."

"Trotsky is well protected. He has a whole private army. Max asked me to help find a way past the guards."

"And you agreed?"

"Naturally," she said briskly. "Trotsky is a traitor, a British agent."

Johnny glanced at her sidelong. She spoke with no sense of irony. She believed it.

"What was the plan?"

"Max showed me a place where some of Trotsky's people met. He told me to cultivate one of them—Trotsky's private secretary—and show him my pictures. I was to offer to paint Trotsky's portrait."

"Did you?"

She shook her head. "The secretary didn't trust me. I think he preferred boys. In the end Max shot him."

"And if they'd let you into the house? What would have happened then?"

"Max had a poison. I was supposed to smuggle it in with my paints. Max said the death would look completely natural, like a heart attack."

"You were prepared to go that far?" Johnny was horrified.

"I don't know for sure," she said thoughtfully. "In the abstract, perhaps. But I didn't see Trotsky's face. I could only know if I saw his face, as close to me as yours."

They rode together in silence for a few minutes. He realized that, despite their enchanted hour in the forest, he would have to be more careful of her than of any of the others.

4

THE boulevard press, as Emil liked to call it, ran horror stories every week about the Red plot to destroy Brazil. There were broad hints planted by the government that old-time politicians—even some who were tied to the coffee barons of São Paulo—were secretly involved.

In the wealthy beach suburbs of the southern zone, Emil and his general staff fired communiqués back and forth, far less troubled by the police than by the uncomforting presence of Max Fabrikant. Emil's reports to Moscow, transmitted by radio via the Soviet Mission in Montevideo, were uniformly optimistic. They inspired Wang Ming, the Chinaman who spoke on behalf of South America at the Congress of the Comintern in Moscow, to declare that an anti-imperialist revolution was at hand in Brazil.

These rival accounts, however exaggerated, were not without foundation. The country's political history had been a chronicle of coups and countercoups, mutinies and regional revolts. There was a floating population of veteran intriguers who were willing to gamble on any new rising against the central government: out-of-work governors who wanted their places back, local dynasts who wanted to stop Rio meddling in their private fiefdoms, restless tenentes (some generals or interventores, virtual dictators of remote states) who were bored with inaction. For some of them, especially those who had marched with Prestes a decade before and still revered his name, the ultimate aims of the conspiracy were of secondary interest; at any rate, as long as the conspirators didn't go around banging their drum too loudly. It was the promise of change—sheer movement, not direction —that made them eager to join up.

For the vast majority of the Brazilian people, who could neither read the newspapers nor place Russia, or perhaps even Rio, on a map, expectations of an impending revolution took exotic forms. Myth traveled further and faster than the speeches of politicians. In the marshy slums of Recife, Father Badó heard a curious rumor that Princess Isabel, who had freed the slaves, had been resurrected to rescue their descendants from the yoke of the landowners and the shopkeepers. In a garrison in the *pampas* country of the Rio Grande do Sul, which had produced both Vargas and Prestes, a young lieutenant told his comrades that the government had insulted the honor of the army and urged them to throw in their lot with a new movement of the patriotic officers that was preparing to claim satisfaction. In Salvador da Bahia, a baker who attended a clandestine gathering of the ANL volunteered to inject a powerful laxative into the bread he supplied to the local barracks, maintaining that this would immobilize the government's soldiers on the day of the revolt. He announced that he was ready to do this to avenge police harassment of spiritists and practitioners of *candomblé.*

Emil sat in his apartment on Rua Paulo Redfern with his fan and his spiked pineapple juice, writing directives in English or German for others to translate. Harry Maitland saw him by chance one morning, taking a stroll along the beach at Ipanema with his taciturn, kinky-haired wife, Lenka. Emil was wearing a felt hat and a baggy suit without a tie. Lenka wore a dress of shapeless brown stuff that trailed to her ankles and a scarf over her lusterless hair. They might have been on the beach at Odessa. They were as utterly remote from the country they had been sent to revolutionize, Harry thought, as visitors from another galaxy.

Yet, as he sifted through the information he gleaned from Johnny and matched it against other, less confidential sources, he worried that Emil might have stumbled on a winning formula. It is generally easier to recruit people *against* an existing state of affairs than *for* some proposed remedy. When the National Liberation Alliance had been banned, attention had been focused on government repression, not the Communist element in its program, and liberals who had previously spurned it took up the cudgels on its behalf. The conspirators did not advertise their objectives. They were willing to latch on to any group that had a grudge against the government, promising money and advancement.

The fact that there was a double agent inside the Comintern team was no guarantee that the revolution would fail. The tsarist secret police had had highly placed agents inside all the opposition groups, including the Bolsheviks; they had also been powerless to stop either of the revolutions of 1917. Colin Bailey had seen fit to remind Harry of this comforting analogy in a recent letter. There were questions Johnny could not answer.

Which of the generals at the Defense Ministry had promised to support a coup? Nilo had made a tantalizing reference to one who could be counted on. What was the new source of funds for the South American bureau that its agents were spending so lavishly? Was Doctor Alcibiades committed to the plot?

If the decision to launch a coup were taken tonight, would Johnny know about it?

This last question worried Johnny as well as his control. Since Max had arrived in Rio, security around Emil and his colleagues had been tightened considerably. Max had gone to ground somewhere; Johnny had been unable to discover his address. Sigrid had a place of her own, a room in a boarding house in Copacabana, where Johnny sometimes stayed overnight. But he knew that she also stayed with Max and at other safe houses dotted around the city. Helene no longer brought documents home. She was more careful than before about what she said to Johnny about her own activities. The Brazilian leaders, including Prestes, had been ordered to change their lodgings. Johnny had been asked to booby-trap a safe for one of them— he had little doubt it was for Prestes himself—but did not know where the safe was being conveyed. For fear of police infiltration, regional leaders, especially Cato's group in the north, had been given much greater autonomy.

Worst of all, it had to be assumed that Johnny was under suspicion. Maitland's meetings with him had become more furtive and less frequent. Since the incident with Hossbach, the two men no longer used the Necrópolis. They used cemeteries a good deal, the graveyard of the rich at Botafogo as well as more anonymous plots up on the hillsides. Brazilians gave graveyards a wide berth at night, when demons and spirits were abroad.

Often Johnny seemed nervous and hypersensitive behind a jocular veneer. He had been in contact with Hossbach again and had been ordered to await instructions for a meeting with the Gestapo man who was arriving from Berlin. If anything came of it, it might serve to divert Max's attention for a bit longer.

But Harry thought he had hit on a more useful way to relieve some of the pressure on Johnny.

5

HARVEY PRINCE, the radio man for the South American bureau, interested Maitland. Johnny had lost contact with the young Californian since their traumatic visit to the northeast. He had heard talk that Harvey was going to be sent home; then that he had insisted on finishing the job he had been sent to do. Johnny thought that Prince must be living in the Southern Zone, because of the speed with which messages were sent and delivered from Emil's apartment. But Johnny did not know the address. The only lead was that Helene had made a disparaging remark about Prince's car. Harvey Prince was posing as an idle American playboy and drove a yellow custom-made convertible. There could not be many cars like it in Rio.

Maitland was on his way to the beach on a quiet Saturday morning when he spotted the car quite by chance in front of a pharmacy on the corner of Copacabana Avenue and the Rua Chile. He parked the Beast in the next block, got out and made a show of inspecting a jeweler's display window. He did not have long to wait. The fair-haired young man who came out of the drugstore wearing sunglasses and a white leisure suit matched Johnny's description.

A car buff could hardly fail to notice the Beast; Harry left it in the parking space and hailed a taxi. The driver had turned his dashboard into an altar with religious medallions and plaster images of the saints.

"Follow that yellow car," Maitland instructed him. "But don't get too close." He remembered Johnny's caution about the number of taxi drivers who had been to the bomb school and added, with a grin, "It's for a bet."

The cabbie smiled back.

Wherever Harvey Prince was going, it wasn't home. They went through the tunnel, out of the Southern Zone and along the breezy embankment. Soon they were heading downtown. The yellow convertible parked near the main post office. Harry told his driver to stop, gave his driver a large bank note and showed him a second.

"Wait for me," he said.

The cabbie nodded happily.

Most of the counters inside the main hall of the post office were already closed. Maitland got into line behind the American; a plump brown woman with four squalling children had taken the place in between.

He could not hear what Prince said to the man behind the counter through the squeals of the children.

But thanks to the tendency of all Brazilian officialdom to reverse English first names and surnames, Prince was having some difficulty making himself understood.

"There's nothing for you, Senhor Gordon," the clerk reported.

"My name isn't Gordon," the Californian said, with some irritation. "It's Wood. Gordon Wood."

The clerk rummaged among his pigeonholes again and produced two airmail letters.

"*Obrigado,*" Prince said curtly, thrusting them into his pocket.

"De nada, Senhor Gordon."

Maitland had intended to purchase some stamps in case the American was watching his back, but the woman ahead of him embarked on a marathon complaint that had something to do with a change of address. So he slipped out of the post office in time to see the yellow convertible sailing away up the Avenida Rio Branco.

"We follow?" his cab driver grinned, turning on a little wire fan for his customer's benefit.

"We follow."

The yellow convertible led them straight back to Copacabana, to a small apartment building on a shady street only a few blocks from the corner pharmacy where Harry had first caught sight of Harvey Prince. The American was neglecting even the most elementary precautions; perhaps he was in a hurry to read his mail. Harry saw the yellow car swing into a narrow lane beside the apartment house that presumably led to a parking area behind.

"Keep on," he instructed the taxi driver.

"Did we win the bet?" the driver asked when he dropped Maitland off a few blocks further on, in front of a *botânico* that sold herbal remedies and religious articles.

"I certainly hope so."

He passed a few minutes in the *botânico,* inspecting potions guaranteed to bring back an errant lover or eliminate a rival and ugly black statuettes of Exú, the devil, with a lolling red tongue and pointy teeth. Then he strolled down to the beach and spent an hour enjoying the spectacle of the most sensuous women in the world parading in various states of near nudity while he contemplated his next moves.

He felt sure that the letters from the United States were personal. Colin Bailey had managed to run a background check on the radio man. Harvey Prince was an orphan. His father, a first-generation immigrant from Galicia, had been active in the Wobblies but had ended his life by blowing his brains out after long years of unemployment and the strain of living with an alcoholic wife who had died, not long after, of cirrhosis. As a teenager, Harvey had been adopted by a wealthy San Francisco art collector who flirted with the local Communist Party; there were strong indications that their relationship had been something other than filial.

He's perfect, Harry thought. A family history of psychological instability, homosexual tendencies that were probably frustrated by the rules he was required to observe in Rio, the recent trauma in the *sertão*—enough to tip any man's balance.

Harry waited until Monday before he revisited Prince's apartment house. As he turned the corner, he saw Helene come out of the building in a hurry. He drove on. He called at his bank before he went to the central post office.

"Anything for Senhor Wood?" he asked a different clerk.

"No, Senhor. Nothing."

"I'd like to rent a mailbox."

He received the expected response: nothing was available. The tactful display of a few banknotes rectified this. He was offered a box almost big enough to hold a body.

"Haven't you got something smaller?"

He signed the form "Gordon Wood" and added the address of the Copacabana apartment house. The rental charge was a fraction of the tip that he left. He received two keys.

He returned in the afternoon to check the box and deposited a plain envelope addressed to "G. Wood."

The next steps would require help.

Maitland was still thinking about them when he got home. The *curupião* barked at him from its cage on the verandah. He responded with a wolf whistle, which it mimicked to perfection. There was a smell of palm oil from the kitchen, but it had to contend with a stronger, fouler odor that made him cough as he entered the living room.

"Luisa!" he called out. "Is something burning?"

Luisa rushed out of the kitchen in her apron, blushing and apologetic. "I'll take it away," she said. "No problem."

She reached for a little incense burner she had slung from the inside door.

"Luisa? What is that stuff?"

"Nothing. It makes the house clean."

"Clean? I thought we were on fire. Let me see that thing." He inspected the contents of the incense burner, a heap of blackened crystals. He sniffed again. "Garlic?"

She nodded.

"Coffee?"

She nodded again.

"What else?"

"A little brown sugar."

"No, there's something more pungent."

"You don't want to know." She smiled, showing all her teeth. Somehow, when she smiled like that, it was quite impossible to be angry with her.

She swirled out to the kitchen.

"Luisa. It's one of your spells, isn't it?"

"It guards the house."

"Against the evil eye, or something like that?"

"Something like that."

"Listen, I've told you before. I don't mind what you do outside this house, but I won't have that mumbo jumbo in here."

"But it's for you, Senhor Harry," she said seriously.

He did not pursue it. He assumed she had been to see her voodoo priestess again—the Mother of the Saint, Luisa called her. You couldn't fight the old religion in Brazil. The Holy Inquisition had tried and lost, and it was unlikely that any of its latter-day competitors would do better. It was a living faith; the images and the rituals, older than those of the Christians, revived by the struggle to preserve them during the brutal exodus from Africa and the harsh centuries of slavery, had not grown tired and worn with hollow repetition. To believers, the *orixás*, the spirit kings who were mediators between men and an unseen, inaccessible god, were present at every turning in life, to protect or to punish. They were also jealous lords who demanded constant propitiation. Hence the chicken or the goat Harry would sometimes find tethered discreetly behind the barn at the back of his house and the rows of candles glimmering under the trees.

They sat together at dinner. The scene would have shocked the crino-lined ladies of the English colony but would probably have startled few Brazilians. Here and in the bedroom they were simply man and woman. Harry wished at times that there could be, in the outside world, some greater equality between them, but Luisa herself would have been the last to demand, or accept, it. In their moments of passion she called him *"meu principe."* He would have been hard put to explain the depth of his feeling for her. It went beyond lust, beyond loyalty and affection, but he would never have dared to call it love. Yet he found it quite impossible to imagine being without her.

Looking at her, he thought of a possible solution to one of his problems.

"That friend of yours—Teresa—" he began. "Didn't you tell me her boyfriend was in trouble with the police?"

"They caught him breaking into an apartment. He told them he was making a delivery and found the door open. He's very clever with locks."

"Did they put him in jail?"

"No. They just gave him a beating, so they could rob the apartment themselves."

"Where is he now?"

"He's got a job as a doorman at one of those places in Lapa." She made a face. "You know the ones."

"I'd like to meet him."

"Why?"

"I'd just like to meet him. Will you arrange it for me with Teresa?"

THE next step required help from a very different quarter. Summerhayes, from the embassy, was flattered to be asked to lunch at A Rotisserie, on the Rua Ouvidor. The restaurant was widely regarded as the city's finest, with prices to match.

Summerhayes wiped his mouth daintily with his napkin after polishing off a desert of crepes doused in Grand Marnier and said, "Your expense allowance from the light company must be a damn sight more generous than HMG's. Or do we have Colin Bailey to thank?"

Maitland eluded the question.

"Actually," he said, "I've got a slight favor to ask."

He explained what he had in mind, and for a moment Summerhayes looked ready to disgorge his excellent lunch.

"Sir Evelyn would have apoplexy!" he protested. "I can hear him now."

"The British Mission does not engage in shady business," Harry volunteered, in a reasonable impression of the ambassador's voice.

Summerhayes stared at Harry in amazement.

"But we owe it to our chap, don't you think?" Harry went on. "After all, we did rather land him in the soup." He added, more confidentially, "I wouldn't be at all surprised if you get a mention in the Birthday Honors List when we pull this off."

"Really?" Summerhayes started to perk up again.

"Sir Evelyn won't know," Harry promised. "I give you my word. We'll even keep Lady Maude in the dark."

Summerhayes began to giggle.

After two glasses of port he said, "There's one thing that still bothers me, Harry. Can we be sure I can meet this chappie without any of his friends spotting me?"

"I'll take care of that," Maitland said as he lit his cigar.

6

IN A modest house on the Rua Sá Ferreira, Helene concentrated on the chessboard. Max seemed distracted. He smoked and stared idly out the window while he waited for her to make her move. She realized that in moving his bishop he had carelessly exposed his queen. She leaped to attack.

"Sorry, Max." She removed his black queen from the board, leaving him with only two major pieces, a rook and the bishop. His mind obviously was elsewhere. He did not even bother to inspect the damage.

"Do you want to concede?" she prodded him.

"Not quite yet."

Barely glancing at the board, he drove the bishop forward, capturing a pawn and placing her in check.

Max got up and stretched his legs, leaving her to work the rest out for herself. She started to move her king to capture the bishop, then realized it was covered by the rook. Her king was hemmed in by her own pieces. It had nowhere to run. In her eagerness to seize the enemy queen, she had neglected the danger.

"The whole secret of chess," Max remarked, "is in the art of sacrifice."

"You knew I couldn't resist the queen."

"Not the first time."

He watched her study his end game before she replaced the chessmen in their original places. She was quick. She wouldn't fall for the same trick twice.

"I want to ask you something," she announced.

"I'm listening."

"Why did you bring Sigrid to Rio?"

"She's useful. Do you object?"

"It complicates things."

"I assume you are referring to Johnny. Are you jealous?"

"Don't be absurd! We haven't got time for these romantic follies, that's all. People make mistakes. It increases the risk to everyone."

"When the wick is lit, the brain goes out," Max recited.

"So why did you give her back to him?"

Of course she is jealous, Max thought. You can throw something away and still want it back when you see someone else using it. This was a weakness he might be able to use.

"I showed you the answer," he said to Helene.

She stared at Max, then at the chessboard. Watching her, he saw that she understood. Max was playing against Johnny, and Sigrid was the queen he had carelessly left exposed.

"What makes you sure that Johnny is a traitor?" Helene challenged him.

"If I were sure, I wouldn't need to test him."

"If you're worried about the Hossbach business—"

"I'm not worried about Herr Hossbach," Max said dismissively. "Not even his masters. But there's a mystery about Johnny. I don't like mysteries unless I create them."

Max had to admit to himself that he had been weak in relation to

Johnny. He had begun to suspect him when Heinz Kordt had made his surprising escape from Hamburg, leaving the corpses of two professional killers behind. Yet Max had always been willing to thrust his suspicions aside. He knew he had given Johnny several reasons to hate him. Yet he felt a curious fondness for the younger man. This emotion was so out of character that it was hard for him to account for it. His vocation required him to doubt every man's motives and convictions; yet he had taken Johnny's on trust. Perhaps he had been vulnerable precisely because, in his world of shadows, he needed to believe in *someone.*

But it was less easy for him now to suppress his doubts about Johnny. British Intelligence had shown its hand in both Copenhagen and Rio. Johnny had been in both places; he was the obvious link. He had warned Max about a Gestapo plot against his life. But that could not clear Johnny of suspicion of a link with the British; there were more than two sides playing this game.

Even now, Max wanted to be proved wrong. He was watching all the leaders of the South American bureau, setting traps. Helene and the Romanian who rented the safe house on Rua Sá Ferreira—a man whose face was unknown to the other Comintern agents—were his eyes and ears. If Johnny was a spy for the British, Max felt sure that one of the two sisters would finally deliver him up: Helene because of jealousy, or Sigrid because lovers grow careless of their own safety.

THE Romanian was bored and felt frayed around the edges. He had spent a whole week tailing various members of Emil's team around the city and had precious little to report to Max. The least interesting of all was the American, Harvey Prince. He stayed shut up in his apartment most of the time. He usually ate lunch alone at a little seafood place round the corner. He seemed to have no contacts outside the bureau. The fuzz on his upper lip indicated he had started to grow a moustache.

Now the Romanian was halfway through a wasted Saturday morning, dozing over a *cafezinho* at a sidewalk cafe diagonally across the street from the American's flat. Ragged brown-skinned boys buzzed around the tables like flies, holding out their palms for money or scraps. A pavement artist set up his easel and offered to produce an instant portrait. The Romanian waved him away. A few tables away, a lanky man in a navy blue blazer lingered over his breakfast rolls, distancing himself from the commotion in the street behind a copy of the London *Times.* He had been there when the Romanian had arrived. The Romanian did not pay him much attention.

When Harvey Prince came out of his building, evidently on his way to lunch, the Englishman folded his paper neatly, settled his bill, and set off across the street. On the far side he quickened his stride to overtake Harvey Prince. His walk was erratic; he appeared to bump into the American. He said something—perhaps an apology—and moved on briskly. Prince had stopped short. He was turning something over in his hands. It was a letter or a small packet. He peered around nervously, stuck it in his pocket and then hurried round the corner into his usual restaurant.

It was nearly three the next morning when Harvey Prince was roused by a violent drumming on his door. He rolled out of bed naked and put on a light cotton robe. He had a raging thirst and the beginnings of a sore throat.

He squinted through the peephole and saw the girl courier, the hard-assed bitch they called Erna, with a man he didn't know. The man looked tough. Prince didn't like his eyes. They seemed to reach out, even through the peephole, to catch him by the throat.

"Jeez, Erna," he complained as he released the bolt. "Don't you people ever sleep?"

He was swinging the door open when it was hurled back so suddenly that it hit him in the face.

A second blow, from the man's gloved fist, brought down on his chest like a hammer, knocked him to the floor.

"Holy shit—"

A swift kick aimed at the kidneys silenced his protest. His dressing gown flapped open. His body was very pale.

Max Fabrikant inspected it with that same brutal stare.

"Look," he said to Helene. "It's pointed, like a dog's."

Harvey brought up his knees and wrapped his arms around them. He seemed to be trying to roll himself into a ball. He was shaking and making little whimpering sounds.

Max sat down on the edge of the bed and started fiddling with a short length of pipe. It dawned on Harvey Prince that it was a silencer.

"I don't believe in lengthy introductions," Max announced. "I'm sure you're not a fool. You will spare yourself—and me—a great deal of unnecessary exertion if you cooperate."

"I don't understand—"

"We'll start with the letter you received this morning. The letter from Mr. Summerhayes."

"I don't know anyone called Summerhayes!"

Max sighed. "You were seen together, outside your apartment."

"But I never saw that man before in my life!"

"You're lying. Is he your boyfriend?"

"What do you think I am?" Prince screamed.

"We both know what you are. I am here to find out what you have done. Where is the letter?" Max had finished screwing the silencer on to the barrel of his pistol.

"I don't know what you're talking about."

Helene looked at Max. "Let me try," she said.

He nodded.

She took the burning cigarette from his lips and went over to Harvey Prince. The American was sweating heavily. He did not want to know what she intended to do with the cigarette.

"In the desk," he said hastily. "The top drawer."

Helene found an airmail envelope addressed to Gordon Wood. "From the United States," she reported to Max.

"Let me see that."

Max scanned the letter—four pages scrawled in a large hand, with exaggerated loops. He scowled over the explicit passages.

"What is this?" he demanded. "Pornography—or a code?"

Harvey's cheeks were scarlet. "It's from an old friend in San Francisco."

"And delivered by Summerhayes of the British Embassy? What is this? The Homintern?"

"I don't know how he came by the letter. It must be a mistake. Or a provocation. My friend writes to me care of the post office."

"All right. You've already confessed to a serious violation of party discipline. Now show me the letter Mr. Summerhayes gave you."

"That's it! I already told you—" his voice rose to a shrill as Helene pressed the burning stump of the cigarette under his scrotum, pinning him with her knee and her free arm so he couldn't wriggle away.

"We're wasting time," Max interjected. "Search the apartment."

Helene looked disappointed. "What about him?"

"I would advise you to stay exactly where you are," Max said to Prince. "The female of the species—"

They found a collection of nude photographs, copies of several secret messages that should have been destroyed, a bundle of love letters from San Francisco, a key and a thousand dollars in U.S. currency.

"Why did you keep these?" Max demanded, shoving the documents under his nose. "To send to your little pen pal in California?"

"I don't know. It must have been an oversight."

"How about the money?"

"I don't know where it came from. I haven't been paid since last month."

Max snorted.

"And this?" he held up the key. "I suppose this is the key to your gas tank."

"I never saw it before."

Helene had lit a fresh cheroot. She nudged Harvey lovingly with it, on the calves and the soles of his feet. He screamed in pain, and somebody in a neighboring flat started to bang on the wall.

"What is it?" Max pushed him. "A safe deposit box?" He glanced at the letter again. "Or a mailbox?"

"I don't have a mailbox." Prince was sobbing. "Oh, Jeez. My mother raised me for this?"

At a more respectable hour of the morning, Max left Helene with the American and went to the post office.

"Excuse me," he said to a clerk. "I found this in my box." He showed the clerk one of the letters to Gordon Wood, carefully resealed. "It's happened before. But I suppose it's understandable. Mister Wood's box is next to mine, isn't it? Three-four-seven?"

The clerk checked his records and shook his head disparagingly.

"No, Senhor. It's five-two-one. I regret the inconvenience."

"That's perfectly all right. Glad to be of assistance."

Half an hour later, Max retrieved both the boomerang letter and a plain envelope, containing an enigmatic postcard and two hundred pounds sterling.

Got him, Max thought. But he wasn't happy. It was all too easy, too amateurish. And why, after all, would Harvey Prince rat on his comrades for money? His adopted father in California was loaded with it. Perhaps he had simply snapped after his ordeal in the north and wanted to take it out on everyone he held responsible. Or else he had been set up.

The Romanian intercepted him on his way back to Harvey Prince's apartment.

"We've got to get away," he said urgently. "The police are all over the place."

"What happened?" Max thought of the irate neighbor, beating on the wall.

The Romanian ran a finger across his throat. "He jumped. Broke his neck."

Harvey Prince's flat was on the third floor. In Max's experience, unless you were six floors up, instant death could not be guaranteed. He supposed they were lucky the American had not lived to explain his reasons to the police.

"What about the woman?"

"She got safe away."

"And the radio?"

"That, too."

Max felt sure that Helene had thought to take the compromising documents with her. They had done a thorough job in ransacking Harvey Prince's apartment. The police would find nothing to tie him to the conspiracy.

The American had killed himself because he had been found out. That seemed to put Johnny and the others in the clear.

Yet Max's mood as he retraced his steps to the safe house on the Rua Sá Ferreira was somber. It had ended so quickly and so neatly. He distrusted neat conclusions. Life, as he had observed it, was extremely untidy.

Eyes of the King

To measure up to all that is
demanded of him, a man must
overestimate his capacities.
—GOETHE

1

THE place was an hour's drive from Maitland's house, in a rough neighborhood on the way to Caxias. Off the main road, the streets soon deteriorated into dried-up creekbeds, meandering strips of baked mud rutted and cratered by the last rains. The car jounced from one pothole to the next. It was like driving on the face of the moon.

The road forked ahead. There was a street lamp at the corner, and a band of young men were clustered under the light, playing pool at an improvised table. They hooted and whistled at the handsome, unfamiliar car.

This was the end of the town. Beyond the pool players, there were no more streetlights. The darkness was complete, save for the occasional glow of a kerosene lamp or candle behind the window of one of the low houses —some little better than mud huts—that fanned out at widening intervals into the tropical forest. Rio Light was not doing much business in these parts.

"Keep left," Luisa instructed him.

She waved at the boys around the pool table as the Beast crawled by, and the whistles multiplied. She had her party dress on her lap, wrapped up in a piece of crepe paper, but she had put on her special beads, blue and white for Yemanjá, the goddess of the waters.

"Are you sure this is the way?" Harry demanded after a jolt that traveled all the way up his spine.

"We're nearly there," Luisa smiled.

Harry was not reassured. She had said this three times since a police patrol had stopped them at the top of the hill. The sergeant had made out he just wanted to give them a friendly warning.

"This is not a healthy neighborhood for a gentleman of your class, Senhor," he had informed Harry. "Not so late in the evening."

He had stared boldly at Luisa, at the beads and amulets at her neck, the fine lace garments that poked out of their wrapping, and demanded in overly familiar terms to know who she was and where she was going.

Luisa had pursed her lips, ready to give the policeman a piece of her mind, but Maitland had interceded.

"We are visiting relatives," he had said smoothly. "And we are running late. Now may we proceed?"

The sergeant had not dared to stop a wealthy foreigner in a Hispano-Suiza. He shrugged and said, "I wouldn't go in there myself, Senhor," and jabbed a finger under his eye to emphasize his point.

"I wonder what that was all about," Harry said as they drove on.

"The police do it all the time," Luisa replied casually. "It is because Ivan's *terreiro* is so famous."

"Do they arrest people for going to the ceremonies?"

"No. Except for the dark side."

"You mean black magic?"

"The *Quimbanda*. Yes. If a man dies because of a spell, then the police come. But they also come to frighten us away."

"Why?"

"Because they're frightened of what they can't see. Because some of their big bosses want a Brazil of white men, nothing of Africa, nothing primitive, everything from countries of snow and ice. Some of them even want to ban Carnival!"

"I can promise you that's something that will never happen."

Harry was mulling over this exchange when a dog lurched out into the glare of his headlights. He jammed his foot down on the brake pedal and came to a stop only a few paces short of the animal, which proceeded to squat down in the middle of the road. It was a bitch and astonishingly ugly. Its splotched yellow-white hide might have been cobbled together from several unmatched pelts. Its swollen teats hung out from its belly like a cow's. Harry honked his horn experimentally. The dog blinked at them and yawned without stirring. It was either dazed by the lights or utterly unaccustomed to cars. He honked again, repeatedly, until the dog raised itself up and hobbled directly across their path. Luisa gasped and clutched at the talisman at her throat when she saw it had only three legs. It disappeared into the deeper shadows at the side of the road.

"It's a bad omen," she whispered as Harry moved the gearshift.

"It wasn't a pretty thing, I'll grant you that."

"It's a message. I don't know if it's for you or for me, or for both of us. We must tell Ivan. He will know what to do."

"Now hold on. I agreed to sit in on your cousin's confirmation. That's all. I have no intention of getting mixed up with any witch doctor."

"He's not—"

"I know, I know. He's the Father of the Saint, and all that. Even if he does call himself Ivan."

"He's a *babalão*," she said seriously. "A man of great power and respect."

"Then you tell him your problems. I'm just the chauffeur."

"There's no need to be afraid."

"My dear, I am not in the least afraid." His tone was patronizing, but he was gripping the steering wheel too tightly. There was a terrible smell in the air, compounded of dried excrement and putrefying flesh.

"It's there," she said, pointing to a low wall with a substantial cement-block building set back among the trees.

"Charming. It smells like a slaughteryard."

He glanced at his watch. It was a few minutes past midnight. Harry's enthusiasm for this nocturnal expedition had begun to wilt even before they had left the house. It was impossible to live fully in Brazil, even for twenty-four hours, without becoming aware of a world of magic and mystery. You might try to avoid looking at it squarely; it was there nonetheless, looking at *you*. A girl he had met at an embassy party, the fashionable widow of a coffee planter, had bribed his previous housekeeper to slip a love potion under his mattress, some concoction sewn up inside the body of a toad. The potion was supposed to make Harry fall in love with his pursuer, but he had detected it from the stench before it had worked its spell. At least that was what Luisa had said when he had told her the story.

In bustling, money-mad São Paulo, Harry had visited a hall as big as St. Paul's where educated, affluent men and women came by the hundreds to hear mediums convey messages from the spirits of the dead. Those who were sick lined up to have their tumors or inflamed appendixes extracted by an illiterate who operated with a rusty kitchen knife without benefit of anesthetics or disinfectants, guided by the spirit of a dead surgeon.

In Copacabana, on New Year's Eve, he had found the beach transformed into a forest of candles. Elegant couples in evening clothes and barefoot kids from the favelas jostled for space. They brought their dreams and their gifts to the water's edge in the hope that Yemanjá would hear them and carry their offerings away in her long tresses, which streamed across the beach like waves. This told the lucky ones their secret desires would be granted.

To hurried visitors from colder climes, this was all hoodoo and hocus-pocus, the sort of thing civilized people had outgrown in the Middle Ages. Major Mackenzie, the choleric Canadian who presided over the fortunes of Rio Light, was fond of observing that "idolatry and moonshine" were proof of the debility of the country's racial stock, and a reason why Brazil, for all its vast natural riches, would never catch up with his native land in its economic development until "practical men"—white men, of course, and Canadians or Scots for preference—took charge.

As he had told Colin Bailey, Harry did not pass judgment on these things. He recognized the power of the African religion in the lives of its initiates, who did not refer to it as voodoo (a bastard word derived from the language of the Fon people of Dahomey, whose slaves had mostly gone to Haiti) but as *candomblé* or *macumba* or *umbanda,* names drawn from the tribal memory of the Yoruba. The gods of *candomblé,* like those of other men, were jealous lords, as unpredictable as the forces of nature to which they were so intimately related. They demanded blood sacrifice. They took possession of their worshipers and rode them like horses. Knowing this much, Harry had never presumed, before that night, to intrude on a gathering of their devotees.

Luisa had talked him into it by describing the night's entertainment as a quite ordinary event in the social cycle, a bit like a child's first communion or a bar mitzvah, an occasion for family festivities. A girl called Elza, Luisa's distant cousin—how distant it was impossible to say, given the uncertainty about their fathers—had spent a month in seclusion, preparing for this final rite of initiation into the cult. Over the past weeks Luisa, playing surrogate mother, had sent live animals and special delicacies, as prescribed by Ivan the witch doctor, to the *terreiro.* Harry had lost patience with her when he learned that she had dipped into her slender savings to pay for a cow and two goats. He suspected that, whatever else was going on, Ivan Pessoa and his friends were not going hungry. He became curious to get a good look at this witch doctor with the Russian forename who had such a reputation—so Luisa claimed—for making and breaking spells.

But he decided to go only at the last moment, when he came home from the office and realized that he was supposed to be dining with the Mackenzies. Stella Mackenzie was a good sort, until the last couple of gins; her breezy, cheerful vulgarity reminded Harry of a barmaid at a pub he liked on the Fulham Road. But Major Mackenzie, with his monocle and his one-eyed opinions, was insufferable. Listening to him was almost enough to make Harry sympathize with the Reds, who wanted to put a bomb under Rio Light. Worse yet, Summerhayes would be in attendance, and Harry had been studiously trying to avoid him since that miserable business involving Harvey Prince. Summerhayes had come beating on Harry's door, quite hysterical, when news of the American's death had appeared in the press. Summerhayes had managed to convince himself that a witness would come forward to identify him to the police and that there would be a dreadful scandal. The prospect of Lady Maude's rage seemed to terrify the poor man even more than the chance—which Maitland considered too slight to be worthy of discussion—that the government would declare him persona non grata. He had refused to take comfort from anything Harry could say, reproaching him with the eyes of a faithful hound that has been beaten for no reason he can comprehend. All in all, Harry was happy to seize on an alternative to Stella Mackenzie's soirée.

He now realized that the slaughterhouse stink was rising from a little cabin that stood on the left side of the path. The cabin was no taller than Harry, but the door was a huge slab of wood hewn from a single trunk and secured with some serious-looking bolts and padlocks.

Harry made a show of holding his nose.

"You can smell Exú," Luisa said, squeezing his arm.

"I smelled him a fair way off."

"He must be fed before the rituals," she added with an air of authority. "And the birds and the animals must all be black. Otherwise he will come and play tricks."

Exú was the devil. At least that was how he was often represented, at the head of a great host of lesser demons. But in this temple, Satan was better-treated than in Christian churches. He wasn't cast out. He was asked very politely to stay in his own house just outside the *terreiro*, guarding the paths.

They passed knots of people smoking and talking in low voices and reached an open space, walled in on three sides. The floor was beaten earth strewn with fresh leaves. There were benches along two of the walls, men sitting on one side, women and girls on the other. The atmosphere was reassuringly, disappointingly normal, even in the uncertain light of the hurricane lamps slung from the ceiling. It might have been a church social, except for the offerings of cane brandy and manioc flour laid out beside the candles in a magic square—and the snakes.

Harry did not notice them until he had almost walked into one. A shadow passed across his eyes. He stopped short and found himself staring into the open jaws of a viper. He stood frozen until a girl started laughing. She was a pretty, catlike little thing in swirling yellow skirts, with a turban wrapped tight around her ears. She saw his eyes move in her direction and stuffed her hand across her mouth, still bubbling over with mirth. The snake had not moved.

Harry let out his breath and ducked his head under the jaws of the dead viper. He saw now that there were snakes suspended from the roof at each corner of the *terreiro*.

Luisa embraced the little brown girl in the yellow skirts and led her over by the hand.

"This is Elza."

Elza looked up at Harry, wide-eyed, and burst out laughing again.

"I must go and dress," Luisa announced. "There is Ivan."

Harry followed her glance. Ivan certainly did not look like a witch doctor. He was short and light-skinned, with curly grey hair and a neat grey beard, wearing a loose cotton shirt that hung down over a copious paunch, smoking and gossiping with his parishioners. Luisa said a few words to him. He turned. His bright, intent eyes seemed to be searching for something behind Harry. He nodded and patted Luisa's cheek.

Harry found a place on the bench reserved for the men and steeled himself for what Luisa had warned would be a long night.

Ivan vanished into one of the rooms that opened off the main hall and reappeared with an iron rattle. He jangled it lazily, and three black men took their places behind the tall, pot-bellied drums. The drums talked for what seemed like an eternity. Over them, the voices of Ivan and the senior drummer rolled monotonously, invoking the *orixás* in their own language. Harry's eyelids began to grow heavy. He glanced furtively at his watch. But little by little, the beat became more insistent, the chorus more peremptory. One by one the initiates rose from their places and joined a conga line. Luisa was among them, dancing between an elephantine black grannie in spectacles and a trim, tidy little Portuguese matron. They shuffled and whirled with surprising grace. The rhythm was subtly infectious. Before he was aware of it, Harry's feet were marking time.

Suddenly a terrible howl went up, and Grannie Elephant fell as if she had been literally bowled off her feet. Her weight carried her through the thicket of arms that was raised to catch her, and her shoulder landed in Harry's lap. The drums talked louder, faster, Ivan's voice rose higher in praise, and the other devotees whisked Grannie Elephant away, removing her spectacles and her shoes so she would not damage herself as she wheeled about, eyes tightly closed, in a strange rolling motion, emitting groans and wails, bent over at the waist as if someone were riding on her back. Harry had not had time to recover from this spectacle when there was a piercing shriek, and Elza went careening across the dance floor. They caught her before she went down, and soon she was stalking about, bent over at the waist, eyes shut, like a hunter in the long grass.

Self-hypnosis, Harry thought. Or very effective playacting. It was horribly contagious. Ivan looked well under. The white man seated next to Harry, who had seemed fairly remote from the proceedings, screamed and lurched out into the circle of the possessed. At the same instant there came a bellow of pain and rage that made Maitland think of a wild animal falling into a pit full of sharpened stakes. To his dismay he realized that this noise was coming from Luisa, who was bucking and prancing, a mount for her savage god.

One by one, the possessed were led out into the *roncó*—the sanctuary —through one of the doors behind the drummers. Some of them returned in procession, under a shower of wildflowers and fresh-cut herbs, decked out in the regalia of their patron saints. Luisa wore blue and white, for Yemanjá, with a silver helmet, a mirror, a sword and a veil of shimmering strands that gusted in front of her face. Her eyes were still closed.

The dancing and singing went on until dawn and climaxed in a deafening ovation that must have carried all the way to Rio. Lesser spirits—the spirits of children and ancestors—now made their entry. Elza came hopping up to Harry with a brace of pacifiers in her mouth, giggling and drooling like a mischievous infant.

"Do you like our *candomblé?*"

"It's charming," Harry said. *"Me encanta."*

"Es encantado!" Elza shrieked and clapped her hands. "He's spellbound!" She skipped away and tried to piggyback on Luisa's shoulders.

To Harry's relief, Luisa looked more or less normal.

"What did it feel like?" he whispered to her.

"I don't remember."

"Well, do you actually see them—these *orixás?*"

"Not see them, not the way you mean. But after—it's difficult to say. It's like feeling a thickness in the air, like seeing colors that don't exist."

He might have pursued this, but Elza darted up and handed him a bottle of beer and a plate of *farofa*, rice and some unidentifiable grey meat.

"Breakfast?"

"Breakfast."

"She's really very pretty," he remarked to Luisa, watching the lilt of the girl's body as she went to serve the others.

"You should see her without her turban. They shaved her head."

He dug his fork into the rice, downed his beer and murmured to Luisa, "Can we go now?"

"First you talk to Ivan," she said firmly. "For the *registro.*"

Ivan received him in a cell-like room, a third of whose space was occupied by a massive wooden sideboard laden with statues of the *orixás,* cauldrons, piled necklaces and curious talismans of wood and iron. The place smelled of blood and incense. Harry did not look too closely at the bones and feathers sticking out of a pot in the corner.

Ivan squatted on one side of a straw mat, his bare feet wide apart, and motioned for Harry—who had been told to leave his shoes at the door—to sit on a low chair opposite, his feet resting between the priest's. There were formalities to be observed; ritual greetings in the language of the Yoruba, an offering to Exú to open the paths. Ivan wrote out Harry's full name on a piece of paper and recited it several times in the course of a long incantation. Then he gave Harry an object to hold in either hand, a seashell and a piece of carved bone. He made Harry rub them quickly together behind his back and then hold out his hands, concealing the contents. Ivan picked one, examined the contents without comment, and cast the cowrie shells. For thousands of years, these had been the most popular oracle of the Yoruba. Each pattern had scores of possible meanings, to be drawn from oral memory—from thousands of verses handed down from one priest to the next—and by testing and retesting, casting the shells over and over again.

"It is not good," Ivan said at last. "There is death and sickness. We must discover the source of the evil."

He cast the shells again.

"One source of the evil is a spirit," he pronounced. "A spirit that was separated from its body too violently, so that it lingers, not knowing where to go."

He looked up sharply. "Have you killed a man?"

"No."

Ivan frowned, and Harry found himself thinking about Harvey Prince, and then about the young tough Bailey had killed in an alley near the Lisbon docks.

"There is danger from others who are living," Ivan went on. "A fire is growing strong, very close to you. You have not yet begun to feel its flames."

He threw the cowries again and started to tell Harry about his family and his earlier life. His statements were remarkably accurate, down to the stillbirth of Maitland's younger brother.

Harry felt increasingly nervous and uncomfortable. Perhaps Ivan does have psychic powers, he thought. Or perhaps I'm reading too much into his guesses.

"You were born with a *caixa de mistérios,*" Ivan announced. "A box of mysteries. You must take care to keep secret what is meant to be secret. The walls have ears."

Ivan's fingers moved back and forth, casting and recasting the shells. He paused to dab his finger in a saucer of some oily vermilion mixture and pressed it against the roof of his mouth. He asked Harry to do the same.

"To make the telling easier," he explained.

The taste was not as offensive as Harry had expected.

"*Xango te defiende,*" Ivan said, with greater force. "Xango defends you. But there is another who is angry. You must appease them both."

Ivan explained what this would entail, and Harry tried hard not to make a face.

Ivan looked hard at him. "This is not a game," he said flatly. "You have invoked a power. It will show itself to you."

AFTERWARDS it was Luisa's turn. Harry drank some more beer and watched Ivan's congregation at play, dancing to music on the radio as if the party were just beginning. He wondered how these people found time to sleep, let alone work. The neighbors were obviously either stone deaf or part of the gathering. He tried to dismiss what Ivan had said. The man was a fortune-teller, admittedly more convincing than the gypsies who read palms or tea leaves at Brighton Beach, but no different in kind.

But when Luisa came back, she looked worried, almost desolate.

She did not speak for a long time after they got into the car. They were climbing toward the house at the edge of the rain forest when she said, "You must do what Ivan said."

"I don't have your way with chickens," he countered, laughing it off. "Besides, I used to give donations to the RSPCA."

"What is RSPCA?"

"Oh, never mind." In his worn-out condition, he did not feel up to explaining the RSPCA and the English reverence for all forms of animal life.

"Another can do it for you," Luisa pursued, "but it won't be the same. There will be consequences."

"Look, we've both had a long night. Let's have a decent breakfast and get some shut-eye, shall we? Thank God it's the weekend."

When she said, "Cook your own bloody bacon and eggs," he realized she had picked up more English than he had given her credit for.

1

EMIL BRANDT padded out of the kitchen in his underwear, carrying a tumbler and a bottle of scotch.

Lenka did not look up from her sewing.

"You said you weren't going to touch hard liquor till the end of the week," she reminded him.

"So I couldn't wait."

She rammed her foot down on the pedal of the ancient Singer sewing machine, and the needle whirred.

"Do you have to do that?" Emil appealed to her, collapsing into the armchair next to the fan. "We're not in Minsk."

"It helps not to look at you," Lenka said savagely.

"So you don't care to look at your husband any more? You're not such a bathing beauty yourself."

"You're falling apart. Who's going to tell you except me?"

He sighed while she followed the needle, hemming a tablecloth they would probably never use.

"You're a hard woman, Lenka."

"So how else would I still be with you?"

He drank and leaned closer to the fan to dry the sweat from his face. The heat was killing him, and the summer still lay ahead. He felt sorry for Lenka but sorrier still for himself. He hardly slept any more. He felt as if insects were crawling under his skin.

It had been worse since the American had died. Max Fabrikant had come storming in, demanding to see copies of every communication that might have passed through the hands of the radio man, ordering the rest of them about like children or mental defectives. Emil had been obliged to report the episode to Moscow, of course. In an attempt to cover himself, he had reported that he had been wary of Harvey Prince for some time and had severely restricted his access. Emil doubted whether this would counteract the poison Max was spreading. Max must have found out by now that Emil had personally recruited Harvey Prince during his stopover in New York. Prince came recommended by one of Emil's most trusted agents, a man he relied on in the old days when they joked that he was the czar of the American Communist movement. Emil had no reason to distrust either Harvey Prince or his sponsor. The boy had his failings, for sure, and he was close to a crack-up after that business in the north, but Emil privately refused to think of him as a traitor. In fact, he suspected something very different: that Max Fabrikant had cooked up the whole affair in order to destroy him.

Emil knew he had powerful enemies in Moscow, people who would never forget that he had once presumed to criticize Stalin's policies and called for a united front with the Social Democrats to stop the Nazis. He had been taught the error of his ways in Moscow, in vertical tombs in the cellars of the Lubyanka where ice formed on the walls and the nights were scarred by the screams of fellow inmates. At the end of his reeducation, he publicly abased himself. He wrote syrupy tributes to Great Stalin, the genius of the age. He crawled before Manuilsky. His persecutors wanted Heinz Kordt, so he gave Kordt to them, along with many others. Betrayal became a habit, even an obsession. Eagerly, he sought out old comrades who dared to challenge Stalin's judgment and denounced them as spies and Trotskyites. In China as in Moscow, he hastened to show he had learned his lessons: that there was no truth except Stalin's; that a Communist would be judged, first and last, by his tireless devotion to the Leader.

I did all this, Emil thought, and they still won't trust me. Is it because I'm German? Or because I'm a Jew? Or because I was already a party organizer when Trotsky and Zinoviev stood at Lenin's right hand?

He had read the resolutions of the Seventh Congress of the Comintern, whose deliberations had extended through most of the month of August. The delegates got to their feet and cheered when Dimitrov announced the start of the Anti-Fascist Decade. With Hitler openly rearming, with Mussolini's legions rolling into Abyssinia and Japanese officers taking snapshots along the Great Wall of China, Moscow had finally approved the policy Stalin had rejected so savagely until now: a broad front against the Fascists. The change came too late to help Germany or those, like Heinz Kordt and a younger Emil, who had been condemned as "premature anti-Fascists." And Emil, suffering the tropical heat in a city thousands of miles from Moscow, wondered whether the change was real. It did not affect his own mission. His orders were the same. Moscow's tone was, if anything, more imperative, more strident.

When Harvey Prince killed himself, Emil confided some of his doubts about the planned revolution—for the first and only time—in a memorandum to Manuilsky. Of course, he attributed the problems he saw to the sloppiness of the Brazilians and the irresolution of his colleagues in the South American bureau.

The reply from the Big House was stinging. The letter was hand carried to Rio from the Soviet Mission in Montevideo by the new wireless operator assigned to replace Harvey Prince. It was signed by Manuilsky himself.

"Loyalty will be judged by results," Manuilsky's letter concluded. "If you fail, no excuse will be sufficient. There are serious charges pending against you."

This passage reminded Emil of a famous dictum of Frederick the Great, one he had once been made to copy out over and over in Gothic script when he had angered a schoolmaster in Cologne: "The world judges our actions not by our reasons but by the success that crowns them."

Manuilsky's letter brought the nightmares closer. Emil woke up between three and four every morning out of howling nightmares in which he was being dragged through the basements of the Lubyanka or across the frozen tundra. His terror was increased by every new report about the purges in Moscow, which had already swallowed up tens of thousands of old party loyalists. It seemed that nobody was safe—at least, nobody who had been imprudent enough to join the party before Stalin had become general secretary. Now Stalin's hatchet man had put him on notice of the penalty for failure in Brazil.

Whatever the cost, he had to go forward. The risk of detection by the Brazilian police paled into insignificance in comparison with Stalin's displeasure.

But who could he trust?

Not the Argentinian, who didn't have the stomach for action.

Not Johnny, who had every reason to hate him.

Not Helene, the bitch informer whose stare could freeze a man's balls off. Helene's transfer was the one good thing to result from Prince's suicide. Max had decided to ship her out, on the grounds that one of the Californian's neighbors might be able to identify her to the police as a regular visitor to the apartment.

But Max still had his woman spy. Sigrid had taken over Helene's work. The younger sister might be the deadlier of the two, Emil told himself. Because she seemed softer, more vulnerable, it was easier to let your guard drop.

Least of all could he trust Max Fabrikant. Max isn't here to help make a revolution, Emil thought. He's here to finish me.

Moscow had sent new men to Rio to reinforce Emil's team: a Lithuanian who specialized in the labor unions, a wireless operator from Tokyo, a Fourth Department man who had gotten himself into some scrape in Denmark and was lucky, by all accounts, to have landed another foreign assignment. None of them had been approved by Emil. More than ever, he felt under hostile eyes.

He banged out to the bedroom and started getting dressed.

"Are you going somewhere?" Lenka called to him.

"I have to meet Nilo."

"That one! That playboy! He's *meshuggeh*. You shouldn't listen to him."

"Who would you have me listen to?" he roared at her, struggling with his tie. "To the Argentinian? All he wants is to go home and eat *empanadas.*"

"Maybe he's got the right idea."

"Nilo's a good boy. He's got guts."

"They're the ones who get you killed."

Emil was not inclined to argue. He had a blinding pain behind his left eye, the result of an abscess above a tooth he should have had pulled out long ago. But who had time for any of that? He had a revolution to make.

THERE was quite a crowd in the waiting room at the clinic on the Rua Chile. But when Emil mentioned his cover name to the receptionist, he was ushered through to the surgery straight away. He raised his hand in salute to the young white-jacketed doctor who was probing around his patient's groin and walked briskly on into the back room. Nilo was stretched out on the sofa, leafing through a copy of the *Psychopathia Sexualis.*

"What did you find out?" Emil demanded.

He had sent Nilo to Recife as his personal emissary, to report on the progress of the revolt. He wanted to believe the stream of gung-ho reports from Cato, the regional chief of the underground, but he needed a second opinion.

"They're straining at the leash. We can't hold them much longer. Cato says that unless we move by the end of the year, the whole thing will blow up in our faces."

"It's Cato's job to keep things under control," Emil commented.

"You have to understand the pressure that is building. The sergeants can't wait much longer. At the end of the year, hundreds of them are going to join the unemployed."

Emil nodded. This was one of the grievances he had set out to exploit. Nervous of left-wing influence in the barracks, the government had decided to retire hundreds of sergeants whose five-year contracts of service expired in December, instead of signing them up for another term. Only a handful of these NCOs were Communist sympathizers, but since word of the impending layoffs had gotten around, plenty were willing to take part in any action that would guarantee them a decent wage.

"We can seize the north tomorrow," Nilo announced. "It's not just the sergeants. Even the army commander in Recife is ready to join us. But we can't afford to delay. We have to catch the tide."

Emil grunted. "And what about Rio?"

"You see where we're sitting."

Emil glanced around at the twin bookcases, one of them filled with jars of pickled specimens, the framed diplomas, the flattering portrait of the mayor above the desk. The clinic had belonged to Doctor Alcibiades before he took charge of the city government. All of its staff were secret party members.

Emil had never met Alcibiades, and did not much like the way he looked in his picture. That face belonged in a silent movie, the kind Valentino played in. How could you count on a man whose eyelashes were that long?

But Alcibiades had proved himself in more important ways than by allowing his old clinic to be used for secret meetings. The mayor had channeled nearly two hundred thousand dollars to the Communist underground. The money was laundered through a charitable foundation dedicated to bettering living conditions in the favelas. Emil was not unaware that most of this cash was supplied by Alcibiades' business friends and that the biggest single donor was Courtland Bull, the American oil millionaire. Bull's yacht had become a familiar sight these past months, basking at the mouth of the Bay of Botafogo like a gleaming white whale.

Emil relished the humor in the situation. Courtland Bull was paying for a revolution that would blow him out of the water. The American obviously thought he was buying himself a president and all the concessions a president could dispense. He was driven by greed, just as Alcibiades was driven by ambition and pride. Emil had had some experience in harnessing those emotions. He intended to do so now.

"What I say now is between the two of us," Emil said to Nilo. "Is that understood?"

"Perfectly."

"I want you to go to Alcibiades as soon as you can manage it without being observed. You will tell him that the date for the rising has been set."

Emil mentioned a Saturday in December, and the Brazilian's face lit up. The man has the confidence of a sleepwalker, Emil thought.

Emil proceeded to list the things he would need from the mayor. On the night of the revolt, the Municipal Guard, which was under the doctor's personal control, was to seize the police headquarters and arrest a number of high officials, including the minister of war and the minister of justice, on the grounds that they were involved in a Fascist plot against the life of the president. Simultaneously, the army and air force officers who were secretly pledged to Prestes would neutralize all armed resistance in the capital, while civilian assault teams took control of the railroads, the telegraph and the docks.

Emil had calculated the odds many times, in discussions with Prestes and the handful of other Brazilians he trusted. He had concluded that the rising had a reasonable chance of success in Rio and in the north, even without mass support. But São Paulo would be contested territory, and the south would probably fight. In a country so immense, so fragmented, the capture of Rio would be merely the prelude to civil war—unless the Communists could disarm their opponents psychologically by presenting themselves as the defenders of the republic against some more sinister force.

He thought he had found a way to do it.

Its shock effect would be tremendous. It would create a national explosion of sympathy for the revolt. But what it required was so alien to the Brazilians' way of doing things, to their celebrated tolerance and *simpatia*, that he did not dare to discuss it even with Prestes. After all, no head of state had ever been assassinated in Brazil.

"There's one thing more," he told Nilo. "We'll need a floor plan of the Guanabara Palace. I want to know where every guard is posted."

Nilo considered this for a moment and said brightly, "There's a back gate. I've seen it myself."

Emil stared at him.

"You can get in through the Fluminense Club. It backs on to the palace gardens."

"What's the Fluminense Club?"

"Honestly, Emil. You've been here half a year and you haven't heard of the national sport?"

"Oh. Yes, of course." Emil looked mildly embarrassed. Fluminense was one of the most popular soccer clubs in the country. "What is the security like?" he pursued.

"At the Fluminense Club? I suppose they have a night watchman. What more would they need?"

"And on the other side of the wall?"

Nilo shrugged. "Maybe a marine or two, having a quiet smoke. Do you want me to find out? It's not difficult. I know one of the coaches at the club."

"Find out everything you can. But don't tell anyone else about this."

"May I say something?"

"Of course."

"If you're planning to grab the president, I'd like to be there in person."

Emil shook his head.

"Why not?"

"Because you don't have a green shirt in your wardrobe."

Emil began to explain what he intended. He found he had not misjudged his man. A smile spread slowly over Nilo's face.

3

Max has put everything into little boxes, Johnny thought, and nailed them up tight.

He suspected that it was because of Max that he had been excluded from several important meetings. He felt he had been relegated to the outer circle, reduced to the role of a mere technician showing Brazilians how to make bombs. Helene's abrupt departure should have allowed him to breathe easier. But the effect was just the opposite. Sigrid had taken her place, and it took far more concentration to keep his guard up with the woman he loved.

He realized the extent of the danger when he came to her room in the night and found her waiting for him in a flimsy negligee, her skin rosy and sweet-scented from the bath.

"Take me now," she breathed. "I can't wait any longer."

He took her in his arms and carried her to the bed. He was about to enter her when she pressed her palm up against his chest and said, "Why do you walk in the cemetery at night?"

His mind reeled. He went to cemeteries to meet Harry Maitland. He always took every possible precaution to insure that he was not being followed. But with Max, every possible precaution might not be enough.

His desire ebbed away. He fell onto the bed by her side, pulling up the sheet because of the sudden chill that had entered the room.

He said, "That's a strange question. Have you been following me? Or did Max tell you to ask me?"

"I need to know the answer."

"All right," he said fiercely. "Here's your fucking answer. I walk by myself at night because I can't sleep. Because I can't forget all the friends I've lost."

"Friends like Harvey Prince?"

"Not him."

"Because he was a British spy?"

"I don't know anything about that!"

"If he wasn't a spy, then why is he dead?"

Because he was born to be a victim, Johnny thought. Like you—unless I can get you out of this.

"If Max wants to interrogate me," Johnny said, "tell him to do it himself."

"I didn't mean to upset you—" suddenly, she was all woman again, snuggling up against him, letting him feel the soft pressure of her body. "I saw you coming out of the cemetery in Botafogo when I was driving back from a meeting."

"And you didn't offer me a lift?"

"I didn't want to embarrass you."

"What do you mean, embarrass me?"

"How could I know what you were doing?"

Liar, Johnny thought. You were never there. But one of Max's watchdogs must have been. If Max knew anything definite, he wouldn't have sent you on this fishing trip. But I'll have to be much more careful.

"Johnny," she implored him, caressing his lower back, "don't hold it against me. It was just something I had to get out of the way. Would you rather I kept these things bottled up?"

"Is there something else you want to ask me?" He looked at her intently. He thought he saw a shadow pass before she buried her face against his chest. Was it shame or fear?

"Just make love to me," she murmured. "I need you so much."

You're not lost to me yet, he told himself.

All real desire had left him, but he worked to make her body sing, until he saw her eyes widen and felt the trembling explosion within her.

When she lay still beside him, he saw Max's face, like a physical presence in the room.

You bastard, he thought. You try to turn all of us into mechanics.

WHEN Max questioned him again, it was not about the cemetery.

The three of them were together in the new apartment Johnny was renting, a stone's throw away from the marina and the Gloria church. Max had brought another recording, an opera in French that Johnny had never heard before. It was Meyerbeer's *Le Prophète*. There was a booklet with the libretto, in the original and in an ungainly English translation. Leafing through it, Johnny found the story of a young man chosen by the Anabaptists—a millenarian religious sect—as their prophet and proclaimed King of Leyden in a violent sixteenth-century crusade. His mother had been forced to deny him; the girl who loved him had killed herself when she saw what he had become. Resolved to destroy the sect, he perished by setting a fire which consumed the palace in which he and the Anabaptists were banqueting.

"Very diverting," Johnny remarked, tossing the booklet back at Max, who was humming and waving his arms about like a conductor. "You have a curious taste in light entertainment."

"I chose it for you, dear boy. Of course, Meyerbeer takes scandalous liberties with the historical record. But it occurred to me you might find his version rather familiar."

"If you're trying to provoke me—"

"I wouldn't dream of it! I should come to you for lessons in provocation!"

Max smiled and held out his glass to Sigrid, who hurried out to the kitchen for another bottle.

Johnny thought, he's playing with me.

"Have you seen your pet Nazi lately?" Max asked.

"I saw Hossbach two days ago. We had a few drinks."

"What happened to the Gestapo man you said they were sending to catch—how did you describe it?—a certain kike from Antwerp?"

"He's here," Johnny reported. "But I haven't met him. Hossbach said the plan has been changed."

Even boozy Hossbach has become careful of me, Johnny reflected.

"But he showed you the photograph, at least?"

"Oh, yes. He showed me the photograph. It was you, all right. Hossbach told me to keep my eyes open."

"I would very much like to meet this friend of Hossbach's who carries my picture around in his wallet," Max said thoughtfully. "Do you suppose you could arrange a meeting?"

"I could try."

He watched Max take his drink from Sigrid. In Johnny's eyes, Max's words and movements were offensively possessive. Max said, "There's a good girl," as if he were petting a domestic animal. What infuriated Johnny most was that Sigrid seemed unconscious of any slight.

At that instant a grisly scene flashed through Johnny's mind: the scene of a shoot-out between Max and the Gestapo, leaving all of them dead.

Why not? he thought. Nobody would be able to blame him—and Sigrid's tether would be broken.

But Max would never let himself be caught so easily.

"I could try," he repeated, more assertively. "Of course, we would have to find the right bait."

"We'll think of something."

The recorded voices of the Anabaptists rose to a crescendo and Max abandoned the conversation to join in the chorus:

> Suivez-nous, amis! Dieu le veut,
> Dieu le veut! C'est le grand jour!

TWO NIGHTS LATER, Johnny kept a rendezvous with Hossbach at the Babylônia Club. The doorman greeted him with a grinning salaam, and a couple of the bar girls blew kisses. He was becoming a regular.

"Hello there, Johnny. Better get that down you quick, before the ice melts."

Johnny took the cocktail that was waiting for him.

"Look at the bouncers on that one." Hossbach smacked his chops, eyeing the new girl, who was attempting to sing "Night and Day." He snapped his fingers for the waiter. "Give the lady a glass of champagne," he instructed. "Tell her to come over here when she's finished the set."

"Very good, sir."

"Well, then." He turned back to Johnny. "What's up? You said on the phone you had something interesting for me."

"Are you still interested in that kike from Antwerp?"

"*Natürlich.* Did you hear something about him?"

"Better. I saw him today."

"How is that possible?" Hossbach narrowed his eyes until the whites were invisible between the folds of flesh. The effect reminded Johnny of Wollweber, the Comintern boss in Copenhagen.

"I was in a jewelry store around the corner from the Copacabana Palace, looking for something to impress a little lady I discovered. Your man walked in and asked for the manager. I saw him go into the back room. I'd bet he was trying to peddle some of those rocks you mentioned."

"You're sure it's the same man?"

"Pretty sure. I never forget a face. He was a few years older than the man in your photo, but I'd swear it's the same one. He had Jew written all over him, and he was dead scared."

"What did you do?"

"I waited till he got outside. He looked ready to run when I approached him, but I spoke to him in English, as if he was an American tourist. I told him the people in the store were thieves and that I'd get him a good price if he had any more stones to sell."

"Did he buy it?" Hossbach's face was damp with excitement.

"He said he'd call me."

"Wait here." Hossbach hauled his weight off the chair and went to use the telephone in the hall.

If they're hungry enough, Max had said, they'll bite.

Hossbach was gone at least fifteen minutes. When he came back, he had a lot of notes scrawled on the back of an envelope. He used them to fire off a series of questions his boss had obviously just dictated, taking more notes as Johnny gave his replies. What were his father's and mother's Christian names? Where had he gone to school in Vienna? Military service?

"It sounds like your boss is a careful man," Johnny remarked, hoping that the cover story of Franz Gruber—the Austrian whose identity he had assumed—was strong enough to withstand a Gestapo investigation in Vienna, at least until this operation was over and he could vanish from Engineer Hossbach's life.

"Listen, it's nothing personal," Hossbach said clumsily. "In my business, we can't be too bloody careful. Here's what we want you to do. If Dorfman gets in touch—" Dorfman was one of Max's many aliases "—tell him to meet you at the Alpino, and make sure you give us at least three hours' notice."

Johnny shook his head. The Alpino had a largely German clientele.

"I told you, the Jew is scared," he pointed out. "He'll want to pick his own time and place."

Hossbach considered this and said, "Okay. But make sure to give us enough warning, so we can set it up right."

"I don't think he'll call," Johnny played the skeptic. "If he's as important in the Communist party as you say, why would he take the risk?"

This little twist helped a lot, because Hossbach became the one defending the whole implausible proposition.

"I know these sons of bitches," the Nazi said. "They like to feather their nests. My guess is he's doing a little business on the side with Uncle Joe's money."

"Speaking of which—"

"You don't need to worry." Hossbach pulled out his wallet and flicked several large banknotes across the table. "I know how to look after my pals. There'll be plenty more if this comes off."

JOHNNY dabbed holy water on his forehead and made the sign of the cross. He bent his knee before the high altar before slipping behind the pews and along the left side of the church toward the confessionals. Light filtered through stained glass made a batik pattern of blues and greens on the stone floor.

He entered the second confessional and leaned his head close to the grille.

"Bless me, Father," he intoned. He added quickly, "I was followed, but I gave them the slip in Cinelandia."

"Max's people or Hossbach's?" Harry Maitland whispered from the priest's side of the confessional.

"Max's, I think." He recounted what Sigrid had said about the cemetery. "Max probably wants to see which way I'll run."

Johnny described Max's plan to deal with Hossbach's employers.

"You can't go through with it," Harry told him. "It's a lunatic scheme. If the thing misfires, you'll get yourself killed."

"That may be one of the attractions for Max."

"I don't understand why Max would be willing to risk the whole Rio operation merely to bag a few Nazi thugs."

"He's not risking the operation," Johnny pointed out, "he's risking *me*. Besides, the Gestapo has got his scent and he doesn't like that."

"Don't go," Harry urged him.

"I have to go. It's a direct order. I think it's also a test. If I do the job right, it may be a bit easier for me to find out what the hell is going on."

"Then at least let me give you some backup."

"What backup? The police? They'd probably arrest me instead of Hossbach's friends. Besides, it wouldn't be very easy to explain."

"I was thinking of myself."

"Thanks for the thought, Harry. But you'd better stay out of this. I don't know where Max will be, but he'll be watching. You can bet on that."

From behind the screen Maitland heard Johnny rising to leave.

"Three Hail Marys," Harry called after him. "And all the luck on God's earth."

IN THE street market under the old aqueduct, the cacophony was immense. It sounded as if all the Furies had been loosed at once. It took a minute or two for Johnny to distinguish the separate elements in the storm of sounds: the shouts of the porters as they shouldered their way through the crowded passages, their wares stacked high on top of their heads or swaying from poles across their shoulders; the shriek of caged parrots and macaws; the rattle and creak of pushcarts; the dull thud of the butchers' meat axes; the clack of cheap wooden clogs; the insistent babble of hawkers arguing over a price; the braying of tethered goats; the squall of a lost child.

Max's instructions had been precise. Johnny was to telephone Hossbach thirty minutes before the meet, thus denying the Nazis time to set up an elaborate ambush. The rendezvous would be on the harbor side of the market, near the wharves where they hauled up freshly caught fish. The long, low building that housed the fish market itself had half a dozen exits.

"Don't carry a gun," Max had warned Johnny. "They may become suspicious and search you. A gun would be hard to explain."

"Don't you want to take them while you have the chance?" Johnny had asked.

"Not immediately."

It seemed that Max's plan was to identify the enemy and have him tailed to his lair. To a counterintelligence mind, Johnny knew, it made sense to leave an identified enemy in place. An identified agent could be monitored. He might be used as a channel for false information. If his weaknesses were learned, he might even be turned against his own masters. If they killed the Gestapo man from Berlin, he would be replaced by an unknown successor, and their advantage would be lost.

But the plan left Johnny highly exposed. It would be up to him to satisfy the Germans, when Max failed to arrive, that he had not been laying a trap. Hossbach swore copiously over the telephone when Johnny told him the arrangements for the meeting. When Johnny set down the receiver, he hesitated for a few minutes before he took the Mauser out of his belt.

I'll be naked without it, he thought, turning the big gun over in his hands. Damn Max's orders. I'm not going into this unarmed.

He tucked the Mauser back into place.

THE stink of raw fish was hard to take on an empty stomach. Slim, dark-skinned men were pulling wriggling eels out of a boat and tossing them into buckets. Outside the blotchy facade of the market building, women squatted behind panniers of bright parrot fish, squid and cuttlefish.

Johnny looked at his watch. He had been waiting nearly twenty minutes.

I'll give it five minutes more, he told himself.

A hawker came up with two buckets of fish slung from a pole. He swung one of the buckets under Johnny's nose. The fish had been dead for a very long time.

"Four for one milreis," he intoned.

Johnny shook his head.

"Five?" the hawker proposed hopefully.

"I'm not interested."

"The fish are fresher inside," the hawker said confidentially. "The fat man told me to tell you."

Johnny toyed with his pipe for a bit—the beauty of a pipe was that it always gave you an excuse for delay—before he strolled into the fish market. The stench inside was overpowering. He blew out clouds of smoke to drive it away. A girl in a maid's cap and apron watched as one of the vendors gutted a large, fatty fish.

Hossbach loomed up out of the shadows. There was a second man with him, nicely turned out in a crisp linen suit and a panama hat.

He looks like a meat porter all the same, Johnny thought.

"This is Dr. Zeller," Hossbach said.

As the stranger came closer, Johnny tried not to stare. There was something horribly familiar about that coarse, bulging face.

I know you, he thought.

"What happened to your pal?" Zeller challenged him.

"Maybe he spotted you," Johnny suggested. "Maybe he just got scared."

"That's two maybes too many." Zeller's tone was less than friendly. "I hope you're not pissing around with me, Gruber."

The way he blustered and pushed himself up too close made Johnny sure. Take away forty pounds and about half as many years and he was looking at Willi Rausch, the schoolyard bully who had killed his father. Willi Rausch, the model Aryan, who had grown up to find there was a seller's market for his talents.

Suddenly Johnny's desire for revenge was all-consuming. His hand crawled towards his back, flirting with the butt of the Mauser.

I could take him now, Johnny told himself. Hossbach too. But there must be others. A coward like Rausch wouldn't risk himself without plenty of backup.

Rausch was squinting at him.

"Haven't we met somewhere?"

"I don't think so."

"I never forget a man," said Rausch. "Weren't you in Hamburg?"

"I've never been in Hamburg."

There's no more time, Johnny realized. I have to do it now.

A flash of movement beyond the archway that led to the loading area caught his eye. There was a chance—just a chance—of narrowing the odds.

"There he goes!" Johnny yelled.

"What? Are you sure?"

"It's Dorfman!" he called over his shoulder. He was off and running between the trestle tables, and the Germans went crashing along after him —two, no, there were four of them now. He had flushed the others from cover.

"Go round the other way and cut him off!" Johnny shouted to Hossbach. "He'll try to get away round the side!"

He heard Rausch and Hossbach barking at each other. He hopscotched over some baskets of crabs and barely escaped a collision with a majestic black woman in the white headdress and voluminous skirts of Bahia. He lurched into one of the tables, producing shrill cries of fear and alarm. His hand closed over something before he careered on. As he neared the archway, he risked a look back. Rausch was stumbling along after him, breathing hard, and a second German had nearly caught up. The others must have gone out the front. The odds were improving.

"He's in there," Johnny announced to Rausch, pointing to a mound of crates that rose to the height of a man's head.

Rausch peered about, clutching a Luger. The porters milling about outside goggled at him.

"Raus!" he snarled at them, brandishing the gun. "Get out!"

The alleyway emptied at once.

"I don't see anything," Rausch said warily. "Kurt—" he motioned to his bodyguard. "You go take a look."

He watched Kurt go zigzagging towards the crates.

"There's something about you I don't like," he said, turning to Johnny. "If you're pissing with me—"

He broke off because for a fleeting moment he saw the glint of light on metal. His scream died in his throat as Johnny drove the point of a fish knife into his neck behind the windpipe. The last sounds he uttered were like those of a cat trying to spit out a hairball.

It was doubtful whether he heard Johnny breathe, "That's for my father."

Johnny dropped to the ground.

Where was Kurt? The bodyguard had vanished behind the crates. There was a truck parked a few yards away, to the left. On his belly, with his Mauser out, Johnny wormed his way towards it.

A shadow fell across his path. He tried to bring the gun up but failed, because at the same moment he felt a shooting pain in his right arm, and his hand went numb.

"*Klugsheisser,*" Kurt swore. He must have seen what had happened and crept around behind the back of the truck. He had stamped his foot down hard across Johnny's wrist.

Johnny lashed out with his good hand, trying to pull the German down, but Kurt jumped away, kicking the Mauser out of reach.

Kurt was evidently undecided whether to shoot Johnny on the spot or wait for Hossbach, who couldn't be far away.

Johnny rose onto his haunches.

"Down!" Kurt jabbed the gun at him. "Get down!"

If this is the end, Johnny thought, I'm not going to meet it on my belly.

In his painful squatting position, he steeled himself for a desperate leap. Kurt was only a few feet away, holding the gun out in front of him like a duelist.

If I can just move fast enough . . .

At the instant he propelled himself forward off his aching calves, the shot rang out. It did not stop Johnny's forward momentum. His head butted into the German's chest, toppling him backwards. He clawed for the throat. The two men rolled together, and Johnny was half blinded by the blood that gushed over his forehead.

With a kind of wonderment, he realized that the blood was not his.

Kurt's face was very white, paler than fish-belly white, around the red crater where one of his eyes had been.

Johnny released the body and retrieved his Mauser. When he peered over the side of the truck, a bullet zinged past his ear, punching a hole in the stucco wall of the fish market behind. The sniper must be in the window of one of the buildings across the alley. He must have a rifle, to be firing at that range. When he stuck his head out again, he was driven back by a second shot.

"Get your ass out of there, you bloody fool!" Hossbach called from somewhere away to his left. "Can't you see it's an ambush?"

Johnny squeezed off a couple of rounds in the general direction of the sniper. Before he made his run for safety through the archway into the market, he risked one more look. He was rewarded with a glimpse of two men at a window. One was squat and swarthy. The other was aquiline, almost elegant as he puffed his cigarette. Max Fabrikant.

As Johnny hurled himself through the doorway, a bullet kicked up the dust where his feet had just been.

"WERE you trying to kill me?" Johnny challenged Max afterwards.

"The better question is, were you asking to be killed?" Max responded calmly. "Nobody told you to play fishwife with the man from Berlin."

"He recognized me," Johnny pointed out. "It was him or me. In any event, I had a score to settle."

"We all have scores to settle. Some of them have to wait."

"Why didn't you kill Hossbach, too?"

"I didn't come to Brazil to hunt Nazis. Nor did you. Actually, I went one better than killing Hossbach. I gave you an alibi."

This was true, up to a point. In the melee and the confusion of flight, it had apparently not occurred to Hossbach to inquire more carefully into the circumstances of Rausch's death. He had appeared to accept Johnny's explanation—that one of the ambushers had been lying in wait with a knife —and, above all, the testimony of his own eyes. He had seen Johnny trading shots with a Red sniper. In a hurried nocturnal meeting, Hossbach had advised Johnny to get out of Rio as soon as possible, and given him an address to contact in Buenos Aires. Naturally, Johnny had agreed to these proposals.

"Come to think of it," said Max, "it might not be such a bad idea if you were to leave. Helene's in B.A. She'll look after you. I can arrange it."

"For Sigrid too?"

"I need her here."

"Why? To hunt Trotsky supporters?"

Max's eyes flashed. For an instant Johnny was reminded of the inexplicable fear he had experienced when this man's gaze was first turned on him in Berlin.

I have many reasons to fear you, Johnny addressed him mentally. But I'll never succumb to you.

Max said, with strange, stiff courtliness, "You presume on our friend-ship."

There was something in the tone that made Johnny feel an unwanted, unexpected stab of sympathy, because it suggested to him that in Max's life, perhaps he really was the closest thing to a friend.

Johnny said, "I'm needed here too."

4

HEEDLESS of reverses, Emil's team forged ahead with the making of a revolution. Prestes spent several weeks writing to old comrades, appealing to shared nostalgia for the days when, as rebel *tenentes,* they had tramped from one end of the country to the other. Some replied apologetically that he had been away from Brazil for too long, that he didn't realize how much things had changed. "I long to join your movement," one major wrote, "but because you have accepted the embrace of the Communists, this would be like loving a girl with syphilis." Others were silent. But there were a few who were ready to rise and who guaranteed the support of whole garrisons. Prestes' confidence in their eventual success remained unshaken.

Bangu, the party boss in Bahia, reported that the people were ready to revolt en masse. Cato sent urgent messages from Recife warning that the pot was bubbling over; revolutionary enthusiasm—whipped up by the bitter strike at the Great Western railroad and the shabby conditions in local barracks—could not be held in check for long. The ANL, officially banned, continued to organize under the slogan of "Bread, Land and Liberty," targeting the land barons and the Greenshirts and the Anglo-American companies like Rio Light and Standard Oil. Cash flowed in via Youamtorg, the Soviet trading company in Montevideo, as well as from the local sources Harry Maitland was trying to investigate. Plans for a general strike were well advanced. The railwaymen were committed; so were the seamen and the workers at the huge Malvillis and Bonfim textile factories in Rio. The graduates of Johnny's training courses were active all over Brazil; pro-government commanders would be surprised in their barracks by a com-bined assault by armed civilians from outside and rebel soldiers from within. At the appropriate time, the capital would be blacked out by bomb attacks on the towers and accumulators of Rio Light, spreading panic and confu-sion in the ranks of the government. Lists of reactionaries who were to be shot were circulating, especially in the north. Under Emil's supervision the conspirators had even drawn up a list of cabinet ministers who would figure in a provisional revolutionary government, to be headed by Prestes. Dr. Alcibiades was to be appointed Minister of Public Health.

Inevitably there were doubters. Toward the end of October 1935, a veteran Brazilian Communist, João Batista Barreto Leite, penned a letter to Prestes counseling caution; he was promptly expelled from the party. Roberto Sisson, the key organizer in the ANL, who had hand-carried secret instructions on preparing an armed rising to regional chiefs in the north, wrote in a similar vein. He knew too much to be kicked out. He was advised that the revolution had been postponed indefinitely and was shut out of all further planning.

There was a doubter even on the Comintern's general staff in Rio. Verdi, the Argentinian, asked Johnny to have a drink with him after a meeting largely concerned with plans to disrupt the Central do Brasil, the railroad that linked the capital with São Paulo.

"I don't understand Emil's confidence," Verdi complained. "Bangu writes from Bahia that the masses are ready to revolt, and Emil swallows it. I went to Bahia. You know who's really in charge there? A mulatto baker who believes in spirits and hates intellectuals. They had a woman on the committee, a popular novelist and beautiful as well. The idiot baker drove her out. He called her into his office and lolled there in his sweaty undershirt, picking his big toe. He told her she had to make sixty-seven changes in her new book because it wasn't sufficiently socialist. I doubt if he could read it. How are we expected to make a revolution with these cretins?"

Verdi took a great gulp of red wine and added, "Either Emil is completely intoxicated or there is a missing element. What do you think?"

"I think he's a man who can't afford to go home empty-handed."

But Johnny was thinking that Verdi was right. Unless Emil had taken leave of his senses, he must have a card up his sleeve—one that neither the Argentinian nor Johnny had been permitted to see.

Verdi mentioned that he had written an editorial for a special edition of the Communist paper, to be issued on the day of the rising. This suggested that Emil had set a deadline. The revolution was going to happen. Johnny's immediate task was to find out when.

HE LAY between sleep and waking, very much alone. After the episode at the fish market Sigrid had spent three full days with him. She was loving and unthreatening, and they even had time to go sailing out in the bay, on a little skiff he rented at the marina.

She lay on the deck, sunning herself, letting the sea breeze stream through her hair.

She said, "I wish we could always be like this," and for a few hours he was completely happy.

But now he was locked in the familiar cycle of absence and distrust. Sigrid disappeared for days at a time, and sometimes he could only guess at what she was doing. She told him once that she had gone to São Paulo with Max. In his mind Johnny connected this with rumors that a leading Trotskyite had arrived in Brazil. Enemies in the family, he reflected, were often the deadliest kind.

As he lay there watching the strip of light under the shutters grow brighter, he thought about others who had been close to him: his father, who had predicted, in his soft, sad way, what would happen to the Communist movement; Heinz, who had seen it come to pass, and whose death still cried out for justice; Helene, who had heard the screams but kept the faith. He tried to picture her in Buenos Aires, tried to fathom what sustained her. Perhaps she was dueling with the Nazis; according to Verdi, Argentina was a hotbed of Gestapo and Abwehr agents. That was what all of them needed —a good clean fight, a just war against unambiguous enemies. Not this dirty war, waged in a permanent penumbra.

He heard the scratch of a key in the lock and sat up in bed.

"Sigi?"

"Good morning." She slipped into the bedroom and kissed him lightly on the side of his face, still crumpled from the pillow. "You look like a child when you're just waking up."

"I'm still asleep," he smiled at her. "You'll have to help me wake up."

He opened his arms to her, and she kissed his lips. She smelled like a sunlit garden.

"Later, sweetheart," she said gently. "I've come to collect you. There's a job Max needs you to do."

"What sort of a job?" he asked warily. He had only recently been reminded that an assignment for Max was most likely to get you killed.

"It's a security job," Sigrid said. "He wants you to booby-trap a safe."

"I'll need to get my stuff." His tools and explosives were stored in Grajaú, at the home of Vasco, the Spanish painter who had blown some of his fingers off playing with bombs on the beach.

They drove to Grajaú, and Johnny emerged from Vasco's house with a bulky black leather bag, like a doctor's.

Their final destination was a modest house in Meier, a working-class district in the northern zone, a long ride from the affluent beach suburbs Emil and the foreign comintern agents preferred. Brown-skinned children ran shouting across the road, chasing a ball, peering in the windows of the car.

A big German shepherd barked at the two Europeans from behind a screen door. As Johnny climbed the steps, it reared up on its hind legs, pawing at the wire, so that its teeth were almost level with his face.

"Down, Príncipe!" a woman called from inside.

The dog went on barking and leaping until she came and hauled it down by the collar. The barks subsided into a low rumble rising up from the belly.

"He's shy with people he doesn't know," the woman apologized, releasing the catch on the door to let them in.

She smiled at Johnny, and he recognized her at once. She was Prestes' woman, the one he had met at Petrópolis. She was wearing a sort of smock over baggy cotton trousers.

"Carlos isn't here," Olga said. "But Max told us you would be coming. The safe is in the next room."

The dog followed at Johnny's heels, sniffing and snarling, his hackles raised.

Johnny turned and held out his hand. The dog shied away, baring his teeth.

"He'll make friends in his own time," Olga said reassuringly.

It was not at all certain the dog agreed. When Johnny took another step towards the bedroom door, Príncipe made a run at him.

"Príncipe!"

Johnny stood perfectly still. The dog drew back and started barking again.

"Look, it would make things a lot easier if you two took him out for a walk," Johnny suggested. "Would you like to go for a walk?" he asked the dog, who kept on snarling but cocked his head in anticipation.

Olga did not look entirely happy about Johnny's suggestion.

"I promise I won't raid the liquor cabinet." He smiled at her.

"All right." She smiled back. "I'll just open the safe for you."

He watched from the door as she dialed the combination, conscious of Sigi and the dog watching him.

"I always thought I had a way with animals," he remarked to Sigrid.

Olga had the safe open. She took a pistol from the top shelf and tucked it inside a capacious handbag.

"How long will you be?" she asked him.

"Less than an hour, I expect."

"We'll be back sooner than that," Sigrid announced, taking Olga's arm.

"Good boy," Johnny said to the dog, and he meant it.

When the women left with Príncipe on a chain, he picked up his bag of tricks and went into the bedroom. The safe was American-made, the same type as Emil's. It would be child's play to wire it up. He started moving papers about to make room for the dynamite.

On top of the stack was a six-page document, a directive from the leadership of the Communist Party of Brazil, addressed to branch organizers around the country. Johnny scanned it quickly. The contents were mostly generalities. The directive announced that the time was propitious for action, that local party officials—hiding their Communist affiliations—should intensify agitation on every level to install a People's Revolutionary Government with Prestes at its head.

He glanced at the paper underneath. It was the draft of a letter, to be signed by Prestes. What it contained was so explosive that Johnny pushed it back into the stack after skimming the first paragraph. He went through the apartment from room to room to check that nobody was in hiding. He peered out the windows to see if anyone was keeping an eye on the place from outside and saw only the children playing ball. Still not satisfied, he went out onto the porch. There was no sign of Olga and Sigrid or of anyone more suspicious than a delivery boy taking groceries into a house nearby. He went back inside and bolted the door.

Now he studied the draft letter more carefully, trying to memorize every detail. It was addressed to the commanding general in Recife. It advised him to be ready to seize full control on December 14, the date set for a general uprising throughout the country. It stated that the courier who brought the letter would provide a verbal report on the preparations that had been made in other army garrisons.

With rising excitement Johnny ferreted through the other documents. There was a notebook with a list of officers and sergeants—some identified by pseudonyms, others by their real names—who had promised to join the revolt. There was enough information to identify some of the couriers. There were sketch maps of Rio and other cities, showing where bombs would be planted and barricades set up, but these were less interesting; he had drawn some of them himself.

Johnny began scribbling notes on a scrap of paper. He allowed himself only ten minutes, realizing that the women might return at any moment. When the time had elapsed, he took off one of his shoes and concealed the information he had stolen inside his sock.

He had not quite finished wiring the safe when he heard the dog bark outside. He hurried to the door, not fast enough to get it open before Olga had tried her key.

"You bolted the door," she challenged him.

"I thought the maid might come," he responded, as casually as he could manage.

"Have you finished?"

"I'll just need a few minutes more."

The dog shouldered his way past the women, bounded over to Johnny and started licking his hand.

"I don't know what you've done to him," Johnny said, looking at Sigrid. "But it seems to have worked wonders."

"I told him to give you the benefit of the doubt."

5

COLIN BAILEY was in his favorite corner of the smoking room, dallying over a glass of port and a copy of the *Economist,* when the club porter came in.

"Telephone call for you, Major Bailey."

The booth was in the lobby, in front of the porter's cubbyhole.

"Yes?"

"It's Norton here, Major. Cecil Norton, at Plunkett's."

"Yes, of course, Mr. Norton. How are you keeping?"

"Very well, thank you kindly, sir. Very well indeed. It's about those shirts you ordered."

"They're ready, are they?"

"Shall I send them round, sir?"

"That won't be necessary. I'll stop in myself."

It was a pleasant stroll up Regent Street, through the white light of November. Plunkett's front window on Savile Row was understated: a couple of bolts of excellent worsted, a striped jacket with the sleeves off, ready for sewing. Bailey went up the stairs and through the cutting room into the tiny back office, where a bright, birdlike little man with a tape measure draped over his shoulders winked at him and produced a Cable & Wireless envelope.

"I was out to lunch when it arrived, Major," Norton explained. "I called you as soon as I came in."

"I'll never have reason to complain about service at Plunkett's, Mr. Norton."

"Always a pleasure, sir."

Communicating with Maitland via the embassy in Rio had become more trouble than it was worth, in Bailey's estimation. Summerhayes, who had seemed a decent enough fellow, though a bit dry, was having kittens over the death of that young American—not without reason, Bailey had to concede. In his opinion, Harry's effort to set up Harvey Prince had been an ill-conceived, amateurish operation with negligible results. He doubted whether it would deceive a professional like Max Fabrikant. Still, his rebuke to Maitland had been coached in the mildest possible language. He couldn't fault the boy for trying. He had told him to use his wits—and he was, after all, an amateur. But Bailey had cautioned Harry to take no further initiatives without proper consultation and to avoid the embassy altogether. Plunkett's was more understanding, by and large, than the Foreign Office.

Bailey went back to Broadway and set about deciphering Harry's telegram, which ran to nearly three pages and must have dug quite a hole in his expense allowance. The cable conveyed both urgency and puzzlement.

Maitland had learned from Johnny that the Comintern had set a date for an armed uprising in Brazil: December 14. It seemed that Johnny had been able to lay hands on extraordinarily detailed information regarding the plans of the conspirators, including the names of senior military officials who had promised to join the revolt. He had come by all these facts in a rather unlikely way. He was a man who was under suspicion, or so he had told Maitland. He had been shut out of policy meetings and believed himself to be shadowed for much of the time. He thought that even his mistress was spying on him. Yet, by his own account, he had been left alone in the flat of the top Communist organizer, at leisure to ransack his private papers. The only explanation he could render was some ridiculous tale of a dog that barked or didn't bark, or both.

What was Bailey to make of all this? He could not rule out the possibility that Max Fabrikant was now in control and was playing Johnny back against the British. Harry was convinced that his agent was telling the truth, so far as he understood it, but Harry might not be in a position to judge. It was equally possible that the episode at Prestes' flat had been a hoax arranged by Max to expose Johnny while feeding false information to Johnny's handlers. The date for the rising could be pure invention, the list of supposed conspirators a concoction designed to send Bailey and the Brazilian authorities—if they were informed—chasing after the wrong hare.

Bailey judged that at least some of the information was authentic and highly compromising. Several of the army officers who were named, and at least one of the couriers, had figured in previous reports from Johnny. But that would fit the profile of a professional deception operation, which required a kernel of truth—a *kanva,* as Max Fabrikant would say—to make the lie believable.

What if Johnny's entire report, including the date of the planned insurrection, was accurate? That opened another question in Bailey's mind. Had his agent simply been fantastically lucky? Or was he *meant* to see the papers in Prestes' safe?

Bailey was a great believer in luck. Unless you were born lucky, in his view, you had no business dabbling in intelligence.

But luck often walked in company with other people's interests. Was it

conceivable that there was somebody else close to the Communist leadership who wanted the conspiracy to fail?

Bailey could not answer his own questions, yet he felt certain the answer
lay with one man: Max Fabrikant. He had tried to fathom that restless
intelligence, to project himself inside Max's mind. But the gulf of character
and circumstance that divided them was immense. Max's behavior since
he had arrived in Brazil had been curiously contradictory. He was clearly
attached to Sigrid, yet he had sent her back to Johnny's bed. He distrusted
Johnny, but he had not taken the simple step of getting him recalled to
Moscow.

Max might despise Emil, the man in charge of the plot, but it was
difficult to imagine the chekist propelled by anything as trivial as personal
spite. Max was a ruthless, highly efficient instrument of his masters; his
whole life represented the triumph of the Russian state party over personal
loyalties, of *raison d'état* over philosophy and morals. He was also a chess
player. If he had staged the scene in Prestes' apartment, it was as a gambit
in a larger play authorized by Moscow.

Bailey sighed. He had concluded early in his career in counterintelligence that one of the worst mistakes was to over-estimate the subtlety of
your opponents.

Max might be baiting a trap. On the other hand, his people might simply
have made a cock-up.

Sitting in London, Colin Bailey could not determine the truth. In the
meantime, the Communists were gearing up for a coup d'état, and Harry
needed guidance.

We have to run with it, Bailey decided.

He picked up his pen and started drafting a reply to Maitland. He
suggested that at this stage Harry should take his friend Colonel Plinio into
his confidence without, of course, disclosing the source of his information.

At the mayor's dinner party in Rio, Colonel Plinio had lyricized his visits
to London, and Bailey had not failed to do his homework. He had found
that his own bootmakers on St. James's Street, made shoes for the colonel
from his personal last. Bailey concluded that a Brazilian with a private last
at the finest bootmaker's in London must be both a confirmed Anglophile
and capable of discretion.

These were desirable qualities for what Bailey had in mind. It was plain
now that there were many influential men in Rio, even in the police, who
could not be trusted. There were those like the mayor who were flirting in
secret with the Communists. There were also the Fascist sympathizers, well
represented in the police, who might seize on new evidence of a Moscow
plot to eliminate anyone they did not like the look of, or even to justify a

coup of their own. De Salis had reported from Berlin that a team of Gestapo officers had left for Rio at the invitation of Colonel Plinio's chief, to provide certain technical instruction for the Brazilians. Bailey had no intention of making Hitler's friends a gift of Johnny's information.

No, Plinio was their man. He was an opportunist, no doubt, but for that very reason he could be easily influenced. It would not escape the colonel's attention that the British could help him to earn a substantial reward from his government, perhaps in the form of his boss's job.

More than a month before, Bailey had started to clear the ground by arranging for the bootmakers in St. James's to furnish Colonel Plinio with an exceptionally fine pair of paddock boots, charged to Bailey's own account. Plinio had not disdained this offering.

In Bailey's mind there was only one satisfactory way for Harry and the colonel to proceed.

"Think of yourself as a midwife," he wrote to Maitland. "Your task is to force an early delivery."

He rather liked his analogy. But to ensure that Harry did not miss the point, he went to some pains to explain it in detail.

He had almost finished encrypting the text when one of the lights at the base of his black telephone flashed on.

"Yes?"

"It's Rowecliff here, Major. There's a young man been waiting for you over half an hour."

"Tell him I'm on my way."

In his excitement over the news from Rio, he had completely forgotten his appointment.

He gave the cable to one of the girls to send off and took a taxi to a house off the King's Road that had had a For Sale sign up for as long as anyone could remember. The real estate agent whose name appeared on the sign was less than helpful when prospective buyers called to ask about it.

Bailey entered the house, using his own key, and found Nicholas twiddling his thumbs in the drawing room at the back, overlooking a small walled garden. Nicholas was one of the new crop of Oxbridge men, slightly baffled by his present environment. He was very good-looking, with curly brown hair worn a little too long at the back. Bailey had interviewed him personally. He thought that the boy would do nicely for an opportunity that had just presented itself on the other side of the world from Brazil. According to de Salis, the wife of the new German Ambassador to Istanbul was a holy terror, given to jumping into bed with any man bold enough to make an advance.

Bailey eyed his new recruit speculatively.

"Do you know Turkey at all?"

"No, sir. I'm afraid not."

"Well, never mind. How would you like to do some fucking on the Secret Vote?"

10

The Bomb Factory

A decision that is quick but
wrong is worth more than one
that is correct but too late.
—LUIS CARLOS PRESTES

1

THE revolution began three weeks ahead of schedule, and the Comintern team in Rio first heard about it over the radio.

It began far away to the north in Natal, the old port city on the bulge of Brazil, on a coast lined with strange, steep sand dunes pleated like skirts that gave way, farther north, to immense salt flats so white that they hurt the eyes.

There had been trouble brewing in the local garrison. On Friday an unpopular lieutenant called Santana had been shot in the back by one of his own men. He had them loaded up like mules in full battle kit, despite the heat. When the shot rang out, his fellow officers came running from the mess. Nobody would admit to pulling the trigger, but the officers placed half a dozen known dissidents under armed guard. They were going to face a court-martial on Monday morning.

The court-martial never took place.

Saturday, November 23, was graduation night in Natal. The new governor and the notables of the town were assembled in the Civic Theater to applaud each other's speeches and hand out prizes to the honors students of the Escola Santo Antonio. The band introduced each speaker with a patriotic tune. It was missing the trombone that evening. Sergeant Quintinho, a self-taught musician who donated some of his free time to the

371

band, had other business to attend to back at the barracks. Everybody liked Quintinho, even if he came from Pernambuco—you might as well say Timbuktu—and held rather advanced opinions for a man who had never set foot in a schoolhouse.

The governor was lost in an interminable sentence. His plight seemed desperate; he had repeated his phrase about "the flower of northern youth" twice over, and there was still no sign of a verb.

The punctuation, when it came, was explosive. Three rifle shots cracked out, then a staccato burst of machine-gun fire. It sounded as if the firing was coming from just outside the doors. Some members of the audience tried to crawl under the seats in front of them. A big man in the second row, a cotton planter, shoved his way to the aisle and stood there brandishing a pistol.

"Show me a Communist!" he bellowed. "I'm ready for those sons of bitches!"

He squeezed off a couple of rounds that blacked out one of the chandeliers and brought down a shower of plaster dust and tinkling glass.

The governor abandoned his hunt for a verb and ordered the band to strike up "Reunir."

The music could hardly be heard above the din. Women screamed as another burst of automatic fire stitched a zigzag line across the double oak doors. The cotton planter, panicking, hurled himself into the frightened mob that was trying to squeeze through the side door, using his pistol as a club.

"They're setting fire to the theater!" someone screamed.

The governor took his wife by the arm and hurried her out through the stage entrance. The police chief and a dozen army and government officials fled after them.

"Go to your posts!" the governor yelled at his followers outside. "I entrust the city to you! Fight to the last man!"

Without further ado the governor rushed to the house of an old business partner whose beautifully engraved cards declared him to be the Honorary Consul of the Republic of Chile.

"I claim political asylum!" the governor shrieked at his astonished friend. "Quick, man! Put out the flag!"

The shots were interspersed with the sound of breaking glass as looters raided the stores.

The honorary consul produced a small, somewhat faded Chilean flag.

"Haven't you got a bigger one?" the governor said doubtfully.

"I'm sorry. But you could go to the French shipping company," the consul added brightly. "They've got a tricolor as big as a house."

"Raul—" The governor's wife squeezed his wrist.

He peeked out the window and saw a squad of soldiers with their caps reversed, rebels from the Twenty-first Battalion, those trouble-makers Vargas had transferred up here from Recife. They had expropriated a supply of hooch and were swilling it from the bottle. There were rowdies in civilian clothes trooping along with them and a few men in the uniforms of the Civil Guard, that gang of political brigands he had just ordered disbanded. Nobody seemed to be resisting them. As he watched, some of them broke down the door of a fine townhouse down the street. He recognized the man who came to argue with them; he was a young engineer, the heir to a wealthy family that supported the governor's party. One of the men in civilian clothes was poking him with his rifle. The engineer's wife tried to push between them. The others dragged her away by the hair and threw her down in the gutter. They shot the engineer right in front of her.

The governor's wife fell into a dead faint.

"Don't think you're not welcome," the honorary consul said to the governor. "But there are two Mexican corvettes in the harbor. You'd be much safer on board."

"If I go, you go too," the governor snapped.

The neck of the decanter shivered against the glass as the consul poured them all drinks.

"I never knew there were so many Communists in Natal," he said unhappily.

WHILE the governor hid behind the flag of Chile, resistance to the rebels centered on the police barracks, whose rear windows looked out over coconut palms and muddy shacks along the Pontengui River.

The white stucco facade had developed eczema; it was scarred and pitted by hundreds of bullets from the rebels who had occupied the houses across the street. They were using the sign for target practice. It used to read "Regimento Policial Militar," but only the initial "R" had survived.

It was hard for the men inside the police barracks to tell what exactly the rebels wanted. Some voices in the mob were cheering the name of the federal defense minister, a notorious reactionary. Others shouted the names of Prestes and the National Liberation Alliance. Somebody was proposing an assault on the Young Ladies' Academy, an expensive boarding school for the the landowners' daughters. This idea was received with enthusiastic roars. It was getting impossible to tell soldiers from civilians; the mutineers from the barracks were arming people at random and swapping clothes with the crowd. Quite a few jailbirds had got hold of rifles. The warden of the state prison was a well-known bleeding heart, little better than a Red (if you asked the police chief's opinion). He had taken to letting some of his prisoners go home every night. It would be no surprise if he were in on the plot.

The chief of police found that fewer than forty of his men had stayed to defend their barracks. They were supplemented by a handful of army officers, including the newly appointed commander of the Twenty-first, a colonel from the south. The colonel was strutting up and down, inspecting everyone as if he were on a parade ground.

"We'll show this rabble what we're made of!" he announced to the chief of police. "Where's your bugler?"

"Noberto!" the police chief barked at a young man who was trying to make himself scarce. "What do you want with him?"

"Get up on the roof!" the colonel ordered the unhappy bugler. "Sound the call to arms!"

Noberto appealed to his chief with spaniel eyes. The police chief shrugged.

"You are a symbol of the heroic resistance," the colonel informed him.

The bugler climbed out the back window and started scaling the wall. They knew when he had reached the top, because the snipers in the houses across the street started blasting away with everything they had—rifles, pistols and machine guns. The men inside the barracks raised a ragged cheer when the strains of "Unido" rang out, only slightly off key. Then the bugle fell silent in the middle of a bar.

Several men rushed to the back windows.

"Did those bastards get him?" the colonel shouted.

"No, sir," someone called back. "He's climbing down the wall."

The colonel rushed over to see. The ground fell away sharply between the street and the river, and the back side of the barracks was a full story higher than the front. Noberto had tossed away his bugle and was crouched on a window ledge, trying to pluck up the courage to jump.

"Get back to your post, you coward!" the colonel bellowed at him, brandishing his service revolver.

This settled things for Noberto. He jumped at the same moment the colonel fired. The bullet went wide, anyway. Some of the other policemen cheered when they saw the bugler fall on his hands and knees in the soft mud, pick himself up and go zigzagging off into the shacks along the river.

"Your men haven't got a pair of balls between them," the colonel informed the police chief.

"Then why don't you go and join *your* men across the street?"

The colonel turned an ugly shade of red and went to inspect the gunners. The defenders' heavy artillery consisted of two Hotchkiss machine guns and an old Maxim gun. From the sound of things and the quantity of shattered glass on the floor, the attackers had superior firepower. But there was no sign of casualties on either side.

One of the policeman had methodically blasted out every pane of glass in the building directly opposite. Satisfied with his accomplishment, he swung the Hotchkiss round to inflict the same demolition on the house next door.

After a whole night of fireworks in which they fired off almost their entire stock of ammunition—a hundred thousand rounds—the defenders agreed to stage an orderly retreat at breakfast time on Sunday. They all took off their uniforms, descended on ropes from the rear windows of the barracks and splashed across the river to take shelter among the stilt shacks on the far side.

The city of Natal was now entirely in the hands of the rebels. In the course of the battle for the police barracks—the only military engagement of any note—the rebels had expended three hundred thousand bullets and wounded a grand total of twelve men. Ten of the twelve had been winged as they fled across the river.

A revolutionary junta set up shop in the Vila Cincinato, a government palace on the outskirts of town. Its apparent chief, a slender mulatto who was a cobbler by trade, presided over meetings with a cavalry saber in his hand. His finance minister, the town postmaster, scented them with his fancy cigars. Sergeant Quintinho, the illiterate trombone player, was appointed minister of defense. A plump, bearded lawyer whom everyone called "Papai Noel," or Father Christmas, was named minister of public works. He was the chief of the Communist underground in Natal, the recipient of secret messages from Recife addressed appropriately, if insecurely, to "Santa."

This Santa was delighted but somewhat bewildered to find himself a member of the first soviet ever formed in Brazil. He had received just three hours forewarning of the rising, when Sergeant Quintinho had hauled him out of his favorite bar in the middle of a lazy Saturday afternoon. "Orders from the top," Quintinho had said. Santa was slightly miffed that the orders had gone straight to the barracks, passing him by. This suggested that the leadership in Rio trusted the sergeants who had joined secret cells inside the army more than properly constituted party officials like himself. But Santa wasn't a man to hold grudges. What did it matter, when the wind was obviously blowing their way? The government of Natal had deflated like a tired meringue. The message would carry clear across Brazil. Santa read the announcement on the radio. It ran on the hour, every hour, in between recordings of the *Internationale* and popular songs of the north.

It was carnival time in the town. Santa came across some kids who were trying to set fire to a streetcar.

"No, no," he intervened. "Don't destroy your own property. The *bondes* are free! They belong to the people!"

The kids got the idea, soon enough. They piled into the tram and shunted off, looking for girls.

The revolution needed a treasury, so Quintinho and the other members of the junta drove down to the local depository of the Bank of Brazil. The manager refused to open the vault. He made out he had swallowed the key. Quintinho sat on his stomach but succeeded only in bringing up the man's breakfast. Someone ran down to the docks and came back with a blowtorch, which the finance minister naturally claimed as an appurtenance of his office. Half an hour later, their pockets stuffed with cash, the members of the junta were ferrying moneybags and gold bars out to their truck. As they made their triumphal progress back to the Vila Cincinato, Quintinho threw fistfuls of banknotes to the crowd.

"Revolution is fun!" he proclaimed.

2

IN THE early hours of Sunday morning, a man on a motorcycle sped through the sprawling industrial zone that lay between Recife and the big new army barracks at Socorro, out near the railyards. The road was almost deserted. Rounding a bend, the courier saw the rear end of a truck, pulled up a quarter of a mile ahead. He had almost caught up to it when the driver pulled out into the middle of the road without bothering to signal. The driver was a real road hog; when the motorcyclist tried to pass, he swung his wheel viciously, blocking off the left lane. The courier sounded his horn and tried to get round the other side. He was almost abreast of the driver's cabin when the truck lurched over to the right, forcing him off the road. His front wheel hit a ditch, and he flew out of his saddle, landing a dozen feet away in a heap of broken bones.

The truck screeched to a halt. A trim man in a pearl grey suit jumped out of the passenger side and made straight for the leather pouch that hung from the saddle of the motorbike. He found what he wanted immediately: a letter in a plain manila envelope. He scanned the contents under his flashlight, refolded the letter and tucked it away inside his breast pocket.

He produced a second letter from his other inside pocket and placed it in the messenger's pouch. Several men who had been concealed in the back of the truck stood around, waiting for him to complete this operation. One of them, a huge mulatto dressed like a stevedore, was holding a Thompson submachine gun. In his hands it looked like a toy.

"Give me that," the man in grey ordered. He took the Thompson and gestured towards the motorbike. "See if it still works."

The black man tried to kick life into the motorcycle. The engine spluttered and died.

"Enough," the man in charge said impatiently. "Take my car. They won't know the difference. Ask for Lieutenant Lamartino. You've got that?"

"Yes, sir. Lieutenant Lamartino. What if someone else is on duty?"

"Say you've got a message from your sister."

The mulatto smiled broadly.

"There won't be any problems," the man in grey assured him. "Most of their officers are in town getting drunk."

There was a big guitar festival in Recife that night, and the officers of the garrison had hired a special bus. They were not likely to hurry back before they had made a thorough inspection of the cantinas and the bawdy houses. Besides, the regional army commander had been summoned to Rio to attend some meeting at the War Ministry.

"Put the motorcycle in the back of the truck," the man in grey ordered his other men.

"What about him?" one of them asked, pointing to the motionless courier.

"Get rid of it."

"Yes, Colonel Falcão."

AT EIGHT that Sunday morning, the duty officer at the Socorro barracks, Captain Mindelo, looked out his window at battalion headquarters and saw a crowd of soldiers with their caps back to front. He recognized some of the usual loudmouths, sergeants and corporals who had been bitching since word got around that they were going to be dumped when their five-year terms expired next month. He had been keeping an eye on them since that incident on the railroad. A week or two before, a platoon had been sent from the barracks to clear the track around the Crab's Bend. The Communists had called another strike and produced a horde of women and children to sit along the railbed and stop the trains from getting through. The platoon commander, Lieutenant Santa Rosa, wasn't going to stand for any nonsense. He ordered the civilians to clear the tracks. This inspired a volley of catcalls and obscene gestures. So he told his men to fire into the air. Shots rang out, and one of them dropped Santa Rosa. He got a bullet between his shoulder blades and died on his way to hospital. The Reds put it around that he was killed by one of his own men. Captain Mindelo didn't know whether to believe this or not—the c.o. had told him in confidence that the fatal bullet was from a pistol, not a rifle—but it did not help anybody's nerves. He had received an anonymous letter warning him that any officer who stood against the people would share the fate of Santa Rosa. Some of his own company sergeants played deaf when he issued commands, so that he had to repeat them in a louder voice, trying not to show rage—or fear. Now the time had come to draw the line.

"What the hell is going on?" he yelled out the window.

"Everardo!" The shout came from one of his friends, Lieutenant Lamartino. They had served together in São Paulo. *"Você e dos nossos!* You're one of us! Join the people! We're counting on you!"

"Have you taken leave of your senses?" the captain shouted back. He was making some quick calculations. He had ten or twelve men in the HQ, including a couple of officers he could rely on. So long as they could hold out, he controlled the arsenal. He ordered his people to load their weapons and cover all sides of the building.

Then he strolled out onto the steps with a swagger stick in the crook of his elbow.

"You're hung over," he said to his friend the lieutenant. "Or still drunk. Go and sleep it off."

A private soldier drove his rifle butt into Mindelo's stomach, and the captain rolled in the dust.

The soldier took aim.

"No!" Lamartino intervened. *"Isso não se faz assim!* It's not done that way!"

Captain Mindelo got to his feet, brushing the dirt from his tunic.

"Kill him like Santa Rosa!" the rebel private urged. "Then the rest will surrender."

"You belong with us," Lamartino appealed to the captain. "The government has fallen. Haven't you heard? Why fight for a lost cause?"

"Go fuck yourself."

Captain Mindelo backed into the headquarters building and was actually inside the door before the shooting started.

He tried the telephone. To his amazement it worked. There was a list of emergency numbers, and he worked through them in sequence. There was no answer from army HQ or the governor's office. Of course, the general was in Rio, and the governor was traveling in Europe. But you would expect someone to pick up their phones. Perhaps Lamartino was not lying. Perhaps the revolution had already triumphed. Nervous and frustrated, Captain Mindelo tried the third number on the list. It belonged to the secretary for public safety.

To Mindelo's relief, his call was answered on the very first ring. The secretary himself was on the other end of the line.

"Falcão."

"Colonel—Your Excellency—this is Captain Mindelo. I am the duty officer at Socorro."

"Well?"

"I'm sorry to disturb you, but there is a revolt in progress."

"How long can you hold out?"

"How long—"

"Give me your exact dispositions," Falcão snapped.

"It's hard to be exact. We are surrounded. Except for the arsenal and the headquarters itself, the barracks is in their hands."

"You will soon receive reinforcements. You will hold out for two hours. You hear me?"

"Yes, Colonel Falcão. Two hours. And then?"

"Then give them whatever they want."

COLONEL FALCÃO, the secretary for public safety of the state of Pernambuco, was no stranger to revolt. As a young army cadet, he had taken part in the rising in Rio in 1922. Two years later, he had been in São Paulo, in the thick of another insurrection. He had joined the revolution that brought Vargas to power and played guerrilla saboteur, cutting telephone lines to stop the loyalists from calling in reinforcements. Twice a loser, once a winner. Thanks to a helpful tip from his friend Plinio Nogueira in Rio, confirmed by news of the mutiny in Natal, Falcão was confident that this time he would even the score—and win bigger than before.

As soon as he received the first telephone call from Captain Mindelo, he rushed around to the home of the acting governor, who came to the door in person in his freshly starched pajamas as if this were the most ordinary Sunday of the year.

Falcão informed the acting governor that a revolution was being attempted and demanded to know what measures he meant to take.

The poor man hesitated and blinked through his thick lenses and burbled something about how there must be no shooting.

"You're under arrest," Colonel Falcão told him.

Within the hour he had locked up two other members of the state cabinet—the secretaries of justice and finance, old adversaries of the colonel—on the grounds that they were secret Communist sympathizers.

He talked to Mindelo every half hour. Amazingly, the rebels had still not cut the telephone lines. Shortly before 11:00 A.M., the colonel learned from Mindelo that the mutineers, several hundred of them, were on their way to the city, accompanied by some of the strikers from the railroad.

Commending himself on his sense of irony, he decided to meet them in the Largo da Paz—Peace Plaza—a large and leafy public square that lay athwart the main road from the barracks to the city center. Falcão had mustered a hybrid force consisting of a couple of companies of loyalist troops from the old Soledad barracks downtown, uniformed policemen and plainclothes detectives, officers of the merchant marine, firemen and streetcar drivers, and a few sporting gentlemen from the Planters' Club. Falcão's men were outnumbered by the rebels and their armed hangers-on. But the colonel knew, as the rebels did not, that thousands of government troops with howitzers and heavy machine guns were already approaching the outskirts of Recife. They came from garrisons in the interior and from as far away as Paraíba and Maceo and João Pessoa. The colonel had wired for help as soon as he received confirmation of the rising in Natal.

In the Largo da Paz a police captain shouted at the rebels through a loudhailer, offering terms of surrender. The police had set up barricades, blocking off the exits that led to the city center. The mutineers responded with bullets. Rebel troops ran into the church on a corner of the square and climbed up inside the bell tower to take potshots at Falcão's men behind their barricades. Others set to digging trenches across the middle of Peace Plaza.

"Shoot to kill," Falcão ordered his men.

He withdrew to a modest hotel nearby to draft a radio message. This was part of his bargain with Colonel Plinio Nogueira, who had supplied such gratifyingly accurate information on the Communist underground in Recife—right down to the location of the secret radio transmitter hidden in the church of the activist priest the locals had dubbed Father Badó.

"The vast majority of the suffering masses of Recife have risen as one man," he scribbled. "Don't fail us now!" He crossed out the second sentence as too plaintive, and substituted, "The hour of victory is at hand!"

He added a few lines and signed the message with the code name of the chief of the regional directorate of the Communist party: "Cato." Cato had left his lodgings in the middle of the night, but Falcão's detectives had kept him under constant surveillance. The colonel was confident the Communist leader would be silenced before he could send a contradictory signal.

Father Badó could hardly object. At that moment, he was enjoying the hospitality of a cell in the House of Detention that the other prisoners described, with reason, as the Matchbox.

3

In Rio it was a perfect Sunday morning. There were sailboats out in the bay. They looked like flying fish beside the gleaming white bulk of the yacht *Slidell,* where the Yankee millionaire Courtland Bull gave parties that had filled the gossip columns for more than a week. By the pool at the Copacabana Palace Hotel, a circle of habitués honed their appetites on seasoned Scotch whisky. The president was at the golf club, in excellent spirits despite the fact that he had managed to land his ball in a sand trap for the third time in as many holes. Roberto Sisson, navy captain (retired) and honorary president of the illegal National Liberation Alliance, was in a less ebullient mood at the House of Detention. Together with a hundred and fifty other suspected "subversives," he had been arrested in a dawn raid by the police. The raid had not stirred a ripple on the placid surface of Carioca life. Many families were still abed, sleeping off Saturday's *feijoada.* The men of the house went to the door in their freshly pressed pajamas to take in the newspapers. The headlines were devoted to new attacks on the mayor by the local version of the League for Decency, which was demanding a halt to casino gambling, and to Mussolini's exploits in darkest Abyssinia. News of the remarkable happenings in the north would not reach the populace at large until late in the day.

Johnny was down at the marina waiting for Sigrid. He had hired a skiff and was checking the rigging. He had a day planned for them that would match the weather, a day of lolling about among the islands, a picnic lunch with some cold white wine, another chance to revisit that afternoon on the Wannsee that first brought them together as man and woman.

There she was now, pushing back her windblown hair with the palm of her hand, casually turned out in a cream cotton jersey and a navy skirt, padding along in rubber-soled shoes. She stood on the edge of the jetty looking down at him, her expression unreadable behind her dark glasses.

"Did you forget our lunch?" he shouted up at her. "I brought the wine!"

"We're not going!" she called back.

He grabbed hold of the capstan and swung himself up onto the pier. "What's the matter?"

"Haven't you heard?" That little vertical line like an exclamation point, appeared between her eyebrows. "It's begun."

"Where?"

"In the north. In Recife. There was a radio message."

"And?"

"You really don't know?"

Harry might have warned me, he thought. No, he corrected himself, Harry was right. It was better that his surprise was real. Harry had hinted that he was going to take steps to "move things along." Johnny could make a fairly good guess at what those steps had been. A word with a government minister, or more likely a friend in the police. An agent provocateur in the north sending false signals in the name of Prestes or Emil . . . the revolution had started according to Colin Bailey's timetable, not Moscow's.

"The police are out in force all over the city," Sigrid reported. "They say the president is going to declare a state of siege. Many people have been arrested."

"Emil? Prestes?"

"No. The leadership is intact. There's going to be an emergency council. They told me to get you."

THE high command of the revolution assembled that night in a doctor's house on Rua Correia de Oliveira. Emil and Nilo were late and Prestes passed the time while the others were waiting for them hunched over a rosewood secretary, scribbling notes to old friends. Johnny glimpsed the contents of one of these messages, addressed to André Trifino Correia, the adjutant of a battalion in Minas Gerais: "We are about to have the revolution. Here we cannot wait longer than two or three days. I am counting on you."

Miranda paced up and down, slapping a balled fist into the palm of his other hand, while Verdi lolled on the sofa, working his way through a bottle of *vinho tinto.* They looked as if they had been up all night.

There was a whistle from the lookout in the street, and a few seconds later Sigrid came through the door. She had tied a scarf around her head and wore a man's loose jacket and culottes.

"Where's Emil?" she asked Johnny.

"Still not here."

Verdi rolled off the sofa. "Is there word from Moscow?" he asked her eagerly.

"The message is for Emil," she said crisply.

So she had come from the radio man. Johnny could picture the scene: a wireless buried under the floorboards somewhere in a house on a hill, carried upstairs at night when they wanted to transmit. It wouldn't be powerful enough to reach Moscow Center. They would try to get messages through via Youamtorg in Montevideo. They must have been signaling frantically since the first news had come through from the north.

"You can give it to me." Verdi smiled at Sigrid, holding out his hand.

She looked at Johnny, over the Argentinian's shoulder.

Johnny said, "What difference can it make?"

"As you like." She took out a folded sheet of paper. Verdi pounced on it.

Johnny followed her out into the hall. "What about Max?" he whispered. "Is he going to cancel the operation?"

She looked at him so sharply he wished he had not asked the question. "What makes you think Max would tell me?" she countered. "Besides, it's not his decision."

"Of course," he agreed. "Are you coming back tonight?"

"I can't say."

He suddenly feared for her, racing back and forth in the new car—the Opel—between the doctor's house and the radio man and Max's bolthole, with the police out in droves.

He said, "For God's sake, be careful."

There was the hint of a smile when she replied, "You're a fine one to talk."

Their lips brushed. Then she was gone into the night.

"You see?" Verdi's voice rose shrilly from the living room. "They've got their heads screwed on right in Moscow! They don't want this thing to go off at half cock!"

He read the contents of the message out loud. It struck Johnny as the reverse of a clear directive. The center requested more detailed information on the progress of the revolt in the north and recommended that Emil or his nominee should return to Moscow as quickly as possible to review the situation. Yet the message allowed Emil plenty of rope to hang himself if he chose. "We have full confidence in the judgment of the South American bureau," it concluded.

There were a couple of low whistles from the lookout, and then Emil came barreling in with Nilo at his heels. It struck Johnny that they were both in suspiciously good spirits.

"Sorry we're late," Emil said briskly. "Let's get to it!"

The revolt was spreading like wildfire in the north, he reported. He had been in radio contact with Cato, in Recife, and Bangu, in Bahia. It would take the government days to mobilize sufficient troops to retake the coastal cities. If the conspirators struck in Rio now, those reinforcements would never be sent.

"In Rio we are unstoppable," Prestes volunteered.

Only Verdi expressed open dissent. He started quoting the signal from Moscow, and Emil snatched it away from him.

"This changes nothing," Emil announced, when he had scanned the contents. "There's no time for consultations. Moscow will back whatever decisions we take."

Verdi complained that the premature risings in the north could be the product of police provocation.

"Suppose you are right," Emil responded. His tone was patronizing, almost insulting. "That would merely prove that the police don't know their business. If the actions in the north were triggered by police spies, they'll find they have started something they can't stop."

"But the raids in Rio this morning—"

"What damage did they do? Answer me that. The police rounded up the usual suspects. They didn't bag a single man we depend on. You see? They're still fumbling in the dark."

"Or leading us on," Verdi suggested gloomily.

"I saw Jorge this morning," Nilo intervened on Emil's behalf. This Jorge was a popular writer of leftist leanings, a supporter of the ANL. "He told me the police raided his apartment. They confiscated every book that was bound in red."

Everyone laughed except Verdi.

Emil made inventory of the units they could count on. There were reliable cells inside the Third Regiment, a short drive away from the presidential palace and the barracks of the Special Police. Communists in the Second Regiment, which supplied guards for the War Ministry, were ready to seize the commanding generals and the army headquarters. Revolutionary cadets and instructors at the Aviation School would neutralize the air force base next door.

Emil asked Johnny to report on his commando teams. In neutral tones, Johnny described how the men he had trained would cut road and rail links to São Paulo and the huge military complex at Vila Militar, and black out Rio Light.

Then Prestes held up the sheaf of letters he had just written to his admirers in garrisons in the interior, directing them to act without hesitation as soon as they received word from him.

"You always leave out the navy," Verdi interjected.

They all recognized that the navy could be a decisive factor in a battle for Rio, with its long-range guns, its planes and its crack corps of marines, who supplied bodyguards for the president. Despite all the propagandizing by Sisson and the other ex-navy men on the council of the ANL—and Johnny's own efforts—the Communists had made few friends in the fleet and almost none within the officer corps. Unlike their counterparts in the army, Brazilian navy officers belonged to an exclusive caste, monied, white and patrician, hostile to ideas of social reform.

"If the navy moves against us, we're sunk," Verdi pressed his point.

Prestes dealt with this. He puffed out his chest and declared, "I can personally guarantee that the navy will join the revolution."

Johnny noticed that even Emil appeared thunderstruck by this intervention.

"I have received certain pledges," Prestes went on. "The navy is on our side."

There was no way for Johnny to tell whether these pledges were real— or whether Prestes was hallucinating.

Johnny said, "That decides it, doesn't it?"

He was rewarded with a look of sheer misery from Verdi, who returned to his bottle, and a broad beam from Emil, who roared, "We move within forty-eight hours! *Wenn schon, den schön!*"

Verdi stifled a belch with his hand. "I beg your pardon?"

"If it's got to be done," Emil translated freely, "do it right!"

WHAT troubled Johnny most was Emil's extraordinary self-confidence. The only reason for it he could fathom—unless Emil himself was a provocateur, which Johnny considered improbable—was that there was a strand to the conspiracy that had been kept hidden even from the other members of the South American bureau.

What could it be?

He stumbled across a possible clue when he went back to Vasco's house, which was being used as an armory for his sabotage squads, to check on the distribution of arms and explosives.

"We're five Thompsons and six revolvers short," the Spaniard reported.

"I don't understand."

"A kid came around with an order signed by Nilo. I couldn't very well send him away empty-handed, could I?"

"What kid?"

"They call him Escoteiro."

Johnny remembered the young tough who had played bodyguard at the meeting in Petrópolis, the one they called Boy Scout. He had been running errands for Nilo for several months.

"A charming young gentleman," Vasco commented with distaste. "He bragged about how he's been given a really big job. You know what he told me? He said he's been preparing for this for months. He said he had a dog, an animal he grew up with. He butchered it, hacked it to bits and disembowelled it. He said he wanted to drive out pity, to harden himself so he can kill without flinching."

"Absolutely charming," Johnny observed. "What would he consider a really big job?"

"He shot off his mouth about sticking a needle up Getulio's backside. But he clammed up when I asked for more. It's hard to believe a kid like that has it in him to do more than make a nuisance of himself on the bleachers. He was dressed like he was going to the game."

"What game?"

"Well, he was sporting a Fluminense tee shirt. I told him he was a bit late for this season."

Johnny could not make much sense out of this, except that Nilo was arming gunmen for purposes that remained obscure to him. But the remark about Getulio—President Vargas—stuck in Johnny's mind. Vargas was still regarded by many Brazilians as a genuine reformer, a man committed to social justice and improving working conditions. His administration included progressives; Doctor Alcibiades was one of his appointees. Though the Vargas reforms had been denounced in the Communist press as a sham, Emil's team privately acknowledged that the President's liberal reputation was a major obstacle to the revolution that was being planned.

Was it possible that Nilo and whoever was behind him—Emil or Max, or the two of them in concert—had decided to remove that obstacle by killing the president?

No, Johnny told himself, such a plot would be madness. The assassination of the president would rally the whole country against his murderers.

He tried to put himself inside Emil's mind, the mind of a desperate man who had been warned by Stalin and his creatures that no excuse would be accepted for failure in Rio, a man who had learned to trample on every moral scruple, every shred of loyalty, in order to pleasure the murderous paranoia that reigned in Moscow.

If I were Emil, Johnny reflected, I wouldn't hesitate about killing a president, if that were the key. But it would have to be done right.

Then he realized how the job might be accomplished.

On the afternoon of Tuesday, November 26, after frenzied preparations, the members of the South American bureau agreed that the revolt would start in Rio at two o'clock the following morning. Prestes signed orders that were to be carried to trusted agents inside the garrison and others that were to be taken to São Paulo and the south by couriers who would leave from the Pedro II station.

The previous day, Johnny had warned Harry Maitland that "the balloon was about to go up." They had taken their normal precautions, meeting in the Gloria church. Now there was no time for elaborate subterfuge. Early

on Tuesday evening, for the first and only time, Johnny risked a visit to Harry's home in Tijuca. He crept round the side, peering in through the windows like a burglar. He saw a handsome mulatto woman singing to herself as she stirred a pot in the kitchen, and then at an upstairs window he saw Harry himself, fiddling with his bow tie. He tossed a small stone at the insect screen. The second one caught Harry's attention.

"What the devil—"

Harry peered down and saw the strongly built figure in the shadows.

"Hold on. I'm coming down."

In urgent, staccato sentences, Johnny explained the last-minute arrangements for the rising. Maitland was relieved to learn the exact locations of the bombs that were to be planted at Rio Light, including one in Major Mackenzie's office. He was pensive when Johnny confided his suspicions of a second plot, concealed from the full membership of the South American bureau. He would suggest to Colonel Plinio that the president's guard should be reinforced, even though there was nothing solid to go on.

Johnny mentioned that Prestes had been trying to set up a personal meeting with Doctor Alcibiades. The conspirators were counting on the mayor to play a decisive role in the plot.

It occurred to Harry that the very best way to monitor the night's entertainments might be to carry on exactly as he had planned. He had been invited to a reception at Doctor Alcibiades'.

But first he had some telephone calls to make.

4

As EVENING deepened, the Cariocas gave themselves over to familiar pleasures. In Lapa they sang serenades of transient love. In the smart casinos the chandeliers blazed on whirring roulette wheels and outrageous décolletés. Along the beaches couples snuggled among the dunes and packs of feral boys—the "captains of the sand"—roamed in search of sport. The city seemed too normal, Harry thought. He wondered whether it had been the same in Paris the night before they stormed the Bastille. As usual, there were a dozen fashionable parties to choose from. But, also as usual, *the* party to be seen at was at Doctor Alcibiades'. Rarely if ever had a bachelor been known to be such a consummate host. But then, with half the women of Rio at his feet, the handsome mayor had no lack of counselors.

Harry drove up to the gates of the villa but was stopped by an apologetic policeman who asked if the Senhor would mind parking farther up the street. He found a space a couple of blocks away, and when he strolled back the same policeman checked his name against a list, making the standard confusion of first name and surname so that Harry had to assist him.

"Your security is very thorough tonight," Maitland remarked, noting that a squad of Special Police, in their bright-red kepis, were patrolling inside the high wrought-iron fence. It occurred to him to wonder whether all the extra guards were there to screen the guests coming in or to stop some of them, and possibly their host, from coming out.

"There you are, dear boy," Desmond Wild assailed him, whisky in hand, as he entered the main salon. The journalist looked subtly different, and Harry realized that this was due less to his startling red cummerbund than to the thing that was perched on top of his pate like a beaver on a rock. Harry could not help staring at it.

Wild was quite unabashed. He patted his hairpiece lovingly. "I got it through the mail," he reported. "Stella Mackenzie says it takes off about ten years. What do you think?"

"I'd say it takes off more than that."

Harry tore his eyes away and examined the crowd. There was the predictable array of beautiful women, some of them competing for the attention of Courtland Bull, who was holding court on the far side of the room near the French doors. Harry spotted a couple of cabinet ministers and several high-ranking officers in dress uniform. He recognized Admiral Wilson Cavalcanti, the navy's chief of operations. There had been a fuss about him only a few days before, when the newspapers published a photograph showing him giving the stiff-arm salute at a Greenshirt rally, and there were calls for his resignation.

The admiral was the center of another little group.

"I see that Cavalcanti is still in circulation," Harry remarked.

"He's in his element. The place is positively crawling with Fascists. See that horse-faced Kraut with him? That's Wolfgang Trott from the German Embassy. He's one of yours."

"I beg your pardon?"

"Cloak-and-dagger type."

"I'll overlook that." Harry scooped a drink from a passing waiter's tray. He wondered how a Fascist admiral fitted into Doctor Alcibiades' lifestyle. Perhaps the mayor was simply playing the old political game, being all things to all men. Or perhaps, if he were secretly involved in the Communist plot, he calculated that a party attended by men like Cavalcanti would supply him with a perfect cover—and an unassailable alibi in the event that the plotters failed.

"I must go and pay my respects to our host," Harry announced. "Have you seen him?"

They both peered around.

"The doctor seems antsy tonight," Desmond Wild observed. "He's been rushing off to the telephone. Do you suppose something's up?"

Stella Mackenzie rescued Harry from the rest of the conversation, squeezing him to her ample bosom as if she intended to smother him.

"Darling Harry," she gushed. "The major's hot for your blood tonight. But I'm going to protect you."

"Come and tell me all about it, Lovie." He winked at Desmond Wild and steered her safely out of earshot. One more gin, he thought, and they would have to carry Stella out.

"The local constabulary are all over head office," she explained jerkily. "They put one of the major's engineers in the jug. Something about a bomb, was it? They said you knew all about it. The major's on the warpath because he wasn't informed."

"I'll sort it out in the morning. There's really nothing to worry about."

"But it's not the bomb that got him so upset. It's the buses."

Harry glanced around nervously, but nobody seemed to be paying any heed to what Stella was saying. Colonel Plinio had called him in some agitation just before he had left for the party, to report that saboteurs had done a pretty good job of knocking out the motor pool at Vila Militar, smashing up transmissions and gear shifts and setting a fire in the main garage. This would delay the arrival of loyalist troops for hours if things got out of hand downtown. Harry had promptly volunteered to put Rio Light's fleet of buses at the disposal of the government. He had tried to telephone Major Mackenzie to prevent a blow-up but had learned from Stella's maid that his boss had already left home. It was bad luck to run in to the Mackenzies at Alcibiades' party, and he had no intention of risking a scene with the major, whom he could see advancing resolutely through the throng.

"That drink looks pretty sick," he said to Stella, seizing her glass, now empty except for the last said ice cubes. "Let me get you the other half."

Stella rewarded him for this gesture with a wet kiss.

He got to the other side of the room and pointed a waiter in Stella's direction. Then he slipped out onto the patio, where he caught sight of a man who struck him as almost as unlikely a guest as Admiral Cavalcanti, a muscular fellow with heavy-lidded eyes who had turned up in a lounge suit instead of black tie. He looked more German than Brazilian. He would have looked all wrong in any kind of civilian rig, except maybe a pair of boxing shorts. Harry had seen him once or twice at official functions, always in uniform. He knew him by reputation as the most feared interrogator in Rio. He was Captain Honorio Schmidt, the head of the Special Police, that athletic corps of bruisers the local wits had dubbed the Tomatoheads.

"Good evening, Harry."

Maitland turned to the source of this port-flavored voice and found Colonel Plinio smoothing his moustache. Unlike Schmidt, the colonel was in uniform, with his cap under his arm.

"I see your men are out in force tonight," Harry remarked to him. "You've even got Honorio Schmidt guarding the back door."

"So we do." Plinio acknowledged the captain with the most distant of nods, and it was plain to Maitland that these two were very far from being friends.

This encouraged Harry to whisper, "I thought Schmidt spent most of his time torturing people."

"Tsk, tsk." Plinio clucked the mildest of reproaches. "You have lived in South America long enough to understand that here a man is put in jail so that he can confess."

"Unfortunately, that philosophy is not unique to South America."

"You are absolutely right. My good friend Honorio, as you may have observed, is a student of the German philosophy. Did you happen to notice Herr Trott?"

"I did."

"He has been sent here to assist us at the recommendation of Captain Schmidt."

"Trott is Gestapo, then?"

Colonel Plinio sighed and consulted his watch. "Nearly eleven," he said. "We still have over three hours to wait."

"I wonder how many of Alcibiades' guests will still be here."

"You may well ask."

"I've been trying to work out why they were all invited in the first place. Admiral Cavalcanti, for example. It's hard to imagine that he has anything much in common with the mayor. And shouldn't he be at navy headquarters, if there's a general alert?"

The Colonel played with his whiskers. "You're missing something that's perfectly obvious, my dear Harry."

"Which is?"

"The common denominator. They weren't invited to the other party. Either by Prestes or the president. We are attending a *salon des refusés.*"

Much as he enjoyed Plinio's bon mot, Maitland's curiosity wasn't slaked by it. He felt certain that their absent host was embroiled in the Comintern plot—though he had only the most circumstantial of evidence to go on— and that the guest list was somehow connected.

"Did you find the bomb?" Harry asked under his breath.

"All three of them. I don't think Alcibiades' chandeliers will go out before the party is over."

"Where did they plant them?"

"Exactly where you said. One in Major Mackenzie's office. Two at the generator."

"I'm trying to avoid the major. He's upset about the buses."

"I'm sure the government will be happy to pay for the gasoline."

"And there's no sign of trouble yet?"

"Not a squeak. We picked up two couriers at the railroad station." He caught Harry's look and added quickly, "We're not altogether novices, Harry. We let them board their trains. If anyone was covering them, he will report to Prestes that they are safely on their way to Minas and São Paulo. The guard at the War Ministry and the Vila Militar has been changed. The duty officers were part of the conspiracy, as you thought. It was all done with perfect discretion. The war minister has put out a general alert, to take effect after midnight. We've sent out word that it's a routine fire drill. You don't look happy, Harry. Have I left anything out?"

"I don't know." Maitland had a crawling sensation at the back of his neck. Johnny's instinct could be right. The vital element might still be missing.

"Where is the president?" he said suddenly.

"I believe he went to the theater. It's Toscanini tonight. Did you know Toscanini once conducted at the Teatro Municipal? The president has a special fondness for his work. The performance must be ending about now. You know, the president is concerned to give the impression that everything is exactly as normal. He has been quite impeccable in that."

"I'm delighted to hear it. And after the theater?"

"He'll go home to bed. He's not a man for late-night parties."

"Who's guarding the palace?"

"The marines, of course. I think he likes their white uniforms. But they're good men. The best the military have."

"And they belong to the navy, as in England."

"Naturally."

"And that means that Admiral Cavalcanti gives them their orders."

"Well, the marines have their own commander."

"But the chief of naval operations is his superior, isn't he?"

"Look here, Harry. I'm not an authority on matters of navy protocol. Why don't you go and ask the admiral himself?"

Maitland frowned.

"Is there something you're driving at?" Colonel Plinio asked him.

"I just can't seem to put my finger on it. You remember I told you about one of Prestes' men, the one the others call Boy Scout?"

"I do."

"Were you able to find out anything more about him?"

"Your description would have fitted a hundred young men who have burned out half their brain cells on alcohol or ideology. Thank you." He took a glass of champagne from a waiter. "Does he matter so much?"

"I keep thinking about his threat."

"Not very specific, was it?"

"Listen, it had to do with the president. That may be what we've missed."

"You mean an assassination attempt?"

"Yes."

Plinio allowed himself a gentle smile.

"I don't see that the idea is particularly funny."

"Forgive me," the Colonel said. "You live among us, but you don't think like us. I know my Brazilians. Carlos Prestes may be a Communist, he may be ready to lie down and lick the dirt off Stalin's toecaps, but he would never authorize the murder of Getulio Vargas. He's a Brazilian, and a Brazilian of a certain class. Within that class we're not given to killing each other. This may, I admit, be a serious political defect. But it's not un-English, is it? Assassination is for Spaniards and Russians. And possibly Germans," he added, glancing at Honorio Schmidt, who had been joined by Trott, the Gestapo representative. "People who burn with the absolute. Besides, the Communists know that if they killed the president, the whole country would unite to mourn him and bury them."

"The leaders of the revolt aren't Brazilians," Harry said quietly. "They're countrymen of Herr Trott."

Plinio tweaked his moustache. "Hmmm. Well, we'll find out soon enough, I suppose. I may drop by the palace and check that Xuxu's tucked up properly for the night. I expect that, like the rest of us, he won't want to miss a thing."

Harry found it odd that the chief of the secret police referred to his president by the same pejorative nickname—Xuxu—as the Communists Johnny was dealing with.

Colonel Plinio put his cap on his head, clicked his heels and gave a comical salute.

"By the way," he said, as an apparent afterthought, "are you coming to see the fireworks?"

"I wouldn't miss them for the world."

5

THE beach was a narrow strip of sand in the cleft between the Sugarloaf and a rocky promontory that struck out into the ocean like a giant paw. The sand, now white under a crescent moon, was pink in the afternoons in the light reflected from the sheer, polished slopes above the royal palms, so they called the place Praia Vermelha, the Red Beach. To Prestes' supporters in the Third Regiment, whose barracks faced the sea, the name seemed auspicious.

Chief among them was a high-strung, voluble captain from the south. He had a knack for holding an audience, even though he delivered his lectures in a monotonous, rather tinny voice and his stature was less than heroic. With his small, squat body, his tiny head and jutting beak of a nose, he strongly resembled the macuco bird, and the nickname Macuco had stuck to him. His influence over the soldiers was the more surprising because he did not belong to the regiment. On the contrary. He had been sent to Praia Vermelha under guard, sentenced to twenty days' detention for spreading sedition among the garrisons of the south. The Fascists had tried to shoot him in Porto Alegre after the court-martial, so his family had prevailed on the General Staff to let him serve out his sentence in the capital.

The regiment treated him with the respect owed to an officer and a gentleman. He dined in the mess. He was allowed to take up residence in a family apartment in Copacabana and to come and go from the barracks as he pleased. He soon made contact with the handful of Communists and the larger amorphous group of Prestes admirers in the barracks. He arranged to circulate Communist broadsheets especially aimed at the sergeants and corporals whose terms of service were about to expire and at the ill-equipped conscripts who were crowded into ramshackle wood-and-stucco pavilions put up for the famous Exposition of 1908 and never expected to last. He singled out the men with the stomach for a fight and schooled them, in one-on-one meetings, in the techniques of insurrection.

Fewer than a dozen men out of the seventeen hundred in the regiment had any exact notion of what was being planned. Fewer than four dozen, despite Macuco's efforts, could be counted on to give instant support to an armed rising. But the little captain from the south was not intimidated by the odds against the conspirators. He was a student of Lenin and Mussolini. His bible was a well-thumbed volume of Curzio Malaparte's essay on the coup d'état, which he had read aloud to some of his recruits. He was convinced that revolutions, of whatever hue, had nothing to do with the masses; the ones that succeeded were the work of a small and dedicated elite advancing to power over a bovine majority that lacked the imagination and the will either to join or to resist. In this vision of things Macuco found a soul mate in Nilo.

While Harry Maitland took the air on the mayor's patio, Macuco was on his way back to the regiment on a bicycle after attending a secret meeting near his flat in Copacabana. In his pocket he carried the letter Nilo had pressed into his hands. He was so elated by its contents that he whistled as he pedaled along. The letter, signed with the magical name of Prestes, appointed Macuco to the command of the Third Regiment of the People's Revolutionary Army. His new commission would take effect at 2:00 A.M., when he was charged with seizing the barracks. At 3:00 A.M., he was to lead an assault on police headquarters and the presidential palace.

The Urca casino, across the avenue from the barracks, was ablaze with lights. The place was a Venus fly-trap for off-duty officers who preferred philandering to politics. Macuco's grin broadened as he saw it looming up. If he had his way, some of his brother officers would see more of the casino than they had contemplated tonight.

As he jumped off his bicycle, he noticed that there were a lot more sentries about than usual. A whole platoon with machine guns was deployed along the street side of the barracks.

Macuco started walking his bike through the line, and a fresh-faced conscript trotted up with his rifle at the ready.

"Halt!"

"*Boa noite, calouro,*" Macuco said casually. "Hello there, greenhorn. Don't you know me?"

"Password!"

"Password? We don't bother with passwords! What do you think this is, a boys' club?"

He heard the rattle of the rifle bolt and began to feel distinctly unhappy. The kid was nervous and green enough to let that thing in his hands go off. It might just be a training exercise, he thought. But if there were an alert and they searched him and found the letter—

His only recourse was to brazen it out.

"Where's your officer?" he demanded. "I'm carrying special orders."

He took out the compromising envelope and waved it in the boy's face. The soldier looked confused but did not give way.

Macuco saw the duty officer striding briskly across the patio. He was delighted to recognize Lieutenant Otelo, his closest friend in the regiment. Apart from Macuco, there were only two commissioned officers in the regiment who belonged to the party; this lieutenant was one of them.

"*Tudo bem,*" the lieutenant said to his jittery sentry. "The captain is expected."

"What's going on?" Macuco whispered to him as they walked towards the barracks.

"They've ordered a general alert."

"And put you in charge of the guard? That's a bit of luck."

"Not just luck. The colonel picked Avelino for duty officer. But he started bitching that he had a date, so I offered to swap places with him."

"They locked up the arms, I suppose?"

"That's the bad news. Julião's in charge of the arsenal. He'll fight us."

"Only if he gets the chance." Macuco grinned. "I'll take care of him myself."

"So we're going to do it?" The subaltern's face was shiny with excitement.

Macuco showed him the letter. "Go to David and Alvaro," he ordered in an undertone. "Tell them to spread the word. I'll go to the others."

When Macuco came out of the barracks, it was almost 1:00 A.M., a clear, bright night. Everything was black and white—the sentries, the revelers coming and going from their cars to the casino across the way—as distinct as in a movie. But Macuco did not spot the colonel until he loomed up from somewhere among the palms, in uniform, with his service revolver at his belt.

"It's a bit late for you, isn't it, Captain?" Colonel Ferreira challenged him. "Don't you have better things to do this time of night?"

"I don't sleep so well, sir."

"What are you doing here?"

"The same as you."

"I beg your pardon?"

"Well, there are plenty of rumors floating around. I thought I'd see if any of them are true."

"You'd do better to get a good night's sleep." Colonel Ferreira's tone was not unkindly; it was almost avuncular.

Macuco mimicked it to perfection. "At your time of life, you're the one who ought to worry about getting your rest."

"Damned impertinence!" the colonel erupted. "Go to your lodgings before I forget you're a guest and have you locked up."

"I'm afraid you're in no position to give that order."

"Lieutenant!" Ferreira called.

Otelo hurried over to them.

"This officer is to be placed in solitary confinement."

The lieutenant swallowed and looked at Macuco.

"I am assuming command," Macuco said coolly. "Colonel Ferreira will be *our* guest tonight."

The revolution in Rio was starting nearly an hour ahead of schedule because of a social indiscretion. So much the better, Macuco told himself. Even if there had been a leak, they would have plenty of time to secure Red Beach before the other side was ready for them.

6

HARRY MAITLAND lingered at the mayor's party long after Colonel Plinio left. At Doctor Alcibiades' villa, nobody took account of the clock. It was nothing unusual for his entertainments to last until dawn. One of the guests was playing "Lili Marlene" on the baby grand. Harry was surprised to see that the pianist was Courtland Bull. He played more delicately than Stella Mackenzie sang. She swayed over towards Harry, moaning the chorus in a tone that reminded Harry of a dog trying to move on an injured leg. He caught her arm before she had sloshed more than an inch of gin and tonic over his white dinner jacket.

"Kiss me, Harry," Stella said, puckering her lips and throwing herself backwards in a parody of Hollywood passion so that he had to fling his arms around her to save her from falling.

He got her upright, gave her a chaste peck on the corner of the mouth and beat a hasty retreat.

Harry noticed that Admiral Cavalcanti had disappeared. So had several of the army officers and the German attaché, Wolfgang Trott. Then Captain Schmidt came marching briskly through the salon, sidestepping the dancers. Instead of going out into the front hall, Schmidt veered right and disappeared down a corridor that led to the library and the private wing. Harry presumed the policeman had gone in search of a lavatory or a telephone. But Schmidt had not returned when, several minutes later, a man who looked more like a bodyguard than a servant came out of the same hallway, crossed the salon, and whispered something to Courtland Bull that caused the American to cease his piano playing. Bull kissed the hands of his claque of lady admirers and followed the messenger back the way he had come. Harry got a better look at the servant this time and thought he had seen him in the background the night Alcibiades had shown off his snake house. The servant was a real charmer: flat-faced, swarthy skin, woolly eyebrows that met in the middle and resembled a hairy caterpillar crawling across his low forehead.

It looked as if Alcibiades had summoned the oil millionaire to a meeting somewhere in the private wing. The mayor had made only a couple of fleeting appearances in the course of the entire evening, interrupting the merrymaking at one point to deliver a brief word in praise of the immense philanthropic efforts of the Bull Foundation and of Mr. Courtland Bull personally. These had allegedly brought new hope to the poor of Rio de Janeiro.

Harry was still puzzled by the connection between Doctor Alcibiades and the oil baron. He had little doubt that Courtland Bull had returned to Rio in high hopes of making a financial killing. He had done his homework with some help from Desmond Wild and an American press cuttings service and knew that Bull was not renowned in his home state of Texas for either philanthropy or progressive leanings. At an oilmen's gathering in Houston, he had publicly berated President Roosevelt for his "good neighbor" policy in South America, which ruled out the use of military force. In Bull's opinion, the Roosevelt approach was a license for "communism and the theft of U.S. property" all over the continent. Yet the Bull Foundation was making generous donations to Doctor Alcibiades' community clinics. The obvious explanation was that Courtland Bull saw the mayor as a coming man in Brazil and wanted to get him in his debt—so deeply in his debt that, if he got greater power, he would have no option but to hand over whatever concessions the Texan demanded. Desmond Wild had heard stories that Bull was mixed up with a consortium that was trying to sell the Brazilian navy some fancy new destroyers and minesweepers. That might explain what Admiral Cavalcanti was doing at the party. South of the Rio Grande—and north of it, too—money tended to talk louder than ideology.

Yet Harry could not satisfy himself with this simple line of reasoning. He felt instinctively that something much deeper and more dangerous was involved. Whatever was taking place in Alcibiades' private rooms must be bound up with the conspiracy that was unfolding in the rest of the city. Was Courtland Bull aware of the Communist plot? Had the mayor invited his strange collection of Nazis and right-wing admirals and generals in order to immobilize them—or to use them in some way?

It was past 1:00 A.M., Harry saw, and he sensed that it was now urgent to have the answers to these questions. He set off down the corridor in the footsteps of Courtland Bull. The hallway ended abruptly in another that led off both to right and left. There was an old German woodcut on the wall. It showed St. Denis, the patron saint of the French and of syphilitics, receiving the supplication of pockmarked reprobates. A memento of Alcibiades' former life.

Maitland hesitated. The library was off to the left, he remembered. The door was slightly ajar, and there was a light on within. He edged towards it.

"The Senhor wishes something?"

He wheeled round at the sound of the gruff voice and found Caterpillar behind him.

"I thought I might use the telephone," Harry said.

"The senhor will find a telephone in the main lobby."

"Perhaps I might see Doctor Alcibiades," Harry changed tack.

"The Doctor is not available."

There was no chance of talking his way round this brute, Harry concluded. He would have to backtrack and start again.

He was moving back along the corridor with Caterpillar shadowing his every step when he heard an inhuman wail.

It seemed to be coming from the other direction, from the end of the hall that led out into the back garden and the reptile house.

The wail turned into a low groan, punctuated by a few human syllables.

Maitland slipped by the guard and hurried towards the source of these sounds. Caterpillar was behind him but made no further move to block him until he got out the side door on to the verandah.

The groans were more distinct now. Maitland fancied that he heard a few words in English, even his own name being called.

"The Senhor must go back inside the house," Caterpillar announced, interposing his bulk on the path that led to the snake house.

"Somebody's been hurt," Maitland protested. "We must go and see."

Caterpillar drew a knife. The moonlight danced along the blade. He signaled for Harry to go back inside.

Instead, Harry struck out with his right foot. He had calculated the distance nicely. The toe of his patent leather shoe clipped the servant's humerus. He squealed, and the knife tumbled from his hand; his lower arm flopped down uselessly, as if the limb had snapped at the elbow. But he looked as if he might still have some fight in him, so Harry delivered another kick to his groin that laid him out on his back.

"You there! What are you doing?" a new voice challenged him. Harry saw a young officer in a red cap advancing between the trees and kicked the knife away into a pool of shadow under the shrubbery.

"This man is a thief," Maitland announced to the policeman. "He's been stealing from the guests. Find Senhora Mackenzie and ask her to make the identification."

His tone was sufficiently haughty and his tailoring so faultless that the young police officer swallowed any objections. He left the semiconscious Caterpillar in charge of one of his men and set off in search of Stella. Harry calculated that her condition might divert the policeman for a good few minutes more.

The groans had stopped. Harry rushed to the reptile house and found it padlocked. He pressed his ear to the door. He could hear a faint, rasping sound from within. It might have been somebody's hoarse breathing. He crept around the corner of the pavilion and peered in through a small window, streaked with dirt. Not enough light filtered through for him to make out anything very clearly. He could identify some of the glass cages, a cactus plant or two, a hairy thing on the floor just below him that must be one of the rodents or small animals the Doctor fed to his pets. A careless keeper must have let it out by mistake.

Then Harry realized that what he was staring at was not an animal. It was Desmond Wild's astonishing mail-order toupee.

He tapped on the window pane. "Desmond?"

He was rewarded with another groan, fainter than before.

He went back to the door and examined the padlock more closely. It was stout but badly rusted. With his penknife he soon managed to prise it open.

He found Desmond Wild lying on his belly, sweating hard, with a nasty blue pallor about his face.

"Harry—thank God—"

"What happened?" Harry managed to roll him over and got his back propped up against a planter.

"Bloody snakes—"

Maitland could see the bite marks now, at least two sets of them, on the left hand, and another at the side of the neck. He slashed at the neck wounds with his pocket knife and tried to suck out the poison, spitting blood over the concrete floor.

"Too late—" Wild moaned. "Got to stop them—"

Was he talking about the pit vipers? Between his ministrations, Harry glanced carefully around the darkened pavilion. He saw no sign of a snake on the loose.

He repeated his exercise on Wild's hand, wondering how long it took a double dose of the jararaca's venom to finish a man. There was only one hope: that Doctor Alcibiades had an antidote ready to hand. He must find the mayor at once. Desmond Wild was already delirious.

"Fluminense," he was raving, as if he were barracking at a football game. "Fluminense."

"Hang on, old man. I'll be back in a couple of minutes."

Maitland hastened back inside the villa. As he headed towards the library, he thought he could guess at least part of what must have happened. Wild had stuck his nose into something, and Alcibiades—or one of his guests—had gone to desperate lengths to silence him. He knew that by going directly to the mayor, he risked exposing himself to similar treatment. But Wild's life was at stake.

"Ah, there you are, Maitland! Where in damnation do you think you're off to? I've got a bone to pick with you!"

It was Major Mackenzie, lurching along the hallway. He seemed in only a marginally steadier condition than Stella. For once Harry was delighted to see him. It would be no bad thing to have a witness. There was surely a limit to the number of guests who could vanish at the mayor's party.

"How are you, Major? Why don't we both go and pay our respects to our host?"

"That's all very well, but about my buses—"

"I think he's in the library."

Harry took the major's arm and escorted him, protesting, up the corridor to the library door, which was now closed.

Without hesitating Maitland turned the knob. As he swung the door open, he sensed that the whole scene inside had been frozen. An extraordinary group was assembled within those paneled walls, and every member of it was staring at the intruders. There was Doctor Alcibiades, of course, his back to the bay window; Admiral Cavalcanti and two men from the General Staff; Captain Schmidt and the German attaché; and Courtland Bull, who was stretched out on a studded leather chesterfield, holding up a cigar between finger and thumb as if he had been using it to emphasize a point.

Doctor Alcibiades was addressing the group in an overdramatic voice, and Harry had no doubt that he had embarked on this soliloquy for the benefit of the new arrivals.

"The name of the disease derives from a Latin poem of the sixteenth century," the mayor was saying. "A poet-physician called Fracastorius invented a shepherd called Syphilis who was cursed with the pox because —so we are told—he raised forbidden altars on the hill. An engaging conceit. Wouldn't you agree, Major Mackenzie?"

"Well, I, er—" The Major took refuge in a mild coughing fit.

"Are you enjoying the party, Harry?"

"Very much so, Doctor. I'm sorry to intrude, but one of your guests needs urgent medical attention. He seems to have been bitten by a snake."

The men in the library mastered themselves pretty well, assuming they had something to hide. Their faces expressed the appropriate blend of curiosity and concern. But Harry noticed that the mayor exchanged a quick glance with Admiral Cavalcanti before saying, "I'll come at once."

As they left the library, Harry saw Cavalcanti pick up the telephone.

Major Mackenzie was flustered. "What's this about snakes?" he demanded. "And what is my wife doing with that policeman?"

There, indeed, was Stella, hanging on the shoulder of a Special Police lieutenant.

"It's some frightful mix-up," she yawned. "I think it's to do with the buses."

They all trooped along behind Harry and the mayor, who stopped to unlock a small room that smelled like a laboratory and removed a vial from a glass case.

If this was an antidote, it came too late to help Desmond Wild. Doctor Alcibiades felt the journalist's pulse, rolled back his eyelids and pronounced him dead.

He then made a great show of searching for a viper, presumably escaped from one of the containers.

"I can't think what your friend was doing messing about in here," he remarked to Harry. "These reporters like to pry into everything."

Maitland picked up Wild's hairpiece and arranged it on top of his skull. It looked slightly more realistic now that the poor fellow was dead.

"I'm afraid we shall all have to wait for the coroner," the mayor informed them. This was obviously absurd, with the police already on the scene of what appeared—at least to the Mackenzies—to be a tragic accident. Doctor Alcibiades was trying to detain them for his own purposes. The major started to protest.

"I'll just go and call Desmond's wife," Harry announced in the midst of Mackenzie's outburst.

"I didn't know Wild was married," Alcibiades said warily.

"Oh, he never showed her in public much." Harry raised an imaginary glass to his lips. As he hurried back to the villa, he saw an officer in white dress uniform—Cavalcanti—striding off towards the stables and the private parking area. Harry avoided the library and returned to the main salon, which was fast emptying. He used the phone in the front lobby to call Colonel Plinio, who answered at the second ring.

"I'm glad I caught you."

"Harry? I can't talk to you now."

"What's happened?"

"The shooting has started. It seems the Reds at Praia Vermelha can't tell the time."

"Well, it's started here, too. One man is dead. The admiral left in a hell of a hurry."

"I don't understand."

"There's no time for that now." He could see Doctor Alcibiades watching him. Fortunately, the mayor had been detained by some of his other guests. "What does Fluminense mean to you?"

"It's a football club."

"Yes, but is there some other significance?"

"Well, some Cariocas think it's a religion, like Manchester United fans. It's an odd time to be talking about it, Harry."

Fluminense. It had been Desmond Wild's last word. And according to Johnny, it was the logo on the jersey that Boy Scout had been wearing when he came to collect his submachine gun. Was there a link?

"Where is the Fluminense Club?"

"Harry—"

"This could be important."

"All right. Surely you've seen it. The club is just behind the Guanabara Palace."

"That must be it!" Maitland exclaimed.

"I simply don't have time for this."

"Meet me there as fast as you can. If you can't make it, send me some of your best men and tell them to look out for me."

He hung up and was out the door before the mayor caught up with him. He tried to slow his step as he weaved through the crowd of leave-takers among the fountains. He heard a voice calling his name but ignored it. There was safety in the crowd. Surely Alcibiades would not risk ordering the guards to stop him in front of so many people who knew him.

He got out into the street and ran east, towards his car. Nobody tried to stop him. He jumped behind the wheel, and the Beast roared away in the direction of the presidential palace. He took the avenue along the embankment and saw a company bus hurtle past, heading for Praia Vermelha.

They were going to kill the president. He was sure of it now. It had also dawned on him that Prestes' crowd were not the only people who were plotting a coup. There were at least two conspiracies, not one; Doctor Alcibiades was the hinge between them.

THERE were troops out in force in front of the little barracks across the street from the German Embassy. As Harry cruised up the Rua Farani toward the palace, he saw an official car coming through the gates. The marine guards saluted; one of them stepped out into the road and waved for Harry to stop and let the limousine pass. He recognized the War Minister in the back. The government was starting to take things in hand.

He slipped the Beast into gear. Glancing into the rearview mirror, he saw an American car behind him. The driver turned in at the gate. One of the marines came up to question him. The guard looked in the back of the car and saluted smartly. Harry could see the white dress uniform, the soft, blurred features that lay too much to one side, as if a sculptor molding the head from clay had tired of his work and pushed it away with the flat of his hand. It was Admiral Cavalcanti, and the marines were letting him through.

There's nothing I can do about it, Harry told himself. If he tried to explain his suspicions, even Colonel Plinio would think him insane.

He drove to the end of the street, rounded the corner and pulled up near the members' entrance to the Fluminense Club. The sidewalk was deserted. The door to the club was locked, the windows shuttered and barred. His pen knife would not work this time. There was no sign of life inside the main building. He walked up the street, inspecting the high fence. It might be possible to shimmy over and get into the grounds.

I'm probably making a complete fool of myself, he thought.

He made a tentative jump at the fence, got a hand on the ledge, but was nicked by something sharp—probably broken glass—and let himself fall back.

At the same instant a truck came screeching around the corner. The driver swung up onto the pavement, so that Harry had to flatten himself against the wall to avoid getting hit. Half a dozen men in civilian clothes tumbled out of the back. Harry looked at the odds and decided to leave his gun in his pocket. It was better to try to bluff his way out. But if this was Boy Scout's mob, that would not be easy.

A black sedan double-parked next to the Beast.

To his relief, Harry saw Colonel Plinio get out.

"I'll handle this one," he shouted to the men who were menacing Maitland with their pistols.

"Breaking and entering, Harry?"

"I wasn't sure you'd come."

"O ye of little faith. Allow me to introduce Doctor Mota, the manager of the club."

Harry shook hands with a tall, saturnine man with slicked-down hair. The club manager did not look amused at being rousted out at two in the morning.

"I told Doctor Mota that you had information about a break-in," Plinio said.

As the manager fumbled with a bunch of keys, the colonel asked in a whisper, "What's all this about a dead man?"

Harry explained what had happened to Desmond Wild. "And Cavalcanti went straight from the mayor's house to the palace," he added. "I saw him go inside."

"What of it? A patriotic officer, guarding his president from a Red revolt? The admiral's trying to make his comeback, that's all. I hope you're not wasting our time."

Doctor Mota had managed to open the door. He led them into the trophy room, where he satisfied himself that nothing was missing.

"I can't think what else anyone would want to steal."

"If we wanted to get into the palace from here, how would we do it?" Harry asked.

"There's a door on the basement level," the manager reported. "But it's locked and bolted from the other side. The president's secretary has the key."

"Will you show us where it is?"

Their heels clattered on the stone steps. There was a strong odor of chlorine and wet towels, but no indication that anyone had been down there since nightfall. The manager kept switching on lights.

The door to the palace gardens certainly looked like a formidable obstacle. It was lined with sheet steel. Harry noticed a faint smell of oil, as if the hinges had been lubricated not long before.

He tried the handle. The heavy door swung open silently, and they looked out across sculpted gardens towards the pillared facade of Guanabara Palace.

"It's unthinkable!" Doctor Mota exclaimed. "And where are the guards?"

"I think I see one of them," Harry remarked. He pointed to a pair of boots jutting out from under a clump of bushes.

The colonel's men pulled the body out into the moonlight. The marine had been stripped to his underwear.

"He's been garroted," Maitland announced, inspecting the thin red line around the neck. "Piano wire, I should think."

Colonel Plinio turned to one of his men. "Euclides, go back into the club and telephone the president's secretary. Tell him we're coming in."

"What if they're already holding the palace?" Maitland interrupted. "Remember, at least one of the attackers is wearing marine uniform."

Plinio thought about this for an instant and said, "You're right. We'll have to chance it." He detailed Euclides to call for reinforcements and to check the state of affairs at the guardhouse at the street entrance to the palace.

"You'd better clear out," he said to Maitland. "This business isn't for foreigners."

"Not on your life. Who brought you here in the first place?"

Colonel Plinio's retort was swallowed up by a sudden burst of fire from the palace.

"Stay behind me," he instructed Harry. Then they were all running along flagstoned paths, splitting into two groups at the foot of the terrace, where two broad flights of steps led up to the top.

A bullet whined past Harry's ear, and he looked up and saw a pretty, dark-haired girl taking aim at him from an upstairs window.

"Comunistas miseráveis!" she screamed above the shooting. "Communist bastards!"

Harry recognized the president's younger daughter. "Don't shoot!" he called up.

The First Family appeared to have barricaded itself on the second floor. A gun battle was raging around the main staircase. It was hard to tell friend from foe in the thick pall of smoke; some of the drapes had caught fire. Men in marine uniforms and a few in civilian clothes were trying to storm the stairs. They were being held off by a smaller group on the landing, in the same medley of attire. Neither the attackers nor the defenders seemed sure whose side Plinio's men were on, and the policemen were equally confused.

There was a pause in the shooting while everyone tried to assess the new odds.

"Look at that one!" Maitland pointed to one of the marines crouched in the stairwell. "He's wearing street shoes!"

"Give yourselves up!" Plinio ordered the attackers, using his best baritone. "Your cause is lost!"

This was received with a volley of fire that failed to drop a single policeman. The colonel's men took cover behind the furniture and blazed away as if they were in competition to see who could exhaust his ammunition first.

"Where's the rest of the guard?" Plinio muttered.

"You might also ask, where is Cavalcanti?" Harry responded.

Caught in a crossfire, the attackers soon lost their fight. Several made a run for the doors, were wounded or intercepted and gave themselves up. There was a young one, a better shot than the rest, who seemed bent on holding out. He had crawled away to reasonable cover behind the banisters and winged two of Plinio's men. But soon he was the only one left fighting. There was a door behind him, now riddled with bullet holes. He had not yet tried to use it for escape.

"I'll bet that's Escoteiro," Harry whispered to Plinio. "Let's try to take him alive. If you cover me, I'll try to get around behind him."

Crouched low, Harry made a zigzag dash for the corridor behind the staircase. He found a terrified maidservant who showed him how to get into the drawing room on the far side of the staircase.

He saw that the drawing room door opened inwards. He turned the handle and was gingerly pulling it towards him when several bullets splintered the wood. One of them cut a neat slit in the sleeve of his dinner jacket. He threw himself to the floor.

At the same instant the door flew towards him, just missing his head, and a solid weight dropped on his shoulders. The reek of blood and urine filled his nostrils. He rolled onto his back and found himself clutching Boy Scout's head to his chest. The boy terrorist stared at him out of one glassy eye. The other had been blown away. Harry's hands were sticky with blood and grey matter and ooze that he did not care to analyze. He started to wriggle free of the body, trying not to throw up.

Then, through the smoke, he saw something that made him forget the state of his stomach. The lobby was full of white uniforms, and at their head Admiral Cavalcanti was leveling his revolver at Harry. He held the gun like a duelist, his right arm outstretched, his left folded away in the crook of his back.

Harry rolled again, but his foot snagged in the belt of Boy Scout's stolen uniform. Cavalcanti's finger tightened on the trigger.

His attention riveted on Maitland, the admiral did not see Colonel Plinio until he struck. Very precisely, Plinio cracked the butt of his own gun against the admiral's wrist.

The bullet went wide, and Cavalcanti dropped his revolver, cursing violently.

"I'm sorry, Admiral," Plinio said blandly. "But you nearly made an irreparable mistake. This is one of our friends."

Maitland got to his feet and met Cavalcanti's eyes. They were pink with hate. He wondered if the admiral had really made a mistake.

"Did you kill this one?" Harry challenged him, tapping Boy Scout's body lightly with the toe of his shoe.

"What of it?"

"Was it necessary?"

"He was Communist scum. Who cares how they lose their skins?"

Colonel Plinio took out his cigar case and offered it to Harry and Cavalcanti. The admiral shook his head impatiently.

"You might dismiss your men now," Plinio remarked to him. "The police have everything under control. By the way, where were your marines when the president was under attack?"

"The Reds staged a diversion at the front of the palace."

"That's very interesting. We obviously missed quite a lot."

Colonel Plinio noticed the president's secretary trotting down the stairs and excused himself.

He returned almost immediately with a beatific smile on his face.

"I regret to inform you, Admiral, that it is my duty to place you under arrest."

"I am answerable only to the military authorities!"

"And to the President of the Republic."

"What is the charge?"

"Treason and attempted assassination."

"This is a farce! You have no evidence!"

"On the contrary. The president has just received a personal telephone call from Doctor Alcibiades, our honorable mayor. I believe you know him. Doctor Alcibiades made the denunciation."

Cavalcanti gaped, then exhibited a mastery of nautical abuse that awed everyone within earshot.

"Are you ready, Admiral?" Plinio pursued. "Or would you prefer to be left alone with your revolver? I believe that way is preferred by officers of the old school in some countries. No?"

Cavalcanti glowered at him, and Plinio motioned for the detectives to disarm him.

"You see," the colonel murmured to Harry as they made their exit together. "We're Brazilians. Even the worst of us. We don't kill the bull."

1

On a damp day in London in early December, Colin Bailey put aside Maitland's report and pictured the man who had written it. He imagined Harry, on his verandah in Tijuca, listening to the birdcalls in the forest and puffing at his cigar while the lovely Luisa brought *caipirinhas*. Or perhaps he had gone south to his ranch, to fish for *dourado* with a bright spoon on the end of his line—silver, of course, was best—or to chase roebuck through the pampas grass in a mock-up of a West Country hunt. He had certainly earned a holiday, and Bailey would have liked nothing better than to chuck the London drizzle and join him.

Only two military units in Rio joined the Communist rising in the early hours of November 27. One was the Third Regiment, which never managed to leave Praia Vermelha. The commandant managed to get away from the rebels and held them pinned down for a time with the aid of a loyal machine-gun company, while the government sent reinforcements round in the buses of the power company. The War Minister took personal charge, talking to the commandant from a public telephone at a gas station on the corner of the Avenida Pasteur. The rebel chief, a bantam captain they called Macuco, refused an offer of conditional surrender. At first light, the government sent warships and fighter planes to shell and strafe the barracks into submission. The flimsy wood and stucco pavilions caught fire like dry tinder. At about one in the afternoon, the surviving rebels gave up the ghost. They were marched through Botafogo in front of jeering crowds. Macuco and the other ringleaders were locked up in an old prison ship, the *Pedro I,* that was resurrected for the occasion.

The other unit that rebelled was the School of Military Aviation out at Campo dos Afonsos, fifteen miles west of the city, next to the headquarters complex in the Vila Militar. This was a cadets' affair led by a Communist instructor. The Air Force regulars at the base next door were alerted in good time. But the school was hard to isolate, because the security gate was unfinished and there was not even a simple fence around most of the perimeter. Captain Socrates drove in at the wheel of a roadster packed with his friends. Though apparently drunk, he arranged the seizure of arms and training planes, shot a loyalist lieutenant and marched off at the head of his cadets to capture the air base next door. His party was met by government troops, shot up pretty badly and the whole business was over by sunup.

The revolt never got started in the Second Regiment or at Army HQ, because the leads from Johnny enabled the authorities to arrest all the key conspirators before the deadline arrived at their destination. Prestes' couriers to garrisons outside Rio never left.

The population at large was never involved. Confronted with the prospect of imminent rout, Communist labor organizers disregarded their orders to lead a general strike. The special edition of the Red paper, *A Manhã,* calling for a mass rebellion was seized by the police before it could be distributed. There were a few acts of sabotage—the vital switch point at Barra do Pirai on the Rio–São Paulo line was blown up—but they had no effect on the outcome of events.

The defeat of the coup attempt in Rio coincided with the collapse of the risings in the north that had triggered it. The ragtag army that invaded Recife's Largo da Paz was shot to pieces by regular army units with field guns. The most notable achievement of the revolt in Recife was that the celebrated German airship, the *Graf Zeppelin,* en route to the city on a journey that had started in Bathurst, had to alter its flight plan.

Hearing rumors of disaster, the festive junta that had held power in Natal since Saturday night boarded a merchant ship in the harbor and tried to make off with the money it had looted from the local bank. They were pursued and overtaken by two navy cruisers. "Santa," the Communist chief, was found to have his share of the loot sewn up inside his trouser cuffs. Rebels fleeing inland were hunted down by gunmen hired for the job by the local land barons.

What was the meaning of the whole affair? Bailey had one version in front of him—a torn-out page from the New York *Times* forwarded by a friend in Manhattan. The *Times'* man on the spot, a certain J. W. White (filing from Buenos Aires to avoid Brazilian censorship), gave the Communists a clean bill of health. In his judgment, the revolt was "not communistic, as reported by the federal authorities. It was socialistic and strongly nationalistic." The demands of the rebels were said to be "mild."

Bailey had read far too much of this sort of thing over the years to let it anger him. He had read it in cables from ambassadors as well as newspaper articles. Sometimes he detected the hand of a Goebbels or a Willi Münzenberg. More often it was a matter of people believing what they wanted to believe and screening out conflicting evidence. This was known to happen in intelligence, as in other trades; hence the difficulty he experienced in persuading some of his colleagues that Hitler was as much of a menace as Stalin, or vice versa. There were relatively few people, in Bailey's experience, who found much satisfaction in unearthing facts that flouted their preconceptions. Yet a willingness to confront facts of that kind —even a delight in so doing—was, in his estimation, one of the hallmarks of an intelligence professional.

So he sat mulling over the questions that Harry's report, though masterly in its way, had left hanging.

One thing was clear: Johnny had played his role superbly. Thanks to his information, a police agent had triggered the mutiny in Natal weeks before the revolt was supposed to begin. A clever bit of provocation by the police chief in Recife had ensured that the second barrel went off, forcing the hand of the Comintern chiefs in Rio. Thanks to Johnny again, the planned coup in Rio was dead in the water hours before it began.

Yet the affair could have ended in tragedy if the assassination plot had succeeded.

There were several things that intrigued Bailey.

Was there a Gestapo agent—perhaps Nilo—inside the South American bureau?

What role, if any, had Max Fabrikant played in the events of November 27?

Had the Fascists mounted a provocation of their own, hoping to use the murder of the president by Reds as a pretext to seize power for themselves?

Whose side was Doctor Alcibiades on?

Bailey had not exhausted the list when C. called him on the direct line. "Would you care to stop in for a spot of tea?"

Bailey stowed his papers away, shut up the filing cabinet and reversed the little cardboard sign that read "Open" on one side and "Locked" on the other.

"Norton at the Foreign Office sent round another billet-doux from their chap in Rio," C. said casually, when they were settled on either side of the teapot.

"Sir Evelyn Paine?"

"Quite so."

"Is he bleating again?"

"On the contrary. He seems to be pleased as punch. The president called him in to express his undying gratitude to His Majesty's Government for saving the country, or words to that effect. Sir Evelyn would be glad to be told, at some point, exactly what he did."

"I'll look into it."

"I gather your young friend Maitland has done rather well. Bring him over so I can get a look at him next time he's in London."

"With pleasure."

"But you might tell him to try not to behave quite so much like something out of John Buchan's thrillers."

Diplomatically, Bailey allowed this to pass without comment.

"Your chap Johnny doesn't cease to astonish me," C. went on. "I thought we might do something for him, to show appreciation and all that."

"What did you have in mind? A bonus?"

"Good heavens, no. I thought I'd ask the prime minister to get him a gong in the Birthday Honors. Naturally, we couldn't allow any mention of it in the papers. But the gesture would count for rather a lot, don't you think?"

"Johnny had an Iron Cross once," Bailey observed. "I believe he chucked it overboard."

C. looked at him as if he had just broken wind.

"I am referring to the Order of the British Empire," C. said grimly.

"It would mean something to Johnny if the King presented it in person."

"Good God! The man's a bloody foreigner!"

"Quite so." Bailey's expression was respectful but unyielding.

Part III

THE PATH OF
THE DEAD

(1936)

We Communists are all dead
men on leave.
——EUGÈNE LEVINÉ,

leader of the
1919 Munich revolt,
shortly before he faced
the firing squad

11

The Chinese Method

I was not averse to the idea of
shooting a property owner simply
because he was a property owner,
so it was reasonable that the
propertied class should punish me
for my intentions.
—GRACILIANO RAMOS,
Memórias do Cárcere

1

THE days slipped by, and Rio returned to its normal pursuits. Driving along
the Avenida Atlântica, it was hard to believe that the country had just
escaped a revolution. Even the principal conspirators were not acting like
hunted men. Harry Maitland made a tour of the beach suburbs and caught
a glimpse of Emil and his wife taking their constitutional along the beach.
Emil had his jacket over his arm and had rolled up his sleeves. He wore
suspenders and a grey felt hat tilted back from his forehead. He was an alien
presence, a world removed from the copper-skinned beauties lazing on the
beach. But he did not look like a man about to jump into a ditch. He might
have been taking his summer holiday at Sochi, on the Black Sea.

Harry was puzzled that Emil and his team had not simply cut and run
after the failure of the revolt. What were they waiting for?

Johnny brought some of the answers in the early days of December.
They met at one of their old haunts, a crowded gaming room in the
Necrópolis, at the back of the Copacabana Palace Hotel.

He's nervous, Maitland thought, watching Johnny from across the roulette table. He wasn't surprised when Johnny bet on red, signaling that he

wanted a personal meeting somewhere else. Maitland placed some chips on number four, one of several locations both men had memorized. Johnny bet on twenty-four, which gave them the hour.

Their rendezvous took place at midnight in a seamen's tavern near the docks.

"Are you all right?"

Johnny was swaying a bit.

"A drink too many," he said. "I'll live."

"Is Max on to you?"

"He has suspicions."

"Nothing more?"

"That's enough, isn't it?" Johnny came back savagely. "He'll move when he's ready. Not before."

"What's going on? Why haven't they tried to get out?"

"They think they're still in business."

"What?"

"You heard me. They're planning to try again."

"Who?"

"Emil. Prestes. Nilo."

"They're crazy."

"Perhaps. But Emil has persuaded Moscow to back them."

"I can't believe it."

"Believe what you like. I brought you a copy of his report." He handed over a squat manila envelope.

"How did you get it?"

Johnny gave him a lopsided grin. He said, "I've been in this business for longer than you. No offense, Harry."

"Of course not."

PLAY it long, Colin Bailey urged in his cables. If you jerk on the line, the big fish will break it.

But Harry didn't like it. Johnny refused the stack of white five-pound notes he offered, the bonus Colin Bailey had finally extracted from C. and the misers in the accounts department. Perhaps Johnny's disinterest was a professional reflex. What was he going to do with the cash in Rio? But Johnny also seemed reticent and evasive. He refused point-blank to talk about Sigrid now, which Maitland thought was a bad sign. Maybe shared adversity was pulling him closer to old comrades.

The Comintern network began to fall apart a few days before Christmas, on the night Vasco's house went up in smoke. Johnny had described the Spanish painter's home in Grajaú, where explosives were hidden in the cellar and under the stairs and the walls were covered with surrealist canvases of melting clocks and women whose bottoms turned into cellos. By Johnny's account, Vasco had to be awarded full marks for guts, if not for brains. Since he'd lost three fingers from his painting hand in that accident on the beach, he had been training himself to hold a brush in the other hand. He even practiced gripping a brush between his toes. According to Johnny, his footwork was pretty good.

In the wake of the mass insurrection that never took place, Vasco had been left sitting on top of three hundred homemade bombs and a truckload of dynamite. Harry first learned what had happened from his morning copy of *O Globo.*

It wasn't clear how it started. A cigarette, carelessly dropped on the floor, sparks from the charcoal stove in the kitchen, a lamp overturned in a domestic squabble, a child playing with matches . . . Johnny's hunch was that canisters holding the two components for a binary explosive, the chemicals he had described to illiterate recruits as "rat poison" and "salt and pepper," had been allowed to get damp in the closet under the stairs. The soggy cardboard was eaten away, the chemicals mixed—and the roof of Vasco's house blew off.

The Spaniard rolled out of the place with his clothes on fire and a terrified child in his arms. Distraught neighbors, their own houses ablaze, called the fire brigade and the police, who went in for Vasco's two-year-old daughter. She was charred like a nicely barbecued chop but still living. The neighbors were ready to tear the little Basque limb from limb, though he swore blind that he thought the boxes he was storing contained only fruit and eggs. The police probably saved his life. They hauled him off for a spiritual session on the *morro* of San Antonio, the headquarters of the Special Police.

Vasco knew quite a few of the Comintern bosses, at least by sight, because of all the boozing and talking that had gone on in his upstairs living room. And of course he knew Johnny, though only by the cover name "Pedro" that he used among the party's military cells.

When Harry learned of Vasco's arrest, he concluded that the time had come to roll up the Comintern team in Rio, and advised Bailey accordingly.

With Vasco and hundreds of local Communists in jug, it was surely only a matter of time before Emil's group accepted defeat and scattered to the four winds. Harry wanted to catch them before they got away. They had a good deal to answer for.

There was still a risk that Johnny could be blown. But in Maitland's view the risk of using the most sensitive information from his agent—the covers and hideouts employed by Emil and his team—was much less than before.

If the Russians wanted to find an informer, there would be a long list of suspects to choose from, starting with the little Spaniard. Max Fabrikant would not be easy to shake off. But with any luck Max would soon be enjoying the hospitality of one of Colonel Plinio's lockups.

Bailey agreed with this assessment. His cheerful response came back by cable: "Shop the buggers!"

1

BETRAYAL is easier for little men, Harry thought. Easiest for those, like Iago, who were so stunted in spirit that they could consume their lives in the service of the "green-eyed monster," jealousy, or in pursuit of trivial advancement. Johnny was built to larger proportions.

In the months he had known the German, even though most of their meetings were hurried and furtive, Harry had found much to admire and even more to identify with: the restless appetite for adventure, the readiness to gamble against the odds. He had never known Johnny to be mean-spirited, even in discussing the men he had most reason to hate.

So Maitland was not altogether surprised when Johnny balked at the final stage of betrayal. The Englishman had anticipated a long conversation and a deal of soul-searching, so he had prepared his ground carefully. He had rented a flat in Flamengo with a view of the bay and filled one of the kitchen cupboards with single-malt scotch.

"The place is yours whenever you need it," he told Johnny.

Maitland cooked dinner himself. It was spaghetti bolognaise, one of the few dishes he was confident about preparing. He was not offended when Johnny showed more interest in the whisky than the food.

"Colin and I both feel that it's time to roll things up," Harry said tentatively. Johnny listened while he rehearsed his reasons.

Then he astonished the Englishman by quoting one of Iago's lines from *Othello:* "I follow him to serve my turn upon him."

He laughed at Harry's expression. "You see, my visits to the Richmond Theater weren't entirely wasted."

Johnny's smile faded. He had heard grim stories about what the police were doing to the Communists who had been rounded up. The Brazilians might eschew capital punishment, but they were quite inventive when it came to torture. It was one thing to betray the plan for the revolution; it was quite another to deliver up comrades to the certainty of physical abuse. In many ways it would be easier for him to shoot Emil or Max himself— he had thought of doing so, more than once—than to turn them over to the police.

He said to Harry, "Who do you want?"

"All of them. The whole South American bureau."

"Prestes, too?"

"Prestes most of all."

No, Johnny thought. I won't give them Prestes. The man is washed up, whether he knows it or not—a sleepwalker stumbling about in a violent dream. Let him run back to Moscow, if Stalin still wants him.

Johnny said, "I don't know where he lives."

Maitland was fairly sure he was lying but resolved not to push the issue. In part of his being, Harry realized, Johnny still belonged to the revolutionary cause. There were people and things he would never betray.

Emil was not one of them. In Johnny's eyes, Emil had blood on his hands —the blood of Heinz Kordt and of thousands of young Chinese herded to the slaughter. If Johnny had had second thoughts, they would have been academic; he had already given Maitland the address of Emil's luxury apartment in Ipanema.

Nilo also deserved whatever was coming to him, Johnny thought. Miranda was one of those—Johnny now knew—who had helped talk Manuilsky and the Comintern into believing that Brazil was ripe for revolt. Johnny would lose no sleep over him. Verdi, the *simpático*, eloquent Argentinian, had proved more clear-sighted than the others, which possibly made him more dangerous.

Johnny was drinking too much whisky and knew it. But he didn't slow his intake. He didn't like playing God with people who had shared the same trenches.

One more name was unavoidable.

Harry mentioned it first. "What about Max?"

"I don't know where to find him," Johnny responded. This time his answer was truthful. He had not seen Max since before the brief, premature spasms of the risings in the north. From what Sigrid had let drop he was convinced that Max was still in Rio, but had no idea where he had gone to ground.

"We have to deal with Max," Harry observed.

"You mean, before he deals with *us,*" Johnny completed the thought for him.

"Exactly."

"Did you have anything particular in mind?"

"Sigrid." Harry watched him as closely as a surgeon making an incision. He knew he was cutting into the most sensitive part of Johnny's life, the part he had always refused to expose.

Johnny shied away angrily. "I won't have her involved," he said flatly.

"She's our only way to Max." Since Johnny did not contradict him, he risked the next sentence. "And this is the only way you can get her away from Max."

"What do you want to do?" Johnny's words came slowly and painfully.

"Put a tail on her."

"No!" Johnny shouted. "You can't expose her to the police! If it has to be done, I'll do it myself."

"Please think it over, Johnny. She's bound to spot you. She's a professional. She's been trained by the best. A man your size and color can't just blend into the Carioca street scene. Brazilians might have a chance."

"No," Johnny repeated, shaking his head.

"It doesn't have to be the police," Harry said patiently. "I'll organize everything myself. I can hire a few smart kids. I'll make out I'm a jealous husband. They don't have to know anything more than that."

Johnny thought this over for a bit, pacing round the room. He reminded Maitland of a large animal circling its cage.

Suddenly, Johnny rounded on him.

"You could do it anyway," he said. "You could set watchers on me and follow Sigrid when she leaves me."

"I could," Harry agreed, "but I won't. Not unless you give your consent. You matter a damn right more to me than Max Fabrikant."

This must have been a turning point, because the next time Johnny spoke, he said "I'll help you. But you must promise me you'll get her away safely."

"You have my word."

This will be the end of it, Johnny pledged himself, and Sigrid. We'll leave together, and that will be the end of betrayals.

But the figure of a player on a Richmond stage loomed up out of memory, mocking him. He heard the actor's lines as clearly as if he were squeezed into those cramped front stalls instead of standing at the window before the shadowed, sensuous curve of the Sugarloaf:

> So I will turn her virtue into pitch
> And out of her own goodness make the net
> That shall enmesh them all.

3

THE police took Emil and his wife in the flat in Ipanema. Emil watched with a bemused smile as they tinkered with the safe. When they attacked the steel door with a blowtorch, he squeezed Lenka's hand. He had watched

Johnny booby-trap the safe with enough explosives to blow all of them into the sea. There were worse ways to die, he thought.

His smile faded when they opened a hole in the steel shell and there was still no explosion. There were more than a thousand documents inside, plus his address book and receipts for payments to agents in Brazil.

"Johnny," he murmured under his breath.

"What's that?" one of the policemen rounded on him.

"Nothing."

I'll give them nothing, Emil promised himself. Not even that. If I start talking, it will never end.

He tried to take Lenka's hand again, but they tore her away.

In the police barracks, when the questioning began, he puffed out his chest and said, "I could tell you these things, but I won't. You can do what you like. I have been tortured by the police before. Even in China."

The one behind the table with a face like a skull gave a thin smile of recognition.

"We are an underdeveloped country," he said. "But not in this."

THEY took Miranda and his girl. They caught Verdi. They got the Romanian. The surviving conspirators roamed the city like vagabonds, from one transient address to the next.

The police released Miranda's mistress, Elza, after only a few days in captivity. She was a pretty, illiterate country girl, little more than a child. Nilo, who had managed to elude the police dragnet, was convinced that she had been blackmailed into working as a police spy. She seemed to be allowed extraordinary access to her man inside the House of Detention; this weighed against her more heavily than anything else. Nilo claimed she was passing on whatever she gleaned about the Communist underground to the Department of Political and Social Order.

The girl was lured to a safe house rented by Nilo and interrogated for several hours. Max was the chief inquisitor, but he remained offstage. Sigrid drove back and forth between his hideout and Nilo's flat with lists of questions and rough transcripts of what the girl had said.

In the early hours of the morning Max pronounced the death sentence.

There were five men present in Nilo's apartment when it was carried out. Nilo wanted to garrote her; he maintained that this was the quietest way and would sow terror among other potential police spies. They found a length of clothesline in the laundry and looped it around Elza's neck. But they were rank amateurs at the business of killing. The first man who tried to choke off the girl's life lost his nerve. Nilo poured strong liquor for all of them and told another to try again, while Elza lay gasping, blue-faced, on the floor. The second executioner was so terrified he lost control of his bowels. It was quite a long evening before they were ready to bury the body, rolled up in a rug, in a garbage dump up in the hills.

Johnny was not invited to this entertainment.

He heard about it from Sigrid. She was oddly detached, as if she were describing a scene from a film, as if the murdered girl existed only on celluloid.

"Was it really necessary?" he asked.

"She knew the punishment." She frightened him when she added, "I would have done the same."

You can't mean that, he pleaded with her silently. This is the madness that Max has induced. At the same moment he was trying to push away the sense of guilt that twisted his stomach. He had given the police Miranda—and the Communists had claimed Miranda's girl, who meant the world no harm.

Later Sigrid responded naturally, even ardently, to his caresses. But he found that his sexual desire was less potent than the image of the terrified girl with the rope sawing at her neck.

When Sigrid left him in the early morning, Harry Maitland's men were watching.

Left alone in the apartment, Johnny felt chilled to the marrow, despite the muggy heat. He threw his head back against the pillows, because everything in the room was churning. He was trying to stay afloat in an empty, hostile sea.

It wasn't easy to follow a car in Rio without being spotted. Private automobiles were still a rarity; even the wealthiest Cariocas patronized the streetcars (first-class, to be sure) or took a taxi. Harry Maitland had allowed for this. He had engaged four trackers: one on a bicycle, posted at the corner nearest Johnny's flat, two in taxis, one in a Ford. It would have been easier and certainly less costly to turn the whole affair over to Colonel Plinio. But Harry did not want to break faith with Johnny. He had to be the one person in Rio Johnny could trust unconditionally.

In any event, Harry's painstaking preparations paid off: by the end of the morning his trackers had identified three separate addresses that were new to Maitland. By the end of the day he was reasonably certain that one of them, on the Rua Guerreiro, was Max's bolthole.

At this point keeping faith with Johnny involved one further complication. Johnny had insisted that, when the police closed in on Max, Sigrid must be with *him*, safely removed from the scene.

Harry intended to keep that promise, too.

*   *   *

ALMOST a week later, Johnny lay on the sofa of the apartment in Flamengo that Harry had rented for him, listening to the rain. It fell in sheets, blocking off his view of the bay. It had even silenced the drums rehearsing for Carnival. A sour taste of tar bubbled up from his pipe, and he tossed it aside.

She must come soon, he told himself. It's been nearly three hours.

He had managed to persuade Sigrid to come for a drive up into the hills, out of the sweltering city.

The sudden, torrential rain had turned their side road into a mudslide, and they had had to reverse back down. He had clutched at one excuse after another to prolong their outing. He had found a little restaurant whose outside walls were adorned with murals depicting its specialties—turkey, suckling pig, rabbit—and ordered two bottles of wine to give himself an excuse to dawdle at the table. She'd become impatient, driving too fast for the wet road, so that they'd skidded on the way back to the city and dented the right fender on a slow-moving oxcart, whose owner had to be pacified with enough *milreis* to pay for a new bullock.

When they parted, he prayed that the thing was over: that the police had come and gone from the house on the Rua Guerreiro, that Max had been exorcised from their lives for good. That she was coming back to him. He had told her to meet him at the new address in Flamengo. Harry was the only other person in Rio who knew it. Max's people couldn't touch them here.

He heard the scratch at the door, like a cat asking to come in, and rushed to open it.

She was holding a little umbrella but was soaked to the skin. Her eyes were wild, her breathing shallow and too fast. She looked on the edge of tears.

"What's happened?" His alarm was unfeigned.

"The police—oh, God. I think they took Max."

"You saw them?"

"They were in the street, outside the house."

"You came straight here?"

"Of course not. I went to Danton." This was a code name for the new radio man, whom Johnny had never met.

"And?"

"The same story."

He fussed over her, fetching towels from the bathroom, pouring stiff drinks, trying not to show the tremendous sense of relief that suddenly possessed him.

It's over, he thought. Within twenty-four hours, two days at most, they would both be on a boat bound for Buenos Aires. They might run into Helene; Johnny had learned that, after Max had sent her south, she had stayed on in Buenos Aires to run the Comintern liaison office there. But there was no reason for Helene to suspect anything. She would know by now that the whole operation in Rio had ended as a rout. He and Sigrid would be accepted as two of the survivors.

After Argentina, Europe. He would take Sigrid to England. He would have to tell more lies to begin with, but later she would understand. She had to.

He felt her forehead. She was running a fever. But already she was on her feet, picking up her bag and umbrella.

"I can't stay," she said. "I have to go back, to make sure—"

"You're not leaving," he said firmly. "I'll go. I want you to lie down."

"Johnny?"

"Yes?"

"What will they do to Max?"

"He'll get by. He's a professional. Eventually Moscow will arrange a trade." He said whatever came into his head. But he realized as he spoke that it was all too glib. His rosy sense of relief had ebbed away, giving place to more complicated, less complacent emotions. In part of himself he was sorry for Max, sorry for what the interrogators would do to him, sorry that Max had survived more formidable opponents to end up in a Brazilian cell. But fear was the larger emotion: fear that Sigrid would never be free of Max's mystique, fear that he would always have to lie to her.

He watched her staring around at the unfamiliar surroundings, the low-slung leather chairs, the colored prints of sailing ships on the walls.

"How long have you had this place?" she asked.

"Not long." He didn't like the tilt of her question. "Listen," he said, "I want you to take a nice hot bath and go to bed. I'll go and check on Max." He remembered, just in time, to ask, "What's the address?"

No AMOUNT of bad weather could stop Carnival. The Avenida Rio Branco was afire with plumes and satins and sequins. Even inside the penitentiaries, they took up the chorus of *Cidade Maravilhosa* and *Pierrot Apaixonado*.

Max Fabrikant was hundreds of miles removed from this scene, comfortably ensconced in a suite at the Crillón in Buenos Aires, a fitting address for a Belgian businessman of evident means. He had explained to a sympathetic clerk that his luggage was being sent on after him. He could pick up the basic necessities at the elegant emporiums along the Calle Florida, behind the hotel.

He had eluded the police trap that Harry Maitland and Colonel Plinio had laid for him in Rio by purest chance—luck, if you were a gambler at heart. Max had taken his morning stroll later than usual and had paused to read the newspapers over a *cafezinho* at a restaurant around the corner from his apartment on the Rua Guerreiro. Even a novice would have found it difficult not to notice the four men who got out of the unmarked car that pulled up directly opposite his building.

Max indulged in a second coffee, sipped it slowly and read the editorials before he resumed his stroll. He observed that plainclothes detectives were covering both the front and back of his building.

He walked on in the most leisurely way in the world but his mind clamped down like a steel trap.

Johnny, he told himself. It had to be Johnny.

He had changed his lodgings after Emil was arrested. Only Sigrid knew where to find him. He was certain that she hadn't consciously betrayed him. That same morning, shortly before he had left his apartment, she had telephoned to report that Johnny had a new address—something Max was quite sure no one in the party had authorized. At the time he had accepted the information merely as proof that Johnny's survival instinct had not atrophied. Now it enlarged all the other question marks over Johnny's activities in Rio. What had Johnny been doing in the cemetery in Botafogo after dark? Why hadn't Emil's safe blown up?

I abandoned my duty, Max reproached himself. I sheltered Johnny because I became an emotional fool, because I imagined I saw something in him I once had, because he is worth—even now—a thousand sniveling Emils. He betrayed the revolution, and I smelled it. But I still refused to interrogate him—I even avoided seeing him—because he was the one person in my life I needed to believe was above suspicion.

I'm going to make all of that right, Max promised himself.

Max left Rio the same day on a steamer registered in Panama and bound for Buenos Aires. The police were all over the docks, but he met the captain of the boat in a waterfront tavern and bribed him to have his passenger smuggled on board inside a packing crate. Deliberately, Max did not entrust his fortunes to any of the Communist cells that survived around the docks. In the age of Stalin and Hitler, he had learned, faith was uncertain; the venal side of man was one thing you could count on.

Now Max's room at the Crillón was quiet except for the scratch of his pen against the writing paper. He waited for the ink to dry, then folded the letter and tucked it inside a plain envelope.

He straightened his tie, put on his hat and took the elevator down to the marbled lobby.

The uniformed doorman ushered him out.

"Would you like a taxi, sir?"

"No. I think I'll walk."

"Perfect day for it, sir."

The girls along the Calle Florida wore light summer dresses and exuberant hats. He picked out one of the boys who were ogling them and beckoned with his finger.

"Señor?"

"Would you like to earn some money?"

"Sí, señor."

"I want you to deliver this for me, as quick as you can." He held out the envelope and an Argentinian banknote with an impressive number of zeroes.

The boy goggled at it.

"All right?"

"Macanudo, señor!" the boy exclaimed happily. He raced off after only the briefest glance at the inscription on the envelope. It was addressed to the military attaché at the German Embassy.

"I'M GETTING you out tonight," Maitland told Johnny on the last day of Carnival. Colonel Plinio had told him of Max's escape. Colin Bailey agreed that it had become too dangerous for Johnny to stay on in Rio.

"Sigrid comes, too," Johnny said.

"Naturally." Maitland cleared his throat. "Does she know—anything?"

"I haven't told her."

"Will you—I mean—"

"Maybe. When she's ready."

Harry wondered then, as he had wondered often during the time they had spent together in Brazil, at the hidden reserves that kept this man going, that enabled him to withstand the appalling loneliness of his double life.

He gave Johnny the address.

"You must be there no later than six in the morning. I'll see you on board myself. How will you introduce me?"

"I'll think of something. She knows I have my own contacts. She won't ask too many questions. After all, she's a professional."

JOHNNY told Sigrid to meet him at the Babylônia Club. It was a place where a single woman wouldn't raise eyebrows. He had gone there with Hossbach. The fact that the place had a sizable German clientele was an asset rather than a liability, in Johnny's estimation. It wasn't the sort of place where the police would expect to find Communists on the run.

He had told Sigrid nothing about the boat, nothing about the escape plan. He preferred to face whatever questions she might raise at the last minute. Besides, he knew she had been to see Olga. He couldn't risk letting anything slip.

In the early evening—the eve of Ash Wednesday—Johnny fought his way through laughing crowds to the safe house in Flamengo. He wanted to pick up a few of his belongings and destroy any papers he would no longer need.

He made a bonfire in a metal wastepaper basket. It gave out more smoke than he had expected. As he struggled with the broken sash of the window above the sofa, he saw them in the street below, their red caps bobbing as they piled out of their truck. Special Police.

They might have been coming for one of his neighbors, but instinct told him they had come for him.

I must have been followed, he thought. Only two people knew that address: Sigrid and Harry Maitland. Whatever Sigrid might suspect, she would never tip off the police.

But she might have told Olga, Johnny realized. Or Max. Could she have told Max? Johnny thought back to the morning they had stopped at a rustic café on the winding road to Petrôpolis, the morning Max was supposed to be arrested. Sigrid went to the rest room and was gone for what seemed like a very long time . . .

This is madness, he told himself. The police weren't coming for him. They were going to somebody else's apartment.

But he could hear the clatter of their boots on the concrete steps. He peered down the fire escape. They were coming up that way, too. They must have his building surrounded.

A terrible, debilitating lassitude crept over him.

Let them come. Let it end.

He trained his thoughts on the girl he loved, waiting for him alone and scared among the dubious clientele of the Babylônia, and his energy began to seep back.

There was still a way out. He had tested it before. He had never liked to live in a place that had only one back door. He flung himself out the back window, onto the little platform at the top of the fire escape, and was greeted with a volley of rifle shots that ricocheted off the wall.

He clutched at the pipe running up to the roof and started to haul himself up, hand over hand.

Then he was running stooped across the rooftops, trying to keep his balance as he weaved to avoid the shots from below. There was a sudden, searing pain across his leg. He gasped and felt himself slithering down the steep angle of the roof. He flailed out with his arms, seeking support. His legs shot out into space. He was gone. No, not quite. He grabbed hold of the gutter. It creaked but held. A bullet drove brick dust into his eyes. Mustering all his strength, he heaved himself back onto the roof, threw himself at a chimney and clung to it. Then he was off again, willing himself not to feel the pain, not to remember that one of his legs was dragging, a dead weight that could no longer support him. The red caps were jumping up and down in the street, trying to follow his passage.

Afterwards it was hard to imagine how he had made it to the end of the row of houses, down another fire escape and through the swirl of samba dancers into the side door of the church before they caught up with him.

Inside the church there was the smell of incense, the sweet melodious chime of organ music. Lighted candles sputtered in a brass stand at the back. Johnny took a spill from the box, lit it and placed it beside the others.

He saw a rubicund priest, preceded by shiny altar-boys swinging censers, moving towards the altar to conduct evening Mass. The pews were mostly deserted; the last night of Carnival was no time for Portuguese priests. Johnny slipped past the side altar, with its great gilded image of the Virgin, and found the door to the vestry. The largest cassock in the closet failed to cover his calves, but it would have to do.

The rest of the night had a dream quality tinged with the musky scent of the *lança perfumes* the young swells in their flash convertibles were spraying into the sashaying crowd.

Johnny emerged from the church as a mock priest in his stolen cassock and lurched toward Lapa. As he approached the door of the Babylônia Club, the pink lights of the sign overhead stained his face like grenadine in a milky cocktail.

The dream turned to a nightmare when he entered the club and saw Sigrid sitting with Hossbach and a second German.

His first instinct was that whoever had sent the police for him must have sent the Gestapo for her. But he could not walk away and leave her. He resolved to brazen it out. He calculated that the Germans wouldn't risk a gunfight in public. He would find a way to get Sigrid to safety. When he joined the table, Hossbach's drunken maunderings and the other German's distant curiosity began to persuade him they both had a real chance. Hossbach seemed to suspect nothing. The encounter was purely accidental.

Johnny's first instinct was sounder; there is a limit to coincidence. He learned that as dawn broke on Ash Wednesday, lying flat on his back inside a ring of Special Police, with the muzzle of his own pistol jammed against his teeth, so that the end of Carnival tasted of blood and gunmetal.

4

SIGRID made sure the police had gone before she slipped out of the Babylônia Club. The rain was coming down in buckets, washing out the last night of Carnival. She huddled in the doorway while the doorman ran to the end of the street to fetch her a taxi.

She watched the red fez bobbing back towards her under the huge candy-striped umbrella, minus the taxi.

"I'm sorry, Senhora," Zé apologized. "With the rain, and all the people going home . . . perhaps one of the gentlemen could take you." He glanced back at the door to the club.

"It's all right. I can walk." She clutched her light stole to her throat.

"But your beautiful hair!" Zé was mortified. "Wait!" He rushed back inside and returned with a handsome umbrella with a mahogany handle banded with silver. "Take this."

She saw the monogram. "But it belongs to someone."

"The cheapskate hasn't given me a tip in weeks. You take it."

"You're marvelous," she said, and gave him a peck on the cheek.

Zé Pimenta beamed and saluted with his pasteboard scimitar.

She lingered as if waiting for the downpour to ease.

"The police gave everybody a scare," she remarked.

Zé spat. "The boss must have forgotten to give someone his squeeze."

"Did they arrest anyone?"

"Not here."

"I saw a priest as well. I thought somebody must have died."

Zé laughed until he was doubled up. "If somebody died in the sack," he confided when he was sufficiently recovered, "they'd drag him up the street." He pointed to the entrance of a rival establishment. "Bad for business." He started chuckling again. "And that wasn't a priest. That was Senhor Gruber. He's a real joker."

"Did he leave alone?"

"He had his pals with him. A couple of Germans in their bibs and tuckers. It looked like they were out to make a real night of it."

Zé watched appreciatively as the girl trotted off. That one was a looker, all right. A lot more class than you usually saw at the Babylônia. It was a crime to let a girl like that walk herself home.

The rain stopped as suddenly as it had started, as she crossed into Cinelandia, pursued by wolf whistles from the elegant young rowdies in a passing convertible. One of them tried to spray her with cologne. She smelled musk and tired lilacs.

A drunk came out of a doorway with his pants around his knees and staggered after her, mouthing obscenities. She tried to walk faster, but her high heels snagged in the cracks of the broken mosaic sidewalk. She took her shoes off and padded on in her stockinged feet.

Her chest was tight, her breathing shallow, when after a few false turns she found the address Johnny had given her. She hesitated at the foot of the steps. The place looked like a sailors' dosshouse. There was a blue light in the front window, behind a torn shade. The hallway reeked of urine and stale beer. There was something sprawled across it, a mound of flesh that shook and shivered with its snores.

She looked back along the street and saw two men in tight-waisted suits and fedoras, like the detectives from the club.

She gripped the furled umbrella and stepped gingerly over the sleeping hulk. It gave a terrific snort and rolled over on to its back, so that she had to skip sideways to avoid a flopping arm. At the same instant a hand reached out of the shadows and clamped her shoulder.

"You'd better come in here."

The voice was quietly authoritative. She moved with it, into the room with the blue lamp. The other furnishings consisted of a bed with an iron frame, a scuffed dresser with a bottle of whisky on top and an armchair with the stuffing hanging out. There was a pile of soiled sheets in the corner, partially concealed by a tan leather suitcase.

"Not quite the Ritz, I'm afraid."

The man was about Johnny's height but younger, with a warm, open face. You didn't learn his kind of English in a language course. She knew there was something very wrong about that.

She felt ready to drop, but she stayed on her feet, close to the door, when he offered her the chair. A moth was trying to batter itself to death against the lamp.

"Would a drink help?"

"I don't think so."

"I could try to rustle up some breakfast," he said doubtfully.

She was trying to read him from his eyes, his hands, the way he crossed his legs when he sat down on the end of the bed. There was nothing threatening about him. The hands were sensitive, the hands of a painter or a surgeon.

"Who are you?"

"A friend of Johnny's."

"The nameless kind?"

"You can call me Harry, if you like. I do think you ought to sit down and rest." He was eyeing her muddy stockings.

She lowered herself into the armchair. It was the first concession.

"Where is he?"

"I don't know. We met at the Babylônia Club. There was a police raid. He said it would be safer if he left first."

"Go on."

"He'd been shot."

"Shot?"

"Not seriously. But he lost a lot of blood. And he was dressed like a priest."

Maitland frowned. Johnny must have fled into the church where they sometimes met—it was only a few blocks from the safe house. Had he tried to leave a message?

She repeated what the doorman had said about the Germans. She remembered that one of them was from the embassy. Maitland made her describe them, just to be sure. There was no doubt about it. Johnny had left the club in the care of the Gestapo. It was not encouraging news. However dim-witted, Hossbach had had plenty of time to mull over what had gone wrong at the fish market and to formulate some questions Johnny might have trouble fielding.

Sigrid asked, "Is he safe?"

"I'm sure everything will be fine," Harry sought to reassure her. "He's a hard man to stop." He looked at his watch. "Besides, we've got plenty of time. Why don't you curl up for a bit? I'm sure Johnny will turn up."

She shook her head, but he could see she was fighting to keep her eyelids open. She accepted a swallow of whisky, and ten minutes later, she was fast asleep in the armchair. It wasn't an easy dream. Her teeth chattered a bit, and her head rocked against her shoulder. Gently Maitland took the cover from the bed and draped it over her.

When he raised the blind almost two hours later to let the morning light into the room, she woke immediately, sitting up wide-eyed like a cat.

"Johnny—"

Maitland had had time to go over all the possibilities. That Johnny was being held at the German Embassy or a Gestapo hideout. That he had been turned over to the police. That Max's people were onto him. That he was safe but forced to lie low for the time being.

Since he knew nothing for certain, except that the boat for Buenos Aires would be leaving within the hour, he decided it was best to lie a little.

"He's been held up," Harry said. "He wants you to go on ahead. He'll be joining you soon."

"You saw him?" she asked eagerly.

"There was a message."

"Why didn't you wake me?"

"I thought you needed your strength. Look, we'll have to get our skates on."

"Skates?" This colloquialism eluded her.

"I promised Johnny I'd put you on that boat."

"But my clothes—" She looked ruefully at her rumpled party dress, her ruined shoes and stockings.

"The morning after Carnival, people make allowances. You'll find everything you need for the voyage in here." He hoisted the suitcase. "I hope they fit." He handed her an envelope. "Money, tickets, passport. There won't be any problems," he rushed on, leaving no space for objections. "You know who to contact in Buenos Aires?"

She obediently recited the Comintern cover address Max had told her to memorize, a language school on the Calle Florida.

"There is something you must do first," Harry instructed her. "As soon as you arrive—before you talk to *anyone*—you are to call on this man." He showed her a card and let her study it until they were both satisfied she had committed the contents to memory. The name was one of those funny English ones that belonged in a cottage with a rose garden and a privet hedge: Bradbeer.

"I won't leave without Johnny," she said defiantly.

"You must," Harry said patiently. "It's what he wants."

"Then let him tell me himself!"

He saw the fear and suspicion in her face and assumed it was all bound up with Johnny. "I'll get him out," Harry promised. "He means a lot to me, too."

She finally acquiesced, but her expression did not change.

She's got every right to be bloody scared, Harry thought. Johnny disappears with a pair of Gestapo hoods, and now she's being batted around between unexplained Englishmen.

He got her on board the boat and tipped the steward to take her flowers and champagne. He lounged around the harbor till he saw the steamship leave. He hoped that Bradbeer would have sense enough to know how to play her. It was a damn tricky thing to spell out in a telegram.

He had something more pressing to worry about now. What had become of Johnny?

5

IF JOHNNY stood on tiptoe, he could touch the ledge of the tiny barred window high up on the wall. If he pulled himself up, like a gymnast on the parallel bars, he could see the spire of a church planted on top of a rocky hill. He had attempted this exercise only once, because the guard who kept watch behind the Judas hole in the steel door had rushed in and beaten him about the kidneys and on the inside of the knees with a rubber truncheon. The guard had gone on thwacking at the soles of his feet when Johnny had fallen to the ground; he had had to bite his lip till it bled so as not to cry out.

He had been made to stand in the middle of that vertical tomb with its shiny walls, rocking lightly from side to side, wishing that he were a horse that could sleep on its feet without falling. It was the second day; he could tell that from the light outside. He was not completely alone, because he could hear the clatter of the wooden clogs—the *tamancos*—of other prisoners in the exercise yard, and at night his neighbors would tap on the wall in a simple, interminable alphabet code. Three taps for the letter C, then sixteen for O, and he had to memorize each number, swaying on his aching legs, in order to work out that someone who believed in him just because he was here was spelling out COURAGE.

The furnishings of the cell consisted of a canvas hammock with the ropes removed in case the prisoner thought of hanging himself and a stinking, open latrine in the concrete floor, which he had been permitted to use only once, before the first interrogation. He had flung the useless hammock over the hole; it did not relieve the stench.

He rocked on his heels like a pendulum, back and forth, back and forth, each time closer to the wall, till his shoulder was scraping it, till he let his weight relax against it, till he was sliding down onto the floor. The clammy concrete under his backside felt better than a feather bed. He did not hear the clack of boots along the corridor, the jangle of keys against the lock; he was lost to all that.

"On your feet!" the warder screamed.

They were beating him again on his feet, his buttocks. They slapped him across the face repeatedly because he still wouldn't wake up, and he tasted salt. They got him by his armpits and hauled him up, but when they let go, he fell down again. They kicked him in the balls, not hard enough to make him black out completely, just hard enough to make him yell and get his eyelids open.

"That's enough!" another voice called out. "The captain's ready for him!"

Somebody thrust some clothes into his arms—not his own but a pair of filthy pajamas several sizes too small and *tamancos* that chafed his toes. They pushed him out the door, along the hallway, down the flight of metal steps that rang under their heels. Through the gaps Johnny could see the creature they kept in a cage under the stairs. There was a bald patch on the top of his head, pink and round like a monk's tonsure, from which the matted strands of hair stuck out like straw; he had his hands over his ears, trying to shut out the clash of metal. When Johnny and his escorts reached the foot of the steps, the creature crouched against the bars of his cage, a big man whose force was spent. He stuck his palm out between the bars, begging for food or cigarettes, and the guards jeered at him.

"Emil?" Johnny croaked, not quite believing.

"Know this one, do you?" One of the guards moved to the cage, thrust his fist under Emil's chin, and forced the head up so that Johnny could see his eyes. They rolled in their sockets, milky and unfocused as marbles.

"Come on then," the guard taunted the man in the cage. "Say something to your friend."

"Oh, God—" Johnny stared at the hand, still held out in supplication, at the rigid, hooked fingers, at the blackened, suppurating scabs where two of the nails had been pulled out. "I never meant this," he mumbled in a low voice, in German. Emil Brandt gave no sign of recognition. One of the jailers spat into his cupped palm. As they shunted Johnny away, he craned his head back and saw Emil dab a finger into the spittle and sample it with his tongue. His face was full of wonder.

The interrogation room was like any other. Indifferent to day and night, windowless, the harsh blue-white glare of a high-wattage bulb stabbing at the prisoner's eyes.

They made him stand in front of the table, and the same thin-faced policeman who had taken down his answers the first day droned through the same set of questions.

"Name?"

"Franz Gruber."

"Birthplace?"

"Vienna, Austria."

"Family?"

"An estranged wife. Erna Gruber."

"Occupation?"

"Importer."

"Religion?"

This is where they bogged down before.

"I have no religion," Johnny said, as he had said the first time.

"That is not an answer. I am not permitted to leave any of the spaces blank."

"Put down seeker, then," Johnny said, remembering what he had told the *cachaça* priest in Recife and wondering whether Father Badó had ended up any better than Emil.

"*Pesquisador?*" the thin man looked up from his paper. His face in the shadow was that of a hungry carp butting the glass of an aquarium. "*Que espécie de culto é?*"

"Just put it down."

"I'll put down Pentecostal," the carp said brightly. "They've heard of that."

The next instant he was on his feet.

"Leave us," Honorio Schmidt said curtly, flicking a riding crop across the palm of his idle hand.

Thoughtfully the chief of the Special Police tilted the lamp away so it was no longer shining directly in Johnny's face. He picked up a straight-backed chair and set it in front of the table.

"Sit," he instructed Johnny, taking his own place on the other side of the table. "I believe you smoke." He offered his leather cigar case. "Whisky?"

Johnny refused none of these offers. He suspected none of them would be repeated.

Captain Honorio pushed a tumbler of scotch across the table. Johnny took one gulp, then another. It was stupid to drink on an empty stomach, but he didn't care. He wanted to blot out the image of Emil reduced to a dribbling idiot in a cage. His fatigue was not enough to overcome it. His hatred for Emil and what he represented was not personal enough to justify it. So he sucked at his glass and puffed at his cheroot as if he expected them to be snatched away at any moment.

"You spoke to your friend, Herr Brandt," the policeman said softly. "What did you say to him?"

"I don't know what you're talking about."

"When he came to us, he was very arrogant. Like you. I put a few questions to him, and do you know what he said? He said, 'I know but I shall not tell.' He said he had experienced every kind of torture in many countries. Even the Chinese method. He defied me to do better. You see the result. He underrated us. I hope you do not make the same mistake. Have some more whisky."

Johnny drank it, though his head was starting to swirl.

"I want you to know that I respect you. Not your exalted political convictions but you, the man. Others have identified you. Your little Spanish friend, the one you taught to make bombs, talks about you like a lost lover. We have documents—heaps of them—that mention a certain Pedro. We know that is one of the names you use. We even know the name you were born with, Herr Lentz."

Johnny kept his lips glued to the glass. It was a long time since he had heard anyone address him by his family name. It hardly belonged to him now.

"I am going to ask very little of you," Captain Honorio pursued. "A capable stenographer is waiting to take down your confession. In case you are tired, I have prepared an abbreviated version for you—" He held up the document. "All it requires is your signature. Here." He handed over several closely typed pages.

"This is absurd," Johnny said after several minutes. "I've never heard of most these people." His prepared confession named various prominent Brazilians as members of the conspiracy. Some of the names were strange to him; others were simply bizarre. Among the alleged plotters was Colonel Plinio Nogueira, the head of the political police. Honorio Schmidt was playing some game of his own. The really puzzling thing was that the document referred to various crimes Johnny had supposedly committed in Germany.

"It's a joke," Johnny went on. "Even if I sign, who would believe any of it?"

"We don't need to fuss with all of that. Here, use my pen. Then you can get some sleep between real sheets."

Johnny struggled to reason through the fog of exhaustion and cheap whisky. What harm would it do to sign? Sigrid was safe—well she must be, mustn't she? Or else Schmidt would have mentioned her. Harry Maitland would see her through. Harry was the man he needed now. Harry would sort it all out with the government and put this cocky mock-German back in his box.

Why wasn't Harry here?

Was it possible he didn't know what had happened?

"You're making a mistake," Johnny said to his interrogator. "It's clearly a case of mistaken identity. I'm a simple businessman. There is—"

He did not finish the sentence because Captain Honorio erupted from behind the table and kicked his chair from under him. His cheek came to rest in a puddle of whisky.

"Someone—will vouch—" Johnny groaned.

"Yes."

"There's someone—who will vouch—"

"For you?" Captain Honorio was engaged in polishing the toes of his boots on his prisoner's buttocks. This appeared to give him considerable satisfaction. "Who is this simpleton? Well? I'm waiting!"

There was no response from the captive, who was lying on his belly, making a noise between a moan and a snore from which it was no longer possible to segregate syllables.

The policeman cracked his riding crop across the prisoner's face. It drew blood but no clearer message.

"It would have been easier to sign," Honorio said to an audience of one. He strode back to the table and pressed the buzzer.

His assistant came in and ventured a floppy salute.

"Has His Excellency arrived?"

"Yes, Captain."

"Then please show him in."

Wolfgang Trott, who had taken to styling himself Graf von Trott in the company of Brazilians of German stock, came into the chamber at a brisk march and greeted Honorio with a floppy version of the Hitler salute.

He inspected the large body laid out on the floor and remarked, "He looks ready for shipment. Are you finished with him?"

"Not quite. He hasn't signed yet."

"Perhaps I might be of some slight assistance."

Captain Honorio inclined his head.

"We don't have a great deal of time," Trott went on. "My superiors are very anxious to spend some time with your friend. There is a German ship leaving for Hamburg on Thursday."

"There are some formalities that must be concluded—"

"I do trust there will be no unnecessary delays."

6

MAITLAND allowed himself several hours before he called Colonel Plinio.

He started with the safe house in Flamengo. It had been swept clean. You would never have guessed that the flat had been ransacked from top to bottom, unless you were looking for the telltale signs: the slight indentation in the rug where a heavy wardrobe had been moved, the floorboard that had been nailed down too firmly, so you could see the fresh impress of the hammer.

He went to the church. He dropped a few cruzeiros in the slot, took a spill from the box and lit it with a match. As he placed the burning candle in the tray beside the others, he probed the narrow crack at the back of the marble ledge. He found a sticky wad of chewing gum. Nothing for him.

He tried their other mailboxes, including the niche behind the wounded lion in the Cemetery of John the Baptist. Nothing.

He called home. Luisa sounded flustered but relieved to hear him. Some strangers had been to the house. Something to do with fixing the electric meter. That didn't sound right. He wasn't aware of any fault in the meter.

"What did they look like?"

"Like cops. They didn't take anything. I never let them out of my sight."

He drove out to Copacabana, to Hossbach's boarding house, not sure what he hoped to accomplish. He was rewarded with a glimpse of the German sitting on the verandah with his landlady, eating sandwiches and drinking beer. This reminded Harry that it was lunchtime and that he was supposed to be helping to entertain some visiting Canadians in the private dining room at Rio Light.

When he whipped into a no-parking space on the Avenida Marechal Floriano, in front of the company building, it was past 2:00 P.M.

A spinsterish secretary followed him into his office.

"You look like something the cat threw up," she said with evident satisfaction.

"Any messages, dear?"

"The major called down three times. He didn't sound very happy."

Harry could hear the voice. When Major Mackenzie gave vent to emotion, his teeth rattled. It made him sound as if he were crunching ice cubes.

The pink message slips and the envelopes on the desk were all routine. The long face of Olga, Prestes' companion, peered mournfully out of a newspaper photograph. "Have You Seen This Woman?" He wondered who had given them the picture.

He got rid of the secretary and tried Colonel Plinio's direct number. The colonel was not in his office. Like half of Rio's population, he was probably at home, giving up work for the beginning of Lent.

He hesitated before dialing Plinio's home number.

If the police were holding Johnny, then the colonel must know about it—and should have called Harry. With the wave of arrests, Johnny was more and more vulnerable. Any one of his comrades might betray him under interrogation. One recourse might have been to confide completely in Colonel Plinio, who had been sniffing after Harry's source. But Colin Bailey had ruled this out on the grounds of the lack of security inside the Brazilian police, and Harry, remembering the ambiguous role that Captain Honorio had played on the night of the coup, thoroughly agreed with him.

He had instructed Johnny that, if he were ever captured by the police, he should ask for Colonel Plinio Nogueira by name and tell him that Maitland would vouch for him as a legitimate businessman.

The fact that Plinio had not been in touch suggested either that Johnny had not been arrested or that the policeman was trying to dredge as much as he could out of him through his own delicate devices.

I'm declaring an interest and probably not gaining a bloody thing, Harry told himself.

But what choice did he have? If the Gestapo—or Max's boys—had Johnny hidden somewhere in the city, he was going to need help to find him. And if he wasted too much time, he risked finding his man too late to save him.

Plinio answered his home telephone in person. He sounded pleasurably dozy.

"My dear Harry. Why aren't you sleeping it off, like everyone else?"

"I'm afraid my employer doesn't recognize hangovers."

"Oh, yes. Your galloping major. What can I do for you?"

"I was wondering if you made any interesting arrests last night."

"None that I heard about. The usual crop of drunks. Have you got any particular reason for asking?"

"A chum of mine seems to have turned up missing. I thought he might have had a few too many."

"Not quite my parish. But of course I'd be happy to make inquiries. What is the name of your friend?"

"Gruber. Franz Gruber."

"He's German, then?"

"Austrian, actually. He's rather good on cigars."

"It will be a pleasure to make his acquaintance. Can you give me a description, just in case?"

Harry did his best to oblige, not leaving out the priest's disguise, which seemed to appeal to the colonel's sense of humor. He wondered, as he talked, whether Plinio was toying with him. He had just hung up when Major Mackenzie barreled into his office.

"Jolly nice of you to grace us with your presence, Maitland!"

"I'm sorry about the lunch—"

"I think we ought to have a chat about your future with this company." The major jammed his monocle into his face.

Harry got up from his desk. "Certainly, sir. Perhaps at a more convenient time—"

"It's convenient now, thank you very much! Two buses damaged beyond repair by your Brazilians," he snarled, "and no sign of compensation!"

Harry didn't dare look at him for fear of bursting out laughing. He looked out the window instead—and saw several men in uniform engaged in trying to hook up the Beast to a tow truck.

"Bloody cheek!"

"Are you talking to me, Maitland?"

"No, sir. Some idiots are trying to tow my car away."

"I gave strict instructions that the street in front of the building is to be kept clear," the Major said primly. "Since the bomb scare, you know."

Which would have been a damn sight more than a scare if I hadn't scotched it, Harry thought.

"But that's my car!"

"We all live by the same rules here," Mackenzie said, with pure malice. "But if you're worried about your paintwork, I dare say someone will drive it to the lot for you."

"I'll do it myself." Harry was rapidly losing his sense of humor.

"No, you won't. We have a few larger things to settle. Agatha!"

The spinster secretary tripped in.

"Mr. Maitland is going to give you his car keys. There we are. Be a good girl and take them down to Jaime, won't you? Tell him Mr. Maitland will pay the fine when he comes down."

The secretary smirked.

"What fine?" Harry was ready to explode.

"Company policy. If you spent any time at all in the office, you might have heard about it."

Maitland sighed and slumped back into his chair.

God, I'm tired, and I've got a slab of pig iron jouncing up and down above my eyes, and I've lost Johnny, and I have to listen to this idiot preach about company manners.

I wonder if Jaime can even drive.

He craned his head round so he could see down into the street, two floors below. The company detective, all smiles, was climbing into the Beast. He made a little bow to the passers-by.

"Maitland. I say, Maitland! Are you listening to me?"

"Oh, yes, sir. Every word."

"You could show a bit more—"

The next word was no doubt "respect," since the major's style was nothing if not predictable, but it was choked off by a roll of thunder that blew out the window behind Harry's head and set the desk shaking.

The shock of the explosion threw the major off his chair. He picked himself up, minus the monocle, and rushed to the window.

The Beast was a pile of junk metal. The headless trunk in the front seat was recognizable as human only because of the arm that dangled over the side of the car. The other arm was gone. The bystanders were scattered across the pavement like fallen leaves. A security guard was doubled up against a lamppost, heaving his guts out.

"They p-put a bomb in your car," the major stammered.

Maitland was picking splinters of glass out of his hair. He could feel a trickle of blood down the back of his neck.

They could have done it with a timer, he thought. They must have planted it somewhere else. It was too public here, and besides, he'd only been in the building half an hour. Unless they had simply lobbed the thing from a passing car. He would have to talk to the people outside. Either way, he was being followed by someone who meant to stop him.

He experienced the odd sense of calm that comes at the heart of a crisis.

"I don't think you'll have any trouble stopping people from parking outside," he remarked to Major Mackenzie, who stared at him as if he had gone utterly insane.

1

THEY had Johnny swinging on an iron bar. It ran inside his knees, biting into the flesh. They had his wrists and his ankles tied together behind his back, so that if he relaxed his grip, he spun round like a top until his head ached.

He tried to think of anything except the questions they repeated over and over.

Where was the girl known as Sigrid or Firelei?

Where were Prestes and his woman?

What were his relations with Harry Maitland?

He tried to imagine himself on the Wannsee with Sigrid in the time before his world blew up in his face.

He was dimly aware that they had brought him a visitor.

"Very colorful," the man remarked to the police captain.

"How are you, Johnny?" he addressed the prisoner in perfect German, with a trace of a Silesian accent. "How do you like the parrot's perch?"

Johnny's leg muscles relaxed for an instant, and he saw Wolfgang Trott leering at him upside down.

"We have devised certain refinements that may be of use to you," Trott remarked to Honorio Schmidt.

He took something from his pocket; Johnny couldn't make out what it was.

"Would you have such a thing as a hammer?"

Schmidt went to the door and called out an order. An athletic young man stripped to the waist came in with the hammer. Honorio and his guest both looked fondly at his pectorals.

"Cut him down and I'll show you," Trott said.

Honorio nodded. Tarzan untied Johnny's bonds and let him fall onto the concrete.

"Now you see—" Trott held up a small convex disk of black plastic. "You fit the cap over the pupil, like so." He jammed his thumb and forefinger into the socket of Johnny's right eye, forcing the lids apart. He inserted the cap, and the light died.

"You must do this very tenderly. Like an act of love," Trott continued his lecture. "Otherwise you will blind the suspect and very quickly drive him out of his wits."

He tapped very gently, and it seemed to Johnny that a red-hot poker was being driven through the eyeball into his brain.

"Now we'll test the results," Trott said. "Which question is at the top of your list?"

Honorio was on the point of replying when there was a rap on the door, and a sergeant in a red cap came in and saluted.

"I ordered no interruptions!" Honorio screamed.

"I'm sorry, sir, but—"

"Get out!"

A dapper figure in a wide-brimmed panama hat tripped around the sergeant, preceded by a white cloud of cigar smoke.

"I wouldn't dream of interrupting your sport, my dear Honorio, but could you possibly spare me a minute?"

"This is not your department." Schmidt glowered at Colonel Plinio.

"That's precisely what I wish to discuss. Preferably among Brazilians." He cocked an eyebrow at Wolfgang Trott. "We *are* still on Brazilian territory, aren't we?"

Trott, red-faced, seemed to be looking for a place to hide the hammer.

"Graf von Trott is here in an advisory capacity," Schmidt said woodenly.

"Quite so, quite so. But you will forgive us, I trust, Herr Trott?"

Trott clicked his heels. "Let me know when it is convenient," he mumbled to Honorio Schmidt.

"You mean, to take delivery of your property?"

Trott's embarrassment increased. He rushed out of the interrogation room.

Blood was running out of Johnny's eye.

"Get that seen to straight away, will you?" Plinio ordered Schmidt's half-naked assistant, who led the prisoner out once his boss gave the nod.

"So you found out about the deportation order," Honorio said when the two of them were alone. Plinio was perched delicately on the edge of a straight-backed chair, his hands folded over the ivory knob of his cane, his trousers hitched up a fraction to preserve their immaculate crease.

"You were in rather a hurry, weren't you?"

"I have the chief's approval, and the justice minister's signature. It's out of your province."

"But my dear fellow, it was never in my province. That's where you made a big mistake. You've overstepped your authority. Political information is my bailiwick. Your people are merely mechanics, employed to assist in extracting it. This prisoner—this Gruber—belongs to me."

"It's my operation from start to finish. If you don't like it, you can go and talk to the chief."

It was no secret in Rio that the chief of police was much closer, personally and politically, to Captain Honorio Schmidt than to the colonel. The chief was a frequent dinner guest at the German Embassy.

"I must congratulate you," Plinio said urbanely.

"I beg your pardon?"

"I was thinking that your spiritual sessions with Gruber must have been stunningly successful, if you're ready to turn him over to our German friends so quickly. May I see the interrogation reports?"

They went to Honorio's office. Half an hour later, several long, closely typed pages were produced.

"During the subversive events that lately deflagrated in this capital," the document opened in the recorder's rotund style, "the subject claimed to be a merchant of tobaccos, living in sybaritic luxury in the Southern Zone."

"There's nothing here," Plinio pronounced after a quick glance. "He's told you nothing."

"Our investigation is still at a preliminary stage—"

"And you're putting him on a boat to Hamburg on Thursday!"

"You're well informed."

Colonel Plinio saw no reason to disclose that his source was the muscular young man whom he had sent out of the interrogation room. One of Plinio's detectives had caught him engaging in acts of public lewdness with other men among the dunes at the Leme end of Copacabana beach. The colonel had spared the young Special Police athlete any embarrassment in return for occasional scraps of information.

"What I'd like to know," Plinio pursued, "is what Herr Trott promised you. A death's head tiepin? An audience with Himmler? Or is it a matter of something you both wish to hide?"

"You're being childishly offensive." Honorio's jug ears, never his best feature, had turned bright pink. "You can read the deportation order for yourself." He pushed it across the desk. "It is a perfectly straightforward matter. Lentz, alias Gruber, alias Pedro and other names, entered Brazil illegally, using forged papers, and is being deported to his native country, where he is wanted for murder."

"I see." Plinio found the deportation order more informative than the interrogation report. It seemed the Gestapo had quite a dossier on the man Harry Maitland had described as his friend. He was wanted on several counts of murder. "I'll tell you what we'll do," the colonel went on. "We will settle this like civilized men. You let me have the prisoner for a few days, and I'll see if he wants to sing to me. Then you and Trott can play with him as long as you wish. Agreed?"

"I told you, I have special authority—"

"I have a few friends of my own, Honorio. Shall we call one of them?"

He scrawled a telephone number over Schmidt's pristine blotter. The captain studied it. It was one of the direct lines to the palace.

Honorio accepted that for the moment he was outgunned.

They strolled out into the courtyard. As his escorts took delivery of the prisoner, Colonel Plinio spotted Honorio's athletic assistant, still shirtless, hurrying towards the garage.

"Do you really think you should let your playmates run around during working hours without their clothes?" Plinio asked pleasantly.

THAT evening, Colonel Plinio received Maitland at home. The house was out beyond the golf club, modest but newly painted and full of happy children, who were shooed out of the sitting room but peeked in through the crack in the door at the tall, sandy-haired stranger.

The colonel proposed champagne or cognac.

"I drink nothing else at home," he declared. "Life has taught me to know my blood group."

The brandy, a very superior Hine, arrived chilled to the point where it had lost all bouquet. Harry was surprised by the colonel's lapse. His taste in all other respects was impeccable.

"You'll find it rides easier in this heat," Plinio remarked, reading his guest's expression. "It would be a crime to dilute it, don't you agree?"

Harry suppressed his misgivings. The cognac slipped down smoothly, all right, but he thought the flavor was barely distinguishable from that of Coca-Cola. It might, of course, have been his palate that was at fault; he was hardly in the mood for a wine tasting.

"I found your friend Gruber," Plinio suddenly announced. "He actually asked for you by name."

"Where is he?"

"At this precise moment, he's on his back in the infirmary. I'm afraid Honorio didn't lose any time before putting him on the grill."

"Is he badly hurt?"

"He'll live. At least, as long as he's in Brazil."

"What do you mean?"

"The Gestapo wants him sent to Germany. The justice minister has actually signed the deportation order. I saw it myself."

Harry froze. Deportation to Germany was a death sentence.

"We've got to stop it," he said. "We'll go to the president if we have to. Dammit, Johnny just saved your government. You ought to be giving him a medal."

"That wouldn't make him very popular with his Communist friends,"

Plinio observed, pleased that Maitland had admitted what he had guessed from the first phone call—that this Gruber was the agent Harry had refused to identify.

"Plinio, I want him out of jail tonight. It's not much to ask."

"It may be more than you think. I doubt if he's fit to travel. But in any event, my hands are tied. My chief gave me a direct order this afternoon. I am to deliver your friend into the custody of Herr Trott on Friday."

"Then call the palace. Go to the president. Explain the situation to him."

"The president is in Porto Alegre. And if I bypass my chief, he'll have me thrown out of my office."

Harry bit his lip. It was obvious why the Gestapo wanted Johnny back in Germany: they wanted to pay him back in their own sweet time for what he had done to Willi Rausch and milk him for whatever he had to yield on comrades who were still at large. Why Plinio's superiors were so accommodating was rather more of a mystery. The most likely explanation was that money had changed hands. But it was also possible that someone high up was scared that Johnny knew something that could destroy him, something about the plot to kill the president.

I could try to mobilize Sir Evelyn and the embassy, Harry thought. Cable Colin and ask him to get the Foreign Office to make a fuss. It would all involve time and bluster and the inevitable leaks—which would pretty much guarantee that Johnny's cover would be blown for good.

No, there was only one satisfactory solution.

He explained it to Plinio, who professed to be scandalized. After another brandy and two glasses of champagne, however, the colonel allowed that he might be swayed by the prospect of a handsome contribution to his personal insurance plan.

"With all this buzz and ferment," he conceded, "a man in my position can never tell where he's going to be next week. I sometimes think there would be worse places to come to roost than a cottage in one of the sunnier home counties. But of course, England is so expensive—"

They shook hands on it.

"I don't suppose you found out who wrecked my car," Harry said before they parted company.

"I am afraid that for once, the city is mute. It is a most unusual thing." But he confided that he had assigned detectives to keep a discreet watch on both Herr Trott and Engineer Hossbach.

8

AT NIGHT, in the infirmary, he woke screaming from a nightmare in which they were trying to gouge out his eyes and screamed again when he realized that his sight was gone. The orderly came running to quiet him.

"There," he murmured, loosening the bandage, so that Johnny could see a stripe of light under his left eye. "There." The right eye was heavily padded.

He lay back in the dank sheets and listened. He heard a train whistle and the thrum of pistons from somewhere nearby and, from nearer still, what sounded like amateurs' night on the radio. Except that they would never sing "The Hymn of the Poor Brazilian" on the government radio. That was marginally less popular with the regime than the *Internationale*.

The singing stopped, and a rotund, humorous voice rang out across the exercise yard the prisoners had dubbed Red Square.

"Tonight, dear friends and comrades, Radio Libertadora will instruct you in the high metaphysical Theory of the Two Suppositions, according to which everything must turn out for the best. If you will only learn this theory, you will understand that there is no reason at all to be apprehensive. None whatsoever. We will either, *primo*, be released, or *segundo*, remain in jail. If the first, well and good. If the second, we will be tried and either *primo*, be acquitted or *segundo*, be condemned. If the second—"

Johnny's attention wandered. He wondered why the guards did not interrupt the prisoners' entertainment. Security at this prison was obviously rather more relaxed than in the barracks of the Special Police. They called the place the Pavilhão dos Primários, which made it sound like a primary school.

The absurd-sounding name deepened the black irony of his situation. The same men who were driving Emil insane were planning to hand him over to the Gestapo, trussed and basted like a chicken. Yet *they* would have been the ones in the cells—as prisoners, not jailers—if he had not ensured the failure of the revolution. He knew he could not afford to dwell on this. He thought of Harry with his freckled, open face, so boyish and so brave.

Whatever lies they had told him in the interrogation room, Sigrid must be safe. Harry had promised that. Harry would keep his word.

He told himself, Harry will get me out of this.

"—if we are executed," the rotund voice was rounding up, "we will either *primo*, go to Heaven, or *segundo*, to the other place. If the first, well and good. If the second, we will meet all our friends. It could happen to anyone."

There was laughter and heckling from the windows across the yard. It darkened Johnny's mood; this solidarity did not include him.

In the morning he persuaded the orderly to change the bandage so he could see out of one eye, at least. The coffee they brought him for breakfast was sickly sweet, probably heavily laced with bromides. He tossed it back all the same. But he couldn't swallow the bread. He tried to divert himself by molding a set of tiny chessmen out of the crumbs. A wave of fatigue rose up and engulfed him before he had finished. When he rose out of it, he found a swarm of cockroaches devouring the last of his pieces.

From the window of the infirmary he could see the coppery glint of water under palms and recognized the Mangue canal, which he had first explored with Nilo on his tour of the city's low life. Nilo, the millionaire terrorist, had survived the wreckage better than he.

He dozed off again and was roused by the clatter of wooden clogs, to find one of the *faxinas*—common criminals whom the guards allowed to perform services for tips—hovering at the foot of his bed.

"These are for you." He thrust a brown paper bag into Johnny's arms.

Johnny looked inside and found two packs of cigarettes, a clean shirt, a loose pair of cotton trousers and a pair of canvas shoes.

"I don't have any money—"

"It's taken care of," the trustie winked at him. The lumps on his bald cranium would have made a phrenologist's day. "Harry says you're to meet him outside at ten tonight."

"I don't understand—"

The *faxina* winked again and gestured towards the double doors that led to the prison pharmacy. "Through there."

Johnny still did not understand, and hardly dared to hope. He slapped a hand to his wrist, to check the watch that was no longer there.

"Wait," he said helplessly. "How will I know when it's ten?"

"It's when the radio starts, isn't it?" The trustie shrugged and shuffled off in advance of an orderly.

HE WAS alone in the infirmary when a shrill whistle from across the exercise yard, followed by rhythmic clapping, announced that Radio Libertadora was on the air.

He eased himself out of bed, put on his new shoes and hobbled over to the double doors. The pharmacy was deserted, too. The outside door was secured, but the key had been left in the lock.

It was raining outside. The guard who should have been stationed in front of the building was probably inside, keeping dry.

"Johnny!"

The call came from a taxi with its light off and the engine running. Harry Maitland opened the back door and helped him inside.

"Here. Put this on."

Harry handed him a coat and hat. Johnny felt the weight of a gun or a bottle in the pocket. There were a hundred questions he needed to ask.

"Sigrid—"

"She's safe. I promise." Then Harry put a finger to his lips and they rode in silence to the Pedro II station.

The night train for São Paulo was actually on time; the vintage engine had a splendid copper-bound smokestack, enormous driving wheels and an old-fashioned cowcatcher in front.

An official whose uniform would not have shamed a field marshal inspected their tickets at the gate. He cast his eye over Johnny's attire.

"I profoundly regret that the Senhor is not permitted to board the train."

Johnny tensed and thrust a hand into his pocket.

"Is there some problem?" Maitland asked calmly.

"It is a company regulation. Gentlemen passengers must be correctly dressed." He looked pointedly at Johnny's bare neck.

"*Muito boa,*" Harry rose to the occasion.

He fished in his holdall and produced a Winchester tie. It looked rather loud to Johnny with its bold stripes of red, brown and blue. But Harry winked at him, and he knotted it hastily around his neck.

The station official smiled his approval and ushered them through.

"I knew there must be a reason I've held on to that thing," Harry said when they were comfortably ensconced in a Pullman.

"I don't imagine I look much like someone who went to an English public school," Johnny remarked, pulling the tie away from his throat.

"Perhaps not," Harry smiled. "But I have the feeling we're classmates just the same."

12

Manhunt

Like a woman, a horse does not
like the weak; still less does it
respect them.
—ALVISI,
Aphorisms

1

FROM among the flowering trees above the house, a sound rang out like the clang of a blacksmith's hammer striking the anvil. The hammer fell again, and Puck, the roly-poly tomcat who had adopted Harry and Luisa, jumped off the pillow and bellied underneath the bed for cover, the way he did during thunderstorms.

Luisa laughed at his timidity but got out of bed to check, for the third or fourth time, that all the doors were locked. The call of the *ferreiro*, the blacksmith bird, was an evil omen; it presaged violence, the clash of metal. And Ivan had warned that the greatest danger to both of them would come in this season, in the darkening of the moon.

She hated to be alone in the big, echoing house. Her whole family could have fitted into the kitchen wing, at the back, where she slept in a little room whose window overlooked her herbal garden. Harry had called from the office to say he was going to be away for a few days to look at horses at his ranch in the south. She had never set eyes on this estate, but he had once showed her photographs of a cluster of neat, whitewashed bungalows and himself in a funny round cap and white breeches, drinking a stirrup cup in a circle of horsemen dressed in the same outlandish style. In one of the pictures was a gate and a painted sign that displayed a bushy-tailed animal she had never seen. It was a red fox, he explained. One of his partners had been a Master of the Hunt in Somerset, which was somewhere in his own country, on the other side of the ocean, where it was the custom for gentlemen to pursue these small, clever animals on horseback.

Luisa asked, "Do you eat them?"

"Of course not," Harry said, in high indignation.

"Then it's a *despacho*. A sacrifice."

Harry chuckled and gave up trying to explain, leaving her puzzled and somewhat frightened, because these Englishmen were obviously homesick for their own country, which meant that one day, inevitably, Harry would leave her for the strange place beyond the waters where men wore red coats and called them pink.

Dudley, Harry's German shepherd, was lying in the coolest spot he could find, at the end of the hall. He gave a tremendous yawn as she padded out of the bedroom but dragged himself to his feet and came puffing along behind her. Dudley belonged in a different climate. The heat sapped all of his strength, and every time he went outside, she had to spend twenty minutes picking the ticks out of his coat. Still, his presence was comforting, especially tonight.

She checked the bolts on the front door and peeped out the bay window. The neighbors' lights were out, and the sky hung down like a black shroud. She could not see as far as the low stone wall at the end of the lawn. Behind her, Dudley staggered around in narrowing circles, ready to flop down.

She told herself not to be such a child, scared to be alone in the dark. She switched off the light and called the dog from the hallway.

"Come, Dudley. You can sleep with me."

But Dudley did not obey. He stiffened. A low rumble came from his throat. Then he started barking, a deep-chested, serious bark guaranteed to deter all but the most determined visitors. He woke up the *curupião* in its cage on the verandah, and it tried to mimic him.

"Dudley?"

Hackles raised, the dog was nudging and pawing the front door. Luisa turned on the porch light and went back to the window. Beyond the pale circle of light, the darkness was impenetrable.

The dog would not be quieted.

It's an animal, she told herself, resolved to be sensible. A squirrel or a stray cat. Or even an armadillo. She had nearly tripped on one of them once, tending her garden.

Dudley's growls alternated with whimpers of frustration. He butted at the door so hard that the glass in the panels shook.

"All right." She unlatched the door. "Go seek."

He barged past her and charged off into the night, his hackles so high he seemed to have sprouted a hump. The air was full of invisible midges. She brushed her arm across her face and retreated inside the screen door.

The dog was barking and snarling. He was going to wake people up.

"Dudley!"

The barking ended with a yelp, followed by a ragged, high-pitched whimper. Then nothing. The stillness that descended was unnerving. She listened carefully and could hear only the whine of mosquitoes, the feathery thud of the moths assaulting the lamp on the porch, the murmur of the wind among the leaves.

"Dudley?"

Nothing. Her hand was trembling as she locked the door.

I have to look for him, all the same.

He might have got stuck in the storm drain, chasing a smaller animal. Or in a trap. The people in the house on the north side had threatened to put out traps after something had killed two of their chickens. What would Harry say if the dog had been hurt badly and she let him lie out there until morning?

She found a flashlight in the kitchen and put on the white silk robe Harry had given her for her birthday.

The heat rose up out of the wet grass. She followed the wavering thread of light into the copse on the northern side of the property, where Dudley's barks had been coming from.

She moved among the trees. Suddenly, she stopped short, biting her lip so as not to cry out.

There was a man standing on the far side of the trees, a burly man with a weapon, a rifle or a shotgun, cradled in his arms.

He must have seen the flashlight. Should I run?

"What the hell is going on?" the man shouted out rudely. "Don't you *Ingleses* ever go to bed?"

It was only Porcão, the neighbor.

"Have you seen our dog?"

"If I see that mutt near my chickens, I'll send him home full of holes."

Luisa was too relieved to care what Porcão said. More confidently, she went back into the copse, jabbing at the undergrowth with her flashlight.

Something glinted white in the arc of the flashlight. She hunted for the spot, found it. And dropped the flashlight.

For an instant she had seen Dudley's face, the jaws partly opened over his shiny alligator teeth, the swollen tongue lolling out at the side. She had also seen the black hollow at his throat, the jagged vent that ran down to the belly, the entrails that spilled out like writhing eels.

She opened her mouth to scream, but the sound was suffocated by a strong hand that was clamped over her lips, while a muscular arm tightened around her waist, hoisting her sideways and upwards till her feet were off the ground. Helpless, gagging, she saw the awkward shape of Porcão shambling back towards his house.

A long, bony face pushed up close to hers. It looked like a death's head. "Where's the *Inglês?*" the skull whispered in Portuguese. "In the house?"

She shook her head.

"Bring her inside," Skull ordered his companions. She could see two more rising up out of the bushes. Plus the man who had her pinioned.

When they got her inside, she saw that one, at least, was a foreigner. His face was pink and sweaty. He had close-cropped blonde hair and no earlobes to speak of. The man who had grabbed her was a huge mulatto, darker than she.

The bony one, who seemed to be in charge, flashed some kind of pass in front of her face.

"Special Police," he breathed. "If you don't want trouble, you'll tell me what I want to know."

"She's just the maid," someone else said. "What can she tell us?"

"I wouldn't mind a maid like that," the mulatto chipped in, with a coarse laugh.

"Where is Senhor Maitland?" Skull demanded.

"He's gone away for a few days."

"Where?"

"I don't know."

"Have you seen this man?"

They showed her a photograph with a police identification number across the bottom.

She shook her head.

"Why did you kill the dog?" she said to them, between tears and rage.

For an answer, their leader hooked a finger over the neck of her silk robe and tore it from her shoulders. Her dark nipples were clearly visible under the nightie. The mulatto stuck his lips out obscenely and blew her a wet kiss.

"You want her, Jaime? Have her! It may loosen her tongue."

He ripped the nightie away from her body. She tried to cover herself with her hands, and Skull laughed at her.

The mulatto hesitated. He was staring at the *guias,* the ritual beads— blue and white for Yemanjá—around her throat.

"What's the matter? You don't like her any more?"

Luisa cowered before them, her eyes shut tight, invoking Yemanjá and the other *orixás*. Lady of the waters, take this from me. Carry me away in the foaming tresses of your hair.

This is not my body, she told herself. Nothing they do can touch me. I will feel nothing.

But she felt a violent hand tear at the *guias*, breaking the strings so that the sacred beads went rolling away in all directions.

Other hands were laid on her, probing and defiling.

"Go on, Hossbach!" Skull cried out merrily. "I can see you want to!"

But they stabbed at her secret places with something sharper than human flesh, with metal or glass, until she could no longer see the colors that could not be named or withstand the calvary of a body that was undeniably hers and was reduced to blurting out everything she knew or could imagine about Harry. They were particularly interested in the hollow inside the chimneypiece where they found his private papers and the mention of a *fazenda* in the south, on the borders of São Paulo and Paraná, with the carved face of a red fox on a sign.

2

"FORMÉ!" the wrangler shouted. He flicked his whip for the benefit of the persistent black flies rather than the horses.

The horses knew just what was expected of them.

They formed up in a rough circle inside the corral, their tails brushing the rails, their heads pointing to the center.

"Now," the wrangler called to Harry, "do you want to see if he still knows you?"

Maitland dropped from his perch on the rail, whipped his straw sombrero from his head and advanced, with the hat outstretched, toward a handsome grey gelding. He was big for a Brazilian horse, fifteen hands at least, with a broad chest and good quarters and a silver-black mane, left shaggy to keep off the flies. He cocked his ears forward and pawed at the red dirt with his neat black hooves as Harry approached.

"Hello, Winston," Harry called to him, holding his hat upside down by the brim. The horse danced forward and nuzzled inside the hat.

"You cheated!" the wrangler reproached him with a grin.

Winston, disappointed at finding nothing inside the hat, was trying to graze inside Harry's shirt. Maitland brought a lump of *rapadura*—raw brown sugar—out of his trouser pocket and let the horse eat it out of his hand.

Johnny came over. He had gained strength these past days at the ranch, but he still wore a patch over one eye. It gave him a piratical look.

"What is he?" Johnny asked. "A thoroughbred?"

Inocencio laughed. The wrangler was a frontiersman, a mixture of Brazilian, Spaniard and Guarani Indian, lithe and quick, with a scrubby beard and skin like saddle leather.

"He's a mongrel, like me," Inocencio said. "Creole, mostly. Some racing blood on the father's side. He's fast, and he's a stayer. But he hasn't been ridden for a couple of months," he added for Harry's benefit. "You'd better watch him."

"Have you still got my saddle?"

"We might be able to find it. What about your friend?"

Maitland turned to Johnny. "Do you feel up to a ride?"

"I'm not in your league."

"You could try Hilde," the wrangler suggested, leading out a stocky little bay mare.

"But she's too small for me."

"She's stronger than you might think," Maitland interjected. "She's a *coralera*. They breed them in Mato Grosso. Best horse you could want for cross-country hacking in these parts. And a lovely temperament to go with it."

The little mare was snuffling and licking Johnny's hand.

He said, "I'll give it a try."

Inocencio produced a Texas saddle with the tree cut down and strapped it on over a soft, loose-woven blanket.

"Don't jerk," the wrangler cautioned. "She's got a mouth like velvet. You only have to *think* what you want her to do."

Maitland was already out of the corral, pressing his knees against Winston's flanks. The horse suddenly leaped into the air and jackknifed till its back legs and forelegs almost met. It was the best Harry could do to stay on, clinging to the mane.

Winston bucked sideways, and Harry hugged his neck, muttering old endearments and trying to get his left foot back into the stirrup.

Johnny trotted past on the coralera mare, looking as if he had been born in the saddle.

"Need any help?" he called back to Maitland, who smiled through his gritted teeth.

He clapped at Winston's sides with his ankles, and they galloped out across a sea of grass, where a herd of humpbacked zebu cattle, oddly Asiatic, were grazing placidly. They did not stop till they reached the bank of a shallow stream. Harry drove his mount on through the muddy water and over a lazy sandbank to the steep, slippery clay on the far side, hanging on to its tail with his left hand and looking out for caimans. When they raced back to the *fazenda,* they were driven by a single will.

Johnny trotted up on the little mare from the opposite direction and swung smoothly down from the saddle.

They took whisky and sodas on the verandah, and Harry said, "I must say, you do seem to have made a remarkable recovery. What would you say to a spot of shooting tomorrow? Inocencio says he saw a ten-point stag in the swamps."

"I can't waste any more time," Johnny responded quietly. "I have to get to Buenos Aires. Have you heard anything about Sigrid? Is she all right?"

He had asked the same question twenty times since they had boarded the train in Rio.

"She's fine," Harry assured him. "Probably a bit disoriented, but you'll sort that out. Bradbeer's a good man. He'll keep her out of trouble until you arrive."

Harry expressed more confidence than he felt. He didn't like the tone of the cable he had finally received from Bradbeer that same morning. Bailey's man said there had been complications in Buenos Aires, without specifying what had gone wrong. Bradbeer strongly recommended that Johnny should take the roundabout route to the Argentine capital, via Paraguay. The British agent was going to arrange for a contact to meet them on the other side of the Paraná River, which Harry remembered as a nest of gamblers and contrabanders. With that evil-looking patch over his eye, Johnny would fit in beautifully.

Harry had yet to break the news of this unexpected detour.

"When do we leave?" Johnny asked.

"We've got a couple of choices. There's a British ship leaving from Santos the day after tomorrow."

"Would that be quickest?"

"If we get through. I've been informed that our friends from Rio have got the ports pretty well covered. It would be safest to skip across the border into Paraguay. No one is looking for us there. We wouldn't lose very much time, because we can fly direct from Asunción to Buenos Aires. There's a mail plane twice a week."

"So your vote is for Paraguay."

"I think it makes sense, don't you?"

Johnny was frustrated by the prospect of a further delay before he caught up with Sigrid. But he tried to make light of the situation.

"I think you're being less than candid, Harry. I think you want to go overland to Paraguay so you can bag a few more deer."

"It never hurts to keep one's hand in," Harry grinned.

3

Luisa scrubbed herself until her palms and the inside of her thighs were chafed, and still did not feel clean. She dug a shallow grave under the bougainvillea and buried what was left of Dudley. Then she took another bath and put on her prettiest dress and her butterfly hat. She took the housekeeping money and walked down the hill to the bus stop. Some hired hands bouncing along in the back of a horse-drawn cart whistled after her.

"I'm in love with you!" one of them called. "I'll make an honest woman of you!"

"So what do you call your wife?" another baited him.

She did not hear them. She was going to Caxias, to Ivan's *terreiro*. She was going for revenge.

She would give Ivan all the money she had and tell him the strange, foreign name she had heard in the night. She would plead with him to speak the terrible name of Exú Caveira, Exú Skull, the dark power that closed off a man's paths and snuffed out his life like a candle.

4

It was two days' ride to the Paraná River, Inocencio said, unless the rains came again. In their saddlebags they stowed enough beef jerky, beans and rapadura to last a week. But in that country, no man who could shoot need ever go hungry. The woods and the marshes were teeming with wild pigs and tapirs, deer and muscovy ducks. As they followed a red dirt trail through the rain forest, Inocencio would lean from the saddle to scoop an orange or papaya from a branch.

Leaving Fox Hill, they had traveled for a time through massive stands of conifers—Paraná pines, Harry explained—with a distant view of a vast coffee plantation on the hills to the south. Now, they were surrounded by true jungle, laced with lianas woven together in the high canopy, far above their heads, so that they rode through a patchwork of light and shade.

Each of the three men had a rifle slung behind his saddle—the short-barreled .44 Winchester that Harry favored because it was light and the flat-nosed lead bullets were easy to find anywhere between here and Asunción.

Twenty miles west of Fox Hill Farm, they dismounted and left the horses in a clearing to graze at will. Harry's little mare, no mean forager, made straight for a *maté* plant; to a horse in these parts, the fruit of the *yerba maté* (as the Spaniards across the border called the plant) was as irresistible as catnip to your average feline.

Maitland and Johnny followed Inocencio for half a mile or so into a shallow, stinking marsh teeming with water fowl.

"The deer love it in here during the day," he whispered, showing Johnny where to crouch. "They get away from the ticks."

Johnny was squatting in the stagnant water when Inocencio put a finger to his lips. A regal stag, six points at least—no, eight—was advancing among the trees. He stopped short and started butting his head against the branches. What was he up to?

Johnny watched the animal over the sight of his Winchester. The stag, not sensing danger, had paused to make his toilette; he was rubbing the fur off his antlers against the rough bark.

"He's yours." Harry reached over and squeezed Johnny's shoulder.

Johnny watched the stag. There was a kind of majesty about him. The way he shook his head, the way he stood up with his chest thrown out, reminded Johnny of someone. Was it Heinz Kordt?

There was a scuffling among the leaves—perhaps a sloth changing position—and the stag reared up his head. The next instant, he was bounding away, across Johnny's line of fire.

Johnny swung the rifle, keeping the sight trained a few yards ahead of the deer. That was the trouble with a .44 Winchester. It threw its bullets rather slowly. You had to aim well in advance of your target.

Johnny went through the motions. At the last possible moment he tightened his finger and squeezed the trigger halfway back, then released it. He lowered the rifle and watched the stag complete his escape.

"You had him," Maitland said, disappointed.

"But I didn't want him."

Maitland shot him a quick glance and turned to Inocencio.

"I don't think venison agrees with our guest. Can we rustle up something else for supper?"

They bagged a *cateto*, a wild pig, back in the woods, and roasted it on a spit that night over a blazing campfire. The sweet-sour reek of the forest seemed more intense after sundown, but the stink from the roasting pig overwhelmed it.

Johnny wrinkled his nose.

Inocencio guffawed and said, "He's got musk glands there—" he pointed to the short ribs "—like a skunk. Good eating, though. You'll see."

He was right. It was better than any pork Johnny had ever tasted, though they all had to pay for it afterwards by picking the ticks off their bodies that had migrated from the drying hide of their dinner.

They couldn't sleep on the ground because the tiny blood-sucking ticks were everywhere. Inocencio slung his hammock at a discreet distance, on the other side of the fire, so the two foreigners could talk in English and drink *pinga* deep into the night.

Maitland lay back in his hammock with his hands behind his neck and a cigar in his teeth and looked up at the distant lights of the Southern Cross.

"Bradbeer's been told to organize a boat to England for you," he remarked to Johnny through a veil of white smoke.

Johnny grunted and reached for the flask of cane brandy.

"I'm sure Colin will understand if you decide to pull out at this stage," Maitland said gently, removing the cigar.

"It's not my decision to make," Johnny responded curtly.

"I'm sure Colin won't put any obstacles in your way. After all you've been through."

"I wasn't thinking of Colin."

Of course not, Harry thought. He was thinking of the girl. Maitland prayed that Bradbeer had handled her with some degree of subtlety. She must be very confused and very frightened—and must by now have guessed part, if not all, of Johnny's secret role. It worried Maitland that Bradbeer had made no direct mention of the girl in the telegram that had been carried on horseback from the post office at Londrina.

"Did your man in Buenos Aires say anything about Max?" Johnny asked.

"No. I assume there hasn't been a sighting. Max would have gone back to Europe straightaway, wouldn't he?"

"Not necessarily. Not before taking care of unfinished business."

"You think it was Max who got you arrested, don't you?"

"He was returning a favor."

"How can you be sure?"

"It had to be Max. He must have obtained the address from Sigrid."

"You might have been followed."

Johnny shook his head. "We were always very careful."

"But Honorio Schmidt's information came from the Gestapo. Isn't it possible they started checking up on you after that business with Willi Rausch?"

"It's possible," Johnny conceded. "But they had information about me —party work names, personal things—that the Gestapo could only have known from an insider."

"Are you suggesting that Max sent your dossier to the Gestapo?"

"Something like that. I'm sure he's done it to others." He told Harry what he had learned in Copenhagen about the systematic betrayal of Stalin's critics inside the German Communist underground to Hitler's secret police.

Max Fabrikant was an enigma to Maitland. He was a man with blood on his hands, including the blood of some of the most vigorous anti-Nazis in Germany. Max had played his own game of provocation and betrayal in Brazil for ends that were still obscure.

"Have you ever considered that Max might be a double agent working for the Gestapo?" Harry asked suddenly.

"I've considered it," Johnny replied. He thought of how Max had nearly got him killed in the shoot-out with the Gestapo at the fish market in Rio and then, at the last minute, had saved his life. "I don't believe Max is working for the Germans," he went on. "The funny thing is, he couldn't have done much more damage if he were."

IN THE dream, Johnny was walking with Sigrid in a warm northern countryside, perhaps in Portugal. The place was beautiful, but there was a stifling sense of unseen oppression. The land was occupied by some hostile presence. They were surrounded by children, not their own, yet children for whom he was responsible. They passed through formal gardens into a vast, many-storied mansion with endless galleries and corridors. Johnny knew this great house, its staff and its secrets, quite well; once he had been trusted here. But the house was troubled. There was some terrible, unidentified danger growing close at hand. He realized they were being hunted. He and Sigrid were suddenly running through the house, looking for a way out. They stumbled through a labyrinth of hallways and stairs before they found an ancient elevator and rode down inside its rickety cage to a flagstoned lobby, where each of the massive doors had half a dozen panels, each with its own locks. All the locks had to be opened simultaneously by the deft manipulation of a bewildering series of catches and keys. Johnny found he could manage this surprisingly easily. Outside, in a walled garden of fleshy plants and running fountains, he sensed that he was nearing the source of the danger. Beyond the wall rose the foreboding bulk of another great house, or a castle. Sigrid and the children backed away, making for the far wall. But Johnny made them hold hands and led them towards the danger. He joked at the top of his voice and burst into snatches of song, as if, by presenting himself as anything other than a fugitive, he would not be taken for one. He saw armored cars and truckloads of enemy soldiers moving away from them in a cloud of dust. There was a wonderful sense of imminent liberation.

Then a shadow fell across his eyes. Something was choking him, blocking his mouth and his nose.

He opened his eyes. The clearing was dappled with morning light. Something warm and furry was dragging itself across his face. He could not see it clearly, because it was on the cheek under his bad eye. The movement tickled, yet suddenly he wanted to scream.

"Don't move," Maitland said softly. He was standing next to Johnny's hammock, holding his rifle by the barrel.

The thing edged down the angle of Johnny's jaw. He felt its hairy legs scrabbling for a purchase on the slope of his neck. Beads of sweat broke out across his forehead. He dug his nails into the palms of his hands until he broke the skin.

The thing dropped off his neck on to the hammock.

"Now!" Maitland ordered.

He did not need a second invitation. He flung himself off, leaving Maitland to swing the butt of his rifle down savagely, once, twice, till the cords of the hammock broke and the tarantula was a sticky black lump among the leaves.

Johnny took a series of deep breaths.

"If Schmidt had used one of those," he said later, "I would have told him anything he wanted to hear."

FROM the rise they could see the peaceful, muddy expanse of the Paraná River, still many miles to the west. Inocencio produced an old brass telescope. Through it Johnny saw a flock of ibises, a couple of Indian canoes and a powerful motor launch that Inocencio pronounced to be a rum-runner's boat.

"There's a little river port downstream," Maitland announced. "We'll ride down in the morning and hire a boat to take us across."

Inocencio did not like the mention of this particular town. The people were all thieves and bloodsuckers, he muttered, worse than the ticks.

"What he means to say," Harry interpreted with a grin, "is that one of his girlfriends' husbands ran him out of town."

They camped near a stream. Maitland magicked a bottle of champagne out of the depths of his saddlebag and placed it in the running water to chill.

"It's your last night in Brazil," he explained to Johnny. "I thought it called for a celebration."

They had an hour of daylight left, and Maitland proposed bagging a few ducks for the dinner table.

A strange, striped bird with a high black comb, two-pronged like devil's horns, fluttered away through the trees as they moved along the water-course. Higher over the treetops, vultures sailed on their great wings.

Johnny scored the first hit. The bird dropped like a stone, somewhere on the far side of the stream. They sloshed across to the other bank and were still searching the undergrowth when Inocencio stopped and motioned for the others to remain still.

He stretched out full length and pressed his ear to the ground.

"What is it?" Maitland asked.

"Listen."

They felt it before they heard it: a faint, rhythmic vibration under the leaves.

"Horses?"

Inocencio nodded. "Six. Maybe more. One far ahead."

"Two parties, then?"

"Or one, with a tracker."

"Are they tracking us?" Johnny asked, his face lined with tension.

"They could be bandits, after the horses," Maitland said. "We'd better get them. Inocencio doesn't like to walk," he added, trying to make light of it. Inocencio was already on his feet, running almost noiselessly through the woods. "Johnny, I think you should wait here."

"No. I'm coming, too."

They could hear the riders clearly now, approaching at a fast clip.

They led the horses deeper into the woods. Winston was shying a bit. Maitland fed him a lump of rapadura to quiet him down and tied his reins to a tree, just in case.

They watched the trail from the cover of thick scrub.

The first rider to appear wore a red bandanna and the flapping grey pants of a gaucho, and a hat with bobbing corks hanging below the brim to keep the flies off his face.

"I know that bastard," Inocencio whispered. "They call him Throat Slitter."

"What is he?"

"He's a bloodhound. He works on a German *fazenda* near Maringá. He killed three men in a fight."

Throat Slitter got off his horse, a big bay, and inspected the remains of the camp. He sniffed the air and peered into the forest. Johnny could see his eyes, hard and glinty, like obsidian. The man seemed to be staring straight at him.

They heard the drumbeat of many hooves, saw a haze of red dust.

Throat Slitter put two fingers in his mouth and let out a piercing whistle.

The riders following him reined in just short of the clearing. There were eight or nine of them, lean, weathered and sunbrowned, except for the one who appeared to be in charge. He was wearing a sun helmet and an army officer's tropical kit with the badges of rank removed. He was too big for his horse, though the horse was a sturdy Arab grey. His face was bright scarlet from the heat and the exertion.

"Hossbach," Johnny murmured.

Hossbach and his men dismounted, leaving their horses to forage. Most of them carried rifles. While Hossbach conferred with his guide, the others started fanning out into the brush.

Maitland would have liked to put a bullet between his eyes then and there—not just because of what had happened in Rio, but because he recognized several of the horses. They had been stolen from Fox Hill. One of them was a promising two-year-old he had hoped to enter in the Grande Prémio some day. Her rider was using a wicked snaffle bit of twisted wire. Her mouth would be ruined. Harry doubted she would ever see a racetrack after the way she had been used on that punishing trail.

He guessed that Hossbach must have flown down from Rio in a light plane. The German Embassy had a two-engine job he could have borrowed. Some of the big *fazendas* had landing strips. The German had boasted to Johnny about the number of Nazi sympathizers in the state of Paraná. He must have touched down at one of their ranches, hired his gang of toughs and set off overland by car or truck for Fox Hill, where he had picked up their scent—and Harry's horses.

Harry knew they had to make an instant decision. They could make a fight of it, but they were badly outnumbered. They could try to get away through the forest, but then they would have to abandon their mounts and try to hack their way to the river on foot. There was only one way they had a fighting chance.

"Inocencio."

Inocencio was silently fuming. He clearly had his own notions about the correct treatment for horse thieves.

"Senhor Gruber and I will draw them after us. See if you can get round behind them and drive off the horses. Then we'll make a bolt for it."

Inocencio slipped away through the dense vegetation. The vines parted and closed behind him again like a curtain.

Hossbach hated the jungle. It stank, and it was full of biting, sucking things you couldn't see. It pressed in around you, closing in like the walls of a medieval torture chamber, till you were gasping for air. Twenty yards from the trail, he was lost. He stumbled along, breathing hard, terrified that he would lose sight of Throat Slitter's bobbing red bandanna and never find his way out.

He had volunteered for this job because he had a score to settle. Johnny Gruber duped him and murdered one of their best agents. Also, Trott had

promised to recommend him for an important job in Europe if he succeeded. It had seemed straightforward enough: a surprise raid on a horse
farm in a part of the country where half the ranchers spoke German. He
hadn't reckoned with *this.*

Someone was calling him by name.

There it was again. "Psst! Hossbach!"

The voice was coming from nearby. Hadn't the others heard it? Damn.
Throat Slitter had vanished among the trees.

"Johnny?"

"Here! Over here!"

He fired in the direction of the sound twice, three times. There was no
echo. The silence of that green hell seemed to mock him.

"Hossbach!"

He fired again and yelled for Throat Slitter and the others, who were
pushing their way through the jungle to get to him, drawn by the shots.

He swung round to shout his orders, and that sudden motion may have
saved him, because a rifle bullet hissed past his ear and got one of his men,
who collapsed like a punctured balloon, in the chest.

Scared and sweating hard, Hossbach waved the others forward and
staggered along after them sideways, covering the rear.

There was a tremendous volley from the other direction, over to the east,
followed by the whinnying and stamping of hooves.

Throat Slitter came running back, shouldering his way through the rest
of the men.

"Back!" he yelled out. "Back! It's a trick."

"Wait!" Hossbach cried out.

One of the men who hesitated was felled by a bullet between the
shoulder blades. He dropped like a tree under the woodcutter's axe.

Hossbach was blundering after the others, tripping over roots and fallen
branches.

He regained the trail in time to see his horse fly past, with the others
stampeding behind. A mestizo on a black horse galloped along at their
heels, firing his rifle into the air.

Hossbach took aim and squeezed off a couple of rounds, but the rider
flung himself down against his horse's neck, so the bullets went wide. He
aimed for the horse, but the trigger snapped on an empty chamber.

Hossbach swore. His men opened fire as two horsemen came darting out
of the woods, but neither of them fell. He watched Johnny and the Englishman racing into the sunset.

"They're probably headed for Esperança," Throat Slitter suggested.

"How far?"

"Fifteen, twenty miles."

"Is there anywhere we can find horses in this godforsaken jungle?"

The guide rubbed his stubbly chin. "Not unless we catch them ourselves."

They started walking west, jangling spurs. They had a stroke of luck. They came across a saddleless straggler—a pretty palomino mare—chewing her way through a *maté* bush. Throat Slitter got a rope round her neck and unwound his Indian belly-belt, a dozen feet of tough, knitted wool that he wore around his waist. He tied one end of the belt around the horse's neck, just behind the ears, and made a turn around the nose. Gripping the other end, he had an improvised rein.

"I'll take her," Hossbach announced.

Throat Slitter gave him a surly look but handed over the rein.

At his first attempt to hoist his bulk up onto the mare's bare back, Hossback slipped and fell heavily in the dirt. The men laughed.

Throat Slitter vaulted on to the mare's back and reached out a hand. "Here. You can ride pillion if you want."

There was pink murder in Hossbach's eyes, but he accepted.

5

MAITLAND was in excellent spirits, although the fisherman had charged him a small fortune to rent out his boat. It was a broken-down tub reeking of bilge water and gutted fish, but the diesel engine seemed serviceable enough. It was the best thing on offer in Esperança, a huddle of adobe huts with a couple of cantinas on a main street that was a blur of red dust and black flies. If Hossbach managed to follow them that far, he would be hard put to follow them any further in an Indian canoe or a leaky dinghy. On the strength of that, Harry had decided to sail all the way downstream to a point just above the Iguaçu Falls, within easy striking distance of their rendezvous at the Paraguayan town of Acaraí. He had trailed a couple of lines over the side of the boat. There were dourados in these waters, and nothing in the world tasted better. There were piranhas, too, as he warned Johnny when he stripped off, intending to take a dip.

They had left Inocencio in Esperança with the horses. Harry had told him to go back to Fox Hill by a different route and alert a friendly officer in the state police that they had been attacked by horse thieves. Here on the frontier, you weren't forgiven for stealing a man's horse.

They caught a couple of dourados and cooked them on the primus stove at the end of the day. In the falling light, dark, vertical clouds bristled above the rain forest like spears. Harry could tell that the falls were near, from the swarms of butterflies with vivid black and red wings that danced across their bow. One of them perched above the wheel. When its wings were folded, the pattern resembled the number eight or the symbol of infinity. The falls had a magnetic attraction for these creatures. Harry fancied he could hear the distant thunder of the waters and calculated that they were half an hour, at most, from their landfall.

Johnny was throwing fish bones over the side.

He looked back and said, "We have company."

Maitland followed the pointing hand and saw the sleek motor launch he had watched through a telescope the day before. The one Inocencio had said belonged to contrabanders. The launch was coming on fast; nothing he had seen on the Paraná River would match it. He wondered whether the skipper was making for the same anchorage.

He slapped the side of his cheek. He had forgotten how ferocious the mosquitoes were on the Paraguayan side.

The launch was almost within hailing distance. There were a lot of people on board. Maybe they were pleasure trippers, not smugglers, as Inocencio, with his sour view of human nature, had maintained.

Maitland raised his arm above his head and waved.

The response was less than friendly.

The first shot, from a high-velocity rifle, cracked the glass in the sole surviving window of the wheelhouse, just beside Maitland's ear. The other bullets flew high and fell short.

Johnny was already hunkered down, sighting along his Winchester, waiting for the launch to get within range. Now they could see Hossbach in his desert tan and Throat Slitter's red bandanna. Hossbach's gang must have hijacked the launch at Esperança, or bought the captain.

Maitland tried to coax more speed out of the engine, till he heard an ominous clanking and the deck started to shudder underfoot. They could never outrun Hossbach's boat.

He took off his belt and used it to lash the wheel into place. Then he crawled along the deck, close to Johnny, and traded shots with the pursuers. It was hopeless. The launch was almost alongside, and the German had got hold of a Hotchkiss gun. It spat lead across their deck, driving wood splinters into Harry's legs and hands.

The launch came at them full throttle.

"They're going to ram!"

Johnny, the sailor, took charge. He yelled to Maitland to cover him and leaped for the wheel. He wrenched the boat around till they were hugging the Paraguayan shore. He saw a jumble of tin-roofed shacks and a sagging jetty—the place where he had intended to land—drift past. Muscovy ducks flapped, squaking, out of the mangroves.

The boat was gathering speed, but for the wrong reason. The current was tugging them along, down to the falls. The crash of the waters blotted out the thrum of the engines. In a few minutes, Johnny realized, he would have to run the boat aground or risk being dragged over the precipice.

Maybe he could lure Hossbach on to a sandbar. The big launch must have a deeper draught than the fishing boat. He veered round to the landward side of an island, into a shallower channel. The launch did not follow. He lost sight of it behind a wilderness of palms and lush tropical plants. The light was fading fast. Everything was indistinct except for the shimmering haze up ahead, the spray from the seething waters of Iguaçu.

The island dropped behind, and the launch hurtled at them, shuddering against their hull. Johnny heard a crash behind him. One of Hossbach's men had flung himself onto the deck. He grabbed the boathook and lashed out with it. He caught the boarder along the side of the jaw and knocked him over the side. He wrestled with the wheel, driving the boat in towards the shore. Their bow scraped against a basalt rock, but the pull of the river was now irresistible. The boat was being swept along like a cork towards the falls.

Johnny heard a cry of alarm from the bigger boat.

He called to Maitland, "Jump!" Land was only a few yards away.

But Maitland was struggling with another boarder, lashing out with feet and fists. Hossbach took a blow to his chest but recovered and was after him with a knife, a kind of knife Johnny had only seen once before, in a Fourth Department weapons course. He did not throw the thing, he fired it. As Maitland's leg shot out again, aiming for the groin, Hossbach released a catch. The razor-sharp blade hissed from its socket and embedded itself deep in Harry's thigh.

Maitland gasped and fell backwards, so his head was dangling in the river.

Hossbach was scrabbling around among ropes and fishing lines for the Winchester. He glanced up, and his mouth dropped open as he saw Johnny thrusting down at him with the boathook. His last thoughts were lost as the hook tore his throat out.

On the other boat they were trying desperately to reverse engines. It was a lost cause. The falls were calling them.

"Harry!"

Maitland was trying to draw the knife blade out of his leg. It sliced into his hand, even through the folded handkerchief.

"Leave that! We have to jump now!"

"I don't think I can."

There was a stubby promontory ahead, with branches that overhung the river. Johnny snatched up a coil of rope, tied one end around Harry's waist and twisted the other round his forearm.

He climbed up onto the roof of the wheelhouse. There would only be one chance. None, unless the branch held.

"Get to the side!" he shouted down to Maitland.

He saw the black silhouette looming up and flexed his leg muscles, willing himself not to feel the ache in his feet, still swollen from the beatings. He bent at the knees, like a diver. When he made his leap, he sensed it would fall short. They had taken too much of his strength. His fingertips grazed the branch he was aiming for, and he was falling, into that murderous current. He went under. He came up again, gasping for air. But the river was sucking him down. Then something slammed into his chest. He clutched at it and felt wood—a submerged root, or a tree trunk. It held his weight. He made the rope fast around it and tugged for Harry to follow.

He saw the Englishman fall, rather than jump, off the boat. He pulled him in, hand over hand.

They clawed their way up onto the rocks and watched the two boats, like lovers clasped in a suicide leap, sail over the falls.

6

JOHNNY pushed open the frosted glass doors of the Casino Acaraí. Inside, they were playing a scratchy record of El Ultimo Beso on the phonograph. A pair of short, dumpy Indian girls in bright prints waited for custom at the bar. The raw light favored neither them nor the peeling walls. Most of the patrons were clustered around the roulette table, slapping down wads of Brazilian, Argentinian and Paraguayan currency which the head croupier accepted imperturbably and distributed between the cash slot and his own pockets. He was a villanous-looking character with a pencil moustache, slicked-down hair and a static, risorius grin.

"How will I know the contact?" Johnny had asked Maitland.

"Bet on twenty-two," was the answer. "Only on twenty-two. Bet big, and at least three times."

It was a variation of the old wheeze they had used at the Necrópolis in Rio.

At that moment Harry was in bed under a mosquito net they had had to acquire for themselves in a dosshouse that styled itself the Hotel Acaraí. Johnny had pulled the knife blade out of Harry's leg with his teeth and bound up the wound as best he could with a handkerchief and a strip off his own shirt. The gash would need stitches, but Maitland refused to trust the local medical profession or to run the risk of attracting curiosity. In the meantime he was numbing the wound—and himself—with liberal shots of a local *aguardiente* labeled Gotas d'Oro, or Drops of Gold.

Johnny studied the group around the roulette wheel, to see if he could spot Bradbeer's contact. They were an unpromising bunch: a portly dowager loaded down with flashy jewels and accompanied by an obvious gigolo; a near hysteric who turned away with his hand over his eyes each time they spun the wheel; a clutch of Argentinian sightseers. The head croupier had no fewer than three assistants. Each time he spun the wheel, they all pressed in around it, so that it was all but impossible for the players to see where it jumped.

Johnny squeezed through the crush and handed the croupier a fistful of Brazilian money. He received a small stack of mauve plastic chips. He placed about a third of them on twenty-two.

"Bolas!" the stage villain called, flourishing his croup close to the knuckles of a player who was trying to rearrange the chips he had already deployed.

Johnny didn't see where the ball landed and didn't much care.

His chips were whisked away.

He bet again. The winning number this time was thirteen. Nobody had it. The dowager started to blubber—whether because of her losses or because of the way her escort was feeling her up in public, it was impossible to say.

Nobody gave Johnny any sign of recognition.

He placed his remaining chips on the same number. This time, he paid attention as the ball bounced around the rim of the wheel. From his height he could see over the shoulders of the assistant croupier, who was stationed so as to block the patrons' view. The ball came to rest on twenty-two. It would be worth quite a bit to him, with the stake he had put down. He glanced at his pile of chips and counted eight of them.

"Veinte-ocho," the stage villain called out.

Johnny waited for them to shell out. Instead, he saw one of the assistants haul away his chips, with all the others.

"Espere—" he burst out.

"Veinte-ocho," the head croupier repeated, with that permanent leer. "Twenty-eight."

Johnny peered at the wheel. Sure enough, the ball was resting at twenty-eight. They had moved it.

The other players started spreading their chips. They didn't know the game was rigged. Or else they knew and didn't care.

Johnny was disgusted, because there was absolutely nothing he could do. He wasn't here to make a killing at the tables. Even if he were prepared to make a scene, it could only succeed in getting him arrested; the house had four witnesses to support its story.

He went to find the men's room. There were slices of lime in the urinal. He watched the steam rise from them and wondered about the contact. Perhaps Bradbeer's agent hadn't come that night or hadn't yet arrived. After all, no time had been set for the meeting.

He had not quite finished when the door opened. A man walked straight to the urinal and started unbuttoning his flies.

"Mr. Maitland, I presume?" he said in excruciating English.

Johnny glanced sideways and met the plaster grin of the croupier who had stolen his money.

THE croupier was well connected and evidently well on his way to becoming a very rich man. He supplied Johnny with a new set of papers, a ride to the capital and a seat on a plane bound for Buenos Aires. The plane turned out to be a four-engine French flying boat en route to Paris from Santiago via various South American capitals. The same company, unknowingly, had flown Prestes to Brazil to start his revolution.

Bradbeer met Johnny at the airport. He would have passed for a merchant banker, slightly at sea in his present surroundings.

As they drove into the city, he asked after Maitland, expressed the appropriate concern over his injury and then turned to practical matters. He had laid on a room for Johnny at the Crillón—damn the expense and all that, Johnny had bloody well earned it. Besides, it was a very decent pub and an easy walk from Bradbeer's flat. He had reserved a cabin on a British steamship, the *Mandalay,* leaving for Southampton and points south within the week. Now, would Johnny like to check into the hotel and rest up for a bit, or would he care to stop in at Bradbeer's place for a drink?

"Where is she?" Johnny demanded coldly.

Bradbeer cleared his throat. "She never made contact," he said.

"*What?*"

Bradbeer started to fidget. "She did arrive safely. I looked into that. But you know what the instructions were. She was supposed to initiate contact."

"You mean she simply disappeared?"

"I imagine she took up with her old gang. I mean—"

"You lost her. Damn you. You lost her."

"Now, hang on a bit. I didn't have a hunting license, you know. I couldn't very well go rattling the cages of the local constabulary either, now could I?"

Johnny sat grimly with his arms folded. He was attacking Bradbeer because Bradbeer was there. It wasn't this Englishman's fault.

"It's still the same place, isn't it? In the Zona Rosa?"

"You can't just barge in there," Bradbeer protested.

"No, of course not," Johnny agreed, once he had confirmed the address. "We'll talk about it after I get some rest."

Bradbeer looked distinctly relieved when he dropped him at the Crillón.

The porter affected not to notice that Johnny's sole luggage consisted of an overnight bag he had picked up in Asunción.

He made a brief inspection of his lodgings and found that, on this occasion, the Firm had spared none of the little touches. He had a whole suite to himself, with a patio and a miniature fountain in which a cherub with a serious bladder problem widdled around the clock. There was a bottle of scotch with an ice bucket and two glasses.

The second glass, useless because there was no one to share, enraged him. He picked it up and dashed it against the pink marble of the mantelpiece.

1

"I'VE BEEN waiting for you, Johnny. I've been waiting for a very long time."

The flashing lights of the honky-tonk across the street drew blue and orange bars across her face.

"You look different in glasses."

She touched the rims defensively with her free hand.

"We're both older," she said, keeping the pistol leveled at his chest. "You're going grey. Keep your hands where I can see them. Higher. That's better."

She felt around inside his jacket for the Mauser. She checked the magazine and exchanged his gun for her own, which she tucked under her belt.

"You walked in like a choirboy," Helene said, with a note of professional reproach.

"Where is she?"

Helene laughed. That hoarse, deep-throated smoker's laugh, like a frog's mating call.

"I don't think you ever understood women, my love. She's tougher than you. Maybe you picked the wrong one."

"What are you saying?"

"She told me all of it. Your Englishman in Rio. Your Mr. Bradbeer. How do the Americans say it? She fingered you."

"May I sit down?"

Helene waved him toward the bed. She sat on the edge of the desk, looking down on him. They were in the Comintern liaison office in the Zona Rosa. Helene had been stationed here since Max had ordered her out of Rio. She had spent the last weeks rescuing boat people from Brazil— the revolution had collapsed completely with the arrest or flight of all its leaders—and waiting for Johnny.

Helene shook a cigarillo out of its pack and lit it with one hand.

She said, "You don't look good, Johnny."

"I've felt better. Do you have to point that thing at me?"

"It helps to remind me we're on different sides," she replied.

"We don't have to be. I've never done anything to harm you. Or Sigrid."

"Here," Helene interjected curtly. "She left you a letter. Read it if you want."

He took the envelope. The letter inside covered less than a page. It was typed, so he could decipher nothing of the mind of the writer from the script. It appealed to nostalgia, to his most precious memories. Sigrid wrote about the black panther in the cage in the Berlin zoo, about the sonnet by Rilke that he had recited to her.

"Come to me quickly," Sigrid wrote. "Without you, I am behind bars."

The words wounded him. He had to assume that she had left this message on Max's instructions, to lure him into a trap. But why had she invoked something so personal, something that belonged only to the two of them? Was she signaling that she still wanted to be with him, that she was literally a prisoner behind bars?

His hand was shaking when he gave the letter back to Helene.

"What have they done with her?" he demanded.

"Max took her to Paris," Helene reported, watching him intently. "There's more. They sent this after she left."

He glanced at the second message. It was briefer even than the first: the six-line transcription of a radio signal from Moscow Center. It congratulated him on his performance in Brazil and ordered him to proceed to Paris to receive new instructions.

It was all so transparent he wanted to laugh out loud. Did they believe he was so witless he would buy this at face value?

"I imagine you know what it means," Helene commented.

"I know."

It meant more interrogations, a forced march to Moscow, torture at the hands of secret policemen more expert than any Brazilian, the chance of a show trial, the certainty of execution. Unless—

He stared at Helene. There were no accusations in the letter or the telegram. Max wanted to lull him into a sense of false security, using his feelings for Sigrid to bait the trap. Max must have ordered Helene to play along. But she had disobeyed orders.

"You're not playing your part very well, are you?" Johnny challenged her. "You were supposed to receive me with open arms and shunt me off to Paris as if everything was absolutely fine. You're letting Max down, my love."

"Leave Max out of this!" she snapped at him. "I want to know why you did it."

"It's a long story," he began, conscious that there was no longer any point in trying to dissemble. His best chance was to appeal to the bond that still existed between himself and this woman. "It started with Heinz," he went on. "When Heinz told me that Stalin and Hitler were natural allies, I didn't believe him. When he showed me how the party was opening the door to the Nazis in Germany, I still didn't want to believe. Heinz had to die before I was ready to understand. You know how he died? Max split his skull open with a sledgehammer because Heinz was one of the few men left in Germany—or the whole world Communist movement—who wasn't afraid to tell the truth."

"That's a lie!" There were bright patches of color in Helene's cheeks, and her chest was heaving.

She knows, Johnny thought. She's heard the screams too. She wouldn't be so agitated if she weren't trying to deny them.

"Heinz wasn't a special case," he proceeded, keeping his voice low and calm. "In fact, his fate was entirely predictable. Why do you think they are butchering the Old Bolsheviks in Moscow? Why do you suppose Wollweber in Copenhagen gives the Gestapo lists of comrades in Germany who, once in their lives, made the mistake of criticizing the party bosses, or the big boss in the Kremlin? Do you believe the revolution has to be built on the corpses of those who sweat in its service, like the Great Wall of China? Do you imagine that what you are doing for the Russian secret police has *anything* in common with socialism?"

"Shut up!" she yelled at him.

"Because you don't believe me, or because you do?"

It was the first time he had ever seen her look terrified. Even in Shanghai, he had never seen her like this.

"You know I'm right," he said softly. "You don't belong with these people any more than I do."

She jumped up and brandished the gun at him.

"Shut your face!"

"Or what?"

The hand with the gun was trembling. She pressed the other hand over it to hold it still.

".You betrayed all of us. I don't want to hear any more about the reasons. You have lives to answer for."

"And some that I saved."

She was crying. She swept the back of her hand across her eyes angrily, to brush this sign of frailty away.

"There is only one honorable solution." As she stood up, it struck him that—consciously or not—she must be seeking to impersonate her putative Prussian sire.

She held the gun out to him, butt forward.

"What precisely would you like me to do?" he said. "Do you want me to blow my brains out?"

She said nothing.

"Revolutionaries don't have a code of honor," he taunted her. "Max taught me that we were supposed to practise Bolshevist elasticity."

"Do it for her sake," Helene implored him. "They'll drag her through all of it otherwise. Her life will be wrecked."

"You had all of this worked out, didn't you? That's why you waited. I'm not a Prussian cavalry officer, darling. I'm not going to do it."

Her lips were trembling. Her eyes goggled as if she were on the brink of a seizure.

"I won't do it," he repeated. "But if you shoot me with my own gun, I suppose it might look like suicide." He got off the bed and advanced slowly towards her.

"Come on," he coaxed her. "We haven't been together in a long time. Let's stop this charade and talk things over calmly."

"Don't come any closer. I'm serious."

"Go ahead then. You'll probably do me a favor."

He moved closer, till he could feel the pressure of the gun barrel against his chest. She still didn't shoot.

"Let's lose that, shall we?"

Gently, not rushing her, he took her wrist. At that moment he felt a tremendous warmth towards this woman he had once held and loved. She was a victim, too. He sensed that she was approaching the same crossroads he had reached when he had learned how Heinz had died.

"There's no fight between us," he said gently, moving his fingers to pry the gun loose.

She began shaking uncontrollably.

"No!" The word was a bellow of pain, neither male nor female, barely human.

He forced her arm back, so that when she fired, the bullet drove into the plaster above their heads. She was fighting back, clawing at his face.

He did not want to hurt her. He kept murmuring her name like a lover.

She heaved towards him with her lower body and kneed him in the groin.

He buckled in a spasm of unbearable pain but remembered the gun. She was lowering the barrel, aiming for his face. He wrenched savagely at her wrist at the instant she pulled the trigger.

At last she dropped the gun, and fell into his arms.

"Oh, my love. I never meant this."

The pistol had gone off at the base of her chin, ripping away flesh and bone and vocal cords. She died without a scream.

He rocked with the body like a dancer, careless of the blood that was oozing over his shoulder and the tears that made salty furrows down his cheeks.

He repeated aloud, "We're both victims."

13

The Gift

. . . neither do the spirits damned
Lose all their virtue.
—MILTON,
Paradise Lost

1

THE black-headed gulls had returned in twos and threes to St. James's Park. These were the ones that were barren, Bailey thought, or had lost their eggs or their young. Beyond a white, fragrant cloud of meadowsweet, tufted ducks swam in the pond among their broods. The inconstancy of ducklings had always intrigued him. Cut off from the brood, they would waddle off to join anything with wings. They seemed to have no sense of a separate identity.

Johnny, perhaps, had too much.

Bailey had met the boat at Southampton. Johnny was tanned and gaunt, his leanness exaggerated by the suit that Bradbeer had loaned him, which was too wide and too short. His dark blonde hair had turned gunmetal grey. He was wearing dark glasses, and one of their first calls in London was to an optician who told him he would never see more than shadows out of his left eye. Johnny accepted this with apparent indifference. They went to the Army and Navy Store, where Bailey picked out a few suits that fitted Johnny well enough.

"You can't go to Paris," Bailey told him over sandwiches at the flat in South Audley street. "Besides, you've got a date with the King. He's going to pin a medal on you."

"You can keep your bloody medal."

Johnny was evasive about what had happened in Buenos Aires, which was a bad sign. After many questions, he said that Helene had killed herself. He could not explain why she had done this with his gun, and Bailey let the subject drop. He could sense that Johnny was tortured by what had happened.

Johnny had plenty of questions of his own about Rio.

"There's some good news," Bailey reported. "Captain Schmidt has been relieved of his duties."

"What about Prestes and the others?"

"The police got Prestes. Something to do with his dog. You did say he had a dog, didn't you?"

"Yes. Príncipe."

"He loved the dog too much. Not a bad quality, I suppose. But not very professional."

There were conflicting accounts of the arrest, Bailey explained. The one he favored was that, even in hiding, the rebel leader wanted his dog to eat only the best. The police knew that his lair was somewhere in the working-class district of Meier and started keeping a watch on butcher shops in the neighborhood. They spotted a young black maid who was regularly buying choice cuts of meat and asking for bones. They tailed her to a house on the Rua Honorio and stormed the house in the early hours of the morning. Prestes himself came to the door in his pajamas. A strapping German girl thrust herself between him and the police, shouting "Don't shoot! We're not dynamiters!"

"That doesn't sound much like Olga."

"That's the information we have."

"What about Nilo?"

Bailey shook his head. "No trace."

"That son of a bitch has a lot to answer for," Johnny growled. He was thinking of the pretty little Bahian girl strangled with a clothesline in Nilo's apartment, and the double game Nilo had played with Doctor Alcibiades and the Fascists.

"They did lock up the snake charmer," Bailey volunteered.

Johnny merely grunted. Doctor Alcibiades, the most duplicitous of all the Brazilians, was no longer of much consequence to him.

"What will they do with her? With Olga?"

Bailey took a sip of beer. "I'm afraid there's talk of deporting her."

Johnny clenched his fists. "You've got to stop it!"

Bailey thought, he's identifying Prestes' woman with Helene—and with what the Gestapo intended to do to him.

"I don't see that there's much we can do. Except possibly to indicate polite concern. It's not exactly HMG's style to stick up for Stalin's agents. And you told us yourself that Olga is a dedicated Communist."

"Can't Harry—"

"Harry's on his way back to England," Bailey said firmly.

But Johnny wouldn't let it rest. "A German Jew, a Communist—Can't you imagine the party the Gestapo will have with her?"

"I can imagine."

A hundred and sixty pounds of tortured flesh was something other than human. It was on the way to becoming something else: a hero, or an informer, or a madman, like Emil Brandt. Johnny had traveled part of that road. He knew. But his grief and anger over Olga's fate was more personal, more specific.

In part of himself he still belongs to them, Bailey thought. He is at war with the ideology and the regime, but he won't abandon comrades who shared the same trenches when he still believed. And he identifies Prestes' woman with his own. If he could conquer this instinct, he would make a more professional agent. And less of a man.

"I'm going to Paris," Johnny repeated.

"Yes. Of course you are."

1

THE vaulting roof of the Gare du Nord could not contain the din. Porters rammed trolleys piled high with expensive luggage through the crowd. The first-class travelers who eddied along in their wake babbled about the excitements of the fall collections, the fabulous embroideries of Jeanne Lanvin, the daring cut of Madeleine Vionnet's crepe evening gowns, the fastidious touch of Mainbocher, the prodigy from Chicago. There were flocks of German and Polish refugees with their possessions on their backs and under their arms. There were men who were racing against the clock and men who were too obviously idling, watching others or watching to see if someone had his eye on *them*. Some of them were vaguely familiar to Johnny, couriers he had seen in one or other of the Comintern offices in the old days. But there was not a face he could put a name to.

Out in the street somebody pushed a leaflet into his hand. It sang the virtues of the Popular Front, the alliance of Socialists and Communists that was on the verge of taking power. Working men in dungarees trooped past on their way to a union meeting or a demonstration. They chanted the

Internationale quite openly, interspersed with bursts of the *Marseillaise,* and some of the bystanders took up the chorus.

He walked to the Comintern hotel on the Rue d'Alsace. Nothing much had changed. Nobody had touched up the paint or fixed the cracks in the masonry. Only the posters on the outside wall had been updated. In one of them—a caricature of a bourgeois politician sitting in Hitler's pocket— he thought he saw Sigrid's touch. The theme was crude, but the wildness of the design gave it unusual power.

It gave him an idea.

The man at the reception desk was the one he remembered. He never seemed to look you in the face, and his fingernails were still sorely in need of attention.

"*Bonjour. Est-ce que Monsieur Münzenberg reste toujours ici?*" he asked in his faulty French.

"Monsieur?"

He repeated the question. During his last stay in Paris, Willi Münzenberg, the Westbureau's propaganda boss, had been living quite openly in this establishment. Everyone addressed him by his own name.

But the clerk affected never to have heard of anyone called Münzenberg.

"I need to reach him urgently. It's a party matter."

The clerk turned his back on Johnny to rummage among the pigeonholes behind the desk. Without turning around, he said, "Your name?"

"Mattern. Fritz Mattern."

It was the name he had used inside the German party. It was the name Willi Münzenberg would remember, if he remembered at all.

"Wait."

The clerk shuffled into the back room. Through an opaque glass door, Johnny could see his silhouette. He was talking—to somebody, or into a telephone. Remembering how Sigrid had once gone looking for Münzenberg at the publishing house and had found Max instead, Johnny almost succumbed to a sudden impulse to rush out the door.

The clerk came back with a travel brochure and slapped it down on the top of the reception desk.

"This will show you the Métro stations, Monsieur," he said in a loud, disgusted voice, the voice of a man worn out by inane inquiries from tourists.

"Thank you," Johnny responded in English, equally loud.

He strolled out of the hotel, turned south past the old prison of St. Lazare and then swung east along the Rue du Paradis. When he was fairly sure that nobody had followed him from the Rue d'Alsace, he turned over the brochure. On the inside back cover he found a scribbled address.

He took the Métro. The line went direct to Odéon, but he made a diversion, changing trains at Chatelet and Jussieu, before he walked up into the perfect spring sunlight of the Boulevard St.-Germain. A girl in a floppy beret was playing Mozart on a violin. A quartet of mimes, their faces chalk white, turned handstands and held out their bowler hats for coins. Tourists and boulevard philosophers thronged the tables along the sidewalk. It was all stunningly normal, which made him feel conspicuous.

He hurried to the Rue Jacob, the address the clerk had given him. It struck him, as he turned the corner, that the house was barely a stone's throw away from the GPU office on the Rue de Seine.

Trap or no trap, he told himself, I'm not going to stop now.

There was an intercom hitched up to the bell beside the door.

"Mattern." He gave the same name he had used on the Rue d'Alsace. "Mattern!"

The buzzer sounded and he pushed his way in, to find himself standing in a mousetrap, a boxlike foyer with a sealed door on the other side, from behind which they were presumably taking a good look at him through the peephole.

The door opened and a feral girl with frizzy red hair and a prognathous jaw gave him the once-over.

"Credentials!"

"I don't have them with me."

Her lips curled back in a most inhospitable way. But Willi Münzenberg appeared from some other room, looking like an abstracted professor with his lank hair and rumpled corduroys.

"It's all right, Cilly," he reassured his assistant. "I know him."

"I ought to say, I used to," Münzenberg added for Johnny's benefit, as he squired him past rows of clacking typewriters into a private office. "You're different. I would never have recognized you."

"We've all changed."

"That's true enough. Especially in Paris. You've come to the right place, Fritz Mattern. Before we know it, the Communists will be sitting in the Hôtel de Ville and the Elysée! For the first time in our lives, we're respectable!"

"Then why all the security?"

"That's because of the Fascists, more than the police. With any luck, we'll soon be running the police." He lowered his voice and went on, "I only wish we'd had the sense to do this in Germany when there was still time."

Johnny said nothing. He stared at the posters and woodcuts on Münzenberg's walls, glorifying the alliance of Socialists and Communists that Stalin had banned in Germany. How long would it last in France?

"I heard you were in South America," the Comintern propaganda chief said.

"Brazil."

"Ah. That was a nasty business. We have countermeasures organized. Solidarity committees in support of the victims of reaction. We even have some titled English ladies who have agreed to sail to Rio to intercede with the government."

"You must try to do something for Olga."

"I want to make her the focus of the campaign. There are some bureaucratic problems, of course."

"There are?"

"Well, there are people close to the top who would rather not advertise our role in Brazil."

He means Manuilsky, Johnny thought. Manuilsky and the big boss, Stalin. They got us into Brazil, then they lost their nerve. Now they don't want to hear about anyone associated with the operation. Let the Gestapo have them. Does a man like Münzenberg, who has more brains, and more guts, than the whole Executive Committee of the Comintern put together, still believe in this gang? How can he? Johnny would have liked to ask, but he had come for something else.

"What can I do for you?" Münzenberg asked.

"I've just come back," Johnny rehearsed his hastily concocted tale. "My companion—Sigrid—has moved from her old address. She told me she would be doing some work for you. I thought you might be able to put me in touch with her."

Münzenberg's face clouded. "I think you've come to the wrong department, friend."

"But I know she's doing work for you. I've seen her posters in the street."

"She's done a few things," Münzenberg conceded. "But it's just a sideline, a hobby. Pity. She has unusual gifts."

"Do you know where she lives?"

Münzenberg rubbed his nose. He could smell that something was wrong. Johnny counted on the fact that he had no high regard for the chekists.

"You might ask Ana," he suggested. "She's in the artists' group. The two of them used to be friends."

The new address was an atelier in Montparnasse, down the street from the Closerie des Lilas, where the Symbolists had discussed a revolution of the imagination and where Lenin and Trotsky had plotted a more tangible one in the world before the war.

Johnny took a table in the window and ordered Pernod and black coffee. Waiting for the gate to open between trains at the Sèvres-Babylone Métro station, he had sensed someone watching him intently. When he whipped around, he caught a fleeting glimpse of a quite ordinary man in a dark grey suit and matching hat, who disappeared in the rush of passengers as the automatic gate swung open. He did not see the man again.

Bailey had offered to cover him. He had refused. Once Max's people picked up his scent, they would spot the tail immediately.

There was a cyclist across the street, taking too long to adjust his clips. He waved to a second cyclist, a girl with straw-colored hair tied up in a scarf. They pedaled away together. Perhaps it was nothing.

His eyes were hot and sore, despite the dark glasses. He couldn't hold the coffee cup steady. His skin was moist, his body racked intermittently by malarial spasms. He forgot the French cigarette that was glued to his lower lip, and the ash crumbled over his shirt front.

In my mid-thirties, he thought, I'm already an old man.

Seeing him like this, would she feel pity, or simply contempt? He didn't want either. He wanted some kind of a life. Since their reunion in Brazil on the heights of the Tijuca rain forest, he had known that she had to be part of that life. He had enough money in a London bank account to support them both in reasonable comfort for the rest of their days. They had fought their battles. They both bore the scars. They had earned the right to some measure of happiness.

But would she come? On the boat train from England he had tried to script in his head what he would say to her if he could find her before Max found him. There were tricks he could play, lies he could tell. He had even thought of arranging a setup to convince her that Max was in the pay of the Gestapo. These ruses might get her out of Max's reach, but they would turn on him later, like hissing snakes, and poison whatever trust had survived between them.

His only chance was tell her the truth and hope that the love they had both been schooled to suppress would prove stronger than doubt.

A girl was coming out of the atelier. Svelte, bobbed hair, dark rain cape. She had a bicycle chained to a railing. She bent to open the padlock.

Johnny tossed some money onto the table and hurried out of the bistro.

"Excuse me. You must be Ana."

"Have we met?"

She looked wary, and he took off the dark glasses. "I'm Johnny. Sigrid's friend."

"Oh. She mentioned you." Her expression changed to mild curiosity. She looked Johnny up and down as if assessing his potential as a lover.

He smiled. "I've got a surprise for her. Do you know where she is?"

"I don't know where she lives." Wary again.

"It's a surprise that absolutely won't wait." Johnny winked.

"Well, in that case—we often go sketching together on Tuesdays, and have lunch afterwards. At the zoo."

"The zoo at Vincennes."

"Yes. I told her I couldn't go today, because I've got a date."

"That's a shame. I hope I get to know you better. Maybe next week?"

"Why not?"

IT TOOK half an hour to find her in the sprawling park. She had set up a folding easel under the trees, in a grassy expanse where African antelopes roamed freely. She had attracted a gaggle of schoolchildren, who were craning over her shoulder to see the picture coming alive.

He came up from behind and started reciting the last stanza of Rilke's poem about the panther—

> *Nur manchmal schiebt der Vorhang der Pupille*
> *sich lautlos auf . . .*

and the charcoal broke against the heavy paper.

Some of the children giggled. A solemn little boy in glasses retrieved the stub of charcoal and offered it to the artist.

"You!" The points of color in her cheeks exaggerated her pallor.

A teacher came bustling over, full of apologies, and shepherded the children away.

"I promised I'd come for you."

Her lips opened and closed, but no words came out.

"Also, I got your letter."

"How—how could you? Are you mad?" She looked around nervously at a couple eating ice cream on a bench, at a busload of American tourists festooned with cameras, trooping along behind their guide.

She said, "This city is death for you."

"I've come for *you.*"

She shied from him like a frightened horse.

"I've come to take you away. Since that night at the Babylônia Club, I've lived only for this."

"Don't talk that way! You don't have the right!"

"Come." Gently but firmly, he took her arm. "Let's talk."

Reluctantly she packed up her easel, and they sat under a sun umbrella among the school parties and the holidaymakers. He ordered a citron pressé. She left hers untouched.

"What happened to your eye?"

He explained—the prison, the Gestapo, the jailbreak, the chase down-river. He omitted Harry Maitland.

"You were luckier than the ones you betrayed," she flew at him. "How many lives have you destroyed?"

"I didn't set out to destroy anyone's life. I did what I had to do." Jerkily, trying to hold her with his eyes, he began to tell the whole story, starting with the death of Heinz Kordt. He talked of how his glowing belief in the world revolution had been trampled down by Stalin's secret police, of how the Soviets and the Nazis were joined in an unholy alliance to create a world fit only for slaves.

"You can sit here in France and say things like that!" she burst in. "Here, when the Popular Front is about to change everything!"

"The Popular Front is only a phase, a zigzag along the way. You'll see. The only man Stalin trusts is Hitler. They're made for each other."

Furious, she slammed her fist down on the table, spilling her drink.

"Shit! You're talking shit!" The coarse word seemed truly foul from those lips. "You think any of this fiction justifies what you've done? You sold us to the British for a hundred pounds a month!"

"They don't pay quite that well. And I didn't do it for money."

"Then why?"

"Because a man must have a place on which to stand."

She stared off into the distance.

"And because I heard the screams."

She was breathing in long, deep drafts, perhaps to master her emotions. When she turned, her face was different. Her features were set. She seemed to have come to a moment of resolution.

"Give me a cigarette."

It always made him uneasy to watch her smoke. The cigarette was awkward, even obscene, in her fingers. She took shallow puffs that did not reach her lungs.

"Where would we go?" she asked suddenly, and hope fluttered inside him like a wounded bird.

"We'll go anywhere you want," he said eagerly. "We'll change our names, make a new life. We'll have money, no need to go short—" He broke off. No, better not to dwell on money. "We'll turn our backs on all of them. You'll be able to paint. I'll go fishing, set up a little business. We'll live like normal people."

"How soon?"

"We can go today. Tonight. Whenever you like."

She threw the cigarette onto the paving stones, stood up and ground it underfoot.

"I have some things to collect. I'll meet you at the Gare du Nord—there's a coffee shop—"

"I know the one."

"Seven o'clock." She said all this without meeting his eyes. She let him clasp her to him, briefly. Their mouths brushed. But there was no life in her. It was like holding a mannequin.

"Sigrid. Are you sure?"

"Oh, yes."

"What made you decide?"

"I heard the screams, too."

3

A MAJOR train station is not the ideal place for a clandestine meeting. The police tend to be more vigilant than in other parts of the city, and it is harder to spot a tail among droves of transients. But this was not what troubled Johnny as he retraced his steps to the Gare du Nord in the lengthening shadows.

She didn't ask about Helene. Is it possible she doesn't know?

Mingling with the last flock of commuters, he made a leisurely circumnavigation of the great station. At 7:00 P.M. sharp, he was seated on a stool within sight of the café, reading *L'Aurore,* while a boy in a sailor cap polished his shoes.

Around the edge of the newspaper, he saw her arrive. She was carrying a small suitcase.

She sits down. The waiter comes, with his napkin over his arm. She orders coffee. No, the waiter brings cognac. She looks at the clock behind the counter. Then she looks at her watch. She is nervous, flustered. That's as it should be. There is nobody following her. Nobody I can see.

He gave the bootblack a couple of coins.

"How would you like to earn five francs more?"

The boy looked uncertain. *"Monsieur est pédé, non?"*

"Non." Johnny molded his most reassuring grin. "Monsieur is *not* a pederast. I want you to take a note to the lady in the café. The one sitting by herself."

"That's all?"

He scratched a couple of lines on a scrap he tore from an envelope.

"Meet me at platform seven. Five minutes. No cage can hold us. J."

He handed the boy the message and a five-franc bill. "Don't talk to her. Just give her the note and leave."

He slipped away through the crowd and took shelter behind a telephone kiosk.

He saw her take the note and try to call the boy back.

She's read it. She frowns and summons the waiter. She is leaving. She has not communicated to anyone. Everything is going to be fine.

He trailed her to platform seven, not daring to be sure. She was at the gate, looking lost. She was wearing a blue suit of a brisk, almost military cut and a little matching hat with a visor. She looked like anything but a Comintern agent on the run. She might have walked straight off the Schiaparelli stand at the fashion show. She was superb. She was the only woman in Paris.

He started swimming towards her, through the tide of people.

She glanced up and saw his head, floating above the others.

He was almost close enough to touch her when she put a cigarette in her mouth and snapped a thin gold lighter he had never seen her use before.

In the next instant, two bulky men bracketed him.

"Police," one of them grunted.

He looked at the bulging face, the dumpling nose. They didn't make faces like that in Paris.

He wrestled with them, trying to break away.

He felt a sharp jab just above the kidneys. His knees sagged. They were hoisting him up, half-dragging, half-carrying him away.

"Excuse, please. Our friend is sick," a voice wafted out of an echoing pit.

In his last flicker of consciousness, he saw a woman in blue, walking briskly away. She did not look back.

"I'M DISAPPOINTED in you, Johnny. I once thought of you as my most brilliant protégé. You end up as a lovesick calf. I warned you against that woman the first time I met her. You should have listened to me then."

Max was sitting at the end of a long refectory table. A brass chandelier hung down from a domed ceiling. The walls were white and uncomforting, bare except for a few somber oils of men in dark robes. The place had the air of a former monastery.

They had propped Johnny up at Max's right hand, in a tall, ladder-backed chair. He was still groggy from the needle they had stuck him with at the station. His abductors were transformed, for the night, into waiters. The service was sloppy, the food of no interest to Johnny. But he noticed from the labels on the wines—a pouilly fuissé, followed by a médoc and a venerable armagnac—that no expense had been spared. "It's our Last Supper," Max had announced. The note of blasphemy was enhanced by the spymaster's appearance. He was wearing a white silk turtleneck inside his black sweater.

Max smoked between courses, during courses, incessantly.

"What have you done with her?" Johnny croaked.

"Me? I've done nothing. She's gone back to Moscow, with my blessing. End of story. Now we have to decide what to do with *you*."

"How long did you know?"

Max blew out smoke and watched the circles rise above the chandelier.

"I suspected for a long time. I didn't have proof until Sigrid gave it to me."

"You suspected in Brazil. Yet you let me remain in place. Why?"

Max signaled for the two burly waiters to go.

"We are all capable of mistakes," Max said serenely.

"Nothing is that simple with you. You wanted Emil destroyed. Didn't you?"

"You needn't exorcise yourself about him." Max steepled his hands.

"You sit there like a defrocked priest!" Johnny exploded at him. "I hated Emil. Then I saw what those bastards did to him—"

"A fit of conscience? From you? That's rather quaint. I'm afraid it won't affect your sentence."

Johnny subsided. Max was right. His outburst was grotesque.

"I was once in Siberia," Max resumed. "Did you know that? No, I was never a prisoner, if that's what you're thinking. But I was out of favor. It was a few years after our first meeting. I had not quite adjusted to the new order of things. I still imagined that Trotsky was some kind of genius. I hadn't learned whose back to scrub. So in order to educate me they sent me to run a logging camp in the northeast, where the temperature drops to eighty below. I made one friend, just one, in almost twelve months. He was a Chukchi. Have you ever met a Chukchi?"

"No."

"Well, never take one on in a fight, at least not on his own terrain. They're an arctic people, primitive, superstitious. They live like wolves in places you would think could never support human lives. One day my Chukchi friend—he was a chief or shaman among the rest, face like a Buddha—invited me to come and watch the wolves. He said there was a lot to be learned from wolves, said they are more like us than any other species. Only a wolf can look a man straight in the eye and sometimes stare him down. I was shit scared, I don't mind admitting it, but I went with him all the same, in a fur-lined parka and snowshoes, loaded up with guns and ammunition and vodka.

"He took me up into some ranges where you could see for miles and miles. All I could make out to begin with was a white wilderness. I couldn't tell north from south. Then he pointed out the ravens—the ravens follow the wolves in hopes of feeding off their kills—and then we saw the pack itself. Magnificent, their legs rolling smoothly as wheels.

"There were two wolves loping along behind the rest. They were what the old man had brought me to watch. They were lone wolves, both trying to join the pack. One was an outcast, driven out of the pack for some reason, probably illness. Wolves sense any contagious infection. When they were resting, the outcast would nip at his backside, as if he had worms. The other wolf had come out of the white void. If he got too close to the others, they would bare their teeth and run at him, driving him away. They weren't inclined to share their food or their territory.

"The whole drama was played out. While the pack was resting, the pariah put his tail between his legs and made another bid for acceptance. He approached the others with his ears flattened back, and we saw him try to lick the muzzle of the alpha wolf. They nipped and snarled at him till he ran away yelping. He saw the lone wolf, the outsider, and all at once his posture changed. His legs stiffened, his jaws opened, and the next second he was hurling himself on the outsider's neck. They tussled for quite a long time. The pack kept out of it. The pariah took some vicious bites, but finally he had the outsider at his mercy. He killed the way wolves generally kill. By ripping the guts out and letting the victim bleed to death.

"As we watched, he limped back to the pack. He must have thought he had vindicated himself in the eyes of his old comrades by killing the intruder. He didn't strut. He cowered and fawned, as before. When the alpha wolf snapped at him, he even rolled over on his back, and put his legs in the air. And you know what his old comrades did? They tore him to pieces."

Max paused and filled two wineglasses to the brim with armagnac.

"Drink," he urged Johnny. "To our cousins the wolves!"

Johnny took a swallow.

"Do you know why I told you that story?"

Johnny waited.

"Because it's about Emil. He killed the outsider, he rolled on his back, and they would still have torn him to bits in Moscow if the Brazilians hadn't got him first."

"It sounds to me as if the story is about *you*," Johnny said quietly. "You did the killing. Heinz Kordt. Miranda's girl—"

"At whose orders?" Max screamed at him, all his urbanity fled. "At whose instigation?"

"The Gestapo would have given the same orders. There are times when a man has to say no to his orders, or become your wolf."

Max hurled his glass at Johnny's head. Johnny bent to one side, and it smashed against the wall.

"I dedicated my life to the cause." He was on his feet, breathing hard. "When you were crapping in your nappies, I was fighting for the revolution—"

"Do you still believe in it?"

"That's a stupid question."

"Do you still believe?"

"It doesn't matter what I believe. There are only two sides, and I am on the side of the party."

"That's a stupid answer."

"You're not entitled to any answers! I could shoot you now."

"Go ahead. I wouldn't lose any sleep over it, anyway." Johnny's indifference wasn't feigned. He felt leached of emotion, even fear.

Max sat down and reached for another glass. He gulped the fine Armagnac like water.

"Why did you kill Helene?"

"I didn't kill her. It was an accident."

It struck him now that this was what Sigrid was talking about, when she said she had heard the screams.

He stared at Max, who was leaning into the table, his chin resting on his arms.

"Do you believe me? Not that it matters."

"I would like to believe you," Max said. "For your own sake. That one loved you better, in her way, than the other. The worst mistake you made in your life was to choose the wrong sister."

THEY talked far into the night, and little of the conversation had the quality of an interrogation. Max was violent, nostalgic, philosophic by turns, and his mood shifts became more vertiginous when the Armagnac was gone and he started working his way through a fresh bottle of vodka. By the end of it Johnny found it hard to keep his eyes awake, even though he knew what followed a Last Supper.

He was finally allowed to fling down on the bed in a room with heavy wooden shutters that were bolted from the outside. When he awoke, the room was still dark, and he was amazed to see from his watch that it was past 10:00 A.M. It seemed odd that neither of Max's house goons had come to rouse him.

He banged on the door. No answer. He rattled the handle and found the door was unlocked. That was even stranger. Surely he had heard the key turn in the lock the night before.

He dressed and set off down the corridor. The house seemed deserted. When he descended the grand staircase and went to the front door, no one came to challenge him. He looked out over a wide terrace to a formal garden that was being rapidly recovered by nature. The lawn was bright with dandelions.

He considered making a break for it, then and there.

No, he told himself. They want an excuse to shoot me in the back, to avoid embarrassments in Moscow.

He went back inside and began exploring the house more methodically. Not a retired convent, after all, to judge by the lady in a wimple whose bosom was bursting out of her bodice in a cracked canvas in the hall. He followed the smell of coffee and warm pastry into the kitchen, and found Max Fabrikant breakfasting alone. He was still drinking—lukewarm vodka, out of a tumbler. He looked and smelled as though he had been up all night.

"Eat. Drink." Max gestured to a chair.

"Where are Rosencrantz and Guildenstern?"

"I gave them the day off. So we could continue our chat." Max could probably drink half the population of Greater Russia under the table, but his speech was furry, and his eyes looked out of focus. "I thought you might want to hear another story." The last word ended in a belch, which he made no effort to suppress.

"Of course." Johnny poured coffee from the pot. Like the vodka, the coffee proved to be lukewarm. Judging that vodka tasted better than coffee at room temperature, he joined Max in a glass.

"One of the greatest witchfinders of medieval Europe," Max began, "was Nicolai Remigii, the hanging judge of the Duke of Lorraine. When old Nick sat on the bench, he had eight hundred women burned at the stake for witchcraft. He had an infallible technique for telling the guilty from the innocent. He would have his suspect bound hand and foot and thrown into a pond. If the woman sank, she was judged innocent. If she floated, she was consigned to the fire. Elegant logic, wouldn't you agree? Not unknown in our century, for that matter."

He drank some more.

"In his dotage, Master Nicolai reached the conclusion that he himself was able to cast magic spells. He was of course a stickler for due process, not to mention a punctilious kraut, my dear Johnny. So he registered himself with the court as a master of witchcraft. And what do you think happened? Did they burn him at the stake? Of course they did. Don't you find that uncommonly illuminating?"

In his excitement, he had seized Johnny's wrist.

He's running a fever worse than mine, Johnny realized.

"Are you going to tell me who this story is about?"

"Ah!" Max sprang up and started hopping around in a lunatic jig. "It's about all of us!"

Johnny waited for him to subside. When Max flopped down, the light went out of him. He rested his head on the table.

After a while, Johnny began to worry that he had blacked out and got up to investigate. But Max snapped back. He sat bolt upright and carried on as if there had been no interruption.

"I don't have friends, Johnny. You know that. Trust is a weakness in my profession. You were perhaps the closest I had to a friend. You and one other. I don't think you ever met him. I called him Mishka. He got on the wrong side of Yezhov. Now he has confessed that he was involved in the assassination of Kirov. He wasn't even in Russia at the time. And he is a Leningrad man. Kirov was his hero. They will shoot him. Naturally."

The story was almost humdrum compared with what both men had lived, what each could be held accountable for. What intrigued Johnny was that the fate of this unknown Mishka—presumably a fellow chekist—had touched Max in a way that the fates of Heinz and Werner had not. Could it be because he believed that Mishka's fate presaged his own?

"Max. Something has happened, hasn't it?"

Fabrikant shrugged and reached for the vodka.

"They're coming at noon," he said drowsily.

"Who?"

"I've been summoned back to Moscow. It's not a friendly invitation." He swilled the booze around inside his cheeks like a mouthwash. "They planned to spring it on me as a surprise. Fortunately, I still have a few people who owe me favors. I got a call during the night."

"What will you do?"

Max lifted the crumpled napkin on the table in front of him, exposing a Makarov service pistol.

"Not that."

Max wiped his mouth with the napkin and laughed. "No, I don't think so. I haven't made up my mind."

"What about me?"

"Take a lesson from old Nick of Lorraine. Be the one that sinks without trace. The door is open, Johnny."

Johnny started walking toward the door, not quite believing. In the doorway he turned back toward Max.

"Did Sigrid really leave for Moscow?"

Max's laugh was a dry rattle. "Forget her. Marry an English girl with
—how do they say?—peaches and cream in her cheeks. Give her a nice
warm fuck for me."

4

"THEY shot Max," Colin Bailey told him. "Put him down like a horse with
a broken leg."

Several months had passed. Time enough for the European dictatorships
to find themselves a handy little proving ground in Spain and for Johnny
to have his audience with the dying King; he went on to a celebration
dinner at the Savoy at which Harry Maitland turned up in tails and insisted
on snaring the prettiest girl on the dance floor to partner Johnny.

Bailey had taken Johnny down to the cottage in Devon for a few days,
sensing that the German was nearing a new emotional crisis. The Firm had
given him a few jobs to do. He had conducted a short training course for
recent recruits on sabotage techniques and Comintern methods, which had
most of the new boys excited. He had been encouraged to jot down his
memoirs, for the files at least; but this literary project seemed to be withering on the vine. The symptoms of Johnny's malaise were easy to read. He
missed the action, and he needed a woman. More than a woman, a friend.

Diana, God love her, had put Johnny on a horse and carted him off to
a show, where he caused quite a stir among some of the county girls—at
least after Diana hinted that he was a titled archduke traveling incognito.
This produced a batch of promising dinner invitations and a rumored affair
which was the talk of the county for a week or so, but it wasn't even half
a step toward solving what a man who had lost his woman and his cause
was going to do with the rest of his life.

Bailey was mulling this over one morning when he picked up his black-
thorn stick and said to Johnny, "Let's get some air."

They drove down to Dartmoor in Diana's cheeky red roadster. Driving
it always made Bailey feel as if he were just coming down from college.
Johnny must have caught the spirit. He was smiling and joking by the time
they arrived at Two Bridges, which was just an inn and a thatched cottage
making eyes at each other from opposite sides of the road.

Johnny's mood darkened when he heard the news about Max. Bailey had
saved it up for a few days, since he had taken the train down from London,
not sure how Johnny would react. The man had the right to rejoice. Max
Fabrikant had been mixed up with most of the tragedies in his life, includ-

ing the loss of Sigrid. Yet he reacted to the news as if something in himself had died.

Bailey led them off at a brisk pace, marking the rhythm with his stick, along the river bank to a blackened cottage. Now their way ran beside an ancient wall of granite lumps patched with lichen, held together over the centuries by the gaps the wind whistled through. This was lean, rough country. A few bighorn sheep, their faces black, grazed among deformed clumps of gorse. Crows and ravens turning slow circles overhead greeted the travelers with a parched cackle that reminded Johnny of Max's parting phrase.

They picked their way over swampy downs to a stile and then a wooden ladder over a farther fence where tufts of sheep's wool hung down from the rusty prongs of the barbed wire. It was only midafternoon, and yet night was closing in. A great, blanketing mist dropped suddenly over the valley, swallowing Beartown Tor, away to the left. From the crest of a hill, peering over the moors, Johnny followed Bailey's pointing arm and made out what seemed to be a giant oak forest in the far distance.

But there was something awry. The trees tilted crazily down the tilt of the valley, cowering under some irresistible force. Closer up, Johnny realized that the oaks were dwarves, the biggest only three times his height. The wood had survived for centuries, scorned—or, more properly, feared —by the tin miners who had plundered the surrounding moorlands for fuel. The trunks of the tiny oaks were bent over, parallel with the ground. The roots snaked around granite boulders, probing far to find the sparse soil and safe moorings for their eccentric loads. Inside the forest, a cobwebby green haze covered everything.

"They call this Wistman's Wood," Bailey explained.

Johnny had to bend almost double to follow him under the dwarf oaks. They found a comfortable perch on a rock and shared a tobacco pouch.

"Is it true that Harry Maitland is joining the Firm?" Johnny asked after a time.

"Yes. As a matter of fact, it is. We're lucky to get him."

Bailey did not see fit to add that it had taken a certain amount of arm-twisting. He had not been above suggesting to Major Mackenzie via circuitous channels that, while HMG was duly grateful for the role played by Rio Light and Harry in particular in the recent distressing events in Brazil, it would be no bad thing if young Maitland were sent back to England. He had acquired some powerful enemies, and the change would do him good. Bailey gathered that Maitland had had woman trouble of his own. Luisa had packed up and left, gone back to the steep cobbled streets of Salvador da Bahia, leaving a puzzling message about how they belonged to the gods of their own peoples. With any luck an eligible young bachelor like Maitland, caught up in the social whirl of the West End, would get over it soon enough. Hadn't Bailey once done the same?

It would be harder for Johnny.

The German turned to look at him through the haze of pipe smoke.

"Was it worth it?" Johnny asked.

"Don't doubt that for a minute," Bailey responded fiercely. "If war comes, as it is bound to come—"

"Your politicians in London seem to doubt that."

"Then damn the politicians! You and I know better. *When* war comes, we will need Brazil. Not just for the rubber and the coffee, but because it's the stepping-stone to North Africa, and that is the key to southern Europe. I don't know what the Americans will do when we have to get rough with Hitler, but just imagine what a difference Brazil would make to them if it were owned by Stalin's boys. Or Hitler's."

He thought about Courtland Bull, the elusive Texan millionaire, financier of Brazilian plots. Bailey's man in Washington had reported that Bull was now lobbying to get himself appointed Ambassador to the Court of St. James's. Bailey intended to put paid to that notion.

"Brazil was a sideshow, all the same," Johnny said.

"The sideshows are often the best things at a carnival. I rate this one of the very best."

A silence fell between them, punctuated only by the continuous low drone from minuscule winged insects, scaled down like the oaks, barely distinguishable from grains of dust in the filtered light but insistent, aiming for the eyes.

"I need a job," Johnny announced.

"I've been giving that some thought. You know, I had it in mind to send Harry to the Hague. You two got along together pretty well, didn't you? You might even be able to teach him to order from a German menu."

Johnny showed no particular interest till Bailey added, "Wolfgang Trott has been appointed first secretary at the German Embassy in the Hague."

"When do I leave?"

"Steady on. I'll have to cut through a mile of red tape."

He sensed Johnny beginning to relax, with the promise of action again in his sights. They smoked and enjoyed the comfortable silence of people who share a language beyond words.

Johnny broke it by asking casually, "Why is this place called Wistman's Wood?"

"Oh, it's a hoary old West Country yarn. The Wisht-Man was Old Nick, or something very close. He had a pack of bloodthirsty dogs called the

Wisht-Hounds, and the locals thought they spied them ranging these moors by night. A dreadful load of piffle, truly. The trail they took—we followed it part of the way—was called the Path of the Dead. You see, they used to carry the coffins along that route for burial in holy ground at Lydford. I suppose it made quite a sight in the dead of winter, those lonely columns of serfs staggering along with the boxes on their shoulders."

"The Path of the Dead," Johnny repeated.

It wasn't a scene from West Country folklore that he saw. It was a series of faces rising up out of the mist of his own past. Heinz Kordt. Emil Brandt. Helene. Max Fabrikant. Sigrid. And then came faces scarcely formed, things from the future, the first rough pummeling of the sculptor's clay.

He raised himself to his full height, pushing back the foliage.

He said, "We're on the right track."

Historical Note

THIS is a work of fiction, but it is based on fact. There was a double agent code-named Johnny who worked for the British in the thirties. One of his many aliases was Franz Gruber. His real name was Johann Heinrich de Graaf, and he was born in the little town of Nordenham, across the River Weser from the port of Bremerhaven, in 1894. His work as an agent inside the Comintern and Soviet military intelligence resulted in some of the greatest—and hitherto unrecorded—successes of British secret intelligence in the era between the two world wars.

Through Johnny, the British were able to penetrate Soviet espionage rings in London, Copenhagen, Paris and Shanghai. He provided critical intelligence on Stalin's bid to make an alliance with Hitler and the Nazi military buildup, although it was ignored by the appeasers who subsequently came to power in Britain. Johnny helped to sabotage Stalin's ambitious plot to turn Brazil into the first Communist state in the Western Hemisphere.

Like many of the most valuable agents, Johnny was a "walk-in." He volunteered his services to the British intelligence chief in Berlin in 1933 out of bitter disillusionment with Soviet policy. He had had firsthand experience of how Stalin had helped to destroy the anti-Nazi forces in

Germany and was secretly collaborating with Hitler many years before the signing of the infamous Nazi-Soviet Non-Aggression Pact that ushered in World War II. He had come to regard communism and fascism as twin evils and spent the rest of his life fighting both, often at great personal risk.

He loved two sisters, both Soviet intelligence operatives, although in real life, only one of them actually went to Brazil.

Johnny had a happier fate than many of his comrades. In 1940, when Hitler and Stalin were openly allied, the Soviet secret police herded 530 German Communists, including some of his former friends, over the bridge at Brest Litovsk in Poland and into the hands of the Gestapo. Readers who are curious to know more about the love affair between Stalin and Hitler and what it meant to Johnny's generation will find fascinating material in the memoirs of a number of Soviet intelligence operatives and Communist organizers who ended up sharing his disenchantment. These memoirs include Walter Krivitsky's *In Stalin's Secret Service,* Alexander Orlov's *The Secret History of Stalin's Crimes,* Ruth Fischer's *Stalin and German Communism,* Eudocio Ravines' *The Yenan Way* and Jan Valtin's *Out of the Night,* all of which provided valuable background for my novel.

On the recorded events of 1935–36 in Brazil, an indispensable source is the magisterial series by Professor John W. F. Dulles, the doyen of Western scholars in this area. His books include *Vargas of Brazil, Anarchists and Communists in Brazil* and *Brazilian Communism, 1935–1945,* all published by the University of Texas. Among the Brazilian works I found helpful were Hélio Silva's *1935: A Revolta Vermelha,* Graciliano Ramos' *Memorías do Cárcere,* a marvelous guide to the personalities involved in the Communist revolt, and the recent sympathetic biography of Prestes' companion, *Olga,* by Fernando Morais. Ivan Pedro de Martins, who was in 1935 the youngest member of the Central Committee of the Brazilian Communist Party, was generous enough to share with me some of the vivid recollections that will be published in his forthcoming autobiography.

For the record, Rudyard Kipling did visit Brazil (in the late 1920s) and immediately fell in love with the country, like many visitors before him and since. His charming travelogues were published by Doubleday in New York in 1940 in a slim volume entitled *Brazilian Sketches* that is not included in the major editions of his collected works.

Unhappily, Johnny did not write his memoirs. But I have been privileged to talk with people who remember him and with others who played a role in the events described in the novel. In the course of several trips to Brazil I have interviewed some of the survivors of the 1935 revolt and examined the police archives from that time, which contain hundreds of Communist documents from the safes—booby-trapped by Johnny—that failed to blow up when they were forced open.

But *Carnival of Spies* is, of course, a novel, not a historical dissertation. For dramatic purposes I have taken a few liberties; for example, the Fascist coup attempt in Brazil actually postdated the Communist rising by about three years. Many of the characters are fictional. They rub shoulders with various historical figures. Among the latter are:

Stalin
Dimitrov, Comintern leader
Manuilsky, Stalin's hatchetman in the Comintern
Piatnitsky, head of the Orgbureau of the Comintern
Berzin, chief of Soviet Military Intelligence
Yezhov, OGPU chief and organizer of the Great Purge
Harry Pollitt, British Communist leader
Getulio Vargas, president of Brazil
Luis Carlos Prestes, Brazilian Communist leader
Olga Benario, his companion
Lampião, Brazilian bandit chief
Ernst Wollweber, German Communist leader active in Copenhagen
Otto Braun, Comintern adviser in China
Von Seeckt, head of Hitler's military mission to Chiang Kai-shek
Tu Yu-seng, criminal overlord of Shanghai
Willi Münzenberg, the brilliant Comintern propagandist who pioneered the art of using "peace" slogans and "solidarity" campaigns to recruit liberals for Communist causes. Münzenberg eventually broke with Stalin over his policy of collaboration with Hitler. He was found dead with a wire garrote around his neck in the woods of Cagnet in southwestern France in 1940—a victim of Stalin's secret police or the Gestapo, or both.

Three Soviet agencies involved in covert operations abroad are described in the novel. A word on each:

The Comintern

THE Communist International, or Comintern, was founded in Moscow in March 1919. According to its program, "It is the aim of the Communist International to fight by all available means, including armed struggle, for the overthrow of the international bourgeoisie and the creation of an international Soviet republic as a transitional stage to the complete abolition of the State . . . The Communist International must, in fact and in deed, be a single Communist Party of the entire world. The parties working in the various countries are but its separate sections."

Comintern advisers had extraordinary powers over local Communist parties, and in the course of the twenties they organized a wave of armed insurrections around the world, including the Hamburg revolt recounted in this book. All these military adventures failed; some brought the deaths of many thousands of party members. The Comintern ran training courses for foreign revolutionaries, notably at the Lenin School, just outside Moscow, which had 500 students in 1935, and in the M-schools, like the one at Bakovka mentioned in this novel, where Red Army instructors taught bomb making and assassination techniques.

In Stalin's time the Comintern—purged of its early, internationalist leaders—became simply an arm of the Soviet state, ruthlessly subjected to every cynical shift in Moscow's policy by the secret police and Stalin's trusted hatchetman, Dmitri Zacharovich Manuilsky, the son of a Greek Orthodox priest who turned up at the United Nations after the war in the guise of a delegate from the Ukraine.

The "heart of the Comintern," according to Walter Krivitsky, was the OMS—the *Otdel Meshdunarodoi Svyasi,* or International Relations Department. This was the most secret section of the Orgbureau, headed by Osip Piatnitsky, the remarkable "Old Bolshevik" described in the book who perished in the Stalin purges. The OMS arranged covert funding, transport and fake documentation and was charged with the security of Comintern operatives abroad.

The Comintern's regional directorates included the powerful Westbureau, which functioned from behind the cover of a publishing house on the Wilhelmstrasse in Berlin—as described in this book—until Hitler took power, when its staffers scattered and regrouped in Paris and Copenhagen.

The South American bureau, based in Buenos Aires until 1928 and afterwards in Montevideo, was the command center for the Rio plot. For many years its dominating figure was August Guralski, a supple, sophisticated Lithuanian Jew who played a key part in recruiting Luis Carlos Prestes to the Communist cause. In Rio in 1935 the South American bureau was headed by a triumvirate that used the amusing acronymn GIN. The "G" was for "Garoto" (or "Kid"), one of the code names for Prestes, who returned to Brazil on a fake Portuguese passport. The "I" was for "Indio," a party name for Rodolfo Ghioldi, a leading Argentine Communist. The "N" was for "Negro," a nom de guerre for Arthur Ewert (who often called himself Harry Berger), who had headed Comintern operations in Shanghai in 1932–34 and, like the fictional Emil, was not the least tragic figure in the Brazilian episode.

The attempted coup in Brazil was the Comintern's last ambitious experiment in overthrowing a target government by force of arms. For a few years afterwards, Stalin's reluctant decision to endorse Popular Front tactics—

made public in the summer of 1935 by the Seventh Congress of the Communist International in Moscow—brought political and propaganda success, especially in France. But at the same time, the Comintern's most courageous and committed agents were falling victim to the purges in Moscow, and the signing of the Nazi-Soviet Pact threw the worldwide Communist movement into utter disarray. After Hitler invaded the Soviet Union, forcing Stalin to align himself with the West, the Comintern became an embarrassment; it had been involved in too many plots against the Western allies. It was officially disbanded in 1943.

However, the Comintern is very much alive to this day in the guise of the International Department (ID) of the Central Committee of the Communist Party of the Soviet Union, which seeks to manipulate foreign political parties—not only Communist parties—for Soviet ends and has its own operatives posted at important embassies.

Soviet State Security

THE Soviet secret police was formally organized in December 1917 as the All-Russian Extraordinary Commission for Combating Counter-Revolution and Sabotage, or Cheka for short. The word "chekist" (or "honorable chekist," in Soviet publications) is still used to describe members of the KGB. The first Soviet intelligence chief, Feliks Dzerzhinsky, described the role of his agency in the following terms in 1918: "We stand for organized terror . . . The Cheka is obliged to defend the revolution and conquer the enemy even if its sword does by chance sometimes fall upon the heads of the innocent."

Since the abolition of the Cheka in 1922, the Soviet secret police has been known by a bewildering chain of initials: GPU, OGPU, NKVD, MVD and KGB. To avoid confusion, Max Fabrikant's organization is referred to throughout this novel as the OGPU. The initials stand for "Obiedinyonnoye Gosudarstvennoye Politicheskoye Upravleniye," or Unified State Political Administration. This was the title used by Soviet state security between November 1923 and 1934.

Nikolai Ivanovich Yezhov, who is seen visiting Stalin and interrogating Johnny in the book, is, of course, a historical figure. He became chief of Soviet state security in September 1936 and presided over the bloody purges that claimed the lives of veteran Comintern organizers, Red Army generals and countless thousands of party faithful.

Max Fabrikant is a fictional character, but some of his European exploits are loosely modeled on the career of a Soviet master spy of Latvian origin who used the alias Michel Avatin and personally executed a number of alleged "traitors." For the record, a senior member of Avatin's service was dispatched to Rio in the fall of 1935 to ferret out spies within the Comintern team, and recommended the murder of the mistress of "Miranda," the secretary-general of the Brazilian Communist Party.

Soviet Military Intelligence

AGAIN, for the sake of simplicity, Soviet military intelligence (today known as the GRU) is described as the Fourth Department (of the General Staff). It was this organization, rather than the forerunner of the KGB, that was responsible for most of the Soviet espionage coups between the two world wars. It produced spies of the caliber of Richard Sorge. It forewarned Stalin of Hitler's impending attack. However, Stalin preferred not to believe its reports; as Johnny reflects in the novel, Hitler was perhaps the only man the Soviet dictator was willing to trust.

General Jan Berzin, the Latvian head of the Fourth Department in this book, is another historical figure. He died in the purges, along with nearly all of his headquarters staff. According to the account of one Soviet intelligence defector, Berzin's death was a slow one; in the cells of the Lubyanka, his testicles were nailed to a block of wood.

ABOUT THE AUTHOR

ROBERT MOSS is the author of *Moscow Rules* and *Death Beam* and the coauthor of *Monimbó* and *The Spike*, all international best sellers. Born in Australia in 1946, he was a history professor at the Australian National University before joining the staff of *The Economist* in London. He worked as a foreign correspondent and a syndicated columnist for twelve years, covering wars and revolutions all over the world. For six years, he was editor of the *Economist*'s influential intelligence bulletin, *Foreign Report*. His nonfiction books include *Urban Guerrillas*, a pioneering study of terrorist techniques. Moss lectures widely at U.S. colleges and NATO military academies, and his articles have appeared in many American publications, including *Parade, The Wall Street Journal, The New Republic, The New York Times Magazine,* and *Commentary*. Moss has interviewed many of the important Soviet bloc intelligence defectors. Moss has a wife and two daughters and, when he is not traveling on field research for his books, he lives on a farm in upstate New York.